A HISTORY OF ARCHITECTURE

S. Paul's Cathedral, London, from the west (1675–1710). See p. 1014

SIR BANISTER FLETCHER'S

A HISTORY OF ARCHITECTURE

Eighteenth Edition

revised by

J. C. PALMES

Hon. F.R.I.B.A., formerly Librarian of the
Royal Institute of British Architects

NEW YORK

CHARLES SCRIBNER'S SONS

1975

Eighteenth edition published in the U.S.A. and Canada by
CHARLES SCRIBNER'S SONS
597 Fifth Avenue, New York 10017
New York

Library of Congress Catalogue Card No. 74-25545
SBN 684-14207-4

Set in Monotype Plantin by
GLOUCESTER TYPESETTING CO LTD

Printed and bound in Great Britain by
JARROLD AND SONS LTD
NORWICH

PREFACE

In the seventeenth edition (1961) Professor Cordingley took the first calculated step towards a practical reassessment of the form and content of 'Banister Fletcher', by greatly extending its range, especially developing those chapters concerned with the later aspects of architectural history, and by making a number of improvements to the balance of the whole, scrupulously preserving none the less the system of analysis and comparison by which the work is distinguished. This method of presentation required each style or period to be considered under five sections: the Influences which shaped it; Architectural Character; Examples of typical buildings; a Comparative Analysis of principal features; a Bibliography of reference sources. In the eighteenth edition we have moved a stage further and, in the face of potential criticism, omitted the Comparative Analysis section in every case. In deciding upon this controversial course, we were influenced by two factors: the need, imperative in our opinion, to offer a much broader conspectus of the world's architecture, while retaining the history's single-volume format; and the fact that, in the majority of chapters, the Comparative Analysis consisted of little more than a restatement, sometimes in identical words, of matters amply discussed under the Architectural Character section.

This considerable change has made it possible to cover a great deal of fresh ground. For the first time there are chapters devoted to Renaissance architecture in Scandinavia, in Russia, and outside Europe; to the indigenous architecture of Sri Lanka (Ceylon); of Burma, Cambodia, Thailand and Indonesia; of Tibet, Nepal and Afghanistan; to Pre-Columbian architecture in America; and, moving forward to our own day, to the 'Modern Movement' and its international evolution since the First World War. In addition, all the chapters of the seventeenth edition which are incorporated in the present volume—some thirty in number—have been revised, and twenty-two have been substantially recast, extended or re-written.

Such a far-reaching programme has entailed the services of a large team of specialists, and I have been wonderfully fortunate in the quality of my collaborators, to whom I extend my very particular thanks, gratefully acknowledging their learned contributions, which are here briefly specified after their names:

JOHN H. G. ARCHER, M.A., R.I.B.A.: nineteenth-century architecture in Britain.

CHARLES A. BURNEY, PH.D., M.A.: the architecture of Egypt and the ancient Near East.

THOMAS H. B. BURROUGH, R.W.A., R.I.B.A.: Renaissance architecture in Scandinavia and Central Europe.

DONALD R. BUTTRESS, M.A., DIP.ARCH. (MANCHESTER), F.S.A., R.I.B.A.: Gothic architecture in Britain.

BERNARD H. COX, F.R.I.C.S., R.I.B.A.: Renaissance architecture in Russia.

MINNETTE DE SILVA, R.I.B.A.: the architecture of the Far East, including new chapters on Sri Lanka; Afghanistan, Nepal and Tibet; Burma, Cambodia, Thailand and Indonesia.

MICHAEL R. HERBERT: Early Christian and Byzantine architecture.

FRANK I. JENKINS, B. ARCH., M.A. (DURHAM), M.S. (ARCH.)(ILLINOIS): architecture in Pre-Columbian America; nineteenth-century Continental Europe; nineteenth-century America.

RICHARD A. KAYLL, DIPL. ARCH.(UCL), R.I.B.A.: Renaissance architecture in Italy, France and Britain.

RUTH PLANT, A.A.DIPL., M.LITT., R.I.B.A.: Rock churches of Ethiopia.

HOWARD E. STUTCHBURY, PH.D., M.A. (MANCHESTER), DIP. T.P. (LONDON), F.R.T.P.I., R.I.B.A.: Romanesque architecture in Italy, France, Central Europe, Spain and the Holy Land, Britain and Scandinavia.

WILLIAM TAYLOR, A.A.DIPL., R.I.B.A.: Greek and Roman architecture.

JOHN C. T. WARREN, M.LITT., B.ARCH. (DUNELM), A.M.T.P.I., R.I.B.A.: Islamic architecture.

For the alterations and additions to the remainder of the text, as also for the general plan and supervision of the book, I am of course responsible; and here again I am deeply aware of the value of the part played by others. To Professor A. G. Dickens, Director of the Institute of Historical Research, University of London, I take this opportunity of recording my appreciation of the sensibility and acumen with which he amended historical inaccuracies in certain chapters. I am no less indebted to the R.I.B.A. Librarian, David Dean, and to John Harris, Curator of the R.I.B.A. Drawings Collection, and their respective staffs, for their patience and invariable good humour in responding to my constant requests and inquiries. I owe much to the resources and librarians of Guildford and Dorking Public Libraries, while to the constructive advice, discerning criticism and active help of expert friends and friendly experts in this country and abroad my debt is immeasurable, far greater indeed than many of them modestly suppose. I think in particular of Michel Gallet, Conservateur-adjoint du Musée Carnavalet, Paris; Adolf Placzek, Avery Librarian, Columbia University, New York; Phyllis Hemingway and her Scandinavian connections; Anil De Silva-Vigier, of UNESCO, and other members of that organization and its associated agency, ICOMOS; Karl Krämer and Jürgen Joedicke, of Stuttgart (for pointing the way to so many reliable information sources); Professor Peter Murray, Head of the Department of the History of Art, Birkbeck College, University of London (for a characteristically prompt and scholarly solution to an otherwise intractable problem); the staff of Finland House and of the Cultural Department of the Brazilian Embassy, London; members of the R.I.B.A. Professional Literature Committee; Cervin Robinson, New York (for aid beyond the call of professional duty); Constance Constable of the Architectural Press; the indefatigable Lionel Bell; Gabriel Harty and Inez Pugh and the production staff of the Athlone Press, to whom has fallen the exceedingly demanding task of preparing this massive work for publication. I would also like to thank Michael Ely, who drew the maps and the chart on p. 407, and Alfreda Wilkinson and Anthony Raven, who prepared the index.

With equal reason I am grateful to those who have drawn attention to mistakes of date or attribution in earlier editions. Wherever feasible, corrections have been made, but in a few instances, such is the inconstancy of architectural taste, there appeared no acceptable reason for mentioning the buildings in question in the current volume. The evidence, however, has been carefully noted, in the expectation that the pendulum of fashion will one day swing in the appropriate direction.

JAMES C. PALMES

CONTENTS

SOURCES OF ILLUSTRATIONS

The publishers wish to express their thanks to the great number of institutions, commercial firms and private persons who have supplied photographs for use in this book or who have given permission for copyright material to be used in the preparation of plans and drawings.

Where acknowledgment is made to published works mentioned in the bibliographies at the end of the chapters the numbers in parentheses refer to the pages of the *History of Architecture* where the full titles may be found.

ABBREVIATIONS   N.B.R.   National Buildings Record
                          N.M.R.   National Monuments Record
                          R.C.H.M. Royal Commission on Historical Monuments
                          R.I.B.A.   Royal Institute of British Architects

FRONTISPIECE

A. F. Kersting

EGYPTIAN ARCHITECTURE

15A, after Emery, 1939 (p. 46); 15B, after J. Garstang, *Mahasna and Bêt-Khallâf*, London 1902; 15C, after A. Badawy, *A History of Egyptian Architecture*, vol. i. Giza 1954; 15D, after (i) F. Benoit, *L'Architecture d'antiquité*, H. Laurens, Paris 1911, (ii) A. Rowe, *Museum Journal of the University of Philadelphia*, xxii, No. 1, Philadelphia 1931, (iii) A. Scharff, *Handbuch der Archäologie, Ägypten*, 1939; 15G, after Lange and Hirmer (p. 46); 15H, after L. Borchardt, *Die Entstehung der Pyramide an der Baugeschichte der Pyramide bei Mejdum nachgewiesen*, Berlin 1928; 15J, after Reisner (p. 46); 15K, L, after (i) D. Hölscher, *Das Grabdenkmal des Königs Chephren*, Leipzig 1912, (ii) A. Badawy (as 15C), (iii) Edwards (p. 46); 15N, after L. Borchardt, *Das Grabdenkmal des Königs Sahu-Ré*, Leipzig 1910–13, and Edwards (p. 46); 18, drawings and reconstructions by J. P. Lauer; 19, after E. Drioton, J. P. Lauer, C. M. Firth and J. E. Quibell (p. 46); 23F, in part after Edwards (p. 46); 24, from Lange and Hirmer (p. 46, Phaidon Press Ltd, 3rd ed. 1961, original German edition by Hirmer Verlag, Munich); 26A, Aerofilms Ltd; 26B, from G. Jéquier, *Les Temples memphites et thébains des origines à la XVIIIᵉ dynastie*, Éditions Albert Morancé, Paris 1920; 28A, after H. Ricke, *Beiträge zur Ägyptischen Bauforschung und Altertumskunde*, Cairo 1950, and Baedeker, *Egypt and the Sudan*, Allen and Unwin Ltd, London 1908; 28B, after A. M. Calverley, *The Temple of King Sethos I at Abydos*, ed. Sir Alan Gardiner, vol. i, 1933, by permission of the Egypt Exploration Society and the Oriental Institute, University of Chicago; 28C–F, after Baedeker, *Egypt and the Sudan*, Allen and Unwin Ltd, London 1908 and 1929 editions; 28G, after Lange and Hirmer (p. 46); 33A, Metropolitan Museum of Art, New York, bequest of Levi Hale Willard, 1883; 33B, Lehnert and Landrock, Cairo; 34A, from Lange and Hirmer (p. 46); 36B, Courtauld Institute of Art; 38A, Aerofilms Ltd; 38B, C, 39B, A. F. Kersting; 40A, Oriental Institute, University of Chicago; 40B, Lehnert and Landrock, Cairo; 42B, A. F. Kersting; 44, 45, from Emery, 1965 (p. 46, Hutchinson).

ARCHITECTURE IN THE ANCIENT NEAR EAST

54A, after (i) Parrot, 1946 (p. 85), (ii) Frankfort, 1954 (p. 84, Penguin Books), (iii) Noldeke *et al.*, *Vorläufiger Bericht über die Ausgrabungen in Uruk-Warka*, Berlin 1937; 54B, after Parrot, 1946 (p. 85) and Sir Leonard Woolley, *Ur Excavations V, The Ziggurat and its Surroundings*, London 1939; 54C, R. Ghirshman; 57A, B, Oriental Institute, University of Chicago, reconstructions (A) by Hamilton Darby and (B) by H. D. Hill; 60, 61, after Mallowan, 1966 (p. 85, Collins); 64C, after Loud (p. 85) by permission of the Oriental Institute, University of Chicago; 65F, after Luschan *et al.* (p. 85); 65G, after *Mitteilungen aus den Orientalischen Sammlungen, Heft XXV; Ausgrabungen in Sendschirli IV*, Königliches Museum, Berlin 1911; 66A, Vorderasiatisches Museum, Berlin, by permission of Generalverwaltung der Staatlichen Museen zu Berlin; 66B, from Mallowan (as 60); 66C, from Loud (p. 85) by permission of the Oriental Institute, University of Chicago; 69A, after Seton Lloyd, *Early Anatolia*, Pelican Books, Harmondsworth 1956, and Puchstein (p. 85); 69B, after Gurney and Puchstein (pp. 84, 85); 69C, Oriental Institute, University of Chicago; 69D, after K. Bittel, R. Naumann, H. Otto, *Yazilikaya*, Leipzig 1941; 69E, after K. Bittel, *Die Ruinen von Bogazköy*, Berlin 1937; 73A, from B. B. Piotrovskii, *Urartu: the Kingdom of Van and its art*, Adams and Dart, Bath 1967; 73B, from *Anatolian Studies X*; 75A, courtesy of Altan Cilingiroglu; 75B, C. Burney; 76A, from T. Özgüç, 'The Urartian Architecture on the Summit of Altintepe', *Anatolia VII*, 1963; 76B, from *Anatolian Studies XVI*; 76C, from E. Bilgiç and B. Oğun, 'Excavations at Kefkalesi, 1964', *Anatolia VIII*, 1964; 80C, after Schmidt (p. 85) by permission of the Oriental Institute, University of Chicago; 81A, B, Oriental Institute, University of Chicago; 81C, from Ghirsham, 1954 (p. 84).

ARCHITECTURE IN INDIA AND PAKISTAN

95B, Department of Archaeology, Government of India; 96B, A. F. Kersting; 96C, Department of Archaeology, Government of India; 99A, B, A. F. Kersting; 100A, B, Department of Archaeology, Government of India; 100D, A. F. Kersting; 103B, Victor Kennett; 104A, B, A. F. Kersting; 106C, Radio Times Hulton Picture Library.

ARCHITECTURE IN SRI LANKA

113A, Douglas Dickins; 113B, 114A, B, Archaeological Department, Government of Sri Lanka; 115A, Douglas Dickins; 115B, Archaeological Department, Government of Sri Lanka; 115C, Douglas Dickins; 115D, Archaeological Department, Government of Sri Lanka.

ARCHITECTURE IN AFGHANISTAN, NEPAL AND TIBET

121A, Unesco/photo A. Lézine; 121B, Unesco/photo Cart; 121C, D, 122A, Douglas Dickins; 122B, Unesco/photo Cart.

ARCHITECTURE IN BURMA, CAMBODIA, THAILAND AND INDONESIA

128A, C, from Hugo Munsterberg, *Art of India and Southeast Asia*, Harry N. Abrams, Inc., New York 1970, original German edition by Holle Verlag GmbH, Baden-Baden; 128B, Copyright R.I.B.A.; 134A, B, Unesco/photo C. Baugey; 135A, B, Douglas Dickins; 136A, B, Unesco/photo C. Baugey; 136C, D, Douglas Dickins; 136E, Unesco/photo D. Davies; 142A, from Hugo Munsterberg (as 128A, C); 142B, Unesco/photo D. Davies; 142C, Unesco/photo Cart.

ARCHITECTURE IN JAPAN

165A, Douglas Dickins; 165B, reproduced by permission of the publishers of *Chambers's Encyclopaedia*; 166A, B, Douglas Dickins; 166C, Ministry of Education and National Commission for the Protection of Cultural Properties, Japan.

ARCHITECTURE IN PRE-COLUMBIAN AMERICA

174A, Unesco/photo R. Garraud; 174B, Mexican Embassy; 174C, D, F, Douglas Dickins; 174E, Wayne Andrews; 178A, D, Victor Kennett; 178B, Grace Line Inc; 178C, L. Hervé; 178E, Courtauld Institute of Art.

GREEK ARCHITECTURE

187A, after Sir Arthur Evans, *Palace of Minos at Knossos*, Macmillan, London 1928; 187B, after Pendlebury (p. 255, Max Parrish, London); 188C, W. Taylor; 190A, B, after Dinsmoor (p. 255, Batsford) and Piet de Jong; 190C, after Lawrence (p. 255, Penguin Books, 1957 ed.); 197G, after Dinsmoor (as 190A); 199A, after Lawrence (as 190C); 199B, 200A, B, after Berve, Gruben and Hirmer (p. 255, Thames and Hudson) by permission of Hirmer Verlag München; 203, in part after Dinsmoor (p. 255, Batsford), and T. Wiegand, *Achter vorläufiger Bericht über die von den Staatlichen Museen in Milet und Didyma unternommenen Ausgrabungen*, Berlin 1924; 205F, after Dinsmoor (p. 255, Batsford); 211E, after A. Furtwängler *et al.*, *Aegina: das Heiligtum der Aphaia*, Bayerische Akademie der Wissenschaften, Munich 1906; 212A, N. Hiscock; 212B, after A. Furtwängler (as 211E); 214A, from Berve, Gruben and Hirmer (as 199B); 214B, Agora Excavations, American School of Classical Studies, Athens; 215, in part after Dinsmoor (p. 255, Batsford); 218A, B, Agora Excavations, American School of Classical Studies, Athens/photo Alison Frantz; 218C, W. Taylor; 220B, C, F, in part after Lawrence (as 190C) and F. Krischen, *Die Griechische Stadt*, Berlin 1938; 224A–C, 231F, after Dinsmoor (p. 255, Batsford) and W. J. Anderson and R. P. Spiers, *Architecture of Ancient Greece and Rome*, Batsford, London 1907; 232A, Agora Excavations, American School of Classical Studies, Athens/photo Alison Frantz; 232B, N. Hiscock; 233, A. F. Kersting; 234A, B, W. Taylor; 238N, after T. Wiegand (as 203); 244A, W. Taylor; 244B, from Martin (p. 255, Macdonald); 246A, from T. Wiegand *et al.*,

Milet: Die Ergebnisse der Ausgrabungen und Untersuchungen, Walter de Gruyter and Co., Berlin 1906; 247, from F. Krischen, *Antike Rathäuser,* Gebr. Mann Verlag, Berlin 1941; 248A, W. Taylor; 248B, Trustees of the British Museum; 248C, Agora Excavations, American School of Classical Studies, Athens; 253A, B, after T. Homolle *et al., Exploration archéologique de Délos,* Paris 1902, by permission of the Ecole française, Athens, and Editions Boccard, Paris.

ROMAN ARCHITECTURE

262A, from Boethius and Ward-Perkins (p. 343, Penguin Books), Istituto di Etruscologia e di Antichita Italiche, Rome University; 262B, Josephine Powell; 264A, Alinari; 264B, C, Alterocca, Terni; 273A, from Gatteschi, *Restauri della Roma Imperiale,* Rome 1924; 273B, after plan by H. C. Bradshaw from Anderson, Spiers and Ashby (p. 343, Batsford); 282A, Fototeca Unione, Rome; 282B, from D. S. Robertson (p. 344, Cambridge University Press), by permission of Staatsbibliothek Bildarchiv, Berlin; 284A, after Anderson, Spiers and Ashby (p. 343, Batsford); 285A, Fototeca Unione, Rome/drawing by Gatteschi; 285B, Alinari; 287A, Leonard von Matt; 289A, B, Fototeca Unione, Rome; 289C, D, Leonard von Matt; 292A, from G. Picard (p. 344, Office du Livre, Fribourg); 292B, Leonard von Matt; 292C, from Wheeler, 1964 (p. 344, Thames and Hudson), drawing by William Suddaby; 294A, C, from G. C. Boon, *Roman Silchester,* Max Parrish, London 1957; 294B, from Quennell (p. 344, Batsford); 297, Foto Marburg; 299, Fototeca Unione, Rome/engraving by Cecil C. Briggs; 300A, after Wheeler, 1964 (as 292C); 300B, Fototeca Unione, Rome; 304A, Alinari; 304B, from D'Espouy (p. 343); 305A, Alinari; 305B, Fototeca Unione, Rome; 306A, A. F. Kersting; 306B, Fototeca Unione, Rome; 310A–C, W. Taylor; 315A–C, Alinari; 316E–G, after S. R. Pierce, *Journal of Roman Studies,* xv (1925); 317A, after R. A. Cordingley and I. A. Richmond, *Journal of the British School at Rome,* x (1927); 317B, after S. R. Pierce (as 316E–G); 317C, Fototeca Unione, Rome; 317D, 321A, A. F. Kersting; 321B, 322A, Alinari; 322B, A. F. Kersting; 328A, Fototeca Unione, Rome/ drawing after G. Tognetti; 332C, E, after Robertson (p. 344, Cambridge University Press), T. Wiegand and H. Schrader, *Priene,* Berlin 1904; 334, from Boethius and Ward-Perkins (as 262A); 336A, after Wheeler, 1964 (as 292C), drawing by Martin Weaver; 336B, Fototeca Unione, Rome; 337A, Alinari; 337B, C, Fototeca Unione, Rome; 338A, model by Gismondi/ photo Alinari; 338B, from G. Calza, 'le origine latine dell' abitazione', *Architettura e Arti Decorative,* III (1923), model by Gismondi; 338C, after G. Calza, *Ostia,* n. 1, Guide-Books to the Museums and Monuments of Italy, Istituto Poligrafico dello Stato, Libreria dello Stato, Rome 1949; 340A, 342A, C, Alinari.

EARLY CHRISTIAN ARCHITECTURE

348B, 350A, B, Alinari; 355B, Foto Marburg; 357A, Fototeca Unione, Rome; 357B, Alinari; 359A, from H. Decker, *Venice,* Anton Schroll and Co., Vienna 1953: 359B, C, A. F. Kersting; 362A, Antonello Perissinotto; 362B, C, after Texier and Pullan (p. 402); 363A, Alinari; 363B, G. H. Forsyth, Kelsey Museum, University of Michigan/reproduced through the courtesy of the Michigan-Princeton-Alexandria Expedition to Mount Sinai; 365A, A. F. Kersting; 365B, from G. Last and R. Pankhurst, *A History of Ethiopia in Pictures,* O.U.P., Addis Ababa 1972; 365C, Alinari; 366B, from P. Verzone, *From Theodoric to Charlemagne,* Methuen, London 1968, by permission of Holle Bildarchiv, Baden-Baden.

BYZANTINE ARCHITECTURE

373, from D. Talbot Rice, *The Art of Byzantium,* Thames and Hudson, London 1959; 374, from Fossati (p. 402); 377A, D, F, after Texier and Pullan (p. 402); 377B, C, E, after O. Demus, *Byzantine Mosaic Decoration,* Kegan Paul, London 1947; 381D, F, after Jackson (p. 402, Cambridge University Press); 385A, from M. Hürlimann, *Istanbul,* Thames and Hudson, London 1958; 385B, A. F. Kersting; 385C, Mansell Collection; 385D, Josephine Powell; 387A, B, after George (p. 402, published by the O.U.P. for the Byzantine Research Fund); 388A, from M. Hürlimann (as 385A); 388B, Office of the Press Counsellor, Turkish Embassy, London; 390A–E, after Millingen, 1912 (p. 402, Macmillan); 392A, Alinari; 392B, from L. Price, *Interiors and Exteriors in Venice,* London 1843; 394A, Alinari; 394B, Testolini; 395B, Agora Excavations, American School of Classical Studies, Athens; 397A, Mansell Collection; 397B, National Tourist Organisation of Greece, London; 398A, Josephine Powell; 398B, A. F. Kersting; 398C–E, Foto Marburg; 398F, Courtauld Institute of Art; 400A Antonello Perissinotto; 400B, from D. R. Buxton, *Russian Mediaeval Architecture,* Cambridge 1934.

ISLAMIC ARCHITECTURE

417A, Middle East Archive, London; 417B, J. Warren; 417C, A. F. Kersting; 420A–C,

423A, J. Warren; 423B–D, 426A–C, 429A, B, A. F. Kersting; 429C, D, Foto Mas; 432A, D, Office of the Press Counsellor, Turkish Embassy, London; 432B, Thames and Hudson/photo Roger Wood, London; 432C, A. F. Kersting; 436A, B, Novosti Press Agency; 436C, from A. V. Pope, *A Survey of Persian Art*, O.U.P., 1938; 436D, Douglas Dickins; 436E, A. F. Kersting; 436F, Roger Wood, London; 440A–E, Office of the Press Counsellor, Turkish Embassy, London; 440F, J. Warren; 443A, C, A. F. Kersting; 443B, J. Warren; 447A, B, Douglas Dickins; 447C, J. Warren; 450A, C, 453A, B, A. F. Kersting; 453C, 454A, J. Warren; 454B, from F. Stark, *The Southern Gates of Arabia*, John Murray, London 1971.

ROMANESQUE ARCHITECTURE IN ITALY

471A–C, 472A–C, 474A, B, Alinari; 476A, Omniafoto, Turin; 476B, 477A, B, Alinari; 477C, J. B. Price; 478A–D, 481A, B, 482A, B, Alinari; 483A, B, Fototeca Unione, Rome; 484A–C, A. F. Kersting.

ROMANESQUE ARCHITECTURE IN FRANCE

493B, Foto Marburg; 493C, A. F. Kersting; 496B, Combier Imp. Mâcon; 498A, Archives photographiques, Paris; 498B, Courtauld Institute of Art/photo G. C. Druce; 501A, Foto Marburg; 502A, C, Combier Imp. Mâcon; 502D, Giraudon.

ROMANESQUE ARCHITECTURE IN CENTRAL EUROPE

504A, Foto Marburg; 509, from Conant (p. 460, Penguin Books, 1959 ed.); 513A–D, Foto Marburg; 514D, A. F. Kersting; 515A, Foto Marburg.

ROMANESQUE ARCHITECTURE IN SPAIN, PORTUGAL AND THE HOLY LAND

525A, after K. J. Conant, *The Early Architectural History of the Cathedral of Santiago de Compostela*, Harvard University Press, copyright 1926 by the President and Fellows of Harvard College/1954 by Kenneth J. Conant; 525B, D, E, after Bevan, 1938 (p. 544, Batsford); 525C, after Clapham (p. 460, O.U.P.); 526A, Foto Mas; 526B, A. F. Kersting; 531A, Foto Mas; 531B, Courtauld Institute of Art; 531C, 532A–C, 535A, Foto Mas; 535B, C, A. F. Kersting; 536A–D, Foto Mas; 537A, B, after Bevan, 1938 (as 525B); 540A, B, H. E. Stutchbury; 540C, 541A, B, A. F. Kersting; 541C, Institut Français d'Archéologie, Beirut; 542A, Aerofilms Ltd; 542B, C, A. F. Kersting.

ROMANESQUE ARCHITECTURE IN THE BRITISH ISLES AND SCANDINAVIA

552B, C, E–G, after Webb (p. 583, Penguin Books); 555A, Thomas H. Mason and Sons Ltd; 555B, photograph by J. R. H. Weaver; 564B, Crown copyright, reproduced by permission of the Department of the Environment; 564C, Crown copyright, N.M.R.; 564D, A. F. Kersting; 573A–E, Aerofilms Ltd; 573F, Crown copyright, N.M.R.; 574A, B, Aerofilms Ltd; 579A, Royal Norwegian Embassy, London; 579B, Swedish Tourist Traffic Association, Stockholm; 579C, D, Riksantikvaren; 580A, The Danish Tourist Board, London; 580B, Refot; 580C, Sören Hallgren; 581A, B, after Clapham (p. 460, O.U.P.); 581C, Riksantikvaren; 581D, after Paulsson (p. 583, Leonard Hill).

GOTHIC ARCHITECTURE IN FRANCE

595A, B, 597C, Foto Marburg; 598A, Roger-Viollet; 598B, A. F. Kersting; 598C, 599B, C, Foto Marburg; 602A, A. F. Kersting; 602B, Foto Mas; 602C, J. Austin; 602D, 603C, D, A. F. Kersting; 606B, Archives photographiques, Paris; 606C, Giraudon; 606D, A. F. Kersting; 608B, J. Austin; 610C, Aéro-photo; 611A, L. Hervé; 615A, Archives photographiques, Paris; 616B, Giraudon.

GOTHIC ARCHITECTURE IN THE BRITISH ISLES

630A, A. F. Kersting; 630B, Gordon Fraser Gallery/photo Edwin Smith; 630C, N.B.R./Weaver; 634A, A. F. Kersting; 634B, School of Architecture, University of Manchester/photo G. Sanville; 634C, Crown copyright, N.M.R.; 639A, Aerofilms Ltd; 639B, Crown copyright, R.C.H.M.; 639C, 646, 649, A. F. Kersting; 650A, Aerofilms Ltd; 650B, A. F. Kersting; 650C, Crown copyright, N.M.R.; 651A, B, A. F. Kersting; 651C, Crown copyright, N.M.R.; 652A, Aerofilms Ltd; 652B, C, 655, 656B, Crown copyright, N.M.R.; 657, Perfecta Publications/photo S. Newbery; 658B, A. F. Kersting; 659A, C, D, Crown copyright, N.M.R.; 659B, A. F. Kersting; 660A, Aerofilms Ltd; 660B, C, Crown copyright, N.M.R.; 664A, B, A. F. Kersting; 664C, Crown copyright, N.M.R.; 665A, A. F. Kersting; 665B, 666A, Crown copyright, N.M.R.; 666B, Perfecta Publications/photo S. Newbery; 669A, from Cox, 1937 (p. 582, Batsford); 669B, School of Architecture, University of Manchester/photo G. Sanville; 670A, B, Crown copyright, N.M.R.; 670C, 671A, A. F. Kersting; 671B, from Braun, 1970 (p. 704, Faber); 671C, D, Crown copyright, N.M.R.;

672A, N.M.R./copyright Rev. J. P. Sumner; 672B, School of Architecture, University of Manchester/photo G. Sanville; 672C, Crown copyright, R.C.H.M.; 675A, Crown copyright, N.M.R.; 675B, D, School of Architecture, University of Manchester/photo G. Sanville; 675C, Crown copyright, N.M.R.; 676A, B, 679A–E, Aerofilms Ltd; 680A, Crown copyright, reproduced by permission of H.M. Stationery Office/Alan Sorrell reconstruction drawing; 680B, Crown copyright, R.C.H.M.; 680C, Crown copyright, N.M.R.; 683H, after Garner and Stratton (p. 704, Batsford); 684A, *Country Life*; 684B, from J. Nash, *The Mansions of England in the Olden Time*, London 1839; 687A, B, N.B.R.; 687C, from J. Nash (as 684B); 688B, after Belcher and Macartney (p. 1070, Batsford); 689A, Crown copyright, R.C.H.M.; 689B, *Country Life*; 689C, A. F. Kersting; 690A, J. Allan Cash; 690B, Crown copyright, R.C.H.M.; 693A, N.B.R.; 693B, Crown copyright, R.C.H.M.; 693C, F. C. Morgan; 694A, B, 695A, B, Aerofilms Ltd; 696A, from D. Loggan, *Cantabrigia illustrata*, Cambridge 1690; 696B, Crown copyright, R.C.H.M.; 697A, Crown copyright, N.M.R.; 697B, N.M.R./copyright Batsford; 697C, Crown copyright, N.M.R.; 698A–C, Crown copyright, Ministry of Works; 701A, Crown copyright, reproduced by permission of the Department of the Environment; 701B, A. F. Kersting.

GOTHIC ARCHITECTURE IN THE NETHERLANDS

713A–C, Rijksdienst voor de Monumentenzorg; 714A, B, copyright A.C.L. Brussels.

GOTHIC ARCHITECTURE IN CENTRAL EUROPE

725A, C, D, 726B–D, 727A, B, Foto Marburg.

LATE MEDIAEVAL ARCHITECTURE IN ITALY

739A, A. F. Kersting; 739B, 740A, B, 741A–C, 742A–C, 749A, Alinari; 749B, A. F. Kersting; 749C, Alinari; 750A, B, A. F. Kersting; 750C, 752A, B, Alinari; 753A, A. F. Kersting; 753B, 754A, B, 755A–C, 756A–C, Alinari; 759A, A. F. Kersting; 759B, C, Alinari.

GOTHIC ARCHITECTURE IN SPAIN AND PORTUGAL

760A–C, 765A, A. F. Kersting; 765D, 766B, Foto Mas; 766C, Foto Marburg; 766D, 771A, A. F. Kersting; 771C, Foto Mas.

RENAISSANCE ARCHITECTURE IN ITALY

789A, from *Journal of the American Institute of Architects*, August 1917, American Academy in Rome/drawing by K. J. Conant; 789B, Phaidon Press Ltd; 790A, B, 794A–D, 805A, 806A–D, Alinari; 807A, A. F. Kersting; 807B–E, 811A–F, 812A, B, Alinari; 813, from *Architettura*, 7 (1961), 276–7; 814, from *Architettura*, 6 (1960), 851; 817A, Courtauld Institute of Art; 817B–D, 818A–F, 829A–C, 830A–F, 835A–C, 836A, B, Alinari; 841E, F, after P. M. Letarouilly, *The Vatican*, I, Alec Tiranti, London 1953; 843A, Alinari; 843B, Courtauld Institute of Art/Piranesi; 844A–D, Alinari; 844E, A. F. Kersting; 844F, 847A–D, Alinari; 848A, B, after Wittkower, 1966 (p. 869, Penguin Books); 848C, after Portoghesi, 1968 (p. 869, Thames and Hudson) by permission of Electa Editrice, Milan; 848D, after *Architettura*, 12 (1967), 752; 849A–C, 850A, B, Alinari; 850C, from *Architettura*, 12 (1967), 752; 856B, C, Alinari; 860A, E, G–J, after Haupt (p. 869, Batsford, vol. ii); 867A, B, 868A, B, Alinari.

RENAISSANCE ARCHITECTURE IN FRANCE

870A, Giraudon; 879G, after Ward, 1926 (p. 917, Batsford); 884A, Giraudon; 884B, after Ward, 1909 (p. 917, Batsford); 885A, Giraudon; 885C, Archives photographiques, Paris; 887A, B, A. F. Kersting; 888A, Archives photographiques, Paris; 893A, Giraudon; 893B, Foto Marburg; 893C, D, Archives photographiques, Paris; 894A, Roger-Viollet; 894B, Foto Marburg; 896A, Aero-photo; 896B, Foto Marburg; 899A, after Ward, 1926 (as 879G); 899B, after Blondel (p. 916); 900A, Foto Marburg; 900B, Giraudon; 900C, Archives photographiques, Paris; 901A, Foto Marburg; 901B, French Government Tourist Office, London; 902A, B, Foto Marburg; 902C, from T. Shotter Boys, *Picturesque Architecture in Paris and other Places*, London 1839; 903A, Archives photographiques, Paris; 903B, Chevojon/copyright by S.P.A.D.E.M., Paris; 903C, J. Austin; 904A, A. F. Kersting; 904B, *Country Life*; 909A, Archives photographiques, Paris; 910B, C, Foto Marburg; 911A, Giraudon; 911B, Foto Marburg; 912A, Giraudon; 912B, Foto Marburg; 912D, A. F. Kersting; 913B, Giraudon.

RENAISSANCE ARCHITECTURE IN GERMANY AND CENTRAL EUROPE

925A, Courtauld Institute of Art; 925B, 926A, B, Foto Marburg; 926C, A. F. Kersting; 926D–F, 927A–C, Foto Marburg; 928A, Deutsche Fotothek Dresden/photo Handrick; 928B, Foto Marburg; 928C, Deutsche Fotothek Dresden; 931A, Bundesdenkmalamt,

Vienna/photo Eva Frodl-Kraft; 931B, Foto Marburg; 932A, C. N. P. Powell; 932B, C, 933A, Foto Marburg; 933B, Bundesdenkmalamt, Vienna/photo Eva Frodl-Kraft; 934A–C, Foto Marburg; 934D, A. F. Kersting; 935A–D, 936A, Foto Marburg; 936B–D, A. F. Kersting.

RENAISSANCE ARCHITECTURE IN BELGIUM AND THE NETHERLANDS

944A, Press Bureau, Belgian Embassy, London; 944B, 947A–D, copyright A.C.L. Brussels; 947E, F, 948A, Rijksdienst voor de Monumentenzorg; 948B, copyright A.C.L. Brussels; 949A, B, Rijksdienst voor de Monumentenzorg; 950A, copyright A.C.L. Brussels; 950B, Rijksmuseum, Amsterdam/photo-Commissie; 950C, copyright A.C.L. Brussels; 950D, Rijksdienst voor de Monumentenzorg.

RENAISSANCE ARCHITECTURE IN SPAIN AND PORTUGAL

957A–C, 958A, C, 959A, B, 960A, B, Foto Mas; 962A, B, after Prentice (p. 972, Batsford); 964A, B, A. F. Kersting; 964C, Mario Novaes; 965A, B, 966A–C, 969A–D, Foto Mas; 970A, A. F. Kersting; 970B, C, Foto Mas; 970D, Alvão, Oporto.

RENAISSANCE ARCHITECTURE IN BRITAIN

989A, Crown copyright, R.C.H.M.; 989B–D, A. F. Kersting; 989E, 991A, Crown copyright, N.M.R.; 991B, A. F. Kersting; 992A, N.B.R.; 992B, A. F. Kersting; 993A, Crown copyright, reproduced from the Ministry of Works's *Official Guide Book to Kirby Hall*, 1955, by permission of the Controller of H.M. Stationery Office; 993B, *Country Life*; 993C, Crown copyright, R.C.H.M.; 994A, after J. A. Gotch, *Old Halls and Manor Houses of Northamptonshire*, Batsford, London 1936; 994B, C, after J. A. Gotch, *Early Renaissance Architecture in England*, Batsford, London 1914; 994E–J, after J. A. Gotch, *Architecture of the Renaissance in England*, Batsford, London, 1891–4; 998B, C, N.B.R.; 999A, A. F. Kersting; 999D, *Country Life*; 1000A, B, A. F. Kersting; 1000C, D, Crown copyright, R.C.H.M.; 1001B–D, 1002D, after J. A. Gotch (as 994E–J); 1006A, National Maritime Museum; 1006B, A. F. Kersting; 1007A, Crown copyright, reproduced by permission of the Controller of H.M. Stationery Office; 1007B, A. F. Kersting; 1008B, D, E, 1009E, F, after Belcher and Macartney (p. 1070, Batsford); 1011A, E, N.B.R.; 1011B, C, *Country Life*; 1011D, Crown copyright, R.C.H.M.; 1012A, B, *Country Life*; 1012C, N.B.R.; 1015A, Crown copyright, N.M.R.; 1015B, A. F. Kersting; 1015C, Crown copyright, R.C.H.M.; 1015D, A. F. Kersting; 1019A, B, Crown copyright, N.M.R.; 1020A, Crown copyright, R.C.H.M.; 1020B, Crown copyright, N.M.R.; 1020C, D, A. F. Kersting; 1024D, after G. H. Birch, *London Churches of the XVIIth and XVIIIth Centuries*, London 1896; 1027A–D, H, after Belcher and Macartney (as 1008B, D, E); 1028A, A. F. Kersting; 1028B, *Country Life*; 1028C, Crown copyright, R.C.H.M.; 1029A, B, A. F. Kersting; 1029C, Crown copyright, R.C.H.M.; 1030A, A. F. Kersting; 1030B, Crown copyright, N.M.R.; 1030C, N.B.R. and the Wren Society; 1031F, 1033A, C–E, after Belcher and Macartney (as 1008B, D, E); 1034A, A. F. Kersting; 1034B, Crown copyright, R.C.H.M.; 1034C, Crown copyright, N.M.R.; 1039A, A. F. Kersting; 1039B, Crown copyright, N.M.R.; 1040A, N.B.R., 1040B, *Country Life*; 1041A, A. F. Kersting; 1041B, J. B. Price; 1041C, N.M.R., by permission of Lady Cholmondeley; 1045A, B, *Country Life*; 1046A, A. F. Kersting; 1046B, *Country Life*; 1046C, D, N.B.R.; 1047A, from Neale, *Views of the Seats of Noblemen and Gentlemen*, 2nd series, vol. i, London 1824/N.B.R.; 1047B, *Country Life*; 1048A, Aerofilms Ltd; 1048B, from N. Nicolson, *Great Houses of Europe*, Weidenfeld, London 1961, by permission of the Trustees of the Newdegate Settlement; 1048C, *Country Life*; 1049A, N.B.R.; 1049B–D, A. F. Kersting; 1051A–E, after Belcher and Macartney (as 1008B, D, E); 1057A, B, D, A. F. Kersting; 1058A, Birmingham Post and Mail Ltd; 1058B, D, A. F. Kersting; 1058C, Crown copyright, N.M.R.; 1059A, *Country Life*; 1059B, N.B.R./photo Gerald Cobb; 1059C, 1060A–C, A. F. Kersting; 1060D, 1063A, N.B.R.; 1063B, E, Judges Ltd, Hastings; 1063C, 1064A, B, A. F. Kersting; 1064C, Raphael Tuck and Sons Ltd; 1064D, The Trustees of Sir John Soane's Museum; 1065A, C, A. F. Kersting; 1065B, N.B.R.; 1066A, A. F. Kersting; 1066B, Crown copyright, N.M.R.; 1066C, from A. E. Richardson, *Monumental Classic Architecture in Great Britain*, Batsford, London 1914; 1067A, A. F. Kersting; 1067B, Radio Times Hulton Picture Library; 1068B, A. F. Kersting; 1068D, British Museum.

RENAISSANCE ARCHITECTURE IN SCANDINAVIA

1077A, T. H. B. Burrough; 1077B, D, Refot; 1077C, Stockholms Stadsmuseum; 1078A, Nationalhistoriske Museum, Frederiksborg; 1078B, Royal Danish Embassy, London; 1083A, B, 1084A, Refot; 1084B, C, 1085A–D, Ronald Sheridan; 1086A, Refot; 1086B–E, Nationalmuseet, Copenhagen; 1089A, Ronald Sheridan; 1089B, C, Nationalmuseet, Copenhagen; 1090A, D, Norsk Folkemuseum, Oslo; 1090B, Eric de Maré; 1090C, E, F, Riksantik-varen; 1091A, B, 1092A, B, Finnish Embassy, London; 1092C, A. F. Kersting.

RENAISSANCE ARCHITECTURE IN RUSSIA

1099A, B. Cox; 1099B, C, Novosti Press Agency; 1100A, B. Cox; 1100B, C, Novosti Press Agency; 1100D, E, B. Cox.

RENAISSANCE AND POST-RENAISSANCE ARCHITECTURE OUTSIDE EUROPE

1105A–E, Wayne Andrews; 1106A, from Kelemen (p. 1118, Macmillan, New York); 1106B, G. E. Kidder Smith; 1106C, Sawders from Cushing; 1106D–F, from T. E. Sanford, *The Story of Architecture in Mexico*, W. W. Norton, New York 1947; 1109A, B, Brazilian Embassy, London; 1109C, E, F, Wayne Andrews; 1109D, Library of Congress; 1110A, Colonial Williamsburg photograph; 1110B, City of Philadelphia; 1110C, Wayne Andrews; 1115A–C, India Office, London; 1116A, The Michaelis Collection/photo Arthur English; 1116B, Australian Information Service, London/photo J. Fitzpatrick.

ARCHITECTURE IN BRITAIN 1830–1914

1121A, B, from E. R. Robson, *School Architecture*, 1877; 1122A, from *Transactions*, vol. xxx, 1955–7, by permission of The Newcomen Society; 1122B–D, 1135A–C, A. F. Kersting; 1136A, N.B.R.; 1136B, D, A. F. Kersting; 1136C, from *Survey of London*, vol. xxx, Athlone Press 1960, by permission of London County Council; 1136E, after *Civil Engineer and Architect's Journal*, Dec. 1840; 1139A, B, A. F. Kersting; 1139C, after Barry (p. 1182); 1140A, N.B.R.; 1140B, A. F. Kersting; 1140C, after A. W. Pugin, *The Present State of Ecclesiastical Architecture in England*, 1843; 1142A, B, N.B.R.; 1142C, *Country Life*; 1142D, from W. H. Pyne, *The History of the Royal Residences*, vol. iii, London 1819; 1142E, *Country Life*; 1142F, J. Austin; 1143A, *Country Life*; 1143B, Sir John Summerson; 1143C, by permission of the British Transport Commission; 1144A, N.B.R.; 1144B, Fox Photos Ltd; 1147B, Manchester Central Library; 1147C, Leeds Metropolitan District Council; 1147D, A. F. Kersting; 1147E, T. and R. Annan; 1147F, Crown copyright, Victoria and Albert Museum; 1148A, A. F. Kersting; 1148C, R. A. Cordingley; 1149A, N.B.R.; 1149C, from Eastlake (p. 1182); 1150A, from Pevsner (p. 1183, Penguin Books); 1150B, Crown copyright, N.M.R.; 1150C, after M. H. and C. H. B. Quennell, *A History of Everyday Things in England*, Batsford, London 1934; 1153A, Elsam, Mann and Cooper; 1153C, N.B.R.; 1154A, B, A. F. Kersting; 1154C, D, *Country Life*; 1155A, C, A. F. Kersting; 1155B, T. and R. Annan; 1155D, N.B.R.; 1155E, Eric de Maré; 1156A, A. F. Kersting; 1156B, R.I.B.A. Drawings Collection; 1159A, E, *Country Life*; 1159B, R.I.B.A. Drawings Collection; 1159C, A. F. Kersting; 1159D, N.B.R.; 1160A, A. F. Kersting; 1160B, R.I.B.A. Drawings Collection; 1162A, A. F. Kersting; 1162B, N.B.R.; 1162D, *Country Life*; 1163A, Robert Roskrow Photography; 1163B, Crown copyright, N.M.R.; 1163C, Edwin Smith; 1164B, N.B.R.; 1164C, Elsam, Mann and Cooper; 1164D, A. F. Kersting; 1167A, after Girouard (p. 1182, O.U.P.); 1167B, after Hitchcock, 1970 (p. 1183, Penguin Books); 1167C, after Sir Lawrence Weaver, *Small Country Houses of Today*, vol. 1, London 1910; 1167D, after H. Muthesius (p. 1183, 1908 ed.); 1168A, from *The British Architect*, vol. 30, 1888; 1168B, *Country Life*; 1169A, N.B.R.; 1169B, J. Archer; 1169C, D, from Howarth (p. 1183, Routledge); 1169E, R.I.B.A. Library, by permission of C. Cowles-Voysey; 1169F, Birmingham Post and Mail Ltd; 1170A–C, T. and R. Annan; 1170D, from H. Muthesius, *die Englische Baukunst der Gegenwart*, Leipzig and Berlin 1900; 1173, School of Architecture, University of Manchester; 1174A, B, Eric de Maré; 1174C, Rupert Roddam; 1174D, David Wrightson; 1175A, B, *Country Life*; 1176B, Sellers Collection, by courtesy of Norman H. Sellers; 1176C, Manchester Central Library; 1179A, J. Archer/photo G. Wheeler; 1179B, Kodak Ltd; 1179C, P. A.-Reuter Photos Ltd; 1179D, *Country Life*; 1179F, London Transport; 1180A, Crown copyright, N.M.R.; 1180C, *Architectural Review*/photo Dell and Wainwright; 1181A, from *Survey of London*, vol. xxx, Athlone Press 1960, by permission of the Archives Department, Westminster City Library; 1181B, R.I.B.A. Press Office/photo Kenneth Prater; 1181C, D, N.M.R./copyright *The Architect*.

ARCHITECTURE IN AUSTRALIA AND NEW ZEALAND 1830–1914

1184A–C, Australian Information Service, London.

ARCHITECTURE IN CONTINENTAL EUROPE 1830–1914

1195A, J. Allan Cash; 1195B, Roger-Viollet; 1195C, Deutsche Fotothek Dresden; 1195D, Periklis Papahatzidakis, Athens; 1196A, from *Builder*, vol. xv, 1858; 1196B, from K. F. Schinkel, *Sammlung architektonischer Entwurfe*, Berlin 1819; 1196C, from J. J. Sweeney and J. L. Sert, *Antoni Gaudi*, Architectural Press 1960; 1197A, Austrian Embassy, London/

photo Bildarchiv d. Öst. Nationalbibliothek; 1197B, A. F. Kersting; 1198A, Roger-Viollet; 1198B–D, Foto Mas; 1198E, from Pevsner, 1960 (p. 1223, Penguin Books); 1198F, Austrian Embassy, London; 1201A, Staatliche Landesbildstelle Hamburg; 1201B, Chevojon/copyright by S.P.A.D.E.M., Paris; 1201C, Austrian Embassy, London; 1201D, from P. Lavedan, *Architecture française*, Larousse, Paris 1944; 1202A, Archives photographiques, Paris; 1202B, Chevojon/copyright by S.P.A.D.E.M., Paris; 1203A, Foto Mas; 1203B, C, Swedish Tourist Traffic Association/photos Heurlin; 1203D, Strüwing; 1204A, B, Foto Marburg; 1207A, Thorvaldsens Museum, Copenhagen; 1207B, A. F. Kersting; 1208A, Bulloz; 1208B, from J. Guadet, *Eléments et Théorie de l'Architecture*, Paris 1901-4; 1209A, Chevojon/copyright by S.P.A.D.E.M., Paris; 1209B, C, from Giedion (p. 1223, Harvard 1954); 1210A, Bulloz; 1210B, C, Chevojon/copyright by S.P.A.D.E.M., Paris; 1211, from J. Guadet (as 1208B); 1213A, copyright A.C.L. Brussels; 1213B, Rheinisches Bildarchiv, Cologne; 1214A, Netherlands Government Information Service/aero-photo Nederland; 1214B, J. Allan Cash; 1215A, A. F. Kersting; 1215B, Alinari; 1215C, Bulloz; 1216A, Netherlands Government Information Service/photo E. M. van Ojen; 1216B, Kunstgewerbemuseum, Zurich; 1217A, Swedish Tourish Traffic Association/photo Wigfusson; 1217B, Swedish Tourist Traffic Association/photo Crispien; 1218A, Foto Marburg; 1218B, Alinari; 1218C, Netherlands Government Information Service; 1218D, E, Archives photographiques, Paris; 1218F, copyright A.C.L. Brussels; 1221A, B, Archives photographiques, Paris; 1222A, Alinari; 1222B–E, Chevojon/copyright by S.P.A.D.E.M., Paris; 1222F, Bildarchiv Stadt Stuttgart/photo Ludwig Windstosser.

ARCHITECTURE OF THE AMERICAS 1790–1914

1224A, Museum of Modern Art, New York; 1224B, Charles Phelps Cushing; 1224C, Wayne Andrews; 1224D, Empire State Building Corporation; 1229A, photo by Abbie Rowe, courtesy National Park Service; 1229B, 1230A–D, Wayne Andrews; 1230E, Chicago Architectural Photo Co.; 1233A, Wayne Andrews; 1233B, Philip Turner for the Historic American Buildings Survey; 1234A, B, Wayne Andrews; 1237A, B, Brown Brothers; 1237C, The J. Clarence Davies Collection, Museum of the City of New York; 1237D, courtesy Supreme Council 33°, Southern Jurisdiction, Washington, D.C.; 1237E, Wayne Andrews; 1238A, Public Archives of Canada; 1238B, C, City of Philadelphia; 1238D, U.S. Department of the Interior; 1238E, F, Chicago Architectural Photo Co.; 1241A, D, Wayne Andrews; 1241B, C, E, Chicago Architectural Photo Co.; 1241F, Hedrich-Blessing; 1242A, from Kimball (p. 1244); 1242B, from A. Bush-Brown, *Louis Sullivan*, George Braziller, Inc., New York, 1960.

INTERNATIONAL ARCHITECTURE SINCE 1914

1251A, Chevojon/copyright by S.P.A.D.E.M., Paris; 1251B, copyright A.C.L. Brussels; 1251C, from H. Kulka, *Adolf Loos*, Anton Schroll and Co., Vienna 1931; 1251D, Koninklijke Maatschappij tot Bevordering der Bouwkunst Bond van Nederlandsche Architecten, B.N.A.; 1251E, Netherlands Government Information Service/photo E. M. van Ojen; 1253A, B, L. Hervé; 1254A–C, 1256A, B, Chevojon/copyright by S.P.A.D.E.M., Paris; 1256C, Bernhard Moosbrugger; 1257A, L. Hervé; 1257B, Chevojon/copyright by S.P.A.D.E.M., Paris; 1257C, Josef Josuweck; 1259A, The Architectural Association/ F. R. Yerbury; 1259B, Dyckerhoff and Widmann; 1260A, Swedish Tourist Traffic Association/photo Pöppel; 1260B, Dyckerhoff and Widmann; 1260C, Finnish Embassy, London/ photo G. Welin; 1261A, C, The Architects Collaborative, Inc.; 1261B, R. D. L. Felton; 1261D, Netherlands Government Information Service/photo Rousel; 1262A, G. E. Kidder-Smith; 1262B, C, Chevojon/copyright by S.P.A.D.E.M., Paris; 1263A, Pier Luigi Nervi/photo Oscar Savio, Rome; 1263B, Unesco/photo Barretty; 1263C, L. Hervé; 1265A, from Pevsner (p. 1309, Penguin Books); 1265B, Fagus-Werk Karl Benscheidt Verkaufs-GmbH; 1267A, Swiss National Tourist Office/photo Mischol; 1267B, Junkers-Luftbild; 1268A, Chevojon/copyright by S.P.A.D.E.M., Paris; 1268B, Netherlands Government Information Service/photo E. M. van Ojen; 1268C, Stockholms Stadsmuseum; 1269A, R. D. L. Felton; 1269B, Pier Luigi Nervi/Foto Vasari, Rome; 1269C, Omniafoto, Turin; 1270A, B, Strüwing; 1270C, Pier Luigi Nervi/photo Moisio, Turin; 1270D, Radio Times Hulton Picture Library; 1272A, B, Hedrich-Blessing; 1274A, B, 1275A, B, Wayne Andrews; 1275C, Black Star/Armin Haab; 1276A, from F. Gutheim, *One Hundred Years of Architecture in America*, Reinhold Publishing Corporation, New York 1957/photo Moulin Studios; 1276B, Thomas Airviews; 1276C, Wayne Andrews; 1276D, courtesy of Johnson's Wax; 1276E, Black Star/Carl Frank; 1276F, Ezra Stoller; 1278A, B, Wayne Andrews; 1278C, Cervin Robinson; 1280A, from Howarth (p. 1309, Routledge); 1280B, F, *Architectural Review*/photos Dell and Wainwright; 1280C, Denys Lasdun; 1280D, Basil Ward; 1280E, Aerofilms Ltd; 1282A, Fry, Drew and Partners/copyright *Architectural Review*/photo Dell

I

EGYPTIAN ARCHITECTURE

Circa 3200 B.C.–A.D. first century

INFLUENCES

GEOGRAPHICAL

Egypt, the land of the Pharaohs, consists of a narrow strip of fertile, alluvial soil along both banks of the Nile, flanked by shelves of barren land and rugged cliffs, beyond which lie arid, desert plateaux. In its lower or northern part, the river divides to form a great delta of sluggish outlets to the Mediterranean Sea, while to the east, and roughly parallel with its course, extends the Red Sea. Egypt was the only country of the ancient world which, by means of these two seas, commanded outlets and inlets for both western and eastern foreign trade. The Nile itself was of untold value, not only as a trade route and unfailing means of communication but also because its overflowing and fertilizing waters made desert sands into fruitful fields. On its banks therefore, from time immemorial, the Egyptians sited their villages, cities and cemeteries.

GEOLOGICAL

The natural products, such as timber, brick, clay and stone, largely determine the character of the architecture of a country. Stone is abundant in Egypt in quantity and variety, and was used not only for buildings and their embellishment, but also for vases, and even for personal ornaments, as the country was poor in metals, apart from copper, gained chiefly from the Sinai Peninsula. Tin was at length imported for the making of bronze. Iron, extremely rare, was of meteoric origin, and not mined. For building, the chief kinds of stone were limestone, sandstone and some alabaster; among the harder stones, granite, quartzite and basalt. Porphyry was little used before Roman times. Foremost in use in the earlier periods was a fine limestone from famous quarries at Tura and Ma'sara in the Mokattam Hills, a few miles south of modern Cairo, but as this was unsuitable for long beams it was supplemented by the red or grey granite (syenite) found at Aswân, much farther south. The limestone rocks extend up-river from the Mokattam Hills as far as Edfu, and there are other ancient quarries along the river valley. Beyond Edfu the formation changes, and at Silsila was quarried much of the sandstone of which Ancient Egypt's finest temples were built. It is partly owing to the durable nature of these building materials that so many monuments still exist. The gigantic scale which distinguishes Egyptian architecture was made possible not only by the materials, but also by the methods of quarrying, transporting and raising enormous blocks of stone into position. Quarrying was done with copper tools and by the use of timber wedges which, when swollen by water, split the blocks away from the natural rock. Massive blocks of the harder stones were often obtained by laboriously pounding trenches around them with balls of dolerite, a very tough, greenish stone. Dolerite also was used for dressing the hard stones. Drilling and sawing were known from early times. Palaces, houses and most buildings other than tombs or temples were constructed of large, sun-dried bricks, which when protected against the weather on the external face were strong and lasting: burnt bricks were very rare before the coming of the Romans. There was very little building timber, but acacia served for boats and sycamore for mummy cases; while the indigenous date palm, whose fruit is a staple food of the people, was sometimes used, in logs, for roofing. Cedar and other woods were imported. Palm leaves, reeds and rushes and similar light materials, used to frame or reinforce mud-brick constructions, or as mats for such as panels, partitions and fences, had a great and permanent influence on the form and character of stone architecture.

CLIMATIC

Egypt has been said to have but two seasons, spring and summer. The climate is equable and warm; snow and frost are unknown, while, except in the Delta, storm and even rain are rare, and these conditions have contributed to the preservation of buildings. Such a climate, with its brilliant sunshine, conduced also to simplicity of design; for as sufficient light reached the interior of temples through doors and roof slits, there was no real need for windows, and thus unbroken massive walls not only protected the interior from the fierce heat of the sun, but also provided an uninterrupted surface for hieroglyphics or pictorial representations of religious ritual, historic events and daily pursuits. During the inundation (July to October) the ground could not be tilled, so the vast population was available for building work. Roof drainage was not an important consideration, and flat roofs of stone slabs sufficed to cover the buildings, and exclude the heat.

HISTORICAL AND SOCIAL

The Egyptian civilization is among the most ancient of which we have any clear knowledge. Our information is derived from ancient literary sources, from records on papyri and tablets, but more particularly from Egyptian buildings and their inscriptions. It was the custom to record matters of history on temples, and of domestic and social interest on tombs and stelae.

Social and industrial conditions in Egypt were largely determined by the inflexible rule of an omnipotent government, which while employing large staffs of trained craftsmen continuously, levied vast armies of labourers for the erection of monumental buildings when the annual inundations made agriculture impossible. Prisoners of war were also turned on to the same work, and during the reign of Rameses II there were so many captives and foreigners in the country employed in public works that, as recorded in Exodus (i. 9–11), the natives viewed with alarm the growing power of these strangers in their midst. The Biblical account of the captivity of the Children of Israel in Egypt (perhaps c. 1360–1230 B.C.) throws a vivid light on the system of labour, on the tyranny of overseers, on the tasks imposed, and on the social conditions of the labourers employed by the Pharaohs to build these enduring monuments of Old Egypt. Social life is also graphically depicted in wall-sculptures of tombs, such as that of Thi (p. 15F), a court official, which portray the Egyptians at war, at play, at the chase, on the farm and in the weaving shed and workshop, as well as at business. Craftsmanship was very highly developed, particularly in the royal workshops, and the Egyptians attained great skill in weaving, glass-blowing, pottery-turning, metal-working, and in making musical instruments, jewellery and furniture. The pursuit of learning, astronomy, mathematics and philosophy was continuously carried on, especially by the priests, and much Egyptian literature has been preserved on papyri made from the pith of the once-abundant papyrus plant.

The kings of Ancient Egypt are known as Pharaohs, a name given to them by the

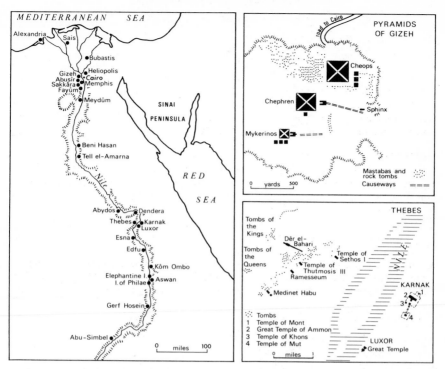

Ancient Egypt: the Great Pyramids: Thebes

Hebrews and derived from the Egyptian Per-aa, the 'Great House'. The Pharaohs, like the Colossi of Memnon, are silhouetted against the mysterious desert background; sometimes they appear as gods and demi-gods, often as mystery priests, generally as builders, but rarely as fathers of their people. A study of the social system in Ancient Egypt conjures up a forbidding picture of an almighty Pharaoh, with his court, officials and priesthood at one end of the scale and the strenuously-toiling peasantry at the other. Of this system the royal pyramids and the frowning temples are the outward and material testimony to this day.

The Pharaohs have been divided into thirty dynasties by Manetho, an Egyptian priest who, about 300 B.C., compiled a history of Egypt in Greek. These dynasties are here, for convenience, grouped into three divisions, with dates which are quite approximate up to 1580 B.C., but progressively more firm thereafter. As is plain from the remains which archaeologists have uncovered, the Egyptian civilization was already well advanced when the first dynasty was inaugurated by Menes, who united Upper and Lower Egypt in a single kingdom.

1. *Ancient Kingdom* (Dynasties I–X), 3200–2130 B.C., nowadays commonly subdivided as follows: the *Archaic period* (Dynasties I–II); the *Old Kingdom* (Dynasties III–VI); the *First Intermediate period* (Dynasties VII–X). Menes, the first dynastic king, is reputed to have founded Memphis, at the southern extremity of Lower Egypt, where it could command Upper Egypt too. Memphis was the capital throughout the great pyramid-building age, extending from the Third to the Sixth Dynasty; but from the dark period of anarchy which then ensued, in which the arts

came to be so despised that, for a time, earlier masterpieces were defaced and monuments pillaged and even destroyed, it was Thebes that emerged, in the Eleventh Dynasty, as the chief city. During the First and Second Dynasties, civilization progressed; the art of writing and the hieroglyphic system already were being developed. The tombs of the kings and nobles were of the 'mastaba' type, rectangular, with flat tops, and these, like the houses, were built of sun-dried bricks. In the Third Dynasty the royal mastaba evolved towards the true pyramid, as is shown by the 'Step' Pyramid of the Pharaoh Zoser at Sakkâra. This was of stone, as were also by this time many of the mastabas, which were to continue as the customary form of tomb for the less great personages. But it was in the Fourth Dynasty that, after further experiments at Meydûm and Dahshûr, the royal pyramid became fully evolved, and the culmination of achievement is represented by the famous three at Gizeh; the Great Pyramid, built by the Pharaoh Cheops; the Second, by Chephren; and the Third, by Mykerinos. Many other pyramids followed, chiefly at Abusîr and Sakkâra in the Fifth Dynasty, among which that of Sahura at the first place and that of Unas at the second are to be remarked. Sakkâra was again the favoured location for the pyramids of Sixth Dynasty kings, but in the latter part of the period pyramids give evidence of a decline, heralding the political and social upheavals of the Seventh and later Dynasties.

2. *Middle Kingdom* (Dynasties XI–XVII), 2130–1580 B.C., often divided into the *Middle Kingdom* (Dynasties XI–XII) and the *Second Intermediate period* (Dynasties XIII–XVII). The Eleventh Dynasty saw a progressive recovery of political stability and of mastery of the arts. Under Mentuhetep II the country was unified again. He built an elaborate, terraced mortuary temple at Dêr el-Bahari, in which was combined a small, completely solid pyramid, raised on a high base, with a rock-cut tomb driven deep into the base of the sheer cliffs behind. Thereafter pyramids usually were of crude brick, faced with stone; and in the New Kingdom period royal tombs were without exception rock-cut, secreted in the Theban hills, their funerary temples being completely detached and standing on the rocky shelf westward of the cultivated land. Amenemhat I of the Twelfth Dynasty was energetic and enterprising. He consolidated the administrative system, made a survey of the country, set boundaries to the provinces, carried out irrigation, re-opened the quarries at Tura, restored the temples and founded the great temple at Karnak. There were other kings, three more of the same name and three Senusrets, who fostered commerce and built temples and pyramids; the latter still grand in dimensions but inferior in construction to the stone-cored pyramids of the III–VI Dynasties. Senusret I erected at Heliopolis the earliest-known instance of a large obelisk. Amenemhat III, a man of many parts, fostered art and industry, irrigated the Fayûm, and probably built there the Labyrinth described by Herodotus. To the Eleventh and Twelfth Dynasties belongs a series of open-fronted tombs at Beni Hasan. Then followed five Dynasties of such confusion that even the succession of kings is uncertain. As a consequence of a great movement of peoples taking place in nearer Asia at this time, nomad tribes swept through Syria and Palestine and overran the Delta, and their leaders became the Hyksos or Shepherd Kings who, though they adopted the Egyptian language and religion, were so hated by the peoples that there was no rest in the land until the usurpers were finally driven out at the beginning of the Eighteenth Dynasty. It was the Hyksos peoples who introduced the horse and chariot to Egypt.

3. *New Kingdom* (Dynasties XVIII–XXX), 1580–332 B.C. In the two earlier Dynasties of this period, Egypt was glorious alike in the arts of peace and war. Her fortunes were varied thereafter, but never again reached the same peak. Amasis I, founder of the epoch, completed the expulsion of the Hyksos from the Delta and

pursued them into Palestine, thus inaugurating Egypt's dominion over her Near-Eastern neighbours. Thebes was the capital, and many buildings were erected. Thothmes I (1530 B.C.) began those additions to the Temple of Ammon, Karnak, by which successive Pharaohs made it the most imposing building in Egypt, and he was the first Pharaoh to be buried in the rock-cut 'corridor' Tombs of the Kings in the Theban mountains. Egypt prospered under the firm rule of kings who had now overcome the power of petty rulers at home. A remarkable figure was Queen Hatshepsut, who patronized the arts of peace, re-established religious rites, and built below the mountain-side her fascinating terraced funerary temple at Dêr el-Bahari. Thothmes III was one of the greatest of the Pharaohs and is renowned alike for foreign wars and home reforms, while he rebuilt and decorated many temples. Amenophis III built the greater part of the temple at Luxor, dignified that at Karnak by pylons and sphinxes, and erected the renowned Colossi of Memnon. Amenophis IV, who in the fourth year of his reign changed his name to Akhnaten, daringly broke away from dynastic and religious traditions, deserted Thebes and founded his capital at Tell el-Amarna, laid out on formal lines and with a great palace and a temple to the sole god Aten, whose symbol was the 'solar disc'. A heretic Pharaoh is a striking anomaly in a country bound by such strong chains to tradition and orthodoxy. The Tomb of Tutankhamen, who was shortly to follow, was discovered in A.D. 1922. Rameses I (1314 B.C.), the founder of the Nineteenth Dynasty, began the great Hypostyle Hall at Karnak. Seti I continued his father's work at Karnak, restored many shattered monuments, built his great Temple at Abydos and his own sepulchre among the Tombs of the Kings. Rameses II (1301 B.C.), called by early Egyptologists 'the Great', is known now to have been given to usurping the achievements of his predecessors; yet undoubtedly he finished and erected many temples, such as the Rock Temples at Abu-Simbel, the Hypostyle Hall at Karnak and the Ramesseum at Thebes, but craftsmanship had begun to deteriorate in this and following reigns. Apart from the first, all the kings of the Twentieth Dynasty (1200–1085 B.C.) were named Rameses; their power waned as that of the priests of Ammon increased. It is significant of the times that, while the temples of the gods were still respected, the tombs of the kings were desecrated. Mediocrity marks the following dynasties, until, with the Twenty-sixth (663–525 B.C.) a period of good government and trade prosperity ensued. Psammetichus I, the first king, completed the rout of the invading Assyrians, and encouraged the immigration of Greeks, who brought in new ideas. Egypt again extended her Mediterranean trade, developed the arts and crafts of bronze-casting, pottery and portrait-painting, and attained a high standard in commercial and legal procedure. Necho (609 B.C.) attempted a canal between the Red Sea and the Nile, but the undertaking was only completed by Darius (522–486 B.C.). From 525 B.C. Egypt was a Persian province for about a hundred years.

4. *The Ptolemaic Period* (332–30 B.C.). Alexander the Great rescued the Egyptians from the Persians and founded Alexandria as the capital, which became the centre of Greek culture. On his death in 323 B.C., Egypt fell to his general Ptolemy, and for three centuries the lower valley of the Nile was the seat of a prosperous and powerful kingdom. Greek customs and methods of government crept in, but the Ptolemies upheld the gods, built temples of the native type and patronized native art. The reign of Ptolemy II is famous for the Pharos, or light-house, the history by Manetho, and the production of the Septuagint. Ptolemy III founded the Great Serapeum of Alexandria, which, after being re-built in the Roman period, was among the most magnificent buildings of the ancient world. Ptolemy V was so great a benefactor of the temples that the priests accorded honours to him and his ancestors in a threefold inscription in hieroglyphic, demotic and Greek writing on

the Rosetta stone, dug up in A.D. 1798 and now in the British Museum, which has provided a valuable key to the hieroglyphic records of Egyptian history. Struggles with Rome were continuous, and on the death of Cleopatra Egypt became a Roman province.

5. *The Roman Period* (30 B.C.–A.D.395). Egypt under Caesar entered on another phase of prosperity. From this period dates the famous 'Pharaoh's Bed' at Philae. Under Constantine, Roman control in Egypt extended even to religion, when in A.D. 324 Christianity was declared to be the recognized religion of the State and the Bible was translated into Coptic. When Theodosius the Great issued his edict in A.D. 381, decreeing that the whole of the Roman Empire should be Christian, many temples were either diverted to Christian use or churches were built within their precincts. Thus a change passed over the spirit of Old Egypt and dealt the death-blow to her indigenous and traditional architecture, which no longer served its original purpose and became merely a relic of the past.

6. *Later Periods* (A.D. 395 to the present day). The Byzantine Period (A.D. 395–640). Changes of Empire influenced politics and art even in the distant provinces, and when Egypt was ruled by the Eastern Roman emperors from Constantinople (now Istanbul), Christian churches were erected in the Byzantine style, another mingling of east and west, which has placed domed Byzantine churches side by side with trabeated Egyptian temples.

Egypt under the Arabs (A.D. 640–1517). The country fell under the influence of those social customs which are bound up with the Moslem religion; conditions which from 1517 onwards were further enforced under Ottoman rule.

Egypt passed in the nineteenth century under French influence until, in 1881, it became virtually a British Protectorate, from 1914 presided over by a Sultan. In 1922 Egypt became an independent State.

Apart from internal social and historical influences, there are those arising from military and commercial contact. The earliest historical incidents are connected with the Sudan, the country of the Nubians or Ethiopians. The Palermo Stele tells us that Seneferu, first king of the Fourth Dynasty, raided the Sudan and brought back prisoners and loot from that vast territory, with its gold, copper and turquoise mines. Amenemhat I, founder of the Twelfth Dynasty, subjugated four tribes in the coveted Sudan; his son, Senusret I, exacted tribute there, worked the copper mines and built a fort and a temple at Wadi Halfa; while Senusret III finally conquered that country and built forts along the Nile to protect the transport of gold. The latter also made a determined sally into Palestine. Various kings sent expeditions to Sinai for copper, that territory having been exploited by Egypt from early dynastic times. Later, the incursions of nomadic tribes resulted in centuries of hated Hyksos rule, until they were finally expelled by Amasis I. He restored Nubia to Egypt and exacted more tribute, as did also the next three Pharaohs. Egyptian power penetrated too into Western Asia as far as the Euphrates. Queen Hatshepsut carried out a trade expedition to 'Punt' (perhaps in south-west Arabia) to secure ebony, ivory, gold and myrrh: the expedition is recorded on the walls of her temple at Dêr el-Bahari. Thothmes III waged victorious wars in Phoenicia, in the upper Euphrates valley and in the Sudan, and the treasure he secured was devoted to temple building, including a great Hall of Columns at Karnak, where his successes are proudly recorded. Amenophis III, the Memnon of the Greeks, carried on friendly intercourse with Asia, and through inter-marriage introduced a foreign element into Egypt, which largely found expression in the monotheistic tendencies of his son Amenophis IV, later to call himself Akhnaten. Akhnaten's religious bigotry brought him into stern conflict with the priesthood, whose power it was part of his policy to check; but though tenacious in his religious opinions and gifted as a builder, his rule was disastrously weak. He built a fine new capital at Tell el-Amarna in central Egypt, but while he was busy building it and a temple for the god of his choice, he lost hold over the Empire in Asia. Years later, Seti I reverted to raids on the Sudan for gold and expeditions to Sinai for copper, and successfully clashed with the Hittites, then dominant in Syria. His son, Rameses II, the Great, after bitter struggles came to amicable terms with the Hittites over rights in Syria, and joined in a treaty which brought peace to nearer Asia for some fifty years.

Merneptah, who succeeded him, quashed a revolt in Palestine, but found sterner work in resisting the inroads of the Libyans, on the west. Egypt then suffered internal dynastic and social troubles for a decade or two. Rameses III vigorously restored order again, but had to withstand the ferocious attacks upon Egypt by a confederation of 'Peoples of the Sea', displaced from the northern parts of the Mediterranean by pressure from still farther north. Both by land and sea, Rameses conquered these militant hosts. Nevertheless, Egypt thereafter gradually declined in vigour till the end of the Twentieth Dynasty. Government was poor or bad, and the populace went increasingly in need, so that in the reign of Rameses IX tomb robbery and the desecration of temples were rife. Decadence and the disintegration of effective control were the keynotes too, of the Twenty-first Dynasty. Then in the Twenty-second, Shishak I, a chieftain of Libyan origin, ushered in a Libyan royal succession which, though split for a long period into two overlapping dynasties, endured for over two hundred years. Shishak I, a capable leader, had re-established Egyptian rule in Syria, Nubia and Palestine, and pillaged Jerusalem. The Nubians, constituting the Twenty-fifth Dynasty, next seized the succession; but the Assyrian Empire now threatened the peace of Egypt and Esarhaddon defeated the Egyptians and took Memphis (671 B.C.), while Ashurbanipal, his son, invaded the country and sacked Thebes (663 B.C.). The withdrawal of the Nubian rulers into their own lands left the kingdom to Psammetichus I, founder of the last notable independent Egyptian dynasty, the Twenty-sixth (663–525 B.C.). Psammetichus began his reign as a mere vassal of Assyria, but with the help of Greek and other mercenaries he threw off the foreign yoke and chased the Assyrians into Palestine. Prosperity was restored and, again with much Greek help, trade re-established. This commercial intercourse introduced new ideas, and once more the Delta, with Sais as the capital, became the centre of Egyptian power. Necho (609 B.C.) emulated his father in supporting trade and briefly re-conquered Syria, but retired after a disastrous encounter with Nebuchadnezzar. Prosperity attended the following reigns, and art flourished, emulating' the characteristics of Ancient Kingdom masterpieces. Then, in 525 B.C., Egypt fell under Persian rule. Cambyses II dethroned Psammetichus III, who had reigned for scarcely a year, and for well over a hundred years, Egypt was a Persian province, prosperous under Darius, oppressed under Xerxes the Great, and in revolt under Artaxerxes I. Egyptian resistance secured eventual success by the opportunism of Amyrtis, the only Pharaoh of the Twenty-eighth Dynasty (404–398 B.C.). Two further dynasties of uneasy rule followed, with eight kings in less than sixty years, concluding with the defeat of the last native Pharaoh, Nectanebus II, and succeeded by a second, though brief, Persian domination (341–332 B.C.). In the latter year, Alexander the Great, having conquered Darius III, was invited to undertake the protection of Egypt. His capital, Alexandria, became the centre for Greek scholars and artists, and under the new impetus, architecture and the arts flourished again.

The first of the Ptolemies, the Greek general who succeeded Alexander, encouraged the influx of Jewish traders, and this increased the prosperity of the country. So the tale of the Ptolemies went on with occasional wars and expeditions, but it came about that Ptolemy XIII and his wife and sister Cleopatra were, in the will of their royal father, placed under the protection of Rome. Court intrigues and trouble with Rome followed, with the ultimate result that Egypt was declared a Roman province (30 B.C.). So Greek officials gave way to Roman, and Egypt was exploited as the granary of Rome, while Nubia was invaded for her mineral wealth. Nero even succeeded in diverting via Egypt the trade from India and Arabia. Under Nero too, it is said that Christianity first reached Egypt, where it soon entered on many conflicts and, as elsewhere, suffered many vicissitudes. At times, many Christian or Coptic churches were either erected or adapted, and by the time of Hadrian, architecture had assumed a Graeco-Roman style. During the reign of Constantine the Great (A.D. 324–337) the government of Egypt was reorganized, and on the division of the Roman Empire, Egypt came under the Eastern Emperor at Constantinople. Under Justinian (A.D. 527–565), a new and more stable administration was formed, but in A.D. 616 the country was captured by the Persians, and in A.D. 640 passed to the Moslems. Art in Ancient Egypt continued strangely unchanged through the various phases of foreign influence from Assyria, Persia, Greece and Rome; and, through all, the indigenous architecture maintained that solemn dignity so suited to the immense stretches of surrounding desert.

RELIGIOUS

The close connection between religion and architecture is everywhere manifest; for the priesthood was powerful, invested with unlimited authority and equipped with all the learning of the age. The religious rites of the Egyptians were traditional, virtually unchangeable, and mysterious, and these traits are reproduced in the architecture, both of tombs and temples. The religion was monotheistic in theory, but polytheistic in practice through the cult of many gods representing natural phenomena and the heavenly bodies, such as the sun, moon and stars, and by the worship of animals as personifications of gods. Egyptian mythology was further complicated by the multiplication of local gods for different centres. The keynote of the Egyptian religion was that of awe and submission to the great power represented by the sun, while the chief worship was for Osiris, the man-god, who died and rose again, the god of death, and through death of resurrection to eternal life. Elaborate preparations were made for the care of their bodies after death, and the wealthy built themselves lordly tomb-houses. The deceased Pharaoh was transported across the Nile to the Western Bank where was the Domain of the Dead, and the religious ceremonies were conducted in a funerary temple or chapel (p. 15L).

In Egypt there was no strict dividing line between gods and kings; no need for the doctrine of the divine right of kings; for kings were ranked, both by themselves and by their people, as actual divinities. Often they filled the double function as kings of their people and priests of their gods, and yet again were themselves gods, commanding priestly service. On the other hand the gods themselves were invested with superhuman and therefore with inventive powers, as when the art of writing was regarded as the invention of the god Thoth. The gods they frequently associated in triads; thus Ammon the sun-god, Mut his wife, the mother of all things, and Khons their son, the moon-god, were the great Theban triad; while Ptah, a creator, Sekhmet, goddess of war, his female counterpart, and Nefertem, their son, formed the Memphis triad. Other gods were the powerful Osiris, god of the dead; Isis, his wife; Horus, the sky-god; Hathor, goddess of love; Set, dread god of evil, and Serapis, a bull-god, representing that strange cult of the sacred bulls. All these and many more, totalling many hundreds, occur in turn or in combination, and the unchanging, traditional architecture of ancient Egypt appears and reappears in all the jealously closed temples, erected for the use of kings and priests in the service of the gods. The outstanding feature of the religion of the Egyptians was their strong belief in a future state, hence the erection of such everlasting monuments as pyramids for the preservation of the dead. The dwelling-house was regarded as a temporary lodging, and the tomb as the permanent abode. This religious attitude is typified in the two predominant types of buildings, the solemn and mysterious temples of the gods and the enduring tomb pyramids of the early kings.

ARCHITECTURAL CHARACTER

The primitive architecture in the valley of the Nile consisted of readily-available tractable materials like reeds, papyrus (now practically extinct) and palm-branch ribs, plastered over with clay. With bundles of stems placed vertically side by side and lashed to a bundle placed horizontally near the top, walls or fences could be made. Alternatively, palm-leaf ribs were planted in the ground at short intervals, with others laced in a diagonal network across them and secured to a horizontal member near the top, the whole being daubed with mud afterwards. Buildings with circular plans could have domical coverings of similar construction, or, if rectangular, could have a tunnel-shaped covering or a flat roof. The pressure of the flat reed-and-mud roofs against the tops of the wall reeds may have produced the characteristic Egyptian 'gorge' cornice (p. 11J), while the 'kheker' cresting less frequently appearing in later architecture may have originated in the terminal tufts of a papyrus-stalk wall (p. 11B). The horizontal binders and angle bundles survived in the roll moulding of stone cornices and wall angles of the historic period (p. 11J). A type of pavilion or kiosk which came to have a special religious significance in connection with the 'Heb-sed' or jubilee festivals of the Pharaohs—though originally commonly used on Nile boats as well as on land—consisted of a light, rectangular structure, open-fronted and with a porch carried on two slender angle-shafts and having a slab-like roof arching from the back to the front. In the Heb-sed ceremony, held at definite intervals of years in the king's reign, the Pharaoh seated himself on a throne beneath such an awning, raised on a high podium and approached by a flight of steps at the front. Timber, once quite plentiful, also was used for the better buildings, in square, heavy vertical plates, lapping one in front of the other and producing an effect of composite buttresses joined at the head and enframing narrow panels, in the upper parts of which window-vents might occur. Palm logs, rounded on the underside, were sometimes used for roofs. All these various forms of construction produced their effects on matured art and architecture, and apart from timber, which had become scarce by dynastic times, never entirely went out of use. Stone was not much employed before the Third Dynasty, except as rubble and as a stiffening or foundation to mud solid walls. Sun-dried mud-brick walling never ceased to be employed, for it was only for the finest buildings of religious character that cut stone became normal. Even palaces remained always relatively frail. Made of Nile mud and mixed with chopped straw or sand, and thoroughly matured by exposure to the sun, the mud bricks were very long lasting, and large, about 356 mm (14 ins) long, 178 mm (7 ins) wide and 102 mm (4 ins) thick. For stability, walls diminished course by course towards the top, chiefly because of the alternate shrinkage and expansion of the soil caused by the annual inundation. As the inner face of the walls had to be vertical for ordinary convenience, it was the outer face only which showed this inward inclination, or 'batter', which remained throughout one of the principal characteristics of Egyptian architecture whether in brick or stone. Sometimes fibre or reed mats were placed between the brick courses at intervals up the walls, to reinforce them, particularly at a building's angles; and a late development was the use of sagging concave courses, for alternate lengths of a long wall, built in advance of the inter-

A CONTINUOUS COIL SPIRAL

B QUADRUPLE SPIRAL

C LOTUS & PAPYRUS

D GRAPE ORNAMENT

E ROPE & FEATHER ORNAMENT

F SACRED BOAT : THEBES

G ROPE & PATERÆ ORNAMENT

H OSIRIS PILLARS RAMESSEUM : THEBES

J DOORWAY IN PYLON, PHILÆ

K WINDOW : MEDINET HABU

L WINGED SOLAR DISC.

M GRANITE SPHINX : LOUVRE : PARIS

N INCISED WALL SCULPTURE : KARNA

vening stretches, to allow of the drying out of the inner brickwork, since walls such as those around the great temple enclosures were very thick, between 9 m (30 ft) and 24.5 m (80 ft). Though the true arch was never used in monumental stone-work, the principle was known very early on: there are brick vaults as early as the beginning of the Third Dynasty. Frequently, the arch rings were built in sloping courses, so that no 'centering' or temporary support was needed, and usually there were two or more arched rings arranged concentrically, the one lying upon the other. The Romans adopted the method of building arches in concentric, super-posed rings, though they did not slope them but used centering in the normal way. The surface decoration of the masonry walls is also held to have been derived from the practice of scratching pictures on the early mud-plaster walls, which manifestly did not lend themselves to modelled or projecting ornament, though their flat and windowless surfaces were eminently suitable for incised relief and explanatory hieroglyphs (pp. 10, 12)—a method of popular teaching which has its parallel in the sculptured façades and stained-glass windows of mediaeval cathedrals. Egyptian columns (p. 11) have a distinctive character, and a very large proportion of them plainly advertise their vegetable origin, their shafts indicative of bundles of plant stems, gathered in a little at the base, and with capitals seemingly derived from the lotus bud (p. 11G), the papyrus flower (p. 11C), or the ubiquitous palm.

Egyptian monumental architecture, which is essentially a columnar and trabeated style, is expressed mainly in pyramids and other tombs and in temples, in contrast to the Near Eastern, its nearest in age, in which tombs are insignificant and spacious palaces assume an importance rivalling that of temple structure. Egyptian temples (p. 31), approached by impressive avenues of sphinxes— mythical monsters, each with the body of a lion and the head of a man, hawk, ram or woman—possess in their massive pylons, great courts, hypostyle halls, inner sanctuaries and dim, secret rooms, a special character; for typically, temples grew by accretion or replace-ment according to the increasing requirements of a powerful priesthood, or to satisfy the pious ambition of successive kings. Greek temples were each planned as one homogeneous whole, and the component parts were all essential to the complete design, while some of the greatest Egyptian temples were but a string of successive buildings diminishing in height behind their imposing pylons (p. 31E).

Egyptian architecture persistently maintained its traditions, and when necessity dictated a change in methods of construction or in the materials used, the tradi-tional forms, hallowed by long use, were perpetuated in spite of novel conditions. It is impressive by its solemnity and gloom as well as by its ponderous solidity, which suggests that the buildings were intended to last eternally. The idea is not without foundation when we realize that the avowed purpose of the pyramids was not only to preserve the mummy of the Pharaoh for the return of the soul in the infinite hereafter, but also to be the centre of the cult of the royal dead, and as a consequence, the dominant element of the vast monumental complex.

EXAMPLES

TOMB ARCHITECTURE

The tombs were of three main types: (a) Mastabas, (b) Royal Pyramids and (c) Rock-hewn tombs.

(a) *Mastabas*. Since the Ancient Egyptians believed so strongly in an after-life, they did their utmost, each according to his means, to build lasting tombs, to preserve the body, and to bury with it the finest commodities that might be needed for the sustenance and eternal enjoyment of the deceased. As early as the First

Dynasty bands of linen were used to wrap round the limbs of the body, to aid its preservation, though embalming was not fully developed until the New Kingdom. In the Archaic period (Dynasties I–II) the king and other leading personages normally had two tombs, one in Lower Egypt and the other in Upper Egypt, the two kingdoms united by Menes, the first of the Pharaohs. Only one tomb, of course, could take the real burial, the other being a cenotaph. The royal cemetery was at Sakkâra, overlooking the capital Memphis, the cenotaphs being far to the south at Abydos. Until the closing years of the First Dynasty these tombs and cenotaphs were surrounded by rows of burials, evidently those of retainers sacrificed to accompany their masters: this custom soon died out in Egypt proper.

By the First Dynasty, the more elaborate graves had come to simulate house plans of several small rooms, a central one containing the sarcophagus and others surrounding it to receive the abundant funerary offerings (p. 15A). The whole was constructed in a broad pit below ground, the wooden roof being supported by wooden posts or crude brick pillars, and the entire area covered by a rectangular, flat-topped mound of the spoil from the excavation, retained in place by very thick brick walls. The outer faces were either serrated with alternate buttress-like projections and narrow recesses—the so-called 'palace façade' arrangement—or plain, and sloped backwards at an angle of about 75°. The 'palace façade' design, perhaps derived from timber panelling, equally had its origins in the mud-brick architecture of Mesopotamia in the Uruk and Jemdet Nasr periods, at a time when Mesopotamian influences on Egyptian civilization, then in its formative phase, have long been recognized. Frequently these façades were painted in bright colours, represented by splashes of paint on the plinths at their base and hinted at by the decoration of later wooden coffins. Such tombs are nowadays known as mastabas, from their resemblance to the low benches built outside the modern Egyptian house. Closely surrounding them was an enclosure wall. Subsequent changes in the design of the mastaba may be summarized as the attempt to achieve greater security for the body of the dead owner and the goods buried with him by concentrating resources on cutting even deeper into the rock, abandoning the elaborate layout of rooms in the superstructure found in the First Dynasty tombs.

Typical of the Second and Third Dynasties is the 'stairway' mastaba, the tomb chamber, with its attendant magazines, having been sunk much deeper and cut in the rock below (p. 15B). Normally, the main axis of the tomb lay north and south, and steps and ramps led from the north end of the top of the mastaba to connect with a shaft which descended to the level of the tomb chamber. After the burial, heavy stone portcullises were dropped across the approach from slots built to receive them, and this was then filled in and all surface traces removed. Externally, the imitation of panelling was usually abandoned in favour of the plain battered sides, except that there were two well-spaced recesses on the east long side. This was the front towards the Nile. The southernmost of the two recesses was a false door (p. 15E), allowing the spirit of the deceased to enter or leave at will, and in front of it was a table for the daily offerings of fresh food.

It was here that about the Fourth Dynasty a small offering chapel developed, tacked on to the mastaba, or an offering room was constructed within the mastaba itself (p. 15C). Tomb chambers were sunk more deeply still, approached by a short horizontal passage from a vertical shaft sunk from the north end of the top of the superstructure. There are many such 'shaft' mastabas at Gizeh (p. 15D). By this time the majority of the mastabas were of limestone, which had been used only sparingly for floors and wall linings in the finest of the brick mastabas of early dynastic times. With the Fifth and Sixth Dynasties the offering room or chapel at ground level tended to become increasingly elaborate (p. 15F, G). In the most

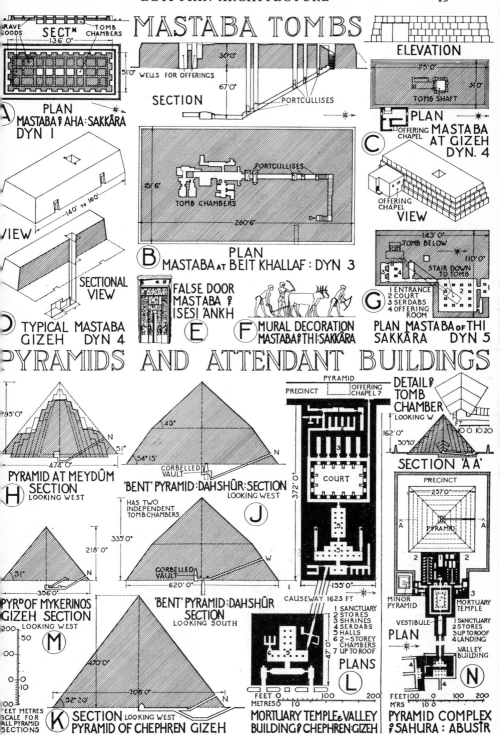

MASTABA TOMBS

SECT^N GRAVE GOODS — TOMB CHAMBERS
136' 0"
51'0"

PLAN
A MASTABA ? AHA : SAKKÂRA
DYN I

SECTION
30'0"
WELLS FOR OFFERINGS
67'0"
PORTCULLISES

ELEVATION
75'0"
31'0"
TOMB SHAFT

PLAN
OFFERING CHAPEL
C MASTABA AT GIZEH DYN. 4

OFFERING CHAPEL
VIEW

151'6"
PORTCULLISES
TOMB CHAMBERS
280'6"

PLAN
B MASTABA AT BEIT KHALLAF : DYN 3

VIEW
140' to 160'

SECTIONAL VIEW

D TYPICAL MASTABA GIZEH DYN 4

E FALSE DOOR MASTABA ? ISESI 'ANKH

F MURAL DECORATION MASTABA ? THI : SAKKÂRA

143' 0"
TOMB BELOW
110' 0"
STAIR DOWN TO TOMB
1 ENTRANCE
2 COURT
3 SERDABS
4 OFFERING ROOM

G PLAN MASTABA of THI SAKKÂRA DYN 5

PYRAMIDS AND ATTENDANT BUILDINGS

PYRAMID
PRECINCT — OFFERING CHAPEL ?

DETAIL ? TOMB CHAMBER
LOOKING W
0 0 10 20

95'0"
N
51°
474'0"

H PYRAMID AT MEYDÛM SECTION LOOKING WEST

43°
54°15'
CORBELLED VAULT
N

'BENT' PYRAMID : DAHSHÛR : SECTION
LOOKING WEST

162'0"
30'10"
COURT
372'0"

SECTION 'A A'

HAS TWO INDEPENDENT TOMB CHAMBERS

J

335'0"
218'0"
CORBELLED VAULT
620'0"
W

'BENT' PYRAMID : DAHSHÛR SECTION
LOOKING SOUTH

155'0"
CAUSEWAY 1623 FT

PRECINCT
257'0"
A — A
PYRAMID

51°
396'0"
N

PYR^D OF MYKERINOS GIZEH SECTION
LOOKING WEST

M

200
50
00
0 0
10
100
FEET METRES SCALE FOR ALL PYRAMID SECTIONS

470'0"
32°20'
708'0"
N

K SECTION LOOKING WEST PYRAMID OF CHEPHREN GIZEH

1 SANCTUARY
2 STORES
3 SHRINES
4 SERDABS
5 HALLS
6 2-STOREY CHAMBERS
7 UP TO ROOF

47'0"
PLANS
L

FEET 0 100 200
METRES 0 10

MORTUARY TEMPLE & VALLEY BUILDING ? CHEPHREN : GIZEH

MINOR PYRAMID
MORTUARY TEMPLE
VESTIBULE
PLAN
1 SANCTUARY
2 STORES
3 UP TO ROOF
4 LANDING
VALLEY BUILDING

N

FEET 100 0 100 200
M'RS 0

PYRAMID COMPLEX ? SAHURA : ABUSÎR

sumptuous examples, there might be a group of rooms, within or adjacent to the mastaba mound, including a columned hall, the walls lined with vividly-coloured reliefs, depicting scenes from the daily life of the deceased. Important among the rooms was the 'serdab'—sometimes there was more than one—completely enclosed except for a slot opposite the head of a statue of the deceased contained within. In the offering room was a 'stele', an upright stone slab inscribed with the name of the deceased, funerary texts and relief carvings intended to serve in the event of failure in the supply of daily offerings. An offering-table stood at its foot.

The **Mastaba of Aha, Sakkâra** (p. 15A), the ruler who can most probably be identified with Menes, unifier of Egypt and founder of Memphis and the First Dynasty, takes the form of a shallow pit, subdivided by crude brick walls into five chambers, the centre one for the body of the king and the others for his intimate possessions. Above them, the brick superstructure covered a broader area and had twenty-seven compartments containing other grave goods, including jars for food-stuffs, ceiled with timber and covered with brick or débris. The exterior had the 'palace-façade' decoration of serrated vertical projections and recesses, the first of the series of such tombs at Sakkâra. Two girdle walls closely surrounded this mastaba. Various types of bonding were used in the mud-brick walls of this and later tombs and other structures, sometimes reinforced by layers of reeds or of sticks at intervals, serving also to help to dry out the brickwork. On the north side of the tomb of Hor-Aha was a group of small model buildings, evidently store-houses, and a large brick-built grave for a solar bark. This illustrates the importance even at this early date of the cult of the sun god, always closely associated with the royal court. By the last reign of the First Dynasty, the tomb of the king, Ka'a, shows immense developments in design: the exterior of the brick superstructure was of the usual panelled type, with multi-coloured paintings of geometrical patterns imitating mats and hangings; a passage led down to the rock-cut burial chamber and store-rooms; surrounding the superstructure was a large enclosure wall, and inside this, on the north side of the tomb itself, was a complex of rooms and passages comparable with the mortuary temples of the pyramids. Thus already there had appeared the prototype of the later pyramid complexes.

The **Mastaba K.1 at Beit Khallaf** (p. 15B) is a massive 'stairway' tomb of crude brick, typical of the Third Dynasty. The stairs and ramp, guarded by five stone portcullises, lead to a rock-cut, stone-lined tomb chamber surrounded by a knot of magazines for the funerary offerings. Above ground, the mastaba is plain and virtually solid.

The **Mastabas at Gizeh,** mostly of the Fourth and Fifth Dynasties, number two or three hundred, arranged in orderly ranks, and adjoin the famous pyramids there (pp. 3, 15C, D, 26A). Fourth Dynasty examples illustrate, on the one hand, the development of the offering chapel (p. 15C), and on the other, the typical 'shaft' mastaba (p. 15D) with deep, underground tomb chambers and a sloping-sided superstructure having two widely spaced recesses on the long east side, the southern of which served as a false door (p. 15E) and for offerings.

The **Mastaba of Thi, Sakkâra** (p. 15G), a high dignitary of the Fifth Dynasty, has all the elaboration of its time. A large pillared court is attached to the north end of the east side, approached from the north by a portico which has a serdab along-side. A passage connects the court with a small chamber and an offering-room, with two pillars, lying inside the mastaba itself. This is equipped with two stelae and an offering-table against the west wall; and south of it is a second serdab, with three slots through the intervening wall corresponding with the three duplicate statues of Thi enclosed there. The low-relief sculptures of this tomb are among the finest and most interesting in Egypt (p. 15F). The actual tomb chamber is below the south end of the mastaba, behind the west wall of the offering-room but at a much lower level. It is reached from a passage slanting diagonally to connect with a stairway emerging in the centre of the court.

(b) *Royal Pyramids.* The great pyramids of the Third to Sixth Dynasties are on sites distributed intermittently along the west side of the Nile for about fifty miles southward of the apex of the Delta, standing on the rocky shelf clear of the cultivated land. Early royal tombs were of the mastaba type, from which the true pyramid evolved, the most important stages being demonstrated by the early Third Dynasty 'Step' pyramid of the Pharaoh Zoser at Sakkâra (pp. 17–20). Further stages of development are marked by one at Meydûm and by two at Dahshûr by Seneferu, first king of the Fourth Dynasty, including the so-called 'Bent' pyramid. The finest true pyramids are the famous three at Gizeh, built by the Fourth Dynasty successors of Seneferu. Pyramids did not stand in solitary isolation but were the primary part of a complex of buildings. They were surrounded by a walled enclosure, had (i) an offering chapel, with a stele, usually abutting the east side of the pyramid but occasionally on the north; (ii) a mortuary temple for the worship of the dead and deified Pharaoh, on the north side in Zoser's complex but normally projecting from the enclosure on the east side; (iii) a raised and enclosed causeway leading to the nearer, western edge of the cultivation where stood (iv) a 'Valley Building' in which embalmment was carried out and interment rites performed. A canal was built to connect the Valley Building with the Nile, by which the funeral cortège magnificently arrived. Pyramids were built with immense outlay in labour and material, in the lifetime of the Pharaohs concerned, to secure the preservation of the body after death till that time should have passed when, according to their belief in immortality, the soul would once more return to the body. Infinite pains were taken to conceal and protect the tomb chamber and its contents, as well as the approach passages, but all precautions proved to be vain, for they were successively rifled first in the period of chaos which followed the Sixth Dynasty and again in the Persian, Roman and Arab periods. Pyramids were founded on the living rock, levelled to receive them, and were of limestone quarried in their locality, faced with the finer limestone coming from Tura on the opposite, eastern, side of the Nile. Granite, in limited use for such as the linings of the chambers and passages, was brought from up-river at Aswân. Tomb chambers and their approaches were either cut in the rock below the monument or were in its constructed core. Entrances normally were from the north side and the sides were scrupulously orientated with the cardinal points. In all known cases, pyramids were built in a series of concentric sloping slices or layers, around a steep pyramidal core, so that the whole mass first appeared in step-like tiers; until, in the case of the true pyramidal form, the steps had been filled in with packing blocks and brought with finely finished facings to their ultimate shape, at the chosen angle of inclination. Nevertheless, all the inner layers were built more or less at the same time, course by course, so that as it proceeded, the top was always approximately level. The final meticulous dressing of the finished faces was from top to bottom, and the apex stone probably was gilded. The Egyptians did not know of the pulley, and their principal tool for raising and turning stone blocks was the lever. To transport them overland, wooden sledges were used, with or without the aid of rollers dropped in turn in front of a sledge and picked up again behind. Blocks for the pyramids were hauled up great broad-topped, sloping ramps of sand or earth, reinforced with crude brick walls, such ramps being placed at right angles to the most convenient of the faces.

The **Step Pyramid of Zoser, Sakkâra** (2778 B.C., beginning of Third Dynasty) (pp. 18, 19) is remarkable as being the world's first large-scale monument in stone. King Zoser's architect, Imhotep, was greatly revered both in his own and

A. Restored view of the pyramid and enclosure from the flooded Nile valley

B. Aerial view of the pyramid and enclosure (restored model)

C. Processional corridor (restored)   D. Angle of Great Court

Step Pyramid of Zoser, Sakkâra (2778 B.C.). See p. 17

STEP PYRAMID OF ZOSER: SAKKÂRA

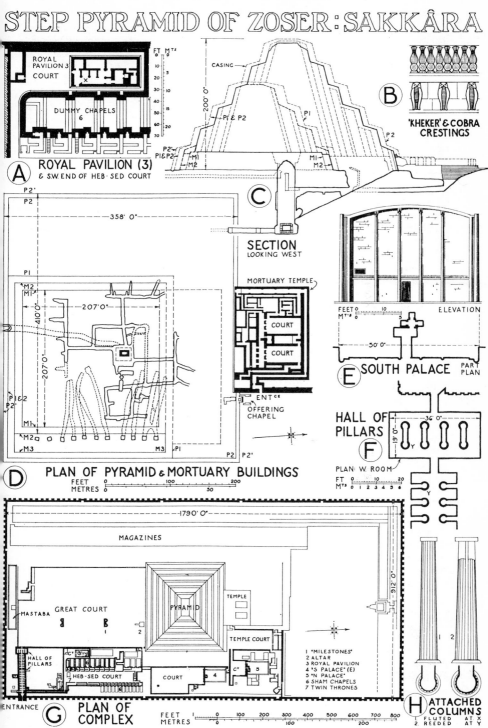

A ROYAL PAVILION (3)
& S.W. END OF HEB-SED COURT

ROYAL PAVILION 3
COURT
DUMMY CHAPELS 6

B 'KHEKER' & COBRA CRESTINGS

CASING

C SECTION LOOKING WEST

D PLAN OF PYRAMID & MORTUARY BUILDINGS
FEET
METRES

MORTUARY TEMPLE
COURT
COURT
ENT^ce
OFFERING CHAPEL

E SOUTH PALACE PART PLAN
FEET
ELEVATION

F HALL OF PILLARS
PLAN: W. ROOM

G PLAN OF COMPLEX
FEET
METRES
ENTRANCE

MAGAZINES
MASTABA
GREAT COURT
PYRAMID
TEMPLE
TEMPLE COURT
HALL OF PILLARS
HEB-SED COURT
COURT

1 "MILESTONES"
2 ALTAR
3 ROYAL PAVILION
4 "S PALACE" (E)
5 "N PALACE"
6 SHAM CHAPELS
7 TWIN THRONES

H ATTACHED COLUMNS
1. FLUTED AT X
2. REEDED AT Y

later times, and in the Twenty-sixth Dynasty was deified. The pyramid itself shows no less than five changes of plan in the course of building. It began as a complete mastaba, 7.9 m (26 ft) high, unusual in having a square plan, of 63 m (207 ft) sides. It was then twice extended, first by a regular addition of 4.3 m (14 ft) to each of its sloping sides and next by an extension eastwards of 8.5 m (28 ft). At this stage the whole was used as a basis for a four-stepped pyramid, made up of layers inclined against a steep-sided core, and again enlarged at the same time so that its plan became a rectangle of about 83 m × 75 m (272 ft × 244 ft). A further enormous addition on the north and west, followed by a quite slight one all round, brought it to its final dimensions of 125 m (410 ft) from east to west by 109 m (358 ft) wide and 60 m (200 ft) high, and added two more steps to the height, making six in all. In this stepped form it remained. Usually, underground tomb chambers were finished before the superstructure had been begun, but there were here two stages owing to the successive enlargements above. A pit of 7.3 m (24 ft) side and 8.5 m (28 ft) deep was the counterpart of the first mastaba, approached by a horizontal tunnel emerging at the north side in an open ramp; but this pit was deepened to 28 m (92 ft) at the pyramid stage of development, and had an Aswân granite tomb chamber at the bottom above which was a limestone-walled room containing a granite plug to stop a hole at the top of the tomb-chamber when the burial had been completed. The approach tunnel too was deepened and converted to a ramp entering the pit at a point some 21.5 m (70 ft) above its base. From the bottom of the pit four corridors extend irregularly towards the four cardinal points, connecting to galleries running in approximate parallel with the four sides of the pyramid, and having spur galleries thrusting from them. Independent of the main subterranean system is a series of eleven separate pits, 32 m (106 ft) deep, on the east side of the original mastaba. These were tombs of members of the royal family. The tomb entrances were sealed by the third extension of the mastaba.

Surrounding the pyramid was a vast rectangular enclosure, 547 m (1,790 ft) from north to south and 278 m (912 ft) wide, with a massive Tura limestone wall, 10.7 m (35 ft) high, indented in the manner of the earlier mastaba façades (pp. 18, 19). Around the walls were bastions, fourteen in all, and each had stone false doors. The only entrance was in a broader bastion near the southern end of the eastern face. In the fact that there is a small offering chapel (with stelae, offering table and a statue of Zoser) and a well-developed mortuary temple, containing two courts, a maze of corridors and many rooms, the buildings inside the enclosure show some relation to earlier developments of the mastaba; but these two buildings abut the north face of the pyramid, instead of the east as was to be the common practice, and all the rest of the structures are quite exceptional and unique to this complex. They are dummy representations of the palace of Zoser and the buildings used in connection with the celebration of his jubilee in his lifetime. Most of them therefore are solid, or almost so, comprised of earth or débris faced with Tura limestone. They are grouped around courts. The entrance to the great enclosure leads to a long processional corridor lined with reeded columns—this site provides the only known instances of the type—which bore architraves and a roof of long stones shaped on the underside like timber logs (p. 18C). At the inner end of the corridor is a pillared hall, with reeded columns attached in pairs, beyond which is the Great Court (p. 18D), where there are two low B-shaped pedestals, used in the royal ceremonial, an altar near the pyramid south face and, on the south side of the court, a mastaba, unusually aligned east-west. Just inside the enclosure entrance a narrow corridor runs deviously northwards to the Heb-sed Court, the principal scene of this festival, lined with sham chapels, each with its small forecourt, those on the western side representing the provinces or 'nomes' of Upper Egypt and those on the eastern, of Lower Egypt. These virtually solid structures had segmental-arched roofs; as also had two similarly-solid large halls of unequal sizes farther north, each facing southwards into its own court and which might have symbolized the two kingdoms. The façades of all of them, chapels and halls, bore three slender, attached columns. Near to the Heb-sed Court, to the west, is the so-called 'Royal Pavilion', within which are three fluted, attached columns. In Zoser's complex as a whole, the masonry technique and the almost total absence of free-standing columns, together with the small spans of the stone beam roofs, indicates the novelty of stone as a building material at this time. The architectural forms show clearly their derivation from earlier structures in reeds, timber or sun-dried brick.

The **Pyramid at Meydûm** (p. 15H) is attributed to Huni, last king of the Third Dynasty. Though eventually completed as a true pyramid, it is definitely known that at one stage it was a seven-stepped structure, contrived by building six thick layers of masonry, each faced with Tura limestone, against a nucleus with sides sloping steeply at 75°; and that there was then an addition of a fresh layer all round, raising the number of steps to eight. These again were faced with Tura limestone, dressed only where the faces showed. Thus both the seven- and the eight-step pyramids had at the time been regarded as finished. But there was yet a further development, in which the steps were packed out and the sides made smooth with finely-dressed Tura stone. Of this ultimate true pyramid, 144.5 m (474 ft) square on base and 90 m (295 ft) high, with sides sloping at 51°, the lower portion still survives, but the upper part has been oddly denuded into a shouldered, tower-like structure. The simple, corbel-roofed tomb chamber was at ground-level in the heart of the masonry. Around the pyramid was a stone enclosure wall, 233 m (764 ft) from north to south, by 209 m (686 ft), within which were a small pyramid on the south side and a mastaba on the north. Also, abutting the centre of the east face of the pyramid, was a small offering-chapel, with an offering-table, flanked by two stelae, in its inner small court. There was no mortuary temple, but a causeway from the eastern wall led to the Valley Building, now submerged.

The **Bent, or South Pyramid of Seneferu, Dahshûr** (2723 B.C.) (p. 15J) has the peculiarities, firstly, that the angle of inclination of the sides changes about half-way up from 54° 15′ in the lower part to 43° in the upper, where it shows hasty completion; and secondly that it has two entirely independent tomb chambers, reached one from the north side and one from the west. The change in slope had the object of lightening the weight of the upper masonry, as the walls of chambers and passages began to show fissures. The plan is square, 187 m (620 ft), and the height about 102 m (335 ft), the materials being the usual local stone with Tura limestone facing, well-preserved. The tomb-chambers are covered by corbelled roofs with gradually in-stepping courses from all four sides, that over the lower chamber concluding with a 305 mm (1 ft) span some 24 m (80 ft) above the floor. Corbelling, as instanced here and at Meydûm, is thus one of the earliest experimental devices for constructing a stone vault. Around the pyramid there was a double-walled rectangular enclosure, an offering chapel and a mortuary temple on the east side and a causeway leading to the Valley Building. The subsidiary structures here probably provide the first instance of what was to be the customary complement and arrangement.

The **North Pyramid of Seneferu, Dahshûr,** made after the abandonment of the Bent Pyramid, was the actual place of burial of Seneferu, for nearby are tombs of the royal family and officiating priests; also, it was designed and completed as a true pyramid, the earliest known. The pitch of its sides, however, is unusually low; 43° 36′, instead of the usual 52° or so, and thus is very similar to that of the upper part of the Bent Pyramid. For the rest the pyramid is normal.

The **Great Pyramid of Cheops** (Khufu), **near Cairo** (pp. 3, 23, 26A). Cheops was the son of Seneferu, and the second king of the Fourth Dynasty. His pyramid, largest of the famous three on this site, was originally 146.4 m (480 ft) high and 230.6 m (756 ft) square on plan, with an area of about 13 acres, or more than twice that of S. Peter, Rome. The four sides, which, as in all periods with only a minor exception, face the cardinal points, are nearly equilateral triangles and make an angle of 51° 52′ with the ground. There are three separate internal chambers, due to changes of plan in the course of building. The subterranean chamber and the so-called 'Queen's Chamber' are discarded projects, abandoned in turn in favour of the 'King's Chamber' where the granite sarcophagus is located. The entrance is 7.3 m (24 ft) off-centre on the north side, and 17 m (55 ft) above ground level, measured vertically, leading to a corridor descending at about 26° to the original rock-cut chamber. In this descending corridor, after the first change of plan, an ascending corridor was cut in the ceiling, about 18.3 m (60 ft) along, rising to some 21 m (70 ft) above ground, at which level the Queen's Chamber was constructed. But before it was entirely completed, the approach was sealed off and the ascending corridor extended into what is now known as the Grand Gallery (p. 23D), a passage 2.1 m (7 ft) wide and 2.3 m (7 ft 6 ins) high, covered by a ramped, corbelled vault of seven great courses, rising to a height of 8.5 m (28 ft) vertically from the floor, where the surviving span of 1.1 m (3 ft 6 ins) is closed by stone slabs. At the top, the Grand Gallery gave on to the King's Chamber 5.2 m (17 ft 2 ins) from north to south, 10.5 m (34 ft 4 ins) long and 5.8 m (19 ft) high which like its vestibule, is lined in granite. In the vestibule there were originally three massive granite slabs, let down in slots in the side walls to seal the chamber after the burial. The covering of the chamber is most elaborate. Five tiers of great stone beams, nine to a tier and together weighing about 400 tons, are ranged one above the other, with a void space between the layers. Above them all is an embryonic vault of pairs of great stones inclined against one another. This latter device occurs also over the Queen's Chamber and again over the pyramid entrance, where just within the former casing there are pairs of inclined stones superposed in two tiers (p. 23C). Two shafts, 203 mm × 152 mm (8 ins × 6 ins), leading from the King's Chamber to the outer face of the pyramid, may have been for ventilation or to allow the free passage of the Ka or spirit of the dead king. There are similar shafts from the Queen's Chamber, left incomplete like the chamber itself. Built solidly of local stone, the pyramid originally was cased in finely-dressed Tura limestone blocks and the apex stone perhaps gilded, but only a few stones at the base now survive. The average weight of blocks is 2500 kg (2½ tons); they are bedded in a thin lime-mortar, used as a lubricant during fixing rather than as an adhesive, laid with amazingly fine joints. Little trace of the pyramid enclosure wall now exists, nor does there much remain of the customary attendant buildings. The offering chapel abutted the centre of the pyramid east face, and the mortuary temple stood axially in front of it, joined by a causeway which led askew eastwards towards the Valley Building. Flanking the temple on east and west are two boat-shaped pits cut in the rock, and there is a third alongside the north flank of the causeway. Whether these actually contained wooden boats for the king's transport in his afterlife is not definitely known. In A.D. 1954 two more pits were discovered adjacent to the south side of the pyramid, covered with stone beams as originally the others had been, in which wooden boats, 35.5 m (115 ft) long, were disclosed intact and in a remarkably fine state of preservation. At a little distance south-east of the east face of the pyramid are three subsidiary pyramids, with chapels on their own east sides, tombs of Cheops' queens.

The **Pyramid of Chephren** (Khafra) (Fourth Dynasty) (pp. 3, 15K, L, 26A) is

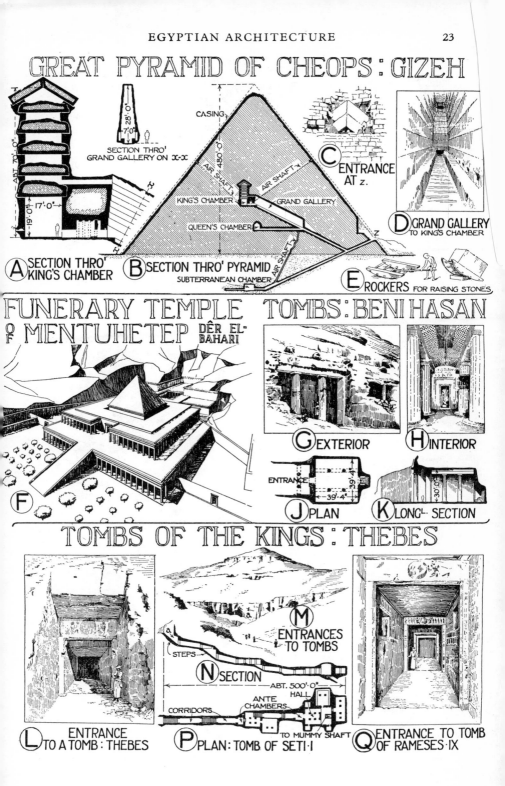

GREAT PYRAMID OF CHEOPS : GIZEH

SECTION THRO' GRAND GALLERY ON X-X

28' 0"

CASING

AIR SHAFT

AIR SHAFT

KING'S CHAMBER

GRAND GALLERY

QUEEN'S CHAMBER

480' 0"

17' 0"

19' 0"

(C) ENTRANCE AT z.

(D) GRAND GALLERY TO KING'S CHAMBER

(A) SECTION THRO' KING'S CHAMBER

(B) SECTION THRO' PYRAMID
SUBTERRANEAN CHAMBER

(E) ROCKERS FOR RAISING STONES

FUNERARY TEMPLE OF MENTUHETEP DÊR EL-BAHARI

(F)

TOMBS : BENI HASAN

(G) EXTERIOR

(H) INTERIOR

ENTRANCE

39' 4"

39' 4"

30' 0"

(J) PLAN

(K) LONG'L SECTION

TOMBS OF THE KINGS : THEBES

(M) ENTRANCES TO TOMBS

STEPS

(N) SECTION

ABT. 500' 0"

HALL

ANTE CHAMBERS

CORRIDORS

TO MUMMY SHAFT

(L) ENTRANCE TO A TOMB : THEBES

(P) PLAN : TOMB OF SETI·I

(Q) ENTRANCE TO TOMB OF RAMESES·IX

The Sphinx, Gizeh, near Cairo, with the pyramid of Cheops in background (*before* 2600 B.C.). See p. 25

the second of the three at Gizeh and only a little less large than the Great Pyramid, 216 m (708 ft) side and 143 m (470 ft) high, but has a steeper slope (52° 20′). There is only one chamber at the core, partly in the rock and partly built-up, but two approaches to it from the north; one through the stonework and the other subterranean, these joining halfway. Near the apex of the pyramid much of the original limestone casing is preserved, and there are fragments to show that the two base courses of the facing were of granite. The remaining buildings of the complex too, are better preserved than in other cases. The offering chapel and the mortuary temple were in the normal positions axial on the east face. The latter, 113.3 m (372 ft) from east to west and 47.2 m (155 ft) wide, was of limestone, lined internally with granite. Flanking it were five boat-shaped pits, three on the south and two on the north. It was extremely solid and barren of features externally. To the west of a great open court, with twelve statues against the piers between the many openings leading to a surrounding corridor, were five deep chambers for statues of the Pharoah, the central one wider than the rest, whilst behind them were corresponding stores, serdabs, and the only entrance to the pyramid enclosure. East of the court was a fore-temple, very similar in plan to the Valley Building, with twin pillared halls and long serdabs on the wings. From an entrance corridor there opened in the north-east corner of the block a series of four rooms in alabaster, where there were alabaster chests containing elements of the viscera, and in the south-east corner, two rooms in granite which received the two royal crowns. Despite the essential symmetry of the plan, the entrance was insignificant and off-centre, leading aslant to the causeway from the Valley Building, which survives substantially intact. The Valley Building (p. 15L) is 44.8 m (147 ft) square and 13 m (43 ft) high, of massive construction in local stone between granite facings, battered outside and vertical within. In this building and on its roof, various ceremonies of purification, mummification and 'opening of the mouth' were conducted. Dual entrances lead from a landing place to a transverse vestibule, and thence to a T-shaped granite-pillared hall, around which were ranged twenty-three statues of the king, the hall being lighted by slots in the angle of wall and ceiling (as p. 32E). Off the southern arm of the hall, there are three chambers in two tiers, while on the opposite flank, an alabaster stair turns through angles to the roof, cutting across the approach to the causeway in the process. A little to the north-west of the Valley Building is the **Great Sphinx of Chephren** (pp. 3, 24, 26A), the colossal enigmatic monster carved from a spur of rock left by Cheops' quarry-masons. It bears the head of Chephren, wearing the royal head-dress, false beard and cobra brow-ornament, and has the body of a recumbent lion. The sculpture is 73.2 m (240 ft) long and 20 m (66 ft) maximum height, the face being 4.1 m (13 ft 6 ins) across. Deficiencies in the rock were made good in stonework. Between the forepaws is a large, inscribed granite stele, recording a restoration made by Thothmes IV (1425 B.C.), of the Eighteenth Dynasty.

The **Pyramid of Mykerinos** (Menkaura) (Fourth Dynasty) (pp. 15M, 26A) is much smaller than its two predecessors at Gizeh, 109 m (356 ft) square and 66.5 m (218 ft) high, with sides sloping at 51°. Much of the casing is preserved, and is mainly Tura limestone but includes sixteen base courses in granite.

The principal pyramids of the Fifth and Sixth Dynasties (2563–2263 B.C.), all built at Abusîr and Sakkâra, were inferior in size and construction to those of the previous dynasty, and tomb chambers and their corridors were simpler and more stereotyped in arrangement.

The **Pyramid of Sahura, Abusîr** (Fifth Dynasty) (p. 15N), is remarkable for the triple series of enormous paired-stone false arches which cover its tomb chamber. It is representative of Fifth and Sixth Dynasty practice in several important

Pyramid of Mykerinos   Pyramid of Chephren   Pyramid of Cheops

A. The Pyramids, Gizeh: aerial view from S.E., with the Sphinx and Valley Building of Chephren in the middle foreground (*c.* 2723–2563 B.C.). See pp. 22–25

B. Tombs at Beni Hasan (2130–1785 B.C.). See p. 27

particulars. Its complex still has the old elements of valley building, causeway and mortuary temple, but the offering-chapel is now incorporated in the temple. A subsidiary small pyramid is included in the south-east angle of the enclosure; this was not a burial place for a queen but had a ritual significance. Relative to the Fourth Dynasty, there is a considerable increase in the number of store-chambers, which tend to enlarge and complicate the plan of the mortuary temple. In decoration, wall reliefs are profuse—a circumstance which applies also to contemporary mastabas (e.g. the Mastaba of Thi, p. 15F). Particularly important architecturally was the use now of granite, free-standing columns, with reeded or plain shafts, and lotus, papyrus or palm capitals, replacing the wholly plain and square pillars of Fourth Dynasty buildings.

(c) *Rock-hewn tombs.* These are rare before the Middle Kingdom, and even so, are at that time a type serving for the nobility rather than royalty; pyramids, though of indifferent construction, remain the principal form of royal tomb.

The **Tombs, Beni Hasan,** numbering thirty-nine, are of the Eleventh and Twelfth Dynasties (2130–1785 B.C.) and belonged to a provincial great family. They are wholly rock-hewn and consist of a chamber behind a porticoed façade plainly imitating wooden construction in the character of the eight- or sixteen-sided, slightly-fluted and tapered columns, their trabeation and the rafter ends above (pp. 23G–K, 26B). Some tombs, like that of Khnemhetep, have slightly-vaulted rock ceilings, supported on fluted or reeded columns, and walls in general were lightly stuccoed and painted with pastoral, domestic and other scenes.

The **Tombs of the Kings, Thebes** (p. 23L–Q) are in the arid mountains on the west side of the Nile. They witness a complete abandonment of the royal pyramid tomb during the New Kingdom in favour of a corridor type, in which stairs, passages and chambers extend as much as 210 m (690 ft) into the mountain side and up to 96 m (315 ft) below the valley floor. The sarcophagus usually lay in a concluding rock-columned hall, and the walls were elaborately painted with ceremonial funerary scenes and religious texts. The most important tombs are those of Seti I and Rameses III, IV and IX. The tombs served only for the sarcophagus and funerary deposits; the mortuary temples stood completely detached (e.g. the Ramesseum, that at Medînet-Habu and Queen Hatshepsut's temple at Dêr el-Bahari), sited in the necropolis adjacent to the western, cultivated land, where there were similar but smaller tombs of high-ranking persons. The temple of Mentuhetep II at Dêr el-Bahari (Middle Kingdom) is transitional, being conjoined with the rock-cut tomb, whilst also having a small pyramid in its confines.

TEMPLES

Temples were of two main classes; the mortuary temples, for ministrations to deified Pharaohs; and the cult temples, for the popular worship of the ancient and mysterious gods. The mortuary temples developed from the offering-chapels of the royal mastabas and pyramids, assuming early permanence and ever greater importance. In the Middle Kingdom, when royal burials began to be made in the hillside, they became architecturally the more important of the two elements; and in the New Kingdom, stood quite detached from the then-customary corridor tombs. Thereafter, their special character tended increasingly to merge into that of the cult temples, and distinction between the two types was eventually lost. Cult temples began in the worship of multifarious local deities. The original essentials were a rectangular palisaded court, entered from a narrow end flanked by pennon-poles and having centrally within them an emblem of the deity. Inside the further end of the court was a pavilion, comprising vestibule and sanctuary. Owing to

TEMPLE PLANS: NEW EMPIRE | PTOLEMAIC AND ROMAN

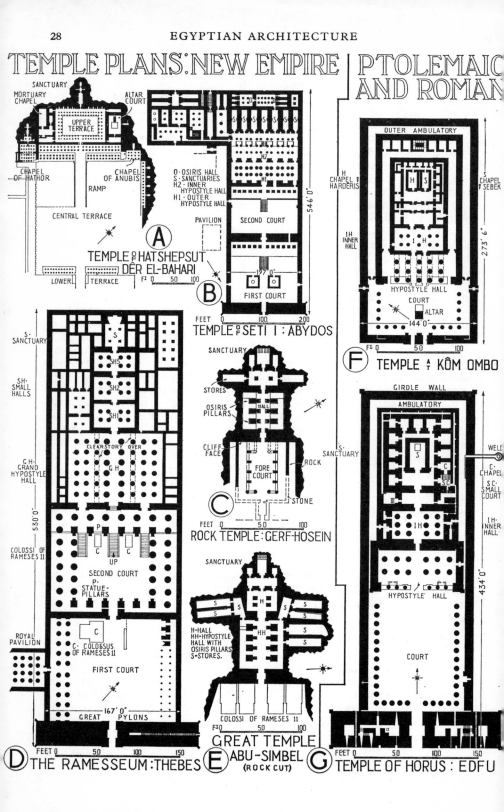

A. TEMPLE OF HATSHEPSUT, DĒR EL-BAHARI

SANCTUARY
MORTUARY CHAPEL
UPPER TERRACE
ALTAR COURT
CHAPEL OF HATHOR
CHAPEL OF ANUBIS
RAMP
CENTRAL TERRACE
LOWER TERRACE
FᵀO 50 100

B. TEMPLE OF SETI I : ABYDOS

O · OSIRIS HALL
S · SANCTUARIES
H2 · INNER HYPOSTYLE HALL
H1 · OUTER HYPOSTYLE HALL
PAVILION
SECOND COURT
197'0"
FIRST COURT
54'6"0"
FEET 0 100 200

C. ROCK TEMPLE : GERF-HOSEIN

SANCTUARY
STORES
OSIRIS PILLARS
CLIFF FACE
FORE COURT
ROCK
STONE
S · SANCTUARY
FEET 0 50 100

D. THE RAMESSEUM : THEBES

S. SANCTUARY
SH · SMALL HALLS
G.H · GRAND HYPOSTYLE HALL
CLEARSTORY OVER
G H
COLOSSI OF RAMESES II
SECOND COURT
P · STATUE-PILLARS
ROYAL PAVILION
C · COLOSSUS OF RAMESES II
FIRST COURT
GREAT PYLONS
167'0"
530'0"
FEET 0 50 100 150

E. GREAT TEMPLE ABU-SIMBEL (ROCK CUT)

SANCTUARY
H · HALL
HH · HYPOSTYLE HALL WITH OSIRIS PILLARS
S · STORES.
COLOSSI OF RAMESES II
FᵀO 50 100

F. TEMPLE OF KŌM OMBO

OUTER AMBULATORY
CHAPEL OF HARŌERIS
CHAPEL OF SEBEK
1H · INNER HALL
HYPOSTYLE HALL
COURT
ALTAR
144'0"
273'6"
FᵀO 50 100

G. TEMPLE OF HORUS : EDFU

GIRDLE WALL
AMBULATORY
WELL
C · CHAPEL
S.C · SMALL COURT
1H · INNER HALL
HYPOSTYLE HALL
COURT
434'0"
FEET 0 50 100 150

successive rebuildings upon these ancient sites, the stages of development are difficult to trace. Apparently, little but the sanctuary and attendant apartments was being built in stone at the opening of the Eighteenth Dynasty, but somewhat later in the New Kingdom, the influx of wealth and universal spread of favoured cults brought the cult temples into full flower. By this time, both mortuary and cult temples had most features in common, yet still bore a resemblance of arrangement to the most venerable shrines. Along a main axis, not specifically orientated, there was a walled open court, with colonnades around, leading to a covered structure, comprising a transverse columned vestibule or 'hypostyle hall' and a sanctuary beyond (or more than one if the temple had a multiple dedication) attended by chapels and other rooms needed by the priesthood. An impressive axial gateway to the court was traditional; it now was extended across the whole width of the court to form a towering, sloping-sided pair of pylons, with tall portal between, equipped with pennon-masts, gorge cornice and roll-moulded outer angles. Temple services were held thrice daily, but none but the priesthood was admitted to them, though privileged persons might sometimes be admitted to the court for certain ceremonies. In the cult temples, processions were a feature, particularly during the periodic festivals, so free circulation was required through or around the sanctuary. Numerous festivals were celebrated during the year, some of which might last for days; at times, shrines of the gods were carried by land or water, to other temples or sacred sites in the neighbourhood, and it was only on such occasions that the populace in general took any kind of part. The whole temple itself stood within a great enclosure, and about it were houses of the priests, official buildings, stores, granaries and a sacred pool or lake (p. 40A).

The **Temple of Khons, Karnak** (1198 B.C.) (pp. 3, 31, 32A), a cult temple, may be taken as the usual type, characterized by entrance pylons, court, hypostyle hall, sanctuary, and various chapels, all enclosed by a high girdle wall. The entrance pylons, fronted by obelisks, were approached through an imposing avenue of sphinxes. The portal gave on to the open court, surrounded on three sides by a double colonnade and leading to the hypostyle hall, to which light was admitted by a clear-storey, formed by the increased height of the columns of the central aisle. Beyond was the sanctuary, with openings front and rear and a circulating passage around, and beyond this again was a four-columned hall. The smaller rooms flanking the sanctuary and at its rear mostly were chapels or served for purposes of the ritual. The temple was protected by a great wall of the same height as the halls themselves, and like them therefore, decreased in height towards the sanctuary end.

The examples which follow are arranged in approximate chronological order.

1. Middle Kingdom (2130–1580 B.C.)

The **Temple of Mentuhetep, Dêr el-Bahari, Thebes** (2065 B.C.) (p. 23F) is exceptional in that it is a mortuary temple directly related to a corridor tomb. It is terraced in two main levels, at the base of steep cliffs. The upper terrace, faced with double colonnades, is approached from a tree-planted forecourt by an inclined way. On the upper terrace a small, completely solid pyramid, raised aloft on a high podium, is wholly surrounded by a walled, hypostyle hall which has further double colonnades outside it. The pyramid was really a cenotaph, for in the rock below it is a dummy burial chamber, approached by an irregular passage from the forecourt. In the rear of the temple is another pillared hall, recessed into the rock face, preceded by an open court from the centre of which a ramp leads down to Mentuhetep's 152.5 m- (500 ft)-long corridor tomb. Like the Ancient Kingdom pyramids, this temple had a causeway, shielded by walls, leading down to a Valley Building three-quarters of a mile away.

2. New Kingdom (1580–332 B.C.)

The **Temple of Hatshepsut, Dêr el-Bahari, Thebes** (1520 B.C.) (pp. 28A, 34A) was built by her architect, Senmut, alongside that of Mentuhetep, of 500 years previously. It is terraced similarly, but her place of burial lay far away in a corridor tomb in the mountains beyond, and this was solely a mortuary temple, dedicated to Ammon and other gods. A processional way of sphinxes connected the temple with the valley. The terraces, approached by ramps, are in three levels, mounting towards the base of the cliffs, their faces lined with double colonnades. The upper terrace is a walled court, lined with a further double colonnade, flanked on the left by the queen's mortuary chapel and on the right by a minor court containing an enormous altar to the sun god Ra. The chief sanctuary lies axially in the rear of the upper court, cut deep in the rock. To right and left of the face of the middle terrace are sanctuaries of Hathor and Anubis. The wall reliefs in this temple are exceptionally fine, and include representations of the queen's trade expedition to Punt (p. 12A), and of her allegedly divine birth. Many pillars are of the eight- or sixteen-sided types reminiscent of the Greek Doric.

The **Great Temple of Ammon, Karnak, Thebes** (1530–323 B.C.) (pp. 3, 32, 33A, B), the grandest of all Egyptian temples, was not built upon one complete plan, but owes its size, disposition and magnificence to the work of many kings. Originally it consisted of a modest shrine constructed early in the Middle Kingdom, about 2000 B.C.; the first considerable enlargement was made by Thothmes I (1530 B.C.). It occupies a site of 366 m × 110 m (1,200 ft × 360 ft), and is placed in an immense enclosure along with other temples and a sacred lake, surrounded by a girdle wall 6.1 m to 9 m (20 ft to 30 ft) thick, while it was connected by an avenue of sphinxes with the temple at Luxor. The temple had six pairs of pylons, added by successive rulers, and consists of various courts and halls leading to the sanctuary, and a large ceremonial hall by Thothmes III in the rear. A great court, 103 m × 84 m (338 ft × 275 ft) deep, gives entrance to the vast hypostyle hall, by Seti I and Rameses II, some 103 m × 52 m (338 ft × 170 ft) internally. The roof of enormous slabs of stone is supported by 134 columns in sixteen rows; the central avenues are about 24 m (78 ft) in height and have columns, 21 m (69 ft) high and 3.6 m (11 ft 9 ins) in diameter, with capitals of the papyrus-flower or bell type, while, in order to admit light through the clear-storey, the side avenues are lower, with columns 13 m (42 ft 6 ins) high and 2.7 m (8 ft 9 ins) in diameter, with papyrus-bud capitals (pp. 32B–F, 33A)—a method of clear-storey lighting more fully developed during the Gothic period in Europe. The effect produced by this forest of columns is most awe-inspiring; the eye is led from the smaller columns of the side avenues, which gradually vanish into semi-darkness and give an idea of unlimited extent, to the larger columns of the central avenues. Incised inscriptions and reliefs in colour, which cover the walls, column shafts and architraves, give the names and exploits of the royal personages who contributed to its grandeur, and praise the gods to whom it was dedicated. In these ancient carvings we find the germ of the idea which, centuries later, led in Christian churches to the employment of coloured mosaics and frescoes, stained-glass windows and mural statues to record the incidents of Bible history and the lives of saints and heroes.

The **Temple at Luxor,** Thebes (1408–1300 B.C.) (pp. 3, 34B), though founded on an older sanctuary, and like most temples, altered and repaired subsequently, is substantially the work of Amenophis III, apart from a great forecourt, with pylons, added by Rameses II. It was dedicated to the Theban triad, Ammon, Mut and Khons. The illustration shows remains of the forecourt, with papyrus-bud capitals and a seated colossus of Rameses, connected by twin colonnades, 53 m (174 ft) long, to a lesser court by Amenophis in the distance. The twin colonnades

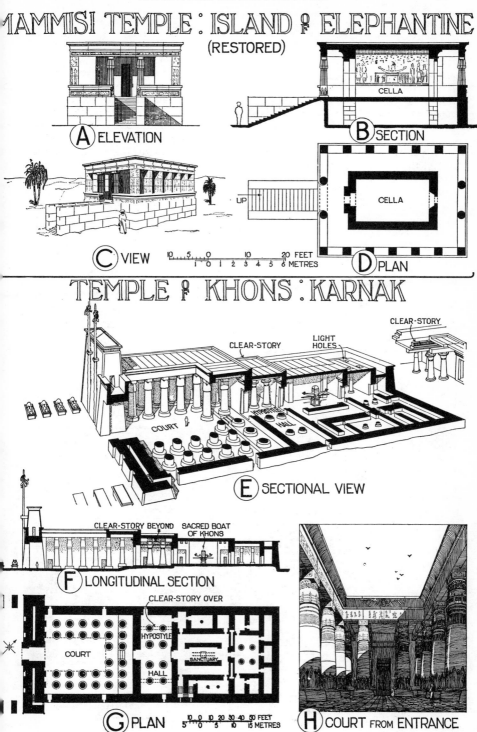

MAMMISI TEMPLE : ISLAND ? ELEPHANTINE
(RESTORED)

A ELEVATION

B SECTION

CELLA

C VIEW

10 5 0 10 20 FEET
1 0 1 2 3 4 5 6 METRES

UP

CELLA

D PLAN

TEMPLE ? KHONS : KARNAK

CLEAR-STORY

CLEAR-STORY LIGHT HOLES

COURT

HYPOSTYLE HALL

E SECTIONAL VIEW

CLEAR-STORY BEYOND SACRED BOAT OF KHONS

F LONGITUDINAL SECTION

CLEAR-STORY OVER

COURT

HYPOSTYLE

SANCTUARY

HALL

G PLAN

10 0 10 20 30 40 50 FEET
5 0 5 10 15 METRES

H COURT FROM ENTRANCE

GREAT TEMPLE OF AMMON : KARNAK

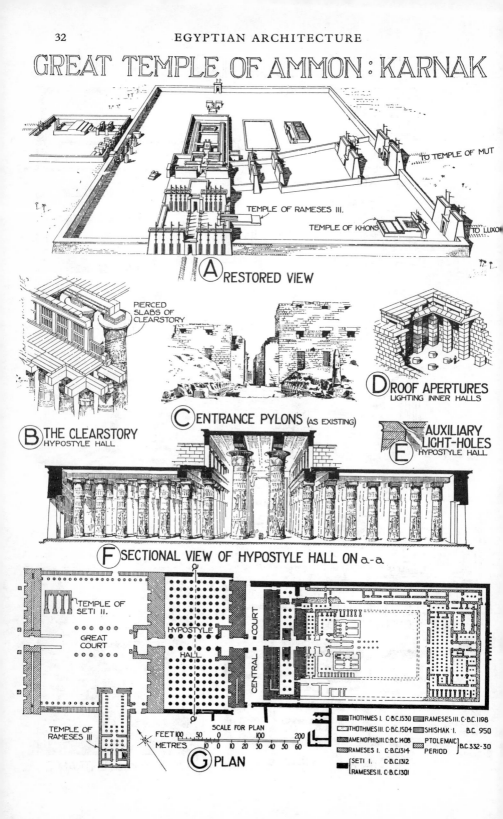

TO TEMPLE OF MUT

TEMPLE OF RAMESES III.

TEMPLE OF KHONS

TO LUXOR

(A) RESTORED VIEW

PIERCED SLABS OF CLEARSTORY

(D) ROOF APERTURES
LIGHTING INNER HALLS

(C) ENTRANCE PYLONS (AS EXISTING)

(B) THE CLEARSTORY
HYPOSTYLE HALL

(E) AUXILIARY
LIGHT-HOLES
HYPOSTYLE HALL

(F) SECTIONAL VIEW OF HYPOSTYLE HALL ON a-a

TEMPLE OF
SETI II.

GREAT
COURT

HYPOSTYLE

HALL

CENTRAL COURT

TEMPLE OF
RAMESES III

FEET 100   50   0   100   200
SCALE FOR PLAN
METRES 10   0   10   20   30   40   50   60

(G) PLAN

THOTHMES I. C·B.C.1530   RAMESES III. C·B.C.1198
THOTHMES III. C·B.C.1504   SHISHAK I.   B.C. 950
AMENOPHIS III. C·B.C.1408 PTOLEMAIC
RAMESES I. C·B.C.1314   PERIOD   B.C.332-30
SETI I.   C·B.C.1312
RAMESES II. C·B.C.1301

A. Great Temple of Ammon, Karnak: Hypostyle hall (restored model)
(*c.* 1312–1301 B.C.). See p. 30

B. Great Temple of Ammon,
Karnak: view across Hypostyle
Hall. See p. 30

C. Temple of Seti I, Abydos:
second Hypostyle Hall (*c.* 1312
B.C.). See p. 35

A. Temple of Queen Hatshepsut, Dêr el-Bahari (*c.* 1520 B.C.). See p. 30

B. Temple of Ammon, Luxor (*c.* 1408–1300 B.C.). See p. 30

of bell-capital columns, 12.8 (42 ft) high, were the only part ever built of a grand hypostyle hall projected by Amenophis, or by the last king of his dynasty, Horemheb. Amenophis III also built a mortuary temple on the west bank at Thebes, but little survives except the twin seated statues of himself, originally 20.8 m (68 ft) high, famous from ancient times as the **Colossi of Memnon.**

The **Temple, Island of Elephantine** (1408 B.C.) (p. 31), destroyed in A.D. 1922, was one of the small so-called Mammisi temples or Birth Houses which often stood in the outer enclosures of large temples and were subsidiary to them. They were sanctuaries perpetuating the tradition of the divine birth of a Pharaoh from a union of the god Horus and a mortal mother, and Hathor, the mother-goddess, or the god Bes, protector of the newly born, usually attended the event. The Birth Houses comprise a single room, or little more, surrounded by a portico of pillars or columns and sometimes stand on a raised podium, approached by a flight of steps from one end. Design for external effect is not typical of Egyptian buildings, but there are instances from the early Eighteenth Dynasty onwards, and the tendency increases in the Ptolemaic and Roman periods.

The **Temple of Seti I, Abydos** (1312 B.C.) (pp. 12B, 28B, 33C) has two pylons, two forecourts and two hypostyle halls, and is unique in having seven sanctuaries side by side, each roofed with stone, corbelled courses cut in the shape of a segmental arch on the underside. Another unusual feature of the temple is a wing of chambers projecting at right angles to the main structure, following the shape of the eminence on which the temple stands. The reliefs on the walls of close-grained limestone are among the finest in Egypt (p. 12B). Seti I built a second mortuary temple on the west bank at Thebes, his successor, Rameses II, adding the finishing touches to both.

The **Ramesseum, Thebes** (1301 B.C.) (pp. 10H, 28D) by Rameses II, is as typical of New Kingdom mortuary temples as is that of Khons, Karnak, of the cult type, though the differences of principle are not very great. In such temples the Pharaoh was worshipped and offerings were made, while his tomb lay far in the mountains behind. The front pylons were 67 m (220 ft) wide, and led to two columned courts, the second having Osiris pillars on the front and rear walls; and so to a grand hypostyle hall, succeeded by three smaller columned halls, which preceded the sanctuary at the far end of the building. There are no arrangements for processional circulation around the sanctuaries of mortuary temples. The hypostyle hall is much smaller than that at Karnak, 30 m × 60 m (98 ft × 196 ft), possessing only 48 columns, including 12 with bell capitals, but like it had an elevated roof over the three axial avenues and an equally well-developed clear-storey. Around the temple, ruins of the temenos walls and the brick-built priests' houses, granaries, stores, etc., still survive. There are fragmentary remains of another mortuary temple by Rameses II at Abydos; and one by Rameses III (1198 B.C.) at **Medînet-Habu** which closely resembles the Ramesseum, and similarly still has evidences of its temenos and brick-built subsidiary buildings surviving (p. 40A).

The **Great Temple, Abu-Simbel** (c. 1301 B.C.) (pp. 28E, 36A, B) is one of two rock-hewn temples at this place commanded by the indefatigable Rameses II, and quite the most stupendous and impressive of its class. An entrance forecourt leads to the imposing façade, 36 m (119 ft) wide and 32 m (105 ft) high, formed as a pylon, immediately in front of which are four rock-cut seated colossal statues of Rameses, over 20 m (65 ft) high. The hall beyond, 9 m (30 ft) high, has eight Osiris pillars and vividly-coloured wall reliefs. Eight smaller chambers open off asymmetrically to right and left, while on the main axis is a smaller hall with four pillars, leading to a vestibule serving three apartments, the central one being the sanctuary and containing four statues of gods and a support for a sacred boat.

A. Great Temple, Abu-Simbel (*c.* 1301 B.C.). See p. 35

B. Great Temple, Abu-Simbel.
See p. 35

C. Small Temple, Abu-Simbel
(*c.* 1301 B.C.). See p. 37

The **Small Temple, Abu-Simbel** (*c.* 1301 B.C.) (p. 36C), by Rameses II, close to the Great Temple, was dedicated to his deified Queen, Nefertari, and the goddess Hathor. The façade here is 27.4 m (90 ft) wide and 12.2 m (40 ft) high, and comprises six niches recessed in the face of the rock and containing six colossal statues, 10 m (33 ft) high; two represent Rameses and one Nefertari on each side of the portal, which leads to a vestibule and a hall, 10.4 m × 8.2m (34 ft × 27 ft), with six pillars bearing the sculptured head of Hathor.

The **Rock-cut Temple at Gerf Hosein** (*c.* 1301 B.C.) (p. 28C), is still another example due to Rameses II. It is of interest in that it retains quite a little of its forecourt, the walls of which are in part rock-cut.

3. Ptolemaic and Roman Periods (332 B.C.–A.D. first century)

The **Temple of Isis, on the island of Philae** (pp. 10J, 38, 39) marks an ancient sacred site. Minor parts of the surviving buildings belong to the Thirtieth Dynasty (378–341 B.C.) but most are by the Ptolemies II–XIII (283–47 B.C.). The irregularities of the plan are due to piecemeal building. The principle of arrangement, however, remains much the same as at the height of the New Kingdom period, a thousand years earlier—a progressive concentration of effect from outer and inner courts and pylons to the ultimate sanctuary in the temple nucleus. Such changes as there are, largely concern details. Column capitals are coarser and more ornate, varied in design from column to column, and have very deep abacus blocks; colonnades appear more frequently on the exterior of buildings, their columns linked by screen walls reaching about half-way up (p. 38B). Such characteristics are notable in the 'Birth House' or Mammisi temple on the west side of the inner court. Also, in a pavilion known as the 'Kiosk' or 'Pharaoh's Bed', standing on the east side of the island; though this is of Roman date (*c.* A.D. 96) (pp. 38A, 39A). It is roofless, and has four columns on the ends and five on the flanks. The two portals axial on the short sides are designed without a central part to the lintels, so as to permit the passage of banners and effigies carried in procession. The whole island nowadays is submerged during a part of the year, leaving only the tops of the buildings visible.

The **Temple of Horus, Edfu** (237–57 B.C.) (pp. 28G, 42A, B), is a fine, well-preserved example of the period. It was built in three stages, with protracted intervals between; first the temple proper by Ptolemy III, then the outer hypostyle hall (140–124 B.C.), and finally the perimeter wall and pylons. It is plainly a processional cult temple. There is a passage surrounding the sanctuary, which serves also to give access to thirteen small chapels, and another completing the entire circuit of the enclosing wall. All the inner rooms were completely dark and windowless. The grand pylons are some 62.6 m (205 ft) across and 30.5 m (100 ft) high. Though in the main the temple demonstrates the tenacity of the ancient traditions, there are here again those distinguishing features of the period, particularly notable in the main hypostyle hall; the foliated or palm capitals, varying in design in pairs astride the axis, the deep abaci, the screen walls between the columns, and the 'broken' lintel of the central portal.

The **Mammisi Temple, Edfu** (116 B.C.), standing in the outer enclosure of the Temple of Horus, is typical of all externally-colonnaded birth-houses, and similar to others at Elephantine, Philae (see above) and Dendera, where there are two, one Ptolemaic and the other Roman.

The **Temple of Hathor, Dendera** (110 B.C.–A.D. 68) (p. 40B) is most imposing, standing in a brick-walled temenos 290 m (951 ft) by 280 m (918 ft) wide. Except in lacking pylons, it closely resembles that at Edfu, and, as there, the hypostyle hall was added to the Ptolemaic nucleus in Roman times, along with the peripheral

A. Island of Philae: aerial view from E. when not submerged: Kiosk in foreground (*c.* A.D. 96); pylons, Temple of Isis and Mammisi Temple on farther side of island (283–47 B.C.). See p. 37

B. Temple of Isis, Philae: columns　　　C. Temple of Isis, Philae: second pylon

A. Temple of Isis, Philae (283–47 B.C.), with Kiosk (*c.* A.D. 96) partly submerged

B. Temple of Isis, Philae: entrance court, showing pylons. See p. 37

A. Mortuary Temple of Rameses III, Medînet-Habu (1198 B.C.) showing surrounding brick-built buildings in temenos. See p. 35

B. Temple of Hathor, Dendera (110 B.C.–A.D. 68). See p. 37

wall, which stands sufficiently clear of the temple to allow a complete processional circuit. The four-sided, Hathor-headed capitals of the hypostyle hall, carrying a conventional representation of the birth-house on the deep abaci above, are typical of the period. Many narrow chambers are concealed in the thickness of the massive outer walls, and stairs lead to the roof, where ceremonies took place.

The **Temple of Sebek and Haroeris at Kôm Ombo** (145 B.C.–A.D. 14) (p. 28F) is peculiar in having a double approach to its twin sanctuaries and two peripheral processional circuits.

OBELISKS

The obelisks, originating in the sacred symbol of the sun god of Heliopolis, and which usually stood in pairs astride temple entrances, are huge monoliths, square on plan and tapering to an electrum-capped pyramidion at the summit, which was the sacred part. They have a height of nine or ten times the diameter at the base, and the four sides are cut with hieroglyphs. The granite for obelisks was quarried by the very laborious method of pounding trenches around the tremendous block with balls of dolerite, a very hard stone, as the more normal method of splitting from the parent rock by means of timber wedges, which expanded after soaking, was too hazardous for so long a unit. Mural reliefs show that obelisks were transported on sledges and river-barges, and erected on their foundations by hauling them up earthen ramps, and then tilting them into position. Many were removed from Egypt by the Roman Emperors, and there are at least twelve in Rome alone.

The **Obelisk** in the Piazza of S. Giovanni in Laterano was brought to Rome from the Temple of Ammon at Karnak, Thebes (p. 30), where it was originally erected by Thothmes III, and is the largest known. It is a monolith of red granite from Aswân, 32 m (105 ft) high without the added pedestal, 2.7 m (9 ft) square at the base and 1.9 m (6 ft 2 ins) at the top, and weighs about 230 tons.

'Cleopatra's Needle', the obelisk on the Thames Embankment, London, originally at Heliopolis, was brought to England from Alexandria in 1878. It bears inscriptions of Thothmes III and Rameses II. It is 20.9 m (68 ft 6 ins) high, 2.4 m × 2.3 m (8 ft × 7 ft 6 ins) at the base, and weighs 180 tons.

DWELLINGS

Clay models deposited in tombs indicate that ordinary dwellings were of crude brick, one or two storeys high, with flat or arched ceilings and a parapeted roof partly occupied by a loggia. Rooms looked towards a north-facing court. Remains of barrack-like dwellings for workers exist at the pyramid sites of Chephren at Gizeh (Fourth Dynasty) and of Sesostris II at Kahun (Twelfth Dynasty) on the eastern edge of the Fayûm; and again at Tell el-Amarna, where the Pharaoh Akhnaten (Eighteenth Dynasty) built his ephemeral new town, occupied only for about fifteen years (c. 1366–1351 B.C.). Each workers' establishment constituted a considerable village, laid out on rigidly formal lines. More freely planned was a village at Dêr el-Medina, constructed for those engaged upon the Theban royal corridor-tombs, and which endured for four centuries. Though in the towns even the better houses were on constricted plots and therefore might be three or four storeys high, where space allowed mansions stood in their own grounds, laid out formally with groves, gardens, pools and minor structures surrounding the rectangular, crude-brick dwelling, this having its door and window openings dressed around in stone. Columns and beams, doors and window frames were made from precious timber. Typically, there was a central hall or living-room, raised sufficiently high with the help of columns to allow clear-storey light on one or more sides,

A. Temple of Horus, Edfu (237–57 B.C.). See p. 37

B. Temple of Horus, Edfu: portico with screen between columns

for first floors were only partial. Regularly there were three fundamental parts; a reception suite, on the cooler, north side of the house; service; and private quarters. Archaic palaces were faced with overlapping vertical timbers, giving the so-called 'palace façade' effect which left its decorative impress upon funerary stone architecture for some time. The 'white walls' of Memphis, famed in later records, were perhaps more probably of mud brick faced with mud plaster and white-washed, although the long tradition of stone-working at Memphis may suggest they were of limestone, thus being glaring white in the strong Egyptian sun. Relatively little is known of later dynastic palaces, of which the most impressive was perhaps that of Amenhotep III at **Malkata,** on the west bank of Thebes and south of the temple of Medînet-Habu. The whole complex comprised a number of large, rambling buildings facing on to wide courts or parade grounds, without any easily discernible plan for the whole: stone was used only sparingly, for column-bases, door-sills and the flooring of baths; mud brick was the material used for the walls, with wood for columns and roofing beams. Tomb paintings reveal the gorgeously canopied thrones in the audience halls of this period; and at Malkata lavish use was made of painted decoration, including plants and water birds around a rectangular pool, on the floors, and likewise too on the walls and ceilings. The central palace at Amarna shows development in the reign of Akhnaten from his father's palace at Malkata, being laid out on a more monumental scale and with greater use of stone in the state rooms. It is, however, significant that in the reign of Amenhotep III, at the height of the Eighteenth Dynasty, the king's chief palace was of brick rather than stone. The pictures at Tell el-Amarna of the royal palace and temples provide very useful evidence for correlation with the excavated remains. Later New Kingdom palaces include those of Merneptah at Memphis and the modest palace of Rameses III within his mortuary temple complex at Medînet-Habu, at a time when the chief centre of government had been moved from Thebes to Lower Egypt.

FORTRESSES

Egyptian penetration of Nubia is now known, through excavations carried out before the completion of the High Dam at Aswân, to have begun by the Fourth Dynasty, a town site of the Old Kingdom having been excavated near the later **fortress of Buhen** (pp. 44, 45). The best preserved of the architectural monuments of the Twelfth Dynasty, the Middle Kingdom, are not in Egypt proper but in Nubia. Here great fortresses were built by successive kings, especially Senusret III, in whose reign Egyptian control of Lower Nubia, between the First and Second Cataracts, was finally made secure. Most of the fortresses are on the west bank of the Nile or on islands. There was close communication between one fortress and the next, with the headquarters at Buhen, the largest stronghold. The military architecture revealed here and at the other fortresses shows astonishing sophistication. At Buhen the main wall stood 4.8 m (15 ft 8 ins) thick and 11 m (36 ft) high, reinforced along its exterior by projecting rectangular towers. At wider intervals along the revetment of the paved rampart beneath the main wall there were semi-circular bastions, having triple loopholes with single embrasures, through which archers could cover the ditch below them by cross-fire (p. 45B). This ditch was dry, with a scarp, and about 9 m (30 ft) wide by 7 m (23 ft) deep. On the outer side of the ditch was a counterscarp surmounted by a narrow covered way of brickwork, beyond which was a glacis sloping down to the natural ground level. The great West Gate (p. 44A), facing the desert and the long roads leading to the mines and quarries, was especially strongly fortified. The use of the scarp or glacis must have been primarily to hinder the advance of an attacking force, and also to prevent

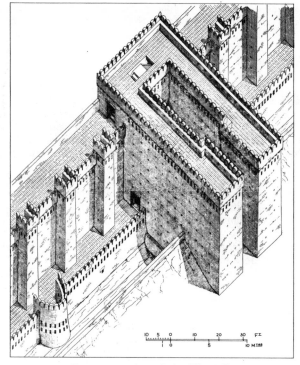

A. Reconstruction of the West Gate

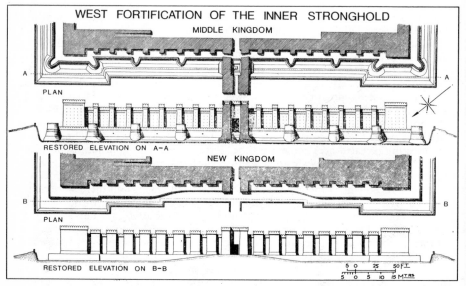

WEST FORTIFICATION OF THE INNER STRONGHOLD

MIDDLE KINGDOM

PLAN

RESTORED ELEVATION ON A-A

NEW KINGDOM

PLAN

RESTORED ELEVATION ON B-B

B. West fortification of the inner stronghold

Fortress of Buhen (2130–1580 B.C.). See p. 43

A. Buhen Fortress: west fortification (2130–1580 B.C.). See p. 43

B. Buhen Fortress: loopholes of the lower ramparts

undermining of the massive walls. There is no question of their being designed against chariotry, since the horse was not introduced into Egypt from Asia until the Hyksos conquest in the seventeenth century B.C. The organization and skill of the local tribes must have been formidable, to necessitate such fortresses. After the collapse of Egyptian rule in Nubia in the period following the Twelfth Dynasty, this was re-established without much difficulty in the early Eighteenth Dynasty. The fortifications of Buhen, once again probably the military and governmental headquarters of Nubia, were rebuilt on a larger scale but of irregular shape, with wide salients, the largest being on the west side. Within it was a great gatehouse with a rock-cut causeway across the ditch, the main entrance to the fortress, facing the desert. The fortress on Uronarti Island had a gate at each end, with an administrative building with store-rooms inside each, and there were houses for the garrison and their families. The best use was made of the restricted space, and little change took place with the reoccupation in the New Kingdom.

BIBLIOGRAPHY

ALDRED, C. *The Development of Egyptian Art*. London, 1952.
BREASTED, J. H. *A History of Egypt*. New York, 1905.
—. *Ancient Records of Egypt*. 5 vols. Chicago, 1906–7.
CARTER, H., and MACE, A. C. *The Tomb of Tut-ankh-Amen*. 3 vols. London, 1923–33.
CLARKE, G. SOMERS, and ENGELBACH, R. *Ancient Egyptian Masonry*. London, 1930.
Description de l'Égypte (known as 'Napoleon's Egypt'). 23 vols. Paris, 1809–22.
DRIOTON, É., and LAUER, J. P. *Sakkarah. The Monuments of Zoser*. Cairo, 1939.
DRIOTON, É., and VANDIER, J. *Les Peuples de l'orient mediterranéen (l'Égypte)*. Paris, 1952.
EDWARDS, I. E. S. *The Pyramids of Egypt*. Harmondsworth, 1947; revised ed., 1961.
EMERY, W. B. *The Tomb of Hor-Aha*. Cairo, 1939.
—. *Archaic Egypt*. Harmondsworth, 1961.
—. *Egypt in Nubia*. London, 1965.
EMERY, W. B., and others. *Great Tombs of the First Dynasty*. 3 vols. London, 1949–58.
FAIRMAN, H. W. 'Town Planning in Pharaonic Egypt', *Town Planning Review*, vol. xx, no. 1. 1949.
—. 'Worship and Festivals in an Egyptian Temple,' *Bulletin of the John Rylands Library*, vol. 37, no. 1. 1954.
FIRTH, C. M., QUIBELL, J. E., and LAUER, J. P. *The Step Pyramid*. Cairo, 1935.
GARDINER, A. H. *The Temple of King Sethos I at Abydos*. Vols. i–iii. London and Chicago, 1933–8.
'Les grandes découvertes archéologiques de 1954', *La Revue de Caire*, vol. xxxiii, no. 175, Numéro Spécial.
LANGE, K., and HIRMER, M., trans. Boothroyd, R. H. *Egypt*. London, 1956; revised 4th ed., 1968.
LUCAS, A. *Ancient Egyptian Materials and Industries*. London, 1948.
NAVILLE, E., and CLARKE, G. SOMERS. *The XIth Dynasty Temple at Deir el-Bahari*. Parts I and II. London, 1907, 1910.
PETRIE, W. M. FLINDERS. *Egyptian Architecture*. London, 1938.
PORTER, B., and MOSS, R. L. B. *Topographical Bibliography of Ancient Egyptian Hieroglyphic Texts, Reliefs, and Painting*. 7 vols. Oxford, 1927–51; amplified 2nd ed., 1960–4.
REISNER, G. A. *The Development of the Egyptian Tomb down to the accession of Cheops*. Cambridge (Mass.), and London, 1935.
STEINDORFF, G., and SEELE, K. C. *When Egypt ruled the East*, 1942; revised ed., 1957.
SMITH, W. STEVENSON. *The History of Egyptian Sculpture and Painting in the Old Kingdom*. London, 1946; 2nd ed., 1949.
—. *The Art and Architecture of Ancient Egypt*. Harmondsworth and Baltimore; revised ed., 1965.
WOLDERING, I. *Egypt: the Art of the Pharaohs* (Art of the World series). London, 1963.

2

ARCHITECTURE IN THE
ANCIENT NEAR EAST

Circa 5000 B.C.–A.D. 641

In the Near East, apart from Egypt, the main centre of urban communities was at first in southern and central Mesopotamia, the lands of Sumer and Akkad, with a gradual extension of city life up the valleys of the Tigris and Euphrates into Assyria and Syria. The earliest settlements of all, however, were not in Mesopotamia but in the Levant and Anatolia, with early village settlements also in the Zagros highlands on either side of the present Iraq–Iran frontier. The development of city life in Palestine, Anatolia and Iran, however, was resumed in the third and second millennia B.C. only after a long period of cultural stagnation following the initial flowering of Neolithic art and architecture. Meanwhile, from *c.* 4000 B.C. and even earlier, the development of cities had become firmly rooted in Sumer, and the economic primacy of Mesopotamia may be said to have continued unbroken until the triumph of Hellenism with the conquests of Alexander the Great.

INFLUENCES

GEOGRAPHICAL

Three broad zones comprise the greater part of the Near East. To the south lies the Arabian peninsula, with its desert extending northwards into Syria; in a great arc extending from the Mediterranean coastal plain of Palestine through north Syria to the head of the Persian Gulf stretches the zone of grasslands, steppes, piedmont country and alluvial river plains termed the Fertile Crescent; and for 2,400 km (1,500 miles) from west to east extends a chain of mountains and plateaux from the Taurus range and central plateau of Anatolia through the mountains and lakes of eastern Turkey and north-west Iran to the parallel ranges of the Zagros highlands, dividing the wide Iranian plateau from the plains of Mesopotamia. The coastal regions of the Aegean, southern Turkey and the Levant are typically Mediterranean, once forested but now largely denuded of trees. A heavily forested zone stretches along the Pontic coast, the Black Sea littoral, while the south coast of the Caspian Sea is sub-tropical in vegetation. To the north the Caucasus range forms a clearly-defined frontier of the Near East, both environmentally and culturally.

The fertile plains of the twin rivers, Tigris and Euphrates, were given the name of Mesopotamia (Gk *mesos* = middle + *potamos* = river). Unlike Egypt, Mesopotamia lacks natural defensive boundaries; on the west it shades gradually into the undulating steppes of the Arabian desert, while on the east the valleys and foot-hills of the Zagros ranges were sufficiently fertile to nurture neighbouring peoples watchfully envious of the richer living offered by the lush Mesopotamian plains. The Tigris and Euphrates rise in the highland zone to the north, and are reinforced by tributaries. After the melting of the snows, the Tigris floods in the spring and the Euphrates a few weeks later, in May. The gentler current of the Euphrates is one explanation of the earlier spread of urban communities, slower to establish themselves in the upper Tigris valley, where the river afforded a less easy means of communication and trade. To check the inundations and to irrigate the plains, the Sumerians and their successors constructed a network of canals, storage basins and ditches, which, besides conserving the rivers in their courses, gave a marvellous fertility to the alluvial land. The abundant harvests of grain, fruit and vegetables, the fish and fowl and animal husbandry were a source of astonishment to visiting travellers and writers. One of the causes, perhaps the main one, of the ultimate decline of Mesopotamia was the growing salinity of the soil resulting from excessive irrigation, with rapid evaporation in the heat of the summer. The canals and rivers served as waterways, too, and made roads largely unnecessary.

North Syria was especially open to influences from all directions, in that its situation gave it access to the maritime trade across the Mediterranean; it was also on the highway from the Anatolian plateau to Egypt, and lay athwart the middle reaches of the Euphrates, thus being accessible to and from the cities of Mesopotamia. Consequently this region and likewise the Lebanon and Palestine to the south were ever open to conquest by one or another neighbouring great power. Incursions from the northern steppes into the Near East included that of the Hittites, who arrived and settled in central Anatolia from *c.* 2000 B.C., in a region always vulnerable to marauding highlanders living immediately to the north.

GEOLOGICAL

The Mesopotamian plain is mostly alluvial, and before systematic control of the flood waters contained much marshland. Reeds and rushes could always be had in profusion, but for building timber, although the ubiquitous palm could be made to serve, reliance had to be placed almost wholly on imports, either from the slopes of the eastern or northern mountains or, for the finest supplies, from the Amanus mountains beside the Amuq (Antioch) plain, where cedars grew as famous in early historical times as those of the Lebanon were for Egypt. Apart from occasional boulders carried down with bygone floods, stone too was lacking; the small amount of limestone and alabaster that was employed had to be transported laboriously from the uplands. So also had the minerals: copper, tin, lead, gold, silver and, later, iron. The one building material universally available was the clay from the soil itself, well suited for the making of bricks, which were either sun-dried or, when intended for the facing of important structures, kiln-fired, and for decorative purposes glazed in different colours. Chopped straw was mixed with the clay for the sun-dried bricks to improve their cohesion. Burnt bricks were sometimes laid in lime mortar, but more often in bitumen, a natural material readily available.

Beyond Mesopotamia, on the plateaux of Anatolia and Iran, the geology is completely different. Stone was available throughout the highland zone for building purposes; and in Anatolia timber was obtainable, in greater quantity and size than today. Consequently distinctive architectural traditions appeared, with the timber-frame structure being the prototype of buildings in mud brick. This change occurred at different periods, beginning as early as the seventh millennium B.C. The local resources of copper and other metals were at first exploited more by visiting Mesopotamian merchants than by the native peoples, although by the second millennium B.C. the Hittites have been credited with being perhaps first in the exploitation of iron; Trans-Caucasian sources of metals also became increasingly important from *c.* 2300 B.C.

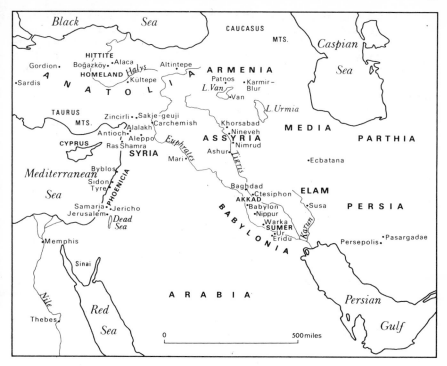

The Ancient Near East

CLIMATIC

Except for the humid Black Sea and Caspian littorals, most of the Near East is subject to extremes of temperature between winter and summer, the prevalence of heat or of cold being determined principally by altitude. Only in northern districts is there enough rainfall to permit dry farming without irrigation, essential for the survival of central and southern Mesopotamia. In much of the highland zone, especially from the upper Euphrates to Lake Urmia, winter is longer than summer and the climate more akin to that of parts of Canada than that of the Persian Gulf. The 'megaron', with its entrance at the end rather than in the long side, was thus suited to the climate of the Anatolian plateau; and perhaps too the dry, exhilarating air of the Iranian plateau—Persepolis stands at an altitude of 1,800 m (6,000 ft)— may account for the frequency of light, columned halls and porticoes in the Persian royal buildings.

HISTORICAL, SOCIAL AND RELIGIOUS

(a) *Mesopotamia*. Since it was in Sumer that writing was first invented, in the fourth millennium B.C., it is here that the longest historical records can be found, though most of the surviving cuneiform tablets are concerned with trade, accounts, or religious texts rather than annals of political or military events. The archaeological evidence suggests that the Sumerians, an 'Asiatic' people, had been occupying the land from the first settlement of Eridu, by historical tradition and material evidence the oldest city of Sumer. Newcomers arrived from time to time, but not until the incursion of the Semitic Akkadians, who came to political ascendancy under Sargon of Agade (c. 2340 B.C.), was there any major change in the population of the alluvial plains of Mesopotamia; and even then the Sumerians regained power under Ur-nammu (c. 2125 B.C.), the founder of the prosperous Third Dynasty of Ur. Before Sargon the cities of Mesopotamia had been ruled by individual governors. In spite of political disunity, there was a strong sense of a common civilization, without which the traditions of Sumerian literature and the very art of writing, could scarcely have been transmitted from one city to another, still less from one generation to the next. With the Akkadian dynasty, especially strong under Sargon and his grandson Naramsin, three new developments occurred: first, political unity was imposed by force on the warring city-states; second, the status of the ruler was deliberately exalted, with the claim to divinity by the king in his lifetime; third, the expansion of Sumero-Akkadian trade beyond the confines of Mesopotamia was stimulated by expeditions led by the king, their purpose being as much economic as military. Moreover, the Semitic peoples, always predominant north and north-west of Sumer and Akkad, now became mingled with the Sumerians, whose script, religion and art they adopted; but they added their own contributions and their own Akkadian language, which became the language of diplomacy as far afield as Egypt and played a dominant role in the Near East, until the rise of Aramaic in the last century of the Assyrian empire.

The mainspring of the growth of cities in Mesopotamia was the temple, the source of that communal organization and authority which each community required to achieve the status and permanence of a city. Irrigation especially demanded such organization; and it likewise necessitated the formulation of a body of practice which in due course became law. Monopoly of writing gave the Sumerian priests as much power in society as the clergy and monks possessed in early mediaeval Europe. Thus the cohesion of each city often ensured its survival, and the conditions of Sumerian society were reflected in its religion, each city being protected by its own god: Anu, the sky god, was patron of Warka; Sin, the moon god, of Ur; Ea (or Enki), god of the waters, of Eridu; Enlil, lord of the Sumerian pantheon, of Nippur; Ningirsu, of Lagash. In later centuries Marduk and Ashur, the national gods of Babylon and Assyria, were to achieve yet greater prominence. Just as religion dominated the thoughts of men and their daily life, so its architectural embodiment in the temple stood out above the surrounding houses, a landmark in the flat alluvial plain. From the temple on its platform evolved the 'ziggurat', or temple tower, itself the sacred mountain. The religion of the Sumerians and their Semitic contemporaries and successors was sombre in its outlook, with an ever-present apprehension that the will of the gods might have been imperfectly foreseen, and thus the need for the higher skills in medicine, divination, mystic interpretation and religious ritual in time produced a powerful class of astrologer-priests. The temple was also the major landowner, its corporate identity protecting it from the changes and chances of secular life; it also engaged its resources and expertise in external trade.

The Old Babylonian period (c. 2016–1595 B.C.), whose best known figure is Hammurabi of Babylon (c. 1792–1750 B.C.), saw considerable commercial activity. The code of Hammurabi sheds light on the rules governing trade, land tenure, feudal service, taxation, slavery and the organization of labour, and emphasises the powers of the secular ruler and the growth of his power in relation to that of the temples, whose role in trade was on the decline too. Babylon was one among many prosperous cities, attaining political supremacy only in the final years of the reign of Hammurabi. Soon after Hammurabi's death the marshes at the head of the Persian Gulf fell into the hands of the dynasty of the Sea Lands. The last century of the First Dynasty of Babylon was one of growing debility, until the raid by Mursilis I, king of the Hittites, and his capture of Babylon (c. 1595 B.C.). Meanwhile, two groups of newcomers from the highland zone, the Hurrians and the Kassites, were making themselves increasingly prominent in northern and central Mesopotamia respectively, until the latter took over political control in the Mesopotamian plain after the Hittite raid had ended the rule of Babylon. In architecture the relative decline in the power of the temples is perhaps to be seen reflected in the emphasis on restoration of older buildings rather than the construction of new ones. The very long but increasingly supine rule by the Kassites lasted until c. 1171 B.C.

Meanwhile the Assyrians, a small but energetic people of only partly Semitic affinities, had re-emerged from the obscurity which had descended on them after the reign of Shamshi-Adad I, the contemporary of Hammurabi in his earlier years. In the fourteenth century B.C. they had successfully challenged and in due course absorbed the kingdom of Mitanni, centred in the Khabur basin. After incessant battles they developed an independent state in the upper Tigris valley. Tukulti-Ninurta I (c. 1250–1210 B.C.) overcame Babylon; but this was only the beginning of an intermittent struggle between the two powers, which was in the end one of the factors leading to the downfall of Assyria (612 B.C.). Both Assyria and Babylon declined greatly in the eleventh and tenth centuries B.C., owing to pressure from Aramaean and Chaldean tribes. While Assyria's military recovery began with Adad-Nirari II (911–890 B.C.), it was not until the reign of Ashurnasirpal II (883–859 B.C.) that the Assyrian dynasty had time for building activity, with the removal of the capital to Nimrud (Calah). The Assyrian kings showed great energy in scientific and literary pursuits, including the amassing of a library at the final capital of Nineveh. After the reign of Shalmaneser III (859–824 B.C.) Assyrian power declined, until the throne was seized by Tiglath-Pileser III (745–727 B.C.). Failure by successive Assyrian kings to secure control of the north-east frontier of their empire, where the Median tribes united to constitute a formidable power in the seventh century B.C., was a fatal error, compounded by involvement—especially under Esarhaddon (681–669 B.C.) and his son Ashurbanipal (668–633 B.C.)—in the short-lived annexation of Egypt. Finally, the 'brothers' war' between Ashurbanipal and Shamash-shum-ukin (later renowned as Sardanapolus), and the sack of Susa (c. 640 B.C.), left the way open to the Medes and reduced the man-power of the Assyrian army. The economy of the great cities of Assyria was like that of the cities to the south in Babylonia, with their guilds of craftsmen occupying their own quarters. Power was in the hands of the nobility, under the king, a small élite evidently too few to serve all the needs of the state. Native Assyrians had in fact become a minority in their own land during the last century of the empire. The kings, dominant as they were, never claimed the divine status given to themselves by the Akkadian kings many centuries before. Their deeds in war and the chase, their rituals and their dress are illuminated by the astonishing succession of reliefs which adorn their palaces. Many of these reliefs provide interesting evidence on military architecture, the defences of cities and methods of warfare. The siege of Lachish in Judah by Sennacherib (c. 700 B.C.) is documented in the famous reliefs from Nineveh, now in the British Museum.

The Neo-Babylonian period (c. 626–539 B.C.) began with the rise of Babylon in alliance with the Medes against Assyria; then came the reign of Nebuchadnezzar II (605–563 B.C.), of Biblical fame; he is lastingly associated with the wonders of Babylon, its palaces, hanging gardens and towered walls. The dynasty ended with Nabonidus, who was defeated by the Persian king, Cyrus (539 B.C.).

(b) *Anatolia, the Levant and Iran.* The archives of the Hittite capital Hattušas (Boğazköy) are the main source of knowledge of the history and civilization of the Hittite state in the second millennium B.C. There emerges an impression of a mingling of several races, and of the continuing influence of Sumero-Akkadian literature. The Hittite state reveals features distinctively Indo-European in its social structure, the assembly of the nobility and the nature of its laws; but during the New Kingdom, after the expansion of the Hittite power southwards into Syria, the monarchy took on more of the character of other states in the ancient Near East. The Phoenician cities of the Levant coast, with their international outlook necessitated by their dependence on maritime trade, contrast strongly with the inward-looking traditions of the Hebrews as revealed in the Bible. The Amarna tablets and other Egyptian sources are relevant to the history of the Levant in the second millennium B.C. A major disruption occurred with the invasion of the Sea Peoples (c. 1200 or a little later), bringing the Philistines to occupy part of the land which has ever since retained their name, Palestine. The most significant result of this event was the development of iron-working. Many cities destroyed by the Sea Peoples, including Ugarit, were never rebuilt, and the Hittite state disappeared.

In the early first millennium B.C. a number of cities rose to prosperity in Syria, especially Carchemish and Hamath. Culturally these cities were the heirs of the Hittite state of the Late Bronze Age, with an admixture of Aramaean influence, and they were eventually absorbed by the expansion of the Assyrian empire. Meanwhile they had looked, with only brief success, to the kingdom of Van (Urartu) for support. This state is known mainly from its monuments and from references in the Assyrian annals: they reveal a dynasty which rose to power in the early ninth century B.C., which contrived to hold the kingdom together through times of adversity after expansion, which secured a renaissance in the seventh century B.C., and which out-lived by a few years its Assyrian neighbour and erstwhile foe. The Iranian plateau, however, remained in the darkness of pre-history until the rise of the Achaemenian state under Cyrus the Great.

(c) *The Persian Empire*. From a relatively small state in south-west Iran, Cyrus the Great, founder of the Achaemenian empire, established the basis of his power by the defeat of his grandfather, Astyages the Mede, at Pasargadae (550 B.C.). The westward expansion of his empire was secured with his defeat of Croesus, the Lydian king, and his capture of Sardis (546 B.C.). Babylon fell without resistance in 539 B.C., and with it the Babylonian possessions in the Levant. Preparations for the conquest of Egypt had to be carried out by Cambyses II (525 B.C.). It seems that the impression produced by the marvellous buildings of Memphis and Thebes, perhaps even more than the sight of the Greek cities of the Ionian coast, popularized columnar architecture among the Persians. Next came Darius I (522–486 B.C.), a capable and enterprising administrator, who built a network of arterial roads and reorganized the empire into satrapies or provinces, twenty in all, each under a satrap or governor. The rule of the Persians was not harsh; customs and religions of the conquered peoples were respected. Craftsmen of many races, including Greeks and Egyptians, migrated to the heart of this new world empire, ruled initially from Babylon but afterwards from Susa and from other centres, especially Persepolis, the new royal seat of government founded by Darius I not far from Pasargadae, itself the unfinished capital established by Cyrus the Great. Hamadan was another major centre, the ancient Ecbatana. The religion of Zoroaster had meanwhile gained a footing in Iran: this was a system of ethical forces representing good and evil at war from the beginning of time. The two protagonists were Ahuramazda, the sky god and creator of good, and Ahriman, the destructive spirit, or power of evil. There was thus a strong tendency towards monotheism, Ahuramazda being supreme, but the popular religion continued to recognize lesser gods, among whom Mithras, the sun god, became the most famous.

The first serious reverses suffered by the Achaemenian empire were in its efforts to conquer Greece, which met with final failure under Xerxes at the battles of Salamis and Plataea (480–479 B.C.). After the rise of Macedon under Philip and his subjugation of the Greek cities, the way lay open to his son Alexander the Great (336–323 B.C.) to carry the war into Asia. With the battle of Gaugamela, in Assyria (331 B.C.), Alexander crushed Darius III, the last king of the Achaemenian dynasty: the empire founded by Cyrus the Great and extended by Cambyses II and Darius I thus fell into Alexander's hands. After his death, Persia passed successively under the Seleucid (312–247 B.C.), Parthian (247 B.C.–A.D. 226) and Sassanian (A.D. 226–641) dynasties, finally being conquered by the Arab armies bringing Islam.

ARCHITECTURAL CHARACTER

In the alluvial plains of the Tigris and Euphrates stone and timber suitable for building were rare or unobtainable except by importation. There was, however, an abundance of clay which, compressed in moulds and either dried in the sun or kiln-fired, provided bricks for every kind of structure. Besides massive, towered fortifications, the outstanding constructions were temple-complexes or palaces, temples being typical of Babylonian architecture and palaces of Assyrian. Buildings were raised on mud brick platforms, and the chief temples had sacred 'ziggurats' (p. 54), artificial mountains made up of tiered, rectangular stages which rose in number from one to seven in the course of Mesopotamian history. Apart from the fortifications and the ziggurats, buildings of all types were arranged round large and small courts, the rooms narrow and thick-walled, carrying brick barrel-vaults and sometimes domes. The roofs were usually flat outside, except where domes protruded. Alternatively, in early or commonplace buildings, palm logs supported rushes and packed clay served for coverings, or, for the best work, cedar and other fine timber was laboriously imported. Burnt brick was used sparingly for facings or where special stress was expected. Walls were whitewashed or, as with the developed ziggurat, painted in colour. Essentially, architecture was arcuated, the true arch with radiating voussoirs having been known by the third millennium B.C. For want of stone, columns were not used, except in a few instances in late Assyrian and Neo-Babylonian work. Towers or flat buttress strips were commonly vertically panelled and finished in stepped battlements above and stone plinths below, with colossal winged bulls guarding the chief portals; in palaces the alabaster plinths or dadoes of state courts and chambers bore low-relief carving, the walls above them being painted internally with bands of continuous friezes on the thin plaster coverings. Facing with polychrome glazed bricks, introduced by the Assyrians, was another mode of decoration, especially favoured by the Neo-Babylonians in lieu of sculptured stone slabs, since in Babylonia stone was scarcer than in Assyria.

The architecture of the Persians was columnar, and thus vastly different from the massive arcuated architecture of the Mesopotamian peoples they conquered. Flat timber roofs rather than vaults served for coverings, which allowed columns to be slender and graceful, while with their help rooms could be large where necessary, and of square proportions rather than elongated as the Mesopotamian brick vaults demanded. For ceilings, wooden brackets and beams carried by the columns supported a covering of clay on a bedding of reeds on logs or planks (p. 80A). The use of double mud brick walls for stability, as at Persepolis, may have allowed small windows just below ceiling level without their appearing on the severe external façades. Stone was plentiful on the upland sites, but used sparingly for such purposes as fire-temples and palace platforms, door and window surrounds, and for richly ornate columns and relief sculpture, often with figures on a modest scale. The

ZIGGURATS

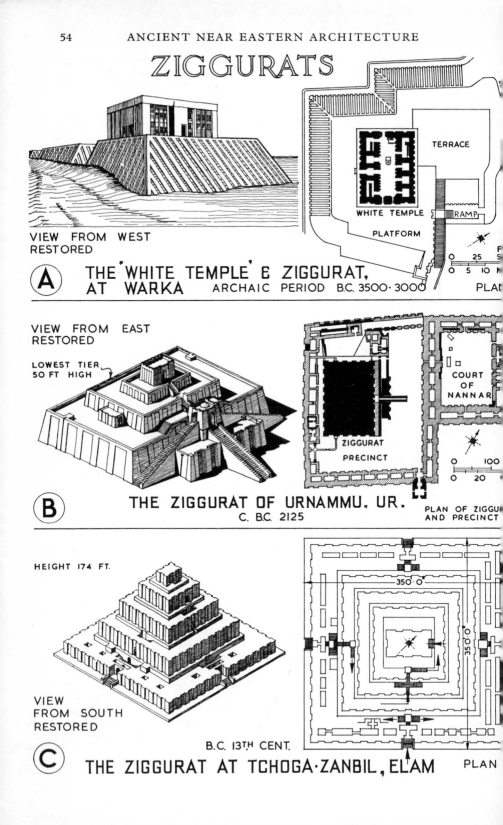

VIEW FROM WEST
RESTORED

TERRACE

WHITE TEMPLE RAMP

PLATFORM

25

5 10

(A) THE 'WHITE TEMPLE' & ZIGGURAT, AT WARKA ARCHAIC PERIOD B.C. 3500·3000 PLAN

VIEW FROM EAST
RESTORED

LOWEST TIER
50 FT HIGH

COURT
OF
NANNAR

ZIGGURAT
PRECINCT

100

20

(B) THE ZIGGURAT OF URNAMMU. UR. C. B.C. 2125 PLAN OF ZIGGU AND PRECINCT

HEIGHT 174 FT.

350·O

35·O·O

VIEW
FROM SOUTH
RESTORED

B.C. 13TH CENT.

(C) THE ZIGGURAT AT TCHOGA·ZANBIL, ELAM PLAN

Persians were at first relatively inexperienced craftsmen, and drew upon the superior skills of the peoples of their empire; many of the usages and features demonstrate derivation from Egyptian, Mesopotamian, Syrian, Ionian Greek and other sources. It would be accurate to claim that the architectural character of the major buildings erected during many centuries in Mesopotamia, and during the Achaemenian period in Iran, exemplify the two main traditions of the Near East as a whole, that of the alluvial river plains and that of the whole highland zone respectively. These were the traditions of clay and wood.

EXAMPLES

The architecture of the ancient Near East is considered under the following headings:
Early Mesopotamian (fifth to second millennia B.C.)
Assyrian and Neo-Babylonian (*c.* 1859–539 B.C.)
Early Anatolian and Hittite (*c.* 3250–*c.* 1170 B.C.)
Canaanite, Phoenician and Israelite (*c.* 3250–587 B.C.)
Syro-Hittite (*c.* 1170–745 B.C.)
Urartian (*c.* 850–*c.* 600 B.C.)
Phrygian (*c.* 750–*c.* 650 B.C.)
Median and Persian (*c.* 750–*c.* 350 B.C.)
Seleucid, Parthian and Sassanian (312 B.C.–A.D. 641)

EARLY MESOPOTAMIAN ARCHITECTURE

Eridu is the first significant example of the initial association of the Mesopotamian tradition in architecture with that of the Sumerians. A succession of remains of temples has been excavated dating back probably earlier than any yet known elsewhere in Sumer. Temple XVI, the earliest to be uncovered in its entirety, already reveals the central feature of the typical Mesopotamian temple, the 'cella' or sanctuary, with an altar in a niche and a central offering-table with traces of burning. The later temples in this sequence at Eridu are on a much larger scale, with the emergence of the tripartite plan, having subsidiary rooms on either side of the cella: this plan was to become standard. Here too was first manifested the embellishment of the exterior by alternating niches and buttresses. The exact orientation of a Mesopotamian temple was of great religious significance from this time onward. The predilection for established sites led to enduring continuity in the sites of temples, themselves the nucleus each of its own city.

Warka (Uruk: the Biblical Erech) was by far the largest of the Sumerian cities which eventually, in the Early Dynastic Period (*c.* 2900– 2340 B.C.), had a perimeter of over 9 km (6 miles). About one-third of this great area was occupied by temples and other public buildings. The two major areas of the city with important buildings were the Eanna and the Anu precincts, associated with the mother goddess and the sky god respectively, and dating back to the late fifth millennium B.C. By the late Uruk (or Protoliterate A and B) period the Eanna precinct had become an impressive grouping of temples, larger than any previously built. Cones of baked clay were set in mud plaster over many of the wall faces in the Eanna precinct temples, forming a distinctive mosaic decoration. One of the most striking examples of this is the so-called **Pillar Temple,** which stood on a terrace or platform and included two rows of massive columns, 2.6 m (8 ft 6 ins) in diameter. Their great girth and the primitive way in which they are constructed, with bricks laid radially to form an approximate circle, suggest a hesitant and experimental approach to an advance in building techniques, this being the oldest surviving evidence of free-standing columns. However, the pattern of cone mosaics clearly suggests imitation of a palm trunk. The Anu 'ziggurat' is more typically Mesopotamian in its tripartite plan for the temple: it is in fact not a ziggurat at all, but a series of temples, each built on top of the preceding one and each on a high platform. The **White Temple** (p. 54A), the best preserved in the Anu series, may be said to illustrate the origin of the ziggurat, or temple-tower, in the prehistoric Mesopotamian temple set on its platform. The concept of the ziggurat may well have combined two separate functions, the religious one being the recreation of a sacred mountain in the flat alluvial plain, and the secular one being to provide a permanent reminder to the populace of the political, social and economic pre-eminence of the temple. The White Temple platform had sloping sides, three of which had flat buttresses; a subsidiary broad square platform of similar height overlapped the north corner, served by a long flight of easy steps from which a circuitous ramp led off from an intermediate landing. The temple, originally white-washed, had an end-to-end hall of a span of 4.5 m (15 ft), flanked on both sides by a series of smaller rooms, three of which contained stairways leading to the roof. Of four entrances, the chief was placed asymmetrically on one long side, giving a 'bent-axis' approach to the sanctuary, marked by an altar platform 1.2 m (4 ft) high, in the north corner of the hall. Centrally nearby was a brick offering table, adjoined by a low semicircular hearth. Shallow buttresses formed the principal decoration of the hall and external walls. The platform stood 13 m (42 ft 6 ins) high, an impressive podium.

The **Ziggurat and Precinct of Ur** (p. 54B), already very old, were extensively remodelled by Urnammu (*c.* 2125 B.C.) and his successors. The complex comprised the ziggurat and its court; a secondary court attached to it, and three great temples. All these stood on a great rectangular platform at the heart of an oval-shaped walled city, itself about 6.1 m (20 ft) above the surrounding plain. The ziggurat, 62 m × 43 m (205 ft × 141 ft) on base, and about 21 m (70 ft) high, carried the usual temple on its summit and had the normal orientation. The ziggurat at Ur had a solid core of mud brick, covered with a skin of burnt brickwork 2.4 m (8 ft) thick, laid in bitumen and with layers of matting at intervals to improve cohesion.

The **Temple Complex, Ischali** (p. 57B), of the early second millennium B.C., was of the terrace type, without a ziggurat. It was rectangular in plan, with a large main terrace court and an upper one in which the temple lay at right angles to the chief axis. On the corresponding side of the main court there were two minor courts, and all were lined with rooms.

The **Temple Oval at Khafaje** (p. 57A), north-east of Baghdad, was an unusual complex, dating from the Early Dynastic period. There was one enclosure within another, 100 m × 70 m (328 ft × 230 ft) overall. Despite the unorthodox shape, the group affords an excellent illustration of the parts of a temple complex of the terrace type normal in the Early Dynastic and subsequent periods. Within the ovals the layout was rectilinear, the corners orientated to the four cardinal points. Of three ascending terrace levels, the lowest made a forecourt approached through an arched and towered gateway from the town, with a many-roomed building on one side, either administrative or a dwelling for the chief priest. The second terrace, wholly surrounded by rooms used as workshops and stores, had at its further end the temple platform, about 3.6 m (12 ft) high. Near its staircase, against the side of the temple terrace, was an external sacrificial altar, while elsewhere in the court were a well and two basins for ritual ablutions. Some special sanctity seems to have attached to the Temple Oval, for before its construction the whole area was dug down to virgin soil, through the accumulated depth of earlier building levels, and then filled with clean sand; foundations of a depth greater than structurally requisite were laid in the sand, and clay packed down against the walls.

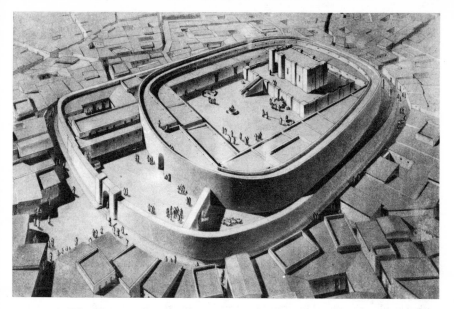

A. The Temple Oval at Khafaje. Third millennium B.C. See p. 56

B. The Temple Complex at Ischali. Early second millennium B.C. See p. 56

Thus the purity of the soil beneath the temple was assured. The later temple at Ischali had largely similar arrangements, though not within an oval perimeter. Just north-east of the Temple Oval stood the Temple of the moon god Sin at Khafaje, with ten successive phases, five dating to the late prehistoric (Jemdet Nasr) period and five to the three phases of the Early Dynastic period. Thus Khafaje illustrates the northward extension of urban life centred upon the city temple, from its first beginnings in Sumer.

At **Tepe Gawra** in northern Mesopotamia, at a time approximately contemporary with the earliest levels at Warka, the first important manifestation of monumental religious architecture appeared, where in Level XIII three contiguous temples, the Northern Temple, the Central Temple and the Eastern shrine formed a group unique at that early date. The hallmark of Sumerian architecture in the Early Dynastic period, but neither before nor after, was the plano-convex mud brick: these were laid in herring-bone pattern, or sometimes with three diagonally laid courses, all leaning in one direction, followed by two or three courses laid flat, with their convex sides upwards, thus acting as an imperfect bonding. Bricks of a special size were used for the three temples of Gawra XIII.

The **Royal Cemetery at Ur** (Early Dynastic III period) displays at its best the engineering skill of Sumerian architects. The stone used in the royal tombs, at a time when brickwork was more and more superseding stone, was limestone, never dressed and only roughly split after quarrying. This use of rubble masonry makes all the more remarkable the ability of the Sumerian builders to roof a tomb chamber with a vault or dome. The true arch was known, and so too was the true barrel vault, in stone, mud brick and burnt brick. Where the tomb itself, set at the foot of a shaft, had more than one room, the connecting doors were often spanned by an arch. However, no chronological sequence of the royal tombs at Ur can be drawn up on the basis of the construction of their roofs: corbel-vaulting, a more primitive method than the true barrel vault, was used not only for some of the royal tombs but also very extensively in the Third Dynasty of Ur. In one of the royal tombs of the Early Dynastic III cemetery at Ur a wooden frame was found on the floor, perhaps used as centering. Two examples of the use of an apse were found. The dome is best illustrated by one tomb chamber found intact: just as the principle of the true arch had been mastered by the Sumerian architects, so too had the use of pendentives.

The **Palace at Mari** was founded in the late third millennium B.C. and endured until its destruction by Hammurabi of Babylon (c. 1757 B.C.). This great building combined within its walls the functions of royal residence, centre for receptions and audiences, offices and a school for the civil service, servants' quarters and numerous store-rooms; in some rooms were found the thousands of cuneiform tablets constituting the royal archives, one of the major sources of historical evidence uncovered in the ancient Near East. There was the indirect access characteristic of palaces in the ancient Near East, preventing the shooting of missiles from without into the great forecourt. The section of the palace devoted to the private apartments of the royal family was embellished with mural paintings displaying contacts with the Minoan civilization of Crete, then at its height. Next to this section were the offices of the civil service, including two rooms with brick benches and yielding tablets showing that here the young recruits were taught the slow, painful mastery of the Akkadian syllabary. The layout of the palace as a whole exemplifies the typical Mesopotamian arrangement of rooms round a succession of courtyards, providing light, air and means of access. Rooms must have been gloomy inside, but doorways were high and only partially covered with matting; most of the palace was probably of one storey only.

The four centuries of Kassite rule in Babylonia (*c.* 1595–1171 B.C.) were un-distinguished in art and architecture generally, being marked by restorations at Ur and elsewhere, but at the new capital of **Dur Kurigalzu,** 32 km (20 miles) west of present-day Baghdad, the royal palace has some new features, including a court bordered on two sides by an ambulatory with square pillars. To the east lay the kingdom of Elam, with its capital at Susa. Nearby was the **Ziggurat of Tchoga-Zanbil** (p. 54C), of the thirteenth century B.C., built by Untash-Gal. The remark-ably complete remains give a fuller and more authentic picture of the upper parts of a ziggurat than were previously available. There were five tiers, the lowest shallower than the rest, each mounted on a plinth. The base is 107 m (350 ft) square and the total height was about 53 m (174 ft). Flights of stairs, recessed in the mass, led to the top of the first tier on the centre of each front, but only that on the south-west led to the second tier, while the rest of the height had to be scaled on the south-east, the principal façade.

ASSYRIAN ARCHITECTURE

In the second millennium B.C., covering the Old Assyrian and Middle Assyrian periods, the Assyrian state had to struggle for its existence. Though its art and architecture were closely bound to those of the south, distinctive traits began to manifest themselves. Polychrome ornamental brickwork, introduced by the Assyrians, had its origins in these early centuries, although the second great innova-tion, the use of high plinths or dadoes of great stone slabs placed on edge and usually carved with low-relief sculpture, did not appear until the reign of Ashurnasirpal II (*c.* 883–859 B.C.). Temples both with and without ziggurats were built in Assyria, but by the Late Assyrian period (911–612 B.C.) palaces were much more numerous and important, emphasising the central role of the monarchy. Recent excavations at Tell Rimah have revealed the use of brick barrel vaulting on a considerable scale.

The **City of Ashur** was the ancient religious and national centre of the Assyrian state, always important wherever the administrative capital might be. Here the ziggurat temple of Ashur, the national god, was restored by Tukulti-Ninurta I (*c.* 1250–1210 B.C.). In his reign and in subsequent generations Ashur displayed the ability of the Assyrian architects to experiment with architectural combinations in a way which demonstrated intentional divergences from the Babylonian prototypes. The double temple of Anu and Adad had twin ziggurats, with their related temples spanning between them. There were two further temples without ziggurats and two enormous palaces, one being primarily for administrative purposes.

The **City of Nimrud** (Calah) (pp. 60–62), was restored and enlarged by Ashurnasirpal II (*c.* 883–859 B.C.), who made it the capital of his kingdom. Excava-tions at Nimrud have been mostly within the citadel (p. 60B), which had an area 550 m × 320 m (1,800 ft × 1,050 ft) and was situated at the south-west corner of the outer town, whose wall had a perimeter of no less than 9 km (6 miles). The North-West Palace (p. 60A, B), was built by Ashurnasirpal II as his chief residence, and comprised a large public court, flanked on the north side by a modest ziggurat with associated temples, and by a row of rooms later used to house administrative records, and on the south side by the huge throne-room and by the private wing of the palace. This was to become the traditional plan of Assyrian palaces, for the first time adorned with slabs carved with scenes of war and the chase and domestic scenes (pp. 60A, 62).

Fort Shalmaneser, Nimrud (p. 61A, B) was built by Shalmaneser III (859–824 B.C.) outside the citadel, which he used as the administrative capital: the Fort served as palace, barracks, arsenal and storehouse. The palace wing included the

A. Gypsum relief from throne room of N.W. Palace, Nimrud (*c.* 879 B.C.).
See p. 59

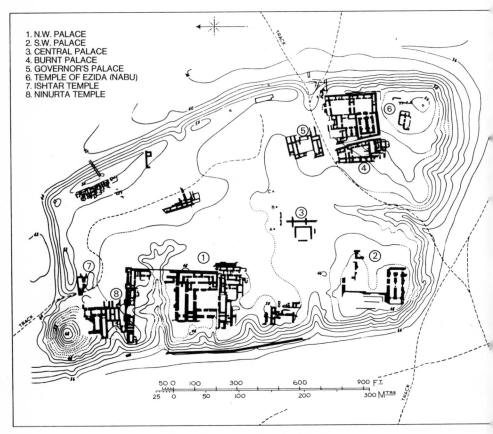

1. N.W. PALACE
2. S.W. PALACE
3. CENTRAL PALACE
4. BURNT PALACE
5. GOVERNOR'S PALACE
6. TEMPLE OF EZIDA (NABU)
7. ISHTAR TEMPLE
8. NINURTA TEMPLE

B. Nimrud: plan of the citadel. See p. 59

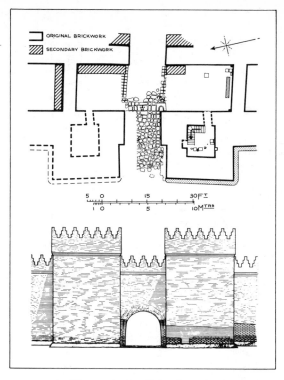

A. Plan and elevation of west gate

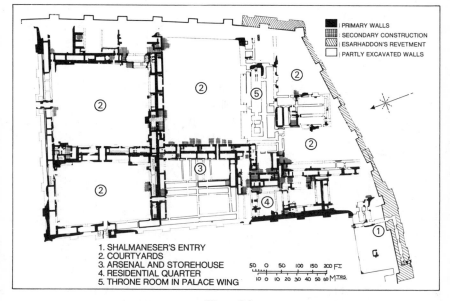

B. Plan of fort

Fort Shalmaneser, Nimrud (mid 9th cent. B.C.). See p. 59

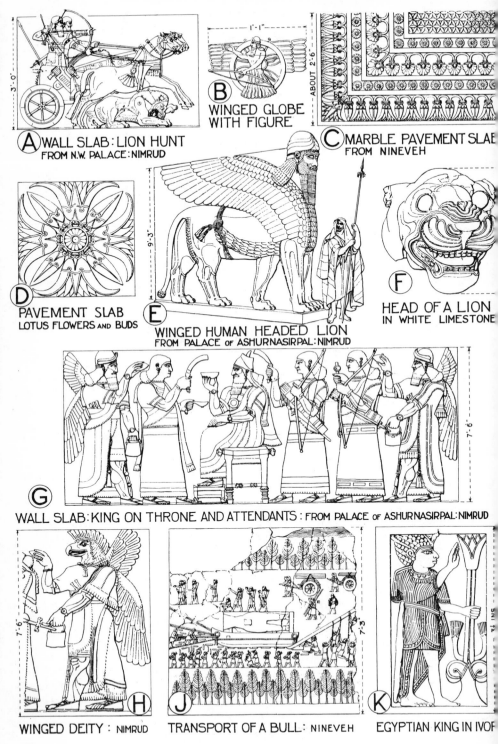

A WALL SLAB: LION HUNT
FROM N.W. PALACE: NIMRUD

B WINGED GLOBE WITH FIGURE

C MARBLE PAVEMENT SLAB
FROM NINEVEH

D PAVEMENT SLAB
LOTUS FLOWERS AND BUDS

E WINGED HUMAN HEADED LION
FROM PALACE OF ASHURNASIRPAL: NIMRUD

F HEAD OF A LION
IN WHITE LIMESTONE

G WALL SLAB: KING ON THRONE AND ATTENDANTS: FROM PALACE OF ASHURNASIRPAL: NIMRUD

H WINGED DEITY: NIMRUD

J TRANSPORT OF A BULL: NINEVEH

K EGYPTIAN KING IN IVORY

usual vast throne-room, and, though in this reign relief sculpture was much less in evidence, there was a magnificent panel of glazed bricks (p. 66B) depicting the king twice, on either side of the sacred tree, a favourite motif of Assyrian art. The rest of Fort Shalmaneser consisted of four quadrants, one entirely of store-rooms and the others surrounded by quarters for the royal guard, including ablutions and 'garages' for the army's chariots.

The **Temple of Ezida, Nimrud** (p. 60B) was built towards the end of the ninth century B.C., and included in its main wing the double sanctuary of Nabu (god of writing) and his consort.

The **City of Khorsabad** (p. 64C) contained the next important buildings in Assyria; it was built by Sargon II (722–705 B.C.) and abandoned at his death. It was square-planned, with a defensive perimeter, and covered nearly one square mile, but this area was never entirely occupied by buildings. There were two gateways in each tower-serrated wall (p. 65D, E), except where the place of one of them on the north-west wall was taken by an extensive citadel enclosure, containing all but one of the town's chief buildings. These comprise a palace for the king's brother, who was his vizier; a temple to Nabu; several official buildings, and, dominating them all, the **Palace of Sargon,** a complex of large and small courts, corridors and rooms, covering 23 acres (p. 64). Each of the buildings was raised upon a terrace, that of the Palace of Sargon reaching to the level of the town walls, which the palace site bestrode, and was approached by broad ramps. The main entrance to the palace grand court was flanked by great towers and guarded by man-headed winged bulls, nearly 3.8 m (12 ft 6 ins) high, supporting a bold, semi-circular arch decorated with brilliantly-coloured glazed bricks. The palace had three main parts, each abutting the grand court. On the left on entering was a group of three large and three small temples; on the right, service quarters and administrative offices; and opposite, the private and residential apartments, with the state chambers behind. The state chambers had their own court, almost as large as the first, round which were dado slabs over 2.1 m (7 ft) high bearing reliefs of the king and his courtiers. The lofty throne-room, about 49 m × 10.7 m (160 ft × 35 ft), was the outermost of the state suite planned around its own internal court. It was probably one of the few apartments to have a flat timber ceiling, for fine timber was rare and costly. The plastered walls bore a painted decoration of a triple band of friezes, framed in running ornament, about 5.5 m (18 ft) high overall, circulating the room above a stone dado or reliefs (p. 66C). Walls were thick, about 6.1 m (20 ft) on average. In the Grand and Temple Courts decoration was contrived by sunken vertical panelling on the whitewashed walls and towers, finishing in stepped battlements above and stone plinths below, plain or carved (p. 64D). Within the mud-brick platforms of the palace there were jointed terra-cotta drains to carry away rainwater, joining larger drains of burnt brick covered with vaults which were slightly pointed and in which the brick courses were laid obliquely, to avoid using wood centering (p. 65C). This device was well known to the Egyptians too. Only stone dadoes so far have been mentioned; at the foot of the façade of the three chief temples there were high plinths projecting from the wall, faced in polychrome glazed bricks portraying sacred motifs and serving as pedestals for high cedar masts probably ringed with ornamental bronze bands, on the most likely reconstruction (p. 64F). The wall behind was panelled with a series of abutted half-columns, a revival of an ancient motif originating in the imitation of palm logs. It is worth noting that the only ziggurat of the city is associated with the palace temples, as at Nimrud, and not with the large Nabu temple nearby. On a square base of 45 m (148 ft) side, the seven-tiered ziggurat rose to the same height (45 m, including the shrine at the top), ascended by a winding ramp 1.8 m (6 ft)

PALACE OF SARGON: KHORSABAD

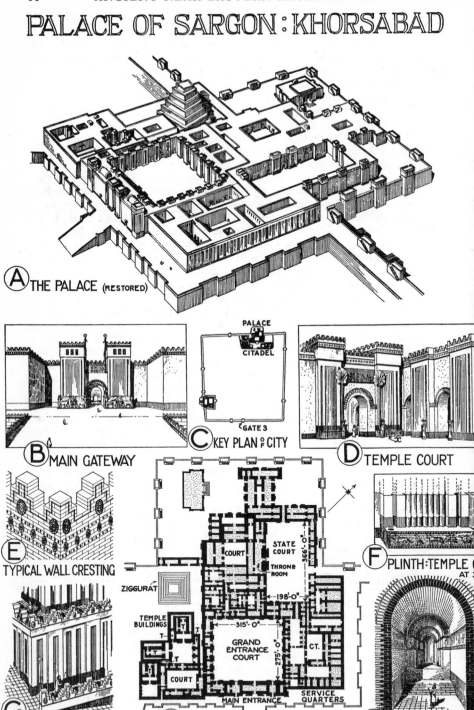

A THE PALACE (RESTORED)

B MAIN GATEWAY

C KEY PLAN OF CITY

PALACE
CITADEL
GATE 3

D TEMPLE COURT

E TYPICAL WALL CRESTING

F PLINTH: TEMPLE C
AT J

G ANGLE OF ZIGGURAT

H PLAN

ZIGGURAT
TEMPLE BUILDINGS
T
T
T
COURT
COURT
STATE COURT
THRONE ROOM
366'-0"
198'-0"
315'-0"
275'-0"
GRAND ENTRANCE COURT
C.T.
SERVICE QUARTERS
MAIN ENTRANCE

J ROOM IN TEMPLE BUILDINGS

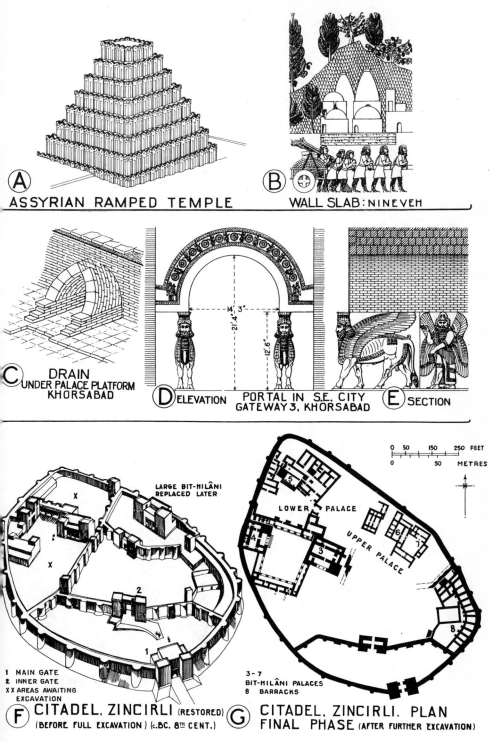

(A) ASSYRIAN RAMPED TEMPLE

(B) WALL SLAB: NINEVEH

(C) DRAIN UNDER PALACE PLATFORM KHORSABAD

(D) ELEVATION PORTAL IN S.E. CITY GATEWAY 3, KHORSABAD

14' 3"
21' 4"
12' 6"

(E) SECTION

LARGE BIT-HILÂNI REPLACED LATER

X

X

2

1

1 MAIN GATE
2 INNER GATE
X X AREAS AWAITING EXCAVATION

(F) CITADEL, ZINCIRLI (RESTORED)
(BEFORE FULL EXCAVATION) (c. BC. 8TH CENT.)

LOWER PALACE

UPPER PALACE

5

3

6

7

8

0 50   150   250 FEET
0   50 METRES

3 - 7 BIT-HILÂNI PALACES
8 BARRACKS

(G) CITADEL, ZINCIRLI. PLAN
FINAL PHASE (AFTER FURTHER EXCAVATION)

A. The Ishtar Gate, Babylon (rebuilt by Nebuchadnezzar II 605–563 B.C.).
See p. 67

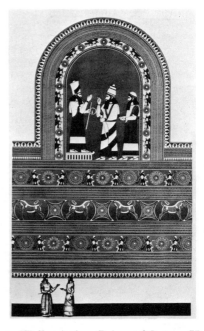

B. Glazed brick panel from throne room suite, Fort Shalmaneser, Nimrud. See p. 63

C. Wall painting, Palace of Sargon II, Khorsabad (722–705 B.C.). See p. 63

wide. The successive tiers were panelled and battlemented and were painted in different colours on the plastered faces (p. 64A, G).

The **City of Nineveh** was made the capital of the Assyrian empire by Sargon's son Sennacherib (705–681 B.C.), who spent the first two years of his reign on the work of raising mighty walls and, on the citadel now called Kuyunjik, building his 'Palace without a Rival' (the South-West Palace). Long inscriptions describing this palace were recovered during the excavations made in the nineteenth century, and the considerable labour of the building operations, especially that of making a secure foundation platform on the mound formed by successive levels of earlier occupation, is stressed therein; it is also depicted in reliefs now in the British Museum (pp. 62J, 65B). Other reliefs show campaigns and hunting in greater detail than ever before. More palaces were built at Nineveh by Sennacherib's immediate successors, Esarhaddon and Ashurbanipal. In the latter's reign relief sculpture in Assyria attained its apogee in scenes of lion hunting and of the bloody campaigns against the kingdom of Elam, culminating in the destruction of Susa (c. 640 B.C.). Soon before the fall of Assyria, Nineveh was given an extra rampart along its vulnerable east side, but this was never finished. The city fell finally only after a prolonged attack by the Medes and Babylonians in 612 B.C., and was never to rise again.

Water supply had long been a major concern of the Assyrian kings: Ashurnasirpal II dug a canal from the river Zab to irrigate the land close to Nimrud, while an arched aqueduct of stone construction, built by Sennacherib at Jerwan, may be said to anticipate Roman achievements of this class.

NEO-BABYLONIAN ARCHITECTURE

Neo-Babylonian architecture was naturally descended from that of the earlier centuries in Mesopotamia, but it derived much also from the architecture of the Assyrians.

The **City of Babylon,** whose ruins differ from those of earlier cities largely because of the use of burnt brick, was rebuilt by Nebuchadnezzar II (605–563 B.C.), for it had been thoroughly destroyed by Sennacherib (689 B.C.). It had an inner and an outer part, each heavily fortified, the inner town was approximately square in plan, of about 1,300 m (4,350 ft) sides, containing the principal buildings, the Euphrates river forming the west side. The few main streets intersected starkly at right angles, terminating in tower-framed bronze gates where they met the walls. Between the main streets tiered dwellings, business houses, temples, chapels and shrines jostled in lively disorder. The principal sites lined the river front, and behind them ran a grand processional way, its vista closed on the north by the Ishtar Gate (p. 66A), glowing in coloured glazed bricks, patterned with yellow and white bulls and dragons in relief upon a blue ground. Hereabouts there were palace-citadels, and connected with Nebuchadnezzar's great palace complex on the water side was that marvel of the ancient world, the Hanging Gardens, 275 m × 183 m (900 ft × 600 ft) overall; among its maze of rooms was a vast throne-room, 52 m × 17 m (170 ft × 56 ft), its long façade decorated with polychrome glazed bricks. The central sites on the river front were occupied by the chief temple of the god of the city, Marduk, and, to the north of it, the expansive precinct where rose the associated ziggurat, the 'Tower of Babel'. The celebrated ziggurat appears to have been one combining the triple stairway approach and massive lower tier customary in early Mesopotamia, with upper stages arranged spirally according to Assyrian practice. The plan was square, of 90 m (295 ft) sides, and there were seven stages in all, the summit temple being faced with blue glazed bricks.

EARLY ANATOLIAN AND HITTITE ARCHITECTURE

The Hittites, although the best-known of the ancient peoples of Anatolia, were not the earliest inhabitants: they inherited on their arrival (*c.* 2000 B.C.) a long tradition of building. In contrast to Mesopotamia, both stone and timber were available in abundance, and in the more densely forest-covered areas timber-frame construction must have been normal. One simple unit which seems to have been Anatolian in origin and which appeared very early was the 'megaron', a rectangular room with central hearth and door at one end, set in a deep porch formed by the prolongation of the side walls to make 'antae'. This unit is too simple not to have been evolved independently in different regions, though it was suited to the extremes of the Anatolian climate. The best known examples have been found at Troy, from the First Settlement (*c.* 3250–2600 B.C.) onwards, and at Beycesultan, in south-western Anatolia. Village houses in much of Turkey today are of mud brick with extensive use of timber, especially for the flat roofs; and where of two storeys, these houses have their living-rooms upstairs, the ground floor being principally for kitchens and store-rooms, and often also for animals. A largely comparable arrangement has been found in the merchant colony established by traders from Ashur at Kanesh (Kültepe), whose houses included an archive for their business records, kept on clay tablets baked in an oven.

Most of the surviving monuments of Hittite architecture date from the fourteenth and thirteenth centuries B.C., the period of the 'Empire'. Mesopotamian influences were strong in Hittite building, but there was much that was individual. In important structures massive stone masonry was used, though the upper parts of walls, even of highland town fortifications, were commonly of sun-dried bricks in timber framing: the chief remains are of town walls and temples.

The **Palace of Beycesultan**, Level V (*c.* 1900–1750 B.C.) is an outstanding example of the use of timber as reinforcement for walls constructed of mud brick with footings of limestone. Some resemblance to the palaces of Minoan Crete is discernible, though not a close one. As in pottery and other artefacts so in architecture this fertile region of south-western Anatolia maintained a tradition distinct from that of the Hittite homeland in central Anatolia.

The outer **Town Walls of Boğazköy** (ancient Hattušas) (*c.* 1360 B.C.) (p. 69B) enclosed some 300 acres. They were of casemate construction, like those of Mesopotamia, being double and connected by cross-walls, the compartments thus formed being packed with rubble. Square towers projected at frequent intervals, and some 6.1 m (20 ft) in front was a lesser wall, with its own minor towers. The outer shell of the main wall was particularly strong, built of large, rock-faced, close-jointed stones up to 1.5 m (5 ft) long, varying in shape from the rectangular to the polygonal. The upper parts of the walls were of brick, and fragments of models provide good evidence that towers and walls finished in crenellations similar to the Mesopotamian. Five gateways partially survive. These were flanked by great towers and had peculiar elliptical openings of which the corbellated upper parts stood on pairs of enormous monolithic stone jambs (p. 69A). Broad archivolts surrounded the portals, and ornamenting the jambs of three of the gates were boldly projecting sculptures. On the 'King's Gate' was an armed figure on the reveal, not in fact a warrior but a god; on the 'Lion Gate', foreparts of lions on the face of the jambs; and on the 'Sphinx Gate' sphinxes not only project forward but show the full body-length on the reveals, thus anticipating the monsters of Assyrian times by some five centuries.

Temple I, Boğazköy (p. 69E) is the largest and oldest of five identified there, which have no regular orientation but show other principal features in common.

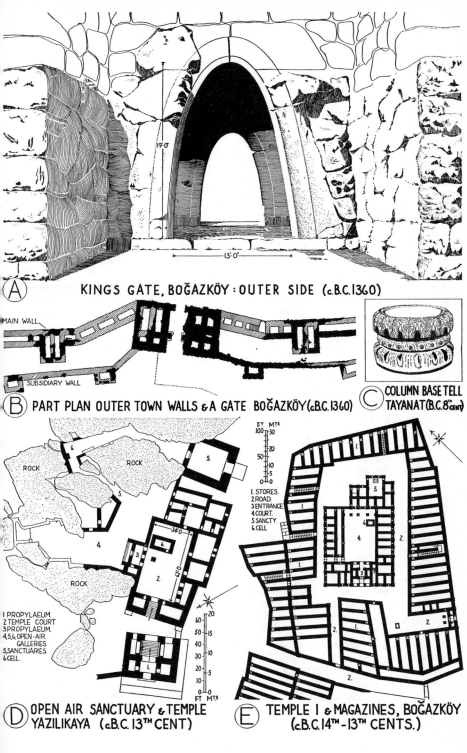

A KINGS GATE, BOĞAZKÖY : OUTER SIDE (c.B.C.1360)

B PART PLAN OUTER TOWN WALLS & A GATE BOĞAZKÖY (c.B.C.1360)

MAIN WALL

SUBSIDIARY WALL

C COLUMN BASE TELL TAYANAT (B.C. 8TH CENT.)

ROCK

ROCK

ROCK

1 PROPYLAEUM.
2 TEMPLE COURT
3 PROPYLAEUM.
4,5,6 OPEN-AIR.
  GALLERIES.
5, SANCTUARIES.
6 CELL.

D OPEN AIR SANCTUARY & TEMPLE YAZILIKAYA (c.B.C. 13TH CENT)

1. STORES.
2. ROAD.
3. ENTRANCE
4. COURT.
5. SANCTY
6. CELL

E TEMPLE I & MAGAZINES, BOĞAZKÖY (c.B.C. 14TH-13TH CENTS.)

They consist of a number of rooms arranged round a central court, with cloister or corridor access on two or more sides. In Temple I the building is girdled by a paved road beyond which are numerous magazines, many still filled with great pottery jars and one containing cuneiform tablets constituting the temple records. Asymmetrically placed was a special unit of several rooms, the largest of all being a sanctuary, only to be reached circuitously through adjacent smaller rooms. The sanctuary projected at one end, so that windows might give side illumination to the cult statue. Unlike Mesopotamian temples, light to most rooms came from deep windows on the external walls. The entrance was also asymmetrical, whether through a simple recessed porch on the flank or, as in Temple I, on the front opposite the sanctuary unit. To one side of the court in Temple I stood a cell built of granite, as was the sanctuary unit, the building elsewhere being of limestone. There was a similar temple at Alaca Hüyük.

The **Open-air Sanctuary, Yazilikaya** (p. 69D), about 1.6 km (1 mile) north-east of Boğazköy, is a deep re-entrant in an almost sheer limestone face, with processions of some seventy gods and goddesses, about 1 m (3 ft) high, carved at eye level on the faces, converging on a rear panel. A lesser sanctuary with reliefs adjoined on the east. Screening the groves was a temple, comprising three buildings in series, linked by walls: a deep propylæum; the temple proper, with rooms on three sides of a court in which stood a walled cell and from which a left-hand turn was made towards the sacred groves through a second, pillared propylæum; and a large sanctuary, independently approached. The propylæum unit occurs also in the architecture of Minoan Crete and Mycenaean Greece (p. 189).

CANAANITE, PHOENICIAN AND ISRAELITE ARCHITECTURE

The architecture of the Levant in the second millennium B.C., of the regions now included within the south-eastern fringes of Turkey, Syria, Lebanon, Jordan and Israel, cannot strictly be described under the above heading. Indeed, the Hurrians formed an important element in the population, especially in north Syria.

The two **Palaces at Tell Atchana** (ancient Alalakh), in the plain of Antioch, may be ascribed to the Hurrians more than to any other group. The earlier of these was built by Yarim-Lim, ruler of the minor kingdom of Yamkhad and a contemporary of Hammurabi. It is in essence a private house, with the public rooms in the north wing and the private rooms in the south, including traces of wall paintings from the upper storey. Perhaps the most interesting features of Yarim-Lim's palace is the use of basalt orthostats in the north wing, the earliest example of a tradition later occurring, as mentioned above, in Hittite and Assyrian buildings. In its extensive use of timber to reinforce the mud-brick superstructure this palace was more in the Anatolian than the Mesopotamian tradition. The larger palace of Niqmepa, built almost three centuries later, represents a refinement of the design of the earlier palace and a larger, more public building.

The **Palace at Ras Shamra** (ancient Ugarit), the prosperous city on the north Syrian coast, seems to be transitional in plan between the palaces of Yarim-Lim and Niqmepa, being less advanced than the latter, although Ugarit was a much more important city than Alalakh. The undoubted achievements of the city-states of the Levant were never adequately reflected in their architecture, at least as hitherto revealed by excavations. It is noteworthy that a group of fourteen family vaults at Ugarit, all with a short dromos with descending stairway and a rectangular funerary chamber with a corbel-vaulted roof, and outstanding in design and execution, can undoubtedly be ascribed to an Aegean element in the city's population, presumably merchants. Rather earlier (probably of the fifteenth century B.C.) were the fortifications of Ugarit, of rough stone masonry and including a well-built postern tunnel for sorties in time of siege. To the thirteenth century B.C. belong palace buildings in dressed stone, which provide the earliest parallel with the better type of masonry used in Palestine, first in the United Kingdom of David and Solomon and later especially in Israel, from the tenth century B.C. onwards. The missing link between these two periods was through the Phoenicians, for whose achievement reliance has still largely to be placed on the Old Testament: the Phoenician cities, mostly concealed beneath remains of Graeco-Roman cities and Crusader castles, have yet to be extensively investigated.

At **Samaria,** founded by Omri (c. 880 B.C.) and captured by the Assyrians (c. 720 B.C.), when the kingdom of Israel was absorbed into the Assyrian empire, excavations have given the most coherent record of the material civilization of Israel, of which it was the capital. Six architectural phases have been distinguished for this period, the first two being marked by the use of finely jointed and dressed masonry, the courses even and horizontal.

At **Jerusalem** nothing has survived of the Temple of Solomon, built by Phoenician craftsmen, with cedar beams imported from the Lebanon. However, the excavations have revealed much of the long and complex succession of defences of the city in the Jebusite period and after David made it the centre of his kingdom, although little has been found surviving of the buildings within the city's walls. Hezekiah's tunnel in the city and cisterns in the barren Negev testify to the continuing concern of the Judaean kings for water supply, a serious weakness of Samaria.

Megiddo and **Hazor** in the northern kingdom, and **Lachish** and **Tell Beit Mersim** in the southern were among the major sites. At **Ezion-Geber,** later called Elath, situated at the head of the Gulf of Aqaba, a smelter for refining the copper from the Wadi Arabah was built, surrounded by workers' quarters and by a protective wall, this being originally founded in the time of Solomon.

SYRO-HITTITE ARCHITECTURE

The porched house, or 'bit-hilâni', so characteristic of Syria, may have had its origin as early as the palace of Yarim-Lim at Alalakh, although it is not until the early first millennium B.C. that this unit can be discerned in developed form in the context of Syro-Hittite civilization. Cultural continuity in Syria was never entirely broken after the end of the Hittite empire; unfortunately, however, the excavations at Carchemish, which had a strong Hittite element in the population, have been sufficient only to establish the sequence of the town's defences and the relative chronology of several groups of relief-sculptured orthostats. The Long Wall of sculptures depicts the victory procession of the ruler of Carchemish at that time, Katuwas (c. 900 B.C.).

At the **Citadel of Zincirli** (p. 65F, G), because far more excavated, the layout is much clearer, which was of oval plan, standing centrally on a mound in a walled town which, like so many in ancient West Asia, was completely circular. The construction of the citadel walls was typical of the period in being of timber-framed, sun-dried brick, standing on two courses of cut masonry on rubble foundations. Internally, the citadel was divided into defensive zones by cross walls, securing the approaches to an 'Upper' and a 'Lower' Palace, of about the eighth century B.C. Each comprised bit-hilâni, two of which are particularly plain in the plan of the Lower Palace (p. 65G). These stood on opposite sides of a large cloistered court, and each had a two-columned porch, with a stair on the right, leading to a transverse hall or throne room, beyond which was a range of smaller rooms including bedroom and bathroom. In front of the throne was a circular hearth, while a hall in the Upper Palace had a moveable iron hearth on bronze wheels. The porch columns were of wood, with stone bases shaped either as a pair of lions or monsters, or in triple ornamented stone cushions having some likeness to the earliest versions of the bases of the Classical Greek Ionic Order (p. 221). Instances of both occur at Tell Tayanat, west of Antioch (p. 69C). Following the old Hittite tradition and partly contemporary Assyrian practice, gates were protected by stone monsters and decorated by orthostats carved in relief.

The **City of Hamath** was distinguished during its most prosperous period (*c.* 900–720 B.C.) by monumental buildings on the citadel, including two gateways, a probable temple and two palaces, only one of which (Building II) was entirely uncovered. The main gate (Building I) had a long staircase, with a landing on the threshold, but the plan is simpler than in the cities of north Syria, such as Carchemish. Though there is the same use of orthostats, they are plain, the work of the sculptors at Hamath being almost confined to the provision of guardian lions. There are no guard rooms on either side, though there are flanking towers. The palace had a buttressed façade notably lacking a columned portico. Traces of gold leaf and fragments of red, blue and white plaster give a hint of the richness of decoration in the living quarters of the palace, on the upper floor; from here too probably came the throne and window grille, both carved in basalt, found thrown into the central court. The staircase evidently had two flights, only the lower one surviving, which gave the main evidence for the excavators' reconstruction of the height of the palace as some 14.4 m (47 ft), with the upper storey being 7 m (23 ft) high; a fallen pier of brickwork from the upper storey was of 48 courses. Hamath is a good example of many sites in the ancient Near East whose poor preservation makes it difficult to grasp immediately the achievements of their architects. Hamath was then, as now, one of the leading cities of inland Syria. Its prosperity, and that of Syro-Hittite cities in general, rapidly declined with the growth of Assyrian power after 745 B.C.

URARTIAN ARCHITECTURE

The origins of the architecture of the Kingdom of Van, known to its Assyrian enemies as Urartu (Ararat), are as obscure as those of the kingdom itself.

FORTRESSES

The most typical buildings so far known in Urartu are the numerous fortresses, many of them strategically sited round Lake Van, others being further afield, round Lake Urmia in north-west Iran, and especially in the Araxes valley. Massive stone masonry of cyclopean character was used for the lower parts of the fortress walls, with buttresses or towers at regular intervals (p. 75A), while mud brick was used for the superstructure. Timber was available for roofing, though not so abundant as in Anatolia. Store rooms containing huge jars for wine, oil or corn are also a usual feature.

The **Citadel of Van,** the capital of Urartu, must have been impregnable; it has a cliff along the south side, and some 90 m (300 ft) of the Urartian walls (*c.* 800 B.C.) (p. 75A) survives among much later work. At the foot of the west end of the citadel of Van stands a massive stone podium, perhaps a shrine but more probably a form of barbican protecting the entrance to the citadel and its water supply from a spring: this was built by Sarduri I, the founder of Van as capital of the kingdom, and some of the blocks are 5.2 m (17 ft) long, being about 1.2 m × 1.2 m

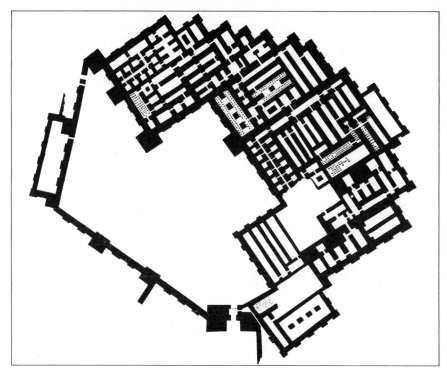

A. Karmir-Blur: plan of the citadel (*c.* 685–645 B.C.). See p. 74

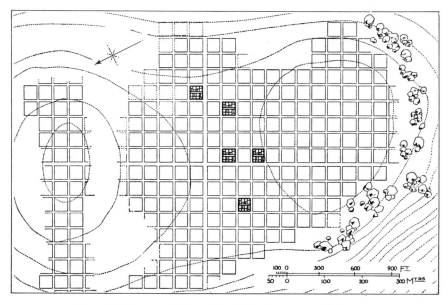

B. Zernaki Tepe: grid-plan site (8th–7th cent. B.C.). See p. 74

(4 ft × 4 ft) in section. The fortifications of the citadel above, like many of the fortresses of Urartu, were almost certainly the work of Menua, whose reign (*c.* 810–786 B.C.), together with that of Rusa II (*c.* 685–645 B.C.) saw the two main periods of building activity that seem to have occurred in the history of Urartu.

Karmir-Blur (ancient Teishebaini) (p. 73A), just outside Erevan, is an outstanding example of an Urartian fortress and governmental centre, with towered and buttressed perimeter wall, massive gateway, parade ground within the wall and ground floor entirely occupied by store-rooms.

The **Citadel of Kefkalesi,** above Adilcevaz on the north-west shore of Lake Van, is of similar date (seventh century B.C.). Less typical is the large fortified enclosure at the foot of Anzavur, near Patnos, whose situation makes it all the more likely to have been a military compound. Probably also intended for military use, though never finished, was the remarkable grid-plan site of **Zernaki Tepe** (p. 73B), on the north-east shore of Lake Van.

At **Çavuştepe,** south-east of Van, there stands a long, narrow citadel crowning the summit of a rocky ridge in the middle of the Hoşap valley, and it is one of the few buildings which show that although massiveness rather than finesse seems the chief characteristic of Urartian architecture, it does include examples of a higher standard than the average Urartian building indicates. At Çavuştepe the perimeter wall is of limestone masonry whose joints are largely oblique, but which is finely dressed throughout. With its temple, this site belongs to the reign of Sarduri II who, before his defeats by Tiglath-Pileser III of Assyria, had brought Urartu to the zenith of its power.

TEMPLES

The most characteristic manifestation of Urartian architecture is the temple, whose original appearance must have resembled a tall, fortified tower. There is a standard plan, square and with shallow corner buttresses; the footings are usually of very fine, smoothly-dressed basalt ashlar, of an altogether finer quality than the walls of the fortresses.

The **Temple at Kayalidere,** which is of rougher masonry, has a façade over 12 m (40 ft) long, with walls 3.2 m (10 ft 6 ins) thick, while the interior of the sanctuary is barely 5 m (16 ft 4 ins) square. Such massive walls themselves imply great height, and although an Assyrian relief depicting the temple of Haldi, chief god of Urartu, at the city of Muşaşir, suggests much squatter proportions, this was due to the confined space of the register in the relief. The Achaemenian Fire Temple at Naksh-i-Rustam (p. 81C) suggests that the proportions of the standard Urartian temple may well have been a double cube, and if, as the relief of the Muşaşir temple suggests, the Urartian temples had gabled roofs, these may have resembled that of the Tomb of Cyrus at Pasargadae (p. 79), though in wood instead of stone.

Apart from the temple at Kayalidere, there are temples of the standard plan at **Anzavur** (with the annals inscription of Menua), **Çavuştepe, Toprakkale** and **Altintepe** (pp. 75B, 76A) (with a colonnade running round the court in which the temple stands). Open-air rock-cut shrines occur at Van and elsewhere.

The **Temple at Toprakkale** is also worthy of mention for its rusticated masonry, the centre of each block being left rough and the joints recessed and smooth. Though this occurs at Ugarit in the second millennium B.C., there seems no adequate evidence to suggest that the Urartians did not develop this independently. At Toprakkale stones of different colours, limestone and basalt, were used inlaid to achieve a contrast.

The characteristic **Urartian tomb** was cut out of the solid rock, with niches in the walls for lamps or offerings: such are the tombs in the south side of the citadel

A. Urartian masonry, Citadel of Van (*c.* 800 B.C.). See p. 72

B. The Temple, Altintepe (7th century B.C.). See p. 74

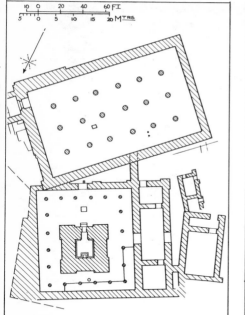

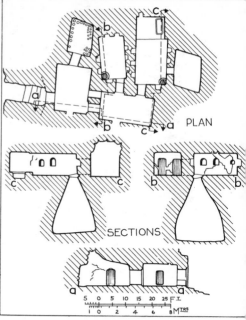

A. Altintepe: plan of temple and
audience hall (7th cent. B.C.). See pp. 74, 77

B. Kayalidere: plan and sections of tomb
(c. 700 B.C.). See p. 77

C. Kefkalesi: Urartian relief with inscription of Rusa II (c. 685–645 B.C.) and
background of a battlemented fortress. See p. 77

of Van and at Kayalidere. At Altintepe there are tombs of comparable design, but of masonry and built into the hillside just beneath the summit of the citadel. False vaults occur in the Altintepe tombs; at **Kayalidere** there are bottle-shaped shafts accessible only through an opening in the floor of the chamber above (p. 76B).

The **Shamiram Su** (Semiramis Canal) is the most famous of the canals and cisterns which formed a major part of the works of the successive Urartian kings, and was constructed by Menua to bring water from the valley of the Hoşap river south-east of Van to the fields and gardens round the capital. This canal is largely visible to this day.

Sculpture was little manifest in Urartu and late in appearance. At Kefkalesi a relief (p. 76C) includes a representation of battlements, windows of narrow slit form and doorways. A bronze model from Toprakkale provides similar evidence of the mud brick superstructure typical of an architectural tradition of which the stone footings alone normally survive, except where fire (as at Kefkalesi and Karmir-Blur) has preserved some of the brickwork.

PALACES

The **Palace of Argishti I** (*c.* 786–764 B.C.) at **Arin-Berd** (ancient Erebuni), the city which he founded close to the later Karmir-Blur, is the most important Urartian palace known. It was decorated with mural paintings in the formal court style, adapted from that of Assyria, with some examples of a freer genre, owing little or nothing to outside influences. This palace included a throne room with two entrances, and a courtyard with a wooden gallery supported by fourteen wooden columns on stone bases.

At **Giriktepe,** close to Patnos, a smaller palace has been excavated: its large hall, decorated with doubly recessed niches, shows similarities to the architecture of the large **citadel of Hasanlu** (*c.* 1000–800 B.C.), a major site just south of Lake Urmia, in a region from which the expanding kingdom of Urartu may have drawn some inspiration for its architecture, at least in mud brick.

At **Altintepe** (p. 76A), near Erzincan, situated by the north-west frontier of Urartu, a palace has been excavated with an audience hall 43.7 m × 24.7 m (143 ft × 81 ft), with six rows of three columns having their superstructure of mud brick, not wood. The diameter of the column bases of stone was almost 1.5 m (5 ft), and they are spaced nearly 5.2 m (17 ft) apart. This hall seems to date from the seventh century B.C., a period of revival in Urartu not long before its final eclipse.

PHRYGIAN ARCHITECTURE

At **Gordion,** the Phrygian capital, the architecture uncovered by excavations includes houses built on the 'megaron' plan, with its essential features of a front porch flanked by antae prolonging the line of the main walls, and leading into a large room with a hearth at or near its centre. This was suited to the extremes of the Anatolian climate. At one time, perhaps through comparisons with modern Turkish village houses, it was doubted whether these ancient megara had anything but flat roofs. The great width and absence of central pillars might alone have suggested otherwise; the proof of gabled roofs is provided by graffiti on walls of megara, by the roof of the timber tomb chamber of the great tumulus at Gordion, supported by three gables, one in the middle and one at each end, and by at least ten of the rock monuments of Phrygia, including those of the so-called Midas City. This group of monuments comprises not tombs but shrines, since the Phrygians had introduced the custom of burial in tumuli. The great gateway of Gordion has a pronounced batter to its façade, and, with the absence of niches and buttresses at regular intervals and the relatively small size of the stones used, these fortifications are quite different in style and construction from the Urartian.

At **Midas City** the carved façades show the timbers crossing at the apex of the gable, as on the graffiti at Gordion, and reveal other architectural features too. One chamber is carved to imitate a house built of logs; in the so-called Tomb of Midas's Wife there are two shuttered windows carved in the gable; doors are represented as opening inwards; the so-called Broken Tomb has a large chamber hewn out of the rock to represent the interior of a house, with benches along three sides, and in the Lion Grave there is a carved bed inside the chamber.

A distinctive feature of Phrygian architecture was the use of terra-cotta tiles as ornament, represented by examples from Gordion and from Pazarli, in central Anatolia; they may also be rendered as geometric patterns on the façades of two of the shrines of Midas City. These tiles seem to have been used as a frieze beneath the pediment of gabled buildings. Vertical and horizontal beams and cross-ties were used in the wooden framework of some of the Phrygian buildings of Gordion. Together with the chamber of the great tumulus and the ornate furniture found there they attest to the wide variety of Phrygian wood-working and the high level of skill achieved in an essentially Anatolian civilization, owing much to Assyria, and perhaps also to Urartu, but at the same time preserving its own identity.

MEDIAN AND PERSIAN ARCHITECTURE

The architectural achievements of the Medes and Persians before the reign of Cyrus the Great have recently been recognized in buildings of the eighth–seventh century B.C. excavated in western Iran, at Godin Tepe, Baba Jan and Nush-i Jan.

At **Godin Tepe,** Level II, the upper citadel originally comprised a fortified manor, or minor palace, which centred around a larger and a smaller columned hall, with additional smaller rooms and rows of magazines; the whole was protected by a fortification wall with bastions, a tower and arrow slots.

At **Baba Jan,** in Levels II and I, the manor must have presented a formidable façade, being defended by eight rectangular towers, one of which was replaced in Level I by a columned portico as the main entrance: the space within the towered wall comprised a rectangular court, later roofed, with a long room on either side. A contemporary building in another part of the same site had one room decorated in a style unknown elsewhere, with heavy painted wall tiles. Columns were also a feature of a large citadel building, approximately contemporary with the manor of Baba Jan, at Haftavan Tepe, in the Urmia basin of north-west Iran.

At **Tepe Nush-i Jan,** near Hamadan (Ecbatana), well-preserved mud brick buildings of Median date have been uncovered in Level I (c. 750–550 B.C.). In one building the earliest known example of a fire altar has been discovered. Unusual mural decorations, suggesting long experience in the use of mud brick, include recessed crosses, blind windows and holes with the appearance of serving to support a scaffold. Another building was a fort, with ramp leading to a staircase, turning round a central pier and roofed with a mud brick corbel vault. The palaces and tombs of the Persians show that many features of their remarkable columnar architecture were derived from the older civilizations: the gorge moulding from Egypt; the sculptured monsters, relief-carved orthostats and polychrome glazed brickwork from Mesopotamia; the style of masonry indirectly perhaps from Urartu.

The site of **Pasargadae** comprises four groups of structures scattered over a plain, centred round the citadel, the residential palace, the tomb of Cyrus and the sacred precinct respectively. Rusticated masonry is a feature of the great platform of the citadel (Takht-i-Suleiman), whose ambitious plan was abandoned, presumably at the death of Cyrus (530 B.C.), in favour of a more modest scheme in mud brick. Multi-toothed chisels were introduced later in the reign of Darius I, so that the absence of their traces on the masonry of the first period gives support to the historical evidence of the foundation of this city by Cyrus. The **Tomb of Cyrus,** a simple box-like monument of limestone 3.2 m × 2.3 m (10 ft 6 ins × 7 ft 6 ins), gabled, and standing on a platform of six steps, is typically Achaemenian in its use of large blocks, accurately cut, smoothly dressed, without mortar but reinforced by swallowtail clamps of lead and iron. Its design, based on an early type of gabled house, is paralleled in the southern Zagros highlands by the tomb of Gur-i-Dokhtar, and has possible antecedents in the underground tombs with gabled roofs in Luristan and in central Iran at Tepe Sialk, near Kashan. A continuing tradition of gabled roofs is suggested by their occurrence in all the finished chambers of the rock-cut tomb of Darius I.

Susa, ancient city of Elam, became the Persian capital in succession to Babylon with the building there of a citadel and palace complex by Darius I (522–486 B.C.). A most illuminating building inscription tells how the resources and skills of the whole empire were utilized in the construction of the palace buildings. Cedar was brought from Lebanon, teak from the Zagros mountains and southern Persia, while the baked bricks were made by the Babylonian method. Most significant of all, craftsmen were drawn from the Assyrians, Babylonians, Egyptians and Ionian Greeks. The remarkable compound of features which constitute the unique and gracious architecture of Persia is thus explained. From this palace and a later one by Artaxerxes II (404–358 B.C.) come the famous glazed-brick decorations, portraying processions of archers, lions, bulls or dragons (p. 80F, G).

The **Palace of Persepolis** (pp. 80A–E, 81A), begun in 518 B.C. by Darius I, was mostly executed by Xerxes I (486–465 B.C.) and finished by Artaxerxes I about 460 B.C. The various buildings stood on a platform, partly built up and partly excavated, faced in well-laid local stone bound with iron cramps, about 460 m × 275 m (1,500 ft × 900 ft) in extent and rising 15 m (50 ft) above the plain at the base of a rocky spur. The approach on the north-west was by a magnificent flight of steps, 6.7 m (22 ft) wide, shallow enough for horses to ascend. A gatehouse by Xerxes had mud-brick walls, faced with polychrome bricks, and front and rear portals guarded by stone bulls. A third doorway on the south led towards the 'Apadana', a grand audience hall, 76.2 m (250 ft) square and with thirty-six columns within its 6 m (20 ft)-thick walls, begun by Darius but completed by his two successors. It stood on its own terrace, 3 m (10 ft) high; had three porticoes, each with double colonnades; stairways on the north and east sides; and minor rooms across the south side and in the four angle towers. The Palace of Darius, small by comparison, lay immediately south of the Apadana, near the west terrace wall. This might have been finished in his lifetime, as also the terraced 'Tripylon', which lay centrally among the buildings and acted as a reception chamber and guard-room for the more private quarters of the palace group. Also by Darius was the 'Treasury', in the south-east angle of the site, a double-walled administrative and storehouse building with columned halls of different sizes and only a single doorway. The buildings of Darius were arranged in the loose fashion of earlier times. Xerxes added his in between. He built his own palace near the south-west angle, connected with an L-shaped building, identified as the women's quarters (harem) which completed the enclosure of a court south of the Tripylon. He also commenced the famous 'Hall of the Hundred Columns' (finished by Artaxerxes I); this is a Throne Hall, 68.6 m (225 ft) square, with columns 11.3 m (37 ft) high, supporting a flat, cedar roof (p. 80A, C). The walls were double, except on the north side, where a portico faced a forecourt, with its

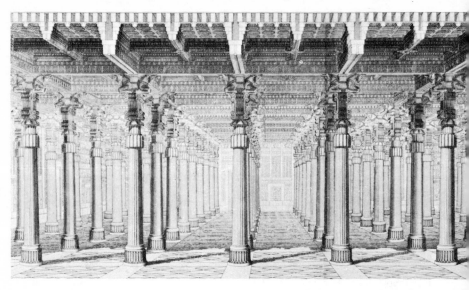

A. Persepolis: Hall of the Hundred Columns (restored) (c. 518–460 B.C.). See p. 79. Other details of the palaces at Persepolis are given below

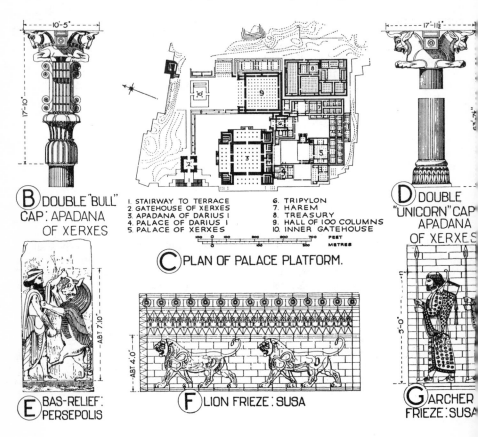

B DOUBLE "BULL" CAP. APADANA OF XERXES

1. STAIRWAY TO TERRACE
2. GATEHOUSE OF XERXES
3. APADANA OF DARIUS I
4. PALACE OF DARIUS I
5. PALACE OF XERXES
6. TRIPYLON
7. HAREM
8. TREASURY
9. HALL OF 100 COLUMNS
10. INNER GATEHOUSE

C PLAN OF PALACE PLATFORM.

D DOUBLE "UNICORN" CAP APADANA OF XERXES

E BAS-RELIEF: PERSEPOLIS

F LION FRIEZE: SUSA

G ARCHER FRIEZE: SUSA

A. Stairway of the Tripylon, Persepolis (518–486 B.C.). See p. 79

B. Tomb of Darius, Naksh-i-Rustam (485 B.C.). See p. 82

C. Fire Temple, Naksh-i-Rustam. See p. 82

own gate-house, separated from the Apadana forecourt by a stout wall. The Throne Hall had two doorways and seven windows on the entrance wall, matched on the other three sides except that niches substituted the windows. All were framed in stone surrounds in the 3.4 m (11 ft)-thick brick wall. From Persepolis have been recovered many wonderful architectural sculptures. All the monumental stairs were lined with reliefs, as also the Apadana terrace, where they were arranged in triple tiers or 'registers', separated by bands of rosettes. Nobles, courtiers, chieftains, tribute-bearers and guardsmen advanced in dignified procession, and traditional subjects filled the awkward angles of the stairways and the deep jambs of the doorways (p. 80E). Stepped battlements crowned the parapet walls. All these sculptures were originally in brilliant colour. Columns of the lesser apartments had wooden shafts, thickly plastered and decoratively painted, but those of the Halls were of stone throughout. They have a character all their own, with moulded bases, fluted shafts and curious, complex capitals with vertical Ionic-like volutes and twin bulls or dragons supporting the roof beams (p. 80B, D).

The **Tomb of Darius, Naksh-i-Rustam** (485 B.C.) (p. 81B), 13 km (8 miles) north of Persepolis, is one of four rock-hewn sepulchres of the great Achaemenian kings. Its façade, 18.3 m (60 ft) wide, appears to reproduce the south front of Darius' palace at Persepolis, with four columns of the double-bull type, central doorway with Egyptian-like cornice, and upper compartment in which an elaborate throne, 2.7 m (9 ft) high, is supported by two rows of figures, above which the king stands before a fire altar. Near the tomb stands a **Fire Temple**, a stone square tower containing a single room, approached by an outside stairway (p. 81C).

SELEUCID, PARTHIAN AND SASSANIAN ARCHITECTURE

The Seleucid Empire, founded in 312 B.C. after the death of Alexander, began to disintegrate about 247 B.C., and after 140 B.C. was confined to the region west of the Euphrates, finally giving way to the Romans in 64 B.C. Meanwhile there was a considerable influx of Macedonian and Greek settlers, who built many new towns, including Seleucia, near Babylon, and Antioch, in Syria. In Bactria, on the eastern border, they spread Greek civilization to India; but in general, their influence was uneven, and in art and architecture it was sometimes the Hellenistic and sometimes the local Persian character that prevailed. The Parthians, who wrested the eastern and Mesopotamian territories piecemeal from the Seleucids, respected the Hellenistic culture and institutions and under their long rule the new Greek cities flourished. Yet as integration proceeded, the arts profoundly declined. With the Sassanian dynasty (A.D. 226–642), when the principal city was Ctesiphon, near Babylon, vigour sprang anew and a number of fine buildings were erected which form a connecting link between the old Mesopotamian architecture on the one hand and Byzantine on the other. Palaces were the dominant type.

The **Palace, Feruz-abad** (south of Persepolis) (c. A.D. 250) (p. 83), built of stone rubble faced with plaster, has a deep, open-fronted arched entrance leading to three domed halls, forming a reception suite, beyond which is a court surrounded by private chambers. The domes are seated over the three square halls with the help of 'squinch' arches thrown across the angles (p. 83C), while the internal walls below them are ornamented with niches having plaster archivolts and enframements of a classical complexion but capped with cornices of the Egyptian 'gorge' type (p. 83C, F).

The **Palace of Shapur I, Bishapur** (west of Persepolis) (c. A.D. 260), was a remarkable building built of plastered stone rubble, with a cruciform plan,

PALACE ⸸ FERUZ-ABAD

50 100 150 FEET
SCALE FOR ELEVATION & SECTION

(A) PRINCIPAL FACADE (RESTORED)

COURT

154'-0"

SCALE FOR PLAN
50 100 150 FEET

(B) EXTERIOR (RESTORED)

(C) TRANSVERSE SECTION

(D) PLAN

(E) ARCH CONSTRUCTION

(F) RECESSES

PALACE ⸸ SARVISTAN

(G) VIEW FROM S.W. (RESTORED)

COURT

X

Y

140'-0"

112'-0"

(H) PENDENTIVE IN HALL "Y"

(J) PLAN

(K) COLUMN IN HALL AT "X"

PALACE ⸸ CTESIPHON

112'-6"

16'-6"

(L) RESTORATION ONE BAY

(M) VIEW OF EXISTING RUINS

(N) RUINS FROM S.

83'-0"
60'-0"
312'-0"
170'-0"

(P) PLAN

dominated by a central dome of elliptical section springing from floor level. The coloured-plaster wall-decoration of modelled architectural features again had a classical character.

The **Palace, Sarvistan** (vicinity of Persepolis) (c. A.D. 350) (p. 83) was fronted by the typical deep barrel-vaulted porches, behind which rose a bee-hive dome, carried on squinch arches (p. 83H), marking the principal apartment. The dome was pierced with openings for light and ventilation. Two long side chambers had barrel vaults supported on massive piers which themselves stood on pairs of stumpy columns (p. 83K), a most ingenious method of reducing the effective span and obtaining powerful abutment to the vaults.

At Feruz-abad and Bishapur there were towered fire-temples, used in connection with open-air ceremonies, similar to that at Naksh-i-Rustam (see above).

The **Palace, Ctesiphon** (p. 83) is usually attributed to Chosroes I (A.D. 531–579) but is probably of the fourth century A.D. As it is in the Mesopotamian plain, it is of brick. The principal part surviving is a vast banqueting hall, open-fronted like the reception tents of tribal sheiks in nomadic days, with flanking private wings screened by an enormous wall, 34.4 m (112 ft 6 ins) high. The latter is ornamented with tiers of attached columns and arcades, an arrangement betraying Roman influence. One wing of the façade fell in 1909 after an exceptional Tigris flood. The elliptical barrel vault over the hall, 7.3 m (24 ft) thick at the base and rising 36.7 m (120 ft) from the floor to cover the 25.3 m (83 ft) span, equalled if it did not surpass the mightiest structural achievements of Ancient Rome. The lower part of the vault is constructed in horizontal courses—Sassanian domes were usually constructed wholly in this manner—but substantially the vault is made up of arch rings sloped against an end wall, so as to avoid the necessity of temporary wood centering. This is a practice which we have seen to have been adopted for brick vaults equally in Ancient Egyptian and in Assyrian architecture.

BIBLIOGRAPHY

ARIK, R. O. *Les Fouilles d'Alaca Hüyük.* Ankara, 1937.
BELL, E. *Early Architecture in Western Asia.* London, 1924.
BITTEL, K. *Boğazköy-Hattušas.* Berlin, 1952.
—. *Hattusha: The Capital of the Hittites.* New York, 1970.
BOTTA, P. E., et FLANDIN, E. *Monuments de Ninive.* 5 vols. Paris, 1849–50.
CHILDE, V. G. *New Light on the Most Ancient East.* 4th ed. New York, 1953.
CONTENEAU, G. *Everyday Life in Babylon and Assyria.* Trans. K. R. and A. R. Maxwell-Hyslop. London and New York, 1954.
—. *Manuel d'archéologie orientale.* 4 vols. Paris, 1947.
DIEULAFOY, M. *L'Art antique de la Perse.* 5 vols. Paris, 1884–9.
FERGUSSON, J. *The Palaces of Nineveh and Persepolis Restored.* London, 1851.
FRANKFORT, H. *The Art and Architecture of the Ancient Orient.* Harmondsworth, 1954.
—. *The Birth of Civilization in the Near East.* London, 1954.
GHIRSHMAN, R. *Iran.* Harmondsworth, 1954.
—. 'Report on the Ziggurat at Tchoga-Zanbil', *Illustrated London News,* 8 September 1956.
GURNEY, O. R. *The Hittites.* 2nd ed. Harmondsworth, 1961.
KELLER, W. *The Bible as History.* London, 1956.
KENYON, KATHLEEN M. *Archaeology in the Holy Land.* London, 1965, 1969.
—. *Jerusalem: Excavating 3,000 Years of History.* London, 1967.
LAMPL, PAUL. *Cities and Planning in the Ancient Near East.* London, 1970.
LAYARD, A. H. *Monuments of Nineveh.* 2 vols. London, 1849.
—. *Nineveh and its Palaces.* 2 vols. London, 1849.
LLOYD, SETON. *Ruined Cities of Iraq.* 3rd ed. London, 1946.
—. *Mounds of the Near East.* Edinburgh, 1963.

—. *Early Highland Peoples of Anatolia.* London, 1967.

LOUD, GORDON. *Khorsabad.* 2 vols. Chicago, 1936–8.

LUSCHAN, F., and others. *Ausgrabungen in Sendschirli.* 5 vols. Berlin, 1893–1943.

MACQUEEN, JAMES G. *Babylon.* London, 1964.

MALLOWAN, M. E. L. *Twenty-five Years of Mesopotamian Discovery.* Brochure. London, 1956.

—. *Nimrud and its Remains.* 2 vols. London, 1966.

MELLAART, JAMES. 'Notes on the Architectural Remains of Troy I and II', *Anatolian Studies,* ix, 1959.

OLMSTEAD, A. T. *History of the Persian Empire: Achaemenid Period.* Chicago, 1948.

PARROT, A. *Archéologie Mésopotamienne.* 2 vols. Paris, 1946–53.

—. *Ziggurats et Tour de Babel.* Paris, 1949.

—. *Mission archéologique de Mari II: Le Palais. 1. Architecture. 2. Peintures. 3. Documents et Monuments.* Paris, 1958–9.

PERROT, G., and CHIPIEZ, C. *History of Art in Chaldea and Assyria, Persia, Phrygia and Judaea.* 5 vols. London and New York, 1884–92.

PLACE, VICTOR. *Ninive et l'Assyrie.* 3 vols. Paris, 1867–70.

PUCHSTEIN, O. *Boghazköy. Die Bauwerke.* Leipzig, 1912.

SCHMIDT, E. F. *Persepolis I.* Chicago, 1953.

SMITH, SIDNEY. *Alalakh and Chronology.* Brochure. London, 1940.

SPIERS, R. P. *Architecture East and West.* London, 1905.

TEXIER, C. *L'Arménie, la Perse et la Mésopotamie.* 2 vols. Paris, 1842–52.

WOOLLEY, SIR C. L. *A Forgotten Kingdom.* Harmondsworth, 1953.

—. *Ur of the Chaldees.* Harmondsworth, 1954.

WRIGHT, G. E. *Biblical Archaeology.* Philadelphia and London, 1957.

YADIN, YIGAEL. *The Art of Warfare in Biblical Lands.* London, 1963.

3

ARCHITECTURE IN INDIA AND PAKISTAN

(HINDU, BUDDHIST AND JAIN)

Circa 500 B.C. to present day

INFLUENCES

GEOGRAPHICAL

India and Pakistan, together with the outlying countries of Afghanistan, Nepal, Tibet, Sri Lanka, Burma, Indo-China, Malaysia and Indonesia form the southern fringe of Asia. The main triangular peninsula, comprising the first two countries, is about fifteen times the size of Great Britain. On the north, a barrier is formed by high mountain ranges stretching from the Hindu Kush in the west, through the Pamirs, Karakorams, and the Himalayas to the mountains of Szechwan in China, in the north-east. On the east, south and west, the area is bounded by the sea. In the earliest times, influences entered the area mainly from Central Asia through the passes of the north-west and north-east: there was also a strong tide of influence from Persia and Western Asia (Graeco-Roman), via Baluchistan (or what is now Afghanistan). Good harbours along the coast are few; intercourse by sea was, therefore, less important in early days, although by the first century A.D., there was a thriving maritime trade with the Roman Empire. The great rivers in the north, the Indus and Ganges and their tributaries, provided trade ways, and many of the area's most important cities were founded along them. Delhi, the 'Rome' of India, on the River Jumna, has been the capital of India, at various times, over a period of a thousand years: around it still are the remains of at least seven separate 'cities' scattered over nearly fifty square miles. (Archaeological surveys have exposed the ruins of the legendary cities of the epic period, c. 1000 B.C., similar to the discoveries of Troy and Mycenae which established the historicity of the Greek epics.) Its importance was due to its commanding position at the junction of the four trade routes from the Lower Ganges, the Hindu Kush, the Indus Valley, and the Gulf of Cambay. The chief commercial city of Pakistan is Karachi, a port founded in the eighteenth century and the sea gateway to the Indus Valley. Excavations at Mohenjo-Daro and Harappa, and in Rajasthan, indicate close links between the so-called 'Indus Valley-Harappan culture' and ancient Mesopotamia. It is only in the south and east of the peninsula that the stream of influences seems to have been diffuse, in spite of Roman trading stations on the coast of the Bay of Bengal.

GEOLOGICAL

The lack of building stone along the Indus and Ganges Valleys, and the easily available timber which was floated down the rivers from the mountains have influenced architecture in the area from the earliest times. In the north, architectural forms, at least until the eighteenth century A.D., tended to be simply the translation into stone of carpentry techniques. There is good white marble in Rajasthan, widely used in buildings, and fine red and cream sandstone from the neighbourhood of Agra; generally speaking, however, these are used mainly as facing materials for rubble walling behind. In the centre and south, the 'trap' and granite of the Deccan and the volcanic potstone of Halebid made their own contributions to the development of regional characteristics. In the Western Ghats, the horizontal rock strata which rise in perpendicular cliffs, made possible the rock-cut sanctuaries of Karli (p. 96A), Ajanta (p. 96C) and Elephanta (p. 104B). At Mamallapuram and Ellora (p. 104A) rock-cut temples, known as 'Raths', were hewn out of amygdaloidal trap formations. As far as timber is concerned, hard teak is found in Burma and in the eastern and western coastal mountains. An excellent softwood, deodar, is found abundantly in the northern mountain ranges; shisham, a hardwood somewhat inferior to teak, grows everywhere in the river valleys of the north. In the riverine plains of Bengal, Uttar Pradesh and the Punjab, the alluvial soil makes good bricks which were, and are, used extensively in these areas. Terra-cotta has been used from the earliest times; the ease with which the plastic clay can be pressed into moulds or carved, before firing, may be responsible (together with the traditions of wood-carving), for the exuberance of decoration in subsequent periods. Lime for building was obtained by burning limestone, shells and kankar, a nodular form of impure lime found in the river valleys.

CLIMATIC

Although slightly more than half the area lies within the Tropic of Cancer, the climate varies widely. In the east, there is a small variation of temperature between summer and winter, a very heavy rainfall in the monsoon season (May to August), and a moderate rainfall throughout the year. This produces a climate generally warm and humid, but not excessively hot. In the bulk of the peninsula, the temperature is fairly equable throughout the year, but the distinction between dry and wet seasons is more clearly marked. In the plains of the north, temperatures rise high in the summer months (May to July) and drop markedly about the winter solstice. The rainy season comes later than in the east, and is shorter. The general character of the climate is dry, with a cooler winter. In the north-west, the hot season and the cold season are nearly equal in length, the former being severe (temperatures rising to 120° F), and the latter also sharp with night-frosts and sleet: the summer rainy season is short and late, and the winter rains are more marked than in the Gangetic Plain. This great variation of climate has less general effect on architecture than might be expected, as protection against heat, even in the north-west, seems to have received more attention than winter comfort. Pierced, or latticed, windows to exclude sunlight and heat are general: and canals, reservoirs and tanks, for ceremonial use, for irrigation, and for comfort, are features of all important religious and secular buildings. The high angle of the sun over much of the area, and the frequency of sunny days, may well have helped to produce the characteristic external carved decoration which takes much of its effect from the contrasts of light and shade. The flat roof, for summer sleeping, is almost universal except in the east, where the need to deal with heavy and continuous rain produced steeply-pitched roofs. Major climatic changes have taken place at least in parts of the area in historic times: excavations at Mohenjo-Daro, for example, clearly indicate that the Lower Indus Valley, now largely semi-desert, once supported the rich animal and vegetable life normally associated with tropical jungles. This may explain, in part, the replacement of wood by stone as a basic building material.

The Indo-Pakistan sub-continent and Sri Lanka

HISTORICAL AND SOCIAL

The earliest defined civilization in the sub-continent is that of the so-called 'Indus Valley-Harappan culture' (2500–1500 B.C.), which was related to the Sumerian cultures of Western Asia. The most famous excavated sites of this period are those at Mohenjo-Daro (in Sind) and Harappa (about a hundred miles south of Lahore); but recent excavations in the Rajasthan area of Western India indicate that this civilization was more widely spread than its present name indicates. All remains discovered so far are of archaeological rather than architectural interest.

Successive incursions, military and economic, into the area from 2000 B.C. until the nineteenth century A.D., brought art and architecture into contact with many influences; Aryan, Persian, Graeco-Roman, Sassanian, Moslem, Portuguese, French and English. The strength of these varied considerably: the first four exercised a deep influence, the next three more purely local ones, and the last, again a strong one. Between the periods of internal weakness marking these incursions, indigenous empires and kingdoms rose and declined. From the point of view of the Hindu, Buddhist and Jain cultures, the most important of these were:

(a) The Mauryan Buddhist Empire in the north, c. 300 B.C., influenced by Alexander the Great's short-lived 'empire'. Cultural influences from Achaemenid Persia (e.g. the Persepolitan type of memorial pillar or 'lath' erected by Asoka) are indicated by the descriptions by a Chinese pilgrim in A.D. 400 of the wooden palace of Asoka at Pataliputra, then still surviving. The first dressed stone architecture dates from the reign of Asoka.

(b) The Bactrian Buddhist kingdoms of Gandhara in the north-west, breaking away from the Mauryan Empire in about 200 B.C. Close cultural affinities with the Graeco-Roman world existed, through trade and cultural exchanges with Asia Minor and the Asian Greek cities founded by Alexander the Great.

(c) The Satavahanas, Andhra and Sunga kingdoms in Central and South India, from about 185 B.C. These areas were less under external influences, and their art was more indigenous in character, reflected in beautiful Buddhist architectural remains (e.g. Barhut and Sanchi stupas), the early flowering of a synthesis of Indian art which led to the classical Gupta period.

(d) The Kushan Empire, founded by a tribe of Central Asian nomads in the north-west, and in existence for the first three centuries of the Christian era. The greatest ruler was Kanishka (c. A.D. 78), whose capital was at Peshawar. This period shows a continuing cultural influx from the Graeco-Roman world of Asia Minor and Sassanian Persia, Central Asia and China. Important centres of art at Gandhara and Mathura (near Delhi) produced the first Buddha images. There are 'architectural' remains of this period in the excavated city of Sirkap (Taxila); in rock-cut shrines with important architectural detail at Bamiyan and the remains of a Greek city, Ai-Kha-Noum (fourth century A.D.) on the banks of the river Oxus, both in North Afghanistan (see p. 119).

(e) The Gupta Empire, embracing the northern areas from the Jumuna River in the west to Assam in the east, and south to the Narbadda River. During this period (fourth to sixth century A.D.), there was maritime expansion to the Far East, carrying with it artistic influences which flowered later in Cambodia and other places. To this phase belong the earliest substantial architectural remains that survive.

(f) In the south, five orthodox Hindu states were successively dominant: the Pallavas (sixth to ninth century), whose influence spread to South-East Asia; the Cholas (late tenth to thirteenth century), whose power reached Burma and Ceylon; the Early Pandyan (eleventh to fourteenth century) in the far south; the kingdom of Vijayanagar, south of the Kistna River, founded in the first half of the fourteenth century and destroyed in 1565; and the Later Pandyan Nayak dynasty of Madura (seventeenth to eighteenth century).

After the middle of the eighteenth century, the disintegration of the Mughal Empire in the north, and the Hindu states in the south, combined with the arrival of European fashions through France and England, virtually put an end to any further development of Hindu architecture. Some self-conscious attempts at a 'revival' since 1947, when India and Pakistan became sovereign states, have produced little of importance. Some religious implications of the organization of society into castes are indicated below, and these divisions still remain clearly marked in spite of recent efforts to break them down. Apart from forming social divisions into classes, the caste system had a racial significance in that Brahmans and Kshatriyas claimed descent from the Sanskrit-speaking Aryan invaders, the Vaisyas were held to be of mixed blood and could therefore lay no claim to racial aristocracy, and the Sudras were the defeated aboriginals. Apart from these, there was a large Moslem population claiming descent from Arab and Persian invaders, but in fact drawn mainly from converts to Islam: these were mostly concentrated in Pakistan and Bangladesh. The sub-continent cannot be viewed as an entity either socially or artistically, for there is as great a divergence of language, social custom, climate, and ethnographic types as may be found within Europe from Scandinavia to the Mediterranean: thus a simple picture of architectural development is impossible. Ordinary domestic buildings of any very great age do not exist; wealth, until recently, was concentrated in the hands of feudal landlords who built palaces for themselves or temples for their gods. In an order where life on earth is looked upon mainly as a preparation for something more enduring after death, it is not surprising that temples are more important monuments than palaces.

RELIGIOUS

In these lands, religion impinged more strongly and continually on everyday life than was normal in the West. The basic doctrines of Hinduism have been modified by the impact of Buddhism and Jainism, which are both, fundamentally, non-conformist sects of Hinduism. The former sect has moved much further from the parent doctrine than the latter, and has now largely disappeared from the country of its origins, although there are Buddhist communities in Bangladesh. Jainism still attracts many devotees in India.

Hindu. The Hindu religion seems to have evolved from a combination of the faiths of the indigenous Dravidians and the Aryan invaders: the Dravidian cult of 'bhakti' (devotion to an incarnation, and so to images) modifying the Aryan preference for abstract principles. These Aryan principles are incorporated in the 'Rig-Veda', a series of hymns composed some time between 1500–800 B.C. About the beginning of the Christian era, the Vedic gods were superseded by the trinity ('Trimurti') of modern Hinduism: Vishnu, the preserver; Siva, the destroyer; and Brahma (the prime being of the trinity), soul and creator of the universe. Vishnu and Siva appear in various forms ('avatars') and for this reason the triune aspect of Hinduism has often been misrepresented as multiple idol worship. Hindu worship is essentially an individual act, and except on certain specified occasions communal worship is foreign to it. This has produced the basic difference between the Hindu temple, and the Moslem mosque (p. 411 ff.).

From the earliest days of Hinduism, an orthodox Hindu's daily life has been governed by religious practice in its minutest details. Any major occasion demands the services of one of the Brahman priesthood, who alone have the authority to officiate. Before the advent of Buddhism, the Brahman caste had thus so concentrated power in their own hands that this early period of Hinduism is known as the Brahmanical period, and the Brahmans' abuse of their power produced the challenges of both the Buddhists and the Jains.

Buddhist. Siddartha, or Gautama Buddha, was born about 563 B.C. on the borders of India and Nepal. He belonged to the princely Kshatriya caste, who had obvious reasons to dispute Brahman domination. Buddha's basic doctrine was that salvation, being attainable by the individual's actions, was within the reach of all regardless of caste, and did not depend on Brahmanical intercession. It followed that the Buddhist religious buildings became concentrated in monasteries (where the contemplative life could be lived in communion with fellow spirits), and in shrines where relics of those who had achieved salvation ('nirvana') were deposited. These shrines took the form of 'stupas', or domical mounds which, grouped with their rails, gateways, processional paths, and crowning 'umbrellas', came to be regarded as symbols of the universe. The monasteries became places of international pilgrimage and dissemination of learning. With the passage of time, the original asceticism of Buddha's doctrines practised by the Theravada Sect became modified, and another, the Mahayana Sect, developed. Buddhism declined in India after the seventh century A.D., but continued in Sri Lanka (Ceylon), South-East Asia and the Far East.

Jain. Jainism was traditionally founded by Mahavira (roughly a contemporary with Buddha) who was himself a Brahman. The goal is salvation through successive re-births, the ideal being rigid asceticism and the avoidance of injury to every living creature, which might be some soul in the process of purification. Jain temples differ little in essentials from the normal Hindu temple, but are distinguished by the extraordinary richness and complexity of their sculptural ornament. Mahavira and twenty-four other saints who had achieved salvation before him are worshipped, sometimes in the form of the animals which are attributed to them.

ARCHITECTURAL CHARACTER

BUDDHIST ARCHITECTURE

(Fourth century B.C.–ninth century A.D.)

Buddhist shrines differ from those of the Hindus and Jains in that they are all designed for congregational use. Monasteries, meeting halls ('chaityas'), and stupa shrines are all planned to accommodate large groups of worshippers. The major examples are in the north-west (i.e. the old Bactrian kingdoms), in the mountains of the Western Ghats above Bombay, and in the north-central east regions. In the rock-cut chaityas of the Western Ghats, the main forms and the details of the wooden prototype buildings, now vanished, have been preserved. Although no structural roof of the period survives, the rock-cut chaityas and raths at Mamallapuram, as well as paintings at Ajanta and the descriptions of Chinese pilgrims, clearly show that roof structures were of wood, covered normally with thatch. In Kashmir, there are a few surviving examples of steeply-pitched pyramidal roofs of stone, on square buildings, but it seems likely that these were masonry reproductions of wooden originals: a very similar type of wooden structure may still be found in temples in the remoter parts of the Kangra Valley in the Himalayas. Decorative detail is used more in the Western classical tradition—to emphasize structure—than in Hindu and Jain buildings, where it conceals structure like a jungle growth. This is even more noticeable in the north-west, where near-replicas of Hellenistic buildings occur (e.g. the Zoroastrian temple at Jhaulian, Taxila), and where both Corinthian and Ionic Orders occur in a distorted but plainly recognizable form. Virtually no secular buildings remain, but the excavated parts of the city of Sirkap (Taxila) (fl. 200 B.C.–A.D. 200), show a city neatly laid out on a rectangular grid and dominated by an 'acropolis' containing a monastery and stupa. The acropolis appears again in other civil settlements, such as Mingaora (Swat state).

In all three styles mouldings have a bulbous character, often heavily undercut. The height and brightness of the sun produce strong shadow lines, and any subtlety of moulding would be lost. In Buddhist Graeco-Bactrian mouldings, in particular, the lack of refinement is noticeable, when compared with their Greek or Roman originals. A moulding made by overlapping rectangular slabs is often used. In other cases, a semicircular openwork moulding, like basketwork, and also the torus, are found. The double convex shape, into which the cross-pieces of Buddhist railings are cut, forms bands of light and shade, taking the place of mouldings (p. 105E).

In marked contrast to Hindu and Jain ornament, Buddhist ornament is restrained both in character and extent, although in later periods and outlying places (such as Indo-China and Java) it became almost Hindu in its exuberance. In the Bactrian work of the north-west, familiar Hellenistic motifs (such as garlands carried by cupids, gryphons and acanthus ornaments) are combined with more exotic ones, like the double-headed eagle, elephants, and flying divinities. In the Central Indian monuments (e.g. Sanchi and Ajanta) the indigenous love of ornament asserts itself more strongly: the female figure in its most voluptuous form is often used, with an apparent disregard for Buddhist rules of asceticism. A female holding the bough of a tree in an upraised hand, which becomes a familiar figure in later periods, first appears in Buddhist work: the origins of the motif are mysterious, but may represent Queen Maya holding a branch while giving birth to the Buddha. Painted wall decoration was widely used, and ranged from purely architectural forms to the very elaborate and beautiful 'genre' paintings on the cave walls at Ajanta, which provide invaluable social and architectural records of the period, together with the various sculptured bas-reliefs depicting scenes from the daily life of the times through the story of Buddha.

JAIN ARCHITECTURE

Early Jain (*c*. third century B.C.). The earliest rock-cut caves were ordered by Emperor Asoka for the use of Ajivika (Jain) ascetics, and were exact copies in rock or wood of thatch structures, a technique inspired by Persepolitan types with highly polished mirror walls. These were the beginnings of the development of rock architecture of later times, and of motifs and forms of expression seen in all later Buddhist architecture: sloping jambs and a semicircular arch with carvings and a stone latticed architrave, a barrel-vaulted hall with a circular cell at the end with a central doorway and a hemispherical domed roof with an overhanging cave like a thatch.

Late Jain (A.D. 1000–1700). Jain temples are found over most of the area, but mainly in the northern central part of the peninsula. There were revivals of architectural activity in the fifteenth century A.D., but the work from this period has little life and shows no real development. The central shrine, covered by a dome or spire, is introduced by a pillared portico, usually in the form of an octagon set within a square (p. 105B). There are thus twelve pillars supporting the roof, which is formed of successively diminishing squares laid diagonally to each other. Although Jain temples are seldom simple units (see Ranpur, p. 98) the most elaborate examples are but a multiplication of the basic form. The main difference between the Jain and the Hindu temple is the lighter and more elegant character of the former. The Jains, also, paid particular attention to the siting and environment of their monuments, creating temple cities on sacred mountains. Although both Hindu and Jain temples are basically enclosed shrines introduced by a more open porch, specifically Jain are ceilings in the form of flat domes, and stonework so elaborately carved that it often loses all its own character and can be compared to petrified foliage. The construction was of successively diminishing courses of stone. In the case of the flat dome, these courses were either laid diagonally each to the next, or, in the larger examples, in circular courses laid horizontally and gradually diminishing in diameter. The concentric rings are elaborately carved, and the single capstone at the apex of the dome is often developed as a pendant.

HINDU ARCHITECTURE

Hindu temples may be roughly grouped into three regional types, although these are not clear cut and a rigid division cannot be assumed.

(*a*) *Northern:* A.D. 350 to the present, which can be further sub-divided into:
(i) East: Orissa (Kalinga), A.D. 800–1250.

(ii) North-West: Kashmir, A.D. 600–1300. An extension of the Gandhara style at Martand, Avantipur and Malot, and previously Buddhist: no remains survive.

(iii) Early Central, A.D. 350–650, which includes the Early and Late Gupta periods; and Late Central, A.D. 950–1050, during the Khajuraho Chandela Dynasty.

(iv) West: Gujarat, A.D. 941–1600, under the Solanki dynasty. The Mount Abu temples, representing the final Baroque phase, date from the thirteenth century.

(b) *Central Deccan*, consisting of:

(i) Early Chalukyan, A.D. 450–750, and Pattadakal, eighth century.

(ii) Later Chalukyan-Hoysalan, A.D. 1000–1325.

(c) *Southern Dravidian*, A.D. 600–1750, which falls into:

(i) Pallava, A.D. 600–900, during the Early phase of which temples were wholly rock-cut, and during the Later wholly structural.

(ii) Cholan, A.D. 700–1150, which was a development of Pallava with Chalukyan influence from the Deccan.

(iii) Early Pandyan, A.D. 1000–1350, an intermediate style, during which temples were expanded.

(iv) Vijayanagar, A.D. 1350–1565, during which elaborate Baroque-style temples were built, a prelude to the Maduran style, while palaces were Hindu with Moslem influences.

(v) Later Pandyan, c. sixteenth to eighteenth century, was the final phase of the Madura style, far south. During the Nayak dynasty a new Dravidian capital was built at Madura.

(vi) South West, Kerala, A.D. 1100–1500, typical of which are the gable-roofed temples of Mudabidri and Mangalore.

In all types the fundamental plan consists of a small unlit shrine called the 'garbha-griha', crowned with the spire-shaped 'sikhara' roof, formed of horizontal courses of stone, and introduced by one or more porch-like halls ('mandapas') used for religious dancing and music. With roofs of flatter pyramidal coverings to the mandap, the span is often reduced either by the introduction of wide-spreading brackets above the column capital, or by successive corbels as in Jain buildings. The vault never seems to have been used at any period, however large the building. This form seems to have evolved about the fourth century A.D. The sanctuary as a whole is the 'vimana'. Except in the south, the vimana is seldom designed to take a congregation of worshippers; its entire self becomes an object of worship. This explains the importance attached to the sculptural decoration of the exterior, and also the sanctity traditionally ascribed by Hindus to the art and to the practitioners of temple building. The vertical sikhara makes a very marked contrast with the low, flat roof-lines of the average Indian village, and proclaims the holy place as unmistakably as does the church-tower in the English countryside. Variations of the simple plan are such as those at Brindaban (p. 105G) where accommodation was necessary for crowds of pilgrims, and at Bellur (p. 105J) where the mandap has become a theatre for ritual dances. In (a), the *Northern Indian* temple, the sikhara is very dominant: it is conical in form, with convex curved sides; and there is normally a finial ('kalasa') of vase or 'melon' form. The 'mandap' or porch-hall is usually more or less enclosed with walls or screens. The general plan form of the vimana is a combination of simple rectangles (e.g. Aihole, Badami). Temples of (b), the *Central Deccan* type, later combined features of the Northern (e.g. the sikhara) with those of the Dravidian (e.g. the stellate plan form). Generally speaking, temples of this type are more florid and exuberant in form and decoration than those of the north. In (c), *Southern Dravidian* temples, the form of the spire becomes a flatter pyramid with straight or (later) concave sides: the term 'sikhara' in this type is given only to the top storey of the spire, which becomes much elaborated and follows either the Buddhist stupa or chaitya form (pp. 96A, 106C). These crowning spires are often grouped in miniature repetitions round the lower stages of the building. Peculiar to the later Dravidian temples are the many-columned halls, tanks, and courtyards surrounding the inner sanctuary. The enclosing walls of the courtyards have gigantic gateway towers ('gopurams') which replace the sikhara as the dominating features of the temple group (p. 106D). The intention of this arrangement is to heighten the emotional impact of the approach to the shrine, and to display the wealth and power of the temple and its servants. The sculptural and decorative details are of little importance compared with those of earlier temples: compare the dry, lifeless carving in the **Temple at Tadpatri** (seventeenth century A.D.) (p. 106B) with that at Bellur (twelfth century A.D.) (p. 103B).

The column at Baroli (p. 100C) shows many characteristics of the Hindu column; the deeply cut bell-form capital (cf. Elephanta, p. 104B), the garland decoration below the capital, the chain-and-bell ornament modulating the transition from the circular to polygonal shaft section, the four apsuras (female divinities) below, and finally the heavy base with its deep-cut mouldings. The typical Hindu column does not exist, but this is a good example of an often-found type. In Dravidian temples, the heavy cushion capital often appears (p. 104A). In later periods decoration becomes so lavish that the column loses its identity as a supporting member (p. 105F, K), and assumes the character of free-standing sculpture (cf. Greek caryatids, p. 233).

Jain and Hindu ornament, in contrast to the severely classical restraint of the Buddhist north-west, is immensely exuberant and based on an appreciation of human and animal forms in their most sensual manifestations. At its best, this sculpture is highly emotive and very beautiful; but it too easily descends, first into sheer virtuosity, and thence into mechanical repetition. Much of the highly elaborate Jain sculpture is an example of this. In the earlier, and finest, examples (e.g. Halebid) the sculptured ornament, although keeping its vitality and interest, is perfectly related to the buildings it adorns. But this is rare, and more often the building is little more than a support for a completely dominant cloak of decoration.

EXAMPLES

BUDDHIST ARCHITECTURE

(Fourth century B.C.–ninth century A.D.)

(1) *Stambhas* or *Laths*. These are monumental pillars, standing free without any structural function, with circular or octagonal shafts. Inscriptions were carved on the shaft. The capital, which was usually Persepolitan in form (cf. p. 82), was bell-shaped and crowned with animal supporters bearing the Buddhist 'chakra' or 'wheel of the law'. The emblem of the Republic of India is the capital of the 'stambha' at **Sarnath.** There are others at **Allahabad,** and further north at **Lauriya Nandangarh** (p. 100A).

(2) *Stupas*. The most important group of these domical mounds is at **Sanchi** in the former state of Bhopal. The **Great Stupa** here dates, in its present form, from the end of the first century B.C., and preserves its stone enclosing railings (pp. 95A, 105E) and the four ceremonial gateways ('toranas') (p. 105A) at the cardinal points of the compass. These ancillary features must have been common to all important stupas. The toranas resemble, and may have inspired, the Chinese 'pai-lou' (p. 155) and the Japanese 'torii' (p. 164). At the base of the stupa is a

A. The Great Stupa, Sanchi, from E. (late 1st cent. B.C.). See p. 94

B. Monastery at Takht-i-Bhai (3rd cent. A.D.). See p. 97

A. The Chaitya, Karli: interior (78 B.C.). See p. 97

B. The Chaitya, Ellora (c. 7th cent.):
interior. See p. 97

C. The Chaitya, Ajanta: façade
(c. A.D. 250). See p. 97

processional path above a platform 4.3 m (14 ft) high. The stupa is of solid brick-work, 32 m (106 ft) in diameter and 12.8 m (42 ft) high. Originally, it was faced with stone, and the crowning feature was a three-tiered stone 'umbrella', similar to that still in place (though damaged) on the stupa within the hall at **Karli** (p. 96A). Other important stupas are at **Barhut** (second century A.D.), and **Amaravati** (A.D. 200). Many sculptured panels from Amaravati are in the British Museum, and a full-size reproduction of the Sanchi railings is in the Indian Museum, South Kensington.

There are many lesser stupas throughout north-west Pakistan; at **Mankiala** near Rawalpindi, at **Taxila,** and in the **Khyber Pass.** The great stupa built by Kanishka at Shah-ji-ki-Dheri, on the outskirts of **Peshawar,** has disappeared, but it was carefully described by Chinese pilgrims of the sixth century as rising to a height of 214 m (700 ft) (including the wooden superstructure). Excavations on its site in 1908 revealed an important bronze relic casket (now in Peshawar Museum), decor-ated with debased Hellenistic motives, and signed by the Greek-named maker, Agesilas.

(3) *Chaityas* or Assembly Halls. No free-standing chaityas of any importance remain, but rock-cut examples at **Bhaja** (250 B.C.), **Nasik** (129 B.C.), **Karli, Ellora,** and **Ajanta,** show clearly the form of the original structure (p. 96A, B, C). The latest of these dates from A.D. 250. The plan consists of an apsidal-ended hall with closely-spaced pillars at each side, forming aisles or ambulatories. A stupa shrine is placed in the apse, furthest from the entrance. The roofs are semicircular in section, and ribs representing the original timber members of the prototypes are cut from the rock. The façade normally contains, above a low entrance portico, a horseshoe-shaped window filled with rock-cut or wooden tracery (p. 96C), which admits light to the interior.

The **Chaitya, Karli** (78 B.C.) (p. 96A), is 38.5 m (126 ft) long, and the height and width are 13.7 m (45 ft). The Persepolitan-type columns are octagonal, and the capitals are formed by pairs of elephants. The bases, shaped like inverted vases, seem to be an indigenous development; it has been suggested that they derive from stone or earthenware sockets to protect the wooden columns from water and insects. The roof ribs, in this case, are actually of wood, inserted after the roof was cut. A fine lath, crowned with four lions, stands at the entrance of this chaitya.

(4) *Viharas* or Monasteries. These consist of a quadrangle surrounded by a verandah on to which open simple square cells. Adjacent to this 'cloister' was the courtyard containing the main stupa, which was usually crowded with smaller votive stupas. Communal rooms, like dining halls and kitchens, adjoined the cloister as the site allowed. Most of the existing viharas are in the north-west of Pakistan and in Afghanistan. There were several fine remains around **Taxila** (second cen-tury B.C. to second century A.D.) and near **Mingaora** in the Swat valley. That at **Takht-i-Bhai** (p. 95B) is typical of these. A number of simple cells are ranged round a quadrangle; the main stupa is placed adjoining this quadrangle in a second courtyard which is crowded with smaller votive stupas. There are several larger chambers for assembly or dining. Walls are built of stone blocks, dressed to a fair face on the outside surfaces, but not squared along the sides. The interstices are filled with much smaller fragments of stone, firmly wedging the large blocks. All appear to have been laid dry, and were probably originally thickly rendered with lime stucco. All roofs have disappeared—they were of wood and thatch, or tile—as has most of the painted stucco with which the masonry was originally faced. Apart from that on the stupas and their bases, there seems to have been little carved orna-ment on buildings. The Corinthian column appears frequently in miniature in the carved aedicules on stupa bases, and also as full-sized fragments detached from

their original contexts. The monastery at **Nalanda** (Bihar) which flourished in the seventh and eighth centuries A.D., represents the last phase. Of great size, it served as a Buddhist university. A stupa excavated there retains little of the Graeco-Roman characteristics of the earlier types: the simple rectangular base with the drum supporting a dome, all that remains of the hemispherical stupa-mound, has been raised on a high four-tiered rectangular plinth, forming an ambulatory terrace around it. Mahayana Buddhist influences from Nalanda spread to South-East Asia. From Buddhist Indonesia (Sumatra), a Srivijaya king founded a monastery for Indonesian pilgrims studying at Nalanda (ninth century).

There are rock-cut viharas adjoining some of the chaitya caves, notably at **Bhaja** (second century B.C.); they consist of a simple group of cells without adornment.

JAIN ARCHITECTURE
(Third century B.C.–seventeenth century A.D.)

Examples of Early Jain (third century B.C.) include the rock-cut caves in the **Barabar Hills**, at **Gaya, Bihar,** one of which is the **Lomas Rishi Cave.** Rock-cut monasteries are to be found in the **Khandagiri** and **Udaigiri Hills, in Orissa,** consisting of cells with a pillared, arcaded verandah (sometimes two-storeyed) around a courtyard, prototypes of later monasteries. There are about thirty-five excavations, the largest and most important being the **Rani Gumpha** (Queen's Cave), **Bihar.**

The most important group of temples of the Later Jain period, in its final Baroque phase (eleventh to seventeenth century A.D.), is at **Mount Abu** (p. 99A), below the peak of this name at the south-western end of the Aravilli range in Rajasthan. Typical of this group is the **Dilwarra Temple** (1032) (p. 99B), built of white marble. There is a large portico-hall, the columns of which are highly decorated and crowned with bracket capitals, carrying the raking struts and a second corbelled capital supporting the roof beams, which are peculiarities of Jain building. These struts evidently derive from a timber form; wall openings have corbelled brackets supporting lintels (adopted in Akbar's Mughal architecture), and the interior of the corbelled dome roof is so highly carved that the marble assumes the character of lacework. In common with the majority of Jain temples, the artistic quality of the carved ornament falls short of the technical achievement.

The **Temple, Ranpur** (1439), on the side of the Aravalli Mountains in Rajasthan, gives the completest picture of a Jain monument. It stands on a high substructure some 60 m (200 ft) square, surrounded by eighty-six cells, each of which is covered by a sikhara-shaped roof. There are five shrines, one at each angle of that in the centre, with four open light courts between. Twenty domes, 6.4 m (21 ft) in diameter, supported on over four hundred columns, are placed symmetrically in groups of five round the angle shrines. The central dome of each group is three storeys high and 11 m (36 ft) in diameter. The domes are all formed in the usual way; of horizontally-corbelled courses of masonry elaborately carved. The multiple repetition of parts, and the virtuosity of the craftsmanship, are typical of Jain temples in general.

HINDU ARCHITECTURE
(a) *Northern Indian* (A.D. 350 to the present)

(i) *East.* **Temples** in **Orissa** (800–1200) on the east coast form a series which presents the finest examples of this type. The typical plan is square; the lofty

A. The Jain temples, Mount Abu (1000–1300). See p. 98

B. Dilwarra Temple, Mount Abu (1032): interior. See p. 98

A (*left*). The Lath (Lion column), Lauriya Nandangarh (243 B.C.). See p. 94

B (*right*). The Parasuramesvara Temple, Bhuvaneshwar (750). See p. 101

c. Column and temples, Baroli (9th cent.). See p. 94

D. Kandarya Mahadev Temple, Khajuraho (*c.* 1000). See p. 101

sikhara covering the 'garbha-griha' or shrine has convex curved sides, the mandap or porch-hall is without columns, and has a lower, stepped roof. Each façade has rectangular projections in the centre, which become triangular in plan in later examples. The elaborate gateways and enclosures of Dravidian temples are entirely missing. Of these Orissa temples, the best known are at **Bhuvaneshwar** (p. 100B). The strong contrast between the emphatic vertical lines of the sikhara and the horizontality of the mandap is softened by the horizontal lines of sculpture, each separated by an incised band, running round the former: these, from a distance, produce an effect reminiscent of rustication. The melon-shaped finial is particularly dominant, and increases in importance as the type develops.

The **Dharmapala Temple and Monastery, Paharpur,** in Bengal (late eighth century) was built under the Pala–Sena dynasty during the Buddhist–Hindu Renaissance (eighth to thirteenth century), and is closely related to Javan temples of Loro Djongrang and Candi Sewu at Prambanam, and Barabudur. It has a vast square court with 300 m (1000 ft) sides, surrounded by cells. In the centre is a shrine rising to over 30 m (100 ft), with recessed superimposed terraces supporting a square cella with projecting porticos on each side, approached by a north stairway leading up to the cella level. Decoration is provided by plaques in terra-cotta relief fixed to the brick façades.

The **Black Pagoda, Kanarak** (thirteenth century) (p. 105C, D) is the ruin of a huge, uncompleted temple to the sun. The cell was never raised above its basement courses. The mandap is so large as to be a virtual assembly hall, and it has been suggested that the problem of supporting the weight of the sikhara, which would have been 60 m (200 ft) high if it were in normal relation with the mandap, was the main reason for the building's incompletion. The sculptured decoration is arranged to form horizontal bands running round the mass of the building (as in the Bhuvaneshwar temples), but all on a proportionately larger scale.

(ii) *North-West* (Kashmir). The **Sun Temple, Martand** (eighth century), was a model for later Brahmanical temples. Beautifully sited on a high plateau with distant mountains behind, it has a shrine placed in the centre of a rectangular court embraced by cells, and a portico for sun-worship ritual, with a smaller room connecting with the cella, which was originally covered by a pyramidal roof rising 23 m (75 ft). It has a decorated pediment, fluted Doric pilasters, and a trefoil arch holding a statue. Also in Kashmir is the **Siva Temple, Pandrethan, Srinagar** (twelfth century).

(iii) *Central.* Early Gupta style (A.D. 350–650) temple prototypes are at **Sanchi** (Buddhist) and **Tigawa** (Hindu), **Jubbulpore,** both of the fifth century, and both with column iconography. Of the Middle period, the **Siva Temple, Deogarh, Jhansi** (sixth century) is the culmination of the earlier Hindu temple, with four porticos, the shrine tower conspicuous above the flat roof, and with an elaborately carved doorway and side niches. This style influenced Cambodian architecture.

The **Kandarya Mahadev Temple, Khajuraho** (c. 1000) (p. 100D), of the Late Central period, is typical of a large group of temples in Central India. A series of mandaps leads to the garbha-griha, but the whole is grouped on one firmly defined base. This, together with the strong horizontals of both sculptural and architectural details, and the carefully considered relationship of the ascending sikharas roof, produce a satisfying unity in the whole mass. The verticals are dominant, but the skilful counterpoint of horizontals prevents monotony. The sides of the main sikhara are enriched by miniature reflections of the whole spire: a common feature in Dravidian temples. There are nearly a thousand figures on the temple, half life-size, and all of a uniformly high artistic standard.

(iv) *West*. **The Sas Bahu Temple, Gwalior** (1093) (p. 103A), comprises only the mandap, the garbha-griha and the sikhara having vanished; the feeling of horizontality (to contrast with the vertical sikhara) is present, and a low-pitched pyramidal roof. The canopied balconies found at Khajuraho (p. 100D) are here developed into features of major importance. The plan is a cross, and the mandap is in three storeys of open galleries surrounding the main central chamber. Other temples of this type are the **Jagannath Temple, Puri** (eleventh century), and those at **Chandravati,** in Rajasthan (ninth century), **Baroli** (ninth century) (p. 100C) and **Udaipur,** Rajasthan (eleventh century). See also under Jain temples.

The **Golden Temple of the Sikhs, Amritsar** (1766) is very strongly influenced by Mughal buildings; it consists of a hall to hold congregations at the reading of sacred books, standing in an artificial lake surrounded by older ancillary buildings.

The **Birla Temple, New Delhi** (1938) is an attempt to translate traditional forms into contemporary idioms in reinforced concrete.

(b) Central Deccan (*Chalukyan–Hoysalan,* 1000–1325)

The **Hoysaleswara Temple, Halebid** (1141–1182) (p. 106A) consists of unfinished twin temples standing side by side on a terrace 1.5 m (5 ft) high, with detached, pillared porches. The walls are covered with friezes of extremely elaborate carving, 214 m (700 ft) long, of elephants, lions, horsemen, geese, and scenes of the conquest of Ceylon. The window openings are filled with elaborately pierced marble slabs.

The **Great Temple, Bellur** (1117) (pp. 103B, 105J), has the typical star-shaped garbha-griha and an elaborately pillared mandap, all covered with highly ornate carvings. It served as a theatre for ritual dances.

The **Temple, Somnathpur** (1268), like that at Halebid, has more than one shrine: in this case there are three, radiating from a central hall. The sikharas have not the emphatic vertical lines of the Northern temples, and the horizontal bands of carving are more marked. On the other hand, the domical top storey, found in Dravidian types, is absent.

(c) Southern Dravidian (600–1750)

(i) *Pallava* (A.D. 600–900). At **Mamallapuram,** near Madras, a series of huge granite rocks was carved into small temples or 'Raths' between 625–674. They are reproductions in solid rock of vanished prototypes; although so early, they contain all the fundamentals of the fully developed Dravidian type, including the domed (stupa-shaped) crowning storey to the sikhara. There is also a chaitya-type roof, and a pyramidal thatch-like roof on a square base; all these are cut in the rocks.

The **Temple, Kanchipuram, Vellore** (eighth century), has the garbha-griha enclosed with a courtyard wall containing gateways crowned with complex structures which foreshadow the great eighth-century gopurams at Madura and elsewhere. The form of the sikharas is based on that of the largest Rath at Mamallapuram.

The rock-cut **Kailasa Temple, Ellora** (750–950) (p. 104A), stands free within a huge artificial basin in the mountain side, 89 m (290 ft) long and 46 m (150 ft) wide. The whole temple stands on a podium 7.6 m (25 ft) high to raise it above the basin floor. All the familiar elements are present: the garbha-griha, the mandap, and a detached shrine in front of the latter for the Siva bull-image. The mandap is larger than those in Northern temples, and indicates what was to follow later at Madura. The pillars are typically Dravidian, seen in their latest form in the rock-cut

A. The Sas Bahu Temple in the Fort, Gwalior (1093). See p. 102

B. The Great Temple, Bellur, from E. (1117). See p. 102

A. The Kailasa Temple, Ellora (750–950). See p. 102

B. Rock-cut temple, Elephanta: interior (9th cent.). See p. 107

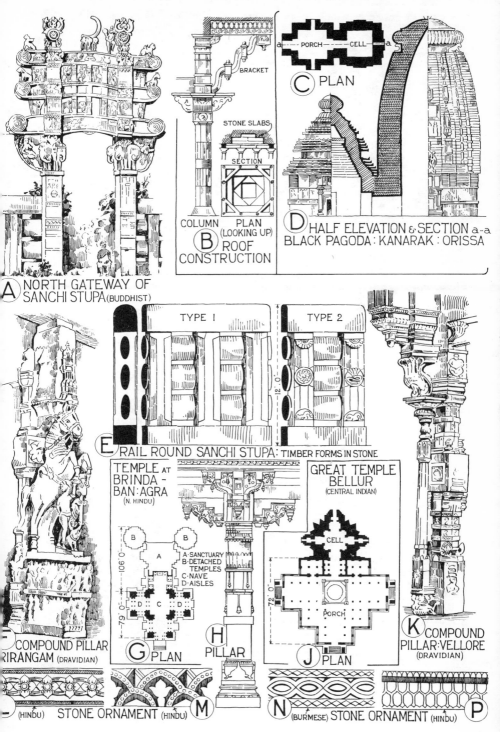

A NORTH GATEWAY OF SANCHI STUPA (BUDDHIST)

B COLUMN PLAN (LOOKING UP) ROOF CONSTRUCTION

BRACKET

STONE SLABS

SECTION

C PLAN

PORCH — CELL

D HALF ELEVATION & SECTION a-a BLACK PAGODA : KANARAK : ORISSA

TYPE 1

TYPE 2

12'-0"

E RAIL ROUND SANCHI STUPA : TIMBER FORMS IN STONE

TEMPLE AT BRINDA-BAN : AGRA (N. HINDU)

A · SANCTUARY
B · DETACHED TEMPLES
C · NAVE
D · AISLES

G PLAN

106'-0"

79'-0"

H PILLAR

GREAT TEMPLE BELLUR (CENTRAL INDIAN)

CELL

PORCH

72'-0"

J PLAN

COMPOUND PILLAR SRIRANGAM (DRAVIDIAN)

K COMPOUND PILLAR : VELLORE (DRAVIDIAN)

(HINDU) STONE ORNAMENT (HINDU) M

N (BURMESE) STONE ORNAMENT (HINDU) P

A. The Hoysaleswara Temple, Halebid:
doorway (1141–82). See p. 102

B. The Old Temple, Tadpatri: portion
of entrance (17th cent.). See p. 94

c. The Great Temple, Tanjore (1000).
See p. 107

D. The Gopuram, Madura (1623).
See p. 107

temples on **Elephanta** island in Bombay harbour (ninth century) (p. 104B). The heavy, curved cornice is also typical, and re-appears for a thousand years.

(ii) *Cholan* (A.D. 700–1150). The **Great Temple, Tanjore** (1000) (p. 106C), is 55 m (180 ft) long and the sikhara of thirteen storeys is 58 m (190 ft) high. The form of the crowning member of the tower, a single stone weighing 80 tons, is based on the Buddhist stupa. The basic forms are used repeatedly in the decoration of the tower; this, and the very beautiful proportions, produce a feeling of great repose.

(iii) *Later Pandyan*, Madura style (*c*. sixteenth to eighteenth century). The later temples, such as those at **Madura** (1623) (p. 106D), **Srirangam** (seventeenth century) (p. 105F), and **Tinnevelly**, in spite of their apparent complexity, preserve the simple fundamentals of the traditional plan. But the garbha-griha and its sikhara are dwarfed by the successive giant gopurams (there are fifteen of these gateway towers at Srirangam), and the small mandap has developed into a series of huge halls, reminiscent of Egyptian hypostyle halls, containing forests of columns; at Madura, there are over 2,000 of them.

SECULAR ARCHITECTURE

Apart from archaeological sites, the earliest extant secular buildings date from the mediaeval period. A notable example is the brilliantly colourful **Man Mandir** palace of **Gwalior Fort** (*c*. 1500), built for Maharaja Man Singh in an indigenous manner, a Mughal-influenced Hindu architecture. Also, in northern India, are the palaces of **Bikanir, Jodhpur, Orchcha, Datia, Udaipur** and **Amber** (Jaipur), the latter of the seventeenth century; while in the south are **Vijayanagar** (sixteenth century) and **Madura Tanjore Fort** (*c*. 1700), which also shows traces of European precedent in the pillared halls. In the west, at **Sarkhej, Ahmedabad** (*c*. 1450), there survives, although sadly neglected, an exquisite synthesis of Hindu-Mughal architecture—basic Hindu structures and details combined with the Mughal genius for ensemble planning on a grand scale.

In Indian towns, the formal plan according to the ancient law books (the Manasara), with its four main avenues aligned at right angles and zoning of buildings, is rarely seen today except at **Jaipur** (eighteenth century). Generally houses alternate with temple façades and noblemen's residences. In the narrow streets the ground floor of many buildings is fronted with awnings and kiosks serving as shops; the upper storeys apparently (but seldom actually) overhang to provide some measure of shade.

Other typical buildings are the 'ghats' or public bathing places, inseparable from town or village life, ablutions playing an essential part in Hindu social and religious ritual. They consist of broad flights of steps leading down to a tank or river. At **Benares** the ghats stretch for nearly 5 km (3 miles) along the banks of the Ganges river-front. Above them the fortress-like palaces present massive ramparts, with rounded bastions of masonry to withstand the action of flood water. The upper storeys have overhanging balconies, light and fanciful latticed windows and pillared loggias. Step-wells or 'baolis' are another characteristic Indian construction, found where wells are deeply sunk. The steps, flanked by two pavilions, are wholly below ground and descend as low as 30 m (100 ft) to the water. A screen rises from water to ground level, separating the stairs from the well-shaft, up which water is drawn by pulleys, a system which seems to have been in use for nearly a thousand years. The dams of the artificial lakes necessary for irrigation were often of great magnificence, with steps, temples and pavilions interspersed with fountains and sculpture, as at **Udaipur.** A number of observatories were built in the seventeenth century, of which there are fine examples at **Jaipur, Benares** and **Delhi,** reflecting a romantic approach to geometry.

BIBLIOGRAPHY

ACHARYA, P. K. *A Dictionary of Indian Architecture.* London, 1927.
—. *Manasara Architecture and Sculpture.* London, 1933–4.
Annual Reports of the Archaeological Survey of India. 1902–30.
BASHAM, A. L. *The Wonder that was India.* New York, 1959.
BATLEY, C. *Indian Architecture.* London, 1934.
BROWN, P. *Indian Architecture: Buddhist and Hindu.* Bombay, 1959.
—. *Indian Architecture: Islamic.* Bombay, 1959.
BURGESS, J. *The Ancient Monuments, Temples and Sculptures of India.* London, 1911.
Cambridge History of India. 6 vols., 1922.
CODRINGTON, K. DE B. *Ancient India.* London, 1926.
COHN, W. *Indische Plastik.* Berlin, 1923.
COOMARASWAMY, A. K. *History of Indian and Indonesian Art.* New York, 1927.
CUNNINGHAM, SIR A. *Archaeological Survey of India.* 23 vols. (2 vols. Cunningham only, 1762–5). Simla and Calcutta, 1871–87.
DE FOREST, L. *Indian Domestic Architecture.* Boston, 1885.
DEY, MUKUL. *My Pilgrimages to Ajanta and Bagh.* London, 1925.
FERGUSSON, J. *Picturesque Illustrations of the Ancient Architecture of Hindostan.* London, 1948.
—. *Illustrations of the Rock-cut Temples of India.* London, 1845.
—. *Architecture of Ahmedabad.* London, 1866.
—. *History of Indian and Eastern Architecture.* 2 vols., revised by Jas. Burgess and R. Phene Spiers. London, 1910.
FOUCHER. A. *L'Art Gréco-Bouddhique du Ghandara.* 2 vols. Paris, 1942.
GANGOLY, O. C. *Indian Architecture.* 2nd ed. Calcutta, 1946.
GOETZ, H. *Art of the World: India.* London, 1959.
—. *Early Wooden Temples of Champa.* Leiden, 1956.
HAVELL, E. B. *The Ancient and Mediaeval Architecture of India.* London, 1915.
KAK, R. C. *Ancient Monuments of Kashmir.* London, 1933.
KRAMRISCH, S. *The Hindu Temple.* Bombay, 1948.
LA ROCHE. *Indische Baukunst.* 6 vols. Berlin, 1921–2.
LE BON, G. *Les Monuments de l'Inde.* Paris, 1893.
Marg, Bombay. Articles by various writers from 1947 onwards.
MARSHALL, SIR J. *Taxila.* 3 vols. Cambridge, 1951.
—. *The Monuments of Sanchi.* Government of India Press, 1938.
—. *Mohenjodaro and the Indus Civilization.* London, 1931.
Memoirs of the Archaeological Survey of India. Vols. 1–40.
MORELAND, W. H., and CHATTERJEE, SIR A. C. *A Short History of the Indian People.* London, 1936.
PIGGOTT, S. *Prehistoric India.* Harmondsworth, 1950.
RAY, A. *Villages, Towns and Secular Buildings in Ancient India: 150 B.C.–A.D. 350.* 1964.
RICHARDSON, A. E., and CORFIATO, H. *The Art of Architecture.* Revised ed. London, 1946.
ROWLAND, B. *The Art and Architecture of India: Buddhist, Hindu, Jain.* Harmondsworth and Baltimore, 1953.
SANKHALIA, H. D. *The University of Nālandā.* Madras, 1934; Bombay, 1962.
SMITH, V. A. *A History of Fine Art in India and Ceylon.* 2nd ed. revised by K. de B. Codrington. Oxford, 1930.
VOLWAHSEN, A. *Living Architecture: Indian.* 2 vols. London and Fribourg, 1969.
WHEELER, SIR M. *Rome Beyond the Imperial Frontiers.* London, 1954.
—. *The Indus Civilization.* Cambridge, 1953.

4
ARCHITECTURE IN SRI LANKA

Third century B.C. to present day

INFLUENCES

GEOGRAPHICAL

Sri Lanka or Ceylon, the latter a corruption of 'Sinhala', the ancient name used in Sanskrit and Sinhalese literature, is a large island in the Indian Ocean 32 km (20 miles) off the southern tip of the Indian peninsular, 5° to 9° north of the Equator (see map on p. 88). It was once a part of the continental land mass. Throughout recorded history Ceylon has been a centre of international trade, due to its strategic position on the west-to-east sea routes and its fine natural harbours.

GEOLOGICAL

Many kinds of building material are exploited: granite, limestone, laterite and sandstone; clay for bricks, roof tiles and pottery, widely used in the wet districts, which also encourage the quick growth of soft and hard timber, bamboo, grasses for thatch and mats, and coconut trees, the wood of which is used for posts and roofs, the leaves for thatch and decoration. The dry areas have teak, satin and other beautiful hardwoods, all of which have been, and still are, used in the building crafts. The topography was utilized in the past to enhance architectural effects: tanks were built round rock outcrops, and cities, palaces and temples were constructed on hills and high rocks.

CLIMATIC

Ceylon is divided into three climatic zones, which have given rise to special building characteristics: a dry hot zone, mainly in the north and east, where in early civilizations vast irrigation tanks were built to conserve rain water; a central wet region, cool and invigorating; and a low-lying hot wet zone in the south and south-west, with a very heavy rainfall and high humidity, where buildings are solid-walled, with wide projecting eaves and verandahs, and steeply-pitched roofs to ward off rain and sun.

SOCIAL AND HISTORICAL

The recorded history of Ceylon covers about 2500 years, for most of which there is a continuous stream of evidence from both native and foreign sources. There were three significant periods in the development of the island's cultural and political life.

The Anuradhapura period (*c*. fourth century B.C. to tenth century A.D.). During this period the foundations were laid for political, social and artistic traditions, which were to continue almost intact for many centuries. Among the several Sinhalese kings of this era noted for their great building works one stands out above the rest, Kassapa I (sixth century A.D.), who left Anuradhapura to create a unique city constructed on and around an immense rock-hill, Sigiriya. In the latter part of the first millennium A.D. Ceylon's development and affluence was such that she was able to withstand many invasions and even to counter-invade south India.

The Polonnaruwa period (eleventh to thirteenth century). After years of invasions and occupations from Cholan, south India, and the sacking of Anuradhapura, the capital was removed to Polonnaruwa, no doubt because it commanded the main roads and trade routes. The building of this city was the principal architectural undertaking of King Parakrama Bahu 'The Great' (twelfth century), who had re-established sovereignty over the whole country. The glory of Polonnaruwa, with its palaces, monasteries, temples, parks, lakes and irrigation works, lasted only to the thirteenth century, by which time it had been reduced to ruins from constant attacks by foreign invaders, and the court moved again, to a series of impermanent settlements: Yapahuwa, Dambadeniya and Kotte (thirteenth to fifteenth century).

The Kandyan period (fifteenth to nineteenth century). This third period of signi-ficance saw the division of the country into several kingdoms, with the capital of the most considerable at Kandy (a corruption of Kandenuwara .. hill-city), in an area initially undisturbed by foreign interference. The adjacent maritime provinces, however, were occupied by the Portuguese in the sixteenth century, by the Dutch in the seventeenth and, last, by the British, who also succeeded in annexing the Kandyan kingdom in 1815, bringing the whole of the island into the British Empire until 1947, when Ceylon became independent. The Portuguese and Dutch intro-duced the late Renaissance and Baroque into the colonial styles, influences still evident today, while the British brought a 'Colonial Georgian' and, later, the Royal Engineers' 'Colonial Classic', to be seen in official buildings and influencing the style of private construction. Moslem merchants and seafarers had little influence on architecture.

In the twentieth century Ceylon, like the whole of the East, is striving to synthe-size European and American ideas and technology with indigenous ways of living and traditional expression.

RELIGIOUS

Ceylon is known as the 'Dharma-Dipa'—the island of the (Buddhist) doctrine. In the third century B.C. the Indian Emperor Asoka sent his son Mahinda Thera to preach Buddhism and to establish the order of Buddhist monks. Later he sent his daughter Sanghamitta Theri with a branch of the sacred Bhodi tree, which was planted at Anuradhapura and is still living, one of the oldest trees in the world. Ever since then Ceylon has remained predominantly Buddhist, with the Tamils of the island faithful to their Hindu origins, and the (Arab) Moors and Malayan settlers Moslem. Christianity, introduced by the European colonizers four hundred years ago, is followed by a small, but influential, minority. Pre-Buddhist folk supersti-tions and, later, Hindu cults and ceremonies were woven into the Buddhist ritual and expressed in the arts, crafts and architecture.

ARCHITECTURAL CHARACTER

In Ceylon, as in Burma, architectural history begins with the introduction of Budd-hism from India in the third century B.C., when durable buildings in brick and stone appeared, as opposed to perishable wood.

Anuradhapura period. The earliest remains are the natural rock chambers, built for the hermits, with drip-ledges to carry away rain water. Later these were deve-loped with walls to form an enclosure (i.e. rock temples). Anuradhapura itself, which was the capital for 1200 years, was a great city, extending 30 km² (12 square miles), with tree-lined roads, palaces, parks, monasteries, stupas, irrigation works and tanks (reservoirs). It is remarkable among Buddhist cities in retaining an almost complete picture of its greatness. Buried in the jungle for some five hundred years, its very desolation and isolation may have protected it from vandalism and well-meaning restorers. Numerous remains of moulded and dressed stone plinths, pillars and lintels survive as evidence of the framed structural system used and the skill of masons and sculptors. Pillars have a significant place in the peristylar architecture of Anuradhapura. Square or octagonal in section, the capital, socketed into the top, is of a plain hexagonal vase shape, with a carved abacus above and mouldings between; sometimes the shaft and capital were cut in one piece. A noteworthy feature of Sinhalese architecture, already apparent in Anuradhapura, was the sensitivity shown towards the natural landscape and its intimate relationship to the buildings. This 2000-year-old tradition is now unhappily dead.

Polonnaruwa period. The city of Polonnaruwa already existed before Parakrama Bahu began his grand building schemes in the twelfth century. Sinhala architecture of this time was mainly a development of the classic Anuradhapura style, coeval with Pagan (Burma), Angkor Vat (Cambodia), and the Sailendra-Srivijaya Empire (Malaysia, Sumatra, Java), with all of which there were religious and commercial contacts. The most important trend was the expansion of the temple to enshrine colossal Buddha images, with interior corridors for processions, as seen in the Lankatilleke temple (Alāhana complex). The outstanding architectural creation, however, was a cetiya-ghara, the 'Wata-da-ge' (circular relic-house), built in stone and brick. The Polonnaruwa example (p. 114A) is exquisitely proportioned, a quality conspicuous in many of the buildings of the period, which produced some of the most beautiful architecture in south-east Asia. Although art and architecture declined after the abandonment of Polonnaruwa, there were exceptions. One such was Yapahuwa (fourteenth century) (p. 114B), indicative of a continuing tradition of the palace city as a mountain fortress (cf. Sigiriya). The gateway, stairways and sculptured lions and beasts recall Cambodia and Java. Close to one of the 'temporary' capitals of this era, Gampola, near Kandy, are two impressive architectural monuments which at once herald the Kandyan style and reflect an earlier manner: the temples of Lankatilleke and Gadaladeniya, near Kandy, both sited on rocky eminences and visible from far away across the paddy fields.

Kandyan period. Kandy, the old hill-city and capital from the sixteenth to the nineteenth century, set romantically in a narrow valley 500 m (1600 ft) up and surrounded by hills, mirrors the last phase of true Sinhala architecture. In its typical form the Kandyan style is an architecture of wood (which has always been indigenous to Ceylon), catering to the needs of a simple but well-to-do agricultural civilization. The Anuradhapura traditional framed structure of pillars and beams is continued but in timber, richly carved with the traditional motifs (the old stone carving was a copy of ancient timber carving). Roofs are high-pitched with wide eaves, slightly curved, finished with small flat (shingles) terracotta tiles and eaves-tiles (with bas-reliefs), all of an ancient pattern. These roofs are a striking feature in the landscape; many levelled, high-peaked and visible from afar. There are many building types existing: mostly monasteries with their temples; 'ambalamas' (rest houses for travellers); parts of the last royal palace (now a museum), and the ancillary buildings—the Audience Hall (now a law-court), the Queen's bathing pavilion (now a library), and the famous Dalada Maligawa, Temple of the Tooth Relic. The decorative craftwork is important: ancient motifs are used as an integral part of the building, such as windows with lacquered wood bars, carved timber doorways, ornamental metalwork door furniture, painted walls, terracotta bas-relief wall-plaques and eaves tiles (as valance boards). All these arts are still practised, with ancient lion, lotus, geese and makara motifs. In the later buildings European influences are evident, with modified Doric columns, true semi-circular arches, and the half-round Roman or Spanish roof-tile.

EXAMPLES

Anuradhapura period

The **Thuparama Dagaba** and the **Ruwanveliseya Dagaba, Anuradhapura** (p. 115A, B) (*dagaba* = tooth-relic chamber) are important Sinhala stupas, which tend to be very large. The Thuparama (third century B.C.) is possibly the oldest extant Buddhist structure. These solid brickwork tumuli, plastered white, are differentiated in Ceylon by the shape of the domical 'mound'. The Thuparama example was originally a 'paddy-heap' (cone-shaped), but was converted into a bell-shape when restored in 1842. There are four concentric rows (of receding height) of monolithic, square to octagonal, stone pillars round the stupa. The Ruwanveliseya Dagaba (second century B.C.), with a basal diameter of 90 m (294 ft), was originally more than 92 m (300 ft) high. A bubble-shaped solid brick dome of the orthodox pattern stands in the centre of two spacious square terraces, one above the other, the sides facing the cardinal points, with a pillared portico and steps on one side of the lower terrace.

The dagaba was usually the focal point of a monastic establishment which, as in India, had a temple, a 'bhodi-ghara' (a shrine enclosing a sacred Bhodi tree), ceremonial, meditation and preaching halls, a court, a priory, and ponds and bathing places for drinking and ablutions.

The **Monastery of Mihintale** (second century B.C.) stands on a hill-top 300 m (1000 ft) up, rocky and forested, nearly 13 km (8 miles) north-east of Anuradhapura. It was here that Mahinda Thera, the Emperor Asoka's son, preached to the court in the third century B.C., and the monastery, regarded as the cradle of Sinhalese Buddhism, has many associations with the royal missionary. An unusual feature is the **Naga Pokuna** ('snake' bathing pool), 40 m (130 ft) long, hewn out of the rock with an immense carved five-hooded cobra poised over the pool. A magnificent architectonic stairway, with 1,840 steps carved out of granite and natural rock, leads to the summit of the hill. The whole place has a quality of timeless solitude and peace, a tangible distillation of Buddhist ideals.

The **Reservoir of Kalawewa** (fifth century A.D.) is an outstanding example of the technical virtuosity of Sinhalese engineers in the handling of water. It covers an area of 25 km² (10 square miles), and supplied water by a canal 87 km (54 miles) long to Anuradhapura, at an incline varying between 19 and 9.5 cm per km (12 and 6 ins per mile). Most of the vast irrigation tanks of this period, as well as many from the Polonnaruwa period, have been restored for agricultural use today. Other characteristic water-works were the bathing tanks, beautifully constructed in stone, with flights of stone steps and decorative stone vases, as in the **Kuttam Pokuna** (twin tanks), **Anuradhapura** (p. 113A), and the pleasure-garden baths, exemplified by those of **Ran Masu park, Anuradhapura** (eighth century and earlier), which have been preserved. Boulders are used as part of the architecture, water cascades down the rock over bas-reliefs of elephants sporting in a lotus-pool. One bath is partly hewn out from beneath a boulder and partly built up. The whole effect of this romantic composition is enchanting and invites comparison with a Roman fountain by Bernini of a thousand years later.

Sigiriya (sixth century A.D.), a romantically-situated rock fortress palace, was developed into a splendid city, with terraced pleasure gardens, pools with cascades

A. Kuttam Pokuna (twin tanks), Anuradhapura. See p. 112

B. Lankatilleke Temple, Polonnaruwa (12th cent.). See p. 116

A. The 'Wata-da-ge' (circular relic-house), Polonnaruwa (12th cent.). See p. 116

B. Stairway and entrance to Yapahuwa Rock Fortress (14th cent.). See p. 111

A. Thuparama Dagaba, Anuradhapura
(3rd cent. B.C.). See p. 112

B. Ruwanveliseya Dagaba,
Anuradhapura (2nd cent. B.C.).
See p. 112

C. Standing and recumbent Buddhas, Gal Vihara (12th cent.). See p. 116

D. Dalada Maligawa, Kandy (18th cent.). See p. 117

(anticipating Renaissance Italy), and immense rock boulders, used as shelters underneath (with painted ceilings) and above as elevated terraces with elegant pavilions. Some of the frescoes survive in a gallery on the west side of the rock. Sigiriya was an amazing feat of engineering, as well as a brilliant architectural achievement.

Polonnaruwa period

Alāhana Monastery, Polonnaruwa (twelfth century), is another example of the Sinhala flair for site planning. A slight eminence has been used for the principal buildings, the surrounding slopes being terraced for lesser structures such as residential quarters for monks, refectory, library, etc. Ponds reflected the architecture, and boulders and other natural features were exploited to enhance the effect. **Lankatilleke Temple** (p. 113B), in red brick, is 52 m (170 ft) long and 20 m (66 ft) wide at the shrine end. The walls, nearly 3.6 m (12 ft) thick, are 17 m (55 ft) high, lime plastered, with paintings of which traces remain. There is a shrine, an antechamber in an opening in the wall, a vestibule and a porch. The entrance is flanked by two solid polygonal turrets with the 'dwarapalas' (door-keepers) in high-relief, and carved stone steps with guard-stones. The interior is restricted by the massive walls. The total height of the temple to the roof pinnacle, which is missing, would have been 30 m (100 ft). The shrine contains a brick and stucco Buddha 12 m (40 ft) high.

The **Gal Vihara Rock Temple** (twelfth century) (p. 115C), north of the Alāhana monastery in a forest setting, has four colossal Buddha figures—standing, seated (two), and recumbent—carved out of the rock, each originally enclosed to form a shrine. They represent the supreme achievement of Ceylon's sculptors, an inspired expression of Buddhist peace and compassion. The recumbent figure, which represents the dying Buddha entering 'nirvana', is 14 m (46 ft) long.

The **Great Quadrangle complex**, Alāhana, contains the **'Galpota'**, a beautifully composed stone slab, upon which the acts of King Nissanka Malla are inscribed, with a carved border of sacred geese (frequent in Buddhist iconography), and a carved sunken panel of twin elephants. The **Lata Mandapa** is an exquisitely designed baroque pavilion for hearing the chanting of sacred texts and worship of the Tooth Relic, with stone pillars like symbolic lotus stalks twisting upward, curled leaf ornament, and capitals in the form of opening buds (comparison with the baldachino of S. Peter's, Rome, may not seem too fanciful). The **Wata-da-ge** (p. 114A) has a round platform, which is 36.5 m (120 ft) in diameter, surrounding the circular stupa-shrine of 17.7 m (58 ft). At the centre is a small brick dagaba with seated Buddha images and altars at the four cardinal points. The inner ambulatory round the shrine had two concentric rows of pillars which supported a timber and tiled roof. Stairways on the four sides have the typical Sinhala carved moonstone thresholds, elephant-trunk-shaped 'makara' balustrades and guard-stones. The repeated rhythm of circular lines (some carved) of plinth, pillars, walls and stupa is delightful. **Thuparama Temple** is an oblong, massive-walled brick building, with a low square tower over the inner shrine, carried on corbelled brick arches.

Sutiyaghara Cetiya, Dadigama, in the western central province (*c*. thirteenth century), was built to commemorate the birthplace of King Parakrama Bahu the Great. In the 'Lotus' shape, it is remarkable in having escaped destruction or looting, and thus gives a clear idea of the interior of such relic houses.

Kandyan period

Embekke Temple (fourteenth century) is a prototype of more important later buildings in the Kandyan timber architectural style.

The **Palace, Kandy** (sixteenth to nineteenth centuries), of which only a part remains: the Queen's Palace, now a museum, and the Audience Hall, the latter epitomizing Kandyan wood construction. The long open-sided pavilion with a shallow stone plinth and stone floor, and four rows of wooden columns, richly carved, comprises a central nave and side aisles. The columns which have square shafts with sunken octagonal sections and carved lotus bracket-capitals, support a roof of heavy beams and king-post trusses. The post-plates are elaborately carved, and the functional, patterned rafters extend into wide eaves, the roof pitch being less marked over the aisles, thus giving a graceful concave effect (the 'bird's-wing' roof of the ancient chronicles).

The **Dalada Maligawa** (Temple of the Tooth Relic), **Kandy** (sixteenth century, restored in the late 1700s) (p. 115D), is adjacent to the royal palace group (above). The oldest part, a finely proportioned shrine, stands in an inner courtyard on a high oblong stone plinth carrying stone pillars with carved wood capitals, which support the carved wood beams of the upper floor housing the Relic. This upper storey has a verandah with balustrades of turned and lacquered wood. Near by is the striking eighteenth-century Pattiripuva ('Octagon'), sited above the lake.

BIBLIOGRAPHY

Annual Reports of the Archaeological Survey of Ceylon.
BAREAU, A. *La vie et l'organisation des communautés Bouddhiques modernes du Ceylan.* Pondicherry, 1957.
BURROW, S. M. *Buried Cities of Ceylon.* London, 1906.
CAVE, H. W. *Ruined Cities of Ceylon.* London, 1900.
Ceylon—Paintings from Temple, Rock and Shrine. UNESCO World Art Series, New York, 1957.
COOMARASWAMY, A. K. *Mediaeval Sinhalese Art.* London, 1908.
DEVENDRA, D. T. *Guide to Yapahuwa.* Colombo, 1951.
GEIGER, W. (Translator). *The Mahawamsa,* and *The Chulawamsa.* Ceylon Government Information Department, Colombo, 1953.
—. *The Mediaeval Period in Ceylon Culture.* Wiesbaden, 1960.
GOONETILEKE, H. A. I. *A Bibliography of Ceylon.* 2 vols. Zug (Switzerland), 1970.
GRISWOLD, A. B. *Siam and the Sinhalese Stupa.* Colombo, 1964.
Guides published on behalf of the Archaeological Department of Ceylon.
History of Ceylon from the earliest times to 1505. Vol. 1 (in two parts). University of Ceylon, Colombo, 1959–60. Vol. II, 1973.
HOCART, A. M. Various papers published in Memoirs of the Archaeological Survey of Ceylon.
KNOX, R. *An Historical Relation of Ceylon.* London, 1681, Glasgow, 1911.
MITTON, G. E. *The Lost Cities of Ceylon.* London, 1928.
PARANAVITANA, S. *Sigiri Graffiti.* 2 vols. London, 1956. And many other publications by this author.
PARKER, H. *Ancient Ceylon.* London, 1910.
PERERA, S. G. *The Royal Palace at Kandy.* Ceylon Observer Annual, 1935.
ROWLAND, B. *The Art and Architecture of India.* Harmondsworth and Baltimore, 1953.
SMITHERS, J. G. *Architectural Remains, Anuradhapura.* Colombo, 1894.
STILL, J. *Ancient Capitals of Ceylon.* 1907.
TURNER, L. J. B. *Kandy—Historical Sketch.* Colombo, 1924. And other publications by this author.

5
ARCHITECTURE
IN AFGHANISTAN, NEPAL
AND TIBET

AFGHANISTAN

INFLUENCES

GEOGRAPHICAL

Situated in the north-west of the Indo-Pakistan sub-continent, with Iran (ancient Persia) on the west and Russia (in part ancient Bactria) and Central Asia to the north, Afghanistan is mainly a vast high plateau between 1,800 m (6,000 ft) and 4,000 m (12,600 ft) above sea level, with the Hindu Kush mountains to the north presenting a formidable barrier. The narrow valleys of the Khyber and Oxus rivers, which were the only communication routes with ancient north-west India (Gandhara), aided the movement of peoples and armies who, throughout a long history, have bequeathed a miscellaneous residue of influences to a land of towering mountains and parched wastes, where living has never been easy.

SOCIAL AND HISTORICAL

In the fourth century B.C. Afghanistan was part of the Achaemenid empire of Darius. It was next occupied by Alexander the Great's armies (356–323 B.C.), followed by Bactrian Greek colonists, who created a colonial-type Greek city-state in Balkh (northern Afghanistan). There was continual cultural contact with Greece through Asian Greek settlements, with Persia and, by the first century B.C., with India. Subsequent Scythian invasions (Kushan dynasties) left an enduring impression. The city of Kapisa (now Begram), the capital of the Kushans, was a famous Mahayana Buddhist site and cosmopolitan meeting place on the great trade route to the Far East. In the fourth and fifth centuries A.D. the Kushan empire gave place to the Sassanian occupation, which had a profound cultural influence throughout the East, spreading even to China. The Chinese pilgrims Fa-hian (fifth century) and Hiuen Tsang (seventh century) have described the Afghanistan of those days, with its magnificent palaces and monasteries.

RELIGIOUS

Afghanistan has passed through many religious phases—Achaemenid and Parthian, Sassanian (Zoroastrian), Indian Buddhist, Greek Hellenist (with Alexander the Great), and Scythian. The impact of Mahayana Buddhism, however, became the predominant influence, superseding the earlier Buddhist faith, until in the eighth century the Moslem religion penetrated the country and, under a Turkish Ghazni dynasty and after, Afghanistan became a Moslem kingdom.

ARCHITECTURAL CHARACTER

The area of northern Afghanistan known as Balkh belongs culturally to Central Asia, new finds at Ai-Kha-Noum (by the Oxus) being Graeco-Bactrian. The southern part, the Kabul River valley, was bound geographically, culturally and politically with north-west India on the one hand and, on the other, with Persia. This composite stream of influences produced Graeco-Roman and Gandharan Buddhist art and architecture (second century B.C. to fourth century A.D.). Ruined stupa mounds are scattered round Kabul and the Kabul River, the most significant being the monastic remains of Bamiyan, and Hadda (of which the sculpture alone remains, showing strong influences of the Roman Pergamene school).

EXAMPLES

Bamiyan, with its monasteries and temples, is important for its relationship to Persia and Central Asia. Superbly situated, the huge group is carved out of a sandstone cliff face, the interior honeycombed with sanctuaries and assembly halls extending for nearly two km (over one mile), with a painted niche at either end, each sheltering a vast Buddha statue. The eastern image is 37 m (120 ft) high, and the western about 54 m (175 ft) (p. 121A), the former an enlarged third-century Gandhara type, the latter (fifth century) an example of the eclectic cosmopolitan influences on Buddhist art. These statues are proto-types of the colossal image cult, later to appear in China and Japan. The structural technique is that of a body and head roughly hewn from the rock, the features and drapery modelled in mud mixed with straw, with a lime plaster finish painted and gilded. The rock-cut sanctuaries and assembly halls probably reflect the building types once existing in Gandhara, influenced by Graeco–Roman–Sassanian styles. Other features are the cupola roofs spanning with arched squinches the square chamber angles in anticipation of the Sassanian fire-temples, the idiosyncratic lantern roof, and the coffered dome, an elaborate system of hexagons (each containing a seated Buddha image) and triangles rising to a central octagon (cf. the Temple of Bacchus, Baalbek, p. 283).

NEPAL

INFLUENCES

GEOGRAPHICAL

Nepal forms an irregular parallelogram some 720 km (450 miles) long and 240 km (150 miles) in average breadth, extending across the Himalayas and along the northern border of India. It is mainly composed of high mountains, which include Mount Everest, and is sparsely inhabited, except in a small area in the centre, the valley of Nepal. In prehistoric times this was a shallow lake; today it is an undulating tract of land used for the cultivation of rice, millet, oil seed and tobacco, and contains the three old capitals, Katmandu, Patan and Bhatgaon.

HISTORICAL AND SOCIAL

The bulk of the population are Newars and Gurkhas (of Tibetan–Mongol stock), who settled in Nepal in very early times and established an indigenous style in art and architecture, which successive migrations and invasions from India have never materially modified. The arts flourished especially during the reign of the Mulla Rajas (thirteenth to eighteenth century), and, more particularly, in the fourteenth, fifteenth and early eighteenth centuries. In 1768 a Gurkha Raja seized the kingdom and a Gurkha dynasty, Hindu by adoption and intermarriage, calling itself Rajput, has since ruled the country. Real power, however, lay for more than a century in the hands of hereditary prime ministers. Since 1950 there has been a cabinet and an elected parliament.

RELIGIOUS

Records state that in the third century B.C. the Indian Emperor Asoka brought Buddhism to the valley of Nepal and built many stupas to commemorate his mission. We know also that in the fifth century A.D., and again in the seventh century, both Buddhist and Hindu settlements were formed, conversions made and monasteries founded. Since then, Hinduism and Buddhism, with Tibetan Tantric influences, have existed side by side. Tibetan influence is also apparent in the mysticism and symbolism inspired by the great mountains and the lonely grandeur of the country.

ARCHITECTURAL CHARACTER

Lying above and between the two great Eastern civilizations of India and China, Nepal has drawn deeply from both cultures, which are reflected in the exuberant decorative treatment of buildings. Stupas, temples, picturesque townships and intricate native craftsmanship are her characteristic architectural heritage. The oldest monuments are stupas, two being associated with the Emperor Asoka, the Swayambhunath and Bodhnath, both near Katmandu. These preserve the form of the earliest Buddhist structures of this type, the orthodox hemispherical mound faced with brick masonry, surrounded by a brick plinth serving as the processional path. Two kinds of temple survive, the 'sikhara' and the 'pagoda' (p. 121B), the first reflecting Indian and the second Chinese (and Burmese) influences. In either case the temple is a shrine enclosing a cella for the god or divine symbol. A typical formal feature of the Nepalese town is the monumental pillar, generally supporting a metal superstructure adorned with mystic symbols, groups of divinities and, especially, portrait statuary of royalties. Secular architecture is principally of wood, but brick is used for structural purposes and metal for ornament. In the larger townships the street façades of houses, which are usually planned to embrace an internal courtyard, are very elaborately treated. Such buildings are frequently of three storeys: the ground floor, probably serving as a shop, is recessed beneath an overhanging first floor, which in turn is overhung by the top storey. Each floor is supported by brackets and struts, ornately carved and sometimes painted. The windows have intricate lattice screens (p. 121D), and roofs have red curved tiles, metal gutters and a projecting cornice for protection against the rain. Every feature is fancifully decorated with carving, embossing, tinkling bells and hanging lamps. The Nepalese delight in adornment is typified by the 'Makara' form of rain-water spouts, which are characteristic of Buddhist iconography and often works of art.

EXAMPLES

The **Swayambhunath stupa, Katmandu** (p. 122B), originally an Asokan tumulus on a hill rising from a valley, stands on a low narrow plinth and has a mediaeval addition of an immense finial, a conical spire in thirteen diminishing tiers symbolizing the thirteen Buddhist heavens, with a striking umbrella apex. The

A. Statue of Buddha, Bamiyan, Afghanistan
(5th cent.). See p. 119

B. Pagoda roofs, Katmandu, Nepal.
See p. 120

C. The Bodhnath stupa, Katmandu.
See p. 123

D. Window, Palace of Fifty-five Windows,
Bhatgaon, Nepal. See p. 120

A. Pasupatinath Temple, Pasupati, Nepal (17th cent.). See p. 123

B. The Swayambhunath stupa, Katmandu, Nepal. See p. 120

C. Potala Palace, Lhasa, Tibet (1642–50). See p. 124

latter stands on a high square base, which has a large pair of human eyes, symbolizing the 'All-seeing One', embossed in metal and ivory on each of the four sides and seeming to follow the movements of the pilgrim.

The **Bodhnath stupa, Katmandu,** (p. 121C) has been restored in recent times, but the old forms are visible in the plain, austere lines of the three platforms 14 m (45 ft) high, low tumulus, and the 14 m (45 ft) high spire resembling the finial of Swayambhunath.

The **Krishna Temple, Patan,** has the typical 'sikhara' spire, but with clusters of small pavilions on each side of the three arcaded storeys, and a carved stone frieze depicting the romantic Krishna legend.

The **Bhawani Temple, Bhatgaon** (eighteenth century), of the 'pagoda' and Tantric type, has the characteristic five-storey overhung roofs, and stands on a high plinth of five receding terraces with a stairway leading up to the shrine embraced by an arcaded verandah.

The **Sacred Town of Pasupati** (p. 122A) (seventeenth century), the Benares of Nepal, stands on the banks of the Bagmati. Dedicated to Siva, it consists entirely of stone and wooden temples, with a burning ghat by the river.

TIBET

INFLUENCES

GEOGRAPHICAL

Bordered on the north and east by China, to the south by India, Nepal and Bhutan, and on the west by India (Kashmir and Ladakh), Tibet is the highest country in the world, lying at the heart of the Himalayas. Much of this rugged land is a large plateau varying in height between 4,000 and 5,000 m (12,000–16,000 ft). Very thinly populated, the inhabited areas—generally centred upon monastic settlements—are almost exclusively in the south, where sheep and yaks are grazed and some agriculture is possible.

HISTORICAL AND SOCIAL

Small regional kingdoms existed until the seventh century, when the whole country came under the sway of King Sron-Btsang-Gam-Po, whose two wives, Nepalese and Chinese princesses, were both Buddhists. Thereafter Tibetan rulers championed the cause of Buddhism and Tibet's cultural history has been a direct reflection of the development of the faith. Monasteries multiplied and were highly privileged, leading ultimately to a form of theocratic government, in which the chief abbot (the Grand or Dalai Lama) became ruler of Tibet. In 1270 Kublai Khan, the Mongol Emperor of China, had conferred sovereignty over Tibet upon the abbot of Sakya monastery, and Chinese influence, although varying in effectiveness, progressively increased in the succeeding centuries. By the eighteenth Tibet's independence was only nominal and, after enduring various forms of foreign incursion, invasion and interference in the nineteenth and twentieth centuries, the country has become in the past decade an autonomous state of the People's Republic of China, and 1,400 years of Tibetan Lamaist culture have ended.

RELIGIOUS

Tibetans originally followed an animistic faith, Bonpo, which included elements of mysticism and sorcery. In 630 A.D. Mahayana Buddhism was introduced, tempered by indigenous folk cults, and in the next century Tantric Buddhism, prevalent in neighbouring countries, was established by Padma-Sambhava. Three hundred years later the final and lasting form of Tibetan Buddhism was shaped by the patriarch Atisa: the cult of the Bodhisattva (one who has vowed to attain Buddhahood), magic, animism and the belief in a living Buddha.

ARCHITECTURAL CHARACTER

Early Tibetan art was influenced by Indian Buddhism, but after the ninth century, when Tibet had made military inroads into western China, interest turned eastward. Architectural achievement is apparent in the stupas, the monastery complex and the decorative crafts. The usual stupa (chorten) form consists of a small bulbous dome on a many-tiered plinth and, similar to the Nepalese type, a square harmika with a mast supporting a chattra (umbrella) surmounted by a flame finial. The monastery is an original expression of Tibetan architecture, fortress-like, sited on hilltops, often commanding magnificent views, built of stone and sun-dried bricks, not to a regular plan, comprising long lines of cells disposed about courtyards having high white-washed walls and four gates. There is a large central square for assemblies, with the temple, library, meeting hall and mansion of the abbot probably in the middle. The temple is a rectangular stone building, with a continuous vermilion or yellow band under the eaves. The roof of tiles or beaten clay carries a Chinese pagoda-type pavilion. The plan resembles a chaitya with a nave and pillars and side aisles. Pillars and beams are painted yellow or red and painted silks hang from the roof. At the far end of the nave is the shrine. The only daylight enters through the doorways, which have sloping jambs (perhaps an echo of the early caves in Bihar). The walls are covered with frescoes or silks. The absence of stylistic variation through so many centuries reflects the conservative, unchanging nature of Tibetan society.

EXAMPLES

The **Sakya Monastery** (1071), 80 km (50 miles) south-west of Shigatse, and once famous for its collection of Sanskrit and Tibetan manuscripts, is seven storeys high with a spacious assembly hall.

The present **Potala 'Palace', Lhasa** (p. 122C), built for the fifth Dalai Lama between 1642–50, stands on a hill 90 m (300 ft) above the plain. Imposing externally, with skyscraper-like sloping walls, gilded roofs and bells crowning the chortens, it has richly decorated sanctuaries, reception and state rooms. Around the central 'palace' are grouped many smaller buildings for lesser members of the hierarchy, the whole agglomeration recalling a fortified mediaeval hill-town of India or Europe.

BIBLIOGRAPHY

BARTHOUX, J. Les Fouilles de Hadda. Paris, 1930.
BELL, C. Religions of Tibet. London, 1968.
—. Tibet, Past and Present. 2nd ed. London, 1968.
BROWN, P. Picturesque Nepal. London, 1921.
CHAPMAN, F. S. Lhasa, The Holy City. London, 1940.
FILLIPPO, F. DE. An Account of Tibet: The Travels of Ippolito Desideri of Pistoia, 1712–27. London, 1937.
FRANCKE, A. H. Antiquities of Indian Tibet. 2 vols. Archaeological Survey of India, 1914–26.

GHIRSHMAN, R. *Iran: Parthians and Sassanians*. Paris and London, 1962.
GORDON, A. K. *Tibetan Religious Art*. New York, 1952.
GROUSSET, R. *In the Footsteps of the Buddha*. London, 1932.
GRÜNWEDEL, A. *Mythologie des Buddhismus in Tibet*. Berlin, 1910.
HACKIN, J. *Nouvelles recherches à Bamiyan*. Paris, 1931.
—. *Indian Art in Tibet and Central Asia*. London, 1925.
—. and others. *Les Antiquités Bouddhiques de Bamiyan*. Paris, 1928.
—. *Diverses recherches archéologiques en Afghanistan*. Paris, 1961.
HAMILTON, B. *Account of the Kingdom of Nepal*.
LEVI, S. *Le Népâl*. 3 vols. Paris, 1905–8.
OLDFIELD, H. A. *Sketches from Nepal*. 2 vols. London, 1880.
PALLIS, M. *Peaks and Lamas*. London, 1939 and 1946.
POTT, P. H. *Art of the World: Burma, Korea, Tibet*. London, 1964.
ROWLAND, B. *The Art and Architecture of India: Buddhist, Hindu, Jain*. Harmondsworth and Baltimore, 1953.
SNELLGROVE, D. L., and RICHARDSON, H. *Cultural History of Tibet*. London, 1968.
STEIN, SIR M. AUREL. *Innermost Asia*. Oxford, 1929.
—. *Ruins of Desert Cathay*. 2 vols. London, 1912. There are many other publications on Central Asia by this author.
TARN, W. W. *The Greeks in Bactria and India*. Cambridge, 1938.
TUCCI, G. *Tibet*. London, 1972.
WADDELL, L. A. *The Buddhism of Tibet*. Cambridge, 1934. And other publications by this author.
WALDSCHMIDT, E. *Gandhara, Kutscha, Turfan*. Leipzig, 1925.
An important source of information is the periodical *Bulletin de l'École française d'Extrême-Orient*.

6

ARCHITECTURE IN BURMA, CAMBODIA, THAILAND AND INDONESIA

BURMA

INFLUENCES

GEOGRAPHICAL, GEOLOGICAL AND CLIMATIC

Burma, bounded on the north-west by the Indo–Pakistan sub-continent and on the south-east and east by China, Laos and Thailand, lies between 20° and 15° latitude, with a narrow tongue of land extending south to 10°. Her early history (c. first centuries B.C.–A.D.) is confined to the river valleys of Central Burma: those of the Irrawaddy, navigable for over 1,450 km (900 miles), Salween, Sittang and Chindwin, which divide the hills in Upper Burma ranging from 150 m to nearly 2000 m (500 ft to 6,000 ft) and form a delta in the south, opening into the Bay of Bengal and the Indian Ocean, whence Indian culture and Buddhism entered the country. There was also a land route from India to China, which passed through Upper Burma and was certainly used by immigrants. Burma is rich in timber, ores and precious stones, while teak and brick are much used in buildings. The climate is tropical, with south-west monsoon rains in summer.

HISTORICAL AND SOCIAL

Four main periods are recognized in Burmese history, the first of which is known as the *Pre-Pagan* (first century B.C. to the eighth century A.D.). The earliest inhabitants appear to have been the Pyu, of Tibeto-Burman stock, who settled in Upper Burma. The Mon-Talaing, of Khmer origin, with a highly developed culture, settled in Lower Burma around Thaton and further south in Dvaravati (later part of Thailand) and in the eighth century A.D., conquered the Pyu and established a capital at Pagan, in Central Burma, on the Irrawaddy. Indian settlements were also established. The *Pagan* period (ninth-thirteenth century) did not imply anything approaching a unified society until the reigns of King Anawrahta (1044–77) and his successors, during which a Burmese state was created which ushered in the classical phase in art and architecture. All this was to end in the thirteenth century with the invasion of Burma by Chinese Mongols under Kublai Khan. The *Post-Pagan* period (fourteenth–seventeenth century) which followed offers a confused picture of internecine power struggles between Shans, Mons, Thais, Laotians, Chinese and Khmers. During these years several new capitals saw the light, including the Shan-Burmese city of Ava and a splendid city at Pegu (sixteenth century), built during an interlude of restored prestige under the powerful King Dayinnaung. Thereafter the process of disintegration continued, again briefly halted under King

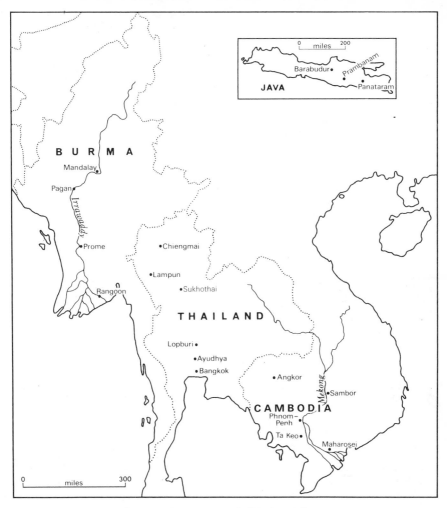

Burma, Cambodia, Thailand and Java

Alaungpaya, who built the port of Rangoon in 1755 (sacked by the Chinese in 1773). By this time British colonization was under way, culminating in the annexation of Burma, which became a province of the Indian Empire in 1886. One of the last Burmese kings, Mindon (1852–78), built his capital city at Mandalay, which constituted a final manifestation of the *Rangoon-Mandalay* period (eighteenth-nineteenth century). Burma declared her independence in January 1948, and is now a republic.

RELIGIOUS

In Burma art and architecture are a reflection of Buddhist devotion. According to the Mawavamsa (Ceylon's historical record), the Emperor Asoka (c. third century B.C.) sent two monks from India to preach the faith, and by the fifth century A.D.

A. Ruins of Buddhist temples and
stupas at Pagan, Burma. See p. 129

B. Shwe Dagon Pagoda, Rangoon,
Burma (16th and 17th cent.). See p. 129

C. Ananda Temple, Pagan, Burma (12th cent.). See p. 129

Buddhism was widely established. Later immigrants brought Nat worship (a pantheon of water and tree spirits, and 'nagas'—snakes), but they were ultimately converted to Buddhism, although Nat superstitions are still general.

ARCHITECTURAL CHARACTER

The development of Burmese architecture follows the four historical periods. Few significant buildings, however, survive from the early centuries. The majority of Burma's important architectural monuments date from the Pagan period, and almost all buildings of real distinction are religious. The basic stupa (zedi, later 'pagoda') form was a massive brick cylindrical construction, built upon a plinth of three or five diminishing terraces; the basic temple form was square in plan with brick walls enclosing narrow vaulted corridors embracing a solid masonry core, which had centrally-placed niches on each side to accommodate Buddha statues, the walls decorated with frescoes or sculptured bas-reliefs. The central core rose in a series of receding storeys, and was crowned with a tapering sikhara-type finial of Orissan–Indian character. The monasteries (Kyaung) and the Ordination Halls (Thein) for monks were derived from wood prototypes. The libraries (Pitakat-Taik), housing the sacred Buddhist texts, resembled the simpler temple designs. Burmese bricks measure about 305 × 203 × 76 mm (12 × 8 × 3 ins), and are set in mud or glue mortar. The true arch was much used in Burma—it was never exploited in India—with radiating voussoirs to form semi-pointed barrel vaults (cf. the Gothic-type great arches of the porticoes of the Ananda Temple, below).

In the Pagan period there are said to have been 5,000 stupas and temples within the boundaries of the capital (p. 128A). In the Post-Pagan era Burma declined architecturally, as well as politically. Chinese influence contributed to the emergence of the 'Pagoda' style, which characterized the seventeenth to nineteenth century. No matter what their particular functions might be, all buildings were treated, constructionally and aesthetically, in a similar manner. Typical of the Burmese feeling for rich and intricate artistry, this architecture of carved wood, lacquer and gilt is essentially a folk art, expressing the native skill, imagination and vitality of the people.

EXAMPLES

The **Mingalazedi Stupa, Pagan** (1274), comprises a high square plinth of three stepped terraces, with stairways in the centre of each side leading to the platform, from which the circular bell-shaped main structure rises. At each angle of the square stands a small replica of the stupa. The design has Javanese precedents (cf. Barabudur, p. 143).

The **Ananda Temple, Pagan** (twelfth century) (p. 128C), represents the supreme attainment of Burmese classical architecture. A massive white brick building, basically square, with finely graduated tiered roofs and, projecting on each side, elaborately decorated portico entrances which give the temple the plan-form of a Greek cross. A golden tapering spire rises over the central masonry block, which also carries similarly gilded smaller spires. Inside are two concentric ambulatories, the inner one passing before four Buddha statues, 9 m (30 ft) high, recessed into each side of the masonry core.

The **Shwe Dagon Pagoda (stupa), Rangoon** (sixteenth and seventeenth century) (p. 128B), built over older foundations and added to many times, reflects Burma's cultural connections with India and China, while expressing the exuberance typical of later phases of Burmese art. In form, the traditional rounded tumulus of the stupa had now evolved into a tall, tenuous structure, rising in this case by repeated enlargements to a height of 113 m (370 ft) above the processional platform. The supporting plinth is multi-planed, its many angles bearing miniature pagodas, the processional platform crowded with carved, gilded and lacquered shrines and spirelets.

King Mindon's capital of **Mandalay** dates only from 1857, but its plan embodied many of the features of Kublai Khan's Peking of the thirteenth century. The lay-out consisted of concentric square enclosures, each with its perimeter wall as a barrier. The palace occupied the central square, and comprised a large number of single-storeyed wooden buildings on a brick platform nearly 1.8 m (6 ft) high, supported on immense wood pillars and extending some 300 m (1,000 ft) on its longest side. All the buildings were profusely decorated with gilding, carving and lacquer, providing a fanciful panorama of roofs, gables, parapets and slender pagoda spires. Mandalay suffered immeasurable destruction during the Second World War.

CAMBODIA

INFLUENCES

GEOGRAPHICAL, GEOLOGICAL AND CLIMATIC

This region of southern Indo-China covers the areas of the Mekong river delta and the China Sea to the south, and the mid-western Mekong region around the latitudes 10° and 15°, bordering the Gulf of Siam in the west and separated on the east from ancient Vietnam by the eastern Moi highlands and, in the north, by the mountains of central Laos. The early history (Funanese period, third–seventh century A.D.) centred round the deltaic region, but subsequently the focus of events shifted further inland to the middle reaches of the Mekong, as far as Bassak and the Roi-Et highlands (during the Khmer period, seventh–fourteenth century). Both these episodes must have contributed to the development of the sophisticated hydraulic works constructed during the later years of the Khmer empire. Timber was the principal building material in the delta area, together with laterite, sandstone and a terra-cotta brick in the hinterland. The cooling rain and wind of the south-west monsoon provides the only break in the tropical humid heat.

SOCIAL AND HISTORICAL

Funanese period (third–sixth century A.D.). Early Indo-China consisted of many small states which ultimately took shape as Cambodia, Laos and Vietnam. The oldest of the trio was Cambodia, corresponding approximately to Funan and founded, according to Chinese tradition, about the second century A.D. by a king Chandan or Kaudinya, who may have been a Kushana of Indo-Scythian stock (their royal title was Chandan), which would account for the marked evidence of Scythian–Persian influences. At its height at the end of the sixth century, the empire of Funan included much of Chenla, Indo-China and parts of Malaya. Chinese records mention the close relations which existed between Funan and India and China, and the high cultural standards, economic strength and impressive social organization of the country.

Later Funanese and Early Khmer period (seventh–eighth century). This period was characterized by political confusion and war. The neighbouring state of Chenla gained suzerainty over Funan and, for the first time, reference is made to the authority exercised by the Khmer kings and people, whose capitals (of Chenla-Funan) near Kampong Thom at Sambor and Prei Kuk survive in an impressive group of pre-Angkor ruins. The dominant power in south-east Asia, however, was exercised by the Srivijaya and Sailendra dynasties of Java and Malaya.

Early Classical Khmer period (ninth century). The primordial role of architecture in Khmer society becomes apparent in this period. King Jayavarman II (800–50) released Cambodia from Javanese thraldom and founded a unified Angkor kingdom, building the first city of Angkor at Phnom Kulen. Among his successors, Indravarman I (877–99) built the Bakong, the first stone temple in the grand style, and introduced the elaborate system of irrigation, which not only became an integral part of subsequent architectural schemes, but a vital element in the economic and social life of the nation. The disintegration of the system caused the final abandonment of the city of Angkor in the sixteenth century. Indravarman's son, Yasovarman I, founded the second city of Angkor and initiated a period of splendour in which Khmer civilization took the form of an aristocratic and intellectual oligarchy under a god-king, with a middle class of artist-craftsmen, and a menial working class.

Transitional Classical Khmer period (tenth–eleventh century). This saw an interlude of dynastic quarrels and the creation of other capital cities. But King Rajendravarman (944–68), who was a cultivated man and an indefatigable builder, returned to Angkor, extending and consolidating Khmer power throughout the region. In the reign of his son and successor, Jayavarman V, the Brahmin royal tutor Yajnavaraha built one of the most beautiful of Khmer temples, the Banteay Srei ('Citadel of Women'), a remarkable exercise in the eclecticism of earlier styles. Suryavarman I (1002–50), who followed, completed the Ta Keo, the first temple to be built of sandstone. Despite the unsettled conditions of the next decades, the magnificent gilded Baphuon Temple-Mountain dates from the reign of his heir, Udayadityavarman II.

Classical Khmer period (twelfth–thirteenth century). This represented a hundred years of pomp and glory before the gradual decline. Suryavarman II (1112–52), most powerful of Cambodian kings, skilled in diplomacy and successful in war, is chiefly remembered for the building of the great Temple-City of Angkor Vat, the supreme achievement of Khmer genius and an architectural expression of the god-king ideal. He also built Angkor Thom, which was almost immediately destroyed in 1177 by marauding Chams, and rebuilt by Jayavarman VII (1180–1218) in a programme unparalleled in the immensity, extravagance and speed of construction, entailing armies of masons, sculptors, decorators and labourers. The king's activities, although he was a mystic and Mahayana Buddhist, were not confined to the building of temples and palaces. He extended his empire by military prowess into Annam, Vientiane, Burma and southern Malaya. Indeed, by the end of his reign the country was exhausted by wars and grandiose architectural schemes, and was ready to welcome Theravada Buddhism, which had no need of magnificent architecture and elaborate ritual, preached the virtues of simplicity and rejected the god-king image. This change in religious and philosophical attitudes marks the end of the Classical Khmer period and was a prelude to the decay of the empire and the eventual conquest of Cambodia by Thailand. Angkor was captured by the Thais in 1437, and the destruction of the reservoirs and hydraulic works had made life in Angkor impossible by the end of the sixteenth century, by which time most of the country had passed into Siamese (Thai) hands. A Cambodian enclave survived in the south, and its capital Phnom-Penh, on the Mekong river, remained the principal city of Cambodia when much of Indo-China became a French protectorate in the nineteenth century.

RELIGIOUS

In the pre-Khmer era the indigenous animistic beliefs of the people in the sacred mountain, the Naga princess (water spirit) and ancestor worship were fused with the Indian religious beliefs of the king, the court and the scholars. Hinduism predominated, with Mahayana Buddhism as a subordinate religion. The worship of Hari-Hara (Siva and Vishnu in a single body, whose image has four faces, and sometimes eight arms) was a particular characteristic. From the ninth century of the Khmer period the cult of the Deva-Raja, the God-King, worshipped in the form of Siva, began to develop, influencing the style of the great pyramid temple-cities of the Angkor region. A great change took place in the thirteenth century, when the process of conversion to Theravada Buddhism (of the Sinhalese sect) assumed the momentum of a popular movement. This particular doctrine involved no elaborate ceremonial, and its missionaries preached self-denial and the simple life. It marked the beginning of the end of the old culture.

ARCHITECTURAL CHARACTER

The earliest recorded capital (c. fifth century A.D.) was Vyadhapura (Angkor Borei) on the lower reaches of the Mekong river, 200 km (120 miles) from the sea and the port of Oc Eo. It was an agglomeration of wooden houses on piles, connected by little canals linked to larger waterways capable of taking sea-going ships. Later Funanese and early Khmer architectural development (seventh and eighth century) was centred upon Sambor and Prei Kuk, in the forests near Kampong Thom, on the road from Saigon to Angkor, and not far from the later Angkor capitals. Wooden buildings gave way to more substantial brick and stone imitations of timber prototypes, which show a mixture of Indian forms grafted on to indigenous elements, and rich decorative sculpture derived from wood carving (harbinger of the exuberant Angkor ornamental art). Examples of temples and shrines still exist, if in a ruined state, at Tat Panom (Sambor) on the Mekong, and Phnom Bayang.

At the beginning of the Early Classical Khmer period three important architectural events occurred, indicating the transitional stages between the pre-Angkor and early Angkor styles, such as the city surrounded and penetrated by moats and artificial lakes; Javanese influence in the emphasis upon the temple-mountain and the concept of the god-king; and the raising of the temple 'cella' to the summit of the stepped pyramid. Of these, the first was the creation of a city and temple-mountain in 800 A.D. on the hill of Phnom Kulen, near Angkor and the lake of Tonle-Sap. The second (chronologically the third) was the building of another capital (893) on the hill and round the temple-mountain of Phnom Bakeng, close to Phnom Kulen, terraced into the hill as a five-levelled pyramid, with isolated towers on the topmost tier and smaller towers at the lower levels. Both cities presaged the typical Khmer town plan: a walled rectangle; the temple at the central intersection of the principal avenues radiating towards gates in the four sides of the moated enclosure, the main gate facing east. The third event, the second in date, was the construction at Roluos, Angkor, of the archetypal Khmer urban irrigation system. An immense artificial lake, 'Baray' Lolei, about 3 km (2 miles) long and 800 m (half a mile) wide was formed by earthen dykes to store water from the Stung Roluos river flowing into a network of moats and waterways. The lake provided for the needs of the whole community, its final task being to irrigate the paddy fields. Such systems could only be realized under a highly centralized authority exemplified, in this context, by the god-king and universal ruler. In the Transitional Classical Khmer period (tenth and eleventh century) the evolution of the temple-mountain was continued in Baksei Chamkrong, Angkor (c. 911), the first to be built-up in stone (laterite) in pyramidal terraces from flat ground, and Koh Ker (921), 64 km (40 miles) north-east of Angkor, constructed on an artificial lake by damming a stream, the normal east-west axis of the city altered to align with it—proof perhaps that the practical needs of the irrigation system were considered more important than a symbolic gesture to religion. As a rule, however, the symbolic axis was respected. A further stage in the evolutionary process came in the Ta Keo (completed *c.* 1010), in which the classical five terraces and five colossal towers were introduced, and still another in the Baphuon (*c.* 1050), in which the style and scale of the temple-mountain became formalized. The culmination of Khmer building art was now in sight.

The Classical Khmer period (twelfth and early thirteenth century) was dominated by two majestic architectural achievements: the creation of Angkor Vat, the temple-city of Suryavarman II (1113–50), and of Angkor Thom, the remodelled capital of Jayavarman VII (1180–1218), the latter a fantastic, baroque manifestation of a declining civilization. Khmer architecture, as expressed in these works, is characterized by grandeur of conception, brilliant landscaping, unsurpassed town-planning in a strictly formal sense, and exuberant sculptural decoration on a grandiose scale, but of exquisite refinement. Building technique, however, remained unsophisticated. Stone was used like wood, and stone walls were often reinforced with concealed timber beams inserted in the hollowed-out centres: when the wood rotted, the stone blocks fell. The corbelled vaulting was never modified and permitted only the spanning of small spaces; hence the confined nature of each 'room', and the grouping together of many such units, and their interconnection by galleries to create an impression of size. To express the verticality of the invariable mountain theme, these galleried groups were placed round and above the central pyramid (cf. the Ta Keo, an early example of 889). No mortar was used: the stone masonry was stabilized by the sheer mass of the construction, and the fine joints of the roofs fitted so perfectly that they remain watertight after several hundred years of neglect. Everywhere sculptural ornament breaks through the architectural lines, often spreading over the whole wall surface. At Angkor Thom this domination of the architecture by sculpture is even more marked than at Angkor Vat.

EXAMPLES

A number of temples and shrines survive from the Late Funanese era, including a Buddhist building of the sixth or seventh century at **Tat Panom** (Sambor), in terra-cotta brick of marked Indian character; another brick structure, the **Temple of Siva, Phnom Bayang** (early seventh century), rectangular and of three receding storeys with a keel-shape roof; and a small sandstone shrine at **Prei Kuk.**

The **Preah Ko Temple** (879) is one of two important temples built by Indravarman I. Situated in the city-water complex, for which the king was also responsible, it is a single-terrace construction (that is, not yet a temple-mountain) with six towers and lavish carving showing strong Javanese influence.

The **Bakong Temple, Roluos** (Angkor) (881) (p. 134A), the second important temple built by Indravarman I, typifies the emergence of the Khmer temple-mountain concept. An architecturally simple stone pyramid, it comprises five superimposed terraces, decreasing in size from an almost square base with sides of 70 m (230 ft) to one with 21 m (69 ft) sides at the top, which is 14 m (47 ft) from the ground. Here again the resemblance to Barabudur (Java) is conspicuous.

Other temples of the Early Classical Khmer period exemplifying the pyramidal superstructure are the **Lolei** (893), set in the Roluos lake, near **Angkor,** and the **Bakheng, Angkor,** of the same date, which largely follows the pattern of Bakong.

A. Bakong Temple, Angkor, Cambodia (881). See p. 133

B. The Royal Palace, Phiméanakas, Cambodia (c. 978). See p. 137

A. Néak Péan shrine, Angkor, Cambodia (12th cent.). See p. 137

B. The Temple of Angkor Vat, Cambodia (12th cent.). See p. 137

A. Central tower,
Temple of Angkor Vat,
(12th cent.). See p. 137

B. The Bayon, Angkor Thom, Cambodia
(early 13th cent.). See p. 137

C. Wāt Phra Sri Sarapet,
Ayudhya, Thailand (c.
1500). See p. 140

D. Throne Room, Royal Palace, Bangkok,
Thailand. See p. 140

E. Tjandi Medhut, Java (9th cent.). See p. 143

Pre-Rup, a red and pale pink three-stepped pyramid with five towers at the summit, came some 70 years later and, like the relatively small, delicate, graceful, subtly-proportioned **Banteay Srei** (967), built 20 km (12 miles) from Angkor, belongs to the Transitional period. A few years after Pre-Rup and Banteay Srei the temple-mountain of **Phiméanakas** (p. 134B) was completed, probably in 978, at the centre of the Angkor of Jayavarman V. It differs from the former in that the long stone chambers of the third terrace have become a continuous covered gallery.

The **Ta Keo Temple** (970–1010) is of more fundamental significance, in that it may be said to epitomize the results of two hundred years of development of the Khmer temple-mountain. Very large, 103 m × 122 m (339 ft × 402 ft) at the base and 48 m (156 ft) square at the top, it has five terraces, the highest being 40 m (129 ft) from the ground, and carrying five colossal stone towers (cf. Pre-Rup).

The **Baphuon temple-mountain** (*c.* 1050) is on the scale of Angkor Vat, and was in many respects a prelude to it. Vaulted stone galleries now enclose the first and second terraces, as well as the third.

The **Néak Péan shrine** (twelfth century) (p. 135A) symbolized paradise floating upon the primeval seas, and fits into no precise category. The circular plinth rises out of a square basin, from which the water flowed through gargoyle fountains, with lion, horse, elephant and human heads, into four symmetrically sited pools (now dried up), and thence through canals to the river, an enchanting conception.

The **City of Angkor Vat** (twelfth century) (pp. 135B, 136A), together with that of Angkor Thom, is one of the prodigious monuments of the last phase of the Khmer civilization at its Classical period. It was built by Suryavarman II (1112–52) as a temple to the god-king image, as a monument to himself, and as his own sepulchre. In plan it is a vast rectangle contained by a moat 4 km (2½ miles) long, and in form it is the familiar stepped pyramid, the third and final level supporting the inner sanctuary and crowned by an immense central conical tower, with four smaller towers of similar design at the corners of the great galleried platform. The Angkor Vat temple-mountain is approached by a paved causeway and entered by a monumental portico leading to a colonnaded and arcaded gallery, which embraces the first terrace. Nearly 800 m (2,500 ft) of the walls of this gallery are decorated with bas-reliefs depicting allegorical tales and legendary events from the Indian epics, the Mahabharata and the Ramayana.

Angkor Thom, the rebuilt capital of Cambodia, laid out by Jayavarman VII (1180–1218), lies a little to the north of Angkor Vat. Planned as an almost square rectangle, with each of its sides over 3 km (2 miles) long and protected by a moat 90 m (300 ft) wide and a laterite stone wall nearly 6.7 m (22 ft) high, it incorporates the two earlier temple-mountains of Baphuon and Phiméanakas. Bridging the moat and leading to five towered gateways were five stone causeways with parapet-balustrades on either side, composed of rows of stone giants holding 'nagas' (symbolic serpents). At the centre of the city the king built his own temple-mountain, the Bayon (see below). His palace, close to the Phiméanakas, has completely vanished.

The **Bayon, Angkor Thom** (early thirteenth century) (p. 136B), symbolizing the god-king cult, originally consisted of a system of vaulted galleries and small pavilions disposed in a cruciform plan. Later similar galleries were added at the corners to form a rectangle, which was then enclosed by outer galleries linked to the inner complex by sixteen chapels, subsequently destroyed. A podium at the centre carried the shrine, which had an image of the Buddha under a naga hood identified with Jayavarman, the Deva-Raja. This motif was reflected on 54 towers, each bearing four Buddha heads carved on each side, which crowned the chapels and pavilions.

THAILAND

INFLUENCES

GEOGRAPHICAL, GEOLOGICAL AND CLIMATIC

Siam—since 1939 the name of Muang T'ai has generally been translated as Thailand—is bordered on the north and west by Burma, and on the north-east and east by Laos and Cambodia. It extends from latitude 20° north to the Malay Peninsula some 1,600 km (1,000 miles) to the south, 5° north of the Equator. The country is immensely rich in durable and decorative timbers, including teak and ebony, suitable for all types of construction work. The other principal building material is brick; stone was little used, except for foundations and during the years of Khmer influence. The climate is tropical, with monsoon rains and winds.

HISTORICAL, SOCIAL AND RELIGIOUS

In the sixth century it appears that the Mon people (Buddhists) from Lower Burma imposed their authority over what is now central Thailand and founded the kingdom of Dvaravati. Early in the eleventh century the Khmers annexed Dvaravati and their influence became paramount in central Thailand, although Dvaravati's prestige as the centre of Buddhist orthodoxy remained largely unimpaired. In the north, where Thai-Syām migrants from south-west China established a semi-independent state with its capital at Chiengsen (modern Chiengmai), a gradual fusion of Mons and Thais led to infiltrations southwards and, in the thirteenth century, to the expulsion of the Khmers and the creation and consolidation of the kingdom of Sukhothai. The centre of gravity, however, continued to move south. In the fourteenth century Ayudhya became the capital, with direct access to the sea and the Cambodian trade routes, a city destined to be renowned throughout the Indo-Chinese world for wealth and luxury, destroyed by the Burmese in 1767 and now a desolate ruin. This was not the first incursion by Burma into Siam. In 1555 Ayudhya had fallen briefly into Burmese hands, but foreign domination has always been short-lived and, apart from the Japanese occupation during the Second World War, Thailand remains unique among the countries of South-East Asia in maintaining a considerable measure of independence throughout her national history. Despite Portuguese, Dutch, French and British commercial intrusion from the sixteenth century onwards, Thailand was always suspicious of European intentions, and managed to evade colonialist occupation. The present capital, Bangkok, was founded in 1782 to take the place of Ayudhya, which lies a short distance to the north. Buddhism came early to this region, via Ceylon and Burma, superimposed upon the indigenous animism, and for fifteen hundred years has remained the prevailing influence on art and architecture.

ARCHITECTURAL CHARACTER

Architecture in Thailand reflects the influences of the Buddhist countries and of the various groups with which she has mingled and associated for two millennia. The resultant complex picture may be divided into:

The Dvaravati period, central Thailand (sixth–tenth century), is characterized by Burman Buddhist forms surviving only in buildings which, strictly speaking, post-date the Dvaravati era, e.g. Lampun and Haripunjaya. There are no other architectural remains, except for fragments of foundations which give some idea of the plans, but not the style of buildings at Nakhon Pathom (later Lopburi), the earliest known capital. Constructed of brick and stone, these plinths, with mouldings similar to those of Buddhist structures from Ceylon to north India of the first millennium, have granite bases with mortise holes for pillars which must have supported timber superstructures.

The Khmer-Lopburi (or Mon-Khmer) period, central and eastern Thailand (tenth–thirteenth century), has been described as a provincial manifestation of the Khmer-Angkor style of architecture, but it also mirrored earlier building traditions of the Mons and Talaings of southern Burma, who brought with them architectural echoes of Pagan. Most of the buildings are in a ruined condition, but well-preserved survivals can be seen at Lopburi and in Sukhothai. The Khmers introduced the use of stone, in place of the traditional brick or rubble bonded with vegetable glue.

The Thai period (thirteenth–seventeenth century) is sometimes subdivided into (1) Sukhothai style, (2) Ayudhya style, and (3) Northern Chiengmai style, although more for convenience than clear differentiation. Sukhothai art and architecture were not inventive, but harmoniously eclectic, employing Indian, Mon-Dravidian, Mon-Pagan, Sinhalese and Khmer motifs. Out of this diversity certain distinctively Thai features emerged, apparent in the typical Buddhist temple complex (Wāt), normally erected on a terrace. These had a central sanctuary, which sheltered a colossal Buddha statue screened by a high wall. The latter had a narrow arched aperture through which the image was viewed and worshipped. Over the sanctuary (reached through a pillared hall) rose a tapering tower, not unlike a minaret. The usually rectangular surrounding stupas carried similar elongated finials, but in the Ayudhya style the stupa was generally circular in plan, ring-based and bell-shaped, as in Ceylon. In the Chiengmai manner of the north cosmopolitan influences were less conspicuous, although here too the custom of copying venerated monuments from abroad as 'reminders' of the need for religious observance was the origin of some of the finest architecture (e.g. Wāt Jet Yot). In all phases of Siamese building the part played by sculpture and, in interiors, by mural painting is important.

The Bangkok style was created in the late eighteenth and nineteenth century. The new capital was designed to emulate the destroyed city of Ayudhya. Many religious buildings and palaces were erected in which traditional forms were overlaid with ornamentation of Chinese character, introduced to Siam by refugees. Surfaces were often finished with porcelain tiles. Sometimes the walls are white stuccoed brick, which contrasts with the brightly-coloured glazed tiles of the multi-levelled over-lapping timber roofs. Gables and bargeboards are decorated with Angkor-Hindu iconography: 'nagas', Vishnu on a 'garuda' (a mythical bird), Siva on a bull, etc. Doors and window shutters are of carved wood, lacquered in black and gold, or painted or inlaid with mother-of-pearl depicting themes of guardian divinities, enchanted forests, ferns, flowers and still life.

EXAMPLES

Wāt Kukut Temple, Lampun (early twelfth century, rebuilt 1218 after an earthquake) represents (and post-dates) the last phase of the Dvaravati style. From a high square platform, with 23 m (75 ft) sides, rises a slender brick pyramid of five diminishing storeys of 28 m (92 ft). On each face of each storey are three terra-cotta Buddha images, making sixty in all.

Wāt Mahadhatu Temple, Lopburi (*c.* twelfth century), restored in the fifteenth century, is a building of the Khmer-Angkor type. It stands in a walled court, and comprises a sanctuary tower (sikhara) and attached portico (mandapa) raised on a high moulded plinth. Especially noteworthy are the heavy arched tympāna above the openings, recalling Angkor.

Wāt Jet Yot Temple, near Chiengmai (*c.* 1455), apparently built to record the 2000th anniversary of the Buddha's death, is a smaller version of the Maha Bodi Temple, Bodhgaya, India, but with added stucco reliefs of celestial beings paying homage. Other examples of the 'copy' type are the **Cetiya Si Liem** (the 'Four-square Reminder'), **Chiengmai** (*c.* 1300), and **Wāt Mahathat** (Great Relic Monastery), **Sukhothai** (fourteenth century).

Among the ruins of **Ayudhya** it is possible to gain some impression of the evolution of the Siamese 'bell' stupa or 'prachedi', normally surrounded by miniature stupas or shrines of similar form. By Buddhist tradition such structures housed the relics of holy men, but at Ayudhya they were no doubt erected as funeral monuments to the kings. Inside the stupas were secret chambers decorated with frescoes and filled with votive objects. Examples include the **Wāt Phra Ram** (*c.* 1369); **Wāt Phra Mahathat** (*c.* 1374); **Wāt Rat Burana** (*c.* 1424); and, the most complete and impressive, **Wāt Phra Sri Sarapet** (*c.* 1500) (p. 136C).

Typical of the Bangkok 'pagoda' manner of later years, a form applied to palaces as well as religious buildings, is the Throne Room of the **Royal Palace, Bangkok** (p. 136D), in which the two main roofs intersect at right angles (i.e. in cruciform plan), with a spire rising at the intersection.

INDONESIA AND THE MALAY ARCHIPELAGO

INFLUENCES

GEOGRAPHICAL, GEOLOGICAL AND CLIMATIC

The Malay peninsula is bounded by southern Thailand in the north, and on the west and south by the Straits of Malacca which separate it from Sumatra, which in turn is separated from Java on the south-east by the narrow Sunda Straits. Java is the first of a chain of islands extending eastward—Bali, Lombok, Sumbawa, Flores, Sumba and Timor, whence a host of smaller islands leads almost to New Guinea. Another group of islands lies to the east of Sumatra and north of Java across the Java sea. The largest in this archipelago is Borneo, separated by the Straits of Macassar on the east from Celebes. To the north of Borneo and Celebes lie the Philippines. Much of this vast heterogeneous region is mountainous. A long curving band of active and extinct volcanoes passes through Sumatra, Java and Bali, and volcanic rock (solidified lava) has been extensively used for construction work. Eruptions have brought down buildings, but it has sometimes been possible to reconstruct important architectural monuments with the original undamaged stones. This is certainly true in part of the ninth-century masterpiece of Barabudur in Java. Indonesia almost bestrides the Equator, with a tropical climate and no great seasonal variation in temperature. The climate is also generally humid and under the influence of both monsoons.

HISTORICAL AND SOCIAL

In the civilization which developed in Sumatra and Java under Indian cultural and religious influence and example, society was divided between court and peasantry. Literature, sculpture and architecture were the prerogative of the 'Kraton', or court. The peasants formed an agricultural community, whose rituals, customs and origins date back to neolithic times and whose lives were almost untouched by the court culture. The first important Indonesian kingdom, and expression of this form of civilization, seems to have been that of King Jayanaga in south-east Sumatra, which coincided with the birth of the Srivijaya Dynasty (seventh to thirteenth century). Srivijaya emerged as a major power with hegemony over the Malayan peninsula, Borneo and western Java, and mercantile connections extending as far as Persia. Unhappily no architectural records survive. Concurrently with the early years of the Srivijaya leadership in Sumatra, two principal dynasties ruled in Java: the Hindu Sanjaya in the central provinces (mid-seventh to tenth century) and the Buddhist Sailendra a little further east. Both have left impressive architectural evidence. It is surmised that the Sailendra line ended with the marriage of a daughter to a Sanjaya king, Rakryan Pikatan, in about the year 840. Thereafter the history of the Srivijaya kingdom in Sumatra is concerned with wars for supremacy over Java, the declining strength of the Sanjaya, and ultimately with defeat (c. 1220) at the hands of the east Javanese dynasties of Singasari and Majapahit, with the former first in the ascendant and the latter inspiring a final renaissance of Javanese art and architecture in the fourteenth century. In the meantime Moslem influence had been gaining ground throughout Indonesia and, by the end of the fifteenth century, the Islamic ruler Balen Pata, himself a Javanese, had assumed control of the whole of Java, including the state of Majapahit. The subsequent evolution of Indonesia is interwoven with the activities of European colonial powers: the Portuguese, the British and, for three and a half centuries, the Dutch. In 1945 the independent Republic of Indonesia came into being, and in 1954 the last tenuous threads which held the Netherlands-Indonesian Union together were severed.

RELIGIOUS

Two interacting movements have moulded the character of Indonesian art and architecture: the ancient indigenous peasant culture of animistic myth and ancestor worship, and the Hindu-Buddhist beliefs brought to the region, and to Java in particular, from the fourth century A.D. by Indian immigrants who, by the seventh century, had made both Sumatra and Java centres of religious learning and pilgrimage. Many years later Islam came to north Sumatra and Malaya, also from India, and by the fifteenth century had spread throughout Java, ousting the Hindu-Buddhist and ancestral spirit cults, which found a lasting haven in Bali.

ARCHITECTURAL CHARACTER

It has already been noted that there are no significant architectural remains in Sumatra, Malaya or Borneo surviving from the Srivijaya empire; but from the contemporary Sanjaya and Sailendra dynasties in middle Java a number of buildings of extraordinary distinction still exist on the high table-lands—the Dieng Plateau and the Kedu plain, dating mainly from the eighth and ninth centuries, and exemplifying a synthesis of Hindu-Indonesian and Buddhist-Indonesian features. It would appear that this architecture, of solid stone walls, corbelled arches and with no load-bearing columns, which reached its consummation with the stupa of Barabudur and the temple complex of Prambanam, was always associated with isolated religious communities and never with large centres of population. The influences of Gupta (Indian) fifth- and sixth-century styles and of Sanchi and Barhut stupa reliefs suggest that there was at this period a wide-ranging movement in Buddhist art from India to the China seas.

A new development began with the shift of power to East Java in the eleventh century, characterized by a lessening of Indian influence and increased evidence of the native Indonesian tradition, reflected especially in the sculpture which already foreshadows the folk-art of the Javanese 'Wayang' puppet drama. This tendency is

A. The stupa of Barabudur, Java (8th–9th cent.): aerial view. See p. 143

B. The stupa of Barabudur, Java

C. Siva Temple, Prambanam, Java (c. 900). See p. 143

even more marked in the Majapahit period (cf. the temple group at Panataram, p. 144). The coming of Islam ended the Hindu-Buddhist architectural tradition in Indonesia, except in Bali, where it has lingered on as a folk art, while the arrival of the Dutch introduced European elements.

Timber is abundant and varied throughout Indonesia, and has always been used for most building types, especially for houses. The traditional dwelling is a 'long house', generally raised on stilts, and often sheltering an entire clan. It is seen at its architectural best in the Menangkabau homes of south central Sumatra, which are carried on carved and decorated wooden pillars, the façades adorned with colour patterns of intertwined flowers in white, black and red, the inward-sloping ridge ('saddle-back') roofs with high gables at each end ornamented with buffalo horns.

EXAMPLES

The **Tjandi Bhima, Dieng** (c. 700) (Hindu) is one of a number of smaller temples and 'Tjandi' (sepulchral monuments) to survive in central Java from the early years of the Sanjaya-Sailendra dynasties. It comprises a simple single-cella shrine, square in plan, beneath a pyramid tower, entered by a prominent porch.

At **Kalasan**, a little further south, there is a Buddhist shrine temple (c. 770) built to hold the ashes of the consort of a Sailendra prince, and planned in the shape of a Greek cross, with projecting wings forming side chapels, each entered through a portico with elaborate pediment surmounted by a 'Kirtimukha', the grotesque mask later so typical of Javanese sculpture. While clearly a development of Tjandi Bhima, Kalasan shows a maturity in execution which presages an Indonesian style.

Tjandi Sewa (ninth century), in the same district, is another Buddhist shrine, but in a far more ruinous condition. In conception resembling Kalasan, but with 250 smaller shrines, it must once have had something of the grandeur of Barabudur and Angkor. **Tjandi Medhut** (p. 136E), of the same date, general plan and structure as the last two monuments, is noteworthy for the well-preserved sculpture, including a renowned Buddha trinity which graces the interior.

The **Stupa of Barabudur** (eighth to ninth century) (p. 142A, B), theatrically sited on the Java plains against a background of smoking volcanoes, is the supreme expression of Indonesian art, and an architectural masterpiece of the Sailendra dynasty. In the form of a shallow stone-clad hill, this extraordinary building symbolizes the world mountain ('Meru') of Indian cosmology and the Mahayana Buddhist cosmic system through the nine stages—there are nine storeys or terraces—which lead to nirvana. Basically square in plan, with a stone plinth-foundation, each 150 m (500 ft) side having five slightly stepped faces (diminishing to three at the higher levels), Barabudur rises through five rectangular closed galleries and three circular open terraces (the latter carrying 72 bell-like stupas) to the crowning central stupa. The galleries display some 1,300 panels of sculpture, depicting the life of the Buddha and legends from the sacred Buddhist texts. Every detail in the design and conception of Barabudur is dictated by religious rather than architectural principles, but the result is spectacular architecture.

At **Prambanam** there is a remarkable complex of 150 shrines ranged about a vast two-tiered terrace, which reflects the decline in Mahayana Buddhism in the ninth and tenth centuries, and a return to the Hindu gods. Most of the shrines are in ruins, but the **Siva Temple of Loro Djongrang** (c. 900) (p. 142C), the main feature of Prambanam, has been considerably restored. Cruciform in plan, on a square base, with four broad formal staircases and a central cella, the temple has much fine sculpture, including a gallery containing forty-two bas-reliefs illustrating the 'Ramayana' epic.

The **temple group at Panataram** (*c.* 1370) is a final manifestation of continuing Hindu culture (Majapahit dynasty) in eastern Java. The Siva 'Tjandi' is particularly interesting and well-preserved: the traditional form of the single cube-like cella and surmounting pyramid is retained, but the treatment is now entirely Javanese. Especially characteristic are the large Kirtimukha masks over the doorways, which anticipate a technique used centuries after in the Wayang puppet plays.

VIETNAM AND LAOS

Vietnam and Laos share the same background, historical, social and religious, as their neighbours in the Indo-Chinese orbit. The special character of Vietnamese building is seen in the 'Kalam' roofs (keel-shaped in the Chinese pagoda style), as at the shrines of **Mi-Son** and **Po Nagar** and in the 'Ly' style (eleventh–twelfth century) of Tonkin province. Southward the influence is Javanese at **Dong-Duang** and **My-Duc**. From the twelfth century the example of Angkor Vat appears in the 'Binh-dinh' style towers at **Nha-trang**. The 'Dinh' (communal meeting-house), built by each village, seemingly continued an ancient tradition of houses built on stilts. By the nineteenth century a Chinese provincial style is apparent in the **Imperial Palace, Hue,** while French influence (especially that of Vauban) guided the city-planners of **Hue, Son-tay, Thanh-hoa** and **Bac-ninh.** In Laos, apart from 'Dong-son' (third–second century B.C.) sites at Luang Prabang and the megaliths of Tran Ninh and Xieng Khouang, an enduring architecture evolved in the late sixteenth century from Thai and Burmese forms, as in **Luang Stupa, Vientiane** and at **Luang Prabang.**

BIBLIOGRAPHY

BURMA

AUNG, U HTIN. *Folk Elements in Burmese Buddhism.* London, 1962.
BEYLIE, L. DE. *Prome et Samara.* Paris, 1907.
COLLIS, M. *The Land of the Great Image.* London, 1943.
DUROISELLE, C. *Guide to Mandalay Palace.* Calcutta, 1931.
GRISWOLD, A. B., KIM, C. and POTT, P. H. *Burma, Korea, Tibet.* London, 1964.
HALL, D. G. E. *Burma.* London, 1950.
HARVEY, G. E. *History of Burma.* London, 1925.
LUCE, G. H. *The Greater Temples of Pagan . . .* Rangoon, 1970.
O'CONNOR, V. C. SCOTT. *Mandalay and other Cities of the Past in Burma.* London, 1907.
ROWLAND, B. *The Art and Architecture of India.* Harmondsworth and Baltimore, 1953.
TIN, U PE MAUNG, and LUCE, G. H. *The Glass Chronicle.* London, 1923.
WIN, U LU PE. *Pictorial Guide to Pagan.* Rangoon, 1955.
YULE, SIR H. *Narrative of the Mission to the Court of Ava in 1855.* London, 1858.
Other sources include the *Annual Reports* and *Memoirs* of the Archaeological Survey of India; the *Reports* of the Superintendant, Archaeological Survey of Burma; the *Journal of the Burma Research Society*; the *Bulletins de l'École française d'Extrême Orient.*

CAMBODIA

BRIGGS, L. P. *The Ancient Khmer Empire.* Philadelphia, 1951.
COEDÈS, G. *Inscriptions du Cambodge.* 6 vols. Hanoi and Paris, 1937–54.
FINOT, L., GOLOUBEW, V., COEDÈS, G. and others. *Le Temple d'Angkor Vat.* 7 vols. Paris, 1929–32.
GITEAU, M. *Histoire du Cambodge.* Paris, 1957.
GLAIZE, M. *Les monuments du Groupe d'Angkor.* Paris, 1963 and Saigon, 1944.
GROSLIER, B. P. *Angkor, hommes et pierres.* Grenoble, 1968.
—. *Art and Civilization of Angkor.* New York, 1957.

—. *Art of the World: Indo-China.* London, 1962.
MALLERET, L. *L'Archéologie du Delta du Mékong.* 3 vols. Paris, 1959–60.
PORÉE-MASPERO, G., and E. *Traditions and Customs of the Khmers.* New Haven, 1953.
RÉMUSAT, G. DE CORAL. *L'Art Khmer: les grandes étapes de son évolution.* Paris, 1912, 1940.
'S.O.S. Angkor', *UNESCO Courier.* December, 1971.
STERN, P. *Les monuments khmers du style du Bayon et Jayavarman VII.* Paris, 1965.
STIERLIN, H. *Angkor.* Fribourg, 1970.
WALES, H. G. QUARITSCH. *Towards Angkor.* London, 1937.

THAILAND

COEDÈS, G. *New Archaeological Discoveries in Siam.* Vol. iv of *Indian Art and Letters.* London, 1930.
EMBREE, J. F., and DOTSON, L. O. *Bibliography of the Peoples and Culture of Mainland South-East Asia.* New Haven, Conn., 1950.
GRAHAM, W. *Siam: A Handbook.* 2 vols. London, 1924.
GRISWOLD, A. B. 'The Architecture and Sculpture of Siam: A Handbook to the Arts . . .', Catalogue of the Exhibition in the USA, 1960–2.
—. *Siam and the Sinhalese Stupa.* Colombo, 1964.
HUTCHINSON, E. W. *Reconstitution d'Ayuthya au temps de Phaulkon.* Saigon, 1946.
LE MAY, R. *Buddhist Art in Siam.* London, 1938.
LOUBÈRE, M. DE LA. *A New Historical Relation of the Kingdom of Siam.* Paris, 1961, London, 1963.
MOUHOT, H. *Voyage dans les royaumes de Siam, de Cambodge, de Laos.* Paris, 1968.
ROWLAND, B. *The Art and Architecture of India.* Harmondsworth and Baltimore, 1953.
SALMONY, A. *La Sculpture du Siam.* Paris, 1925.
WELLS, K. E. *Thai Buddhism: its Rites and Activities.* Bangkok, 1939.
WOOD, W. A. R. *A History of Siam.* Bangkok, 1933.

INDONESIA AND THE MALAY ARCHIPELAGO

COEDÈS, G. *The Indianized States of South-East Asia.* Honolulu, 1968.
COOMARASWAMY, A. K. *History of Indian and Indonesian Art.* New York, 1927.
COVARRUBIAS, M. *Island of Bali.* New York, 1937.
FRÉDÉRIC, L. *Sud-Est Asiatique: ses temples, ses sculptures.* Paris, 1964.
GANGOLY, O. C. *The Art of Java.* Calcutta, 1928.
HALL, D. G. E. *A History of South-East Asia.* London, 1964.
HARRISON, B. *South-East Asia, A Short History.* London, 1954.
HEEKEREN, H. R. VAN. *The Stone Age of Indonesia.* The Hague, 1958.
—. *The Bronze Age of Indonesia.* The Hague, 1958.
HEINE-GELDERN, R. VON. Introduction: Catalogue of the Exposition of 'Indonesian Art'. New York, 1948.
KROM, N. J. *Barabudur: Archaeological Description.* The Hague, 1927.
LOEB, E. M., and HEINE-GELDERN, R. VON. *Sumatra: its History and People.* Vienna, 1935.
MAY, R. LE. *The Culture of South-East Asia.* London, 1954.
MOORHEAD, F. J. *A History of Malaya and her Neighbours.* London, 1957.
ROWLAND, B. *The Art and Architecture of India.* Harmondsworth and Baltimore, 1953.
TWEEDIE, M. W. F. *Prehistoric Malaya.* Singapore, 1955.
WAGNER, F. A. *Indonesia.* London, 1959.
WALES, H. G. QUARITSCH. *Pre-History and Religion in South-East Asia.* London, 1957.
WINDSTEDT, SIR R. *The Malays.* London, 1953.
WITH, K. *Java.* The Hague, 1920.
ZIMMER, H. *Myths and Symbols in Indian Art and Civilization.* New York, 1946.
—. *The Art of Indian Asia.* New York, 1955.
ZOETE, B. DE, and SPIES, W. *Dance and Drama in Bali.* 2nd ed. London, 1952.

7

ARCHITECTURE IN CHINA

Third century B.C. to present day

INFLUENCES

GEOGRAPHICAL

The Republic of China, comprising twenty-three provinces and the autonomous regions of Inner Mongolia and Sinkiang-Uigur, covers an area larger than the whole of Europe and equal to nearly one-thirteenth of the total land area of the world. The great bulk of transport in South China is still carried on inland waterways as it has been for centuries, including the great rivers Yangtze and Si Kiang, and their tributaries supplemented by canals. Wheeled transport supersedes water transport north of the Tsinling Mountains, and has done so ever since the development of the 'Silk Road' from Changan 2,415 km (1,500 miles) to Balkh in Afghanistan at the time of Pan Ch'ao (A.D. 32–102). A programme of railway construction was commenced in the twentieth century and continued in the 1930s with the construction of great trunk lines in the north, while in July 1956 the great Paochi–Chengtu railway, 676 km (420 miles) long, was completed. The country is mountainous, with extensive fertile valleys in the middle and south-east, and great plains in the north. The many excellent harbours promoted maritime contact with South-East Asia in early times, and with the West during the last two centuries.

GEOLOGICAL

Coal is widely distributed, but the country is deficient in iron and petroleum; in the south tin, copper, zinc, antimony, tungsten, manganese and mercury are abundant. The soil in the north is chiefly loess and alluvium with a marked absence of trees; further south on the west of the Yangtze gorges there are many pine trees, chestnuts and maples. Red sandstone is characteristic of Szechwan, where the dominant trees are nanmu, paulownia, catalpa and broussonetia, the paper mulberry tree. South of the Tsinling the bamboo tree is cultivated extensively. Sedimentary rocks exist in South West China on the high plateau, and jungle vegetation is prolific in the valleys. The mulberry tree, which has no direct influence on architecture as a structural timber, created the ancient and prosperous silk industry which initiated Chinese contacts with the Western World at the time the Roman Empire was at its height. Timber is the principal material in Chinese architecture; bamboo, pine and the Persea nanmu, the tallest and straightest of all the trees in China; it was floated down the Yangtze River in trunks to serve as columns in palaces and temples in Peking. Bricks from the clay of the river plains were also used, as well as limestone and sandstone; but brick and stone were never considered as important as timber. A standard work on architecture, *Ying Tsao Fa Shih* (*The Method of Architecture*) published by Imperial order in the year A.D. 1103 refers only to stonework as a material fit for use in thresholds, stairs, balusters, engineering works, etc., and disregards brick altogether. Roofs were covered with clay tiles, coloured and glazed with symbolic colours, black, red, azure, white and yellow.

CLIMATIC

The mountain ranges leave the north unprotected from the cold strong winter winds from Mongolia, which, sweeping down from Asia produce severe winters with an average January temperature in Peking of $-5°$ C. Further south it is warmer, and the winter temperature is equivalent to an English summer. Because the country extends from latitude $45°$ to latitude $20°$ north of the Equator, it experiences a range of climate varying from extreme cold to almost tropical. The north-east and south-westerly monsoons sweep across the country in summer and winter, yielding the heaviest rainfall in the summer, averaging from 1 to 1.5 m (40 to 60 ins) per year. These climatic conditions are partly responsible for the characteristic Chinese roof with its accentuated curved eaves. Heating of buildings was often provided by charcoal burners without flues or fire-places; beds, raised on a dais (kang), were heated underneath with burning charcoal.

HISTORICAL, SOCIAL AND RELIGIOUS

Chinese archaeology is still in its infancy, and scanty records make it difficult to establish accurate dates until about 720 B.C. Before that time dynastic history is legendary and includes the Emperor Fu-hsi (2852 B.C.) who, it is claimed, evolved social order out of chaos. Fu-hsi was followed by Shên Nung, who introduced agricultural implements and discovered medicine. He was succeeded by Huang Ti, the Yellow Emperor, who consolidated the Empire, enlarged its boundaries, and introduced extensive reform and social improvements. Of a succession of emperors that followed, the most outstanding was the great Yao who, with his successor Shun, stands at the dawn of Chinese history as a model of all wisdom and sovereign virtue. The dynasties Hsia (2205–1766 B.C.), Shang or Yin (1766–1122 B.C.) followed, until the Chou (1122 B.C.) and first Emperor Wu Wang, started an era of great expansion of culture and territory; but expansion brought distintegration; the power of central government declined and feudalism flourished, resulting in the break-down of the Empire into a number of warring states similar in many respects to Europe in the Middle Ages. In the sixth century B.C. this political deterioration seems to have contributed to the emergence of theorists, thinkers and schools of philosophy. Among these, Confucius sought to bring a new order by his code of ethics and education, and contemporary with him was Lao Tzŭ, reputed founder of Taoism. There were other influential philosophers of vigorous thought, but the Chou dynasty, which had survived in an effete form and with much-shrunken dominions, continued to decline until it disappeared and was replaced by the Ch'in (255–206 B.C.), the fourth emperor of which, Shih Huang Ti, styled himself the First Emperor, and founded a new and homogeneous empire on the ruins of the old feudal system. He divided the Empire into thirty-six provinces, and built a vast palace by forced labour at Hsien Yang; he also constructed by forced and convict labour fortifications including part of the Great Wall against barbarian invasion. He suppressed opposition and criticism by destroying records of all opposing ideas and doctrines, and imposed his will by harsh discipline. He built roads, extended canals, and laid the foundations of a great Empire, which found full expression in the succeeding dynasty, the Han (206 B.C.–A.D. 220) which so developed the economic and cultural state of the Empire that at the time of the Emperor Kuang Wu Ti, it vied with the Roman Empire of Hadrian as the most powerful state on the face of the earth. During this time trade routes were developed and commerce in silk, cloth, furs, rhubarb and cinnamon was carried on extensively with the Roman Empire, Persia, India and other Asiatic countries, and Eastern Turkestan became a Chinese colony. There was an exchange of ideas, an influx of foreign culture, and the

China

introduction of Buddhism. Confucianism and Taoism were revived, and the capital
was moved first to Changan and thence to Loyang. In A.D. 284 the Roman Emperor
Diocletian sent ambassadors to China. But the dynasty weakened and the Han
was followed by three and a half centuries of disunion, until the Empire was reunited in the T'ang (A.D. 618–907) when, under the leadership of the second
Emperor T'ai Tsung (A.D. 627–49), it became more powerful than before. An
alliance with the Turks was purchased, just as the Emperor Justinian had done in
A.D. 558. Eastern Persia was regained up to the Caspian Sea. Ambassadors from
Persia and Constantinople went on a mission to the Emperor in 645. Foreign
traders came by land and sea, and Chinese goods were on sale in Baghdad; Nesto-
rian Christians, Jews, Moslems and Persians were seen in the streets of Canton.
But the Chinese were forbidden by Imperial rescript from going abroad, and their
architecture consequently suffered little influence from the expansion of trade.
Buddhism reached its peak and stimulated the arts and influenced architectural
form; painting probably reached the highest point in Chinese history with an
emphasis on calligraphy and the use of the brush. Printing was introduced; books
printed in 868 have been found in the grottoes of Tun-huang. The Sung dynasty
followed the T'ang, with capitals at K'aifêng and Hangchow; from 960–1279 the
cultural developments of the T'ang were maintained, and the first book on architecture was issued in 1103. But the dynasty succumbed to the military superiority
of Kublai Khan (Emperor Shih Tsŭ) the Mongol, who founded the Yüan (Mongol)
dynasty which flourished until A.D. 1368. China reached her greatest prestige and,
with the exception of Hindustan, Arabia and Western Asia, all the Mongol princes

as far as the Dnieper were her tributaries. The Grand Canal was completed, and Chinese influence spread further west as a result of the exploration of Marco Polo. With the collapse of the Mongol Empire in 1368 there was a wave of xenophobia, and with the Chinese dynasty of the Ming (1368–1644) foreign trade and influence declined.

The first Ming Emperor was Hung-Wo; he established .his capital at Nanking (southern capital), and his successor Yung-Lo founded the northern capital Peking, and laid out the city as one of the outstanding architectural conceptions of the world. The ban on foreigners was lifted, and penetration by Jesuit missionaries initiated a gradual infiltration of Western culture and ideas, which eventually transformed the social structure of the Empire. Manchus overthrew the Ming, and established the Ch'ing dynasty in 1644, which survived until 1912. K'ang Hsi (1661–1721) added Tibet to the Empire and published the Dictionary of the Chinese language. Ch'ien Lung (1735–95), who received Lord Macartney as Britain's first ambassador, invaded Burma, Cochin-China and Nepal, and crushed a Moslem rebellion. England's declaration of war against China in 1840 marked the beginning of active European intervention. In 1873 foreign ministers secured the right of audience with the Emperor. A noteworthy feature of the Ch'ing is the increasing influence and progressive encroachment of Western traders. To the Chinese the Westerners were barbarians, and their ideas and influences strongly resisted. But, after the formation of the Republic in 1912, China adopted the calendar of the West and began to introduce a system of education substantially inspired by American theories. The old culture and philosophies yielded to Western methods, and industrialization gained a tentative foothold. In 1937 a life-and-death struggle opened with Japan, and in 1941 (so-called) Nationalist China joined the 'Allies' in the Second World War. In 1949 the Nationalist Government collapsed, the Communists seized control and the People's Republic of China was proclaimed. Withdrawing to the island of Formosa (Taiwan) under Chiang Kai-Shek, the Nationalists have continued to seek support from the Chinese on the mainland, but with no success.

The main religious and ethical influences in China have been Confucianism (Confucius, 551–479 B.C.), Taoism and Buddhism. Confucianism was a new code of social conduct and a philosophy of life; it was not a religion as we understand it; it laid stress on the family and ancestor worship; it was a doctrine of the 'Middle Way'. Taoism attempted to transcend Confucianism and was founded at about the same time, probably by Lao Tzǔ in the fourth to the third century B.C., who offered a doctrine of universal love as his solution to social disorder. It encompassed mysticism and superstition and was readily combined with Buddhism when that religion spread to China from India in the second century A.D. by way of the three trade routes from India. By the first century A.D., Buddhist monks and laymen were living in China, and built a temple at Anhui in A.D. 190. Buddhism developed rapidly after the downfall of the Han (A.D. 221) and exerted a great influence on architectural expression. The combination of Confucianism, Taoism and Buddhism has produced concepts of the universe and beliefs about the future closely allied with superstition, astrology and necromancy which have controlled the planning of society and of cities as well as of the design of buildings. A pseudo-science, 'fêng shui', evolved, which was based on a belief that forces exist in every locality which act on all types of buildings, towns and cities, for good or ill, and sites were chosen or adapted accordingly. With the impact of the West, starting with the Jesuit mission in 1582, Christian influence also developed. Confucianism gradually disintegrated and ancestor worship declined. The considerable Moslem minority in China contributed little to architecture.

ARCHITECTURAL CHARACTER

The architecture of China is a faithful index of her civilization, for both were practically stationary for many centuries. Of the fine arts as understood in the West, only painting was recognized by the Chinese; sculpture, architecture and the crafts were regarded as artisan work. The art was poetic rather than material; the Chinese revelled in the beauty of nature and had little feeling for architectural design, which they held subservient to human needs. The Chinese had little religious zeal, and therefore few great temples; no territorial aristocracy and therefore no noble country houses; little of that pride which erects town mansions, while their domestic architecture was trammelled by sumptuary laws to mark the social status of the owner. Yet, within these limitations, Chinese architecture has held its own as an indigenous style from the early centuries until at least the middle of this century.

The roof was the chief feature, supported on timber uprights and independent of the walls, which were often useless for support as were the large traceried windows of the European Gothic style. The roofs contrast strongly with the Greek, Roman and Renaissance styles, in which there is often an evident endeavour to hide the roof, whereas the Chinese roof-ridges are laden with elaborate ornamental cresting and the up-tilted angles are adorned with fantastic dragons and grotesque ornament. It is considered a sign of dignity to place roofs one over the other, and this system also serves to protect the interior from extremes of heat and cold. The framing of the characteristic T'ing roof with 'I'rimoya' gables is of open timber construction and is supported on wooden posts independent of the enclosing walls (pp. 153, 154). Roofs, which are concave in section, are generally covered with enamelled tiles of S shape (pantiles) set in mortar, which is also used to form cover-joints as a protection from the driving winds (p. 153). The roof-framing consists of a system of trusses in rigid rectangles (not triangles as in Europe) formed of bamboos held together by wooden tenons, and thus the weight of the roof acts vertically and no oblique thrust comes on the walls (p. 154H, K). The lightness and strength of bamboo were important factors in influencing a system of construction quite different from the framed European roof-truss. The connection between the roof and the pillars which sustained it is often strengthened by brackets, and the soffits are often divided into square or octagonal coffers by means of raised ribs with brass socketings at their intersection. The use of bright colours, applied in the form of glazed tiles and porcelain, is a characteristic of Chinese buildings; the colours were symbolic of Chinese rites. 'Pai-lous' or gateways, of stone and wood, derived from Indian 'toranas', are features of Chinese architecture and, like many others, were only erected by government permission (p. 153C), sometimes as entrances to temples and tombs, sometimes as monuments to the dead, and sometimes to stand across a street. They consist of two or more upright posts with horizontal frieze, making one, two or three openings, sometimes surmounted by a series of brackets like those under temple eaves. Towers in stone, square like those in the Great Wall, are of early date, and show the influence of Mesopotamia in the use of arch and vault. The pagoda, the most typical Chinese building, is usually octagonal in plan, with thirteen storeys and repeated roofs, highly coloured, and with upturned eaves.

The Chinese built mainly in timber; brick and timber were sometimes combined, and most wooden buildings are raised on a stone or brick platform as a protection against damp, while stone was reserved for special structures and the walls of important edifices. Bricks sometimes have a glazed coloured surface and walls are also faced with glazed tiles or majolica. Walls are often constructed hollow, as described by Sir William Chambers (1757), thus saving material and effecting a more equable temperature in the house. Doorways are square-headed, but varied in outline by fretted pendants from the horizontal timbers. Windows are of similar form, suiting the rectangular framing of timber posts or the lashing together of bamboos. They are frequently filled in with the lining of the oyster shell, which is as transparent as talc and admits an effective subdued light. Rice paper was also used instead of glass in windows.

Chinese building procedure as applied to columns is peculiar, and is the reverse of that in other countries. Instead of first raising the columns and framing the superstructure upon them, the Chinese made the framework of the roof and this determined the position of the columns, which were often of nanmu wood, while the rigidity of the framework and roof-beams was relied on to keep the columns in position on the stone foundations. In short, instead of putting the roof on the columns, they put the columns under the roof (p. 154G, M, N). It was therefore essential that the roof-beams should be tenoned direct at the various heights into the shaft, without the intervention of a second member or capital, which was therefore omitted, but the roof-beams were supported by brackets, often multiplied in number and ornate in character. Chinese columns, whether for temples, pai-lous, palaces or houses, are unique, for in all other styles the capital is one of the most important architectural features. Columns, whether free-standing, as in palace halls, or carried up as an integral part of the wall, were without capitals, and were bound direct to the roof-beams of the rectangular-framed roof which presses vertically down on them, and thus columns and roofs are the chief features of the T'ing type of building, in which the walls are of no constructive value.

Chinese ornament (p. 154) expresses national characteristics. All Eastern nations appear to have a natural instinct for colour, and the Chinese are no exception. Colour schemes form an integral part of Chinese architecture; roofs are covered with brightly glazed tiles in symbolic colours, while the outstanding ridges and hips are emphasized with highly coloured dragons, fishes and grotesque figures in glazed terra-cotta. Coloured ornament is applied to buildings in the form of enamelled glazed tiles, painted woodwork, landscape and figure subjects. The Chinese excel in the minor arts, in silk- and cotton-weaving, in carvings of wood and ivory, and in porcelain ware. The Chinese sense for art found its outlet not in architecture, but in painting, of which from early times there were several great schools. The Chinese were past masters in the use of the brush, with which they produced a wonderful fineness of line, as is seen in their calligraphy, for which they used a soft brush instead of a hard stylo. Thus it was that their decoration in architecture took the form of colour applied to surfaces on which were painted landscapes, birds and flowers. Mahayana Buddhism encouraged mystery and symbolism, and the great yellow dragon and the tiger were freely introduced into decorative colour schemes.

EXAMPLES

TEMPLES

Buddhist temples resemble those of India, consisting of successive open courts and porticoes with kitchens, refectories, and sleeping cells for the priests. The normal type consists of three lofty pavilions of one storey, with parallel open timber roofs, approached by broad flights of steps, gateways and bridges.

The **Temple of Heaven (Ch'i Nien Tien), Peking** (A.D. 1420), circular and triple-roofed, with roofs covered with deep cobalt-blue glazed tiles, dominates the Ch'i Ku T'an or altar of prayer for grain, open to the sky with three tiers of marble steps and balustrades. The temple, facing south, is 30 m (99 ft) high with the upper roof supported by four gigantic columns, and the lower roofs by twelve columns, all straight trunks of nanmu trees. Founded by the Ming Emperor Yung-Lo it has been rebuilt correctly in every detail in recent years. To the south is the **Great Altar of Heaven,** the most sacred of all Chinese religious structures, consisting of marble terraces and nine circles of nine marble stones symbolizing Chinese numerical philosophy. There are other single-roofed temples, of which one is the 'Hall of Central Peace', and another the **Temple of Agriculture** (p. 154D). In all these circular buildings there is the characteristic bracket frieze under the widely projecting eaves.

The **Temple of Honan, Canton** (p. 154N), is a typical Buddhist temple, enclosed by a wall with gateway, porch, ante-chapel, successive halls and sanctuary with the Buddha and seats for the monks, a 'dagoba', offices and kitchens beyond.

The **Temple of the Sleeping Buddha, near Peking,** built of brick in two storeys, is unusual in having circular-headed windows in a clear-storey as well as in the ground storey. The columns are faced with glazed bricks, and between them are niches with the statue of Buddha; the roof has an elaborate cresting with finials and flamboyant dragons (p. 153A).

Most Chinese temples, however, are of the simple T'ing type as exemplified in the **Sacrificial Hall of Yung-Lo** (fifteenth century A.D.) near Peking, consisting of a concave roof on uprights, covered with brilliant coloured tiles, yellow at the temple of the earth, red at the temple of the sun, bluish-white at the temple of the moon. There are monastery temples containing the image of the Buddhist triad— just as in England there were monastic churches—surrounded by a wall and approached through the typical 'pai-lou' or gateway. The whole monastic group consists of temple, 'dagoba' or relic shrine, bell-tower, pagoda, library, and dwellings for the monks. There are also ancestral temples such as the Confucian Temple in the Kuo Tzu Chien, Peking, and mosques which resemble the Buddhist temples.

PAGODAS

The pagodas (t'ai), derived from Indian prototypes, are distributed in considerable numbers over the country and form the most important structures in the temple enclosures (pp. 153B, 154E). They vary from three to fifteen storeys in height, the number being uneven in every case and very often thirteen, sometimes with staircases to each floor, and were probably originally constructed in timber; those that remain are mostly of brick, the timber structures having perished. Pagodas had formerly a religious significance, but those erected latterly are secular in character and are sometimes monuments to victory; they are often associated with fêng-shui to insure good fortune. They are frequently polygonal in plan and the roof slopes to each storey, and are elaborately ornamented.

The **Pagoda, Sung Yüeh Ssü, Honan** (c. A.D. 523), is the oldest pagoda still standing in China; constructed of brick and mud on an octagonal base, it rises to a height of about 27 m (90 ft) in fifteen blind storeys.

The **Porcelain Pagoda, Yüan Ming Yüan, near Peking,** is a fine example of glazed faience after the style of the famous porcelain pagoda at Nanking (p. 154E) which was destroyed by the Taiping rebels in A.D. 1854. The whole of the brick walls and projecting roof eaves are clothed in coloured porcelain tiles, glazed in five colours, deep purplish-blue, rich green, yellow, sang de boeuf red, and turquoise-blue, which were intended to suggest the five jewels of Buddhist paradise. Conspicuous amongst many other pagodas are the Pa Li Chuan Pagoda, near Peking (thirteenth century A.D.) of thirteen storeys; the Nan t'a at Fang Shan, Chih-li

A. Temple of the Sleeping Buddha, in the Summer Palace, near Peking.
See p. 152

B. Typical Chinese pagoda. See p. 152   C. A typical pai-lou. See p. 155

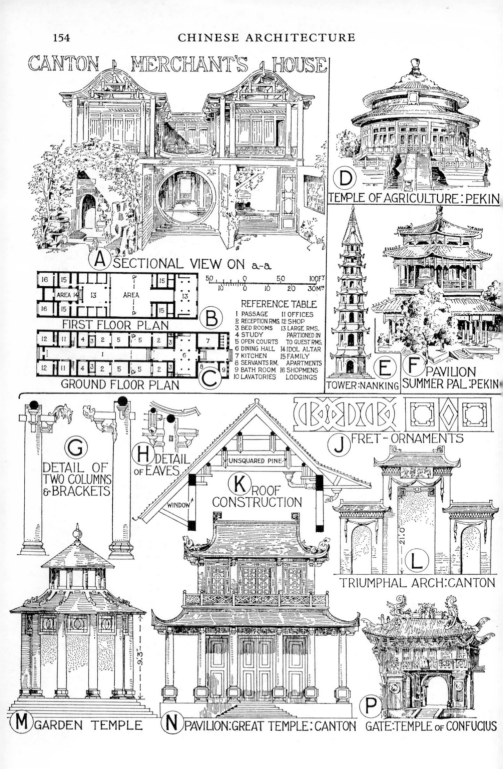

CANTON MERCHANT'S HOUSE

A SECTIONAL VIEW ON a-a

B FIRST FLOOR PLAN

C GROUND FLOOR PLAN

16	15			15
	AREA 14	13	AREA	13
16	15			15

12	11	4	3	2	5	2	5	7
			1		6			
12	11	4	3	2	5	2	5	7
							8	9

50   50   100 FT
10   0   10   20   30 M?

REFERENCE TABLE

1 PASSAGE — 11 OFFICES
2 RECEPTION RMS. — 12 SHOP
3 BED ROOMS — 13 LARGE RMS.
4 STUDY — PARTIONED IN
5 OPEN COURTS — TO GUEST RMS.
6 DINING HALL — 14 IDOL ALTAR
7 KITCHEN — 15 FAMILY
8 SERVANTS RM. — APARTMENTS
9 BATH ROOM — 16 SHOPMENS
10 LAVATORIES — LODGINGS

D TEMPLE OF AGRICULTURE: PEKIN

E TOWER: NANKING

F PAVILION SUMMER PAL: PEKIN

G DETAIL OF TWO COLUMNS & BRACKETS

H DETAIL OF EAVES

J FRET-ORNAMENTS

K ROOF CONSTRUCTION
UNSQUARED PINE
WINDOW

L TRIUMPHAL ARCH: CANTON
21.0"

M GARDEN TEMPLE
9.3"

N PAVILION: GREAT TEMPLE: CANTON

P GATE: TEMPLE OF CONFUCIUS

(eleventh century A.D.) of eleven storeys; the Pei t'a at Fang Shan, Chih-li (eighth century A.D.); the pagoda at Ling Kuang Ssü, near Peking (seventh century A.D.) of thirteen storeys, built of brick upon stone foundations; and others at Hangchow, and Foochow, where the White Pagoda of seven storeys dominates the town. There are the Great Pagoda, the Twin Pen Pagodas—reputed to be 1,000 years old—and the Ink Pagoda, 37 m (120 ft) high, all at Soochow, and others at Shanghai, Ningpo, Nanking and Peking. There is a somewhat lifeless example in Kew Gardens designed by Sir William Chambers, and there are models in the Indian Museum, South Kensington.

PAI-LOUS

The pai-lous of China (p. 153C) bear a family resemblance to the toranas of India (cf. the Sanchi stupa, p. 94) and the torii of Japan, and were erected by special authority as memorials to deceased persons of distinction. They were constructed of wood or stone and have one or three openings, formed by posts supporting horizontal rails bearing an inscription and often crowned with bold projecting roofs of symbolical coloured tiles. The pai-lou which spans the avenue leading to the **Temple of the Sleeping Buddha,** near Peking, is a magnificent example with three arches in sculptured marble, separated by vermilion stucco walls with panelled faience enamelled in yellow, green and blue, in the centre of which is the inscribed marble tablet. The all-timber pai-lou at the lake of the Summer Palace, Peking, is a characteristic example of another form of pai-lou which marks the entrance to a sacred or beautiful place; the marble pai-lou at the **Altar of Heaven, Peking,** shows the type of structure which is one of the most salient features of Chinese architectural design, upon which was lavished all possible richness of decoration.

TOMBS

Tombs, though associated with ancestor-worship and therefore sacred, are not of great architectural value because the pai-lous were the real memorial monuments. Tombs are sometimes cone-shaped mounds surrounded by stones, sometimes cut in the rock or designed in the hillside, with a horseshoe back in stone sloping to the front and covered with symbolic carvings, while mythical animals guard the entrance.

The **Tombs of the Ming Dynasty** (A.D. 1368–1644), north of Peking, are entered through triumphal gateways or pai-lous of white marble and along an avenue a mile in length, flanked by thirty-two monolithic figures some 3.6 m (12 ft) high of camels, horses, priests, elephants, lions and griffins. Each of the thirteen tombs consists of an earthen mound, half a mile in circumference, supported by a retaining wall over 6 m (20 ft) high, and they seem to be founded on such monuments as the Sanchi stupa in India (p. 94).

The **Tomb of Yung-lo, Peking** (A.D. 1425), consists of a tumulus, surrounded by a crested wall with a three-storeyed tower, two entrance gateways, and an ancestral hall of the T'ing type in the entrance court.

PALACES

Imperial palaces and official residences were erected as isolated, one-storeyed pavilions resembling temples in general design, and crowned with the typical roof, but these detached buildings are not imposing as are the large homogeneous palaces of Europe, except for their landscaping.

The **Imperial Palace, Peking,** situated in the centre of the 'Forbidden City', has three vast halls, all similar in design, of magnificent proportions and resplendent in oriental decoration. The 'Tai Ho Tien' Hall of Highest Peace (A.D. 1602) is the most important, with terraces and open verandahs, and is formed of nave and aisles, parallel to the façade, separated by great columns, with the Imperial dais at the centre. A Pavilion (p. 154F) of the Summer Palace, Peking, destroyed A.D. 1860, gives an idea of some of the smaller buildings. Within the enclosing wall there were residences for emperor and officers of state, and the groups of buildings were set amidst pleasure gardens, lakes and grottoes on a magnificent scale.

HOUSES

Houses, generally of one storey like the temples, are constructed with timber supports, filled in with brickwork (p. 150). The building regulations not only governed the dimensions, but also the number of columns, and thus had a marked effect on the plan and arrangement of Chinese houses; for, while the Emperor had his hall of nine bays, a prince was restricted to seven, a mandarin to five and an ordinary citizen to three bays. Roofs are of a steep pitch with boldly projecting eaves and highly ornamented ridges of coloured and glazed tiles, with the angles turned up and finished with grotesque animals or fantastic ornament. The roof-framing in bamboo and other wood is frequently painted red, green or blue. The houses owe much of their character to their environment of gardens, planned to suggest a natural landscape, elaborated with fountains, artificial rocks, woodland scenery, lakes, flower-beds, hanging plants, bridges, watercourses, stepping-stones and garden temples (p. 154M). Town houses of importance are also made up of a collection of isolated pavilions, surrounded by gardens. Houses, like temples, face south; the front door opens into a courtyard with rooms on either side and a hall at the end, followed by another and often by a third or women's court with garden beyond; while all windows, as in French fortified châteaux, face inwards. There are three principal divisions, viz.: (a) vestibule or porter's lodge on the street; (b) audience chamber and family rooms; (c) kitchen and servants' rooms (p. 154A, B, C). The verandah or portico of wooden columns is a special feature of Chinese dwelling houses. Differing from the Japanese and Indian tradition of sitting on the floor with low furniture, the Chinese, from T'ang times at least, have used higher tables and chairs as in Europe.

BRIDGES

Bridges form conspicuous features in a country of rivers and waterways, and constitute the main architectural characteristic of the Chinese landscape; it has been estimated that there are about twelve bridges per square mile in many parts of the country, and about two and a half million altogether. They are of various types of construction and design, pontoon bridges, wooden truss bridges, stone bridges, arched bridges of brick and stone, cantilever bridges and suspension bridges. Pontoon bridges have been in use since the beginning of recorded history, a well-known example being that at Ningpo. Nearly as old as the pontoon bridge is the wooden truss bridge, and in the densely-forested mountainous districts of the country there are countless examples of this form of construction. In the area around the Yangtze delta, where natural stone is plentiful, bridges built of granite are numerous; the Chinese bridge-builders used this material to its maximum capacity, allowing no margin for safety. Stone truss bridges in spans less than 4–5 m (14–16 ft), and 2–3 m (6–10 ft) high above the water were the cheapest form of construction for narrow canals. They were also used for wider spans, such as the 'Bridge of 10,000 Ages', Foochow, built A.D. 1323, 390 m (1,270 ft) long and 4.4 m

(14 ft 6 ins) wide, with thirty-five intermediate piers and thirty-six spans; the 'Bridge of 10,000 Times Peace', at Tsienchowfu, built during the Sung Dynasty, is 1,154 m (3,780 ft) long and 4.9 m (16 ft) wide, with forty-seven spans. Normally, however, bridges of great length were arched; the arch is never skew, and the abutments are nearly always vertical; the arch stones are cut to fit each other exactly but are not radiating voussoirs. Mortar was seldom used either in the arch, abutments or foundations. Arches were usually circular, but pointed arches were sometimes used, as in a bridge at Yachowfu, Szechwan. The 'Jewel Belt' bridge, near Soochow, has fifty-three arches, all semicircular; the 'camel-back' bridge at the Summer Palace, Peking, has a pointed arch. In those parts of the country where tree trunks were easily obtainable, cantilever construction was popular; this incorporated stone abutments supporting piled up cantilevered wooden trunks which carried the horizontal roadway. In Western China, the use of bamboo rope encouraged the construction of suspension bridges with granite abutments and wooden intermediate supports with bamboo ropes; at Kwan Hsien there is a bridge of this kind 215 m (700 ft) long, with its longest span 61 m × 2.7 m (200 ft × 9 ft) wide, which is carried by ten bamboo cables each 164 mm (6½ ins) in diameter. The bamboo ropes have a breaking load of 1,800 kg per cm² (26,000 lbs. per sq. in). The Yangtze River Bridge (completed 1957), is one of the world's largest bridges, of 1,670 m (5,480 ft) total length with a clearance above the water level of 18 m (59 ft), constructed of concrete piers with a double-decker steel-and-concrete decking. It was built in twenty-six months.

THE GREAT WALL OF CHINA

The **'Great Wall'** (214 B.C.) (p. 148), the most famous of ancient Chinese building undertakings, is 2,260 km (1,400 miles) long, 6 to 9 m (20 to 30 ft) high, 7.6 m (25 ft) thick at the base, sloping to 4.5 m (15 ft) at the top. There are square towers at intervals in this immense mileage of masonry which, like Hadrian's Wall in Britain, follows the contours of the country, climbs mountain tops, descends deep gorges, strides across lofty table-lands, and spans wide rivers, like a huge serpent wrought in brick and stone. Recent investigations of the brick arches in the Wall have led to the conclusion that the Wall was originally an earth embankment faced with stone at a later date and that the brick arches in the passages and the watch towers originate from A.D. 1368, when the whole Wall was thoroughly repaired.

EPILOGUE

Since 1949 there has been a vast amount of construction in China, including commercial and industrial buildings, schools and colleges, hospitals, transport buildings, hotels, cinemas, theatres and housing. These buildings show a complete departure from Chinese tradition and exhibit (with a few exceptions) an unimaginative adaptation of Western Renaissance revivalism in concrete and stone. Only in a small number of structures is any semblance of Chinese individuality to be found.

BIBLIOGRAPHY

BOERSCHMANN, E. *Die Baukunst und religiöse Kultur der Chinesen*. Berlin, 1911.
—. *Chinesische Architektur*. 2 vols. Berlin, 1926.
BOYD, A. *Chinese Architecture and Town Planning, 1950 B.C.–A.D. 1911*. London, 1962.
CHAMBERS, SIR W. *Designs of Chinese Buildings*. London, 1757.
CHI, TSUI. *A Short History of Chinese Civilization*. London, 1942.

DE SILVA, A. *Chinese Landscape Painting.* London, 1967.

ECKE, G. *Chinese Domestic Furniture.* Hongkong, 1962.

FUGL-MEYER, H. *Chinese Bridges.* Shanghai, 1937.

GRATTAN, F. M. *Notes upon the Architecture of China.* London, 1894.

HEWLEY, W. M. (Ed.) *Chinese Folk Design.* Berkeley, 1949.

HILDEBRAND, H. *Der Tempel Ta-chüeh-sy bei Peking.* Berlin, 1897.

JONES, O. *Examples of Chinese Ornament.* London, 1867.

LATOURETTE, K. S. *The Chinese Civilization.* New York, 1941.

LI CHIEH. *Ying-tsao Fa Shih.* (Building methods and patterns; the Sung Manual of Architecture.) First produced in 1103; reproduced in colour 1925; printed in smaller format in Shanghai, 1957.

MIRAMS, D. G. *Brief History of Chinese Architecture.* Hongkong, 1940.

MÜNSTERBERG, O. *Chinesische Kunstgeschichte.* 2 vols. Esslingen, 1910–12.

NEEDHAM, J. *Science and Civilization in China.* Cambridge, 1954–.

PALÉOLOGUE, M. *L'Art chinois.* Paris, 1887.

PIRALOZZI-T'SERSTEVENS, M. *Living Architecture: Chinese.* Fribourg and London, 1972.

PRIP-MOELLER, J. *Chinese Buddhist Monasteries.* Copenhagen and London, 1937; Hongkong, 1967.

SICKMAN, L. and SOPER, A. *The Art and Architecture of China.* Harmondsworth and Baltimore, 1958.

SIRÉN, O. *The Imperial Palaces of Peking.* 3 vols. Paris, 1926.

—. *The Walls and Gates of Peking.* London, 1924.

—. *The Gardens of China.* New York, 1949.

SKINNER, R. T. F. (Translator). *Types and structural forms in Chinese architecture. General account of the Chinese House. Ming Dynasty house in Hui-chou.* Building and Public Works Publishing House, Peking, 1957.

SPEISER, W. *Art of the World: China.* London, 1962.

STEIN, SIR M. AUREL. *Ruins of Desert Cathay.* 2 vols. London, 1912.

TOKIWA, D., and SEKINO, T. *Buddhist Monuments in China.* Tokyo, 1930.

WATSON, W. *Archaeology in China.* London, 1960.

—. *China before the Han Dynasty.* London, 1961.

WU, N. I. *Chinese and Indian Architecture.* London and New York, 1963.

8

ARCHITECTURE IN JAPAN

Sixth century A.D. to present day

INFLUENCES

GEOGRAPHICAL

Japan, with its principal island, Honshiu, and attendant islands to north and south, lies off the eastern coast of Asia, from which it is separated by the Sea of Japan. The eastern shores of Japan are bounded by the Pacific Ocean. Geographically Japan has many points of resemblance to Great Britain; both lie opposite populous continents with indented coast-lines providing excellent harbours; both are at the head of important trade routes and across international lines of communication.

GEOLOGICAL

The prevalence of earthquakes in Japan has had a profound effect upon building development. Practically the whole of Japan is rugged hill country, and some four-fifths of the entire area is occupied by forests and wild vegetation. The land however, is one of very great natural beauty. There is probably a greater diversity of trees than in any other country. Bamboo is plentiful, and extensively used in building. Stone is mainly of volcanic origin and unstratified. Granites and porphyries are well represented, but there is a dearth of lime and sandstone. Stone is used for foundation work, or in polygonal form for the lower portions of walling, upon which would be erected an upper timber structure.

CLIMATIC

Japan is influenced by a cold airstream from Asia in winter, and by the incursion of warm moist air from the Pacific in the summer. The mountainous nature of the country, in conjunction with the prevailing airstreams, conduces to exceptionally heavy rainfall, particularly in the summer. Houses, wherever possible, face south and deeply projecting eaves are provided to give protection against the sun, while high courtyard walls screen the northern aspect from the cold winds of winter.

HISTORICAL, SOCIAL AND RELIGIOUS

The early history of Japan is obscure, but she can be credited with a degree of civilization even before the true historic period, which commenced about A.D. 400, when Chinese culture was introduced through Korea. By A.D. 500 the Japanese had become a distinctive race of people, but at a primitive state of development, with the population divided into isolated communities ruled by chieftains. These conditions led to intrigue among the rulers, superstition became rampant and abuses flourished. During the Suiko period (A.D. 552–645), Buddhism became firmly established and the nation tended to become a bureaucratic state with Chinese laws and ceremonial. Early written records, the Kojiki, a 'Record of Ancient Matters' (A.D. 712), and the Nihongi, the 'Japanese Chronicle' (A.D. 720), commence chronology with the Emperor Jimmu, who is reputed to have united Japan in 660 B.C. The

Mikado, as the most powerful chieftain, acquired certain prerogatives with which he eventually acquired full domination over the nation. It is reputed that by about 600, more than four hundred Buddhist temples had been erected. Nara became the capital in 710, and the city was laid out with nine gates, a palace and seven great temples. When Kioto became the capital in 794, the arts of domestic architecture and landscape gardening made great strides. Through many vicissitudes and in the face of open aggression, Buddhism gained in strength and fortified monasteries multiplied. Feudalism, at its height in the thirteenth century, recognized three groups—the Emperor and nobles, the Shoguns with the military caste, and the people. Under the Tokugawa dynasty (1603–1868), the divine descent of the Emperor was emphasized and actively promulgated. After continual strife, which at times resulted in civil war, the last of the Shoguns resigned in 1867. A constitution was formed in 1890 which eventually recognized the rights of the people. The representative government which emerged laid the foundations of the subsequent progressive position of Japan.

The Japanese have in the past tended towards a self-imposed isolationism, with exclusion of all foreign intercourse. Overseas trade was a government monopoly; thus there was no incentive for individual enterprise in foreign commerce. Some intercourse was established with Korea and China as early as the eighth century A.D., but it was not until 1543 that the Portuguese discovered and began trading with Japan. This was the first direct contact that the Japanese had with peoples of the Western World. Christianity was introduced in 1549 by S. Francis Xavier, but this missionary effort led to many conflicts. Envoys from Japan visited Europe in 1582. Korea was invaded by the Japanese in 1592. Despite these tentative contacts with the outer world, Japan reverted to isolationism and in 1614 all foreign priests were expelled. The Spaniards were driven out in 1624, and the Portuguese in 1638. Christianity was finally interdicted on the departure of the Portuguese, and then for a period of almost 200 years, Japan was closed to the outside world. Commercial treaties with America and European countries were, however, entered into in 1854, when Japan felt the effects of American enterprise and English institutions. Following these contacts came wars with China and Russia, while in 1914 Japan joined the alliance against Germany; but in 1941 she sided with the Axis powers.

Shinto was the Chinese name for the indigenous polydemonism which existed in Japan before the introduction of Buddhism. While Shintoism was without any well-defined moral code, it did lay great stress upon ancestor and nature worship. Image worship or elaborate temple buildings were uncalled for. The native Shinto faith was profoundly affected by Buddhism, introduced from the Chinese mainland about A.D. 550. Buddhism encouraged the erection of temples, and its mystic symbolism inspired the artistic Japanese temperament to the production of countless images of every possible size and fantastic form. The priesthood contributed greatly to the development of the country, even in road construction and bridge building, which by aiding communication between isolated localities greatly helped the unification of the country and strengthened the influence of the priesthood. Buddhism gradually became the paramount religious influence, but Shintoism was never extinguished, and in course of time was grafted upon the Buddhist faith. In relatively modern times Shintoism regained predominance, and by its tenets largely contributed to the fervent Japanese nationalism displayed in recent history.

ARCHITECTURAL CHARACTER

The architecture of Japan was largely derived from China, but at all times maintained its own special characteristics of lightness and delicacy. Refinement in

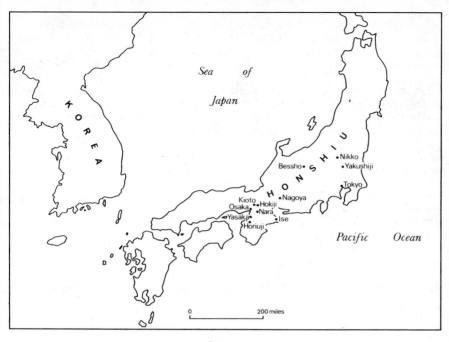

Japan

Japanese architecture, combined with minuteness in carving and decoration, are particularly noticeable in timber construction, where cumulative skill and artistry of generations of craftsmen render work in timber akin to fine joinery.

Notable are the dominant roofs, which form a striking contrast with practice in the Middle East and India, where flat terrace roofs predominate. While Japanese roofs bear a general resemblance to Chinese, they are as a rule simpler in treatment and possess more subtlety and refinement in outline. Characterized by their exquisite curvature, they are supported upon a succession of simple or compound brackets. The upper part of the roof is terminated by a gable placed vertically above the end walls, known as an 'I'rimoya' gable, while the lower part of the main roof is carried round the ends of the building in a hipped form (p. 162A, H). Roof coverings can be thatch, shingles or tiles. Thatched roofs often have a prominent ridge of tiles with an exaggerated cresting, or the ridge may be of stout bamboos, tied with blackened rope and terminated with finials. Tiled roofs have flattish and roll tiles alternately, while cover tiles, often of decorative form, are used to mask joints at the eaves. Ridges and hips are made up of layers of tiles set in mortar, finished with large moulded tile cappings and crestings. A lower roof, known as 'hisashi', is sometimes projected below the eaves of the main roof. Hollowed bamboos are used to form roof gutters and down pipes. Gable ends often have cusped barge-boards with pendants (p. 162H, J, M). Curved brackets ('Kumo-Hijiki') adorn the underside of the overhanging eaves. The subtle curvature of barge-boards and brackets has been compared to the shapes of certain cloud formations, and the resemblance is such as to indicate an inherent appreciation of natural beauty in the minds of the craftsmen.

Columns, which followed the Chinese form, are conspicuous in Japanese temples

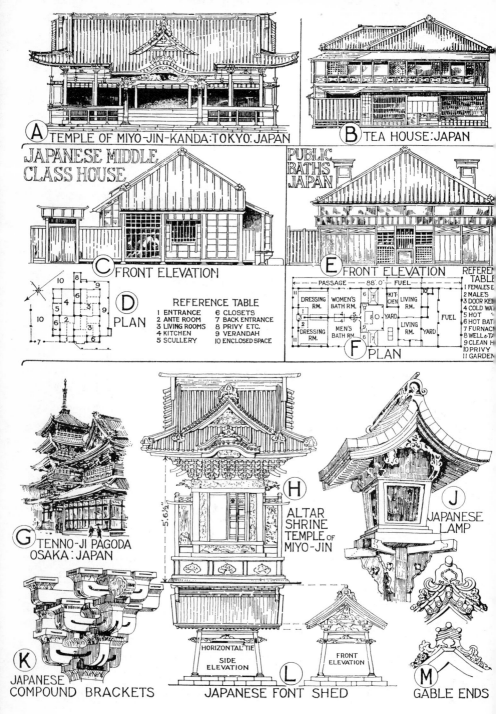

A TEMPLE OF MIYO-JIN-KANDA: TOKYO: JAPAN

B TEA HOUSE: JAPAN

JAPANESE MIDDLE CLASS HOUSE

PUBLIC BATHS JAPAN

C FRONT ELEVATION

D PLAN

REFERENCE TABLE
1 ENTRANCE   6 CLOSETS
2 ANTE ROOM   7 BACK ENTRANCE
3 LIVING ROOMS   8 PRIVY ETC.
4 KITCHEN   9 VERANDAH
5 SCULLERY   10 ENCLOSED SPACE

E FRONT ELEVATION

REFERENCE TABLE
1 FEMALES E
2 MALE'S
3 DOOR KEE
4 COLD WA
5 HOT
6 HOT BAT
7 FURNAC
8 WELL & TA
9 CLEAN H
10 PRIVY
11 GARDEN

PASSAGE — 88' 0" — FUEL

DRESSING RM.   WOMEN'S BATH RM.   KIT-CHEN   LIVING RM.   FUEL
DRESSING RM.   MEN'S BATH RM.   YARD   LIVING RM.   YARD

F PLAN

G TENNO-JI PAGODA OSAKA: JAPAN

H ALTAR SHRINE TEMPLE OF MIYO-JIN

5' 6½"

J JAPANESE LAMP

K JAPANESE COMPOUND BRACKETS

HORIZONTAL TIE
SIDE ELEVATION

FRONT ELEVATION

L JAPANESE FONT SHED

M GABLE ENDS

and in façades to palaces and gateways. Intercolumniation is regulated by the standard of measurement known as the 'ken', which is divided into twenty parts, termed minutes, and each minute being again divided into a further twenty-two parts or seconds of space. Columns, when square, are panelled and when round or octagonal are reeded and often richly lacquered. Even when plain, columns are objects of beauty, as timber was split by wedges and smoothed with a spear-shaped plane known as a 'Yariganna', which left a very beautiful finish.

Most houses are constructed of wood-framing with wood or stout paper infilling, which in an earthquake shock is much safer than stone or brick construction. Temple walling is a strictly trabeated arrangement of timber posts and rails dividing surfaces into regular oblong spaces, filled in with plaster, boarding or carved and painted panels (p. 162A). Light is introduced principally through doorways. A system of cornice-bracketing in both simple and complex forms is a very characteristic feature of Japanese buildings (pp. 162K, 166A). Standardized arrangements of this bracketing constitute various 'orders'. Immediately above the pillars or columns is a highly-decorated frieze, and above this, the bracketing consists of a series of projecting wooden corbels supporting horizontal members and rafters with decorated faces, thus allowing the roof to overhang the wall, often by as much as 2.5 m (8 ft). The disposition of columns, posts, brackets, and rafters forming the cornice is in accordance with well-recognized modules of measurement, while intercolumniation is governed by the 'ken'. Buildings are stilted upon stone piles to a height which would ensure timber being above ground water during the rainy season. The undersides of beams are frequently cambered to avoid any impression of sagging, while piers and columns are given a refined entasis and frequently an inward inclination to mitigate the effects of earthquake shocks.

Owing to the great projection of roofs over exterior walls, there is little direct natural light and the greater part of the light which reaches interiors is reflected from the ground. Window-openings are filled with timber trellis and provided with wooden shutters externally, and paper—usually rice-paper—in light sashes, internally. In all cases, exterior walling is extremely thin; columns receive the main load from the roof and wall panels are entirely non-structural.

Circumstances which led to a comparative absence of mouldings in Chinese architecture, apply also to Japanese work. Wall surfaces were admired for their own intrinsic beauty, and emphasis by surrounding mouldings was not required. The plain cyma and ovolo were introduced in column bases, but as there are no capitals they do not appear as decoration to the head of a column.

Carved and coloured panels formed in enclosure walls, in projecting eaves to roofs, and in the 'ramma' or pierced ventilators below cornices are characteristic. In friezes, panels in high relief occur, representing cloud forms and objects of natural beauty—the chrysanthemum, the stork and pine tree being typical subjects for motifs—which invariably carried a symbolic significance. Ornamental brass caps, usually gilded for preservation, are frequently fixed to the ends of projecting timbers and over connections in wood to hide open joints which may occur through shrinkage. Embossed gilded metalwork is also freely applied to gables and pendants. Colour decoration, introduced from China in the sixth century, is applied to both exteriors and interiors of Japanese temples. Beams, brackets, carvings and flat surfaces are picked out in gilding and bright colours—blue, green, purple, madder and vermilion—the last a particularly beautiful colour when subjected to weathering. Wall paintings frequently appear upon a gold ground, and usually depict animal forms, birds, insects and flowers. Supporting pillars are usually black, red or gold. Lacquering is extensively employed, and is applied with consummate skill. Subjects for decoration are birds, trees attended by idealistic mountain, cloud and water forms. Frequently, natural objects are combined with the weird and grotesque, resulting in a curious mixture of realistic and symbolic forms. Despite rigid conventions and disregard of perspective, Japanese genius for pure decoration has contrived to invest all major works of every period with vitality and dramatic presentation. The Japanese are noted too, for their meticulous treatment of detail. All the accessories of architectural design, lacquer work, ivory carving, enamels, faience and bronzes vie with each other in minute accuracy and softness of colour.

EXAMPLES

TEMPLES

Japanese temples, which were inspired by Chinese influence, do not rely upon monotonous repetition of similar features as in China, but owe much of their distinctive character to a well-balanced symmetry of component parts. Interiors are largely dependent on the justly world-famous decorative art of Japan. Decoration, with lavish use of gold lacquer and brilliant colouring, can cover both walls and ceilings, and is particularly suited to the subdued lighting of temple buildings.

Shinto temples can be distinguished from Buddhist by the characteristic 'torii' or gateways formed by upright posts supporting two or more horizontal beams, under which, it was considered, worshippers must pass for prayers to be effectual. Buddhist foundations are entered through an elaborate two-storeyed gateway, surmounted by a muniment room under an ornate roof (p. 165A). Temples usually have a columned loggia, either round three sides or forming a façade to the main building. Frequently there is a portico over the approach steps which rests upon timber columns, held together at the top by horizontal tie beams. In large temples and halls, the interior columns are provided with elaborate compound bracketing to support the roof.

Buddhist Temples at Horiuji (p. 165A), **Nara and Nikko,** like other examples, underwent little change from Chinese prototypes. The mountainous character of the country made it possible to utilize natural terraces for temple sites, instead of having to rely upon artificial, built-up platforms which are the rule in China. In Japan, avenues of trees, and rows of lanterns in both stone and bronze (p. 166A), produce picturesque and imposing effects in conjunction with buildings when viewed against the sombre background of wooded landscape. Generally, temples comprise isolated structures within concentric enclosures, the outer enclosure formed by a low wall, the second as a promenade for priests, and the third enclosing the main temple building surrounded by a lofty, roofed screen wall. Temples are invariably raised upon a stone foundation to a height of approximately 1.5 m (5 ft), and the sanctuary is reached by steps leading to a verandah covered by the projecting roof of the temple in the centre, a typical example being the **Temple of Miyo-Jin-Kanda, Tokyo** (p. 162A). In 1949, fire destroyed the main portion of the Temple at Horiuji, but this has now been faithfully restored to its original form; an example of Japanese reverence for tradition. Mortuary temples of the Shoguns at Tokyo are regarded as ranking among the more famous buildings of Japan.

The **Buddhist Temple of Hommonji, near Tokyo,** has a two-storey gateway and a reliquary, a library, reception hall and rooms for priests, besides a pagoda. Tiles were used for roofing of Buddhist temples, instead of the thatch customary on Shinto shrines.

The **Shinto shrine of Kamiji-Yama, in Ise** (p. 165B), comprises a series of single-storeyed buildings typical of other Shinto structures. While these shrines are commonly considered as being of little architectural importance, they are significant

A. Main entrance, Horiuji Temple, near Nara (7th cent.). See p. 164

B. The Shinto Shrine of Kamiji-Yama in Ise. See p. 164

A. Kasuga (Shinto) Shrine, Nara: gateway
with stone lanterns in foreground

B. Kofukuji Temple, Nara (1426):
Pagoda. See p. 167

C. Gateway, Tomb of Ieyasu, Nikko (17th cent.). See p. 167

as contributing to the picturesque element in the Japanese scene. The shrines in Ise offer another example of the national homage to tradition, for despite the fact that they are entirely rebuilt every twenty years, the shrines today remain exact replicas of original structures of the third–sixth centuries.

The **Kurodani Temple, Kioto,** is noted for its beautiful garden, and is surrounded by a cemetery with typical monuments.

PAGODAS

Pagodas followed in the wake of Buddhistic influence from China, but those now standing mainly date from the seventeenth century, and are adjuncts of important temples. They are square in plan, mostly five-storeyed and about 45 m (150 ft) in height. In construction, they are virtually suspended around a central timber post, thus providing a measure of stability against earthquake shock. The ground storey contains images and shrines, while the upper storeys serve as 'belvederes'. There are wide projecting roofs to each storey, and the subtle curvature distinguishes them from comparable Chinese examples.

The **Pagoda, Horiuji,** is the earliest example remaining, and is reputed to have been built by Koreans in 607. This pagoda is supported by a great central post, 30 m (100 ft) high and 1 m (3 ft) square at the base, the whole being surmounted by a curious finial, decorated with metal rings and bells.

The **Pagoda, Hokiji** (646), is a particularly beautiful example, and while probably constructed by a Japanese master, it clearly follows the Korean tradition.

The three-storeyed **Pagoda, Yakushiji,** was built only a little later; 680. This is notable not only because it comprises three storeys, but also because it is one of the earliest works by native builders. It is more graceful than the Korean-inspired examples, and introduces the truly national style.

The **Pagoda, Bessho,** is a five-storeyed octagonal structure, while the **Tenno-ji Pagoda, Osaka** (p. 162G) and the **Kofukuji Pagoda, Nara** (1426) (p. 166B), are also fine examples of five-storeyed pagodas.

TOMBS

Reverence for the dead has at all times led to the erection of large and small monuments. Apart from the tombs of the Shoguns, Tokyo, which are world-famous, the **Tomb of Ieyasu, Nikko,** is typical of the larger mausoleum. Flights of steps make an imposing entry to the mortuary chapel and tomb chambers. Besides these structures there are priests' chambers, store houses, and a pagoda. The whole is contained within a triple enclosure, with three 'pai-lou'-style entrances. This tomb, however, belongs to a late period (seventeenth century), and is an example of decadence in design, through over-elaboration with ornamentation tending to lose all restraint and constructive meaning (p. 166C).

PALACES

The Imperial palaces were of a simple type, consisting of a principal hall, joined by corridors to three separate pavilions for the family of the Emperor. From the sixteenth century, palaces were protected by walls of masonry, often formed with a batter, concave on the external face, and with tilted quoin stones, to resist earthquake shocks. A moat invariably encircled the walls.

The **Imperial Palace, Nara,** (eighth century) is the focal point of the city, being situated at the end of a central avenue possessing four parallel streets on either side, crossed by others at right angles—evidence of considered town planning and indicating Chinese inspiration.

When the capital was removed to Kioto in 794, this city too was carefully planned, but on an even more sumptuous scale, being formed with a series of rectangular blocks for buildings similar to many modern American cities.

The **Mikado's Palace, Kioto,** is a typical example, comprising one-storey buildings covered with temple-style roofing, which instead of having one uniform slope has gables in what is known as the 'I'rimoya' style. The pavilions overlook splendid gardens, and are connected by covered corridors. Pavilions are divided internally into rooms by sliding screens 2.1 m (7 ft) high, and as in smaller houses, the rooms are reached by an exterior veranda. Room sizes are governed by the number of floor mats, which for Imperial palaces measure 2.1 m × 1.1 m (7 ft × 3 ft 6 ins). The residential block is about 30 m × 18 m (100 ft × 60 ft) and can be divided into fourteen separate rooms, including a throne room with the Imperial dais, and the Mikado's sleeping apartment.

The **Palaces of the Shoguns** reflect the feudal conditions which prevailed in a later period (1603–1868), and were protected by moats and fortified enclosures like so many of the mediaeval castles of England. They offer a grim reminder of the civil strife which ravaged the country at the time of their erection.

The **Kinkaku-ji** and **Ginkaku-ji, Kioto** (c. 1600), are examples of particularly charming garden pavilions. Originally covered with gold and silver leaf, they represent the Japanese delight in brilliant ornamentation.

HOUSES

Japanese houses are entered through a vestibule, and have a verandah, living, dining and guest rooms, with a recess for flowers and art treasures. There are rooms for host and hostess, but no bedrooms in the usual sense, no distinction being made between living and sleeping apartments. Rooms are regulated in size by floor mats or 'tatami' used as floor coverings, and measuring one 'ken', about 1.8 m (6 ft), by a 'half-ken'. Imperial or royal mats are a little larger. A typical middle-class dwelling, except where a central court is introduced, is planned as a simple rectangle (p. 162C, D), usually one storey high, with entrance, ante-room, living rooms, kitchen (with scullery), store-rooms and garden. A separate small fire-resisting structure, known as a 'go-down', is built for the storage of valuables. Walling is formed by light timber vertical posts and horizontal members covered with weather-boarding. Interior partitions are formed with light movable timber frames, with an infilling of stout translucent paper, 1.8 m (6 ft) in height, the friezes above being plastered or wood-lined. These screens can be slid aside—maximum flexibility in planning being a characteristic of Japanese dwellings, while the external (verandah) partitions can be similarly rearranged, or removed to permit the entire house to be open to the garden. Two main reception rooms form a suite, the second a step higher than the first and having two alcoves or 'tokonamas', a special feature of Japanese houses, used to display a flower arrangement or a selected art treasure. Thatched roofs are employed in rural areas, steeply pitched to ward off heavy rains. Tiled roofing is more common in built-up areas, to give protection from fire. Chimneys are unnecessary, as charcoal braziers are the usual source of domestic heating. In some larger houses, European influence has led to the erection of a separate wing with rooms in the 'Western' style. Japanese houses owe much of their bright and cheerful character to simplicity of design, consummate skill in both selection and working of materials, as well as to well-chosen garden settings. Night illumination by decorative Japanese lanterns produces effects of exquisite beauty.

INNS AND BATH-HOUSES

The typical Japanese inn closely resembles the large private house, but it is invariably planned round a central courtyard. In larger examples, upper floors are provided with connecting galleries on the principle developed in London during mediaeval and later times. The **Shukin-ro, Nagoya,** is an excellent example of Japanese practice.

Appreciation of the importance of personal hygiene is strongly marked in the Japanese character. A typical bath-house is illustrated (p. 162E, F).

TEA-HOUSES

Tea-houses (p. 162B) were developed in the Kamakura period (1185–1335) as a result of the aesthetic doctrine of Zen Buddhism, which permeated Japanese thought and resulted in the 'tea-ceremony', garden cultivation and flower arrangement. The tea-house represents a most exclusive Japanese social institution, and was the resort of the most sophisticated and fashionable world: in no sense can it be identified with a normal public restaurant. Tea-houses are maintained solely for the cult of the tea-drinking ceremony, associated with contemplation and appreciation of the arts. Typically and stylistically indigenous, they are normally small in scale, the size regulated by mats, often down to a single-mat room, barely 1.8 m × 1 m (6 ft × 3 ft), and always with the recess or tokonama. Architecturally, the greatest care is lavished on these structures, while no detail of lighting, ventilation or decoration is neglected. The entry for guests is usually approached by stepping stones through a pleasure garden with tastefully arranged flower-beds. Decorative stone lanterns and skilfully landscaped trees and watercourses contrive to form a delightful setting to the small central fane dedicated to the tea-drinking ceremony.

BIBLIOGRAPHY

A Guide to Japanese Architecture. Tokyo, 1971. Contains descriptions and excellent illustrations of traditional as well as modern buildings.

ALEX, W. *Japanese Architecture.* New York and London, 1963.

BLASER, W. *Structure and Form in Japan.* Zürich, 1963.

CRAM, R. ADAMS. *Impressions of Japanese Architecture and the Allied Arts.* New York, 1905.

HARADA, J. *The Lesson of Japanese Architecture.* London, 1936.

HUISH, M. B. *Japan and its Art.* London, 1936.

KIDDER JR., J. E. *Japan before Buddhism.* London, 1959.

—. *Japanese Temples: sculpture, painting, gardens, architecture.* London, 1964.

KISHIDA, H. *Japanese Architecture.* Tokyo, 1935.

MASUDA, T. *Living Architecture: Japan.* London, 1971.

MINAMOTO, H. *An Illustrated History of Japanese Art.* Kioto, 1935.

PAINE, R. T., and SOPER, A. *The Art and Architecture of Japan.* Harmondsworth and Baltimore, 1957.

SADLER, A. *A Short History of Japanese Architecture.* Sydney and London, 1957.

SANSOM, G. B. *Japan: a Short Cultural History.* New York, 1943.

SOPER, A. *The Evolution of Buddhist Architecture in Japan.* Princeton, 1942.

WALEY, A. (Translator). *The Tales of Genjii.* London, 1952.

9
ARCHITECTURE IN PRE-COLUMBIAN AMERICA

The earliest signs of human life in America date from *c.* 9500 B.C., and it is likely that man came to the continent across what are now the Bering Straits from north-east Asia, when it was joined to North America. Whatever his origins, by the first millennium B.C. the early American had made great cultural advances and, over the next two thousand years, developed a series of remarkable civilizations in Middle America and in the region roughly equivalent to modern Peru.

MIDDLE AMERICA

INFLUENCES

GEOGRAPHICAL AND CLIMATIC

The important areas were central Mexico, including part of the Gulf of Mexico coast and the Oaxaca region, and the territories comprising the Yucatan Peninsula, southern Mexico, Honduras and Guatemala. Climatically, these have little in common, the dry high plains of the former contrasting with the tropical conditions and impenetrable rain forests of the latter.

GEOLOGICAL

Both regions have excellent building stone: in northern Yucatan, limestone which could be easily worked or burnt for lime; and in Mexico volcanic rock of various types, including 'tezontli', a porous stone ranging in colour from black to crimson, much favoured by the Aztec builders. From early times, throughout Middle America, adobe brick made from sun-dried clay was widely used, as it continues to be today, and the forests of the south-east furnished excellent hardwoods.

HISTORICAL, SOCIAL AND RELIGIOUS

The earliest civilization, the Olmec, grew up on the Gulf coast in the first millennium B.C., and extended its influence into Guatemala to the south and the Oaxaca region of Mexico to the west. From it developed the great Maya culture of the Yucatan region, which existed at least as early as 600 B.C., and is usually broken down into three phases: *Pre-Classic*, until A.D. 100; *Classic*, 100–900; and *Post-Classic*, 900–1525.

About 100 B.C. another important civilization came into being on the Mexican Plateau at Teotihuacán, which reached its peak between A.D. 150–350. During the seventh century Teotihuacán entered a decline and was finally abandoned at the beginning of the tenth century. About this time the Toltecs, a warlike people who probably originated in the deserts to the north-west, founded nearby a new centre, Tula, and extended their influence through central Mexico and into Maya territory, where it is dramatically evident in the ruins of Chichén Itzá.

Tula was overthrown about 1170, and for nearly two centuries the area was subjected to a series of invasions until the arrival of the Aztec people in the fourteenth century. The latter founded the twin capitals of Tenochtitlán and Tlatelolco on the site of present-day Mexico City, whence their rule eventually extended to Oaxaca, the Gulf coast and the frontier of modern Guatemala, enduring until the Spanish conquest of the area in 1519–21.

In all the civilizations of Middle America religion played a pervasive part, and the largest and most impressive buildings served a religious purpose. Throughout the region the most important gods were those representing natural phenomena—the sun and moon, rain and corn. The Toltecs worshipped Quetzalcóatl, the Plumed Serpent, and probably introduced human sacrifice, which later characterized the Aztec religion.

Maize was the staple food, but without domestic animals its cultivation was difficult and required an enormous labour force. Similarly, great armies of workmen were necessary to raise the pyramids and other monuments which dominated the religious centres, building feats the more remarkable since neither the wheel nor pulley system was known.

Broadly speaking, the structure of Middle American societies was based on a powerful ruling priesthood, supported by a large peasant or slave population, and in essentials was similar to that of Ancient Egypt. Aztec society was relatively complex and organized in a number of distinct and separate classes—priests, warriors, merchants, craftsmen and serfs—and ruled by a priest-king with absolute powers, elected from the royal family by a council of priests and warriors.

A primitive form of glyphic writing was used in Olmec times and later more sophisticated forms were developed by the Maya and Aztecs. The Maya were highly skilled in mathematics and astronomy and they, and later the Aztecs, possessed an extremely accurate calendar, based on a 365-day year and a concurrent 260-day religious cycle, the two systems coinciding every 52 years. The ending of one 52-year cycle and the beginning of another was regarded as a particularly significant time, marked in the case of the Aztecs by the rebuilding of important religious monuments.

The Maya seem to have been a peace-loving people, unlike the Toltecs and Aztecs, who were accomplished warriors and possessed large, highly-organized armies. That the latter were so quickly overcome in 1519–21 is explained partly by the attitude of their king, Moctezuma II, who believed that Cortez was the Toltec god, Quetzalcóatl, returned to his native land and against whom resistance would be ineffectual; and also by the fact that steel, gunpowder and the horse, all of them unknown to the early Americans, gave the Spanish an overwhelming advantage.

ARCHITECTURAL CHARACTER

The most important building type in this region was the temple pyramid. The temple building itself which surmounted the pyramid was a relatively small structure derived from the house form and serving as the 'house of the god'. Entered by a single door, it consisted of one or two windowless chambers and, in Maya examples, was crowned externally by a high roof-crest or comb. Mexican examples, according to sixteenth-century illustrations, had tall false fronts of wood, decorated with symbols connected with the god of the temple.

The truncated pyramid base, which formed the main part of the structure, was

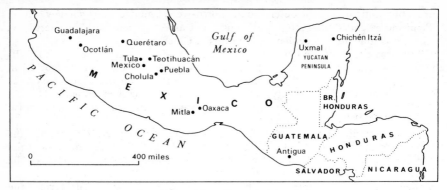

Pre-Columbian Central America

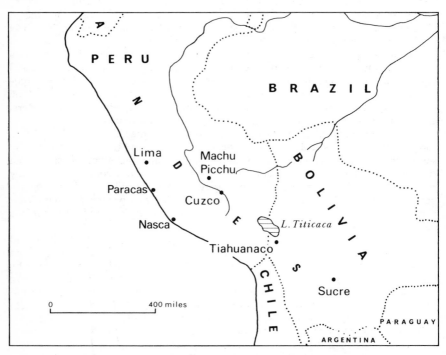

Pre-Columbian South America

stepped and terraced in a variety of ways, and was nearer in form and purpose to the Mesopotamian ziggurat than the Egyptian tomb pyramid. Early examples were of simple form, like that at Cuicuilco, just south of Mexico City, which was built of clay reinforced with large stones, and unusual in its circular plan. More elaborate forms were developed at Teotihuacán and in the Maya centres, where richly carved vertical panels of stone separating the terraces now increased in number. Other examples, like the Pyramid of the Sun at Teotihuacán (p. 174B), were broader in their treatment, the terraces being linked by undecorated inclined masonry walls. The main mass of the pyramid was built of rubble masonry or adobe, which was then faced with stone, colour being added over a plaster coating. The temple pyramids were the foci of the cities and sacred enclosures of Middle America, which were laid out with great skill and show a highly developed feeling for monumental, formal planning.

While adobe brick was used for lesser buildings, for all buildings of importance stone was employed, either finely dressed or carved or laid as roughly-dressed rubble. In coursed work little attention was paid to the staggering of vertical joints. Stone facing panels, carved with formalized representations of jaguars, coyotes and eagles, occur in Toltec work, while geometric patterns formed by projecting stones are found at Mitla (p. 174E), suggestive of woven designs and characteristic of the Mixtec-Zapotec culture.

Roofs were flat, windows were not used, and doorways were square-headed. The true arch was unknown, but in Maya work the principle of the corbel was exploited and corbelled openings and vaults were common, the latter sometimes incorporating wooden ties. Internal walls could be decorated with mural paintings and, in the Aztec and late Maya periods, these were of high quality.

EXAMPLES

The **Temple Pyramid, Cuicuilco** (*c.* 500 B.C.) can be regarded as a forerunner of the later temple pyramids, despite its circular plan. Constructed of adobe reinforced with large stones, it is 19.7 m (65 ft) high and has a diameter at its base of nearly 134 m (440 ft). The original pyramid had two stages, later increased to four, and was surmounted by a small temple building, approached by ramps or staircases on the east and west. The structure is still partly buried under the lava flow from the volcano Xitli which engulfed it about 1,700 years ago.

The **Pyramid of the Sun, Teotihuacán** (*c.* A.D. 250) (p. 174B), forms part of an important complex of buildings centred on a broad avenue 3 km (2 miles) long. The stone-faced pyramid rises in four stages to a height of 66 m (216 ft) and is over 213 m (700 ft) square in plan. The temple building which originally crowned it was approached from the west by a broad stairway.

The **Citadel, Teotihuacán** (*c.* 600) (p. 174B), consists of a large court surrounded by terraced platforms and, at its east end, incorporates a small pyramid. In the latter can be seen the method of dealing with the stages characteristic of Teotihuacán and also found at Chichén Itzá: instead of simple, inclined surfaces, the different levels are separated by deep, strongly framed friezes ('tableros') which overhang relatively narrow inclined bands of masonry ('taluds').

The **Temple Pyramid, Tenayuca** (thirteenth–sixteenth century), originally carried twin temples dedicated respectively to Huitzilopochtli, the war god, and Tlaloc, the rain god. The pyramid has four stages and its sides are steeply inclined and faced with undressed stones of relatively small size, with quoins reminiscent of Anglo-Saxon 'long and short work'. Following the 52-year cycle of the Aztec calendar the pyramid was enlarged five times, in 1299, 1351, 1403, 1455 and 1507. The pyramid rises from a base 42.7 m (140 ft) square to a height of 15.2 m (50 ft).

Temple I (Temple of the Giant Jaguar), Tikal (*c.* 500) (p. 174A), is an impressive example of a Classic Maya temple pyramid. At its base the pyramid is 34 m × 29.8 m (112 ft × 98 ft) in plan and rises in ten stages to a height of 30.5 m (100 ft). The stages are separated by almost vertical walls which give the structure a monumental, towering character. The temple building itself consists of a main

A. Temple I, Tikal
(c. 500). See p. 173

B. Teotihuacán: Pyramid of the Sun (c. 250) to
left, Citadel (c. 600) beyond. See p. 173

C. The Ball Court, Chichén Itzá
(c. 1200). See p. 175

D. The Temple of the Warriors, Chichén Itzá
(c. 1100). See p. 175

E. The Palace, Mitla (c. 1000):
detail of doorway. See p. 175

F. The Palace of the Governors, Uxmal (c. 900
See p. 175

sanctuary, from each side of which open three smaller chambers or recesses, all of which are roofed with corbelled vaults. The temple is approached by a single steep flight of steps and above it rises a high stone roof-comb, making a total height for the pyramid and its temple of 47.5 m (156 ft).

The **Temple of the Inscriptions, Palenque** (c. 550) is unusual in that at ground level, within the mass of the pyramid, there is a large vaulted crypt, which is approached from the summit of the pyramid by a corbel-vaulted stairway. The stairway was blocked up, after building, with rubble, and inside the crypt there is a monolithic sarcophagus.

The **North Pyramid, Tula** (c. 1100) is a five-stage Toltec pyramid, originally faced with stone panels carved with jaguars and coyotes, eagles eating human hearts and symbols of the god Quetzalcóatl. The temple which surmounted the pyramid incorporated four colossal basalt telemones of Toltec warriors, and four square columns carved with reliefs of warriors, which supported the temple roof. A pair of cylindrical columns decorated with the feathered serpent motif flanked the entrance. The temple was approached by a single broad stairway which led from a wide court or atrium, with a double colonnade of square columns, originally roofed, at the base of the pyramid.

The **Temple of the Warriors, Chichén Itzá** (c. 1100) (p. 174D), has a striking resemblance to the North Pyramid at Tula. Like the latter, it was approached through a colonnade of square columns and incorporated square columns in its interior, but its external walls are decorated with projecting trunk-like forms associated with the long-nosed Maya rain god.

The **Ball Court, Copan** (late sixth century) was built for a ceremonial ball game which played an important part in the religions of Middle America from an early date. The court is in the form of a long rectangular space with, at right angles to it, smaller spaces at each end. On the long sides of the main space there are low sloping masonry walls which provided platforms for temples.

The **Ball Court, Chichén Itzá** (c. 1200) (p. 174C) is contained by high walls. On the stone bench running along the base of these are almost life-size relief carvings showing teams of Maya and Toltec players, against a richly carved background of plant and serpent forms.

The **Palace Buildings, Mitla** (c. 1000) (p. 174E). Each of the palaces consists of four rectangular one-room elements of one storey, grouped around a central open courtyard. In some cases, elements are independent and free-standing; in others, they are overlapped to form a completely closed court in the centre, entered through a small opening in one corner. Single or triple entrances in the centre of each element opened to the court and provided the only light source. Externally, the walls are decorated with complex geometric patterns formed by projecting stones, the designs, suggestive of woven forms, being contained in heavy rectangular masonry frames and characteristic of Mixtec-Zapotec buildings.

The **Palace of the Governors, Uxmal** (c. 900) (p. 174F) has a one-storeyed building measuring 98 m × 11.9 m (322 ft × 39 ft) standing on a high base of two stages. It consists of a central mass linked by great triangular corbelled arches to smaller blocks on either side, and contains twenty chambers, all covered by corbelled vaults. The façade of the building is 8.5 m (28 ft) high and is divided into two deep horizontal bands. The lower of these is of plain ashlar masonry, punctuated by eleven rectangular door openings, each with an undecorated architrave set back from the wall face. The upper band, approximately the height of the vaults behind, projects over the lower band and is decorated with intricate patterns in relief reminiscent of woven designs.

PERU

INFLUENCES

GEOGRAPHICAL AND CLIMATIC

Physically, the region falls into two sections: the great mountain range of the Andes, and, between it and the Pacific, a narrow coastal strip, in places no wider than 96 km (60 miles). Except along the rivers, conditions in the latter are arid, rain being precipitated before reaching the coast by the cold Humbold current of the Pacific. Rising rapidly to the east of the coastal strip, the Andes provide some of the wildest and most desolate landscape in the world. The mountains are cut deeply by gorges and steep valleys, fertile pockets in an otherwise bleak and rocky wilderness, and high among them are a number of natural basins, including those of Cuzco and Titicaca.

GEOLOGICAL

In the coastal region, adobe brick was the basic building material, even for the largest structures. In the highlands, three types of stone were in general use for important buildings: black andesite, Yucay limestone and diorite porphyry.

HISTORICAL, SOCIAL AND RELIGIOUS

Relatively advanced civilizations existed in Peru before the first millennium B.C., and at Kotosh in the central highlands the substantial remains of a temple of c. 1800 B.C. have been discovered. Nearby, at Chavin, there are other important remains and the centre has given its name to a culture, based on the worship of man-jaguar gods, which influenced the entire region.

Between 100 B.C. and A.D. 300 a number of new and distinct centres emerged, notably at Paracas and Nasca on the south coast and at Mochica (Moche) on the north coast; and later, about A.D. 600, an especially important one came into being at Tiahuanaco in the Titicaca Basin of the southern highlands. The influence of Tiahuanaco, especially in religious matters, was great and extended throughout Peru, providing a sense of religious and political unity in the area which continued after the collapse of the centre in the eleventh century.

As the power of Tiahuanaca waned, there emerged in the north of the coastal region a new nation, the Chimu, who from their centre at Chanchan extended their territory until they controlled, through an excellent road system, some 960 km (600 miles) of the coast lands. At the same time the Inca people of the central highlands settled in the Cuzco Basin, where they founded their capital. For some two centuries the Inca waged war against neighbouring tribes until their superiority was conclusively established in the mid-fifteenth century. Invading the coastal region, they conquered the powerful Chimu and eventually extended their empire into central Chile to the south, and southern Columbia to the north.

Throughout the region the cultivation of crops was difficult. In the mountains the steep valley sides were terraced into andanas, the precious soil being retained by great masonry walls, while the arid conditions of the coastal strip were overcome by complex irrigation systems. As in Middle America, the wheel was unknown, but the native llama was domesticated at an early date and was employed for agricultural purposes and transport. Another animal, the alpaca, was also of great importance to the Peruvian economy, its long fine hair being used for textiles, in the weaving of which great skill was developed. The civilizations of Peru possessed neither the hieroglyphic writing nor the sophisticated calendar of Central America; they were, however, extremely skilful in the working of gold, silver and copper and their alloys.

Under the Incas, religion and the state were interdependent, the Inca himself being supposedly related to the all-powerful sun god. The Inca governed as an absolute ruler, with below him a series of nobles, members of the royal family and the rulers of states within the empire. The system was extremely rigid, yet through it an enormous area was controlled which, on the arrival of Pizarro's Spanish expedition in 1532, extended from north to south for some 4,000 km (2,500 miles).

ARCHITECTURAL CHARACTER

Adobe brick, as we have seen, was the basic building material in the coastal region, and with it great terraced structures like the Temple of the Sun at Moche and the fortress at Paramonga were built. Roofs were sometimes gabled, openings kept to a minimum, and generally the architecture was one of strong simple forms. At Chanchan, however, the walls of important buildings were richly textured with geometric patterns, cut into the facing of clay plaster. Adobe bricks were made in a variety of shapes at different periods and included conical, hemispherical and cubic forms. Houses were generally of one room, entered by a single door and without windows. Several houses belonging to different members of a family were grouped around a central courtyard, and a typical village was made up of a number of these compounds.

In the highlands simple buildings were usually constructed of rubble, sometimes bonded with clay. For public buildings and fortifications dressed stone was used in a variety of forms, including smooth ashlar, polygonal masonry of large irregular stones, and walling where the edges of the stones were bevelled and their faces dressed into a cushion-like form. In all cases the stones were fitted together with great precision, their abutting faces probably being ground together with sand. Even in coursed work little attention was paid to the staggering of vertical joints. Rich external decoration was lacking in buildings in the highlands, which were characterized by broad simple forms, closely integrated with their sites, and the superb quality of their masonry. At Tiahuanaco, however, decoration is found cut into the great andesite lintol of the Gate of the Sun (p. 178B). Roofs, even in public buildings, were covered with thatch, although in the southern highlands corbelled stone roofs were sometimes used.

EXAMPLES

The **Temple of the Sun, Moche** (c. A.D. 800), has a pyramid, 104 m (340 ft) square in plan and 23 m (75 ft) high, rising from a terraced platform measuring 230 m × 137 m (750 ft × 450 ft) in plan and 18.3 m (60 ft) in height. The whole of this impressive structure is built of adobe brick.

Chanchan (c. 1200), the capital of the Chimu Empire, had an area of over 9.6 square kilometres (6 square miles) and was composed of ten large compounds, each enclosed by walls, in some cases reaching over 9 m (30 ft) in height. All the buildings in the city were constructed of adobe brick, some being decorated with brick mosaics, and others having patterns resembling woven designs, cut into a facing of mud plaster.

The Fortress, Paramonga (c. 1200–1400) (p. 178A) is another impressive example of adobe brick construction, and demonstrates a remarkable grasp of the principles of fortification. Succeeding terraces and walls are arranged to give protection to the lower stages, while projecting corner bastions provide cover to the main walls of the fortress.

The **Gate of the Sun, Tiahuanaco** (c. 1000–1200) (p. 178B) is one of the most

A. The Fortress, Paramonga
(c. 1200–1400). See p. 177

B. The Gate of the Sun, Tiahuanaco
(c. 1000–1200). See p. 177

C. The Fortress, Sacsahuamán (c. 1475). See p. 179

D. Inca Street, Cuzco
(c. 1450–1532). See p. 179

E. Machu Picchu (c. 1500). See p. 179

important monuments of the great ceremonial site in the Titicaca Basin. In effect the gateway is an enormous piece of sculpture, cut from a single andesite block, measuring approximately 3 m (10 ft) high and 3.8 m (12 ft 6 ins) wide, with an estimated weight of 10 tons. Above a rectangular opening, emphasized by a plain recessed band, there is a deep, slightly projecting frieze, in the centre of which is carved a formalized representation of the god Viracocha. Flanking the central figure are forty-eight small rectangular reliefs depicting figures running towards the god.

Sacsahuamán (*c.* 1475) (p. 178C) was built as a fortress to protect Cuzco, the Sacred City of the Incas, which it overlooks, and to provide a place of refuge for its inhabitants in the event of attack. Three stages of terraces, with high retaining walls of Yucay limestone, stretch for more than half a kilometre (a third of a mile). The walls follow a saw-tooth pattern in plan and the three stages together reach a height of 18 m (60 ft). The lowest wall is formed of monoliths measuring as much as 8.2 m (27 ft) high and 3.6 m (12 ft) thick. While some of the stones are roughly squared, others are polygonal, and all are fitted together with great precision.

Cuzco (*c.* 1450–1532) (p. 178D), the capital of the Inca Empire, has numerous examples of superb masonry construction, mostly incorporated into later colonial buildings. The Inca city was centred on a plaza where the most important temple stood. Dedicated to the Sun God, this consisted of a main hall measuring approximately 28 m × 14.3 m (93 ft × 47 ft), and a number of smaller ancillary buildings. Part of a curved wall in fine ashlar masonry belonging to the temple can still be seen, forming the base for later building, as well as other sections of walling from the Inca period, including a particularly fine example which was originally part of the House of the Chosen Women.

Machu Picchu (*c.* 1500) (p. 178E) is a late Inca town, dramatically sited on the saddle between two mountains and overlooking the Urubamba River, which winds 900 m (3,000 ft) below it. Its buildings, all constructed of local stone, use various types of walling, from coursed ashlar to roughly dressed rubble, and incorporate characteristic trapezoidal doorways. Some of the walls have rectangular niches formed on the inner side. Masonry gables still stand and some buildings have small trapezoidal window openings. The steep slopes of the site are terraced with masonry retaining walls to hold soil for gardens, and the various levels of the town are linked by stone stairways.

BIBLIOGRAPHY

BUSHNELL, G. H. S. *Peru.* 2nd ed. London, 1963.
—. *The First Americans.* London, 1968.
COE, M. D. *Mexico.* London, 1962.
—. *The Maya.* London, 1966.
KELEMAN, P. *Medieval American Art.* 2 vols. New York, 1956.
KUBLER, G. *Art and Architecture of Ancient America.* Harmondsworth and Baltimore, 1962.
MASON, J. A. *The Ancient Civilizations of Peru.* Harmondsworth, 1957.
MORLEY, S. J., and BRAINERD, G. W. *The Ancient Maya.* 3rd ed. Stanford, California, 1956.
PETERSON, F. A. *Ancient Mexico.* New York, 1959.
STIERLIN, H. *Living Architecture: Mayan.* New York and London, 1964.
THOMPSON, J. E. S. *The Rise and Fall of Mayan Civilization.* 2nd ed. Norman, Oklahoma, 1966.
VAILLANT, G. C. *The Aztecs of Mexico.* Harmondsworth, 1950.

IO

GREEK ARCHITECTURE

Circa 3000–30 B.C.

INFLUENCES

GEOGRAPHICAL

It was upon the island of Crete that arose the first great sea-power of the Mediterranean, which flourished a thousand years before the Greek civilization reached its peak. This 'Aegean' culture extended to Greece and her islands, and was founded on trade around the whole eastern Mediterranean seaboard, with Asia Minor, Cyprus, Syria, Palestine, Egypt and Libya. Trading vessels also reached South Italy and Sicily. Routes were thus established which, when the Aegean civilization had crumbled, were followed by colonists who were to help to found the Greece of classical times, which comprised not only the motherland itself and the neighbouring islands, but settlements in South Italy and Sicily, western Asia Minor, Cyrenaica and others distributed sporadically elsewhere around the Mediterranean and the Black Sea. Geography determined the fortunes of both the Aegean and the Greek cultures, for the rugged nature of the Greek peninsula and its islands, with mountainous hinterlands which rendered internal communication difficult, made the sea the inevitable means of intercourse. The mountains of inland Greece separated the inhabitants into groups or clans, and thus arose that rivalry which characterized the Greek states, whether in peace or war.

GEOLOGICAL

Greece and her domains had ample supplies of good building-stone, but the mineral of greatest importance to her architecture was her unrivalled marble, the most beautiful and monumental of all building materials, and one which facilitates exactness of line and refinement of detail. This marble is found in abundance, notably in the mountains of Hymettus and Pentelicus near Athens, and in the islands of Paros and Naxos. The Greeks attached so much importance to the quality of fine-grained marble for producing exact outlines and smooth surfaces that, as in the Temples at Paestum, Italy, they even coated coarse-grained limestone with a layer of marble 'stucco' in order to secure this effect, which is the great characteristic of their architecture.

CLIMATIC

The climate was intermediate between rigorous cold and relaxing heat. The clear atmosphere and intensity of light was conducive to the development of that love of precise and exact forms which are special attributes of Greek architecture. The administration of justice, dramatic representations, and most public ceremonies took place in the open air, even in winter, and to this is largely due the limited variety of public buildings other than temples. The hot summer sun and sudden winter showers, together with the Greek love of conversation, probably explain the porticoes and colonnades which were such important features.

GREEK ARCHITECTURE

HISTORICAL AND SOCIAL

The history of the Greek world may be conveniently
periods, but to avoid confusion the terminology used
title Aegean embraces the civilizations of Crete and ma
times to about 1100 B.C. Cretan is commonly known as
King Minos of Knossos, and the mainland civilizati
Mycenaean, after one of the great centres, Mycenae. T
to as Helladic, the precursor of Hellenic (classical Gr

The Aegean civilization centred on Crete was initiat..
nium B.C., by a movement of peoples from Asia Minor. In Crete the,
the original inhabitants, who were of ancient Mediterranean stock. During
Early Period, 3000–1800 B.C., the civilization grew and expanded, developing a
commercial empire protected by naval power. Crafts, pottery, communications and
trade through coastal towns produced a unity of culture and economic stability.
Some form of political unity among the ninety or more towns of Crete was achieved,
first under Phaestos, and later under Knossos, at both of which complex palaces
evolved. Lesser towns also gathered around smaller but no less complex palaces, or
elaborate 'royal villas', and the commonality of palace-towns suggests a federation
of princes or kings perhaps semi-divine in authority. Commerce exported cultural
influences in addition to pottery, crafts and decorative arts, and the inhabitants of
what is now Greece were increasingly affected by the superior trading civilization
of Crete. Unlike Crete, which was protected by the sea and its naval power, the
mainland was subject to incursions of northern peoples. About 2000 B.C. there
occurred a particular invasion of migrant peoples, who may have come originally
from south Russia. They spoke a language something like Greek, and introduced
houses originally designed for more wintry climates. That sort of house ('megaron')
seems to imitate a timber form originating from the forests of northern and eastern
Europe.

Between 1800 and 1600 B.C. the whole Aegean culture developed until by the
latter date it had achieved a power co-equal with the civilizations of Egypt and
Mesopotamia. The palace of Knossos indicates a highly centralized, bureaucratic
system; the evidence of its character and nature supports the notion of an elegant,
sybaritic society, enjoying music, dancing and athletic pursuits. Women took an
important part in social life and participated in most activities, and there was a
total absence of the monumental class structures as compared with Egypt and
Mesopotamia.

Between 1600 and 1400 B.C. the brilliance of the civilization continued, but there
is evidence that the balance of power and influence moved in the reverse direction
and Cretan influence declined after 1500 B.C. In about 1450–1400 B.C. Knossos and
other palace towns were destroyed, and the civilization they represented collapsed
in ruin. Controversy persists as to how and why that destruction was brought about:
whatever the reason, destruction was widespread and thorough. Control of the sea
thus passed to the mainland princes, who now existed in a sort of federation linked
by ties of varying strength.

Mycenaean or Helladic Greece (1400–1100 B.C.). Mainland centres had always
required defence; quarrelling and violence among the towns perpetuated insecurity
and the necessity for protection, and the magnificent but grim fortifications of
Mycenae and Tiryns conjure up an atmosphere of somewhat barbaric cruelty in
strange contrast to the refined architecture, art and living which existed within. The
absorption of Cretan ideas and the use of Cretan craftsmen produced continuity of
architectural characteristics during Cretan supremacy and after its collapse. Citadel

The Central Lands of the Greek World

palaces, around which open townships grew up, became centres of small but powerful land empires, exploiting the heritage of Cretan mercantile supremacy to maintain trading wealth across the sea.

About 1300 B.C. the wealth of Helladic towns began to decline. It is possible that troubles among princely states had become critical, leading to the Trojan War about 1200 B.C. At the same time there were further race migrations and many confused invasions among the Aegean and Near-East peoples. It is likely that the hordes invading the Aegean were the 'Achaeans'—Homer's name for Greeks. Within a century the citadel palaces were destroyed, in the end by the last stream of Greek invaders whom we know as 'Dorians'. Earlier arrivals—Achaeans, Aeolians—fled across the sea to Asia Minor where, as Ionians, they at length developed a prosperous civilization anew. The destruction of Helladic citadels was one of many events which brought about the end of Bronze Age civilization at large. The Iron Age had arrived in Greece, and the virtual extinction of the Bronze Age civilizations of the Aegean produced during the ensuing centuries (Homer's 'Dark Age') an era little understood, and uncertain in reconstruction. Building was small-scale, essentially local and impermanent, and the few remains scarcely clarify the picture. Some centres survived, so that a certain continuity of traditions and standards obtained to give rise to slow development through the age of Homer. Athens was one such centre.

Hellenic Greece (800–323 B.C.). By the eighth century B.C. the city-state ('polis') emerged as the basis of Greek society, and the Greeks adopted an alphabet from the Phoenicians, which had momentous results in the development of language and literacy. Early settlements evolved as small, highly independent communities acknowledging no authority higher than their own. The lack of political unity was to some extent countered by a sort of federal unity derived from common language, customs and religion. The city-state evolved as an autonomous, independent unit, about which the Greeks had definite ideas as to extent, size and its relation to the gods. As the eighth century progressed the constricted setting of the city and its government generated dissatisfaction among an expanding population: an outlet was found in emigration, and eventually new cities were established, particularly in Sicily and south Italy. Freed from homeland conservatism, colonial cities developed with remarkable rapidity, and Paestum in south Italy, and Syracuse, Selinus and Agrigentum in Sicily, among colonial cities in the western Greek world, contributed uniquely to the expression of Greek ideas and produced a brilliant outburst of building and architecture. At the same time, but in their different way, so did the increasingly wealthy commercial cities in Ionian Greece—Didyma, Ephesus and Miletus. The expansionist movement continued through the seventh century, declining only when confronted by the Etruscans established in western Italy, the power of Carthage across the narrows of the Mediterranean from Sicily, and the aggressive Assyrian Empire in the east.

By 600 B.C. the cities of Greece had settled down to their several forms of government—oligarchic, tyrannic or democratic— and by the end of the sixth century the tempo of events and ideas accelerated further. Tyrannical power within Greece was increasingly opposed, while externally the aggressive attitude of the Persian Empire in succession to Assyria became increasingly threatening. The Ionians of Asia Minor became politically involved with the Persian monarchy, and their unwillingness to submit to domination led to the invasion and conquest of the Greek cities. The revolt of the cities (499–493 B.C.) was suppressed and led to a punitive expedition under Darius I into Greece. There followed a brief, and unique, unity among the Greeks to resist attack. Darius was defeated at Marathon (490 B.C.) and a later invasion under Xerxes was also defeated at the naval battle of Salamis, (480 B.C.) and the land battle of Plataea (479 B.C.). The disruption by war, and the final, astonishing victory of a collection of small city-states over the Persian Empire, paved the way for the downfall of tyrannic governments and the development of democratic regimes based on elections. The democratic process was an especially Athenian influence, and in the forty years after the Persian defeat Athenian democracy was to be the crucible in which was synthesised the Greek achievement. The rule of Pericles (444–429 B.C.) marked the climax of Athenian prosperity, and the tremendous outburst of building activity in reconstruction which was to express the ultimate development of Hellenic art and architecture.

The supremacy of Athens, and the methods used to achieve and maintain it, aroused resentment and jealousy, and especially the exasperation of Sparta. Preliminary hostilities provoked the Peloponnesian War (431–404 B.C.) during which Athens was gradually exhausted and the economy of Greece disrupted, and the ultimate defeat of Athens also marked the beginning of the decline of the democratic spirit. Supremacy, for which she was unfit, passed to Sparta.

Despite the political dissensions and military excesses the fifth century witnessed the great flowering of Greek philosophies in many fields of thinking. The late seventh and early sixth century had been a time of law-making, followed during the sixth century by speculation in philosophy and science. Pythagoras is perhaps the best known of those sixth-century philosopher-scientists. The thinkers of the fifth

century, particularly Socrates, were primarily concerned with the nature of knowledge and the human soul, but there was also prodigious study in physics, mathematics, astronomy and music. The close of the fifth century marked the great
flowering of drama, amid the excesses of the Peloponnesian War. Tragic drama
appears to have originated in the festival of the worship of Dionysos, and developed
from those archaic festivities to a dramatic medium for questioning man's relations
with the gods, and thus Greek theatre has a profoundly religious attribute.

Hellenistic Greece (323–30 B.C.). The succession of Sparta was short-lived and
the fourth century saw a sequence of attempts by city-states to dominate Greece.
The confused situation was resolved into a federal system imposed by the supremacy of Macedonia. Under Philip (359–336 B.C.) the unification of Greece was
accomplished, and firmly established under his son Alexander the Great (336–323
B.C.), who then embarked on a national crusade against Persia. Within five years he
completely destroyed the Persian Empire, annexing Egypt and penetrating as far
east as the Punjab. The vast territory became a Hellenistic Empire through which
Greek civilization was extended. New and splendid cities were founded of which
Alexandria was to be the largest and most famous. As a result the centre of the
Greek world shifted east—politically, economically and artistically—and the west
declined in importance.

The early death of Alexander at the age of thirty-two was followed by the
division of the Empire among his generals, who squabbled for more than forty
years before the Hellenistic world more or less settled into three enlightened
monarchies—those of Antigonus in Greece, Seleucis in Asia Minor and Ptolemy in
Egypt. But, brilliant though those states were, they failed to maintain unity:
mutual animosity and economic decline during the third century aggravated disorder and afforded opportunity for intrusion by the centralized, expanding power
of the Romans, bringing with them law, order and unified government, and adopting much of the culture of the Hellenistic world. Greece itself became a Roman
province in 146 B.C., and the Greek states of Asia Minor and Egypt gradually came
under Roman control, the latter in 30 B.C.

RELIGIOUS

The religion of the 'Aegeans' was a nature worship which went through a series of
primitive stages. Though eventually divinities were conceived in human form, and
represented by small idols, rocks and stone pillars and all sorts of trees and animals
continued to be venerated. Mysteries of masculine force were represented by the
sacred bull, symbolized by the 'horns of consecration', and the shield and the
sacrificial double axe also had mystical virtues. The supreme deity was the fertility-
or mother-goddess, Rhea, later identified with Hera by the Greeks. Priestesses,
rather than priests, conducted the religious rites. Worship centred on sacrificial
altars, in open-air enclosures, caves, small chapels or household shrines. Temples
were not needed until after the collapse of the Aegean civilization, when the Greeks
began to represent their deities by large statues. The religious ceremonies of the
Aegeans included sacred games and ritual dances, establishing traditions upon
which the classical Greek athletic contests and arts of the theatre were founded.

The Greek religion also was in the main a worship of natural phenomena, but
more highly developed. The gods were personifications of particular elements, or
were deified heroes, and each town or district had its own local preferences, ceremonies and traditions. There was no regular priesthood. The priests and priestesses
were not members of an exclusive class but led the normal community life.

The principal Greek deities, with their attributes and Roman names, are as
follows:

GREEK (The twelve Olympians)		ROMAN
Zeus	The supreme god, and ruler of the sky	Jupiter (Jove)
Hera	Wife of Zeus, and goddess of marriage	Juno
Apollo	God of law and reason, art, music and poetry; founder of cities	Apollo
Athena	Goddess of wisdom and learning	Minerva
Poseidon	The sea god	Neptune
Dionysos	God of wine, feasting and revelry	Bacchus
Demeter	Goddess of earth and agriculture	Ceres
Artemis	Goddess of the chase	Diana
Hermes	Messenger of the gods. God of commerce	Mercury
Aphrodite	Goddess of love and beauty	Venus
Hephaestus	God of fire, flame and forge. God of handicrafts	Vulcan
Ares	God of war	Mars

Also: Hestia (Vesta), goddess of the hearth (sacred fire); Helios (Sol), the sun god; Selene (Luna), the moon goddess; Pan (Pan), god of the flocks. Two mortals who became gods were Heracles (Hercules), god of strength and labour, and Asclepius (Aesculapius), god of healing.

AEGEAN ARCHITECTURE

(*Circa* 3000–1100 B.C.)

ARCHITECTURAL CHARACTER

The architecture of Crete and the other islands differed from that of the mainland, although in the minor arts, practice was common. The island peoples were partly Asiatic in origin, and their buildings had the flat roofs typical of eastern countries. The flat roofs allowed buildings to be drawn together, when necessary, in large blocks, two, three or even four storeys high, light-wells being used to admit natural light to the inner parts of the blocks. Spacious stairways were developed, in return flights, and the flat roofs formed part of the serviceable accommodation. The mainland peoples, on the other hand, brought their northern practices with them, and used low-pitched roofs, so that, apart from exceptions due to Island influence, their buildings were single-storeyed, and allowance had to be made between the comparatively small units for the removal of rain-water. The characteristic mainland domestic unit was the megaron, which had a deep plan, comprising a columned entrance porch, an anteroom with central doorway, the living-apartment or megaron proper (p. 188A, 6, 8), with central hearth and columns supporting the roof, and normally, a thalamus or sleeping-room behind. The powerful Cretan navy made fortifications largely unnecessary on the islands, and gave freedom in the selection of town sites; on the mainland the liability to hostile irruption made it essential to choose elevated sites, encircled by massive defensive walls. As a whole, houses and palaces are the principal building-types representative of Aegean architecture, with, chiefly on the mainland, an important class of underground tomb. Buildings were constructed of rubble or cut stonework to dado height, the upper parts having a heavy, double frame of timber, the panels being infilled with sun-dried brick or stone rubble. The walls were coated with stucco outside, and either tinted, or, on the islands, painted with patterns inspired by the framed construction which lay behind. Gypsum, plentiful in Crete, also served to make hard, polished floors and roof-deckings carried on rounded logs, or was used in slabs for similar purposes. Masonry technique was well-developed, and particularly on the mainland, ranged from a 'cyclopean' type comprised of great boulder-like stones, used in fortifications, to coarse or fine ashlar of heavy blocks (p. 188B). No mortar was ever employed, though clay sometimes served for bedding in rubble or cyclopean work. Polygonal walling, an advanced technique, was not invented until Hellenic times. False arches of heavy blocks, or of corbels advanced course by course until a triangular head had been formed, covered the openings in stone walls (p. 190H), and the corbel method was normal too for vaults or pointed domes, as in the Treasury of Atreus, Mycenae (p. 190). Square, masonry pillars, with a bracket form of capital, sometimes gave intermediate support on lower floors, but the distinctive type of column was of cypress wood, with a downward-tapering, cylindrical shaft, a slight, disc-like base and a widely-projecting capital with two main parts, a square abacus above, and a circular, bulbous echinus below (p. 190D); not unlike the Doric capital of later times, except that there are here additional small mouldings above and below the echinus. This broad-topped form of column was necessary to collect the weight of the thick, supported walls.

EXAMPLES

In the whole epoch of Aegean art, from c. 3000 to 1100 B.C., followed by a 'Dark Age' up to c. 650 B.C., a climax of achievement was reached in the two centuries 1600–1400 B.C. The architecture of Crete—the originating centre—and the neighbouring Aegean islands, differed in important respects from that of the Greek mainland, which suffered successive northern invasions, and thus had a somewhat different racial complexion. Of the many towns in Crete, Knossos and Phaestos were the most important, and Tiryns and Mycenae represent the mainland. Athens, Orchomenos and Pylos were other important mainland centres.

PALACES

Island towns had few defences, as they were politically unified early, and were protected by the powerful mercantile navy of Crete. Mainland settlements, on the other hand, needed fortified strongholds to protect the agricultural villages from which livelihood was drawn, and to which the villagers could repair in times of danger. The elaborate palaces of the kings or local chieftains and their retinues were the main structures of the period.

The **Palace of King Minos, Knossos** (p. 187), represents the Cretan type and was the chief upon the island, as the other towns were subject to Knossos. It was destroyed about 1400 B.C., and had grown by stages from a series of separate buildings into a continuous complex arranged around an open court, 51.8 m × 27.4 m (170 ft × 90 ft) wide. The whole spanned roughly 122 m (400 ft) each way, and covered about four acres. Additionally, on the west side, there was a paved market-court, and to the north of it, a theatral area, flanked by banks of broad, shallow steps, for public displays and sports. The town proper lay still further to the west. The site of the palace is a slight eminence, but the ground falls more steeply to the south and south-east. The buildings mostly were of at least two storeys, the lower merely 2.44 m (8 ft) high, divided into long narrow store-rooms on the west wing, stocked with enormous earthenware oil jars and with storage bins cut along the centre of their floors. At the northern end were stored the archives, comprised of thousands of inscribed clay tablets: and facing towards the central court in this wing was a 'Throne Room', which appears to have been a chapel for religious observance, containing an alabaster throne for the priest-king with benches on each side for priestesses, all facing towards a colonnaded light-well or lustral tank. Frescoed griffins on the wall behind face towards the throne. The throne room was approached from an ante-room opening from the courtyard by four pairs of folding

PALACE of KING MINOS :
KNOSSOS . CRETE

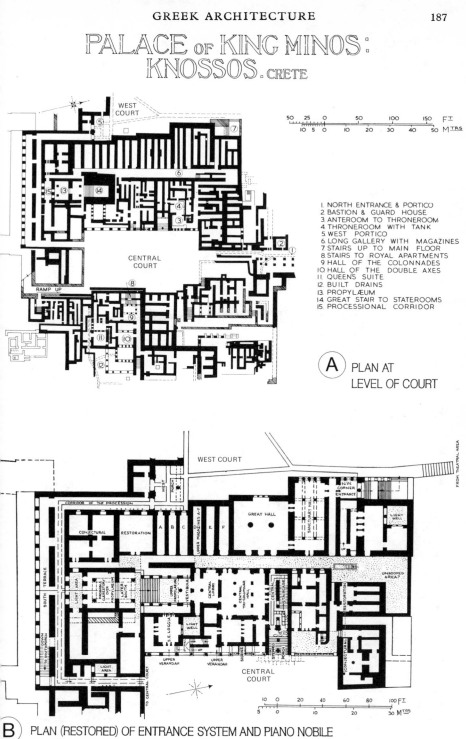

WEST COURT

CENTRAL COURT

RAMP UP

1. NORTH ENTRANCE & PORTICO
2. BASTION & GUARD HOUSE
3. ANTEROOM TO THRONEROOM
4. THRONEROOM WITH TANK
5. WEST PORTICO
6. LONG GALLERY WITH MAGAZINES
7. STAIRS UP TO MAIN FLOOR
8. STAIRS TO ROYAL APARTMENTS
9. HALL OF THE COLONNADES
10. HALL OF THE DOUBLE AXES
11. QUEENS SUITE
12. BUILT DRAINS
13. PROPYLÆUM
14. GREAT STAIR TO STATEROOMS
15. PROCESSIONAL CORRIDOR

A) PLAN AT LEVEL OF COURT

WEST COURT

FROM THEATRICAL AREA

CORRIDOR OF THE PROCESSION

CONJECTURAL RESTORATION

SOUTH TERRACE

LIGHT AREA

GREAT HALL

N.W. CORNER ENTRANCE

SANCTUARY HALL

LIGHT WELL

UPPER MAGAZINES A-F

UNROOFED AREA?

RESTORATION

CONJECTURAL

LIGHT AREA

CENTRAL COURT

TO CENTRAL COURT

UPPER VERANDAH

UPPER VERANDAH

SHRINE

B) PLAN (RESTORED) OF ENTRANCE SYSTEM AND PIANO NOBILE OF WEST PALACE SYSTEM

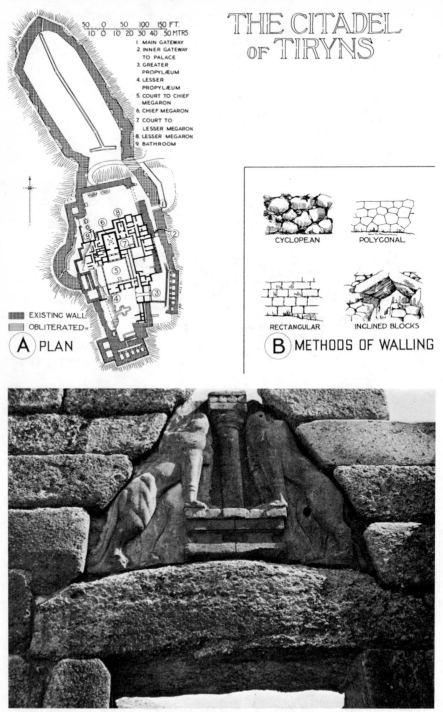

THE CITADEL OF TIRYNS

50   0   50   100   150 FT.
10   0   10 20 30 40 50 MTRS

1. MAIN GATEWAY
2. INNER GATEWAY TO PALACE
3. GREATER PROPYLÆUM
4. LESSER PROPYLÆUM
5. COURT TO CHIEF MEGARON
6. CHIEF MEGARON
7. COURT TO LESSER MEGARON
8. LESSER MEGARON
9. BATHROOM

EXISTING WALL
OBLITERATED„

(A) PLAN

CYCLOPEAN   POLYGONAL

RECTANGULAR   INCLINED BLOCKS

(B) METHODS OF WALLING

c. The Lion Gate, Mycenae (c. 1250 B.C.). See p. 191

doors. In general, the buildings were of cut stone or gypsum blocks in the lower tier, but of sun-dried brick or rubble, laced with timber, in the upper. On the principal (first) floor of the western wing were spacious state-rooms, approached by a circuitous ceremonial approach from the west market-court, via a grand staircase near the south end of the block. The restored piano nobile illustrates the extraordinary and unique arrangement where the function of the palace demanded formality invoking a sense of occasion (p. 187B). On the north or coastward side was an entrance to the central court, protected by a massive guardroom, one of the few evidences of defence on the whole site. To the east of this entrance were the industrial quarters, where pottery, jewellery and other crafts were practised and where oil was refined. Centrally in the east wing at the upper level was a further hall of state. Near the south-east corner of the courtyard the slope was cut away for the royal domestic apartments, three storeys high, the upper at courtyard level and the two lower facing outwards to terraced gardens. They were connected by a stately staircase, in return flights, lighted by a ramped colonnade of wooden columns from an adjacent light-well. Each floor was similar, with the queen's suite secluded from the rest and with no external windows, all the light proceeding from light-wells. Most remarkable were the sanitary arrangements, the queen's rooms having bathroom and water closets (the latter with a flushing device), connected to a drainage system of socketed earthenware pipes which served the royal quarters as a whole. Stairways, light-wells and colonnades of downward-tapering cypress-wood columns are typical of Island palaces, as also are double-folding doors, arranged in close series so that a whole length of wall could be thrown almost completely open. Walls regularly were plastered, and decorated with splendid frescoes. The palace appears at first glance to be a chaos of disorganized development, but its composition was the result of organic growth in its functional character, unity being found in the Minoan preference for linear form in response to the developing needs of living. The palace at Phaestos had almost precisely similar features.

The **Palace, Tiryns** (*c.* 1300 B.C.) (p. 188A) is a hill-top citadel, surrounded by defensive walls upwards of 7.3 m (24 ft) thick. At points where there are storage chambers embodied, the thickness is as much as 17.3 m (57 ft). The masonry is of the cyclopean type (p. 188B), except for short stretches of ashlar done at a later stage. The palace occupies the highest part of the elongated enclosure, and to the north of it were the dwellings of retainers, all these being divided by a defensive cross wall from a lower terrace, bare of buildings and intended as a place of refuge for the villagers and their flocks and herds in times of war; for here, there was no neighbouring town. The circuitous approach to the palace was devised so as to facilitate defence. It led through two gateways and two propylaea before reaching the second of two large, colonnaded courts. These propylaea, each comprising an inner and outer columned porch, sheltering a single portal in the dividing wall, anticipate the famous propylaea of classical Greece, such as that to the Acropolis at Athens (p. 196). Dominant in the plan, facing south into the inner large court, is a large megaron, 9.7 m (32 ft) wide inside, the distinctive domestic unit of the mainland, though here serving a ceremonial purpose as well, for to one side of the main apartment is a throne, raised on steps, facing a fixed, central hearth. The megaron had a low-pitched roof, and in many other features of detail and construction resembled the early temples of Hellenic Greece. A second, smaller megaron, 6.1 m (20 ft) wide inside, may have served as women's quarters. This and a third, still smaller, megaron were cut off from the inner large court and could only be approached by a tortuous route from the outer propylon. Though the palace was essentially one-storey, there were parts with upper floors, due to Island influences. On the western side of the large megaron was a bathroom with a floor of a single

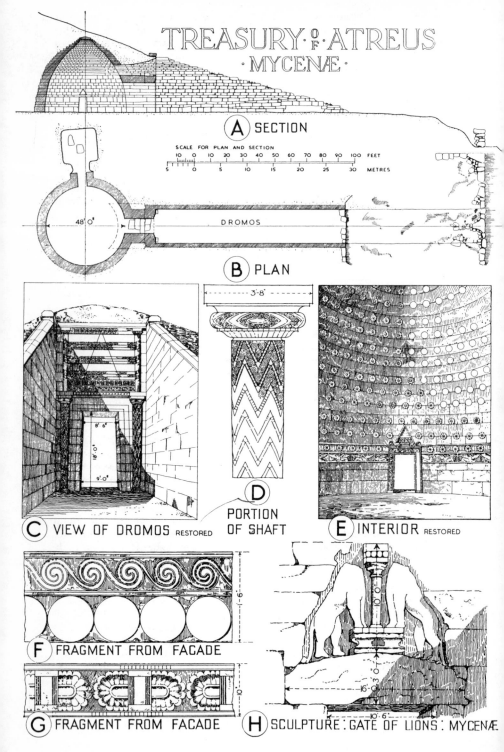

TREASURY·OF·ATREUS
·MYCENÆ·

A SECTION

SCALE FOR PLAN AND SECTION
10 0 10 20 30 40 50 60 70 80 90 100 FEET
5   0   5   10   15   20   25   30 METRES

48'0"   DROMOS

B PLAN

3'-8"

C VIEW OF DROMOS RESTORED

D PORTION OF SHAFT

E INTERIOR RESTORED

8'-6"
18'-0"
9'-0"

F FRAGMENT FROM FACADE

G FRAGMENT FROM FACADE

H SCULPTURE·GATE OF LIONS·MYCENÆ

16'-3"
10'-6"

black stone, measuring 3.9 m × 3.3 m (13 ft × 11 ft). Of the corresponding palace at Mycenae, of about the same date, less evidence survives, but whatever is forthcoming confirms the principles already noted at Tiryns. The recent excavation of the Palace of Nestor at Pylos further substantiates the principles and understanding of the Aegean palace complex.

The **Lion Gate, Mycenae** (*c.* 1250 B.C.) (pp. 188C, 190H) is the most famous feature of the above palace, standing in the circuit of its massive walls, which elsewhere are of the cyclopean type. The gateway, and the adjacent ashlar walls, represent a later modification. It has always stood above ground. Great, upright stone jambs support an immense lintel, spanning 3.2 m (10 ft 6 ins) and measuring 4.9 m (16 ft) long, by 1.06 m (3½ ft) high in the middle, by 2.4 m (8 ft) deep. Above is a triangular relieving opening, formed by advancing stone courses, trimmed to shape and filled with a stone slab, 51 mm (2 ins) thick, bearing a relief carving of two rampant lions facing a central column. This device had a religious meaning. The sculpture records for us the nature of the typical downward-tapering timber column of the Aegeans. It is shown carrying a lintel made up of timber plates trapping rounded logs between them. The triangular void generated a setting for sculpture important in the development of Hellenic architecture.

TOMBS

Of the several forms of tomb used by the Aegeans, two types offer architectural interest. They are found principally on the mainland. One is the rock-cut or chamber tomb, in which a rectangular chamber, about 3.6–6.1 m (12–20 ft) cube, is cut within the slope of a convenient hillside and approached by a passage or 'dromos', open to the sky, leading to a doorway in the rock façade. Similar, but far more elaborate is the 'tholos' type of tomb, a subterranean stone-vaulted construction shaped like an old-fashioned skip beehive.

The **'Treasury of Atreus', Mycenae** (*c.* 1325 B.C.) (p. 190), also known as the 'Tomb of Agamemnon', is the finest of these. It is 14.6 m (48 ft) in diameter and 13.4 m (44 ft) high inside, made up of 34 rings of masonry, capped by a single stone, dressed after completion to the form of a pointed dome. The courses are laid on flat beds, so no centering was needed. There were three metal friezes decorating the lower courses, and metal rosettes studded the vault face elsewhere. The whole construction was built within a cylindrical pit, upon a rammed clay floor, the apex just reaching the ground level of a hillside. A lateral, rock-cut, chamber, 8.2 m (27 ft) square and 5.8 m (19 ft) high, probably lined with heavy marble slabs originally, was the actual place of burial. The approach to the tomb was by a dromos, open to the sky, 6.4 m (21 ft) wide and 35 m (115 ft) long, its masonry walls rising with the hillside to a maximum of 13.7 m (45 ft). These walls were up to 3 m (10 ft) thick, and behind them were further very thick walls of sun-dried brick, to protect them from damp. The impressive façade stood 7.3 m (24 ft) in front of the chamber, and its portal, 2.7 m (9 ft) wide and 5.4 m (18 ft) high, narrowing by 305 mm (1 ft) towards the top, required two enormous lintels in the depth, one of them weighing more than 100 tons. There were triangular relieving openings over this and the side-chamber portals. The façade was embellished with architectural dressings in green, red and white stones, including the relieving opening, and flanking the door were single, green alabaster attached columns, of typical Aegean form, 6.1 m (20 ft) high, tapering downwards from 559 mm to 521 mm (22 ins to 20½ ins), decorated with bands of chevron ornament in relief. One of these columns is now in the British Museum.

Of a number of other such tombs, showing progressive stages of advance, the finest are the 'Tomb of Clytemnestra', Mycenae, and the 'Treasury of Minyas' at Orchomenos, Boeotia. The flanking columns of the former had fluted shafts. Portals in most cases were walled-up between burials, but some had actual doors, turning in pivots in lintel and threshold.

GREEK ARCHITECTURE

(650–30 B.C.)

ARCHITECTURAL CHARACTER

1. *The Hellenic Period* (650–323 B.C.). Greek culture naturally owed much to preceding civilizations, but the Hellenic Greeks, by reason of their innate artistic sense, so profoundly influenced the development of European art that Greece must be regarded as the veritable source of literary and artistic inspiration.

The 'Dark Age' which followed the Aegean civilization broke the continuity of the arts and threw them back to their early beginnings; but because some of the causative factors were similar, early Hellenic architecture had features in common with its predecessor. Though temples were now the chief building type, the earliest resembled the Aegean megaron in plan and in having timber-laced, sun-dried brick walls, stucco-covered, on stone dadoes; timber-enframed portals (the origin of the door architrave), narrowing a little towards the top; timber antae or uprights protecting the free ends of the naos walls where they embraced the pronaos or porch; and a low-pitched roof showing pediments or gables over the narrow ends. Then too, temple enclosures had propylaea, also found in Aegean architecture (p. 188A). But the outstanding difference was that, almost from the first, colonnades appear, surrounding the temple and forming an essential part of it. Greek architecture was essentially columnar and trabeated (*trabs* = a beam), and this gave it that simple straightforward character in which the constructive system is self-evident, uncomplicated by such devices as are involved in arch, vault and dome. From first to last in this period, the wooden roofs were untrussed, the rafters being supported by longitudinal beams—wall-plates, purlins and ridge-piece—laid on the walls and colonnades themselves or propped on struts from cross-beams (p. 212B). As the principle of triangulation was unknown, spans could not be large, unless internal lines of columns were supplied, and these usually were in two superimposed tiers (pp. 210B; 212B). This contrast with the constructive genius of the Romans is most marked (p. 288), and a reminder that the two architectures have to be assessed quite differently. Greek columns and their entablatures were at first entirely of timber, with terra-cotta decorations in the upper trabeation, but were converted into stone quite early in the period, about 600 B.C. The translation was quite direct, timber forms being imitated in stone with remarkable exactness. For this reason Greek architecture sometimes has been called 'a carpentry in marble', though in fact comparatively few buildings were erected comprehensively in marble before the fifth century B.C., this material meantime being sparingly employed for the finer details and for sculpture. The walls, too, became wholly of stone about the same time (600 B.C.), yet the tradition of the dado always survived in the special way the stones were arranged at the base of the wall (p. 212B). Ceilings, sometimes omitted, leaving an open roof, were treated decoratively with timber-panelled coffers, or, within the colonnades around temples, were of flat, stone slabs, coffered to imitate the timber. Almost all kinds of stone walls were used, from coursed rubble to the finest ashlar, well-bonded but always without mortar, unless for the smallest quantity necessary to ensure that the stones were firmly bedded. In the best buildings, such as temples, ashlar was normal, and the greatest precautions

OPTICAL CORRECTIONS IN ARCHITECTURE

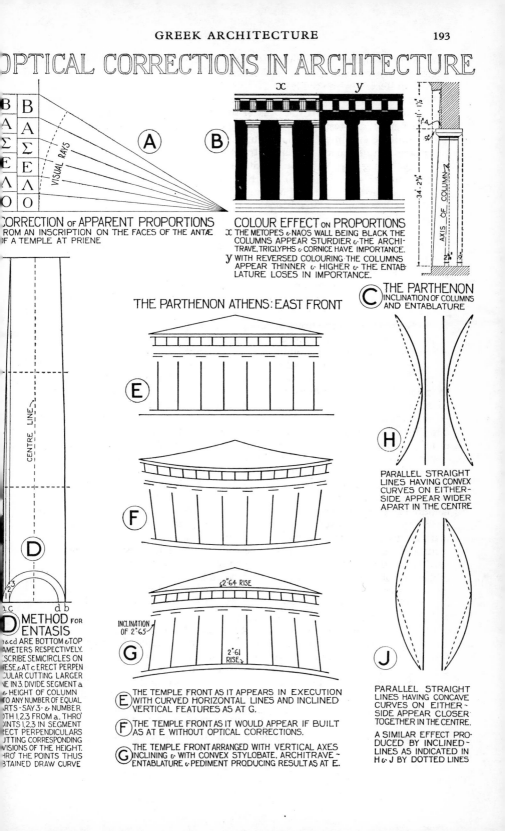

A CORRECTION of APPARENT PROPORTIONS
FROM AN INSCRIPTION ON THE FACES OF THE ANTÆ
OF A TEMPLE AT PRIENE

B COLOUR EFFECT ON PROPORTIONS
x THE METOPES & NAOS WALL BEING BLACK THE
COLUMNS APPEAR STURDIER & THE ARCHI-
TRAVE, TRIGLYPHS & CORNICE HAVE IMPORTANCE.
y WITH REVERSED COLOURING THE COLUMNS
APPEAR THINNER & HIGHER & THE ENTAB-
LATURE LOSES IN IMPORTANCE.

C THE PARTHENON
INCLINATION OF COLUMNS
AND ENTABLATURE

THE PARTHENON ATHENS: EAST FRONT

D METHOD FOR
ENTASIS
a & cd ARE BOTTOM & TOP
DIAMETERS RESPECTIVELY.
DESCRIBE SEMICIRCLES ON
THESE & AT c ERECT PERPEN-
DICULAR CUTTING LARGER
ONE IN 3. DIVIDE SEGMENT a
& HEIGHT OF COLUMN
INTO ANY NUMBER OF EQUAL
PARTS - SAY 3 - & NUMBER
BOTH 1,2,3 FROM a. THRO'
POINTS 1,2,3 IN SEGMENT
CUTTING CORRESPONDING
DIVISIONS OF THE HEIGHT.
THRO' THE POINTS THUS
OBTAINED DRAW CURVE

H PARALLEL STRAIGHT
LINES HAVING CONVEX
CURVES ON EITHER-
SIDE APPEAR WIDER
APART IN THE CENTRE

6.2"64 RISE
INCLINATION
OF 2°65
2°61
RISE

J PARALLEL STRAIGHT
LINES HAVING CONCAVE
CURVES ON EITHER-
SIDE APPEAR CLOSER
TOGETHER IN THE CENTRE.

A SIMILAR EFFECT PRO-
DUCED BY INCLINED-
LINES AS INDICATED IN
H & J BY DOTTED LINES

E THE TEMPLE FRONT AS IT APPEARS IN EXECUTION
WITH CURVED HORIZONTAL LINES AND INCLINED
VERTICAL FEATURES AS AT G.

F THE TEMPLE FRONT AS IT WOULD APPEAR IF BUILT
AS AT E. WITHOUT OPTICAL CORRECTIONS.

G THE TEMPLE FRONT ARRANGED WITH VERTICAL AXES
INCLINING & WITH CONVEX STYLOBATE, ARCHITRAVE-
ENTABLATURE & PEDIMENT PRODUCING RESULT AS AT E.

were taken to minimize the joints, so that they might not impair the architectural effect. In such work, the stones were secured together by wrought-iron cramps and dowels, protected by molten lead.

Several important refinements were practised in Greek architecture, in order to correct optical illusions. At the peak of the period, some of these were of a most delicate nature, and testify to a most advanced sensitivity to form. The Parthenon is the supreme example. The long horizontal lines of such features as stylobates, architraves, and cornices, which, if straight in reality would have appeared to the Greek eye to sag or drop in the middle of their length, were formed with slightly convex outlines (p. 193E, F, G). In the Parthenon, the stylobate has an upward curvature towards its centre of 60 mm ($2\frac{3}{8}$ ins) on the east and west façades, and of 110 mm ($4\frac{5}{16}$ ins) on the lateral façades. Vertical features were also inclined inwards towards the top to correct the appearance of falling outwards; thus the axes of the angle columns lean inwards 60 mm ($2\frac{3}{8}$ ins) and the axes of the columns, if produced, would meet at a distance of 2.4 km ($1\frac{1}{2}$ miles) above the stylobate (p. 193C). Greek columns usually, though not invariably, have an entasis (see Glossary and p. 193H, J). The shafts of the Parthenon have this slight convexity of silhouette—as well as the usual upward taper, or diminution—the deviation amounting to 17 mm ($\frac{11}{16}$ in), in a height of 9.4 m (31 ft) (p. 193D). Entasis is most pronounced in the Basilica at Paestum (p. 209E, H), where it amounts to 54 mm ($2\frac{1}{8}$ ins), and at its most delicate in the North Porch of the Erechtheion (p. 231), where it is less than 6.35 mm ($\frac{1}{4}$ in). Angle columns of temples were not only set closer to the adjacent columns, but were also stouter, as it was found that they appeared thinner against the open sky than those seen against the solid background of the 'naos' wall (p. 193B). In the case of the Parthenon, to heighten the perspective effect induced by the narrowed spacings of the angle columns, the large elements in the frieze, known as triglyphs (p. 205A), were spaced progressively more closely together from the centre outwards on the two short fronts, so that none is precisely above a column. The intervals differ by a maximum of 105 mm ($4\frac{1}{8}$ ins). Another correction was to make the letters of inscriptions, when raised up on buildings, larger in the upper lines than in the lower, so that they might appear all of one size when viewed from below (p. 193A). The finest sculpture completed the most important buildings, and the delicate adjustment and refined treatment, alike of the architecture and sculpture, were made possible by the hard, fine grain of the marble. Early sculptures in stone usually were coloured all over, but when marble came to be employed, bright colours and gilding were applied only to selected parts, so as to emphasize the fine qualities of the material itself. Similarly, in the best buildings, colour was restricted to the architectural detail, the broader, flat surfaces being left plain. Most of the mouldings, particularly those with curved profiles, had their own kind of conventional running ornament painted on, or carved and painted. When marble-masonry was not forthcoming, a coating of hard stucco, made with powdered marble, gave the desired quality of finish to stone-built structures. Mural painting, as on the walls of temples and porticoes, was a highly developed art.

From the original two 'Orders of Architecture', Doric and Ionic, evolved simultaneously by the two main branches of the Greek race, there at length arose a third, the Corinthian, a purely decorative variant which although invented by the Hellenic Greeks was only to attain its full identity in the hands of the Romans. The Etruscans (p. 263) developed the Tuscan, inspired by the Doric and a simpler and cruder version of it; while the last to appear was the 'Composite', a Roman contribution which did not differ greatly from the Corinthian, and which, like it, was an offshoot from the Ionic. These were the 'Five Orders of Architecture' of classical times. An 'Order' consists of the upright column or support, including the capital, and base, if any, and the horizontal entablature or part supported. The entablature is divided into architrave or lower part, frieze or middle part, and cornice or upper part. The proportions of column and entablature vary in the different 'Orders', as do also their mouldings and ornament. The origin and evolution of the different parts of the three Greek Orders are considered under their respective headings in Examples (pp. 202, 221, 235).

The Doric style was practised chiefly in South Italy and Sicily and on the Greek Mainland; Asia Minor was the true home of the Ionic. Cyrenaica, in North Africa, was Doric too, but the surviving monuments there are not as fully recorded as they are elsewhere. Though there are some important remains in Greece of the earliest experiments in Doric Architecture, it was the western colonies that showed the greater vigour in the archaic stages of development. Examples to show the corresponding evolution in Ionic Asia Minor are decidedly fewer in number. The finest buildings of the Hellenic period, in either style, are found on the mainland; and the select few in Athens herself, where they mostly belong to the last sixty years of the fifth century B.C. The reasons for the apparently odd circumstance that Athens should bring to fruition the Ionic as well as the Doric style, have to do with her ancient history—Athens was a stronghold in Aegean times— as well as her political circumstances. In Greece proper, the Doric and Ionic influenced one another to some extent in the process of formative development, but in Asia Minor the Ionic, since it originated there, resisted the innovations introduced on the mainland until the fourth century B.C., by which time there was a general slight decline in Greek taste, compensated however by a progressive widening of the scope of architecture to new types of building and more ambitious and extensive arrangements.

2. *The Hellenistic Period* (323–30 B.C.). In this period, due to the conquests of Alexander, Greek culture was diffused over many Near-Eastern lands, and in newly-founded cities, no less than in the old strongholds in Asia Minor, made fresh and brilliant advances. Athens, despite political vicissitudes, maintained much of her artistic prestige and renown. To this resplendent Grecian world the Romans came as comparative novices in the arts, deeply admiring and avidly assimilating whatever ideas and methods their practical minds deemed of value to their own evolving systems. Roman architecture was taking its own florid shape just at this time, and it was Greek Hellenistic architecture that provided much of the decorative inspiration as well as the embryos of quite a few of the Roman building-types. Even later, in the Roman Imperial age, Rome continued to draw from the art of the old Greek territories almost as much as it gave in the way of brilliant constructional theory and practical procedure.

Greek Hellenic architecture mostly had been of a religious character, but from the fourth century B.C. onwards, public buildings multiplied in type and number and passed into permanent form. Indeed, there were almost as many different kinds as there are today. They were dignified and gracious structures, and a quite new departure was that they now were related formally to one another, instead of being disposed irregularly on undulating natural sites. Civic design developed apace, and entire groups of buildings, themselves quite complex, were laid out on symmetrical lines in orderly schemes, often linked by colonnaded porticoes or 'stoas'. Town planning, an art which had originated as early as the fifth century B.C., became normal for new developments. Trabeated architecture still was usual, but arches began to appear over wall-openings, and large, niche-like recesses in building-plans. Such 'exedrae' previously had only been employed outdoors. Stone vaults, with radiating voussoirs, though used mostly for the coverings of tombs, were no longer uncommon. Of the highest importance was the advent, about the third century B.C., of the roof truss, which allowed large spaces to be covered without the aid of encumbering lines of intermediate pillars; though it was the Romans who were to secure the full advantage of this development. Due to the increased complexity of buildings, all kinds of new situations arose to be met by the Orders of Architecture, and they lost much of their original purity of form and simplicity of use. Taste declined, and the ornate Corinthian gained in popularity at the expense of the Doric, which at length, according to the Roman author Vitruvius, writing in the late first century B.C., came to be considered as unsuitable for sacred buildings. At times, novelty was deliberately sought. Parts were interchanged between Doric and Ionic, and two Orders commonly were used in the same building. They also were superimposed in tiers, sometimes of necessity, as when colonnaded buildings were two storeys high, but at other times solely as a decorative caprice. These departures from the strict canons of the Hellenic period were observed by the Romans and came to be characteristic of their use of the Orders.

EXAMPLES

In Greek cities there was a place apart, usually upon the highest part, for the 'temenos' or sacred enclosure, as at Delphi (p. 200B). Often, topography allowed this to be a citadel too, an Acropolis or upper city, where the principal sacred buildings might stand, both for dignity and safety. These were walled, like the city itself, and sometimes were very irregular in shape, due to the lie of the land. Propylaea, or entrance gateways, marked the approach to the sacred enclosures in many cities, such as Athens, Epidauros, Eleusis and Priene.

The **Propylaea, Athens** (437–432 B.C.) (pp. 197, 198A, B), erected under Pericles by the architect Mnesicles, forms the imposing entrance to the Acropolis, approached by a steep ascent from the plain below. The front and rear hexastyle Doric porticoes are on different levels, and give access to a covered hall with a wide central passage flanked by Ionic columns and with an eastern wall with five doorways of different heights. The projecting wings on either side of the western front have three Doric columns, smaller than those of the main block. The northern wing, provided with windows, was used as a pinacotheca (p. 197H), but the southern wing was never completed, probably to avoid encroaching on the sacred precincts of the Temple of Nikè Apteros. The general appearance, showing the important position of the Propylaea as part of the world-famous group of Acropolis buildings, is shown in the view (p. 198A). The asymmetrical composition, except for the central portico, gives rise to unresolved controversy; conjecturally it may have been designed as a symmetrical composition and unfinished because of the Peloponnesian War. Notwithstanding, its sculptural form and spatial qualities, together with scale, majesty and splendour ensure its unique achievement not only as a gateway but as an enclosure of space.

The **Acropolis, Athens** (p. 198A, B), is the supreme example, foremost among world-famous building-sites. A general idea of the original appearance of the Acropolis can be obtained from the restoration.

Normally, a city temenos contained a principal temple and maybe one or two subsidiary temples or shrines, together with treasuries in which were stored the offerings and processional regalia of other cities that held the presiding deity in esteem. There were also stoas, or colonnaded shelters; altars; statues or votive columns set up in honour of heroes, benefactors or victors in the games; exedrae, i.e. semi-circular seats or walled recesses for rest and contemplation; and sacred groves of trees. **Olympia** (p. 199), **Delphi** (p. 200B), **Epidauros, Corinth, Eleusis** and **Delos** were further towns having a temenos famous in Doric Greece. But temples and shrines were to be found too, adjacent to the Agora, the city

THE PROPYLÆA : ATHENS

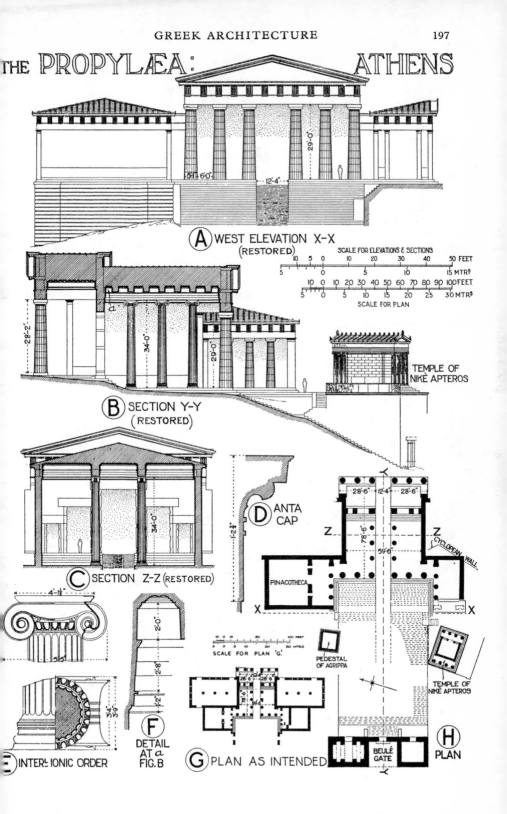

A WEST ELEVATION X-X
(RESTORED)

SCALE FOR ELEVATIONS & SECTIONS

10 5 0   10   20   30   40   50 FEET
5   0   5   10   15 MTRS

10 0 10 20 30 40 50 60 70 80 90 100 FEET
5   0   5   10   15   20   25   30 MTRS
SCALE FOR PLAN

B SECTION Y-Y
(RESTORED)

TEMPLE OF
NIKÉ APTEROS

C SECTION Z-Z (RESTORED)

D ANTA CAP

E INTER- IONIC ORDER

F DETAIL AT *a* FIG. B

G PLAN AS INTENDED

SCALE FOR PLAN 'G'
10 0 10   50   100 FEET
5 0 5 10   20   50 MTRS

PINACOTHECA

CYCLOPEAN WALL

PEDESTAL
OF AGRIPPA

TEMPLE OF
NIKÉ APTEROS

BEULÉ GATE

H PLAN

KEY
1. The Propylaea
2. The Pinacotheca
3. The Erechtheion
4. The Parthenon
5. The Temple of Nikè Apteros

A. The Acropolis, Athens (reconstruction as at *c.* A.D. 161 by M. Lambert). See p. 196

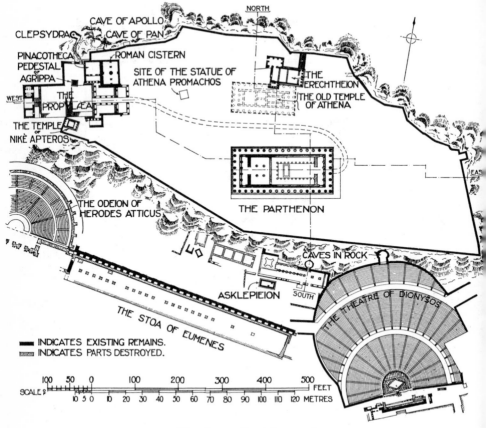

B. The Acropolis, Athens: plan

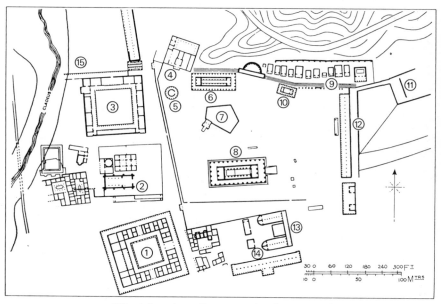

A. The Altis, Olympia (restored). See p. 196

B. Olympia: plan of temenos (2nd cent. A.D.)

1. Leonideum
2. Pheidias' workshop
3. Palaestra
4. Prytaneion
5. Philippeion
6. Temple of Hera
7. Pelopium
8. Temple of Zeus
9. Treasuries
10. Metroum (Temple of Meter)
11. Stadium
12. Stoa of Echo
13. Bouleuterion
14. South Stoa
15. Gymnasium

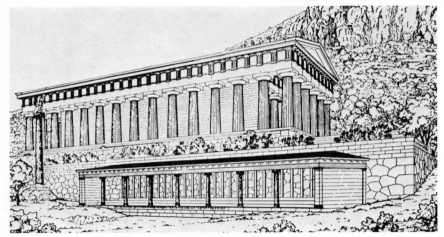

A. Delphi, Athenian stoa. Behind it, the polygonal wall and temple of Apollo VI.
See p. 196

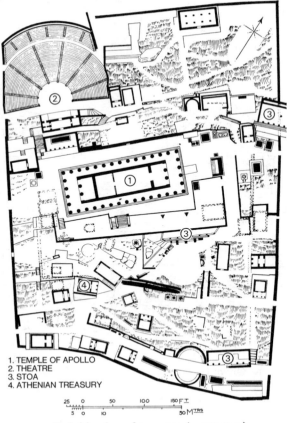

1. TEMPLE OF APOLLO
2. THEATRE
3. STOA
4. ATHENIAN TREASURY

B. Delphi: plan of temenos (*c.* 150 B.C.)
(reconstruction by P. de la Coste-Messelière)

square.or market place, the focus of Greek political, social, business and economic life. About it were the Prytaneion or Civic Hall; the Bouleuterion or Council House, a covered place of assembly; market enclosures of various types and stoas facing towards the Agora and serving miscellaneous functions. Colonnades sheltered the public fountains, and the vital importance of clear, pure water gave the fountain building a high civic prestige. At first, the Agora also served for open-air public meetings, religious assemblies and as a theatral area for contests, games and spectacles, but by Hellenistic times a number of the former uses of the Agora had been relegated to specially designed buildings. There were very fine, formal civic squares at **Priene** (p. 228G), **Miletus** and **Ephesus,** all in Asia Minor.

TEMPLES

Temples were the chief class of building in the Hellenic period, and we now describe their purpose and the different types in use. They were built with special regard to outward effect, since they were not intended for internal worship and the altar stood opposite the east front. They were adorned with fine sculpture in order to form fitting shrines to the deities to whom they were dedicated. They generally stood upon a crepidoma (see Glossary) of three or more steps. The 'naos', containing the statue of the god or goddess, was the kernel of the plan, and there was sometimes a treasury chamber, as well as front and rear porticoes, respectively known as the pronaos and opisthodomos (epinaos). Colonnades wholly surrounded all but the smallest buildings.

With one or two exceptions, Greek temples were not large, but even so, as the principle of the roof truss was not understood before the Hellenistic period, internal double-tiered colonnades were often needed to help support the roof. On the two short ends of the temple, a triangular-shaped pediment, usually filled with sculpture, terminated the simple span roof (pp. 211, 214A). These roofs were constructed of timber members, boarded and covered with terra-cotta or marble tiles, overlapping one another and finished off at the eaves with antefixæ (p. 205H) or, in the case of Ionic temples, stopping behind a crowning moulding ornamented with lion-head sculptured masks which served to eject rainwater (p. 205E). The entrance doors normally were within the pronaos on the east front, and as they were tall, reaching about two-thirds the height of the lofty naos, when open they would allow ample light to illuminate the statue in the naos. Even when closed, metal grilles in the panels of the doors would admit sufficient light for ordinary purposes. Windows were rare in temple buildings, and consequently it was at one time thought that quite a few temples must have been 'hypaethral', i.e. partly open to the sky. A few large ones were, such as the Temple of Apollo at Didyma, near Miletus (pp. 203N, 238), but rarely, and due rather to incompletion than intention, as was, apparently, the case at the Heraeum, Samos (p. 225) and the Temples of Zeus Olympius at Agrigentum (pp. 203G, 209) and Athens (p. 239) at the time when the latter was seen by Vitruvius. Surviving fragments of marble roof tiles from a dozen sites show that light was quite often admitted to roof spaces through holes cut in specially large tiles.

The comparative plans (p. 203) show the different types of temple employed by the Greeks. Rectangular temples are described (*a*) according to the number of columns on the entrance front and (*b*) by the arrangement of the exterior columns of the temple in relation to the naos, as below:

    (*a*) Henostyle—one column   Distyle—two columns
        Tristyle—three columns   Tetrastyle—four columns
        Pentastyle—five columns   Hexastyle—six columns

Heptastyle—seven columns　　　Octastyle—eight columns
Enneastyle—nine columns　　　Decastyle—ten columns
Dodecastyle—twelve columns.

(b) 'In antis' temples have from one to four columns between antae at the front. Two is the usual number.

'Amphi-antis' temples have from one to four columns between antae at front and rear. Two is the usual number.

'Prostyle' temples have a portico of columns at the front.

'Amphi-prostyle' temples have a portico of columns at front and rear.

'Peripteral' temples have a single line of columns surrounding the naos.

'Pseudo-peripteral' temples have flank columns attached to the naos wall.

'Dipteral' temples have a double line of columns surrounding the naos.

'Pseudo-dipteral' temples are like the last, but the inner range of columns is omitted on the flanks of the naos.

Examples are:

(i) Distyle in antis—The Temple of Nemesis, Rhamnus. Doric (p. 203A).

(ii) Amphi-antis distyle—No surviving example, but for type see p. 203B.

(iii) Prostyle tetrastyle—Temple 'B' at Selinus, Sicily. Doric (p. 203C).

(iv) Amphi-prostyle tetrastyle—Temple on the Ilissus, Athens. Ionic (pp. 203D, 228A).

(v) Peripteral hexastyle—Theseion, Athens. Doric (pp. 203J, 215L).

(vi) Pseudo-peripteral heptastyle—Temple of Zeus Olympius, Agrigentum. Doric (pp. 203G, 209K).

(vii) Peripteral octastyle—Parthenon, Athens. Doric (pp. 203M, 217G).

(viii) Dipteral octastyle—Olympieion, Athens. Corinthian (p. 203H).

(ix) Pseudo-dipteral octastyle—Temple 'G.T.', Selinus, Sicily. Doric (p. 203L).

(x) Peripteral enneastyle—'Basilica', Paestum. Doric (pp. 203K, 209H).

(xi) Dipteral decastyle—Temple of Apollo at Didyma, near Miletus. Ionic (p. 203N).

Types (i) and (iii) often served too as treasuries (p. 234B). The larger temples in the Doric style are usually hexastyle or octastyle. Pseudo-peripteral arrangements are very rare before the Hellenistic period, but became the favourite with the Romans. The more important Ionic temples of Asia Minor nearly always are dipteral or pseudo-dipteral and of a more variable and ostentatious nature than the Doric; they normally have a deep pronaos, and a shallow opisthodomos or none at all. The use of the Corinthian Order for the whole of a temple is not common until later Hellenistic times. The Erechtheion, Athens (p. 231F) is an exceptional instance of irregular planning. Greek circular temples usually were peripteral, as the Philippeion, Olympia (pp. 199A, B, 203F), and the Tholos, Epidauros (p. 203E).

THE DORIC ORDER

Though at one time the question was debated, there is now no doubt that the Order had a timber origin (p. 205F). Whilst there are certain resemblances between the Aegean megaron and the earliest temples (see p. 192), these do not concern the peristyles, which are distinctively Greek, and in any case there is evidence that between the Aegean and the Greek periods temple structure goes back to very primitive beginnings and virtually begins anew. Simple structures like those illustrated on p. 205C, D, doubtless continued to be built even while those of a sacred character were being progressively refined for their very special purpose, and indeed close counterparts can still be found among rustic structures today. Evidently, Greek columns began as tapered tree trunks, the function of the square

COMPARATIVE PLANS ᵒᶠ GREEK TEMPLES

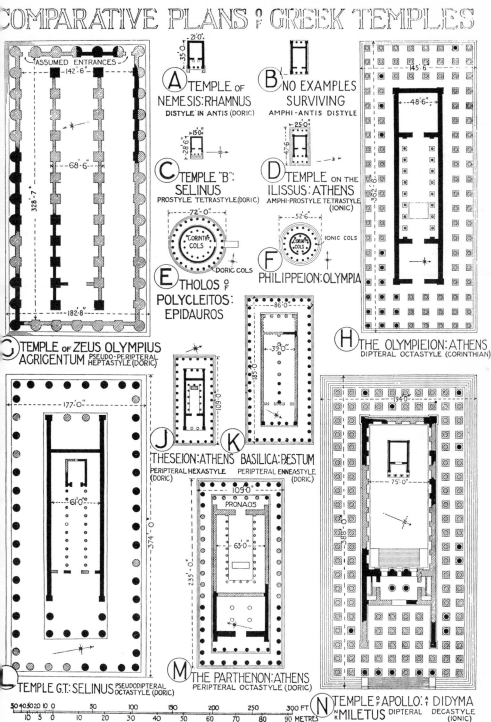

(A) TEMPLE OF NEMESIS: RHAMNUS
DISTYLE IN ANTIS (DORIC)

(B) NO EXAMPLES SURVIVING
AMPHI-ANTIS DISTYLE

(C) TEMPLE "B": SELINUS
PROSTYLE TETRASTYLE (DORIC)

(D) TEMPLE ON THE ILISSUS: ATHENS
AMPHI-PROSTYLE TETRASTYLE (IONIC)

(E) THOLOS OF POLYCLEITOS: EPIDAUROS

(F) PHILIPPEION: OLYMPIA

(G) TEMPLE OF ZEUS OLYMPIUS ACRIGENTUM
PSEUDO-PERIPTERAL HEPTASTYLE (DORIC)

(H) THE OLYMPIEION: ATHENS
DIPTERAL OCTASTYLE (CORINTHIAN)

(J) THESEION: ATHENS
PERIPTERAL HEXASTYLE (DORIC)

(K) BASILICA: PÆSTUM
PERIPTERAL ENNEASTYLE (DORIC)

(L) TEMPLE G.T.: SELINUS
PSEUDODIPTERAL OCTASTYLE (DORIC)

(M) THE PARTHENON: ATHENS
PERIPTERAL OCTASTYLE (DORIC)

(N) TEMPLE OF APOLLO: DIDYMA MILETUS
DIPTERAL DECASTYLE (IONIC)

PRONAOS

abacus and circular echinus comprising the capital being to gather and transmit the load of the entablature to the column shaft. The architrave is readily identifiable as a lintel—in fact, pairs of lintels, plated together—spanning from column to column and sustaining cross beams showing their ends as triglyphs in the frieze. Cross beams were heavy and numerous for the reason already seen; roof trusses were unknown and the beams had to support struts to prop up the sloping roofs. The lowest member of the cornice represents a wooden plate across the tops of the triglyphs to receive the wide, flat rafters, recognizable in stone architecture as mutules, which always retain a slope echoing the pitch of the roof. On their undersides are seen the guttae, stone replicas of wooden pins driven through the mutules to secure the roof boarding, on which were laid terra-cotta tiles bedded on mud or clay. The eaves tiles were specially made so that flanges could droop over the rafter ends to conceal them and present a continuous fascia which survives in stone architecture as the corona, the principal projecting member of the cornice. Just before wooden colonnades were converted into stone, the terra-cotta eaves crestings were very ornate and differed quite a little in design from place to place. There were also decorative terra-cotta plates slotted into the interspaces (metopes) between the triglyphs. These terra-cottas, of which quite a few survive, were richly painted in dark colours. The earliest stone colonnades, from about 600 B.C., had very clumsy proportions, as the capacities of stone were imperfectly known. The Temple of Apollo, Syracuse, Sicily (c. 565 B.C.) had columns little more than four times their own diameter in height and a ponderous stone entablature about half the height of the column. All the details were similarly crude. Afterwards, the Doric Order underwent a progressive lightening of parts which did not halt when the style had been perfected, but went on continuously throughout the two Greek periods. In the case of the Parthenon, the entablature is about one-third the height of the columns. Typical arrangements will now be described.

The **Doric Column** (pp. 205A, 207) stands without a base directly on a crepidoma, usually of three steps, and has a height, including the capital, of from 4 to 6 times the diameter at the base in the Hellenic period and up to $7\frac{1}{4}$ in the Hellenistic. The circular shaft, diminishing at the top from $\frac{3}{4}$ to $\frac{2}{3}$ of this diameter, is divided as a rule into 20 shallow flutes or channels separated by sharp 'arrises', but sometimes there are 12, 16, 18, or, as at Paestum, 24 (p. 207C). With the normal 20, a projection or arris came under the angles of the square abacus above, while a flute lay astride each of the main, rectangular axes. The shaft has normally a slightly convex profile called the entasis, discussed earlier (p. 194), to counteract the hollow appearance which results from straight-sided columns (p. 193D). The shaft terminates in the 'hypotrachelion', usually formed of three grooves in archaic examples and later of one groove, and immediately above it is the continuation of the fluted shaft known as the 'trachelion' or necking. The distinctive capital consists of abacus and echinus. Near the base of the echinus are 'annulets' or horizontal fillets, from three to five in number, which stop the vertical lines of the arrises and flutes of the shaft. The form of the echinus varies with the date of the building. In the earlier temples at Paestum (p. 207B, C) it has considerable projection, and is fuller in outline, approximating to a parabolic section; whereas in mature examples such as the Theseion (p. 207E) and the Parthenon (p. 207F) the projection is less and the profile more subtle, approximating to a hyperbolic curve. In Hellenistic work, when the column has become slender, the whole capital is shallower and the curve of the echinus approaches a straight line. The abacus, which forms the upper member of the capital, is a square slab, unmoulded until very late Greek times, when it begins to acquire a small moulding at the top.

The **Doric entablature** (p. 205A, E) which, in the case of the Parthenon, is $1\frac{3}{4}$

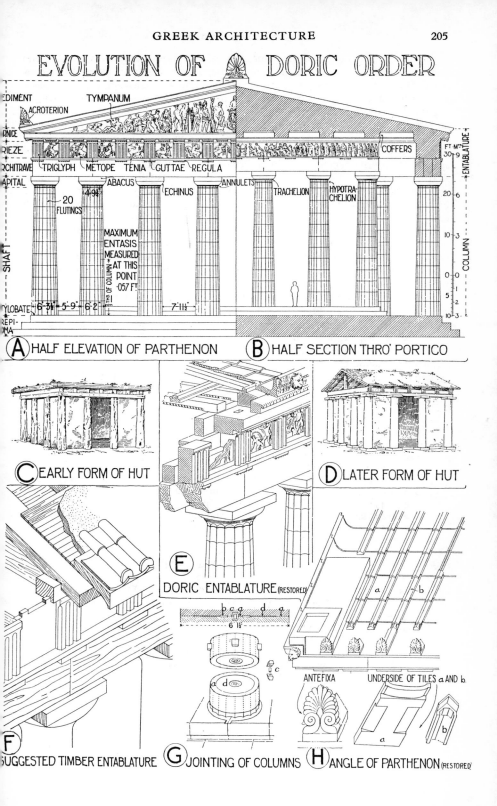

EVOLUTION OF A DORIC ORDER

A HALF ELEVATION OF PARTHENON   **B** HALF SECTION THRO' PORTICO

C EARLY FORM OF HUT

D LATER FORM OF HUT

E DORIC ENTABLATURE (RESTORED)

F SUGGESTED TIMBER ENTABLATURE   **G** JOINTING OF COLUMNS   **H** ANGLE OF PARTHENON (RESTORED)

times the lower diameter of the column in height, varies between the earliest and latest examples from $2\frac{1}{4}$ to as little as $1\frac{1}{3}$, by the same kind of internal measure. An entablature has three main divisions: (a) The architrave or principal beam usually is made up of two or three slabs in the depth, the outermost showing a vertical face in one plane. Capping it is a flat projecting band called the taenia, and under this, at intervals corresponding to the triglyphs, are strips each known as a regula, with six guttae or small conical drops below. (b) The frieze is formed of triglyphs with three upright channels which alternate with metopes or square spaces, often ornamented with fine relief sculpture, as in the Parthenon (p. 219). A triglyph is aligned over each column and there is usually one over each inter-columniation. At the angles of the temple, however, two triglyphs meet with a bevelled edge, and the intercolumniation is less by about half a triglyph in width than that of the others. Where extra convenience was needed, as in the Propylaea, Athens (p. 197A), a central intercolumniation sometimes was made three metopes wide. Also, when in the Hellenistic period the proportions of the Order became very light, it was necessary regularly to increase the number of metopes in each intercolumniation. At Cora, in Italy, a Roman temple built under Hellenistic influence, four metopes were needed to each intercolumniation. (c) The cornice, the upper or crowning part, has at the top a cymatium or gutter moulding resting on a bird's beak moulding, and below this is the corona or vertical face. The soffit or underside of the cornice has an inclination approximating to the slope of the roof, and has flat blocks or mutules, which suggest the ends of sloping rafters. A mutule occurs over each triglyph and each metope, and is usually ornamented with eighteen guttae, in three rows of six each.

The principal Doric temples were in Greece, Sicily and South Italy, as set forth below.

Doric Temples in Greece

c. 590 B.C.	The Heraion, Olympia (p. 208)
c. 540 B.C.	Temple of Apollo, Corinth
c. 510 B.C.	Temple of Apollo, Delphi (p. 200A)
c. 490 B.C.	Temple of Aphaia, Aegina (p. 208)
c. 460 B.C.	Temple of Zeus, Olympia (p. 213)
449–444 B.C.	The Theseion (Temple of Hephaestus), Athens (p. 213)
c. 450–425 B.C.	Temple of Apollo Epicurius, Bassae (p. 219)
447–432 B.C.	The Parthenon, Athens (p. 213)
444–440 B.C.	Temple of Poseidon, Sunium
436–432 B.C.	Temple of Nemesis, Rhamnus (p. 203A)
c. 380 B.C.	Temple of Asclepius, Epidauros
c. 350 B.C.	The Tholos, Epidauros (p. 203E)
c. 300 B.C.	Temple of Apollo, Delos (p. 207G)

Doric Temples in Sicily and South Italy

c. 565 B.C.	Temple of Apollo, Syracuse (p. 204)
c. 550–530 B.C.	Temple 'C', Selinus
c. 530 B.C.	The 'Basilica', Paestum (p. 208)
c. 520–450 B.C.	The Great Temple of Apollo (G.T.), Selinus (p. 203L)
c. 510 B.C.	Temple of Demeter, Paestum (p. 208)
c. 510–409 B.C.	Temple of Zeus Olympius, Agrigentum (p. 208)
480 B.C.	Temple of Athena, Syracuse (p. 358)
c. 460 B.C.	Temple of Hera Lacinia, Agrigentum
c. 460 B.C.	Temple of Poseidon, Paestum (p. 208)
c. 430 B.C.	Temple of Concord, Agrigentum
c. 424–416 B.C.	Temple at Segesta, Sicily

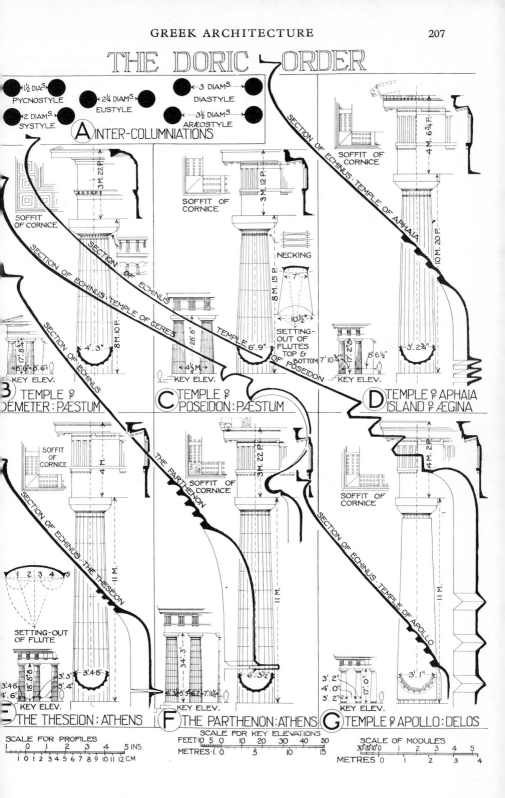

THE DORIC ORDER

A INTER-COLUMNIATIONS

+1½ DIAMS· PYCNOSTYLE
+2 DIAMS· SYSTYLE
2¼ DIAMS· EUSTYLE
+3 DIAMS· DIASTYLE
3½ DIAMS· ARÆOSTYLE

SECTION OF ECHINUS · TEMPLE OF APHAIA
SOFFIT OF CORNICE
4 M. 6¾ P.
10 M. 20 P.
3'. 2¾"
KEY ELEV.

SOFFIT OF CORNICE
3 M. 22 P.
SECTION OF ECHINUS · TEMPLE OF CERES
8 M. 10 P.
4'. 3"
8'. 6"–8'. 6"
17'. 8¾"
KEY ELEV.

B TEMPLE OF DEMETER : PÆSTUM

SOFFIT OF CORNICE
3 M. 12 P.
NECKING
8 M. 15 P.
10½"
SETTING-OUT OF FLUTES TOP & BOTTOM
SECTION OF ECHINUS · TEMPLE OF POSEIDON
TEMPLE 6'. 9"
28'. 8"
4½ M.
7'. 10¾"
KEY ELEV.

C TEMPLE OF POSEIDON : PÆSTUM

SOFFIT OF CORNICE
4 M. 2 P.
8'. 6½"
17'. 2½"
KEY ELEV.

D TEMPLE OF APHAIA ISLAND OF ÆGINA

SOFFIT OF CORNICE
4 M.
SECTION OF ECHINUS · THE THESEION
THE PARTHENON
1 2 3 4 5
SETTING-OUT OF FLUTE
II M.
3'. 48"
4'. 6"
18'. 8¼"
3'. 3"
5'. 4"
3'. 48"
KEY ELEV.

E THE THESEION : ATHENS

SOFFIT OF CORNICE
3 M. 22 P.
II M.
34'. 3"
6'. 3½"
6'. 3½"–5'. 9¾"–2'. 7'. 11¼"
KEY ELEV.

F THE PARTHENON : ATHENS

SOFFIT OF CORNICE
4 M. 2 P.
SECTION OF ECHINUS · TEMPLE OF APOLLO
II M.
3'. 1"
3'. 2"
4'. 0"
3'. 2½"
17'. 0"
KEY ELEV.

G TEMPLE OF APOLLO : DELOS

SCALE FOR PROFILES
0 1 2 3 4 5 INS.
0 1 2 3 4 5 6 7 8 9 10 11 12 CM

SCALE FOR KEY ELEVATIONS
FEET 10 5 0 10 20 30 40 50
METRES 1 0 5 10 15

SCALE OF MODULES
30 20 10 0 1 2 3 4 5
METRES 0 1 2 3 4

The **Heraion, Olympia** (*c.* 590 B.C.) (p. 209C, F), dedicated to Hera, is most interesting as it illustrates the process of transition from timber construction to stone. It stands on a platform of two steps, measuring 51.2 m × 19.6 m (168 ft × 64 ft 6 ins). As usual with early Doric temples, the plan has long proportions. The thick naos walls are of ashlar stone to a height of 1.07 m (3 ft 6 ins), but all the upper walls were of sun-dried brick, strengthened with wooden framing, a method of construction reminiscent of Aegean practice. Inside the temple, alternate columns of a range of eight on each side were attached by spur walls to the naos walls. The internal columns and all those in the colonnades outside were originally of wood, but were replaced with stone from time to time over a period of centuries. Thus they vary very much in their details, and are either monolithic or built-up in a varying number of courses of 'drums'. The entablature remained always of timber, and the antae and the door casings were also of wood.

The **'Basilica', Paestum** (*c.* 530 B.C.) (p. 209E, H), in reality a temple, is unusual in being enneastyle, the central line of eight columns in the naos assisting to divide the width of the temple into four parts, to allow easy support for the roof timbers. For this reason too, the ambulatory is very wide at the sides and the temple consequently almost pseudo-dipteral, while the pronaos is tristyle in antis. The columns have a pronounced diminution and entasis, and the capitals are heavy and wide-spreading. A peculiarity of this temple and the neighbouring **Temple of Demeter** (Ceres) (*c.* 510 B.C.) is the decorative treatment of the trachelion (p. 207B), showing Ionic influence.

The **Temple of Zeus Olympius, Agrigentum** (*c.* 510–409 B.C.) (pp. 203G, 209) also is of archaic, unusual design, with a heptastyle, pseudo-peripteral arrangement and a plan comprising a central naos and two slightly narrower flanking apartments. At the west a portion of the naos was cut off to form a sanctuary. The temple is now in a ruinous condition, but measured 52.7 m × 110 m (173 ft × 361 ft) over the stylobate, so large that its roofing appears never to have been completed. That there were pediments over the short ends is clear from an ancient description and from surviving fragments. The enormous attached, external columns, 4 m (13 ft 3 ins) diameter and over 17 m (56 ft) high, show traces of Ionic influence in having mouldings across the base. In the upper portion of the screen wall, between the outer columns, were giant 'Atlantes', sculptured figures, 7.6 m (25 ft) high, giving intermediate support to the massive entablature. Some authorities place the Atlantes in the naos (p. 209J). Because of the great scale, the Order had to be made up of many stone pieces. The coarse stone was finished with a thin coating of fine marble stucco.

The **Temple of Poseidon, Paestum** (*c.* 460 B.C.) (pp. 207C, 209A, B, D, G, 210), is one of the best preserved of all early Greek temples. Though more mature than the three last-named temples from Doric western territory—the two at Paestum and that at Agrigentum—and now approaching the perfected type, the plan is still rather long and the Order heavy. The columns are about 8.8 m (29 ft) high and thus 4.3 times their lower diameter of 2.0 m (6 ft 9 ins). The temple is peripteral hexastyle, with fourteen columns on the flanks and has the normal crepidoma of three steps, pronaos, naos and opisthodomos. Near the entrance, steps led to the roof space. The columns in the naos, preserved almost intact, are in a double tier, the upper separated from the lower solely by a stone architrave, and not a full entablature. The number of flutes varies; the columns of the outer colonnade have 24, the lower, inner Order the normal 20, and the upper range only 16.

The **Temple of Aphaia, Aegina** (*c.* 490 B.C.) (pp. 211, 212), on an island about twenty-five miles from Athens, like the last example represents the almost perfected temple type, but its appreciably earlier date indicates that mainland

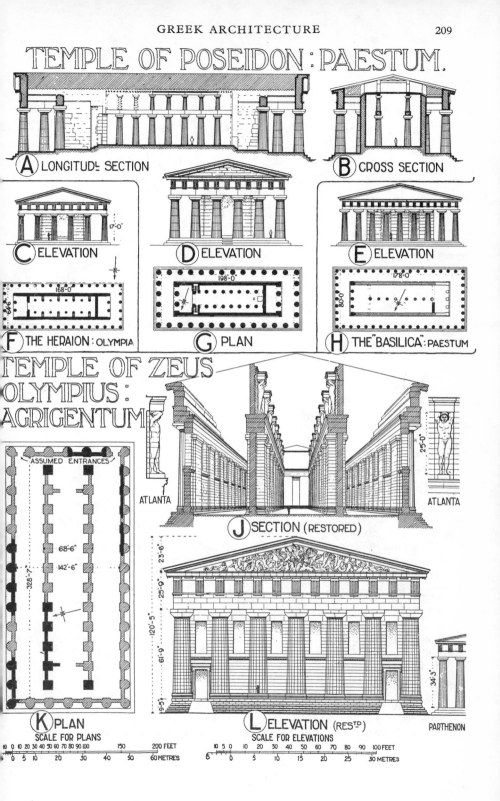

TEMPLE OF POSEIDON : PAESTUM.

A LONGITUD⁴ SECTION

B CROSS SECTION

C ELEVATION

D ELEVATION

E ELEVATION

F THE HERAION : OLYMPIA

G PLAN

H THE "BASILICA" : PAESTUM

TEMPLE OF ZEUS OLYMPIUS : AGRIGENTUM

ASSUMED ENTRANCES

ATLANTA

J SECTION (RESTORED)

ATLANTA

K PLAN

SCALE FOR PLANS

L ELEVATION (RESᵀᴰ)

SCALE FOR ELEVATIONS

PARTHENON

A. Temple of Poseidon, Paestum (*c.* 460 B.C.). See p. 208

B. Temple of Poseidon, Paestum, showing superimposed columns

TEMPLE ᴼꜰ APHAIA : ÆGINA
(RESTORED)

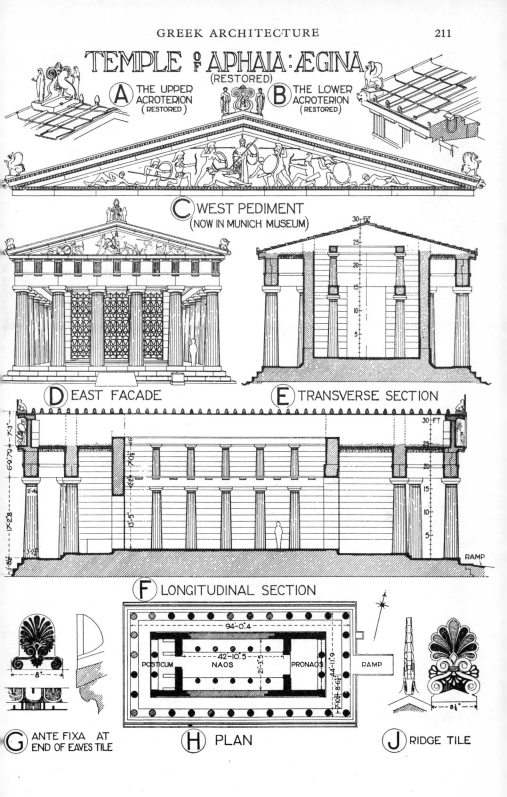

A THE UPPER ACROTERION (RESTORED)

B THE LOWER ACROTERION (RESTORED)

C WEST PEDIMENT (NOW IN MUNICH MUSEUM)

D EAST FACADE

E TRANSVERSE SECTION

F LONGITUDINAL SECTION

G ANTE FIXA AT END OF EAVES TILE

H PLAN

POSTICUM   NAOS   PRONAOS   RAMP

94'·0"·4

42'·10"·5

21'·3"·5

J RIDGE TILE

A. Temple of Aphaia, Aegina (*c.* 490 B.C.). See p. 208

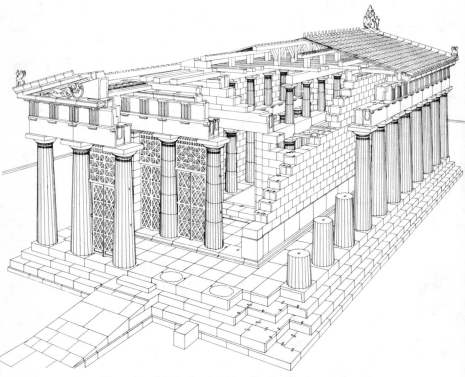

B. Temple of Aphaia, Aegina. Sectional view, restored

Greece by this time was showing the greater initiative. It is hexastyle, with all the normal parts and arrangement, including a shortened plan, requiring only twelve flanking columns. The off-centre doorway to the opisthodomos, though contemporary, was an afterthought. This temple, like the last, possessed a double range of interior columns, separated simply by an architrave. It now seems unlikely that the temple was hypaethral, as sometimes had been thought. All the exterior columns had monolithic shafts, except three adjacent ones on the north side, which were built up in drums after the naos had been completed. The pediment sculptures, the elaborately-carved acroteria, the antefixae and the roof slabs over the pediments and eaves were in Parian marble, the rest of the roof tiles being in terra-cotta (p. 211A, B, C, G, J). The entablature was painted in glowing colours. The pediments contained remarkable sculptures belonging to the latest phase of archaic Greek art, dating from c. 490 B.C., like the temple itself. These sculptures, now in Munich, are shown as disposed in Cockerell's restorations, but later authorities have suggested different arrangements of the figures. The majority of the temple was of local limestone, treated usually with a coat of marble stucco.

· The **Temple of Zeus, Olympia** (c. 460 B.C.) (pp. 199, 214A) designed by Libon of Elis, belongs to the phase of the developed temple of the fifth century. Continuity of pattern and formal organization were achieved in what is arguably the finest manifestation of the Doric temple. It was orthodox in arrangement but grand in its dimensions, being 27.7 m × 62.28 m (90 ft 9 ins × 204 ft 4 ins) over the stylobate— a monumental scale as befitted the supremacy of the God and the location. Mostly, it was built of coarse limestone, faced with marble stucco, but had Parian marble for the sculptured pediments, the carved metopes over the inner porches, the cymatium and all the roof slabs. Appropriately the temple dedicated to the Father of the Gods at the sacred pan-Hellenic centre of Olympia was embellished to the point of completeness within the canon of the Doric idea by sculpture which achieved a serenity and composure of supreme monumental quality. The splendid architectural effect was heightened by picking out the mouldings and ornament in blue, red and gold, the main surfaces being left white. The acroteria were of bronze. About 448 B.C. the temple received the colossal gold-and-ivory statue, 12.2 m (40 ft) high above its base, by Pheidias the famous sculptor who at that time was also working on the colossal statue of Athena for the Parthenon. Inside the naos, once again, were superimposed colonnades. Fragments of large marble tiles, with elliptical holes cut in them, through which light was admitted to the roof space, were found on the site. During the fifth century A.D. the building was wrecked by an earthquake, but the vast platform surrounded by overturned columns and pieces of entablature demonstrate even in total ruin the essential monumentality of the achievement.

The **Theseion, Athens** (449–444 B.C.) (pp. 214B, 215), is now thought to be a temple to Hephaestus. It is very well preserved externally, owing to its having been converted into a church by the Byzantine Greeks who, however, gutted the naos and constructed an apse at the east end. The plan is normal, except for a roomier arrangement within the east front and a crepidoma of only two steps; also, the double tier of inner columns, which hitherto ran the whole length of the naos, here returns across the west end. The building was almost wholly of marble. Relief sculptures once existed in the pediments, but otherwise were limited to friezes over the pronaos and opisthodomos porches, and to metopes across the east front and the neighbouring four on each flank. Much survives of the stone coffered ceilings over the ambulatory, with some traces of the original colouring.

The **Parthenon, Athens** (447–432 B.C.) (pp. 198, 205A, B, H, 207F, 217, 218), erected on the Acropolis, south of the old Temple of Athena (p. 198B), in the time of

A. Temple of Zeus, Olympia (restored) (*c.* 460 B.C.). See p. 213

B. The Theseion, Athens (449–444 B.C.). See p. 213

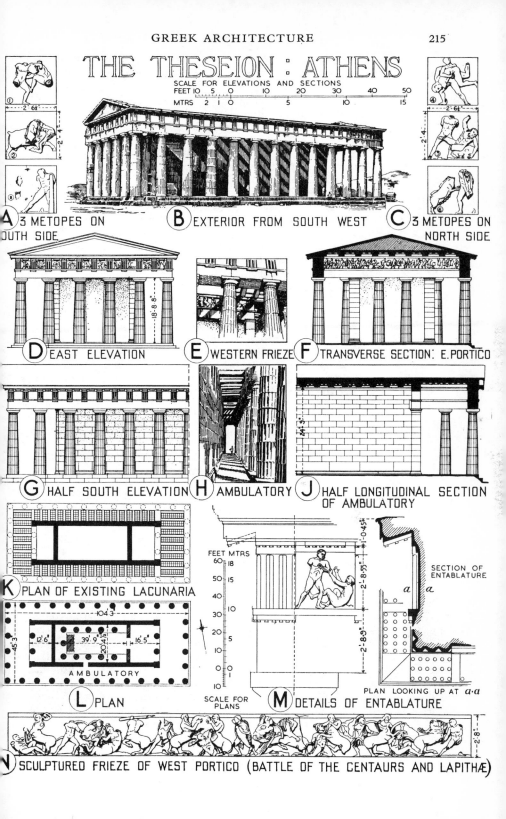

THE THESEION : ATHENS

SCALE FOR ELEVATIONS AND SECTIONS
FEET 10 5 0 10 20 30 40 50
MTRS 2 1 0 5 10 15

A 3 METOPES ON SOUTH SIDE

B EXTERIOR FROM SOUTH WEST

C 3 METOPES ON NORTH SIDE

D EAST ELEVATION

E WESTERN FRIEZE

F TRANSVERSE SECTION: E. PORTICO

G HALF SOUTH ELEVATION

H AMBULATORY

J HALF LONGITUDINAL SECTION OF AMBULATORY

K PLAN OF EXISTING LACUNARIA

L PLAN

AMBULATORY

M DETAILS OF ENTABLATURE

FEET MTRS

SCALE FOR PLANS

SECTION OF ENTABLATURE

PLAN LOOKING UP AT a·a

N SCULPTURED FRIEZE OF WEST PORTICO (BATTLE OF THE CENTAURS AND LAPITHÆ)

Pericles, was dedicated to Athena Parthenos, the virgin Athena. Ictinus and Callicrates were the architects, and Pheidias was the master sculptor. The temple is peripteral octastyle in plan, with seventeen columns on the flanks, and stands on a crepidoma of three steps, which measures 30.9 m × 69.5 m (101 ft 4 ins × 228 ft) along the top, i.e. a relation of breadth to length of about 4 to 9. Each of the steps is about 508 mm (1 ft 8 ins) high and 711 mm (2 ft 4 ins) wide, and as these were too steep to ascend with comfort, intermediate steps were provided at the centre of the east and west ends (p. 217A). The principal doorway on the east led into the naos, known as the 'Hecatompedon', after an archaic temple which had stood upon the site and was so named because its naos had measured 100 Attic feet long. This eastern chamber, 19.2 m (63 ft) wide and 29.8 m (98 ft) long, had Doric colonnades on three sides, forming an ambulatory. They were in two tiers, separated by an architrave, and gave support to the roof timbers. There were ten columns on each side, and five across the west end, counting the angle columns twice. Near the western end stood the famous statue of Athena Parthenos, one of the most marvellous works of Pheidias, representing Athena fully armed with spear, helmet, aegis and shield, and supporting a winged Victory in her right hand. This was a 'chryselephantine' or gold and ivory statue, about 12.8 m (42 ft) high including pedestal, and the gold plates which formed the drapery, armour and accessories over the wooden core were detachable, so that they could be removed in case of danger. The face, hands and feet were of ivory, and the eyes of precious stones. The ceiling of the naos was of wood, decoratively painted, ornamented with sunken 'lacunaria' or coffers. Various suggestions have been made as to how the naos was lighted, but the very large double doors, when open, probably were the sole means of admitting natural light. To the west of the naos was the Parthenon or virgin's chamber, from which the temple took its name. This was entered from the opisthodomos by a large doorway corresponding to the eastern one, and its roof was supported by four Ionic columns (p. 217E, F). As this chamber was shallow and high, a double tier of Doric columns would have appeared exceptionally clumsy, while a single range would have encumbered the floor space unduly. So Ionic columns were used instead, and both Orders are found in the one building, a practice increasingly prevalent from this time onwards. Numerous other evidences of Ionic influence are found in this essentially Doric building. The naos and virgin's chamber were enclosed by walls about 1.2 m (4 ft) thick, and the whole temple was encircled by an ambulatory 2.7 m (9 ft) wide on the sides and 3.3 m (11 ft) in the front and rear. The pronaos and opisthodomos, each about 18.3 m × 3.6 m (60 ft × 12 ft), were arranged in a somewhat unusual manner with six columns about 1.7 m (5½ ft) in diameter and 10 m (33 ft) high, forming a prostyle portico on an upper platform of two steps. Both pronaos and opisthodomos were used as treasuries, and, in order to render them secure, lofty metal grilles extending from top to bottom were fixed between the columns, with the entrance gates in the central inter-columniation.

Externally, the dominant feature is the stately peristyle of fluted marble columns (pp. 193C, 207F). The columns are about 1.9 m (6 ft 2 ins) in diameter at the base and 10.4 m (34 ft 3 ins) high: or, to express their proportions directly, they are nearly 5½ times their own lower diameter in height. The angle columns are a little larger in diameter; 1.9 m (6 ft 3½ ins). All diminish at the top of the shaft to a little more than three-quarters the lower diameter. The columns support an entablature about 3.4 m (11 ft) high (p. 193C), with the usual divisions of architrave, frieze and cornice (pp. 205A, 207F, 217C, 218B). The architrave was ornamented with bronze shields, probably presented by Alexander the Great in 334 B.C., and with dedicatory inscriptions in bronze letters. The joints of the marble roof-slabs above the cornice

THE PARTHENON: ATHENS

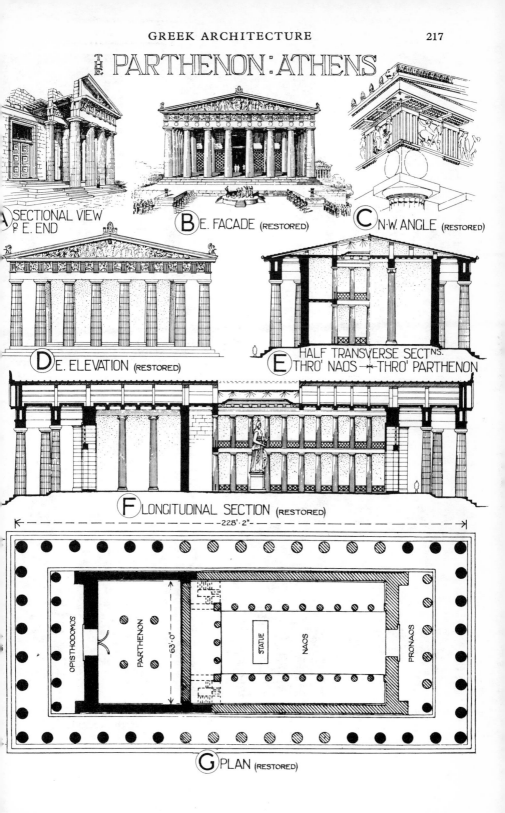

A SECTIONAL VIEW ᵒᶠ E. END

B E. FACADE (RESTORED)

C N·W· ANGLE (RESTORED)

D E. ELEVATION (RESTORED)

E HALF TRANSVERSE SECTⁿˢ. THRO' NAOS ⟶ THRO' PARTHENON

F LONGITUDINAL SECTION (RESTORED)

—228' 2"—

OPISTHODOMOS

PARTHENON

63' 0"

STATUE

NAOS

PRONAOS

G PLAN (RESTORED)

A. The Parthenon, Athens (447–432 B.C.). See p. 213

B. The Parthenon, Athens: view of angle

C. The Parthenon, Athens: south peristyle

were masked by carved antefixae, which formed an ornamental cresting along the sides of the building (pp. 205H, 217C). The pediments, which have an inclination of 13½ degrees, terminated the roof at each end of the temple, and had large floral acroteria, about 2.7 m (9 ft) high, at the apex and lower angles (pp. 205A, 217B, D). The peristyle ceiling was enriched with lacunaria and marble beams. The optical refinements used in the different parts of the Parthenon have already been described (p. 194). The tympana in the pediments were filled with the finest sculpture of Pheidias. That of the eastern pediment represented the birth of Athena and of the west, the contest of Athena and Poseidon for the soil of Attica. The use of sculptured friezes, both inside and outside the temple, is another evidence of Ionic influence. The celebrated Panathenaic frieze was carved along the top of the naos wall just below the peristyle ceiling, and was taken across the east and west ends above the six columns of the pronaos and opisthodomos. It is 1 m (3 ft 4 ins) high, in very slight relief of about 38 mm (1½ ins), and the sculpture is treated in such a way as to be seen effectively by the light reflected up from the white marble pavement below, the shadow being thrown upwards (p. 217A). It represents the Panathenaic procession, which went every fourth year to the Acropolis to present the 'peplos' (shawl) to the goddess Athena, and it portrays the preparations of Athenian knights, and the great procession of cavalry, chariots, men with olive branches, musicians, youths, sacrificial animals, maidens with sacrificial vessels, magistrates and gods, all culminating in a great central group at the eastern end over the principal entrance to the temple, while the imposing chryselephantine statue of Athena in the naos was seen through the open door. Out of the original length of 159.7 m (524 ft), only 102 m (335 ft) are in existence. The western frieze, excepting the three central figures, is in its original position; the greater portion of that belonging to the northern, southern and eastern sides is in the British Museum, while the remainder, with the exception of eight fragments of the eastern frieze in the Louvre, is in the Athens Museum. The sculptured metopes, about 1.3 m (4 ft 5 ins) square, numbering fourteen on each front and thirty-two on each side, are in high relief. Those on the eastern façade represent contests between gods and giants; on the western, between Greeks and Amazons; on the southern, between Centaurs and Lapiths; and on the northern, scenes from the siege of Troy. Traces of bright colours have been found on the sculptures in pediment, metope and frieze. The Parthenon was a real embodiment of,the synthesis of Doric and Ionic cultures. The collaboration of Ictinus, Callicrates and Pheidias had created an Athenian style and reached the apex of the classical temple—the supreme accomplishment of Classical Greece.

In the fifth or sixth century the Parthenon was converted into a Byzantine Christian church, dedicated to the 'Divine Wisdom', and an apse was formed at its eastern end. From about A.D. 1204, under the Frankish dukes of Athens, it served as a Latin church, until, in A.D. 1458 it was converted into a Turkish mosque. Then, during the capture of Athens by the Venetians in A.D. 1687, it was much damaged by a shell which fell into the portion of the building used as a powder magazine. The Venetians withdrew in the following year. In A.D. 1801–3, through the instrumentality of Lord Elgin, many of the sculptures were removed to the British Museum. After some further damage from various causes, including that from an earthquake in A.D. 1894, and some trivial attempts at restoration, the north side was re-assembled from the scattered fragments between A.D. 1921–9. Little survives, however, of the interior.

The **Temple of Apollo Epicurius, Bassae**, in Arcadia (*c.* 450–425 B.C.) (p. 220) is a mainland temple contemporary with the Parthenon, and Ictinus was again the architect. The temple took a long time in building, owing to Ictinus'

TEMPLE ⁰f APOLLO EPICURIUS : BASSÆ

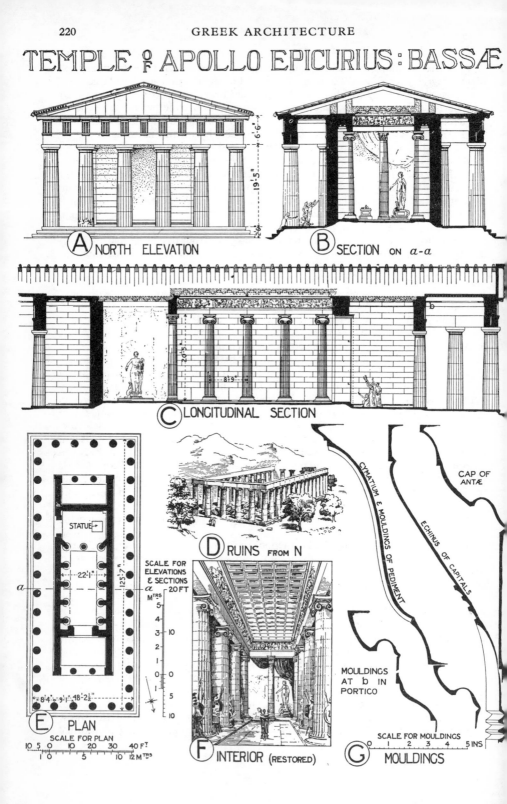

Ⓐ NORTH ELEVATION

Ⓑ SECTION ON *a-a*

Ⓒ LONGITUDINAL SECTION

Ⓓ RUINS FROM N

Ⓔ PLAN

STATUE →

SCALE FOR ELEVATIONS & SECTIONS

SCALE FOR PLAN

Ⓕ INTERIOR (RESTORED)

CYMATIUM & MOULDINGS OF PEDIMENT

CAP OF ANTÆ

ECHINUS OF CAPITALS

MOULDINGS AT b IN PORTICO

SCALE FOR MOULDINGS

Ⓖ MOULDINGS

preoccupation with the Parthenon, begun a year or two later, though completed earlier. A most remarkable feature of this temple is the use in it of all three of the Greek Orders of Architecture—Doric outside and Ionic and Corinthian within; it seems evident that the practice of using different Orders in one building was introduced by Ictinus. The plan is hexastyle peripteral, with fifteen columns on the flanks, all built up in drums. Most of the building is of a hard, fine-grained grey limestone, but marble was used for the sculptures and the more decorative parts, including the ceilings over the pronaos, the opisthodomos and the short sides of the ambulatory, which otherwise were of stone. The temple has other peculiarities. It faces north, instead of east, and the statue of Apollo was placed in an adyton, or inner sanctuary, partially screened off from the naos proper and lighted from a large opening in the eastern, side wall. On both sides of the naos are Ionic half-columns, attached to spur walls, the recesses thus formed with the main naos wall having a stone, coffered ceiling. Between the adyton and the naos was a single, free-standing column, with a Corinthian capital (p. 236F). Until recently it was thought this was the solitary instance in the temple, but Professor Dinsmoor now has disclosed that the adjacent spur walls, splayed diagonally from the main walls, also had partial Corinthian capitals. These three are the first instances known of the Corinthian Order. There is a possibility that Callimachus himself designed them (see p. 235). The entablature was Ionic and continuous with that over the four Ionic half-columns on each side. The capitals of the latter were of unique design, with diagonal volutes, and they had high wide-flaring bases (p. 224C). Professor Dinsmoor shows too, that the naos had a coffered timber ceiling and that there was no hypaethral lighting, although some light was undoubtedly admitted to the roof space through rectangular openings in many of the marble roof tiles. The celebrated sculptured marble frieze over the half-columns, portions of which are in the British Museum, must have been poorly illuminated. It is 611 mm (2 ft) high and ran 30.5 m (100 ft) long, representing battles of Centaurs and Lapiths and Athenians and Amazons.

THE IONIC ORDER

The Ionic Order (p. 224) is specially remarkable for its volute or scroll capital, which, like so many other decorative motifs, may have been derived from the Egyptian lotus (p. 222B), which must have undergone sundry modifications on its way from Egypt through Assyria and divers other Near Eastern countries to Asia Minor (p. 222E). The spiral was also a common motif in Aegean art, and this could well account for its survival in those places which had inherited the Aegean tradition. The early Ionic capitals at Cyprus (p. 222A), Neandria (p. 222M), Lesbos and Larissa exhibit volutes of a distinctly vegetable type with a palmette interposed. Other Ionic capitals at the Greek colony of Naukratis in Egypt (p. 222K), or at Delos (p. 222J), Delphi (p. 222L) and Athens, where they had served as votive offerings, would seem to form a link between these and later types.

The nautilus shell (p. 222D) with its simple spiral and the ram's horns (p. 222G) are examples of nature's spirals which were at hand for the observant architect; and scrolls, quite obviously derived from nature, are seen on Egyptian wall paintings (p. 222F), Cypriot vases (p. 222H), and bronze armour plates (p. 222N). The bracket capital (p. 222C) shows a simple device for decreasing the bearing of an architrave, still frequently employed at the present day. The long and shallow form of many early capitals (p. 222J, L) indicates this kind of purpose and points unmistakably to a wooden origin. There is indeed no doubt that, as a whole, the Ionic Order of Asia Minor, like the Doric Order from further west, evolved from timber forms. Originally, the architrave spanning from column to column was

THE IONIC VOLUTE

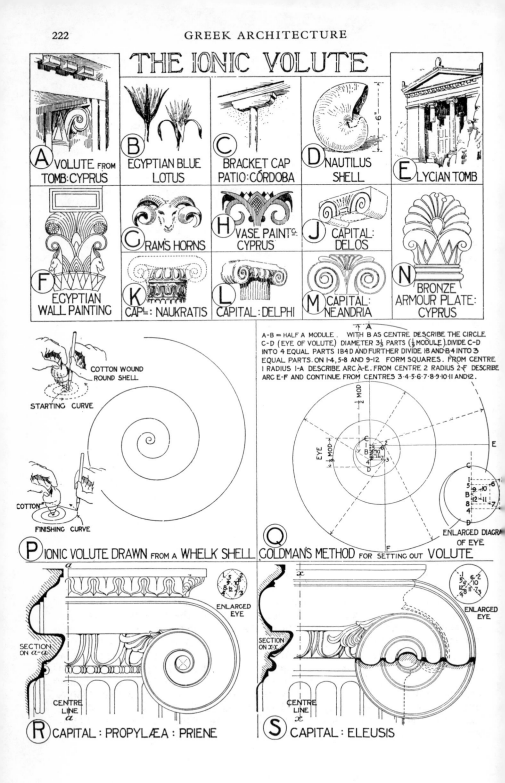

A VOLUTE FROM TOMB: CYPRUS

B EGYPTIAN BLUE LOTUS

C BRACKET CAP PATIO: CÓRDOBA

D NAUTILUS SHELL

E LYCIAN TOMB

F EGYPTIAN WALL PAINTING

G RAM'S HORNS

H VASE PAINTG: CYPRUS

J CAPITAL: DELOS

K CAPL: NAUKRATIS

L CAPITAL: DELPHI

M CAPITAL: NEANDRIA

N BRONZE ARMOUR PLATE: CYPRUS

COTTON WOUND ROUND SHELL

STARTING CURVE

COTTON

FINISHING CURVE

P IONIC VOLUTE DRAWN FROM A WHELK SHELL

A-B = HALF A MODULE. WITH B AS CENTRE, DESCRIBE THE CIRCLE C-D (EYE OF VOLUTE.) DIAMETER 3½ PARTS (⅛ MODULE.) DIVIDE C-D INTO 4 EQUAL PARTS 1B4D AND FURTHER DIVIDE 1B AND B4 INTO 3 EQUAL PARTS. ON 1-4, 5-8 AND 9-12 FORM SQUARES. FROM CENTRE 1 RADIUS 1-A DESCRIBE ARC A-E. FROM CENTRE 2 RADIUS 2-F DESCRIBE ARC E-F AND CONTINUE FROM CENTRES 3·4·5·6·7·8·9·10·11 AND 12.

½ MOD

EYE

⅛ MOD

ENLARGED DIAGRAM OF EYE

Q GOLDMAN'S METHOD FOR SETTING OUT VOLUTE

SECTION ON α-α

ENLARGED EYE

CENTRE LINE α

R CAPITAL: PROPYLÆA: PRIENE

SECTION ON x-x

ENLARGED EYE

CENTRE LINE x

S CAPITAL: ELEUSIS

made up of broad timber plates, laid one on top of the other. On the architrave were laid cross-beams, but these were smaller and more numerous than the Doric triglyph beams, and relatively to the architrave took up far less height. Even with the longitudinal timbers above them providing seating for the rafter and cover for their ends, the whole entablature was much shallower, and therefore lighter, than the Doric; so that after translation into stone, there was less need for sturdy column support. Thus Ionic columns were always comparatively slender, and needed a base at their lower end to spread the weight transmitted. In the entablature there were only two main parts; the architrave, with its fasciae, representing the original plates, and a cornice of which the 'dentils', derived from the closely-spaced cross-beams, formed an integral part. There was no frieze in the entablature of the true Ionic Order of Asia Minor, and none was acquired there until late fourth century B.C. The Ionians, whose architecture always tended towards excessive ornamentation, loved the sculptured frieze, but it was used on the body of the temple rather than as an essential part of the entablature.

Ionic columns, including capital and base, are usually about nine times their lower diameter in height and have twenty-four flutes separated by fillets and not by arrises or sharp edges as in the Doric column. Early examples, however, may have as many as forty (p. 224A), forty-four, or forty-eight flutes, which then are shallow and do meet on a sharp arris. The moulded base evolved by stages into that known as the 'Attic' base (p. 242H), having been brought to this perfected form in Attica. It consists of an upper and lower torus, divided by a scotia and fillets, but until late in the Hellenic period there is no square plinth. The capital has a pair of volutes or spirals, about two-thirds the diameter in height, showing to front and back and joined at the sides by a concave cushion, sometimes plain but usually ornamented with numerous flutes, fillets and beads. The volute scroll rests on an echinus, circular on plan, carved with egg-and-dart and resting on a bead moulding. Methods of setting out volutes are shown (p. 222P, Q, R, S). Above the volute scrolls was a shallow abacus, with moulded edge, which at first was elongated in the direction of the architrave it supported, but which eventually became square on plan. The Greek double-fronted capital represented difficulties at the outer angles of a rectangular building, and in such positions a canted angle volute was used (p. 224B, D, E, F). The four-fronted capital, like that indicated by the Order in the Temple at Bassae (p. 224C), is exceptional in Greek Hellenic architecture though it became increasingly common in the Hellenistic period.

The **Ionic entablature** (p. 224) passed through important stages of development during the Hellenic period. As evolved in Asia Minor, it had only two main parts, architrave and cornice, the latter containing large dentils in the bed-mould. It was therefore very light in relation to the columns, being as little as one-sixth of their height. The Order was soon used on the mainland too, at first only in treasuries, but afterwards importantly in temples, like the Erechtheion (p. 230) and the Temple of Nikè Apteros, Athens (p. 229), which are the finest examples of the style. On the mainland, the influence of the Doric caused a frieze to be inserted in the entablature, but with the consequence that, until late fourth century B.C., the bed-mould was omitted from the cornice except for a minor moulding under the widely-projecting corona. At about this time (late fourth century B.C.), Asia Minor adopted mainland practice and the three-part entablature became universal for the Order, but with the fresh development that henceforward the dentilled bed-mould type of cornice as well as the frieze became established parts of the entablature. Whenever the frieze was present, at whatever stage of the evolution, on the mainland or in Ionia, the entablature still was much lighter than the Doric—about one-quarter the height of the column, i.e. rather more than two diameters high. The

THE IONIC ORDER

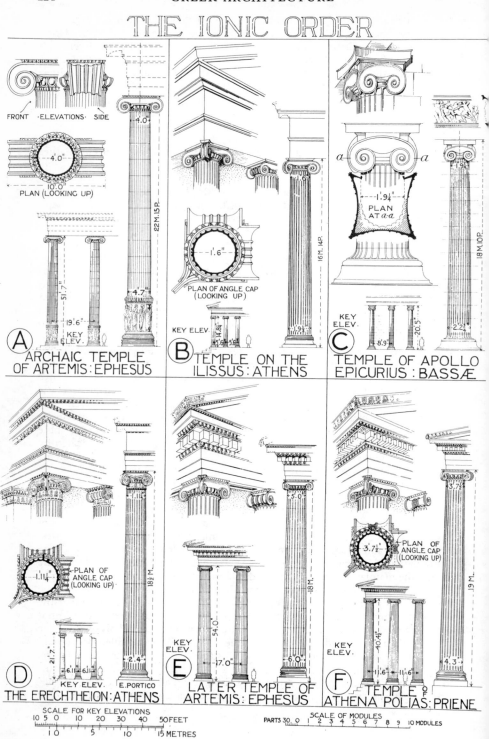

FRONT ·ELEVATIONS· SIDE

PLAN (LOOKING UP)

KEY ELEV.

A ARCHAIC TEMPLE OF ARTEMIS : EPHESUS

PLAN OF ANGLE CAP (LOOKING UP)

KEY ELEV.

B TEMPLE ON THE ILISSUS : ATHENS

PLAN AT a·a

KEY ELEV.

C TEMPLE OF APOLLO EPICURIUS : BASSÆ

PLAN OF ANGLE CAP (LOOKING UP)

KEY ELEV.   E.PORTICO

D THE ERECHTHEION : ATHENS

KEY ELEV.

E LATER TEMPLE OF ARTEMIS : EPHESUS

PLAN OF ANGLE CAP (LOOKING UP)

KEY ELEV.

F TEMPLE OF ATHENA POLIAS : PRIENE

SCALE FOR KEY ELEVATIONS
10 5 0   10   20   30   40   50 FEET
1 0   5   10   15 METRES

PARTS 30 0   SCALE OF MODULES
1 2 3 4 5 6 7 8 9 10 MODULES

Ionic architrave, normally with three fasciae, is capped by a small group of mouldings. The frieze, when present, sometimes is plain, but more often is ornamented with a continuous band of sculpture. Ionic temples do not show antefixae on the flanks; instead, the cymatium or gutter moulding of the inclined cornices at the ends of the temple is carried along the side cornices too, and carved lion heads at intervals serve to eject the rainwater from the roof.

The principal examples of the Ionic Order, found in Asia Minor and on the Greek mainland, are set forth below.

Ionic Temples in Asia Minor

c. 560 B.C.	Archaic Temple of Artemis, Ephesus (below)
c. 525 B.C.	Temple of Hera, Samos (below)
c. 356 B.C.	Later Temple of Artemis, Ephesus (below)
c. 334 B.C.	Temple of Athena Polias, Priene (p. 227)
c. 325 B.C.	Temple of Artemis-Cybele, Sardis
c. 330 B.C.–A.D. 41	Temple of Apollo, Didyma, near Miletus (p. 229)
193 B.C.	Temple of Dionysos, Teos

Ionic Temples in Greece

449 B.C.	Temple on the Ilissus, Athens (p. 229)
c. 450–425 B.C.	Temple of Apollo Epicurius, Bassae (internal Order only) (p. 219)
427 B.C.	Temple of Nikè Apteros, Athens (p. 229)
421–405 B.C.	The Erechtheion, Athens (p. 230)
339 B.C.	The Philippeion, Olympia (external colonnade) (pp. 199A,B, 203F)

The **Temple of Hera, Samos** (*c.* 525 B.C.) was almost contemporary, and only slightly inferior in size, as compared with the Archaic Temple of Artemis, Ephesus (*c.* 560 B.C.) (see below). Samos was one of the scenes of the establishment of a peristyle temple in the seventh century, with emphasis on the front by the introduction of a second row of columns, thus heralding the dipteral form and deeply colonnaded porticoes which appeared in the later temples at Samos and Ephesus. The sixth-century temple measured 50.5 m × 103 m (165 ft × 337 ft) and was dipteral octastyle, though the rear façade contained ten columns, and had a deep columned portico. Scarcely finished, the building was destroyed by fire and replaced (*c.* 525 B.C.) by another, greater structure measuring 54.6 m × 112.2 m (180 ft × 368 ft); dimensions never afterwards exceeded in the Greek world. The portico was octastyle, the rear façade having nine columns (enneastyle), and the double peristyle rows of twenty-four columns. Probably influenced by the recently-built Temple of Artemis at Ephesus, the end colonnades were increased by a third row of columns, making them tripteral. The colossal building was never finished, the colonnades remaining incomplete.

The **Later Temple of Artemis, Ephesus** (*c.* 356 B.C.) (p. 226), was the fifth in succession to stand upon this very famous site. The three earliest had been relatively small; the immediate predecessor, known as the 'Archaic' temple (*c.* 560 B.C.), was burnt down in 356 B.C. and built anew in still more magnificent style, but on an identical plan. The only substantial differences between the old and the new were in the quality of the detail and the fact that the Later Temple stood on a platform of steps, about 2.7 m (9 ft) high, instead of upon a two-step crepidoma, as formerly. Yet owing to the scanty remains, there are uncertainties about the arrangement of the plan, and several somewhat different restorations have been proposed. The temple was dipteral, octastyle at the front but perhaps enneastyle (nine columns) at the rear. The object of an extra rear column would be to evade the very serious difficulties of spanning the exceptionally wide central intercolumniation,

THE TEMPLE OF ARTEMIS:EPHESUS

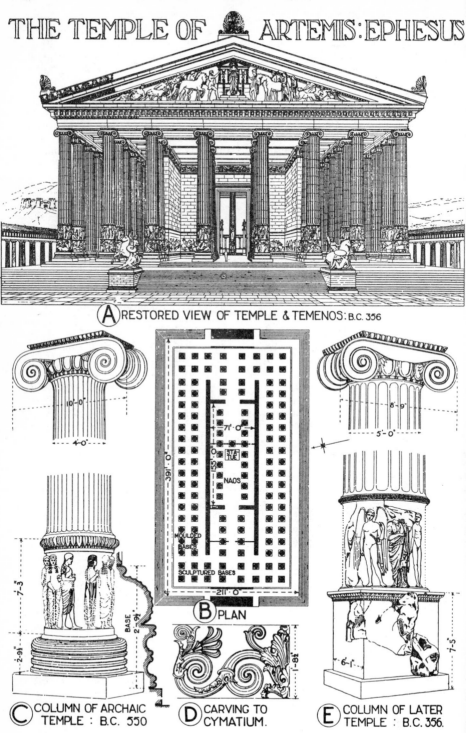

Ⓐ RESTORED VIEW OF TEMPLE & TEMENOS: B.C. 356

Ⓑ PLAN

Ⓒ COLUMN OF ARCHAIC TEMPLE : B.C. 550

Ⓓ CARVING TO CYMATIUM.

Ⓔ COLUMN OF LATER TEMPLE : B.C. 356.

which, although inescapable at the front, was not essential on the rear. The column spacings on the main front were progressively less wide from the centre outwards to the angles, and the central one was more than 8.5 m (28 ft), to be spanned by a marble architrave block about 1.2 m (4 ft) high; for the temple was grand in dimensions, though not the largest in Ionia. Over the stylobate, it measured about 51.8 m × 112 m (170 ft × 366 ft), with the flights of steps in addition. The columns were some 1.8 m (6 ft) in diameter and almost 17.7 m (58 ft) high. The entablature was relatively shallow, being of the usual Asiatic type, comprising architrave and dentilled cornice but no frieze. We have seen earlier that grandiose plans, dipteral as here, or pseudo-dipteral, are typical of the Ionic of Asia Minor. Equally characteristic are the deep pronaos, having several pairs of columns within it, and the shallow opisthodomos, which in some cases is absent altogether. About the internal arrangements of this temple, nothing is definitely known. The orientation is unusual, as for traditional reasons on this site, the temple faced west instead of east. The building was one of the most impressive of Greek temples and was celebrated for its sculptures. The pediment bore a sculptured tympanum representing Artemis mothering her devotees bringing their offerings, while the crowning acroteria portrayed the goddess enthroned. There were 117 columns altogether (interpretations differ), 36 of which bore sculptures on their lower parts. The preceding temple had similar sculptures, and fragments from both periods, along with elements of corresponding capitals and shafts, some of which are in the British Museum, allow us to compare the early and late work (pp. 224A, E; 226C, E). The volutes of the earlier capitals spread widely beyond the column shaft, and the abacus is nearly twice as long as it is wide; in the later examples the volutes are much more compact, and the abacus consequently is almost square. Flutes on the column shafts, numbering up to 48 in the earlier instances, in the later have settled to the normal 24, separated by fillets instead of sharp arrises. It is typical of Asia Minor practice that in neither temple were the columns identical in all respects. The designs varied a little between one column and the next. Thus in the older temple, rosettes might be substituted for the inner part of the conventional volute. Base mouldings in Asia Minor in the Hellenic period commonly had only two main elements, a large torus upon a deep, circular disc, both of them lavishly ornamented with horizontal flutes and reeds, separated by fillets or beads; but it was with the Archaic Temple at Ephesus that a square plinth first came to be associated with the Ionic base (p. 226C). Also, the site evidences early instances of the pedestal under the Order (p. 226E), which henceforward became accepted as an optional element in the classical decorative system. The building of the Later Temple is said to have extended well into the Hellenistic period. Like its predecessor, it ranked as one of the seven wonders of the Ancient World. The original designers were Demetrius and Paeonius of Ephesus, and probably Deinocrates. Famous sculptors, particularly Scopas, were employed in its decoration. The Temple of Artemis was the centre of the Pan-Ionian festival of the Asiatic colonies, as the Parthenon was of the Panathenaic festival in the motherland.

The **Temple of Athena Polias, Priene** (*c.* 334 B.C.) (pp. 224F, 228) is finely proportioned but more modest in plan and scale than other principal Asia Minor temples. Pythius, the architect, wrote a book about it. For once, the plan is peripteral, 19.5 m × 37 m (64 ft × 122 ft) over the stylobate, with a hexastyle front and eleven columns on the sides, almost twice as long as broad. The deep pronaos and shallow opisthodomos are normal, while the column bases have the now usual plinth. The two-part entablature, still omitting the frieze, shows how deep-rooted in Asia Minor was this traditional arrangement (p. 224F). (Restorations showing a frieze, as p. 228, are no longer accepted as correct.) The columns are 1.3 m (4 ft

TEMPLE ON THE ILISSUS: ATHENS

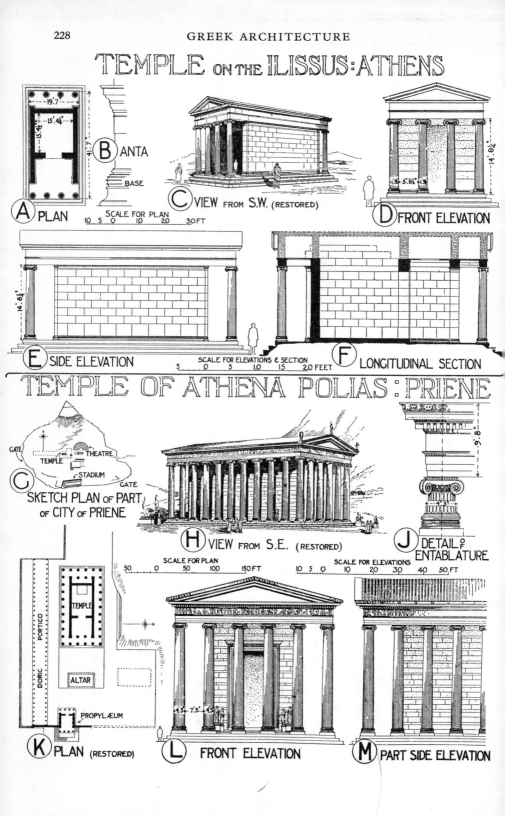

A PLAN

19.7
15'.4½"
15'.4½"
41'.7

B ANTA

BASE

C VIEW FROM S.W. (RESTORED)

SCALE FOR PLAN
10 5 0   10   20   30 FT

D FRONT ELEVATION

14'.8¼"
15'.3.8¾"

E SIDE ELEVATION

14'.8¼"

SCALE FOR ELEVATIONS & SECTION
5   0   5   10   15   20 FEET

F LONGITUDINAL SECTION

TEMPLE OF ATHENA POLIAS: PRIENE

G SKETCH PLAN OF PART OF CITY OF PRIENE

GATE
THEATRE
TEMPLE
STADIUM
GATE

H VIEW FROM S.E. (RESTORED)

J DETAIL OF ENTABLATURE

9'.8¼"
4'.3½"

K PLAN (RESTORED)

DORIC PORTICO
TEMPLE
ALTAR
PROPYLÆUM

SCALE FOR PLAN
50   0   50   100   150 FT

SCALE FOR ELEVATIONS
10 5 0   10   20   30   40   50 FT

L FRONT ELEVATION

4'.3½" 7'.3" 4'.3½"

M PART SIDE ELEVATION

3 ins) in diameter, and had a height of 11.4 m (37 ft 6 ins), supporting an entablature 2 m (6 ft 10 ins) in height, including the cymatium. Fragments of the Order are in the British Museum.

The **Temple of Apollo, Didyma, near Miletus** (*c.* 330 B.C.–A.D. 41) (pp. 203N, 238) was so long under construction as to be essentially a Hellenistic building, and even so, was never quite completed: the great Hellenistic temples were ambitious displays of Ionic monumentality, straining the resources available and slow in building. It was designed by Paeonius of Ephesus and Daphnis of Miletus and of vast size, 51.1 m × 109.3 m (168 ft × 359 ft) at the top of the seven-step crepidoma. The 120 columns were 2.03 m (6 ft 8 ins) in diameter and 19.7 m (64 ft 8 ins) high. The column bases (p. 238M) varied in design, in pairs astride the main axis of the temple. The arrangement was dipteral decastyle (ten columns), and there was the customary deep pronaos, and no opisthodomos. The naos was unroofed to form a deep interior court (adyton) lower than the surrounding peristyle level, an enormous space 53.7 m × 21.7 m × 25 m (176 ft × 71 ft × 82 ft). Two inclined ways led downwards from the pronaos, under staircases flanking a vestibule, to the paved court at the rear of which a small prostyle Ionic temple formed the shrine of Apollo. The walls of the adyton were buttressed by gigantic pilasters 1.8 m (6 ft) wide and 914 mm (3 ft) projection (p. 238J), ornamented in a way unusual for anta capitals in Asia Minor. Leading back from the adyton, an imposing flight of steps gave access to the vestibule through three doorways between which rose two huge Corinthian half-columns (p. 238L, P), the capitals of which lacked the main pairs of volutes and had sharply pointed angles to their abaci. The building was unique in the integration of exterior and interior as an orderly expression of clàssical architecture, and yet contained novel effects of space and illusion.

The **Temple on the Ilissus, Athens** (449 B.C.) (pp. 224B, 228), an amphiprostyle tetrastyle small temple, of Pentelic marble, measured about 6.1 m × 12.8 m (20 ft × 42 ft) over a three-step crepidoma. The architect was Callicrates, who, with Ictinus, was responsible for the Parthenon. It is a developed example of mainland Ionic, showing certain differences which occur there, due to the influence of the Doric. Even in the sixth century B.C., the archaic phase, treasuries built at sacred sites in Greece by Ionian cities represented at the festivals, possessed these differences from the native types; and in two cases, the Cnidian and Siphnian treasuries, both at Delphi, respectively of 565 B.C. and 530 B.C., the in-antis porches had pairs of 'caryatid' sculptured female figures instead of columns, foreshadowing the famous examples of the Erechtheion (pp. 231G, 233). The principal traits referred to however, concern the entablature, which in mainland Ionic possessed a frieze from the beginning, but with a resulting ejection of most of the bed-mould of the cornice, including the distinctive dentils, there remaining only a cyma-reversa moulding in this position. The architrave too, quite often is plain, like the Doric, without the bands or fasciae normal in Asia Minor. Such features are found in this temple; and the column bases are 'Attic', with an extra small torus below the disc—now become a hollow scotia mould—and the upper large torus usual in Ionia at this time.

The **Temple of Nikè Apteros, Athens** (427 B.C.) (pp. 197B, H, 198A, B, 234A), is an exquisite amphi-prostyle tetrastyle small temple of marble, about 5.4 m × 8.2 m (18 ft × 27 ft) over the stylobate, dedicated to 'Wingless Victory', standing picturesquely on the south-western spur of the Acropolis. Callicrates was again the architect. The bastion which forms its site was surrounded on three sides by a marble balustrade, 965 mm (3 ft 2 ins) high, enriched with very fine sculpture. The temple is quite small, the columns being 533 mm (1 ft 9 ins) diameter and 4 m (13 ft 3 ins) high, standing upon a crepidoma of three steps. The columns thus are unusually short in proportion, rather less than eight diameters. Apart from this circumstance and the fact that the architrave has fascia bands, the Ionic Order closely resembles that of the Temple on the Ilissus. The entablature has a frieze, which·bore beautiful relief sculpture, of which there are examples in the British Museum. The temple was taken down by the Turks in 1687, and built into a battery on the Acropolis; but in 1836, the materials were recovered and the temple was reconstructed on the original site.

The **Erechtheion, Athens** (421–405 B.C.) (pp. 198A, B, 224D, 231, 232, 233, 234C, D, 254J), by Mnesicles, stands on the Acropolis north of the Parthenon, next to the site of an older temple of Athena badly damaged in 480 B.C. by the Persians. It is unusual and irregular in plan (p. 231F), having three porches as well as an attached colonnade on the western end, and was constructed at two different levels, the western half of the naos and the ground to the north and west sides of the building being 3.2 m (10 ft 6 ins) below the rest. A flight of steps north of the east portico joined the two levels. The temple was intended as a replacement of the old temple of Athena, on a similar plan; but it having been decided to retain the western half of the naos of the older building, which had suffered less than the remainder from the Persian depredations, the new structure was thrust further north on to an awkward, falling site, where too, there were several sacred spots, much venerated by the Athenians. These had to be preserved intact, and led to severe distortions of the original design. The eastern part of the main block, forming the shrine of Athena Polias, guardian of the city, is at the general Acropolis level, approached from a hexastyle porch, with columns 686 mm (2 ft 3 ins) in diameter and 6.5 m (21 ft 6 ins) high, by a high doorway flanked by a window on each side. Windows are quite rare in Greek temple architecture. The western part of the naos, at the lower level, was divided into three chambers, together comprising the shrine of Erechtheus. The westernmost served as a vestibule to the other two, which were separated by a longitudinal wall. The walls sub-dividing the western part were about 3.9 m (13 ft) high and did not reach the ceiling, which they all shared. In the western vestibule was the tank containing the salt sea of Poseidon. This vestibule also connected the North Portico and that roughly balancing it on the south side, the Caryatid Porch, which, being at the higher level, had the necessary flight of steps within it. The North Porch probably was a substitute for a western portico, for if there had been one in the latter position, it would have encroached upon the sanctuary of Pandrosus, an enclosure outside the west front and in which grew the sacred olive tree of Athens, and impinged upon the tomb of Cecrops which lay adjacent to the west wall. In fact, to escape the latter, the position of the west wall had to be altered after the building had started, withdrawn a little towards the east. On the west wall there was only the semblance of a portico, for its upper part bore an attached colonnade of four columns in antis, while in the lower was a doorway leading from the western enclosed vestibule to the sanctuary of Pandrosus.

A general view of the former appearance of the building, built splendidly in Pentelic marble, is given in the restoration (p. 231A). The main block, measuring 11.5 m × 22.8 m (38 ft × 75 ft), was roofed at a common level, and the east porch and the attached portico on the west shared the same entablature, of the Attic type without dentils, which surrounded the whole building. The anta moulding, as well, continued along the flanks. As the bases of the western attached columns were raised about 914 mm (3 ft) above those of the east porch, the two Orders necessarily had different proportions. The tetrastyle North Porch, two bays deep, has columns 813 mm (2 ft 8 ins) in diameter and 7.6 m (25 ft) high. The Porch stands at the lower level and its entablature fits just below the main one, resembling it in design and, like it, having a frieze of black Eleusinian limestone to which relief sculpture in white marble formerly was attached by cramps. Under the North

THE ERECHTHEION : ATHENS

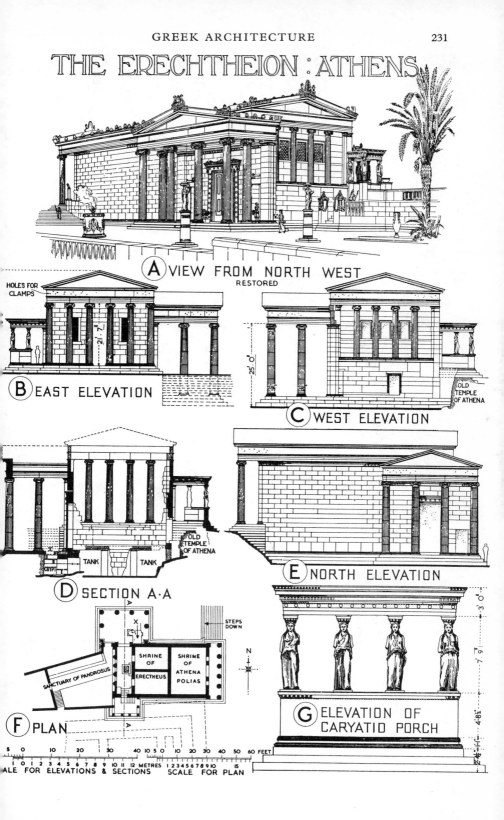

A VIEW FROM NORTH WEST
RESTORED

HOLES FOR CLAMPS

21' 7"

B EAST ELEVATION

25' 0"

OLD TEMPLE OF ATHENA

C WEST ELEVATION

OLD TEMPLE OF ATHENA

TANK   TANK

CRYPT

D SECTION A·A

E NORTH ELEVATION

3' 0"

7' 9"

4' 8½"

2' 4"

G ELEVATION OF CARYATID PORCH

STEPS DOWN

N

SHRINE OF ERECTHEUS

SHRINE OF ATHENA POLIAS

SANCTUARY OF PANDROSUS

F PLAN

5 0   10   20   30   40 10 5 0 10   20   30   40   50   60 FEET
1 0 1 2 3 4 5 6 7 8 9 10 11 12 METRES 1 2 3 4 5 6 7 8 9 10   15
ALE FOR ELEVATIONS & SECTIONS   SCALE FOR PLAN

A. The Erechtheion, Athens (421–405 B.C.). See p. 230

B. The Erechtheion, Athens, from the S.E.

The Erechtheion, Athens (421–405 B.C.): Caryatid Porch. See p. 235

A. Temple of Nikè Apteros (Athena Nikè),
Athens (restored) (427 B.C.). See p. 229

B. Athenian Treasury, Delphi
(510 B.C.). See p. 202

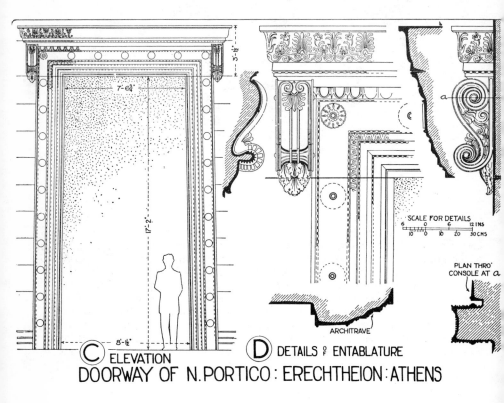

C ELEVATION

D DETAILS ᵒꜰ ENTABLATURE

DOORWAY OF N. PORTICO : ERECHTHEION : ATHENS

Porch floor is a basement, and the marks on its rock floor where the trident of Poseidon had struck could be exposed to the sky through a trap in the basement ceiling and a marble shaft in the porch roof. The North Porch capitals are very fine (p. 232A). The spirals of the volutes are enriched with intermediate fillets, and below them is an ornamental band of anthemion ornament. At the outer angles of the Porch, as on the East front too (p. 224D), the volutes are canted at forty-five degrees to overcome the difficulty of expressing adjacent faces of the capitals. Within the Porch is a famous doorway, excellently preserved (p. 234C, D). The proportions of the columns of the three porches differ, being $9\frac{1}{2}$ diameters on the east front, $9\frac{3}{8}$ diameters in the North Porch and 9 diameters for the half columns on the west front. As originally arranged, the latter columns on the west were attached to piers, between which there were perhaps grilles in metal or wood, but these openings were walled up in Roman times except for windows in the three central inter-columniations (p. 231C). The southern or Caryatid Porch (pp. 231G, 232A, B, 233, 254J) had six draped female figures or Caryatids, 2.3 m (7 ft 9 ins) high, standing on a solid marble wall rising about 2.4 m (8 ft) above the Acropolis level. All the figures face southwards; the three western lean on the right and the three eastern on the left leg, giving an effect of resistance to the weight of the entablature which, because of the special circumstances is of the shallow, Asiatic type of design, lacking the frieze and with dentils in the cornice, though the dentils are less large than the true Ionic type. The second caryatid from the west is in the British Museum, and is replaced by a terra-cotta copy.

The Erechtheion has passed through various vicissitudes, having suffered conversion to other uses and much damage from time to time. Internally, little survives of the former arrangements, but of the rest there are considerable remains, all of which in the present century have been restored to their former place.

THE CORINTHIAN ORDER

The Corinthian Order did not evolve from a constructive basis like the Doric and Ionic Orders, but made its first appearance in Greek architecture in the fifth century B.C. as a decorative variant of the Ionic, the difference lying almost entirely in the column capital. It came to acquire a more distinct identity as time progressed, though it was the Romans who brought it to full maturity in the late first century B.C. There are few Hellenic examples; its popularity increased greatly in the Hellenistic period.

The **Corinthian column,** with base and shaft resembling the Ionic, tended to become more slender, and eventually a proportion of ten diameters was regarded as fitting. The distinctive feature is the capital, which is much deeper than the Ionic, and though of variable height at first, settled down to a proportion of about $1\frac{1}{6}$ diameters high (p. 236). Vitruvius records the tradition (Bk. IV, chap. i) that the invention of the capital was due to Callimachus, a worker in Corinthian bronze, who obtained the idea from observing a basket over the grave of a Corinthian maiden, covered with a tile to protect the offerings it contained. Accidentally, the basket was placed over the root of an acanthus plant, the stems and foliage of which grew and turned into volutes at the angle of the tile (p. 236B). The earlier examples appear to have been in bronze. The perfected type has a deep, inverted bell, the lower part of which is surrounded by two tiers of eight acanthus leaves (p. 236C, D), and from between the leaves of the upper row rise eight caulicoli (*caulis* = a stalk), each surmounted by a calyx from which emerge volutes or helices supporting the angles of the abacus and the central foliated ornaments. Each face of the moulded abacus is curved outwards to a point at the angles (pp. 238L, P; 236F, H, K), or else the abacus is chamfered at each angle (p. 236G). Another and

EVOLUTION OF THE CORINTHIAN CAPITAL

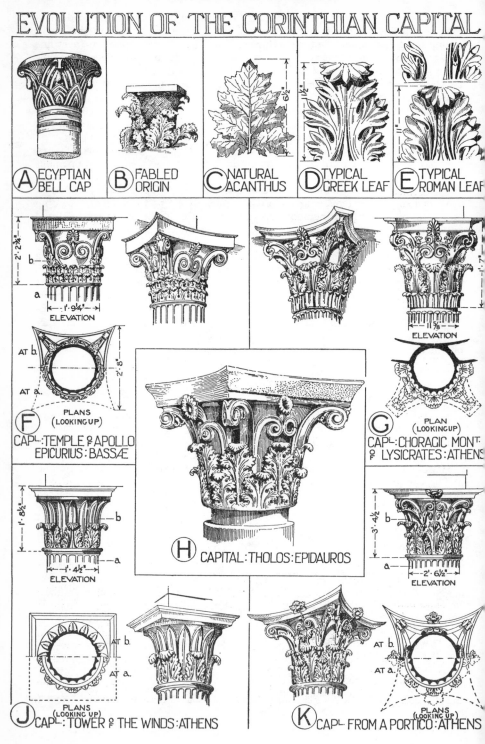

(A) EGYPTIAN BELL CAP

(B) FABLED ORIGIN

(C) NATURAL ACANTHUS

(D) TYPICAL GREEK LEAF

(E) TYPICAL ROMAN LEAF

(F) CAPL: TEMPLE OF APOLLO EPICURIUS: BASSÆ

(G) CAPL: CHORAGIC MONT. OF LYSICRATES: ATHENS

(H) CAPITAL: THOLOS: EPIDAUROS

(J) CAPL: TOWER OF THE WINDS: ATHENS

(K) CAPL: FROM A PORTICO: ATHENS

ELEVATION

PLANS (LOOKING UP)

PLAN (LOOKING UP)

rarer type has one row of acanthus leaves with water leaves above and no volutes, and a moulded abacus, square on plan (p. 236J).

The **Corinthian entablature** is not distinguishable from the Ionic in Greek architecture; in the earliest known instance of the Order, in the Temple of Apollo Epicurius at Bassae (p. 220), Corinthian and Ionic internal columns share the same entablature. Throughout the Hellenic period the Order is used with either the Doric or the Ionic Order in the same building, the notable exception being the Monument of Lysicrates, Athens (below), where also it appears externally for the first time. Invariably there are three parts to the Corinthian entablature, architrave, frieze and cornice, and the latter normally is the developed type, with small dentils in the bed-mould. Eventually, in Roman hands, the Order is enriched by extra small mouldings, and an important 'modillion' band is added to the bed-mould, the modillions being consoles or brackets, giving support to the projecting corona of the cornice.

Corinthian Examples

c. 450–425 B.C.	Temple of Apollo Epicurius, Bassae (internal) (pp. 219, 220, 236F)
c. 400 B.C.	The Tholos, Delphi (internal Order)
c. 350 B.C.	The Tholos, Epidauros (internal Order) (pp. 203E, 236H)
339 B.C.	The Tholos (Philippeion), Olympia (internal Order) (pp. 199, 203F)
334 B.C.	Choragic Monument of Lysicrates, Athens (below)
c. 330 B.C.–A.D. 41	Temple of Apollo, Didyma, near Miletus (internal) (p. 203N)
174 B.C.–A.D. 132	The Olympieion, Athens (p. 239)
c. 48 B.C.	Tower of the Winds, Athens (p. 239)

The **Tholos, Epidauros** (c. 350 B.C.) (pp. 203E, 236H) was a circular building, probably a temple, larger and more elaborate than the Tholos at Delphi (c. 400 B.C.). A peristyle of twenty-six Doric columns encircled the wall, the diameter of the stylobate measuring 21.8 m (71 ft 6 ins). Internally, a free-standing circle of fourteen Corinthian columns elaborated the space and accentuated the circular plan; the capitals were of singular beauty (p. 236H). In addition, ornamental forms were lavished throughout the building, together with experiments in polychromy, to make it one of the most inspired creations of the fourth century, and indicating an increasing indulgence of taste for architectural decoration.

The **Tholos (Philippeion), Olympia** (339 B.C.) (pp. 199, 203F) was begun by Philip of Macedonia and completed by Alexander. The external peristyle consisted of eighteen Ionic columns, and the inner face of the wall was decorated with nine Corinthian half-columns. The diameter of the stylobate was 14 m (46 ft).

The **Choragic Monument of Lysicrates**, Athens (334 B.C.) (pp. 236G, 238), is a type of monument erected to support a tripod, awarded as a prize for athletic exercises, or musical competitions in Greek festivals. There were many of these in the Street of Tripods. Lysicrates had been the leader of a successful chorus, and this elaborate monument was built to commemorate the event. Of its two stages, the lower is a lofty podium of Piraeus stone, 2.9 m (9 ft 6 ins) square on plan, decoratively treated with drafted margins to the masonry joints, with a high, stepped base and a simple, projecting capping. The upper part is a hollow cylinder of white Pentelic marble, 1.8 m (6 ft) in diameter inside, standing upon a base of bluish Hymettian marble, around which are six Corinthian columns, appearing to be attached, though in reality complete, as the curving wall forms panels between them. Between the column capitals there are sculptured bas-reliefs. Above the entablature is a dome shaped from a single block of Pentelic marble, carved to imitate fish-scale tiling, and bearing three sculptured scrolls terminating in a floral ornament, which formerly bore a bronze tripod, its base being 10.3 m (34 ft) above the ground. Marble acroteria, linked together as a decorative cresting, served

THE CHORAGIC MONUMENT OF LYSICRATES : ATHENS

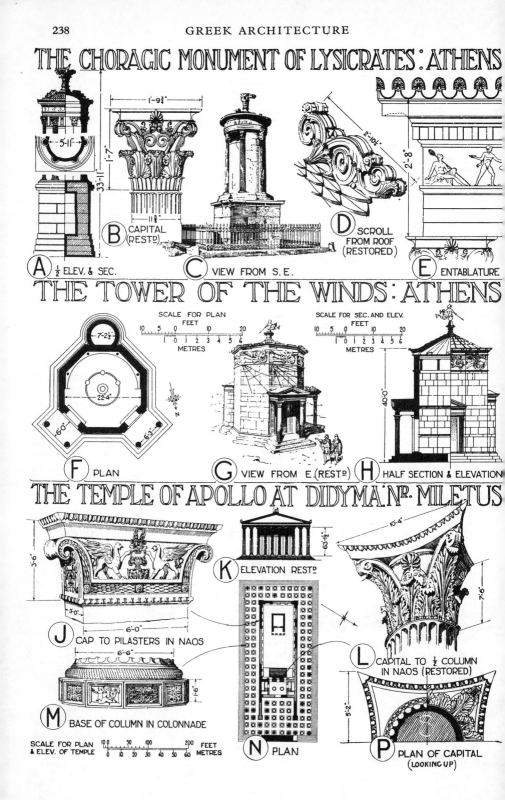

A ½ ELEV. & SEC.

B CAPITAL (REST?)

C VIEW FROM S.E.

D SCROLL FROM ROOF (RESTORED)

E ENTABLATURE

THE TOWER OF THE WINDS : ATHENS

SCALE FOR PLAN
FEET

METRES

SCALE FOR SEC. AND ELEV.
FEET

METRES

F PLAN

G VIEW FROM E.(REST?)

H HALF SECTION & ELEVATION

THE TEMPLE OF APOLLO AT DIDYMA N? MILETUS

J CAP TO PILASTERS IN NAOS

K ELEVATION REST?

L CAPITAL TO ½ COLUMN IN NAOS (RESTORED)

M BASE OF COLUMN IN COLONNADE

N PLAN

P PLAN OF CAPITAL (LOOKING UP)

SCALE FOR PLAN & ELEV. OF TEMPLE
FEET
METRES

in place of the usual cymatium to the cornice. This monument provides the first instance of the Corinthian Order used externally, and of a building employing it as the sole Order. For the first time too, an entablature, whether Corinthian or Ionic, appears with both frieze and dentilled cornice, a type of design which henceforward was to become universal (p. 238E). The columns are 3.5 m (11 ft 7 ins) high and have capitals of graceful if imperfect design which relatively are of unusual depth; 483 mm (1 ft 7 ins), or 1½ diameters. The upper halves of the capitals fit awkwardly upon the lower, and are too narrow-waisted at that point. The flutings of the shafts terminate as leaves, and the channel above them may have had a bronze collar. Between the acanthus leaves of the capitals, which have each only a single range, the place of a lower being taken by water leaves, there are eight-petalled rosettes, which appear to imitate bronze clips such as might have been used in earlier instances to secure metal foliage (p. 238B). The architrave bears an inscription indicating the purpose of the monument, and the frieze is sculptured to represent the myth of Dionysos and the pirates of the Tyrrhenian Sea.

The **Temple of Zeus Olympius (Olympieion), Athens** (174 B.C.–A.D. 132) (p. 203H), stands on a site of an earlier Doric temple commenced in 515 B.C. It was built as the gift to Athens of Antiochus Epiphanes of Syria, from designs by Cossutius, a Roman architect. Yet there was much that was Greek in its conception and execution, so far as it was constructed at that time, and it demonstrates the growing fondness for the Corinthian Order in the Hellenistic period. It remained incomplete, and Sulla in 86 B.C. transported some of the columns to Rome for the Temple of Jupiter Capitolinus (p. 265), where they had an important effect on Roman taste. Work was resumed under Augustus, but it was completed and dedicated by Hadrian, in A.D. 132. It was dipteral octastyle (p. 203H) and measured 44.3 m × 110.5 m (145 ft 6 ins × 362 ft 6 ins), standing in a magnificent peribolus or enclosure of 129.2 m × 207.2 m (424 ft × 680 ft). Vitruvius records that it was hypaethral, but it is probable that it was covered in after his time. The fifteen columns remaining of the former one hundred and four columns of the peristyle bear witness to its pristine grandeur. They were 1.9 m (6 ft 4 ins) in diameter and 17 m (56 ft) high, a proportion of about one to nine. The surviving capitals appear to date from all three periods of construction, though the later maintain the character of the original design.

The **Tower of the Winds, Athens** (c. 48 B.C.) (pp. 236J, 238,) is another Hellenistic building, also known as the Horologium of Andronikos Cyrrhestes, who erected it for measuring time by means of a clepsydra or water-clock internally and by a sundial externally; while it was also provided with a weather-vane. The building, on a crepidoma of three steps, is octagonal, and its eight sides face the more important points of the compass. It is of marble, and measures 6.8 m (22 ft 4 ins) internally, and on the north-east and north-west sides are distyle porticoes with fluted columns 4.1 m (13 ft 6 ins) high, without bases and bearing capitals which vary from the normal Corinthian design, having square abaci, no volutes and a range of water leaves occupying the upper half of the bell, over a single row of acanthus leaves (p. 236J). From the south side projected a circular water cistern, supplying the water-clock. The interior is 12.4 m (40 ft 9 ins) high, and the upper part is encircled by small, fluted Doric columns, standing on a projecting band. The external wall of the octagonal structure is plain for a height of 8.8 m (29 ft) with the exception of incised lines forming the sundial, and above this, boldly sculptured figures on each face represent the eight principal winds. The roof, which was formed of twenty-four radiating, wedge-shaped blocks of marble, was once surmounted by a bronze Triton, pivoting to show with his rod the quarter in which the wind lay.

MOULDINGS

Mouldings are an architectural device whereby, with the help of the light and shade they produce, definition is given to the salient lines of a building (pp. 241, 242). Thus the delicacy of moulded contours is in proportion to the strength of sunlight in any given country, always making due allowance for national tendencies and the possibilities of the material used. Greek love of refinement found full opportunity for expression in graceful mouldings in the sunny climate of Greece; the Roman character, in a somewhat similar climate, displayed itself in more pronounced mouldings; while in grey and sombre England mouldings became coarse and full-bodied to secure sufficient shadow to throw up their lines. Greek mouldings were refined and delicate in contour, due first to the fine-grained marble in which often they were carved, and secondly to the clear atmosphere and continuous sunshine which produced strong shadows from slight projections. Though the sections of these mouldings were probably formed by hand, they approach very closely to various conic sections, such as parabolas, hyperbolas and ellipses. As a general rule the lines of the carved ornament on any Greek moulding correspond to the profile of that moulding and thus emphasize it by the expression of its own curvature in an enriched form. The examples given of mouldings taken from the Parthenon, Erechtheion, and elsewhere may be studied (pp. 241, 242).

The following is a classified list of the most important mouldings compared with the Roman (p. 241).

(a) The cyma recta (Hogarth's 'line of beauty') which is often carved with honeysuckle ornament, whose outline corresponds with the section (pp. 241G, 242Q).

(b) The cyma reversa (ogee) when enriched is carved with the water leaf and tongue (pp. 241H, 242N, Q).

(c) The ovolo (egg-like) when enriched is carved with the egg and dart, or egg and tongue ornament (pp. 241F, 242L, Q).

(d) The fillet, a small plain face to separate other mouldings (p. 241A), is usually without enrichment.

(e) The astragal or bead serves much the same purpose as the fillet, but approaches a circle in section. It is sometimes carved with the 'bead and reel' or with beads, which, in fact, gave the name to the moulding (pp. 241B, 242Q).

(f) The cavetto is a simple hollow (p. 241D).

(g) The scotia is a deep hollow which occurs in bases, and is generally not enriched (pp. 241E, 242H, T).

(h) The torus is really a magnified bead moulding which, when enriched, is carved with the guilloche or plait ornament, or with bundles of leaves tied with bands (pp. 241L, 242H, R, S, T).

(i) The bird's-beak moulding occurs frequently in the Doric Order, and gives a deep shadow (pp. 241K, 242A, E).

(j) The corona, or deep vertical face of the upper portion of the cornice, was frequently painted with a Greek 'fret' ornament (pp. 241C, 242C).

THEATRES

The Greek theatre, an open-air structure, was generally hollowed out of the slope of a hillside, in or near a city, and received definitive architectural form only in the fourth century B.C. Primitive theatres were no more than natural spaces, preferably on sloping ground so that spectators could overlook the flat area, sometimes paved, on which ceremonial chorus and dances were performed around the altar of

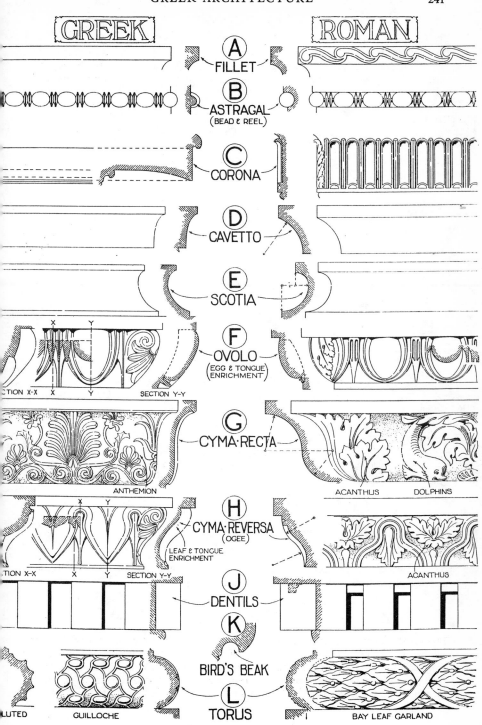

GREEK | ROMAN

A FILLET

B ASTRAGAL (BEAD & REEL)

C CORONA

D CAVETTO

E SCOTIA

F OVOLO (EGG & TONGUE ENRICHMENT)

SECTION X-X   SECTION Y-Y

G CYMA·RECTA

ANTHEMION   ACANTHUS   DOLPHINS

H CYMA·REVERSA (OGEE)

LEAF & TONGUE ENRICHMENT

SECTION X-X   SECTION Y-Y   ACANTHUS

J DENTILS

K BIRD'S BEAK

FLUTED   GUILLOCHE

L TORUS

BAY LEAF GARLAND

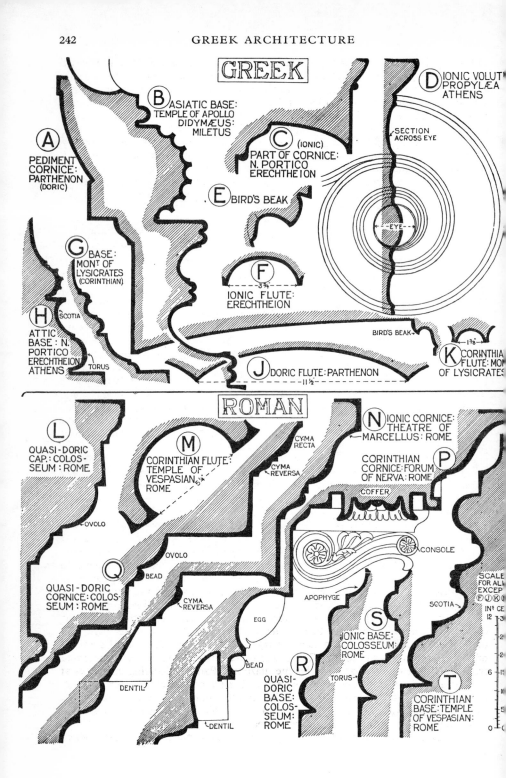

GREEK

A PEDIMENT CORNICE: PARTHENON (DORIC)

B ASIATIC BASE: TEMPLE OF APOLLO DIDYMÆUS: MILETUS

C (IONIC) PART OF CORNICE: N. PORTICO ERECHTHEION

D IONIC VOLUTE PROPYLÆA ATHENS

SECTION ACROSS EYE

EYE

E BIRD'S BEAK

BIRD'S BEAK

F IONIC FLUTE: ERECHTHEION ¾

G BASE: MONT OF LYSICRATES (CORINTHIAN)

H ATTIC BASE: N. PORTICO ERECHTHEION ATHENS

SCOTIA

TORUS

J DORIC FLUTE: PARTHENON 11½

K CORINTHIAN FLUTE: MONT OF LYSICRATES 1⅜

ROMAN

L QUASI-DORIC CAP.: COLOSSEUM: ROME

OVOLO

M CORINTHIAN FLUTE: TEMPLE OF VESPASIAN: ROME 5¼

CYMA RECTA

CYMA REVERSA

N IONIC CORNICE: THEATRE OF MARCELLUS: ROME

P CORINTHIAN CORNICE: FORUM OF NERVA: ROME

COFFER

CONSOLE

Q QUASI-DORIC CORNICE: COLOSSEUM: ROME

OVOLO

BEAD

CYMA REVERSA

EGG

BEAD

APOPHYGE

SCOTIA

S IONIC BASE: COLOSSEUM: ROME

TORUS

DENTIL

R QUASI-DORIC BASE: COLOSSEUM: ROME

DENTIL

T CORINTHIAN BASE: TEMPLE OF VESPASIAN: ROME

SCALE FOR ALL EXCEPT F J K

INS CE.

12

6

0

Dionysos. The worship of Dionysos, in whose honour early archaic frenzy provided the basis out of which Greek drama developed, gave to the theatre a profoundly religious attribute culminating in the achievements of Athenian tragic drama and satyric comedy during the latter half of the fifth century B.C. The supreme achievements of Athenian tragedy were enacted in at best the rudimentary though ancient setting of the Theatre of Dionysos against the cliffs of the Acropolis.

The translation of Dionysiac worship into the art of drama to become a civico-religious festival necessitated some regularization of the traditional natural 'theatre', which then became the simple, canonical elements of formal design. The developed form consisted of three independent elements: the auditorium (cavea) in tiers of stone seats arranged in a horseshoe shape around the circular paved space (orchestra) used by the chorus, and the stage (skene) for actors. The skene was a structure, tangential to the orchestra, affording a backing for simple stage décor. The orchestra was the focal point, for on it the chorus enacted the action of the drama and around it, greater than a semicircle, was organized the arrangement of the seating. The tiers of seats partially enclosing the orchestra to a point beyond its diameter terminated in a retaining wall, along the face of which was a passage (parados) leading to the skene. Early in the Hellenistic period a 'proscenium' came to be built in front of the skene to accommodate changes in dramatic presentation, and with the advent of the proscenium the importance of the orchestra declined. The skene became two-storeyed and elaborate in design, further shifting the focus from the orchestra and thus negating the arrangement of seats flanking the parados. Gradually stage buildings encroached on the orchestra cutting off part of its circular form, and architectural unity of skene and cavea was achieved by bridging the parados with a ceremonial gateway. All Greek theatres were altered in that manner during the Hellenistic period and were further modified in Roman times.

The acoustic efficiency of Greek theatres resulted from an understanding of contributing factors: sound was intensified near the source by reflection from the hard paving of the orchestra and from the skene, sound spread out evenly and without obstacle from source to audience, and there was no reflection back from audience to source. As the theatre was without enclosing walls or roof there was no reverberation, so that increase of loudness did not generate loss of clarity, and by its nature in such a setting classical drama was expressed through a declamatory style of speech. The quality of speech, excellent hearing conditions and a still atmosphere ensured the phenomenal success of the large open-air auditorium.

The **Theatre, Epidauros** (*c.* 350 B.C.) (p. 244), designed by Polycleitos, was the most perfect development of the theatral form. The principles of designing to perfection experienced in building temples were applied to the theatre. Geometrical exactitude of layout was accompanied by variations and adjustments in response to human requirements: only the central two-thirds of the seating is concentric with the circle of the orchestra, and the seats nearer the parados were arranged with a slightly flatter curve as a concession to easier sight lines. The section of the cavea was also designed with proper regard for sight lines, the upper part outside the gangway (diazoma) being at an angle steeper than the lower part. The orchestra, a complete circle, is 20.4 m (67 ft) in diameter, and the overall diameter of the theatre is 118 m (387 ft). The lower cavea has 34 rows of seats, separated from the upper cavea of 21 rows by the diazoma. 'Parodoi' forming entrances at orchestra level separate the cavea from the skene reconstructed about 200 B.C. Sloping ramps, starting from outside the simple stone gateways, led to a high proscenium, providing a stage about 3.00 m (10 ft) deep, faced with an Ionic colonnade and having projecting wings or parascenia at the ends.

The **Theatre of Dionysos, Athens** (reconstructed *c.* 330 B.C.) (p. 198B), which

A. Theatre, Epidauros (c. 350 B.C.). See p. 243

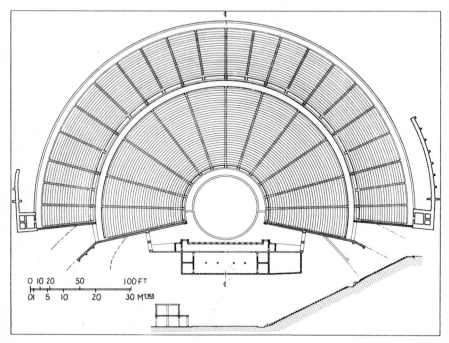

B. Theatre, Epidauros: plan and section

could accommodate eighteen thousand spectators, was founded about 500 B.C. and suffered successive modifications through the Greek and Roman times. It is scooped out of the Acropolis rock, and is tremendously deep, having three banks of seats and two diazomata. On the front row were sixty-seven marble thrones for city dignitaries, of individual design, added about the first century B.C.

A theatre was usual in every Greek town of consequence, as at **Delphi** (p. 200B), **Ephesus, Syracuse, Delos** and **Priene,** but very many were altered by the Romans.

PUBLIC BUILDINGS

The restorations of Athens (p. 248C), Olympia (p. 199) and Delphi (p. 200) give an idea of the distribution of buildings on these famous sites.

The **Agora** (p. 248C), or town square, was the centre of social and business life, around or near which were stoas or colonnaded porticoes, temples, administrative and public buildings, markets, places of entertainment, monuments and shrines.

The **Stoa** (pp. 198B, 199, 248A, C), a long, colonnaded building, served many purposes, as until late times the Greeks could not easily erect complex structures. Stoas were used around public places and as shelters at religious shrines. Important instances are the Stoa Poikilè or Echo Colonnade, Olympia (p. 199B), about 100.5 m × 9.1 m (330 ft × 30 ft), two at Epidauros, three at Delphi (p. 200A), and the Stoas of Eumenes, Athens and Attalos II, Athens (p. 248A, C).

The **Prytaneion** served as senate house for the chief dignitaries of the city and as a place where distinguished visitors and citizens might be entertained. It contained the official banqueting room and also the symbolic communal hearth on which a fire burnt perpetually, associated with the cult of Hestia, goddess of the hearth. Instances occur at Olympia (p. 199B), Athens and Priene.

The **Bouleuterion,** or council house was a covered meeting place for the democratically-elected councils. Early examples necessarily were small and needed many columns to support the roof; Hellenistic examples might accommodate more than five hundred persons, but still needed some intermediate roof supports. They were usually rectangular buildings with banked seats facing inwards on three sides, as at **Priene** (known as the Ecclesiasterion) (p. 247), or arranged in a semi-circle. Those at Olympia (p. 199) and Athens were repeatedly enlarged. That at Miletus (c. 170 B.C.) (p. 246A) accommodated 1,200 people.

Assembly Halls, for citizens in general, were similar, but needed to be larger. Until constructive skill was sufficiently advanced, public assemblies met in the open air, in the case of Athens at the hill-side Pnyx. Covered assembly halls went by special names in different places, e.g. the Thersilion, Megalopolis (c. 370 B.C.) and, the Ecclesiasterion, Priene (c. 200 B.C.) (see above). The Telesterion, or Hall of the Mysteries, Eleusis, served a religious purpose.

The **Odeion,** a kindred type to the theatre, was a building in which musicians performed their works for the approval of the public and competed for prizes. The Odeion of Pericles, Athens (c. 435 B.C.), adjoined the theatre of Dionysos, and served too for rehearsals. It was a square building with eighty-one columns—nine by nine—so placed as to give clear sight lines. The Odeion of Herodes Atticus, Athens (c. A.D. 161) (p. 198B) was very much more ambitious. It resembled a theatre in plan and probably was not wholly roofed over.

The **Stadium** was the foot racecourse in cities where games were celebrated, and had a length of about 183 m (600 ft) between banks of seats founded on convenient natural ground or on the spoil from excavation of flat sites. The starting end was straight, the other semi-circular. The oldest stadium in Greece is that at Olympia (p. 199B), and there are others at Epidauros, Delphi, Ephesus and Athens.

A. Bouleuterion (Council House), Miletus (*c.* 170 B.C.). See p. 245

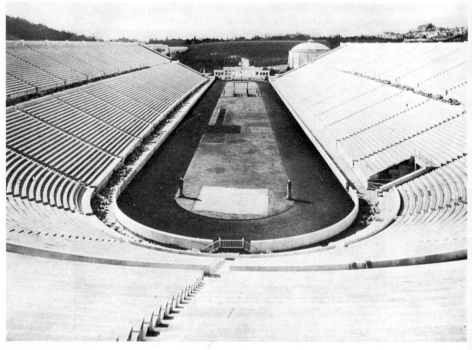

B. The Stadium, Athens, looking towards entrance (reconstructed *c.* A.D. 160 and restored in 1896). See p. 245

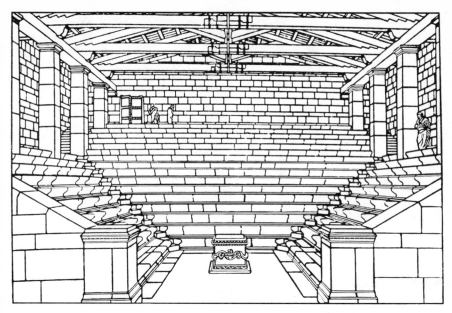

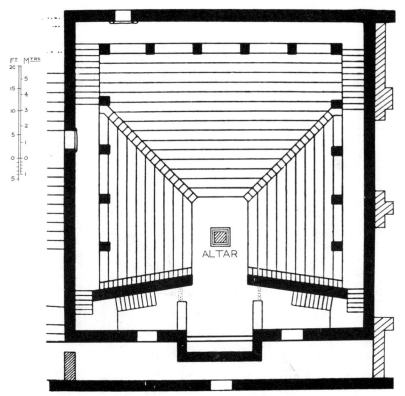

ALTAR

Ecclesiasterion, Priene (*c.* 200 B.C.): restored interior and plan. See p. 245

A. Stoa of Attalos II, Athens (c. 150 B.C.). See p. 245

B. Nereid Monument, Xanthos (restored) (c. 400 B.C.). See p. 249

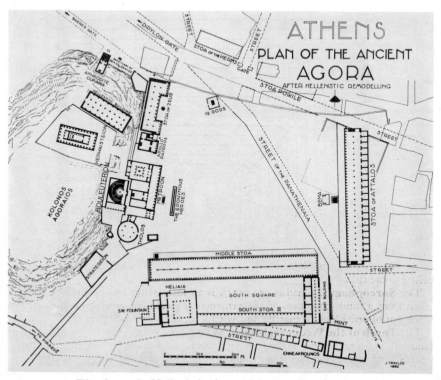

C. The Agora in Hellenistic times, Athens: plan. See p. 245

The latter (p. 246B), commenced 331 B.C. and reconstructed in A.D. 160 by Herodes Atticus, was restored from A.D. 1896 for the Olympic Games of 1906. It is said to accommodate 50,000 spectators.

The **Hippodrome** was a similar, though longer type of building for horse and chariot racing, and was the prototype of the Roman circus. Few traces now remain.

The **Palaestra** was a wrestling-school, but the term is usually used interchangeably with **Gymnasium**, a place for physical exercises of all kinds. Gymnasia, as at Olympia (p. 199B), Ephesus and Pergamon, were prototypes of the Roman thermae, and in the Hellenistic period were formal structures comprising courts for athletes, tanks for bathers, rooms for dressing and toilet, places for rest and conversation, exedrae and other seats for spectators, stores and an ephebeum or club-room which served too for lectures.

Naval buildings included ship-sheds and stores. The Arsenal at the Piraeus, built c. 340 B.C., a long narrow building for the storage of sailing tackle of the Athenian navy, is chiefly important in that the specification survives to show that still at that time the principle of the timber roof truss was not understood. The so-called **Sanctuary of the Bulls, Delos** (third century B.C.) (p. 254C, E, F, H) was similar in form, 67 m (220 ft) long and 9.1 m (30 ft) wide, and was a sacred, commemorative building housing a war galley in a shallow, dry tank. At the far end was a sanctuary approached through an entrance flanked by piers which were half Doric columns and half antae capped by recumbent sculptured bulls.

TOMBS

The **Nereid Monument, Xanthos** (c. 400 B.C.) (p. 248B) typifies Ionian sculptural luxuriance and the use in Greek Asia Minor of a temple form of tomb, elevated on a high podium. The entablature lacks a true frieze, but the architrave is sculptured and there are other bas-relief friezes on the podium. Between the columns stood nereids or marine nymphs. The remains are in the British Museum.

The **Mausoleum, Halicarnassos** (355–350 B.C.) (p. 250), the most famous of all tombs and one of the seven wonders of the world, was erected to King Mausolos by his widow, Artemisia, and from it is derived the term 'mausoleum', applied to monumental tombs. It had a lofty podium and a temple-like upper part surrounded by Ionic columns and surmounted by a pyramidal roof, with a marble quadriga and a group of statuary at its apex (p. 250C, L). The restoration of Newton and Pullan is shown in detail (p. 250A–D, L), and some of the other restorations made of this monument (p. 250E–K). The architects were Pythius and Satyrus, and Scopas was among the famous sculptors employed. Portions of three friezes, the statues of Mausolos and Artemisia, with the horses, quadriga, and other fragments, are in the British Museum.

The **Lion Tomb, Cnidos** (c. 350 B.C.) (p. 251A–F) is unusual for Asia Minor in having Doric columns. Unusual too is their pseudo-peripteral arrangement. This was another early instance of the introduction of the Egyptian, stepped pyramidal crown, from which the terminal crouching lion, which gives the tomb its name, is in the British Museum. The circular interior was roofed with a corbelled dome (p. 251B).

The **Sarcophagus, Cnidos** (p. 251J), is an interesting and beautiful example, taken from a tomb chamber, of the ornamental treatment given to a stone coffin hewn out of one block of marble and with sculptures of a late period.

The **Tomb of the Weepers, Sidon** (350 B.C.) (p. 251K), now in the Museum at Istanbul, is a sarcophagus in the form of a miniature Ionic temple, with sculptured figures of mourners between the columns.

THE MAUSOLEUM : HALICARNASSOS

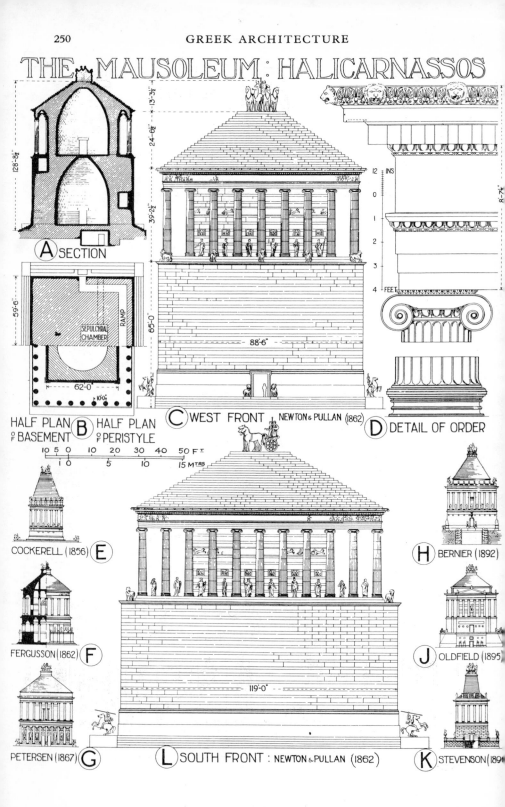

A SECTION

HALF PLAN OF BASEMENT B HALF PLAN OF PERISTYLE

C WEST FRONT NEWTON & PULLAN (1862)

D DETAIL OF ORDER

SEPULCHRAL CHAMBER

RAMP

10 5 0　10　20　30　40　50 FT
10　　　5　　　10　　15 MTRS

COCKERELL (1856) E

FERGUSSON (1862) F

PETERSEN (1867) G

L SOUTH FRONT : NEWTON & PULLAN (1862)

H BERNIER (1892)

J OLDFIELD (1895)

K STEVENSON (189

LION TOMB AT CNIDOS
(RESTORED)

A) SIDE ELEVATION B) SECTION C) FRONT ELEVATION

D) PLAN & BASE E) KEY PLAN F) PLAN OF PERISTYLE

SCALE FOR PLANS

SCALE FOR ELEVATIONS

101'-0"   WALL

LID RAISED ON PROPS

ABT 7'-0"

5'-6" G) H) 10'-4"

THE "ALEXANDER" SARCOPHAGUS: SIDON

J) TOMB AT CNIDOS

K) TOMB OF THE WEEPERS: SIDON

ABT 5'-6"

ABT 9'-5"

The **Alexander Sarcophagus** (330–320 B.C.) (p. 251G, H), also found near Sidon and now in the Istanbul Museum, is the most beautiful and best preserved surviving example of this class of monuments. It is so called because marble sculptures on its sides represent battles and hunting scenes of Alexander.

There are also important rock-cut tombs in Cyrenaica, North Africa, and in Asia Minor (p. 222E), including two from Lycia, now in the British Museum, which illustrate the genesis of the Ionic entablature from a wooden prototype.

The **Stele** (p. 254G) consisted of a slab of stone placed upright in the ground, like a modern headstone, carved in bas-relief and generally terminated with floriated ornament; many of these can be seen in the British Museum, the Metropolitan Museum of Art, New York, and the Boston Museum.

The **Tomb, Mylasa** (p. 316A–D), in Asia Minor, though built in the Roman period, shows the strength of the Greek tradition there. It is of the temple-tomb class, and resembles the Halicarnassos Mausoleum; it has Corinthian tetrastyle colonnades raised on a high podium, and a pyramidal crown of stone slabs, of which the lowest course has diagonal beams across the angles. The angle pillars are square, and the intermediate columns elliptical, their bearing area being increased by the insertion of pilaster strips on each side. The tomb at **Dougga** (p. 316R), near Tunis, is somewhat similar, but has a walled-up colonnade.

DOMESTIC BUILDINGS

The Greeks lived much of their waking life in the public and sacred parts of the city, and their houses were at first modest in scope and materials. The rooms looked towards a small court, the chief apartments being on the north side, facing the winter sun, with others on the east and west sides. Two-storey arrangements were quite common. In Asia Minor, the Ionians long retained the Aegean megaron as a chief element in their houses (p. 332C, E), but the Dorian Greeks developed the 'pastas' house (p. 253), the pastas being a long, shallow room, crossing the house from side to side and partly open on the south towards the court, whilst serving too for access to the main inner rooms to the north. In old parts of towns, houses were irregular and crowded, and still were varied in design when towns came to be regularly planned. Second storeys sometimes were flats, and shops might occupy parts of the frontages. Knowledge of Greek house design comes principally from the planned lay-outs of Olynthos, Macedonia (between 432–348 B.C.) and Priene, Asia Minor (fourth and third centuries B.C.), and from Delos (second century B.C.) on the island of that name. Full colonnaded peristyles began to develop around the internal courts of the Greek house from the third century B.C.

'**House No. 33**', Priene (p. 332C, E), measuring about 29.8 m × 17.3 m (98 ft × 57 ft) overall, is one of the best examples in this planned town (p. 228G) of the survival of the megaron element, usually found in a block of four apartments, in which the megaron and its columned porch, facing south on to the inner court, give access to two further rooms ranged along one flank. All four apartments were as much as 6.1 m (20 ft) high.

The '**Maison de la Colline**', Delos (p. 253) is an unusually regular house, nearly square, illustrating the pastas type which became general and influenced Roman arrangements. The court was fully colonnaded, with a water cistern centrally below it, its north side lighting the pastas which extended the full width of the house. From the latter opened a large room, occupying half the available width, and two other principal apartments of differing sizes. The entrance was on the west, with a kitchen adjoining, and in the south-west corner was a wooden staircase to bedrooms opening from a gallery on a second floor. Other Delian

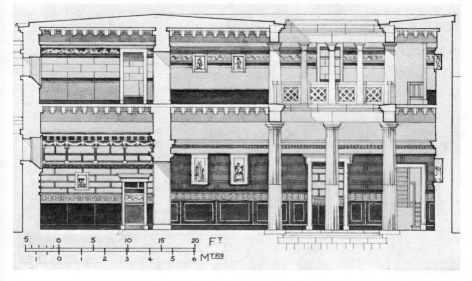

A. Section (restored)

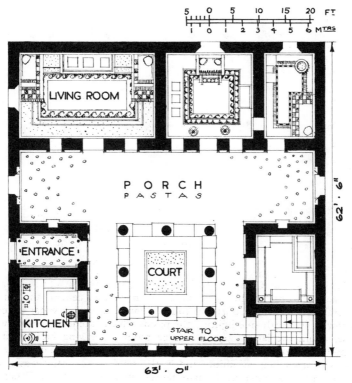

B. Plan (restored)

'Maison de la Colline', Delos (2nd cent. B.C.). See p. 252

A PEDESTAL: PRIENE

4'-0½" 4'-0½" 3'-7"

B AN ACROTERION

C DETAIL OF CAP AT *a*

SIDE FRONT 2'-4½"

D A CANEPHORA

E KEY PLAN

SANCTUARY *a* SUNKEN AREA ABT. 219'-0"

ABOUT 14'-6" 2'-3" ABT 2'-5"

F 3'-9"

G STELE

4'-10½"

H SANCTUARY ᵒᶠ THE BULLS: DELOS: ELEV. AT *a*

J CARYATID: ERECHTHEION

houses, usually with peristyles, were much less formal, and non\
like the typical Roman house at Pompeii (p. 332B).

BIBLIOGRAPHY

ALLSOPP, H. B. *A History of Classical Architecture.* London, 1965.
AYRTON, E. *The Doric Temple.* London, 1961.
BEAN, G. E. *Aegean Turkey: an Archaeological Guide.* London, 1966.
—. *Turkey's Southern Shore: an Archaeological Guide.* London, 1968.
BERVE, H., GRUBEN, G., and HIRMER, M. *Greek Temples, Theatres and Shrines.* London, 1963.
BIEBER, M. *The History of the Greek and Roman Theatre.* London and Princeton, 1961.
BLEGEN, C. W. *Troy and the Trojans.* London, 1966.
BOWRA, C. M. *The Greek Experience.* London, 1957.
CARY, M. *The Geographical Background of Greek and Roman History.* Oxford, 1949.
COOK, J. M. *The Greeks in the East.* London, 1962.
COOK, R. M. *The Greeks till Alexander.* London, 1961.
COTTRELL, L. *The Bull of Minos.* London, 1953.
DINSMOOR, W. B. *The Architecture of Ancient Greece.* 3rd ed. London, 1950.
FINLEY, M. I. *The Ancient Greeks.* London, 1963.
FYFE, T. *Hellenistic Architecture.* Cambridge, 1936.
GRAHAM, J. W. *The Palaces of Crete.* Princeton, 1962.
HEGE, W., and RODENWALDT, G. *The Acropolis.* Oxford, 1957.
HEYDEN, A. A. M. VAN DER, and SCULLARD, H. H. (Editors) *Atlas of the Classical World.* London, 1960.
HUTCHINSON, R. W. *Pre-Historic Crete.* Harmondsworth, 1962.
LAWRENCE, A. W. *Greek Architecture.* 2nd ed. Harmondsworth, 1967.
MARTIENSSEN, R. D. *The Idea of Space in Greek Architecture.* Witwatersrand, 1958.
MARTIN, R. *Living Architecture: Greek.* London, 1967.
MATZ, F. *Crete and Early Greece.* London, 1962.
PENDLEBURY, J. D. S. *A Handbook to the Palace of Minos, Knossos.* London, 1955.
QUENNELL, M., and C. H. B. *Everyday Things in Ancient Greece.* 2nd ed. London, 1954.
RIDER, B. C. *The Greek House.* Cambridge, 1965.
ROBERTSON, D. S. *Handbook of Greek and Roman Architecture.* 2nd ed. Cambridge, 1945.
SCRANTON, R. L. *Greek Architecture.* London, 1968.
SCULLY, V. *The Earth, the Temple, and the Gods.* New Haven and London, 1963.
SELTMAN, C. *Approach to Greek Art.* Cambridge, 1948.
SPIERS, R. P. *The Orders of Architecture.* London, 1926.
STOBART, J. C. *The Glory that was Greece.* 4th ed. London, 1964.
TAYLOR, W. *Greek Architecture.* London, 1971.
TAYLOUR, LORD WILLIAM. *The Mycenaeans.* London, 1965.
WOODHEAD, A. G. *The Greeks in the West.* London, 1962.
WYCHERLEY, R. E. *How the Greeks built Cities.* London, 1949.

II

ROMAN ARCHITECTURE

300 B.C.–A.D. 365, preceded by Etruscan, 750–100 B.C.

INFLUENCES

GEOGRAPHICAL

The comparative simplicity of the long coast-line of the Italian peninsula forms a strong contrast to the complexity of the indented coast-lines of Greece and the innumerable islands of the Archipelago. Italy has few natural harbours and few islands along her shores. The great chain of the Apennines runs like a spine down the centre of Italy and much of the country is very mountainous, but it is not broken up into isolated little valleys to the same extent as is Greece. The central and commanding position of Italy in the Mediterranean Sea enabled Rome to act as an intermediary in spreading art and civilization over Europe, Western Asia and North Africa. The methods adopted by Rome for extending her influence differed from those of Greece: the Romans were not a seafaring people like the Greeks, and depended for the extension of their power, not on colonization, but on conquest. The Roman Empire was ultimately not confined geographically to Italy, but included all those parts of Europe, North Africa and Western Asia which constituted the then-known world (p. 258).

GEOLOGICAL

The mineral wealth of early Italy was concentrated in Etruria, and it was to the iron of the island of Elba, and the copper and tin of the adjacent mainland that the rise of the Etruscan civilization was due. These provided the means of economic exchange and were the principal materials of its manufactures, crafts and arts. For building, there was ample good stone and, at that time, adequate timber.

The Romans, in their turn, took very great pains to exploit natural resources to the full. The geological formation of Italy differs from that of Greece, where the chief and almost the only building materials are stone and marble; whereas in addition to these, the Romans could procure suitable earths for the making of terra-cotta and brick, the latter very extensively used, even for important buildings. In the neighbourhood of Rome building stones included tufa, of varying degrees of hardness, from calcareous deposits in Rome itself and immediate vicinity; peperino, a stone of volcanic origin from Mount Albano; travertine, a hard limestone of fine quality from Tivoli; lava from volcanic eruptions; besides excellent sand and gravel. The building material, however, which led to great structural innovations was concrete, formed of stone or brick rubble and a mortar of which the important ingredient was pozzolana, a volcanic earth, found in thick strata in and around Rome and in the region of Naples. Pliny records that enormous quantities of white and coloured marbles were imported from all parts of the Empire to special wharves on the Tiber. Roman architecture was naturally influenced by the materials found in the widely differing localities where it planted itself; but concrete, which in conjunction with its brick or stone facings was the favourite material, helped to give uniformity of style throughout the Empire and thus local geological influences were to a certain extent at a discount.

CLIMATIC

North Italy has the climate of the temperate region of Europe, Central Italy is genial and sunny, while the south is almost tropical. This variety of climatic conditions is sufficient to account for diversity of architectural features and treatment in the peninsula itself, while the differing climates of the various Roman provinces produced local modifications in details, though Roman architectural character was so pronounced and assertive as to leave little choice in general design.

HISTORICAL AND SOCIAL

In early historical times, Etruria, in west-central Italy, was occupied by the Etruscans. Their antècedents are uncertain, but were probably immigrants from Asia Minor. By the eighth century B.C., when they first came to historical notice, they had subjugated the local inhabitants and thereafter the power of the Etruscans increased until it was the greatest in Italy and at sea to the west. Italy was inhabited by several races; to the north of Etruria were the Ligurians, to the east the Picenes, and to the south the Samnites and Latins. In addition, from the mid-eighth century B.C. onwards Greek colonies were established in South Italy and Sicily. The expansion of Etruscan territory, down the west coast beyond the Bay of Naples and Pompeii, northward into the valley of the Po and eastward towards the Adriatic Sea, created the need for some form of organized administration, and towns or districts were intermittently joined together in leagues. The Etruscans were great builders, redoubtable sailors and skilled craftsmen in metalwork and pottery. They surrounded their towns with walls of superb masonry, displaying a mastery of stone construction. Their art was vigorous, if somewhat coarse, until contact with the Greek cities in South Italy introduced an infusion of Greek refinement.

From its legendary foundation c. 753 B.C., and throughout the sixth century B.C., Rome was little more than an insignificant hill town in South Etruria. It was under Etruscan domination and ruled by Etruscan kings, aided by a form of popular assembly. Towards the close of the sixth century B.C. Etruscan supremacy began to decline and c. 500 B.C. saw the fall of the monarchy and the collapse of Etruscan power in Rome. The foundation of the independent city-republic of Rome separated Etruria from her southern domains, and in 474 B.C. Etruscan power was further undermined by the disaster of defeat in a sea battle by the Syracusans, allies of Cumae, the oldest of the Greek colonies in South Italy. The decline in Etruscan fortunes was countered by the rising influence and increasing dominance of Rome among Etruscan cities, especially after the defeat and conquest of Veii, the nearest of the great Etruscan cities. The declaration and development of a constitutional republic and civil service are indicative of Roman characteristics; they were great organizers, thrifty, patient farmer-soldiers, dutiful to authority and the law and concerned with efficiency and justice. With these qualities they established political leadership through a league of city-states which gradually became dependencies. An expansionist outlook fostered opportunity and fame abroad, temporarily checked in the north of Italy after defeat by the Gauls in 390 B.C. The Gauls also weakened the resistance of the surviving Etruscan towns, though they only fell to the revived aggression of Rome by slow stages. Meanwhile, the Roman conquest of South Italy was accomplished by c. 273 B.C. Expansion of influence generated friction with Carthage, heralding the first war with peoples outside Italy. The first Punic War (264–241 B.C.) against Carthage ended with the annexation of Sicily as the first Roman province. The second Punic War (218–201 B.C.) became

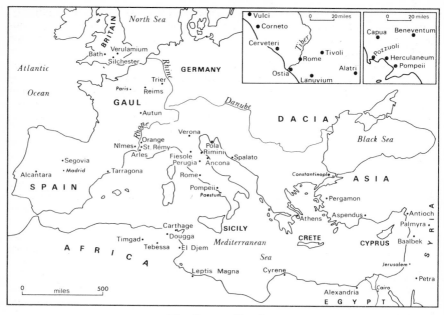

The Roman Empire

a bitter struggle for survival. Hannibal, the great Carthaginian general, entered Italy from the north via Spain and the Alps, defeated the Roman armies and ravaged Italy for years, until recalled to meet a counter-attack of the Romans, under Scipio, upon Carthage itself. Scipio's victory at Zama (202 B.C.) broke Carthaginian power, but a persistent revival engendered Roman determination to destroy Carthage, which was accomplished by the third Punic War (149–146 B.C.). Carthage, with its territory, became a Roman province in Africa. The conquest of Macedonia (168 B.C.) and Greece (146 B.C.) added two more provinces to the Roman Empire, and also stimulated the importation of Greek art and artists to Italy. In its turn, Greece formed a stepping stone to Asia Minor and the Hellenistic monarchies of the eastern Mediterranean world, of which the major part became the Roman province of Asia in 133 B.C., the remainder being gradually incorporated during the ensuing century and a half. In 133 B.C. Spain was conquered; in 64 B.C. the conquest of Syria established the Roman Empire from the Euphrates to the Atlantic.

The prolonged and often desperate wars had a deleterious effect on the Roman personality and on constitutional government. The economic and social dislocations led to the drift of refugees and the dispossessed to Rome, producing social unbalance and class strife which, with the acquisition of territories and the beginning of Empire overwhelmed and broke the system of government devised for a city-state. These troubles were further aggravated by the problems of maintaining large standing armies serving for long campaigns in distant territories. A citizen-soldiery had to be transformed into a professional army, the reform and control of which exasperated ineffective republican government and gave rise to a succession of military dictatorships of which that of Julius Caesar is the most famous. Caesar's brilliant campaigns in Gaul (58–49 B.C.) established Rome's northern frontiers along the Rhine and the English Channel. His attempt to reorganize the republican system was abruptly terminated by his assassination in 44 B.C., when there followed a period of confusion. The Triumvirate, consisting of Marcus Antonius, Caius Octavius (great-nephew of Julius Caesar) and Marcus Aemilius Lepidus defeated attempts to revive republican government, but itself became a battle for supremacy between Marcus Antonius and Caius Octavius, the former being eventually defeated at Actium (31 B.C.). Egypt then became a Roman province in 30 B.C. By his victory at Actium, Caius Octavius became supreme in the Roman world and set about reorganizing centralized government with the need to administer a world empire, and to restore political and economic stability after a century of strife and civil wars.

Curiously, the political bankruptcy of the collapsing republic and the excesses of military dictatorships were marked by a century of progress in the arts. After the conquest of Greece a rapid increase in Hellenistic influences, accompanied by the wholesale acquisition of works of art, stimulated the desire for a veneer of culture not previously conspicuous in the Roman character. Later Republican architecture, which had mainly been utilitarian, consciously adopted Greek influence with a shift of emphasis to the monumental, beautiful and essentially decorative. The last years of the disintegrating Republic also witnessed the high point of Latin culture, in the writings of Cicero (106–42 B.C.), the poetry of Virgil (70–19 B.C.), Horace (65–8 B.C.) and Ovid (43 B.C.–A.D. 17), and the histories of Livy (59 B.C.–A.D. 17).

The reorganization of the Roman world by Caius Octavius led to the formation of the Empire in its true sense. As a result he received the title of 'Imperator', and in 27 B.C. that of 'Augustus', afterwards used as a surname by all Roman Emperors. His long reign (27 B.C.–A.D. 14)—the Augustan Age— was one of the great eras in the world's history, like the Periclean Age in Greece. At such epochs a new spring seems to well up in national and individual life, vitalizing art and literature; and the reorganization and recovery, the establishment of the 'Pax Romana' and the achievements during the reign of Augustus caused later Romans to regard the period as a Golden Age. It was indeed the boast of Augustus that he found Rome a city of brick and left it one of marble. This colourful claim should not be taken too seriously, but his principate inaugurated a succession of vast Imperial building schemes overlaying much Republican architecture. An Imperial style, much affected by Hellenistic influences, was established to 'improve' the capital city of the Empire, the population of which had increased by then to make it the largest city in the Ancient World.

Augustus had no direct heir and the problem of Imperial succession was only uneasily solved while the Imperial family could claim descent from Julius Caesar, as with Tiberius (A.D. 14–37), Caligula (37–41), Claudius (41–54), in whose reign the conquest of Britain was begun, and Nero (54–68). The excesses of these unstable successors to Augustus symbolize an age glutted with power and ostentatious wealth, extravagant pleasure and search for entertainment, providing excuse and opportunity for vast building enterprises. The violent death of Nero left the Imperial succession vacant, and there ensued a year of civil war during which three aspirants to the throne rose and fell. An army commander, Vespasian, eventually restored order and founded the Flavian dynasty. His reign (69–79), and those of his sons Titus (79–81) and Domitian (81–96) were responsible for much Imperial building and further expansion of the Roman frontiers in Britain and Illyria. The murder of Domitian produced yet another crisis, which was settled by the establishment of a coalition between the Senate and Emperors, and the reigns of Nerva (96–98), Trajan (98–117), Hadrian (117–38), Antoninus Pius (138–61) and Marcus Aurelius (161–80), collectively known as the Antonine Age, are witness to the virtues and abilities of those administrators. During the reign of Trajan the Empire reached its greatest extent with the conquest of Dacia and Parthia, and the military extravagances were paralleled by vast Imperial building enterprises. The reign of Hadrian, probably the greatest of all Roman Emperors, may be regarded as a second Golden Age; a policy of retrenchment made the 'Pax Romana' literal in a world of Imperial culture and enlightenment, and enabled a prodigious outburst of building activity, in which Roman architecture achieved its true synthesis.

The social life of the Romans is clearly revealed in their architecture: there were thermae for bathing and games, circuses for races, amphitheatres for gladiatorial contests, theatres for drama, basilicas for lawsuits, state temples for religion, and the apartment house or the 'domus' for family life, while the forum was everywhere the centre of public life and national commerce. Amidst all this diversity of pursuits one constant trait runs through all Roman life, the capacity for obedience, which was the basis alike of society and the state. The 'patria potestas', or supreme power of the father, was the foundation stone of family life, and out of their obedience to authority, whether to the head of the household, or to censors in the state, the Romans developed their capacity as law-makers. Based on slavery, and aristocratic in origin, the Roman system lacked a strong middle class. Roman women were held in high respect, family life was protected, and the Temple of Vesta, the most sacred spot in Rome, has recorded for all time the sacredness attached by the Romans to their family hearth.

The closing years of the reign of Marcus Aurelius were marred by plague and the first of the barbarian inroads on the Danube frontier, and the murder of his unworthy son and successor Commodus (180–92) brought the collapse of the coalition. The following century became a period of political confusion, civil wars and invasions, and economic instability, during which a turbulent populace within the Imperial city, and the maintenance of large armies to check barbarian pressure on the frontiers dominated the affairs of government. With the exception of Septimius Severus (193–211) and Caracalla (211–17), both of whom added their patronage to architecture, and introduced strong measures for a difficult situation, the Emperors of the third century A.D. were inadequate for the times. The political power of the Empire was weakened by social chaos and economic decline, and the murder of Emperors was commonplace, thus disrupting effective government. Diocletian (284–305) effected a thorough and devastating overhaul of the Imperial system, and reorganized the civil service into a more efficient but ruthless bureaucracy. The Emperor now became a divine autocrat. Diocletian's system, involving a co-Emperor, became unworkable after his abdication, and chaos was only averted by the rise to power of Constantine (306–37) who further reorganized the reunited Empire, but at the price of a totalitarian state on eastern models, with recurring crises, constant inflation and increasingly extortionate, omnicompetent bureaucracy. Two of Constantine's acts were of the utmost significance for the future. First, he accepted Christianity (313) as a religion equal with other religions practised in the Empire; secondly, realizing that Rome was no longer central or defensible from frontier threats, in 324 he chose Byzantium as the site for a new city to be the headquarters of the Empire in the east. It was formally inaugurated in 330 as the City of Constantine, or Constantinopolis.

The successors of Constantine were weak and unable to control the growing economic and social collapse, and increasing disintegration of the military system. In 365 it became expedient to divide the Empire into East and West, with one Emperor at Constantinople and one in Italy with his capital at Milan (later Ravenna). Rome itself was no longer important. The severance of the western from the richer and more populous eastern provinces combined with internal dissensions and the progressive collapse of the defensive system to impoverish and barbarize the western half of the Empire. In 407 the Rhine frontier was broken and barbarians occupied Gaul, cutting the lines of communication between Rome and Britain. The fall of the western Empire was now imminent; in 408 the Roman army withdrew from Britain; in 410 the Goths, under Alaric, invaded Italy and sacked Rome, while the western provinces successively passed beyond Imperial control under recurrent waves of barbarian invaders. Rome was sacked again in 455, and in 476 the last Roman Emperor of the west was deposed by the German Odoacer as the first king of Italy.

RELIGIOUS

Since the Romans were originally a mixed people, their polytheistic religion was the fusion of several cults, but owed most to the Etruscans. In contrast to the religion of the Greeks, the Etruscan involved a scrupulous attention to ritual, to conformity, and to the will of the gods in a fatalistic acceptance of their domination. In the course of time many of the chief Roman gods acquired similar attributes to those of the Greeks, but retained their Latin names and rites (see p. 185). The religiosity of the Etruscans clearly manifested itself in the discipline of rules regulating man's relations with the gods, the ritual of ceremonies and sacrifices, and the beliefs and prescriptions concerning life after death. Such rules required divination by a priest class as part of the apparatus of state, which aspect influenced early Roman politico-religious thinking, so that the religion of ancient Rome soon became part of the constitution of the state, and even the worship of the gods was eventually kept up only as a matter of state policy. In Imperial times the Emperor ultimately received divine honours, and may also be described as the head of a pantheon of deities of the various provinces which came under the tolerant and widespread Roman rule. Religious feelings had not so strong a hold on the Romans as on the Greeks, and did not enter into the life of the people to the same degree; nor do we find that it formed a bond of union among the different provinces of the Empire. Dissatisfaction with state religion showed itself from time to time in the introduction to Rome of alien cults from Egypt and the Near East, especially during the crises of the third and fourth centuries A.D. Christianity in particular increased its appeal until, despite periodic persecution, it had become sufficiently widespread to be recognized by the Emperor Constantine in 313 as equal with other religions. The position of the Emperor as Pontifex Maximus is rather indicative of the glorification of the Empire than of religion, and officialism stamped its character even on temple architecture. Sacerdotalism had no place in Roman religion, and the priests were neither powerful nor privileged, but only performed the sacrifices, while augurs ascertained from omens the will of the gods. Every house, whether palace, villa or 'domus' had an altar to the Lares or family gods, and ancestor worship was a recognized part of religious rites; so it came about that Vesta, goddess of the hearth, was exalted to a high position in the Roman pantheon, and vestal virgins, attached to the temples of Vesta, were of greater importance than ordinary priests of sacrifice.

ETRUSCAN ARCHITECTURE

(750–100 B.C.)

ARCHITECTURAL CHARACTER

The Etruscans, who were the early inhabitants of west-central Italy, were great builders, and their methods were taken over by the Romans. They made remarkable advances in the organization of large-scale undertakings, such as the

A. Model of Temple of Juno Sospita, Lanuvium (5th cent. B.C.). See p. 265

B. Falerii Novi: gate in 3rd cent. B.C. town walls. See p. 263

construction of city walls and sewers, the draining of marshes and the control of rivers, and the cutting of channels to regulate the water-level of lakes. They are credited with the earliest use in Italy, if not in Europe, of the true or radiating arch, and with the invention of a new Order of Architecture, called the Tuscan. Etruscan towns were fortified with powerful stone walls, several feet thick, which were alternatively of the Cyclopean type, like that of the Aegeans; of polygonal work, as occasionally used by the Greeks (p. 188B); or, when the available stone was easily worked, of fine squared and bonded masonry laid in alternate courses of header and stretcher blocks sometimes more than two feet high. No mortar was used. Exceptionally, city walls were of very large, partly-burnt bricks, as at Arezzo, where the bricks were approximately $457 \times 305 \times 152$ mm ($1\frac{1}{2} \times 1 \times \frac{1}{2}$ ft), laid in clay mortar through the thickness of the 4.4 m (14 ft 6 ins) wall. A stone city gateway at Volterra, the Porta all'Arco, bears the remains of the earliest known arch above ground, dating from about 300 B.C. Falerii Novi (Santa Maria di Falleri), rebuilt by the Romans after the destruction of Falerii, was surrounded by walls penetrated by arched gateways of sophisticated design (p. 262B). This type of arch, which is detached from the enclosing wall, exemplifies the summation of the Etruscan tradition, and was the type usual until the age of Augustus. Tombs, which exist in great numbers, were located outside the city walls on special necropolis sites, the earliest often taking the form of great, conical tumuli, with stone burial chambers concealed within their earthen mounds. The majority were underground, cut in the soft tufa rock and simulating the interior of the contemporary house. The 'atrium' type of house, characteristic of Roman times, is believed to have originated with the Etruscans, though there is little to show now, for dwellings were of sun-dried brick, covered with terra-cotta-tiled wooden roofs. Temples too were at first of sun-dried brick, but had timber frames and columns to sustain the wide-eaved, low pitched roofs, lavishly ornamented with brilliantly-coloured terracotta slabs and crestings along the pediments, cornices and ridge. Columns themselves sometimes were sheathed in terra-cotta. From the fourth century B.C., walls and columns were of stone throughout, as at all times were the high platforms, or 'podiums', on which the temples stood. Temples were invariably frontal, and usually faced south.

EXAMPLES

The **Cloaca Maxima, Rome,** was first constructed in the late Regal period as an open drain for the valleys between the hills of Rome; which is its only title to be included as an Etruscan example, as nothing of the present remains is so old. The drain was subsequently covered in, and underwent many repairs in ancient times. At its outlet to the river Tiber (p. 266A), it shows a semicircular (Roman) vault of peperino stone, of c. 78 B.C., 3.35 m (11 ft) in span, of three concentric rings of voussoirs, each 762 mm (2 ft 6 ins) high. The oldest known true arch in Rome is that over a similar drain in front of the Temple of Saturn, dating from about the fourth century B.C. Voussoir barrel vaults occur in numerous underground tombs of the third and fourth centuries B.C., in the region of Chiusi and Perugia.

The **Arch of Augustus, Perugia** (late second century B.C.) (p. 266B) is so called because of the inscription 'Augusta Perusia', carved on the arch after 27 B.C. Although Perugia fell to the Romans in 310 B.C., the arch still retains a strong Etruscan character, as do the contemporary city walls, about two miles long, surrounding the ancient city. Both are built of large blocks of travertine stone, without mortar. An earlier arch, partially surviving, is the **Porta all'Arco, Volterra,** of the

The Necropolis, Cerveteri: (*top*) tumulus tomb (*c.* 500 B.C.);
(*centre*) interior of the Tomb of the Stucco Reliefs (3rd cent. B.C.);
(*bottom*) detail, interior of the Tomb of the Frame (5th cent. B.C.). See p. 265

fourth or third century B.C., in walls of roughly-squared, large blocks of sandstone of the sixth century B.C.

The **Temple of Jupiter Capitolinus, Rome** (509 B.C.) (pp. 273A, 285A), the principal example of this type of building, had its cella divided into three chambers for statues of Jupiter, Minerva and Juno, and was nearly square on plan, with widely spaced columns to support timber architraves. It was burnt in 83 B.C., and rebuilt first by Sulla, who used some of the marble Corinthian columns taken from the Olympieion, Athens (p. 239), and later by Domitian in A.D. 82.

The **Temple of Juno Sospita, Lanuvium** (fifth cent. B.C.) (pp. 262A, 266H, J) is restored from the description by Vitruvius (Bk. IV, chap. vii). The plan has three cells for three deities, and a front portico with two rows of four columns, widely spaced and approached by walled-in steps—a type of temple plan afterwards adopted by the Romans, and in contrast to the Greek type. The restored elevation (p. 266J) shows the steps between flanking walls and the portico columns support-ing a terra-cotta-covered timber entablature and pediment. The roof carpentry of an Etruscan temple is included in this reconstruction (p. 266K) and the terra-cotta roof covering of this Temple has been set up in the British Museum (p. 266H), while an interesting Renaissance version of the portico is seen in S. Paul, Covent Garden, London (pp. 1004, 1009G–J).

The **Temple, Alatri** (third century B.C.) (p. 266L), remains of which were found in A.D. 1882, has been re-erected in the court of the Villa of Pope Julius, Rome. This small Etruscan temple rests on a podium, and a sloping ramp gives access to a portico of two columns from which the central doorway opens into the cella. It is now known that there was no rear porch. The typical entablature of enriched terra-cotta, pediment with acroteria, and eaves with antefixae, resemble those from Lanuvium. Greek influence is probably responsible for the return to the single cella. Alatri is not in Etruria, but in the centre of Latium.

Etruscan Tomb, Corneto-Tarquinia. Of many rock-cut tombs at Etruscan Tarquinia, near the present Corneto, some twenty-three are especially renowned for their vivid wall paintings, which retain a remarkable freshness. One tomb shows architectural importance as well (p. 266F, G). The entrance leads to an outer cham-ber, somewhat resembling the atrium of an Etruscan house as described by Vitruvius, with a rock roof carved in imitation of rafters sloping up to a central opening which admitted light through a vertical shaft. A doorway leads to a smaller, inner chamber at a lower level.

The **Necropolis, Cerveteri** (p. 264), is one of the most remarkable burial sites. The tombs are laid out systematically along paved streets, like a town for the living. The oldest tombs, which include the seventh century B.C. Regolini-Galassi example, where rich treasures were found in A.D. 1836, are distributed irregularly in the neighbourhood, whereas the great tumulus mounds and the underground rock-cut chamber-tombs, chiefly of the sixth and fifth centuries B.C., are grouped compactly together to save space. Most famous among the latter are the late-seventh century Tomb of the Shields and Stools and the fifth century Tomb of the Frame, which reproduce in rock the interior features of houses; and the Tomb of the Stucco Reliefs, third century B.C., where the personal and household possessions of the deceased noble and his wife are modelled in stucco on the walls.

The **Necropolis, Vulci.** The ancient city site has long been deserted, but the tombs of its necropolis were discovered and despoiled of their priceless store of jewellery and painted vases in the nineteenth century. But there, as elsewhere, tombs were often adorned with architectural features, as well as wall paintings. A tomb from Vulci, discovered in A.D. 1833, has been reconstructed in the British Museum. It includes a short, sturdy column with a capital (p. 266D) which is

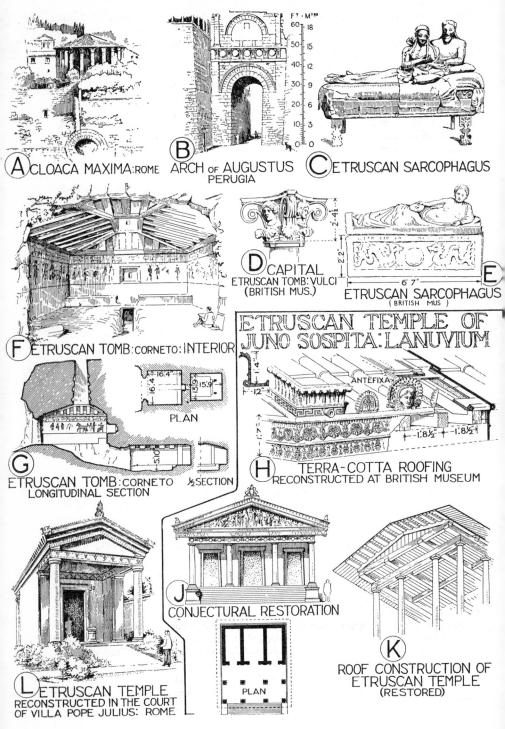

(A) CLOACA MAXIMA: ROME

(B) ARCH OF AUGUSTUS
PERUGIA

(C) ETRUSCAN SARCOPHAGUS

(D) CAPITAL
ETRUSCAN TOMB: VULCI
(BRITISH MUS.)

(E) ETRUSCAN SARCOPHAGUS
(BRITISH MUS)

(F) ETRUSCAN TOMB: CORNETO: INTERIOR

(G) ETRUSCAN TOMB: CORNETO
LONGITUDINAL SECTION

PLAN

½ SECTION

(H) ETRUSCAN TEMPLE OF
JUNO SOSPITA: LANUVIUM

ANTEFIXA

TERRA-COTTA ROOFING
RECONSTRUCTED AT BRITISH MUSEUM

(J) CONJECTURAL RESTORATION

PLAN

(K) ROOF CONSTRUCTION OF
ETRUSCAN TEMPLE
(RESTORED)

(L) ETRUSCAN TEMPLE
RECONSTRUCTED IN THE COURT
OF VILLA POPE JULIUS: ROME

distinctively Etruscan, with upspringing volutes at the corners, and carved human heads between. It derives from a primitive type from the Near East, but the heads are an Etruscan addition; used quite frequently too for the decoration of the keystones of arches. The acanthus leaves show the influence of the Greek Corinthian Order. We have seen that the Etruscans imitated the Greek Doric Order and produced from it their own 'Tuscan' variant. They also had their versions of the Greek Ionic, as seen in the Arch of Augustus, Perugia (p. 266B).

Etruscan Sarcophagi. Both ordinary burial and cremation were practised in Etruria. The receptacles grew increasingly large, until in the fourth century B.C., sarcophagi of stone, alabaster and terra-cotta were used in very large numbers. The deceased were normally represented as reclining on a couch. The sarcophagus from the British Museum (p. 266E) has marine monsters on the side, and the reclining figure holds the plate for the coin to be paid to Charon for ferrying the departed across the Styx. The example from Cerveteri, now in the Villa of Pope Julius Etruscan Museum, Rome (p. 266C) is in terra-cotta, and in portraying man and wife together, shows the high status which women enjoyed in Etruscan society.

ROMAN ARCHITECTURE

(300 B.C.–A.D. 365)

ARCHITECTURAL CHARACTER

Roman building work retained its Etruscan character for some time after the Republic had been founded in 509 B.C., but in the third century B.C. began to derive much of its external complexion from Greek sources. By about 200 B.C., its own identity was well established, though experiments with building method, and the exploitation of building materials, were to progress continuously until well into the Christian era. The mightiest achievements belong to the period of the Roman Empire, growing increasingly daring as time progressed.

The Romans adopted the columnar and trabeated style of the Greeks, and developed also the arch and the vault from the beginnings made by the Etruscans. This combined use of column, beam and arch is the keynote of the Roman style in its earliest stages. The Colosseum, Rome (p. 307), everywhere throughout its structure, displays these two features in combination, for piers strengthened and faced by attached half-columns support arches, which in their turn carry the entablature. In works of an engineering character, such as aqueducts, the arch was supported on piers without the facing column. Thus the Orders of architecture which, as used by the Greeks, were essentially constructive were frequently employed by the Romans as decorative features which could be omitted, although the Romans also used them constructively in temple colonnades and basilicas (p. 291A).

The Doric, Ionic and Corinthian Orders of architecture were used by the Greeks (p. 194), and the Etruscans and Romans added respectively the Tuscan and Composite Orders, making five in all. The Tuscan Order (p. 266J, K) is a simplified version of the Doric Order, about 7 diameters high, with base, unfluted shaft, and simply-moulded capital, and with a plain entablature. Actually, in ancient times it was used only with the wooden entablatures of the Etruscans, and there is no certain Roman example. Vitruvius, the Roman authority on architecture in the late first century B.C., recorded it, and it was revived with a stone entablature in Renaissance days. The Composite Order was not evolved until the first century A.D. The proportions of the various Orders are illustrated on p. 1052.

Temples were the predominating buildings of the Hellenic and Hellenistic Greeks and were of one storey, but the complex civilization and varied needs of the

Romans introduced other types and necessitated the use of several storeys, which were frequently ornamented, as in the Colosseum, by attached half-columns super-imposed one above the other. The architectural aims of the Romans were essentially utilitarian, and thermae, amphitheatres, basilicas, aqueducts and bridges all testify to the great constructive ability they possessed.

The Romans continued and developed the Etruscan method of using large blocks of stone without mortar during the Republic, but their practical mind eventually hit upon greater economy of materials by the use of concrete, a hard composition which consists of small fragments of stone, such as tufa of its various kinds, peperino or travertine, or again, broken bricks, laid in an excellent mortar of lime and well-selected sand. The 'sand' was, in fact, usually pozzolana, a special earth which abounds in the volcanic regions of Italy. The important parts of the work were done by skilled craftsmen, who built up the outer carcase of the ponderous walls and saw to the erection of the temporary wooden centerings for arches and vaults. Under their direction, the purely mechanical tasks of dumping alternate layers of mortar and broken stones or brick, which would solidify into concrete, were performed by local slaves liable to statute labour on public buildings or, in the case of military works, by soldiers of the Roman legions.

Roman walls, both of stone and concrete, are of special character and must be described in detail. Walls of 'opus quadratum', i.e. rectangular blocks of stone, with or without mortar joints but frequently secured with dowels or cramps, still continued in use. In the best work, the stones were very regular, $4 \times 2 \times 2$ Roman feet in dimensions (the Roman foot is 12.7 mm ($\frac{1}{2}$ inch) less than the English), laid in the usual alternate courses of headers and stretchers. Sometimes, such walls were solid throughout, at others, used as a facing to the concrete core, as in the case of temple podiums. Roman concrete walls presented a succession of face effects. Good mortar of lime and sand first began to be used extensively in the third century B.C., and when its virtues had been realized, stones became quite small, and on the wall faces appeared in a loose pattern roughly resembling the polygonal work from which the techniques derived. This pattern is known as 'opus incertum' (p. 269B). Gradually, it became more regular, until by the time of Augustus it had assumed the net-like effect of 'opus reticulatum' (p. 269C), with fine joints running diagonally, so that each stone unit was precisely square, though set lozenge fashion. In both the incertum and the reticulate work, the stones were only 102 mm (4 ins) or so across the face, and tailed into the wall pyramidally for about 203–254 mm (8–10 ins). Specially cut stones were used at outer vertical angles. Reticulate work in its turn was superseded by brick facing, or 'opus testaceum' (p. 269D), which became the hall-mark of the Imperial period in Italy and elsewhere. Wall cores then sometimes were of broken brick too, but generally, stone fragments still continued to be used. The 'bricks' were in fact old roofing tiles, upwards of 38 mm ($1\frac{1}{2}$ ins) thick and of considerable but irregular length, raggedly broken to tail back into the wall: only in the second half of the first century A.D. were triangular bricks specially made for facing the walls. Except in the case of opus incertum, the wall faces were necessarily laid a little in advance of the core of a wall, in better mortar, and they consequently tended to come adrift. Hence bonding courses of large square tiles or 'bipedales', two Roman feet square were soon introduced to pass back into or even right through the wall, distributed at frequent intervals up the height. A variant kind of facing appeared for a while about the time of Hadrian, in which panels of reticulate work were enframed in horizontal and vertical strips of brickwork. A final type, 'opus mixtum', an alternation of courses of brickwork and small, squared stone blocks, began to be used towards the end of the Empire period. These several kinds of facing to concrete walls were not used everywhere; in many

CONSTRUCTION of WALLS and ARCHES

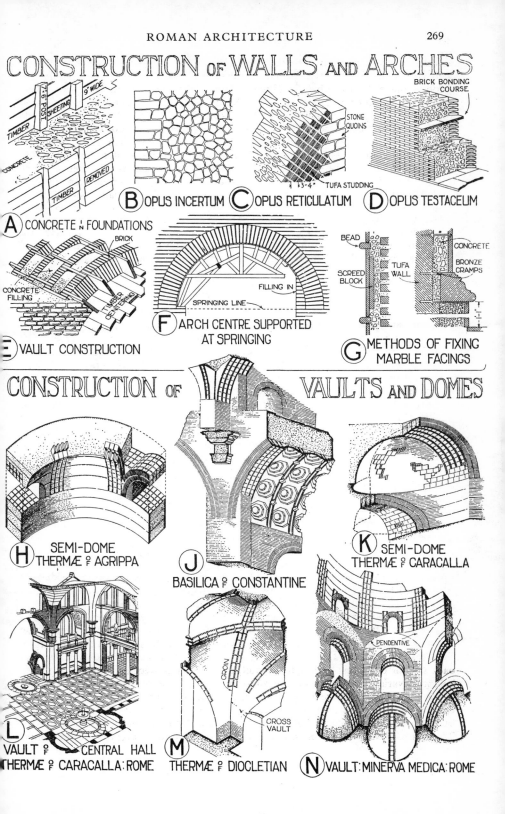

A CONCRETE in FOUNDATIONS

B OPUS INCERTUM **C** OPUS RETICULATUM **D** OPUS TESTACEUM

E VAULT CONSTRUCTION

F ARCH CENTRE SUPPORTED AT SPRINGING

G METHODS OF FIXING MARBLE FACINGS

CONSTRUCTION of VAULTS and DOMES

H SEMI-DOME THERMÆ of AGRIPPA

J BASILICA of CONSTANTINE

K SEMI-DOME THERMÆ of CARACALLA

L VAULT of CENTRAL HALL THERMÆ of CARACALLA: ROME

M THERMÆ of DIOCLETIAN

N VAULT: MINERVA MEDICA: ROME

of the Roman provinces, Britain included, a coursed-rubble facing of squared units only a few inches high was usual. No special facings could, of course, be employed when the concrete was laid against earth or boarding in foundations or vaults (p. 269A, E).

It was upon the capacity to span over enormous spaces that the character of Roman architecture largely depended. The Greeks of Hellenic times had been limited to what could be achieved by simple beams of wood, and so had had to introduce double lines of superimposed columns inside even their temples, to support the roof timbers, whenever extra space was needed. It was not till about the third century B.C. that the Greeks began timidly to employ the principle of triangulation of the elements of wooden roof trusses. The Romans seized upon the idea, and developed it apace: Vitruvius, the Augustan architect, tells us of the wooden-roofed basilica he built at Fano, in North Italy, where the central unimpeded space was 18.29 m (60 ft) wide by 36.58 m (120 ft). Similarly, the Romans developed the stone arch of the Etruscans; and already before the end of the Republic could bridge a span of 24.38 m (80 ft), as in the Pons Fabricius at Rome. But it was, above all, the use of concrete which allowed the Romans to build vaults of a magnitude never equalled till the introduction of steel for buildings in the nineteenth century. Concrete vaults had the advantage over stone in that they could be accommodated to complicated plan forms without involving difficult and laborious stone cutting. The vaults were supported on 'centering' or temporary wooden framework until the concrete had set. In important cases, such vaults were constructed of brick ribs, with concrete filling, the object being to lighten the load imposed on the centering and to guard against cracks (p. 269E). The various vaults used in Roman buildings were as follows (p. 269): (a) The semicircular or waggon-headed vault, otherwise known as the 'barrel' or 'tunnel' vault, was borne throughout its length on the two parallel walls of a rectangular apartment (p. 627A). (b) The cross-vault (pp. 627B, 628A), which was formed by the intersection of two semicircular vaults of equal span, was used over a square apartment and the pressure was taken by the four angles. When cross-vaults were used over long halls or corridors, the hall was divided by piers into square bays, each of which was covered with a cross-vault, which allowed of the insertion of windows in the upper part of the walls, as in the central hall of the Thermae of Caracalla (pp. 269L, 297) and the Thermae of Diocletian, Rome (p. 302A). The lines of intersection of these cross-vaults are known as 'groins'. (c) Hemispherical domes or cupolas (*cupa* = a cup) (p. 287) were used over circular structures, and semi-domes for exedrae or semicircular recesses (p. 269H, K).

In all these vaulting forms, concrete was the important factor, for it was economical of skilled labour and had much greater cohesion than vaults made up of separate stone units. Yet it remained necessary to buttress the oblique sideways thrusts exerted against the walls by the enormously heavy concrete vaults, which even at the crown, were several feet thick. The barrel vaults over the side aisles or recesses of the Basilica of Constantine, Rome, for instance, each of which spans 23.16 m (76 ft), were 2.44 m (8 ft) thick at the top (p. 269J), and the dome of the famous Pantheon, 43.28 m (142 ft) across, is more than 1.22 m (4 ft) thick in its upper part (p. 288A). To a certain extent the ponderous walls absorbed these stresses, but the Romans took no chances and devised an elaborate buttressing system. The fact is not always apparent, for in complex buildings the thrusts of one vault were balanced against those of another, as in the Thermae of Diocletian (p. 302D), where the enormous central hall was surrounded by lesser apartments with their walls aligned against the points where the stresses of the groined triple vault were received. Also, the Romans usually concealed their buttresses with a masking wall.

The art of buttressing was developed in the course of early engineering works, which frequently required the retaining of masses of earth. Three principal types of buttress were used. (i) The hemicycle or niche, which is the best of all buttresses for retaining earth. This type was used on an enormous scale in the Forum of Trajan, on the north-east side, where the hemicycle cuts into the foot of the Quirinal. Galleries of shops and offices in three tiers conceal its utilitarian purpose. (ii) The ordinary 'Gothic' type of 'spur' buttress, familiar in countless Mediaeval buildings. The niche type was not very suitable for buildings where large openings for windows and doors were needed—though a pair can be seen flanking the portal between the central hall and the frigidarium of the Thermae of Diocletian (p. 302D) —so for convenience in normal buildings it was squared-off into spur buttresses and a linking wall in which windows could be placed. The connecting wall, however, was put across the outer edge of the buttresses so that the space between them could be covered over with a vault and included in the useful interior accommodation. The aisles of the Basilica of Constantine utilize the space between the great buttresses in this way (p. 291D, E, F), and the latter can be seen, with their sloping tops, rising above the vaults of the aisles to catch the thrusts of the main vaults where they are concentrated in the pockets above the columned pillars (p. 291D). Instances of flying buttresses are also known. (iii) The principle of the pinnacle too, was extensively used. Pinnacles were placed on the tops of spur buttresses to help by their weight to drive the oblique thrusts more steeply down to earth. They are of very great size at the Thermae of Diocletian (p. 302B), but, as is almost invariably the case in Roman architecture, their mundane purpose is disguised by architectural ornament; in this instance by canopied sculptures. In buildings of which the walls were not too much broken up by window or other openings, the same principle was applied, but the extra load then ran continuously along the top of the wall outside the base of the vault, as an abutment, to reduce the danger of its collapsing outwards.

The Pantheon at Rome, the finest of all illustrations of Roman construction, embodies every form of Roman buttress. It will be noted there (p. 288A) that the building is two tiers high to the springing of the hemispherical dome inside, but there is an extra tier on the outside, providing rigid and weighty haunches to prevent the dome from splitting outwards; and, as an extra precaution, a further series of steps of concrete rises two-thirds the height of the dome. It is for this constructional reason that Roman domes are always saucer-shaped outside, though hemispherical within. Very adroitly in this building, the weight of the vault is reduced by omitting a portion at the crown—the most difficult part to construct—to provide an 'eye' which is the sole source of natural light. The 6.1 m (20 ft) thick walls are not by any means solid; the decorative recesses inside are contrived within spur buttresses linking inner and outer shells, and between these recesses are constructional niches which run the full three-tier height and are crowned with semi-domes at the top of each tier; in the upper tiers they are split in half by spur buttresses (p. 288A, B). Thus all the forms of buttress used later in developed Mediaeval architecture were anticipated by Roman architects, but with the difference that the Roman were far less light and compact, and seldom plainly exposed to view.

Concrete vaults often were lightened by recesses or 'coffers' on the underside, but concrete does not lend itself to carved enrichment, like stonework, and walls and vaults normally received a decorative sheathing of plaster, stucco, marble or mosaic. Various plasters of lime and sand were used outside, and plaster or stucco within. The latter was of marble dust and lime, and frequently was modelled into shallow, geometrical patterns, the panels thus created being ornamented with low-relief figures and foliage, and painted in attractive colours. In such cases the stucco was as much as 76 mm (3 ins) in thickness. When bold mouldings or entire columns were required in this material, as in the peristyles of houses, they would have a concrete or brick core. Alternatively for walls, especially in domestic work, the stucco was carefully prepared, in as many as five successive coats, to receive elaborate and brilliant paintings in fresco, tempera or encaustic. A special mixture, 'opus signinum', of ground terra-cotta and lime, with or without sand, was used for the lining of water-channels, aqueducts and reservoirs and in damp situations.

Marble was rarely used solidly throughout a wall; and only the white was so employed, never the coloured. Normally it was just a facing, up to 305 mm (1 ft) or so thick when the marble was the native 'Luna' from Carrara, but in mere veneers down to 12.7 mm ($\frac{1}{2}$ inch) thick in the case of coloured marbles. Marble, porphyry, jasper or granite veneers were laid against a stucco backing and secured to the walls by iron or bronze cramps (p. 269G); they were arranged in geometrical patterns of different varieties ('opus sectile'), and were used in this manner too for floors. Coloured marbles were too expensive for universal use, and on walls, the pattern was frequently simulated in paint instead. When the Orders of architecture were constructed in marble as a whole, as in the case of temple porches, it was only the column shafts that might be of the coloured varieties; and to show their veinings or textures to best advantage, they were unfluted monoliths, shaped at the quarry before shipping. The omission of fluting in such instances affected usage in general, and as often as not the flutes were omitted even when the shafts were built up in stone, whatever the Order employed.

Marble mosaics were employed to some extent for walls and vaults, but above all, for floors, in an infinite variety of geometrical and pictorial patterns. A humbler type of paving was 'opus spicatum', made of small bricks set in herring-bone pattern. Glass mosaics made a brilliant decoration for vaults and were excellent for structures and situations liable to damp, such as garden ornaments and pavilions, fountains and semi-subterranean porticoes and grottoes. Gilding was sometimes applied to wood ornaments and to bronze-covered roofs of important buildings, such as the Pantheon (p. 290).

The abundance of statues brought from Greece led to the formation of wall niches for their reception, and these were either semicircular or rectangular, and were occasionally flanked by columns supporting a pediment, or were fronted by a screen of columns, as in the Pantheon (pp. 287B, 288A,B).

EXAMPLES
FORUMS

The forum, corresponding to the agora in a Greek city, was a central open space used as a meeting-place, market, or rendezvous for political demonstrations. In towns which had grown from small beginnings, forums were often somewhat irregular in shape, but when towns were newly founded or for some reason partially rebuilt, the forums were laid out systematically, on formal lines.

The **Forum Romanum, Rome,** the oldest and most important in the city, was sited in the valley between Rome's famous hills. It is not strictly rectangular; it was originally an all-purpose forum, but as the city grew its shops were removed elsewhere and the contests and displays which once had taken place there were relegated to the theatre, amphitheatre and circus. Only the chief public buildings then were grouped around it, and its appearance in the heyday of ancient Rome, adorned with pillars of victory and statues and surrounded by porticoes, colonnades, temples and basilicas, must indeed have been imposing (p. 273).

The **Imperial Forums.** Rome, with its great Empire, required more civic space

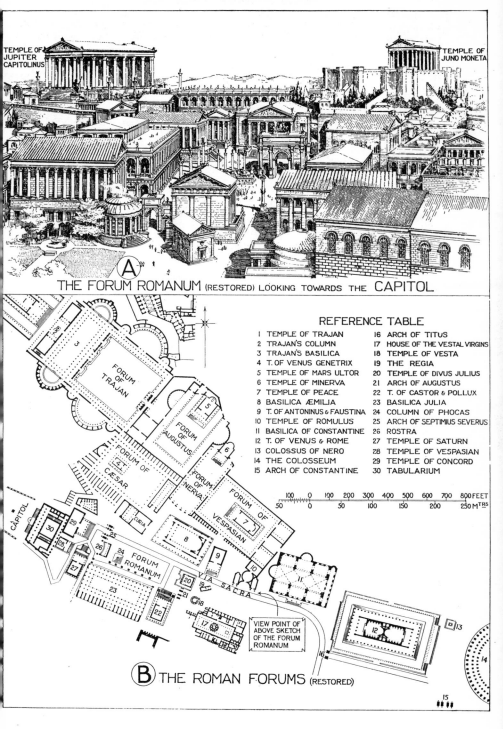

TEMPLE OF JUPITER CAPITOLINUS

TEMPLE OF JUNO MONETA

Ⓐ THE FORUM ROMANUM (RESTORED) LOOKING TOWARDS THE CAPITOL

REFERENCE TABLE

1	TEMPLE OF TRAJAN	16	ARCH OF TITUS
2	TRAJAN'S COLUMN	17	HOUSE OF THE VESTAL VIRGINS
3	TRAJAN'S BASILICA	18	TEMPLE OF VESTA
4	T. OF VENUS GENETRIX	19	THE REGIA
5	TEMPLE OF MARS ULTOR	20	TEMPLE OF DIVUS JULIUS
6	TEMPLE OF MINERVA	21	ARCH OF AUGUSTUS
7	TEMPLE OF PEACE	22	T. OF CASTOR & POLLUX
8	BASILICA ÆMILIA	23	BASILICA JULIA
9	T. OF ANTONINUS & FAUSTINA	24	COLUMN OF PHOCAS
10	TEMPLE OF ROMULUS	25	ARCH OF SEPTIMIUS SEVERUS
11	BASILICA OF CONSTANTINE	26	ROSTRA
12	T. OF VENUS & ROME	27	TEMPLE OF SATURN
13	COLOSSUS OF NERO	28	TEMPLE OF VESPASIAN
14	THE COLOSSEUM	29	TEMPLE OF CONCORD
15	ARCH OF CONSTANTINE	30	TABULARIUM

FORUM OF TRAJAN

FORUM OF AUGUSTUS

FORUM OF CÆSAR

FORUM OF NERVA

FORUM OF VESPASIAN

CAPITOL

CURIA

FORUM ROMANUM

VIA SACRA

100 0 100 200 300 400 500 600 700 800 FEET
50 0 50 100 150 200 250 MTRS

VIEW POINT OF ABOVE SKETCH OF THE FORUM ROMANUM

Ⓑ THE ROMAN FORUMS (RESTORED)

than the Forum Romanum allowed, and successive Emperors laid out imposing new symmetrical forums which were at the same time monuments to themselves. Julius Caesar added the first; then the Emperors Augustus, Vespasian, Nerva and Trajan in turn (p. 273B).

The **Forum of Trajan, Rome** (A.D. 98–113) (p. 273B), was the largest of these. It comprised four parts: (i) the forum proper, with large hemicycles on either side, screened off by colonnades, containing tiers of shops; (ii) a marketing area comprising shops and a two-storey vaulted hall on the slopes of the Quirinal Hill beyond the north-eastern hemicycle; (iii) the Basilica of Trajan and two adjoining libraries separated by a court from which rose Trajan's commemorative column; and (iv) a peristyled enclosure containing the Temple of Trajan.

Apart from these forums, others, such as the **'Forum Boarium'** (p. 285B), served as specialized markets. The forums of Rome and the provinces provide many instances of well-considered town-planning, and there were fine examples even in the outskirts of the Empire, as at Palmyra, Samaria, Damascus, Antioch, **Baalbek** (p. 281A, F) and Bosra in Syria; Pergamon in Asia Minor; Timgad and Tebessa in North Africa; and at **Silchester** (p. 294) and elsewhere in England; in all of which there were colonnaded streets to give shelter from the sun.

RECTANGULAR TEMPLES

Roman temples are an amalgamation of Etruscan and Greek types; for while in many respects they resembled the Greek, the typical prostyle portico and podium were derived from Etruscan temples (p. 263). There are several types, of which the most characteristic is pseudo-peripteral (p. 275B, H), which, instead of side colonnades, has half-columns attached to the walls with a prostyle portico in front. The steps to the principal entrance were flanked by massive, low walls which were an extension of the lateral podium, and they frequently supported groups of statuary (p. 275G). Greek peripteral temples were normally twice as long as their width, but Roman temples were much shorter in proportion, while the cella itself, used as a treasure house and as a museum for Greek statuary, frequently occupied the whole width of the building. The intercolumniation was sometimes wider than in Greek temples, and then the architrave and frieze were built in voussoirs as flat arches, but this treatment was unnecessary where walls supported the entablature. Most rectangular temples were simple structures compared with buildings erected for public relaxation, like theatres, amphitheatres and thermae, and the latter types are more truly representative of Roman architectural taste and constructional skill. Nevertheless, temples quite clearly evidence Roman ability to cover large spaces without the aid of intermediate supports. Spans of 15.2 m or 18.3 m (50 or 60 ft) were common. Normally, the roofs were of trussed timbers, like the basilicas, and probably were elaborately coffered with wooden panelling on the underside. Some few temples were vaulted, as the Temple of Venus and Rome at Rome (p. 279C, E). Roman temples sometimes were partially or wholly isolated in precincts, like those in the Imperial Forums at Rome (p. 273B), though most were intended to be seen from the forum which they faced, and the entrance was emphasized by the deep portico and steps. There was no attempt at orientation, as in the Greek temples, which regularly faced east, or the Etruscan, which usually faced south.

The **Temple of Fortuna Virilis, Rome** (c. 40 B.C.) (pp. 275A, B, C, 285B) is pseudo-peripteral tetrastyle with the deep portico common in Roman temples and which illustrates the retention of Etruscan practice. The Ionic Order used, however, shows Hellenistic Greek influence in almost all its details. The capitals are two-faced, so there had to be a canted volute on those at the angles, as in the East

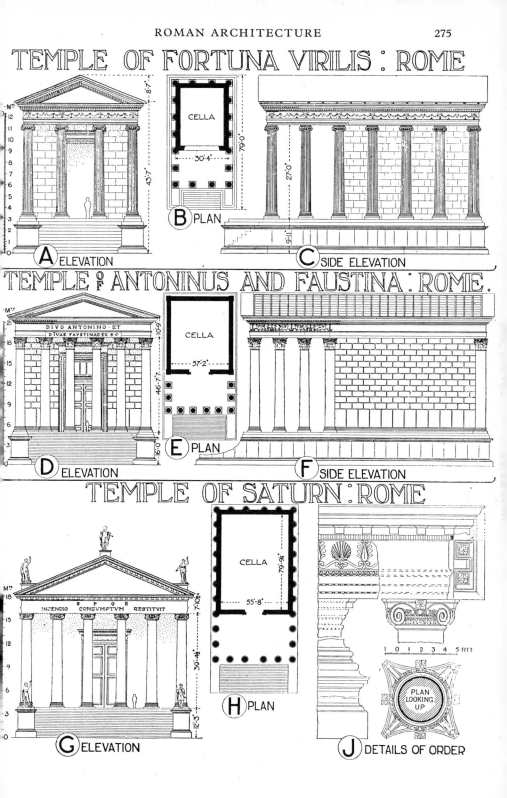

TEMPLE OF FORTUNA VIRILIS : ROME

A ELEVATION

B PLAN

CELLA

30'-4"

79'-0"

8'-7"

43'-7"

27'-0"

9'-11"

C SIDE ELEVATION

TEMPLE OF ANTONINUS AND FAUSTINA : ROME

DIVO ANTONINO · ET
DIVAE FAVSTINAE EX · S · C

D ELEVATION

CELLA

57'-2"

46'-7"

10'-9"

16'-0"

E PLAN

F SIDE ELEVATION

TEMPLE OF SATURN : ROME

INCENDIO CONSVMPTVM RESTITVIT
S · P · Q · R

G ELEVATION

7'-10½"

12'-3"

CELLA

55'-8"

79'-9½"

39'-4½"

H PLAN

PLAN LOOKING UP

1 0 1 2 3 4 5 FEET

J DETAILS OF ORDER

Portico of the Erechtheion, Athens (p. 224D), but the front wall of the cella raised a special difficulty, as the two attached columns which mark its position had to have canted volutes too. The temple demonstrates Roman selective use of materials according to their respective properties, for whilst the majority of the building is faced in tough travertine, the shafts of the intermediate attached columns on the side and rear walls, the cella itself and the portion of entablature above it are of tufa stone, and the podium core is concrete.

The **Temple of Mars Ultor, Rome** (14–2 B.C.) (pp. 273B, 277), in the Forum of Augustus, was dedicated to Mars the Avenger by Augustus in fulfilment of his vow to avenge the death of Caesar. It was one of the largest and finest of temples; from the artistic point of view, Roman architecture reached its climax in Augustan times, though the great constructional achievements had then barely commenced. Quite a little of the temple survives. Apart from its being attached to the forum wall, it was peripteral and had Corinthian columns 17.68 m (58 ft) high. The walls were of peperino stone, faced with thin slabs of Luna marble, tied back at intervals up the height by solid marble bonding courses, whilst for the podium there were upright large facing slabs of marble about 305 mm (1 ft) thick. The cella, nearly square, had internal columns and pilasters, and an apsidal recess—one of the earliest instances of a feature afterwards adopted in Early Christian churches. It stood in front of the Quirinal Hill in a peribolus surrounded by a wall some 30.48 m (100 ft) high, of peperino stone and ornamented with niches for statues (p. 277A).

The **Temple of Concord, Rome** (7 B.C.–A.D. 10) (p. 273B), had a very large cella, unusual in being wider than deep—45.11 m × 24.99 m (148 ft × 82 ft)—due to its cramped position against the base of the Capitol Hill. Its deep hexastyle prostyle porch occupied the centre of one of the longer sides, and the whole stood on a platform about 6.1 m (20 ft) above the roadway. The cornice of this temple affords one of the earliest instances in Rome of the use of 'modillions' or scrolled consoles, later an orthodox part of the Corinthian entablature (cf. p. 278).

The **Temple of Castor and Pollux, Rome** (7 B.C.–A.D. 6) (pp. 273B, 278) had been dedicated in 482 B.C. to the twin gods in gratitude for their aid at the battle of Lake Regillus in 496 B.C. This peripteral temple had an octastyle portico on a raised podium, 6.7 m (22 ft) high, faced with Pentelic marble and filled in solid except for vaulted small chambers below the side intercolumniations which served as strong-rooms for storing the temple treasure and for testing weights and measures. The three existing columns of Pentelic marble are 14.76 m (48 ft 5 ins) high and have unique Corinthian capitals in which the central volutes intertwine, and between these and the angle volutes rises a tendril from which foliage is carried along the abacus (p. 278D). The entablature, 3.82 m (12 ft 6½ ins) high, has an architrave with carved mouldings, a plain frieze, and a cornice enriched with modillions, dentils and cymatium, and lion heads throw off rain-water. The angle (p. 278C) shows a clever arrangement of ornamental features.

The **Maison Carrée, Nîmes** (16 B.C.) (p. 277) is the best preserved Roman temple in existence, and is externally complete. It represents the ultimate of Graeco-Etruscan design interpreted in monumental Augustan architecture, correct in the canons of design and incorporating a rich, well-detailed Corinthian order. It is raised on a podium 3.66 m (12 ft) high, with steps only on the entrance (west) façade, and it is pseudo-peripteral prostyle hexastyle. The deep porch has three open bays on each side, and half columns extend around the sides and rear of the cella. The Corinthian columns support a rich entablature incorporating a frieze of tendril pattern and an early instance of a modillioned cornice. Originally the podium stood on a platform surrounded by porticoes which defined the forum.

TEMPLE OF MARS ULTOR : ROME

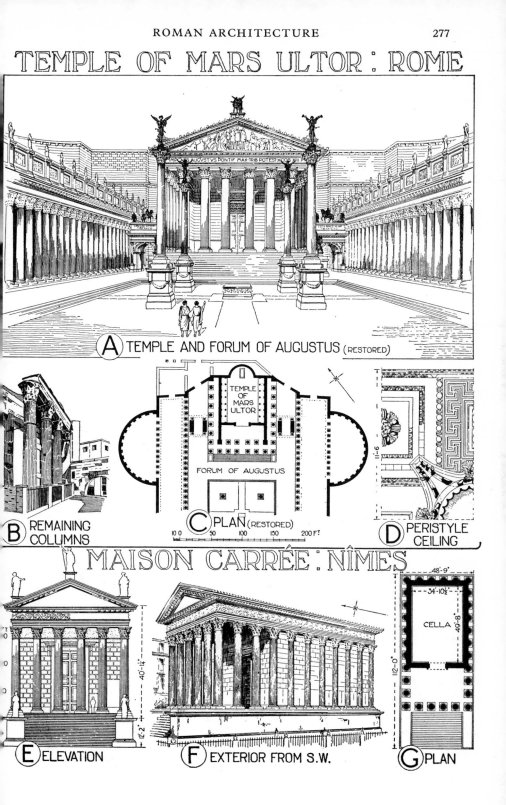

(A) TEMPLE AND FORUM OF AUGUSTUS (RESTORED)

TEMPLE OF MARS ULTOR

FORUM OF AUGUSTUS

(B) REMAINING COLUMNS

(C) PLAN (RESTORED)

10 0   50   100   150   200 FT

(D) PERISTYLE CEILING

MAISON CARRÉE : NÎMES

CELLA

(E) ELEVATION

(F) EXTERIOR FROM S.W.

(G) PLAN

TEMPLE OF CASTOR & POLLUX: ROME

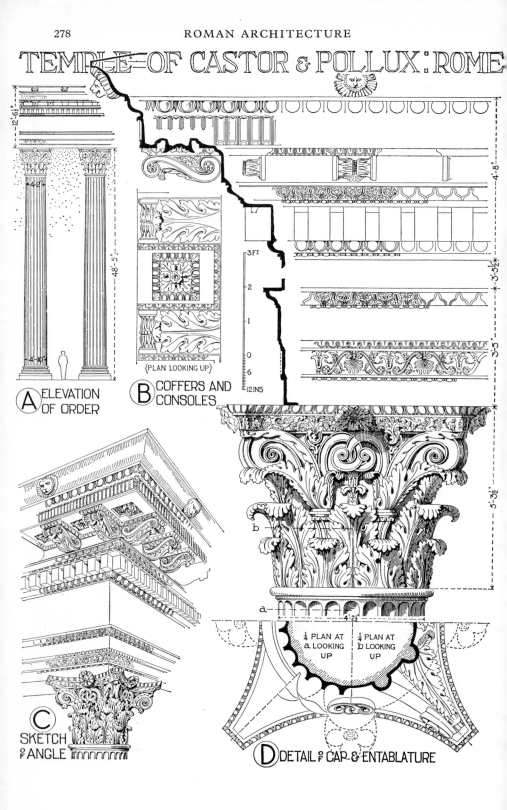

A ELEVATION OF ORDER

B COFFERS AND CONSOLES

(PLAN LOOKING UP)

C SKETCH OF ANGLE

D DETAIL OF CAP & ENTABLATURE

¼ PLAN AT a LOOKING UP   ¼ PLAN AT b LOOKING UP

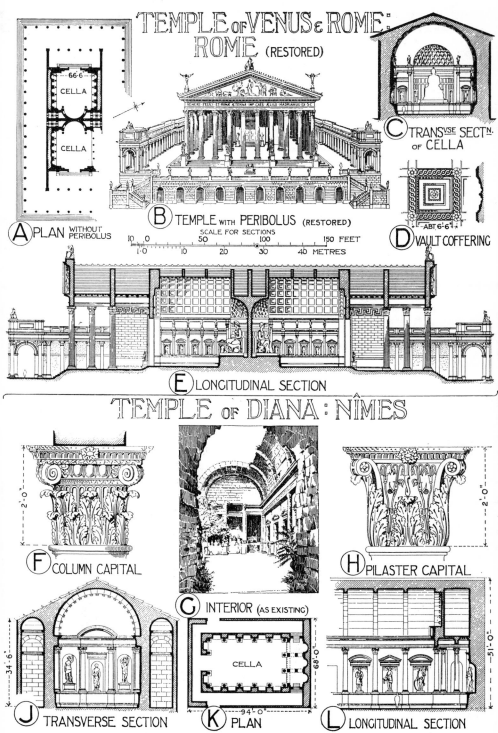

TEMPLE of VENUS & ROME: ROME (RESTORED)

A PLAN WITHOUT PERIBOLUS

66·6

CELLA

CELLA

B TEMPLE with PERIBOLUS (RESTORED)

VENERI FELICI ET ROMÆ ÆTERNÆ IMP CÆS ÆLIUS HADRIANUS EX S C

C TRANS.VSE SECT.N of CELLA

D VAULT COFFERING

ABT 6·6

SCALE FOR SECTIONS

10 0 50 100 150 FEET

1·0 10 20 30 40 METRES

E LONGITUDINAL SECTION

TEMPLE of DIANA: NÎMES

F COLUMN CAPITAL

2·0

G INTERIOR (AS EXISTING)

H PILASTER CAPITAL

2·0

J TRANSVERSE SECTION

34·6

K PLAN

CELLA

68·0

94·0

L LONGITUDINAL SECTION

51·0

The **Temple of Diana, Nîmes** (c. A.D. 130) (p. 279), is a misnomer for a grand staircase hall which dignified the approach to a baths establishment at a higher level. The walls of the hall have internal columns, enframing niches, with capitals that can be interpreted either as Corinthian or Composite, and an entablature from which springs a stone-ribbed barrel vault, the thrust of which is counteracted by continuous vaults over the side aisles. Above the vaults was a solid, pitched roof covered with stone slates (p. 279J). In these arrangements, the building was probably a prototype of many southern French Romanesque churches (p. 488).

The **Temple of Vespasian, Rome** (A.D. 94) (pp. 242M, T, 273B) was erected by Domitian, beside the Temple of Concord. It had a prostyle hexastyle Corinthian portico, of which only three columns remain, and portion of an ornate entablature with a heavily sculptured frieze.

The **Temple of Venus and Rome, Rome** (A.D. 123–35) (pp. 273B, 279), of which little remains, was designed for Hadrian by Apollodorus of Damascus, and was raised on a platform about 164.6 m × 103.63 m (540 ft × 340 ft), which was entered through gateways in a surrounding colonnade of nearly 200 columns of Egyptian granite and porphyry, which formed a magnificent frame to this imposing temple (p. 279B). The plan was pseudo-dipteral decastyle, and was still more unusual in that it had two cellas with apses placed back to back, and there was a pronaos at each front. The cella walls, which internally had monolithic columns framing niches for statues, were of extra thickness to take the thrust of the semi-circular coffered vault, and the two apses for the statues of Venus and Rome had semi-domes which still exist. The plan (p. 279A) gives the usually accepted arrangement of this building. The restoration (p. 279B) shows the peribolus of columns surrounding the temenos, and the temple centrally within, with its Pentelic columns, sculptured pediments, and a great roof, covered with gold-plated bronze tiles, which were stripped off by Pope Honorius (A.D. 625) to cover the basilican church of S. Peter.

The **Temple of Antoninus and Faustina, Rome** (A.D. 141) (pp. 273B, 275D, E, F) is prostyle hexastyle, and has a deep portico, reached by steps between the podium walls, leading into a spacious cella, 17.42 m (57 ft 2 ins) wide, with plain external walling without attached columns. The pediment was destroyed and the upper part altered when it was converted into the Church of S. Lorenzo in Miranda in A.D. 1602.

The **Temple of Saturn, Rome** (A.D. 284) (pp. 273B, 275G, H, J) is a pseudo-peripteral prostyle hexastyle example of a debased type, in a commanding position close to the Capitol. The temple is raised on a podium 3.73 m (12 ft 3 ins) high and steps lead to the portico of granite columns, 12 m (39 ft 4½ ins) high, of which only eight remain, with Ionic capitals having typical angle volutes, but the pediment no longer exists. The architrave mouldings were omitted along the front to admit of the inscription (p. 275G).

The **Temple of Jupiter, Baalbek** (p. 281), was commenced about A.D. 10, the forepart undertaken by Antoninus Pius (A.D. 138–61) and the entrance portico not completed till c. A.D. 249. The whole structure, built of hard limestone, forms part of the magnificent temple group which rears its massive form high above the plain, below the hills of Lebanon. It was raised on a high platform, approached by steps which led to a dodecastyle Corinthian portico 'in antis'. Three doorways opened into a hexastyle forecourt with rectangular exedrae on either side, each fronted with four columns. Another three-fold portal led into the main court, 115.97 m (380 ft 6 ins) square, with rectangular and semicircular exedrae on three sides, all fronted with columns. The wall enclosing the main court rises 21.34 m (70 ft) above the plain, and the substructure of the actual temple is formed of gigantic blocks of

TEMPLES AT BAALBEK : LEBANON

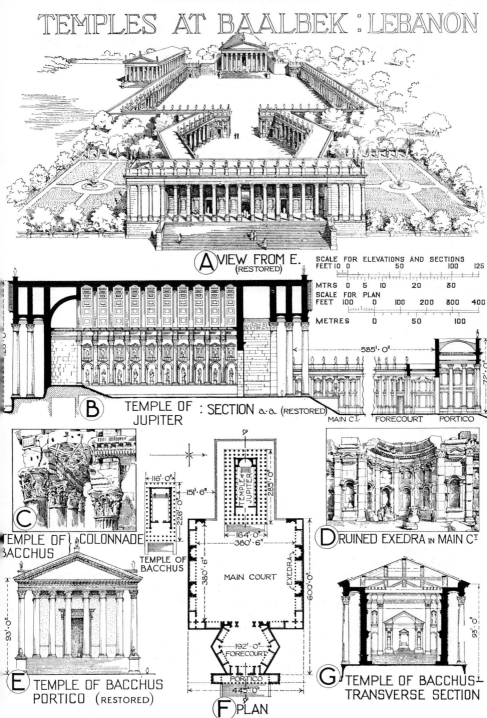

Ⓐ VIEW FROM E. (RESTORED)

SCALE FOR ELEVATIONS AND SECTIONS
FEET 10 0   50   100   125

MTRS 0 5 10   20   30

SCALE FOR PLAN
FEET 100   0   100   200   300   400

METRES   0   50   100

Ⓑ TEMPLE OF : SECTION a·a (RESTORED)
JUPITER

585'·0"   72'·0"

MAIN Cᵀ   FORECOURT   PORTICO

Ⓒ TEMPLE OF COLONNADE
BACCHUS

116'·0"
151'·6"
226'·0"

TEMPLE OF
BACCHUS

285'·0"

TEMPLE
JUPITER

164'·0"
380'·6"
380'·6"
MAIN COURT
600'·0"
EXEDRA

192'·0"
FORECOURT

PORTICO
445'·0"

Ⓓ RUINED EXEDRA IN MAIN Cᵀ

Ⓔ TEMPLE OF BACCHUS
PORTICO (RESTORED)

93'·0"

Ⓕ PLAN

Ⓖ TEMPLE OF BACCHUS-
TRANSVERSE SECTION

95'·0"

A. The Temple of Bacchus, Baalbek (2nd cent. A.D.): interior of cella. See p. 283

B. The Temple of Bacchus, Baalbek: interior of cella (restored)

stone on the western side. Three of these are known as the Trilithon, and are about 19.51 m (64 ft) long, 3.43 m (11 ft 3 ins) thick, and 4.50 m (14 ft 9 ins) high, and 725 tons in weight. The temple itself, also constructed of large blocks without mortar, faced the main court, and stood on a podium 5.18 m (17 ft) above it. It was dipteral decastyle, and the unfluted Corinthian columns, of which only six remain, are about 19.81 m (65 ft) high and 2.13 m (7 ft) in diameter, carrying an entablature 4.04 m (13 ft 3 ins) high. The temple was much damaged by Theodosius the Great (A.D. 379–95), and later by Arabs and Turks.

The **Temple of Bacchus** (so-called), **Baalbek** (second century A.D.) (pp. 281, 282), beside the Temple of Jupiter, is a singular building. It stands on a high podium and is approached on the east by steps between wing walls. The colonnade, of unfluted Corinthian columns, is peripteral octastyle with fifteen columns on each side, and it contains a deep porch six columns in width. The intercolumniation is remarkably narrow. The peristyle is roofed with a convex, coffered ceiling of monolithic blocks richly carved with medallions and busts of gods and emperors. In contrast to the Greek tradition of the exterior, the interior of the building is remarkably ornate. The elaborately decorated entrance, flanked on each side by a staircase tower giving access to the roof level, opens into the cella lined by Corinthian pilasters surmounting a dado, and enlarged by Corinthian half-columns on pedestals supporting a returned entablature. Between the pilasters are superimposed tiers of niches, the lower with arcuated architraves and horizontal cornices, the upper with triangular pediments. At the inner end of the cella a monumental flight of steps rose to an elaborate vaulted sanctuary which framed the statue of the deity. The whole interior, roofed by a coffered, timber ceiling, was an astonishingly luxuriant concept, and by reason of its state of survival holds a unique place as an example of its kind in the history of architecture.

CIRCULAR AND POLYGONAL TEMPLES

The **Temple of Vesta, Rome** (A.D. 205) (pp. 273B, 284), in the Forum Romanum, was the most sacred shrine in the Imperial city, and here under the custody of the Vestal Virgins the sacred fire was kept alight which signified the home hearth as the centre and source of Roman life and power (p. 261). It was founded in 715 B.C., but was frequently destroyed by fire and repeatedly rebuilt, finally by Septimius Severus in A.D. 205 (p. 284C). According to recent excavations, it seems to have had a podium 3.05 m (10 ft) high supporting a circular cella, 9.14 m (30 ft) in diameter, surrounded by eighteen Corinthian columns, 5.33 m (17 ft 6 ins) high, and fragments of columns have been found with fillets for the insertion of metal screens.

The **Temple of Vesta, Tivoli** (c. 80 B.C.) (p. 284) is circular peripteral with a podium supporting a cella 7.32 m (24 ft) in diameter, surrounded by a peristyle of eighteen Corinthian columns 7.16 m (23 ft 6 ins) high. The cella has two windows and a doorway approached by steps. The columns are nearly 9¾ diameters high, and the capitals, with large and unusual central flower and foliage derived from a crinkly variety of the 'acanthus mollis', are one diameter in height. This early temple, like that of Portunus, Rome, shows Hellenistic influence very strongly.

The **Temple of Portunus, Rome** (p. 285B), formerly known as the Temple of Vesta, now S. Maria del Sole, is not later than the time of Augustus. It is situated in the Forum Boarium on a circular platform of eight marble steps. It is of Parian marble and is circular peripteral with twenty Corinthian columns, 10.54 m (34 ft 7 ins) high and 0.97 m (3 ft 2 ins) in diameter and therefore nearly eleven diameters high, which surround a cella 8.53 m (28 ft) in diameter. The capitals

TEMPLE OF VESTA: ROME (RESTORED)

A PLAN — 18'·6"

B THE ORDER

C ELEVATION — 21'·6"

TEMPLE OF VESTA: TIVOLI.

D PLAN — 24'·0"

E CAPITAL — 2'·5"

F ELEVATION (RESTORED) — 23'·6"

TEMPLE OF VENUS: BAALBEK (RESTORED)

G PLAN — 32'·0"

H EXTERIOR FROM N.W.

½ SECTION   ½ ELEVATᴺ   J

A. Temple of Jupiter Capitolinus, Rome (restored).
(Dedicated 509 B.C., and as rebuilt in A.D. 82 by Domitian). See p. 265

B. Temples of Portunus (*left*) (*c.* 31 B.C.) (p. 283) and Fortuna Virilis
(*c.* 40 B.C.) (p. 274), in the Forum Boarium, Rome

have acanthus leaves V-shaped in section and with sharp-pointed lobes which generally indicate Greek craftsmanship. The roof was probably of timber rafters covered with bronze tiles.

The **Pantheon, Rome** (pp. 287, 288, 289, 292A) is in the most perfect preservation of all ancient buildings in Rome; much has been removed, much has been restored, but the walls and vaulting of this great circular structure with its magnificent colonnaded porticò still remain. It belongs to two different periods. Its site was previously a large open place, 2.44 m (8 ft) below the present level, on to which faced the south front of the predecessor of the Pantheon, a temple completed in 25 B.C. by Agrippa, son-in-law of Augustus. Agrippa's temple was broad and shallow, 43.74 m (143 ft 6 ins) wide × 19.81 m (65 ft) deep, and probably of the three-celled Etruscan type. It was severely damaged by fire late in the first century A.D. The Rotunda was erected (A.D. 120–4) by the Emperor Hadrian on the forecourt to the older temple, but at the higher level and in such a manner that the podium of the latter could serve for the foundations of a boldly projecting porch, now facing north instead of south. The portico of Agrippa's temple too was re-used, but made octastyle instead of decastyle, the pediment consequently having a steeper pitch than before. Agrippa's original inscription still appears on the frieze, along with an addition made by Severus and Caracalla, recording a restoration of A.D. 202. The Corinthian octastyle portico, 33.53 m (110 ft) wide × 18.29 m (60 ft) deep in the centre, forms an imposing entrance to this grandest of all circular temples. The unfluted monolithic columns of Egyptian granite, with Corinthian capitals of white Pentelic marble, are 14.15 m (46 ft 5 ins) high, 1.51 m (4 ft 11½ ins) in diameter at the base, and 1.31 m (4 ft 3½ ins) at the top (p. 288C, D, E). They support an entablature 3.35 m (11 ft) high, and a pediment which originally had a bronze relief, as is indicated by the holes for fixing it which still remain (p. 288A). The eight front columns with the others form a triple colonnade, as in Etruscan temples (p. 288B). At the back of this portico are niches in which stood colossal statues of Augustus and Agrippa, and in the thickness of the wall behind these niches stairs lead to the upper parts of the building (p. 288B). The ancient bronze doors which, with the fanlight, were originally plated with gold, still remain, but the bronze plates of the original segmental vaulting were removed in 1626 and recast for the baldachino in S. Peter's (p. 843B) and for the cannon of the Castle of S. Angelo.

The Rotunda is circular, with an internal diameter and height each of 43.43 m (142 ft 6 ins). A massive circular foundation, 4.50 m (14 ft 9 ins) deep, supports the wall of brick-faced concrete, which, as we have seen (p. 271), was not solid but comprised an elaborate constructive system, carefully devised to meet every kind of stress and strain to which it was likely to be subjected. Internally, the wall was lined with marble and porphyry. There are eight great recesses, one of which forms the entrance, while the others—three of which are semicircular and four rectangular exedrae, probably contained statues of the gods of the seven planets. Each of the exedrae, except that opposite the entrance, which has a semi-dome, has two monolithic marble columns in antis, 10.61 m (34 ft 10 ins) high, with their lower third reeded and their upper portion fluted, and Corinthian capitals supporting an entablature (pp. 287B, 288A). Above these columns are hidden relieving arches. The eight piers have three tiers of constructive niches concealed within them. The marble facings to these piers, as well as the pedimented altars projecting from them, are later additions. The pavement of granite, porphyry and marble was restored in the nineteenth century. The attic, or upper part of the circular wall, was originally faced with marble pilasters (six of the capitals of which are in the British Museum) and panelling of giallo antico, serpentine and pavonazzetto, but in 1747 this was replaced by stucco decoration.

A. Exterior (A.D. 120–4: portico reconstructed from an earlier temple of 25 B.C.)

B. Drawing of interior by Piranesi

The Pantheon, Rome (A.D. 120–4). See p. 286

THE PANTHEON : ROME

BRONZE MOULDING TO EYE OF DOME

2'·6"

EYE (UNGLAZED)

4'·0" THICK

43'·1"

A SECTION THRO' PORTICO AND ROTUNDA

85'·7"

24'·11"

4'·1"

24'·10"

142'·6"

10 5 0 10 20 30 40 50 60 70 80 90 100 F⁻

5 0 5 10 15 20 25 30 M⁻⁵

B PLAN

CENTRAL VOLUTES

ANGLE VOLUTES

CAULICOLUS AND ACANTHUS LEAVES

1'·9"

1'·4¼"

3'·1½"

a

b

c

4'·3½"

5'·1"

PLANS OF CAPITAL (LOOKING UP) AT a · b & c.

a

b

b

c

4'·11½"

2'·7½"

46'·5"

10'·11"

4'·11½"

C PORTICO ORDER D DETAILS OF CAPITAL E DETAILS ᵒᶠ PORTICO COLUMNS

A. Interior from the entrance

B. Interior showing restored attic

C. Interior showing coffered dome

D. Interior showing floor

The Pantheon, Rome (A.D. 120–4). See p. 286

In effect, the Rotunda is a cylinder, three tiers high; the hemispherical dome, fitted inside, springs from the top of the second tier, so that the third stage forms an abutment to its base. The inner surface of the dome is coffered in five ranges, in each of which the mouldings are adjusted or foreshortened with regard to their appearance from below and were originally embellished with central ornaments of stucco. The coffers not only ornament the surface of the dome, but also serve to reduce its weight. The Pantheon is an instance of the Roman skilful variation of the composition of concrete according to the function it has to serve. Researches carried out in 1929–34 have shown that the hand-laid courses of the brick-faced walls are alternately of travertine and tufa stone lumps in the lowest tier, and of tufa and brick in the second and third, there being large bonding tiles at intervals. The tufa and brick alternation continues in the lower part of the dome, but turns to a lighter alternation of tufa and pumice above the top of the third range of coffers. The courses everywhere are horizontal. The lighting of the building is effected by one circular unglazed opening, 8.23 m (27 ft) in diameter, in the crown of the dome, and it still retains its original bronze cornice (pp. 287B, 288A). This method of lighting produces the most solemn and impressive effect. It is a matter of no small surprise that from this one single source ample light should be thrown round all parts of the building, even when the great bronze doors are closed.

Originally, the lower storey of the Pantheon was faced externally with large slabs of gleaming white Pentelic marble and its two upper storeys were coated with stucco. The dome, the lower portion of which is formed in steps, was covered with gilded bronze plates, till they were removed to Constantinople in A.D. 655 and replaced by lead. The octastyle portico contained in its pediment a magnificent bronze relief representing a 'gigantomachy' or battle of the Titans and various deities, while the massive attic behind supported imposing groups of bronze statuary as restored in the Metropolitan Museum of Art, New York.

The Pantheon has survived many centuries of change, both temporal and spiritual, but is still devoted to the service of religion. In A.D. 608 it was dedicated by Pope Boniface IV to S. Maria ad Martyres, when many loads of martyrs' bones were brought here from the Catacombs. It is now known as S. Maria Rotonda and is shorn of statuary, marble sheathing, iridescent bronze, and glittering gold which rendered it magnificent in the days of Imperial Rome, but it still compels worldwide admiration by reason of the severe simplicity and unity of the design.

The **Temple of Venus, Baalbek** (A.D. 273) (p. 284) has a cella, 9.75 m (32 ft) in diameter, raised on a podium and approached by steps. It is surrounded by Corinthian columns 10.26 m (33 ft 8 ins) high, some having five-sided capitals, six of which are well advanced from the cella wall and occupy positions resulting from the division of the circle into seven equal parts (p. 284G). The line of the entablature supported by these six columns is curved inwards between the columns towards the cella wall, forming a decoratively-treated buttressing system to a stone dome, which, however, has fallen. The entrance is placed centrally between two divisions of the circle, and has a column on either side. The external wall of the cella has Corinthian pilasters behind the columns, with semicircular niches for statuary between them; while internally it has superimposed Ionic and Corinthian Orders.

Christian baptisteries were evolved from such little circular buildings (see also the Mausoleum of Diocletian, p. 314), which therefore hold an extremely interesting position in architectural evolution (p. 364).

BASILICAS

Basilicas, which were halls of justice and commercial exchanges, indicate clearly,

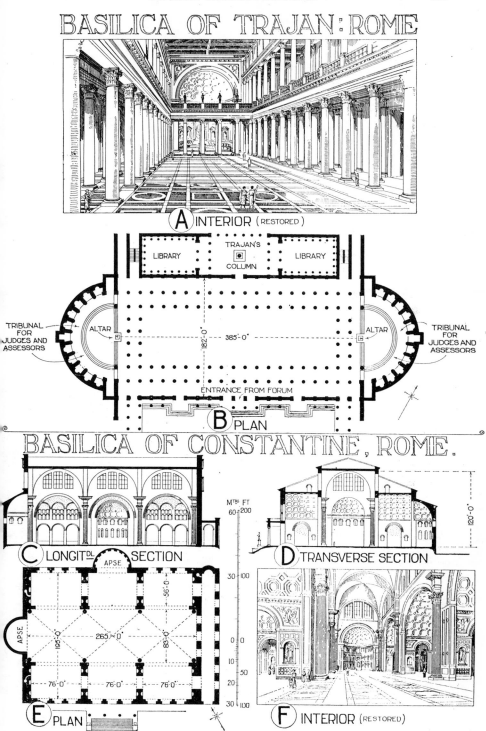

BASILICA OF TRAJAN: ROME

A INTERIOR (RESTORED)

B PLAN

TRAJAN'S COLUMN

LIBRARY

LIBRARY

TRIBUNAL FOR JUDGES AND ASSESSORS

ALTAR

ALTAR

TRIBUNAL FOR JUDGES AND ASSESSORS

182'-0"

385'-0"

ENTRANCE FROM FORUM

BASILICA OF CONSTANTINE, ROME.

C LONGITᴰᴸ SECTION

APSE

D TRANSVERSE SECTION

120'-0"

E PLAN

APSE

APSE

56'-0"

195'-0"

265'-0"

83'-0"

76'-0"

76'-0"

76'-0"

MᵀᴿˢFᵀ

F INTERIOR (RESTORED)

A. The Pantheon, Rome (A.D. 120–4):
interior showing Order. See p. 286

B. Basilica of Constantine, Rome
(A.D. 310–13): surviving vaulted north
aisle. See p. 293

C. Basilica of Constantine, Rome (A.D. 310–13): reconstructed interior

by their central position, the importance of law and business in Old Rome. These buildings, which are of a pronounced type, are a link between Classic and Christian architecture (p. 352). The usual plan of a basilica was a rectangle twice as long as its width. Either two or four rows of columns forming a 'nave' and two or four aisles ran the whole length, and there were sometimes galleries over the aisles. The nave roof was raised above that of the aisles, so that the windows might be placed in the upper walls between the two levels. The entrance was either at the side or at one end. The tribunal, opposite the entrance, was on a raised dais, generally in a semicircular apse, and sometimes separated from the main building by a screen of columns or by a low balustrade. Ranged round the apse were seats for the assessors, with a raised seat in the centre for the praetor, and in front was the altar where sacrifice was offered before transacting business. The roof was generally of wood, which the Roman knowledge of the principles of the roof truss permitted them to use over very large spaces, when required. Basilicas usually presented a simple and unadorned exterior: they were sometimes without walls at the sides.

Trajan's Basilica, Rome (A.D. 98–112) (pp. 273B, 291), by Apollodorus of Damascus, was entered through a portico from Trajan's Forum (p. 291B). Adjoining the Basilica were the Greek and Latin libraries with Trajan's famous Column in an open court between them (p. 291B). It had a central nave (p. 291A), 117.34 m (385 ft) long and 26.51 m (87 ft) wide, with double aisles, each 7.24 m (23 ft 9 ins) wide, and the total internal height was about 36.58 m (120 ft). The columns separating nave and aisles were of red granite from Syene, with white marble Corinthian capitals, and they supported galleries over the side aisles, above which came the clear-storey and simple timber roof. At each end were raised tribunals with semicircular apses and sacrificial altars in front.

The **Basilica of Constantine, Rome** (A.D. 310–13) (pp. 273B, 291, 292B, C), also known as the Basilica of Maxentius or Basilica Nova, adjoins the Forum Romanum. It consists of a central nave, 80.77 m × 25.30 m (265 ft long × 83 ft wide), and was crowned at a height of 36.58 m (120 ft) by an immense groined vault in three compartments. North and south are aisles also in three compartments, each roofed with a great semicircular vault, 23.16 m (76 ft) in span, springing from walls which are at right angles to the nave and pierced by openings, and these walls, steadied by the pressure of the aisle vaults, supported the nave vault. Monolithic columns stood in front of these transverse walls and supported entablatures from which sprang the nave cross-vaults (p. 291F). There were two apses, that on the north being an addition made by the Emperor Constantine, who finished the building, brought almost to completion by his predecessor, Maxentius. Light was introduced in the upper part of the nave over the aisle vaults by lunettes in the wall formed under the intersecting vaulting. The building is similar to the central halls of the thermae (p. 295) and with them, manifestly foreshadows the planning and structural organization of the greatest of Byzantine buildings, S. Sophia, Constantinople (p. 383). It is too, in many respects a prototype of a Gothic structure, in which the thrust and weight of intersecting vaults are collected and brought down on to piers built to receive them. The vaults to the northern aisle remain with their deep coffering, and show a series of embedded brick arches, spanning the vaults from side to side (pp. 269J, 292B), intended to localize cracks which might arise in the concrete. The main vault had similar 'box' ribs of brickwork, and other ribs following the groins, which greatly eased construction. Such ribs were a feature of many vaults of the later Imperial period, but they were reserved for the best work. A portion of the main vault still overhangs in mid-air, showing the extraordinary cohesive quality of concrete.

Other basilicas at Rome were the **Basilica Porcia** (184 B.C.), the first to be built

A. The Forum and Basilica, Silchester (2nd cent. A.D.) (reconstruction)

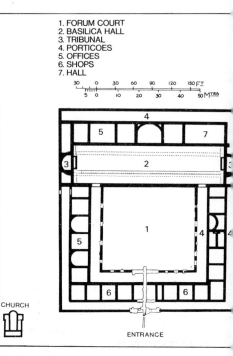

1. FORUM COURT
2. BASILICA HALL
3. TRIBUNAL
4. PORTICOES
5. OFFICES
6. SHOPS
7. HALL

B. The Basilica, Silchester: interior. See p. 295

C. The Forum and Basilica, Silchester: plan

in the city; the **Basilica Julia** (46 B.C.) (p. 273B); and the **Basilica Æmilia** (p. 273B). The Basilica, Pompeii, and those at Trier, Timgad, and **Silchester** (p. 294) in England, are other examples.

THERMAE

The Thermae (Gk. *thermos* = hot) or palatial public baths of Imperial Rome, which were probably derived from the Greek gymnasia, portray, even in their ruin, the manners and customs of the pleasure-loving populace, and are as characteristic of Roman civilization as are the amphitheatres. The principal ruins of thermae in Italy are at Rome and Pompeii. The thermae were not only designed for luxurious bathing, but were resorted to for news and gossip, and served, like a modern club, as a rendezvous of social life besides being used for lectures and athletic sports, and indeed entered largely into the daily life of the Imperial City. A small entrance charge of a quadrans ($\frac{1}{4}$ farthing) was sometimes made, but in later times they were opened free to the populace by emperors in search of popularity. The thermae were under the management of the 'aediles'; there were also 'balneatores' to take the entrance money, and janitors to guard the doors, with a staff of attendants, including anointers, manicurists, barbers, shampooers, besides stokers, lamplighters, and hundreds of slaves to make the process of bathing a luxurious relaxation.

The thermae were generally raised on a high platform within an enclosing wall, and underneath were the furnaces and rooms connected with the service of the establishment, which usually consisted of three main parts, as shown in the Thermae of Caracalla (p. 296B) and Diocletian (p. 302D).

(*a*) A main building. In this was a dominant central hall, about which all other rooms were symmetrically arranged, having on its cross axis the three chief apartments of the whole thermae—the 'tepidarium', or warm room, through which was reached the 'calidarium' or hot room, each with heated-water baths; and, on the other side of the central hall, the 'frigidarium', containing an unheated swimming bath. The rest of the rooms were duplicated. On each side there might be a 'laconicum' ('sudatorium'), or dry sweating room; and invariably there were 'apodyteria', or dressing rooms, and 'unctuaria' for oils and unguents, where the 'aliptor' shampooed, oiled, sanded and anointed the bathers and scraped the skin with the 'strigil'. Invariably also, there was a palaestra, for physical exercise, comprising an open peristyle court and attendant surrounding rooms including, sometimes, a bath for athletes. Large heated rooms usually needed a vault, and glass or translucent marble windows, to contain the heat.

(*b*) A large open space. This was a park-like enclosure surrounding the central structure, planted with trees and ornamented with statues and fountains. Part of it was used as a stadium, for foot-racing, with raised seats at the side for spectators.

(*c*) An outer ring of apartments. These included lecture rooms and exedrae for philosophers, poets, and statesmen; while colonnades, a feature of all open spaces in Rome, served as a protection from the sun. A large reservoir fed by a special aqueduct supplied all the water needed for the bath apartments, fountains, and miscellaneous purposes. Other apartments were let off as shops or accommodated the numerous slaves of the establishment.

The **Thermae of Caracalla, Rome** (A.D. 211–17) (pp. 269K, L, 296, 297), with accommodation for 1,600 bathers, give a spendid idea of the size and magnificence of these establishments; for although now in ruins, the relative positions of tepidarium, calidarium, frigidarium, apodyteria, and other apartments can still be traced. The thermae stood on a platform 6.10 m (20 ft) high, measuring over one-fifth of a mile each way, and underneath were the vaulted store-chambers, corridors,

THERMÆ ọf CARACALLA : ROME

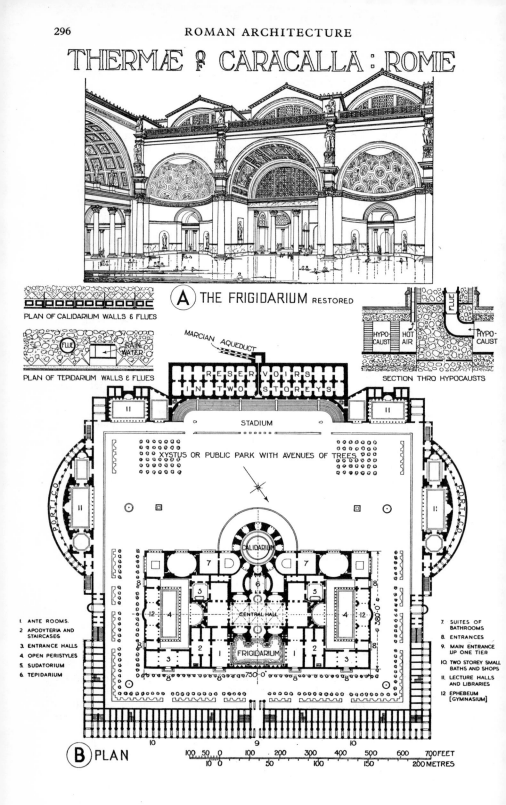

PLAN OF CALIDARIUM WALLS & FLUES

(A) THE FRIGIDARIUM RESTORED

PLAN OF TEPIDARIUM WALLS & FLUES

MARCIAN AQUEDUCT

HYPO-CAUST   HOT AIR   HYPO-CAUST

SECTION THRO HYPOCAUSTS

FLUE

RAIN WATER

FLUE

RESERVOIRS IN TWO STOREYS

STADIUM

XYSTUS OR PUBLIC PARK WITH AVENUES OF TREES

PORTICO   PORTICO

CALIDARIUM

CENTRAL HALL

FRIGIDARIUM

1. ANTE ROOMS.
2. APODYTERIA AND STAIRCASES
3. ENTRANCE HALLS
4. OPEN PERISTYLES
5. SUDATORIUM
6. TEPIDARIUM

7. SUITES OF BATHROOMS
8. ENTRANCES
9. MAIN ENTRANCE UP ONE TIER
10. TWO STOREY SMALL BATHS AND SHOPS
11. LECTURE HALLS AND LIBRARIES
12. EPHEBEUM [GYMNASIUM]

(B) PLAN

100 50 0   100   200   300   400   500   600   700 FEET
10 0   50   100   150   200 METRES

The Thermae of Caracalla, Rome (A.D. 211-17): great hall (restored). See p. 295

furnaces, hypocausts and hot-air ducts for heating the buildings (p. 296). A colonnade on the entrance side screened two storeys forming shops on the ground level and 'slipper' baths on the platform level. The main entrance led to the park-like enclosure, laid out for wrestling and games, around which were grouped halls for dramatic representations and lectures. On the opposite side of the platform and beyond the stadium was the great vaulted reservoir of water supplied by the Marcian aqueduct, carried through leaden pipes to the places needed, and for the hot baths, heated by furnaces in the substructure nearby. The main building block measured 228 m × 115.82 m (750 ft × 380 ft), thus covering an area of 26.480 m² (285,000 sq. ft), i.e. about equal to Westminster Palace, and larger than either the British Museum or the Royal Courts of Justice, London. There were only four doorways on the north-east side, which was exposed to cold winds; but large columned openings to the gardens were a feature of the south-west side. The symmetrical planning of this building on axial lines gave vistas through the various halls and saloons, while exedrae and screens of columns prevented any loss of scale and emphasized the vastness of the building.

The great central hall, around which subsidiary halls were grouped (pp. 296B, 297), was 55.77 m × 24.08 m (183 ft × 79 ft), roofed with an immense semicircular, intersecting vault of concrete, in three compartments 32.92 m (108 ft) high, which rested on eight massive piers of masonry, fronted with granite columns 11.58 m (38 ft) high and 1.63 m (5 ft 4 ins) in diameter, supporting short pieces of entablature (p. 269L). This great hall was lighted by clear-storey windows under the intersecting vaults, which rose above the roofs of adjoining halls, as in the Thermae of Diocletian (p. 302A), and the Basilica of Constantine (p. 291C, D, F). The calidarium had a dome similar to that of the Pantheon, and special attention was given to heating this apartment by wall flues (p. 296). The frigidarium was probably open to the sky, and this open-air swimming-bath formed a welcome retreat during the hot and sultry months in the Imperial City (p. 296A). The interior, unlike the exterior, was evidently elaborately decorated, in marked contrast to Greek methods. Pavements were formed of bright-coloured mosaics in geometrical patterns or with figures of athletes; the lower parts of the concrete walls were sheathed with many-coloured marbles, and the upper parts with painted and modelled stucco; the great columns under the vault springers were of granite, porphyry, giallo antico, alabaster or other rare marbles. Various coloured marble columns were used constructively to support the upper balconies and peristyle roofs, and decoratively to form frames for the superimposed niches in the walls. The great vaults were also richly ornamented with coffering, modelled and painted stucco, or coloured glass mosaic.

These magnificent halls sheltered some of the finest sculpture of antiquity, which was brought from Greece or executed by Greek artists in Rome. During the excavation of the thermae in the Renaissance period many of these masterpieces of art were removed to the Vatican and other museums in Rome, whence later some were carried off to the museums of Europe. Additional interest was given to interiors by the perpetual streams of running water which, issuing from the mouths of lions sculptured in marble or wrought in brightly polished silver, fell into marble basins and produced a delicious coolness in hot, sultry weather. The exteriors of these great thermae appear to have been treated very plainly in stucco, except on the side open to the main gardens, where they were more elaborate.

The **Thermae of Agrippa, Rome** (c. 20 B.C.), which were the earliest, have disappeared, and such fragments as remain belong to later restorations. The **Thermae of Trajan** were still partly standing till A.D. 1795.

The **Thermae of Titus, Rome** (A.D. 80), stood on a great platform, partly over

Thermae of Hadrian, Leptis Magna (A.D. 126–7): frigidarium (restored). See p. 301

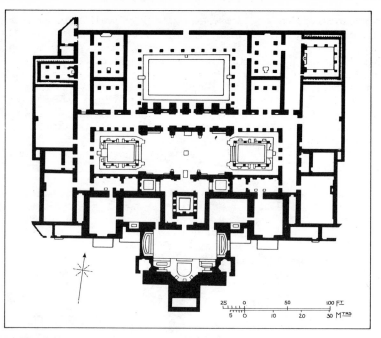

A. Thermae of Hadrian, Leptis Magna (A.D. 126–7): plan. See p. 301

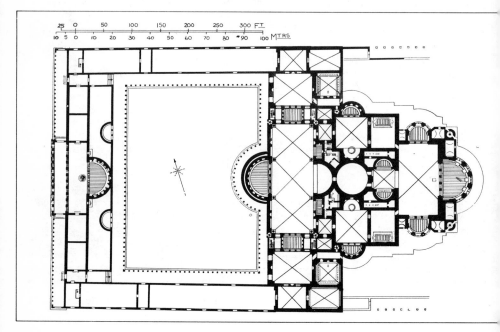

B. Imperial Thermae, Trier (3rd cent. A.D.): plan. See p. 301

the foundations of Nero's Golden House on the Esquiline Hill, and when excavated about A.D. 1500 many remarkable frescoes were discovered, which had considerable influence on the painting of that period; and some of the finest statues of antiquity, such as the Laocoon group, found their way into the art galleries of Europe.

The **Thermae of Diocletian, Rome** (A.D. 302) (p. 302), which accommodated over 3,000 bathers, resembled the Baths of Caracalla in their general distribution (p. 302D). The great central hall, 60.96 m × 24.38 m and 27.43 m high (200 ft × 80 ft and 90 ft high), has the original cross vaulting of concrete (p. 269M), springing from eight monolithic columns of Egyptian granite, 15.24 m (50 ft) high and 1.52 m (5 ft) in diameter, with Composite capitals of white marble, supporting an ornamental entablature (p. 302A). This building is of special interest, first because it gives the general appearance of these great halls, and secondly because Michelangelo converted it in 1563 into the Church of S. Maria degli Angeli (pp. 302A, 839). A choir was added on one side by Vanvitelli (A.D. 1749), which converted the nave into a transept. The restorations of the frigidarium (p. 302B) and the ephebeum (p. 302H) give a good idea of the sumptuous character of the building.

The unbounded licence of the public baths, which were resorted to for all sorts of dissipation, brought them under the ban of the Early Christians, who held that bathing might be practised for cleanliness, but not for pleasure. Then in the fifth century the thermae fell further into disuse and decay, owing to the destruction of aqueducts by the Huns, and also to the decrease of the population. Later they served as quarries for Mediaeval and Renaissance builders.

The **Balneum** or small private bath was very usual in Roman palaces (p. 330D) and houses, and under the Republic gave its name to public baths, which were simpler in character than the later thermae of the Empire, in which bathing became secondary to luxury and entertainment. The **Stabian Baths, Pompeii** (c. 120 B.C.) and the **Forum Baths, Pompeii** (c. 80 B.C.), are on the lines of these small public baths.

Wherever the Romans settled they built thermae for the people, and thus at that notable Roman city of Timgad, North Africa, there are the ruins of no less than eleven of these sumptuous thermal establishments. Also in North Africa, at **Leptis Magna,** are the **Thermae of Hadrian** (A.D. 126-7) (pp. 299, 300A); and at **Trier,** Germany, are the **Imperial Thermae** (third century A.D.) (p. 300B). Both illustrate the universality throughout the Roman Empire of the function and the principles of design and construction of these building complexes. The **Roman Thermae, Bath** (England), the 'Aquae Sulis' of the Romans, are the most remarkable in existence, where the hot water still gushes up and flows through the massive leaden conduit into the great swimming-bath. The Romans also used slipper baths, many of which were beautifully carved.

The **Minerva Medica, Rome** (c. A.D. 260) (p. 382A, B), is now generally regarded as having been a nymphaeum in the sumptuous Licinian gardens, since numerous other remains of important garden buildings have been found in the neighbourhood. The absence of a hypocaust and of flue tiles precludes it from having served for heated baths of any kind. It is decagonal on plan, 24.38 m (80 ft) in diameter, with semicircular niches on nine sides and the entrance on the tenth. The niches are both decorative and constructional. They are reversed compared with those in the walls of the Pantheon (p. 288B), yet they serve, as there, to give stability to the structure. In the angles between them there are spur buttresses which rise up the angles of the building to stiffen an upper tier, in which there is a range of large windows to give light and air to the growing plants, assisted by other windows at the back of a pair of niches on either side. The buttresses proved too weak to retain the concrete dome, despite the aid given by a heavy, stepped haunch rising

THERMÆ OF DIOCLETIAN : ROME

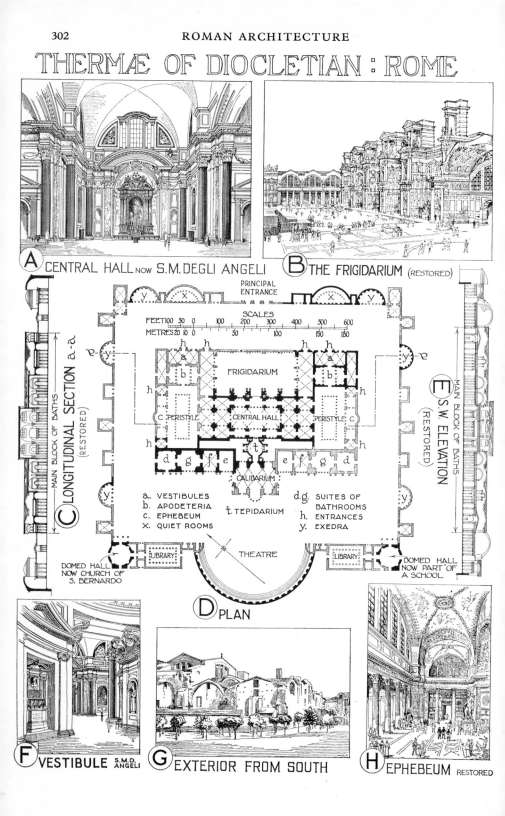

A CENTRAL HALL NOW S.M. DEGLI ANGELI

B THE FRIGIDARIUM (RESTORED)

PRINCIPAL ENTRANCE

SCALES
FEET 100 50 0 100 200 300 400 500 600
METRES 20 10 0 50 100 150 180

FRIGIDARIUM

C LONGITUDINAL SECTION a-a (RESTORED)

MAIN BLOCK OF BATHS

C PERISTYLE   CENTRAL HALL   PERISTYLE C

CALIDARIUM

E S.W. ELEVATION (RESTORED)

MAIN BLOCK OF BATHS

a. VESTIBULES
b. APODETERIA
c. EPHEBEUM
x. QUIET ROOMS
t. TEPIDARIUM
d.g. SUITES OF BATHROOMS
h. ENTRANCES
y. EXEDRA

DOMED HALL NOW CHURCH OF S. BERNARDO

LIBRARY   THEATRE   LIBRARY

DOMED HALL NOW PART OF A SCHOOL

D PLAN

F VESTIBULE S.M.D. ANGELI

G EXTERIOR FROM SOUTH

H EPHEBEUM RESTORED

around the base of the dome in the usual Roman fashion, and almost at once, the building was strengthened on the rear with two tremendous buttresses. These again proved insufficient, and in the fourth century, exedrae were added on both flanks, decorative in appearance but really to give added strength to the too-frail supports. The dome, which bears a remarkable resemblance to S. Vitale, Ravenna (p. 380), is particularly interesting because here roughly formed 'pendentives' are employed to set its circular rim upon the decagonal base (p. 269N), a device further developed by the Byzantines. In the dome are embedded box ribs, laced together by tile horizontal courses, running upwards towards the crown. Such box ribs have been noted at the Basilica of Constantine (p. 293): they first appear in Roman work in barrel vaults at the Colosseum (A.D. 70–82), in groined vaults by the end of the first century and in domes in early second century A.D. Tile ribs made vaults tougher, lighter and easier to build. Although this garden building would be unimportant to the Romans, it marks a definite stage towards the more lightly poised constructional system of the Byzantines, and the evolution of the dome.

THEATRES

Roman theatres were often adapted from the Greek to suit the Roman drama, and for this the auditorium, with its tiers of seats one above the other, was restricted to a semicircle (p. 305B). The central area at the ground level, which in Greek theatres was occupied by the chorus, became part of the auditorium and was assigned to senators and other dignitaries. The stage increased in importance and was raised and brought into immediate connection with the auditorium. Roman theatres were not only hollowed out of a hill-side, but they were also built up by means of concrete vaulting, supporting tiers of seats, under which were the connecting corridors used for retreat in case of sudden showers.

The **Theatre, Orange** (*c*. A.D. 50), in the south of France, is in an unusually good state of preservation, and here the auditorium, which holds 7,000 spectators, is partly constructed and partly hollowed out of the hill-side. It is 103.62 m (340 ft) in diameter between the enclosing walls, and has stairways on either side of the various levels. The stage was 61.87 m (203 ft) wide by 13.72 (45 ft) deep, and is enclosed by return walls at right angles to the wall at the back of the stage. The great wall of the outer façade, 98.75 m (324 ft) long by 35.36 m (116 ft) high, is ornamented with wall arcading, and there still remain the two tiers of corbel stones pierced with holes for the seating of towering masts, from the top of which chains extended to support the front of a wooden sloping awning over the stage. An enormous portico, which once extended across the full width of the façade, has entirely disappeared.

The **Theatre of Marcellus, Rome** (23–13 B.C.) (pp. 304A, 305), was built up on a level site, and the seats of the auditorium were supported not on a hillside, but, like those of the Colosseum, on radiating walls and concrete vaulting. It is the only ancient theatre now in Rome, and, though in a ruinous condition, portions of its auditorium still remain, consisting of two tiers of arcading, with superimposed Doric and Ionic Orders. The third tier has disappeared.

The **Odeion of Herodes Atticus, Athens** (A.D. 161) (p. 198B), connected by an arcade with the Theatre of Dionysos (p. 243), is Roman in plan, partly hewn out of the Acropolis rock and partly constructed, and its marble seats accommodated 6,000 people; while cedar wood, found buried on the site, would suggest that there may have been a roof to the stage. The **'Small Theatre', Pompeii** (80 B.C.) was definitely a roofed building, for an audience of about 1,500.

The **Theatre, Ostia** (p. 304B), the large theatre at Pompeii, as well as those at

A. Theatre of Marcellus, Rome (23–13 B.C.) (restored). See p. 303

B. Roman Theatre, Ostia, near Rome (restored)
(c. A.D. 10; enlarged c. 193–217). See p. 303

A. Theatre of Marcellus, Rome (23–13 B.C.) (reconstruction)

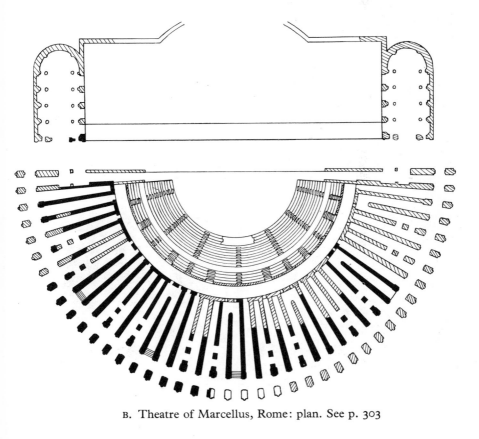

B. Theatre of Marcellus, Rome: plan. See p. 303

A. The Colosseum, Rome (A.D. 70–82): upper storey added 222–4

B. The Colosseum, Rome: the arena and auditorium. See p. 307

Taormina and Syracuse in Sicily, at Fiesole near Florence, at Timgad and Sabratha in North Africa, and Aspendus in Asia Minor, are other Roman examples. The **Roman Theatre, Verulamium** (second century A.D.), near S. Albans, is the only known Roman theatre in England.

AMPHITHEATRES

Amphitheatres, unknown to the Greeks, are characteristically Roman buildings found in every important settlement and are good exponents of the character and life of the Romans, who preferred displays of mortal combats, considered to be a good training for a nation of warriors, to the tame mimicry of the stage. Gladiatorial combats had their origin in funeral religious rites connected with human sacrifices to the *manes* of the dead. The elliptical amphitheatre, with its rising tiers of seats, may be regarded as a compound of two theatres, stage to stage, thus making a continuous auditorium round a central arena. In addition to their normal purposes, they were also used for naval exhibitions, and water-pipes for flooding some of the arenas still exist. Spanish bull-rings of to-day give some idea of the arrangement and uses of Roman amphitheatres. The arena, a Latin word meaning sand or beach, was so called because of the sand with which it was strewn to absorb the blood of the combatants.

The **Colosseum, Rome** (pp. 306, 308), also known as the Flavian Amphi-theatre, was commenced by Vespasian (A.D. 70) and completed by Domitian (A.D. 82). It is situated in the level valley between the Esquiline and Caelian Hills, and in plan it is a vast ellipse, 189 m × 156.4 m (620 ft × 513 ft), with eighty external arcaded openings on each storey, those on the ground floor forming entrances from which the various tiers of seats were reached (p. 308). The arena proper is an oval 87.47 m × 54.86 m (287 ft × 180 ft) surrounded by a wall 4.57 m (15 ft) high, behind which was the podium, with the Imperial throne and seats for the Pontifex Maxi-mus, Vestal Virgins, Senators, Praetors and other officers of state. Behind the podium rose the auditorium seats for some 50,000 spectators, with corridors and stairs beneath, while dens for the wild beasts were under the lowest tier, on a level with the arena (pp. 306B, 308). The seats, which have been removed, were in four main divisions, the two lower or grand tiers for those of equestrian rank and for Roman citizens, separated from the third tier by a high encircling wall, above which was the top range and colonnade, all of which were reached by stairs from the surrounding corridors placed at intervals between radiating walls (p. 308B). The construction is notable for the skilful combination of materials, according to the purpose to which they were applied. The component parts of the concrete vary thus: (i) lava was used for solid foundations, (ii) tufa and brick for the supporting walls, (iii) pumice stone for the vaults to reduce their weight (p. 308B). Travertine blocks, set without mortar and held together with metal cramps, were used in the façade, while marble was employed for the columns, seats and ornament. The supporting mass has been calculated to occupy as much as one-sixth of the whole area of the building, and consists of wedge-shaped piers, radiating inwards and supporting concrete vaults sloping downwards towards the centre, all producing a structure of great inherent strength and consequently difficult to destroy.

The external façade, 48 m (157 ft 6 ins) high, is divided into four storeys; the lower are pierced with arches, and have attached three-quarter-columns of quasi-Doric, Ionic and Corinthian Orders, while the top storey has Corinthian pilasters, with corbels between to support the masts of the velarium which was drawn across the auditorium (p. 308A, B).

Some of the special architectural features of this wonderful building are: (i) the

THE COLOSSEUM : ROME

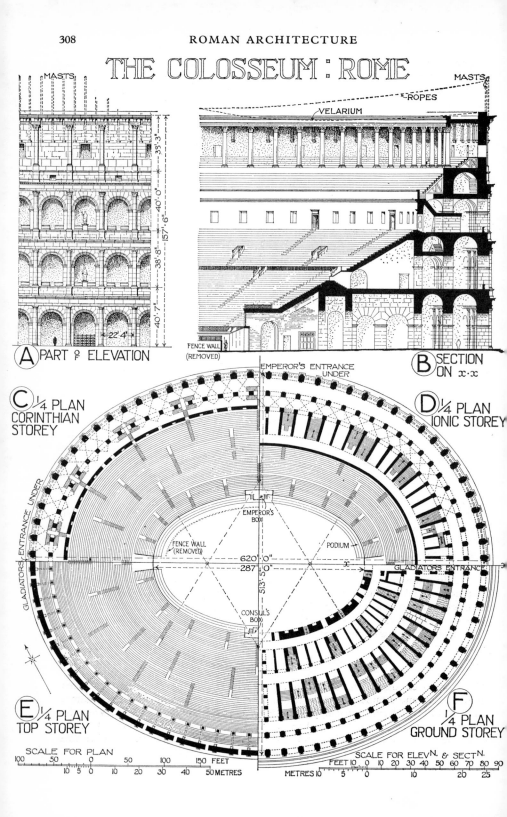

MASTS

A PART OF ELEVATION

35'·3"
40'·0" } 157'·6"
38'·8"
40'·7"

22'·4"

FENCE WALL (REMOVED)

MASTS

ROPES

VELARIUM

B SECTION ON x·x

C ¼ PLAN CORINTHIAN STOREY

D ¼ PLAN IONIC STOREY

EMPEROR'S ENTRANCE UNDER

GLADIATORS' ENTRANCE UNDER

PLAN
EMPEROR'S BOX

FENCE WALL (REMOVED)

PODIUM

620'·0"
287'·0"
513'·5"

CONSUL'S BOX

GLADIATORS' ENTRANCE

x

E ¼ PLAN TOP STOREY

F ¼ PLAN GROUND STOREY

SCALE FOR PLAN
100 50 0 50 100 150 FEET
10 5 0 10 20 30 40 50 METRES

SCALE FOR ELEVN. & SECTN.
FEET 10 0 10 20 30 40 50 60 70 80 90
METRES 10 5 0 10 20 25

massive piers which support the three tiers of apparently countless arcades which encircle the exterior and form covered ambulatories; (ii) the decorative use of the Classic Orders of architecture, which are superimposed and are thus in strong contrast to the Greek use of single Orders; (iii) the grand sweeping lines of the unbroken entablatures round the building (p. 306A). The proportions of the attached columns, which all have the same diameter, are unusual, for the Doric columns are about $9\frac{1}{3}$ diameters high, and the Ionic and Corinthian about $8\frac{3}{4}$ diameters.

The Colosseum is of a type unique among ancient buildings. The structural problems involved were engineering in character, and all the more so because the Romans built up the whole gigantic edifice without that extraneous support which the Greeks secured in theatre building, by scooping the auditorium out of the earth. Here, then, is an entirely new departure made possible by the invention and use of concrete, employed not only in corridors and cells, even in chambers under the arena itself, but also in multitudes of raking vaults, which formed the almost indestructible foundations of each of the four tiers of seats reared one above the other in a great ellipse, to the crowning colonnade. Greek architecture had been simple in appearance and self-evident in design, with columns standing on a crepidoma below and supporting an entablature above. Roman architecture, especially as carried out first in the Theatre of Marcellus and afterwards in numerous amphitheatres, became complex in appearance and hidden in design; for not only were columns placed in front of piers, but there were columns above columns, entablatures above entablatures, and arches above arches, while radiating vaults round the whole building were hidden supports to the auditorium seats. In the Greek theatres the steps which radiated at regular intervals to the various ranges of seats were slabs of marble between the seats; in a Roman amphitheatre the stairs emerged at intervals from the vaulted supporting corridors which swept round the building. Stupendous in proportions, complex in structure, and yet consistent in the constant repetition of the external design, the Colosseum compels alike awe and admiration of a nation who conceived and carried to completion such an immense undertaking to serve popular amusements. The Colosseum is still magnificent, even in its ruin, and recalls the gladiatorial contests, the naval displays, and the martyrdom of Christians which took place within its giant walls before it became a Mediaeval fortress or was plundered to provide building materials for Renaissance palaces and churches.

The **Amphitheatre, Verona** (A.D. 290), is in unusually good preservation, and nearly all the stone seats are intact, although only four complete bays of the upper part of the external wall are standing.

The **Amphitheatre, Pompeii** (70 B.C.), the earliest to be built, and those at Pozzuoli, Capua, Syracuse, Pola, Nîmes, Arles and El Djem (near Carthage), are other examples, besides the remains known as the 'Maumbury Rings' at Dorchester, and the Amphitheatre at Caerleon (Monmouth). The amphitheatre at **El Djem** (ancient Thysdrus, third century A.D.) (p. 310) ranked next in size after the Colosseum, Rome. The exterior is of massive appearance, the width of the piers supporting the arches being greater than the width of the spaces between.

CIRCUSES

The Roman circus, for horse and chariot racing, was derived from the Greek hippodrome, and attained great magnificence. (For foot-racing and athletic games there was the stadium, based upon the Greek stadium, usually included with the amenities of the thermae rather than appearing as a separate building.) Chariot racing was enormously popular, and vast sums were spent upon the training and

A. Exterior from S.W.

B. Exterior arcade   c. Exterior arcade: typical bay detail

El Djem, near Carthage: Amphitheatre (3rd cent. A.D.). See p. 309

selection of men and horses. Famous charioteers were the idols of the day, and though risking life and limb, reaped rich rewards. Four-horsed chariots were usual, but races were varied by using two, three, or sometimes six, eight or ten horses, and by equestrian displays and acrobatic riding. The teams of the four factions or 'stables' of Rome competed against one another. Heavy betting gave intensity to the popular interest, and brought its attendant evils. Until a permanent amphitheatre had been provided in Rome, in the late first century B.C., the hippodrome was also used for the brutal contests of man and beast.

The **Circus Maximus, Rome** (p. 312B, C, D, E), so called from its great size was sited in the valley between the Aventine and Palatine Hills, but has long since disappeared. It was the oldest in Rome and underwent many improvements and restorations. Julius Caesar, from 46 B.C., followed by Augustus, first gave it the monumental proportions for which it is so famous, and later emperors, Claudius, Nero, Titus and Trajan, added their enrichments of costly marbles, columns and statues. From Heliopolis, Egypt, came the obelisk of Rameses II, now standing in the Piazza del Popolo, brought by Augustus to occupy the centre of the spina or dividing wall, which ran down the middle of the arena in a slightly oblique direction, so that the chariots might have more room at the starting end. The restored view (p. 312D), shows its probable appearance in the fourth century A.D. It measured 609.6 m (2,000 ft) long and 198.12 m (650 ft) wide, and seated 255,000 spectators. The twelve 'carceres' held the contestant chariots and horses, and each race required seven laps of the spina, equal to a distance of about $2\frac{1}{4}$ miles. In the time of Caligula, the number of races held in one day of the games was doubled, from twelve to twenty-four. When a race was in progress, the laps were signalled by moving seven large wooden eggs on the spina. Despite the twelve carceres, it seems that not more than four teams raced at a time. The bas-relief and view give a good idea of a racing quadriga (p. 312C, E) and the relief on a lamp shows the triumphant victor in a race (p. 312B). Around the track rose the triple banks of seats, supported on concrete vaults: outside, the circus showed three ranges of marble arcades like those of the Colosseum, under which thronged the excited crowds, importuned by wine-sellers, caterers, tipsters and cheap-jacks who plied their trades there. The last race to take place in the Circus was in A.D. 549.

The **Circus of Maxentius, Rome** (A.D. 311) (p. 312A), of which vestiges still remain, consisted of a long, open, circular-ended arena with a 'spina' on its longer axis, and was surrounded by tiers of marble seats, supported on raking vaults. At one end of the arena were the 'carceres' or stalls for horses and chariots, with a central processional entrance and two side entrances, and at the opposite end was the 'Porta Triumphalis', and the whole was enclosed by a concrete wall.

The circuses of Flaminius and Nero were other examples in the Imperial City.

TOMBS

The Romans practised both forms of burial, cremation and interment, and thus sarcophagi for the body and urns for the ashes are sometimes found in the same tomb chamber. During the first three centuries of the Christian era, the body of nearly every Emperor was burnt on a magnificent pyre, from which an eagle was released to symbolize his escaping soul. In the second century, when cremation became less usual, wealthy citizens were embalmed on their death and placed in massive and costly sarcophagi. Roman law forbade burial inside city confines, and tombs lined the main roads radiating from the town gates, as along the Via Appia, Rome, or the Street of the Tombs, Pompeii, with its fine Gate of Herculaneum or again, at Ostia.

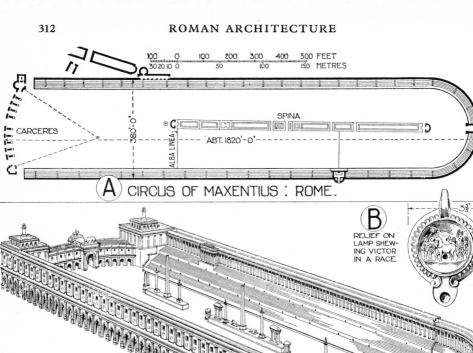

100 0   100 200 300 400 500 FEET
30 20 10 0   50   100   150 METRES

CARCERES

380'-0"

ALBA LINEA

SPINA

ABT. 1820'-0"

(A) CIRCUS OF MAXENTIUS : ROME.

(B) RELIEF ON LAMP SHEW-ING VICTOR IN A RACE

1'-4"

(C) BAS-RELIEF

(D) CIRCUS MAXIMUS : ROME(RESTORED)

E. Circus Maximus, Rome (restored): a quadriga race

The Romans had five classes of burial places: Coemeteria, Monumental tombs, Pyramidal tombs, Temple-shaped tombs, and Sculptured memorials of miscellaneous kinds.

1. *Coemeteria* or subterranean vaults contained both columbaria and loculi. 'Columbaria' (p. 316Q), so named because of their resemblance to pigeon-holes, were niches formed in the rock to receive a vase containing the ashes of the deceased, and with the name inscribed thereon. 'Loculi' or recesses for corpses were sealed with a front slab inscribed with the name, as in the tomb of the Gens Cornelia, Rome. Sarcophagi, often beautifully carved with figures and festoons, and surmounted by lids like roofs terminating in scrolls, were also placed in the vaults (p. 316P). Later these vaults were called Catacombs from 'ad Catacumbas', the place-name of a district in Rome, where many are found.

2. *Monumental tombs* are the most typical Roman class, descended from the Etruscan tumuli, with their embracing ring of stones or rock. They consisted of large cylindrical blocks, often on a quadrangular podium, topped with a conical crown of earth or stone.

The **Tomb of Caecilia Metella, Rome** (*c.* 20 B.C.) (pp. 316J, 317C), is on the Via Appia. It has a podium, 30.48 m (100 ft) square, supporting a circular mass, 28.65 m (94 ft) in diameter, at the core of which was the tomb chamber containing the sarcophagus, now in the cortile of the Farnese Palace, Rome. The exterior, faced with travertine, was crowned by an entablature, the frieze of which is carved with ox-skulls and festoons, above which there was probably a conical earthen mound.

The **Mausoleum of Augustus, Rome** (*c.* 25 B.C.) (p. 317A), erected for himself and his heirs, was a huge cylinder, 88.39 m (290 ft) in diameter, faced in travertine, supporting a mound of earth, 44.20 m (145 ft) high from the ground, planted with evergreen trees and surmounted by a bronze effigy of Augustus. The interior was subdivided into tiers of compartments, some of them vaulted, by a complex system of ring and radial concrete walls, all of them finely finished with opus reticulatum facings although all the compartments were filled with earth, except for the sepulchral chamber and the passages leading to it. Behind the façade wall, a series of hemicycle buttresses completed the precautions for retaining and dividing the pressures of the great load of earth. A central pillar cored the system and supported the crowning statue. In the twelfth century the monument was converted into a fortress by the Colonna family; in its later history its ruins served in turn for a formal garden, a bull ring, a theatre and a concert hall, the latter removed in 1934.

The **Mausoleum of Hadrian, Rome** (*c.* A.D. 135) (pp. 316E, F, G, 317B), one of the most important of these tombs, is now the Castle of S. Angelo. It originally consisted, as shown in the conjectural restoration, of a square podium 86.87 m (285 ft) each way and 12.80 m (42 ft) high, below a drum-shaped mass, 70.10 m (230 ft) in diameter and rising to over 30.48 m (100 ft). Then a mound of earth, planted with funerary trees, capped by a massive, cylindrical tower, provided a platform, 54.86 m (180 ft) from the ground, for a sculptured quadriga. The facing of the structure was Parian marble, and there were marble or gilded bronze equestrian groups at the angles of the podium as well as marble statues around the drum. The monument was surrounded by a bronze railing, adorned with gilt-bronze peacocks. In lateral dimension (300 Roman feet) it accords with the Mausoleum of Augustus, but was in every way a superior design. The barrel-vaulted tomb chamber, in which was the porphyry sarcophagus of Hadrian, was right at the heart of the building, its floor 13.41 m (44 ft) above the entrance level and reached by a rising corridor which made a complete circuit of the drum before turning inwards, over the entrance passage, to reach the tomb chamber. There is evidence here again in this monument of structural compartmentation to divide the loads and stresses; the podium portion is entirely made up of narrow, structural chambers, radiating from the drum. The monument has been much despoiled by the Goths and later Vandals, and also much altered, for during the Middle Ages it was converted by the Popes into a fortress, was afterwards used as barracks, and is now a museum.

3. *Pyramidal tombs* were probably due to the introduction of Egyptian ideas after the conquest of Egypt (p. 6). The **Pyramid of Caestius, Rome** (12 B.C.) (p. 316K), is formed of concrete faced externally with white marble, and has a tomb chamber, the vaults and walls of which are decorated with figure paintings.

4. *Temple-shaped tombs* usually consisted of a mortuary chapel, often having a colonnaded portico or peristyle, standing on a podium in which was the sepulchral vault. In the chapel were niches containing statues of deities and portraits or busts of deceased members of the family. When there was no podium, the niches served for the cinerary urns too. Rock-cut tombs, which are numerous in the East, as around Palmyra, Jerusalem, Petra (Syria) and Cyrene (North Africa), often had temple-like façades in one or two storeys, with the sepulchral chamber cut in the rock behind.

The **Tomb of Annia Regilla, Rome** (c. A.D. 143) (p. 315A), 7.93 m (26 ft) square on plan, had a broad flight of steps on its north side, leading to a mortuary chapel, standing over a podium containing the sepulchral chamber. Both chambers had groined vaults. Externally, it is a fine and well-preserved example of Roman polychrome brickwork, with russet-red bricks for the pilastered order and yellow ochre for the walls between. There are four Corinthian pilasters on the west and south sides, but on the east, the inner two are expressed as hexagonal columns, sunk into wall recesses. Centrally below them is the entrance to the vault. Originally, the podium was covered with a thin coating of stucco, painted brilliant plum-red and with white lines to imitate the very brickwork which lay underneath.

The **Tomb of the Caetennii, Rome,** is the richest among a score or so of chamber tombs recently excavated below the nave floor of the great church of S. Peter, where they had first been sealed from the light of day by its predecessor, Constantine's basilican church of A.D. 330 (p. 352). They date from the second century A.D. up to that time, and many wonderful art treasures have been disclosed, including a very early, Christian mosaic vault. They were closely ranged along a narrow street-way, their walls painted and white-lined to simulate with greater pungency the true brickwork behind. The Caetennii tomb, 5.18 m (17 ft) wide and 5.5 m (18 ft) deep, had a marble-faced dado below a continuous range of alternating square and semicircular niches, framed with stucco dressings, which held the cinerary urns. Frescoes decorated the lunettes of the groined vault, itself richly ornamented with low-relief stucco panelling, as were the similar vaults of the **Tombs of the Valerii** and **Pancratii** on the Via Latina, Rome (p. 315B, C).

The **Mausoleum of Diocletian, Spalato** (Split) (c. A.D. 300) (p. 330C, D), standing in his palace, is elaborate, as befits an Emperor's tomb. It is octagonal externally, and is raised upon a podium containing the sepulchral chamber. Around it, there is a low peristyle of Corinthian columns. Internally, it is circular, 13.31 m (43 ft 8 ins) diameter, with four semicircular and four rectangular recesses, including with the latter the one containing the entrance. Between the recesses stand eight granite Corinthian columns, carrying an entablature broken back around them. Above them are eight more columns, much smaller and alternately Corinthian and Composite. But the remarkable feature is the hemispherical dome, which is of two contiguous shells of brickwork, each about 305 mm (1 ft) thick, the inner one being made up entirely of brick arches, arranged fishscale fashion. This dome represents the ultimate achievement in Roman vaulting, presaging Byzantine construction, massive concrete having given way to compact, wide-jointed brickwork,

A. The Tomb of Annia Regilla, Rome (*c.* A.D. 143). See p. 314

B. Tomb of the Valerii, Via Latina, Rome: stuccoed vault (1st cent. A.D.). See p. 314

C. Tomb of the Pancratii, Via Latina, Rome: stuccoed vault (2nd cent. A.D.). See p. 314

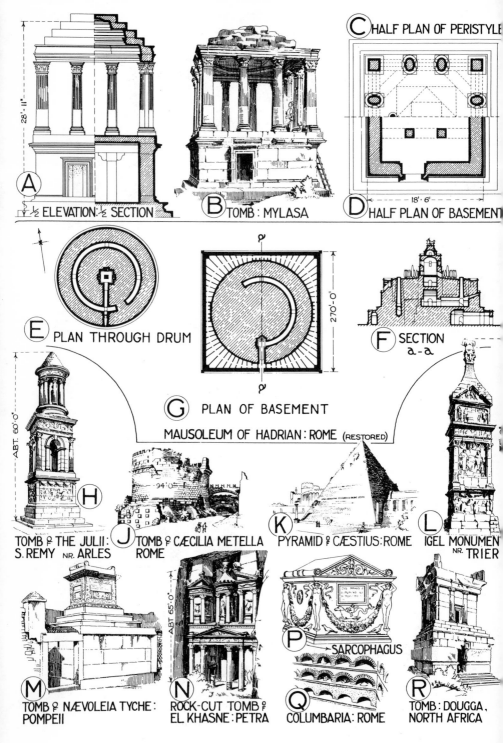

A   ½ ELEVATION: ½ SECTION

B   TOMB: MYLASA

C   HALF PLAN OF PERISTYLE

D   HALF PLAN OF BASEMENT

E   PLAN THROUGH DRUM

F   SECTION a-a

G   PLAN OF BASEMENT

MAUSOLEUM OF HADRIAN: ROME (RESTORED)

H   TOMB OF THE JULII: S. REMY NR. ARLES

J   TOMB OF CÆCILIA METELLA ROME

K   PYRAMID OF CÆSTIUS: ROME

L   IGEL MONUMENT NR. TRIER

M   TOMB OF NÆVOLEIA TYCHE: POMPEII

N   ROCK-CUT TOMB OF EL KHASNE: PETRA

P   SARCOPHAGUS

Q   COLUMBARIA: ROME

R   TOMB: DOUGGA, NORTH AFRICA

A. Mausoleum of Augustus, Rome (restored) (*c.* 25 B.C.). See p. 313

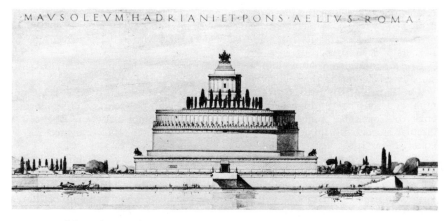

B. Mausoleum of Hadrian, Rome (restored) (*c.* A.D. 135). See p. 313

C. Tomb of Caecilia Metella, Rome (*c.* 20 B.C.). See p. 313

D. Tomb of 'El Khasne', Petra (*c.* A.D. 120). See p. 318

systematically laid through the whole thickness of the vault. Above the brick shells however, light concrete was used to sustain an octagonal, pyramidal roof (p. 330C).

The **Tomb of 'El Khasne', Petra** (c. A.D. 120) (pp. 316N, 317D) is one of the most interesting rock-cut tombs in that district, which number over 750. The façade, 19.81 m (65 ft) high, is of a debased type of architecture; the lower storey has a hexastyle Corinthian portico from which central and side doors lead into tomb chambers, while the upper storey also has columns supporting a broken pediment and a central circular structure surmounted by a conical roof and urn.

5. *Sculptured Memorials*. Minor tombs were extremely varied in their forms, but though comparatively small, might be richly ornate outside. Many represented an altar, with a sepulchral chamber contained in a high base; others appeared as semi-domed niches, commemorative arches, pillars or as semicircular benches or walled and paved enclosures.

The **Tomb of Naevoleia Tyche, Pompeii** (p. 316M) is of the altar type, the sepulchral chamber in the base having a large niche opposite the doorway and others elsewhere in the walls. In them, cinerary urns were discovered, as well as upon stone benches at the foot of the side walls. Three of the urns were of glass, protected by lead containers. The marble-faced altar above was raised upon a flight of three marble steps, its front and sides decorated with reliefs, surrounded by borders of acanthus scrolls.

Cenotaphs or memorial monuments to persons buried elsewhere were also occasionally erected, as in the following instances:

The **Tomb of the Julii, S. Rémy** (c. 40 B.C.) (p. 316H), in Provence, is a cenotaph, and consists of a high pedestal ornamented with bas-reliefs and supporting engaged Corinthian angle columns with arched openings between. Above is a circular storey with fluted Corinthian columns and entablature, crowned with a conical stone roof.

The **Igel Monument, near Trier** (A.D. 250) (p. 316L), is of similar design, erected by the Secundini family. A sculptured podium about 4.88 m (16 ft) square supports an intermediate stage with an Order of Corinthian pilasters, enclosing a large sculptured panel above which comes an attic surmounted by a sculptured pediment and crowned by a curved pyramidal roof, terminating at a height of 22.86 m (75 ft) above the ground.

TRIUMPHAL ARCHES

Monumental arches first occur about 200 B.C., but few now surviving are much earlier than the reign of Augustus. Chief among them are the triumphal arches erected to emperors and generals, commemorating victorious campaigns. Such arches were adorned with appropriate bas-reliefs and usually carried gilt-bronze statuary on an attic storey, the latter having a dedicatory inscription on its face. They had either one or three openings, two of the latter being footways, and the piers were ornamented with Corinthian or Composite pilasters or columns: slightly detached, full columns often were used after the early second century A.D.

The **Arch of Tiberius, Orange** (c. 30 B.C.) (p. 324A). In A.D. 25, Tiberius added his inscription to this monument, built before his reign. Triple openings, which appear here, are rare before the second century A.D. The arch is very ornate, with a double attic, and has Corinthian three-quarter columns flanking the central opening and at the outer angles. There also are attached columns at the side, and, remarkably for its early date, the inner pair carries a false arch above an entablature broken back sympathetically to receive it.

The **Arch of Titus, Rome** (A.D. 82) (pp. 273, 319, 321A), with a single opening

THE ARCH OF TITUS : ROME

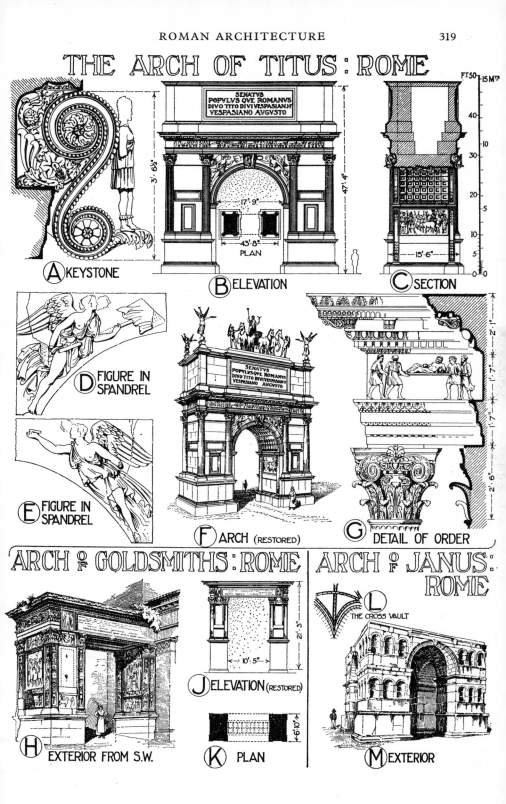

A KEYSTONE

SENATVS
POPVLVS QVE ROMANVS
DIVO TITO DIVI VESPASIANI F
VESPASIANO AVGVSTO

17' 9"

43' 8"

PLAN

3' 6½"

47' 4"

15' 6"

B ELEVATION

C SECTION

D FIGURE IN SPANDREL

E FIGURE IN SPANDREL

F ARCH (RESTORED)

SENATVS
POPVLVS QVE ROMANVS
DIVO TITO DIVI VESPASIANI F
VESPASIANO AVGVSTO

G DETAIL OF ORDER

ARCH ⁰⸍F GOLDSMITHS : ROME

ARCH ⁰⸍F JANUS : ROME

H EXTERIOR FROM S.W.

J ELEVATION (RESTORED)

10' 5"

21' 3"

6' 10"

K PLAN

THE CROSS VAULT

L

M EXTERIOR

ARCH OF SEPTIMIUS SEVERUS : ROME

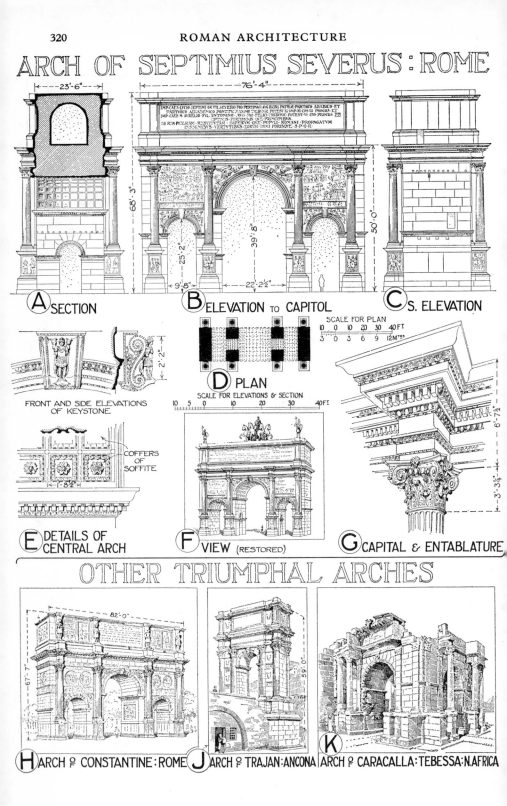

A SECTION

B ELEVATION TO CAPITOL

C S. ELEVATION

FRONT AND SIDE ELEVATIONS OF KEYSTONE

COFFERS OF SOFFITE

D PLAN

SCALE FOR PLAN
10 0 10 20 30 40 FT
3 0 3 6 9 12 M^TRS

SCALE FOR ELEVATIONS & SECTION
10 5 0 10 20 30 40 FT

E DETAILS OF CENTRAL ARCH

F VIEW (RESTORED)

G CAPITAL & ENTABLATURE

OTHER TRIUMPHAL ARCHES

H ARCH ♀ CONSTANTINE : ROME

J ARCH ♀ TRAJAN : ANCONA

K ARCH ♀ CARACALLA : TEBESSA : N. AFRICA

A. Arch of Titus, Rome (A.D. 82). See p. 318

B. Arch of Septimius Severus, Rome (A.D. 203). See p. 323

A. Arch of Trajan, Beneventum (A.D. 114). See p. 323

B. Arch of Constantine, Rome (A.D. 312). See p. 323

commemorates the capture of Jerusalem. On each main face attached columns flank the opening and at the outer angles, and these are the earliest known examples of the fully-developed Roman Composite Order (p. 319G). The soffit of the archway is ornamented with deeply recessed coffers, and a relief in the centre represents the apotheosis of Titus. On one side of the opening is a carved relief of the Emperor in a triumphal car, and on the other is a representation of the spoils taken from the Temple at Jerusalem. The keystones, which project considerably to support the main architrave, are also richly carved and are faced with figures of Roma and Fortuna (p. 319A). The attic storey, with the dedication, was originally surmounted by a bronze quadriga (p. 319F).

The **Arch of Trajan, Ancona** (A.D. 113) (p. 320J) was erected astride a causeway in honour of that emperor, who had made the harbour. It is of marble and is well preserved, although its bronze enrichments have disappeared. It is approached by a flight of steps and has a high podium with an archway 3.05 m (10 ft) wide, flanked on both sides by pairs of fluted Corinthian columns on pedestals, supporting an entablature and attic stage for inscriptions. The total height is 18.59 m (61 ft).

The **Arch of Trajan, Beneventum** (A.D. 114) (pp. 322A, 629D), one of the best-preserved Roman structures in South Italy, is similar in arrangement to the arch of Titus, Rome, and like it, has Composite column-capitals. It is of Greek marble; and the profuse bas-reliefs commemorate Trajan's Dacian wars and triumphs.

There are other single arches at Pola (*c.* 30 B.C.), Rimini (27 B.C.), Aosta (25 B.C.), S. Rémy (*c.* 25 B.C.) and Susa (7 B.C.). The archways in London at Hyde Park Corner (p. 1068E) and Constitution Hill are modern examples of the type.

The **Arch of the Goldsmiths, Rome** (A.D. 204) (p. 319H, J, K), erected in honour of Septimius Severus, is not a triumphal arch, nor is it of arched construction, for the opening is spanned by a horizontal entablature; while the workmanship is poor and over-elaborated. It adjoins the Campanile of the Church of S. Giorgio in Velabro.

The **Arch of Septimius Severus, Rome** (A.D. 203) (pp. 273, 320A–G, 321B, 629E), of the triple-arch type, was dedicated to the Emperor and his two sons to commemorate their Parthian victories. It is of white marble, and the three archways rest on piers, in front of which are detached Composite columns on pedestals. The central archway, with a richly coffered semicircular vault, has lateral openings to the side archways. On the summit, all in bronze, were statues of the Emperor and his two sons, Caracalla and Geta, in a six-horse chariot, with soldiers on either side.

The **Arch of Constantine, Rome** (A.D. 312) (pp. 320H, 322B), built in honour of Constantine's victory over Maxentius, is of fine proportions, with eight monolithic detached Corinthian columns supporting an entablature returned back to the wall, and on the attic storey a quadriga. Much of the decorative sculpture was brought from earlier monuments of the time of Trajan, and represents incidents of his reign.

Commemorative arches sometimes were erected on bridges, as at Saintes (A.D. 17), where there were twin passageways, or the Roman bridge at Alcantara (A.D. 105–16) (p. 341).

TOWN GATEWAYS AND ARCHWAYS

Town gateways were of three main types: (1) those forming part of the protective wall circuit, usually simple, but sometimes elaborated into commemorative monuments; (2) ornamental portals to forums, market places or other large enclosures; (3) arches built at main street intersections, particularly when the main streets were colonnaded, as in many towns in North Africa and Syria. Gateways of the first

A. Arch of Tiberius, Orange, France (*c.* 30 B.C.). See p. 318

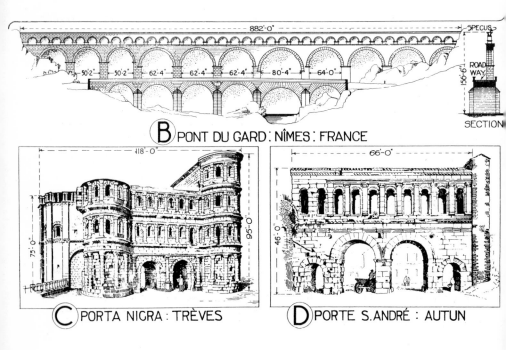

B PONT DU GARD : NÎMES : FRANCE

C PORTA NIGRA : TRÈVES

D PORTE S.ANDRÉ : AUTUN

type, in town walls, might have one main archway and a footway on each side, or, more often, two main archways, with or without a pair of side footways.

1. The **Porte S. André** (p. 324D) and the **Porte d'Arroux, Autun,** probably of the time of Augustus, have four archways, two for vehicles and two for pedestrians. Above the openings are arcaded galleries, connecting the ramparts on either side, decorated with pilasters of the Ionic Order in the case of the Porte S. André, and of the Corinthian in the other.

The **Porte de Mars, Reims** (first century A.D.), which now lacks its entablature and upper parts, is of grand dimensions, about 32.92 m (108 ft) wide. It has three openings, those on the flanks almost as large as that in the centre. The piers are decorated with pairs of Corinthian attached columns on both back and front, and as too there is a pair of attached columns on the sides, the arch must always have been free-standing and is not an ordinary gateway.

Little survives of the gateways of the walled towns of Roman Britain, such as London, York, Chester, Colchester and Lincoln.

The **Porta Nigra, Trier (Trèves)** (c. A.D. 300) (p. 324C), though ornamented with tiers of crudely-carved Tuscan attached columns, enframing arcades above the lowest stage, is truly a defensive gateway, with a double archway equipped with portcullises and leading to an unroofed court which could be defended against besiegers. Flanking semicircular towers form part of the structure, which is 35.05 m (115 ft) wide and reaches 28.96 m (95 ft) at its highest part.

2. The **Portico of Octavia, Rome,** erected by Augustus as a reconstruction of an older arrangement, had a fine double colonnade, but only five columns are still standing. The portico formed part of a rectangular peribolus comprising 300 smaller columns, surrounding an enclosure in which stood temples of Jupiter and Juno.

3. The **Arch of Caracalla, Tebessa** (A.D. 214) (p. 320K), formerly stood at the meeting of four roads in the centre of this ancient town in Algeria, but is now attached to the city walls built by Justinian in A.D. 535. It occupies a square of 10.97 m (36 ft) with archways 4.88 m (16 ft) wide on each front, flanked by detached Corinthian columns surmounted by an entablature having a frieze of unusual depth in order to receive the inscription.

There was a similar four-sided arch at Palmyra, famous for its colonnaded streets, as were Gerasa, also in Syria, and Timgad, in North Africa.

The **Arch of Janus Quadrifrons, Rome** (c. A.D. 315) (p. 319M), in the Forum Boarium, is another example of a four-way arch, but is of poor design. It has a simple cross-vault (p. 319L) with embedded brick box-ribs at the groins, affording a further instance of the progressive character of Roman constructive techniques: such ribs are possibly the prototypes of Gothic ribbed vaults.

PILLARS OF VICTORY

Trajan's Column, Rome (A.D. 113) (pp. 273B, 291B, 326), was adjacent to his Basilica and stood in an open colonnaded court carrying galleries at different levels, from which the bas-reliefs on its shaft could be viewed (p. 326B). It is a Roman Doric column, entirely of marble, with a total height of 35.23 m (115 ft 7 ins). In the pedestal, ornamented with sculptured trophies, is an entrance to the tomb chamber of Trajan. The shaft, 3.71 m (12 ft 2 ins) in diameter, contains a spiral staircase lighted by small openings and was originally surmounted by a bronze eagle, replaced by a bronze statue of Trajan after his death. This in turn was removed at some time unknown, and the present statue of S. Peter has crowned the column since 1588. The bas-reliefs illustrating incidents of Trajan's war with the

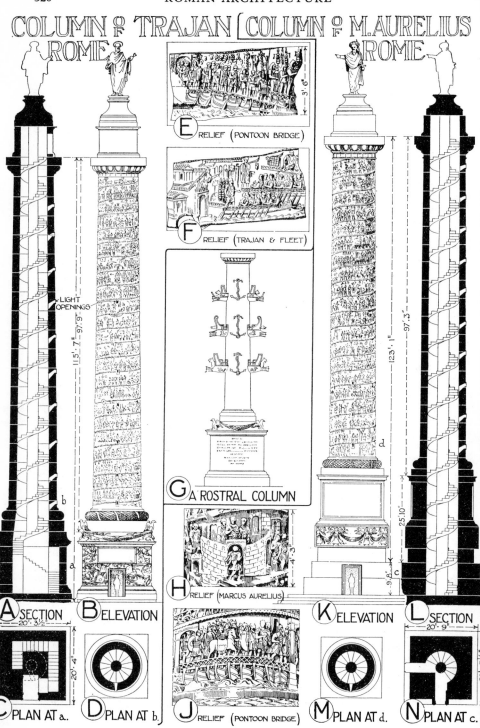

COLUMN OF TRAJAN ROME
COLUMN OF M.AURELIUS ROME

E RELIEF (PONTOON BRIDGE)

F RELIEF (TRAJAN & FLEET)

G A ROSTRAL COLUMN

H RELIEF (MARCUS AURELIUS)

J RELIEF (PONTOON BRIDGE)

A SECTION

B ELEVATION

K ELEVATION

L SECTION

C PLAN AT a.

D PLAN AT b.

M PLAN AT d.

N PLAN AT c.

LIGHT OPENINGS

Dacians were probably intended to represent the unwinding of a parchment scroll (p. 326E, F). There were 2,500 human figures, full of dramatic vigour, and many incidents of military campaigning by land and water, all carved on a spiral band over 244 m (800 ft) long and about 1.17 m (3 ft 10 ins) wide. There is a full-sized plaster reproduction in the Victoria and Albert Museum.

The **Column of Antoninus Pius, Rome** (A.D. 161), of which the pedestal now stands in the great hemicycle of the Giardino della Pigna of the Vatican (pp. 838B, 843A) was founded on the design of Trajan's column.

The **Column of Marcus Aurelius, Rome** (A.D. 174) (p. 326), which stands in the Piazza Colonna, commemorates the Emperor's victory on the Danube. It resembles Trajan's column and formerly stood in front of a temple dedicated to the Emperor. The marble pedestal is surmounted by a shaft 29.64 m (97 ft 3 ins) high and 4.01 m (13 ft 2 ins) in diameter, carved with remarkable spiral reliefs. The top is reached by 197 steps and was crowned by the statue of Marcus Aurelius till it was replaced (A.D. 1589) in the time of Pope Sixtus V by the existing statue of S. Paul. The spiral band winds round the column in twenty tiers, and represents the campaigns of Marcus Aurelius against the German tribes north of the Danube. One relief (p. 326H) shows Marcus Aurelius, and another (p. 326J) represents a pontoon bridge over which Roman troops with baggage are passing.

Rostral columns (p. 326G) were frequently erected in the time of the Emperors to celebrate naval victories, and took their name from the rostra, or prows of captured ships, with which they were embellished, while an inscription recorded the deeds which led to their erection.

PALACES

The **Palaces of the Emperors, Rome** (p. 328), are impressive even as ruins, of which enough remain to show their vast extent and imposing character. Excavations on the Palatine Hill have revealed remains of a group of magnificent palaces to which successive emperors, notably Augustus, Tiberius, Caligula, Domitian and Septimius Severus, made their contribution. The palaces, which crowned the Palatine and looked down on the centre of civic life in the valley below, were approached from the Forum Romanum by sloping ways of which the chief was the Clivus Palatinus, which branched off from the Via Sacra, west of the Arch of Titus.

Quite a little still survives of the modest house of the second half of the first century B.C. which Augustus purchased for his own occupation (p. 328B 16) and extended; but a substantial part of the remains on the Palatine are due to new buildings and drastic reconstructions carried out for Domitian by his architect, Rabirius. The main elements of Domitian's palace (p. 328B) were the State Suite (21); the private apartments (the so-called 'Palace of Augustus') (10), which at a lower level had a grand segmental portico and stepped terraces overlooking the Circus Maximus lying below the south-west slope of the hill; and a large walled garden (8), with a great hemicycle (7) on one long side, behind which were baths buildings. The latter were partly rebuilt by Septimius Severus, who also made massive additions in this locality (9).

Domitian's palace affords a splendid instance of Roman axial planning, with the magnificent vistas it allowed, and of the devices used to mask awkward changes of alignment. The grandest part of the palace was the State Suite. The north-eastern portico (p. 328A; B 21 H), of cippolino columns, led into the public halls, the Tablinum or throne-room (21 F), flanked on one side by the Temple of the Lares or Imperial household gods (21 E), and on the other by the Basilica or Hall of Justice (21 G). Thus, according to tradition, the Imperial power was firmly planted,

A. Palace of Domitian on the Palatine Hill, Rome

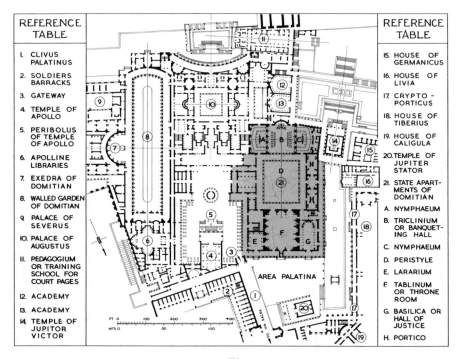

REFERENCE TABLE	
1.	CLIVUS PALATINUS
2.	SOLDIERS BARRACKS
3.	GATEWAY
4.	TEMPLE OF APOLLO
5.	PERIBOLUS OF TEMPLE OF APOLLO
6.	APOLLINE LIBRARIES
7.	EXEDRA OF DOMITIAN
8.	WALLED GARDEN OF DOMITIAN
9.	PALACE OF SEVERUS
10.	PALACE OF AUGUSTUS
11.	PEDAGOGIUM OR TRAINING SCHOOL FOR COURT PAGES
12.	ACADEMY
13.	ACADEMY
14.	TEMPLE OF JUPITOR VICTOR

REFERENCE TABLE	
15.	HOUSE OF GERMANICUS
16.	HOUSE OF LIVIA
17.	CRYPTO-PORTICUS
18.	HOUSE OF TIBERIUS
19.	HOUSE OF CALIGULA
20.	TEMPLE OF JUPITER STATOR
21.	STATE APARTMENTS OF DOMITIAN
A.	NYMPHAEUM
B.	TRICLINIUM OR BANQUETING HALL
C.	NYMPHAEUM
D.	PERISTYLE
E.	LARARIUM
F.	TABLINUM OR THRONE ROOM
G.	BASILICA OR HALL OF JUSTICE
H.	PORTICO

B. Plan

The Palaces of the Emperors on the Palatine Hill, Rome (restored)
(commenced A.D. 3 and continued by the Emperors till A.D. 212). See p. 327

in architectural planning at any rate, between religion and justice. Directly beyond the throne-room was the Peristyle (21 D), a rectangular garden surrounded by marble colonnades designed for court life and pageantry. This, in its turn, opened into the Triclinium or Banqueting Hall (21 B), with its three couches for reclining guests. This social sanctum of time-honoured hospitality was remote from the distraction of the public courts and looked out into the peristyle and two nymphaea or open gardens with flowering plants, playing fountains and running water. Not only were the Imperial palaces on the Palatine imposing in extent, plan, and proportions, but both within and without they were decorated on the grand scale and in a manner made familiar to us by the revelations of the buried city of Pompeii. The floors were worked in conventional and pictorial mosaics for which the craftsmen of Italy are still famous; the walls were relieved by marble columns and painted with frescoes, and the ceiling vaults were modelled in low-relief stucco picked out with bright colours, while everywhere there were niches for the splendid statues brought from conquered Greece.

The **Golden House of Nero, Rome** (A.D. 65), built after the great fire in the city, has become a synonym for all that is magnificent in royal palaces, but it was destroyed by the Flavian Emperors and made room for the Colosseum and Imperial Thermae. Pliny describes the lavish ornamentation and fittings, and Raphael drew inspiration from its buried frescoes.

The **Palace of Diocletian, Spalato** (Split) (A.D. 300) (p. 330) forms the greater part of the Mediaeval town of Spalato in Dalmatia, which has therefore been called a city in a house. This magnificent palace, with its imposing arcade, stretches along the sea-front of the Adriatic and may be described as a royal country house, or a château by the sea. Its original appearance can be well understood from the restored view (p. 330C). The plan of the palace was approximately rectangular, occupying 3.24 hectares (8 acres), almost equal in extent to the Escorial in Spain (p. 963). There was a square tower at each angle, and in the centre of the north, east, and west sides were the 'golden', 'silver', and 'iron' gateways, flanked by octagonal towers with sub-entrances to broad, colonnaded avenues, 10.97 m (36 ft) wide, which met in the centre and gave the palace the character of a Roman camp. The two northern portions were probably for guests and principal officers of the household; while across the southern portion there were the Imperial apartments, flanked by two courts in one of which stood Diocletian's Mausoleum, described earlier (p. 314), and in the other, a temple dedicated to Jupiter. A vestibule, circular inside and preceded by a porch of four columns in antis led to a suite of spacious rooms fronting south on to a grand arcaded gallery, 159.72 m (524 ft) long and 7.32 m (24 ft) wide, overlooking the sea, which probably contained works of art besides serving for leisurely promenades (cf. Elizabethan gallery, p. 995). Centrally below the gallery was a watergate, the Porta Aenea or Brazen Gate. Elsewhere, the outer walls of the palace were lined internally on three sides with cells for slaves and soldiers of the Imperial retinue. Besides the novel construction of the vault of the mausoleum (p. 314) there are other features of this fortress-like building which give it a transitional character and foreshadow future developments. Its architecture is still classical, but is debased and hints strongly of the Byzantine, especially in the flattened profile of the mouldings and in the fretted running ornament (cf. p. 401). Also, the arch form appears here in a connection for which there are very few precedents in earlier Roman work. Above the northern gateway there are decorative arches springing directly from the capitals of columns (p. 330A), and the portal itself has a decorative archivolt above a flat lintel made up of joggled voussoirs. Similarly, the Corinthian columns flanking the approach to the vestibule of the Imperial apartments carry arches from their capitals, and over the central

PALACE OF DIOCLETIAN : SPALATO

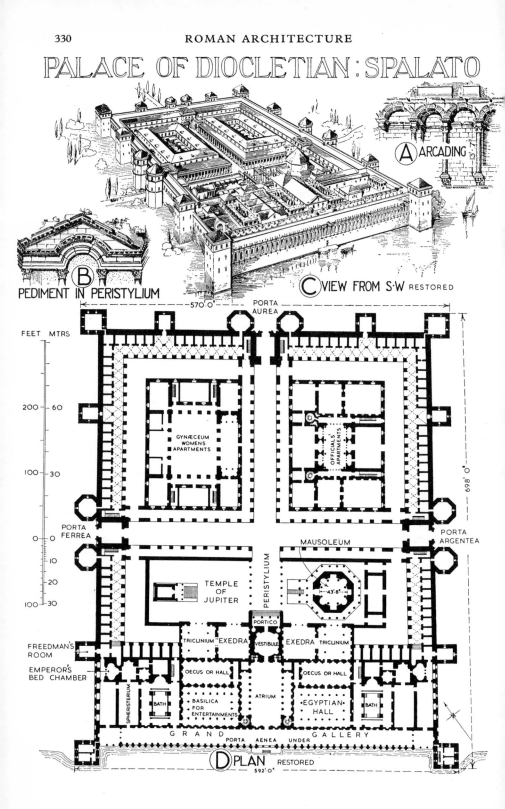

A ARCADING

B PEDIMENT IN PERISTYLIUM

C VIEW FROM S·W RESTORED

PORTA AUREA

FEET   MTRS

GYNÆCEUM WOMEN'S APARTMENTS

OFFICIALS APARTMENTS

PORTA FERREA

PORTA ARGENTEA

MAUSOLEUM

TEMPLE OF JUPITER

PERISTYLIUM

43' 8"

FREEDMAN'S ROOM

EMPEROR'S BED CHAMBER

PORTICO

TRICLINIUM EXEDRA VESTIBULE EXEDRA TRICLINIUM

OECUS OR HALL

OECUS OR HALL

SPHERISTERIUM

BATH

BASILICA FOR ENTERTAINMENTS

ATRIUM

EGYPTIAN HALL

BATH

G R A N D   G A L L E R Y

PORTA AENEA UNDER

D PLAN RESTORED

592' 0"

570' 0"

698' 0"

intercolumniation of the porch the whole entablature is turned into an arch (p. 330B). Thus here are early instances of a principle which was carried to its logical conclusion in the Romanesque and Gothic styles.

ROMAN HOUSES

Roman dwelling-houses are of three types: (a) The domus or private house; (b) the villa or country house; and (c) the insula or many-storeyed tenement.

(a) The *domus* or private house combined the features of the old Italic or Etruscan dwelling with other elements derived, about the second century B.C., from the Greek house. An atrium formed the more public portion of the building and beyond was the peristyle of Greek origin, the centre of the family apartments.

The **'Atrium Vestae', Rome** (c. A.D. 66) (p. 273B) or House of the Vestals, much modified in the late second century A.D., was a special kind of dwelling near the Forum where lived the six Vestal Virgins who tended the sacred fire in the adjacent Temple of Vesta. Rooms were arranged in two storeys alongside a great colonnaded court, 54.86 m × 14.63 m (180 ft × 48 ft), with a large, vaulted hall and other principal apartments across the rear short end.

The **House of Livia, Rome** (c. 55 B.C.) (p. 328B 16), on the Palatine, which the Emperor Augustus purchased for his own use, is the most interesting of the remains of a domus in the Imperial city.

Pompeii and Herculaneum were provincial towns buried by deposits of volcanic ash at the devastating eruption of Vesuvius in A.D. 79. Pompeian houses were thus remarkably preserved. Excavations show how the lay-out of the town was greatly enlarged, c. fifth century B.C., either by the Etruscans or the Samnites, who secured power in turn, from a small and irregular settlement of the Oscans, the earliest inhabitants, into an extensive but still modest market town of some 64.75 hectares (160 acres). The new part had a regular 'grid-iron' street arrangement, cutting the building sites into rectangular blocks. The streets were very narrow, 2.44 m, 3.66 m or 4.57 m (8, 12 or 15 ft) wide, while the widest were 7.16 m (23 ft 6 ins) with a roadway 4.11 m (13 ft 6 ins) and paths 1.52 m (5 ft) wide. Houses were spaciously laid out at first, but as the town became congested, small houses and shops grew up around them and lined the street frontages, while second storeys became increasingly common. The Romans had become masters in 80 B.C. By Imperial times Pompeii had become thoroughly Latinized, and Greek influences, which had been important throughout, gave place to the Roman. In the last phases before the eruption, commerce and industry were encroaching upon the dwellings of the patricians, and they and the wealthy citizens had begun to move out beyond the obsolete defensive walls to nearby suburbs and villas.

The rooms of a Pompeian mansion were lighted by openings on to internal courts, as in Mediaeval times in England and France, and as in Eastern houses to this day; some of the courts were small, but the light is strong in sunny Italy. Braziers were used for heating. The domestic water supply was drawn from wells or was rainwater collected from roofs until in the first century B.C. a branch aqueduct was made; profuse supplies then were carried in leaden pipes to domestic taps in all but the smallest dwellings, and to street and garden fountains and basins. Despite the three public baths in the town, most of the larger houses had their own bathroom suites.

The **House of the Surgeon, Pompeii** (fourth century B.C.), represents the oldest type of house, as yet unaffected by Greek influence. All its chief rooms were arranged around an 'atrium', a covered court of which only a small central portion was open to the sky.

HOUSE OF PANSA : POMPEII

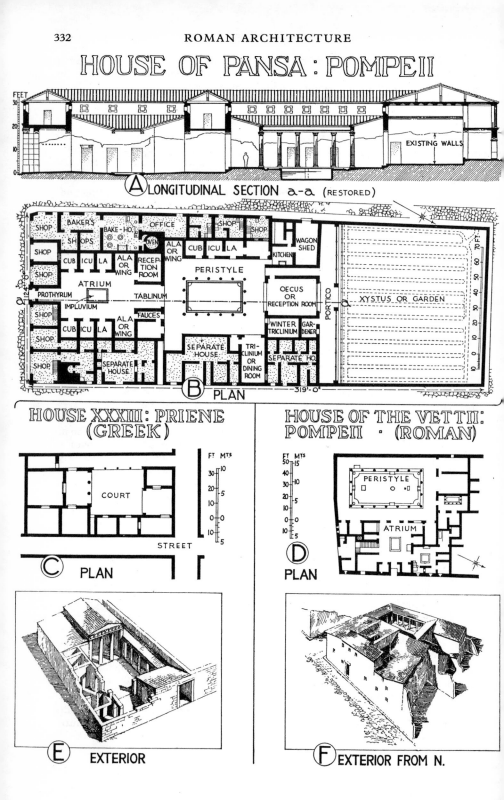

FEET
30
20
10
0

EXISTING WALLS

Ⓐ LONGITUDINAL SECTION a-a (RESTORED)

Ⓑ PLAN — 319'-0"

SHOP · SHOP · SHOP · SHOP · SHOP · SHOP · SHOP

BAKER'S · SHOPS · BAKE-HO. · OFFICE · OVEN · SHOP · SHOP

CUB ICU LA · ALA OR WING · RECEP-TION ROOM · CUB ICU LA · KITCHEN · WAGON SHED

ATRIUM · PERISTYLE

PROTHYRUM · TABLINUM · OECUS OR RECEPTION ROOM · PORTICO · XYSTUS OR GARDEN

IMPLUVIUM · FAUCES

CUB ICU LA · ALA OR WING · WINTER TRI-CLINIUM · GAR-DENER

SEPARATE HOUSE · TRI-CLINIUM OR DINING ROOM · SEPARATE HO

SEPARATE HOUSE

70 FT · 60 · 50 · 40 · 30 · 20 · 10 · 0

HOUSE XXXIII : PRIENE (GREEK)

COURT

STREET

FT MTS
30 · 10
20 · 5
10
0 · 0
10 · 5

Ⓒ PLAN

HOUSE OF THE VETTII : POMPEII · (ROMAN)

FT MTS
50 · 15
40
30 · 10
20 · 5
10
0 · 0
10 · 5

PERISTYLE

ATRIUM

Ⓓ PLAN

Ⓔ EXTERIOR

Ⓕ EXTERIOR FROM N.

The **House of Pansa, Pompeii** (second century B.C.) (p. 332), illustrates the typical domus or family mansion, fully developed. It comprises two main portions; the atrium, or forepart, which served for formal occasions as well as normal use; and a rear or 'peristyle' portion, which was the more intimate, private part. The first of these, the atrium, is the traditional Italic house, which in the House of the Surgeon represents the entire dwelling; the second, the colonnaded peristyle, is an additional chief element derived from the Greek house, becoming common from the early second century B.C. From this latter time too, Greek influence caused columns sometimes to be used to support the margins of the roof opening or 'compluvium' of an enlarged atrium, which in the original lacked columns. Privacy was assured for the whole house since all the rooms, with rare exceptions, faced inwards towards atrium or peristyle, light being gained for them through tall doorways with metal grilles within their doors or hung with curtains. Window glass was rare, even in Pompeii's last days. Encircling the House of Pansa on three sides were shops, bakeries and three smaller dwellings. A 'prothyrum' or entrance passage led from the street to the atrium, where a central, shallow rectangular basin or 'impluvium' was sunk in the pavement directly below the compluvium opening in the 'lean-to' roof above, which sloped down four ways towards it. The atrium also contained the shrine of the family gods, and near to the impluvium there stood a marble table, a traditional survival of the ancient banqueting board. An open living-room or 'tablinum' was curtained off between the atrium and the peristyle, and at the side was a passage, the 'fauces'. The peristyle enframed by sixteen Ionic columns, was laid out with flower beds and graced with statuary, fountains and water-basins. 'Cubicula' or bedrooms, 'triclinia' or diningrooms with different aspects for summer and winter, the 'oecus' or reception-room, and 'alae' or recesses for conversation surrounded the peristyle. Dining-rooms were fitted with three couches for nine people, the recognized number for a Roman feast. Floors were decorated with mosaics and walls with fresco paintings. The kitchen and pantry were at the side of the peristyle, farthest from the entrance, but convenient for the side street. There was a series of small upper rooms round the atrium and peristyle.

The **House of the Vettii, Pompeii** (A.D. first century) (p. 332D, F) differs from others in that the atrium, owing to the restricted site, adjoins the peristyle. The kitchen, with its cooking apparatus still *in situ*, and the triclinium, with its wall frescoes representing Classical myths, are typical of many other houses.

The **Houses of the Faun, Diomede, Sallust, and the Tragic Poet** are typical residences, with floors, walls, and vaulted ceilings decorated in the characteristic Pompeian style, and furnished with candelabra, lamps, vases, statues, and fountains, many of which are now in the Naples and Pompeii Museums. The floors were of patterned mosaic, either in black and white or in coloured marbles. The walls were painted, unpretentiously at first, but from c. 200 B.C. in fresco decorations in a series of 'styles'; the *first* imitated coloured marble veneering, in paint and modelled stucco (second century to 80 B.C.); the *second* shows either architecturally-enframed panels of large paintings or the realistic and robust representation of architectural elements, in the shape of arcades, colonnades and other spatial scenes (80 B.C.–A.D. 14); in the *third*, wall panels have architectural frames but of unrealistic, slender and often grotesque 'Egyptian' elements surrounding small, isolated pictures of Greek character, though vistas still appear, especially in the frieze (A.D. 14–63); and in the *fourth*, vistas of fantastically slender and fragile shrines, porticoes and similar structures occupy the whole body of the wall (overlaps with the third style—A.D. 50–79). Ceilings and vaults, covered with stucco, had frescoed decoration related to that of the walls. Roofs were covered

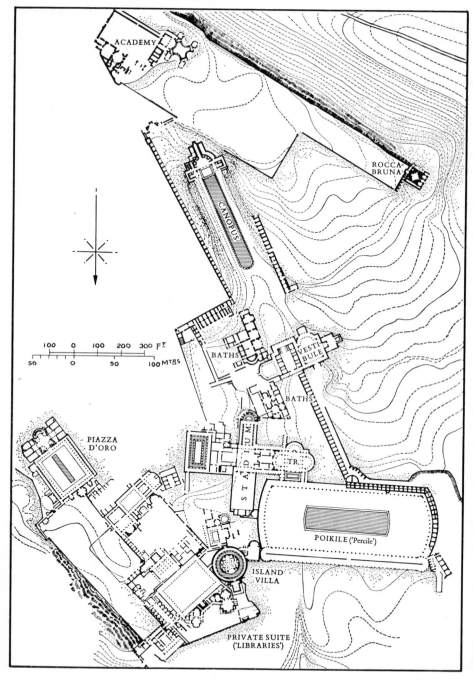

Hadrian's Villa, Tivoli (A.D. 124): plan. See p. 335

externally with tiles. The remains of these houses, as excavated in such cities as Pompeii and Timgad, reveal in the details of their arrangement the everyday life of Roman citizens.

(b) The *villa* or country house. **Hadrian's Villa, Tivoli** (A.D. 124) (pp. 334, 336A, 337) with its surroundings and gardens, occupied about eighteen square km (seven square miles). The vast complex is predominantly a large park scattered with extraordinary buildings ingeniously linked to exploit the possibilities of the undulating site, and constructed in such a manner as to demonstrate imaginative mastery of concrete faced with brick. Colonnaded courtyards and vestibules contrast with circular and octagonal apartments and halls with astonishing virtuosity and variety as curves, countercurves and curvilinearity are invoked. The great Piazza d'Oro (p. 336A) is flanked on two sides by apartments of extraordinary plan. On the north is a structure of eight compartments, four apsidal alternating with four rectangular bays supporting a dome which, like the Pantheon, had a central opening. To the south is a large hall of equally unusual plan; eight piers support arches which probably supported a dome, and between the piers are recesses with alternately convex and concave fronts, each front being supported by pairs of columns. The Island Villa (Teatro Marittimo) (p. 337B, C) contains within a triple circle of surrounding wall, colonnade and moat an astonishingly unique arrangement of apsidal, convex and concave rooms arranged around a central courtyard containing a central colonnaded fountain. Besides the Imperial apartments there were terraces, colonnades, palaestrae, theatres and thermae, all combining to epitomize the attitudes to design and the techniques of construction in Imperial architecture stimulated by Hadrian and his epoch.

The **Villa of Maximian, Piazza Armerina, Sicily** (early fourth century A.D.) (p. 336B), was built as the country retreat of Maximian, colleague of the Emperor Diocletian, and it was the almost exact counterpart of the palace at Spalato. It is characteristic of the age that the requirements of an emperor in retirement should have been expressed so differently. At Piazza Armerina the seclusion of a valley precluded the need for defence, and in contrast to the compact planning of Diocletian's Palace at Spalato the Villa of Maximian sprawled in a relaxed manner reminiscent of the Italian country villa quintessentially interpreted in the Villa of Hadrian, Tivoli. A monumental triple entrance and horseshoe-shaped forecourt gave access to the main body of the villa; in succession a peristyle court flanked by living quarters, a transverse corridor and a large apsidal audience chamber. South of the audience chamber and accessible from the corridor was a private suite of two bedrooms and a triclinium flanking a small semicircular courtyard. To the south and west was a large independent ceremonial hall opening on to an oval peristyle court, and projecting obliquely from the north-west corner of the main peristyle court was a bathing establishment. As at Tivoli, planning was organized as a loose arrangement of suites of rooms exploiting undulations of the site to produce juxtapositions of contrasting axes, but unlike Tivoli it developed an introspective character and dissociation from the surrounding landscape. Symmetry and axiality were employed only incidentally as elements of the composition rather than the essential axial vistas of conventional classical planning.

Apart from these exceptional palatial examples, villas abounded in the more attractive parts of the Empire, once peaceful conditions had been securely established. In type they ranged from luxurious country retreats, replete with every urban innovation, to modest farmsteads with a minimum of residential refinement. Few villas were erected in Britain primarily for pleasure. The average villa, however, combined comfort with utility, the elegant suite of rooms of the well-to-do owner being segregated from the working parts, operated by slaves in the charge of

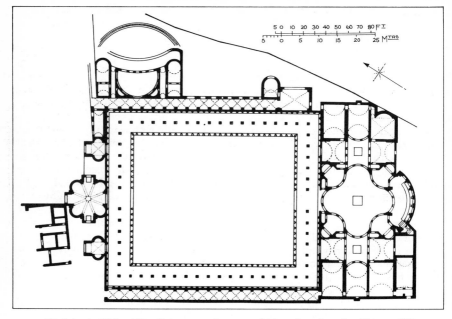

A. Hadrian's Villa, Tivoli (A.D. 124): part of plan showing the Piazza d'Oro.
See p. 335

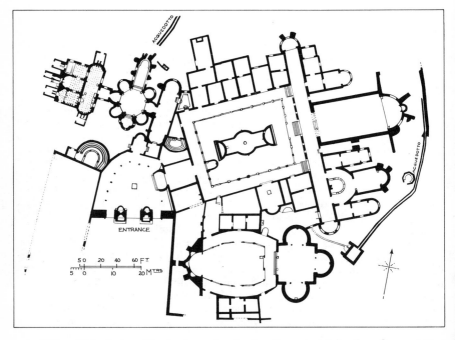

B. Villa of Maximian, Piazza Armerina (early 4th cent. A.D.): plan. See p. 335

A. The Canopus

B. Island Villa (Teatro Marittimo)   C. Island Villa: colonnade

Hadrian's Villa, Tivoli (A.D. 124). See p. 335

A. Block of flats at Ostia (restored). See p. 339

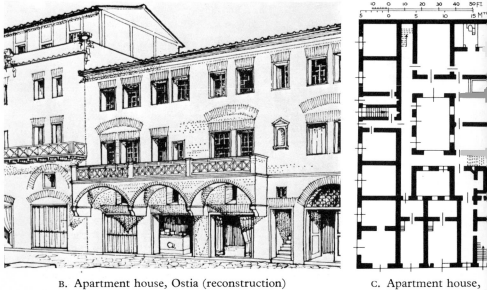

B. Apartment house, Ostia (reconstruction)

C. Apartment house, Ostia: plan

an overseer. Buildings were arranged around a court or a peristyle, or, after the first century A.D., were often of the 'corridor' type in which a single bank of rooms was connected by open or closed porticoes running externally. Adaptations were made for climatic conditions; a bath house was regularly present in the later villas of Roman Britain.

(c) The *insula* or apartment block was far more common than the domus in Rome, where space was very precious; and also in **Ostia,** the port of Rome, where large numbers of workers had to be adjacent to the docks (p. 338). Flat blocks rose four, five and even more storeys high, and Augustus and Nero in turn vainly placed restrictions of 20.73 m (68 ft) and 17.68 m (58 ft) upon them. Built economically of brick-faced concrete, with architectural dressings in a deeper colour, their appearance was surprisingly modern. Continuous balconies in concrete or timber, sometimes enclosed, were a frequent feature (p. 338A, B). Rooms of each flat were reached one through the other from common stairs (p. 338C), and numerous large windows faced both ways to surrounding streets and alleys and on to large internal, garden courts. Window glass was rare, and folding shutters or hanging cloths must largely have been used. Ground floor flats sometimes were occupied by the wealthy, but otherwise served, as at Pompeii, for workshops and bakeries or for 'tabernae', shops or miniature dwellings of one open-fronted room, with a wooden-floored loft over it, reached by means of a few stone steps and a ladder. Well water sufficed until the aqueducts came, but even then, water did not reach upper floors and their tenants had to use street fountains and public baths and latrines. Fire risk was very high. Heating and cooking were by brazier and stove.

AQUEDUCTS

Ruined aqueducts throughout the Empire show the importance attached by the Romans to an adequate water supply. Immense quantities of water were required for the great thermae and for public fountains, to say nothing of the domestic supply for the large population, and it has been computed that 1,610 million litres (350 million gallons) were daily poured into Rome through the eleven great aqueducts. The Romans were acquainted with the simple hydrostatic law that water rises to its own level in closed pipes, and in towns, water was distributed to public buildings, street fountains, workshops and the ground floor of dwellings by lead pipes (or sometimes of terra-cotta or wood) from large reservoirs and cisterns located in suitable positions for the regulation of supplies. Occasionally too, the trunk supply was siphoned across deep valleys, the water being divided for the purpose into nine or ten small-bore 38 mm (*c.* 1½ ins) lead pipes between reservoirs at each side; for the Romans were unable to make cast-iron pipes or to devise other trustworthy means of withstanding the great pressures occasioned in the process. Usually, since labour was abundant, it was more practicable to build tiers of stone or concrete arches, sometimes 30.48 m (100 ft) high, over ravines and low-lying places, to make tunnels through obstructions of earth or rock, and otherwise by the most direct means to maintain a slight but consistent fall for the water-conveying duct or 'specus' from the springs or rivers at the source to the reservoir where distribution began. Circuitous routes were often necessary. Across plains, particularly outside towns, an aqueduct had to be raised high enough to give a sufficient 'head' to the supply, and the use of arches obviated obstruction to traffic. The ducts varied in dimension according to need—from 0.46 m to 1.22 m (1½ ft to 4 ft) wide and from 0.61 m to 2.44 m (2 ft to 8 ft) high—and were lined with a very hard hydraulic cement.

The **Aqua Marcia, Rome** (144 B.C.), forms part of a triple aqueduct which, by

A. The Aqua Claudia, Rome (A.D. 38–52). See p. 341

B. The Pont du Gard, Nimes (c. A.D. 14). See p. 341

the Porta S. Lorenzo, carried the Aqua Marcia, the Aqua Tepula (127 B.C.), and the Aqua Julia (33 B.C.)—an economical arrangement by which several channels, one above the other, are carried by one series of arches.

The **Aqua Claudia, Rome** (A.D. 38) (p. 340A), built by the Emperors Caligula and Claudius, brought water to Rome from Subiaco, 72 km (45 miles) distant; part of its length is or solid masonry, and for 15.2 km (9½ miles) it is borne on lofty arches, great lengths of which remain in the Campagna. It is probably the finest of all Roman aqueducts, and some of the arches are over 30.48 m (100 ft) high. Five km (3 miles) from Rome it is joined by the Anio Novus (A.D. 38), 99 km (62 miles) in length.

The **Pont du Gard, Nîmes,** France (c. A.D. 14) (pp. 324B, 340B), forms part of a magnificent aqueduct, 40 km (25 miles) long, constructed to bring water to Nîmes from the neighbourhood of Uzes. It is well preserved, 268.83 m (882 ft) long, and formed of three tiers of arches, crossing the valley 47.24 m (155 ft) above the river Gard. In the two lower tiers the arch above the river is the widest and the others vary in width, while in the uppermost tier there are thirty-five arches of 4.27 m (14 ft) span, supporting the 'specus' or water channel. Except for the top tier, the masonry is laid dry, without mortar, and some of the arch voussoirs of the intermediate tier were made to project to carry the temporary wooden framing or centering on which the arch was formed (p. 340B).

Aqueducts at Tarragona, Segovia (c. A.D. 10), Spalato, and elsewhere testify to the importance attached to a good water supply, and the regulations throw a light on Roman administrative methods in the Imperial City and Roman Provinces.

BRIDGES

Roman bridges were simple, solid and practical in construction and designed to offer a well-calculated resistance to the rush of water. The roadway usually sloped upwards a little at the approaches, but otherwise was level. Early bridges were of timber, which was used too for the lesser constructions at all times, though often with stone piers. The finest were of stone. Very great spans were achieved when necessary; the arch of an Augustan bridge near Aosta, in north-west Italy, was 35.66 m (117 ft) across.

The **Pons Sublicius, Rome,** was for long the only bridge across the Tiber, and Livy records its destruction by the Roman garrison when the Etruscans were advancing upon Rome; while Macaulay has immortalized the incident of its defence by Horatius Cocles.

The **Pons Mulvius, Rome** (109 B.C.) (p. 342A), now known as the Ponte Molle, has semicircular arches over massive piers with protecting 'starlings' or cut-waters and extra arches above them to allow the flood waters to pass through. It was here that Cicero arrested the Gaulish ambassadors and Maxentius met death and defeat at the hands of Constantine (A.D. 312).

The **Pons Fabricius, Rome** (62–21 B.C.), with its flood water aperture and starlings, is one of the best preserved Roman bridges. Each of its twin arches spans about 24.38 m (80 ft).

The **Bridge of Augustus, Rimini** (A.D. 14–20) (p. 342C), is the best preserved and one of the finest ancient structures in Italy, with its stretch of five arches over the river Marecchia.

The **Roman Bridge, Alcantara** (A.D. 105–16) (pp. 323, 342B), the larger arches of which are nearly 27.43 m (90 ft) wide, exemplifies one of two impressive types found in Spain, that is (a) the many-arched type, of which that at Salamanca, of extreme length, is an example; (b) the single-arched type, such as the later Moorish

A. The Pons Mulvius (Ponte Molle), Rome (109 B.C.). See p. 341

B. Roman bridge over the Tagus, Alcantara, Spain (A.D. 105–16). See p. 341

C. Bridge of Augustus, Rimini (A.D. 14–20). See p. 341

and Gothic bridge at Toledo which, with the romantic sweep of its gigantic arch, spans the rocky valley of the Tagus.

FOUNTAINS

Public fountains, which were numerous, amounting to many hundreds in the various Roman cities, were designed either as a large basin of water ('lacus'), or as spouting jets ('salientes'), or the two were combined with marble columns and statues. Private fountains existed in great numbers, mainly in the courts and gardens of houses, with great variety of design in coloured marbles and porphyries, and were often decorated with bronze statuettes. The water sometimes issued from fishes, shells or other objects supported by a figure of a nymph and sometimes from lions' heads in wall niches lined with mosaics, as at Pompeii.

BIBLIOGRAPHY

ALLSOPP, H. B. *A History of Classical Architecture.* London, 1965.

ANDERSON, W. J., SPIERS, R. P., and ASHBY, T. *The Architecture of Ancient Rome.* London, 1927.

Atlas of the Classical World, ed. A. A. M. VAN DER HEYDEN and H. H. SCULLARD. London, 1960.

AURIGEMMA, S. *Villa Adriani.* Rome, 1962.

BIANCHI BANDINELLI, R. *Leptis Magna.* Rome, 1963.

BIEBER, M. *The History of the Greek and Roman Theatre.* London and Princeton, 1961.

BLAKE, M. E. *Ancient Roman Construction from the Prehistoric Period to Augustus.* Washington, 1947.

—. *Roman Construction in Italy from Tiberius through the Flavians.* Washington, 1959.

BLOCH, R. *The Etruscans.* London, 1958.

—. *Etruscan Art.* London, 1959.

—. *The Origins of Rome.* London, 1960.

BOËTHIUS, A. *The Golden House of Nero.* Ann Arbor, 1960.

BOËTHIUS, A., and WARD-PERKINS, J. B. *Etruscan and Roman Architecture.* Harmondsworth and Baltimore, 1970.

BROGAN, O. *Roman Gaul.* London, 1953.

BROWN, F. E. *Roman Architecture.* London and New York, 1961.

CARCOPINO, J. *Daily Life in Ancient Rome.* London, 1946.

CARY, M. *Geographic Background of Greek and Roman History.* Oxford, 1949.

COURTOIS, C. *Timgad.* Algiers, 1951.

D'ESPOUY, H. *Fragments de l'architecture antique.* 2 vols. Paris, 1899.

D'ESPOUY, et SEURE. *Monuments antiques.* 4 vols. Paris 1900–.

DI VITA, A. *Sabratha.* Basel, 1969.

DUDLEY, D. R. *Urbs Roma.* Aberdeen, 1967.

GRANT, M. *The World of Rome.* London, 1960.

HANSON, J. A. *Roman Theater-temples.* Princeton, 1959.

HARDING, G. L. *The Antiquities of Jordan.* London, 1959.

HAVERFIELD, F. *Ancient Town Planning.* Oxford, 1913.

HAYNES, D. E. L. *The Antiquities of Tripolitania.* Tripolitania, 1959.

LEACROFT, H., and R. *The Buildings of Ancient Rome.* Leicester, 1969.

LIVERSIDGE, J. *Britain in the Roman Empire.* London, 1968.

MACDONALD, W. L. *The Architecture of the Roman Empire, I: an introductory study.* Yale University Press, 1965.

MEIGGS, R. *Roman Ostia.* Oxford, 1960.

MINOPRIO, A. 'A Restoration of the Basilica of Constantine, Rome', *Journal of the British School*, Rome, vol. xii, 1933.

NASH, E. *Pictorial Dictionary of Ancient Rome.* 2 vols. 2nd ed. London, 1968.

PALLOTTINO, M. *The Etruscans.* Harmondsworth, 1965.

PICARD, G. *Living Architecture: Roman*. Fribourg, 1965.
PLOMMER, H. *Ancient and Classical Architecture*. London, 1956.
QUENNELL, M., and C. H. B. *Everyday Life in Roman Britain*. 3rd ed. London, 1947.
RICHMOND, I. A. *The City Wall of Imperial Rome*. Oxford, 1930.
—. *Roman Britain*. Harmondsworth, 1963.
RIVOIRA, G. T. *Roman Architecture*. Oxford, 1925.
ROBERTSON, D. S. *A Handbook of Greek and Roman Architecture*. Cambridge, 1945; reissue 1969.
SORRELL, A. *Roman London*. London, 1969.
SPIERS, R. P. *The Orders of Architecture*. London, 1926.
STARCKY, J. *Palmyre*. Paris, 1952.
STOBART, J. C. *The Grandeur that was Rome*. 3rd ed. London, 1938.
VIGHI, R. *The Pantheon*. Rome, 1955.
VITRUVIUS. *De Architectura libri X*. Translated by M. H. Morgan. Cambridge, 1914. Various English translations.
VOGT, J. *The Decline of Rome*. London, 1967.
WHEELER, R. E. M. *Rome beyond the Imperial Frontiers*. Harmondsworth, 1954.
—. *Roman Art and Architecture*. London, 1964.
—. *Roman Africa in Colour*. London, 1966.
ZSCHIETZSCHMANN, W. *Hellas and Rome*. 1959.

12

EARLY CHRISTIAN ARCHITECTURE

313–800

INFLUENCES

GEOGRAPHICAL

Christianity had its birth in Judaea, an eastern province of the Roman Empire, but directly it became a living organism it was naturally carried by S. Peter, S. Paul and other missionaries to Rome, as the centre of the World-Empire. There at the fountain-head of power and influence, and in spite of opposition and persecution, the new religion took root and grew, till it was strong enough to become the recognized universal religion of the whole Roman Empire. Early Christian architecture in Rome was influenced by, and was the logical outcome of, existing Roman art, and it was modified in other parts of the Empire according to the type already recognized as suitable for the geographical situation of those countries, such as Syria, Asia Minor, North Africa and Egypt.

GEOLOGICAL

Geological influences may be said to have acted indirectly rather than directly on Early Christian architecture, for the ruins of Roman buildings often provided the quarry whence materials were obtained. This influenced the style, both as regards construction and decoration; for columns and other architectural features, as well as fine sculptures and mosaics from older buildings, were worked into basilican churches of the new faith.

CLIMATIC

The climate of Italy, the most important centre of building activity in this epoch, has been dealt with in the chapter on Roman architecture (p. 257). The climatic conditions of such Roman provinces as Egypt, Syria and North Africa where Christianity was established naturally modified the style. The fiercer sun and hotter climate necessitated small windows and other eastern features.

HISTORICAL AND SOCIAL

The Early Christian period is generally taken as lasting from Constantine to the coronation of Charlemagne (800). The incursions of the Huns into Europe about 376 eventually brought about invasions from the north into Italy, and in 410 Rome itself was sacked by the Goths under Alaric. So many conflicting forces were at work in Europe that the spread of the new religion was arrested during this period of change and upheaval, until 451, when the defeat of Attila, king of the Huns, at the battle of Châlons aided in the consolidation of Christianity in Europe. In 568 the Lombards penetrated into Italy and held the northern part for 200 years. Then in 800 Charlemagne was crowned by the Pope in Rome, and from this date the

Empire was styled the Holy Roman Empire, a title which survived until 1806. From 800 to 1000, the dominant architectural influence was no longer Rome but Lombardy, and the style which developed there was Romanesque (pp. 456 ff.).

Constantine changed the capital of the Empire from Rome to Byzantium in 330, when the old Roman political system came to an end, and this royal convert reigned as an absolute monarch till his death in 337. Besides the troubles caused by Julian the Apostate, Christianity suffered further disabilities during the unsettled conditions consequent upon the division of the Roman Empire, which first took place in 364 when Valentinian became Emperor of the West and his brother Valens of the East. Theodosius the Great (379–95) reunited, for a time, the Eastern and Western Empires, and in 438 Theodosius II published his legal code, an important work on the constitutions of the Emperors from the time of Constantine. The series of Emperors in the West came to an end in A.D. 476, and the Eastern and Western Empires were nominally reunited by Zeno, who reigned at Constantinople. Then again the seat of power was changed, and Theodoric the Goth reigned in Italy (493–526) during a period of peace and prosperity. In the wake of this change, Byzantine art influenced Early Christian art by way of Ravenna, which rivalled Rome in importance and was the capital of the Gothic rulers, 493–553, with the exception of a short period when it was subdued by Justinian (537). Kings were now elected for the separate states of Spain, Gaul, Northern Africa and Italy. The emancipation of Western Europe from direct Imperial control resulted in the development of Romano-Teutonic civilization, which facilitated the growth of new states and nationalities, gave a fresh impulse to Christianity, and eventually strengthened the power of the bishops of Rome. The formation of these new states resulted also in the growth and development of Romance and Teutonic languages, which, for general use, largely replaced Latin. It is clear that these many social changes and political disturbances could not fail to be reflected in the architecture of a period in which great formative forces were at work.

RELIGIOUS

In all human history there is no record so striking as that of the rise of Christianity, and no phenomenon so outstanding as the rapidity with which it was diffused throughout the civilized world. Not only in this period but also in all subsequent ages, Christianity has inspired the building of some of the greatest architectural monuments. The number of Christian communities established by the Apostle Paul in his missionary journeys round the Eastern Mediterranean, in Syria, Asia Minor, Greece and Italy, might lead us to expect many more ruins of Early Christian basilican churches throughout these districts. However, it must be remembered that unlike those of the old Greeks and Romans which were built to shelter the statues of the gods, the purpose of the Christian church was to shelter worshippers who met for prayer and praise to an unseen deity, and, during the unsettled conditions at the beginning of Christianity, various places were adapted for this worship. Thus the building of pagan temples ceased before any attempt was made to build Christian churches. In 313 Constantine and Licinus issued their celebrated Edict of Milan, giving Christianity equal rights with other religions, and in 326 Constantine made it the official religion of the Roman Empire. Fortified by its official position and thus freed from the need for unity within, which had been engendered by persecution from without, the Church was soon divided by doctrinal differences and the Council of Nicaea (325), called by Constantine, was the first of several such councils for the settlement of disputes about heresies. The steady progress of Christianity was temporarily arrested by a reaction (361–3) under Julian the Apostate, and then for several generations religion suffered an eclipse as a power

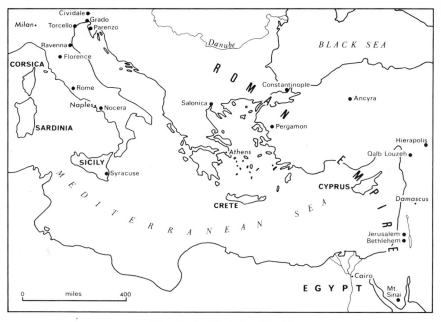

The Early Christian World

in European civilization, and the whole continent was given over to war and anarchy. Pope Gregory the Great (590–604) employed the Imperial army of Constantinople to defend Rome against the Lombards, and thus, by making common cause with the people, early laid the foundations of the temporal power of the Papacy, which steadily increased, especially under Popes Adrian I and Leo III. Throughout the whole Early Christian period the power of the eastern, or Byzantine, half of the Empire, with Constantinople as its centre, had been growing, and rivalry between East and West led to a schism in the Church which culminated in the coronation of Charlemagne in 800, under the title of Emperor of the Romans.

ARCHITECTURAL CHARACTER

The character of Early Christian architecture is chiefly to be seen in buildings of the fourth to the ninth century, though the style persisted in Rome up to the Renaissance.

Each age of human development inevitably modifies the art it has inherited, in its effort, sometimes conscious and sometimes unconscious, to adapt the art of the past to express the outlook of the present. Thus in architecture one style is generally evolved from that preceding by a series of gradual changes. The early Christians, as Roman craftsmen, continued old Roman traditions, but prosperity was declining and it was natural that for their new buildings they should utilize as far as possible the materials from Roman temples which had become useless for their original purpose. Further, in their churches, modelled on Roman basilicas, they used old columns which by various devices were brought to a uniform height (p. 350A). On this account, although extremely interesting from an archaeological point of view,

A. The basilican church of S. Apollinare in Classe, Ravenna (534–9). See p. 358

B. The basilican church of S. Apollinare in Classe, Ravenna. Nave looking E.

S. CLEMENTE : ROME

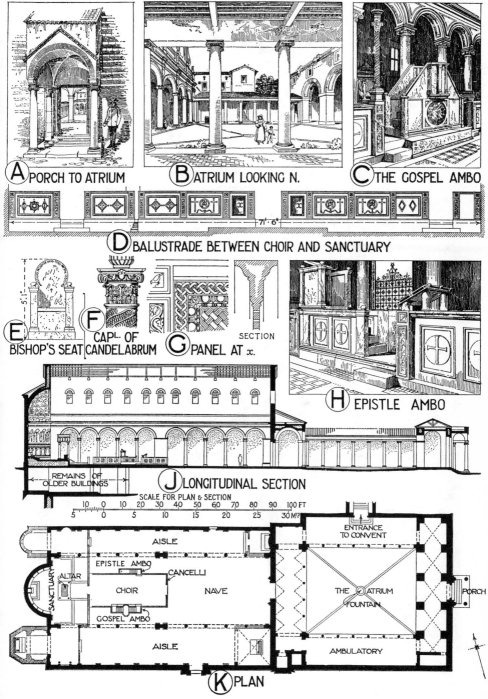

A PORCH TO ATRIUM

B ATRIUM LOOKING N.

C THE GOSPEL AMBO

D BALUSTRADE BETWEEN CHOIR AND SANCTUARY

7'·6"

E BISHOP'S SEAT

5'·1"

F CAP^L OF CANDELABRUM

G PANEL AT x.

SECTION

H EPISTLE AMBO

J LONGITUDINAL SECTION

REMAINS OF OLDER BUILDINGS

SCALE FOR PLAN & SECTION

10 0 10 20 30 40 50 60 70 80 90 100 FT
5 0 5 10 15 20 25 30 M^TS

K PLAN

ENTRANCE TO CONVENT

AISLE

EPISTLE AMBO

CANCELLI

SANCTUARY

ALTAR

CHOIR

NAVE

THE ATRIUM

FOUNTAIN

PORCH

GOSPEL AMBO

AISLE

AMBULATORY

A. The basilican church of S. Clemente, Rome
(rebuilt 1099–1108 over a 4th cent. church). See p. 352

B. The basilican church of S. Maria Maggiore, Rome
(432, with later alterations). See p. 354

Early Christian buildings hardly have the architectural value of a style produced by the solution of constructive problems. Basilican churches had either closely spaced columns carrying the entablature (p. 350B), or more widely spaced columns carrying semicircular arches (p. 350A). The basilican church with three or five aisles, covered by a simple timber roof, is typical of the Early Christian style (p. 357B), as opposed to the vaulted Byzantine church with its central circular dome placed over a square by means of pendentives (p. 376).

The architectural character of the basilican churches is rendered impressive and dignified by the long perspective of columns which carry the eye along to the sanctuary; a treatment which, combined with the comparatively low height of interiors, makes these churches appear longer than they really are, as is seen in S. Paolo fuori le Mura (p. 353F), and S. Maria Maggiore (p. 350B). An 'arch of triumph', figurative of the transition through death to eternal life, gave entrance to the sanctuary with the high altar in the centre standing free under its baldachino upheld by marble columns. The vista was rounded off by an apse lined with marble slabs and crowned with a semi-dome encrusted with glittering golden mosaics in which Christ appears surrounded by prophets, saints and martyrs (pp. 348B, 350A).

Timber roofs (pp. 356A, H, 357B) covered the central nave, and only simple forms of construction, such as king and queen post trusses, were employed. It is believed that the decoration of the visible framework was of later date, as at S. Miniato, Florence (pp. 472A, B, 473), and a casing of richly gilded coffers was often added in the Renaissance period (p. 350A, B). The narrower side aisles were occasionally vaulted and the apse was usually domed. Walls were still constructed according to Roman methods of using hand-laid rubble-concrete faced with brick or stone and sometimes plaster (p. 348A). Mosaic decoration was added internally (p. 348B), and sometimes also externally on west façades; though little regard was paid to external architectural effect (p. 356G).

The introduction of colour with the use of glass mosaics gave richness and mystery to interiors. The Early Christian basilicas were usually decorated with mosaic in the apse semi-dome and wall (p. 348B), on the triumphal arch (p. 348B), and on the walls above the nave arcades (p. 350B); sometimes piers and arch soffits were likewise treated. In the period when most of these basilicas were decorated there were no set rules of iconography to govern the composition and position of the pictures, as in the Byzantine churches from the eleventh century onwards (p. 380). The mosaics were set up purely for decorative purposes, rather than as a pictorial explanation of the bible, and indeed much of the subject matter was of a dedicatory, votive or ceremonial nature. The early mosaics, with lifelike figures set in landscapes, gave way to frontally posed figures with large staring eyes and brilliantly coloured vesture, below which dangled the feet. They appeared set in colourful frames, as in S. Demetrius, and later against plain gold backgrounds. The method of execution was coarse and bold, and no attempt at neatness of joint or regularity in the bedding of the mosaic appear to have been made; but such apparent lack of care resulted in the vitality and iridescence which characterize the best examples of this art. Pavements were formed from the abundant store of old marbles in Rome, and slices of columns were laid as centres to surrounding bands of inlay in intricate geometric patterns (p. 355A) as at S. Lorenzo (p. 369Q) and SS. Giovanni e Paolo (p. 369T).

EXAMPLES

BASILICAN CHURCHES

Basilicas (Gk. *basilikos*=kingly) or Roman halls of justice probably served the early Christians as models for their churches, which thus form a connecting link between buildings of pagan Classic times and those of the Romanesque period which followed. Some authorities, however, believe Early Christian churches to have been evolved from Roman dwelling-houses, where the community had been in the habit of assembling, from the 'scholae' or lecture rooms of the philosophers, or even from pagan temples (p. 277C). Others trace the general plan and arrangement to the catacombs outside Rome, where some of the earliest Christian services were held. A basilican church was usually erected over the burial-place of the saint to whom the church was dedicated. The approach to the church was through an atrium or open forecourt surrounded by arcades. Next came the covered narthex, between the atrium and the church, which was assigned to penitents. The narthex opened into the nave, lighted by a clear-storey of small windows, with an aisle on either side, usually half the width of the nave. Occasionally there are two aisles on each side of the nave, as in the basilicas of Old S. Peter (p. 353B, C), S. Paolo (p. 353E, F), and S. Giovanni in Laterano. Galleries for women were sometimes placed over the aisles, as at S. Agnese (p. 356A, C, D, E) and S. Lorenzo, Rome (p. 355A), but otherwise the sexes sat on opposite sides of the nave. There is no 'bema' (Gk. platform) in S. Clemente, but this feature is found in other basilicas such as S. Peter's, Rome (p. 352), and may have been the germ of the Mediaeval transept which later converted the plan into a Latin cross. Some consider, however, that this cruciform plan was derived from buildings which had been erected for sepulchral purposes, as, for example, the Tomb of Galla Placidia (p. 367). A choir, which became necessary owing to the growth of ritual, was enclosed by low screen walls or 'cancelli' (hence 'chancel') and was provided with an 'ambo' or pulpit on either side, dating from the first church, from which the Gospel and Epistle were read (pp. 349H, K, 350A). In the apse or sanctuary the bishop took the central place, which had been that of the 'praetor' in the Roman basilica, and the presbyters, or members of the church council, occupied seats on either side corresponding to those used by the Roman 'assessors'. The altar, in front of the apse, which in the basilica had been used for libations or sacrifices to the gods, was placed immediately over the burial place of the titulary saint and adapted for the celebration of Christian rites. A ciborium, also known as a tabernacle or baldachino, was erected on columns over the altar.

S. Clemente, Rome (1099–1108) (pp. 349, 350A), was rebuilt over a much earlier church, some of the foundations of which still survive in the crypt. The present church retains the original arrangement and fittings and shows the suitability of the basilican plan for Christian ritual and for sheltering a number of worshippers. An atrium or open rectangular forecourt (p. 349B), surrounded by arcades, forms an imposing approach to the church, and in the centre is a fountain of water for ablutions. This is followed by the narthex, or entrance porch, which opens into the nave and single aisles. In the apse semi-dome is an early twelfth-century mosaic depicting the triumph over the cross. The church is now decorated in Baroque style.

The **Basilican Church of S. Peter, Rome** (330) (p. 353A–C), erected by Constantine near the site of the martyrdom of S. Peter in the circus of Nero, was pulled down to make way for the present cathedral (p. 839). The atrium led through the narthex to the great nave with double aisles terminating in five arches, the central

BASILICAN CHURCH ⁑ S. PETER : ROME

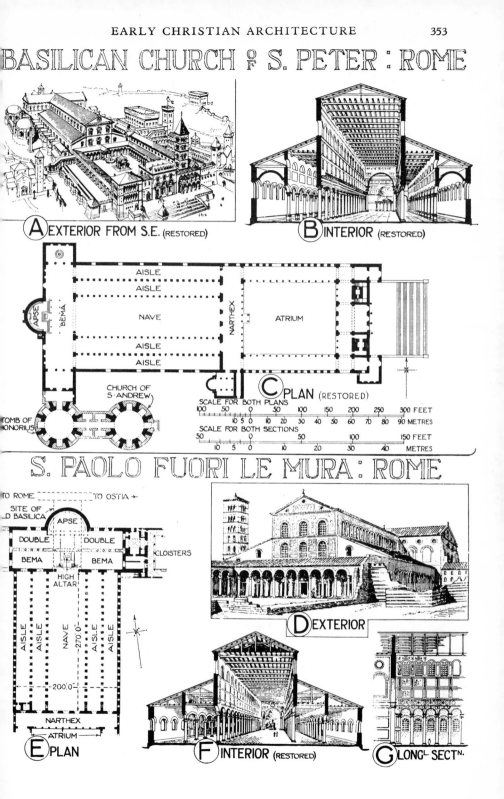

Ⓐ EXTERIOR FROM S.E. (RESTORED)

Ⓑ INTERIOR (RESTORED)

AISLE
AISLE
NAVE
AISLE
AISLE
APSE
BEMA
NARTHEX
ATRIUM

CHURCH OF S·ANDREW

TOMB OF HONORIUS

Ⓒ PLAN (RESTORED)

SCALE FOR BOTH PLANS
100   50   0   50   100   150   200   250   300 FEET
        10 5 0   10   20   30   40   50   60   70   80   90 METRES

SCALE FOR BOTH SECTIONS
50   0   50   100   150 FEET
     10 5 0   10   20   30   40 METRES

S. PAOLO FUORI LE MURA : ROME

TO ROME   TO OSTIA →
SITE OF OLD BASILICA
APSE
DOUBLE   DOUBLE
BEMA   BEMA   CLOISTERS
HIGH ALTAR
AISLE AISLE NAVE AISLE AISLE
        270'·0"
        200'·0"
NARTHEX
ATRIUM

Ⓔ PLAN

Ⓓ EXTERIOR

Ⓕ INTERIOR (RESTORED)

Ⓖ LONGL· SECTN·

of which was called the arch of triumph (p. 353B, C). Beyond was the bema and the sanctuary or semicircular apse with the Pope's seat against the centre of the wall. The priest, as in all Early Christian basilican churches, stood behind the altar and faced east, as the chancel was in this case at the west end (p. 353C).

S. Giovanni in Laterano, Rome (330) is also a double-aisled basilica, but has been so much altered at various times, particularly in the mid-seventeenth and late nineteenth centuries, as to have lost its original Early Christian character.

S. Paolo fuori le Mura, Rome (pp. 353D-G, 369G), founded in 380, was destroyed in 1823, but was rebuilt on the original design, and is the largest and most impressive of all basilican churches. The nave has eighty great columns of Simplon granite, with mosaic mural medallions of the Popes above. The arch of triumph with fifth-century mosaics, the double bema, the apse with mosaics of the thirteenth century, and the remarkable high altar with its double baldachino over the confessio of S. Paul, all contribute to the grandeur of the interior.

S. Maria Maggiore, Rome (432) (p. 350B), was built by Pope Sixtus III and is the only church of which there is evidence that it was originally a pagan basilica. The interior (p. 350B) is the most beautiful of the single-aisled basilicas, with its ranges of Ionic columns of Hymettian marble and entablature surmounted by the original mosaics of Sixtus III, some of which were destroyed when the transepts were added in 1290. The mosaic panels deal with Old Testament history, and among the twenty-seven that remain are scenes such as the Crossing of the Red Sea and the Fall of Jericho. On the triumphal arch are bands of mosaic depicting the childhood of Christ according to an apocryphal infancy gospel. The present apse dates from 1290 and the coffered ceiling of the nave was added in 1500.

S. Lorenzo fuori le Mura, Rome (p. 355A), is the product of two churches with their apses placed back to back, as in the temple of Venus and Rome, Rome (p. 280). The two churches, of which one was founded in 432 and the other rebuilt in 578, were joined in 1216 by the removal of the apses and insertion of columns. There are some mosaics on the faces of the arch at the intersection of the buildings and an inscription recording the enlargement of the church. Because of differences in the level of the two churches, the eastern half was provided with a gallery.

S. Sabina, Rome (422-32) (p. 357A, B), although often altered, retains its original character. The basilican plan has nave and aisles separated by twenty-four Corinthian columns of Proconnesian marble supporting semicircular arches, plain clear-storey walls and a simple open timber roof. The mosaics in the apse date from 822 and portray female personifications of the Churches of the Jews and Gentiles.

S. Agnese fuori le Mura, Rome (625-38) (pp. 356, 369A), was founded by Constantine in 324 over the tomb of S. Agnese. It shares with S. Lorenzo fuori le Mura the peculiarity of having aisles in two storeys. Between nave and aisles are sixteen ancient columns supporting arches, with smaller gallery columns above. The apse with altar and baldachino is at the western end, and mosaics in the semi-dome (1525) represent S. Agnese between two popes (p. 369A). The exterior, with simple clear-storey windows, is plain and the apse in flanked by a campanile (776) (p. 356B).

S. Stefano Rotondo, Rome (468-83) (pp. 355B, 366), is the largest circular church in existence, having a diameter of 64 m (210 ft). A central circular area is encompassed by concentric inner and outer ambulatories. The outer of these is divided into eight segments by the four chapels which radiate, in cross-formation, from the inner ambulatory; the general appearance of the building is a cross within a circle. The high central and inner ambulatory roofs are supported by two rings of columns from older buildings; the outer range supports arches and the inner a

A. S. Lorenzo fuori le Mura, Rome. Interior looking towards sanctuary. (Two churches dating from 432 and 578 respectively, joined together in 1216.) See p. 354

B. S. Stefano Rotondo, Rome (468–83): interior. See p. 354

S. AGNESE FUORI LE MURA: ROME

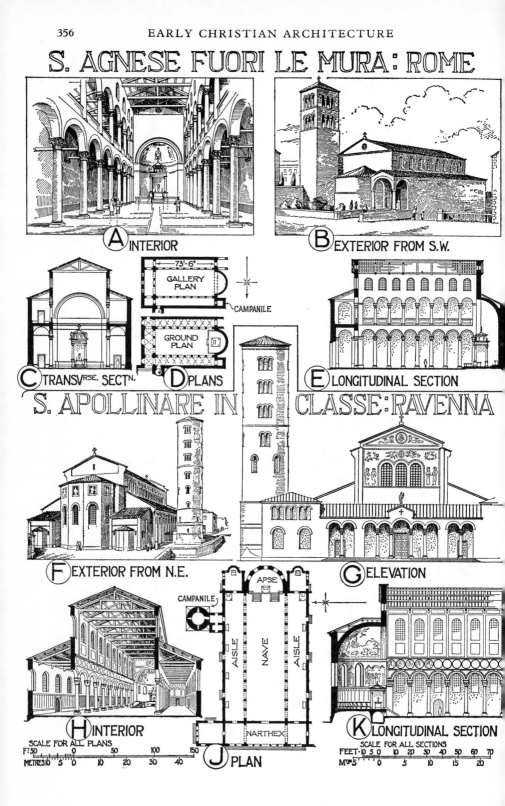

(A) INTERIOR

(B) EXTERIOR FROM S.W.

(C) TRANSVᴿˢᴱ· SECTᴺ·

GALLERY PLAN — 73'-6"

CAMPANILE

GROUND PLAN

(D) PLANS

(E) LONGITUDINAL SECTION

S. APOLLINARE IN CLASSE: RAVENNA

(F) EXTERIOR FROM N.E.

(G) ELEVATION

(H) INTERIOR

CAMPANILE

APSE

AISLE NAVE AISLE

NARTHEX

(J) PLAN

(K) LONGITUDINAL SECTION

SCALE FOR ALL PLANS
FT.50 0 50 100 150
METRES 10 5 0 10 20 30 40

SCALE FOR ALL SECTIONS
FEET 10 5 0 10 20 30 40 50 60 70
Mᵀˢ·5 0 5 10 15 20

A. The basilican church of S. Sabina, Rome (422–32). See p. 354

B. S. Sabina, Rome: interior

horizontal architrave. Two central columns and a cross wall give additional support to the main roof timbers. It is possible that originally the central space was roofed by a dome of very light materials. This, and the arrangement of the outer ambulatory, can be seen in the suggested reconstruction (p. 366B).

S. Apollinare Nuovo, Ravenna (493–525), was erected by Theodoric the Great adjacent to his palace. It is a single-aisled basilica with a nave which terminates in an apse that has been rebuilt, in recent times, less its decorations. The nave has a coffered ceiling and is greater in height than in breadth. These proportions, together with an ample admittance of light, create an atmosphere of spaciousness within the church. Above the nave arcades are the world-famous mosaics, the lower bands of which portray processions of saints. On the north wall twenty-two female saints, led by the Magi, advance towards the Virgin and Child; on the opposite wall twenty-six male martyrs process from Theodoric's Palace to the enthroned Christ at the end of the frieze. The church has a magnificent cylindrical campanile with windows which increase in width from single to double, and finally to treble, openings at the top of the tower.

S. Apollinare in Classe, Ravenna (534–9) (pp. 348, 356, 369E, H, J), was erected by the Emperor Justinian on the site of a temple of Apollo and, like the church S. Apollinare Nuovo, was probably built by Byzantine craftsmen, for here the influence of Constantinople was strong. The simple plan forms a single-aisled basilican church, 45.7 m (150 ft) × 30 m (98 ft). The atrium has disappeared, but a narthex leads into the church. The eastern apse, which is circular internally and polygonal externally, is raised above the crypt and contains a high altar with ciborium. On the north is one of the earliest circular campanili, of the same date. The interior is impressive with nave arcade of cipollino columns, Byzantine capitals, and dosseret blocks (pp. 348B, 369E, J) supporting arches, above which is the band, 1.5 m (5 ft) high, of portraits of bishops of Ravenna. The aspidal mosaics, among the finest in Ravenna, are of the sixth and seventh centuries. In highly symbolical form the Transfiguration and the Last Judgement share the apse semi-dome.

Torcello Cathedral (rebuilt 1008) (pp. 359A, B, 394B), is dedicated to S. Maria Assunta. It still has the foundations of the original bishop's throne flanked by six rising tiers of seats in the main apse, which gives a good idea of Early Christian arrangements. There are some fine mosaics in two of the apses and on the west wall of the nave, the latter depicting the Last Judgement in a series of imaginative and macabre scenes. This church, with the towering mass of the campanile and the Byzantine church of S. Fosca (pp. 393, 394B), compose an historic group.

Syracuse Cathedral, Sicily (p. 359C), still clearly shows how a pagan temple of Athena (p. 206) was converted in 640 into a Christian church, by the construction of a wall between its peristyle columns and the formation of openings in its cella walls.

The Church of the Nativity, Bethlehem (330) (p. 360A–D), founded by Constantine over the traditional birthplace of Christ and rebuilt 527–65, is one of a number of basilican churches in Palestine and Syria erected between the third and seventh centuries, before the Moslem hordes overran the country. It is surrounded by a high wall which encloses the precincts of the Latins, Greeks and Armenians, who jointly own the church. This historic building, with the monolithic Corinthian columns, 5.8 m (19 ft) high, of the nave and double aisles, and the three apses of the sanctuary, is still, in spite of restorations, grand in its simplicity of plan and must have been peculiarly suitable to receive the immense number of worshippers at the birth-shrine of the founder of Christianity. There are some seventh- and eleventh-century mosaics in the sanctuary and nave.

The Church of the Holy Sepulchre, Jerusalem (p. 360E–G), erected by Constantine over the reputed tomb of Christ, defaced and damaged by the Persians and

A. Torcello Cathedral, near Venice (rebuilt 1008). Apsidal end. See p. 358

B. Torcello Cathedral: interior
showing screen and sanctuary

C. Syracuse Cathedral. Converted
(640) from Greek Doric Temple of
Athena (c. 480 B.C.). See p. 358

CHURCH OF THE NATIVITY : BETHLEHEM

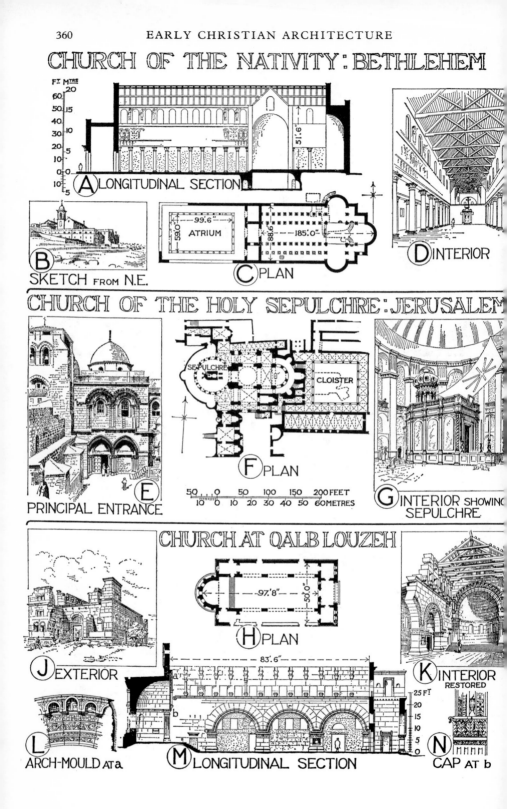

A LONGITUDINAL SECTION

B SKETCH FROM N.E.

C PLAN

99'.6"
ATRIUM
59'.0"
88'.6"
185'.0"

51'.6"

D INTERIOR

CHURCH OF THE HOLY SEPULCHRE : JERUSALEM

E PRINCIPAL ENTRANCE

F PLAN

SEPULCHRE
CLOISTER

50 0 50 100 150 200 FEET
10 0 10 20 30 40 50 60 METRES

G INTERIOR SHOWING SEPULCHRE

CHURCH AT QALB LOUZEH

H PLAN

97'.8"
50'.0"

J EXTERIOR

K INTERIOR RESTORED

L ARCH-MOULD AT a

M LONGITUDINAL SECTION

83'.6"

25 FT
20
15
10
5
0

N CAP AT b

Moslems, rebuilt by Crusaders and often restored, appears to date from the twelfth century, for its architecture resembles that of Sicily in that period. The entrance (1140) (p. 360E) leads into the transept, to the left of which is the rotunda, rebuilt by the Crusaders 1099, with the Holy Sepulchre itself, reconstructed in recent times; while on the right is the church of the Crusaders. This circular type was copied at S. Gereon, Cologne (p. 723); Little Maplestead, Essex; S. Sepulchre, Cambridge; Northampton; Ludlow Castle Chapel, and the Temple Church, London.

The **Church at Qalb Louzeh** (sixth century) (p. 360H–N), in Syria, has a basilican plan with entrance flanked by two towers, and nave separated by piers carrying semicircular arches. Above are corbels supporting short columns to carry the roof trusses. The church exhibits many points common to all Syrian churches, which broke away from the Roman type owing to distance from the capital.

S. Francesco, Ravenna (560) (p. 363A) was erected by Bishop Neone, and is divided by two rows of columns of Greek marble. From 1261–1810 it was in the hands of Franciscan friars who gave it its name, and during this period it was remodelled. Further restoration took place in 1921.

S. George, Salonica (c. 300) (p. 362), a circular edifice, was built close to the triumphal arch and palace of Galerius. A dome 24.4 m (80 ft) in diameter covers the building internally but does not show externally, as a shallow conical timber roof with tiles was placed over it—one of the earliest examples of an inner dome covered by a timber roof. Eight barrel-vaulted recesses almost penetrate the full thickness of the walls (p. 362B); above these is a ring of windows with a further series of small arches just below the dome. In about 400 it was converted for use as a Christian church, when the eastern recess was enlarged and extended to form a chancel and apse. An ambulatory was erected round the building and the end walls of the other recesses were pierced to open into it. A narthex was added to the west. The lower zone of the dome is decorated with a band of mosaic depicting sixteen martyrs set against an architectural background; inscribed beside them are their names, their roles in life and festival months. The Rotunda, as it is also called, was used as a mosque during the Turkish occupation of Salonica, and a minaret was added. The ambulatory and narthex no longer exist, and the building is now a museum.

S. Demetrius, Salonica (475–500) (p. 365A), is a basilican church with a central nave flanked by double aisles and crossed by transepts at the bema. All of the aisles have galleries and each has a separate roof. Though severely damaged by fire in the seventh century and again in 1917, it has on each occasion been reconstructed to the plans laid down in the late fifth century. Such materials as were spared by the last fire have been used in the rebuilding of the present church, and some of the very fine mosaic panels have been set up again.

The **Church of the Virgin, S. Catherine's Monastery, Mt Sinai** (mid-sixth century) (p. 363B). The complex of church, conventual buildings, and barracks for the protecting garrison, is enclosed within a high wall. It was built by Justinian's order as a fortress shrine on the traditional site of the Burning Bush on Mount Sinai. A narthex, flanked by towers, leads into the well preserved double-aisled basilica, which still has the original carved and inscribed beams to the nave roof, which is of open timber construction. Each aisle has a separate roof, though they have been merged into one on part of the south side. The church is an example of the way in which rather coarse local architecture has been embellished with decorations of the highest technical and artistic merit; in this case probably executed by mosaicists from Constantinople. The mosaic in the apse semi-dome depicts the Transfiguration; this scene is bordered by medallions of prophets, apostles and the

A. Exterior

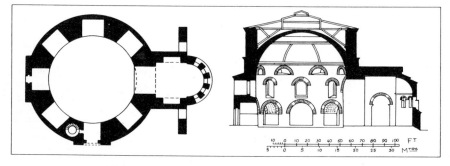

B. Plan   C. Longitudinal section

S. George, Salonica (*c.* 300). See p. 361

A. S. Francesco, Ravenna (560). See p. 361

B. S. Catherine's Monastery, Mount Sinai (mid-6th cent.). See p. 361

Abbot Longinus, in whose time, states the integral inscription, this work was carried out. Because of S. Catherine's remoteness from the capital it escaped the ravages of the Iconoclast movement (726–843), and so mosaics from the most flourishing period under Justinian were preserved.

In Asia Minor, as at Ancyra, Pergamon and Hierapolis; in North Africa as at Algiers; and also in Egypt, where the early Christians were known as Copts, there are a number of basilican churches of the period, but in all the style died out owing to the Moslem conquest in the seventh century.

ETHIOPIAN ROCK CHURCHES

Aksum, in the Tigre province of Ethiopia, was the centre of a notable civilization from the first to the tenth century A.D. The Aksumite kings were converted to Christianity, beginning with Ezana in 341. In the tenth century a foreign invasion under a semitic queen, Judith, led to the destruction of many monuments, although a number of stelae, cut from solid granite and carved, survive from the Aksumite age. In the twelfth and thirteenth centuries Zagwe rulers settled in Lasta (a little to the south of Aksum), creating a centre at Roha, now called Lalibela after a king of that name (1190–1222), who directed the cutting of eleven rock churches in one complex, and countless more in the surrounding mountains. With the replacement of the Zagwe dynasty by the Solomonid line in 1270, the building of churches revived in the Tigre, but almost all were razed by fanatic Moslem hordes in 1525–40, leaving only those indestructibly carved from the rock.

The churches at and around **Lalibela** (twelfth to fourteenth century) are of volcanic tufa; some, like **Giorgis Church** (p. 365B), are monolithic, others have only the façades cut free. The interiors, columns, lintels and arches are decorated, often with Aksumite detail. In the Tigre 130 rock churches (fourteenth to fifteenth century) of limestone and sandstone are still in use, only three with façades hewn from the rock. Abreha, at Atsbeha; Cherkos, at Wkro; and Mike'al, at Amba are five-aisled in width and at least three bays in depth, with high transverse barrel vault and crossing. Jesus, Archnao Saharti; Maryam, Korkor; Mike'al, Barka; Maryam, Wkro; Gabriel, Wukien, and many others, are three-aisled with three, four or five bays, centre apse and chapels. One or more arks are a feature (the Ark of the Covenant is traditionally believed to have been brought to Ethiopia by the son of King Solomon and the Queen of Sheba). Sometimes the walls have paintings and the rock roofs may be carved with patterns derived from wooden lantern roofs. There are stepped, square-cut or bracket capitals, with chamfered columns, in the finer examples.

BAPTISTERIES

Separate buildings used only for the sacrament of baptism were a feature of Early Christianity. For this rite, Roman circular temples and tombs were occasionally used. As the rite was administered only on three great Christian festivals—Easter, Pentecost and Epiphany—these buildings had to be of considerable size, and until the end of the sixth century of our era they sometimes adjoined the atrium or forecourt of the church; but after this period, and especially with the introduction of infant baptism, the baptistery was replaced by a font in the church, close to the entrance. When circular Roman temples or tombs were modified to meet the new requirements, these sometimes had to be enlarged. It was difficult to cover the enclosed area with one roof supported only by outside walls, and therefore, whereas the Romans had used internal columns attached to the walls in a decorative way,

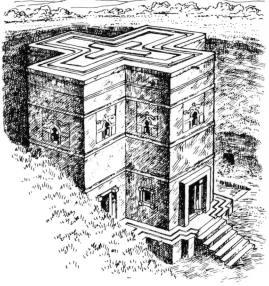

A. S. Demetrius, Salonica (475–500): nave. See p. 361

B. Giorgis Church, Lalibela, Ethiopia. See p. 364

C. Tomb of Galla Placidia, Ravenna (c. 425). See p. 367

S. STEFANO ROTONDO : ROME

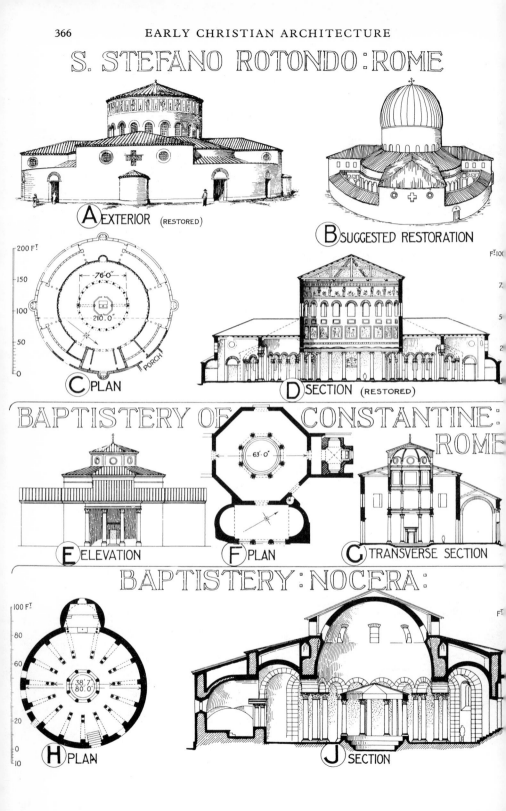

Ⓐ EXTERIOR (RESTORED)

Ⓑ SUGGESTED RESTORATION

Ⓒ PLAN

Ⓓ SECTION (RESTORED)

BAPTISTERY OF CONSTANTINE : ROME

Ⓔ ELEVATION

Ⓕ PLAN

Ⓖ TRANSVERSE SECTION

BAPTISTERY : NOCERA :

Ⓗ PLAN

Ⓙ SECTION

the Early Christians used columns constructively to support the central roof, and surrounded the whole with a one-storeyed aisle enclosed by an outer wall, which supported a lower roof (p. 366E–J).

The **Baptistery of Constantine, Rome** (432–40) (p. 366E, F, G), built near the Lateran church by Sixtus III, and not by Constantine to whom it is generally attributed, is among the oldest of Italian baptisteries, of which it was probably the model. It is octagonal and the roof is supported by a two-storeyed ring of eight porphyry and marble columns taken from old pagan buildings, while in the centre is an old Roman bath of green basalt converted into a font.

The **Orthodox Baptistery, Ravenna** (400–450), was completed and decorated under Bishop Neone for the Orthodox community. It is octagonal with two internal wall arcades one above the other, similarly placed to the superimposed columns in the Mausoleum of Diocletian, now the Cathedral, at Spalato (Split) (p. 314). The upper arcade is subdivided into triple arches under each main arch, the earliest example of a treatment which became so usual in the Romanesque period (p. 465D). The dome, constructed of hollow tiles, has fine fifth-century mosaics representing the baptism of Christ.

The **Baptistery, Nocera** (p. 366H, J) is various dated from the mid-fourth to the sixth century. It is 24.4 m (80 ft) in diameter and has a ring of thirty antique columns, in pairs, supporting the dome which is covered externally by a wooden roof. A barrel-vaulted ambulatory encircles the central domed area. In the middle of the building is an octagonal font with eight columns and steps descending into it.

TOMBS

Up to the fourth century, burial within city boundaries was usually prohibited by law, but the Christian objection to cremation and insistence on burial in consecrated ground, together with the desire to provide monumental tombs which were at once an expression of the Christian faith in immortality and a memorial to the dead, led to the erection of imposing structures, which were usually domed and often enriched with lavish mosaic decorations.

S. Costanza, Rome (330) (p. 368A, B, C, D, E), erected by Constantine for his daughter Constantia, was converted into a church in 1256. The entrance leads to the central space, 12.2 m (40 ft) in diameter, encircled by twelve pairs of coupled granite columns which support the dome, and it has a surrounding aisle covered with a barrel vault, ornamented with mosaics of the fourth century representing the vintage.

The **Tomb of Galla Placidia, Ravenna** (c. 425) (pp. 365C, 368F, G, H, J), is a very early example of a building cruciform in plan, and extremely interesting, as the sarcophagi still remain in their original positions in the arms of the cross. Of simple appearance externally, the walls of brickwork are relieved by shallow blind arches. A square tower, roofed by a shallow pyramid, conceals the unusual dome in which both dome and pendentives are a part of the same sphere (p. 378B). The walls are lined with marble slabs and the dome and vaults still retain the original mosaics on a blue background.

The **Tomb of Theodoric, Ravenna** (530) (p. 368K, L, M), is in two storeys, of which the lower, a decagon externally 13.7 m (45 ft) in diameter, encloses a cruciform crypt, while the upper storey is circular internally and has traces of an external arcade. The extraordinary roof is formed of one huge slab of stone weighing 470 tons and hollowed into a flattish dome, 10.7 m (35 ft) in diameter, on which stone handles are formed for hoisting it into position. The ashes of the founder were deposited in an urn above the dome.

S. COSTANZA : ROME

20 M^{TES}

F^{T} 60 — 50 — 15 — 40 — 10 — 30 — 20 — 5 — 10 — 0

40'-0"

(A) ELEVATION

(B) SECTION ON a·a

F^{T} 100 — 30 M^{TES} — 80 — 25 — 60 — 20 — 15 — 40 — 10 — 20 — 5 — 0

74'-0"
40'-0"

(C) SECTIONAL VIEW

(D) PLAN (RESTORED)

(E) INTERIOR

TOMB OF GALLA PLACIDIA : RAVENNA

KEY DIAGRAM OF DOME

33'-0"

(F) EXTERIOR

(G) PLAN

(H) TRANSVERSE SECT^{N}

(J) INTERIOR

TOMB OF THEODORIC : RAVENNA

UPPER CHAMBER   LOWER CHAMBER

(K) EXTERIOR

(L) PLAN

(M) SECTION

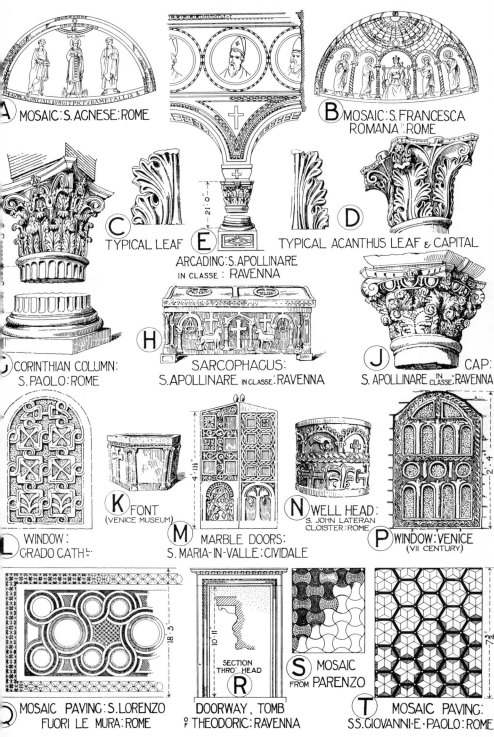

A MOSAIC: S. AGNESE: ROME

B MOSAIC: S. FRANCESCA ROMANA: ROME

C TYPICAL LEAF

D TYPICAL ACANTHUS LEAF & CAPITAL

E ARCADING: S. APOLLINARE IN CLASSE: RAVENNA

21'·0"

G CORINTHIAN COLUMN: S. PAOLO: ROME

H SARCOPHAGUS: S. APOLLINARE IN CLASSE: RAVENNA

J CAP: S. APOLLINARE IN CLASSE: RAVENNA

K FONT (VENICE MUSEUM)

L WINDOW: GRADO CATH.

M MARBLE DOORS: S. MARIA-IN-VALLE: CIVIDALE

4'·11¾"

N WELL HEAD: S. JOHN LATERAN CLOISTER: ROME

P WINDOW: VENICE (VII CENTURY)

2'·4"

Q MOSAIC PAVING: S. LORENZO FUORI LE MURA: ROME

18'·3"

R DOORWAY, TOMB OF THEODORIC: RAVENNA

10'·11"

SECTION THRO' HEAD

S MOSAIC FROM PARENZO

T MOSAIC PAVING: SS. GIOVANNI·E·PAOLO: ROME

7¾"

BIBLIOGRAPHY

BROWN, G. BALDWIN. *From Schola to Cathedral*. Edinburgh, 1886.

BUNSEN, C. C. J. *Die Basiliken des christlichen Roms*. Munich, 1843.

BUTLER, A. J. *The Ancient Coptic Churches of Egypt*. 2 vols. Oxford, 1884.

BUTLER, H. C. *Ancient Architecture in Syria: Expedition 1904–5*. 2 vols. Leyden, 1907–20.

BUXTON, D. R. 'The Christian Antiquities of Northern Ethiopia.' *Archaeologia XCII*, London, 1947.

—. 'The Rock-hewn and other Mediaeval Churches of the Tigre Province.' *Archaeologia CIII*, 1971.

CLAUSSE, G. *Les monuments du christianisme au Moyen Age*. 2 vols. Paris, 1893.

CORTE, A. MONTI DELLA. *Lalibela: Le Chiese Ipogee e Monolitiche e gli altre monumenti medievale del Lasta*. Rome, 1940.

CUMMINGS, C. A. *A History of Architecture in Italy*. 2 vols. New York, 1901; London, 1928.

DAVIES, J. G. *The Origin and Development of Early Christian Architecture*. London, 1952.

FROTHINGHAM, A. L. *Monuments of Christian Rome*. New York, 1908.

GERSTER, G. *Kirchen im Fels*. Stuttgart, 1968; English translation, 1971. Has important bibliography.

HARVEY, W. *Church of the Nativity, Bethlehem*. Oxford and London, 1935.

—. *Church of the Holy Sepulchre, Jerusalem*. Oxford and London, 1935.

HODDINOTT, R. F. *Early Byzantine Churches in Macedonia and Southern Serbia*. London, 1963.

HUBSCH, H. *Monuments de l'architecture chrétienne depuis Constantin jusqu'à Charlemagne*. Paris, 1866.

KRAUTHEIMER, R. *Early Christian and Byzantine Architecture*. Harmondsworth, 1965.

LEROUX, G. *Les origines de l'édifice hypostyle*. Paris, 1913.

MARUCCHI, O. *Basiliques et églises de Rome*. Paris, 1902.

MEER, F. VAN DER, and MOHRMANN, CHRISTINE. *Atlas of the Early Christian World*. English translation by Mary F. Hedlund and H. H. Rowley. London, 1958.

MICHEL, A. *Histoire de l'art*. Vol. i, pt. i. Paris, 1905.

PLANT, R. 'Rock Churches of the Tigre Province.' *Ethiopia Observer* XIII, no. 2, 1970.

—. 'Notes on 17 newly discovered rock-hewn churches of the Tigre.' *Ethiopia Observer* XVI, no. 1, 1973.

RIVOIRA, G. T. *Lombardic Architecture*. English translation by G. McN. Rushforth. 2 vols. London, 1910.

SOTIRIOU, G., and M. *I Basiliki tou Agiou Dimitriou, Thessalonikis*. Athens, 1952.

STEWART, CECIL. *Early Christian, Byzantine and Romanesque Architecture* (vol. ii of Simpson, F. M., *History of Architectural Development*). London, 1954.

STRZYGOWSKI, J. *Orient oder Rom*. Leipzig, 1901; *Kleinasien*. Leipzig, 1903; *Byzantinische Denkmäler*. 3 vols. Vienna, 1891–1903; and *Early Church Art in Northern Europe*. London, 1928.

VOGÜÉ, MARQUIS DE. *Les églises de la Terre-Sainte*. Paris, 1860.

—. *Syrie centrale*. 2 vols. Paris, 1865–7.

WULFF, O. *Altchristliche Kunst*. Berlin and Potsdam, 1914.

XYNGOPOULOS, A. *I Basiliki tou Agiou Dimitriou*. Thessalonika, 1946.

13

BYZANTINE ARCHITECTURE

330–1453 and later

INFLUENCES

GEOGRAPHICAL

Byzantium, renamed Constantinople* after Constantine the Great, its Imperial founder, and also called 'New Rome', was inaugurated as capital of the Roman Empire in 330. It stood at the junction of the Bosphorus and the Sea of Marmora, where Europe and Asia are divided by only a narrow strip of water. This gave it a commanding and central position for the government of the eastern and most valuable part of the Roman Empire. It was also at the intersection of two great highways of commerce, the water highway between the Black Sea and Mediterranean, and the trade route between Europe and Asia; and thus it controlled the corn trade from the northern shores of the Euxine. The natural harbour of the Golden Horn possesses unusual advantages for commerce; for it is four miles in length, unaffected by tides, and of sufficient depth to render its quays accessible to ships of deep draught. Byzantine art pervaded all parts of the Eastern Roman Empire and was carried by traders to Greece, Serbia, Russia, Asia Minor, North Africa and further west, where it is found in Venice, Ravenna, and Périgueux, and it had considerable influence on the architecture of these districts. Venice, by her situation, was a connecting link between the Byzantine and Frankish Empires, and a depot for merchandise from both East and West.

GEOLOGICAL

Constantinople had no good building stone, and local materials such as clay for bricks and rubble for concrete were employed. Other materials more monumental in character had therefore to be imported; marble was brought from the quarries in the islands and along the shores of the Eastern Mediterranean to Constantinople, which was the chief marble-working centre and supplied all parts of the Roman Empire. Byzantine architecture was further considerably influenced by the multitude of monolithic columns of such sizes as were obtainable from the different quarries. These were even introduced into the underground cisterns for the water storage of this Imperial city.

CLIMATIC

The Romans adapted their methods of building to suit the needs of the new eastern capital and to those conditions of life which had there already created traditional forms of art: thus flat roofs for summer resort were combined with oriental domes, and these, with small windows often high up in otherwise unbroken walls, formed the chief features of the style, and sheltering arcades surrounded the open courts.

* The name Constantinople is retained in the text of this chapter, although the city has been renamed Istanbul.

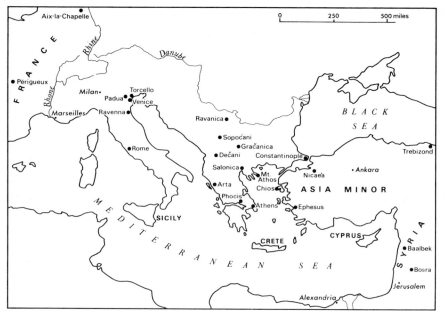

The Byzantine Empire

HISTORICAL AND SOCIAL

Byzantium was founded as a Greek colony *c*. 660 B.C., and in A.D. 330 became the capital of the Roman Empire. On the death of the Emperor Theodosius I (395) the Empire was finally divided, and Byzantium continued to be the capital of the Eastern Empire, and throughout the Middle Ages was the bulwark of Christianity against the attacks of Slav barbarians on the west, and of Moslems on the east. Honorius (395–423), the first Western Emperor of the newly divided Empire, removed his residence from Rome to Ravenna on the east coast of Italy (404), and consequently there was great building activity in that city, which, from its position, was peculiarly susceptible to Byzantine influence. A further impetus was given to building when Ravenna became an archiepiscopal see in 438. During the reign of Justinian (527–565) Sicily and Italy were recovered to the Eastern Empire, and this new connection promoted a revival of building in Italy; here again Byzantine influence came into play, and from before 584 to 752 Ravenna was the seat of the exarch or representative of the Byzantine Emperors, and its buildings of this period became of a still more pronounced Byzantine type. The history of the Byzantine Empire from the fifth to the eleventh century is one of fluctuating and gradually declining fortunes. It first lost its western provinces in the fifth century, some of which, including Italy and Sicily, were regained in the sixth century under Justinian; while again in the following century its strength was greatly reduced by conflict with the Persians, but yet once more in the eighth century the Empire somewhat recovered itself, till in the ninth century it was again strong enough to carry on fierce contests against the Moslems, who were long kept at bay on the eastern side. In the eleventh century the decline was accelerated because, besides having enemies on the east and north, the Empire was now attacked by Normans and

S. Sophia, Constantinople, from S.W. (532–7). See p. 383.
The minarets are a Turkish addition

S. Sophia, Constantinople: interior looking towards apse (532–7). See p. 383

Venetians, till the 'Latin occupation' of Constantinople was accomplished in 1204 and lasted to 1261 (see Chapter 19). The old Empire still lingered on for nearly two hundred years, but its vitality had been sapped by internal dissensions and continuous warfare against the Persians and Turks, and it was finally captured by Ottoman Turks in 1453. Nevertheless, the spirit of the Byzantine Empire persisted even after the Empire had fallen, especially in Russia and in the Balkans. Constantinople has continued up to the present day as the seat of a Patriarch of the Orthodox Church.

Constantine reviewed the attempt initiated by his predecessor Diocletian (284–305) to provide adequate civil government and military protection throughout the widespread Roman Empire and showed his statesmanship in his manner of dealing with this political problem, just as he did in securing support for himself from the growing power of Christianity by establishing it as the state religion. Diocletian's attempt, however, to solve the difficulty of managing the Eastern Empire from the west of Italy by instituting three seats of government, in addition to that of Rome, had proved ineffectual and open to abuse, and therefore when Constantine in his turn was confronted with the same difficulty he took the bold course of transplanting his capital from Rome to Byzantium (330) because he recognized the political value of its central position in the Empire. Byzantium was an old Greek city, and so the new Imperial buildings were executed by Greek craftsmen untrammelled by Roman traditions. Within the fortifications of Constantine, the new city was laid out on Roman lines, so far as the hills and site allowed. There was the central dividing street running through a succession of six forums of which the original Augusteum was adjoined, not only by S. Sophia, the greatest glory of early Christendom, but also by the Imperial palace, senate house and law courts. The Forum of Constantine, with its great porphyry column, was the centre of commercial life, while, in the Hippodrome hard by, the chariot races took place which were the chief amusement of New Rome, as gladiatorial combat had been of Old Rome. The Hippodrome held the same position in the social life of New Rome as the Colosseum and thermae did in Old Rome, and was indeed used for all purposes and on all occasions—for the election of emperors, burning of martyrs, execution of criminals, and for triumphal processions—and so was truly termed the axis of the Byzantine world. The emperors paid the same attention to the water supply of their new as of their old capital, for water was brought by aqueducts and stored in enormous underground cisterns with roofs upheld by many hundreds of columns. As time went on and the population increased the city of Constantine was extended, and the Great Wall with its famous military gates and many towers was built by Theodosius II (413) to set a circle of land and water fortifications against the attacks of Huns and Goths.

Constantine (306–337), a strong and despotic ruler, was followed by emperors who were too weak to assert their authority, and in 364 the Empire was divided into East and West, with two Emperors. After Theodosius, the first emperor who emerged into prominence was Justinian (527–65), who codified the Roman laws, was a great patron of architecture, and was responsible not only for the rebuilding of S. Sophia, but also for many other churches in the city and in Syria and Palestine. During the Macedonian dynasty (867–1057) and the Comnenian dynasty (1081–1185) there was a remarkable outburst of building activity. In spite of its culture, commercial prosperity and industrial activity, the Byzantine Empire's increasingly isolated situation as a bulwark of Christian civilization, and its exposure to attacks by barbarians from the north and Moslems from the east, led in the end to its destruction. Decay from within facilitated defeat from without. The final crash came when the capital was captured by the Ottoman Turks in 1453.

RELIGIOUS

In the year 313 the Edict of Milan was issued, which granted toleration to Christians, and in 330 Constantinople became the capital of the first Christian Empire. It follows that the chief buildings erected in the new capital were churches for the new religion. At first they were of the basilican Early Christian type, but later the domical Byzantine style was developed. Disputes and differences soon sprang up in the Church and became so rife that the Council of Nicaea (325) was only the first of a series called to suppress heresies. The political division, too, between East and West was followed by a division of the Churches, due in part to the 'Filioque controversy' which developed in the ninth century and eventually culminated in the 'Great Schism' in 1054. The Eastern and Western Churches had been further divided by the 'Iconoclastic movement', which resulted from the decree of the Eastern Emperor, Leo III (717–41), who, fearing that idolatry would be fostered by the use of sculpture, forbade all representations of human or animal forms. Many Greek artists thereupon left Constantinople for Italy, where, under Pope Gregory II, they could carry on their art unmolested by Imperial decrees. This movement resulted in the admission of painted figures in the decoration of Eastern churches, but all statues were still excluded. These controversies and other differences in ritual have vitally affected Byzantine church architecture up to the present day. Byzantine architecture, devoid of statues, has always been and still remains the official style of the Orthodox Church of Greece and eastern Europe which has conserved unchanged its doctrines and ritual. Therefore the architecture also became stereotyped in form through all periods, in sharp contrast with the changes and additions which characterize the developments of mediaeval architecture to suit it to the varying requirements of church economy and ritual in western Europe.

ARCHITECTURAL CHARACTER

The character of Byzantine architecture, which dates from the fifth century to the present day, is determined by the novel development of the dome to cover polygonal and square plans for churches, tombs and baptisteries. The practice of using a domical system of roof construction is in strong contrast to the Early Christian timber trusses and the Romanesque system of stone vaults. It may be broadly stated that the basilican type of plan belongs to Early Christian architecture (Chapter 12) and the domed, centralized type of plan to the Byzantine. At the same time, during the first few centuries of the Byzantine Empire one may find domical constructions in Italy and basilican plans in the Eastern Empire. The system of construction in hand-laid concrete, introduced by the Romans, progressively had become more like regular brickwork, and in this form was adopted by the Byzantines. The carcase of brickwork was first completed and allowed to settle before the interior surface sheathing of unyielding marble slabs was added, and this independence of the component parts is characteristic of Byzantine construction (p. 378G, M). Brickwork, moreover, lent itself externally to decorative caprices in patterns and banding, and internally it was suitable for covering with marble, mosaic and fresco decoration. The Byzantines therefore took great pains in the manufacture of bricks, which were employed alike in military, ecclesiastical and domestic architecture. The ordinary bricks were like the Roman, about 38 mm ($1\frac{1}{2}$ ins) in depth, and were laid on thick beds of mortar. This general use of brickwork necessitated special care in making mortar, which was composed of lime and sand with crushed pottery, tiles or bricks, and much of it remains as hard as that in the best buildings of Rome. The decorative character of external façades depended largely on the arrangement

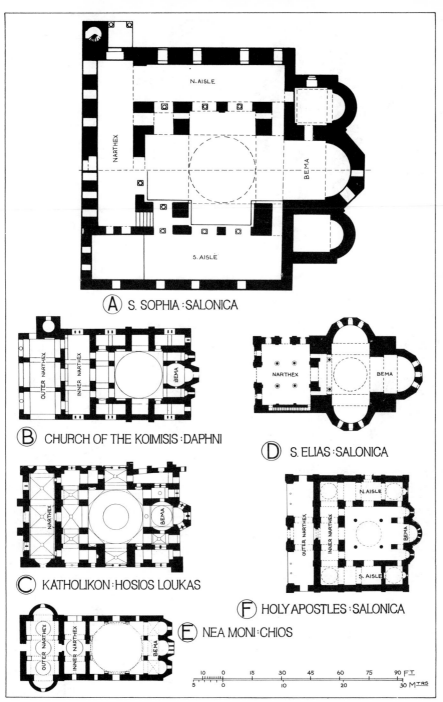

Ⓐ S. SOPHIA : SALONICA

Ⓑ CHURCH OF THE KOIMISIS : DAPHNI

Ⓒ KATHOLIKON : HOSIOS LOUKAS

Ⓓ S. ELIAS : SALONICA

Ⓔ NEA MONI : CHIOS

Ⓕ HOLY APOSTLES : SALONICA

Comparative plans of Byzantine churches

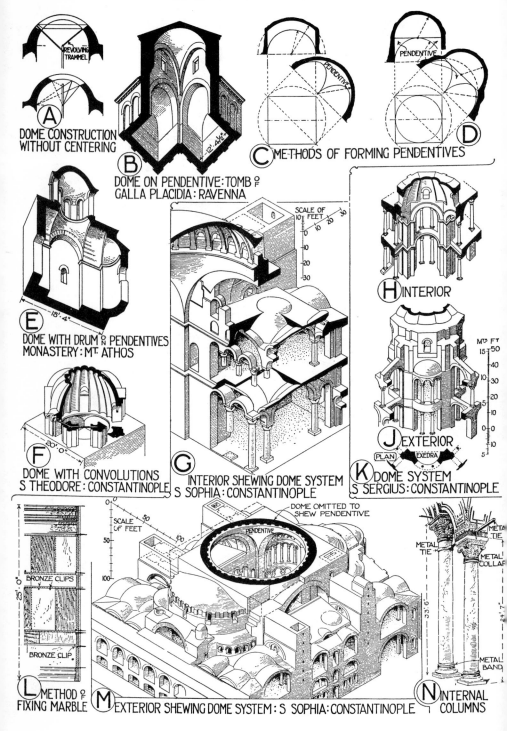

A DOME CONSTRUCTION WITHOUT CENTERING

B DOME ON PENDENTIVE: TOMB ᵒᶠ GALLA PLACIDIA: RAVENNA

C METHODS OF FORMING PENDENTIVES

D

E DOME WITH DRUM ᴺ PENDENTIVES MONASTERY: Mᵀ ATHOS

F DOME WITH CONVOLUTIONS S THEODORE: CONSTANTINOPLE

G INTERIOR SHEWING DOME SYSTEM S SOPHIA: CONSTANTINOPLE

H INTERIOR

J EXTERIOR

K DOME SYSTEM S SERGIUS: CONSTANTINOPLE

L METHOD ᵒᶠ FIXING MARBLE

M EXTERIOR SHEWING DOME SYSTEM: S SOPHIA: CONSTANTINOPLE

N INTERNAL COLUMNS

of the facing bricks, which were not always laid horizontally, but sometimes obliquely, sometimes in the form of the meander fret, sometimes in the chevron or herring-bone pattern, and in many other similar designs, giving great variety to the façades. An attempt was also made to ornament the rough brick exteriors by the use of stone bands and decorative arches.

The dome, which had always been a traditional feature in the East, became the prevailing motif of Byzantine architecture, which was a fusion of the domical construction with the Classical columnar style. Domes of various types (p. 378) were now placed over square compartments by means of 'pendentives' (pp. 374, 378, 384, 391), whereas in Roman architecture domes were only used over circular or polygonal structures. These domes were usually constructed of bricks or of some light porous stone, such as pumice, or even of pottery, as at S. Vitale, Ravenna (p. 382D). Some Byzantine domes and vaults were, it is believed, constructed without temporary support or 'centering' by the simple use of large flat bricks, and this is a quite distinct system probably derived from Eastern methods; that more conventional methods of dome construction were used is evidenced by the survival of a centering board, and imprints of others, in the eleventh-century church of S. John at Ligourio in Greece. Windows were formed in the lower portion of the dome which, in the later period, was hoisted upon a high 'drum'—a feature which was still further developed in western Renaissance architecture by the addition of an external peristyle. At S. Sophia the haunches were strengthened by a ring of small buttresses to compensate for the weakening effect of the window openings (pp. 373, 384A). The grouping of small domes or semi-domes round the large central dome was effective (pp. 373, 378M), and one of the characteristic features of Byzantine churches was that the forms of the vaults and domes were visible externally, undisguised by any timbered roof (p. 384A, D); thus in the Byzantine style the exterior closely corresponds with the interior. There are, however, a number of Byzantine churches which have features quite contrary to this characteristic. At S. Mark, Venice, there are tall bulbous wooden-framed domes above the true domes (p. 391B). Some domes do not show outwardly at all, as with the bema dome at Hosios Loukas (p. 397A), or the dome above the eso-narthex at Nea Moni (p. 396). In S. Sophia is seen the perfect expression of the Byzantine style: for the columns are not merely ornamental, but really support the galleries, and semicircular arches rest directly on columns with capitals suitable for supporting the springers of arches of which the voussoirs were rectangular blocks, not set in receding moulded planes as in mediaeval architecture (p. 465A, B). The Byzantine capital was shaped to form a simple transition from the square abacus to the circular shaft. The numerous columns in S. Sophia exhibit the remarkable and beautiful structural expedient of surrounding the shafts, both under the capital and above the base, by bronze annulets (pp. 378N, 385A, B). Monolithic shafts which, owing to the height required, had to be set up contrary to the stratification of the quarry, were therefore liable to split, and these bronze annulets not only overcame this danger, but also prevented the lead 'seating' from being forced out by the superincumbent weight. Although marble columns from old buildings were utilized, the importation of newly-quarried columns and rare marbles for decorative purposes continued, and the Theodosian code encouraged and regulated this industry, so that coloured marbles were employed to a greater extent than in preceding styles. The interiors were beautified by pavements in 'opus sectile' or 'opus Alexandrinum' (p. 466K), and in domes and apses by coloured mosaics, which were of glass rendered opaque by oxide of tin, an invention which had also been employed in the Early Christian architecture. Marble and mosaic were used broadly to make a complete lining for a rough carcase, and mouldings were replaced by decorative bands formed in the mosaic. This use of mosaics resulted in the rounding of angles and, with the absence of mouldings and cornices, the designs and pictures continued uninterrupted on a universal golden ground over apses, walls, arches and pendentives upwards to the dome. In late examples fresco painting was often used instead of mosaic. Invariably the pictures were arranged in a special order: the bust of Christ usually occupied the dome and the four Evangelists were set in the pendentives; the Virgin and Child were customarily located in the apse, while all round the walls were representations of the saints and incidents in the life of Christ. The churches of Constantinople, Salonica and the Monastery of Hosios Loukas show the perfection to which this scheme of decoration was carried.

The character of Byzantine architecture shows development in its three main periods: (1) 330–850, including the reign of Justinian; (2) 850–1200, including the Macedonian and Comnenian dynasties; (3) 1200 to recent times. The character was also affected by local influences, as seen in examples found in Turkey, Italy, Greece, Macedonia, Armenia, Syria, Russia, Serbia and France.

The Greek church in Moscow Road, London, designed by Oldrid Scott, and the Roman Catholic Cathedral, Westminster, by John F. Bentley, are modern examples of Byzantine treatment in England.

EXAMPLES

CHURCHES

Byzantine churches are distinguished by the centralized type of plan, having a dome over the nave which, in early examples, is sometimes supported by semidomes. In later examples the churches are much smaller and the dome is raised upon a high drum with, occasionally, additional smaller domes rising at a lower level. There is usually a narthex, or entrance porch, at the west end, and the east end is cut off from the nave by an 'iconostas', or screen of pictures.

SS. Sergius and Bacchus, Constantinople (525–30) (pp. 381, 398A, B), erected by Justinian, is nearly square on plan, 33 m × 28 m (109 ft × 92 ft), and the arrangement of the interior is similar to that of S. Vitale (p. 382C), but it has only four colonnaded exedrae to the central octagon. The church would resemble S. Sophia in plan if it were cut in two, and a dome on pendentives placed over an intervening square and the whole doubled in size. The dome over the central space, 16 m (52 ft) in diameter and 21.2 m (69 ft 6 ins) high, is visible externally, and has a peculiar, melon-like form with ridges and furrows from base to summit (p. 378H, J, K).

S. Vitale, Ravenna (526–47) (p. 382), was commissioned during the episcopate of Ecclesius (521–32) at a time when Ravenna was under Ostro-Gothic domination. An inner octagon of 16.6 m (54 ft 9 ins) is enclosed by an outer octagon of 35 m (115 ft). The apsidal chancel is successfully designed to open direct from one side of the inner octagon, while the other seven arches enclose columns, in two tiers, placed on a semicircle, and these are reminiscent of the exedrae of S. Sophia (p. 385B) and SS. Sergius and Bacchus (p. 378H–K). The lower columns carry the gallery usual in eastern churches and the upper columns terminate in squinches adjacent to the arches referred to above. It is upon the eight great arches and piers of the inner octagon that the dome and drum rest. The dome is curious in that it is constructed of earthen pots fitted into each other, those in the upper part being laid horizontally, thus producing a lightness of structure which did not require the arches and buttresses found necessary in SS. Sergius and Bacchus and S. Sophia, Constantinople. This remarkable construction in pottery is protected by a timber roof, thus differing from Roman usage and approximating to the practice

SS. SERGIUS & BACCHUS : CONSTANTINOPLE

(A) EXTERIOR FROM S.E.

SPRINGING OF DOME

TURKISH PORTICO

NARTHEX

BARREL VAULT

BARREL VAULT

52' 0"

BARREL VAULT

BARREL VAULT

MINARET

(B) PLAN

(C) SECTION a·a

S. THEODORE : CONSTANTINOPLE

(D) EXTERIOR FROM N.W.

(E) S.E. ELEVATION

INNER NARTHEX

OUTER NARTHEX

57' 6"   29' 0"

MINARET

(F) PLAN

(G) LONGITUDINAL SECTION

LITTLE METROPOLE CATHEDRAL : ATHENS

25' 7"

38' 0"

(H) PLAN

26' 6"

(J) E. ELEVATION

(K) EXTERIOR FROM N.W.

36' 0"

(L) LONG. SECTION

SCALE FOR ALL PLANS
FEET 10 0 10 20 30 40 50 60 70 80 90
M™5 5 0 5 10 15 20 25

SCALE FOR ALL ELEV.NS. & SECT.NS.
10 FT. 0 10 20 30 40
1 0 5 10 METRS.

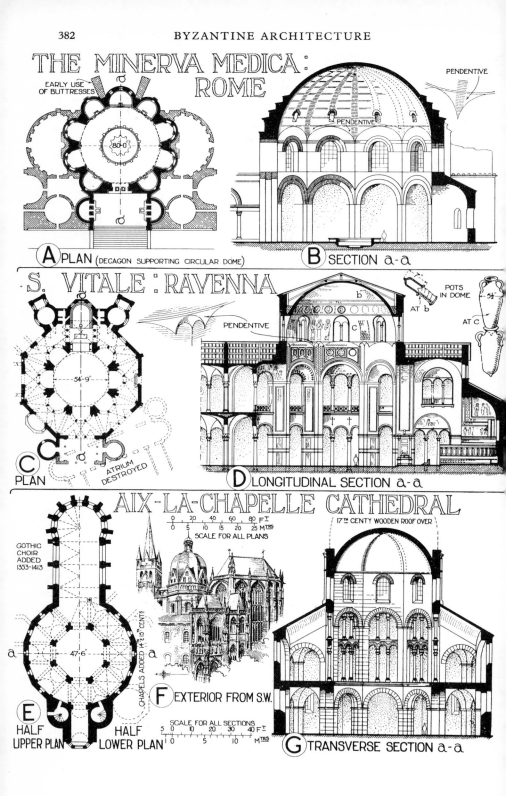

THE MINERVA MEDICA : ROME

EARLY USE OF BUTTRESSES

80'·0"

PENDENTIVE

PENDENTIVE

Ⓐ PLAN (DECAGON SUPPORTING CIRCULAR DOME)

Ⓑ SECTION a-a

S. VITALE : RAVENNA

54'·9"

PENDENTIVE

POTS IN DOME — 5½"

AT b

AT c

Ⓒ PLAN

ATRIUM DESTROYED

Ⓓ LONGITUDINAL SECTION a-a

AIX-LA-CHAPELLE CATHEDRAL

GOTHIC CHOIR ADDED 1353-1413

47'·6"

CHAPELS ADDED 14TH·15TH CENTS

0   20   40   60   80 FT
0   5   10   15   20   25 MTRS
SCALE FOR ALL PLANS

17TH CENTY WOODEN ROOF OVER

Ⓔ HALF UPPER PLAN   HALF LOWER PLAN

Ⓕ EXTERIOR FROM S.W.

SCALE FOR ALL SECTIONS
5   0   10   20   30   40 FT
0   5   10 MTRS

Ⓖ TRANSVERSE SECTION a-a

which prevailed among mediaeval architects (p. 382D). It is also worthy of notice that the walls, being carried up to support the timber roof, act as haunches and assist in directing the thrust of the dome downwards. The interior is remarkable for the beauty of its carved capitals with dosseret blocks (p. 401C), while the mosaics which line the walls of the sanctuary are unique in this form of Christian art inasmuch as they are a most valuable record of the costumes of the period. Here are life-size figures of Justinian and the Empress Theodora at the consecration of the church in all the glittering array of state panoply and surrounded by the ladies of the Court. Prominent in the centre of the apse is the commanding figure of Christ seated on an azure globe and holding the Crown of Life and the seven-sealed book. The exterior in large thin bricks with thick mortar joints is characteristic of the simple external treatment of so many Byzantine buildings. The cathedral of Aix-la-Chapelle (Aachen) (p. 382E, F, G) much resembles S. Vitale, and probably was derived from it (p. 510), while SS. Sergius and Bacchus is also similar in plan, but consists of an octagon enclosed in a square (p. 381B).

S. Sophia, Constantinople (*Hagia Sophia* = divine wisdom) (532–7) (pp. 373, 374, 384, 385A, B), was built for Justinian by the architects Anthemius of Tralles and Isidorus of Miletus, on the site of two successive basilican churches of the same name, erected respectively by Constantine (*c.* 335) and Theodosius II (415). It was the most important church in Constantinople. The noble atrium forming the approach to the church led through the great triple portal to the outer narthex; beyond is the imposing main narthex, 61 m × 9 m (200 ft × 30 ft), which is in two storeys, the lower of which was used by catechumens and penitents, while the upper forms part of the gallery to the church. The plan consists of a central space 32.6 m (107 ft) square, with four massive stone piers, 7.6 m × 18.3 m (25 ft × 60 ft), pierced by arches for aisles and gallery, supporting four semicircular arches upon which rests the dome, 32.6 m (107 ft) in diameter and 54.8 m (180 ft) above the ground. East and west of this central area are great hemicycles, crowned with semi-domes, the space thus enclosed forming a great oval nave, 68.6 m × 32.6 m (225 ft × 107 ft), being about 8.5 m (28 ft) wider than the huge vaulted tepidarium of the Thermae of Caracalla. The great hemicycles are flanked by exedrae with semi-domes, and at the extreme east is the apse. North and south of the nave are two-storeyed aisles over 15.2 m (50 ft) wide, the upper storey being the 'gynaeceum' or women's gallery, reached from the outside by ramps at each corner and by stone steps in the interior. These aisles bring the main building approximately to a square which, excluding the eastern apse and the narthex, measures 76.2 m × 67 m (250 ft × 220 ft). North and south, forming continuations of the four great piers already mentioned, are huge buttresses 7.6 m (25 ft) wide by 18.3 m (60 ft) long, which take the thrust of the main arches and central dome on the two sides where there are no semi-domes (p. 378M). The two principal semi-domes, east and west, abut against the great supporting arches and thus act as buttresses to the central dome.

The monumental interior (p. 374) gives the impression of one vast domed space, but the detailed effect, with the great hemicycles and smaller exedrae, is one of extreme intricacy, in spite of the simplicity of the general scheme. Scale is obtained by the gradation of the various parts, from the two-storeyed arcades of the aisles to the lofty dome which rests, with little apparent support, like a canopy over the centre, or, as Procopius described it, 'as if suspended by a chain from heaven'. Gigantic pendentives to the central dome overhang about 7.6 m (25 ft) and are themselves over 18.3 m (60 ft) high (p. 384C), above which the dome itself rises only 15.2 m (50 ft). The dome is constructed of bricks about 686 mm (27 ins) square in the lower part and 610 mm (24 ins) square at the crown, and 50 mm (2 ins) thick, with mortar joints of nearly the same thickness. The joints do not radiate from the

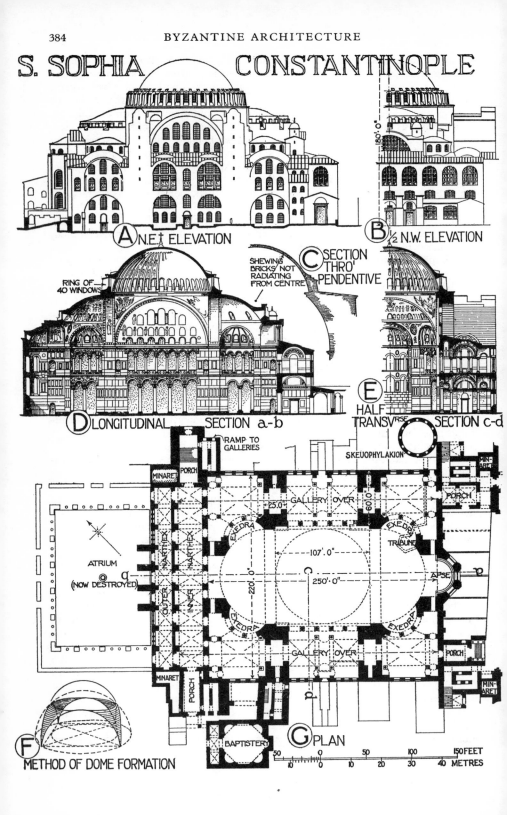

S. SOPHIA   CONSTANTINOPLE

(A) N.E.† ELEVATION

(B) ½ N.W. ELEVATION

180'. 0"

SHEWING
BRICKS NOT
RADIATING
FROM CENTRE

(C) SECTION
THRO'
PENDENTIVE

RING OF
40 WINDOWS

(D) LONGITUDINAL   SECTION a-b

(E) HALF
TRANSVᴿˢᴱ   SECTION c-d

RAMP TO
GALLERIES

SKEUOPHYLAKION

MINARET

PORCH

MIN-ARET

PORCH

25.0'

GALLERY OVER

60'.0"

ATRIUM

q

(NOW DESTROYED)

OUTER NARTHEX

INNER NARTHEX

EXEDRA

EXEDRA

TRIBUNE

107'. 0"

220. 0'

250'. 0"

APSE

p

EXEDRA

EXEDRA

MINARET

PORCH

GALLERY OVER

PORCH

MIN-ARET

p

(F) METHOD OF DOME FORMATION

BAPTISTERY

(G) PLAN

50   50   100   150 FEET

10   0   10   20   30   40 METRES

A. North aisle, looking east   B. Interior from an exedra

S. Sophia, Constantinople (532–7). See p. 383

C. Exterior from S.E.   D. Interior looking E.

S. Irene, Constantinople. Built by Justinian 532, rebuilt 564, and again in 740.
See p. 386

centre of the dome, but have a flatter inclination, in order to diminish the thrust. Walls and piers are sheeted with marbles of Phrygian white, Laconian green, Libyan blue, Celtic black, besides Thessalian and Bosphorus marbles, all fixed by metal clips (p. 378L). Floors are laid with large rectangular marble paving slabs. The greater part of the interior above the springings of the great arches, in the dome, semi-domes and arches and vaults of the galleries, is still covered in Turkish plaster and decorated in the style when the building was used as a mosque. There are examples of the original sixth-century mosaics, which were simple decorative patterns including Christograms and crosses, on a plain gold ground, in the inner narthex, the aisles, and a few other areas. There are some wonderful pictorial mosaics, dating from the ninth to the twelfth centuries, set up in various parts of the building.

To support the groined vaults 107 columns of marbles are used constructively under the galleries, and moulded bronze rings encircle the column shafts at their junction with capitals and bases, while the outward pressure of the arches is counteracted by tie-rods (pp. 378N, 385A, B). The lower storeys of the aisles north and south of the central space are supported by four columns of dark-green marble, while the upper storeys have six columns of the same marble. Each of the four exedrae (p. 385B) has two large columns of dark-red porphyry, and six smaller columns in the gallery (p. 384D). The capitals (pp. 378N, 385A, B) are mostly of the cubiform type, with small Ionic angle volutes and delicately incised carving, in which is sometimes woven the monogram of Justinian, while a variation of the dosseret block on the lines of the Classical abacus is generally used above the capital. The lighting is partly effected by forty small windows in the lower part of the dome (pp. 373, 374) and by twelve windows grouped in the spandrel walls north and south under the great arches (p. 374) which support the dome, while there are windows in the lower part of the domes of the exedrae and of the apse. Many of the windows are small and spanned by semicircular arches; others are more elaborate, as in the 'gynaeceum' in which large semicircular-headed openings are divided into six by columns in two heights, between which marble lattice screens admit light through glazed openings about 180 mm (7 ins) square (p. 401K).

The exterior (p. 373) is less impressive than the interior, for the brick walls are plastered over and distempered conveying a drab effect at close quarters. The actual shape of the domes and semi-domes is visible, as there is only a covering of lead, 6.35 mm ($\frac{1}{4}$ inch) thick, resting on wooden battens placed immediately on the outer surface of the brick domes. The immense buttresses and the deeply recessed spandrel wall between them are imposing features in an exterior which depends for effect entirely on the massiveness and general symmetry of its proportions. The lofty minarets were added by the Turks after the capture of Constantinople (1453), and they frame in the subsidiary buildings of the Turkish period. S. Sophia is the supreme monument of Byzantine architecture, and provided the model for many of the great mosques which were built after the Turkish capture. The building is now a museum.

S. Irene, Constantinople (740) (pp. 385C, D, 387), is a domed basilica built first in 532 on the site of a former church. It was rebuilt in 564 and again in 740, when it underwent major structural alterations, mainly to the nave, which is flanked by galleried aisles and terminates in an apse at the east end. Changes made to the vaulting of the western part of the nave, and the placing upon it of a shallow dome, made it similar to the already domed eastern half. At the same time the eastern dome was rebuilt on a drum pierced with windows, and is thought to be the earliest example of a dome so mounted. This was found to give dignity to the church and so became the usual treatment. The mosaics in the apse semi-dome, a blue

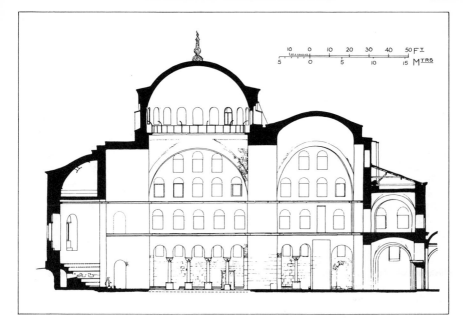

A. Longitudinal section looking south

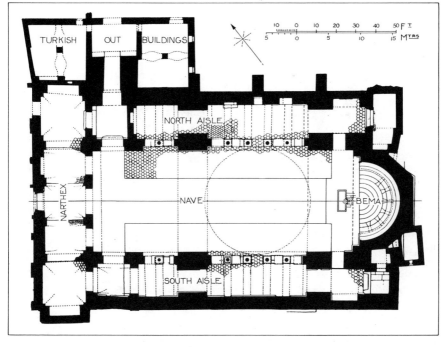

B. Ground floor plan

S. Irene, Constantinople. See p. 386

A. S. Saviour in the Chora, Constantinople, with Turkish minaret (founded
4th cent., but rebuilt *c.* 1050). See p. 389

B. S. Mary Pammakaristos, Constantinople: the parekklesion, *c.* 1315, from
the south. See p. 389

cross on a plain gold ground, typify religious art of the Iconoclast period (726–843) when such designs were set up in place of figural compositions which were banned.

S. Theodore, Constantinople (*c.* 1100) (p. 381D, E, F, G), now the Kilisse Mosque, is a perfect specimen of a typical small Byzantine church. It has a double narthex crowned with domes leading into a nave 9 m (29 ft 6 ins) square, with central dome formed with curved flutings and set on a drum 4 m (13 ft) in diameter (p. 378F), and with an apse semicircular internally and polygonal externally. The plan is what is commonly known as the 'cross-in-square' and is characteristic of the later development of the style. The basis of the design is a dome and drum raised upon pendentives over a square which is usually defined by four columns. From this square project four arms, which are usually barrel-vaulted. At each internal angle is a smaller area, roofed at a lower level, so that the building has a square ground plan but is cruciform above. Sometimes, as here there is an additional bay at the east end, and usually a narthex at the west end. The very elaborate exterior is of brick and stone in bands, with columns supporting semicircular arches surmounted by windows within a second tier of similar arches recessed in rings, while over the outer narthex are the three octagonal tile-covered domes on high drums.

S. Saviour in the Chora, Constantinople (*c.* 1050) (pp. 388A, 390), and equally well known as the Kariye Djami, was founded in the fourth century. The present building is an eleventh- and early twelfth-century structure which was added to, restored and decorated during the years 1303–21 by the Grand Logothete Theodore Metochites, who is portrayed in a mosaic in the church. The central area has a dome on a high drum, 5.3 m (17 ft 6 ins) in diameter, pierced by windows, and triple windows set in blind arches on three sides of the nave. Domed nartheces afford access to the nave and also to the parekklesion, which runs the full length of the south side of the building. The church is famous for its decorations; frescoes in the nave and parekklesion, and brilliantly coloured mosaics, displaying detail and realism, cover the lunettes, arches and domes of the nartheces.

The **Church of the Apostles, Constantinople,** founded by Constantine the Great, was rebuilt by Justinian and destroyed in 1463 to make way for the mosque of Sultan Mohammad II. With its cruciform plan and five domes it is said to have been the prototype of S. Mark, Venice (below) and S. Front, Périgueux (p. 393).

A number of Byzantine churches in Constantinople have been well preserved, considering their conversion into mosques, and are excellent examples of the smaller structures on the typical Byzantine plan of a Greek cross with a central dome. These include **S. Mary Pammakaristos** (eighth century) (p. 388B), now the Fetiyeh Djami; **S. Theodosia** (ninth century), much altered by the Turks when converting it into a mosque—the Gul Djami; and **S. Saviour Pantokrator** (early twelfth century), a triple church founded by the Empress Irene, now the Zeirek Djami.

S. Mark, Venice (1063–85) (pp. 391, 392, 394A), reflects the art of Byzantium which so largely influenced the architecture of Venice, situated midway between East and West. The glittering, resplendent façade of the narthex faces the great Piazza of San Marco, whose vast open space, paved in marble, forms a great public atrium to the church dedicated to the sea-city's patron saint. This famous edifice stands on the site of the original basilican church, which was founded in 830 to receive the body of S. Mark, and partially burnt down in 976. Between 1063 and 1085 the plan was completely transformed to resemble that of the Church of the Apostles, Constantinople (above): transepts were added, the sanctuary was extended, the narthex was continued round the sides, and the interior altered from the basilican to the Byzantine plan of a Greek cross surmounted by domes. The plan (p. 391C) has a central dome, 12.8 m (42 ft) in diameter, and a dome over each

S. SAVIOUR IN THE CHORA CONSTANTINOPLE

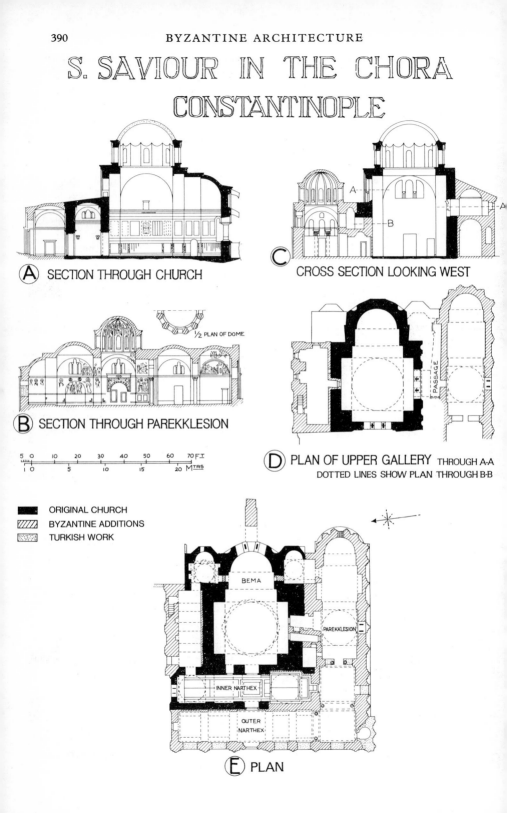

(A) SECTION THROUGH CHURCH

(C) CROSS SECTION LOOKING WEST

1/2 PLAN OF DOME

(B) SECTION THROUGH PAREKKLESION

PASSAGE

(D) PLAN OF UPPER GALLERY THROUGH A-A
DOTTED LINES SHOW PLAN THROUGH B-B

5   0   10   20   30   40   50   60   70 F.T
1   0   5   10   15   20 M.TRS

■ ORIGINAL CHURCH
▨ BYZANTINE ADDITIONS
░ TURKISH WORK

BEMA

PAREKKLESION

INNER NARTHEX

OUTER NARTHEX

(E) PLAN

S. MARK : VENICE & S. FRONT : PERIGUEUX

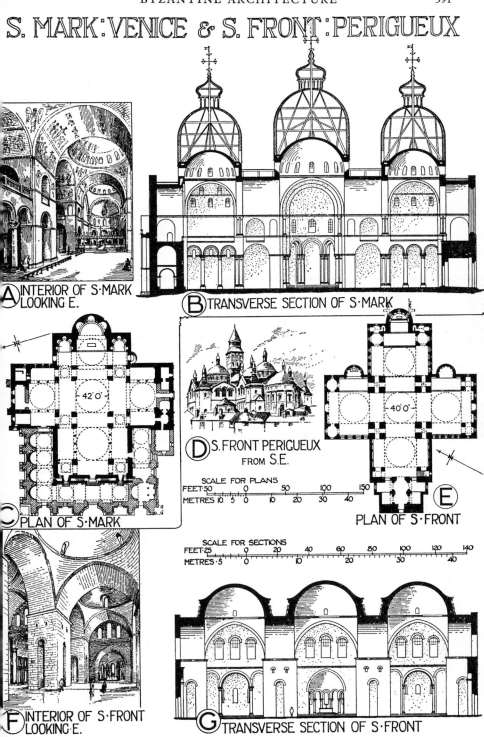

A INTERIOR OF S·MARK LOOKING E.

B TRANSVERSE SECTION OF S·MARK

C PLAN OF S·MARK

D S. FRONT PERIGUEUX FROM S.E.

E PLAN OF S·FRONT

SCALE FOR PLANS
FEET·50   0   50   100   150
METRES·10 5 0 10 20 30 40

SCALE FOR SECTIONS
FEET·25   0   20   40   60   80   100   120   140
METRES·5   0   10   20   30   40

F INTERIOR OF S·FRONT LOOKING·E.

G TRANSVERSE SECTION OF S·FRONT

A. S. Mark, Venice: west façade
(12th cent.; gilded domes 13th cent., and 15th cent. additions). See p. 389

B. S. Mark, Venice: interior looking E. (1063–85; cancelli erected 1393).
See p. 389

arm of the cross. The great square piers, 8.5 m × 6.4 m (28 ft × 21 ft), which carry the dome are pierced on both the ground and gallery levels, and arcades support passages connecting the central piers to the extremities of the nave and transepts. The addition of the narthex and baptistery makes the church approximately square on plan.

The interior (p. 392B) is gorgeous in coloured marbles and brilliant glass mosaics which, extending in one continuous surface over vault and dome, picture the story of the Creation, the fall of man and the Redemption, the miracles of Christ and the legends of the saints, all enshrined in a glowing golden background. Mosaic constitutes here, as also in the vaulted narthex, the real and essential decoration, to which all architectural detail is subordinated, and it is used like the stained glass of mediaeval churches to produce a popular representation of incidents from the Old and New Testaments.

The exterior, dating partly from the twelfth century, with its five entrance portals (p. 392A), was much enriched by mosaic and marble decoration during the Renaissance. Above the most northerly of these portals is the only survivor of the original exterior mosaics, which is of particular interest as it shows the church as it was in 1204 (p. 394A). The exterior has indeed a character peculiarly its own; for it is a marvellous blending into one homogeneous whole of a variety of features from many foreign lands. Bronze horses from the triumphal arch of Nero, columns of porphyry, alabaster, and verde-antico from Constantinople and Alexandria, coloured marble facing from Eastern cities, all form part of the world-wide contribution which, in the twelfth century, commanders of warships and captains of trading vessels were alike bidden to levy and bring in as votive offerings for success in commerce and victory in war. In the thirteenth century a crown of gold was given to the building by the unique timber domes (p. 391B), and finally, in the fifteenth century, the façade was further embellished by Gothic canopied niches, ogee arches and crocketed pinnacles, all of which form a delicate stone framework to the glittering mosaics below. S. Mark depends for beauty externally not only on delicate sculpture, but also on subtle, variable, and indescribable colour, produced by transparent alabaster, polished marble and lustrous gold mosaic.

S. Front, Périgueux (1120) (p. 391), is an interesting product of Byzantine influence carried west along trade routes by Venetian merchants, and is an almost identical copy in plan of S. Mark, Venice. The entire absence of mosaic, however, shows by contrast how much Byzantine interiors owe to that art, for this French version appears bare and plain in comparison with the pure Byzantine original.

S. Fosca, Torcello (1108) (p. 394B) forms with the old cathedral and campanile a picturesque group rising from this island in the lagoons of Venice. It is based on the Byzantine plan, with the scant remains of a central dome supported by eight columns; externally an arcade on five sides forms a semi-octagon. The details indicate that this simple building was constructed by Byzantine Greeks who also worked on the rebuilding of S. Mark, Venice.

The **Little Metropole Cathedral, Athens** (c. 1250) (p. 381), is the smallest cathedral in the world, for it measures only 11.6 × 7.6 m (38 ft × 25 ft), and the dome, supported on a high octagonal drum, is only 2.7 m (9 ft) in diameter. Its façades contain many miscellaneous marbles from old Greek buildings.

The **Kapnikarea Church, Athens** (875), and **S. Theodore, Athens** (1060–70) (p. 395A), both have small central domes raised on octagonal drums.

The **Church of the Apostles, Athens** (c. 1020) (p. 395B) is a cross-in-square church which has been restored in recent years. Apsidal endings to the arms of the cross penetrate the walls of the building on three sides, and give it a polygonal appearance outwardly. There is a central dome on an octagonal drum pierced by

A. S. Mark, Venice: mosaic showing church as in 1204. See p. 389

B. S. Fosca, Torcello (1108). See p. 393
The basilican cathedral and campanile on the left. See p. 358

A. S. Theodore, Athens (1060–70). See p. 393

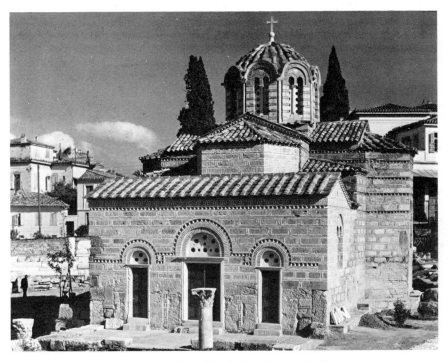

B. Church of the Apostles, Athens (c. 1020). See p. 393

windows framed by arches. As the spaces between these arches are not levelled off, the dome, thus rising from a base line of semicircles, acquires the scalloped edge so characteristic of middle-Byzantine Greece. The walls are of Byzantine brick and stone construction.

The diminutive proportions of these churches are due to the simple ritual of the Greek Orthodox Church and to the absence of instrumental music and of chairs for the worshippers—an influence which did not apply to churches in the Byzantine style erected, like S. Mark, Venice, for Catholic ritual.

The **Two Churches of the Monastery of Hosios Loukas, Phocis,** in Greece (eleventh cent.) (pp. 377C, 397A, 401L). The Katholikon (*c.* 1020), the larger of the two churches, is famous for the mosaics which line vaults, arches and half-domes, in contrast to the marble sheets of varied colours fixed to the walls. Here is exemplified, so admirably, the iconographic layout of middle-Byzantine church mosaics. Four great L-shaped piers, crowned by squinches and bridged by arches, rise to form an octagonal base to the drum of the dome. Basically a cross within a square, the interior appears to be very complicated, with its system of galleried transepts and corner chapels. The domed bema ceiling is covered externally by a pent-roof (p. 397A) and the narthex has an upper storey. The Church of the Theotokos (*c.* 1040) abuts on to the north wall of the Katholikon, and it is in this church that the monastic community worships. The dome and drum rise up on pendentives supported by four columns. Barrel-vaulted cross-arms radiate to the outer walls, and corner chapels fill up the square which terminates in triple apses. The interior decorations are very simple and there are no mosaics. Externally, bands of dog-tooth friezes relieve the walls and the octagonal drum is decorated with ornamental window arches and carved marble panels.

Nea Moni, Chios (1042–56) (p. 377E) is one of a few churches of its type to have survived. The square nave, without cross-arms, is roofed by a dome which spans to the outer walls of the building. The dome is a concrete replacement of the original, which fell during an earthquake in 1881. The drum of the dome is carried on eight squinches, deep and narrow in the four corners and broad and shallow in the axes, which in turn rise up from eight pilasters projecting from the nave walls. The pilasters also divide the walls into three bays, rectangular in the lower zone and higher up conforming to the curves of the squinches which crown them. Triple apses lead off from the eastern end of the nave, which is preceded in the west by two nartheces. The exo-narthex has apsidal projections at either end, and is roofed by three domes which are all visible externally. The eso-narthex has a domed centre bay, flanked by barrel-vaulted chambers; a tiled pent-roof obscures this dome outwardly. Mosaics and marble panels embellish the interior, the mosaics displaying unusual features such as mountains in outline only and an unconventional use of colour. The Christological cycle in the squinches includes the rarely found Deposition scene. The eso-narthex is covered in mosaics, among which are a series of Stylites and the warrior saints. Externally, the white plastered brick walls are relieved by shallow blind arches; the main dome, with scalloped edge, rises upon a high drum pierced with windows.

The **Church of the Koimisis, Daphni** (*c.* 1080) (pp. 377B, 397B), is similar to the Katholikon at Hosios Loukas in the arrangement of the L-shaped piers at the corners of the central square; each supports a squinch which, when coupled with the four great arches bridging the piers, contributes to the formation of an octagon on which rests the drum and dome. Four cross-arms radiate from below the dome, and corner chapels and aisles complete the 'square'. There the similarity to S. Luke's Katholikon ends; at Daphni there are no galleries, triple apses project from the eastern façade, and there are two nartheces, the outer one having no roof.

A. Monastery of Hosios Loukas, Phocis, from S. (11th cent.). See p. 396

B. Church of the Koimisis, Daphni, from E. (c. 1080). See p. 396

A. SS. Sergius and Bacchus, Constantinople, from E. (525–30). See p. 380

B. SS. Sergius and Bacchus, Constantinople: interior

C. Aghia Parigoritissa, Arta, from N.W. (1282–9). See p. 399

D. Aghia Parigoritissa, Arta: interior looking N.

E. Katholikon, Lavra Monastery, Mount Athos, from N.E. (early 11th cent.). See p. 399

F. Holy Apostles, Salonica, from E. (1312–15). See p. 399

The walls are constructed of stone blocks framed with bricks. The church is decorated with a fine cycle of mosaics arranged in strict iconographic order; in the dome there is a rather awesome portrayal of Christ Pantokrator. Despite the presence of mosaics the interior appears somewhat bare, as all those surfaces once covered with marble panels or mosaics have either been plastered over or left with exposed brickwork.

Aghia Parigoritissa, Arta (1282–9) (p. 398C, D) is a cube-shaped structure surmounted by five domes and a tempietto, and there are five apses projecting from the eastern wall. Windows in two tiers pierce the walls of stone blocks to illuminate the galleries of the narthex and side aisles. As the central core of the church is enclosed on three sides, the admittance of light to this very dark interior would rely solely on the windows of the dome, were it not for openings in the inner walls of the gallery above the narthex and aisles. The dome and drum are supported in an unusual manner. Eight sets of piers and cantilevered columns, arranged in pairs at the corners of the central square, rise up in three stages to carry pendentives, the latter bifurcated at their bases by deep narrow squinches (p. 398D). Four barrel-vaulted cross-arms radiate beneath the dome, the eastern arm being elongated to the main apse. The interior decorations have suffered greatly, with bare brick and stone predominating, save for some mouldings, a fresco in the apse, and some mosaics.

The **Katholikon of the Lavra Monastery, Mount Athos** (early eleventh century) (p. 398E), is a domed cruciform church with barrel-vaulted cross-arms. In addition to the usual eastern apse, there are apses at the ends of the northern and southern arms of the cross to provide space for the monks of the choir. The Lavra Katholikon was the first Athonite church to be built on a trifoliate plan, which has since been adopted for monastic katholika on the Holy Mountain. Another example is the **Church of the Prophet Elias** (c. 1360), **Salonica** (p. 377D).

S. Sophia, Salonica (c. 700) (p. 377A), has a galleried narthex and side aisles enclosing, on three sides, the central dome and four barrel-vaulted cross-arms. The eastern arm is elongated to the main apse, which is flanked by the Prothesis and Diaconicon. Fine mosaics of the eighth to the eleventh century adorn the apse, bema and dome, the latter with an Ascension scene. Careful study of the apse mosaic, an enthroned Virgin, has revealed that it replaced earlier mosaics, the first of which was pre-Iconoclastic, and therefore the church must have been built before 726. It was used as a mosque for three centuries, damaged by fire in 1890 and rebuilt in the years 1907–10.

The **Church of the Holy Apostles, Salonica** (1312–15) (pp. 377F, 398F) has five domes set on high drums, the central one being carried on pendentives supported by columns. Outer and inner nartheces and side aisles enclose the naos of the church on three sides. The four arms of the cross are barrel-vaulted. The church is built entirely of brick with intricate patterns worked into the eastern wall (p. 398F). The mosaics are rather fragmentary, but are important as they are the last examples of this art-form as practised by the Byzantines.

The **Churches at Bosra** (512) and **Ezra** (515) in Syria follow a favourite plan of a circle or octagon within a square with niches in the angles. They are considered to be prototypes of Byzantine churches like SS. Sergius and Bacchus, Constantinople (p. 381B), and San Vitale, Ravenna (p. 382C).

The **Church at Gračanica** (1321) (p. 400A), in Serbia, with its characteristic exterior of brick and stone and its domes on high drums grouped around the dominating central dome, is probably the most remarkable of all the churches in that country, where the architecture was midway between two influences, arising respectively from Constantinople on the east and Rome on the west, the former

A. Gračanica Church from S.E. (1321). See p. 399

B. S. Sophia, Novgorod (1052). See p. 402

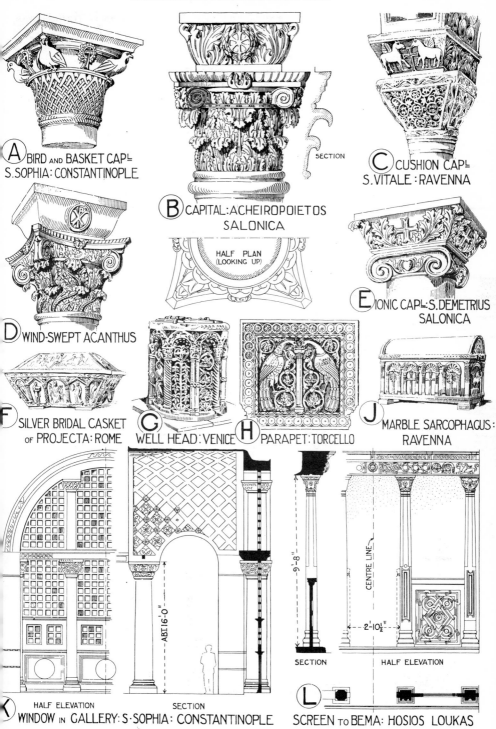

A BIRD AND BASKET CAP.ᴸ
S.SOPHIA: CONSTANTINOPLE

B CAPITAL: ACHEIROPOIETOS
SALONICA

HALF PLAN
(LOOKING UP)

SECTION

C CUSHION CAP.ᴸ
S. VITALE : RAVENNA

D WIND-SWEPT ACANTHUS

E IONIC CAP.ᴸ: S. DEMETRIUS
SALONICA

F SILVER BRIDAL CASKET
OF PROJECTA: ROME

G WELL HEAD: VENICE

H PARAPET: TORCELLO

J MARBLE SARCOPHAGUS:
RAVENNA

K HALF ELEVATION
WINDOW IN GALLERY: S·SOPHIA: CONSTANTINOPLE
SECTION
AB.16'-0"

L SCREEN TO BEMA: HOSIOS LOUKAS
SECTION
HALF ELEVATION
9'-8"
2'-10½"
CENTRE LINE

prevailing. The churches at **Nerezi** (1164), **Mileševo** (1234), **Staro Nagoričane,** a remodelled basilica (1313), **Dečani,** a domed basilica (1330), **Ravanica** (1375) and **Kruševac** (1380) are other Serbian examples of note in the Yugoslavian Federative Republics of Serbia and Macedonia.

The churches in Russia are a development of Byzantine architecture. **S. Sophia, Kiev** (1037–46) has thirteen domes and the mosaic decorations are set up in the prescribed positions governed by Byzantine iconographic rules. At **S. Sophia, Novgorod** (1052), the top surface of the dome is steepened, partly to throw off snow and partly for aesthetic reasons (p. 400B); later, considerable emphasis seems to have been laid on the skyline, for the domes have a curious bulbous shape and are raised on tall, cylindrical drums. The most striking example of the style is **S. Basil,** in the **Red Square in Moscow** (1554), where there are eight bulb-like domes, each different and all painted in the most brilliant colours.

BIBLIOGRAPHY

BEYLIÉ, L. DE. *L'Habitation byzantine*. Grenoble and Paris, 1902–3.

CHOISY, A. *L'Art de bâtir chez les Byzantins*. Paris, 1883.

COLASANTI, A. *L'arte bisantina in Italia*. Milan, 1912.

DALTON, O. M. *Byzantine Art and Archaeology*. Oxford, 1911.

DIDRON, A. N. *Christian Iconography*. 2 vols. London, 1886.

DIEHL, C. *Manuel d'art byzantin*. Paris, 1910.

EBERSOLT, J. *Monuments d'architecture byzantine*. Paris, 1934.

ERRARD, C., et GAYET. *L'art byzantin*. 4 vols. Paris, 1901–11.

FOORD, E. *The Byzantine Empire*. London, 1911.

FOSSATI, G. *Aya Sofia, Constantinople*. London, 1852.

GEORGE, WALTER S. *The Church of S. Eirene at Constantinople*. London, 1913.

GURLITT, C. *Die Baukunst Konstantinopels*. 2 vols. Berlin, 1907–12.

HAMILTON, J. ARNOTT. *Byzantine Architecture and Decoration*. London, 1933.

JACKSON, SIR T. G. *Byzantine and Romanesque Architecture*. Cambridge, 1920.

KNIGHT, H. G. *Ecclesiastical Architecture of Italy*. 2 vols. London, 1842–4.

KRAUTHEIMER, R. *Early Christian and Byzantine Architecture*. Harmondsworth and Baltimore, 1965.

LETHABY, W. R. *Church of Sancta Sophia, Constantinople*. London and New York, 1894.

MATHEWS, T. F. *The Early Churches of Constantinople: Architecture and Liturgy*. Philadelphia, 1972.

MICHEL, A. *Histoire de l'art*. Vol. i, pt. i. Paris, 1905.

MILLET, G. *Le Monastire de Daphne*. Paris, 1899.

MILLINGEN, A. VAN. *Byzantine Constantinople*. London, 1899.

—. *Byzantine Churches in Constantinople*. London, 1912.

ONGANIA, F. *Saint Mark's, Venice*. Several vols. Venice, 1881.

ORLANDOS, A. K. *I Parigoritissa tis Artis*. Athens, 1963.

PORTER, A. K. *Mediaeval Architecture*. 2 vols. New York and London, 1909.

RICE, D. TALBOT. *Byzantine Art*. London, 1954.

SALZENBURG, W. *Alt-christliche Baudenkmäler von Constantinopel*. 2 vols. Berlin, 1854–5.

SCHULTZ, R. W., and BARNSLEY, S. H. *The Monastery of St. Luke of Stiris in Phocis*. Folio. London, 1901.

SOTIRIOU, G. A. *The Byzantine Monuments of Cyprus*. Vol. i. Athens, 1935. (In Greek.)

SPIERS, R. *Architecture East and West*. London, 1905.

STEWART, CECIL. *Early Christian, Byzantine and Romanesque Architecture* (vol. ii of Simpson, F. M., *History of Architectural Development*). London, 1954.

STRZYGOWSKI, J. *Kleinasien*. 4to., 1903; *Byzantinische Denkmäler*. 2 vols. Vienna, 1891–1903.

TEXIER, C., and PULLAN, R. P. *Byzantine Architecture*. London, 1864.

UNDERWOOD, P. *The Kariye Djami*. 3 vols. London, 1967.

14

ISLAMIC ARCHITECTURE

Seventh century to the present day

Islam is the third great monotheistic religion to have sprung from the Semitic peoples. It was established in the seventh century of the Christian era by the prophet Mohammed who died at Medina in A.D. 632. By the end of the century the religion had spread to the Western Mediterranean and into Central Asia. Thereafter Islamic rulers and their peoples created various distinctive styles of building with many important common characteristics. These styles, now generally known as Islamic, are also variously called Moslem (or Muslim) and Mohammedan, and were earlier described as Saracenic and Moorish. The several individual styles are generally identified by the name of a ruling dynasty (e.g. Ummayad, Abbasid, Fatimid, Seljuk, Mughal, Ottoman et al.).

INFLUENCES

GEOGRAPHICAL

The Moslem faith flourished principally in the countries of southern Asia and North Africa, and in consequence many of the characteristics common to the various Islamic styles reveal a strong regional individuality. The diagram on p. 407 attempts to illustrate the historical and geographical relationship between the more productive of the Moslem dynasties. In modern (but necessarily approximate) terms the following countries were governed by Islamic rulers and largely populated by Islamic peoples during the periods indicated:

Africa north of the Sahara

Morocco Algeria Tunisia Libya Egypt	}	seventh century onwards

Sahara and Eastern Africa

Spanish Sahara Mauretania Mali Northern Nigeria Niger Chad Sudan Somali	}	ninth and tenth centuries onwards

Asia and Asia Minor

Saudi Arabia and states of the Arabian Peninsula	
Syria	
Israel	
Jordan	seventh century onwards
Lebanon	
Iraq	
Iran	
Asiatic Turkey	tenth century onwards
Afghanistan	ninth century onwards
South Russia (the Soviet Socialist Republics bordering on the Caspian and Aral Seas, also the Soviet Socialist Republics of Kirgizkaya and Tadzhikskaya)	seventh to ninth century onwards (western section of this area eleventh century onwards)
Mongolia (part of) Pakistan and northern India	eleventh century onwards
Philippines and Indonesia	fourteenth century onwards

Other important communities were established in isolation outside this geographical block, in places such as Zanzibar, Madagascar and China, while twentieth-century mobility has brought Islam to outposts throughout the world, with architectural consequences in apparently unlikely places as far apart as Sydney and South Shields.

The spread of Islam has been frequently associated with military conquest, racial movements, and in some cases with the consequent displacement of established populations. The most important of these movements were the Arab expansion northwards and westwards out of the Arabian peninsula, and the drive of Turkish and Mongol groups south, south-east and south-west out of Central Asia. The resulting important architecture has very largely been associated with religious civic complexes. In many instances Moslem rulers were content to make use of the established cities as capitals, but there are frequent examples of the establishment of new towns, generally administrative and palatial cities housing the Moslem élite.

GEOLOGICAL

The countries into which Islam first expanded were already rich in building tradition, and the important techniques of exploitation of natural resources for building work and trade in building materials had long been established. Brick making and pisé walling was almost universal in the alluvial plains; in the stone-bearing areas the arts of selecting and working stones were strong; marble was generally available as an article of trade if not native to the locality and often from the same source the limes for manufacture of mortars and plaster were readily procurable. Building stones occur in variety throughout the Islamic world, and knowledge of the more sophisticated techniques applicable to building was based on locally produced materials, in some cases supplemented by supplies from distant sources. There was a long tradition of ceramic production, use of gypsum plasters, glass manufacture and the various forms of metalwork needed for building. With the exception of the Lebanon, Northern Iran, the Balkans and parts of Asia Minor, timber was of limited type and quality. In many areas it was scarce; its use in building was, however, universal and frequently skilled. The prevalence of earthquakes in the

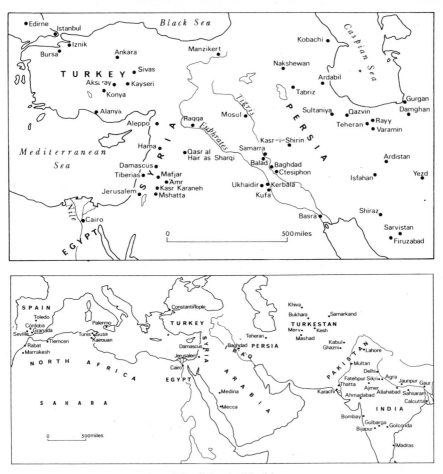

The Islamic World

near and middle-eastern countries resulted in the employment of some long-established, specialized structural techniques.

CLIMATIC

Much of the territory historically dominated by Islam tends to be fertile by virtue of irrigation, rather than direct rainfall. Although some of the most important areas fall within the Mediterranean climatic region (with warm moist winters, hot dry summers), the greater part of the Moslem world lies within the grip of some form of 'continental' climate, with extremes of temperature and modest rainfall. Generally excessive sunshine has produced a tendency towards wide eaves and sheltering arcades, while window openings are minimized and rainwater disposal neglected. Heating of buildings has generally been regarded as of little importance, but the cooling effect of structures with very heavy walls and high rooms has been widely exploited. Unprotected circulation areas are common.

HISTORICAL

Moslem chronology dates from A.D. 622, the year of the Hegira (Hijrah), when Mohammed moved from Mecca to Medina. In the succeeding ten years of his life Mohammed established the framework of the religion and the beginnings of the military organization charged with spreading the faith. Immediately after his death in 632, the concerted efforts of the Arabian tribes carried them as conquerors into central Asia and westwards towards the Atlantic. Islam spread more slowly into Africa and along the trade routes through the Indian Ocean. Later, when Arab energies had been absorbed by the vast new territories which they controlled, added impetus was given to its expansion by the conversion of groups of Turks and Mongols. Wherever it penetrated, Islam established a cultural tie with its Arabian heartland, annually renewed in the great pilgrimage to Mecca, enjoined on every Moslem as a sacred duty to be performed if possible at least once in his life. This cultural concentricity did much to unify the thought and architecture of the Islamic peoples.

The explosive expansion of Islam was led by the first Caliphs, who mounted a series of desert-based attacks which were almost invariably successful. The initial advance out of the Arabian peninsula was a straightforward northward movement through the barren fringes of the fertile lands of the Mediterranean littoral (present day Israel, Lebanon and Syria). The desert-moving armies struck westwards from the security of the desert first at Jerusalem, then at Damascus and finally but unsuccessfully towards Constantinople. Their northward advance was deflected eastwards as it reached the southern foothills of the mountains of Asia Minor. Still basing their operations on the deserts they extended their attacks into the Tigris-Euphrates basin and engaged the Sassanian Empire in its heartland.

Militarily shattered in 641 at Nihivand, the Sassanians crumbled. In the west, however, the Byzantine Empire, which had lost only its Palestinian provinces, established an erratic frontier with Islam where mountains and desert met (the present border of Syria and Turkey), and despite an audacious direct seaborne attempt on Constantinople, the Byzantines held the Arabs at bay, apart from a series of deep raids into Asia Minor. The success of the Arab armies was primarily the often-proved superiority of fast-moving military concentrations over widely-extended static defences. What was new was the religious zeal that gave the spur to the strategy, and the tenacity of the Arab movement, together with the system of religious government that gave order and stability to the conquered territories.

Blocked by Byzantium in the north-west, stretched perilously far in the north-east, the Arabs opened a new field of operations by turning westwards. In 640 they conquered Egypt, and within thirty years had gained control of the whole of the Mediterranean coast of North Africa. By 711 they were established in southern Spain, and fifty years later had conquered almost all the Peninsula, striking deep into southern France before being halted in 732 by a major defeat at Poitiers at the hands of Charles Martel, the 'Saviour of Europe'. This event marked the limit of Arab expansion, their capacity for conquest being exhausted in the immense territory within their grasp by the middle of the eighth century. By this time, however, control of much of the Empire had passed from the Arab (Ummayad) dynasty to the Persian-orientated (Abbasid) dynasty ruling in Baghdad. The Abbasids were in many ways the successors of the Sassanians, although militarily they became progressively dominated by the Turkish mercenary caste with which they surrounded themselves.

During the tenth, eleventh and twelfth centuries a series of Turkish groups moved continuously out of central Asia into Persia and Asia Minor, and gradually came to control the power structure of Islam. They were thus brought into military conflict

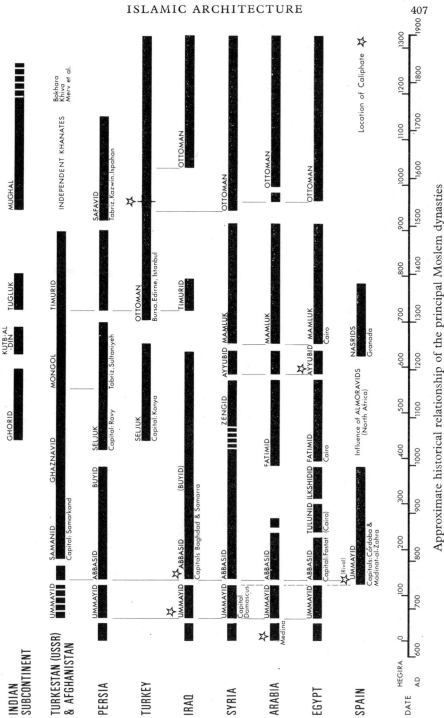

Approximate historical relationship of the principal Moslem dynasties

with Byzantium. The challenge culminated in a major defeat of the Byzantine Emperor at Manzikert in north-west Anatolia in 1027. The Asian provinces of Byzantium then fell piecemeal to the Turkish invaders, who by the twelfth century had reached the Ionian coast.

From the mountains of Afghanistan another Moslem dynasty of Turkish stock carried Islam into northern India, where it was effectively established from the beginning of the eleventh century. Meanwhile, the Moslem kingdoms in Spain were pressed increasingly hard by their Christian neighbours to the north, who, inspired with crusading fervour, had also established a precarious foothold in Palestine. Occasionally bolstered, but as often embarrassed, by reinforcements from the west, these Christian kingdoms (Edessa, Outremer, Jerusalem, etc.) survived into the thirteenth century. In 1291 Acre fell and the sea-sustained power of the Frankish knights was driven from the coast to dwindle in Cyprus, Rhodes and ultimately Malta. The conflict had important architectural consequences however (see Chapter 19). Conversely, at the western extremity of Islam, Arab power in Spain was forced to contract until it consisted of only the tiny Emirate of Granada, which survived to the end of the fifteenth century.

The slow process of infiltration of Turkish elements from Asia Minor was followed in the middle of the thirteenth and fourteenth centuries by a series of catastrophic military eruptions, first under Genghis Khan and his sons, and then under a Turk, Tamerlaine. The Mongol horsemen swept from central Asia into Persia, Iraq, Syria and Turkey, and struck westwards with terrifying rapacity through the Crimea into Europe. A cultural heritage that had been virtually continuous from Sassanian into Islamic times and had raised Baghdad to its peak of magnificence, was brutally assaulted and in a large part annihilated by armies whose object was utter destruction. Under Genghis Khan the Abbasid Caliphs and their capital, Baghdad, were ruthlessly wiped out in 1258, and after a final series of devastations the Mongol armies under Tamerlaine dominated the whole of the northern Islamic world from India to Anatolia. Every local dynasty in these areas tumbled, the defeat of the rapidly rising Ottoman dynasty at Ankara in 1400 being particularly significant in that it allowed the Byzantine emperors a short respite from an apparently imminent doom.

Although the Mongol incursions were inherently destructive, the sudden upsurge of their power was not entirely sterile in architectural terms. Islam flourished in central Asia, and a series of important buildings was constructed in cities such as Bukhara and Samarkand. Mongol dynasties in Persia and northern India began to create where once they had destroyed, while on the south-western fringe of Europe the Ottomans quickly recovered, capturing Constantinople in 1453. Within a hundred years this upstart dynasty had mastered the whole of western Islam from the gates of Vienna to the Barbary coast, from Egypt and the Hejaz to the Crimea. In the east they reached and held Baghdad in the early sixteenth century, and during this period their creative energies found expression in a new and significant facet of Islamic architecture.

In Asia a series of minor dynasties stabilized their territories around principal cities, such as Merv, Khiva, Samarkand and Bukhara; and Persia, which began the sixteenth century divided, was united by conquest under the Safavid Dynasty. The Safavids gave the country more than two centuries of stable government, in which a distinctively Persian variant of Islamic architecture reached a peak of magnificence. In India the earlier dominance of a Pathan dynasty, which had established its capital in Delhi in 1206, declined after the death of Mohammed Shah in 1316. A series of independent states, with capitals at Jodhpur, Ahmadabad, Mandu, Gaur, Gulbarga, Golconda and Bijapur were effectively autonomous until their gradual absorption into the Mughal dominions. This dynasty, whose first emperor was Babur (1526–56) had its capital at Delhi, and under Akbar the Great at Agra. Akbar also founded the short-lived capital of Fatehpur Sikri, which survives almost intact. He was succeeded by three equally powerful emperors before the dynasty crumbled in the eighteenth century.

The story thenceforward is dispiriting throughout the Islamic world. General territorial stability in the eighteenth and nineteenth centuries was the concomitant of the increasing influence of European commercial and technological superiority. In India the Mughal dynasty yielded to the ascendancy of the British East India Company, and the absorption of the Indian sub-continent gradually but inevitably into the British Empire brought with it English colonial architecture and a lack of confidence in native styles, which inhibited important further development. Afghanistan and Persia retained their independence, but made no architectural advance. The Khanates of Central Asia, while relatively isolated from European influence were equally inhibited by their economic stagnation until the nineteenth century, when they fell victim to Russian territorial expansion.

Constantinople, the heart of the Ottoman Empire, fell increasingly under the cultural influence of France and Italy, and in the nineteenth century became dependent on technical help from Germany. A distinctive hybrid form of Islamic architecture developed in Constantinople, in which Renaissance and Ottoman Islamic forms were merged. The provinces of the Ottoman Empire from Iraq to Egypt made neither effective economic, political nor architectural progress. The most western provinces on the North African coast came under French suzerainty, where positive architectural achievement was essentially European in tradition.

Major political changes in the twentieth century resulted in the creation of the largest Islamic state—Pakistan, founded in 1947, and the break-up of the largest Islamic Empire—Turkey, defeated in the First World War. Turkey became a republic in 1920 and thereafter was territorially confined to Thrace and Anatolia. With the exception of parts of the U.S.S.R. all Islamic countries achieved total self government after the Second World War. In many places the traditions of Islamic building have been applied to the needs of expanding communities and changed situations. The combination of traditional forms and the technological opportunities of twentieth–century architecture has proved difficult. The vigour of much of the endeavour indicates that in due course a more coherent style could emerge.

SOCIAL

The Arab groups, which were the spearhead of the advance of Islam, were essentially tribal, and in consequence the behaviour patterns and cultural attributes of emergent Islamic societies were based on the traditions of the desert. Overrunning lands that had for many years known more sophisticated forms of civilization, the Arabs accepted the patterns of organization which they encountered where these were not in conflict with their own requirements. As Moslem communities become stabilised over the succeeding centuries, a clear social pattern emerged in which public life was reserved for men. Women played a secondary role, almost inevitably assuming a major share of the domestic, and sometimes of the agricultural, burden. Only among nomadic groups did the Moslem world accept any degree of equality between the sexes in public life; for the rest, the woman's place was in the private part of the household—the harem. In public she was protected by the anonymity of the veil. Men performed the significant public duties and controlled all public affairs, and this social structure had direct architectural consequences in the layout of domestic and public buildings.

Islamic states made provision for the existence within them of self-contained groups of different religions. These separate communities were 'peoples of the book'—Jews and Christians—whose beliefs were based on revelations and teachings contributory to Islam. Such peoples were entitled to a protected status, in which they retained freedom of worship and internal self-government. Thus the social pattern of Moslem states must be seen as having included substantial and sometimes even majority populations of protected peoples, while several of the Islamic empires, notably the Turkish and Mughal, governed extensive territories in which major groups of non-Moslems lived. Government was normally direct, by a despotic ruler or his deputy, and the law was based on the teachings of the Prophet, interpreted by a theologically-trained judiciary. Conversion was not normally forced and was occasionally discouraged, though apostasy was rare and usually perilous.

RELIGIOUS

Islam is the last of the three great religions of the Middle East. Its essence is contained in a simple sentence, which is both the profession of faith and the credo of its adherents: 'There is only one God and Mohammed is his prophet.' The Faith is held to be the ultimate revelation of God's will for creation. It is a complete philosophy of life and government, and there is no differentiation in Islamic thinking between religious and secular matters: consequently Islamic precepts apply equally to all behaviour and all buildings. The Faith is also held to be the logical successor to Jewish and Christian teaching, and preaches a doctrine of tolerance towards these earlier-founded religions.

Moslem thought is codified in three works. Of these, the Koran is regarded as revelation through the medium of the Prophet Mohammed; the Hadith is a collection of his sayings or injunctions, and is of lesser weight; while the Law is extracted from the Prophet's instructions, from tradition and example. On these basic compilations rests the whole philosophical structure of the Islamic world.

The Prophet's successors were the Caliphs, but with the exception of the first four (the 'rightly guided') Caliphs, their authority was of no real consequence in moulding the religion. There was an early·dispute over the succession, and there were at times rival Caliphs in different parts of the Islamic world. The direct line of Caliphs ruled in Medina, Damascus, Kufa, Baghdad, Samarra, Raqqa, Cairo and Constantinople, the last holder of the office being the Ottoman Sultan deposed in 1920. The office itself was abolished in 1922. One influential line of descent from Mohammed continues in the Aga Khan.

Within forty years of the Prophet's death, a major division of belief occurred in the Moslem world. The essential dispute hinged upon the method of determining the succession to the leadership, and to this dispute can be traced the powerful schism that divides the Islamic world into Sunni and Shia persuasions. For architectural purposes, it can be said that the more orthodox sect is the Sunni, strongest in Turkey and North Africa: Shia beliefs have traditionally been strongest in Persia and Iraq.

The Islamic faith produced in successive generations of its followers a way of life and a set of attitudes which had great influence on their architecture. These may be summarised as: an acceptance of the dominance of Islam and the immutability of its revelations; an acceptance of the transitory nature of earthly life; personal humility; an abhorrence of image-worship. The effects of these beliefs on Islamic architecture can be seen in the following characteristics: there is no essential differentiation in techniques between buildings with a directly religious connotation and other buildings; that important architectural endeavour is normally expended on buildings having a direct social or community purpose, including that of worship; that decorations tend towards the abstract, using geometric, calligraphic and plant motifs, with a preference for a uniform field of decoration rather than a focal element; and that a basic conservatism discouraged innovations and favoured established forms.

TERMINOLOGY

A number of basic terms are inevitable since they have no direct equivalent in other sections. The terms themselves may vary between countries, in which case the relevant country is indicated in parentheses.

(1) Building types. *Masjid* (Persia, India), *Jami*: mosque, principal place of worship, the word Jami indicating the use of the building for Friday prayers. *Mesjid* (Turkey): small prayer house. *Madrassah* (Egypt), *Medrese* (Turkey): religious college and mosque. *Saray*, *Serai*: palace.

(2) Building components. *Mihrab*: niche orientated towards Mecca. *Mimber*: raised platform for ceremonial announcements. *Iwan*, *Ivan* (Persia): open-fronted vault facing on to a court. *Bab*: gateway. *Sahn*: courtyard of a mosque, also described as 'ablutions court' (Turkey). *Minaret*: tower from which call to prayer is made. *Harem*: women's or private quarters of a house or palace. *Selamlik*: men's or guests' quarters. *Kibla*, *Kible*: axis orientated towards Mecca. *Chattri* (India): kiosk.

(3) Personnel. *Muezzin*: caller who summons the faithful to prayer. *Imam*: man who leads the congregation at prayer. *Caliph*: successor to the Prophet as military, judical and spiritual leader of Islam.

ARCHITECTURAL CHARACTER

Islamic architecture, insofar as it can be defined, is not the product of any one place or people. It is the product of a major historic event—the rapid conquest of diverse territories by a people with no architectural tradition, and the consequent synthesis of styles under one philosophy but in many different circumstances.

The majority of Islamic buildings are fundamentally related to a principal axis. This axis (and secondary axes) frequently extended into a formal landscape which is an integral part of the design. While the prime axis was the kibla, the general concept was derived from the line of balance and symmetry implicit in the concept of perfect creation. This was the basis of the formal disposition of gardens, buildings, parts of buildings and of articles as small as rugs.

The discipline inherent in Islamic architecture is apparent in the slow evolution of form and the relatively limited repertoire of elements employed. Most commonly these were arcades, domed spaces, courts and very large portals, perhaps incorporating a 'great' niche, the iwan. Islamic architecture is fundamentally centred upon God. At its heart is the mosque, an inward-looking building whose prime purpose is contemplation and prayer. It is a space removed from the immediate impact of worldly affairs. It is not, however, designed to be spiritually uplifting, nor to produce a sense of exaltation, and there is no positive object of attention or of adoration.

Above all things the mosque is essentially democratic; in it all have equal rights, and it may serve many functions other than prayer. It is still commonly used as a school, transactions may be made there and treasures stored. Official notices are given out there and newly-arrived caravans normally repaired to the mosque where travellers have the right of shelter; and though many of these functions have become comparatively unimportant in modern society, the mosque remains the focus of Moslem life—something between a forum and a prayer house.

The mosque was a novel conception, of which the first example was the court-yard of the Prophet's house at Medina. The earliest consist of open courts sur-rounded by arcades (as in Syria) or by trabeated timber colonnades with flat roofs. An early innovation was the minaret, a tower from whose top the Muezzin gave the call to prayer (a form of summons adopted in deliberate distinction to the clapper used by early Christians).

The form of some of the earliest mosques appears to have been derived almost accidentally. The mihrab, a concave niche occupied by the Imam leading prayers, was first introduced by the Caliph Al Walid in rebuilding the Prophet's Mosque at Medina. It may have its origins with the Coptic workmen employed there. The first minarets were the extant towers of the temenos of the Hellenistic temple which became the Great Mosque at Damascus. These served as the prototypes for the first purpose-built minarets, which appear to have been those of the mosques of Omar, Bosra and 'Amr, Fustat. The size of the earliest Iraqi mosques followed the precedent of the first mosque at Kufa (638) whose boundaries were determined by successive arrow-casts in four directions. Converted churches, sometimes shared with their original owners, set the pattern of the Syrian mosques. In these eastward-orientated churches Moslems were obliged to pray across the line of the nave and aisles, setting a precedent for the cross-arcading of many congregational mosques on the western side of the Arabian Desert.

The early custom of building the governor's residence and treasury against the kibla wall of the mosque followed a burglary. In consequence the Caliph instructed that the two should be joined, so that users of the mosque would constitute a watch 'by day and night'.

These casual influences, combined with the work of local craftsmen steeped in the pre-Islamic tradition, produced distinctive architectural styles on the eastern and western sides of the Arabian Desert. During the Ummayad period the styles bore a close relationship to each other and to preceding Sassanian and Byzantine work. During this period the theological proscription of imagery had not become formalized, and within decorative limits figurative representation was used quite freely, although it never became iconographic. Indeed its principal use was secular.

The mosque was of such central importance to the life of the community that it became the dominant building type, and its form is echoed in structures built for other purposes. It is always conceived round an axis directed towards Mecca and, with the exception of the earliest instances, this axis is terminated on the inner face of the mosque by the mihrab—a niche where the leader of the congregation (the Imam) makes his prayers. This act, which involves prostration, must be observed from other parts of the prayer chamber and lateral vision is, therefore, important. The congregation assembles in lines traversing the main axis and takes its cue from the Imam, or from those in the centre of the line in a position to observe him. Thus a multi-columned hall with transverse aisles is acceptable. Since there is nothing sacrosanct about the mihrab, secondary mihrabs are often placed in other positions of convenience, for the use of smaller congregations or individuals. The prayer space is almost unfurnished; in a congregational mosque it is normally provided with a mimber—a platform approached by a steep flight of steps—from which formal pronouncements can be made. A part of the prayer space may be railed off or fitted with a balcony for special uses—those of a dignatory or ruler, or of Muez-zins or women. There is sometimes also a fixed reading desk or preaching stool which can take various forms.

The congregational mosque usually has a courtyard, which precedes the prayer chamber and contains a tank or fountain for ritual ablution. In harsher climates this is not as a rule held to be an integral part of the prayer space, and footwear is permitted: in more temperate regions the reverse is the case. In the larger mosques the courtyard is generally surrounded by an arcade. All but the meanest and earliest mosques have a raised place for the use of the Muezzin, and in the majority of cases this takes the form of a tapering tower, frequently equipped with balconies. Mosques with more than one such minaret were by almost universal tradition built by members of the ruling house; four is the normal maximum, a mosque with six is exceptional, while the Ka'aba at Mecca is unique with seven. Although the position of the minaret varied widely, several clear tendencies are apparent: a single minaret associated with the main entrance (Mesopotamia and North Africa); coupled minarets associated with the entrance gate (Seljuk and post-Seljuk Persia); a single minaret off-centre between courtyard and prayer chamber, usually on the south side (Turkey). In the more important buildings multiple minarets were disposed symmetrically about the prayer chamber. The relationship between prayer chamber and minarets is subject to many variations, from the dominance of a massive tower over an anonymous courtyard wall, to the elegant counterpoint of a slender needle against the powerful mass of a great dome.

The courtyard which is so fundamental a feature of the mosque is also in its several variations the principal element of other building types, the college (medrese, or madrassah), the hostel (han or caravanserai), the palace and the house. According to their function the courtyards were cloistered and arcaded and the sides were punctuated with gateways, prayer chambers or arched porches (iwans). The other important element is the single building cell. At one extreme this might be the simple kiosk used in isolation as a little ornamental pavilion, emphasizing a roof, or providing a focus in a pleasure garden; it might take the form of the massive tomb, high and domed, or it might be repeated to form a cloister, terrace or court. It is an almost universal rule in Islamic building that each cell of a complex building structure is individually expressed, in plan and in volume. Rarely, except in domestic examples, is a concealing envelope wrapped around a multi-cellular construction.

All traditional constructional techniques were employed, including baked and unbaked bricks, timber framing with brick or plaster infill, rubble and worked stone. A wide variety of facings and castings was used. The technique of striated masonry (alternate bands of brick and stone) was borrowed from Byzantium.

The most important form of opening was the pointed arch, which was principally two- and four-centred and generally constructed as a true arch, though corbelled examples were common in India. Arches were generally tied. It is now apparent that the use of the two-centred arch was established both in Syria and Mesopotamia in the sixth century A.D. and that its use in Islam represents a continuation of an evolutionary trend already under way at the time of the Arab invasion. Trabeated construction was largely confined to work in timber, except in some parts of India. Window openings were frequently small and traditionally closed with wooden shutters, iron bars, marble grilles or plaster lights set with clear glass. The construction of doors tended to be complex for decorative reasons, and to depend upon the skilful assembly of a large number of small components. The relieving arch was frequently used, often in conjunction with a lintel, when the lunette might be glazed or filled with a decorative panel.

In Europe and parts of Asia Minor flat and pitched roofs were normally constructed of timber. Elsewhere they often consisted of close assemblies of pole joists, frequently of poplar or palm. Stone slab roofs were largely confined to India and parts of Syria. Barrel-vaulting or cross-vaulting was extensively used for minor spans, particularly for caravanserais, bazaars, military work and cisterns, and often also included in the less significant parts of major public buildings. Domes were widely used throughout the Islamic world: Persian, Mughal and Egyptian domes tended to be pointed in contrast to the hemispherical Turkish version. Pitched roofs in the Mediterranean countries were generally covered with Roman tiles, while domes were sheathed in marble in India, ceramic tiles in Persia and Iraq and lead in Asia Minor and Europe. Flat roofs were rendered, paved, sealed with bitumen or compacted clay.

Ancient Greek and Roman columns were often re-used by Moslems, and thus became models for new work, particularly in Turkey. Fluted columns were not employed, but tapering circular shafts, with entasis, were common, except in parts of Persia where Sassanian influence continued, and in India, where a square form occurs derived from Jain models. A wide variety of mouldings and friezes is found; Ottoman architecture in particular is distinguished by a rich vocabulary of mouldings often used in isolation from other forms of ornament. Moslem architecture is also characterized by friezes and crestings, often associated with the mouldings. Abstract and geometric motifs were basic constituents of Islamic ornament. Decoration of Moslem buildings was extensive and made use of the following techniques: carving in bas-relief, stone inlay, stone mosaic, structural assembly of contrasting stone, patterned brickwork, carved stucco, ceramic facing, ceramic mosaic, glass mosaic, painting, timber inlay and pietra dura. Motifs were derived from calligraphy, floral abstraction and geometric interlacement. At its best Moslem architecture achieves great distinction in the use of ornament which, however brilliant, rich in colour, extensive or skilful, is always secondary in function to architectural form and never the focus or raison d'être of the work.

Among precise architectural features, the following are the most frequently recurrent and characteristic: arcading, both timber and masonry; the pointed arch; the true dome; columns, similar in proportion to Graeco-Roman models or their derivatives; squinches, stalactite corbelling and pendentives. Of structural and decorative techniques those of which Moslems make the most significant use are: banded or striated masonry (including brick and stone coursing); decorative bonding for brickwork; interlocked and inlaid stone masonry; metal or timber ties to arches; bas-relief carving in stone, timber and plaster; ceramic cladding and facing; interlocking panelled geometric timber construction; screens or pierced grilles in marble, metal or timber for window openings, internal window lights in stained glass set in plaster; colonettes, particularly at quoins; stalactite decoration.

The pointed arch, sometimes stilted, was used from the earliest stages in Moslem development, producing a series of forms: two-centred, four-centred, horseshoe, cusped, foliated and ogee. Initially used only as a two-centred form with separations of upwards of one tenth, a more pronounced form with separations of one fifth became standard in the eighth century after which the four-centred types came into use.

An important structural and ornamental device, the stalactite, is peculiar to countries dominated by Islam. It can be used as a corbel to close an opening, as a frieze, as a pendentive and to reduce a square to a chamfer on an arris or capital. Inverted, it is occasionally used to transpose a circular or multi-faceted shaft to a square base. A similar purpose is served by the 'Turkish Triangle', an arrangement of slender triangles, interlocked and with their planes at variance. The use of stalactites (also known as muqarnas), which is something between a decorative and a structural technique, requires description. The construction is a form of corbelling in which the corbel is set at an angle to the main wall, the arris of the corbel being the furthest projection. This supports in turn similar corbels placed above the first and on either side of it, so that their line of junction continues the arris of the first corbel. The process repeated successively produced a continuous corbelling which can be elaborated and decorated to an astonishing degree. It has provided

Islamic artists with a device capable of application to many materials, on the largest and smallest scale. It has been used to dazzle and delight the beholder, to display the virtuosity of the artist and the wealth of his patron and in the process has become more peculiarly identified with Islam than any other feature.

The influence of Islamic architecture had consequences in Europe, particularly in the introduction and development of the pointed arch and vault, in various aspects of military architecture, in types and techniques of ornament and in plan forms such as the cloister. These skills were apparent to Sir Christopher Wren who wrote (in his history of Westminster Abbey, 1713) 'This we now call the Gothick manner of architecture . . . tho' the Goths were rather destroyers than builders I think it should with more reason be called the Saracen style; for those people wanted neither arts nor learning.' 'Those people's' architecture was a compound of the religious philosophy of Mohammed and the legacy of Hellenistic and Sassanian arts of building. The resultant style, developed under Arabic, Syrian, Persian, Turkish and Mughal inspiration reached peaks of accomplishment that rank high among man's achievements.

EXAMPLES

THE ARAB PENINSULA, SYRIA AND MESOPOTAMIA

Apart from some fragmentary remains of a few Yemeni buildings, the evidence for any tradition of fine architecture in Arabia at the time of the Prophet is virtually confined to literary indications of the composite timber and stone construction adopted in the building of the sacred object at Mecca—the Ka'aba. On this slender basis it would appear likely that the Red Sea States of the Arabian Peninsula were in pre-Islamic times using structural methods then common in Abyssinia. There is no substantial evidence that in the seventh century the Arabs of Mecca and Medina possessed either architectural knowledge or tradition beyond the simple vernacular. To meet the religious and administrative needs in lands they had conquered and to establish their dominant political position in visual terms, the Arabs, therefore, made use of local craftsmen. They did not impose a style, having none to impose, and consequently the local traditions and techniques continued.

Kufa is a new town founded within six years of the death of Mohammed, and stands on the desert fringe of the Tigris-Euphrates basin. Its great mosque and palace were short-lived, but the complex is important, both in establishing a type and in demonstrating an immediate acceptance of Sassanian influence. The **Great Mosque** (c. 640) was a primitive building whose courtyard was marked only by a ditch. On its southern or kibla side a covered colonnade extended across the full width. There was no mihrab. The **Dar al-Imara** (Palace) ultimately consisted of a double enceinte wall, buttressed by half-round attached towers on the square plan of a Roman frontier fort. The central area contained a complex of buildings around a great court terminating in a columned, aisled hall which led to a domed chamber.

Kubbet es-Sakhra (the Dome of the Rock), **Jerusalem** (688–92), (p. 417A) is probably the most fundamentally important Islamic structure. Though sometimes described as a mosque it should properly be thought of as a shrine. It consists of a great central dome covering the summit of Mount Moriah, whence the Prophet is believed to have made his night ride to Heaven. Its double timber dome is carried on a great masonry arcade, which is surrounded by arcaded aisles on an octagonal plan. The interior is richly finished in quartered marble and glass mosaic. A Corinthian colonnade carries the great arcade of two-centred arches, and inner and outer aisles are separated by a second colonnade of Corinthian columns, surmounted by an arcaded wall structure. The exterior wall surface, now sheathed in sixteenth-century Turkish tiles, was originally faced with glass mosaic. The dome, although subsequently reconstructed, has always consisted of an approximately concentric cross-braced inner and outer timber framework. From the first its sheathing has been faced with gilded plates of copper. In concept the building is similar to the Byzantine Holy Sepulchre at Jerusalem which it was designed to emulate (p. 358). In structural technique it closely follows Syrian precedent, and in decoration it is a continuation of the traditions of Hellenized Syria. Built by the Ummayad Caliph Abd Al-Malik, although in its features the building seems entirely Syrio-Byzantine, it has an underlying quality which anticipates the aesthetic of succeeding Islamic work, and the influence of its high dome on later Islamic architecture can hardly be overstressed.

The **Mosque of Al-Aqsa, Jerusalem** (710 and later) is the most ancient mosque in Jerusalem, and stands adjacent to the Dome of the Rock and aligned upon it. A primitive structure was replaced about 710–15 by the Caliph Al-Walid. The original probably consisted of an aisled hall with colonnades parallel with the kibla axis. Subsequent reconstructions in 780 and 1035 have produced a multi-aisled prayer space, in which the central aisle is flanked by Corinthian colonnades of Roman proportions, carrying an arcaded wall complete with triforium and clearstorey, and terminated by a dome over what, in so church-like a structure, it is tempting to call the sanctuary. The rebuilding was carried out under the Abbasid Caliph Al-Mahdi in 780 but the workmanship is local and shows no trace of Persian influence.

The **Great Mosque, Damascus** (p. 417B, C) is the earliest mosque to survive intact. The original temple of Damascus stood in a walled temenos (sacred enclosure). At each corner of its rectangular plan there stood a square tower. In the Christian era a church was built within the enclosure, occupying a small part of the centre, probably the temple itself. After the Arab conquest another part of the enclosure was simultaneously used as a mosque. In 705 the Caliph Al-Walid, needing a mosque adequate for the large congregation of his capital, took over the entire temenos, and constructed on its long south side a series of parallel arcades, carrying pitched roofs and intersected by a central aisle on the mihrab axis. A dome was carried on a high drum built over the middle of this central aisle, and arcades were added on the remaining sides of the temenos. Piers and Corinthian columns carried the mixed pointed and semicircular arcades, which are surmounted by a secondary arcade half the height of the lower. This is the first of many examples of the use of superimposed arcades to give greater height to a mosque interior. Despite the clearly Romano-Byzantine techniques of construction and decoration, the building is obviously designed for Moslem purposes and has a strong Islamic quality. In particular it possesses important early decorative elements in its geometric window grilles and the extensive mosaic decoration in the arcades of the courtyard, where tellingly literal landscape is employed as an even field of decoration. The Great Mosque at Hama, Syria, is strikingly similar, though on a smaller scale.

The **Mosque of the Prophet's House, Medina.** The house of Mohammed was enlarged and rebuilt as a full congregational mosque in 707–9 by Greek and Egyptian craftsmen augmenting local labour. The introduction of one of the first two mihrabs in Islam (the mosque at 'Amr was contemporary—see below) has given rise to the suggestion that the mihrab may have a Coptic origin. The mosque was rebuilt in stone with a colonnade on the kibla wall, and has since been much reconstructed. It contains the simple tomb of the prophet.

The Arab Ummayad dynasty and its court was composed of men long-bred to

A. Kubbet es-Sakhra (Dome of the Rock), Jerusalem (688–92). See p. 415

. The Great Mosque, Damascus:
courtyard (c. 706–15). See p. 416

C. The Great Mosque, Damascus:
interior

the traditions of the desert. As a complement to and release from an irksome urban life, they built themselves a series of 'retreats' on the desert fringes of the lands they had conquered. Generally modelled on Roman frontier forts, these comprised a complex of buildings contained within a high, defensive external wall, buttressed by three-quarter and half-round towers. Their plans normally depend upon successive internal subdivision into compartments composed of three equal sections.

The **Palace of Minya, Tiberias,** in Syria (c. 715) consists of a square enclosure just over an acre in extent, with one great entrance flanked by rounded towers. Within the enclosure two-storeyed buildings surround a central courtyard. The outer wall was crenellated and many of the ceremonial rooms of the building were richly decorated with marble facings and mosaic floors.

Kasr Karaneh, Jordan (probably early seventh century) (p. 420A) stands on the Syrian side of the desert and exhibits the typical tripartite subdivision which leaves a small central courtyard surrounded by a two-storeyed structure of interlinked rooms. The character of the detailing is quite remarkably Sassanian in quality for a position so far west.

The **Small Palace, 'Amr,** in Jordan (712–15) is less formal and regular in plan. It does not have the typical defensive aspect of other contemporary buildings, and appears to have served as a hunting lodge and baths. It is interesting on account of a complex tripartite vaulting system and the very early use of pointed arches. Its massive construction and comparative isolation have preserved it remarkably intact, the entire series of domes and vaults remaining. The principal fame of this little building rests on the remarkable surviving fresco paintings, which are the most extensive secular pre-Romanesque paintings in existence and are very largely figurative in character, portraying wild animals and dancing girls. A building of similar purpose but later in date is the **Bath of As Sakrah.** Both these buildings probably served as the centre of the court encampment, possibly for quite long periods. Their use was particularly favoured during the spring pasturage when the desert had been watered by the scant winter rains.

Qasr al Hair as Sharqi (728–9), in Syria, is situated in thin grassland northeast of Palmyra, and is a particularly fine survivor of a typical walled estate containing irrigated gardens and pastures. Two fortified, buttressed rectangular enclosures stand side by side, the first of greater mass and more compact exhibiting the typical Ummayad tripartite subdivision of succeeding stages: the second, larger and more loosely planned, appears to have been a slightly later rationalization of the encampment which grew up outside the gate of the fortified palace. A large part of the shallow valley in which the buildings stand was enclosed by a three mile wall to form a 'Hair' or game preserve. The mosque in the larger enclosure continues Byzantine traditions of detailing and the group contains possibly the first example in Islamic art of the joggled voussoir; the building also includes an early example of the defensive feature later so important in the Middle East and Mediaeval Europe, the machicolation.

Khirbet an-Mafjar, Jordan (743–8) is a monumental palace complex which stood in walled gardens. The principal buildings were a great bath, an elaborate residential palace and a mosque. The façade of the palace, with its blind arcading, betrays the influence of buildings such as Ctesiphon and foreshadows the later great Abbasid palaces. Sumptuous mosaic floors and almost obsessively rich ornamentation reflect the intermingling of Roman and Sassanian influences.

The **desert palace of Mshatta,** Jordan (745 and later) was under construction at the same time and incomplete at the fall of the Ummayad dynasty. It stood on the western fringe of the deserts and was the most ambitious of its type, exhibiting the typical planning process of successive division into three parts with the main axial approach on the centre line. Typically a great centre court was flanked by ranges of interlinked buildings, contained within a square boundary wall, reinforced with half-round buttress towers, with three-quarter round towers at the corners. Superb workmanship and a high degree of finish raise the bas-relief dados and panels to a peak of achievement for the period. Their inclusion externally indicates that the defensive mien of the structure was of little practical importance. In the detailing Sassanian and Hellenistic influences are so fused that a recognizably Islamic style has been defined. The building was never finished.

The revolution that swept the Ummayad dynasty from power (and with one exception to death) carried the centre of government eastward into Mesopotamia, into the heartland of the earlier Sassanian Empire, where Persian attitudes, Persian power and Persian influence relatively quickly relegated the Arab into second place. Even militarily the Arabs were replaced by a Turkish caste gradually brought in from Central Asia.

The **City of Baghdad** Iraq (762 onward). A few miles up the Tigris from the decaying Sassanian capital Ctesiphon, the triumphant Caliph Al-Mansur established a new capital as the centre of the Islamic world. Circular in plan, moated and walled, with four great entrances on the principal axes, its diameter was nearly 2,743 m (9,000 ft) and the surrounding great wall was almost 18.3 m (60 ft) high. The palace at the centre was built on intersecting cross axes radiating from the four gates at the cardinal points. The whole of the centre of the city was given over to the palace, which accommodated the administrative buildings and was crowned by a high green dome that came to symbolize the capital. The residential quarters formed a ring immediately inside the great wall. For the first time in Islam the new Abbasid city gives evidence of a ruler insulated from his people in palatial pomp within the capital itself. Nothing now survives of the round city, and its character must be deduced from fragmentary descriptions and comparative work at Samarra (see below).

Ukhaidir, Iraq (possibly 780) (p. 420B). Variously described as a palace and fortress the remarkable ruin of Ukhaidir is something of both. It stands by a small Wadi on the eastern fringe of the Arabian Desert and appears to be associated with two other isolated ruins of similar character, the tower Minar Mujdeh and the brick-built Khan At'Shan. Ukhaidir consists of a high buttressed rectangular enceinte over 168 m (550 ft) square standing within a low walled compound. The subdivision into courtyards includes a court of public reception and a mosque. The interior structure is entirely rough rubble, with elliptical and pointed vaults built without centering and the whole building was faced in a coarse stucco. While its impressive massing derives from its function, much of the internal quality demonstrates a vigorous architectural style that is of Sassanian inspiration, no doubt reflecting contemporary Baghdad.

The **City of Raqqa,** Syria (c. 774 and later) was founded on the banks of the Euphrates. Its walls, in the style of Baghdad, had an irregular circular form except for the southern side, which followed the profile of the river bank. In addition to sections of the mud-brick wall and fragments of the palace an important vaulted gateway survives, the Baghdad Gate, exhibiting a magnificent interplay of patterned brickwork. The gate is of particular importance in that it incorporates the earliest surviving major four-centred arch. The arch construction is typically Abbasid with opposed rings of voussoirs. The arrangement of the gate (probably tenth century) is an important early example of the oblique entrance, which forced the attacker to pass from an outer to an inner gate past defended works.

The **City of Samarra,** Iraq (836) was founded by the Caliph Al-Mu'tasim. It stands on the Tigris upstream of Baghdad and was intended to remove the Caliph's

A. Kasr Karaneh, Jordan (probably early 7th cent.). See p. 418

B. The fortress-palace of Ukhaidir, Kerbala, Iraq (possibly 780). See p. 419

C. The Great Mosque, Samarra, Iraq (848 and later). See p. 421

Turkish army from the immediate vicinity of the population of Baghdad. The town was constructed in haste, largely in unbaked brick on a regular plan, being extended northwards along the east bank of the river. The huge city is not walled and has outlying buildings on the west bank of the river. It was built in three phases. Samarra was abandoned after about eighty years, when the Abbasid court returned to Baghdad, with the exception of a small walled town that grew up around the shrine of one of the twelve Shia Imams. Three distinct styles of ornament are distinguished, the first carved and precise, fresh, lively and of Hellenistic inspiration, the second modelled and transitional. By the third period a wholly new style had been synthesized in which powerful repetition of abstract moulded forms had supplanted the previous naturalism. The first palace, the **Bulkawara** was planned on a series of intersecting axes, the subdivisions accommodating gardens, courts and pavilions, at the centre of which stood the throne building facing an enormous flight of steps leading down to a riverside terrace. The immense wealth of the Caliphs was reflected in the luxurious decoration. The carved marble dados, carved and gilded timber roofs, walls elaborately painted in fresco, all had origins as diffuse as the empire from which Al-Mu'tasim had summoned his craftsmen. Apart from the painted brick-vaulted throne room it was generally a single-storey structure of masonry, with flat timber roofs carried on pole-joists.

The **Great Mosque or Malwiya, Samarra** (848 and later) (p. 420C), now disaffected, was the largest mosque ever built. It was the work of the Caliph Al-Mutawakkil, who also built the nearby mosque of Abu Dulaf (below). The Malwiya consisted of an immense walled courtyard on a ratio of three to two, 155 m × 238 m (510 ft × 780 ft) overall surrounded by four aisles, except on the south, where their number was increased to nine. The internal structure of mud-brick piers and pole-joisted roofs has long disappeared but the massive brick outer walls remain, buttressed at intervals of 15.2 m (50 ft) by half-round towers. The dramatic and evocative feature of this building is the enormous helicoidal minaret at the northern end, isolated from the mosque, but on the main axis. The notion of a winding ramp encircling a diminishing tower derives originally from the ziggurats of Mesopotamia (see p. 53), of which at least one example had survived to this period, though it appears to have been a Moslem innovation to apply the idea to a circular tower. The **mosque of Abu Dulaf** (860–1), a few miles north, was similar in design though not quite so large, but here the mud-brick outer wall has disappeared leaving the burnt brick arcades in isolation.

The **Qubbat as-Sulaibiya, Samarra,** (c. 863) was constructed over the grave of the Caliph Al-Muntasir. This is the first known mausoleum of Islamic history and was constructed on the orders of the Caliph's Greek mother, on a low hill on the west bank of the Euphrates and aligned upon the Great Mosque. It comprises an octagonal ambulatory around a square chamber which was originally covered with a dome. The grave was set beneath the plastered block structure, whose style set an important precedent for the octagonal tomb structures first popular in Central Asia and spreading thence into India and Turkey.

As a result of the abandonment of the city, the surviving ruins of Samarra provide one of the earliest important and coherent instances of the form of early Moslem domestic architecture. The houses here consisted of courtyard structures, usually on a proportion of three to two, presenting blank walls to the street, with the principal chambers (often T-shaped) at the further end. They were single-storeyed and flat roofed, constructed of mud-brick, with pole-joisted roofs, surfaced with compacted mud. Later Abbasid work after the abandonment of Samarra can be illustrated by some of the few buildings that survived the later destructions of Baghdad, principally **al-Mustansiriye** (1233) (p. 423A), a restored Madrassah comprising four iwans fronting on to a great court, impeccably executed in carved brickwork. This building and the similar **Amin-ed-Din Caravanserai** (1358) are mature examples of a well-established type important throughout the Abbasid and Safavid periods. One great gate of the city, **Bab-el-Wastani** survives consisting of a vaulted gatehouse on an island with linking bridges. A further important brick built bridge, the **Jisr-Harb, Balad** (1232) survives some 87 km (54 miles) north of Baghdad. It is typical of late Abbasid work in its use of the four-centred arch, carved and moulded brickwork and powerful modelling. A calligraphic frieze runs the entire length of the bridge.

The later buildings of Iraq, Palestine and the Arabian peninsula, though in many instances memorable, reflect developments elsewhere in Islam under Seljuk, Mamluk, Safavid and Ottoman dynasties, and are treated under the relevant sections. Later developments are illustrated by the nineteenth-century palace **Beit-el-din** in the Lebanon, a mountain retreat for a local semi-autonomous ruler. The plan is based on a fountain court open on one side, and the construction involves an elaborate decorative scheme of interlocking inlaid marble blocks. Despite sumptuous detailing minor European influence and a lack of stylistic dynamism mark this as a typical building of later Islamic work in the area.

EGYPT AND NORTH AFRICA TO TUNISIA

The **Mosque of 'Amr, Fustat.** The town of Fustat had been established by the Arab general 'Amr on his conquest of Egypt in 640. The earliest mosque was rebuilt in 673, when a minaret was added. No visually important part remains of the original mosque, which appears to have been of the basic Arabian pattern, with arcades surrounding a courtyard, the prayer hall being several aisles deep. It is known to have contained, after its second reconstruction, one of the earliest minarets and mihrabs. The mosque as it stands today is largely composed of thirteenth-, fourteenth- and eighteenth-century work. At present the arcades of the prayer hall run at right-angles to the kibla wall: in the ninth century they ran parallel to it in the Syrian manner. Its roof was always flat, the arcades being carried on Corinthian columns.

In 869 Ahmed Ibn Tulun (from Samarra) was appointed Governor first of Cairo and then of the whole of Egypt and, finding Fustat too small for his purposes, founded a new capital adjacent to the present citadel of Cairo.

The **Dar al-Imara and Mosque of Ibn Tulun, Cairo** (876–9) (pp. 423B, 425A, B) has many features related to the Great Mosque at Samarra. Rectangular walls enclose a courtyard, surrounded on three sides by a compound in which stands, almost on axis, a minaret enwrapped by a spiral ramp. The plan of the minaret is now, however, square. The arcade of the mosque itself is double on three sides and is carried on piers, while a similar multiple arcade forms the prayer space on the kibla wall. Though smaller than the earlier mosques of Samarra, it is a large building which retains its original form despite several restorations. Construction is in red brick, faced with stucco in which the friezes are incised. The modification of the basic Corinthian capital to the colonnettes of the arcade piers, the vine-leaf friezes and the intricate geometric window grilles, indicate a high level of architectural development. The admixture of several different types of ornament found separately at Samarra is taken to show that the mosque of Ibn Tulun was not only an essentially Iraqi building in type, but that it was built by craftsmen from Samarra who had arrived in Egypt a relatively short time before.

The **Mosque of Al-Azhar, Cairo** (970 and later) is the earliest surviving Fatimid structure and is a direct sequel to the mosque of Ibn Tulun. Successive alterations have very largely obscured the original design, but it had a rectangular court

A. The al-Mustansiriye Madrassah, Baghdad (1233). See p. 421

B. Mosque of Ibn Tulun, Cairo (876–9). See p. 422

C. Madrassah of Sultan Qaytbay, Cairo (1472–4). See p. 427

D. Madrassah of Sultan Qaytbay, Cairo: interior

flanked on three sides by a flat-roofed prayer space. The structure of the whole roof area consisted of a series of arcades of two-centred arches, carried on Corinthian colonnades tied transversely and longitudinally with wooden tie-beams, and running parallel to the kibla wall in all cases, except for the arcades on either side of the central aisle, which were extended above the roof in a clear-storey and terminated with a dome. This arrangement derived from the great Mosque of Kairouan (see p. 428) whence the Fatimids had come to Egypt. About twenty years later a similar mosque, that of **Al-Hakim** (finished 1013) was built with brick piers in place of columns to carry the arcades. The other surviving Fatimid mosque of importance in Cairo is the **Al-Aqmar Mosque** of 1035 (completed in 1125). The massive and elaborate entrance exhibits magnificent ribbed, hooded portals which contain very early examples of stalactite detailing.

The **Citadel, Cairo.** By the middle of the eleventh century the Fatimid Caliphs, like their Abbasid predecessors in Baghdad, were threatened by the growing power of the Turkish slaves brought in as body-guards. Seeking to strengthen their position, the Caliphs, particularly Al-Mustansir, rebuilt much of the mud walling of the city in magnificent masonry. One of the great gates built by his Armenian architects, the **Bab al-Futuh,** survives to demonstrate the architectural and military skills of northern Syria. Two great rounded bastions, with deep blind arcades, thrust forward to encompass a vaulted entrance which combined architectural magnificence with military impregnability.

The **Mosque of Sultan Baybars, Cairo** (1267–9) was the first mosque built by a Mamluk Sultan. It was of an interesting transitional type, with great iwans fronting its courtyard. The entrance gate carried the single great minaret. The arcades surrounding the courtyard ran parallel to the adjoining external wall in all cases and were constructed both of columns and piers. In front of the mihrab, a massive structure of masonry piers carried a large dome. The mosque thus becomes an important example of the transition of emphasis from the colonnaded hall to the domed central space, reflecting perhaps the northern origins of the new rulers.

The **Mosque and Tomb of Sultan Barkuk, Cairo** (1399–1412) forms a distinctive group in which twin domes and twin minarets are balanced about the central axis. The proportions of the dome structure, carried on massive cubes of masonry diminished by steps at the upper corners, carry very much further the now apparent urge to verticality, reflected also in the profile of the domes themselves. These are carried on high drums and move smoothly with unmarked transition into a flowing curve reflecting the two-centred arch. The minarets are remarkably delicate and constructed in diminishing stages.

A remarkable Fatimid work survives in Sicily, illustrating the extent to which Fatimid influence spread across the Mediterranean. The roof of the **Palatine Chapel at Palermo** built by Cairene craftsmen in c. 1138 for Roger II is a masterpiece of painted stalactite vaulting which is quite the equal of contemporary work in Baghdad.

With the end of the Fatimid Caliphate and the reintroduction of Sunni Orthodoxy into Egypt in 1171, a new building type appeared in Egypt, the Madrassah, or collegiate mosque.

The **Madrassah of Sultan Salih, Cairo,** is the earliest surviving example and typical of its kind, with an indirect entrance to the central courtyard on to which face four iwans, in the form already long established in Persia and Iraq.

The **Madrassah complex of Sultan Qala'un, Cairo** (1284–5) (p. 426B) is characterized by greater height in relation to width than its predecessors, and represents a sophisticated development of the Cairene style. The group contains a hospital and the founder's tomb, in addition to the madrassah. Within the tomb a

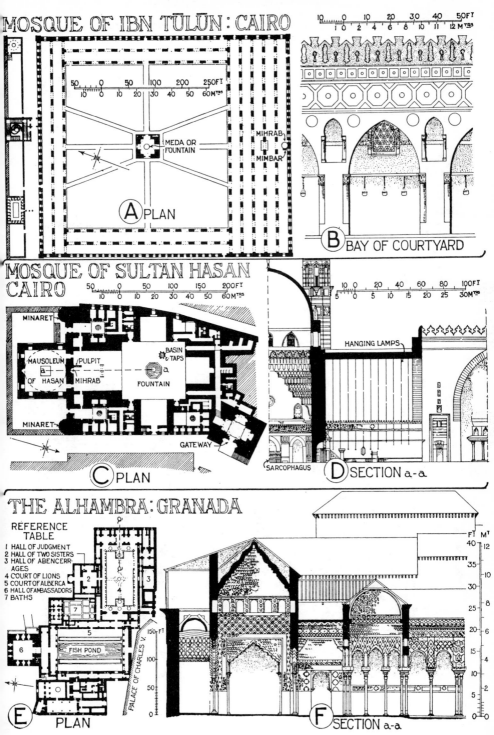

MOSQUE OF IBN TŪLŪN : CAIRO

50   0   50   100   200   250 FT
10   0   10   20   30   40   50   60 MTRS

MEDA OR FOUNTAIN

MIHRAB
MIMBAR

Ⓐ PLAN

10   0   10   20   30   40   50 FT
1   0   2   4   6   8   10   11   12 MTRS

Ⓑ BAY OF COURTYARD

MOSQUE OF SULTAN HASAN CAIRO

50   0   50   100   150   200 FT
10   0   10   20   30   40   50   60 MTRS

MINARET

MAUSOLEUM OF HASAN
PULPIT
MIHRAB
BASIN & TAPS
FOUNTAIN

MINARET

GATEWAY

Ⓒ PLAN

10   0   20   40   60   80   100 FT
5   0   5   10   15   20   25   30 MTRS

HANGING LAMPS

SARCOPHAGUS

Ⓓ SECTION a-a

THE ALHAMBRA : GRANADA

REFERENCE TABLE
1 HALL OF JUDGMENT
2 HALL OF TWO SISTERS
3 HALL OF ABENCERR-
  AGES
4 COURT OF LIONS
5 COURT OF ALBERCA
6 HALL OF AMBASSADORS
7 BATHS

FISH POND

PALACE OF CHARLES V.

150 FT
100
50
0

Ⓔ PLAN

FT   MT
40   12
35   10
30
25   8
20   6
15   4
10
5   2
0   0

Ⓕ SECTION a-a

A. The Great Mosque, Kairouan, Tunisia (c. 725). See p. 428

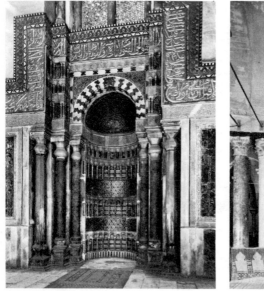

B. Madrassah of Sultan Qala'un,   c. The Great Mosque, Kairouan: interior
Cairo (1284–5): interior. See p. 424

Corinthian order carries a complicated octagonal arcade of pointed horseshoe arches; the high walls are lit by a triple series of windows whose upper members have a curious affinity with northern-European Romanesque. It is perhaps the most richly finished and evocative work of its period in North Africa.

The **Madrassah and Tomb of Sultan Hasan, Cairo** (1356–63) (p. 425C, D), has all the characteristic elements of the Egyptian madrassah on an impressive scale. A tortuous entrance passage leads obliquely into the central court, fronted by four large iwans. The sense of enclosure is here further emphasized by the scale of the 30 m (100 ft) high walls. On the main axis behind the mihrab stands the founder's tomb. The great entrance portal on the street is of similar size and scale, with handsome stalactite-headed opening and strongly modelled decoration.

The **Madrassah of Sultan Qaytbay, Cairo** (1472–4) (p. 423C, D), single-domed with horizontally-striated masonry, strongly vertical in emphasis, is situated in a tightly packed quarter of the city. It has a tall circular minaret of diminishing stages with elaborately decorated stalactite-corbelled balconies. The sub-structure of the dome chamber is now half as high again as it is wide, and the dome is carried on a tall drum from which it rises with a high profile to a point. The picturesque aspect of the asymmetric exterior is heightened by the striated facing whose colours are picked up in the elaborately banded, inlaid decoration of arches, friezes and crestings. The external surface of the dome of the mosque is carved with a deep-cut interlacement of bars, intertwined with floral motifs in a design that is both brilliant and typical of the extreme of elaboration achieved in this period. The interior is distinguished for its intricate inlay and carving, fine windows and handsome proportions.

At the end of the fifteenth century Cairo was both a prosperous mercantile city and the centre of the Caliphate. After the Ottoman conquest in the early sixteenth century the stylistic characteristics of important buildings altered, the most important patrons being Turkish, although Cairo remained a provincial capital with hundreds of mosques and many fine houses.

The influence of domestic ceremonial and tradition seems to have produced an element of continuity between Sassanian and Abbasid domestic building which was carried over into Tulunid Egypt and up to the nineteenth century. Two of the most distinguished houses of this tradition are the **Bayt al-Qady** (1495) and **the house of Jamal ad-din As-Zahabi** (1637). In the latter, as in a madrassah, a relatively small door to the street gives an oblique approach to the central court, from which a stair leads up to a loggia. This loggia is in effect an entrance hall leading to the principal public room, which consisted of a central well fronted by a dais on each side. In a grander building this reception space would be cruciform. Private rooms opened off this room and off the loggia, and a rigid segregation existed between harem (women's quarters) and selamlik (men's quarters and reception areas). These houses were all designed to be seen from within, the street façade being no more than a wall containing the minimum possible opening.

SPAIN AND WESTERN NORTH AFRICA

Apd ar-Rahman I was the only Ummayad leader to escape death at the hands of the Abbasids. From Syria he fled first to Tunisia and thence to Spain, accompanied by large numbers of Syrians, including no doubt leaders of political and social life. Their arrival raised what had been a distant and relatively unimportant province to a centre of intellectual and creative energy. The importance of Syrian influence in Ummayad Spain can hardly be overstressed, but before this there had been a series of important provincial developments in North Africa, chiefly in Tunisia.

The **Great Mosque, Kairouan,** Tunisia (c. 725) (p. 426A, C), founded in the late seventh century, is important for its minaret, the earliest complete surviving example of a structure built for the purpose. The architectural origin of this minaret can be traced to the square-shafted tapering stone church towers of Syria and the preceding Roman towers of the region. The tower itself consists of a massive, slightly tapering first stage, topped by two reduced, arcaded sections, the last being later in date (1294). It stands on axis over the main entrance to the mosque. The mosque itself has a near-rectangular courtyard, flanked by multi-columned arcades carrying a flat roof. Its incorrect southward orientation reveals its Syrian origins, and a similar reason probably accounts for the distinctive arcades of the prayer hall, which run at right angles to the kibla wall—a feature first found in the Al-Aqsa mosque at Jerusalem and immediately afterwards at Córdoba. In each of these cases the central aisle is lighted by a clear-storey and terminated in a dome (see also the Cairene mosques of Al-Azhar and Al-Hakim above). The building has several times been reconstructed, notably in 863 and 1294.

The **Great Mosque, Córdoba** (785 and later) (p. 429A, B, C) was begun in 785 by Apd ar-Rahman I. This first stage of the mosque displays a positive and vigorous quality that sets the pattern for the three major additions of 848 (Apd ar-Rahman II), 961 and 968 (Al-Hakam), and 987 (Al-Mansur). These were to make the mosque inferior in size only to the Malwiya and Abu Dulaf Mosques in Samarra. The minaret added by Apd ar-Rahman III (950) was of the square-towered Syrian type. The arcades set parallel to the main axis, are carried on a great variety of classical columns. Their height being inadequate for the mosque interior, its Syrian builders adopted the device previously used in the Great Mosque in Damascus of setting a double arcade on the columns. At Córdoba this was constructed by bringing the upper structure directly down on to the column in a stilt and throwing the lower arch across as a bracing member. The arches are round and constructed of alternating stone and multiple brick voussoirs, whose complexity and repetition produces an apparently endless flickering interplay, typical of the repetitive patterning traditional in Moslem architecture. In the successive additions this motif was elaborated, horseshoe and cusped arches made their appearances and finally their interlacement became even more complex, with secondary bracing arches springing from the crests of their lower counterparts. A number of minor domes were also introduced, carried on interlocked squinch arches, and the quality of decoration was brought to the highest levels of refinement. Under Al-Hakam, mosaic workers were even brought from Constantinople by arrangement with the Byzantine emperor. Though now a cathedral, the Great Mosque of Córdoba remains relatively unaltered, and stands as one of the supreme achievements of Islamic architecture.

The **Great Mosque, Susa (Sousse),** Tunisia (855) comprises a rectangular courtyard surrounded by barrel-vaulted arcades. The prayer-space, now six aisles deep and vaulted throughout, originally had only three aisles. While the overall form is typical of the multi-pillared congregational mosque, this is a major early example of vaulting applied to such a structure. Other early examples are the **Bu Fatata Mosque** (839), **Susa,** and the **Cistern at Ramla** near **Jerusalem** (789).

Madinat-al-Zahra. Apd ar-Rahman III built a new palatine city near Córdoba in 936. Although totally destroyed before it was a century old, it was a noble and carefully designed complex with much Syrian content, both in the masonry and in ornament and detail. Essentially it was a palace and administrative centre, with domestic ancilliaries. It is remembered principally for the brilliant precision of its bas-relief carving and its remarkable similarity to late Ummayad work in Syria 200 years earlier. A great rectangular compound wall enclosed three terraces covered with pavilions, courts, gardens and halls. The structural characteristics of the

A. The Great Mosque, Córdoba
(785 and later). See p. 428

B. The Great Mosque, Córdoba:
Capella de Villaviciosa (961–9)

C. The Great Mosque, Córdoba:
work of Apd ar-Rahman I

D. The Alhambra, Granada:
Court of the Lions (1338–90).
See p. 430

buildings seem to have been essentially those of the second phase of the building of the mosque at Córdoba, but such wealth and skill was expended on these structures that the city must have been the greatest achievement of Islamic Spain.

San Cristo de la Luz, Toledo (960), built as a mosque but subsequently used as a church, demonstrates an important change in character in Moslem building in Spain. As in the development of Egyptian mosques, so in Spain there was a tendency for proportions to become attenuated, with growing emphasis on the vertical. The mosque in Toledo was essentially a square compartment containing four columns, dividing the space into nine smaller squares. The central unit was roofed with a high dome, its springing being about four diameters above the floor. It was flanked by secondary domes, all constructed in variants of the interwoven arch technique. The upper openings in the compartment walls were heavily cusped and the great lower arches are all of a pronounced horseshoe form.

In the eleventh century Ummayad power in Spain declined into an alliance of petty princedoms eventually governed by a north African dynasty, the Al-Moravids. With their rule came a change towards a lighter and more decorative quality in building. Between 1135 and 1143 the **Qarawiyin Mosque in Fez** was extended. Part of the work involved the addition of plaster vaults on a wooden structure, an incongruity that illustrates an emotional rather than a rational approach to design. At the same time the **Mosque of Tlemcen** was lavishly improved, again with an emphasis on a lighter technique. Within a few years (soon after 1150) it was followed by the **Kutubiyya Mosque at Marrakesh** and then by the **Great Mosque at Tenmal.** These buildings collectively exhibit a concentration of effort on decorative elements and a consciously stylistic approach that has given an image of stalactites and horseshoe arches to Moroccan architecture, but is of secondary worth.

The **Alhambra, Granada** (1338–90) (pp. 425E, F, 429D) was, like Madinat-al-Zahra, a fortified palace with a complex of buildings set in gardens. Though Moslem power in Spain had already passed its peak when the Nasrid dynasty came to build their great palace at Granada, it flourished for just over a century as a brilliant finale, and the building survives as one of the most elaborate and richly decorated of extant Islamic palaces. The most important section dates from the middle and latter half of the fourteenth century. The principal part of the palace consists of two rectangular courts, one reserved for the use of the sovereign and his entourage and the other for public ceremonial. The latter, the Court of the Lions (p. 429D), 35 m × 20 m (115 ft × 66 ft), is surrounded by an arcade, in which very slender columns with high dosseret blocks carry a perforated arcade-structure of stucco, incredibly pierced and interlaced to give it a filigree-like delicacy. At the eastern end of the court is the Hall of Justice, while other halls terminate the cross axes. The domed structure covering each of these chambers is elaborated with a remarkable complexity of stalactite detail, executed with perfect discipline. The vertical surfaces of the chambers are covered with endless fields of interwoven arabesque ornament in carved stucco, and the walls of the Hall of Justice itself are treated with an elaborate display of stalactite arch, miniature columns, arabesque interlacings and calligraphic friezes. The Court of Myrtles, 42 m × 23 m (138 ft × 75 ft), has as the northern termination to its axis the massive tower of Komares, containing the Hall of Ambassadors, an almost symmetrical cubic chamber crowned by a polygonal dome; on each of three sides, triple openings lead through the profusely decorated walls to viewing balconies high above the city. The Alhambra, perhaps the most extraordinary achievement of Islamic architecture, is possessed of an almost ethereal quality, springing from its decorative complexity. A lack of structural validity and the relatively fragile nature of some of the materials (painted wood and plaster) are redeemed by the elegant handling and brilliant execution of the extremely refined design.

PERSIA (IRAN) AND TURKESTAN

The Arabs dominated Persia from the time of their whirlwind destruction of Sassanian military power at Nihevand in 641 until 750. With the ascendancy of the Abbasid Caliphs in Baghdad there arose a new political structure, in which roles were effectively reversed and Persian thinking and political power became dominant. Although in 962 the Gaznavid dynasty introduced the first wave of Turkish influence, Persian art and literature continued to flourish both in central Asia and present day Afghanistan and Iran throughout this and the succeeding rule of the Seljuk dynasty (1037 onwards). Mongol invasions under Genghis Khan in 1220, Hulagu Khan in 1258 and Tamerlaine in 1380 asserted the political dominance of central Asia and did tremendous damage to the established culture. In the Mongol homeland, however, there was an important cultural resurgence which suffered no subsequent defeat, although it went into gradual decline in the fifteenth century. In the early part of the sixteenth century rivalry with Ottoman Turkey strengthened and reunited Persia under the Safavid Dynasty, producing a cultural renaissance of which substantial architectural works survive. The Sassanian Kingdoms which had preceded the Moslem invasion had produced architecture of a high order: its intellectual brilliance was equalled by superb structural techniques, particularly in brickwork. Outstanding examples survived for many centuries, a great crumbling fragment of the colossal parabolic brick arch of Ctesiphon existing even today. It is misleading, however, to judge the succeeding early Islamic architecture in Persia by its few remains. Evidence indicates that there were three early types of mosque: the dome over a square structure of four arches on piers (an adaptation of the Sassanian fire temple), a simple barrel structure open at one end (essentially an iwan, a traditional Parthian and Sassanian form); and the Arabic open courtyard plan with a colonnade at one end. These elements were merged in various ways.

The **Tarik-han Mosque, Damghan** (early eighth century) is the oldest surviving Moslem building in Persia. Its plan is essentially 'Arabian' and comprises a colonnaded courtyard with a multi-columned prayer hall at one end, and a detached minaret. The chief features of the building are the massive circular piers 1.8 m (6 ft) in diameter and 3.6 m (12 ft) in height, from which spring equally ponderous parabolic arches carrying shallow domes. These arches were not remarkable in their time, but are an almost unique survival of a form deriving from the same source as the vast arch of Ctesiphon and leading to the introduction of the pointed arch. The mosque also contains four-centred pointed arches to the secondary spans.

The **Tomb of Ismail the Samanid, Bukhara** (c. 907) (p. 432C). A great cultural resurgence took place under the Samanid dynasty which ruled from Bukhara and Samarkand in the tenth century. Though its architectural remains are scanty, one important building survives, the relatively small domed mausoleum of Ismail constructed in highly decorative brickwork. The building is an almost perfect cube, on which is superimposed a hemispherical masonry dome. The main body of the structure is built in brick, the entire external surface carrying a series of complex patterns of basket-weave type, formed by elaborate brick bonding. The design is well-articulated and boldly modelled, with attached corner columns and a deep frieze of arched openings. The interior is as elaborate as the exterior, the entire finished surface being in brickwork. The building exemplified a highly-developed architectural form and is the precursor in character and structural

A. Inje Minare Medrese, Konya (1258). See p. 434

B. Gunbad-i-Qabus, Gurgan (1006). See p. 433

C. Tomb of Ismail the Samanid, Bukhara (c. 907). See p. 431

D. Chifte Minareli Medrese, Sivas (1271). See p. 434

content of a series of important Moslem tombs. A notable similar tomb is that of **Jalal ad-din al-Hussayni, Karakanid, Usgen** (1152).

The **Masjid-i-Jami, Nayin** (*c.* 960) is important for having the earliest surviving plaster work in Persia. Though a relatively unimportant building of its period the almost universal later destructions focus attention on it as an example. The mosque consists again of a central court surrounded by colonnades, although these are rather more complex and much larger in relation to the size of the court than those of the mosque at Damghan. The distinctly pointed arches, again carried on rounded piers are much taller and have elaborately carved stucco decoration on the columns, soffits of arches and around the mihrab. The ornament is remarkably free and has a much softer and more lyrical quality than the vigorous patterning of the tomb of Ismail. It seems likely that this building reflected the many more important buildings of the period, such as the Masjid-i-Jami in Shiraz.

Gunbad-i-Qabus, Gurgan (1006) (p. 432B). From the eleventh century onwards a series of great tomb towers were built as mausolea; of these the tall, simple, tapering cone-topped tomb built by Qabus in 1006–7 is much the most impressive. It stands 50 m (167 ft) high and is constructed entirely of brick, with no ornament save two spare bands of Kufic inscription. No other mausoleum was so tall or stark, and almost all were much more heavily decorated. Among the more important were: **Pir-i-alamder** (1021) and **Chihilpuktaran** (1058), both at **Damghan; Ala-ad-din, Varamin** (1287); the tomb of **Bayazit, Bistam** (1313); **Gunbad Abdullah, Damavend** (twelfth century); and the tomb of **Doghrul, Rayy** (1139).

Seljuk architecture became clearly established in the late eleventh century, developing in Turkestan, Persia, northern Iraq and eastern Turkey into a distinctive art form.

The **Masjid-i-Jami, Isfahan** (1071) is perhaps the most sumptuous and monumental of Persian Seljuk buildings. As it stands today it is an accretion of several different periods, but the eleventh-century Seljuk work is clearly distinguished and reaches its peak of achievement in the dome of Malik Shah, a great chamber which fronts the mihrab. Its structure is essentially brick and comprises a high pointed dome on an octagonal drum, incorporating squinches set on a cubic chamber. In this building the forms had become attenuated, the entire chamber being broken down into a series of high pointed arched segments, each forming a face of the octagon though set upon a square plan. For the first time in surviving Moslem art the adaption of a rectangular plan to a domed covering was achieved by a structure which displays a coherent emotive purpose. The plan of the mosque itself reflects Sassanian tradition and is an important departure from the previously universal Arabian type. Four iwans open on to the great central court, which is surrounded by two-storey arcades. The iwan of the prayer hall opens into a domed prayer chamber at the south of the building. The whole comprises a complex of vaults, cross vaults and domed chambers, covering an area of 122 m × 90 m (400 ft × 300 ft), the majority of which dates from the eleventh and twelfth centuries. It is built almost entirely of brick, and provides a brilliant demonstration of Seljuk mastery of the building of two- and four-centred arches, squinches, domes, ribbed and groined vaults and structural stalactites (muqarnas).

Rabat-i-Malik, Khurasan (eleventh century) is a desert caravanserai in an isolated region which illustrates the immensely resourceful handling of brickwork by the Seljuks. One great wall only remains, of which the central portion consists of massive drums, surmounted by stalactite-type arches and topped by a great carved Kufic frieze.

The **Masjid-i-Jami, Ardistan** (late twelfth century) comprises a four-iwan courtyard with the southernmost iwan opening into a domed prayer chamber, and is in many ways structurally similar to work at Isfahan. It is, however, smaller in scale, less extensive, and contains a wealth of incised brickwork and some ceramic friezes, replacing the pure patterned brickwork of Isfahan.

The **Haydariya, Qazvin** (twelfth century), a building of similar date and structural techniques, is an important early example of the madrassah type of plan, later to become so integral a part of Turkish architecture. A square courtyard, formed of a series of cells, focused on a square domed chamber in the centre of of the kibla wall. The mosque boasts a superb Kufic frieze in stucco.

The **Mausoleum of Sultan Sanjar, Merv** (1160) follows the form of the tomb of Ismail Samanid which here is greatly expanded into a monumental brick structure. Both the drum of the dome and the upper levels of the main chamber are elaborated with great arcades, and the main structure is built in a series of groined vaults, expressed on the face of the building. The construction is again entirely of brick, but the interior exhibits the extraordinary though surprisingly common technique of a plain brick face coated in plaster, which was subsequently incised in imitation of decorative brickwork.

The **Inje Minare Medrese, Konya** (1258) (p. 432A) is among the many remarkable buildings of the western Seljuks, who dominated Asia Minor, together with the **Buyuk Karatay Medrese** and the **Ala-ed-din mosque,** also at Konya. The Inje Minare Medrese was a monumental building possessing an extremely tall minaret, now destroyed, and the finest entrance portal in the whole of Seljuk architecture. The minaret was faced in ceramic brickwork and modelled with a series of vertical ribs. The gateway stands forward boldly in an isolated portal of overwhelming magnificence: its entire forward-facing surface is enlivened with calligraphic bands, boldly carried across the contours of the several recessed planes of the façade and complemented by moulds and friezes of astonishing virtuosity.

The Seljuks of Asia Minor centred on Konya form a partially isolated parallel development to that of the dynasty that controlled Persia. Influenced on the one hand by the Byzantines, and on the other by Syrian Moslems, their important works are spread widely through Asia Minor and include the **vaulted shipyards at Alanya** (1226) by an architect from Aleppo, and the great caravanserais such as that of **Sultanhan, Aksaray,** near Konya (1229–36). An important series of surviving tombs demonstrates an almost universal tendency towards the construction of multi-angular (octagonal or dodecagonal) towers, containing the tomb chamber in the basement, surmounted by a high prayer chamber, capped by a pointed conical roof. A prime example, typical in all its details is the **Döner Kümbet, Kayseri** (1276). Seljuk buildings in Asia Minor tended to be more modest in scale than their Persian equivalents: they were very numerous, however, and at their best monumental. An important late Seljuk work is the **Chifte Minareli Medrese in Sivas** (1271) (p. 432D), where two identical geometrically-ornamented minarets rise from a great stalactite-headed entrance portal in typical Persian style.

At the other extreme of Seljuk influence, in Turkestan, the twelfth century was marked by a number of buildings constructed under very direct Persian influence. Majestic minarets were raised over great mosques, two of the most important survivors being that of **Vabkent** (1196–8) and the **Kalan Minaret, Bukhara** (1127–9) (p. 436B). Both are tall, circular banded minarets, carrying high enclosed galleries, elaborately decorated with patterned brickwork. Other survivals include a series of twelfth-century mausolea at Uzkend, which continue in decoration and form the features that distinguished the earlier tomb of Ismail the Samanid. Mongol destruction in the thirteenth century, extending from India to Turkey, was succeeded by a new phase of building. The new rulers and their lieutenants embraced both branches of the Islamic persuasion, as well as Buddhism and Christianity. Their important surviving buildings, however, are Moslem.

From 1295 to 1305 Ghazan Khan built a new capital city at Tabriz of which only a part of one building—the **Mosque of Ali Shah** (1300) survives. In 1305 Sultan Oljeitu moved the capital to nearby Sultaniya. This in turn suffered almost total destruction apart from the damaged huge brick **Tomb of Oljeitu, Sultaniya** (1306–12) (p. 436c), a great octagonal structure, with a dome 24.4 m (80 ft) in diameter and almost 55 m (180 ft) in height. Faced in blue tiles and rising from an octagonal body, whose rhythmic arcading heightens its impressive scale, the building is perfectly detailed and proportioned. Its part-ruined state exposes the ingenious system of ribs and vaults that carried the great pointed dome high above the two-storey octagon of the tomb chamber.

The **Masjid-i-Jami, Varamin** (1322) was built on the typical Persian plan with four iwans opening on to a rectangular court. Much of the vaulted entrance gate to the courtyard, the iwan to the prayer hall and the great domed chamber of the prayer hall itself remains. The fine vaulting in brickwork and the careful skill in its proportioning is worthy of Seljuk work at its peak. In addition to the ornamental brickwork, simulated brickwork, faience facing and richly modelled stucco are all used with effect.

The **Masjid-i-Jami, Yezd** (1324–64) has a very high portal supporting a pair of cylindrical minarets whose soaring quality, together with the elaborate and sophisticated use of ceramic facings, particularly in the prayer chamber, mark a transition to the ultimate phase in Persian design.

The **Shah-i-Zinda Necropolis, Samarkand** (fourteenth and fifteenth centuries) (p. 436A) consists of sixteen domed mausolea sited in two groups, at either end of a ceremonial path. While conforming to the basic pattern, they present a series of variations in dome contour and finish which illustrate important changes and precedents: tall ribbed domes on high drums, bulbous profiles, ceramic mosaic facings and bold use of patterned brickwork all find their place in this architectural proving-ground. The typical tomb has a shallow iwan as its portal. Turquoise, cobalt and green tilework is used with powerful effect, augmented in the later stages with yellow and black.

At the end of the fourteenth century Tamerlaine (Timur) despoiled the territories of northern Islam to enrich his capital, Samarkand, where the civic square, the Registan, was the centre of an immense civic complex.

The **Gur-i-Mir, Samarkand** (1404) (p. 436E) is Tamerlaine's family mausoleum. Apart from its size and brilliant ceramic cladding it is remarkable for an elongated circular drum, which carries a stilted bulbous ribbed dome, a structure whose extraordinary proportions may reflect the ruler's personal idiosyncrasies (he had earlier, it is said, executed the architect of the Masjid-i-Jami in Samarkand because the building was not sufficiently impressive). The plan form of this mosque, with a minaret at each corner of its rectangular courtyard, was an important precedent for subsequent Mughal building in India.

The end of the fifteenth century was marked by the rise of the Safavid dynasty which was destined to see Persian architecture carried to a final peak. Most of the initial works were, however, carried out in the west of the country, an area later devastated by the Persian-Ottoman wars, and by a series of earthquakes. The earliest important Safavid monuments date from the middle of the sixteenth century, under Shah Abbas I, who made Isfahan his capital. At its height the city could count its mosques, colleges, baths and caravanserais by the hundred. The great mosque on the Meidan was not begun until the seventeenth century.

The mosque of **Sheik Lütfüllah, Isfahan** (1601–8) which also faces on to the

A. Shah-i-Zinda Necropolis, Samarkand
(14th and 15th cent.). See p. 435

B. Kalan Minaret,
Bukhara (1127–9).
See p. 434

C. Tomb of Oljeitu, Sultaniya (1306–12).
See p. 435

D. Masjid-i-Shah, Isfahan
(1612–38). See p. 437

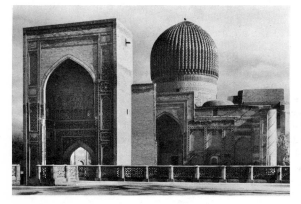

E. The Gur-i-Mir, Samarkand (1404). See p. 435

F. The Masjid-i-Shah
and the Meidan, Isfahan
(1612–38). See p. 437

Meidan, is a simple building, consisting of an iwan from which an angled approach leads into a domed cubical chamber. The transition from square to octagon is carried out by a single squinch and the simplicity of the building is matched by the perfect balance of its components and the brilliance of the ceramic tile cladding which covers every surface.

The **Masjid-i-Shah, Isfahan** (1612–38) (p. 436F) forms the terminal feature of the great public square of the city, the Meidan, which was surrounded by great arcades and flanked on its other sides by the Sheik Lütfüllah mosque, a palace and the royal caravanserai. The main axis of the mosque is necessarily at an angle to that of the Meidan. The building itself comprises a further courtyard, on to which face the great iwans, the last leading into a domed prayer hall. Tall twin minarets stand above the entrance gate. A second similar pair mark the iwan leading to the prayer chamber. The entrance iwan, minarets and dome are all clad in blue faience overlaid with whirling arabesques and rhythmic geometric patterns. A similar decoration is found inside the dome, in the iwans and in the arcades to the courtyards. This mosque of Shah Abbas combines stylistic perfection with brilliant decoration, and absolute control of all the elements. Apart from the staggering virtuosity of the ceramics, the handling of every detail from window grilles to stalactites reveals complete mastery of form.

The **Shrine of Imam-Riza, Mashad** (early seventeenth century), where restoration work began in 1601, now comprises some thirty buildings ranged around four major and eight minor courts. The same control of basic elements and inventive ceramic work typified the many seventeenth-century restorations and additions. The principal architectural features consist of a series of monumental iwans facing the courtyards, which are surrounded variously by single and double arcades with the axes terminating in domed chambers.

The **Madrassah Madir-i-Shah, Isfahan** (1706–14), is the greatest of the eighteenth-century mosques of Persia. It was built around two courtyards and continued the traditional plan with a principal iwan leading into a domed prayer chamber. It is distinguished by its extreme regularity of planning, while reflecting in character and detail work of a full century earlier.

While this is perhaps the last great Persian building, architecture in the country did not go into a sudden decline though it slowly lost creative vigour and became imitative. Among important and interesting later buildings are the eighteenth-century **Vakil Mosque, Shiraz**, whose twisting-pillared prayer hall is roofed with intricate brick vaults, and the great contemporary fortress in the same city whose towers are deeply patterned with complex geometric brickwork, continuing the long-established tradition of deliberately beautifying a purely utilitarian structure.

In Iraq the Shia population grew gradually less inhibited as the Turkish (Sunni) overlordship became less oppressive. Development of the major Shia shrines at **An Najaf, Kerbala, Khadimain** (Baghdad) and **Samarra** continues the essential tradition to the present day.

In the independent Khanates of Turkestan, Moslem architecture likewise followed a declining course punctuated with occasional resurgence. In one of the most active centres, the town of **Khiva**, considerable building took place in the eighteenth and nineteenth centuries, including the **Tash-hauli Palace** (1833–5), and the contemporary **mausoleum of Pahlavan Mahmud**. In both these buildings traditional plans, structural forms, and techniques of decoration demonstrate the continuity of traditional influences. A great minaret, the **Khaltah Minar** of a slightly later date, is geometrically patterned with ceramic-faced brickwork, and as late as 1908 another similar structure, the **Koca Islam minaret** was built.

TURKEY

Ottoman architecture properly begins with the emergence of a small princedom in Asia Minor at the beginning of the fourteenth century, but its distinctive qualities really emerge late in the fifteenth century. Major buildings followed the capture of two important Byzantine towns, Bursa and Iznik (Nicaea). Two principal types of mosque immediately emerged: the multi-pillared hall covered with a series of domes, and a single dome-on-cube building preceded by a porch.

The **Alla-üddin Mosque, Bursa** (1326) comprises a hemispherical dome on a near-cubic prayer chamber, preceded by a small porch with a small dome at the centre. It reveals Ottoman acceptance of a modified Seljuk form.

The **Yeshil Mosque, Iznik** (1378) (p. 440A) is of a similar type, with the entrance porch crowned by its central dome rising to the full height of the body of the prayer chamber. Although the main dome is impressive and the building highly finished, its proportions are clumsy by comparison with later works. The minaret is richly faced with green glazed bricks, and the surface is modelled with projecting bricks in a manner typical of the period.

The **Ulu Mosque, Bursa** (1395–9) has twenty equal domes covering the great prayer space, ranged in four ranks of five. The structural technique which was to become the hall-mark of Ottoman architecture is here fully developed. Rectangular piers carry slightly pointed arches, between which pendentives rise to carry a lighted drum surmounted by a hemispherical dome.

The **Yeshil Mosque, Bursa** (1421) represents an intermediate type, in which a central dome covered a prayer space linked to three iwans with floors raised above that of the central area. A fountain was placed under the central dome and the iwan on the east (kibla) side was much elaborated. This mosque has a complex pattern of minor rooms built into the main structure, including royal apartments. A series of galleries opened into the mosque at upper level. The walls are largely faced with hexagonal ceramic tiles, and the whole lofty interior has the sophisticated elegance of a mature architectural style. The tomb adjacent to the mosque is an early example of the type favoured by the Ottomans in succeeding centuries. A multi-faceted lower structure rises by pendentives to a ring carrying a simple dome on a low drum, and in this case the dome is pointed, though later examples were almost universally hemispherical. The tomb is ceramic-faced inside and out, and the interior, particularly, possesses exceedingly intricate ceramic mosaic, which in execution and quality of design is fully equal to contemporary Persian work. The preceding mosques at Bursa on a similar pattern are those of Murad (1363) and Yilderim Bayazit (1390).

The **Uch Sherefeli Mosque, Edirne** (1438–47) represented a major advance, combining for the first time the essential elements of the Ottoman Imperial mosques —an entrance courtyard surrounded by a domed arcade, and linked to the mosque by a porch much lower in height than the great rectangular prayer chamber covered by a major dome. In this case the dome is carried on a hexagonal 'ring', necessitating the construction of two large piers inside the prayer space. Four subsidiary domes complete the prayer hall.

The **Fatih Mosque, Istanbul** (1463–71), the original Conqueror's Mosque, was begun within ten years of the conquest of Constantinople and replaced by a building of different design in the eighteenth century. It consisted of an entrance courtyard and a rectangular prayer space covered by a major dome buttressed by a half-dome over the mihrab. This arrangement was not new to the Ottomans, for earlier buildings in Asia Minor illustrate a similar structural combination. The Fatih Mosque was contained within a compound surrounded by a series of colleges, forming the largest early civic group in Ottoman architecture.

The **Chinli Kiosk, Istanbul** (1472) (p. 440B) is an unusual and lovely building on a plan much influenced by Persian structures. A cruciform central space is surmounted by a dome and surrounded by other domed chambers and verandahs. The entrance face is formed by a long arcaded verandah of great elegance, almost unique in its Persian character.

The **Mosque of Sultan Bayazit, Edirne** (1484–8) is the earliest complete work that fully illustrates the pure Ottoman style, and is a building of remarkable completeness and purity. Behind the rectangular colonnaded ablutions court stands a simple cubic prayer chamber surmounted by a hemispherical dome. Low wings extend from the prayer chamber and from them rise identical slender minarets. Immediately adjacent, a complex of courtyards and domed structures accommodates a mental hospital, a college and living quarters. The whole group benefits from the austere simplicity of its white limestone masonry, with lead-sheathed domes and steeples carrying a minimum of ornament.

The **Mosque of Bayazit, Istanbul** (1508) is the earliest surviving Imperial Mosque in the Ottoman capital. The prayer hall contains four great piers, which carry the major dome buttressed by two opposed half domes on the long axis. It was the first substantial Ottoman building to reproduce the structural form of S. Sophia (p. 383). The side aisles are covered by secondary domes rather than by vaulted galleries, and are closely integrated with the main prayer space. A domed arcade surrounds the ablutions court and two remarkable lateral wings project from the prayer chamber, terminating in towers carrying the tall slender minarets. The mosque possesses the earliest surviving fully-developed Ottoman minarets—multi-faceted, stalactite-balconied, pencil-slim and topped with tall leaded steeples.

The **Shehzade Mosque, Istanbul** (1544–8) built for Sultan Suleyman by the architect Koca Sinan, exhibits perfectly the classical relationship between the component parts of the Ottoman mosque; the rectangular ablutions courtyard, surrounded by a domed arcade and cloister, is succeeded by a great domed prayer chamber, from the western-most corners of which rise two slender minarets. Beyond the prayer chamber stands a tomb garden where, in an almost central position, stands the tomb of Prince Shehzade—an octagonal tower, faced with decorative stone inlay and capped with a ribbed dome. The Shehzade Mosque is particularly remarkable for the symmetry of the prayer chamber, in which half-domes buttress the central dome on all four sides and four subsidiary domes complete the covered area. The building is also notable for a high degree of ornamentation for its period, expressed in stalactite-headed doorways of incredible precision and complexity, multi-coloured stone inlay in the elaborate crestings and unique bas-relief carvings on the minarets.

The **Suleymaniye Mosque, Istanbul** (1551–8) (p. 440F), like the several preceding mosques, is the centre of a civic complex. Around the compound containing the mosque itself are grouped baths, schools, several colleges, a hospital, groups of shops, public restaurants, various living quarters and houses for officials and holders of civic and religious offices. The entire complex, designed by Sinan, was built in less than a decade. In structural form the mosque echoes the nearby Bayazit Mosque and the Church of S. Sophia, although in the handling of volume and mass it demonstrates a very precise application of mathematical systems of proportioning. To the two normal minarets is added a further pair at the extreme western end of the ablutions courtyard. Although the Suleymaniye is a large building—the dome has a diameter of 26 m (85 ft) and a height of 51.8 m (170 ft)—its quality derives from a very clear expression of the structural form, extensive use of limestone ashlar contrasted with intensive decoration and bold modelling based on carefully calculated proportioning. In this it was both typical of the style and the

A. The Yeshil Mosque,
Iznik (1378). See p. 438

B. The Chinli Kiosk, Istanbul (1472).
See p. 439

C. The Selimiye Mosque,
Edirne (1570–5). See p. 441

D. The Mosque of Sultan Ahmed, Istanbul
(1610–16). See p. 441

E. The Nuro-Osmaniye
Mosque, Istanbul (1754–6).
See p. 441

F. The Suleymaniye Mosque, Istanbul
(1551–8). See p. 439

peak of its achievement. Ceramic tiles, made in Iznik (Nicea), reached a second phase of extensive use in Ottoman architecture by the middle of the sixteenth century. Used modestly but with careful precision in the mosque itself, they are included abundantly and brilliantly in the octagonal tombs of the Sultan and of his wife Roxelana, in the cemetery immediately behind the prayer chamber.

The **Mosque of Rustem Pasha, Istanbul** (1560), also stands among a group of caravanserais, baths, shops and warehouses, the last one forming the massive vaulted substructure of the mosque. It is one of the first of a widespread type in which a single large dome is carried on a hexagonal or, as in this case, on an octagonal arrangement of supporting piers within a rectangular chamber. The interior is lavishly covered with ceramic wall tiles.

The **Mosque of Mihrimah at Topkapi, Istanbul** (c. 1560) represents an extreme of refinement in the single dome-on-cube type of mosque. The prayer chamber has low side aisles and is preceded by an unusually large forecourt. Its distinctive feature is the size of the great arches in the four walls carrying the dome. The very large number of windows within the arches produces a remarkably brightly-lit interior.

The **Selimiye Mosque, Edirne** (1570–5) (p. 440C), with its two integral colleges, was designed to stand in isolation on a hilltop within the city. Its great dome, deliberately larger than that of S. Sophia, is carried on eight massive piers, contained within a rectangular envelope. At each corner of the rectangle stands a tall, triple-balconied minaret, with boldly modelled shafts of supreme elegance. The dome is almost 30 m (100 ft) in diameter and 45 m (150 ft) high at the base of the finial, and the minarets approach 75 m (250 ft) in total height. The building is complex and refined in construction, elegant and simple in massing. The decoration is judicious and the workmanship exemplary; the architect Sinan regarded it as his greatest achievement.

The **Mosque of Sokulla Mehmet Pasha, Istanbul,** contemporary with the Selimiye, is a particularly fine example of the same architect's frequent use of a hexagonal supporting structure to carry a great dome over a square prayer chamber. It is particularly high for its type and perfect in detail. The mihrab wall is faced with ceramic tiles of the finest quality, and the small group (which includes a dervish monastery and college) is ingeniously adapted to a steeply sloping site.

The **Mosque of Sultan Ahmed, Istanbul** (1610–16) (p. 440D), on a prominent site on the Hippodrome complementary to that of S. Sophia, is distinguished by its six minarets. Four enormous piers dominate the interior and carry a central dome which is buttressed, as in the Shehzade Mosque, by four subsidiary half-domes. The Sultan Ahmed Mosque perhaps marks the end of the classical period of Ottoman architecture. It is noted for its predominantly blue Iznik tilework—whence it derives the name 'The Blue Mosque'.

The **Nuro-Osmaniye Mosque, Istanbul** (1754–6) (p. 440E), while deriving from the basic form of the classical tradition is in its detail and superficial character an example of the hybrid style known as Turkish Baroque, which resulted from the assimilation of Renaissance influences in the eighteenth century. The structural scheme and proportions resemble those of the Mihrimah Mosque, but the ablutions courtyard is reduced from the rectangular to a half-rounded shape and the outward form is dominated by the curvilinear tendencies of the period.

In the late nineteenth and early twentieth century there was a reaction and return to the purely classical models of the sixteenth century, of which the **Shishli Mosque in Istanbul** (1910) is a representative example. The style of the capital was produced throughout the Empire, in Greece, the Balkans, southern Russia, Mesopotamia and Palestine. Significant examples are at the **Ka'aba in Mecca**

(c. 1560), **Osman Pasha, Trikkala** (c. 1570), the **Suleyman Tekke, Damascus** (1560), the **Kurshunlu Mosque, Kayseri** (1571), the **Mosque of Al Malika (Saffiya) Cairo** (1610), and the **Mosque of Mohammed Ali, Cairo** (1824–7). Much Turkish domestic building was built in timber and has as a result proved somewhat ephemeral. Examples have survived from almost all periods, however, demonstrating techniques of timber framing often infilled with brick and sheathed in boarding, which at its best reached high levels of refinement. The best achievements of this type of building can be seen in the elegant palaces and kiosks built on the Bosphorus. The **Emirgan Yalisi, Istanbul** (seventeenth century) is a particularly fine example: the principal chamber (selamlik) has a marble fountain in the centre of a cruciform plan, three of whose arms are sofas or reclining areas. Its wide eaves, powerful timber brackets and projecting screened balconies are typical of Turkish domestic building, whether in the yalis (seaside pleasure houses) or in the four- and five-storeyed houses packed densely into narrow city streets.

THE INDIAN SUB-CONTINENT

Moslem architecture in India divides itself into two periods, the second of which is the more productive, original and important. Work in the earlier period is attributable to minor dynasties. In 1193 a late ruler of the Persian house of Ghazni, Mahmed-el-Ghori, with his general, Qutb-al-Din, conquered northern India and established a new capital at Delhi in the name of Islam. Thenceforward various members of this dynasty ruled principalities in northern India. To consolidate their conquests, the Moslems immediately built several important mosques, including one each in their principal capitals of Delhi and Ajmer. The conquerors were primarily soldiers and administrators, however, and though the works were executed in the essentially Islamic discipline of their homeland the local craftsmen, trained in Hindu building crafts, contributed elements which led to a composite style. The Jain temples of the country were in many ways similar to the arcaded courtyard mosque and there was, therefore, an immediate affinity in building type.

The **Quwat al-Islam (or Qutb) Mosque, Delhi,** in the Punjab (1193 and later) (p. 443A) was built on the site of a Hindu temple, making use of a large number of its columns. Basically an Iraqi type of mosque, it comprised a colonnaded courtyard with a minor dome over the entrance gate. The courtyard measured 43 m × 33 m (142 ft × 108 ft). An outer courtyard, approximately four times greater in area, shared one common wall, the kibla or western wall, which was arcaded in the Hindu manner. In the outer court stood a giant minaret, the Qutb Minar, built about 1225. It is circular in plan, 15.2 m (50 ft) in diameter at the base, and carries four balconies on stalactite corbels. With its pronounced taper, calligraphic banding and powerful ribs with pointed arrises, it is essentially Persian in concept, as is the nearby **Tomb of Iltutmish** (1235–6)—a richly decorated octagonal chamber designed to carry a dome over a central cenotaph. The entire internal surface is striated with bas-relief friezes and sets an important precedent for the extensive use of calligraphic decoration in the sub-continent.

The Mongol invasions of the twelfth century interrupted building in India, as elsewhere, but early in the thirteenth century local Moslem rulers were again building significantly in northern India.

The **Mosque of Ajmer, Delhi** (thirteenth century) is a converted building comprising a rectangular courtyard surrounded by a domed colonnade of Jain detail and workmanship. The Mohammedan contribution is a massive screen of seven pointed arches, which precedes the principal prayer hall and once carried two minarets on its high portal, in the central Asian manner. The screen is

A. The Quwat al-Islam Mosque, Delhi (1193 and later). See p. 442

B. The Rukn-i-Alam, Multan (1231). See p. 444

C. Tomb of Humayun, Delhi (1565–6). See p. 446

decorated with powerful calligraphic friezes, and by virtue of both date and quality of design is of great importance. The arches, however, are constructed by the essentially native technique of corbelling, though the four-centred and cusped profiles are essentially Islamic.

In 1321 Ghias u-din, the first of the Tugluk Shahs, founded a new capital at Delhi. His buildings had qualities of simplicity, boldness of proportion and precise adherence to sound structural principles that indicate central Asian origins. Nevertheless much contemporary work was composite in character and Hindu materials were frequently incorporated in nominally Islamic buildings. Tombs usually took the form of an octagonal tower carrying a pointed central dome, surrounded in the more elaborate examples by small pavilions originating from the little Persian turrets, common in such positions. These turrets eventually developed into the distinctively Indian chattris.

Tugluk I came of a Turkish dynasty with a probable admixture of Mongol blood. He rose to power as governor of the lower Punjab and there built himself a tomb now known as the **Rukn-i-Alam, Multan** (1231) (p. 443B). Leaving Multan to govern from Delhi, Ghias u-din made over the building to his spiritual tutor. It is a tall octagonal domed structure in two storeys. The innovatory lower octagonal chamber flanked by buttress towers carries a scarcely diminished second stage rich with predominantly blue tilework panels, friezes and crestings contrasting with carved and plain brickwork.

Persian influence is plain in the several tombs of this period in Multan, as in the lower Indus valley, at Thatta in Sind. In the more easterly provinces of Moslem India native influences were very much stronger.

The **Adina Mosque, Gaur** (c. 1360) and the **Mosque at Gulbarga, Bengal** (c. 1367) are both notable as mosques of the type in which a large number of small domes were used repetitively to cover multi-columned halls. In the latter the courtyard has been incorporated into the immense covered prayer hall, 65.9 m × 51.8 m (216 ft × 170 ft).

The **Tomb of Tugluk I, Dehli,** in which Ghias u-din, the first of the Tugluk dynasty, was buried, stands in the ruin-strewn plains of Delhi on an outwork of his new capital. A fortified podium protects the square bastion, its battered panelled sides set with blind arcades. A high pointed dome is carried above it on a low octagonal drum. The whole building shows a remarkable freedom from Hindu influence. Under Ghias u-din's son Mohammed Tugluk and his cousin Firuz, who succeeded him, the architectural influence of Persia and Turkestan remained predominant. Among the principal surviving buildings of the period are a college and tombs in the **Hairz-i-Khas, Firuzabad, Delhi** and the subsequent **Begum Puri Mosque.** An important example of early fourteenth-century detailing is the **Alai Darwaza** addition to the **Mosque of Quwat al-Islam, Delhi** (1310). The complexity of its calligraphic friezes and the brilliant execution of the very elaborate detailing are a convincing demonstration of the growing maturity of Moslem architecture in India.

Political fragmentation encouraged localized styles in states such as Jaunpur. The **Jami Masjid, Jaunpur** (1438–78) is a courtyard-type mosque. Five-aisled colonnades, doubled on the inner and outer rows, carry domes and bracketed stone-slab eaves—a typical Hindu method of construction. The great portal fronts a domed entrance chamber. A similar but earlier portal, in effect a great iwan, was built in 1408 as the entrance to the prayer chamber of the **Atala Mosque, Jaunpur.** The damaged multi-staged pylons supporting the great arch are so massive as to completely obscure the multiple domes over the chamber behind it. Heavy corbels and lintels are extensively used in place of the arch.

The **Jami Masjid, Ahmadabad** (1411–24) is perhaps the most important example of a series of fifteenth-century buildings produced in the capital of another independent state—Gujarat, in a similarly composite style. The main prayer hall of the mosque is roofed with two hundred and sixty columns supporting fifteen symmetrically arranged stone domes of corbelled construction—typically Hindu in structure and in some details of finish.

Other contemporary similar mosques in Ahmadabad are those of **Muhfiz Khan, Sidi Sayyid** and **Rani Sipari.** Among the most important tombs are those of **Sayyid Usman** (1460) and **Sayyid Mubarak** (1484). Elsewhere the **Jami Masjid, Mandu** (1405–40) has a square courtyard enclosed by arcades, each of eleven pointed arches supported on red sandstone piers and roofed with numerous domes; and the **Jami Masjid, Champanir** (1500–8), one of the largest and most imposing mosques in India, has a spacious court, a many-domed sanctuary and two minarets flanking the central entrance gateway.

The growth of the power of the Mughal dynasty can be traced to the lessons learned by the Emperors Babur and Humayun in Afghanistan and central Asia and their use of improved artillery under foreign, often Turkish, advice. In 1526 Babur Shah, advancing from Kabul through the Punjab, defeated Ibrahim, Sultan of Delhi, and opened the way to the domination of the greater part of India by his dynasty until the death of Aurangzeb in 1707. Babur had preoccupations other than building and his son Humayun was the first of the dynasty to indulge in monumental architecture, though his work has been largely effaced and it is to a contemporary native prince, Sultan Sher Shah, that the important surviving works of the period are due.

The **Mosque of Sher Shah, Delhi** (1540–5) known as the Kila-i-Kuhna, is a simple but impressive building, lacking a minaret and comprising a multi-domed prayer chamber, behind a very simple entrance court. Each of the five bays of the entrance front contains a shallow iwan, surmounted by a rigid cornice and cresting above which rises the low dome. The central bay is emphasized with calligraphic friezes, panelling and mouldings and the whole front is inlaid with marble. The importance of the building lies in its massing and form, and it appears to have had considerable influence on subsequent buildings.

The **Tomb of Sher Shah, Sahsaram** (1542–5) is the culminating edifice of pre-Mughal tradition in India. Standing on a monumental pedestal in an artificial lake, the mausoleum itself is octagonal, each side except that of the mihrab having an entrance. Both the main body of the tomb and its surrounding arcade carry a series of small chattris at each angle. The central dome is rather low, although the extreme complication and size of the finial substructure creates a visually compensating vertical emphasis. The dome is 21.6 m (71 ft) in diameter. The upper structure is sandstone and the lower granite.

At **Bijapur,** the capital of an independent Kingdom outside the Mughal Empire until 1686, a remarkable florescence occurred between 1565 and 1686. Works of this period include the unfinished **Jami Masjid** (c. 1576) (p. 449G, H), measuring 100 m × 79 m (330 ft × 260 ft) and roofed with a number of small domes over square compartments and a central dome 17 m (57 ft) in diameter, carried on interlacing pointed arches—an example of Moslem skill recalling a technique used in Spain six centuries earlier. Also at Bijapur, a compound entered by a lofty gate contained the **Royal Garden of Ibrahim Rauza,** built between 1626 and 1633. The buildings within the garden include the tomb of Ibrahim II, kiosks and a handsome mosque. Ibrahim's successor, Mahmud, lies in the tomb known as the **Gol Gombaz** (1636–59). This is a boldly proportioned and magnificent building whose dome has a span of 38 m (125 ft) supported on high intersecting arches and apparently modelled on the earlier Jami Masjid. It was under Babur's grandson, Akbar the Great (1556–1605), that political and economic conditions had altered sufficiently to encourage the Mughals into a consistent architectural effort which led to the development of a distinct style and their highest achievements.

The **Tomb of Humayun, Delhi** (1565–6) (p. 443C) in which Akbar buried his father, the second Mughal emperor, stands in a handsome formal garden set on a podium 6.7 m (22 ft) high, faced with an arcaded red sandstone wall. The structure both of the tomb and the arcaded podium is heightened by an inlay of white marble which outlines doors, arches and spandrel panels. From the podium rises the domed tomb itself, 49 m (160 ft) square and 38 m (125 ft) high. In plan this great block is a central domed octagon, buttressed by four octagonal towers and grouped around a central cenotaph to form the main body of the mausoleum. Faced with red sandstone, it is picked out with white marble, also used to face the dome. The centre of each face is marked by a great iwan, flanked by arcaded panels and lesser iwans in each face of the corner towers. A powerful cresting contains the whole of the lower block. Small chattris surmount each corner tower, and behind them and above them rises a dome of Safavid proportions, double-shelled and higher in profile than any of its predecessors. The dome stands on a high drum reminiscent of the domes of Samarkand. It is low, however, compared with later works, and the handling of the corner pavilions renders them insignificant. Nevertheless in this building, with its loftier proportions, positive massing and the delineation of sectors of the façade with white banding separating the polychrome inserts, the Mughal style had been established. The building is set in gardens whose axial lines prolong the axes of the building into the landscape. In this respect also, Akbar's tomb for his father is the precursor of greater mausolea to follow.

The **Red Fort, Agra** (1564–80) was rebuilt by Akbar the Great, who began the immense work early in his reign. Its red sandstone enceinte wall 21.3 m (70 ft) high, fronting a 10-m (33-ft) ditch and over a mile long is pierced by two intricate and sophisticated multiple gates. On its eastern side a great terrace fronts the river Jumna. Though further work was done to the great fort by his grandson, Shah Jehan, it was Akbar who surrounded the original brick fortress of the Lodi rulers with its vast sandstone walls and complicated entrances. With similar forts in Lahore and Delhi, this huge structure convincingly demonstrates the great power and wealth of the Mughal rulers. Significant care was given to architectural scale and detail, even in so inherently practical a work. Many of the polygonal towers are vigorously decorated with inlaid panels, string courses and domed pavilions, while the massive and carefully aligned crenellations, with their pointed arched heads, have a relationship to the cresting so frequently used which may not have been entirely accidental. The forts at Delhi and Lahore were similarly enlarged at this period.

Fatehpur Sikri (1569 to c. 1580) is the surviving deserted capital city built by Akbar the Great. Not content with the palace complex contained in the Red Fort, Akbar followed what amounts almost to a tradition among Mughal rulers in building a new administrative capital. It was perhaps less of a city than a palace complex, with living quarters for the personnel needed by the palace and government: it was deserted primarily on account of the poor water supply, and survives as a remarkable and virtually unaltered monument to Mughal architecture at its height. One of its most fascinating buildings is the **Diwan-i-Khas** (p. 447E), the unique ceremonial throne room, a square, two-storeyed building, surmounted on each corner by chattris. An elaborate column in the centre of the chamber supports a throne and is approached by four bridges of fretted marble spanning from the centre point to corbels in each corner of the room, where the chief ministers sat. The device has an obvious relationship to a formal Mughal garden. The cubic interior is otherwise

A. Tomb of Sheik Salim
Chistee, Fatehpur Sikri
(c. 1575). See p. 448

B. The Panch Mahal, Fatehpur Sikri.
See p. 448

C. Mosque of the
Wazir-Han, Lahore
(1634). See p. 452

D. Diwan-i-Am, Agra Fort, from S.W.
(1628–58). See p. 451

E. Diwan-i-Khas,
Fatehpur Sikri (1569–75).
See p. 446

F. Taj-Mahal, Agra: Great Gateway to
garden court (1630–53). See p. 451

void, though its finish and detailing is of remarkable quality. Akbar's spectacular city, 3.22 km (2 miles) long and 1.61 km (1 mile) broad, contains a series of other buildings of great importance, among them a palace for his Turkish wife, and the **Panch Mahal** (p. 447B), a five-storey pavilion of unknown purpose. The private buildings of the city included the monumental residence of **Rajah Birbal**; an elaborately panelled and ornamented, wide-eaved, two-storey structure topped with twin domes. The city itself was bounded on one side by an artificial lake and walled on the other three sides. While different buildings show varying degrees of Persian and Hindu influence, its importance lies in the stylistic synthesis which represents Mughal architecture at its peak and in remarkably complete survival.

The **Jami Masjid, Fatehpur Sikri** (p. 449C), is a large courtyard mosque, measuring 132 m × 112 m (433 ft × 366 ft), surrounded by arcaded cloisters surmounted by a series of domes and a cresting of chattris, all isolated, but placed so close as to seem interconnected. The mosque has an immense entrance gateway, the **Buland Darwaza** (p. 453A), 40 m (130 ft) high, and is approached by a massive flight of steps. In proportion and character the portal is a great iwan framed in bands of calligraphic ornament. A corresponding iwan occurs in front of the dome to the prayer chamber proper. The great gateway with its half-octagonal front stands in the centre of the southern side dominating the town. A lesser gateway is placed on the east, and on the north stand two important tombs, those of **Nawab Islam Khan** and of **Sheik Salim Chistee** (pp. 447A, 449C–F). The latter, a low marble dome, stands on a small podium carved and inlaid with the utmost delicacy. Between the posts of the bays of each side a series of filigree marble grilles of remarkable extent form screens. The building has a jewel-like quality and is sheathed entirely in white marble, dating from the reign of Shah Jehan, which contrasts with the massive red sandstone walls of the mosque. This mosque of Akbar is the earliest example of the standard pattern of great Mughal mosques, in which the prayer chamber carries a great central dome flanked by two domes not much smaller in size.

The **Tomb of Akbar, Sikandra, Agra** (1593–1613) represents a new departure in tomb building, comprising a series of square, superimposed terraces ornamented with pavilions and chattris. Although entirely Mughal in detail, it appears probable that the basic structural form had Hindu origins. Under the massive structure a series of vaults lead down to the central tomb chamber. Each of the terraces above is surrounded by arcaded cloisters and the topmost, containing the cenotaph, is enclosed with dazzling pierced marble trelliswork. The tomb stands in a formal garden which is approached through a massive red sandstone gateway (p. 453B).

The **Itimad-ud-Daula, Agra** (early seventeenth century), one of the few buildings for which Akbar's son Jehangir was responsible, is a gem-like building illustrating the high level of skill of his craftsmen. It stands in a formal garden and comprises a square white marble structure with low minarets at each corner and a square pavilion raised above the central chamber. Its marble screens, panelling, and elegant detailing are executed with the utmost perfection. For the first time in Mughal art there appears the 'pietra dura' technique of inlaying precious and semi-precious stones into marble, which appears to have been made fashionable in India by itinerant Italian craftsmen.

The **Tomb of Jehangir, Lahore** (1630) is a notable instance of the Mughal concept of the creation of a complete environment, a world apart contained within a walled compound. The building was set in a series of formal gardens with water courses and axial approach paths, each vista terminated by a great gateway. The tomb of Jehangir is a low broad pavilion of restrained elegance, whose multiple piers are sheathed in white marble containing elaborate perforated screens and

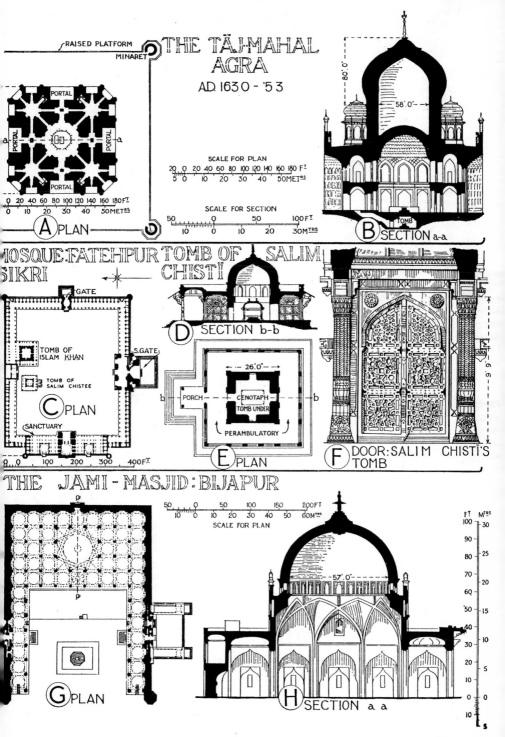

THE TĀJ·MAHAL
AGRA
A.D. 1630 - '53

RAISED PLATFORM
MINARET
PORTAL

SCALE FOR PLAN
20 0 20 40 60 80 100 120 140 160 180 FT
5 0 10 20 30 40 50METRS

SCALE FOR SECTION
50 0 50 100FT
10 0 10 20 30MTRS

0 20 40 60 80 100 120 140 160 180FT
0 10 20 30 40 50METRS

(A) PLAN

80'.0"
58'.0"

(B) SECTION a-a
TOMB

MOSQUE·FATEHPUR
SIKRI

GATE

TOMB OF
ISLAM KHAN

TOMB OF
SALIM CHISTEE

S.GATE

(C) PLAN

SANCTUARY

0 0 100 200 300 400FT

TOMB OF SALIM
CHISTĪ

(D) SECTION b-b

26'.0"

b PORCH CENOTAPH b
TOMB UNDER

PERAMBULATORY

(E) PLAN

(F) DOOR: SALIM CHISTI'S
TOMB

9'.6"

THE JAMI · MASJID : BIJAPUR

50 0 50 100 150 200FT
10 0 10 20 30 40 50 60MTRS
SCALE FOR PLAN

(G) PLAN

57'.0"

(H) SECTION a a

FT MTRS
100 30
90
80 25
70 20
60
50 15
40
30 10
20 5
10
0 0
10
5

A. General view of Mausoleum

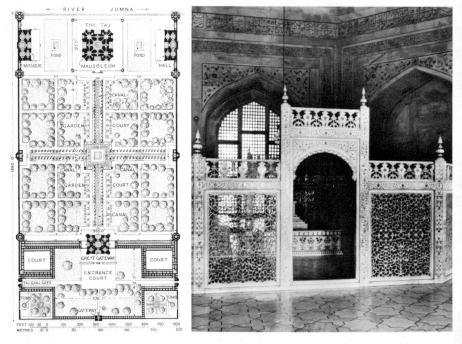

B. Plan showing entrance court,
gateway, garden court
and Mausoleum

C. Marble screen enclosing tombs

The Taj-Mahal, Agra (1630–53). See p. 451

pietra dura inlay. Work of similarly refined character and quality is to be found in the mosque and pavilions of the nearby **Fort at Lahore**. This building was, effectively the first of a series of glorious achievements under the Emperor Shah Jehan, a man whose cultural tastes and yearning to build was matched by enormous resources which, however, he eventually outran. Under his 'reign of marble' existing buildings were marble-clad and the new arose sumptuous in the soft grey and white sheen of the stone.

The **Fort and Palace, Delhi** (1639–48). Although much has been altered and destroyed within the fort, sufficient remains to display the dazzling techniques and immense building energies of Shah Jehan, who was responsible for so much work, principally at Lahore, Agra and Delhi. The palace within Akbar's fort occupies an area of about 490 m × 980 m (1,600 ft × 3,200 ft), the largest part laid out in a series of great courts, aligned on intersecting axes with formal gardens, kiosks, colonnades, arcades, great gateways and an immense entrance hall, forming a vaulted bazaar. Although much damaged in the nineteenth century, it remains one of the greatest palaces of the Islamic world. Among the surviving buildings are the throne room, the **Diwan-i-Khas**, and the **Rang Mahal**. Each is perfect in conception and detail. The buildings are completely sheathed in white marble, and the pierced marble screens are of incredible refinement, elaborate pietra dura inlay having superseded all other forms of decoration. The Italian provenance of this technique is evident from the motifs employed in the Diwan-i-Khas. The Moti-Mahal, the Hira-Mahal and the Rang Mahal are all pavilions of the most delicate beauty, adorned with fountains and formal water courses, perforated marble screens and a sculptural perfection that marks them as the culmination of a carefully conceived, sumptuous and magnificently executed design.

The **Jami Masjid, Delhi** (1644–58) was also built by Emperor Shah Jehan. A congregational mosque with a courtyard 99 m (325 ft) square and a pair of minarets 40 m (130 ft) high, it stands on a high podium and on the three principal axes has great gateways. On the fourth axis facing the courtyard, a massive iwan of Persian proportions fronts a prayer hall dominated by triple domes. These, like other seventeenth-century Mughal domes, have a perceptibly bulbous profile. The building gains great effect from the podium, each gate being approached by pyramidal flights of steps, and each angle of the building terminating with a tower and capped with a domed pavilion.

The **Moti Masjid, Agra** (The Pearl Mosque) (1646–54) was built by Shah Jehan within the palace of the Red Fort. It is an elegant triple-domed marble building fronting a court 46 m (150 ft) square. The prayer hall of the mosque is preceded by an arcade of cusped pointed arches, similar to those in the palace at Delhi, and the prayer chamber itself is surmounted by triple domes, similar in character to those at the Delhi Mosque. A series of chattris enlivens the façade to the court. The building displays a high degree of finish, although it is less exuberant in detailing than other contemporary works. The noble **Diwan-i-Am** (p. 447D), a multi-pillared audience hall, measuring 63 m × 23 m (208 ft × 76 ft) is stylistically similar, but without the domes. Other buildings added to the palace included the Nagina Masjid in the women's quarters and the Diwan-i-Khas (1637).

The **Taj-Mahal, Agra** (1630–53) (pp. 447F, 449A, B, 450), in the tradition of Mughal tombs stood in a formally laid out walled garden, with kiosks, and entered through pavilion gateways. It was the culminating work in the life of the Emperor Shah Jehan, erected to the memory of his favourite wife, Mumtaz-i-Mahal. The mausoleum itself is 57 m (186 ft) square in plan and the structure consists in effect of four complex, but basically octagonal, towers linked together to carry a great dome spanning the central space between them. Smaller domed pavilions cap each tower, and circular tapering minarets stand at each corner of the podium on which the structure stands. The central inner dome is 24.4 m (80 ft) high and 17.7 m (58 ft) in diameter, but it is surmounted by an outer shell nearly 61 m (200 ft) in height. The general massing and form of the structure are in a direct line of development from the earlier tomb of Humayun, but in the Taj-Mahal the proportioning and control of mass has reached perfection. The tombs of Shah Jehan and his wife are enclosed with a marble screen of incredible elaboration and delicacy. The interior of the building, dimly lit through pierced marble lattices, contains a virtuoso display of inlaid marble decoration. The entire building derives an ethereal quality from its facing of white marble. The setting reflects the quality of the building, though it is remarkable in that the main structure stands almost on the bank of the river Jumna. In consequence the formal gardens lie to one side. This asymmetrical arrangement is explained by Shah Jehan's intention to build his own similar, complementary mausoleum in black marble in a corresponding position on the other side of the river. A cruciform pattern of canals, a series of rectangular gardens and three additional structures, a mosque, a hall, and a gateway in red sandstone picked out with inlay and dressings in white marble complete the building complex.

The **Mihrta Mahal, Bijapur** (1620) typified one of the distinctively different fusions of Hindu and Moslem elements in the further parts of Mughal-dominated India, in this case a regional style in the Deccan. While the general structural pattern remains constant the gateway to the mosque is resplendent with delicate balconies and two slender minarets. Also at Bijapur the **Tomb and Mosque of Ibrahim II** (1627) is an example of the same provincial style, with a bulbous dome set above a rectangular wide-eaved pavilion.

The **Mosque of the Wazir-Han, Lahore** (1634) (p. 447C), in the Punjab, illustrates a more distinctly Persian influence. The architectural quality is altogether much firmer and less sumptuous, though the buildings were brilliantly clad in ceramic mosaic, in which lively yellow grounds were prominent. The influence of Timurid architecture is pronounced. Lower down the Indus a purer Persian style is apparent at this period in Multan, while further south again, in Sind, a similar freedom from Hindu influence is apparent. Typically Timurid shapes are made to look even more derivative by the distinctive use of blue-green tiles, particularly on an important range of tombs at Thatta.

Shah Jehan's successor, Aurangzeb, though a fervent Moslem, was no patron of architecture, his most significant building being the **Moti Masjid in Delhi** (1659). While later Moslem work in India must not be discounted, it did not again reach the heights of the works of Shah Jehan.

The **Badshahi Mosque, Lahore** (1840) a very large congregational mosque, simple in concept and severe in detail, follows the pattern of the Imperial Mughal mosques. The courtyard is reached through a massive entrance portal surmounted by three white marble-faced domes of slightly bulbous profile. Two tall, multi-faceted, tapering minarets are placed at the extreme western corners of the courtyard. These are replacements of four earlier minarets, which stood at the corners.

The tomb of **Sir Mohammed Iqbal, Lahore** (twentieth century) is a single-storey wide-eaved pavilion, standing in a formal garden. It is representative of consciously scholarly Islamic design, following Mughal precedent and reflecting particularly the influence of the nearby tomb of Jehangir.

ISLAMIC VERNACULAR ARCHITECTURE

The vernacular building of the Islamic world deserves consideration principally for the distinctive and complex urban groupings characteristic of the East. The

A. The Buland Darwaza, Fatehpur Sikri (*c.* 1575). See p. 448

B. Gateway, Tomb of Akbar, Sikandra (*c.* 1600). See p. 448

C. 'Beehive' village, near Aleppo, Northern Syria. See p. 455

A. Kasbah: Ait Ben Haddon, Morocco. See p. 455

B. Shibam, in the Hadramaut, Southern Arabia. See p. 455

settlements are typically very tight-knit, with irregular streets of minimal width bounded by high walls behind which lies a dense matrix of courtyard dwellings. Entire streets are frequently covered to form shopping arcades (bazaars or suqs). Particularly significant examples exist in Istanbul, Aleppo, Damascus, Baghdad and Isfahan. Off the streets enlarged courtyards accommodate workshops, markets, caravanserais and mosques. Traditionally and frequently even today the complicated urban fabric surges against the walls of even the most important buildings. Necessarily, therefore, many vernacular urban buildings are courtyard-orientated and lacking in external elevations. The architectural significance rests in the quality of the whole compact agglomerate. Nevertheless some very distinctive architectural forms have emerged, notably the domed structures of Northern Syria and Central Persia (p. 453C), the tall, cantilevered timber structures of the Balkans, Istanbul and Kashmir, the towered cities of Southern Arabia such as Shibam, in the Hadramaut (p. 454B), and the fortress-like Kasbahs of Algeria and Morocco (p. 454A).

BIBLIOGRAPHY

ASLANAPA, O. *Turkish Architecture.* London, 1971.

BELL, GERTRUDE. *The Palace and Mosque at Ukkhaidir.* Oxford, 1914.

BROWN, PERCY. *Indian Architecture: the Islamic Period.* Bombay, 1942.

CRESSWELL, K. A. C. *A Short Account of Early Muslim Architecture.* Harmondsworth and Baltimore, 1958.

—. *Early Muslim Architecture.* Part I. Oxford, 1962.

—. *Early Muslim Architecture.* Part II. Oxford, 1962.

—. *The Muslim Architecture of Egypt.* Oxford, 1952.

ESIN, E. *Mecca the Blessed, Medina the Radiant.* London, 1963.

GOODWIN, G. *Ottoman Architecture.* London, 1971.

GRUBE, E. *The World of Islam.* London, 1969.

GUILLAUME, A. *Islam.* London, 1960.

HAMBLY, G. *Cities of Mughal India.* London, 1968.

HILL, DEREK, and GRABAR, OLEG. *Islamic Architecture and its Decoration.* London, 1967.

HITTI, P. K. *The History of the Arabs.* London, 1946.

HOAG, JOHN D. *Western Islamic Architecture.* London and New York, 1963.

HOURANI, ALBERT H., and STERN, S. M. *The Islamic City.* Oxford, 1970.

HRBAS, and KNOBLOCH. *The Art of Central Asia.* London, 1965.

KUHNEL, ERNST. *Islamic Art and Architecture.* London, 1966.

KURAN, APTULLAH. *The Mosque in Early Ottoman Architecture.* Chicago and London, 1968.

LE STRANGE, G. *Lands of the Eastern Caliphate.* Cambridge, 1930.

LEWIS, B., PELLAT, C., and SCHACHT, J. (Eds.) *The Encyclopaedia of Islam.* Leiden, 1959–.

MAYER, L. A. *Islamic Architects and their Works.* Geneva, 1956.

POPE, A. UPHAM. *Persian Architecture.* London, 1965.

RIVOIRA, G. T. *Moslem Architecture.* Oxford, 1918.

SMITH, E. *Mughal Architecture of Fatehpur Sikri.* Allahabad, 1898.

TALBOT-RICE, D. *Islamic Art.* London, 1965.

TALBOT-RICE, T. *The Seljuks in Asia Minor.* London, 1961.

TOY, SIDNEY. *The Strongholds of India.* London, 1957.

VOGT, GÖKNIL ULYA. *Living Architecture: Ottoman.* London, 1966.

WILBER, D. N. *Architecture of Islamic Iran.* Princeton, 1955.

15

ROMANESQUE ARCHITECTURE IN EUROPE

From the ninth century

INFLUENCES

The decline of the Roman Empire in the West led to the rise of the independent states and nations of Europe. The coronation by the Pope of the Frankish king Charlemagne (in 800) as Holy Roman Emperor marked the beginning of a new era, with the establishment of a pan-Germanic Christian state, politically ordered and bound by both ecclesiastical and political ties to Rome. The Carolingian Renaissance was based upon a Germanic culture allied with late Roman traditions and subject to Byzantine and Oriental influences. Many important Romanesque architectural features were discernible before the time of Berengar, the last Carolingian Emperor, and they reflect the rise of the power of the Empire in Aquitania, Burgundy, Lombardy and Saxony. The great monastic foundations proliferated and expanded, being closely linked with economic revival, the fusion of Latin and Teutonic communities, and the survival of Roman Law in the monastic rule. Many architectural problems posed in building religious houses were quite new, and monastic architectural development tended to take the lead in changes of fashion and technique. After the middle of the tenth century, an increasing number of major buildings were vaulted, partly to guard against fire-risks, partly to create strong structures to resist the raids of the Norsemen in North-West Europe, of the Hungarians in Central Europe, and of the Moors in Catalonia. The earliest construction of this kind is probably that of the ninth century in Asturia, but the earliest revival of the complete Roman tradition took place in areas where many ancient buildings had survived: Lombardy, Provence, Languedoc and ducal Burgundy. Many nations of Europe had by this time struggled into existence. France and Spain were powerful enough to throw off the rule of the Holy Roman Empire, which even in Germany had a precarious hold over its subordinate rulers. By the end of the eleventh century stable Christian kingdoms were established in Scandinavia and Norman England, while the Crusaders set up states in the Holy Land with less durable prospects.

Christianity, the chief source of education and culture, was gradually spreading throughout northern Europe, and the erection of a church often resulted in the foundation of a city, for the Papacy had been rising to great power and influence, rivalling or controlling such civil government as existed. Justinian's Pragmatic Sanction of 554 had already conferred authority on bishops over provincial and municipal governments, and this had increased the power of the Church, which now often dominated public affairs. Bishops and abbots were also by reason of their feudal possessions military chiefs who sometimes took the field in person. Everywhere the power and prestige of the Church increased. Religious enthusiasm and zeal found their material expression in the magnificent cathedral churches and monastic buildings, which were an even more significant outcome of this period than were the castles of feudal chiefs. This same religious fervour led to the Crusades against Moslem occupation of Palestine and the Holy Places, and this intermittent warfare (1027–1292) between Christians of the West and Moslems of the East was not without its effect on Western art. Monastic communities had existed since the fourth century and by 800 the spread of Benedictine houses was being promoted by Charlemagne and other rulers. The eleventh century proved especially remarkable for the great development of the monastic system which encouraged new methods in agriculture and exercised its influence on architecture; indeed, until the middle of the twelfth century science, letters, art and culture were largely the monopoly of the religious Orders. The schools attached to monasteries trained youths for the service of religion; monks and their pupils were often the designers of cathedrals.

The principal religious Orders were:

(1) The Benedictine Order ('Black Monks'), founded early in the sixth century at Montecassino in southern Italy by S. Benedict of Nursia. Possessions were held in common, but the absence of particular vows of poverty actually facilitated charitable works and agrarian enterprise. Benedictine houses were commonly sited in towns, part of the church being devoted to offices for the laity.

(2) The Cluniac Order, founded by Abbot Odo in 910 at Cluny in Burgundy.

(3) The Carthusian Order, founded by S. Bruno at the Grande Chartreuse near Grenoble in 1086, returned to eremitic and ascetic principles, which had elsewhere been relaxed. The Charterhouses, often remotely sited, provided separate cells for the monks, generally grouped around a cloister garth, and the community served a simply-planned church; Carthusian architecture is notably severe and unadorned.

(4) The Cistercian Order ('White Monks'), founded in 1098 at Cîteaux by S. Stephen Harding, and at Clairvaux by S. Bernard. After 1134 all Cistercian churches were dedicated to the Virgin and had no separate Lady Chapel, which in churches of other Orders most commonly formed an eastern extension of the choir arm (as at Norwich, p. 641D), at the west end of the nave (as at Durham, p. 641E), or occasionally by extension of the choir aisle. The ascetic aims of the Cistercian Order produced an architecture which was at first simple and severe. In mature Cistercian planning, the monks' frater, or refectory, was sited at right angles to the south walk of the cloister, with the kitchen adjoining it to the west, and the frater of the 'conversi', or lay brethren, beyond. In early examples and in the later Middle Ages, when the numbers of conversi were reduced, the monks' frater was built parallel to the south cloister walk and occupied it for most of its length in the Benedictine manner. The usual form of Cistercian chapter house was an aisled hall, in contrast to those of the Benedictine and Augustinian Orders, which were either rectangular (as at Bristol, p. 643K), apsidal (Durham, p. 641E) or circular (Worcester, p. 641A).

(5) Secular canons, serving principally cathedral and collegiate churches.

The Orders of Canons Regular:

(6) Augustinian Canons ('Black Canons regular'), established in about 1050. They undertook both monastic and pastoral duties in houses often sited in towns, and planned similarly to those of the Benedictine Order.

(7) Premonstratensian Canons ('White Canons regular'), founded around 1100 by S. Norbert at Prémontré in Picardy.

(8) Gilbertine Canons, an exclusively English Order founded in the twelfth century by S. Gilbert of Sempringham, usually combining a house of canons of

Augustine rule with another of nuns of Cistercian rule, in conventual buildings separately planned, attached to a common church divided axially by a wall.

The Military Orders:

(9) The Knights Templar, founded in 1119 to protect the Holy Places in Palestine and to safeguard the pilgrim routes to Jerusalem. Templars' churches were modelled upon the Rotunda of the Anastasis in the Holy Sepulchre Church in Jerusalem (p. 360E–G).

(10) The Knights Hospitallers, organized in about 1113 (the Knights of S. John of Jerusalem) under Augustinian rule. The Order eventually held a great deal of property in Europe, but developed no characteristic architecture of its own.

(11) The mendicant Orders of Friars, founded during the thirteenth century and headed by the Franciscans and the Dominicans. The functions of friary churches were sufficiently distinctive to demand planning of a characteristic kind, but they developed when Gothic architecture was already succeeding Romanesque throughout most of Europe. Their houses were usually sited in towns, where the friars preached and did charitable works among the common people. Some also played an important part in the rising universities throughout Europe.

ARCHITECTURAL CHARACTER

The mature Romanesque style of the tenth to the twelfth centuries was remarkable for the tentative use of a new constructive principle: the deliberate articulation of structure, in which each constructive part played a designed role in establishing equilibrium. This new system, which was accompanied by the use of dressed stones of comparatively small size connected by thick beds of mortar, led in the thirteenth century, after many experiments, to the full development of the Gothic system of architecture, in which elasticity and equilibrium were jointly employed. The general architectural character of the Romanesque style is sober and dignified, while formal massing depends on the grouping of towers and the projection of transepts and choir. In different countries regional tendencies were encouraged by local conditions; but in all the character depends on the employment of vaulting, based initially on Roman methods.

Roman cross-vaults (pp. 627B, 628A) were used throughout Europe till the beginning of the twelfth century, but they were heavy and difficult to construct and were gradually superseded by 'rib and panel' vaulting, in which a framework of ribs supported thin stone panels. The new method consisted in designing the profile of the ribs to which the form of the panels was adapted; whereas in Roman architecture the shape of the vault itself determined the groin, which was formed by the intersection of the vaults. Romanesque architects therefore first decided the profile of the transverse, longitudinal and diagonal ribs. Groins had previously been settled naturally by the intersection of the vault surfaces; this arrangement produced the quadripartite (four-part) vault. If the cross-vaults were semi-cylindrical the diagonal groin would be a semi-ellipse (p. 628D), but Romanesque architects did not resort to the use of ordinates as was afterwards done in the Renaissance period; instead, they surmounted the difficulty arising from the different spans of diagonal and transverse ribs in various ways. In France and Germany the vaulting ribs of a square vaulting compartment were usually semicircular curves starting from the same level; therefore the diagonal rib, having the longest span, rose to a greater height than the transverse and longitudinal ribs, and when the panelling was filled in on the top of these ribs each vault was domical (p. 628F). In England vaults were generally constructed with continuous level ridges, instead of in this domical form, and the differences in height between diagonal and transverse ribs in a square vaulting compartment was equalized by 'stilting' the latter or by making the diagonal rib a segment of a larger circle than that of the longitudinal and transverse ribs, which were semicircular, as shown on p. 627G. In vaulting an oblong compartment the difference between the heights of diagonal and transverse ribs was still greater than in a square compartment and produced an awkward waving line of the ribs on plan (p. 628B), but little attempt was made to vault any but square compartments. At Worms (p. 512J), and S. Michele at Pavia (p. 475E), the difficulty of vaulting oblong nave compartments was partially surmounted by including two of them to make one square bay of vaulting, each corresponding with two square compartments of the side aisles. In some instances, as in the Abbaye-aux-Hommes, Caen (p. 500A) the intermediate pier was carried up as a vaulting shaft to support a rib which altered the quadripartite vaulting compartment into six parts, known as 'sexpartite' vaulting (p. 627E). The main piers were usually more massive than the intermediate because they supported the chief weight of the vaulting. The difficulty of equalizing the height of ribs of different spans, especially in oblong compartments, was finally surmounted by the introduction of the pointed arch (p. 627F), when the system of 'rib and panel' vaulting was further elaborated by the addition of various supplementary ribs.

The Roman basilica had been the model for Early Christian churches, the plan of which was subject to new developments during the Romanesque period. The addition of transepts and the prolongation of the sanctuary of chancel made the church a well-defined cross on plan, as at S. Michele, Pavia (p. 475E). Transepts were generally the same breadth as the nave, which was usually twice the width of the aisles. The choir was often raised on piers above the level of the nave and over a vaulted crypt, in which saint or martyr had been buried, as at S. Miniato, Florence (p. 472B). In later churches aisles were sometimes carried round the chancel to form an ambulatory as in Santiago de Compostela (p. 525A). Towers, square, octagonal or circular, are prominent features of most Romanesque churches, either over the crossing, at the west end centrally with the nave, or at the east end, sometimes arranged in pairs at the west end and at the ends of the transepts or at the eastern ends of the aisles, often rising to a great height in well-marked stages pierced with windows.

Roman methods of craftsmanship still influenced constructive art in Europe. Walls were often roughly built, and were relieved externally by shallow buttresses or pilaster strips, connected at the top by bands of horizontal mouldings or by a series of semicircular arches on corbels (pp. 489C, 511C, 512D, F). Attached columns, with rough capitals supporting semicircular arches, formed wall arcading, which was a frequent decorative feature (p. 489G).

Arcades consisted of massive circular columns or piers which supported semicircular arches, as in the naves of Norman cathedrals (p. 564D). Door and window openings are very characteristic, with jambs or sides formed in a series of receding moulded planes known as 'orders', in which are set circular shafts surmounted by a continuous abacus. The semicircular arch above was also constructed in receding concentric rings (p. 465B), which followed the lines of the recesses below. A rose or wheel window was often placed over the west door, as at S. Zeno Maggiore, Verona (p. 476A). Glass seems not to have come into general use till the ninth century.

In Italy, the traditional monolithic column, often of Roman origin, was usual, but in the West, and especially in France and England, the columns were generally cylindrical and of massive proportions, built up with ashlar masonry and having a rubble core. These were treated with flutings or with spiral, trellis or chevron patterns (p. 564D). Variations of Corinthian or Ionic capitals were used, as in S. John's Chapel, Tower of London (p. 562A), and elsewhere (pp. 466E, F, 490C, G), and in later times the capital was often of a cushion (cubiform) shape, as also in S. John's Chapel, Tower of London (p. 575C), and Winchester (p. 561C), and was sometimes richly carved and scalloped (pp. 561B, D, E, 562A–C).

Mouldings were often elaborately carved (p. 559A). The base of the column was generally an adaptation of the old Attic form, but the circular moulding often projected over the square plinth below, at the angles of which flowers or animals were occasionally carved to fill up the triangular part (p. 561H). The abacus above the capital (p. 561E) was distinctive in form; it was higher, but projected less than in the Classical column and was moulded with alternate fillets and hollows.

Ornament, into which entered vegetable and animal forms, was treated conventionally, and carving and sculpture were often rough (pp. 466, 490, 508, 579C, D). For interiors, frescoes were more usual than mosaics, which had been such a feature of Early Christian churches.

BIBLIOGRAPHY

BUSCH, H., and LOHSE, B. *Romanesque Europe*. London 1960.

CLAPHAM, A. W. *Romanesque Architecture in Western Europe*. Oxford, 1936.

CONANT K. J. *Carolingian and Romanesque Architecture, 800–1200*. 2nd ed. Baltimore and Harmondsworth, 1966.

CORROYER, E. *L'Architecture Romane*. Paris, 1900.

EYGUN, F. *Romanesque Architecture*. London, 1932.

FOCILLON, H. *Art of the West in the Middle Ages*. 2 vols. Vol. i: *Romanesque Art*. 2nd ed. London and New York, 1969.

FRANKL, P. *Die Frühmittelalterliche und Romanische Baukunst*. Potsdam, 1926.

HELIOT, P. *Du Carolingien au Gothique (XIe–XIIIe S.)*. Paris, 1966.

HUBERT, J. *L'Art pré-Roman*. Paris, 1938.

JACKSON, T. G. *Byzantine and Romanesque Architecture*. 2 vols. Cambridge, 1913.

KUNSTLER, G. (Ed.) *Romanesque Art in Europe*. London, 1969.

LETHABY, W. R. *Mediaeval Art*. 1904. Revised and edited by D. Talbot Rice. London, 1949.

MOORE, C. H. 'Romanesque Architecture', *Journal R.I.B.A.*, 3rd series, xxi, 1913–14.

NEBOLSIRE, G. *Journey into Romanesque*. London, 1969.

OURSEL, R. *Living Architecture: Romanesque*. London, 1967.

PORTER, A. K. *Mediaeval Architecture: its Origins and Development*, with lists of monuments and bibliography. 2nd ed. New York, 1966.

PUIG Y CADAFALCH, J. *La Géographie et les Origines du Premier Art Roman*. Paris, 1935.

SAALMAN, H. *European Architecture, 600–1200*. 2nd ed. New York and London, 1968.

TIMMERS, J. J. M. *Handbook of Romanesque Art*. London, 1969.

16

ROMANESQUE ARCHITECTURE IN ITALY

Ninth to twelfth century

INFLUENCES

GEOGRAPHICAL

The long, narrow peninsula of Italy stretches from the Alps on the north, right down through the waters of the Mediterranean, almost to Africa on the south. These geographical variations were accompanied by other differences which influenced architecture in such varying degrees that it may be most conveniently considered under:

(a) *Central Italy*. The central region lies between Florence, commanding the passage of the Arno, in the north; Pisa, the maritime power to the west; and Naples, the naval port on the south. Rome, rich in ancient pagan monuments and Early Christian churches, here exercised a paramount influence on architecture.

(b) *North Italy*. Milan, the capital of Lombardy, enjoyed great prosperity on account of its proximity to several Alpine passes and its situation in the fertile plains of Lombardy. Venice and Ravenna, which were connecting trade links between East and West, fell geographically under the influences of Byzantine art.

(c) *South Italy and Sicily*. South Italy, including Calabria, was by position specially susceptible to influence from the East, and, after passing under Greek and Roman rule, it formed part of the Byzantine Empire under Justinian. Sicily, facing Greece on one side, Italy on another, and North Africa on the third, was exposed to influences from all three countries.

GEOLOGICAL

(a) *Central Italy*. Tuscany possessed great mineral wealth and an abundance of stone. Various building materials were used in Rome, including bricks, volcanic tufa or peperino, travertine stone from Tivoli, and marble from Carrara and from Paros and other Greek islands. Much material was also obtained from the ruins of Classic buildings.

(b) *North Italy*. The low-lying plains of Lombardy supplied clay for making bricks, which, used with marble from the hills, gave a special character to the architecture. Venice on the Adriatic imported marbles in her merchant vessels.

(c) *South Italy and Sicily*. The mountains of South Italy and Sicily supplied calcareous and shelly limestone as well as many kinds of marble, while the sulphur mines, especially of Sicily, largely contributed to that prosperity which was conducive to building enterprise.

CLIMATIC

(a) *Central Italy*. The brilliant sunshine demanded, as in the Roman period, small windows and thick walls, both in cities of the plain and in cities built on the hilltops. The climate varies not only from north to south, but also from east to west according to the proximity to the Apennines, which are often snow-clad, or to the sea-board.

(b) *North Italy*. The climate resembles that of Central Europe, and varies between extremes of heat and cold. The towns from Milan on the west to Venice on the east lie below the Alps, and thus in the winter they are swept by the ice-winds from the mountains; while in the summer these same mountains protect them from the north winds, when the heat in the plains is often excessive.

(c) *South Italy and Sicily*. The climate is almost sub-tropical; on the southern coasts of Italy buildings have flat roofs and other features of Oriental cities.

HISTORICAL, SOCIAL AND RELIGIOUS

(a) *Central Italy*. Pisa, like Genoa in the north and Amalfi in the south, sent merchant fleets to the Holy Land for the Easter Fair at Jerusalem, and so the Pisans were brought into contact with Eastern art. At the beginning of the eleventh century Pisa was the rival of Venice and Genoa as a great commercial and naval power, and took the lead in the wars against the infidels, defeating the Moslems in 1025, 1030 and 1089. The Pisans also captured Palermo in 1062, and this contact with the Moslems probably accounts for the characteristic Pisan use of striped marbles. The Pisans were defeated by the Genoese in 1284, and this was the beginning of their decline. The rise of Florence dates from 1125, when the inhabitants of Fiesole moved there, owing to the destruction of their city, and in the following century Florence rivalled Pisa in commerce. Lucca, another important city during this period, was rent by the feuds of the Guelphs, supporters of the Popes, and the Ghibellines, who sided with the Emperors. These internal feuds are traceable in architectural features of the city, such as the battlements of castles and fortifications. The artistic activity of Tuscany in the eleventh century showed itself chiefly in architecture, which provided a setting for the arts of painting and sculpture. The growth of an industrial population, the increase of commerce, and the rise of ruling families promoted the foundation of independent and fortified cities, such as Pisa, Lucca and Pistoia, all rivals in architectural achievements.

During this period the Popes, although they had only small temporal dominions, began to exercise influence in Italian politics. Pépin, king of the Franks, sided with Pope Stephen II against the Lombards, and restored to him Ravenna, the chief city of the Exarchate. In 755 Central Italy became independent under the Pope, and so inaugurated the temporal power of the papacy. Then Charlemagne, invited by Pope Adrian I (772–95), advanced into Italy in 773, defeated the Lombards and entered Rome for the first time in 744. He bestowed the dukedom of Spoleto on Pope Adrian, the wealth of the Church rapidly increased, and from this period the papal connection with Byzantium was broken off.

(b) *North Italy*. In spite of the intervening Alps, the invaders who had occupied the valley of the Po kept up commercial communications with those on the Rhine by means of the Alpine passes. Thus Milan was subject then as afterwards to German influence in art, but the old Roman influence re-asserted itself in the eleventh and twelfth centuries, which witnessed great building activity in Lombardy.

The inroads made by the Goths into the North Italian plains led to the gradual rise of the powerful Venetian state; for the hardy northern traders planted their new colony on the islands of the lagoons. There, safe from serious attacks, they settled on a republican form of government, which afterwards became an oligarchy under the Doge, who was invested with supreme authority. Commerce and art were the special care of the Venetians. Their close alliance with Byzantium (Constantinople) greatly increased their commerce, so that by the end of the eleventh

Italy in the tenth century

century it extended along the Dalmatian, Croatian and Istrian coasts to those of the Black Sea and the western Mediterranean. They raised glorious buildings, and brought precious freights from the East, including relics from the Holy Land. Thus did the East triumph in the West through its influence on the buildings of the Queen of the Adriatic. All the free cities, or independent commonwealth of Italy, such as Milan, Pavia, Verona and Genoa, vied with one another in the beauty of their public buildings, and this spirit of rivalry encouraged the most remarkable structural advances in all Italy.

(c) *South Italy and Sicily*. In 827 the Moslems landed in Sicily and gradually overran the island, which had formed part of the Byzantine Empire. The latter part of the tenth century was their most prosperous period, but bloody religious struggles ended in the downfall of the Moslem dynasty. From 1061 to 1090 the Normans, under Robert and Roger Guiscard, were engaged in the conquest of the island, and in 1130 a descendent of the latter was crowned at Palermo. During the succeeding years Sicily was again prosperous, as may be judged by the number and beauty of the buildings of this period, and her fleet was powerful enough to defeat the Arabs and the Greeks.

Under Moslem rule even church façades were ornamented with geometrical patterns, because the Moslem religion forebade the representation of the human figure (see Chapter 14). The Moslem and the earlier Byzantine influence persisted even after the Norman conquest of the region in 1061. The traditional use of mosaic in decoration was fostered by the Norman kings, who established a school of mosaic at Palermo. Southern Italy, which always maintained a close connection with Sicily, has yet to be fully explored for traces of its architectural development.

ARCHITECTURAL CHARACTER

(a) *Central Italy*. The basilican type of church was closely adhered to during this period; Italians were slow to adopt a new system of construction and preferred to concentrate on beauty and delicacy of ornamental detail, while the architectural character was much governed by Classic traditions. The most pronounced features of façades were the ornamental arcades which rose one above the other, sometimes even into the gables (pp. 469A, 470). This decorative use of arcaded galleries is one instance of the employment of an architectural feature having a constructive origin. When a wooden roof was placed over a vault there was no need to continue the solid external walls above the springing of the vault, as wooden rafters exerted little thrust (p. 366J); hence this upper portion of the wall could be pierced or arcaded (p. 465E, G), and this arcading came to be used, especially by the Pisans, as a decorative feature, and sometimes even entirely covered the western façade (p. 469A). In a similar way the battlemented parapet, primarily designed for defence, was used as a purely decorative feature. By carrying the external walls above the springing of the vault, an additional load was provided which usefully deflected the vault thrust. The use of marble for facing walls distinguishes Romanesque architecture in Italy from that of the rest of Europe (p. 472A). Churches had, for the most part, simple open timber roofs ornamented with bright colouring. Quite commonly naves were divided from aisles by antique columns (p. 469C). The choir was occasionally raised above a crypt reached by steps from the nave. In consequence of the brilliant climate, while arcades are universal, doors and windows are small and unimportant, with 'jambs' in rectangular recesses or 'orders' filled in with small shafts, crowned with semicircular arches (p. 465B, C, K) in contrast with the classic architrave. Window tracery was at no time employed to any great extent in Italy, and even wheel windows are only rudimentary in pattern. Timber roofs over naves are of the simple, open basilican type with rafters and tie-beams often effectively decorated in colour (p. 472B); while aisles occasionally have groined vaults of small span, divided into compartments by transverse arches. A vast number of columns from ancient Roman temples were utilized in the new churches, and this retarded the development of the novel types which were introduced in districts more remote from Rome (pp. 469C, 472B). In some places, as at Tuscania, rudely carved Corinthianesque columns carry round-arched arcades instead of entablatures. The finely carved and slender twisted columns in the cloisters of S. Giovanni in Laterano and S. Paolo fuori le Mura, Rome, are delicate variations of the Classic type (p. 465H). There are rough imitations of old Classic mouldings, but elaborate variations of a more pronounced Romanesque type in recessed planes were used in doorways and windows (p. 465B–E, K). Classical precedent in ornament was followed so as to suit the old fragments incorporated in the new buildings, and rough variations of the Roman acanthus scroll are frequent (p. 466D, J). The rows

A COMPARATIVE TREATMENT OF CLASSIC ARCHITRAVE.

ARCH MOULDINGS

JAMB MOULDINGS

BASES

SCALE
12 9 6 3 0   12 INS.

B DETAILS OF DOORWAY: S. CRISTOFORO: LUCCA

C DOORWAY: S. CRISTOFORO: LUCCA

D RINGHIERA: BROLETTO: MONZA

E APSE: S. MARIA MAGGIORE: BERGAMO

F E. END: S. ABBONDIO: COMO

G APSE: S. FEDELE: COMO

H CLOISTERS: S. PAOLO: ROME

J PORCH: S. ZENO MAGGIORE: VERONA

K DOORWAY: BAPTISTERY: PISA

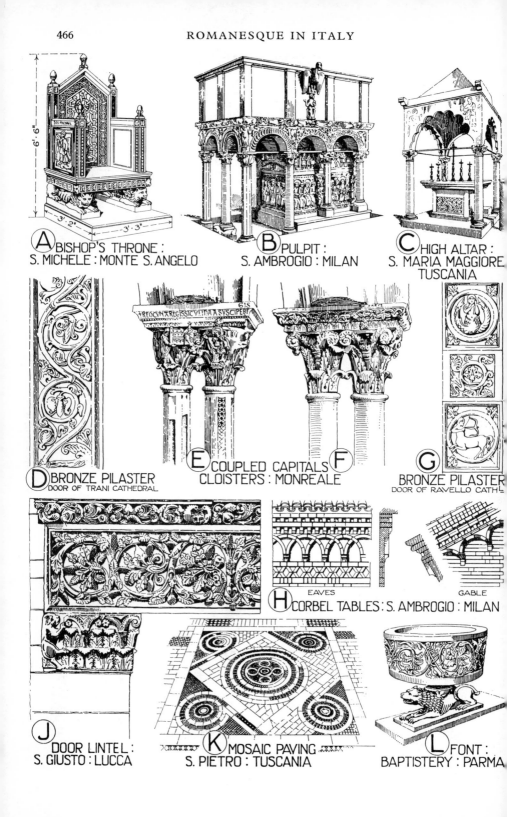

A BISHOP'S THRONE :
S. MICHELE : MONTE S. ANGELO

B PULPIT :
S. AMBROGIO : MILAN

C HIGH ALTAR :
S. MARIA MAGGIORE
TUSCANIA

D BRONZE PILASTER
DOOR OF TRANI CATHEDRAL

E COUPLED CAPITALS
CLOISTERS : MONREALE

F

G BRONZE PILASTER
DOOR OF RAVELLO CATH!

H CORBEL TABLES : S. AMBROGIO : MILAN

EAVES   GABLE

J DOOR LINTEL :
S. GIUSTO : LUCCA

K MOSAIC PAVING
S. PIETRO : TUSCANIA

L FONT :
BAPTISTERY : PARMA

of Apostles on doorway lintels, as at Pistoia, are similar in style to Byzantine ivories. In all parts of Italy Christian symbolism now entered into decorative carving and mosaics. The monogram of Christ, the emblems of evangelists and saints, and the whole system of symbolism, represented by trees, birds, fishes and animals, are all worked into the decorative scheme. At Tuscania, the high altar in S. Maria Maggiore and the mosaic paving in S. Pietro (p. 466C, K) are characteristic of the region and of their period. Byzantine influence was strong in Ravenna and Pisa, which developed their own individual styles. Campanili or bell-towers, which seem to have originated in the sixth century, henceforward gave a special character to ecclesiastical architecture (pp. 469A, 470A–D).

(b) *North Italy*. It was in Lombardy that the most important developments took place. The principal innovation was the development of the ribbed vault which brought about the adoption of many new constructive features. The churches are basilican in type, but naves as well as side aisles are vaulted and have external wooden roofs. Aisles are often two storeys in height, while thick walls between the side chapels act as buttresses to resist the pressure of the vaults. The flat, severe entrance façades stretch across the whole church, thus masking externally the division of nave and aisles. There is often a central projecting porch, with columns standing on the backs of crouching beasts and a wheel window above to light the nave (p. 465J). The gable is characteristically outlined with raking arcades and there are also arcades round the apse under the eaves. The general character becomes less refined, owing to the increased use of stone and brick instead of marble, and ornament shows a departure from Classic precedent, and portrays, with an element of the grotesque, the rough outdoor life of invaders from the north. The Comacine masters, a privileged guild of architects and sculptors originating in Como, carried out church building and characteristic decoration during the eleventh century, not only in the north, but also in other parts of Italy. There were many baptisteries, usually octagonal or circular, such as the one at Novara, which is connected to the Cathedral by an atrium similar to the famous atrium at S. Ambrogio, Milan. Open arcades round the apses, with the arcaded octagonal lantern at the crossing, give great charm to the buildings externally (p. 465E, G). Projecting porches, which were preferred to recessed doorways, are bold arched structures often of two storeys, flanked by isolated columns on huge semi-grotesque beasts, as at Verona (p. 477C). Towers are straight shafts, often detached, as at Verona (p. 476A), without buttresses or spires (pp. 465F, 471B, 474A). The composition of façades usually relies upon simple pilaster strip decoration, running from the ground and ending in small arches under the eaves, as at S. Abbondio, Como (p. 465F). Sometimes there is a large circular window over the entrance, and usually this front extends the whole width of nave and aisles and terminates in one wide-spreading gable filled in with open arcaded galleries which spring either from horizontal or from stepped bases, as at Pavia (p. 475F). Internally, sturdy piers faced with attached half-columns took the place of the Classic column, as supports to the heavy stone vaulting (p. 475B, D). The half-columns on the side towards the nave were carried up as vaulting shafts, and this was the beginning of a system which was destined in the Gothic period to transform the shape of piers. Roughly carved grotesques of men and beasts occur, along with vigorous hunting scenes and incidents of daily life. Crouching beasts support columns of projecting porches and of bishops' thrones (p. 466A). The font (p. 466L), similarly supported, and the corbel tables (p. 466H) are typical.

(c) *South Italy and Sicily*. The changing architectural character can be traced through Byzantine, Moslem and Norman rule, and each successive period carried with it something from the past. Byzantine influence is evident in the mosaic decoration of interiors and predominates in the plans of such buildings as the church of the Martorana at Palermo, where the dome, supported on four columns, covers the square central space. Moslem influence is especially seen in the application of stripes of coloured marbles and in the use of stilted pointed arches. The Norman character is displayed in the planning and construction of the cathedral of Monreale, which has a cruciform plan, is decorated with mosaics and has a nave arcade of stilted pointed arches. In South Italy domes rather than vaults were adopted, but timber roofs were the rule in Sicily under Moslem influence and had stalactite ceilings, rich in design and colour. Lateral walls were occasionally decorated with flat pilaster strips connected horizontally by small arches springing from corbels. Wheel windows, as in the churches of Palermo, are often made of sheets of pierced marble, and are highly elaborate. Greater variety in columns and capitals was brought about by changes which resulted from the successive introduction of Byzantine, Moslem and Norman art, of which the nave arcade columns (p. 481A) and the coupled columns in the cloisters at Monreale (pp. 466E, F, 481B) are good examples. In South Italy elaborately modelled bronze doors are characteristic externally, while coloured mosaics add to the beauty of the interiors of Palermo churches. Colour, in spreading masses of geometric design, was the predominant note of internal decoration of South Italian and more especially of Sicilian churches, while the bronze pilasters (p. 466D, G) clearly indicate the influence of the Classic tradition.

EXAMPLES

CENTRAL ITALY

Pisa Cathedral (1063–1118 and 1261–72) (pp. 469, 470B) with Baptistery, Campanile and Campo Santo, together form one of the most famous building groups of the world (p. 469A). The cathedral is one of the finest of the Romanesque period and has a strongly marked individuality. It resembles other early basilican churches in plan, with long rows of columns connected by arches, double aisles, and a nave which has the usual timber roof (p. 469C). The exterior has bands of red and white marble, and the ground storey is faced with wall arcading, while the entrance façade is thrown into relief by tiers of open arcades which rise one above another right into the gable end. The transepts, with an apse at each end, were an advance on the simple basilican plan. The elliptical dome over the crossing, or intersection of nave and transepts, is of later date (p. 469D). The building depends for its interest on its general proportions and on the delicacy of its ornamental features, rather than on any new structural development, such as may be seen in Northern Italy.

The **Campanile, Pisa** (1174–1271) (pp. 469A, 470A–D), is a circular tower, 16 m (52 ft) in diameter, rising in eight storeys of encircling arcades. This world-famous leaning tower, which is the most arresting feature of this marvellous group, has been the subject of much discussion, but there is little doubt that its inclination, which recent measurements proved to be on the increase, is due to subsidence in the foundations. The upper part of the tower now overhangs its base more than 4.2 m (13 ft 10 ins), and it thus has a very unstable appearance. The belfry was not added until 1350.

The **Baptistery, Pisa** (1153–1265) (pp. 469A, D, 470E–G), was designed by Dioti Salvi, on a circular plan, with a central space or nave, 18.3 m (60 ft) in diameter, separated by four piers and eight columns from the surrounding two-storeyed aisle, which makes the building nearly 39.3 m (129 ft) in diameter. Externally it is surrounded on the lower storey by half-columns, connected by semicircular arches, under one of which is the door (p. 465K), with, above, an open arcade of small

PISA CATHEDRAL

Ⓐ THE PISAN GROUP FROM S.W.

Ⓑ PLAN

SCALE FOR PLAN
FEET·100 50 0 50 100 150
METRES 10 0 10 20 30 40

Ⓒ INTERIOR LOOKING E.

Ⓓ BIRD'S-EYE VIEW FROM CAMPANILE

Ⓔ TRANSVERSE SECTION $x \cdot x$

Ⓕ LONGITUDINAL SECTION

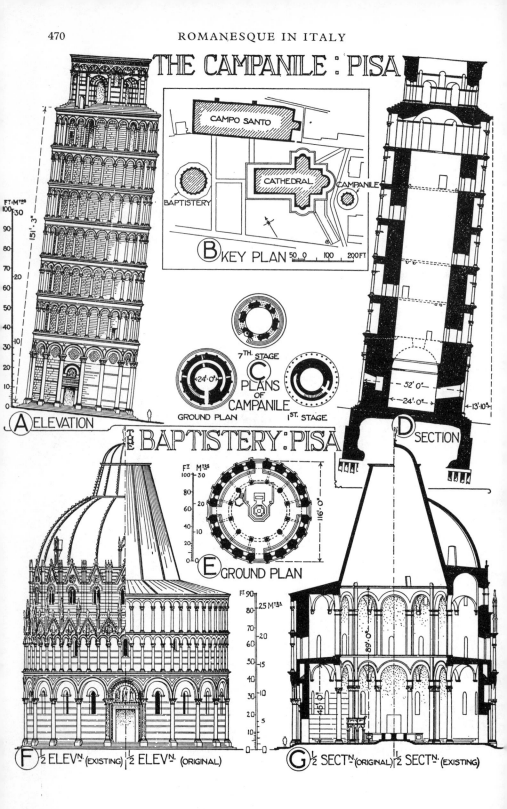

THE CAMPANILE : PISA

B KEY PLAN 50 0 100 200FT
CAMPO SANTO
CATHEDRAL
BAPTISTERY
CAMPANILE

C PLANS OF CAMPANILE
7TH. STAGE
GROUND PLAN — 24'.0"
1ST. STAGE

A ELEVATION — 151'.3"

D SECTION — 52' 0" — 24'.0" — 13'.10½"

THE BAPTISTERY : PISA

E GROUND PLAN — 116'.0"

F ½ ELEVᴺ. (EXISTING) ½ ELEVᴺ. (ORIGINAL)

G ½ SECTᴺ. (ORIGINAL) ½ SECTᴺ. (EXISTING) — 89'.0" — 45'.0"

A. Pistoia Cathedral (13th cent.). See p. 473

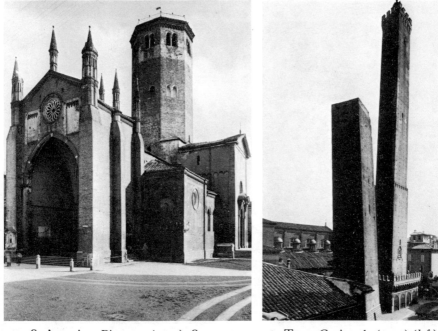

B. S. Antonino, Piacenza (1104). See p. 473

C. Torre Garisenda (1100) (*left*) and Torre Asinelli (1109), Bologna. See p. 480

A. S. Miniato al Monte, Florence (1018–62). See p. 473

B. S. Miniato al Monte, Florence:
nave looking E.

C. The Baptistery, Cremona (1167).
See p. 479

detached shafts. This arcade is surmounted by Gothic additions of the fourteenth century, which disguise the original design. The structure is crowned by an outer hemispherical roof, through which penetrates a truncated cone capped by a small dome, covering the central space (p. 470F, G). This Baptistery resembles the church of S. Donato (ninth century) at Zadar, Dalmatia, in which, however, the central space is only 9 m (30 ft) in diameter.

S. Martino, Lucca (façade 1204) and **S. Michele, Lucca** (1143 and later), with a façade (1288) of which the gables are mere screens, are very similar in style to the buildings of the Pisan group, because at the time of their erection Lucca had fallen under the power of Pisa.

Pistoia Cathedral (thirteenth century) was also built under the influence of the Pisan school, and with its porch and arcaded façade in black and white marble followed the style of other churches in the city (p. 471A), including **S. Andrea** and **S. Giovanni fuor Civitas** (late twelfth century).

The **Cloisters of S. Giovanni in Laterano, Rome** (1234) and of **S. Paolo fuori le Mura, Rome** (c. 1200) (p. 465H) are of special interest, since they are among the few instances of Romanesque art in Rome which show any progressive character, owing to the survival of the Classical tradition; besides which, the use of Roman architectural fragments still gave the churches a basilican character. The delicate twisted twin columns, inlaid with patterned glass mosaics, are the special features of these cloisters, and are a triumph of craftsmanship which has given to these coils of stone the subtlety of living forms. The coupled columns carry semicircular arches in groups of five or more openings between the recurrent piers, and form an arcade round the four sides of the cloister.

S. Miniato al Monte, Florence (1018–62) (p. 472A, B) is important as showing some innovations; for the length of the church is divided by piers and transverse diaphragm arches into three main compartments, of which the raised eastern portion has a crypt open to the nave and containing the tomb of the saint. This division seems a prelude to the idea of vaulting in compartments, and is a departure from the basilican type of long, unbroken ranges of columns and arches. The novel panelling and banding in black and white marble, both of exterior and interior, were carried further in the Gothic period in Italy. The sanctuary has translucent marble, instead of glass, in the window openings. The open timber roof, with its bright colour decoration recently restored, gives an excellent idea of the effect produced by the use of simple colour on these basilican roofs.

NORTH ITALY

S. Antonino, Piacenza (1104) (p. 471B), rebuilt on the site of an earlier cathedral, is noted for its later Gothic porch, Il Paradiso (1350).

S. Ambrogio, Milan (c. 1080–1128) (p. 474), founded by the great S. Ambrose in the fourth century, raised on its present plan (c. 850) and partly rebuilt with vault and dome in the twelfth century, has a proud history, and set a type for Lombard churches, as did its founder for Lombard ritual, which included the metrical chanting of the Mass. Here S. Augustine was baptized, the Emperor Theodosius was excommunicated, and Lombard kings and Germanic emperors were crowned. The plan includes the only existing atrium among Lombard churches, a narthex flanked by towers, vaulted nave and aisles with an octagon over the crossing, triforium gallery, raised choir over the crypt, and an apse. The interior (p. 474B) is severely plain and impressive. The pulpit (p. 466B), which is built over a sixth-century sarcophagus, consists of an arcade with characteristic Lombard ornamentation of carved birds and animals.

A. S. Ambrogio, Milan, showing atrium (*c.* 1080–1128). See p. 473

B. S. Ambrogio, Milan: nave looking E.

S. MICHELE : PAVIA

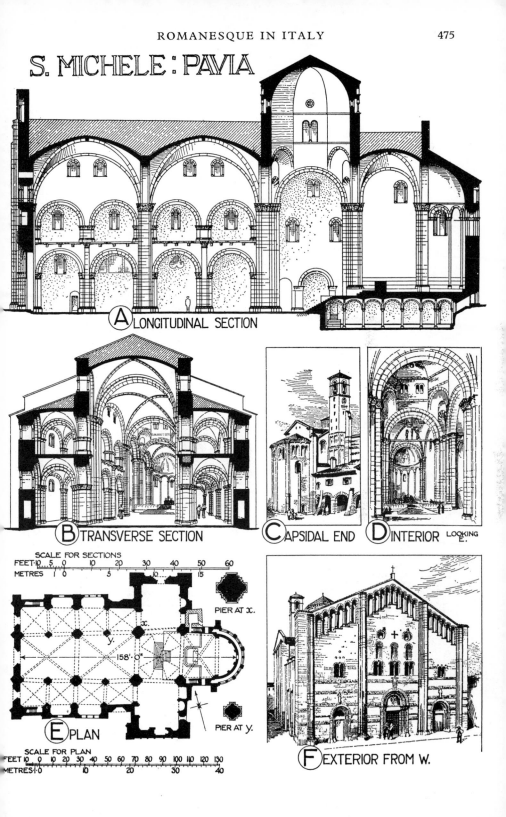

Ⓐ LONGITUDINAL SECTION

Ⓑ TRANSVERSE SECTION

Ⓒ APSIDAL END

Ⓓ INTERIOR LOOKING E.

SCALE FOR SECTIONS
FEET·10 5 0 10 20 30 40 50 60
METRES 1 0 5 10 15

PIER AT x.

158'·0"

PIER AT y.

Ⓔ PLAN

SCALE FOR PLAN
FEET·10 0 10 20 30 40 50 60 70 80 90 100 110 120 130
METRES·1·0 10 20 30 40

Ⓕ EXTERIOR FROM W.

A. S. Zeno Maggiore, Verona (*c.* 1123 and later). See p. 479

B. S. Zeno Maggiore, Verona: nave looking E.

A. Fondaco dei Turchi, Venice (12th cent., but largely rebuilt). See p. 480

B. Monreale Cathedral (1174–82):
apses at east end. See p. 480

c. S. Zeno Maggiore, Verona
(c. 1123 and later): porch. See p. 479

A. Exterior   B. Interior

The Baptistery, Parma (1196–1270). See p. 479

C. The Capella Palatina, Palermo: interior (1129–43). See p. 485

D. La Zisa, Palermo (1154–66). See p. 485

S. Michele, Pavia (*c.* 1100–60) (p. 475), is a version in stone of the structural system of S. Ambrogio, which itself is an advance on the divisions, marked only by piers, in S. Miniato; for here not only is the nave divided into square bays by transverse arches but the dividing piers are of a clustered character, shaped to receive the vaulting ribs. This church is cruciform in plan with well-defined transepts and a raised choir, under which is a vaulted crypt. The side aisles, which are two storeys in height, are also vaulted in square compartments, two of which correspond to one vaulting bay of the nave. The flat façade shows little play of light and shade, with its three simple, recessed portals and four vertical pilaster strips from ground to gable, almost akin to buttresses. The wide-spreading gable stretches across nave and aisles and is emphasized by a characteristic raking arcaded gallery which is the only prominent feature of this simple design (p. 475F).

S. Zeno Maggiore, Verona (*c.* 1123 and later) (p. 476), has a façade which is stern in its simplicity. The fine projecting porch has two free-standing columns, which rest on the backs of crouching beasts and support a semicircular vault, over which is a gabled roof (p. 477C). Above is the great wheel window which lights the nave, one of the earliest in Italy, and the whole façade is relieved by pilaster strips connected by corbel tables under the slopes of the centre gable and side roofs. The interior (p. 476B) has a nave arcade of compound piers with uncarved capitals, and the nave shaft is carried up as if to support a vault. Intermediate columns with carved capitals support semicircular arches, surmounted by a wall banded in red brick and stone. There is no triforium, but a clear-storey, and above this is a wooden ceiling of trefoil form. The choir, 2.1 m (7 ft) above the nave floor, has a high pointed fourteenth-century vault and an apse, and beneath is the crypt, in seven aisles, with the shrine of S. Zeno. This is a development of the traditional arrangement of high choir over crypt in pilgrimage churches which can be traced back through S. Ambrogio (p. 474B), S. Pietro at Agliate (*c.* 875), S. Apollinare in Classe at Ravenna (pp. 348B, 356K) and the seventh-century adaptations of the east end of Old S. Peter's in Rome. The campanile (p. 476A) is detached, as is usual in Italy, has no buttresses, and is of alternate courses of marble and brick, terminating in open arcades to the bell-chamber, angle pinnacles and a high-pitched roof. The sturdy tower formerly belonged to a residence of the Mediaeval German emperors and is finished with Ghibelline battlements.

Baptisteries are a special feature of Italian architecture and represent a period of Christianity when the baptismal rite was carried out only three times a year— Easter, Pentecost and the Epiphany—and therefore required a large and separate building. The **Baptistery, Cremona** (1167) (p. 472C), is octagonal, and has a projecting porch and the usual pilaster strips, corbel tables and arcading. The **Baptistery, Asti** (1050), and the **Baptistery, Parma** (1196–1270) (p. 478A, B), are octagonal, modelled on that of Constantine, Rome (p. 366E–G).

The *Campanili* or bell-towers are a product of the period, and, unlike the church towers of England, France and Germany, generally stand alone, though they were sometimes connected by cloisters with the church. Campanili of North Italian towns are often civic monuments rather than integral parts of churches, and, like the civic towers of Belgium (p. 717), were symbols of power, and served also as watch-towers. They are square in plan, without the projecting buttresses which are usual north of the Alps, and their design is generally simple, broken only by windows which light the internal staircase or sloping way. The window openings increase in number with the height of the tower and often form an open loggia at the top, through which may be seen the swinging of the bells, and the whole is often surmounted by a pyramidal roof, as in the rebuilt campanile of S.

Mark, Venice (pp. 744, 730A), originally built 888, and also in that of S. Zeno Maggiore, Verona (p. 476A), which dates originally from 1172.

The **Torre Asinelli, Bologna** (1109), 69 m (225 ft) high, and the **Torre Garisenda, Bologna** (1100) (p. 471C), 40 m (130 ft) high, date from the time when the town was prominent in the struggles of the period, and are the leaning towers referred to by Dante, while **San Gimignano** (p. 756C), with its thirteen towers, built for defence and ostentation, has the appearance of a Romanesque city so often pictured by Raphael in later times.

The **Fondaco dei Turchi, Venice** (p. 477A), a twelfth-century mercantile palace (since rebuilt) on the Grand Canal, is an example of the high level which domestic architecture reached in Venice as the outcome of her prosperous trade with the East. The **Palazzo Farsetti** and the **Palazzo Loredan** (twelfth century) are in the same style, with cubiform capitals carrying semicircular arches which are sometimes stilted.

SOUTH ITALY AND SICILY

S. Nicola, Bari (*c.* 1085–1132) (pp. 482, 483A), a Benedictine church, was the prototype of the Romanesque of the late eleventh and twelfth centuries in Apulia. It has an aisled western arm, transepts, three eastern apses and two western towers. The most distinctive and influential feature is the structural organization of the nave, with its main arcade on piers and grouped columns, triforium and clear-storey generously proportioned. The nave has added diaphragm arches and a flat timber ceiling, and the groined aisle vaults support a gallery. This composition seems to have been derived from closely contemporary ideas current in Emilia. With its Apulian progeny, this church shares fine masonry details, including projecting porches, wheel windows, and a refinement of carved decoration which is in the Greek tradition. Most of the Apulian churches modelled upon S. Nicola are cathedrals, and they include those of **Bari** itself (*c.* 1160 and later), **Trani** (*c.* 1139 and later), a pilgrimage church with basilican nave, a large crypt and some Lombard detail, **Bitetto** (early twelfth century), **Ruvo** (twelfth century), and **Bitonto** (1175–1200).

Cefalù Cathedral (1131–1240) (pp. 483B, 484), founded by Count Roger (King Roger II of Sicily) as a royal pantheon, was served by Augustinian canons. It is externally the most distinctly Romanesque church in Sicily, and has a basilican nave with groined aisle vaults, columnar arcades, a high transept and a tri-apsidal east end with later ribbed vaulting over presbytery and south transept. The two western towers, of minaret proportions, enclose a columned porch.

Monreale Cathedral (1174–82) (pp. 477B, 481) stands on the heights south-west of Palermo, and is the most splendid of all the monuments erected under Norman rule in Sicily. The plan is basilican in its western part and quasi-Byzantine in its eastern part, with a choir raised above the nave and with eastern apses. The nave columns have capitals of Byzantine form with 'dosseret-blocks' encrusted with mosaic, to support pointed arches, which are not in recessed planes as in northern Romanesque buildings, and in the aisles there are pointed windows without tracery. The walls are covered with mosaics in gold and colour, representing scenes from Biblical history with a figure of Christ in the apse, framed in arabesques; while a high dado of white marble slabs is bordered by inlaid patterns in coloured porphyries. The open timber roofs, intricate in design, are brightly painted in the Moslem style. The interior is solemn and grand, an effect produced by the severity of the design, enhanced by the coloured decoration. The low, oblong central lantern and the antique bronze doors add to the beauty and distinction of this famous

A. Monreale Cathedral: interior looking E. (1174–82). See p. 480

B. Monreale Cathedral: the cloisters (1172–89)

A. S. Nicola, Bari: west front (*c.* 1085–1132). See p. 480

B. S. Nicola, Bari: interior

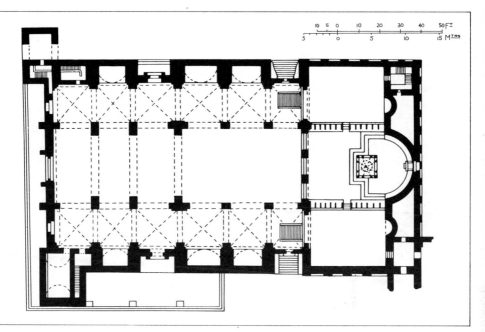

A. S. Nicola, Bari: plan (*c.* 1085–1132). See p. 480

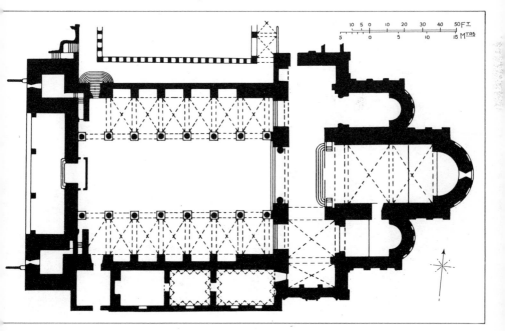

B. Cefalù Cathedral: plan (1131–1240). See p. 480

A. Cefalù Cathedral from the S.E. (1131–1240). See p. 480

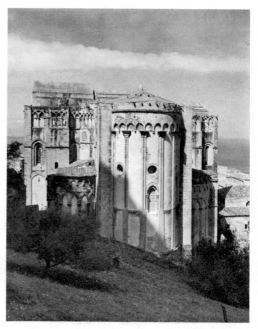

B. Cefalù Cathedral: west door   C. Cefalù Cathedral from E.

church. The cloisters (1172–89) (p. 481B), the only remaining portion of the Benedictine monastery, are the finest of the style. They consist of coupled columns, in some cases inlaid with glass mosaics, supporting pointed arches, and have beautiful Corinthianesque capitals (p. 466E, F), one of which represents William I of Sicily offering the Church to the Virgin.

The **Capella Palatina, Palermo** (1129–43) (p. 478C), the chapel in the Royal Palace, has gilt and coloured mosaics in the interior, and a dome, 5.5 m (18 ft) in diameter, indicative of Byzantine influence, while the carved stalactite ceiling, pulpit, candelabra and organ gallery show Moslem craftsmanship.

S. Giovanni degli Eremiti, Palermo (1148–), **La Martorana, Palermo** (1143–51) (S. Maria del Ammiraglio), and **S. Cataldo, Palermo** (1161–) are other churches which, in the arrangement of their domes and ornamentation, show the blending of Moslem and Byzantine art.

La Zisa, Palermo (Arabic, *El Aziza*=Palace of Delights) (1154–66) (p. 478D), is a three-storeyed Norman castle with battlemented parapet, and shows the influence of Moslem art. The vestibule is rich in marble columns and coloured tiles, while the stalactite vaults over the alcoves recall the glories of the Alhambra, Granada.

BIBLIOGRAPHY

ARATA, G. U. *L'Architettura arabo-normanna in Sicilia.* Milan, 1914.
ARSLAN, W. *L'Architettura Romanica Veronese.* Verona, 1939.
AVENA, A. *Monumente dell' Italia meridionale.* Rome, 1911.
CESILU, C. *Architettura Romanica Genovese.* Milan, 1945.
CUMMINGS, C. A. *A History of Architecture in Italy.* 2 vols. 2nd ed. New York and London, 1928.
DECKER, H. *Romanesque Art in Italy.* London, 1958.
GURLITT, C. *Denkmäler der Kunst in Dalmatien.* 2 vols. Berlin, 1910.
KRONIG, WOLFGANG. *The Cathedral of Monreale and Norman Architecture in Sicily.* Palermo, 1965.
MAGNI, M. C. *Architettura Romanica Comasca.* Milan, 1960.
MARTIN, C., and ENLART, C. *L'Art Roman en Italie.* Paris, 1912–24.
NORWICH, J. J. *The Normans in the South: 1016–1130.* London, 1967.
PORTER, A. K. *Lombard Architecture.* 3 vols. New Haven and London, 1915–17.
—. *The Construction of Lombard and Gothic Vaults.* New Haven and London, 1911.
RICCI, C. *Romanesque Architecture in Italy.* London, 1925.
RIVOIRA, G. T. *Le Origini della Architettura Lombarda.* 2 vols. Rome, 1901–7; London, 1910.
SALINI, M. *L'Architettura Romanica in Toscana.* Milan and Rome, 1927.
VENTURI, A. *Storia dell' Arte Italiana.* Vols. ii and iii. Milan, 1902–4.

17
ROMANESQUE ARCHITECTURE IN FRANCE

Ninth to twelfth century

INFLUENCES

GEOGRAPHICAL

France has great natural highways along the valleys of the Rhône, Saône, Seine and Garonne which connect the Mediterranean with the Atlantic Ocean and the English Channel. The different territories into which the country was divided at this period had strongly marked characteristics in architecture, as in all else, partly due to the difference in geographical position. Roman civilization had spread through France along the historic highway of the fertile Rhône valley, where the influence of Roman architecture is everywhere evident. Somewhat later, the trade route from the Mediterranean along the Garonne valley carried Venetian and Eastern influence across the south-west of France to Périgueux, in Aquitaine, the centre of an area endowed with a large group of churches showing Eastern Mediterranean inspiration which can be traced specifically to Venice and Cyprus. North of the River Loire is seen the influence of the Norsemen who came by sea, and of the Franks who stretched across the country from the Rhine to Brittany.

GEOLOGICAL

France has an abundance of good stone, easily quarried and freely used for all types of buildings. In the north the fine-grained Caen stone was available throughout Normandy. In the volcanic district of Auvergne the coloured pumice and tufa were not only used for walls and inlaid decoration, but were so light in weight that they were also employed in large blocks for the solid stone vaulted roofs peculiar to the district.

CLIMATIC

The climatic variations between north and south regulate door and window openings, which decrease in size towards the south. The climate also determines the pitch of roofs which, from being steep in the north to throw off snow, become almost flat in the sub-tropical south, and these features largely control the general architectural style.

HISTORICAL, SOCIAL AND RELIGIOUS

Caesar's conquest of Gaul (58–49 B.C.) was followed by the systematic Romanization of the country, which had begun with the making of a road system centred upon Lyons, and the development of thriving commercial colonies which adopted the Roman social system in their independent municipalities. The 'Pax Romana' was established, and by the early third century, social conditions were very stable; thereafter Roman administration and industrial and commercial development were progressively undermined by barbarian incursions and by the increasing power of great landowners. In A.D. 250 Frankish barbarians began their attacks, and strife continued till Goths, Franks and Romans united to defeat Attila, king of the Huns (451). Then Clovis, king of the Salian Franks, defeated the Romans (486) at Soissons, absorbed the kingdom of Burgundy, drove Alaric II, king of the Visigoths, out of Aquitaine (507), united the Frankish tribes and established the Merovingian dynasty, and so achieved the Frankish conquest of Gaul. Christianity was first established in the Rhône valley, where Lyons contributed martyrs to the cause. The Moslems overran southern France (719–32), but Charles Martel defeated them at Poitiers (732) and changed the future of Western Europe. The Carolingian dynasty followed, and Pépin was crowned as the first Carolingian king by Pope Stephen II (754), to whom he presented the Exarchate of Ravenna. The Roman monarchical principle was now supplanted by the feudal system in France. After two and a half centuries of civil war and conflicts between kings and nobles, King Pépin (752–68) united the four kingdoms of the 'Ile de France', the area around Paris. Charlemagne, Pépin's son, king of a united France (768–814), also arrogated to himself all Western Europe as the Holy Roman Empire. Under his strong rule and patronage learning, art and architecture all made striking advances. Yet by the time of Charlemagne's death France was already being ravaged by the Northmen, and later the Empire ceased to embrace Europe. Louis the Pious (814–40) left it to his three sons, and the Treaty of Verdun (843) divided it into three kingdoms, with Charles the Bald as King of France. Subsequently the Middle Kingdom was partitioned between France and Germany, the latter retaining the title of Holy Roman Empire. The Northmen insistently penetrated up the rivers, the French monarchy grew weaker, and feudal lords became strong enough to elect the king. Charles III ceded Normandy to Duke Rollo (911), and this foreign influence reacted on the architecture of northern France. Hugh Capet brought in the Capetian dynasty (987) which, with its centre in the Ile de France, was hemmed in by powerful enemies, but under Philip I (1060–1105) the king's power was increased, because the conquest of England by the Normans withdrew their attacks from his kingdom. In 910 the Cluniac Order had been founded in Burgundy, and was followed in 1098 by the Cistercian Order at Cîteaux. The severity of this rule as to simplicity in church buildings caused a reaction from the decorative treatment found at S. Gilles and S. Trophîme, Arles (p. 495A). Attention was then concentrated upon producing grand and severe rather than ornate buildings. Paris became the capital of Hugh Capet's kingdom in 987, but his authority extended little beyond Paris and Orleans, as the greater part of France was held by the independent lords of Aquitaine, Auvergne, Provence, Anjou, Burgundy, Normandy and Brittany. In 1066 Duke William conquered England, and numerous churches and castles in Normandy reflect the prosperity of his duchy.

The eleventh century was marked by a widespread desire to withdraw from the world and embrace the monastic life; this resulted in the foundation of many religious houses, which gave an impulse to architecture and also fostered art and learning. Religious zeal was not, however, confined within monastic walls, but adventurously mingled with secular ambitions to produce the Crusades, which began in 1096 and were continued under Louis VII (1147). This intercourse with the East reacted in its turn on the art of the West. The crusading king, Louis, aided by his minister Abbot Suger of S. Denis, also displayed his religious zeal in church-building. On the other hand, he weakened his kingdom by divorcing Eleanor of Aquitaine (1152), who then married Henry of Anjou, king of England, thus giving the English king rule over more than half of France. The country rallied again under Philip Augustus (1180–1223), who was strong enough to subdue the feudal

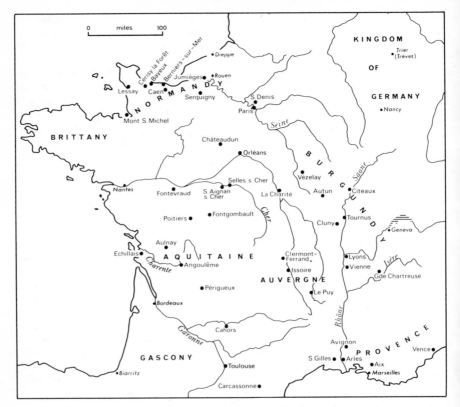

France in the eleventh century

lords and attack Henry II of England. These were among the complex forces which went to the making of the French people; while the influence of Roman civilization is specially noticeable during the period when monasticism produced the grand series of Romanesque buildings in France.

ARCHITECTURAL CHARACTER

In the south, churches were usually cruciform in plan and frequently had naves covered with barrel vaults whose thrust was taken by half-barrel vaults over aisles in two storeys (p. 500C). Buttresses are internal and form the divisions between the chapels which flank the nave, as at Vienne Cathedral. Towers are sometimes detached, like Italian campanili. Cloisters are treated with the utmost elaboration, as at S. Trophime, Arles (p. 489F), and form a special feature in the plan of many churches of the period. Circular churches are rare, but the development of the semicircular east end as an ambulatory, with radiating chapels, is common in southern France. In the north, plans were of the basilican type with nave and aisles. The use of high nave vaults changed the setting-out of the bays, which were brought to a square by making one nave vaulting compartment equal to the length of two bays of the aisles (p. 500D), until the introduction of the pointed arch solved the problem of vaulting oblong compartments with ribbed vaults.

S.ESTEPHE

B FIREPLACE & CHIMNEY: ABBEY OF SENANQUE: S.GILLES

C WEST FAÇADE: E.CHILLAIS

D MONASTIC KITCHEN: FONTEVRAUD

OISTERS: S.TROPHÎME: ARLES

G APSE: S.PIERRE: AULNAY

NAVE PIERS: LESSAY H

JAMB

9'-10"

5'-5½"

DOORWAY: SERQUIGNY

K PORCH: S.TROPHÎME: ARLES

L DOORWAY: FONTGOMBAULT

M

5'-6'

N CERISY-LA-FORET

7'-3½'

P S.GILLES

5'-2½'

Q ABBAYE AUX DAMES CAEN

4'-9'

R BERNIERES-SUR-MER

LY NAVE PIER

NAVE PIERS

(A) CAPITAL: FLEAC

(B) TYMPANUM: LA CHARITÉ-S^R-LOIRE

(C) CAPITAL: S. AIGNAN-S^R-CHER

(D) TWIN CAPITALS: S. SERNIN: TOULOUSE

(E) APSIDAL END: SELLES-SUR-CHER

(F) CARVING: VENCE

(G) TWIN CAPS CLOISTER S. TROPHIME: ARLES

(H) BASES: AIX CATH^L

(J) SCULP^D FRIEZE: ANGOULÊME CATH^L

(K) PIER AND COLUMNS: CLOISTER: AIX CATH^L

(L) DOORWAY: S. GILLES

(M) SCULP^D SPANDREL BAYEUX CATHEDRAL

The south is remarkable for richly decorated church façades and graceful cloisters, and for the use of old Roman architectural features which seem to have acquired a fresh significance. Roman buildings at Arles, Nîmes, Orange and other places in the Rhône valley naturally exerted considerable influence throughout Provence. In Aquitaine and Anjou the aisleless naves, covered with domes on pendentives (p. 494), or vaulting supported only by the massive walls of the recessed chapels, recall the great halls of Roman thermae. The development of vaulting (p. 458) progressed, and naves were often covered with barrel vaults (p. 501A), whose thrust was resisted by half-barrel vaults over two-storeyed aisles, thus suppressing the clear-storey, as at Notre Dame du Port, Clermont-Ferrand. Nave wall arcades of aisleless churches are semicircular, with mouldings in recesses or 'orders' (p. 494A, B, F), while cloister arcades are elaborated with coupled columns in the depth of the walls, and with carved capitals which support the semicircular arches of the narrow bays, which were left unglazed as in Italy (p. 489F). The western portals of such churches as S. Trophîme, Arles (p. 489K), and S. Gilles (p. 495A) recall the columns and horizontal entablatures of the Romans, but in other cases doorways have recessed jambs as usual in this period (p. 489J, L). Narrow windows with semicircular heads and wide splays inwards suffice to admit light, especially in the south (p. 489G).

Naves were first covered by barrel vaults (p. 501A) buttressed by half-barrel vaults over aisles, which were sometimes two storeys high and thus left no space for a clear-storey. The vault was sometimes pointed (p. 502D), and this had the advantage of lessening the superincumbent thrust of the stone roofing slabs which, especially in Auvergne, were frequently laid direct upon the vaults and were given the low pitch suitable to the south. The narthex or antechapel of S. Madeleine, Vézelay (1132) (p. 495B), has one of the earliest pointed cross-vaults in France. Southern climatic conditions required that roofs need only be low in pitch, but other factors entered into the nature of their construction; for in the volcanic district of Auvergne the light nature of the stone resulted in stone-covered vaults; while in Aquitaine, Eastern Mediterranean influences promoted the use of domical construction, as at Angoulême. Piers were derived from the Roman square pier, with attached columns to which were added nook shafts, and on the nave side the half-round shafts were carried up to the springing of the vaults (p. 496B). These piers, as at Lessay (p. 489H), were the prototypes of the richly clustered Gothic piers. Capitals, as at Aix, clearly show the influence of Classic buildings (p. 490K).

In the north, where Roman remains were less abundant, there was greater freedom in developing a new style, and western façades of churches, especially in Normandy, are distinguished by the introduction of two flanking towers, while plain, massive side walls with flat buttresses emphasize the richness of the façades. Naves are covered by ribbed vaults which are often sexpartite and in square compartments or 'severies', the ribs being constructed independently and supporting the panels (pp. 500D, F, 501B). The gradual change to the Gothic system was promoted by repeated attempts to cover oblong compartments with 'rib and panel' vaults, a problem which was eventually solved by the introduction of the pointed arch, first used in the south of France and introduced into the north in the twelfth century. The solution to the many problems which had faced the Romanesque designers was found in the building of the choir of the Abbey of S. Denis (1137–44), near Paris, where the ribbed vault, pointed arch and flying buttress are successfully combined. Nave arcades are spanned by semicircular arches which are repeated in the deep triforia, as at the Abbaye-aux-Hommes. Imposing western doorways (pp. 496A, C, 501C) with sculptured tympana were the forerunners of the magnificent sculptured entrances of the Gothic period. Windows with semicircular heads are sometimes grouped together and enclosed in a larger arch, as in the nave wall or clear-storey immediately beneath the vault (p. 501B). The height of clear-storeys was increased by means of intersecting ribbed vaults whose thrust was taken by buttress arches under the aisle roofs (p. 500C)—a step towards the later external flying buttresses. In the north, also, the most important developments in stone vaulting technique took place, with the introduction of the rib and panel system. The vaults were usually covered by wooden framed roofs, finished with slates and of steep pitch to throw off snow and water (p. 502B).

The massive walls characteristic of this period were, in both south and north, of rubble faced with squared stone. Sculptured and moulded ornament was concentrated on wall arcades, especially on western façades, which thus stand out in contrast to the general simplicity of the external wall treatment (p. 496C). Façades were often divided by string courses or horizontal mouldings into storeys relieved by single, coupled or grouped windows, and frequently had arcading as at Echillais (p. 489C). Buttresses were wide strips of slight projection (p. 501C) or half-round shafts (p. 489G); while flying buttresses, admitting of high clear-storey windows to light the nave, were introduced in the latter half of the twelfth century (p. 502B). Towers were generally square with pyramidal or conical roofs (p. 489A). Cylindrical piers, as at Jumièges, (p. 498B), were frequent, surmounted with carved capitals of Corinthianesque type and square abacus, from which the vaulting shafts start awkwardly.

Mouldings executed in stone are coarser than those in the marble of Italy. In the south, Classic tradition is reflected in the graceful moulding contours. Capitals and bases are either rough imitations of the old Roman Corinthian type (p. 490C, H) or have considerable variations, due to the introduction of animal figures. In the north, the jambs are formed in receding planes, with recesses filled with nook shafts fluted or carved with zigzag ornament. Capitals are frequently cubiform blocks, sometimes carved with animal subjects (p. 490A). Corbel tables of great richness, supported by grotesquely carved heads, often form the wall cornices (p. 490E). Façades of churches of the Charente district in Aquitaine have elaborate carved ornament representing foliage, or figures of men and animals (p. 490J), and capitals of columns on the ground storey are often continued as a rich, broad frieze across the building (p. 490L). In the north, stained glass, which was more suitable to large openings, was only gradually developed. The diaper work in the spandrels of arches is supposed to be an imitation in carving of the colour-pattern work or stuff draperies that originally occupied the same position, while the period is rich in carving of zigzags, rosettes and billets (p. 490F, M). Carved tympana, dealing with Biblical subjects, are frequently of considerable distinction (pp. 490B, 495B).

EXAMPLES

ECCLESIASTICAL ARCHITECTURE

Southern France includes Aquitaine, Auvergne, Provence, Anjou and Burgundy, each with its special architectural peculiarities.

S. Sernin, Toulouse (1077–1119 and later) (p. 493A, B), in Aquitaine, is cruciform with nave, double aisles and transepts. The nave has a round-arched barrel vault, with plain square ribs, supporting the roofing slabs direct, and the high triforium chamber has external windows which light the nave, for there is no clearstorey. The central octagonal tower (1250) with a spire (1478), 66 m (215 ft) high, belongs to the Gothic period (p. 609). Santiago de Compostela, Spain (p. 534) is similar in many respects.

A. S. Sernin, Toulouse, from S.W. (1077–1119 and later). See p. 492

B. S. Sernin, Toulouse: nave looking E.

C. S. Denis, near Paris: S.W. bay of narthex (c. 1135–44). See p. 499

ANGOULÊME CATHEDRAL

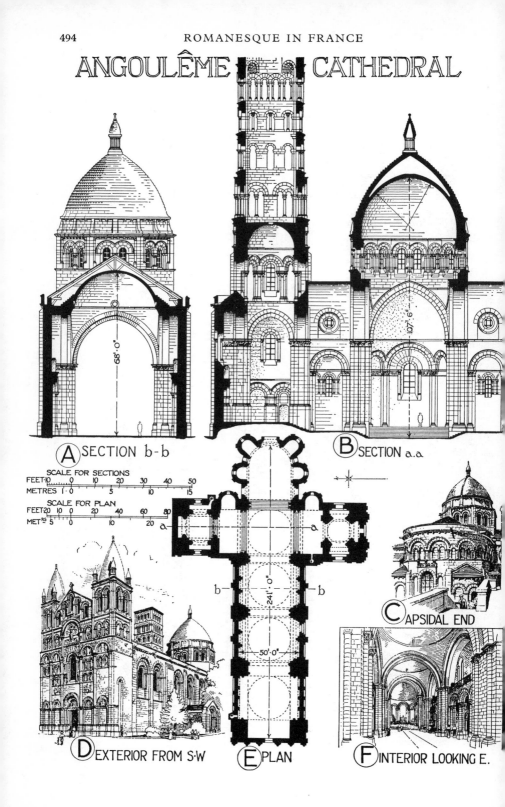

Ⓐ SECTION b-b

SCALE FOR SECTIONS
FEET·10 0   10   20   30   40   50
METRES 1·0   5   10   15

SCALE FOR PLAN
FEET·20 10 0   20   40   60   80
MET⁵ 5   0   10   20

Ⓑ SECTION a.a

Ⓒ APSIDAL END

Ⓓ EXTERIOR FROM S·W

Ⓔ PLAN

Ⓕ INTERIOR LOOKING E.

A. S. Gilles-du-Gard, near Arles: west façade (*c.* 1135–95). See p. 497

B. S. Madeleine, Vézelay: the narthex (*c.* 1132). See p. 497

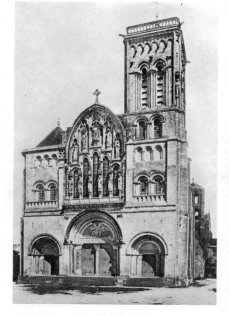

A. The façade   B. The interior

S. Madeleine, Vézelay (*c.* 1104–32 and later). See p. 497

C. Notre Dame la Grande, Poitiers (*c.* 1130–45). See p. 497

Angoulême Cathedral (*c.* 1105–28 and later) (p. 494), in Aquitaine, has a long aisleless nave, 15.2 m (50 ft) wide, transepts with lateral chapels, and an apsidal choir with four chapels, forming a Latin cross on plan. The nave is covered with three stone domes on pendentives and a double dome over the crossing raised on a drum with sixteen windows and crowned by a finial. Both transepts originally had towers, but the southern one was destroyed in 1568. The western façade (p. 494D) is rich with tiers of arcades divided into five bays by lofty shafts. Over the entrance is a high window framed in sculpture, and there are two flanking western towers.

Cahors Cathedral (1119), in Aquitaine, is an aisleless church crowned by two domes on pendentives, and somewhat resembles S. Irene, Constantinople (p. 386).

Notre Dame du Port, Clermont-Ferrand, S. Austremoine, Issoire, and **Le Puy Cathedral,** all in Auvergne and of the twelfth century, have local character imparted to them by the light stone vaults, and inlaid decoration of different-coloured lavas of the Puy de Dôme district.

Notre Dame, Avignon, in Provence, is one of the numerous churches of the eleventh and twelfth centuries in which pointed barrel vaults were used, and which show Classical influence.

S. Trophîme, Arles (1150), has beautiful cloisters with coupled carved capitals (p. 489F) and a fine porch (p. 489K), based on a Roman triumphal arch, but with modifications, such as deeply recessed jambs and columns resting on lions, behind which are sculptured saints; the entablature carries a row of figures and the sculptured tympanum represents Christ as Judge of the World.

The **Church of S. Gilles-du-Gard** (*c.* 1135–95), near Arles, has probably the most elaborate sculptured façade in Provence (pp. 490L, 495A), with three porches connected by colonnades perhaps suggesting the façade of S. Mark, Venice (p. 389).

Notre Dame la Grande, Poitiers (*c.* 1130–45) (pp. 496C, 501A), in Anjou, has a fine sculptured west front and imposing conical dome over the crossing, while the interior (p. 501A) has neither triforium nor clear-storey, but is covered by a barrel vault with prominent unmoulded transverse ribs.

Fontevraud Abbey (*c.* 1100–19 and later) (p. 498A) also in Anjou, resembles Angoulême Cathedral in its nave and general arrangement.

The **Abbey Church, Cluny** (1088–*c.* 1121), formed part of the most famous monastic establishment in Burgundy, which influenced the design of the churches, many of which, like Cluny itself, have been destroyed. It was the longest in France, 136 m (443 ft), with nave and choir, each with double aisles, double transepts and a chevet of five apsidal chapels. The pointed arch, among the earliest in Europe, was employed in the nave arcades, and the nave was covered with a great barrel vault, while the aisles probably had groined vaulting, but little now remains.

Autun Cathedral (*c.* 1120–32 and later) (p. 502C, D), another Burgundian church, has a nave covered with a pointed barrel vault on transverse arches which spring so low down as almost to squeeze out the clear-storey windows. At the east end there are three apses, and the portals of the west front are rich in sculpture (p. 502C).

S. Madeleine, Vézelay (*c.* 1104–32 and later) (pp. 495B, 496A, B), in Burgundy, has a most remarkable narthex (*c.* 1132) with nave and aisles crowned by one of the earliest pointed cross-vaults in France; this leads into the church, which also has nave and aisles, the transepts, choir, and chevet being completed *c.* 1170. The nave has no triforium, but a clear-storey with small windows between the immense transverse arches of the highly domical, groined intersecting vault (p. 496B). The central portal (p. 496A), with two square-headed doorways, separated by a Corinthianesque column, is spanned by a large semicircular arch containing a relief of the **Last Judgement.** Left and right are side portals, and in the upper part of the

A. Fontevraud Abbey, from N.E. (*c.* 1100–19 and later). See p. 497

B. Jumièges Abbey (1050). View of nave showing alternation of clustered piers and columns. See p. 492

façade is a large five-light window richly sculptured and flanked by towers, that on the left rising only to the height of the nave.

S. Philibert, Tournus (c. 950–1120), in Burgundy, once the Abbey Church of the Benedictine monastery, has arches which span the nave laterally from pier to pier, and support barrel vaults under which windows were formed (p. 502A).

Northern France includes Normandy, the Ile de France and Brittany.

The **Abbey of Bernay** (c. 1017–40) was probably the first important Norman church. It had a nave of seven bays, of which five are still intact, divided into arcade, triforium and clear-storey. The choir and side aisles terminated in apses and there were transepts, and over the crossing a tower.

The **Abbaye-aux-Hommes, Caen** (c. 1068–1115) (pp. 500, 502B), known as S. Étienne, is one of the many fine churches in Normandy of this period, which were the product of the prosperity and power of the Norman dukes. It was begun by William the Conqueror, and is of the vaulted, basilican type which was developed into the complete Gothic in the thirteenth century, and may have been modelled on the Romanesque cathedral of Speyer (p. 516). Its original eastern apse was superseded in 1166 by the characteristic chevet (pp. 500D, 502B). The western façade, flanked by two square towers, crowned by octagonal spires which with angle pinnacles were added in the thirteenth century, was the prototype of later Gothic façades. The nave provides a significant example of 'sexpartite' vaulting (pp. 459, 500F). Here, over the large square bays, intermediate transverse ribs are introduced which cut the diagonal ribs at their intersections and thus support them. This method was superseded on the introduction of the pointed arch, when each compartment, whatever its shape, could be vaulted without reference to the neighbouring one, because the difference between the width of the nave and the distance longitudinally between the piers could easily be surmounted by pointed arches of different radii manipulated so as to equalize the height of the ribs. The thrust of this nave vault, one of the earliest, was counteracted by a semi-barrel vault over the triforium gallery, protected externally by a timber roof, and forming, as it were, a concealed flying buttress, which later in the thirteenth century was emphasized externally as a feature of the design. The Abbaye-aux-Hommes has nine spires, a remarkable instance of the use of spires as architectural features.

The **Abbaye-aux-Dames ('La Trinité'), Caen** (1062–c. 1110) (p. 501B, C), founded by Matilda, wife of William the Conqueror, has a fine western façade with two square towers in arcaded stages, strengthened at the angles by flat buttresses and formerly crowned by spires. The massive walls of the nave and aisles with slightly projecting buttresses and the square tower over the crossing complete this homogeneous design. The interior (p. 501B) has a remarkable intersecting pseudo-sexpartite ribbed vault, in which two bays are included in each vaulting compartment, with semicircular diagonal and transverse ribs and intermediate ribs which support a diaphragm wall.

In addition to the abbeys mentioned above there are a number of smaller churches, of which the most important are **Bernières, Ouistreham** and **S. Georges, Boscherville**, all of which are vaulted, and have interesting towers built in stages and culminating in pyramidal stone roofs.

The **Abbey of S. Denis** (c. 1135–44) (p. 493C), near Paris, was built by the Abbé Suger and is one of the few buildings in this style in the Ile de France. The Abbey Church is of great interest as the burial-place of the French kings. The original choir and two internal bays still remain, and a Gothic nave and transept (c. 1231) have been wedged in between them. The west front includes an early

ABBAYE-AUX-HOMMES (S. ETIENNE):CAEN

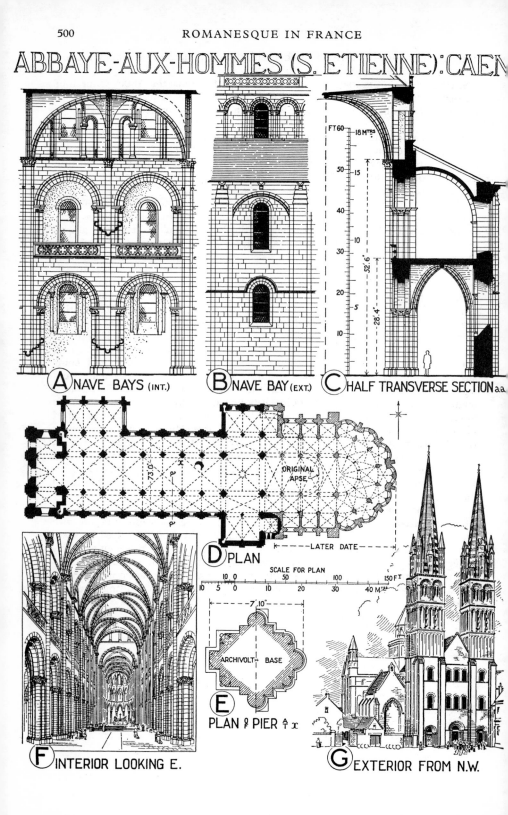

A NAVE BAYS (INT.)

B NAVE BAY (EXT)

C HALF TRANSVERSE SECTION aa

FT 60   18 MᵀRˢ
50   15
40   10
30
20   5
10

52.6'
28.4'

D PLAN

73.0

ORIGINAL APSE

LATER DATE

SCALE FOR PLAN
10 0   50   100   150 FT
5 0   10   20   30   40 MᵀRˢ

E PLAN OF PIER ½ x

7'10"

ARCHIVOLT   BASE

F INTERIOR LOOKING E.

G EXTERIOR FROM N.W.

A. Notre Dame la Grande, Poitiers (c. 1130–45): interior. See p. 497

B. The Abbaye-aux-Dames, Caen (vault 1100–10)

C. The Abbaye-aux-Dames, Caen (1062–c. 1110). See p. 499

A. S. Philibert, Tournus (*c.* 950–1120): nave. See p. 499

B. The Abbaye-aux-Hommes, Caen, from E. (*c.* 1068–1115). See p. 499

C. Autun Cathedral: main portal. See p. 497

D. Autun Cathedral: interior looking towards sanctuary (*c.* 1120–32)

instance of the use of the pointed arch, while the eastern end, though still retaining many Romanesque features, is probably the earliest truly Gothic structure.

SECULAR ARCHITECTURE

Buildings other than ecclesiastical have not been well preserved, because they were not sacred against attack, because they were generally built for military purposes and so were liable to destruction, and because of the risk of injury by fire and adaptation to changed requirements. **Fortified towns,** like Carcassonne (p. 609), which dates from Roman times: **Bridges,** like the Pont d'Avignon (1177–85) (p. 609), built by the *frères-pontifes* or sacred guild of bridge builders; **Castles,** such as the Château de Châteaudun (p. 617) and the fortified Abbey of Mont S. Michel (p. 609), and the stone **Houses** of the twelfth century still found at Cluny and elsewhere, are types of buildings which were begun in the Romanesque style, but much altered or extended in the Gothic period. The Monastic Kitchen, Fontevraud (*c.* 1115) (p. 489D), with its fine roof, and the fireplace and chimney from S. Gilles (p. 489B), are remnants which illustrate secular work of this period.

BIBLIOGRAPHY

AUBERT, M., and VERRIER, J. *L'Architecture française des origines à la fin de l'époque Romane.* Paris, 1947.

BAUM, J. *Romanische Baukunst in Frankreich.* Stuttgart, 1910; Paris, 1911; London, 1928.

BROWN, E. A. *Norman Architecture in England and France.* London, 1919.

COLAS, RENÉE. *Le Style Roman en France.* Paris, 1927.

ENLART, C. *L'Architecture Religieuse en France.* Paris, 1902.

EVANS, JOAN. *Romanesque Architecture of the Order of Cluny.* Cambridge, 1938.

—. *Cluniac Art of the Romanesque Period.* Cambridge, 1950.

GANTNER, J., and POBÉ, M. *Romanesque Art in France.* London, 1956.

HUDSON, E. W. 'The Beginnings of Gothic Architecture and Norman Vaulting', *Journal R.I.B.A.,* 3rd series, ix, 1902.

LAVEDAN, P. *French Architecture.* London, 1956.

MAIRE, R. LE. *L'Architecture Romane.* Pt. i: *Les Origines du Style Gothique en Brabant.* Paris, 1906.

MARKHAM, VIOLET R. *Romanesque France.* London, 1929.

MARTIN, C. *L'Art Roman en France.* Paris, 1912.

MICHEL, A. *Histoire de l'Art.* Vol. i, pt. i (for article by C. Enlart on Romanesque). Paris, 1905.

PORTER, A. K. *Medieval Architecture.* 2 vols. New York and London, 1909.

REY, R. *L'Art Roman et ses Origines* (Archéologie pré-Romane et Romane). Toulouse and Paris, 1945.

RUPRICH-ROBERT, V. M. C. *L'Architecture Normande aux XIe et XIIe siècles.* Paris, 1884–9.

STYRIE, R. DE LA. *L'Architecture Religieuse en France à l'Epoque Romane.* Paris, 1912; 2nd ed. 1919.

THIOLLER, N., and F. *L'Architecture Religieuse à l'époque romane dans l'ancien diocèse du Puy.* Le Puy, 1900.

UHLER, F. *France Romane.* Neuchatel and Paris, 1952.

Zodiaque Journal. Bourgogne Romane, Paris, 1954. Auvergne, Paris, 1955. Touraine, Yonne, 1957. Poitou, Yonne, 1957. Anjou, Limousin, Roussillon, Val de Loire, Yonne. 1959.

A. S. Gereon, Cologne, from E. (1160).
See pp. 361, 723

B. Mainz Cathedral from S.W.
(1009, 1181 and later). See p. 516

C. S. Gereon, Cologne, from S. (straight-sided choir 1075; towers and apse 1160;
oval nave 1219–27). See pp. 361, 723

18

ROMANESQUE ARCHITECTURE IN CENTRAL EUROPE

Ninth to thirteenth century

INFLUENCES

GEOGRAPHICAL

What is now known as Germany was through many centuries a conglomeration, first of various tribes fighting amongst themselves, and then of various independent states, principalities and powers occupying the great central district of Europe. This country north of the Alps was not geographically so generally accessible to Roman influence as was Gaul, with her sea-ports and great trade routes, but here the Rhine played the same part in civilization as the Rhône did in Gaul, and Roman civilization spread north-west along the fertile Rhineland and into Saxony, while the region to the east was untouched.

GEOLOGICAL

Stone from the mountains along the Rhine Valley was the material used for buildings in this district. Along the Baltic shores and in central and southern Germany there was an ample supply of timber. As there was no stone or timber in the plains of the north, brick was used almost exclusively in the district east of the Elbe, and the style consequently differs from that of other districts.

CLIMATIC

The average temperature of central Germany is much the same as in southern England, but in summer is higher and in winter lower. Roman influence was such that even the northern climate did not exert its full influence on building. Nevertheless there was a distinct tendency to large windows, and to steep roofs to throw off snow.

HISTORICAL, SOCIAL AND RELIGIOUS

Under the influence of Rome Christianity took root in southern Germany and in the Rhineland, while the rest of the country remained pagan. As early as the sixth century the bishops of Trier and Cologne were conspicuous in promoting church building, of which evidences can still be traced. Charlemagne, (768–814), the first Frankish king who became Roman Emperor, was crowned in 800 at Rome by the Pope, and ruled over the land of the Franks, which included central Germany and northern France, and he also established the Frankish dominion over southern France and northern Italy (p. 456). He restored civilization in a great measure to Western Europe, and was a patron of architecture. He forced the people of Saxony to embrace Christianity, and this resulted in the erection of a number of circular baptisteries, as the conversion of the tribes made a great demand for the baptismal rite. Charlemagne died in 814, and after the death of·his son and successor Louis

Central Europe in the twelfth century

the Pious the division of the Empire (843) resulted in an independent German kingdom. The German princes demanded the right to elect their own sovereign, and
Conrad I (911–19) reigned as king of Germany. Henry the Fowler (919–36) drove the
Magyars out of Saxony, subjugated Bohemia and the tribes between the Elbe and
the Oder, thus again establishing a united Germany. Otto the Great (936–73) was
crowned king at Aix-la-Chapelle. His wars, including his conquest of Lombardy
(951), made him the greatest sovereign in Europe, and in 961 he received the
Imperial crown at Rome; but for two centuries after his death the royal authority
remained weak.

　　The social development of these districts was much the same as in Europe generally; feudal lords were intolerant of kingly authority and oppressive towards the
people, who became freemen or fell back as serfs, according as kings and cities prevailed against feudal tyranny. To an increasing extent Germany split up into
smaller principalities, and the feudal system strengthened, as it appealed to the
desire of the feudal lords to become dukes of independent states.

　　When Conrad II became king of Germany in 1024, Denmark, under Canute the

Great, threatened his power in the north, and Poland and Hungary in the east, but he inaugurated the great Imperial age, by restricting the power of both secular and ecclesiastical princes. After wars between rival claimants, Conrad III in 1138 became the first of the Hohenstaufen dynasty and was followed by Frederick Barbarossa (1152–90), who was also crowned Emperor at Rome. He defeated Denmark and Poland, secured the alliance of Hungary and negotiated with France and England, but his interference in papal schisms brought disaster, till emperor and pope were reconciled under Gregory VIII. The Imperial cause was again asserted in Europe by the brilliant Frederick II (1218–50), who united in himself the crowns of the Holy Roman Empire, Germany, Sicily, Lombardy, Burgundy and Jerusalem. The political connection of the Hohenstaufen (or Swabian) emperors (1138–1254) with Lombardy is evidenced in the similarity of the architecture of the two countries during the later part of the period.

ARCHITECTURAL CHARACTER

Romanesque architecture in Central Europe exhibits a continuous combination of Carolingian tradition and Lombard influence. In later and larger examples, the resulting composition in external mass and formal arrangement is as distinguished as in any of the great Romanesque achievements in other European regions. The significant structural developments in the High Romanesque of Burgundy, Normandy and Lombardy, were followed in Germany with reluctance, however, and pointed arcades and ribbed vaults made only a late appearance.

In monastic churches particularly, the principal features of Carolingian planning (p. 509), survived strongly. They include a choir at the west end, the Nun's Choir, or Winter Choir, often accommodated in a Western apse (pp. 512A, J, 515A), but occasionally provided in a square west end with either transept or tribune (p. 511D). This western choir was commonly built over a crypt in the manner of the Lombardic high choir. In France this arrangement appears very rarely, merely as the result of rebuilding on a Carolingian substructure. This western work in the German examples sometimes was supplemented by the traditional narthex (p. 515A), and both East and West transepts are frequently furnished with both crossing towers (originally timber-built in diminishing stages) and with customary Carolingian cylindrical staircase towers (p. 512F). A distinctive characteristic of the architecture of the lower Rhineland, and of the valleys of the Moselle and Main, during the later eleventh and twelfth centuries, is a three-apse plan of trefoil form (p. 511D). This appears to be an idea imported from early Christian Lombardy. Nave arcades are frequently unmoulded and the semicircular arches spring from piers (p. 512B), or cylinders, while alternate piers are sometimes carried up to support the vault ribs (pp. 511A, 512B). Cloisters often have small columns supporting arches in groups of three (p. 508P). Arcaded eaves galleries to apses, towers, and aisles are very common (pp. 504A, 511C, 512A, C) and are clearly derived from Lombardy (pp. 465E, 475F). They are sometimes carried entirely round the body of the church, as at Speyer Cathedral (p. 514C, D).

In the Rhineland the semicircular cross-vault of the nave is of a domical nature, owing to the use of semicircular ribs, which rise to a greater height over the diagonal of the compartment. The system of including two bays of the aisle in one nave vaulting compartment was generally adopted (pp. 511A, B, 512B, C). Timber roofs were also employed for naves with large spans, as at Gernrode. Square towers, divided into storeys by moulded courses, frequently terminate in four gables with hipped rafters rising from the apex of each, and the roofing planes intersect at these rafters and thus form a pyramidal or 'helm' roof with four diamond-shaped sides

A CAPITALS ABBEY-CHURCH, CONRADSBURG.

B

C CAPITALS ILSENBURG : D CONRADSBUR

E CAPITALS: LIMBURG

F

G ORNAMENT: LIMBURG.

H WINDOW: GERNRODE.

J COLUMN HECKLINGEN

K W. TOWERS: LIMBURG CATH.

L COLUMN ILSENBURG.

M WINDOW: LAACH

N PORTAL: BÂLE.

P CLOISTERS: ASCHAFFENBURG.

Q TOWER: S. COLUMBA, COLOGN

JAMB

5' 8"

R DOORWAY S. MARTIN, WORMS.

S DOORWAY: STRASBOURG CATH.

T N.E. PORTAL: BAMBERG.

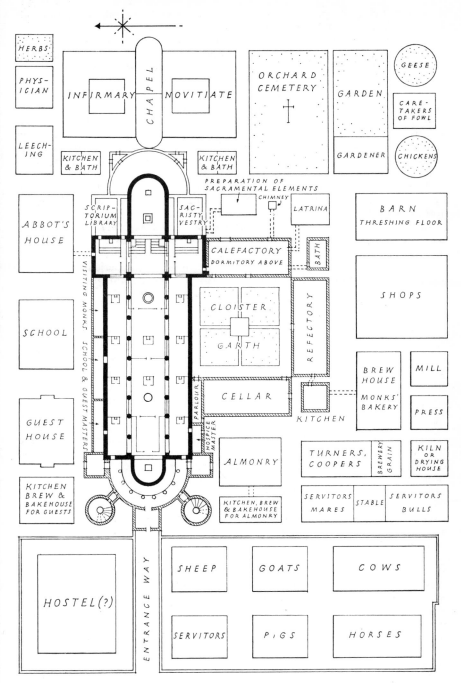

The Monastery of S. Gallen (*c.* 820): plan. See p. 510

meeting at the apex (pp. 508K, 511C). Polygonal towers have similar roofs, but with valleys between the gables (p. 511C, E).

The plain wall surface is relieved by pilaster strips, connected horizontally at different stages by ranges of arches on corbels which, owing to the smallness of scale, have the appearance of moulded string courses (pp. 508K, 511C, 512F). Doorways are frequently in the side aisles instead of in the west front or transepts, and have recesses with nook shafts (p. 508R, S, T). Windows are usually single, but occasionally grouped (p. 508M), and sometimes have a mid-wall shaft (p. 508H, Q).

In nave arcades square piers with attached half-columns were usual, though sometimes varied by the alternation of compound piers and cylinders crowned by capitals bold in execution and well designed (p. 508A, B, C, D). The shafts and capitals in doorways were frequently elaborately carved with figures of men, birds and animals (p. 508E, J, L, N).

There is a general absence of mouldings in nave arcades. When these occur, they are as a rule of indifferent design, and those of capitals and bases take a distinctive form intermediate between Roman and Gothic.

Internally the flat wall surfaces may have been painted originally, but the general effect today is extremely bare. Characteristic carving in bands was employed (p. 508G), and in the north, lines of coloured bricks were used externally. The sculpture is often well executed (p. 508N), and the craftsmanship of this period is seen in the bronze doors of Hildesheim Cathedral (A.D. 1015), which are wrought in wonderful detail to represent the Creation, the Fall and the Redemption.

EXAMPLES

Aix-la-Chapelle (Aachen) Cathedral (792–805) (pp. 382E–G, 383, 513A), built by the Emperor Charlemagne as his tomb-house, resembles S. Vitale, Ravenna (p. 382C, D). The entrance, flanked by staircase turrets, leads into a polygon of sixteen sides, 32 m (105 ft) in diameter. Every two angles of this polygon converge on to one pier, and thus form an internal octagon, the eight piers of which support a dome 14.5 m (47 ft 6 ins) in diameter, rising above the two-storeyed surrounding aisles. The building has been much altered since the time of Charlemagne, for the Gothic choir was added (1353–1413); the gables date from the thirteenth century and the lofty outer roof of the octagon from the seventeenth century. The surrounding chapels are of the fourteenth and fifteenth centuries and the western steeple has been added in recent years (p. 513A). The building is of historic interest as the prototype of other similar churches in Germany, but especially as the place of coronation of the Holy Roman Emperors.

Gernrode Abbey (S. Cyriakus) (961 and later) has a nave, covered by a wooden roof, aisles and a fine triforium, and is probably the earliest instance of a church with an apse at both ends.

The **Monastery of S. Gallen** (c. 820) (p. 509), in modern Switzerland, is a typical German Benedictine monastery of the period. A complete plan found in the seventeenth century appears to have been prepared by Eginhardt, Charlemagne's architect, and shows a double-apse church with cloisters, abbot's lodging, school, refectory, dormitory, guest-house, dispensary, infirmary, granaries, bakehouses, orchard and cemetery.

S. Godehard, Hildesheim (1133–72) and **S. Michael, Hildesheim** (c. 1001–33 and later), have nave arcades in which square piers and columns are used to support semicircular arches.

The **Church of the Apostles, Cologne** (c. 1190 and later) (pp. 511, 513B), is one of the series of trefoil churches in that city. The plan forms a broad nave, aisles

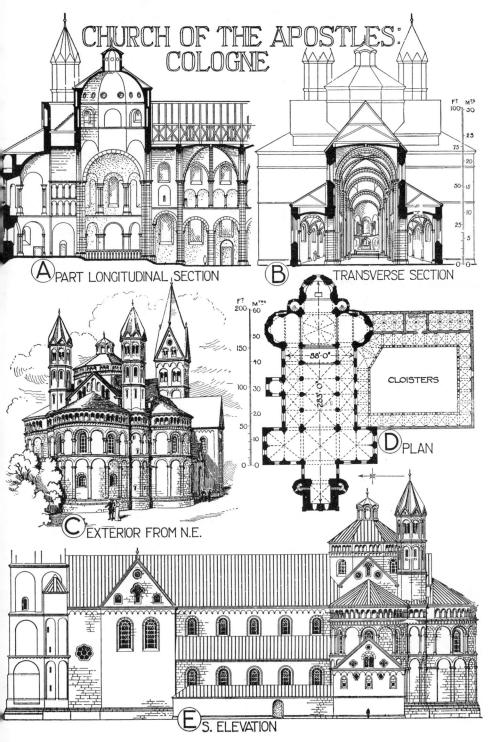

CHURCH OF THE APOSTLES: COLOGNE

A PART LONGITUDINAL SECTION

B TRANSVERSE SECTION

C EXTERIOR FROM N.E.

D PLAN

CLOISTERS

88'·0"

283'·0"

E S. ELEVATION

WORMS CATHEDRAL

SCALE FOR SECTIONS &c.

Ⓐ WESTERN APSE   Ⓑ NAVE BAY (INT.)   Ⓒ TRANSVERSE SECTION x·x

Ⓓ CORNICE (EXT.)

Ⓔ NAVE PIER
ELEVATION
PLAN
--6'·5"--

Ⓕ EXTERIOR FROM N.E.

Ⓖ EXTERNAL ANGLE OF CHOIR

WESTERN APSE   EASTERN APSE

SCALE FOR PLAN

Ⓗ JAMB OF N. DOORWAY
ELEVATION
PLAN

Ⓙ PLAN

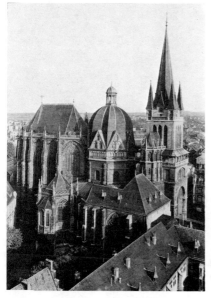

A. Aix-la-Chapelle (Aachen) Cathedral from N.W. (792–805 and later). See p. 510

B. Church of the Apostles, Cologne, from N.E. (c. 1190 and later additions). See p. 510

C. Exterior from W.

D. Exterior from S.E.

Worms Cathedral (11th–12th centuries). See p. 516

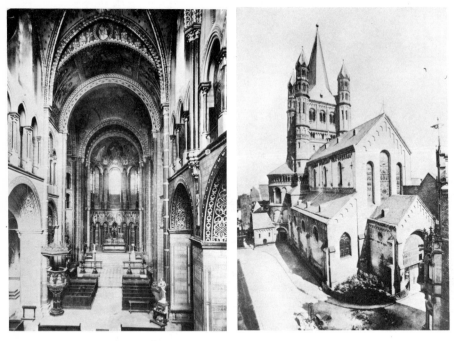

A. Nave looking E. B. Exterior from N.W.
S. Martin, Cologne (1185 and later). See p. 516

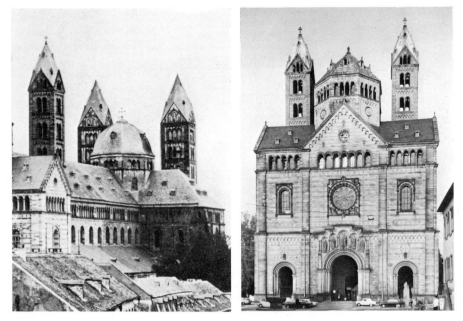

C. Exterior from N.E. D. West façade
Speyer Cathedral (1031–61 and later). See p. 516

A. Maria Laach Abbey Church: exterior from N.W. (1093–1156). See p. 516

B. Trier Cathedral (1016–47) and the Liebfrauenkirche (1242–53), from W.
See pp. 516, 723

half its width, western transepts, and a triapsidal choir, while over the crossing a low octagonal tower gives dignity to the effective external grouping (p. 513B). The entrance is by a northern porch, and there is no great western portal as in France, the west end being occupied by a tower (p. 511D) flanked by stair turrets, crowned with a typical Rhenish roof, consisting of a steep gable on each face from which ride the ridges of a pyramidal roof. An Anglo-Saxon example can be seen at Sompting, Sussex (p. 551E). The trefoil end has wall arcading in two storeys crowned with the characteristic eaves arcade, and on the south side are the cloisters.

S. Maria im Capitol (c. 1040–65) and **S. Martin** (1185 and later) (p. 514A, B) are other trefoil-plan churches in **Cologne**. Further examples occur at **Neuss, Roermond** and **Bonn**.

Worms Cathedral (eleventh to twelfth cent.) (pp. 512,513C, D), **Speyer Cathedral** (1031–61 and later) (p. 514C, D) and **Mainz Cathedral** (after 1009, 1181 and later) (p. 504B), are representative of the greater churches of the period. The plan of Worms is apsidal at both ends, with eastern and western octagons, while one vaulting bay of the nave corresponds with two of the aisles, and cross-vaults are employed in both cases (p. 512C, J). Twin circular towers containing stairs flank the eastern and western apses, and the crossing of the nave and transept is covered with a low octagonal tower, crowned with a pointed roof. The entrances are in the aisles, a position favoured both in Germany and England. The lateral façades have circular-headed windows, between the characteristic flat pilaster strips.

Maria Laach Abbey (1093–1156) (p. 515A) is a Benedictine church. The plan differs from most others because on either side of the western apse, which is used as a tomb-house, are entrances from the cloistered atrium which still exists, and there are also three eastern apses. The vaulting bays of nave and aisles are of the same width, which shows an advance towards the Gothic system. The church is built chiefly of local lava and the exterior is a fine grouping of six towers, double transepts, and east and west apses.

Lübeck Cathedral (1173) is an example of the brick architecture of north Germany; but the Gothic choir and aisles were not added till 1335 (p. 729) thus converting it into a 'hall' church (p. 723).

Trier Cathedral (1016–47 and later) (p. 515B) is reminiscent of the importance of this ancient city which, in the fourth century, was one of the residences of Roman Emperors. The cathedral succeeded a basilican church destroyed by Franks and Normans, but rebuilt and enlarged in the eleventh century.

BIBLIOGRAPHY

BUSCH, H. *Germanica Romanica*. Vienna and Munich, 1963.
DEHIO, G. and BEZOLD, G. VON. *Die Kirchliche Baukunst des Abendlandes*. Stuttgart, 1884–1901.
HAUPT, A. VON. *Die Baukunst der Germanen von der Völkerwanderung bis zu Karl dem Grossen*. Leipzig, 1909. 3rd ed., Berlin, 1935.
JANTZEN, H. *Ottonische Kunst*. Munich, 1947.
LEHMANN, E. *Der frühe deutsche Kirchenbau*. Berlin, 1938.
PÜHRINGER, R. *Denkmäler der früh- und hochromanischen Baukunst in Österreich*. Vienna and Leipzig, 1931.

19

ROMANESQUE ARCHITECTURE IN SPAIN, PORTUGAL AND THE HOLY LAND

Ninth to thirteenth century

The mediaeval architecture of the Iberian peninsula, and the architecture of the Crusades in the Eastern Mediterranean, were both produced by a confluence of Christian and Moslem civilizations. The complete opposition of a severe simple Christianity, spreading progressively southward, to the relaxed sophisticated Mediterranean Mohammedan culture, which it eventually replaced in Spain, and which it temporarily displaced in Syria and Palestine, produced anomalies in architecture which are characteristic of both the Romanesque product and the Gothic which succeeded it. Much of the architecture of the period in both regions betrays the influence of Islam continuously, though the Christian elements eventually dominated. There were, however, instances in which the influence of the religious orders, particularly of Cluny in Catalonia and of the Cistercians in both Castile and Portugal, was sufficient to produce church architecture owing nothing to sources outside Western Europe. In the Holy Land, also, there are a few Crusader churches which are derived very largely from specific French and Lombardic sources.

Christian Spain and the narrow territories held by the Crusaders in the Holy Land were at the opposite remote extremities of mediaeval Christendom. They had in common the problems of difficulty of communication and co-operation between separate kingdoms and principalities. Most new ideas were imported from the established and developing cultural centres of Europe, and were grafted on to those already available in Moslem models. The sources of these imported ideas, and some of the ideas themselves, were common to both regions.

INFLUENCES

GEOGRAPHICAL

Spain and Portugal. The Iberian peninsula is isolated from the rest of Europe by the mountainous barrier of the Pyrenees, but communication to the south, providing contact with Africa, is relatively easy across the Straits of Gibraltar. The peninsula is divided into distinct natural regions by the principal mountain ranges which cross it from east to west, enclosing high bare plateau lands. In the Middle Ages, these natural divisions provided boundaries for rival races and kingdoms. Portugal is divided from Spain by the western limits of these high table lands and by the steep gorges of four great rivers. French influence was dominant in the north, but Moorish influence in the south persisted until 1492 in the Emirate of Granada, centred on a fertile plain surrounded by high ranges.

Spain and Portugal in the twelfth century

The Holy Land. The most influential single geographical characteristic of the Latin Kingdom of the Crusades was its shape. From north to south it included the County of Edessa, the Principality of Antioch, the County of Tripoli and the Kingdom of Jerusalem, and this whole territory was nearly 800 km (500 miles) long, but generally very narrow between the Mediterranean coast and the eastern frontier with the semi-desert. Except in the extreme north, between the upper Euphrates and the outposts on the coast south of the Taurus, the lateral extent of the Crusader lands was limited to the depth of the coastal plain and the ranges and river valleys inland containing together the fertile country of the Crescent. While the Crusaders held this territory, they commanded the access routes to the coast and the inland links with the coastal roads and port facilities. At the Homs Gap this width was as little as 40 km (25 miles), and the danger of severance of the northern and southern parts of the Kingdom imposed a continuous threat which promoted some of the intense development of a military architecture which was as consistent and dramatic as any Romanesque work in Europe.

GEOLOGICAL

Spain and Portugal. The peninsula itself is a great rock massif, including the Sierras of Castile in the north, the mountains of Toledo in the centre, and the Sierra Morena in the south. Natural resources in building stone include granite in the north; limestone in the south and the Ebro basin; red sandstone in the Pyrenees and Andalusia, and both eruptive rock and semi-marbles distributed everywhere. Building generally relied upon the use of these stone sources. The eruptive rock served for rubble walling with brick bonding courses and quoins, which was used under Moorish influence with much success, as in the towers and gates of the city

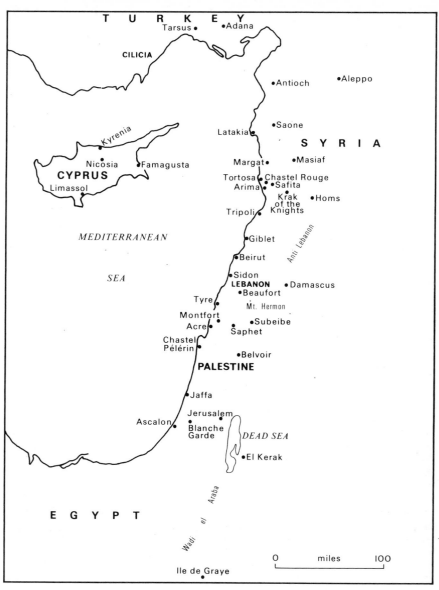

The Holy Land of the Crusaders

of Toledo; while in Valladolid bricks of Roman character are laid in thick mortar beds. There are few forests in Spain, and the conspicuous absence of timber suitable for building accentuates still further the predominance of stone in architecture.

The Holy Land. Here stone materials of eminent suitability for great castles and small churches were abundant, though timber was not as plentiful as in those parts of Europe from which the Crusader builders had come.

CLIMATIC

Spain and Portugal. The climatic variations are as marked as the geographical, and as different as the geological conditions; but there are four chief varieties of climate. In the provinces along the north and north-west sea-coast, the climate is mild, equable and rainy. The most marked variety of climate is that of the great central table-land and the basin of the Ebro, with great extremes of temperature, as in Madrid and Burgos; while the plains of Castile are swept by winds in winter and are torrid in summer. The middle climate along the Mediterranean is moderate and the southern in Andalusia is sub-tropical, with the greatest heat in Córdoba. The sunny nature of the climate influenced the architecture of the peninsula with its small windows and thick walls. Many large Gothic church windows, derived from France, were blocked up in later years to keep out the scorching sun.

The Holy Land. Climatic conditions vary from the harsh arid semi-desert of the south and the eastern fringes, through the oppressive summer of the Jordan valley to the rocky highlands of Syria which are under snow for much of the year. Rainfall is generally concentrated in the late winter months, but is then usually considerable. Water supply in the higher lands, however, as in earlier times, presented problems in those localities developed for strategic strength inland, and led to substantial works for water storage, comparable with those of the Romans in this remote province as much as a thousand years earlier. These strategic positions, in many cases, commanded the coastal route and its connections inland to the traditional roads through the Rift of Wadi Araba, north of the Gulf of Aqaba, the valley of the Jordan, and those of the Litani and the upper Orontes (the alluvial land forming the Buq'eia between the Lebanon and anti-Lebanon ranges, which the Crusaders labelled la Bocquée). These were the ancient caravan routes connecting Mesopotamia with the lower Nile.

HISTORICAL, SOCIAL AND RELIGIOUS

Spain and Portugal. The Visigothic invasions across the Pyrenees displaced the northern tribes of Vandals and Suevi and took nearly complete possession of the peninsula for three centuries until the time of the Moslem conquest of all but Asturia, in 711–18 (p. 406). The Moorish incursions in south-west Europe were brought to an end by Charles Martel at Poitiers in 732, and subsequent mediaeval Spanish history is dominated by successive extensions of Christian influence and the regaining of territory until the very end of the fifteenth century.

Another outstanding feature of Spanish history during this period is the connection of Spain not only with France, her near neighbour, but also with England through royal marriages; with Italy through papal supervision and the quarrels with the Angevins in Naples and Sicily, and with the Moors from Africa. All these links affected in varying degrees the architecture of the Peninsula. The evidence of Moorish influence appears in curious construction and exuberant detail; this occurs quite often even in the Christian north, owing to the demand there for Moorish craftsmen with their superior ability.

The Christian states of Castile, León, Navarre, Aragon and Portugal grew up simultaneously, gradually driving the Moslems into Andalusia. After many intermittent successes, the battle of Tolosa (1212) was the final turning-point in the decline of Moslem influence. As a result of the exultation over the conquest of the Moslems, Christian art received a great impetus, aided too by the plunder taken from the Moors. James I (1213–76), king of Aragon, advanced in the east of Spain until the kingdom of Granada was the only portion left to the Moslems. As to social conditions in Spain, only a small proportion of the population, including citizens of chartered towns, were free; under the system of land tenure the peasants were oppressed throughout the Middle Ages, a condition which produced the peasants' revolts of the fifteenth and sixteenth centuries. Social life in Spain was dominated by the grandees and the clergy: churches and monasteries are the chief architectural monuments, while in domestic architecture there is little of importance except the houses of the nobility.

Christianity had reached the Iberian Peninsula in the second century and flourished for most of the following two hundred years. The constant warfare waged against the Moors, which was religious even more than racial, gave a certain unity to the Christian states of the Peninsula. Throughout the mediaeval period the Catholic Church was the strongest and most constant unifying force in the struggle against the Moors, and it thus obtained great temporal power and possessions. This fact, and the Spanish taste for dramatic ceremonial and ritual, determined the planning of cathedrals and churches with their great sanctuaries and enormous chapels of the noble families. The Moslem religion forbade the human figure in sculpture and decorations, and encouraged geometrical ornament, and the result of this ordinance is seen in the extreme richness and intricacy of surface decoration even in Christian churches, on which craftsmen trained in the Moorish traditions were often employed.

The Holy Land. The Latin Kingdom in the Holy Land was established as a direct consequence of the reaction in Christian Europe following the call by Pope Urban II in 1095 to the First Crusade. Earlier efforts had resulted in premature and ill-organized expeditions which met with great losses, but the response to Urban's call produced a force of 150,000 in Constantinople in 1097, some of which passed through the Cilician Gates, the principal pass in the Taurus range, later in that year. However, when Jerusalem fell in 1099, the Crusader force probably numbered little more than one-tenth of those who had left Constantinople two years earlier. By about 1115, towards the end of the reign of Baldwin I, the Kingdom was fully established, but, in spite of continuous reinforcement from Europe, it suffered from a persistent lack of the armed manpower, and the solution everywhere was to replace soldiers with stonework. Moreover, the Frankish fighting men were in a minority even in their own garrisons, and some of the characteristics of the magnificent military architecture resulted from the necessity for security as much against internal revolt as against external threat. The prosecution of the Holy War through the twelfth century produced buildings not only of military value and wide influence upon later castle architecture in Europe. It is worth emphasising that the building initiative of the Crusades was turned also to the necessary religious functions, and in many cases these were combined: the Templars' hospice buildings in Palestine usually included a fortified church. No complete example remains, but there is a comparable survivor at Luz in the Pyrenees. The great inland castles almost invariably had a chapel, and Tortosa has a cathedral church. Churches were built, or more usually adapted from existing buildings, in many of the holy places. The centres of administration, however, and the communication network, were based upon the castles. Contemporary descriptions indicate clearly the importance of the castles as the secure centres of agrarian communities dependent upon the cultivation of the surrounding land, and owing allegiance to the feudal lord whose fief extended over the country commanded and protected by the castle itself.

When Moslem force was assembled under the united command of Zengi and Nur Ed-Din, the menace came not from the cities on the fringe of the eastern desert but from Mesopotamia. The loss of Edessa in 1144 was serious because it deprived the Kingdom of both extensive corn produce and of a source of auxiliary manpower in the Christian Armenian community. The Second Crusade of 1148 was quite ineffective in compensating for this loss. Saladin's victory at Hattin in 1187 so drastically reduced Crusader strength in the Holy Land that it never recovered. Although Richard I took Jaffa, Acre and Ascalon in 1191 and 1192, and although Crusader defences were further strengthened and their fortunes varied throughout the ensuing century, the result was inevitable: in 1292 the last of the Latins in the Holy Land sailed away from Chastel Pélérin to Cyprus.

ARCHITECTURAL CHARACTER

SPAIN AND PORTUGAL

The consequences of the migration of Germanic tribes at the fall of the Western Roman Empire included the establishment of the Visigothic Kingdom in Spain which lasted for three hundred years, until the great Moslem invasion of the early years of the eighth century. The tangible remains of this period are scarce, but are sufficient to show that Visigothic art provided a link between Eastern and Western Mediterranean cultures long before the Moorish influences were introduced. Some features of church design of this period anticipated the distinctive characteristics of mature Spanish Romanesque architecture. The most important of these was the horseshoe arch (see p. 1310). Church planning, as shown in the few authenticated examples of this time, was varied, and includes instances of both basilican and Greek-cross forms, in both cases with chapels attached to the eastern arm as 'prothesis' and 'diaconicon'. Decorative devices include cable mouldings and some Syrian motifs (rosettes, circumscribed stars) rather crudely executed in low relief. Some of the details suggest occasional re-use of antique Roman material.

Following the Moslem invasion in 711, Christian Spain was reduced by 718 to the Visigothic Kingdom of Asturia, to which Galicia was added by reconquest early in the reign of Alfonso the Catholic. By about 780, a national school of church architecture, painting and sculpture had developed and in the ninth and tenth centuries achieved a stature, largely independently, quite comparable with that of contemporary Lombardy or Saxon England. Early in the reign of Ramiro I (843–50), this isolated northern kingdom suffered the attentions of the Norse raiders who subsequently settled in France, Sicily and England; they gained no foothold in Spain. It is credibly supposed that it was this threat which led to the very early introduction in Asturian church and court architecture of barrel vaulting as a protection against fire. The most typical plan form for these Asturian churches is basilican, with a bema, or lateral chapel projections providing a kind of transept. The east end incorporated sanctuary and square flanking chapels; the apse was unknown. In earlier examples, round arches in brick occur, springing from Carolingian piers instead of from Visigothic columns, and decorative sculpture was confined to the sanctuary. In later examples, carved decoration is more elaborate, but the quality of its execution is inferior to that of contemporary Moslem work.

Churches built for Christian communities under tolerant Moslem control were based principally upon mosque traditions. Together with the churches built for refugees from the later persecution of Apd-ar Rahman II and of Mohammed I during the middle years of the ninth century, these Mozarabic churches stand apart from the Asturian and Galician development toward the maturity of the High Romanesque. Very varied, they have in common a return to the Visigothic form of horseshoe arch, the re-use of ancient materials, and decorative carving of debased classical or Byzantine form, but often of exquisite workmanship.

In Andorra and Catalonia, on both sides of the Pyrenees, Mozarabic architecture was succeeded after the middle years of the tenth century by a truly Continental

Romanesque style created in Lombardy soon after 800. This was imported into Catalan monastic church building by both land and sea as Mediterranean and Oriental trade developed, following the expulsion of the Moors late in the eighth century from this part of Spain. In all the earliest examples, nave and aisles were covered with continuous barrel vaults, and it is significant that these occurred in a region neighbouring that which had already produced vaulted churches, the constructional technique being based upon that of provincial Roman antiquity. The demands of the support of vaults brought about the use of rectangular piers instead of columns in aisled churches, and from the beginning of the eleventh century, transverse arches were introduced. Planning was usually of a basilican pattern, frequently with some form of transept projection. The abbey church at Ripoll (1020–32) (p. 533), is the outstanding example of early Catalan Romanesque, and is of a grander scale than anything which preceded it in Spain. It has been largely restored, but it represents many of the characteristics of its place and period, and the influence of the early Romanesque of Lombardy is clearly evident. These features include eastern apses (seven at Ripoll), with arcaded galleries below the eaves, blind arcading and pilaster strips on the wall faces of apse and aisles, and arcaded gable galleries on the west front. Most of the monastic examples have massive square-plan bell-towers, reproducing the character of Lombardic and Piedmontese towers down to the finest detail. Early Catalan churches were frequently roofed in stone laid directly on the vault, and some eleventh-century examples of cruciform plan have a crossing dome supported on squinch arches and groined aisle vaults with transverse arches supported on cruciform piers. Sculpture and decorative carving were very scarce in the earliest of Catalan Romanesque work, but it developed to a high degree towards the end of the twelfth-century. Where columns were used in arcades, Corinthianesque capitals often simulate the standards set by Mozarabic predecessors. Carved architectural detail and free sculpture in cloisters is particularly fine, and many of the motifs betray Moslem inspiration.

The early Romanesque, largely Lombardic, traditions survived in Catalonia until they were overtaken by Gothic fashions, but in north-western and central Spain after about 1050, French ideas were introduced and led to the development of a mature Franco-Spanish Romanesque style which displaced the native architecture as effectively as did that of Normandy in England. These French ideas were carried across the Pyrenees by pilgrims to Santiago de Compostela, by Cluniac monks (who became very influential in northern Spain), and by itinerant French craftsmen. An incidental but significant phase of Romanesque development in Spain was provided by church buildings in parts of Castile and of Aragon newly-recovered to Christian rule. The craftsmanship and design traditions of the north were adopted both by Christian masons of Mozarabic descent and by Moslems living in these regions. Most of the products of this Mudéjar movement are simple churches without aisles, having sanctuary barrel vaults, timber ceilings elsewhere, and some form of eastern apse, usually polygonal in plan. These small parochial churches were built both economically and skilfully, for the Mudéjars had inherited all the craft skills of their forebears. Most of their churches were built in brick. Much of the later Mudéjar work in Castile is in the form of a brick-built version of the earlier translations from Lombardy in Catalonia, with basilican planning, eastern apses and external blind arcading. But this arcading is set in Moorish panels, and the arches are of horseshoe form. After the beginning of the thirteenth century, arcades became pointed and cusped, though the architecture is still predominantly Romanesque in character. In Aragon, the Mudéjar style developed continuously through the mediaeval period, and even as late as the fourteenth century it referred back to its Romanesque origins.

The first appearance of a mature and seemly vaulted Romanesque Spanish church architecture was in León shortly after the middle of the eleventh century, and it occurred principally in churches marking the stages of the pilgrimage route to Santiago de Compostela. The French influences can be traced back through the routes in France from the Loire—in Touraine and Poitou—from Anjou, Burgundy and Languedoc. Few of the smaller pilgrimage churches survive unaltered, but their general form was aisled, with barrel-vaulted nave, barrel or groined aisle vaults, and either no clear-storey or a very low one. Occasionally bold barrel-vaulted transepts occur, and parallel eastern apses were usual. Twelfth-century churches in Castile and León include several examples without aisles, but with a central cupola supported either upon squinches, as in Lombardy, or upon pendentives in the fashion of Périgord. The province of Salamantina near the western border of León, has a group of distinctive churches of the late twelfth century which portray many of the native Spanish High Romanesque characteristics, and those adapted from imported ideas. This group is sited in the valley of the Douro and immediately to the south, and in each example the simple aisled traditional triapsidal plan occurs, with a short sanctuary and vaulted transept, for the ritual choir in most Spanish cathedral and collegiate churches was accommodated in the east end of the nave and the crossing, just as in the early Cistercian abbeys. The construction of these churches is in very massive ashlar masonry, and most of them have domical ribbed vaults which may have been adapted from either Angevin or Moorish models. The most remarkable common feature in this group is a lantern dome over a pierced drum on pendentives rising from the pointed crossing arches (p. 767D). The cupola in each case is ribbed, the ribs springing from shafts between the window openings in the drum, and although the structural form is Byzantine, the inspiration seems likely to have been in mosque architecture.

The finest achievement of the Spanish High Romanesque is the great church which marked the goal of the pilgrimage to Santiago de Compostela (p. 534). The Old Cathedral was still being finished as late as the eighteenth century, and its late eleventh-century composition has been obscured, particularly externally. It is impossible to consider this design otherwise than in association with the great pilgrimage churches of S. Martin at Tours, S. Martial at Limoges, Ste-Foi at Conques and S. Sernin at Toulouse, which Santiago most closely resembles. Typical of these great churches, it has a long nave of ten bays with groined-vaulted aisles, a gallery with half-barrel vault, and no clear-storey. The high vault is a barrel with transverse arches, which is returned through the wide transepts, together with heavy square piers with attached shafts, the inner ones carried up through the gallery to carry the vault arches. The spacious eastern arm has a Cluniac ambulatory with five radiating apsidal chapels, the central chapel of San Salvador composed in the tradition of Auvergne, with cusped arches sufficient to provide a suspicion of Moorish influence. The original design contemplated nine towers, the full Carolingian complement, including two western towers, the central crossing lantern, and towers in the western transept angles, with paired turrets at the outer faces of the transepts. The central tower is octagonal and supported on squinches. The general design of the Old Cathedral itself influenced greater churches of the twelfth century in Galicia, particularly in its structural organization and its Cluniac chevet. The cathedrals of Lugo, Tuy and Orense reflect many of its characteristics, and the Old Cathedral of Coimbra in Portugal adopted its galleried continuous triforium.

The County of Portugal was recovered as part of Christian Spain between 1055 and 1064, but was not established as a definitive Kingdom until 1263. Meanwhile, as in the recovered territories in the Spanish Kingdoms, there was extensive

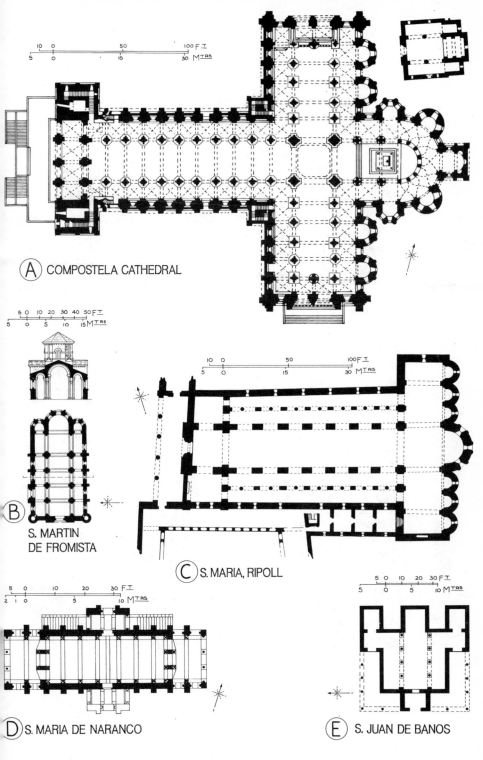

A COMPOSTELA CATHEDRAL

B S. MARTIN DE FROMISTA

C S. MARIA, RIPOLL

D S. MARIA DE NARANCO

E S. JUAN DE BANOS

A. Loarre: Castle exterior (*c.* 1070 and *c.* 1095). See p. 538

B. Ávila, Castile, showing town walls (1088–91). See p. 538

settlement by foreign insurgents, many of them French pilgrims and warriors. The principal influences in Portuguese greater church architecture are those of the pilgrimage and of Burgundy. The cathedrals of Lisbon and Coimbra (Sé Velha) both belong to the middle of the twelfth century (though Lisbon is largely rebuilt), and owe much to Santiago de Compostela, with some of the Burgundian and Languedocian character suppressed in favour of an elegance in detail which probably indicates local respect for Moslem work. Late twelfth-century church architecture in Portugal became in some cases half-Gothic, though in planning, structure and decoration the Romanesque traditions were abandoned with reluctance. It is in Portugal, in the Convento do Cristo at Tomar, that the finest of the Templars' churches in the Iberian peninsula occurs. The Templars developed a high reputation for building work, not least in their several churches derived from the annular planning of the Rotunda of the Holy Sepulchre Church in Jerusalem. A few of these occurred in Spain, notably at Segovia, and at Eunate, near the junction of the pilgrimage routes. A quite distinct contribution to the later Romanesque art of Spain and Portugal was made by the Cistercian abbeys. The finest is at Alcobaça in Portugal, where the abbey church is of an unusual composition with aisles of full height in the form of a 'hall church'. As in the French and English Cistercian architecture of this time, several embryonic Gothic features appeared, including pointed arcades and barrel vaults, grouped lancet openings and deeply-cut arch mouldings.

Spain is well-endowed with mediaeval military architecture, and grand castles are particularly numerous in Castile (which takes its name from them). Most of the remaining examples are those of the feudal nobility of the fourteenth and fifteenth centuries; fortifications of Romanesque date and character are few but impressive. The earliest castles and town walls occur in Andalusia and are related to Moorish work in Morocco. Christian work of early date is very similar, except that stonework was in rubble, which presented difficulty with quoins. Curtain walls were therefore furnished with circular towers, and battlements were usually of Moslem form, having a single block surmounting each merlon weathered to a pyramid form. The finest of Romanesque castles in Spain is at Loarre in Aragon (p. 526A); it incorporates an important Augustinian church. The city walls of Ávila (1088–91) (p. 526B), in central Castile, are of granite, are spendidly preserved, and constitute one of the most distinguished works of military architecture in Europe. They were built by Raymond of Burgundy, using Burgundian craftsmen, though the designer was a Roman. There are eighty-six identical semicircular towers and ten gates. The fortified eastern apse of the cathedral was later incorporated.

THE HOLY LAND

MILITARY BUILDINGS

The castles of the Crusaders were of three kinds, each having a specific function, which depended on geographical situation.

(1) *Pilgrim forts*. Sited and designed to secure the routes from coastal ports to Jerusalem, principally by way of Joppa (Tel-Aviv) and Ascalon, they were generally designed on a Byzantine pattern derived from the ancient Roman *castrum* or legionary fort. The installation included a thin curtain wall with rectangular corner towers of small projection, a large fosse or ditch, and an outer earth rampart. In some cases there was a central citadel. These forts were of no very great strength, and relied upon relatively plentiful manpower. After 1128 the Templars took charge of the forts on the pilgrimage roads, and in many cases they developed a commandery planned in conventual manner.

(2) *Coastal fortifications*. The Levantine coastal ports were fortified to secure the sea links with the West. They include Ascalon, Joppa, Tyre, Sidon, Beirut and Tortosa. They took the form either of a 'bastide town'—a civil settlement under the protection of a castle (which had contact directly with the countryside, as at Giblet (Gibail), or with only the sea, as at Sidon (Saida), which could be isolated by a cut sea-dyke)—or of a coastal castle with no dependent township, like Chastel Pélérin, which had very limited access across the narrow peninsula neck.

(3) *Strategic inland castles*. The principal functions of these great castles were to protect the coast road, as in the case of Margat, above Baniyas in Syria; to safeguard the mountain passes, as Safita and the Krak of the Knights, which commanded the Homs Gap; to secure the river valley routes, as in the case of Beaufort, overlooking the gorge of the Litani; and to provide visual command of the approach routes across the eastern frontier, as Subeibe, on the slopes of Mount Hermon, over-looked the routes from Damascus to Tyre and Galilee, and as Baldwin's Montreal in Idumaea controlled both the caravan route between Damascus and Egypt and the ancient spice route out of Arabia by way of Wadi Araba, and was also within striking distance of the pilgrim road of the Haj to Medina and Mecca.

A large part of the strategic strength of the Crusader castles lay in an elaborate system of communication between them by means of carrier pigeon and visual signalling. Both techniques were probably of eastern origin and were borrowed from Arab and Byzantine practice.

The general form of the large castles makes it possible to divide them into two main types. The first kind are those of the twelfth century, up to about the time of Hattin (1187), when the main strategic process was one of hopeful expansion, and the purposes of the fortifications was primarily offensive. New works were usually relatively simple in form and mostly comprised strong points from which to effect the capture of the ports still under Moslem control, and castles on remote eastern sites, beyond the Jordan, intended to support attacks upon the inland trade routes. Other building work of this period was incorporated in existing extensive castles and fortified towns inherited by both Franks and Armenians by capture from Byzantine and Arab control. The common characteristic of most of the new work of this kind was the tower keep. It was not in itself capable of providing more than a readily defensible base and refuge for armoured knights, and was imported into the Holy Land principally from Normandy, where it had not then reached a high state of development. At the time of the First Crusade, there were only two Norman castles of this type in England, at London and Colchester (pp. 572, 575). The early twelfth-century keep in Crusader work was therefore derived from relatively simple models, and it was adapted to its Syrian setting, usually having a single entrance at ground level (instead of at the first stage with a forebuilding) and was commonly of only two storeys. The upper floor was supported on vaulting, in place of the timber beams of the higher stages of Western European castle keeps of the time, for heavy timbers were not generally available. The keep was usually sited at the most vulnerable part of the castle, where its mass would be most effective, but in some castles on level sites on the coastal plain, it was built centrally in order to afford cover to all parts of the bailey and its surrounding defences. These included a curtain wall corbelled out to carry a wall-walk or 'alure', and punctuated with towers of limited salient which became progressively more numerous and more boldly projecting. The curtain towers in early examples tend to be square in plan, rather than rounded, though practice in this respect was very variable. Where the topography provided a single obvious approach for attack, a fosse was cut, and in some cases became so essential an element of the defences as to involve excavations, sometimes in rock, on a dramatic scale.

The second type of castle belongs mostly to the period of nearly one hundred years after Hattin, and shows the need for increasing defensive strength in place of depleted manpower. Only four important, new castles were built—Chastel Pélérin, Montfort, Margat and Saphet, and two of these are on old sites. The design of these, and the reconstruction of several others, illustrate the most important and influential features of the military architecture of the Crusades. Several were carefully planned in concentric form, having a double rampart system, probably inspired by Byzantine and Moslem town-defence systems. This was combined with the use of round towers of bold salient, grouped at gates and in some cases to provide an inner refuge or donjon for security from a disaffected mercenary garrison. Both curtain towers and the ramparts were often provided with a 'talus' in the form of the classical glacis, a bold sloping thickness of the foot of walls and towers as a deterrent to mining and to deflect missiles. Another device developed with considerable ingenuity is the 'bent entrance', which compelled investing forces to follow a devious and confined route while exposed to lateral fire and the hazards of retaliation by way of meurtrières in the vaults over gatehouses and passages through curtain walls; in some cases the planning of a 'bent entrance' limited the use of a battering ram. This was almost certainly an idea borrowed from Saracen town defences of the kind illustrated by the Great Gate at Aleppo, and in the Damascus Gate (Bab-al-Ahmood) in the walls of Suleiman at Jerusalem. After the end of the twelfth century, as passive defensive devices became more important, archery played an increasing part, particularly as flanking fire-power was augmented by the greater projection of towers, and less of the fighting was conducted from the crenellations of the top of curtain walls. The arrow-slits in the Norman keep were relatively few, but the later castles were equipped with carefully-designed long loopholes and large inner embrasures which allowed a wider field of fire. The general shortage of timber caused difficulties in providing the tops of walls and towers with the projecting brattices and palisades common in European fortification. Instead, later Crusader work includes stone machicolations developed from those of box form found in Saracen town walls. Among the most effective of siege weapons were water shortage and famine, and the capacity of underground storage chambers and cisterns in some of the larger castles was immense. Margat was customarily provisioned for a thousand men to withstand siege for as long as five years; one vaulted cistern at Saone held over three million gallons, while the Krak had a windmill, enormous granary spaces, oil presses, an aqueduct and a well. In spite of these precautions, several of the great castles finally fell because of exhaustion of supplies.

RELIGIOUS BUILDINGS

The Church of the Holy Sepulchre in Jerusalem (p. 358), by its origin and its function, is the most sacred in Christendom, and its holy places were the final objective of the Crusades. As is to be expected, it represents the finest and most ambitious of Crusader church architecture, the sources of which can be traced to Provence, Poitou, Burgundy, Languedoc and to the art of the Santiago pilgrim routes, all overlaid with native Levantine characteristics.

Lesser churches in the Latin Kingdom in several cases are well-preserved, largely because of sound construction in fine masonry. Even in examples of nearly pure Romanesque character, pointed arches are common, both in arcades and wall openings. High vaults are usually of barrel form, with transverse arches, and only occasionally groined, though groin vaults to aisles are not uncommon. A triapsidal east end occurs in Beirut Cathedral, but Tortosa has pastaphories of Byzantine form. Apses quite frequently are enclosed in rectangular masonry masses in Provençal or early Norman manner. The Crusaders left evidence of their art in many buildings which they adapted to church purposes, and were responsible, for instance, for the ornamental iron balustrades in the Dome of the Rock (p. 415) which, with Al-Aqsa mosque in the Haram at Jerusalem, was a church under the control of the Templars. Decoration of the chapels in castles under the care of the military Orders was often exuberant, and included fine examples of the crafts of mosaic, patterned tiles and carved stonework.

EXAMPLES

SPAIN AND PORTUGAL

RELIGIOUS BUILDINGS

S. Juan de Baños de Cerrato (661) (pp. 525E, 531A), of royal foundation, is the finest surviving Visigothic church, planned as a three-aisle basilica with a four-bay nave, originally with a transept with eastern chapels at the outer ends. Outside the nave aisles was a colonnade connected to a western narthex, in a manner similar to that current in Syria and Armenia, and probably to inspire the lateral portico common in later Spanish Romanesque churches. The nave arcade has horseshoe arches springing from varied Corinthian columns, and the arched window openings are small, with horseshoe heads.

S. Julián de los Prados (Santullano), near Oviedo (c. 830) is among the best preserved of the early Asturian churches, and was somewhat restored not long before the Spanish Civil War. It has a typical basilican form, with a wide transverse bay forming a kind of transept, outer lateral chapels, a square sanctuary with flanking chapels (which suggest a triple dedication such as was common in the Coptic church), and a western narthex. Only the eastern chapels are vaulted, and the timber ceilings elsewhere include some original decorated beams.

S. Maria de Naranco (848) (pp. 525D, 531B), was built by Ramiro I next to his palace near Oviedo, and ably represents the structural advances in church architecture of the Visigothic kingdom of Asturia. It has a long rectangular nave with open tribunes at both ends, over a crypt. Both stages and the tribunes are barrel-vaulted with transverse arches and external buttresses. The arch corbels are vigorously carved and the same sort of decoration occurs in the capitals of columns in the tribunes. The building is likely to have been intended principally to provide for sacred royal ceremonial. There is no clear indication of its having had any kind of sanctuary.

S. Cristina de Lena (c. 905) represents a development of the completely vaulted form of Naranco. The nave and square sanctuary have barrel vaults with transverse arches which are carried down below the supporting corbels in decorative bands, and the vault form is repeated in two lateral chapels abutting the nave. The narrow western narthex is vaulted too, but without. arches. The walls are stiffened with external piers and the entire masonry construction is in only roughly coursed work, except for the geometrical transennae and a remarkably decorated three-arch iconostasis on smooth Corinthianesque columns.

S. Miguel de Escalada, near León (913) (p. 531C) is the finest and largest of the Mozarabic churches. It was founded by Córdoban refugees and relies upon some of the craft traditions of the Mosque of Córdoba. It has a basilican plan, with a nave of five bays, and fine horseshoe arcades on antique columns (probably from a late Roman or Visigothic church on the same site) which are returned across the

A. S. Juan de Baños de Cerrato (661): sanctuary. See p. 530

B. S. Maria de Naranco (848). See p. 530

C. S. Miguel de Escalada, near León (913): crossing and sanctuary. See p. 530

A. S. Maria, Ripoll (*c.* 1020–32). See p. 533

B. Monastery of S. Martin-du-Canigou   C. S. Tirso, Sahagún (*c.* 1145).
(1009–26). See p. 533   See p. 533

nave as an iconostasis screen. The three eastern apses are of horseshoe form in plan, with lobed domical vaults, the whole enclosed within a single masonry mass. The high timber ceiling is later in date and decorated in Mudéjar manner. There is a shallow clear-storey with small horseshoe-headed openings, and a southern portico of about 930 of twelve arched bays similar to those of the nave arcades.

Other Leónese Mozarabic churches of importance include **Santiago de Peñalba** (919), which has a nave of two bays, with a lobed dome over the eastern one, lobed vaults over both eastern and western apses, and barrel-vaulted transepts; **S. Maria de Lebeña, near Santander** (924), which has some of the Asturian character of its locality, but the arcades are of horseshoe shape and the detail is in the Córdoban tradition; and **S. Maria de Melque, near Toledo,** a small cruciform church with arches, window heads, and apse plan all of horseshoe shape, but with no evidence of any decorative scheme, which may well have been built before the Christian refugees left Córdoba, and may be dated about 900.

The **Monastery of S. Martin-du-Canigou** (1009–26) (p. 532B), in French Catalonia (Roussillon), has a church of 'hall' form, both aisles and nave barrel-vaulted over a vaulted crypt. The arcades are wide-spaced on simple columns, with compound piers at the centre. There is no clear-storey. The only natural lighting is at the ends of the body of the church, which was probably quite acceptable, since so many of the monastic offices were conducted at night.

S. Maria, Ripoll (*c.* 1020–32) (pp. 525C, 532A) is the finest of the eleventh-century early Romanesque churches. It has a double-aisled basilican nave of seven bays, and the outer arcades alternate to produce double bays in the outer aisles, in the Lombardic manner. The bold transept is modelled on the basilican church bema, and there are seven eastern apses. Externally, the church portrays many of the Lombardic features which accompany its formal derivation from Italian models. These include arcaded apse galleries, blind wall arcading and pilaster strips, and gable galleries on the west front.

S. Vincente de Cardona (*c.* 1020) incorporates many Lombard devices, but the nave has a high clear-storey, the aisles have groined vaults, and the transverse arches bear upon pilasters engaged to arcade piers. At the crossing is a cupola carried on squinch arches. The transepts are of shallow projection, and there are three eastern apses, the central one stilted to form a deep barrel-vaulted bay.

S. Tirso, Sahagún (*c.* 1145) (p. 532C), one of the earliest brick Mudéjar churches, has much of the eleventh-century character of Catalan Romanesque, though with Moorish overtones, such as the horseshoe-headed blind arcading to the apses, set in rectangular panels.

La Lugareja, Arévalo (thirteenth century) (p. 536A) is the finest example of Mudéjar work in brick. A Cistercian church, it has many Lombardic devices, and a bold central tower enclosing a lantern cupola on pendentives.

S. Martín de Frómista (after 1066) (pp. 525B, 535A) is the only complete example of the Spanish 'pilgrimage' style, with a four-bay nave, shallow transept, and three parallel apses. It has barrel vaults throughout but, like Canigou, it approaches 'hall church' form, the aisle vault springing nearly at the level of that of the high vault, so that there is no clear-storey. There is a tall octagonal lantern at the crossing.

S. Isidoro, León (1054–67 and 1101) (p. 767C), built by Ferdinand I of Castile, now includes only the western narthex of his construction, the 'Panteón de Los Reyes', adjoined on two sides by the 'Portico', the burial porch being composed in six columned compartments covered by domed groin vaults. It is Burgundian in style and the carvings of capitals and painted fresco decoration of about 1175 are among the most impressive of early Spanish Romanesque work. The body of this church was rebuilt progressively by French architects and now has a barrel-vaulted nave and transepts, groined aisle vaults, and had a triapsidal east end, of which the central apse has been replaced. The transept arches at the crossing are cusped, and rise through the height of a generous clear-storey.

The **Old Cathedral of Santiago de Compostela** (1075–1128, with later additions and alterations) (pp. 525A, 535B, C), at the end of the pilgrims' route, was unequalled in magnificence and maturity in Spain in its time. The tomb of S. James, son of Zebedee, was recognized in 813. Before the middle of the ninth century, a Benedictine monastery had been established at Compostela, and the international pilgrimage had developed before the end of that century. The international character of the pilgrimage probably sprang partly from a feeling for the Spanish crusade, aimed at recovery of the Moslem-occupied territory in the peninsula, and is clearly illustrated in the architectural similarities of the great pilgrimage churches at Tours, Limoges, Conques and Toulouse. The plan is cruciform, aisled, with galleries which run continuously around the building; when designed, it was the only church in Spain with ambulatory and radiating chapels; the high vault is a barrel with transverse arches, the aisle vaults groined, and the galleries are covered with a half barrel opposing the high vault, and the bays at this level are separated by a diaphragm arch. The structural composition is advanced and assured, and is matched by the quality of decoration, particularly in relief sculpture. The interior survives largely unaltered, except for the loss of the twelfth-century 'coro' at the east end of the nave, and the generally Baroque furnishings and fittings of the choir. Externally, the east end is largely concealed, and the only original façade is that of the south transept, of 1103, the 'Puerta de las Platerías', and even that was altered after a fire in 1116. The 'Portico de la Gloria' at the west front (p. 535C) was added (1168–88) within the vestibule. Modelled upon the inner portal of the narthex of La Madeleine at Vézelay (p. 495B), it is one of the finest works of mediaeval Christendom.

The Gloria at Santiago de Compostela was imitated in the thirteenth-century portico of **Orense Cathedral** (the 'Paraíso'), and in other minor derivatives such as those in the churches of **S. Jerónimo, Compostela; S. Julián de Moraime, Carboerio; Évora** in Portugal, and **S. Martín de Noya**, which is as late as of fifteenth century date. The main features of the structural and planning composition of Santiago de Compostela were also quoted in greater churches of the region: **Orense Cathedral** (1132–94) has triforium galleries and much of the Burgundian quality; **Tuy Cathedral** (1150–80), in Pontevedra, has galleries, including those of the transepts, but the triforium stage is blind; **Lugo Cathedral** (1129) has barrel vaults to the galleries instead of half barrels with diaphragm arches; the **Old Cathedral of Coimbra** (Sé Velha) (1162), in Portugal, is another variant without a clear-storey, and with three parallel eastern apses, but the Cluniac chevet was adopted again in **S. Julián, Carboerio** and in **S. Maria de Cambre** in La Coruña.

The Salamantine group of late twelfth-century churches includes **Zamora Cathedral** (1152–74), the **Collegiate Church at Toro** (1162–1240) (p. 536C), the **Old Cathedral, Salamanca** (1160) (pp. 760A, 767D, F), **Ciudad Rodrigo Cathedral** (1165–1230) (p. 536D), and the abbey church of **S. Martín de Castaneda.** All of these, except S. Martín, have a lantern crossing dome on pendentives (at Salamanca and Toro pierced for double tiers of lights), and domical ribbed vaults on the Angevin pattern, pointed arcades, pointed high barrel vaults (in the cases of Toro and the Zamora transepts), traditional Romanesque basilican triapsidal planning and massive stone ashlar construction with distinctly Moorish overtones in decoration. **S. Vicente, Ávila** (1109 and later), has a characteristic plan of the

A. S. Martín de Frómista (after 1066). See p. 533

B. Santiago de Compostela
(1075–1128, with later additions):
nave. See p. 534

C. Santiago de Compostela:
Portico de la Gloria (1168–88)

A. La Lugareja, Arévalo (13th cent.).
See p. 533

B. S. Vicente, Ávila: principal
doorway (12th cent.). See p. 534

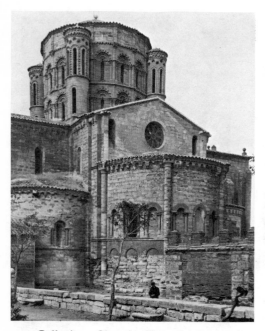

C. Collegiate Church, Toro (1162–1240).
See p. 534

D. Ciudad Rodrigo Cathedral (1165–
1230): crossing looking S.E. See p. 534

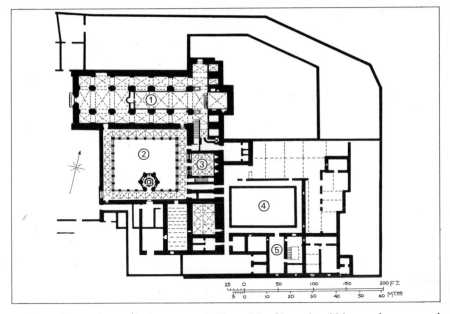

A. Santa Creus, Catalonia (1174–1225). Plan of the Cistercian Abbey and conventual buildings: 1. Abbey Church; 2. Cloister; 3. Chapter-house; 4. Old Cloister; 5. Refectory. See p. 538

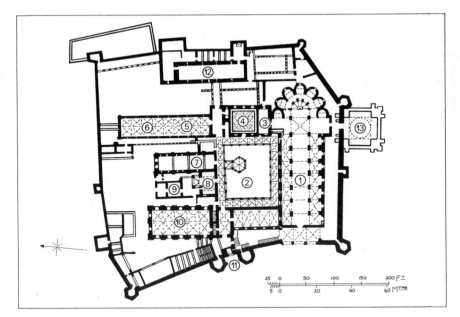

B. Monastery of Poblet, Catalonia (founded 1151; church 1180–96). Plan of the church and conventual buildings: 1. Abbey Church; 2. Cloister; 3. Treasury (above); 4. Chapter-house; 5 and 6. Library, Dormitories above; 7. Refectory; 8. Kitchen; 9. Dispensary; 10. Refectory of lay brothers, later Cellarium; 11. Puerta Real; 12. Old Dormitory (?); 13. Sacristy. See p. 538

same sort, groined aisle vaults and a ribbed high cross vault, with a square crossing tower, and a distinctive western portal (p. 536B) which appears to owe much to both Burgundy and Poitou.

Évora Cathedral (*c*. 1185–1204) is representative of the semi-Gothic character of church architecture in Portugal in the latter half of the twelfth century, with ribbed aisle vaults, and in both planning and detail, Cistercian influence is evident, though much obscured in later rebuilding of the eastern arm. Cistercian architecture in the peninsula generally expresses most of the unifying characteristics of the Order.

Meira, in Galicia, was founded in 1143, but not completed until 1258. It has the most strongly Burgundian character of all Cistercian examples in Spain, for all the arches and the high barrel vault are pointed, the aisle vaults are groined, and the windows are deep-splayed lancets.

Poblet, in Catalonia (p. 537B) was founded in 1151, and the church was built between 1180 and 1196, with a chevet having five radiating chapels, with absidoles attached to the transepts. The aisles have four-part vaults throughout, but nave and transepts are barrel vaulted.

There is an extensive range of notable conventual buildings, mostly of late twelfth and thirteenth century date, lying as at **La Oliva**, on the north side of the church.

Santa Creus, in Catalonia (1174–1225) (p. 537A) has a church of archaic plan form, with a square-ended aisleless sanctuary and square transept chapels. The whole of the church has four-part vaulting, and much of the substantial range of conventual buildings survives to portray planning on the transitional Cistercian pattern. The Portuguese example at **Alcobaça** (1158–1223) provides one of the finest Cistercian church interiors, a 'hall church', ribbed vaulted, light and spacious, and full of half-Gothic precocities. The royal Cistercian nunnery of **Las Huelgas, near Burgos**, retains much of Romanesque general character, though details and structural form are too advanced to merit any label but Gothic, and a substantial portion of internal decoration is Moorish. It was in this church that the architect, almost certainly a foreigner, introduced the eight-part vault characteristic of Anjou. Gothic features occur equally prominently in the Church of the **Convento do Cristo, Tomar** (*c*. 1150–62), one of the finest surviving buildings of the Templars, which has a sixteen-sided ambulatory surrounding an octagonal arched sanctuary. A later example of a similarly planned Templar church occurs in **Vera Cruz, Segovia** (1208), and at **Eunate, in Navarra**, is an octagonal pilgrims' burial chapel planned in the same tradition. Other Templars' churches are those at **Torres, near Logrono, S. Juan de Duero, Soria** and **S. Miguel, Almazán,** which has an octagonal ribbed cupola derived from the great Mosque at Córdoba.

MILITARY BUILDINGS

The finest Romanesque castle in Spain is at **Loarre** (*c*. 1070 and *c*. 1095) (p. 526A), a complex of circular towers and curtain wall incorporating a church of Augustinian canons, sited on a spur overlooking the Gállego valley. The town defences at **Ávila, in Castile** (1088–91) (p. 526B) include a curtain wall 2.5 km (1½ miles) long, with 86 identical circular towers, built in granite by Raymond of Burgundy, largely in a French masonry manner. There are ten gates, each formed by an arched opening between two adjoining towers. There is little of Moslem influence in this work and, because of their remarkable state of preservation, these civic ramparts present one of the most extensive and impressive examples of mediaeval military architecture. At **Berlanga de Duero, Soria,** there are extensive remains of curtain walls with circular towers, and at **Almonacid** in Castile there are double ramparts with similar towers but without loopholes, crudely constructed.

THE HOLY LAND

MILITARY BUILDINGS

The **Château de Mer, Sidon,** in the Lebanon (1228) (p. 540A, B) is the best surviving example of a coastal Crusader castle, separated from its dependent township by a sea-dyke crossed only by a later causeway. It was capable of independent defence after the town had been invested, particularly if support could be maintained for the castle alone by sea. It still possesses substantial remains of a two-storey keep, an imposing land gate with decoratively-carved box machicolations, large storage and domestic buildings within the ward, and clear evidence of the use of ancient column shafts as binders through the curtain wall masonry. Sidon remained a Frankish stronghold almost to the end of the period of Crusader control of territory in the Holy Land.

Giblet, on the site of the Phoenician port of Byblos, was extensively refortified during the twelfth century. The ancient defences were rebuilt as a new curtain wall with square towers, and a substantial two-storey keep.

Chastel Pélérin (Pilgrims' Castle), Atlit, was built in 1218 by the Templars with the help of the Teutonic Knights and of the many pilgrims from whom it derives its name. The castle is now largely in ruins, but its plan is clearly discernible. It stands upon a peninsula commanding the approach to one of the principal passes between the coast and the Palestinian interior. The main defences are on the landward side, and include a stone glacis, a moat which could be opened to the sea, and a double range of ramparts crossing the whole width of the promontory, both furnished with square towers, covering alternating fields of fire. The defences on the sea fronts were provided by a massive curtain of which little now remains. The buildings within it included a church, probably planned on the customary Templar pattern. This was the only castle, apart from Tortosa, never taken by siege.

Margat Castle commands a narrow neck of the coastal plain at Baniyas, south of Latakia, on the seaward side of the Gebel Alawi, the northern extension of the Lebanon mountains. It supported the Assassin (Ismaili) strongholds of Kadmus and Masiaf. It was acquired from the Midi family of Mazoir by the Hospitallers in 1186, and while under their control Margat became the largest of all the Crusaders' castles. The double concentric fortifications enclose an enormous area, and incorporate a narrow outer bailey on the western side, with a large circular tower-keep above a bold circular outer tower in the lower curtain, furnished with a tall double talus and box machicolation. The castle was attacked in 1288 by the Sultan Qala'un, and the outer defences were successfully mined. The keep resisted assault until, after it had been seriously mined, the Hospitallers withdrew to Acre.

Beaufort (p. 541C) guards a pass through the Lebanon mountains. It stands at the head of the gorge of the river Litani on a site readily accessible only from an adjoining plateau, from which it was divided by a shallow rock-cut moat. The square keep is built into the curtain, and a natural glacis is reinforced on the western flank with a built escarpment.

Kerak, in Moab, was part of the eastern line of defensive strongholds, standing on a mountain spur at the junction of two wadis in the high plateau east of the Dead Sea. The castle covers its dependent village from attack based on higher ground to the north, and is isolated from both by a rock-cut fosse in the Byzantine tradition, similar to that at Beaufort, with which it also shares the device of a strong keep in the curtain commanding the most likely approach route.

Saone (pp. 540C, 541A), at the north end of the Gebel Alawi, was built on a site previously fortified by the Greeks in Byzantine fashion, with a thin outer curtain wall punctuated with shallow rectangular towers, and a keep commanding the most

A. Château de Mer, Sidon (1228): east curtain wall and gateway. See p. 539

B. Château de Mer, Sidon: gateway

C. Saone: the fosse and bridge pier. See p. 539

A. Saone: the east curtain wall. See p. 539

B. Krak of the Knights: view from S.W. See p. 543

C. Château de Beaufort: aerial view. See p. 539

A. Krak of the Knights: aerial view. See p. 543

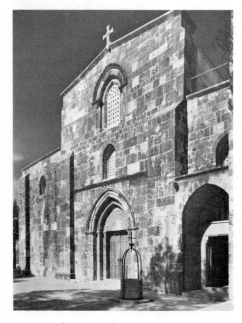

B. S. Anne, Jerusalem (1142):
west front. See p. 544

C. S. Anne, Jerusalem: interior

vulnerable part of the curtain. It was taken during the passage southward of the First Crusade, and became a dependency of the Princes of Antioch. The main Crusader work was carried out soon after 1120, and represents one of the best examples of the earlier phases of castle building in the Latin Kingdom. It stands upon a triangular spur, the ground falling sharply on two sides. On the third side, separating the castle from its outworks, which extend nearly half a mile, is an enormous rock-cut ravine, 20 m (65 ft) wide where it abuts the postern gatehouse towers, and involving the excavation of 172,730 tonnes (170,000 tons) of bed rock. Since it was not possible to span this fosse with a single drawbridge, a pinnacle was left in the excavation to provide central support. Above this fosse stand a square two-storey keep with a single narrow doorway and three round towers, of which two are possibly the earliest of all Crusader towers in this form. The postern gatehouse on the face of the great fosse is formed of two circular towers. Elsewhere in the curtain, the towers are square, and of small salient, without loops, but with an alure at the top, as was customary at their early-twelfth-century date. The main gatehouse on the south side has an entrance in its flank, with a direct approach from the inner face to the ward, which probably represents the first Latin use in the eastern Mediterranean of the 'bent entrance' derived from Moslem town defences. The castle fell to Saladin in 1188, largely because of his successful use of six mangonels, which breached the curtain. Some of his stone projectiles, weighing up to 300 kg (660 lbs), are still identifiable on the ground within the curtain.

The Krak of the Knights (pp. 541B, 542A), described by T. E. Lawrence as 'the best preserved and most wholly admirable castle in the world', is the easternmost of a chain of five castles sited so as to secure the Homs Gap; the Krak was in visual signal communication with Akkar, at the north end of the Litani valley (La Bocquée), and with Safita, Chastel Rouge and Arima, nearer the coast (see map, p. 519). The castle stands upon a southern spur of the Gebel Alawi, on the site of an earlier Moslem 'Castle of the Kurds', which was taken by Raymond of S. Gilles during the First Crusade, but first properly occupied by Tancred of Antioch in 1110. In 1142 it was given by Raymond, Count of Tripoli, into the care of the Knights Hospitallers, and it was they who, during the ensuing fifty years, remodelled and developed it as the most distinguished work of military architecture of its time. The plan is completely concentric, having two lines of defence, the inner ramparts lying close to the outer and continuously dominating them. The single ward of the original eleventh-century castle covered about the same area as the later inner enclosure, and some of the remains of the early work on the crest of the spur are incorporated in the existing building. The outer curtain is furnished on the north and west sides with eight round towers, of which one is later than the Crusader occupation, and of which two form the north barbican, also extended at a later date. The curtain towers are generously provided with carefully-disposed loops, and the whole outer wall walk has loops and merlons above box-machicolations, some of which are part of recent restoration. The main gateway is on the east flank, and gives access to a long ramped and vaulted 'bent entrance', defensible at the gatehouse by moat and drawbridge, machicolations over the external wall, four gates and at least one portcullis; the vaulted ramp itself has meurtrière holes in the roof, and is exposed at three points to flanking assault from the outer ward. The greater part of the inner defences dates from the late twelfth and early thirteenth centuries, though the inner gatehouse, the inner north-west postern tower, and the chapel (of which the apse forms a tower above the outer ward) belong to the Latin occupation before the time of the Hospital. The most remarkable single feature of the inner castle is the colossal glacis on the west and south sides, which the Arabs call 'the Mountain', rising formidably above the great cistern and the outer ward, more than 25 m (80 ft) thick at the base. At the south end of the inner structure is a stronghold formed of three great round towers, linked by a sentry-walk on two tiers of vaults, and containing what was clearly the finest set of apartments, serving as a refuge as much from the hostility of a disaffected mercenary garrison as from that of investing forces. The vaulted loggia in the upper court is a fine early mature Gothic addition. The Krak was attacked unsuccessfully on twelve separate occasions, but eventually, in March of 1271, the Sultan Beibars (the 'Panther') laid siege to the castle, and the knights were brought to surrender, in April, by means of forged instructions. Except for a brief period during the First World War this magnificent castle has been in Moslem hands ever since.

RELIGIOUS BUILDINGS

Crusader church architecture generally followed Cistercian or Burgundian fashion and many examples possess transitional half-Gothic features, though traditional Romanesque planning was customary. **Tortosa Cathedral,** built within the fortified precinct which became the headquarters of the Templars, has a characteristically Burgundian barrel-vaulted nave, groined aisle vaults, and compound piers with foliated capitals, but the sanctuary planning is Byzantine, with pastaphory chapels. **Beirut Cathedral,** now a mosque, has a similar structural composition, though with a clear-storey, and the east end has three apses. Crusader churches at **Tyre, Sebastieh** and **Caesarea** have cruciform plans, and squared apses of Provençal type occur at **Nazareth** and **Ramleh. S. Jeremia at Abu Gosh** has Coptic characteristics. One of the best preserved of the smaller churches of the Crusaders is **S. Anne, Jerusalem** (1142) (p. 542B, C), which commemorates the site held to be that of the home of the parents of the Virgin, and consequently her birth-place. The church was built by the queen of Baldwin I as that of a Benedictine nunnery, and was beautifully restored after 1878 by the White Fathers, to whom it now belongs. It has a typical Benedictine plan, aisled, with a groined nave vault, shallow transepts, three eastern apses, and, unusually, a dome on pendentives at the crossing of exactly the Périgord kind. The arches are generally pointed, and the central west door is a finely-proportioned near-Gothic feature (p. 542B) embellished with moulding enrichments which anticipate the thirteenth-century dog-tooth. The Crusader work on the **Church of the Holy Sepulchre, Jerusalem,** is described in Chapter 12 (p. 361).

BIBLIOGRAPHY

AGNELLO, G. *L'Arquitectura Aragonese-Catalana in Siracusa.* Rome, 1942.
BEVAN, B. *Mudéjar Towers of Aragon.* London, 1929.
—. *History of Spanish Architecture.* London, 1938.
CAMPS Y CORZOLA, E. *Arquitectura Cristina Primitiva Visigoda y Asturiana.* Madrid, 1929.
DESCHAMPS, P. *Le Crac des Chevaliers.* 2 vols. Paris, 1934.
—. *Le Château de Saone.* Paris, 1935.
ENLART, C. *Les Monuments des Croisés dans le Royaume de Jérusalem.* 2 vols. Paris, 1945.
FEDDEN, R., and THOMSON, J. *Crusader Castles.* London, 1957.
FIELCHENFELD, F. W. (Ed.) *Die Meisterwerke der Baukunst in Portugal.* Vienna and Leipzig, 1908.
KING, G. G. *The Way of Saint James.* London, 1920.
—. *Pre-Romanesque Churches of Spain.* London, 1924.
—. *Mudéjar.* London, 1927.
KING, J. CATHCART. 'The Taking of Le Crac des Chevaliers in 1271', *Antiquity*, vol. 23, 1949.

LANGÉ, S. *Architettura delle Crociate in Palestina.* Como, 1965.

LAWRENCE, T. E. *Crusader Castles.* London, 1936. (Limited edition.)

MÜLLER-WIENER, W. *Castles of the Crusaders.* Trans. J. M. Brownjohn. London, 1966.

PERNOUD, R. *In the Steps of the Crusaders.* Trans. M. Case. London, 1959.

POLLEY, G. H. *Spanish Architecture and Ornament.* Boston, 1919.

PORTER, A. K. *Spanish Romanesque Sculpture.* London, 1928.

PUIG Y CADAFALCH, J. *L'Architectura Románica a Catalanya.* Barcelona, 1919–21.

SMAIL, R. C. 'Crusader Castles of the Twelfth Century', *Cambridge Historical Journal,* vol. 10, 1951.

SUBIAS, G. J. *Las Rutas del Románico.* Barcelona, 1965.

VASCONCELLOS, J. DE. *Arte Románica em Portugal.* Lisbon, 1918.

WATSON, W. C. *Portuguese Architecture.* London, 1908.

WHITEHILL, W. M. *Spanish Romanesque Architecture of the Eleventh Century.* Oxford and London, 1941.

20

ROMANESQUE ARCHITECTURE IN THE BRITISH ISLES AND SCANDINAVIA

First to twelfth century

INFLUENCES

GEOGRAPHICAL

In northern Europe, remote from Rome, development depended largely upon a common concern with sea and river routes. The insular situation of Britain had a variable but persistent influence upon the character of her architecture throughout the mediaeval period. The geographical similarities of political divisions of Scandinavia are sufficient to give the whole region a unity which was emphasized by the greater ease of sailing across the narrow waters within the region than of crossing the mountains toward the rest of Europe. Skill in navigation during the early Middle Ages led to the Nordic colonization of Iceland and Greenland, and to cultural and commercial contact with Ireland and Britain, probably to incidental contact with the American mainland. Within the Scandinavian region, the geographical characteristics decided the directions in which cultural influences were to to be exerted: those of the Danes in England and Normandy; of the Norwegians in Scotland and Ireland; of the Swedes in the Baltic and, by way of Russian rivers, to eastern Europe.

Natural resources in Scandinavia provided for principally agrarian products in the south and east, and for forestry and fur-trading in the north. The export of copper and iron ores led to strong mercantile connections with the Continent, centred, for instance, in Götland and southern Sweden. The deep Norwegian valleys dictated both an independent and generally slower rate of evolution, and a wider variety of local building techniques; but connections by sea with north-west Europe ensured an interchange of ideas in building probably greater than the remaining evidence of activity in the earlier part of the period can demonstrate.

GEOLOGICAL

The varied geological formation of Great Britain was responsible for a wider variety of building materials, and in early times the survival of remains from the Roman occupation provided ideas for a variety of methods for using them. In some instances, the Roman buildings provided opportunity for re-use of the materials themselves. The English hardwood forests, particularly in the north-western and south-eastern counties, provided roof-framing material for the more important buildings, and for lesser buildings which were entirely timber-framed. Most of the indigenous building stones contributed to the materials of the more mature military and religious buildings, and local characteristics in masonry developed at an early stage, if only because of the difficulty of transport over long distances otherwise than by water. Consequently, walling in flint is largely confined to East Anglia and the chalk hills in the south (where it is often associated with circular plans because of the scarcity of freestones for quoins); yet stone from Caen in Normandy was brought by means of sea and river transport for some building work under royal patronage. Except for isolated and mostly early instances of the re-use of Roman brick, it was not until after the succession of the high Romanesque by Gothic fashions that brickwork was re-developed as a building material in Britain.

CLIMATIC

The generally low northern light tended to encourage the development of ways of producing larger or multiple openings in walls, and the most sophisticated of mature Romanesque attempts, particularly in Norman England, tended to demonstrate the way toward the more dramatic and later Gothic achievement. Massive masonry construction and steeply-pitched roofs were customary devices for dealing with the more severe northern European climate, though in those parts of Scandinavia where snow could normally be expected to persist for some time, roof pitches were often reduced in order that it should assist in retaining heat within buildings.

HISTORICAL, SOCIAL AND RELIGIOUS

The British Isles

The Roman conquest of Britain was preceded by the landings of Julius Caesar in 55 and 54 B.C. During the military occupation following the Claudian invasion of A.D. 43 progress was made in developing natural resources such as tin, iron and lead; the mineral waters of Bath were exploited. Orderly government was ensured by the Roman legions, and improved methods in agriculture stabilized society. Roman dress and language were adopted by those in contact with the new rulers. The building of towns and later of the large country settlements called villas was necessary to support the civil administration and to propagate the Roman way of life. The latter has been revealed by the excavation of fora, basilicas, thermae, temples and villas, as at Bignor and Fishbourne in Sussex, Darenth in Kent, Corstopitum in Northumberland, Fifehead-Neville in Dorset, Silchester in Hampshire, Chedworth in Gloucestershire and at Bath (p. 301). There are ruins of a Roman lighthouse at Dover and of Roman fortifications in or near the mediaeval city walls of London, York, Lincoln and Colchester; a place-name affix from castra signifies a Roman military settlement, as in Winchester, Leicester, Gloucester and Exeter. Roman roads were important for civil as much as for military purposes. The principal Roman roads in Britain were Watling Street (Dover via London to Wroxeter); Ermine Street (London via Lincoln to York and Catterick); Fosse Way (Exeter via Bath and Cirencester to Lincoln); Icknield Way (Dorchester via Silchester and London to Caistor S. Edmund); Akeman Street (Cirencester to S. Albans).

Christianity first made its way into Britain during the Roman occupation, but during the years of the Anglo-Saxon settlements, after the middle of the fifth century, church building was of historical importance only in Ireland. S. Alban, the first British martyr, died in 305, and in 314 the bishops of York, London and Lincoln are recorded as attending the Council of Arles, but religious influences upon building in Britain were very small until S. Augustine landed in England in 597, converted the Kentish King Ethelbert and other kings of the Saxon Heptarchy, and introduced the Benedictine order. The Seven Kingdoms were based upon the migration of Jutes into Kent, Saxons in Sussex, Wessex and Essex, and of Angles in Mercia, East Anglia and Northumbria. The conversion to Christianity of the Anglo-Saxon kings and their people is evidenced by numerous surviving

The British Isles in the twelfth century

churches, towers and crosses of the seventh and eighth centuries. In Ireland, after about 834, the Scandinavian raiders became settlers, maintaining connections with their homeland, and the earlier timber building tradition (described by Bede in 731) may have influenced building technique in Scandinavia.

The post-Heptarchy period, until the time of the vigorous Norman influence upon the court of Edward the Confessor, was characterized by Benedictine reform and by the monastic revival of the late tenth century, principally supported by King Edgar (959–75), by S. Dunstan, who became Abbot of Glastonbury in 960, and by Ethelwold, Bishop of Winchester in 963. The main effects of monastic reform and revival were to introduce the features of Continental Carolingian building, which had been briefly foreshadowed in Britain only in the northern work of the school of S. Wilfrid of York.

In 1042, Edward, son of the English King Ethelred, acceded to the throne. Norman by association and education, he consolidated the kingdom and, largely by the introduction of Norman favourites into the Court and the Church, assured the Norman influence of England before the Conquest. He appointed Robert, Abbot of Jumièges, as Archbishop of Canterbury in 1051, and had meanwhile begun in about 1045 the building of Westminster Abbey, the church planned in the current Norman Benedictine fashion, and the conventual buildings based largely upon the Cluniac pattern.

The Norman Conquest of 1066 linked England to the Continent and introduced a fully developed feudal system. Yet all land was held from the king, who established the most efficient and centralized government in Europe. Castles were built to strengthen the position of the conquerors. Towns, which grew up around abbeys and castles, became trading centres, and through their merchant guilds laid the foundations of urban government. Villages continued as mere collections of rudimentary dwellings. Settled government prompted the pursuit of learning, based in the twelfth and thirteenth centuries upon monastic schools and upon the two English universities. French was the language commonly used in court circles until the thirteenth century, when, owing to resentment caused by the introduction of Angevin strangers, English gradually supplanted it, and the final fusion of Norman and English occurred. The First Crusade was preached in 1096 by Pope Urban II and Peter the Hermit. The later Crusades induced an exchange of ideas between East and West, and involved England in international movements. Richard I, son of Eleanor of Aquitaine and Henry II, after his experience of the Third Crusade, established a pattern of military architecture in his building of Château-Gaillard at Les Andelys in Normandy. The Crusades gave impetus to the progress of learning and in the foundation (1113–18) of the military Orders which influenced some aspects of church-building later in the Middle Ages. In 1128 the Cistercians built their first English house at Waverley in Surrey, and William of Sens began the rebuilding of Canterbury Cathedral choir.

Scandinavia

Social history in Scandinavia in the early centuries of this era is obscure, but it is evident that kingdoms were established first in Denmark and Norway, and that by about the year 1000 Sweden was united as part of the Svear Kingdom. The Viking expansion of the ninth century, which included the early Danish settlement in north-east England, the colonization of Normandy and the establishment of Svear colonies in Latvia, all brought Northern influences to bear upon European development. The earliest domestic building customs were based upon timber techniques allied to forms probably derived from ancient Greek and Cretan cultures.

The most distinctive building development of the period in Scandinavia followed the conversion of the Northern races, which was started by the Frankish missionary Angar at Hedeby in Denmark in 826, but not completed until the end of the twelfth century. Some North German influences, encouraged by trade, can be traced, but the Norse Church itself was established from Britain, and Christianity was legally maintained in Norway, Greenland and Iceland by the end of the tenth century. In 980 the Danish King Harold made his people Christians, English bishops were introduced, and during the following century Canute and his successors spread their empire to England. In 1030 the Norwegian Christian King Olav Haraldsson was killed in battle, and was later canonized. The Cathedral at Trondheim was built as his reliquary. During the eleventh century Christian centres were established successively further north in Sweden, at Lund, Skara and Sigtuna, and in 1130 a diocese was established at Gamla (Old) Uppsala, after the destruction of the

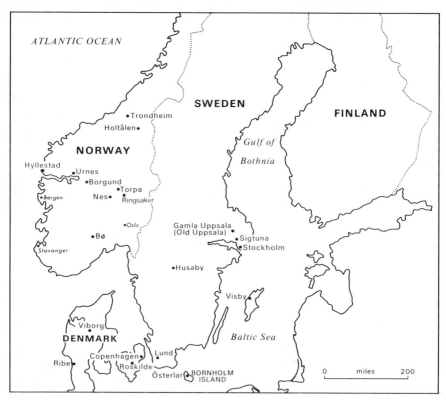

Scandinavia in the twelfth century

pagan temple there at the beginning of the century. The earliest Christian Scandinavian buildings, those of the Frankish missionaries, were certainly timber-built,
and, particularly in Norway, the development of timber techniques continued well
into the thirteenth century. In its earliest forms, it was introduced into both England and Ireland. Subsequent building in stone reflects predominantly German
and Cluniac influences in Denmark (which was a province of Hamburg-Bremen
until 1103), Anglo-Norman origins in Norway, and a compound of these in
Sweden. The monastic orders played an important part in reinforcing Scandinavian links with Europe, and the Benedictine church architecture of Denmark
and Norway followed very closely much of the custom of the Order, though with
some Cluniac modifications, and in both Denmark and Sweden were established
several examples of Cistercian abbeys displaying the simple and robust characteristics of Burgundy, and plan forms derived from both Fontenay and Pontigny.
Smaller churches in mediaeval Scandinavia, even as late as the fourteenth century,
were built in simple Romanesque form. In more remote and secluded areas fashions
in building were usually those of an earlier period in much of the rest of Europe,
and the associated decorative arts depended upon the forms of folk art. In Finland,
for instance, the expansion of Swedish power in the eastern Baltic promoted
church-building in stone after the beginning of the thirteenth century, but the
stylistic characteristics which persisted were predominantly Romanesque.

ANGLO-SAXON STYLE

STORED

A PLAN AT BELFRY STAGE

15'.0"

B EARLS BARTON: TOWER WINDOW

C EARLS BARTON: TOWER

D SOMPTING: TOWER ARCH

E SOMPTING: TOWER

F S. BENET: CAMBRIDGE: IMPOST

G S. MARY THE YOUNGER: YORK: TOWER WINDOW

H WINDOW: WORTH CH. SUSSEX
4'.11"
GLASS   GLASS
PLAN

J DEERHURST: GLO'STERSHIRE: TOWER WINDOW

K BOARHUNT CH. HANTS

L WORTH CHURCH: SUSSEX

M BRADFORD-on-AVON CH: WILTS

N PLAN
59'.6"   18'.6"

P S. BENET: CAMBR°E. TOWER

Q PLAN
PORCH
14'.0"   42'.0"

ANGLO-SAXON CHURCH PLANS

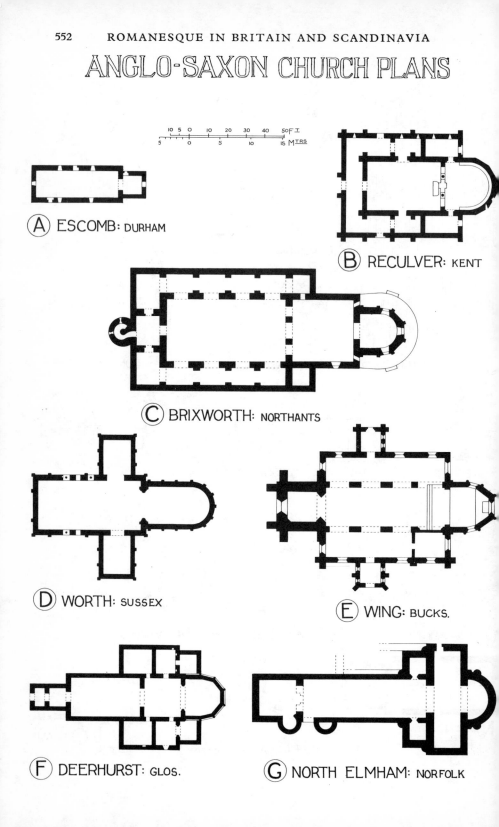

(A) ESCOMB: DURHAM

(B) RECULVER: KENT

(C) BRIXWORTH: NORTHANTS

(D) WORTH: SUSSEX

(E) WING: BUCKS.

(F) DEERHURST: GLOS.

(G) NORTH ELMHAM: NORFOLK

The pattern of mediaeval history in Scandinavia was dependent generally upon the continuing conflict between Denmark and Sweden. Danish solidarity was early reduced by revolt among the peasants and fights between feudal landowners. By the middle of the thirteenth century the Hanseatic League of north German cities was able to intrude along the Baltic shores, and even on the Atlantic seaboard of Norway. In the southern Baltic the merchant interests of the Hansa were widespread, while the feudal administration of the farming classes depended, particularly in Sweden, upon the alliance between the Crown and the feudal lords. The wars of the Danes against their neighbours and the League led to concessions of substantial land interests to German nobles. The consequent lack of concentration of aristocratic wealth gave less opportunity for great display in domestic or military architecture than was possible in other parts of northern Europe.

ARCHITECTURAL CHARACTER

THE BRITISH ISLES

Roman period. The architecture of the Romans in Britain was of the same character as in other parts of Europe, and much still survives, in remains such as those of Hadrian's Wall, and those of urban building in Silchester, Bath, Chester, Corstopitum (Corbridge), Viroconium (Wroxeter) and Verulamium (near S. Albans). Fora, basilicas, baths (p. 301), a theatre (at Verulamium, p. 307), temples—in Aquae Sulis (Bath) and Londinium (the city of London), villas (at Verulamium), and a palace (at Fishbourne) have been uncovered. Examples of mosaic flooring, pottery and sculptures indicate the care which the Romans bestowed on dwelling houses and public buildings. The characteristics of Roman architecture (pp. 267–72) were so virile that they inevitably influenced subsequent Anglo-Saxon and Romanesque architecture in Britain.

The form of the Christian church in Britain before the end of the Roman occupation is exemplified at Silchester (p. 294C). This was a small church, with a basilican plan, built probably early in the fourth century. It had a western apse, for the ritual at this time required that the celebrant face east from beyond the altar, and in this may be compared with S. Giovanni in Laterano (*c.* 324) (p. 354) and S. Reparatus, Orléansville, in Algeria (324). It had transeptal projections in the form of Byzantine 'pastaphories' (a diaconicon accessible from the sanctuary as a sacristy, and a prothesis accessible from the nave as an offertory); and a triumphal arch derived directly from Roman precedent as a sanctuary screen in the form of a Byzantine iconostasis.

Anglo-Saxon period. Domestic building was probably largely dependent upon the use of timber, but little evidence remains of methods of construction. The considerable later development in timber-framing techniques was a characteristic of buildings of all types and found its parallel in ship-building. The masonry of church buildings from about the middle of the seventh century shows signs of dependence on timber prototypes, as in the 'long and short work' in quoins (p. 551C, P), pilaster strips derived from the 'liesenen' of the Carolingian Rhineland (p. 551C, E, M), triangular-headed openings (p. 551J), blind arcading (p. 551M), turned balusters (p. 551B), and midwall shafts (p. 551G, H). Before the period of the Heptarchy, architecture of any pretension free from direct Roman influence was in framed timber (which Bede entitled *more Scottorum* in his description of a church built on Lindisfarne in 582). But a link with earlier stone-built forms was expressed in some more permanent post-Carolingian building in Ireland where, in spite of remoteness from Rome, there were strong early connections with the

Coptic church in Egypt. The Oratory of Gallerus, near Dingle in Kerry (p. 555A) is a monastic cell of the sixth or seventh century, rectangular in plan, in the form of a corbel vault, smooth-worked internally, and with a pointed extrados. There are monastic sites in the Skelligs exhibiting groups of 'clochains' similar in construction, and reminiscent both in form and in masonry technique, of the Mycenaean Treasury of Atreus (p. 190A). The most spectacular group is on Skellig Michael.

The two principal schools of church building during the Heptarchy are Kentish and Northumbrian in provenance. The southern examples follow precedents derived from Mediterranean Gaul in work closely related to the Canterbury Abbey of S. Augustine and to four subordinate Canterbury churches. They can be represented by the church at Reculver in Kent (p. 552B) founded in 669, and having a broad rectangular plan, with eastern apse, two pastaphories, porches on north and south as burial chapels ('portici'), a western porch and narthex, and a three-arch iconostasis. The school of Bishop Benedict Biscop in Northumbria showed the influence of Merovingian Gaul, Celtic timber traditions, and the foundations of S. Columba in Ireland, and is represented by the church at Escomb, of the late seventh century (p. 552A). An instance of the results of the reforms of S. Wilfrid of York is the church at Brixworth in Northamptonshire (c. 675) (pp. 552C, 555B), a four-bay aisled basilica (of which the aisles, probably in porticus form, have not survived), with originally a three-arch opening into a rectangular presbytery, and an eastern apse, polygonal externally. The arches of the main arcade are constructed crudely in re-used Roman brick.

The introduction of Carolingian fashions in church building in England followed Benedictine reforms and the monastic revival of the late tenth century, promoted by King Edgar, by S. Dunstan at Glastonbury and by Ethelwold, Bishop of Winchester. The two main imported characteristics were the claustral plan, of which the archetype was that of S. Gallen in Switzerland (p. 509), and the basilican aisled hall for the body of the church, which had been anticipated in England only in the work of S. Wilfrid. Double-ended plans occurred in the rebuilding in about 960 of S. Augustine's Abbey at Canterbury, and at Sherborne and Ely, and had been occasionally anticipated in lesser churches, as in that at Abingdon, Berkshire, during the seventh century. Aisled naves were not common in lesser churches, but they did occasionally occur in examples such as those at Wing, Buckinghamshire (p. 552E), and at Great Paxton in Huntingdonshire.

Central and western axial church towers appeared commonly during the tenth century, in examples such as those of S. Mary in Castro at Dover, and Deerhurst (p. 552F), which also preserved a polygonal apse of a Carolingian kind. At Barton-on-Humber, Lincolnshire, the three-cell-church had a central tower-nave of the middle tenth century. The slightly later Saxon cathedral at North Elmham (p. 552G) had two axial towers, an eastern apse, and fully-developed transepts either developed from pastaphories or derived through Carolingian Germany from the 'bema' of the early church in Rome, such as that of Old S. Peter's (p. 353A, C).

Tenth- and eleventh-century towers were occasionally terminated in a form of short hipped spire springing from each apex of the four gables on the tower faces. This is patently a device imported from the High Romanesque churches of the Rhineland (cf. pp. 508K, 513B), and an English example, now rare, of this 'Rhenish spire' or 'Saxon helm' is that of Sompting in Sussex (p. 551E). A unique example of pre-Conquest timber building survives at Greenstead-juxta-Ongar in Essex. This church was probably built as a burial chapel for S. Edmund the Martyr in 1013. The nave wall, though restored, is in the form of halved tree-boles, with the plane faces forming the inner face, and the palisade set in mortices in timber head and sill. This form of construction, not unknown also in Ireland, is clearly derived from

A. Oratory of Gallerus, Dingle, County Kerry (6th or 7th cent.). See p. 554

B. Brixworth Church, Northamptonshire (c. 675). See p. 567

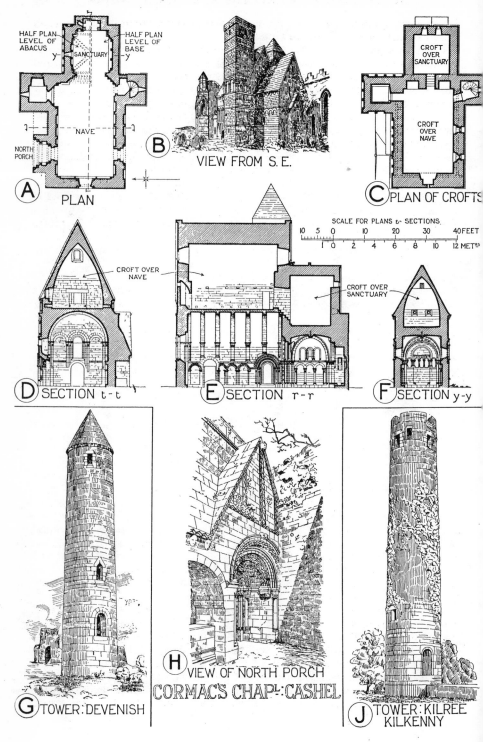

A PLAN

HALF PLAN LEVEL OF ABACUS

HALF PLAN LEVEL OF BASE

SANCTUARY

NAVE

NORTH PORCH

B VIEW FROM S.E.

C PLAN OF CROFTS

CROFT OVER SANCTUARY

CROFT OVER NAVE

D SECTION t-t

CROFT OVER NAVE

E SECTION r-r

SCALE FOR PLANS & SECTIONS
10 5 0 10 20 30 40 FEET
1 0 2 4 6 8 10 12 METRES

CROFT OVER SANCTUARY

F SECTION y-y

G TOWER: DEVENISH

H VIEW OF NORTH PORCH
CORMAC'S CHAPL: CASHEL

J TOWER: KILREE KILKENNY

Scandinavia; a simpler type is exemplified in Sancta Maria Minor in Lund, and an exactly similar form at Hemse in Gotland.

The most sophisticated of Anglo-Saxon masonry building includes the decorative devices of Carolingian Germany probably based on timber forms inherited from Roman antiquity (pilaster strips, triangular arcading and the ubiquitous monolithic arch with impost blocks), but occasionally is associated with ashlar facings and either in-and-out bands or 'long-and-short work' in quoins (p. 551C, K, P). In its most advanced form, the dependence on adaptation of timber-building characteristics disappears in favour of arcading in shallow relief, use of caps and bases, and true stone motifs of a kind well demonstrated in S. Lawrence at Bradford-on-Avon, Wiltshire (p. 551M), a two-cell church with one porticus, founded at the beginning of the eighth century and substantially remodelled in the tenth. No very distinct vocabulary of stone moulding was developed in the British Isles before the eleventh century, but one distinctive characteristic was the use of a projecting hood mould to internal arcades, as in Wing and in S. Benet at Cambridge (p. 551F). This is of some importance, for it survived in Britain well into the period of mature Gothic church architecture, in increasingly vigorous form, and it then provided a clear distinction between the native Gothic and that of the Continent (cf. pp. 563C, G–K, N–R, 599B, 602C, 765D).

There is evidence of direct Norman influence upon English church architecture at least two decades before the Conquest. There are instances of this in decorative carved stonework, particularly in tympana to arched doorways, such as those at Knook, Wiltshire, and S. Matthew at Ipswich. The work is more crude than the best of Saxon stone carving evident in grave slabs, crosses and occasionally in a frieze, such as that at Castor in Northamptonshire, and in the early eleventh-century panels now at Chichester, probably originally in the cathedral at Selsea. A consequence of growing Norman influence, which had an opposite effect, was the survival of modified Saxon fashions into the early twelfth century at the hands of refugees re-settled in Ireland and Scotland. This produced the two-cell churches, each with a square tower, in Cormac's Chapel at Cashel of the Kings (p. 556A–H) and in S. Rule at S. Andrews. The most marked instance of pre-Conquest Norman influence in England followed the beginning of the building of the Confessor's Abbey at Westminster in about 1042. This was a thoroughbred Norman Benedictine abbey church, finished in about 1050, though not dedicated until 1065. The plan of the church seems to owe much to those at both Bernay and Jumièges, and the conventual layout was of a characteristic Continental Cluniac kind.

Norman period. After the conquest, both civil and ecclesiastical administration were soon remodelled upon that of the Duchy of Normandy. During the last three decades of the eleventh century there was an enormous surge of military and church building, centred particularly upon the great Benedictine abbeys. In greater church architecture, the characteristics directly or indirectly inherited from Cluny were the long nave exemplified in Norwich (14 bays) (p. 641D); S. Albans (13 bays) (p. 642F) and Winchester (12 bays) (p. 640C), and also double eastern transepts (the 'patriarchal' plan) as seen in Conrad's work at Canterbury of about 1100 (p. 641B). Features imported directly from Normandy are the typical Benedictine plan having three eastern apses, such as those at Durham (p. 641E), Peterborough (p. 640D), Binham Priory and S. Albans (p. 642F), where also occurred transept apses ('absidoles'), introduced by Archbishop Lanfranc at Canterbury in 1065 (p. 641B); one transept apse survives at Norwich (p. 641D), two at Gloucester (p. 641C), and four in the eastern apses at Canterbury. The multiplicity of apsidal chapels in monastic churches was necessitated by the growing demand for facilities for the individual offices of a Benedictine community. In some cases,

Anglo-Norman church planning followed central French fashion with a main eastern apse and ambulatory, such as those of Norwich (p. 641D), Gloucester (p. 641C) and Battle Abbey. A similar, but more mature form of chevet occurred in Beaulieu Abbey, but this was unusual in Cistercian architecture in the British Isles. It was common, in both secular and monastery churches, to find a central lantern tower over the choir crossing, and Norman examples survive at S. Albans, Norwich, Tewkesbury and Southwell. At Old Sarum in c. 1075 a substantial tower was built over the north transept, Exeter cathedral (p. 642E) retains both transept towers, and Norman work in the western towers survives at Durham (p. 641E), Southwell Minster (p. 642K), and Chichester (p. 642G); at Ely (p. 640A), the western tower is central and was originally complemented to both north and south by flanking octagonal towers.

The earliest Anglo-Norman groin vaults are those over irregular crypt spaces at Winchester (c. 1079) and Gloucester (c. 1089), both revealing planning for an ambulatory above. The choir tribune at Gloucester was built with a semi-barrel vault between 1089 and 1100, and this is still visible behind the early fourteenth-century re-casing of the Norman work. Groined aisle vaults were built in the nave at Ely after 1087 (p. 640A), but no high groin vault was ever attempted in Norman England. The earliest great church designed initially and entirely with a rib vaulting system is Durham cathedral, where work was begun in 1093; the choir aisle vaults, with depressed segmental diagonal ribs, were finished in 1096, the high vault of the eastern arm in 1107, and of the nave by about 1132, probably only very shortly after those of the two churches founded by Duke William and Matilda in Caen, with their sexpartite high ribbed vaults (pp. 500, 501B, C, 502B). The significant difference between these and the quadripartite vaults of Durham is that the English version combines the ribbed vault with single nave bays, having alternating cylindrical and compound piers from the shafts of which spring heavy transverse pointed arches. The alternate pier plan was used in the Lanfranc tradition at Jumièges (p. 498B), but no high vault was achieved there. Variants on Anglo-Norman greater church structural design, without high vaults, survive in the nave at Ely (p. 640A), which has alternating piers of the Jumièges kind, three arcade orders, a fully-developed tribune and lofty clear-storey; and in the twelfth-century work at Peterborough (p. 569D, E, F, H, J), where the composition is similar, but the piers are uniform, and the painted timber nave ceiling is original. In the nave of the secular minster at Southwell (p. 642K), of about 1130, there is a full arcade on cylindrical piers, a full triforium with traces of bar tracery of a probably primitive kind, and a low clear-storey with no vertical shafts—a composition clearly not intended to accommodate a high vault. In Romsey Abbey, a church of Benedictine nuns, the triforium 'bar tracery' survives in the form of open sub-arches within a high arcade embracing the triforium, a device which was quoted in several later instances, notably in the choir of Christ Church at Oxford (pp. 568, 642C), and which originated in the choir of Tewkesbury Abbey. The square east end at Romsey, designed to accommodate the high altar against the east wall, represents a characteristic almost universally adopted in the earlier Cistercian church in England. The Cistercian ritual choir was usually sited in and beyond the crossing so that the eastern arm was often short and without aisles, as at Tintern, built in about 1130. At Rievaulx, founded in 1132, the nave plan is long, the roof was of timber, the aisles covered with lateral pointed barrel vaults and the nave arcade itself pointed. The same characteristics reappeared at Fountains Abbey, which was begun in about 1135 (pp. 570, 571). These Cistercian devices were imported from Burgundy, the home of the Order, where a complete prototype exists at Fontenay, founded in 1119, but in the later and more

COMPARATIVE DOORWAYS

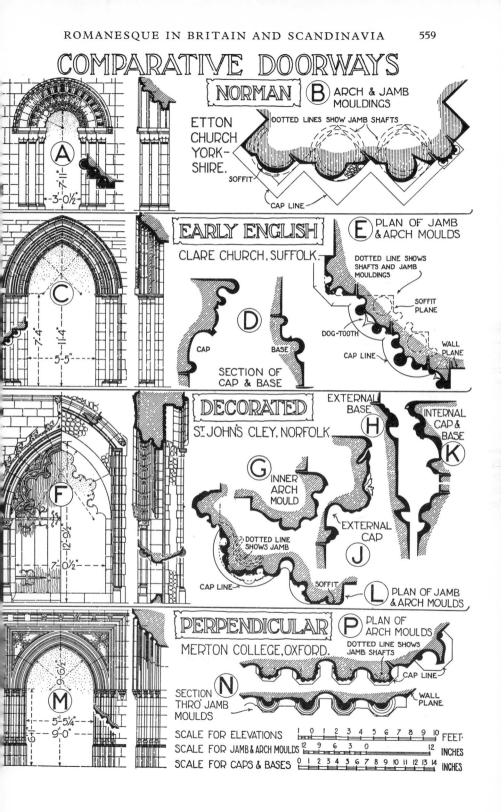

NORMAN — B ARCH & JAMB MOULDINGS

ETTON CHURCH YORKSHIRE.

A

DOTTED LINES SHOW JAMB SHAFTS

SOFFIT

CAP LINE

1'-7½"
3'-0½"

EARLY ENGLISH — E PLAN OF JAMB & ARCH MOULDS

CLARE CHURCH, SUFFOLK.

C

D

DOTTED LINE SHOWS SHAFTS AND JAMB MOULDINGS

SOFFIT PLANE

DOG-TOOTH

CAP LINE

WALL PLANE

CAP   BASE

SECTION OF CAP & BASE

7'-4"
1'-4"
5'-5"

DECORATED — ST. JOHN'S CLEY, NORFOLK.

EXTERNAL BASE

H

INTERNAL CAP & BASE

K

G INNER ARCH MOULD

EXTERNAL CAP

J

DOTTED LINE SHOWS JAMB

CAP LINE

SOFFIT

L PLAN OF JAMB & ARCH MOULDS

F

2'-
1'-2'-9½"
7'-0½"

PERPENDICULAR — P PLAN OF ARCH MOULDS

MERTON COLLEGE, OXFORD.

DOTTED LINE SHOWS JAMB SHAFTS

CAP LINE

SECTION THRO' JAMB MOULDS

N

WALL PLANE

M

9'-6½"
5'-5¼"
9'-0"
6'-

SCALE FOR ELEVATIONS   0 1 2 3 4 5 6 7 8 9 10 FEET

SCALE FOR JAMB & ARCH MOULDS   12 9 6 3 0   12 INCHES

SCALE FOR CAPS & BASES   0 1 2 3 4 5 6 7 8 9 10 11 12 13 14 INCHES

COMPARATIVE WINDOWS

(NORMAN)

Ⓐ WALTHAM ABBEY

(EARLY ENGLISH)

Ⓑ WIVELSFIELD SUSSEX

Ⓒ WILEY WILTS

Ⓓ CASTLE HALL WINCHESTER

(EARLY ENGLISH)

Ⓔ MEOPH. KENT

(DEC)

Ⓕ DUSTON NORTHANTS

(DECORATED)

(DEC)

Ⓖ WALTHAM ABBEY

(DECORATED)

BALL FLOWER ORNAMENT

Ⓗ S. MARY MAGDALEN CHURCH : OXFORD

Ⓙ HOLBEACH CH.: LINCS

Ⓚ BADGEWORTH : GLO

INS 12 0   5   10   15   20 F⸱

SCALE FOR ALL THE   WINDOWS EXCEPT Ⓜ

(PERP.)

(PERPENDICULAR)

Ⓛ WAWNE : YORKS

Ⓜ S. GEORGE'S CHAPEL : WINDSOR

5   0   5   10 F⸱

Ⓝ S. MICHAEL : BASINGS⸱

COMPARATIVE PIERS, CAPS & BASES.

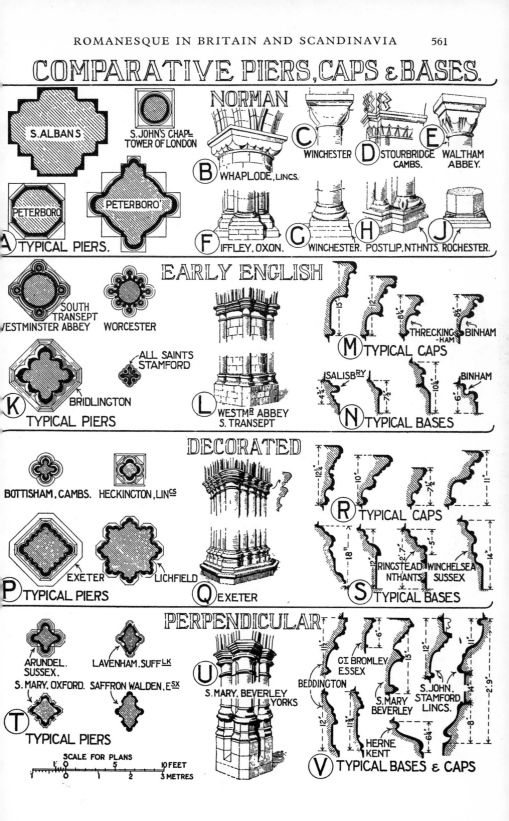

NORMAN

S.ALBANS

S.JOHN'S CHAP. TOWER OF LONDON

PETERBORO

PETERBORO'

(A) TYPICAL PIERS.

(B) WHAPLODE, LINCS.

(C) WINCHESTER

(D) STOURBRIDGE CAMBS.

(E) WALTHAM ABBEY.

(F) IFFLEY, OXON.

(G) WINCHESTER.

(H) POSTLIP, NTHNTS.

(J) ROCHESTER.

EARLY ENGLISH

SOUTH TRANSEPT WESTMINSTER ABBEY

WORCESTER

ALL SAINTS STAMFORD

(K) BRIDLINGTON TYPICAL PIERS

(L) WESTM. ABBEY S. TRANSEPT

(M) TYPICAL CAPS

THRECKING-HAM

BINHAM

(N) TYPICAL BASES

SALISBRY

BINHAM

DECORATED

BOTTISHAM, CAMBS. HECKINGTON, LINCS

(P) EXETER LICHFIELD TYPICAL PIERS

(Q) EXETER

(R) TYPICAL CAPS

(S) TYPICAL BASES

RINGSTEAD NTHANTS

WINCHELSEA SUSSEX

PERPENDICULAR

ARUNDEL. SUSSEX.

LAVENHAM. SUFF LK

S. MARY, OXFORD. SAFFRON WALDEN, E SX

(T) TYPICAL PIERS

(U) S. MARY, BEVERLEY YORKS

GT BROMLEY ESSEX

BEDDINGTON

S.MARY BEVERLEY

S.JOHN. STAMFORD LINCS.

HERNE KENT

(V) TYPICAL BASES & CAPS

SCALE FOR PLANS
10 FEET
3 METRES

COMPARATIVE CARVED CAPITALS

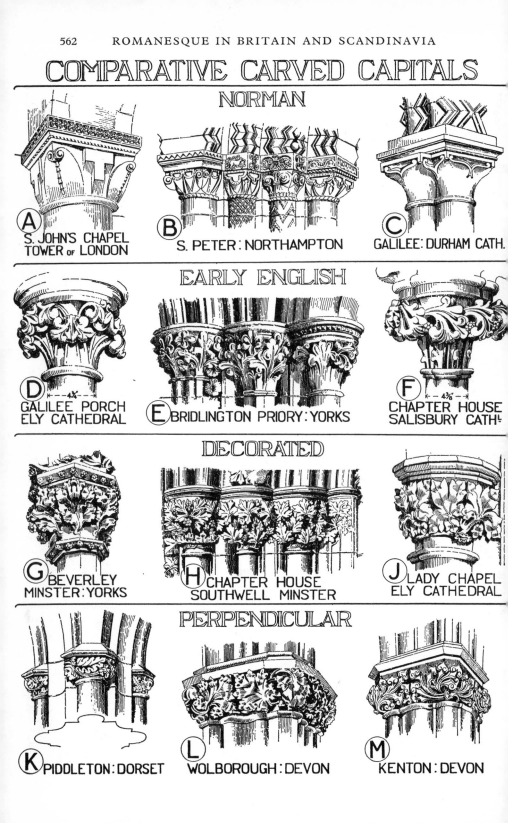

NORMAN

(A) S. JOHN'S CHAPEL TOWER OF LONDON

(B) S. PETER: NORTHAMPTON

(C) GALILEE: DURHAM CATH.

EARLY ENGLISH

(D) GALILEE PORCH ELY CATHEDRAL

(E) BRIDLINGTON PRIORY: YORKS

(F) CHAPTER HOUSE SALISBURY CATH!

DECORATED

(G) BEVERLEY MINSTER: YORKS

(H) CHAPTER HOUSE SOUTHWELL MINSTER

(J) LADY CHAPEL ELY CATHEDRAL

PERPENDICULAR

(K) PIDDLETON: DORSET

(L) WOLBOROUGH: DEVON

(M) KENTON: DEVON

COMPARATIVE MOULDINGS

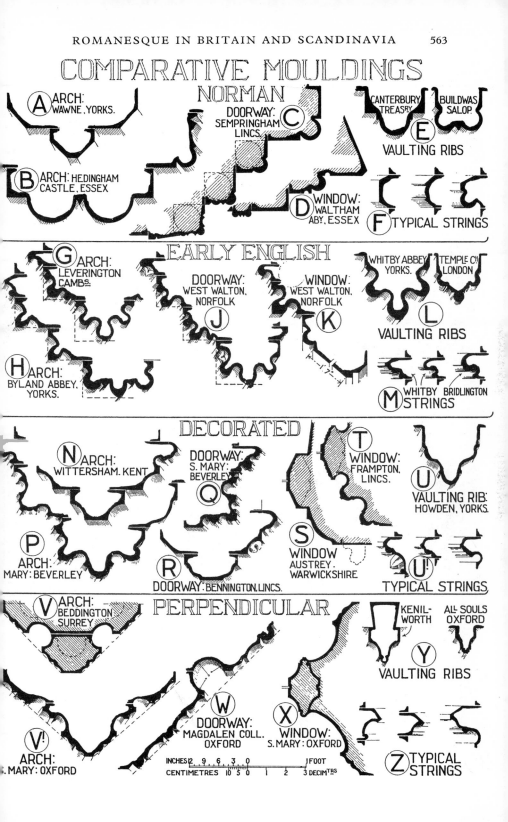

NORMAN

A ARCH: WAWNE, YORKS.

B ARCH: HEDINGHAM CASTLE, ESSEX

C DOORWAY: SEMPRINGHAM LINCS.

D WINDOW: WALTHAM ABY, ESSEX

E CANTERBURY TREASRY. BUILDWAS SALOP.
VAULTING RIBS

F TYPICAL STRINGS

EARLY ENGLISH

G ARCH: LEVERINGTON CAMBS.

H ARCH: BYLAND ABBEY, YORKS.

J DOORWAY: WEST WALTON, NORFOLK

K WINDOW: WEST WALTON, NORFOLK

L WHITBY ABBEY YORKS. TEMPLE Cʰ LONDON
VAULTING RIBS

M WHITBY BRIDLINGTON STRINGS

DECORATED

N ARCH: WITTERSHAM, KENT

P ARCH: MARY: BEVERLEY

Q DOORWAY: S. MARY: BEVERLEY

R DOORWAY: BENNINGTON, LINCS.

T WINDOW: FRAMPTON, LINCS.

S WINDOW AUSTREY. WARWICKSHIRE

U VAULTING RIB: HOWDEN, YORKS.

U' TYPICAL STRINGS

PERPENDICULAR

V ARCH: BEDDINGTON SURREY

V! ARCH: S. MARY: OXFORD

W DOORWAY: MAGDALEN COLL. OXFORD

X WINDOW: S. MARY: OXFORD

Y KENILWORTH ALL SOULS OXFORD
VAULTING RIBS

Z TYPICAL STRINGS

INCHES 12, 9, 6, 3, 0 1 FOOT
CENTIMETRES 10 5 0 1 2 3 DECIMᵀᴿˢ

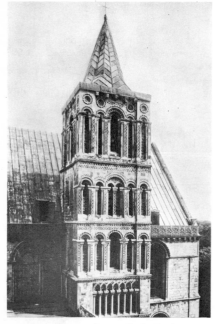

A. Canterbury Cathedral:
Norman tower, S.E. transept
(*c.* 1100–25). See pp. 568, 653

B. Leuchars Church from S.E. (1172–85;
tower 17th cent.). See pp. 565, 700

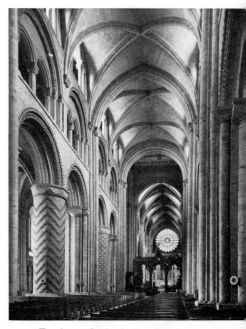

C. S. Bartholomew the Great,
London: choir looking E. (1123–50;
and later additions). See p. 565

D. Durham Cathedral: nave (1110–33)
looking E. See pp. 568, 654

mature English examples Anglo-Norman details occur frequently. Of these details, those which were inherited from pre-Conquest architecture include the hood mould to internal arcades (p. 557) and a bold soffit roll or bowtell moulding (p. 563B). Mouldings generally are enriched by conventional carving with increased vigour through the late eleventh and the twelfth centuries, as in S. Bartholomew, London (p. 564C), and Waltham Abbey. Doorways and windows have jambs in square recesses or 'orders' enclosing nook-shafts. These 'orders' are frequently carved with zigzag and beak-head ornament, as at Etton (p. 559A, B), or elaborately sculptured, as at Barfreston, Kent. Windows are small and the internal jambs are deeply splayed (p. 560A). They are in single lights, often flanked by blind arcading (p. 644A), although double windows with a central shaft occur (often in towers), while three openings, the middle being the largest, are grouped together, as in S. Bartholomew, London (p. 564C), and elsewhere (p. 644).

Piers (p. 561A–J), short and massive, are cylindrical or polygonal, as at Gloucester, Hereford, Southwell and S. John's Chapel, Tower of London (p. 575C), while at Durham lozenge, chevron and vertical channellings were worked on the cylindrical piers (p. 564D). Compound piers, with rectangular recesses containing shafts, as at Peterborough (p. 569J) and Durham (p. 564D), were often used alternately with cylindrical piers, as at Norwich, Durham and Waltham. The shape of piers was influenced by the vaulting shafts which they supported. The small shafts in the recessed 'orders' of doorways and windows were sometimes richly carved. Capitals (pp. 561A–J, 562A–C) are usually cubiform or cushion type, sometimes carved and scalloped, but some, such as the Ionic capital in the Tower of London, are reminiscent of Roman architecture, though the Corinthian type, which occurs at Canterbury (p. 651B) is more frequently seen in France. Carved foliage, especially the acanthus scroll, is clearly due to Roman art, though executed in a bolder and less refined manner. The tympana over many Norman doorways, such as the Priest's Door at Ely, are sculptured with effective though rough representations of scriptural subjects. Arcading of intersecting arches (p. 569F) along aisle walls is frequent, and is often piled up in storeys to ornament the whole wall. The parish church of Leuchars, Fife, has an eastern apse with unusually bold wall arcading on coupled column shafts (p. 564B). Stained glass was now used, though sparingly, in small pieces, leaded together in mosaic-like patterns. The glass panels in the choir at Canterbury (1174) represent Biblical subjects, set in a blue or ruby ground, and framed in brilliantly-coloured scrollwork. Timber roofs were coloured, sometimes with lozenge-shaped panels, as at Peterborough (p. 569H), and the restored roof in Waltham Abbey gives an idea of the original colour treatment. Hanging tapestries gave warmth and interest to interiors, as the famous Bayeux tapestry testifies.

SCANDINAVIA

Truly Romanesque characteristics did not appear in the architecture of Scandinavia until both British and Continental European influences upon church building in stone became effective toward the middle of the eleventh century. In Norway, the early timber techniques were particularly persistent, and significant masonry building was sparse until the early years of the twelfth century. The traditions of ship-building and of timber-built pagan temples (of certainly earlier date than the tenth century) supported the development of a distinctive native architecture of which there is ample early evidence, and which, in its finest fully mature form, is represented by a number of surviving examples. The most highly developed form of stave church has an inner timber colonnade which contributes to a basilican section with a (blind) clear-storey, and a steep scissors-trussed roof. In the Nes church, Hallingdal, the structural design depended upon a single central timber column rising to the main roof ridge, with horizontal supports extending to the upper sills of the outer walls. Both here and elsewhere, the contrast between internal decorative simplicity and the extraordinary vigour of external carved decoration, particularly of the west front and entrance doorway, is very marked. It may well be due to the fact that, in a low northern light, external carving was more fitting, although exposed to effects of the weather which must have been marked in a material so short-lived as softwood timber. A church which reveals most of the characteristics of the code of carved decoration in Norwegian timber churches is that at Urnes (pp. 578, 579D). By the early twelfth century Norwegian contacts with Ireland had been continuous, though uneasy, for more than three centuries, and an Irish character is blended with the Viking tradition in work of a remarkable hybrid strength. Many of the motifs are based on stylized animal forms, combined with interlaced coils sometimes in the form of foliage of an almost Carolingian kind.

Mediaeval dwellings in Scandinavia show a continuous tradition of timber building, particularly in Norway. The customary technique was a form of 'lafting', making use of logs lapped at their ends. In some two-storey versions, the upper storey, and occasionally the outer walls at ground level, were constructed in palisade fashion very much in the form of a cell of a stave church. The Swedish version of this combined structure, which was common throughout south Scandinavia, is known as 'ramloftstuga'. Domestic building in stone followed a pattern of construction and planning derived from southern custom.

Masonry techniques in church building readily revealed an early dependence particularly upon English and Norman models. Churches at Husaby (p. 579B), and at Sigtuna (p. 581B), have axial towers and eastern apses, with either continuous or crossing vaults. A series of round churches on Bornholm represent an incident in Danish progress towards a mature Romanesque architecture. They may reflect the ideas generated by King Sigurd's pilgrimage to Jerusalem in the years 1107–11. The Bornholm examples are all of the twelfth century, and have central vault piers, apsidal projections and bold plan buttresses (p. 580A).

Smaller twelfth-century churches in southern Scandinavia are frequently based upon the two-cell plan of a kind very similar to those of both Celtic and Gallic origin in England of the Heptarchy, but simple barrel vaults and western towers are not uncommon among surviving examples such as that at Venge, the Maria Church at Bergen, and Bø Church in Telemark.

Twelfth-century cathedral churches in Scandinavia show a progressively more mature Romanesque character, incorporating the effects of Norman and German development in masonry techniques and structural design aimed at fully-vaulted composition. Earlier precedents at Roskilde in Denmark were based upon a simple aisled nave, with an aisleless choir and a square west end projecting between two towers. Lund Cathedral (1103) displays a marked Rhine-Lombardic character, emphasized by the western additions of later date. The Norwegian examples at Stavanger (1130) and Kirkwall in the Orkneys are modest interpretations of the northern Anglo-Norman formula. Cluniac influences, operating through Germany and Denmark, were most marked in south and east Norway, and were best represented in Oslo and Hamar, now ruined. They are still evident at Ringsaker, which belongs mostly to the period 1113–30, and has a barrel-vaulted nave, half-barrel aisle vaults, long narrow transepts and a bold crossing tower. In Jutland, the cathedrals of Ribe and Viborg illustrate the continuing German and Lombardic influences upon mature Scandinavian Romanesque churches. Carved decoration of considerable richness, as in Lund Cathedral (p. 580C), is not uncommon in the mature Scandinavian greater church.

EXAMPLES

THE BRITISH ISLES

Pre-Conquest Romanesque architecture in Britain is represented mostly in church building, of which in many cases only fragments survive, either in parts of the structure of churches substantially of later date, or in decorative elements re-used or incorporated in churches completely and subsequently rebuilt. In some instances, only the plan form can be represented by surviving foundations or wall footings.

The most complete examples of early date illustrate the fashions in church building during the Heptarchy. The southern school of S. Augustine is best represented by **S. Peter's at Bradwell-Juxta-Mare, Essex** (c. 660), which has complete main walls with bold regularly-spaced buttresses, constructed largely of reclaimed Roman material, with apparently original plain square window openings and a wide west doorway. The apse at the east end and the pastaphory chapels have disappeared, but there is evidence of a three-arch opening at the east end of the nave, now walled in. The northern school of Benedict Biscop is well exemplified at **Escomb in County Durham** (late seventh century) (p. 552A), which preserves its long, narrow and lofty nave, with entrances on north and south, and with a square east end to the chancel. The nearly contemporary church at **Brixworth, Northamptonshire** (pp. 552C, 555B) represents the effects of the movement promoted by S. Wilfrid, and may be claimed as the earlier English example of basilican church form upon which greater church design subsequently depended.

Later pre-Conquest examples which exhibit more mature masonry detail and which survive sufficiently completely to illustrate church design of the ninth and tenth centuries include churches at **Worth, Sussex** (pp. 551H, L, 552D) (aisle openings, chancel arch and eastern apse), **Bradford-on-Avon, Wiltshire** (p. 551M), and the tower at **Earl's Barton, Northamptonshire** (p. 551A–C).

CATHEDRAL CHURCHES

The cathedral churches of England and Wales may be divided into (a) those of the old foundation, (b) of monastic foundation and (c) of the new foundation.

(a) The thirteen cathedrals of the old foundation which were served by secular clergy were not affected by the reforms of Henry VIII. They are the cathedrals of York, Lichfield, Wells, Exeter, Salisbury, Chichester, Lincoln, Hereford, London and the Welsh Cathedrals of Llandaff, Bangor, S. David's and S. Asaph.

(b) The thirteen cathedrals of the monastic foundation were originally served by regular clergy or monks, and were reconstituted at the Dissolution of the Monasteries as chapters of secular canons. They are the cathedrals of Canterbury, Durham, Rochester, Winchester, Worcester, Norwich, Ely, Carlisle, Peterborough, Gloucester, Chester, Oxford and Bristol. The last five only became cathedrals at the Dissolution. Westminster Abbey was a cathedral church only from 1540 to 1545. When the change in these monastic establishments was made, the abbot became the bishop, the prior the dean, and the monks became canons and choristers, while the personnel generally remained the same.

(c) The cathedrals of the new foundation are those to which bishops have been more recently appointed, viz. Ripon and Southwell, which are old collegiate churches, as well as the parochial churches of Newcastle, Wakefield, Manchester, Birmingham, Truro, Chelmsford and Southwark, the abbey church of S. Albans, Bury S. Edmunds, Coventry, Liverpool, Guildford and others.

Those in which substantial Anglo-Norman work survives include:

Bristol (p. 643K). Augustinian priory. Rectangular chapter house with bold interlaced wall arcades.

Canterbury (pp. 564A, 641B, 651A, B). Benedictine monastery. Confessor's abbey church 1042–50; choir replaced and enlarged 1096–1126; choir rebuilt on remains after fire and extended eastwards 1174–85 by William of Sens and his English successor on a plan contracted in width to preserve chevet chapels. Extensive crypt of 1100–25.

Carlisle (p. 643B). Augustinian monastery. Two Norman bays remain.

Chichester (p. 642G), Norman nave, transitional retro-choir.

Durham (pp. 564D, 641E). Benedictine monastery. Norman work in choir transepts and western towers (1093–1133) among the finest in England; the vaults of the eastern arm are probably the earliest essays in ribbed vaulting outside Italy, and those of the nave the earliest to incorporate pointed ribs.

Ely (p. 640A). Benedictine monastery. Norman nave and transepts with timber roof, lower parts of west front (beyond the Galilee), only the southern part remaining.

Exeter (p 642E). The disposition of the two transept towers, the only surviving Norman work, is unique in Britain.

Gloucester (p. 641C). Benedictine abbey. Norman choir cased early fourteenth century.

Hereford (p. 643H). Extensive Norman remains internally visible in nave, choir and south transept.

Norwich (p. 641D). Benedictine monastery. Long Norman nave, aisleless transepts, choir with apsidal chapels (1096–1145).

Oxford (pp. 630B, 642C). Augustinian priory. Norman nave and choir with triforium gallery within the arcades (1158–80).

Peterborough (pp. 569, 640D, 658A, 660A). Benedictine abbey. Fine Norman interior (1117–93); original nave timber ceiling; choir apse enclosed by late fifteenth-century work.

Rochester (p. 642H). Benedictine monastery. Crypt, nave and west door of Norman church survive.

S. Albans (p. 642F). Benedictine abbey. Norman nave, transepts, choir and central tower showing evidence of re-use of material from both Roman and Saxon buildings.

Southwell (p. 642K). Norman nave, transepts and towers.

Winchester (p. 640C). Benedictine monastery. Norman transepts with early ribbed aisle vaults, and tower; choir and nave (1079–93) cased (1394–1450).

Worcester (p. 641A). Benedictine monastery. Norman crypt and transepts; chapter house on distinctive circular plan.

MONASTIC BUILDINGS

The influence in Britain of the architecture of the religious Orders, as in most of Europe, was very considerable. During the Romanesque period, most of the monastic and military orders established houses in England, but the Orders of friars were established at a later date. The planning and architectural character of buildings of some Orders was quite distinctive, though the general arrangement was most usually derived from the Benedictine prototype illustrated in the plan of the establishment at S. Gallen of about 820 (pp. 509, 510).

The principal Orders and the architectural characteristics of their buildings are described in Chapter 15. The main foundations in Britain include:

(1) Benedictine. **S. Augustine's at Canterbury,** the first Benedictine house

PETERBOROUGH CATHEDRAL

(A) ROSE WINDOW: CENTRE GABLE: W. FRONT

(B) EXTERIOR FROM N.E.

(C) ROSE WINDOW: SIDE GABLES: W. FRONT

(D) EXTERNAL BAY

(E) TRANSVERSE SECTION THRO' CHOIR

CLEARSTORY

TRIFORIUM

CHOIR ARCADE

PASSAGE

56'.0"

78'.0"

31'.0"

84'.0"

52'.0"

78'.0"

82'.3"

FEET 10 0 10 20 30 40 50
METRES 1 0 5 10 15

(F) INTERNAL BAY

(G) W. FRONT

(H) INTERIOR LOOKING E.

(J) S. TRANSEPT LOOKG. S.E.

FOUNTAINS ABBEY : YORKSHIRE

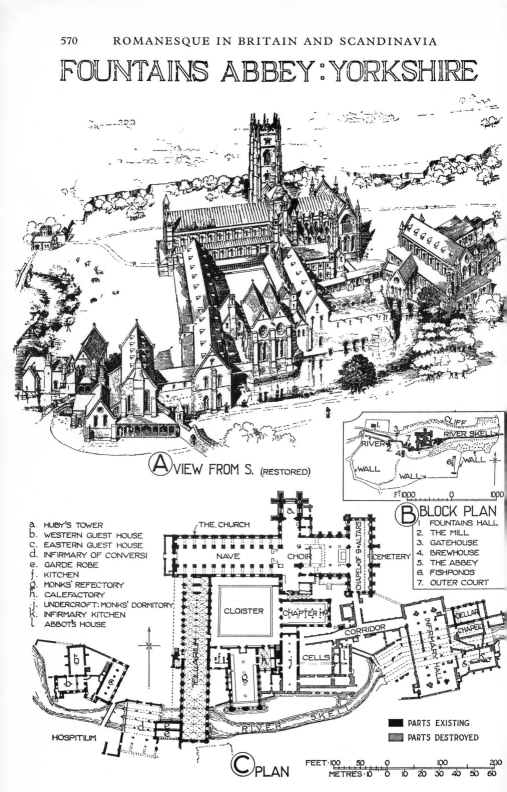

Ⓐ VIEW FROM S. (RESTORED)

Ⓑ BLOCK PLAN
1. FOUNTAINS HALL
2. THE MILL
3. GATEHOUSE
4. BREWHOUSE
5. THE ABBEY
6. FISHPONDS
7. OUTER COURT

a. HUBY'S TOWER
b. WESTERN GUEST HOUSE
c. EASTERN GUEST HOUSE
d. INFIRMARY OF CONVERSI
e. GARDE ROBE
f. KITCHEN
g. MONKS' REFECTORY
h. CALEFACTORY
j. UNDERCROFT: MONKS' DORMITORY
k. INFIRMARY KITCHEN
l. ABBOT'S HOUSE

THE CHURCH
NAVE
CHOIR
CHAPEL OF 9 ALTARS
CEMETERY
CLOISTER
CHAPTER HO.
CORRIDOR
CELLS
CELLAR
CHAPEL
INFIRMARY HALL

HOSPITIUM
RIVER SKELL

PARTS EXISTING
PARTS DESTROYED

Ⓒ PLAN

FEET·100 50 0 100 200
METRES·10 0 10 20 30 40 50 60

in England; **Westminster Abbey,** which exemplifies fully developed Benedictine planning; **Norwich,** and **Durham.**

(2) Cluniac. This Order was not strongly represented in England; **Thetford Priory, Norfolk,** contains an example of the Lady Chapel formed by an extension of the choir aisle.

(3) Carthusian. There were only nine Charterhouses in Britain, of which the first was at **Witham, Somerset.** The remains of the best example are those of **Mount Grace Priory, Yorkshire.**

(4) Cistercian. The first Cistercian monastery was built at **Waverley, Surrey,** followed by **Rievaulx, Fountains** and **Kirkstall,** all in Yorkshire (see also below).

(5) Augustinian. The cathedrals at **Bristol** and **Oxford** were originally founded by this order.

(6) Premonstratensian. **Easby** in Yorkshire, and **Bayham Abbey, Sussex.**

(7) Gilbertine. **Watton Priory** is an example of the double house combining canons of Augustinian rule and Cistercian nuns.

(8) Knights Templar. **S. Sepulchre in Cambridge** (c. 1130) and the **Temple Church in Northampton.**

(9) Knights Hospitaller. The church at **Little Maplestead, Essex** (c. 1119), similar in form to a Templars' church, though later rebuilt and extended, is supposed to have been a church of the Knights Hospitallers.

A representative example of mature, largely Romanesque monastic architecture is **Fountains Abbey, Yorkshire** (p. 570). The community appears to have been founded (1135) soon after Rievaulx, the first Cistercian establishment in that county (1132), and before Kirkstall (1152). It is thought to have been named from the springs in the valley of the Skell. Although in ruins, owing to the care with which the place has been uncovered, it is easy here to make a mental picture of a great monastery (p. 570A, C). The gatehouse (p. 570B) led into the outer court; south of this were the guest house and the infirmary of the conversi, or lay brethren, and east of it was the cellarium, no less than 90 m (300 ft) long, comprising storehouses and refectory of these conversi on the lower floor, with their dormitory above. Opposite the gatehouse is the conventual church, of which the nave and transepts date from about 1147, but the choir appears to have been enlarged between 1203 and 1247, and at the same time the transept known as the 'Chapel of the Nine Altars' was built. The tower, by Abbot Huby (1494–1526), is still the dominating feature in this beautiful valley. The door in the south-east angle of the nave leads into the cloister court, round which were ranged the chapter house, the monks' dormitory and its undercroft, the calefactory or warming house, the monks' refectory, the kitchen with two great fireplaces, and alongside was a washing lavatory, part of which still remains. Still farther east were the cells for refractory monks and the abbot's lodge, north of which a corridor led to the infirmary hall, with adjacent chapel, cellar and kitchen. The chapter house, of which the vaulting is now destroyed, was rectangular, and against the walls were stone benches rising one above another on which the monks sat. The complete monastic establishment must have existed till the time of Abbot William Thirsk (1526–36), after which the estate was sold (1540) to Sir Richard Gresham, whose successor pulled down the infirmary and the stone wall, and built Fountains Hall (p. 570B) on the site in 1611 (p. 999B).

CASTLES

Anglo-Saxon period. There were no castles, as the forts or 'burhs' built at this time were for community use; properly speaking, castles were private strongholds for king or lord, and were an outcome of the feudal system, which did not apply in

England until the Conquest, though one or two earthworks were built under Norman influence before that event.

Norman period. Of some fifteen hundred castles in England, more than twelve hundred were founded during the eleventh and twelfth centuries. Only a few of the most important had stone keeps from the outset; the majority began as 'motte and bailey' earthworks. The motte or mound usually was partly natural, partly artificial, its sides steepened by a ditch dug around its base. The flat-topped crest sometimes was broad enough to accommodate a timber dwelling. In other cases it served solely as a citadel, carrying a wooden defence tower, raised on angle posts. The dwelling and ancillary buildings then were sited in the bailey, this being a zone which looped from the foot of the motte, defined by ditches and earthen ramparts, and which was spacious enough also to provide refuge for dependants, peasantry and stock in times of need. An inclined wooden bridge connected the bailey with the motte. The fringe of the motte crest and the summits of the earth ramparts were lined by palisades of close-set timber baulks, or occasionally by rough stone walls.

Thetford, Norfolk, affords a fine instance, 24.4 m (80 ft) high, of the hundreds of surviving mottes, and there are very many others with later stone buildings upon them, as at **Berkhamsted, Herts; Windsor** (p. 574A); and **Lewes, Sussex,** each constructed before *c.* 1125. Particularly early examples are those at **Cambridge** (1068) and **York,** where there are two (1069, 1069). **Dromore Castle, N. Ireland** (*c.* 1180) (p. 573C) has its motte and bailey almost in pristine condition, and is a relic of the Norman overlordship of Ireland after 1171.

Stone 'curtain' walls soon began to replace the perishable timber palisades, and in the twelfth century, particularly the latter half, mottes assumed that form known as the 'shell-keep', because of the empty-looking crowning ring of high walls. The bailey stone walls rode up the mound to join those of the shell-keep. **Windsor Castle** (p. 574A) has a shell-keep of about 1170 (the upper half and the windows are nineteenth century), with an elongated bailey on each side. Other twelfth-century examples are **Carisbrooke, Isle of Wight** (*c.* 1140–50) (p. 573E); **Launceston,** within which a round keep was built about 1240; **Restormel** (p. 573D); and **Trematon.** The last three are in Cornwall.

The greatest castles of the period had stone 'donjons' (nowadays known as keeps) rather than mottes, and similarly had baileys related to them. The earliest type was the rectangular 'hall-keep', in which the great hall and the private chamber were laid side by side, above a storage floor at ground level; sometimes there was an additional, entrance, floor between the two levels. About 1125 the 'tower-keep' became a frequent variant, the private chamber then being above the hall; and by 1150 practice was turning in favour of the polygonal or circular plan, since the square-angled keep was vulnerable to mining.

The **Tower of London** (*c.* 1086–97) (pp. 574B, 575), a hall-keep, only assumed after several reigns its form as a 'concentric' castle, with successive lines of fortification—a plan probably based on Moslem models. Here, the rectangular keep of three storeys—the upper was divided into two, later on—28 m (92 ft) in height, stands in the centre of an inner bailey, surrounded by a wall with thirteen towers (*c.* 1250), which is, in its turn, enclosed by an outer bailey and wall with eight towers and an encircling moat (*c.* 1280). Other examples, numbering about fifty, include **Colchester** (*c.* 1090), **Corfe, Dorset** (*c.* 1125), and **Castle Rising, Norfolk** (*c.* 1140), also hall-keeps; **Rochester** (1126–39), with wall fireplace and **Hedingham, Essex** (*c.* 1140) (p. 573A), which are tower-keeps; and **Chilham, Kent** (*c.* 1160), **Orford, Suffolk** (1166–72) (p. 573B) and **Conisborough, Yorkshire** (1185–90) (p. 573F) with octagonal or circular plans, each having protruding spurs. Keeps tended to become less magnificent as the strength of the outer defence advanced.

A. Castle Hedingham, Essex:
the keep (c. 1140). See p. 572

B. Orford Castle, Suffolk: the keep
(1166–72). See pp. 572, 674

C. Dromore Castle, N. Ireland
(c. 1180). See p. 572

D. Restormel Castle, Cornwall
(12th cent. and later). See p. 572

E. Carisbrooke Castle, Isle of Wight
(c. 1140–50): aerial view. See pp. 572, 678

F. Conisborough Castle, Yorkshire
(1185–90): the keep. See pp. 572, 674

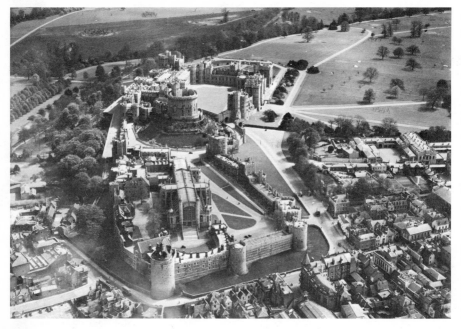

A. Windsor Castle: aerial view from W. See p. 572

B. Tower of London: aerial view (*c*. 1086–97). See p. 572

THE TOWER OF LONDON

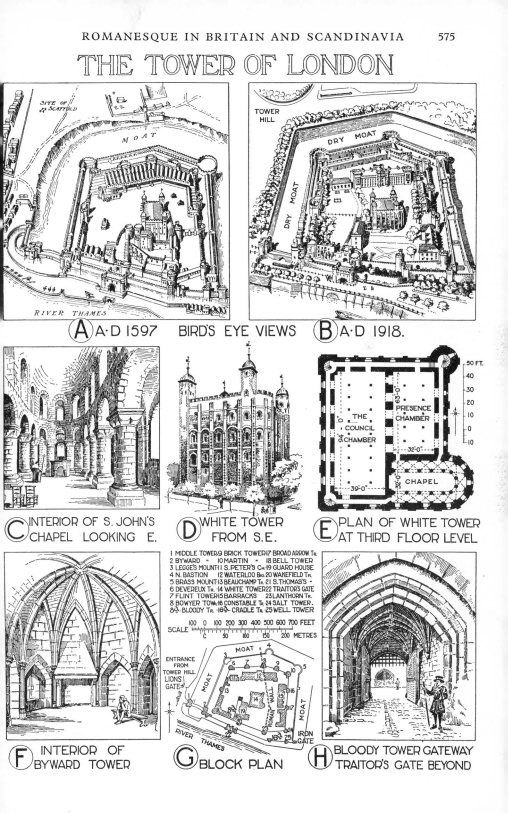

(A) A·D 1597   BIRD'S EYE VIEWS   (B) A·D 1918.

(C) INTERIOR OF S. JOHN'S CHAPEL LOOKING E.

(D) WHITE TOWER FROM S.E.

(E) PLAN OF WHITE TOWER AT THIRD FLOOR LEVEL

(F) INTERIOR OF BYWARD TOWER

(G) BLOCK PLAN

(H) BLOODY TOWER GATEWAY TRAITOR'S GATE BEYOND

1 MIDDLE TOWER·9 BRICK TOWER·17 BROAD ARROW Tr.
2 BYWARD   " 10 MARTIN   " 18 BELL TOWER
3 LEGGE'S MOUNT·11 S. PETER'S Ch.·19 GUARD HOUSE
4 N. BASTION   12 WATERLOO Bks·20 WAKEFIELD Tr.
5 BRASS MOUNT·13 BEAUCHAMP Tr.·21 S. THOMAS'S "
6 DEVEREUX Tr. ·14 WHITE TOWER·22 TRAITOR'S GATE
7 FLINT TOWER·15 BARRACKS   23 LANTHORN Tr.
8 BOWYER TOWr.·16 CONSTABLE Tr.·24 SALT TOWER.
8a. BLOODY Tr. ·16a. CRADLE Tr. 25 WELL TOWER

MEDIÆVAL MANOR HOUSES

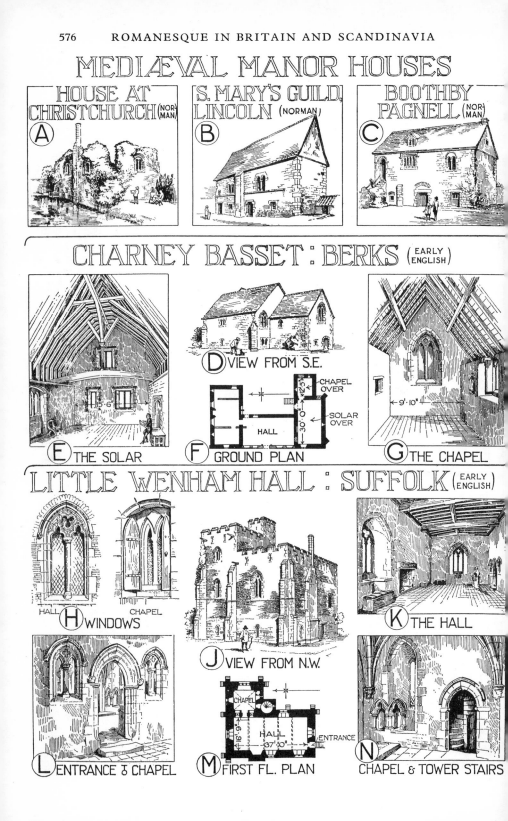

HOUSE AT CHRISTCHURCH (NORMAN)

A

S. MARY'S GUILD, LINCOLN (NORMAN)

B

BOOTHBY PAGNELL (NORMAN)

C

CHARNEY BASSET : BERKS (EARLY ENGLISH)

E THE SOLAR

D VIEW FROM S.E.

F GROUND PLAN

- CHAPEL OVER
- SOLAR OVER
- HALL

G THE CHAPEL

LITTLE WENHAM HALL : SUFFOLK (EARLY ENGLISH)

H WINDOWS — HALL — CHAPEL

J VIEW FROM N.W.

K THE HALL

L ENTRANCE & CHAPEL

M FIRST FL. PLAN — CHAPEL — HALL — ENTRANCE

N CHAPEL & TOWER STAIRS

MANOR HOUSES

One of the earliest types of dwelling in England was the aisled hall, known well before Roman times. Originally the chief form of tribal building, its social status declined temporarily in the Romano-British period, when it might be used in relation to a villa as servants' quarters, as an outbuilding or barn. In Anglo-Saxon times it could be on the one hand a palace or mansion or on the other a husband-man's steading, accommodating corn and fodder in the 'nave', oxen and horses in the 'aisles' and living quarters in the end opposite the entrance. In the Norman period the aisled timber building definitely emerged as a manorial type of residential hall, in each case forming almost the sole accommodation for living, eating and sleeping, privacy not being considered important. Supplementary accommodation, for cooking, stabling and the like was separate and relatively lightly built. The manor was a Norman feudal institution serving for local rural governance, and carrying rights over an extent of land and its tenants. Though the manor house was non-military in purpose, it for long needed defences against forays, disturbances and robbers, and thus was often moated and lightly protected. As time elapsed, standards of convenience and comfort developed, and certain of the original functions of the common hall were dispersed to separate rooms, so that the hall became less important, and building plans more elaborate. Norman castle building led to the use of a second type of manor house, placed on a first floor and thus usually in stone; eventually it merged with the first, during and after the late thirteenth century. Because of the building material, this class has tended to survive more often than the timber ground-floor type. It is also to be noted that there were important differences in methods of structure—particularly of timber roofs —between south-eastern and north-western England, the dividing line being approximately the oolitic limestone belt (see inset map, p. 623), where hybrid types developed, as also in general in the Midlands.

Norman period. Such few examples as remain are mostly in the south-east. They have suffered variously drastic modifications. In the majority, stone-built, the domestic accommodation is raised on a first floor, over an 'undercroft' or storage 'cellar', this type probably reflecting contemporary castle-keep arrangements. **Boothby Pagnell, Lincs.** (p. 576C), **S. Mary's Guild, Lincoln** (p. 576B) and the **Norman House, Christchurch, Hants.** (p. 576A), are instances. On the first floor there might be little more than the one room, the hall, or additionally a smaller private chamber or 'solar', at the opposite end to the entrance. Cooking was probably done outdoors, and supplementary accommodation provided in frail shelters elsewhere in the enclosure. The second type, often wholly in timber, was a 'nave-and-aisles' single-storey srtucture, like a very simple church, all ancillary needs being provided for separately, as before. Roofs in general were of the 'trussed-rafter' kind typical in the south-east, lacking a ridge-piece; in the north-west, there normally were principals spaced down the length of the building, carrying purlins and a heavy ridge.

SCANDINAVIA

RELIGIOUS BUILDINGS

The stave churches represent a most distinctive indigenous architectural pheno-menon of the early Middle Ages in Scandinavia. They were probably most common in Norway, but there are important examples in Sweden and Denmark.

Sancta Maria Minor, Lund (*c.* 1020), now in Sweden, is probably the earliest example of the timber stave churches. Of the simplest type, it is nearly basilican in plan form, having two cells, with the outer palisade walls constructed of halved and splined logs very similar to those at Greenstead in Essex (p. 554).

The **Holtålen** stave church from Gauldal, now preserved in the Folk Museum at Trondheim, is the most typical of the numerous and persistent type of small church. Of late eleventh century date, it has a two-cell plan and stout timber columns at the corners framed into sills, with head beams and a laterally-trussed steeply-pitched roof. In this case the palisade walls are tongued and grooved.

Later examples, exemplified by the group of churches at **Sogne, near Bergen,** have an internal timber colonnade and basilican section. The most celebrated of these is that at **Borgund** (c. 1150) (pp. 579A, 581C), which illustrates the full development of the structural design of the stave church. The chancel has an eastern apse of later date, and the upper gables are embellished with carved dragons' heads, reminiscent of the figureheads of pagan times. Internal decoration is limited to carved heads as capitals to the main columns and foliated carvings of the bracing timbers above the level of the aisled walls. Another of this group, at **Urnes** at the head of the Sogne Fjord (p. 579D), exemplifies the vigorous Celtic character of carved decoration most usually applied in wood carving of the west front, and particularly the west entrance doorway. Although dating from the first half of the twelfth century, it has a decorative style representative of a tradition which flourished one or two generations later, when the original Norse motifs were being modified by the imposition of essentially Christian art forms. Here the influence of the traditions of the Celtic rune-stones and crosses is clearly apparent. A later example from **Hyllestad Church in Setesdalen,** of about 1200 (p. 579C), involves both vine coils and human figures in an allegorical composition of pagan origin, and while much of the detail is archaic, the vigour of the craft tradition was clearly maintained.

Stone-built church architecture in Scandinavia, particularly after the middle of the twelfth century, was most profoundly influenced by Norman and Anglo-Norman Benedictine fashion. Earlier examples, however, such as **Husaby in Skaraborg** (p. 579B), while reflecting some of the Carolingian characteristics of this tradition, such as the axial western tower (c. 1057) and eastern apse, also adopted some of the Anglo-Saxon features of the ninth and tenth centuries, such as mid-wall shafts in window openings.

S. Peter at Sigtuna, on Lake Mälar (p. 581B), probably dating from the end of the eleventh century, although largely ruined has windows with mid-wall shafts, and its plan reveals a design based upon axial towers at both crossing and the west end, a two-aisled nave formed by a central colonnade, and abbreviated but purely Norman Benedictine eastern and transept apses.

Some of the earliest twelfth-century examples are those comprising the group on **Bornholm island,** of which that at **Österlar** is representative (p. 580A). They have much in common with the central planning of the Templars' churches, though usually with a central vault column instead of a ring arcade, and probably derive from the same Jerusalem prototype.

The cathedral churches at **Ribe** and **Viborg, in Jutland,** show in their designs of 1130 and 1140 strong influence of Lombardy through Germany, in wall arcading and pilaster strips. **Ribe** has cross-vaulted aisles, but no high vault seems to have been originally intended, while there is an unusual foreign intrusion of a dome on pendentives at the crossing which can have been modelled only upon those of the Périgord churches (pp. 494, 498A) of slightly earlier date. The south-western tower is of much later date, but is furnished with a fine Rhenish helm.

Lund Cathedral (pp. 580B, C, 581A), then in Denmark, now in Sweden, was built

A. Borgund Church, Sogne Fjord, Norway (*c.* 1150). See p. 578

B. Husaby Church, Skaraborg, Sweden (11th and 12th cent.). See p. 578

C. Hyllestad Church, Setesdalen, Norway (*c.* 1200): detail of doorway. See p. 578

D. Urnes Church, Sogne Fjord, Norway (early 12th cent.): detail of doorway. See p. 578

A. Österlar Church, Bornholm island, Denmark (12th cent.). See p. 578

B. Lund Cathedral, Sweden (begun
c. 1103): west front. See p. 578

C. Lund Cathedral, Sweden:
detail of doorway

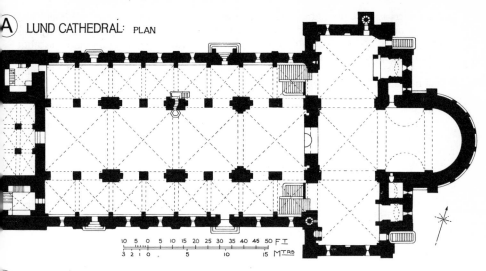

A) LUND CATHEDRAL: PLAN

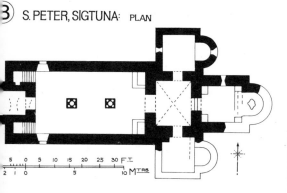

B) S. PETER, SIGTUNA: PLAN

D) HOUSE: TYNNELSÖ:
PLAN AND SECTION

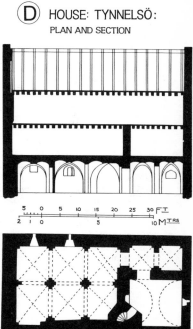

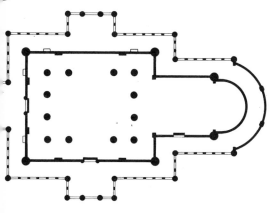

C) BORGUND CHURCH: PLAN

after 1103 to an enlarged design by Donatus, probably a Lombard architect. The plan is organized on a double-bay system, possibly modelled upon that of Speyer (p. 514C, D), and incorporates a western tribune and towers begun about 1150 but completed in Lombardic style in a much more recent restoration. The arcaded eastern apse is strongly Lombardic and probably earlier than comparable Rhineland examples (pp. 512A, 513B) of the same influence. Richly decorated capitals, arches and tympana reflect a continuing Nordic tradition increasingly responsive to southern inspiration, sometimes of classical origin.

The **Cathedral of S. Swithin at Stavanger,** in Norway (c. 1130), has massive cylindrical piers in the nave like those of Durham, but without a vault and with small clear-storey windows pierced in the wall over the arcade piers instead of the crowns of the bold arches themselves.

The **Cathedral of S. Magnus, Kirkwall,** in the Orkneys, a little later than Stavanger, is part of the Norwegian Romanesque succession, but with a full triforium over an arcade in both nave and choir supported again by cylindrical columns, and with square chapels on the eastern side of the transept.

SECULAR BUILDINGS

Early mediaeval minor domestic architecture in Scandinavia generally conformed to the strong tradition of timber construction, and little original work survives. The traditional forms themselves are fairly readily discerned, and the constructional techniques were apparently similar in many respects. Stone-built dwellings followed the continental custom, and must have had much in common with the Norman manor house in England. An example at **Tynnelsö** (p. 581D) may be compared with those at Lincoln and Boothby Pagnell (p. 576B, C). The lower storey is a cross-vaulted undercroft probably used for storage and occasional accommodation of livestock, with a hall and chamber at first-floor level. In Sweden this form of dwelling was more ambitious than in the English examples; at Tynneslö a ceremonial hall was superimposed at second floor. In another case, at **Torpa in Västergötland,** such a house has two upper floors and a base storey, and begins to assume the scale and form of a tower keep.

BIBLIOGRAPHY

ABRAHAMSON, HELGE. *Building in Norway.* Oslo, 1959.
ADDY, S. O. *The Evolution of the English House.* London, 1933.
ALNAES, E., and others. *Norwegian Architecture through the Ages.* Oslo, 1950.
BATSFORD, H., and FRY, C. *Cathedrals of England.* London, 1936.
BOASE, T. S. R. *English Art: 1100–1216.* Oxford, 1953.
BRAUN, H. *Introduction to English Mediaeval Architecture.* 2nd ed. London, 1968.
—. *The English Castle.* 3rd ed. London, 1947–8.
BROWN, E. A. *Norman Architecture in England and France.* London, 1919.
BROWN, G. B. *The Arts in Early England.* Vol. 2. London, 1903.
BROWN, R. A. *English Mediaeval Castles.* London, 1954.
BUGGE, A. *Norske Stavkirke.* Oslo, 1953.
BUTLER, R. M. 'Irish Architecture, Ancient and Medieval', *Journal R.I.B.A.,* 3rd series, no. 38, 1931, pp. 623ff.
CHAMPNEYS, A. C. *Irish Ecclesiastical Architecture.* London, 1910.
CLAPHAM, A. W. *Romanesque Architecture in England.* London, 1950.
—. *English Romanesque Architecture before the Conquest.* Oxford, 1930.
—. *English Romanesque Architecture after the Conquest.* Oxford, 1934.
COX, J. C. *Parish Churches of England.* London, 1937 and other editions.
—. *English Church Fittings.* London, 1933.

CROSSLEY, F. H. *The English Abbey*. London, 1935.
—. *Timber Building in England*. London, 1941.
CRUDEN, S. H. *The Scottish Castle*. London, 1960.
DUNBAR, J. G. *Historic Architecture of Scotland*. London, 1966.
FABER, T. *Dansk Arkitektur*. Copenhagen, 1963.
FISHER, E. A. *Introduction to Anglo-Saxon Architecture and Sculpture*. London, 1959.
FLETCHER, E. G. M., and JACKSON, E. D. C. 'Long-and-Short Work in Saxon Churches', *British Archaeological Association Journal*, 4th series, no. 9, 1944.
GILLESPIE, J. *Details of Scottish Domestic Architecture*. Edinburgh, 1922.
GILYARD-BEER, R. *Abbeys*. London (HMSO), 1958.
GOTCH, J. A. *The Growth of the English House*. London, 1928.
HAHR, A. *Architecture in Sweden*. Stockholm, 1938.
HARVEY, J. H. *English Cathedrals*. 2nd ed. London, 1956.
HENRY, F. *Irish Art*. 3rd ed. London, 1965.
HOWARD, F. E. *Mediaeval Styles of the English Parish Church*. London, 1936.
LANGBERG, H. *Danmarks Bygningskultur*. Vol. i. Copenhagen, 1955.
LEASK, H. G. 'Characteristic Features of Irish Architecture' (from early times to the twelfth century), *North Munster Antiquarian Journal*, 1936.
—. *Irish Castles and Castellated Houses*. Dundalk, 1942.
LINDHOLM, D. *Stave Churches in Norway*. London, 1970.
MACGIBBON, D., and ROSS, T. *Castellated and Domestic Architecture of Scotland*. 5 vols. Edinburgh, 1887.
—. *Ecclesiastic Architecture of Scotland*. 3 vols. Edinburgh, 1896.
MACKENZIE, W. M. *The Mediaeval Castle in Scotland*. 1927.
OLSSON, T., and SILOW, SVEN. *L'Architecture Suédoise*. Stockholm, 1951.
O'NEIL, B. H. ST. J. *Castles* (an introduction to the castles of England and Wales). *London* (HMSO), 1954.
PALMER, R. L. *English Monasteries in the Middle Ages*. London, 1930.
PAULSSON, T. *Scandinavian Architecture*. London, 1958.
QUENNELL, M., and C. H. B. *History of Everyday Things in England, 1066–1499*. London, 1931.
—. *Everyday Life in Anglo-Saxon, Viking and Norman Times*. London, 1926.
RICHMOND, I. A. *Roman Britain*. Harmondsworth, 1955.
ROUSSEL, AAGE. *Norse Building Customs in the Scottish Isles*. Copenhagen and London, 1934.
SALZMAN, L. F. *English Life in the Middle Ages*. Oxford, 1927.
SEDDING, E. H. *Norman Architecture in Cornwall*. London, 1909.
STOLL, R. *Architecture and Sculpture in Early Britain* (Celtic, Saxon, Norman). London, 1967.
TAYLOR, H. M., and J. *Anglo-Saxon Architecture*. Cambridge, 1965.
THOMPSON, A. H. *Military Architecture in England*. London, 1912.
TIPPING, H. A. *English Homes: Period I. 1066–1485*. London, 1901.
TOY, S. *Castles of Great Britain*. 2nd ed. London, 1954.
VRIEM, HALVOR. *Norsk Trearkitektur*. Oslo, 1947.
WEBB, G. F. *Architecture in Britain in the Middle Ages*. 2nd ed. Harmondsworth, 1965.

NOTRE DAME : PARIS

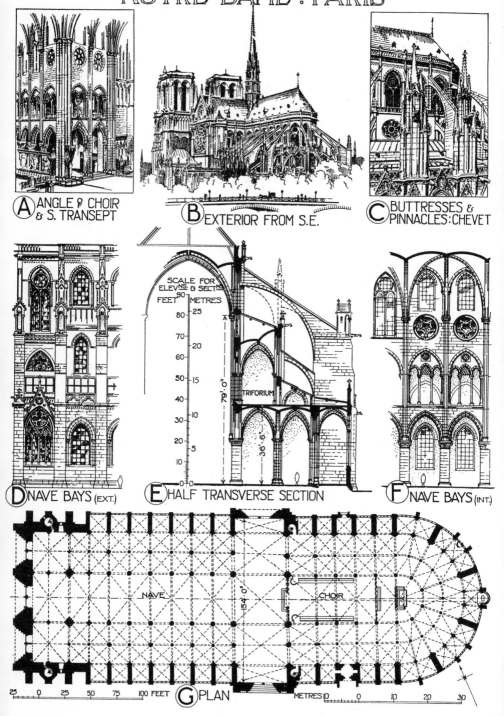

Ⓐ ANGLE & CHOIR & S. TRANSEPT

Ⓑ EXTERIOR FROM S.E.

Ⓒ BUTTRESSES & PINNACLES : CHEVET

Ⓓ NAVE BAYS (EXT.)

Ⓔ HALF TRANSVERSE SECTION

SCALE FOR ELEVNS. & SECTN.
FEET — METRES
90
80 — 25
70 — 20
60
50 — 15
40
30 — 10
20 — 5
10
0 — 0

TRIFORIUM

79'·0"

36'·6"

Ⓕ NAVE BAYS (INT.)

Ⓖ PLAN

NAVE   154'·0"   CHOIR

25 0 25 50 75 100 FEET

METRES 10 0 10 20 30

21

GOTHIC ARCHITECTURE IN FRANCE

Twelfth to sixteenth century

INFLUENCES

GEOGRAPHICAL

France may be considered, from an architectural standpoint, as divided into two parts by the River Loire. With the Franks on the north and the Romance races on the south, architecture was influenced not only by geographical position, but also by racial differences. The buildings of old Roman settlers in Provence and along the fertile Rhône valley not only determined the character of Romanesque in this district (p. 486), but also exercised an influence over the Gothic which followed. In the well-defined valley of the Garonne, which had been a trade-route from Marseilles to Bordeaux for merchants from the East, it is natural that there should be traces of Byzantine traditions, even as late as the Gothic period. Moorish Spain made its contribution too. The north of France, on the other hand, had been exposed to incursions of Norsemen, and this element left an impression on architecture. The 'Ile de France' or Royal Domain—an old district forming a kind of island bounded by the Seine, the Marne and other rivers with Paris as its capital, became, as the headquarters of the kings of France, the district where, after the introduction of the pointed arch by way of Moslem example during the early Crusades, the great French Gothic cathedrals were first built in rapid succession.

GEOLOGICAL

The excellent building stone of France continued as abundant as in the Romanesque period (p. 486), and that found near Caen aided in the development of the northern Gothic style. In the mountainous districts of Auvergne the use of volcanic stone gave a rich chromatic appearance to the buildings; while in the extreme south good local stone helped to continue the Classical traditions handed down through the Romanesque period (p. 488), but are in contrast with the fine marble of Italy.

CLIMATIC

All that it is necessary to add to the note on p. 486 is that the comparatively dull climate of the north permitted, and even invited, the extension of large traceried windows to light the vast interiors.

HISTORICAL, SOCIAL AND RELIGIOUS

Philip Augustus (1180–1223), after declaring King John of England to have forfeited all the fiefs he held of the French crown, proceeded to conquer Normandy and the other English possessions, with the exception of Aquitaine. Philip next defeated the combined English, German and Flemish forces at Bouvines (1214), and it was in his reign that a number of French cathedrals were begun. Louis IX

(S. Louis) (1226–70) further increased the power of the crown, but died at Tunis, when setting out on the ninth or last Crusade. The overthrow of the independent counts of Toulouse by Louis IX, during the religious wars against the Albigenses, obtained for the kingdom of France a triple seaboard on the Mediterranean, the Atlantic and the English Channel, and this consolidation, by which the widely differing regions were gradually absorbed under one king, corresponds with the great cathedral-building epoch of the thirteenth century.

In 1337 the Hundred Years' War with England began, over claims arising from the marriage of Isabella of France with Edward II of England, and in 1346 the Battle of Crécy was won by the English. The French were again defeated by the English at Poitiers in 1356. Henry V of England defeated the French at Agincourt (1415) and entered Paris (1420). During the reign of Charles VII (1422–61) there was a great outburst of national sentiment when Joan of Arc raised the siege of Orléans (1429) and was burnt at Rouen as a witch by the English. In 1453 the English were expelled from the whole of France except Calais. So ended the Hundred Years' War. Charles VII and Louis XI (1461–83) formed a strong standing army, encouraged trade, augmented taxation and worked for the unity of France by annexing Burgundy, Artois and Provence. Charles VIII (1483–98) married Anne of Brittany, and united that province to the French crown. Thus the close of the mediaeval period marks a united France, free from foreign invasion.

Before the establishment of the kingdom of France, when Hugh Capet became 'King of the French' (987), the country had been peopled by races differing in origin who were at war with one another and who perpetuated differences in government, customs and language. The consequent diversity of influences was not without its effect both on Romanesque (p. 487) and on Gothic architecture. The period during which Gothic architecture in France had its growth was marked by all the restlessness that characterizes the style, which is instinct with the intellectual and spiritual aspirations of that age. The feudal system, though it had obvious military and government advantages, was the root from which sprang the tyranny of the lords over the common people as well as the revolt of the same lords against the kingly power. When kings were strong, the nobles were kept in check and the people prospered, and thus kings and traders naturally fostered the towns against the nobles. The twelfth century was remarkable for the continuous struggle of these urban communes to assert their freedom. During the reign of Philip IV (Le Bel) (1285–1314) the Parlement de Paris became the principal law court, and the constitutional power of the central authority grew at the expense of feudal and ecclesiastical powers. The Black Death (1347–49) swept off a large part of the population and inevitably retarded progress in architecture, yet the richness of the soil still continued to supply the prosperity which, on the secular side, built the world-famous châteaux of France and the hôtels de ville of the manufacturing towns, while on the ecclesiastical side a powerful and religious laity erected that wonderful series of cathedrals which are at once the marvel and the glory of France.

The religious zeal of the twelfth and thirteenth centuries, when Christianity was united against the Moslems, was especially manifested in France in the Third Crusade (1189) under Philip Augustus, and the Eighth and Ninth Crusades (1249, 1270) under S. Louis, and was marked by the erection of many grand cathedrals which were the work of the laity and the free communes, in contrast with the monastic church-building of the Romanesque period, such as that of Abbé Suger, minister of Louis VII (1137–80). The clergy, as a corporate body, had reached the summit of their power, largely due to their championship of justice and their adhesion to the royal cause. The papacy, in spite of vicissitudes, was undoubtedly powerful in France during the seventy years (1307–77) of the residence of the

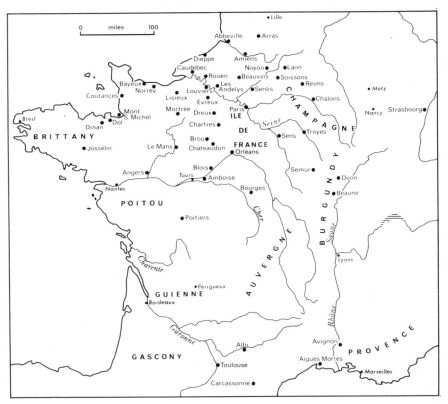

France in the fourteenth century

Popes in their fortress-palace at Avignon. The religious spirit of the age found an outlet in the inauguration of cults of special saints in different localities, and this brought fame to certain shrines which thus acquired wealth and importance as pilgrimage centres, this being reflected in the beautiful architecture and decoration of the churches. The active zeal with which urban populations set about building cathedrals produced almost miraculously rapid results, and with this outburst of building activity transformed the face of France. A crusade against the heretical Albigenses of Albi, Toulouse and Carcassonne was preached by the Cistercians in 1204, and relentless war was waged during the thirteenth century, under papal orders, by the king of France and the nobles of the north against the south, and ended in the destruction of the famous culture of Provence, the humiliation of the princes of the south, and the ultimate extermination of the heresy.

ARCHITECTURAL CHARACTER

The Gothic style, 'l'architecture ogivale' (as it is still called by French traditional-ists), originated in the royal domain of the Ile de France. That much, if little else, is clear. Indeed it is a curious fact that this region, centred upon Paris and now comprising the departments of Aisne, Oise, Seine, Seine-et-Oise, Seine-et-Marne and part of Somme, which is singularly rich in Gothic survivals, can offer little evidence of Romanesque precedents or traditional developments leading to such radical change. Structurally, the point of departure of Gothic architecture is 'la voûte sur croisée d'ogives', a vaulting framework of intersecting stone pointed-arch ribs, which support thin stone panels. The ribs were constructed as permanent 'formwork' and the thin stone panels laid upon them would have been temporarily supported by a movable centre. The vaulting of oblong compartments often produced difficulties, and the semicircular Romanesque arch was for some time retained for the diagonal or longer spans. The earliest known pointed-arch vaults are those above the ambulatory at Morienval, Oise (c. 1120), but the Abbé Suger is generally given credit for introducing the 'Ogival' system, when he applied it to the choir roof of the Benedictine Abbey of S. Denis, on the outskirts of Paris (1144) (p. 499). Certainly the rebuilding of S. Denis inspired the subsequent Gothic 'boom'. The license which Gothic masons allowed themselves in the treatment and disposition of ribs, with which they spun an intricate web of many strands, makes the evolution of Gothic vaulting a most fascinating study. The vault pressures operated both downwards by the weight of the stone, through the action of the law of gravitation, and outwards by the force of the arch voussoirs; both pressures were collected by the meeting of the ribs at the angles of vaulting compartments, and the resultant oblique pressure was then counteracted and transmitted to the ground by buttresses and flying buttresses weighted by pinnacles (pp. 589, 600E, 604D). The weight of the roof, transmitted by the nave arcades, also played its part in directing thrusts to earth.

The Gothic system of buttresses also carried a further implication. Walls were now less necessary as supports and this release of the wall from its age-old load-bearing function no doubt contributed to the invention of coloured (stained) glass, used henceforth to adorn window-walls enclosed under pointed vaults originally adopted for constructive reasons. The stonework of traceried windows in churches thus provided a framework for pictures of incidents in Bible history. In France as elsewhere the storms, wars and neglect of centuries have destroyed much of the best stained glass. But in the cathedral of Chartres, where seventy-five per cent of the thirteenth-century glass has miraculously survived, it is still possible to sense the majesty of a great church in the Middle Ages, and in that supramundane light of prevailing blue merging into violet gain some impression of the effect which Gothic artists (and, more particularly, their masters) intended to create. In northern and central France, and in north Europe generally, the windows stretched from buttress to buttress, providing full scope for the use of glowing stained glass as the chief interior decoration, and it followed that walls were kept uniformly flat internally, so that the coloured windows might be seen by all.

If by no means universal, the semicircular 'chevet', with its garland of chapels and processional aisle, is a characteristic part of the plan of the apsidal east end of major French Gothic churches, while transepts are less prominent and the height and width of naves tend to be greater than in their British counterparts.

Gothic architecture lasted in France from c. 1150–1550, and is commonly divided into: (1) *Primaire* (twelfth century), sometimes called 'à lancettes', a period distinguished by pointed arches and geometric traceried windows, exemplifying the change, if not the processes of transition, from Romanesque, as at Noyon, Sens and Senlis (all c. 1150); (2) *Secondaire* (thirteenth century) or 'Rayonnant', a period characterized by circular windows with wheel tracery, as at Reims, Amiens and Bourges; and (3) *Tertiaire* (fourteenth, fifteenth and part of the sixteenth centuries) or 'Flamboyant', from the flame-like window tracery, as at S. Ouen, Rouen; S. Jacques, Dieppe; Albi; Caudebec; and La Trinité, Vendôme (p. 606D).

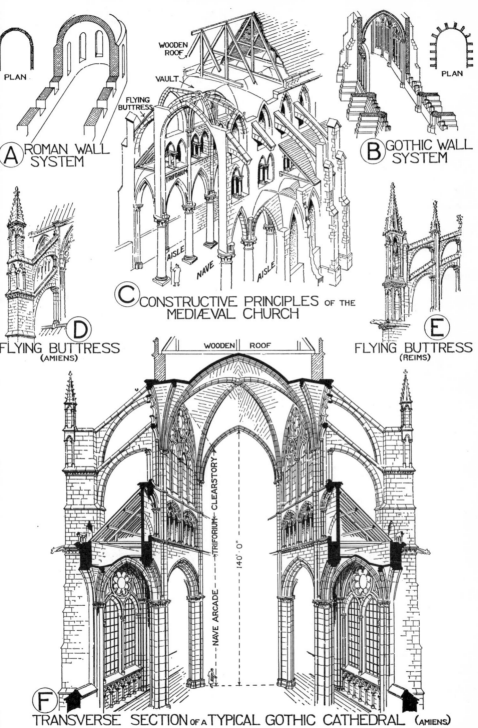

PLAN

WOODEN ROOF

VAULT

FLYING BUTTRESS

A ROMAN WALL SYSTEM

PLAN

B GOTHIC WALL SYSTEM

TRIFORIUM

AISLE

NAVE

AISLE

C CONSTRUCTIVE PRINCIPLES OF THE MEDIÆVAL CHURCH

D FLYING BUTTRESS (AMIENS)

E FLYING BUTTRESS (REIMS)

WOODEN ROOF

TRIFORIUM — CLEARSTORY

NAVE ARCADE

140'. 0"

F TRANSVERSE SECTION OF A TYPICAL GOTHIC CATHEDRAL (AMIENS)

TYPICAL ENGLISH & FRENCH GOTHIC PLANS

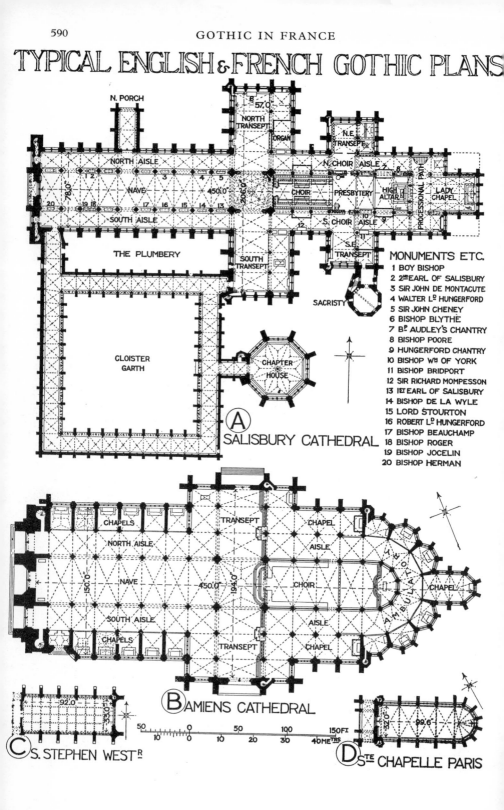

N. PORCH

NORTH TRANSEPT

57.0

ORGAN

N.E. TRANSEPT

NORTH AISLE

N. CHOIR AISLE

NAVE · 450.0

CHOIR

PRESBYTERY

HIGH ALTAR

LADY CHAPEL

PROCESSIONAL PATH

SOUTH AISLE

S. CHOIR AISLE

THE PLUMBERY

SOUTH TRANSEPT

S.E. TRANSEPT

SACRISTY

MONUMENTS ETC.

1　BOY BISHOP
2　2ᴺᴰ EARL OF SALISBURY
3　SIR JOHN DE MONTACUTE
4　WALTER Lᴰ HUNGERFORD
5　SIR JOHN CHENEY
6　BISHOP BLYTHE
7　Bᴾ AUDLEY'S CHANTRY
8　BISHOP POORE
9　HUNGERFORD CHANTRY
10　BISHOP Wᴹ OF YORK
11　BISHOP BRIDPORT
12　SIR RICHARD MOMPESSON
13　1ˢᵀ EARL OF SALISBURY
14　BISHOP DE LA WYLE
15　LORD STOURTON
16　ROBERT Lᴰ HUNGERFORD
17　BISHOP BEAUCHAMP
18　BISHOP ROGER
19　BISHOP JOCELIN
20　BISHOP HERMAN

CLOISTER GARTH

CHAPTER HOUSE

Ⓐ SALISBURY CATHEDRAL

CHAPELS

TRANSEPT

CHAPEL

NORTH AISLE

AISLE

NAVE · 450.0

CHOIR

CHAPEL

SOUTH AISLE

AISLE

CHAPELS

TRANSEPT

CHAPEL

Ⓑ AMIENS CATHEDRAL

Ⓒ S. STEPHEN WESTᴿ

92.0

Ⓓ Sᵀᴱ CHAPELLE PARIS

99.6

50　0　50　100　150 FT
10　0　10　20　30　40 METRS

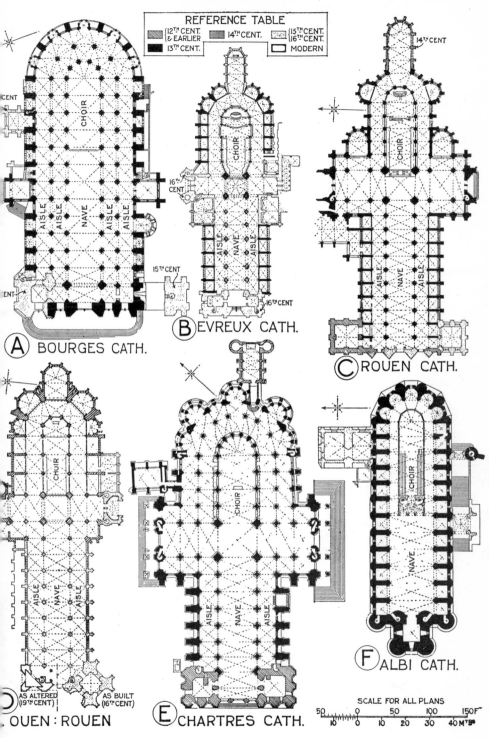

REFERENCE TABLE

{12TH CENT. & EARLIER · 13TH CENT. · 14TH CENT. · {15TH CENT. 16TH CENT. · MODERN

Ⓐ BOURGES CATH.

Ⓑ EVREUX CATH.

Ⓒ ROUEN CATH.

Ⓓ ROUEN: ROUEN

AS ALTERED (19TH CENT) · AS BUILT (16TH CENT)

Ⓔ CHARTRES CATH.

Ⓕ ALBI CATH.

SCALE FOR ALL PLANS

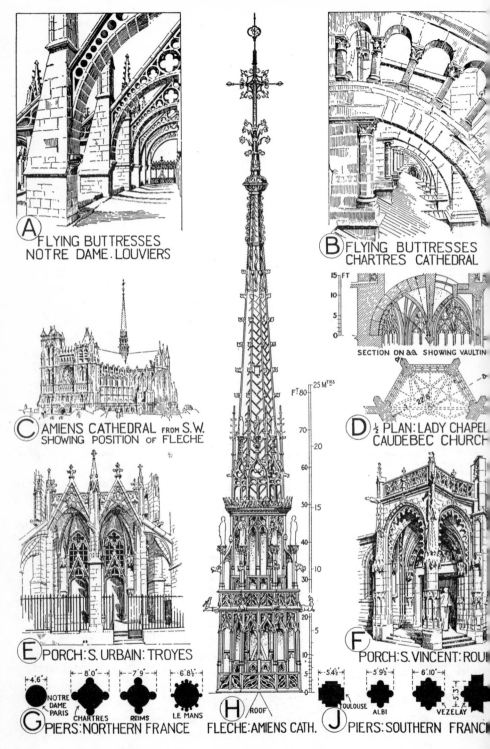

A FLYING BUTTRESSES NOTRE DAME. LOUVIERS

B FLYING BUTTRESSES CHARTRES CATHEDRAL

C AMIENS CATHEDRAL FROM S.W. SHOWING POSITION OF FLECHE

SECTION ON aa SHOWING VAULTIN

D ½ PLAN: LADY CHAPEL CAUDEBEC CHURCH

E PORCH: S. URBAIN: TROYES

F PORCH: S. VINCENT: ROU

G PIERS: NORTHERN FRANCE

NOTRE DAME PARIS

CHARTRES

REIMS

LE MANS

H FLECHE: AMIENS CATH.

ROOF

J PIERS: SOUTHERN FRANC

TOULOUSE

ALBI

VEZELAY

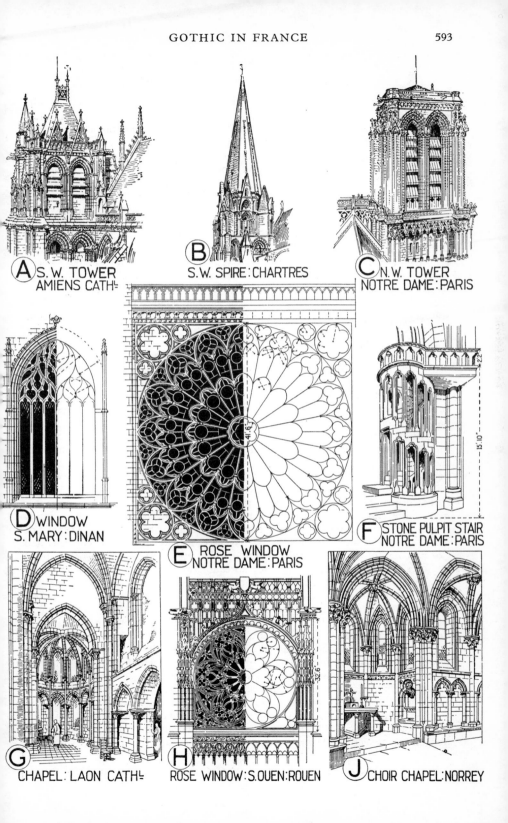

A S. W. TOWER AMIENS CATH.L

B S.W. SPIRE : CHARTRES

C N. W. TOWER NOTRE DAME : PARIS

D WINDOW S. MARY : DINAN

E ROSE WINDOW NOTRE DAME : PARIS

F STONE PULPIT STAIR NOTRE DAME : PARIS

G CHAPEL : LAON CATH.L

H ROSE WINDOW : S. OUEN : ROUEN

J CHOIR CHAPEL : NORREY

EXAMPLES

CATHEDRALS AND CHURCHES

The unique position occupied by cathedrals in the general social and civic life of mediaeval times was nowhere more pronounced than in France. It is important here to remember that the original use and intention of these national monuments was so different from their modern function, which has become purely religious and ecclesiastical, that it is impossible for the reader to appreciate their meaning and value without bearing in mind this wider aspect of old French cathedrals at the time of their building, when there were practically no other public meeting-places. French cathedrals, about one hundred and fifty in number, were erected in the first half of the thirteenth century out of funds provided chiefly by the laity, and since commonly they did not originate as part of monastic establishments they differ considerably from most English cathedrals in purpose and consequently in both plan and design. The situation and surroundings of the cathedrals of France also form a marked contrast with those of England; for French cathedrals were a part of the life of the townspeople and jostled their houses shoulder to shoulder, and were not, as they generally were in England, set apart in a secluded close. Furthermore, these national churches, by means of the painted glass of the interior and the statuary of the exterior, served the citizens as an illustrated Bible when few of them could read.

Notre-Dame, Paris (1163–c. 1250) (pp. 584, 593C, E, F, 595A, B), one of the oldest of French Gothic cathedrals, was begun by Bishop Maurice de Sully. The plan, which either by accident or intention is on a bent axial line, is typical, with wide nave and double aisles, transepts of small projection practically in line with the aisles, and a notable chevet, with double aisles and surrounding chapels (of later date) between the buttresses. The choir, transepts, and all but two bays of the nave were completed by 1196; the latter bays and the main part of the western front by 1220; the upper stage of the west front, containing the rose window, by 1225 and the western towers by about 1250. Considerable modifications then were made to the fully completed building. Between 1250–70 the transepts were extended by the depth of their original buttresses, and chapels afterwards thrown out between the buttresses of the nave, while the former circular upper triforium windows and the clear-storey windows were together replaced by taller clear-storey windows: those nearest the crossing were reinstated by Viollet-le-Duc (p. 584A). The radiating chapels between the buttresses of the choir were constructed from 1296–1325. The impressive but sombre interior has a nave arcade with cylindrical columns and Corinthianesque capitals carrying pointed arches and shafts to support the ribs of the lofty sexpartite vaulting. The wide-spreading western façade (p. 595A) is probably the finest and most characteristic in France, and served as a model for many later churches. It has three deeply recessed portals with successive encircling tiers of statued niches, and the central doorway is divided by a pillar with a statue of Christ, while above and across this stretches a band of statues of the kings of France. This is surmounted by a central wheel window of great beauty, 13 m (42 ft) in diameter, flanked by high coupled windows, over which again a pierced arcaded screen stretches across the façade in front of the nave roof and connecting the two western towers, which have high pointed louvred openings. It is a façade of distinctly harmonious composition and peculiarly suitable to the flat island site from which it rises alone in its impressiveness, without aid from surroundings and position; although it has lost some dignity by the removal of the flight of steps which formed a base. The lateral façades are unimposing, as chapels were later wedged in between the buttresses (1296), which obscure the original design. The

A. West façade   B. Nave looking E.

Notre-Dame, Paris (1163–c. 1250). See p. 594

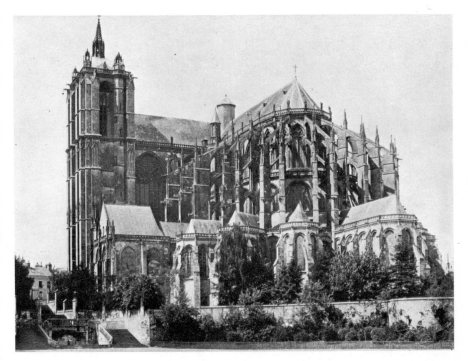

c. Le Mans Cathedral from S.E.
(Nave 12th cent.; S. transept 14th cent.; choir 1217–54.) See p. 596

east end, however, presents a fairylike appearance with slender flying buttresses and chevet chapels which, with the gabled transepts and delicate flèche soaring 90 m (300 ft) above the ground, backed by the western towers, form one of the most striking of cathedral groups (p. 584B).

Laon 'Cathedral' (1160–1225) (p. 598B)—still so-called, though not actually the seat of a bishop since 1789—a Latin cross in plan, is in the early French Gothic style. The nave has an arcade of circular columns with varied Corinthianesque capitals and square abaci to carry pointed arches and shafts to support the ribs of the sexpartite vaulting. The triforium gallery has a high, slightly pointed enclosing arch over two smaller pointed arches resting on a central column; above this and under the clear-storey windows is a second triforium gallery, as at Noyon, thus dividing the nave into four storeys instead of the usual three. The boldly projecting transepts have later two-storeyed chapels, outside the original plan (p. 593G). The sanctuary is unusual in having a square end as in England, instead of apsidal, due to the influence of an English bishop who held the see in the twelfth century. The west façade (p. 598B), imitated later at Reims and certain German cathedrals, is an architectural masterpiece, with three boldly projecting porches, emphasized by gables and turrets and a central rose window surmounted by blind arcading. Two open traceried towers, square below and octagonal above, are adorned with figures of the so-called miraculous oxen, said to have carted the building stone up the rocky rampart on which stands the great cathedral, which reflects in its style the independent spirit of the citizens. If completed, it would have been a still more striking composition, with two western towers, two towers over each transept, and a central tower—a seven-towered building.

Soissons Cathedral (1180–1225), the church of a royal abbey of monks and nuns, is fully-developed early Gothic. The south transept, with clustered columns, narrow pointed arches and shafts which support the vaulting ribs, is unusual in that it is apsidal. The choir, completed in 1212, imitates Chartres, and the interior has the four-storey arrangement with additional triforium.

Le Mans Cathedral is remarkable for an austere nave in the Romanesque style (twelfth century), and for the vast choir (1217–54), which is said to be larger than the whole Cathedral of Soissons. It has nave, double aisles, and a notable chevet, with thirteen chapels of unusual projection (p. 595C).

Bourges Cathedral (1192–1275) (pp. 591A, 597, 598C), ultra-French in type, is remarkable for absence of transepts and shortness in proportion to width, and it has a general resemblance in plan to Notre-Dame, Paris; while the nave has triforium, clear-storey and sexpartite vault, 38 m (125 ft) high (p. 597C). The double aisles, in different heights, are unique in France, resembling Milan Cathedral (pp. 737B, 738D). The exterior presents an imposing appearance owing to its uniform width, unbroken by transeptal projections, while the west façade, 55 m (180 ft) wide, flanked by towers, has five portals approached by a fine flight of steps. The principal portal (p. 597B) has double semicircular-headed doorways, with deeply recessed jambs and trefoil wall arcading, surmounted by richly canopied niches, and those on the right side still contain statues. A wide-spreading pointed arch spans the whole, in six rings, each filled with saints in canopied niches, and the tympanum has an elaborately sculptured Last Judgment—all surmounted by a steep gable enclosing a wheel window and niches. The exterior from the east end reveals a picturesque confusion of innumerable double flying buttresses over the aisles, with pinnacles and other features (p. 597A); while the thirteenth-century stained-glass windows are amongst the finest in France.

Chartres Cathedral (rebuilt 1194–1260) (pp. 591E, 592B, G, 593B, 599, 618D, E, 619A, D, E, G), dominating the town, has an extensive crypt, a remnant of

A. Cathedral from S.E.

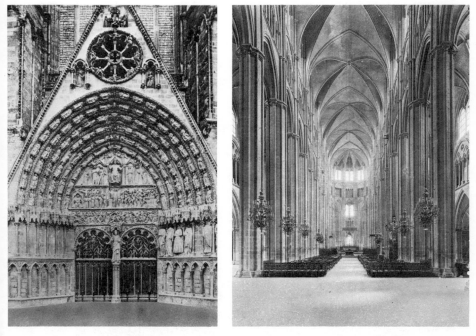

B. West doorway   C. Interior looking E.

Bourges Cathedral (1192–1275). See p. 596

A. Reims Cathedral from W. (1211–   B. Laon Cathedral: west façade
90; towers *c.* 1305–1427). See p. 601   (1160–1225). See p. 596

c. Bourges Cathedral: west façade (1192–1275). See p. 596

A. Cathedral from N.W.

B. Interior looking E.   c. Interior looking W.

Chartres Cathedral (1194–1260; north spire 1507–14). See p. 596

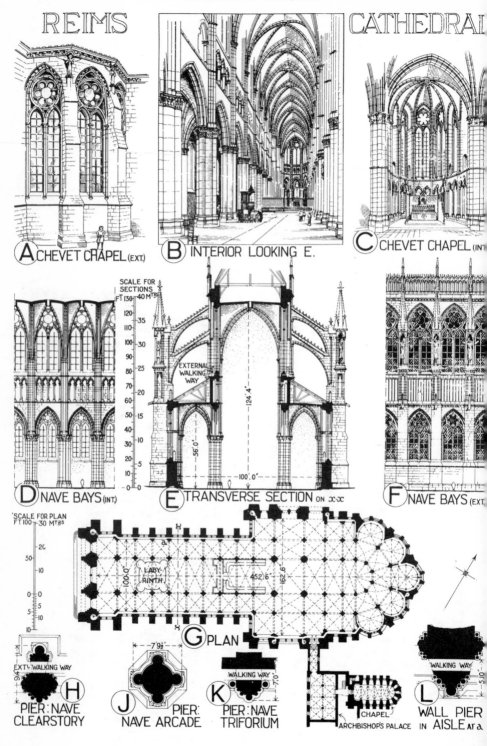

REIMS CATHEDRAL

A CHEVET CHAPEL (EXT.)

B INTERIOR LOOKING E.

C CHEVET CHAPEL (INT.)

D NAVE BAYS (INT.)

SCALE FOR SECTIONS
FT 130 – 40 MTRS
120 – 35
110
100 – 30
90
80 – 25
70 – 20
60
50 – 15
40
30 – 10
20
10 – 5
0 – 0

E TRANSVERSE SECTION ON X-X

EXTERNAL WALKING WAY

124'.4"
56'.0"
100'.0"

F NAVE BAYS (EXT.)

SCALE FOR PLAN
FT 100 – 30 MTRS
20
50
10
0 – 0
5
10
10

LABY-RINTH

100'.0"

452'.6"

162'.6"

G PLAN

EXT'L WALKING WAY

H PIER: NAVE CLEARSTORY

7'.9½"

J PIER: NAVE ARCADE

WALKING WAY
7'.0"

K PIER: NAVE TRIFORIUM

CHAPEL
ARCHBISHOP'S PALACE

WALKING WAY
5'.10"

L WALL PIER IN AISLE AT a.

the Romanesque earlier church, still used for pilgrimages to the shrine of the Vierge Noire. The plan has a short nave, strongly marked aisled transepts, each provided with two towers, which, with the two western and two contemplated eastern towers and a central tower, would have made a magnificent pile of nine important towers. The unusual chevet is built above the crypt of the older church, while the spire (1507–14) of the north tower is one of the most beautiful in Europe, and forms a contrast with the earlier one on the south (1145–70). The interior (p. 599B, c) has a fine nave arcade of circular piers with four shafts, low arcaded triforium surmounted by a clear-storey of two-light pointed windows, all crowned with a quadripartite vault, 37 m (120 ft) high, in oblong bays—probably the first example in which the square bay was abandoned. The cathedral is remarkable, even in France, for the wonderful thirteenth-century stained glass of its one hundred and sixty windows, and for the profusion of fine sculptured figures in the doorways of the west front and in the triple porches of the north (p. 618D, E) and south transepts. The flying buttresses are in three arches one above another, the two lower of which are connected by radiating balusters resembling the spokes of a wheel (p. 592B).

Reims Cathedral (1211–90) (pp. 598A, 600) owes its arrangement to its purpose as the coronation church of the kings of France; for the nave and aisles of the western arm are broadened out in the eastern arm (finished 1241) into a nave and double aisles, so as to include the projecting transepts and thus give space for coronation ceremonies; while the chevet has a ring of five chapels (p. 600A, c, G), similar to Westminster Abbey, the design of which was largely inspired by this building (p. 663D). The names of successive mason-architects are known. The western façade (c. 1255–90), by Bernard de Soissons, more ornate than that of Notre-Dame, Paris, has the usual recessed portals exquisitely carved with some five hundred statues; the tympana are occupied by rose windows instead of sculpture, and each is framed in by five rings of statues and enclosed by richly ornamented gables, of which the central one contains the group of the Coronation of the Virgin (p. 598A). Above the central portal is the magnificent rose window, 12 m (40 ft) in diameter, flanked by high traceried openings; while in the upper stage, instead of the open arcade of Notre-Dame, is a band of tabernacled statues of the kings of France, above which rise the two western towers (1305–1427), 80 m (267 ft) high, with angle turrets and incomplete spires. The interior (p. 600B) gives an impression of vast space, and is grand in the extreme, with its nave arcade of clustered piers (p. 600J) supporting pointed arches, surmounted by shallow triforium, lofty clear-storey (p. 600D), and fine intersecting vault, 42 m (137 ft) above the floor, while in the distance is seen the chevet with its columns. Flying buttresses, over single aisles in the nave (p. 600E) and over double aisles at the east end (p. 589E), show how the thrust of the vault is transmitted by arches to piers weighted by pinnacles and statuary. This great cathedral was much damaged in the 1914–18 war, but has been skilfully restored.

Amiens Cathedral (1220–88) (pp. 589D, F, 590B, 592C, H, 593A, 602, 618H) was begun with the nave, an unusual procedure, designed by Robert de Luzarches and completed in 1236. The choir was next (1236–70), in the charge successively of Thomas and Regnault de Cormont, father and son, and afterwards the transepts. The upper part of the west front and the western towers followed after an interval (1366–1420). The cathedral is typically French, 137 m (450 ft) long and 46 m (150 ft) wide, with transepts only slightly projecting, and a sweeping chevet of seven chapels. The buttress chapels are later additions. The noble interior, spacious in its soaring height, seems to enclose the sky above, and the stone vault, 43 m (140 ft) high, is upheld by cylindrical columns with four attached smaller columns (p. 589F). The great glory of this cathedral—the 'Bible of Amiens'—is the carved

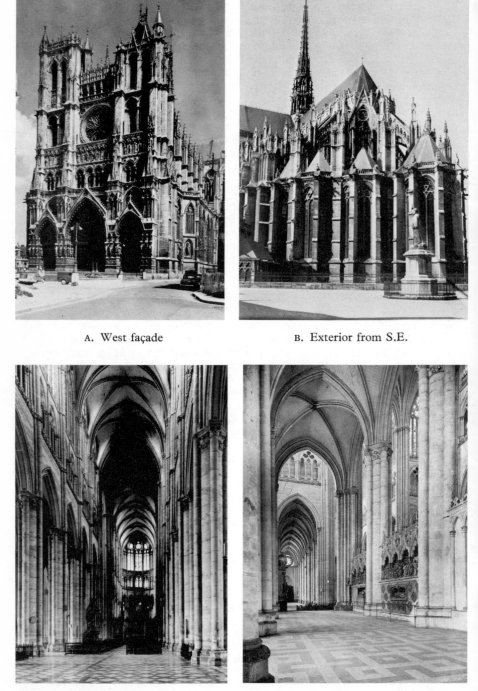

A. West façade

B. Exterior from S.E.

C. Interior looking E.

D. South choir aisle, looking W.

Amiens Cathedral (1220–88). See p. 601

A. Exterior from N.E.   B. East end of upper chapel

La Sainte Chapelle, Paris (1243–8). See p. 605

c. Coutances Cathedral: west
façade (1218–91). See p. 605

D. Bayeux Cathedral from E. (13th–15th
cents.; choir 1230–). See p. 605

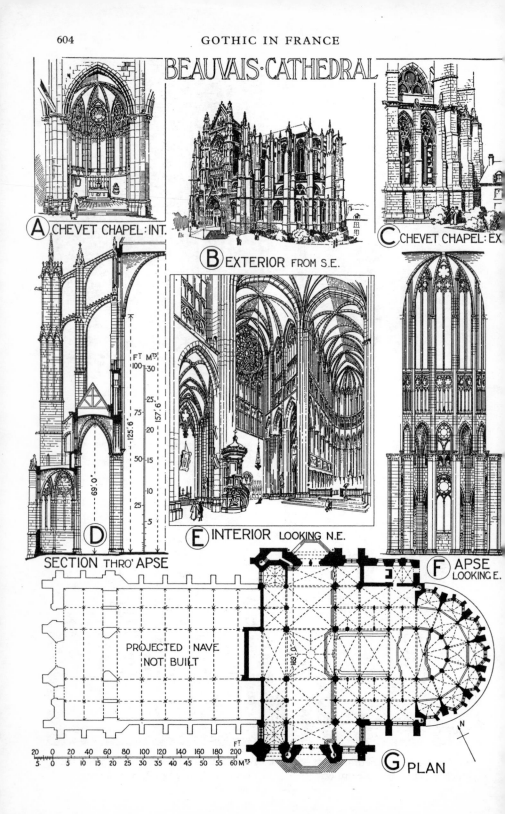

BEAUVAIS·CATHEDRAL

A CHEVET CHAPEL: INT.

B EXTERIOR FROM S.E.

C CHEVET CHAPEL: EX

D SECTION THRO' APSE

E INTERIOR LOOKING N.E.

F APSE LOOKING E.

G PLAN

PROJECTED NAVE NOT BUILT

FT MTS
100 — 30
75 — 25
50 — 20
25 — 15
— 10
— 5

69'.0"
125'.6"
157'.6"

FT
20 0 20 40 60 80 100 120 140 160 180 200
5 0 5 10 15 20 25 30 35 40 45 50 55 60 MTS

woodwork in the choir stalls, which breaks away from studied lines and soars above like the branches of living trees. The western façade is one of the finest in France (p. 602A), and with its serried ranks of statues resmbles Notre-Dame and Reims. The central western doors are separated by one of the noblest of sculptured figures in the world, the 'Beau Dieu d'Amiens'. The ridge of the external wooden roof is over 60 m (200 ft) above the ground. The upper flying buttresses have only one aisle to span (p. 589D). The slender timber flèche (p. 592C, H), rising 55 m (180 ft) above the roof, forms the crowning feature of this beautiful church (p. 602B).

Bayeux Cathedral (thirteenth to fifteenth century) (p. 603D), built on to the remains of a church of c. 1077, had its Romanesque nave transformed in the early thirteenth century, a new choir constructed after 1230 and a central tower added in the fifteenth century. It is remarkable for its twenty-two chapels and immense Romanesque crypt under the sanctuary.

Noyon Cathedral (1145–1228), an early Gothic building combining the German triapsal plan and the French chevet, has a large vaulted triforium.

Coutances Cathedral (1218–91) (p. 603C), on its dominating hill site, is famous for the two western towers and spires, and the beautiful octagonal lantern over the crossing of nave and transepts.

Rouen Cathedral (1202–30 and later) (p. 591C) has a double-storeyed nave arcade and three beautiful towers: the spire of the one over the crossing was rebuilt in cast-iron, 1823–76. The building was seriously war-damaged in 1944.

Evreux Cathedral (1119–1531) (p. 591B), **Troyes Cathedral** (1208–1429) (p. 606A), grand and wide, with five aisles, an ancient choir, chevet and decorated west façade, and **Dol Cathedral** (1204 to sixteenth century), a massive pile with square east end, are other interesting examples. **S. Urbain, Troyes** (1262) (p. 592E), exquisite with triple porches; **S. Pierre, Caen** (1308–1521) (p. 909B) with its bold turreted tower, of which the spire was destroyed in 1944; and **S. Pierre, Lisieux** (1170–1235), raised high on its approaching steps, are some among the number of wonderful buildings which make the church fame of Normandy.

La Sainte Chapelle, Paris (1243–48) (p. 603A, B), built by Pierre de Montreuil, one of the greatest architects of the thirteenth century, with the space between the buttresses occupied by windows, 4.5 m (15 ft) wide and 15.2 m (50 ft) high, is often quoted as a typical Gothic structure. The plan (p. 590D) was in size similar to that of S. Stephen, Westminster (p. 590C). It has a richly vaulted crypt, and such characteristic French features as the apsidal termination and high stone-vaulted roof.

Beauvais Cathedral (1247–1568) (p. 604) was never completed to the west of the choir and transepts (p. 604G), and the site of the proposed nave is partly occupied by the Romanesque church of c. 997 known as the 'Basseœuvre'. The roof fell (1284), and the choir was reconstructed and strengthened by additional piers (1337–47), and in the sixteenth century the transepts were built. There was an open-work spire, 152 m (500 ft) high, over the crossing, which collapsed in 1573, partly because there was no nave to buttress it on the west. The building is of extreme height, 48 m (157 ft 6 ins) to the vault—the loftiest in Europe—and about three and a half times its span, and is perhaps the most daring achievement in Gothic architecture. The structure is held together internally only by a network of iron tie-rods, which suggests that these ambitious builders had attempted more than they could properly achieve, while flying buttresses (p. 604B, D), in three tiers and of immense thickness, take the vault thrust. The polygonal chevet has seven encircling chapels (p. 604A, C), and the rich stained-glass windows (p. 604E) are of the thirteenth, fourteenth and sixteenth centuries. The south transept façade (p. 604B), now denuded of statues, is an ornate design in the Flamboyant style, even

A. Troyes Cathedral: west façade
(1208–1429). See p. 605

B. S. Ouen, Rouen, from S.E.
(1318–1515). See p. 609

C. S. Vulfran, Abbeville
(1488–1539). See p. 609

D. Church of the Trinité, Vendôme
(c. 1500). See p. 588

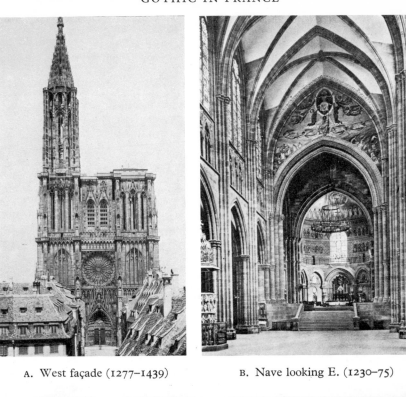

A. West façade (1277–1439) B. Nave looking E. (1230–75)

c. West doorway D. North doorway

Strasbourg Cathedral (*c.* 1230–1365; spire 1439). See p. 609

A. Mont S. Michel from the south. Church; Romanesque nave 1122–35;
Gothic choir 1450–1521. See p. 609

B. Exterior from E.   C. Interior looking W.

Albi Cathedral (1282–1390; S. porch 1520–35). See p. 609

excelling the western fronts of many cathedrals, and the carved wooden doors are masterpieces of Gothic and Renaissance workmanship.

S. Ouen, Rouen (1318–1515) (pp. 591D, 593H, 606B), of which the choir (1318–39) is contemporary with Cologne; **S. Maclou, Rouen** (1432–1500), probably the richest Flamboyant example in France with a fine pentagonal porch (badly damaged, 1944); **S. Jacques, Dieppe** (1350–1440) and **S. Vulfran, Abbeville** (1488–1534) (p. 606C), very severely damaged in 1944, are later examples in the north of France, mostly in the Flamboyant style.

Strasbourg Cathedral (1230–1365) (p. 607A, B, C, D) has a Gothic nave which was added to the Romanesque choir and transepts (1179). The beautiful western façade of 1276–1365 has a recessed portal (p. 607C), richly carved, as is usual in France, surmounted by an open-work gable and tracery in two planes, above which is a rose window, 12.8 m (42 ft) in diameter, flanked with double traceried windows and two western towers, one of which terminates in an open-work octagon and spire, 142 m (466 ft) high, erected 1399–1439. The north doorway (p. 607D) has a crown of triple gables, and pierced parapets with intersecting mouldings. Like many an English cathedral it is the outcome of centuries of work, as one generation succeeded another in adding its part.

In the south of France there are fewer churches of the Middle Ages, partly because of the number erected in the Romanesque period, and they differ from northern churches in plan and design, owing to the proximity and influence of Roman buildings.

S. Sernin, Toulouse (1080–96), a five-aisled Romanesque church (p. 492), has a Gothic tower and spire (p. 493A).

Albi Cathedral (1282–1390) (pp. 591F, 608B, C), a fortress-church, consists of a large impressive vaulted hall, 18 m (59 ft) wide, which is the widest in France, with an apsidal end, a series of flanking chapels separated by internal buttresses, and an unrivalled rood screen of c. 1500. The richly ornate south porch of 1520–35 contrasts vigorously with the sheer mass of the church brickwork.

The **Church of the Cordeliers, Toulouse** (1350), partially destroyed in 1871, was of this type, and has some similarity in plan with King's College Chapel, Cambridge (p. 646). **Angers Cathedral** (1149–1274) and **Poitiers Cathedral** (1162–1379), with its square east end, are notable churches.

FORTIFIED TOWNS

France is rich in many types of secular Gothic buildings. There is a tendency to think that Gothic architecture was confined to churches, but the style was employed for all buildings, whether domestic, military, civil or ecclesiastical, although the purpose naturally influenced the design.

Carcassonne (p. 610A, B) and **Aigues Mortes** are notable thirteenth-century fortified towns. The former has a double wall, of which the inner circuit is partly sixth century; these, with their fifty towers and moat still give an idea of a mediaeval fortress-town, entered through two fortified gateways guarded by machicolations, drawbridge and portcullis.

Avignon (1349–68) (p. 610C), although without its moat, is still encircled by machicolated walls and towers. The town contains the imposing palace with its cliff-like walls (1316–64) (p. 611A), which was the headquarters of the popes from 1309–77. The famous Pont d'Avignon, with its midway chapel (1177–85), was thrown across the river by the *Frères Pontifes*, or guild of bridge-builders, to connect the town with Villeneuve.

Mont S. Michel (thirteenth century and later, restored by Viollet-le-Duc)

A. Carcassonne: entrance to Château with bridge over moat

B. Carcassonne: aerial view of old walled town from W. (13th cent).
Restored by Viollet-le-Duc. See p. 609

Pont d'Avignon

C. Avignon: aerial view from S. showing the Palace of the Popes (1316–64).
See p. 609

A. Avignon: Palace of the Popes
(1316–64). See p. 609

B. House of Jacques Cœur, Bourges:
the courtyard (1442–53). See p. 617

c. Château de Pierrefonds (1390–1400). See p. 613

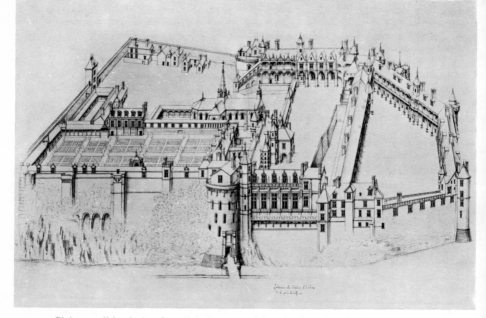

A. Château d'Amboise from N. (1434 and later). Drawing by J. A. du Cerceau in the 16th cent. See p. 613

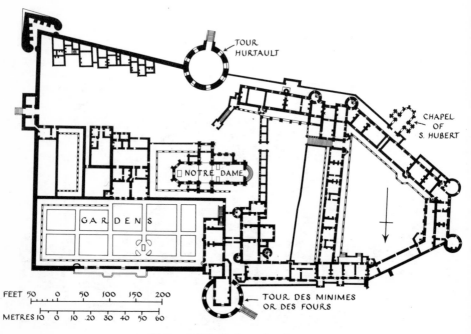

B. Château d'Amboise: plan in 1575

(p. 608A) was a fortified monastery rather than a town, but containing within its walls secular buildings. The main element of the world-famous monastery is the storeyed 'Merveille' (1203–28), with its cloisters and 'Salle des Chevaliers'.

CASTLES

Castles were generally built on mounds above rivers to command valleys and had thick walls and small windows to resist attack. Many castles were adapted to make more convenient residences in the Renaissance period, and there are many such castles along the River Loire.

The **Château Gaillard, Les Andelys** (1196–98), built by Richard Cœur-de-Lion, was a fine castle with a 'donjon', or keep, protected by three lines of outworks and many towers, but little now remains.

The **Château de Pierrefonds** (1390–1400) (p. 611C), restored by Viollet-le-Duc, gives an admirable idea of other castles of this period. It stands on a rocky height above the village, and its cliff-like walls, 6 m (20 ft) thick, rise sheer from the ground, and, like the eight massive round towers, have machicolations and battlemented parapets surrounding an irregular courtyard, while the entrance is guarded by a drawbridge over the moat.

The **Château d'Amboise** (1434 and later) (p. 612A, B), like many other castles is perched above the Loire to command the surrounding valleys, and has early Renaissance additions.

HÔTELS DE VILLE

These are few, as there was little municipal life under the feudal system, and in this France differed from Flanders and Italy. Communal business was probably carried on in the market-place or in churches and cloisters.

The **Hôtel de Ville, Arras** (1510) (p. 615A), has an arcade under a large hall with traceried windows, and a steep roof, containing three storeys of dormer windows; while the giant belfry reached 76 m (250 ft) above the ground; but all has been rebuilt since the Great War of 1914–18.

The **Hôtel de Ville, Bourges** (fifteenth century), is notable for a Flamboyant tower (p. 614C) with tracery, crockets, sculptured figures and windows, while internally the chimney-piece is unusually fine, even for this period (p. 614F).

The **Hôtel de Ville, Dreux** (1502–37) (p. 615C), resembles a square donjon with pyramidal roof, and the **Hôtel de Ville, Compiègne** (early fifteenth century) (p. 615B), is a beautiful example of civic architecture, with mullioned windows, traceried parapet and central tower. It was damaged during the war of 1914–18.

PALAIS DE JUSTICE

These were originally the great halls in which kings and nobles dispensed justice to their vassals, while ecclesiastical courts dealt with matrimonial cases and laws of inheritance; but towns with charters eventually obtained their own magistrates. The **Palais de Justice, Rouen** (1493–1508) (pp. 614B, 616B), severely damaged in 1944, was an exceedingly rich specimen of French municipal architecture and eloquent of the importance of this old city of the Norman kings. The magnificent hall 41 m × 17 m (135 ft × 57 ft) (destroyed), rivalling the Guildhall, London, in size, occupied one side of the building, and had a fine pointed timber roof; while from the centre of the group rose the tower with traceried windows. The late Gothic façades were crowned with a steep roof and dormer windows.

A LE CHATEAU D'O MORTREE

B PALAIS DE JUSTICE: ROUEN

C HOTEL DE VILLE: BOURGES

D TIMBER HOUSE CAEN

E LOUIS XII STAIR: CHAT. DE BLOIS

F STONE CHIMNEY-PIEC HOTEL DE VILLE: BOURGE

G TIMBER HOUSE: BEAUVAIS

H HOTEL DE CLUNY: PARIS

J HALF-TIMBER HOUSE: S.L

A. Hôtel de Ville, Arras (1510; rebuilt
after 1919). See p. 613

B. Hôtel de Ville, Compiègne
(15th cent.). See p. 613

c. Hôtel de Ville, Dreux
(1502–37). See p. 613

D. Hôtel de Cluny, Paris
(1485–98). See p. 617

A. Château de Josselin, Brittany (16th cent.). See p. 617

B. Palais de Justice, Rouen (1493–1508). See p. 613

HOSPITALS

The 'Maisons-Dieu' were attached to monasteries or provided in cities for the treatment of the sick, and for distribution of alms to travellers and pilgrims. The **Hôtel Dieu, Beaune** (1443–51), has old timber galleries round a courtyard for open-air treatment, thus forecasting modern sanatoria. The gabled roofs, in coloured tiles, have dormer windows with barge-boards and tall finials, and a stair-turret is set in the angle of the court.

COUNTRY HOUSES

On the introduction of gunpowder, and with the development of the new social order in the fifteenth century, country houses took the place of fortified castles, though they were still called 'châteaux'. The **Château d'O, Mortrée** (p. 614A), and the **Château de Châteaudun** (rebuilt 1441) are both stately mansions rather than castles. The **Château de Blois** (east wing) (1498–1504) has a thirteenth-century Salle des Etats and gateway to the court, around which later buildings were added (p. 878). The Gothic spiral staircase of Louis XII (p. 614E) was probably the model for the marvellous staircase of Francis I of the early Renaissance period (p. 879A, C). The **Château de Josselin, Brittany** (p. 616A), although dating from the twelfth century, was rebuilt in the early sixteenth century, and with its circular towers, ogee door-heads, mullioned windows, traceried parapet, and steep roof with dormer windows, is typical of many others scattered throughout France.

TOWN HOUSES

The 'maisons nobles' began to rise in the fifteenth century when French nobles ceased to be feudal lords in fortified castles, and erected houses, known to this day as 'hôtels', planned, as in the country, round a court and with an elaborate façade to the street. The **House of Jacques Cœur, Bourges** (1442–53) (p. 611B), is undoubtedly among the finest mediaeval town residences in France. It was built by a merchant prince, partly on the town ramparts, round a central court and has seven turret stairs. The **Hôtel de Bourgtheroulde, Rouen** (c. 1475) is a good example of this type of house, with its enclosed court surrounded by façades somewhat resembling the Palais de Justice in the same city. Juxtaposed in the court is an early Renaissance building of 1501–37, on which the lower bas-relief panels depict the meeting of Francis I and Henry VIII of England on the 'Field of the Cloth of Gold' in 1520. The façades were severely damaged in 1944. The **Hôtel Chambellan, Dijon** (fifteenth century), was one of the great town houses of this period. The central court contains an angle turret stair with newel branching into a richly carved head; while the street façade has some fine figures carved in wood. The **Hôtel de Cluny, Paris** (1485–98) (p. 615D)—now a museum—retains its mediaeval character, and is a fine specimen of late Gothic. The chapel (p. 614H) stands above an arcade which supports on its central pier an oriel window of pleasing proportions with Flamboyant tracery, crockets and finials. In the **Hôtel de Sens, Paris** (1485), the outside walls are pierced with large, symmetrically-placed windows, indicating a marked change in architectural manners and, perhaps, anticipating a more stable urban society.

Smaller domestic buildings still exist, as in Cluny, where doors and windows are of the later Romanesque type; while in S. Lô (p. 614J), Lisieux, Caen (p. 614D), Chartres, Beauvais (p. 614G), and Rouen there are timber houses with carved barge-boards and overhanging storeys; but a large number have succumbed to the ravages of time and fire. They are not generally earlier than the fifteenth century.

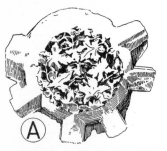

GARGOYLE : ILE DE FRANCE

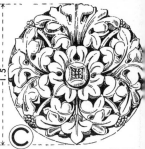

A VAULTING BOSS : DIJON MUS^M   **B** GARGOYLE : S. CHAPELLE : PARIS   **C** BOSS : MONT. S. MICHEL

D NORTH PORCH : CHARTRES CATHEDRAL   **E** NORTH PORCH : CHARTRES FROM N. W

F BASES S. MICHAEL'S CHAPEL. MONTREALE

G FONT URCEL NR. LAON

H DIAPER ON PEDESTAL AMIENS CATHEDRAL

DETAIL OF CROCKET AT a

J CROCKET CAPITAL : SEMUR

A CAPITAL. N. PORCH CHARTRES CATHEDRAL

B JAMB: W. DOORWAY: GRAND ANDELY

PLAN

8'·10½"

C CAPITAL. NOTRE DAME CHALONS·SUR·MARNE

2'3"

SECTION THROUGH PILASTER

SECTION THROUGH PILASTER

SCALE FT.10
9
8
7
6
5
4
3
2
1
0
3 MTRS
2
1
0

D TYMPANUM LEFT DOORWAY OF WEST PORTAL: CHARTRES

14'·8"

14'·8"

E PILASTER S. PORCH: CHARTRES

F TOMB OF PHILIBERT LE BEAU: BROU

G PILASTER S. PORCH: CHARTRES

BIBLIOGRAPHY

AUBERT, M. *L'architecture française à l'époque gothique*. Paris, 1943.

AUBERT, M., and GOUBERT, S. *Cathédrales et trésors gothiques en France*. Paris, 1958.

BASDEVANT, D. *L'architecture française*. Paris, 1971.

BAUDOT, A. DE, and PERRAULT-DABOT, A. *Les cathédrales de France*. 2 vols. Paris, 1905–7.

BONY, J. *Les cathédrales gothiques en France du nord*. Paris, 1951.

BOWIE, T. (Ed.) *The sketchbook of Villard de Honnecourt*. Bloomington, Indiana, 1959 and 1968. Several other illustrated commentaries on this album of annotated drawings by a thirteenth-century architect have been published in French, English and German.

BRANNER, R. *Gothic Architecture*. New York and London, 1961.

—. *Burgundian Gothic Architecture*. London, 1960.

CALI, F., and MOLINIER, S. *L'ordre ogival*. Paris, 1963.

COLOMBIER, P. DU. *Les chantiers des cathédrales*. Paris, 1953.

CROSBY, S. M. *L'abbaye royale de Saint-Denis*. Paris, 1953.

FITCHEN, J. *The Construction of Gothic Cathedrals*. Oxford, 1961.

FOCILLON, H. *Art d'Occident, le Moyen Age roman et gothique*. Paris, 1938 and 1965.

FRANKL, P. *Gothic Architecture*. Harmondsworth and Baltimore, 1962.

GRODECKI, L. *Suger et l'architecture monastique* . . . Paris, 1948.

LASTEYRIE, P. DE. *Histoire de l'architecture religieuse en France à l'époque gothique*. Paris, 1926.

LAVEDAN, P. *L'architecture française*. Paris, 1944; English edition: Harmondsworth, 1956.

LEFRANÇOIS-PILLION, L. *Maîtres d'oeuvre et tailleurs de pierres des cathédrales*. Paris, 1949.

MÂLE, E. *L'art religieux au XIIe et au XIIIe siècles en France*. 2 vols. Paris, 1910 and 1922; English editions of XIII century volume: London, 1913 and 1961, New York, 1958.

SALET, F. *L'art gothique*. Paris, 1963.

SIMSON, O. VON. *The Gothic Cathedral* . . . London, 1956.

VIOLLET-LE-DUC, E. *Dictionnaire raisonné de l'architecture française du XIe au XVIe siècles*. Paris, 1854–68.

WEST, G. H. *Gothic Architecture in England and France*. London, 1927.

WORRINGER, W. *Form in Gothic*. London, 1957.

22

GOTHIC ARCHITECTURE IN THE BRITISH ISLES

Twelfth to sixteenth century

INFLUENCES

GEOGRAPHICAL

The British Isles, while on the outskirts of civilization, were opposite a rich and populous continent, and their history is part of that of Mediaeval Europe as a whole. In the Middle Ages Wales, Ireland and Scotland, although they periodically enjoyed a precarious political independence from England, are in the preliminary sections of the chapter considered together, for it is generally true that in all three the main lines of development corresponded with those in England: examples, however, are listed separately at the end of the chapter. In Ireland the vigorous native Celtic tradition had a marked effect on later mediaeval work, while in Scotland recurrent political contacts with France influenced style, especially in the mid-fifteenth century.

The climatic conditions have been described in Chapter 20, while the influence of geological formation is discussed under the head 'Regional Styles' on p. 637.

HISTORICAL, SOCIAL AND RELIGIOUS

A study of Gothic architecture in Britain must take into account the preceding work of the Normans in the eleventh and twelfth centuries; indeed, the transition from Romanesque to Gothic design is easy to observe in examples, but difficult to define. The rebuilding of the choir of Canterbury Cathedral (c. 1174), by the French mason William of Sens, may be conveniently taken as the start of separate English development, although the raising of the high ribbed vaults at Durham Cathedral in 1093 had been an event of greater constructional innovation. At first English design was almost totally dependent on ideas borrowed from the Continent; later, however, there were several significant national contributions to the art of Gothic Europe as a whole. The development of stone vaulting and roofing in timber are both well known, but there were modest examples in the applied arts too—devotional images in alabaster, the celebrated English embroideries, illuminated books and a splendid fifteenth-century output of painted glass.

A table of some of the principal events occurring between the accession of Henry II (1154) and the death of Henry VIII in 1547, which can be shown to have influenced the development of Gothic architecture in the British Isles, follows.

1151. Henry II (as he became) married Eleanor of Aquitaine, divorced wife of Louis VII of France, a union which had far-reaching effects since Henry then became possessed of more than half of France. Subsequent rivalry led to the Hundred Years' War (1337–1453), but the English victories of Crécy, Poitiers and Agincourt were followed by the French re-conquests of the mid-fifteenth century, which reduced the English possesions to Calais.

c. 1174. Canterbury Cathedral choir was rebuilt by William of Sens.

1189–99. Continued participation in the Crusades, especially during the reign of Richard I ('Coeur-de-Lion'), involved Britain in international military affairs and influenced the development of fortifications.

1221. The Dominicans (Black Friars) came to England, followed in 1224 by the Franciscans (Grey Friars) and in 1240 by the Carmelites (White Friars). All built spacious new churches for preaching.

1265. Simon de Montfort assembled the first Parliament to include both burgesses from the towns and Knights of the shire.

1272–1307. The pacification of Wales by Edward I led to spectacular improvements in the design of border castles.

1314. After the Battle of Bannockburn the Scots achieved a precarious measure of independence from England, not extinguished until the Union of the Crowns under James I in 1604.

1326. By Acts of Parliament the importation of foreign cloths was severely restricted; continental workers were welcomed as settlers, especially in East Anglia, where the textile trade greatly prospered.

1329–37. The reconstruction of the south transept of Gloucester Abbey, followed by the enlargement of the choir to house the tomb of Edward II, murdered at Berkeley in 1327, gave impetus to the development of the late Gothic style.

1330. S. Stephen's Chapel in the Palace of Westminster was rebuilt by the mason William of Ramsey, in a style adopted from that of the French court.

1347–81. The rise of the yeoman class and the free labourer after the Black Death (1348–9), which had swept away one-third of the population, helped to promote social unrest, culminating in the Peasants' Revolt of 1381. Towns continued to increase in importance, and within them the wealthy merchant oligarchies dominated local government.

c. 1376. William Wycliffe (1320–84) criticised the wealth and worldliness of the clergy, and rejected the Papalist dogma of the Mass, while his followers translated the Bible into English.

c. 1450–85. Dynastic conflict between rival Lancastrian and Yorkist supporters, known as the Wars of the Roses, disrupted orderly government until the victory of Bosworth Field put the first Tudor king, Henry VII, on the throne, but the development of social and civil institutions continued. The growth in home trade and foreign commerce was accompanied by the change from villeinage to free labour and the rising importance of the Guilds which controlled craftsmanship. Industrial prosperity (centred mainly in East Anglia and the West Country) helped to create a new and prosperous middle class, and townsmen increasingly controlled their own churches, schools and charities. Lay literacy developed more rapidly with the general adoption of printing, after its introduction into England by Caxton in 1477, and numerous schools were founded, such as Winchester (1382) and Eton (1440). The writings of Colet, More and other humanists followed the Italian thinkers and broke away from mediaeval philosophy and theology. Their work coincided with the last brilliant flowering of Gothic art in England, enriched by the decorative exuberance of the Renaissance.

1515–30. Cardinal Wolsey, the Lord Chancellor, built palaces, patronized art and introduced foreign craftsmen into England. In 1520 Henry VIII and his courtiers visited the French king, Francis I, on the 'Field of the Cloth of Gold'.

1536–40. The monasteries, nunneries and friaries were dissolved by Henry VIII, with the political result that much land was sold to his nobles and gentry. Architectural consequences included the despoliation of many great mediaeval buildings and the loss of the works of art which they contained.

England in the fifteenth century

ARCHITECTURAL CHARACTER

Mediaeval archaeology has developed rapidly over the last fifty years, but it remains true that we observe the material evidence of the Gothic past, especially in England, through a complex framework of styles and characteristics which were set up by nineteenth-century writers who were acute observers of detail, but whose knowledge of wider issues was sometimes limited. In England, the antiquaries of the eighteenth century gradually evolved a sort of dated timetable or sequence of styles which was codified and popularized by Thomas Rickman in his celebrated book, *An Attempt to Discriminate the Styles . . .* , the first edition of which was published in 1817. Inadequate though this system was, since it is based partly on historical periods (i.e. the reigns of monarchs) and partly on architectural character, it has held the field so long in all descriptions of English mediaeval architecture, that it has become an integral part of architectural phraseology. Edmund Sharpe modified the nomenclature a little, suggesting style names for periods based on the evolution he observed in the character of window tracery. Other attempts to remove ambiguities were not successful, and the old names have stuck. It should be remembered that the change from one style to another was uneven and gradual. When the High Gothic style was gaining acceptance in England during the reign of Henry II (1154–89), the techniques of solid Norman work were progressively modified over a number of years. This process is especially obvious, and the period label 'Transitional' was coined. Whilst the character of Saxon and Anglo-Norman work has been described in Chapter 20, the names 'Anglo-Saxon' and Norman are included in the list below to demonstrate that, in early Gothic work especially, the legacy from the preceding period was pronounced. The term 'Elizabethan' is similarly added to recognize the post-mediaeval survivals.

Norman, 1066–1154. Whilst there was considerable Norman influence in building before the Conquest, this period includes the raising of most of the major Romanesque churches and castles.

Transitional, 1154–89. This phase is most obvious in the work carried out in the reign of Henry II. One often finds, for example, pointed arches introduced into structures otherwise Romanesque in character.

Early English, 1189–1307. This period is the English equivalent of the High Gothic of northern France, and is occasionally known as the 'Lancet' style, from the characteristic shape of the long narrow windows, or as 'First Pointed'.

Decorated, 1307–77. Although it includes the reigns of Edward II and Edward III, the style cannot be confined to these limits. Broadly speaking, there is an early phase in which window tracery is usually 'Geometrical' in form, followed by a period of flowing tracery patterns and surface decoration which is normally called 'Curvilinear'. Occasionally the term 'Second Pointed' is used. The French 'Flamboyant' style is in some respects equivalent to later Decorated work in England, but its development on the Continent was more protracted, extending even into the mid-sixteenth century.

Perpendicular, 1377–1485. Sharpe's nomenclature uses the term 'Rectilinear', based on the observed tendency for large windows to be divided by horizontal tracery members or transomes. Some would claim this 'Third Pointed' style as a purely English development.

Tudor, 1495–1558. This period is marked by an increasing application of Renaissance detail to buildings otherwise late Perpendicular Gothic.

Elizabethan, 1558–1603. Whilst the new ideas of the Renaissance took strong hold in this period, a number of traditional mediaeval characteristics still appear; for example, the persistence of the Great Hall in house plans, mullioned windows and the Gothic outline of building masses.

In the brief descriptions of architectural character in the periods Early English, Decorated and Perpendicular, walls, columns, openings and decoration will be described in approximately the same order. Because they are difficult to explain within such a notation, three important topics will be discussed separately, namely: the evolution of stone vaulting in England; a classification and description of timber roofing; regional styles with special reference to local materials.

Early English period. Walls retain the massive character of preceding Norman work, but using less interior rubble and more cut stone. The concentration of roof and vaulting loads on deeper buttresses (pp. 639A, 644E) began the process of reducing the intervening walls to mere enclosing screens. The three-tier structural bay depended on the simple geometrical arrangement of grouped or single arched openings; internally, the arcade was usually half the total height and the upper part divided equally between the triforium and clear-storey (p. 644D, E, F); where flying buttresses occur, they were sometimes placed in a subordinate position, out of sight under the timbers of a triforium roof. Columns were compound, cylindrical (in simple work) or octagonal, sometimes surrounded by detached shafts of Purbeck marble (pp. 561K, L, 639B, C, 651B, 660C), held by rings of stone or metal. Capitals (pp. 561M, 562D–F, 639B, 660C), boldly moulded to give deep shadows, were often carved with upright 'stiff leaf' foliage; the normal abacus was circular on plan and not square as was usual in France. The so-called 'waterholding' base (p. 561N) is very characteristic. Arch mouldings (p. 563G–M) were quite complex and formed into deep recesses and ridges, often undercut and occasionally enriched with furrows of 'dog tooth' or leafed ornament. Whilst stone tracery as such had not yet developed, grouped compositions of 'lancet' windows set under a common hood mould (p. 560C, D) began to include geometrically-arranged piercings and horizontal stone stiffening bars. Decoration of wall surfaces was rare; occasionally spandrels might be filled with restrained ornament.

Decorated period. There was a further reduction in wall thickness, with wider windows between projecting buttresses in offset stages, these ornamented with niches, statuary and finials (pp. 645G, J, H, K, 666B). As vaulting developed, tall tapered pinnacles became common, even where the absence of vaults rendered them structurally unnecessary. These pinnacles were frequently linked together by richly decorated or pierced parapets and moulded string courses. Internally, the arcade and clear-storey of a tripartite bay were maintained, while the triforium tended to diminish (pp. 645G, H, J, K, 655). Columns (pp. 561P–S, 655), sometimes of a lozenge-shaped plan, were surrounded by subsidiary engaged shafts; capitals, not so deeply undercut, were frequently carved with more naturalistic oak, ivy or maple leaves (p. 562G, H, J). Arched openings (p. 563N–U) were generally equilateral and wider than they had been before, and were enriched by somewhat shallower mouldings at wider intervals. Window tracery (pp. 560E, H, J, K, 639C, 645G, H, 656A, B) developed very rapidly; at first the patterns were simple interlocked designs of circles and arcs, but soon with the introduction of cusps and raised mouldings the essential geometry was merged into web-like 'curvilinear' compositions (pp. 560H, J, 666B). Decoration moved away from a reliance on intricate and sumptuous geometry towards an even richer exploitation of surface texture, naturalistic carving and statuary (pp. 650B, 675C). Stained glass, losing the vibrant, mosaic character it had in the thirteenth century, filled the traceried lights of wide windows with translucent figured pictures, displayed in architectural canopies.

Perpendicular period. Late Gothic designs became attenuated, essentially linear, at times over-refined and brittle (p. 670B). As windows grew larger to accommodate brilliant displays of coloured glass, buttresses and the remaining walls (and even columns and arch-soffits) were decorated with tracery-like panels (pp. 646, 657, 670A); the effect might be described as surface ornament stretched over minimum structure. Buttresses were visually important, even in those buildings which were unvaulted, deep at the base and cut back in a series of exaggerated steps, reaching upwards as tall pinnacles between solid or open ornamented battlemented parapets (pp. 651A, 665A). Since roof pitches were generally lower, the skyline silhouette was often important. The arcades and clear-storeys of structural bays were tall and the triforium, if it occurred, was reduced to a mere wall passage (pp. 645M, 657, 664C). Columns were more slender; mouldings often ran without interruption from floor to ceiling or up the shaft and round the arch itself (p. 659C), with capitals reduced to vestigial form or not present at all. Arches, while they continued to be moulded (p. 563V–Z), were simpler, even severe, and like windows tended to be wide, and flat in outline, with four-centred or square heads. Window tracery became stereotyped after the necessary introduction of horizontal transomes for stability. Small lights in the upper parts framed stylized painted glass figures (pp. 560L–N, 646, 665B). The maintenance of strong geometry and variation in tracery thickness sometimes produced designs of great beauty; characteristically some, if not all, mullions (or vertical tracery members) ran up without interruption from sill to window-head. With the common use of silver stain, late Gothic glass achieved great splendour. Significantly, however, the latest work paid little regard to the limiting shapes of the stone divisions; iconographical material expanded pictorially over the whole glazed area (p. 646). Architectural decoration in general was lavish, but ornament was often confined to suitable spaces between mouldings, in cornices and elsewhere, relying for its effect on contrast with adjoining undecorated surfaces (p. 671D). Carved figurework, of an increasingly secular character, and heraldic devices and moulded profiles began to show unmistakeable signs of Renaissance influence that grew rapidly in the sixteenth century (pp. 652C, 664C).

THE EVOLUTION OF ENGLISH GOTHIC VAULTING

The problem for the Mediaeval architect was to construct a stone vault over the lofty nave of a church of the basilican type, while leaving clear-storey windows in the nave walls above the aisle roofs. While Roman vaulting consisted in the design either of semicircular vaults or of semicircular cross-vaults, of which the meeting lines or intersections are known as groins, Mediaeval vaulting was of quite a different type; for the simple groins were now replaced by specially constructed ribs on which the thin vaulting panels were placed. This was an economical form of building; for it dispensed with the large amount of 'centering' required for the temporary support of the heavy Roman vaults, as each rib, when constructed, itself became the support of the vault panel. The weight of the stone vault, high above the ground, exerted considerable thrust and so involved the solution of structural problems and resulted in the employment of responsive features, such as buttresses and pinnacles, to counteract the thrust of this nave vault, while the numerous ribs meeting on the pier capitals had to be supported by piers of appropriate design.

After Saxon and Norman techniques of vaulting in stone had reached a reasonable degree of perfection, culminating in the remarkable achievements over the nave at Durham Cathedral between 1128 and 1133 (p. 564D), English work followed contemporary French examples.

Early English Vaulting (p. 660C). The pointed arch came into general use in the thirteenth century, and, without use being made of stilting or any other contrivances, surmounted the difficulties created by the intersection of semicircular vaults of different spans (p. 627F). The plain four-part (quadripartite) ribbed vault, primarily constructed as a skeleton framework of diagonal and transverse ribs, was chiefly used in this period, as in the naves of Durham, Salisbury (p. 639B) and Gloucester, and the aisles of Peterborough. Intermediate uprising ribs, known as 'tiercerons', were inserted later between the transverse and diagonal ribs to give additional support to the panels, as in the choir of Lincoln Cathedral (p. 656B). Ridge ribs were then introduced to resist the thrust of the opposing 'tiercerons' and keep them in position. In Continental examples the ridge rib is often not continuous and is only used for those ribs which abut obliquely at the summit. Ridge ribs are generally horizontal in England, but on the Continent are arched between the bosses. The courses of the vault panels meet at the ridge in zigzag lines, as in the nave of Westminster Abbey (p. 664B), Lincoln, Exeter and Lichfield Cathedrals, as well as in the churches of south-west France. Wall ribs or 'formerets' enclosing the

EVOLUTION OF GOTHIC VAULTING

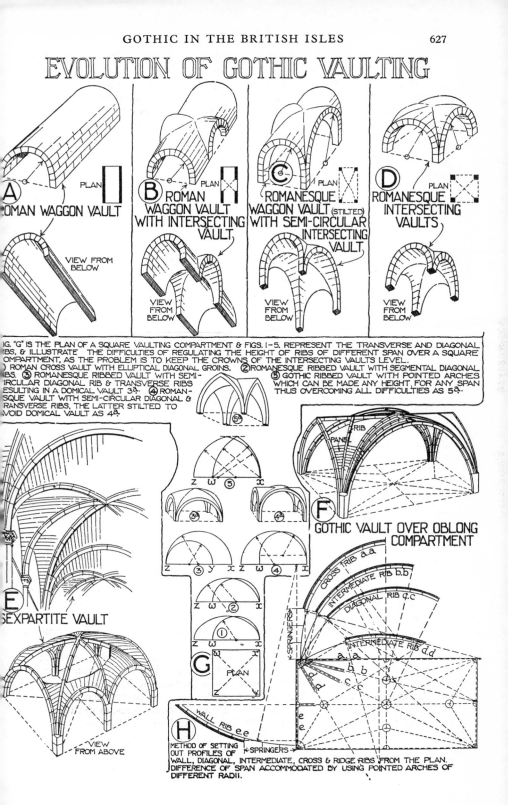

A ROMAN WAGGON VAULT

PLAN

VIEW FROM BELOW

B ROMAN WAGGON VAULT WITH INTERSECTING VAULT

PLAN

VIEW FROM BELOW

C ROMANESQUE WAGGON VAULT (STILTED) WITH SEMI-CIRCULAR INTERSECTING VAULT

PLAN

VIEW FROM BELOW

D ROMANESQUE INTERSECTING VAULTS

PLAN

VIEW FROM BELOW

FIG. "G" IS THE PLAN OF A SQUARE VAULTING COMPARTMENT & FIGS. 1-5. REPRESENT THE TRANSVERSE AND DIAGONAL RIBS, & ILLUSTRATE THE DIFFICULTIES OF REGULATING THE HEIGHT OF RIBS OF DIFFERENT SPAN OVER A SQUARE COMPARTMENT, AS THE PROBLEM IS TO KEEP THE CROWNS OF THE INTERSECTING VAULTS LEVEL.
① ROMAN CROSS VAULT WITH ELLIPTICAL DIAGONAL GROINS. ② ROMANESQUE RIBBED VAULT WITH SEGMENTAL DIAGONAL RIBS. ③ ROMANESQUE RIBBED VAULT WITH SEMI-CIRCULAR DIAGONAL RIB & TRANSVERSE RIBS RESULTING IN A DOMICAL VAULT 3ᵃ. ④ ROMANESQUE VAULT WITH SEMI-CIRCULAR DIAGONAL & TRANSVERSE RIBS, THE LATTER STILTED TO AVOID DOMICAL VAULT AS 4ᵃ.
⑤ GOTHIC RIBBED VAULT WITH POINTED ARCHES WHICH CAN BE MADE ANY HEIGHT, FOR ANY SPAN THUS OVERCOMING ALL DIFFICULTIES AS 5ᵃ.

RIB
PANEL

F GOTHIC VAULT OVER OBLONG COMPARTMENT

E SEXPARTITE VAULT

VIEW FROM ABOVE

z ω ⑤ x
3ᵃ   4ᵃ
z ω ③ y x z ω ④ x
z ω ② x
①
z ω ① x

G PLAN

CROSS RIB a.a
INTERMEDIATE RIB b.b
DIAGONAL RIB c.c
INTERMEDIATE RIB d.d
a.a
b.b
SPRINGERS
WALL RIB e.e
H METHOD OF SETTING OUT PROFILES OF WALL, DIAGONAL, INTERMEDIATE, CROSS & RIDGE RIBS FROM THE PLAN. DIFFERENCE OF SPAN ACCOMMODATED BY USING POINTED ARCHES OF DIFFERENT RADII.
SPRINGERS

COMPARATIVE DIAGRAMS OF VAULTS

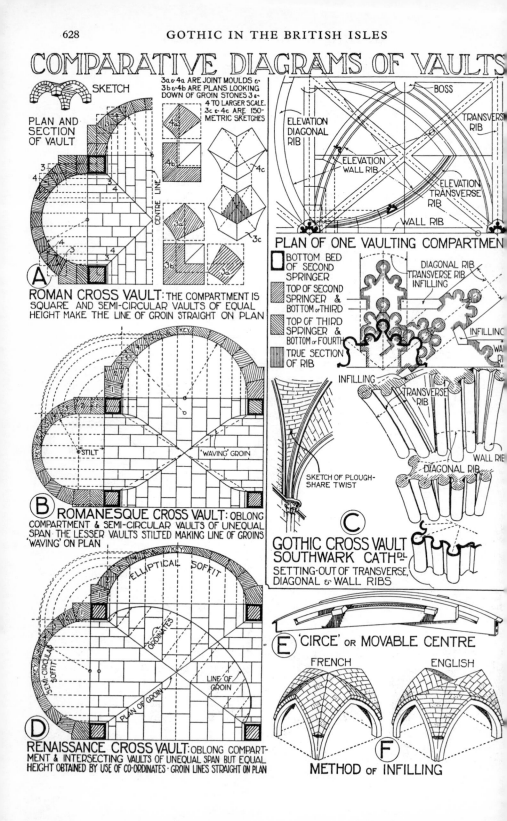

SKETCH

PLAN AND SECTION OF VAULT

3a & 4a ARE JOINT MOULDS & 3b & 4b ARE PLANS LOOKING DOWN OF GROIN STONES 3 & 4 TO LARGER SCALE. 3c & 4c ARE ISO-METRIC SKETCHES

4a
4b
4c
CENTRE LINE
3a
3b
3c

A ROMAN CROSS VAULT: THE COMPARTMENT IS SQUARE AND SEMI-CIRCULAR VAULTS OF EQUAL HEIGHT MAKE THE LINE OF GROIN STRAIGHT ON PLAN

KEY
STILT
'WAVING' GROIN

B ROMANESQUE CROSS VAULT: OBLONG COMPARTMENT & SEMI-CIRCULAR VAULTS OF UNEQUAL SPAN. THE LESSER VAULTS STILTED MAKING LINE OF GROINS 'WAVING' ON PLAN

KEY
ELLIPTICAL SOFFIT
SEMI-CIRCULAR SOFFIT
ORDINATES
LINE OF GROIN
PLAN OF GROIN

D RENAISSANCE CROSS VAULT: OBLONG COMPARTMENT & INTERSECTING VAULTS OF UNEQUAL SPAN BUT EQUAL HEIGHT OBTAINED BY USE OF CO-ORDINATES · GROIN LINES STRAIGHT ON PLAN

BOSS
ELEVATION DIAGONAL RIB
TRANSVERSE RIB
ELEVATION WALL RIB
ELEVATION TRANSVERSE RIB
WALL RIB

PLAN OF ONE VAULTING COMPARTMENT

BOTTOM BED OF SECOND SPRINGER
TOP OF SECOND SPRINGER & BOTTOM OF THIRD
TOP OF THIRD SPRINGER & BOTTOM OF FOURTH
TRUE SECTION OF RIB

DIAGONAL RIB
TRANSVERSE RIB
INFILLING
WALL RIB

INFILLING
TRANSVERSE RIB
WALL RIB
DIAGONAL RIB

SKETCH OF PLOUGH-SHARE TWIST

C GOTHIC CROSS VAULT SOUTHWARK CATH.ᴰᴸ
SETTING-OUT OF TRANSVERSE, DIAGONAL & WALL RIBS

E 'CIRCE' OR MOVABLE CENTRE

FRENCH   ENGLISH

F METHOD OF INFILLING

PRINCIPLES OF PROPORTIONS

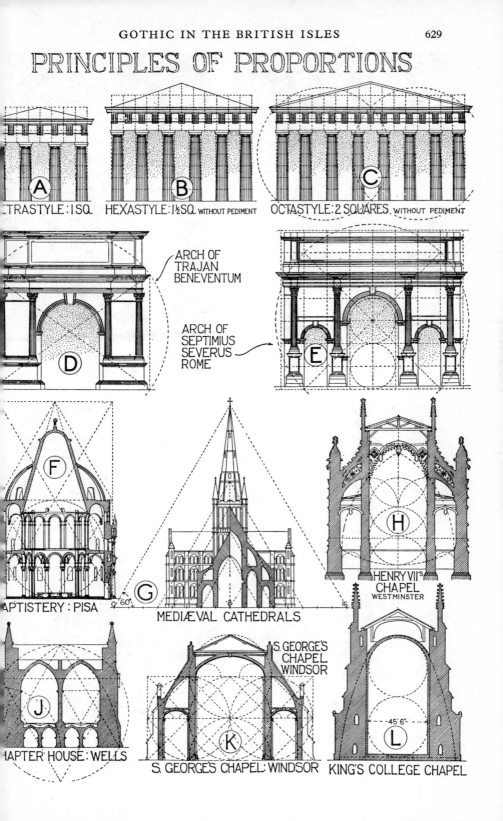

A — TETRASTYLE : 1 SQ.

B — HEXASTYLE : 1½ SQ. WITHOUT PEDIMENT

C — OCTASTYLE : 2 SQUARES WITHOUT PEDIMENT

ARCH OF TRAJAN BENEVENTUM

ARCH OF SEPTIMIUS SEVERUS ROME

D

E

F — BAPTISTERY : PISA

G — MEDIÆVAL CATHEDRALS

H — HENRY VII'S CHAPEL WESTMINSTER

J — CHAPTER HOUSE : WELLS

K — S. GEORGE'S CHAPEL WINDSOR

L — KING'S COLLEGE CHAPEL

45' 6"

A. Christ Church, Oxford: vaulted staircase (1640). See p. 632

B. Oxford Cathedral (Christ Church): interior looking E. (1158–80) (choir vault *c*. 1480–1500). See pp. 568, 632

C. Divinity School, Oxford: interior (1430–55; vault 1480–3). See p. 632

lateral wall space of the vaulting compartment came into use during this period. The 'ploughshare twist', which sometimes occurs in the panels between diagonal and wall ribs, as in Westminster Abbey and Southwark Cathedral (p. 628C), is produced by raising the springing of the wall rib above that of the diagonal rib in order to increase the size of clear-storey windows, whose shape was thus influenced by the vault.

Decorated Vaulting. A general elaboration of vaulting is characteristic of this period, and this is due not only to the greater use of both intermediate and ridge ribs, as in the nave vault of Exeter Cathedral (p. 655), but also to the addition of 'lierne' ribs (French, *lien* = tie or bond)—a term applied to any rib other than a ridge rib which does not start from the springing of the vaulting compartment. Previously each rib marked a change in the direction of the vaulting surface, but 'lierne' ribs merely follow the curved surface of the panel and, by their number and disposition, often give an intricate appearance to an otherwise simple vault. The star-shaped pattern thus produced is called 'stellar' vaulting (pp. 665B, 670A) and there are examples of it in Gloucester (1337–77), Canterbury (1379–1400), Wells, Ely (choir) (p. 645K), Bristol (p. 659C) and Winchester Cathedrals (p. 645M), and also at Tewkesbury Abbey. At Bristol Cathedral the choir aisles are roofed at the level of the springing of the main vault by a unique arrangement of stone arches from which ribbed cross vaulted compartments rise; essentially these support the main span as if they were buttresses beneath the outer roof and give the church a cross section not unlike that of a continental hall church (p. 659D). Vaulting during this period comprised transverse, diagonal, tierceron, ridge and lierne ribs, and this increased number of ribs so decreased the size of the panels they supported that the space from rib to rib was frequently spanned by a single stone. Carved bosses (French, *bosse* = lump or knob) or keystones, which had already come into use in the thirteenth century, had their origin in a constructive use as keystones against which the ribs abutted and also in the need for disguising the awkward mitres made by the meeting of moulded ribs. In the fourteenth century the increase in the number of ribs led to a corresponding increase in the number of bosses, which gave to these Gothic vaults an extremely ornamental and web-like appearance.

Perpendicular Vaulting. The intricate 'stellar' vaulting evolved in the late fourteenth and early fifteenth centuries led, by experimental stages, to the type known as fan, palm or conoidal vaulting, first used in the cloisters at Gloucester (1351–77), in which the rising ribs are formed at equal angles on inverted concave cones and are thus of the same curve, and these are connected at different heights by horizontal lierne ribs. The development was somewhat as follows: in the thirteenth century the vault followed the outline of inverted, four-sided concave pyramids; in the fourteenth century the introduction of more ribs resulted in polygonal pyramids with ribs of different curves, while in the fifteenth century the design was simplified by the introduction of 'fan' vaulting in which all ribs are of similar curve (p. 660B). The reduction of the size of panels, consequent on the increase in the number of ribs, brought about a return to the Roman method of construction; for in fan vaulting the ribs and panels were often formed in the same piece of stone instead of the panels resting as separate stones on the ribs, and thus the ribs lost their structural use. This method seems to have been first adopted in vaults where ribs were most numerous, and in Tudor times both systems are found, as at King's College Chapel, Cambridge (1512–15) (p. 646); while in others, as in Henry the Seventh's Chapel, Westminster, the whole vault has ribs and panels formed out of the same piece of stone. The problem of supporting the flat, lozenge-shaped space in the crown of the vault was comparatively easy in cloisters, where the vaulting compartments were approximately square, but difficulties arose in adapting fan vaulting to the bays of naves which generally measured twice as much transversely as longitudinally. In King's College Chapel the conoids are incomplete, for the sides had to be cut off, thereby forming awkward transverse junctions. Henry the Seventh's Chapel (1503–19) has hidden transverse arches which penetrate above the vaulting and, at a distance from the walls, support pendants or elongated voussoirs, from which spring the conoids, thus reducing the central vaulting space from an oblong to a square (p. 664C). At Oxford Cathedral, by a similar method, the pendants, supported by an upper arch, are placed at some distance from the walls, and from them spring the rib and panel vault (1480–1500) (p. 630B). Fan vaulting is confined to England, as at Sherborne Abbey (1475); the Divinity School, Oxford (1480–3) (p. 630C); Gloucester Cathedral; S. George's Chapel, Windsor (1501–8), and the retro-choir, Peterborough, and the tradition was maintained in the vault over the staircase at Christ Church, Oxford (1640) (p. 630A).

Tudor Vaulting. The four-centred arch (p. 1310, No. 17), so typical of the period, seems to have had its origin in the difficulty of making the various ribs in the oblong vaulting compartments of naves reach the same height. In an oblong Mediaeval vaulting compartment which had a lancet-shaped window in the nave wall, the diagonal ribs are either semicircular or pointed, i.e. struck from two centres in which each side of the arch must be less than the quadrant of a circle; and because the transverse and wall ribs are shorter than the diagonal ribs, they are still smaller segments of a circle. In oblong vaulting compartments of late Gothic vaults, which often had windows in the nave wall crowned with pointed arches of equilateral or, in early Tudor times, even of the 'drop' arch form (p. 1310, No. 13), the diagonal and transverse ribs had to be struck from four centres in order to accommodate their height to that of the window arch. These of necessity were low four-centred arches which started with the same curve as the window arch, but after a certain height the remainder of each rib was struck from another centre in order to bring the apex of all ribs to the same height as that of the window arch. The four-centred arches which were used in late Gothic vaults and conspicuously in fan vaulting were afterwards introduced over doors, windows, fireplaces and wall tombs, as well as in traceried panels, possibly with a desire to harmonize with the vaulted superstructure.

A CLASSIFICATION AND DESCRIPTION OF TIMBER ROOFS

Timber outer roofs were almost always used above a vaulted ceiling; in these cases internal appearance was of no account, and there was hardly any development in the design of such a wooden covering over the period as a whole. Open roofs, that is those meant to be seen from the underside, show a rich variety from the thirteenth century right up to Tudor times, generally most elaborate towards the end of the period. Local styles are often well defined; for example, in the rich camber-beam roofs of the later Middle Ages in Lancashire and Cheshire (p. 657), or the glorious hammer-beam designs commonly found in East Anglia (p. 633F, H, L). Because many early roofs were subsequently replaced, especially after the mid-fourteenth century, when pitches were reduced as lead became a popular substitute for less permanent coverings, evolution is not so clearly apparent as in the case of vaults. There are a few fine wooden ceilings of the Norman period still in existence, for example at Peterborough Cathedral, but few surviving roofs are earlier than the thirteenth century, and the majority are much later. Constructional evolution is more readily demonstrated by the roofs of manor houses or barns. 'Single' roofs (lacking principals), 'trussed-rafter' (p. 633A), 'hammer-beam' roofs

TYPES OF TIMBER CHURCH ROOFS

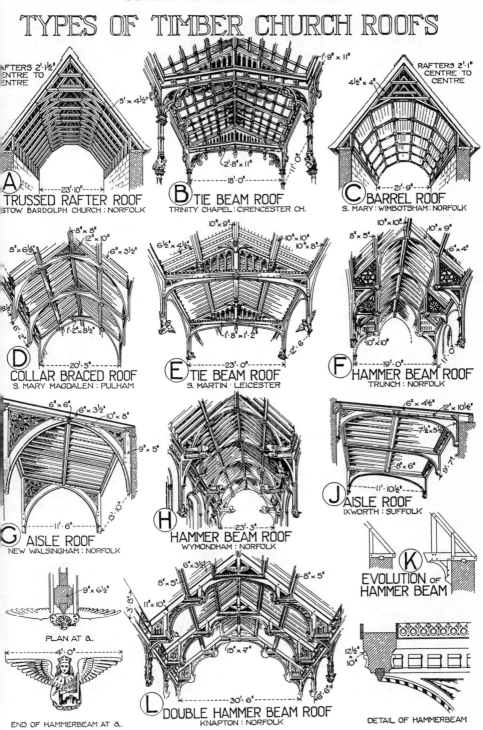

RAFTERS 2' 1½"
CENTRE TO
CENTRE

5' × 4½"

A TRUSSED RAFTER ROOF
STOW BARDOLPH CHURCH : NORFOLK

1'·9" × 11"

4½" × 4"

2'·8" × 11"

B TIE BEAM ROOF
TRINITY CHAPEL : CIRENCESTER CH.

RAFTERS 2'·1"
CENTRE TO
CENTRE

4½" × 4"

C BARREL ROOF
S. MARY : WIMBOTSHAM : NORFOLK

8" × 8"
12" × 10"
8" × 6½"
6" × 3½"

1'·2" × 8½"

D COLLAR BRACED ROOF
S. MARY MAGDALEN : PULHAM

10" × 9"
6½" × 4½"
10" × 10"
10" × 8"

1'·8" × 1'·2"

E TIE BEAM ROOF
S. MARTIN · LEICESTER

10" × 10"
8" × 5"
10" × 9"
6" × 4"

40" × 10"

F HAMMER BEAM ROOF
TRUNCH : NORFOLK

6" × 6"
6" × 3½"
10" × 8"
9" × 5"

11'·6"

G AISLE ROOF
NEW WALSINGHAM : NORFOLK

H HAMMER BEAM ROOF
WYMONDHAM : NORFOLK

6" × 4½"
12" × 10½"
7½" × 5½"
8" × 6"

11'·10½"

J AISLE ROOF
IXWORTH : SUFFOLK

K EVOLUTION OF
HAMMER BEAM

9" × 6½"

PLAN AT a.

4'·0"

END OF HAMMERBEAM AT a.

6" × 3½"
8" × 5"
8" × 5"
11" × 10"
15" × 7"

30'·6"

L DOUBLE HAMMER BEAM ROOF
KNAPTON : NORFOLK

12½" × 10"

DETAIL OF HAMMERBEAM

A. Old Tithe Barn, Bradford-on-Avon (1350). See p. 699

B. Needham Market: nave roof (15th cent.). See p. 637

C. Westminster Hall (1397–9). See p. 636

(p. 633F, H, L), and those having a 'crown-post' (known also as a 'king-post') standing on a tie-beam in order to support a 'collar-purlin', almost invariably belong to the south-eastern half of the country; the dividing line running approximately along the oolitic limestone belt shown in the inset map, p. 623. In the south-east too, the 'principal rafter' of roof trusses serves as a common rafter as well as to support side purlins, tenoned into them. The ridge-piece, if any, runs under the common rafters rather than between them as is modern practice. In the north-western half of the country and in Wales, roofs were almost invariably 'framed', there being well-defined principals supporting purlins and a ridge-piece upon their backs. Frequently, there were 'wind-braces' arching from the purlins to the principal rafters (p. 687A, B). 'Arch-braced' roofs, common from the fourteenth century, are found in both halves of the country. In general, roofs tended to become more elaborate and ornate as time elapsed. There was very much overlap in the types developing in succession.

The English open timber roofs of the Middle Ages (p. 633) may be classified as: (1) Trussed-rafter roofs. (2) Tie-beam roofs. (3) Collar-braced roofs. (4) Hammerbeam roofs. (5) Aisle roofs.

(1) *Trussed-rafter roofs* (p. 633A) are nearly always steeply pitched, averaging fifty-five degrees; they are rare in churches after c. 1400. The fundamental form of roof in the south-east was that composed of 'couples' of rafters, each pair separate, without a ridge-piece; but as the rafters exercised outward thrust they were usually joined together by a collar, or pair of collars, or were stiffened further by braces from collar to rafters, as at Stow Bardolph Church, Norfolk. Sometimes the braces were extended past the collar, scissor-wise, as at Lympenhoe Church, Norfolk, or the scissor braces were themselves considered sufficient. The rafters rested on the outer portion of the wall, and thus left an unsightly ledge on the inside, covered by upright struts, which also added to the stability of the roof. The triangle thus formed is held to be the origin of the hammer-beam arrangement (p. 633K), when principals had been developed. The arched trussed-rafter roof was obtained by the use of curved timbers connecting the rafters and collars, as at Solihull Church, Warwickshire, and it was sometimes lined with boards to form a pentagonal 'barrel' ceiling, ornamented with ribs and bosses (p. 633C).

(2) *Tie-beam roofs* (pp. 633B, E, 657) are found in connection both with steeply-pitched and low-pitched roofs. In early use the tie-beam represents a 'baulk-tie' which joined the wall-posts of timber buildings, and in stone buildings was often haphazardly placed in order to prevent the wall plates from spreading. It came to serve, usually cambered upwards, to carry an ornamental or plain crown-post, which in its turn sustained a collar-purlin, linking the collars and giving rigidity to a roof otherwise belonging to the trussed-rafter class. Even so, the type was rather frail, and many elementary or naïve devices were tried for the purpose of propping-up side purlins from the tie-beam (p. 687A) before true roof principals were evolved. So long as roofs were steeply pitched, the tie-beam obstructed the upper space; when from the thirteenth century roofs were progressively lowered it came into its own again, but then as a part of a truss, with principal rafters supporting purlins and ridge-piece, the triangle thus formed having various arrangements of vertical struts and tracery (p. 633B, E). Curved braces often connected the underside of the tie-beam with vertical wall-pieces, and thus the whole was framed together in the form of a depressed arch, as at S. Martin, Leicester (p. 633E). A final phase (fifteenth and sixteenth century) was to depress the roof-pitch to such an extent, even less than ten degrees, that the roof could be carried on a cambered tie-beam with only a modicum of firring.

(3) *The Collar-braced roof*, which may be said to originate about 1300, is a natural

descendant of the 'cruck-truss' roof of the western half of the country (p. 693C), in which principals of the cruck type—spaced down the length of a building to carry purlins and a ridge, and these the rafters—are raised upon walls instead of starting from the ground, as formerly. In the process, the curved 'blades' or principal rafters of the crucks tend to be straightened out, and the former tie-beams appear as a collar connecting them together. When, as is usually the case in prime examples, braces are added below the collar to link it with the principal rafters, the outcome is what is known as an 'arch-braced' truss. Among domestic buildings, Stokesay Castle hall, Shropshire, has a straightforward and very early example (thirteenth century). The roof pitch usually is steep—about fifty-two degrees, descending to below fifty degrees in the fifteenth century. In south-west England, where the 'framed' principle of roof construction was not so strongly traditional as in the north-west, arch-braced church roofs often lacked a ridge-piece; and in south-eastern England (including East Anglia), where it was quite alien, it was nevertheless soon adopted but very frequently to produce hybrid forms in which the 'single' and the 'framed' methods of construction of the roof members were confused (p. 633D). This mixture of practice is particularly marked in such secular examples as Sutton Courtenay in Berkshire (fourteenth century) and Cobham, in Kent (sixteenth century). In the same region in the fifteenth century, as well as in Somerset and Devon, arch-braces sometimes swept to the roof apex without the intervention of a collar, or were omitted altogether. In all the variants of the type, there normally were arch-braces too at the feet of the principal rafters, connecting with wall-posts to carry the roof load down the inner wall faces and giving a pointed-arch profile to the lower edge of the roof trusses.

(4) *The Hammer-beam roof*, found principally in the south-eastern half of the country, was evolved during the fourteenth century, perhaps from the triangle at the foot of the trussed-rafter roof (pp. 633F, H, L, 634B, C). It consists of a series of trusses, repeated at intervals, to support the intermediate purlins and rafters, and its object is to transmit the weight and thrust of the roof as low down as possible in the supporting wall. The component parts of each truss are the two principal rafters and hammer-beams with struts, curved braces and collars which vary in number and design. The hammer-beam itself is merely a lengthened sole piece (p. 633K), of which the projecting part is supported by a curved brace from the wall piece, and in its turn it supports a vertical strut to the principal rafter. This rigid system of timbers, all tenoned and pinned together, is designed to resist the outward pressure of the rafters, and is supplemented in the Gothic period by external buttresses. It has been suggested that the hammer-beam was the result of cutting away the centre of the tie-beam after the introduction of the curved brace, but there is little in common between a hammer-beam and a tie-beam roof, except that, in both, the trusses are at intervals. Moreover the tie-beam was used even in conjunction with the hammer-beam, as at Outwell, where the alternate trusses have hammer-beams. The chief varieties of the hammer-beam roof are: (*a*) those with hammer-beams, struts, collars and curved braces, as at Little Welnetham, Suffolk; (*b*) those in which the collar-beam is omitted and curved braces are carried up to a wedge-shaped strut at the ridge, as at Wymondham, Norfolk (p. 633H), and Trunch, Norfolk (p. 633F); (*c*) those in which short hammer-beams support curved braces instead of struts, with collar-beams above, as at Capel S. Mary, Suffolk, and at Hampton Court Palace, London; (*d*) those in which curved braces rise from hammer-beam to ridge, as at Palgrave, Suffolk; (*e*) those with an arched rib which, springing from wall piece to collar, gives additional rigidity, as at Eltham Palace, in Kent (1481), and in that most magnificent of all timber roofs at Westminster Hall, by the distinguished master-carpenter, Hugh Herland, which dates from 1397–9

(p. 634C); (*f*) double hammer-beam roofs, as at S. Margaret, Ipswich, Knapton (p. 633L), Needham Market, Suffolk (p. 634B) and Middle Temple Hall (1572), which have a second range of hammer-beams further to stiffen the principals and transmit the weight through the first range to the wall: they appear from the fifteenth century onwards.

(5) *Aisle roofs* (p. 633G, J) usually reflected the design of the main roofs. Roof pitches changed in concert with those of the high roofs, except that they quite frequently were at a less angle in order to facilitate clear-storey lighting of naves.

REGIONAL STYLES

A band of oolitic freestone, including the well-known Bath stone, stretches diagonally across England from Somerset to Lincolnshire and South Yorkshire, and supplies such excellent materials for all types of building in its vicinity that this geological influence is seen in the cathedrals along its course, the fine manor houses of Somerset (p. 684A) and Northamptonshire, as well as in a series of spectacular parish churches. The granites of Cornwall, Devon and parts of Scotland, and the gritstones of Lancashire and Yorkshire in the north were both so hard in texture as to admit of little sculptural ornament, and this gives severity to the architecture of these districts. In Wales and over most of Ireland good stone was difficult to obtain, so that thick massive walls of layered slate were dressed with smaller quantities of better material when used for quoins and at openings. The flint work of Norfolk, Suffolk and part of the south coast gives pronounced local character to the churches of these districts, especially since towers had to be round in shape without large stones to turn the corners (p. 671B). When, as especially in the Tudor period, the flints were 'knapped' or split and set in panels of traceried freestone, flush with the wall face, the disabilities of this shortage of normal mason's stone could produce architectural decoration of a high order.

Whilst it is probably true that in most places timber was the common material for houses and less important structures, in Lancashire, Cheshire, Shropshire and Sussex the fine old oak forests encouraged the development of more sophisticated wooden construction. A few important timber mansions in the west (p. 687C), some good barns and houses remaining in the south and west, and many belfries and towers, for example, in Essex are survivors of a kind of building once much more common than it is now (pp. 671C, 693B). Brickwork, a product of the river valleys and used by the Romans during their occupation of Britain, later fell into disuse, until revived in and around London and the low-lying eastern counties at the end of the thirteenth century, before becoming an almost universally popular material from about 1500 onwards (p. 689A, B, C).

As communications improved, local distinctions tended to disappear. Early road transport was difficult and costly, so carriage by sea or river was often preferred, and English stone was easily supplemented by Caen stone from Normandy, if the work was important enough. A few exotic, decorative materials were often brought great distances—marble from Tournai, used in tombs and fonts, Purbeck stone from Dorset for use in clustered column shafts, especially in the thirteenth century, and alabaster, chiefly from Nottinghamshire, which in the fifteenth century was the basis of a prosperous industry in the manufacture of altarpieces, tombs and screens, sometimes exported to Europe.

Local differences in design and construction were much affected by the peculiar organization of the building trades. Masons, carpenters and others were contracted to work for a series of masters. For example, if important new construction was on hand at a great abbey or cathedral, numbers of craftsmen would be attracted to the area, and were available for other work, if the major undertaking slowed down or ceased altogether. Again, a local group of masons might become well known and be invited to another place of work. Marked similarities in different buildings can often be explained in this way; for example, some of the great towers of the fifteenth century in Somerset, the perpendicular rebuilding at Edington Priory in Wiltshire and at Winchester Cathedral; or, in a remoter situation, the strikingly similar fortifications at S. David's Palace, Lamphey Palace and Swansea Castle.

In spite of iconoclastic losses after the Reformation and the zeal of restorers, many fittings and works of art survive showing similar regional characteristics (p. 672A). The vigorous work of the late Romanesque carvers of Herefordshire continued into the Gothic period. The counties of Wales and East Anglia have splendid collections of wood carving in screens and lofts. East Anglia has much good late Gothic panel painting (p. 672B), and related groups of joiners and carvers are thought to have worked on the choir stalls at Manchester, Ripon, Beverley and elsewhere in the fifteenth century. The study of the design of surviving fittings is an essential part of an understanding of the work of the period as a whole (p. 675B, C.)

EXAMPLES

GREATER CHURCHES

Although Gothic architecture is properly understood in terms of structure, that is, in the problems of stability of a series of stone vaulting compartments, it is generally true that the major English churches were only modest achievements in this sense. The towers of a west front or the spacing of piers and buttresses fulfil a structural purpose, but the interest of an English cathedral or abbey lies in three factors. Firstly, with the exception of Salisbury, they were constantly in the process of construction and alteration, and so show continuous architectural development. Secondly, liturgical practices produced a particularly varied series of solutions in the planning of the eastern part of the church; and thirdly, they contain, in a reasonably intact state, a range of original fittings without parallel in Europe.

Great churches may have been cathedrals (see p. 567), attached to monasteries or, later in the Middle Ages, have had a collegiate constitution. Architecturally, these different functions might make little difference, since in each kind of foundation there would be a large church with domestic and administrative buildings adjoining it (pp. 570A–C, 652A). Because many bishops' sees were established within monasteries, close to or within large towns, many churches are withdrawn into a precinct formed around the usual conventual buildings; dormitories, infirmary, guest houses, cloisters and the like. Should the church have been served by secular canons, the arrangement would not be very different; Salisbury (p. 639A), Wells (p. 658B) and Lincoln Cathedrals all stand inside a close, and have other quasi-monastic features, such as cloisters, chapter houses and strong gateways. There were distinctive features associated with the various monastic Orders, both in the church proper and in the disposition of the conventual buildings; for example, Cistercian choirs were usually simple in plan and without elaborate east ends, while the Charterhouses of the Carthusians centred upon their cellular cloisters, and not on a church. The preaching friars often built large auditory naves, adjoining their choirs, in the centres of populous towns.

Until the thirteenth century a major church was likely to have a simple plan, but an ambitious rebuilding scheme might then begin at the east end and progress westward, showing a corresponding development in style. Occasionally, as in the naves of Westminster (p. 664B) or Beverley, an original thirteenth-century design

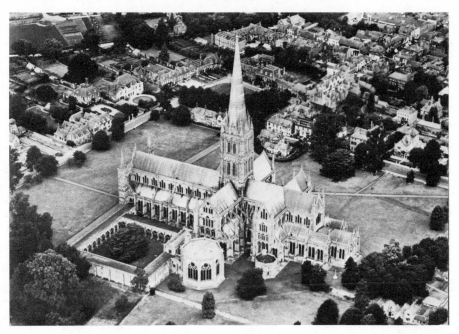

A. Aerial view of Cathedral from S.E.

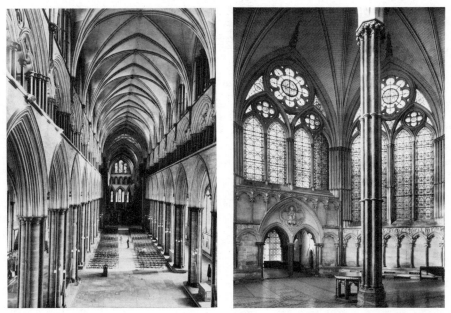

B. The nave looking E.   C. The chapter house (1263–84)

Salisbury Cathedral (1220–65). See p. 661

COMPARATIVE PLANS OF ENGLISH CATHEDRALS

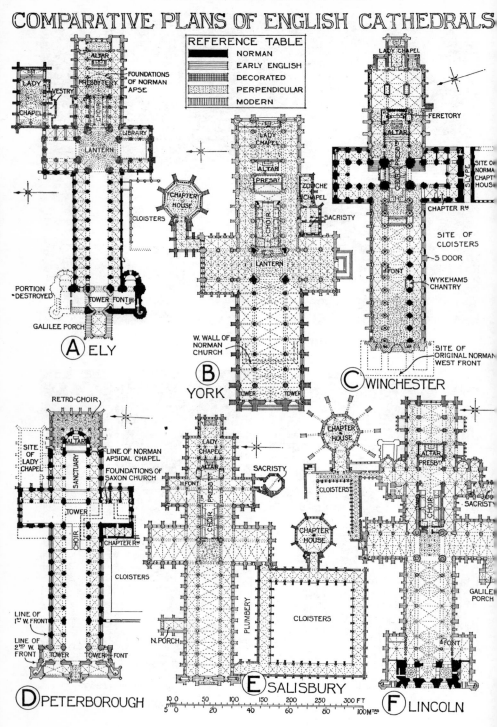

REFERENCE TABLE

▓	NORMAL
≣	EARLY ENGLISH
▦	DECORATED
░	PERPENDICULAR
▤	MODERN

A ELY

B YORK

C WINCHESTER

D PETERBOROUGH

E SALISBURY

F LINCOLN

COMPARATIVE PLANS OF ENGLISH CATHEDRALS

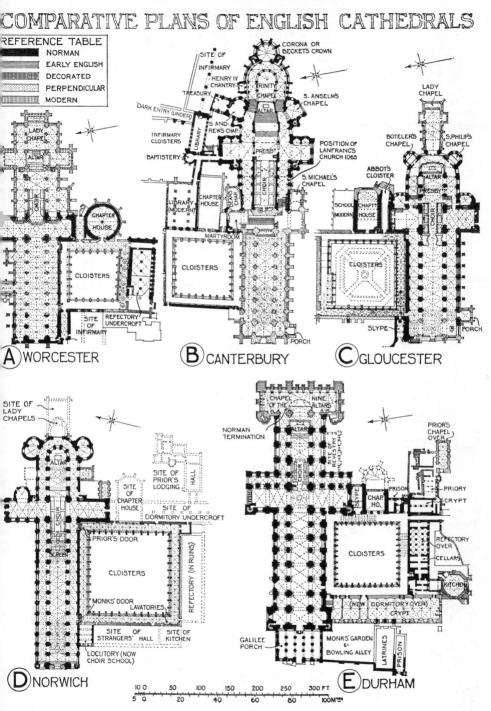

REFERENCE TABLE
- NORMAN
- EARLY ENGLISH
- DECORATED
- PERPENDICULAR
- MODERN

Ⓐ WORCESTER

Ⓑ CANTERBURY

Ⓒ GLOUCESTER

Ⓓ NORWICH

Ⓔ DURHAM

COMPARATIVE PLANS OF ENGLISH CATHEDRALS

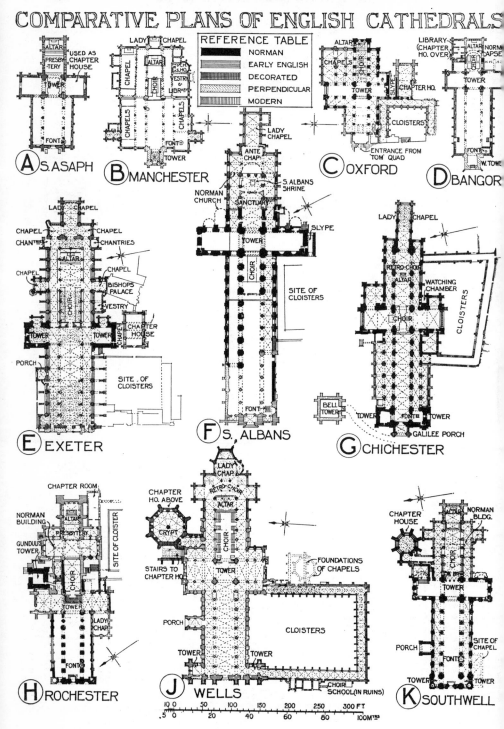

REFERENCE TABLE

▮	NORMAN
	EARLY ENGLISH
	DECORATED
	PERPENDICULAR
	MODERN

(A) S. ASAPH

(B) MANCHESTER

(C) OXFORD

(D) BANGOR

(E) EXETER

(F) S. ALBANS

(G) CHICHESTER

(H) ROCHESTER

(J) WELLS

(K) SOUTHWELL

COMPARATIVE PLANS OF ENGLISH CATHEDRALS

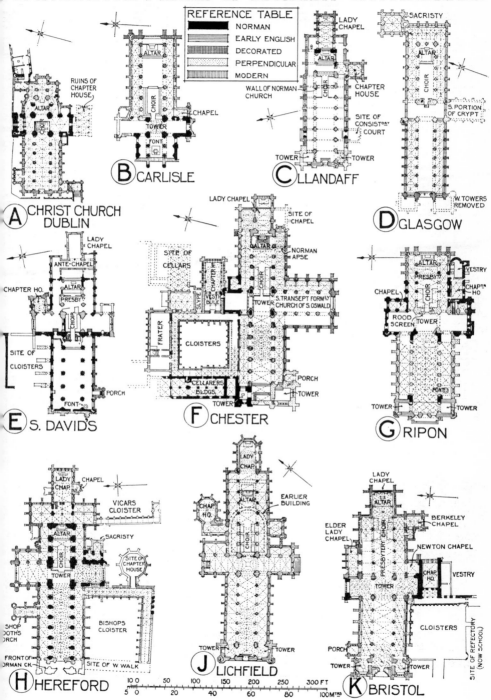

REFERENCE TABLE
NORMAN
EARLY ENGLISH
DECORATED
PERPENDICULAR
MODERN

A CHRIST CHURCH DUBLIN

B CARLISLE

C LLANDAFF

D GLASGOW

E S. DAVID'S

F CHESTER

G RIPON

H HEREFORD

J LICHFIELD

K BRISTOL

THE COMPARATIVE TREATMENT OF
NORMAN   TRANSITIONAL   EARLY ENGLISH
(LANCET)

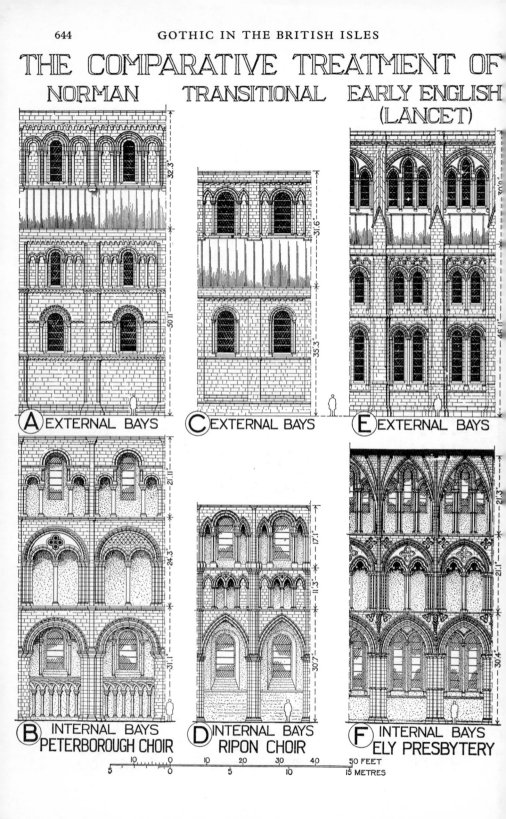

(A) EXTERNAL BAYS

(C) EXTERNAL BAYS

(E) EXTERNAL BAYS

(B) INTERNAL BAYS
PETERBOROUGH CHOIR

(D) INTERNAL BAYS
RIPON CHOIR

(F) INTERNAL BAYS
ELY PRESBYTERY

ENGLISH GOTHIC CATHEDRALS

DECORATED (GEOMETRIC⁴)   DECORATED (CURVILINEAR)   PERPENDICULAR (RECTILINEAR)

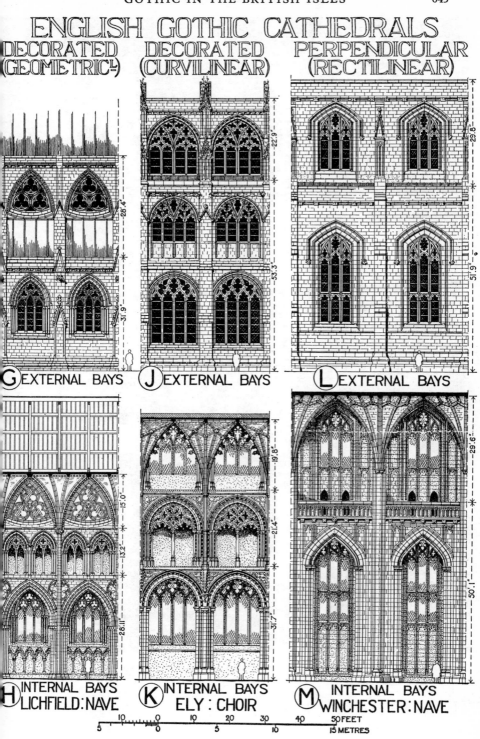

G EXTERNAL BAYS   **J** EXTERNAL BAYS   **L** EXTERNAL BAYS

H INTERNAL BAYS LICHFIELD:NAVE   **K** INTERNAL BAYS ELY : CHOIR   **M** INTERNAL BAYS WINCHESTER:NAVE

King's College Chapel, Cambridge (1446-1515): nave. See p. 653

was continued after the space of two centuries, with only minor details of capitals and mouldings betraying their actual dates. Superficial repairs in any part of a church would substitute the latest tracery or decoration without basic changes to the structure. At Winchester Cathedral (p. 645L, M) an up-to-date stone skin was applied to the massive Norman nave during the second half of the fourteenth century, but the most spectacular reconstruction of an older building took place at Gloucester Abbey (p. 665A, B), when the choir was recased and enlarged upwards as a great lantern of glass and stone, between 1331 and 1367. At Ely (p. 652A) and Southwell the old Romanesque naves survive because the rebuilding schemes begun at the east end never reached them.

In line with continental practice most English churches at first had semicircular or polygonal choir endings. At Westminster (pp. 663D, 664A) a French sort of chevet took the place of an earlier Norman round apse; at Norwich (p. 651C) the twelfth-century lower parts carry a tall perpendicular superstructure of about 1472, whilst Peterborough (p. 660A, B) has a curious combination, with the old apse (c. 1116) surrounded at the base by a spacious retro-choir, fan-vaulted, added between 1496 and 1508 by the mason John Wastell. These examples are exceptional since after 1200 most east ends were built square, and—broadly speaking—fall into two categories: first, those in which the high ridge of the main roof continues unbroken from the crossing to the end of the choir or presbytery (p. 650A) and, secondly, those with a lower roof level east of the high gable of the choir proper (p. 639A). At Beverley (p. 650A) the aisles are withdrawn one bay westwards (the Lady chapel being housed in the central projection); whereas at both Selby (p. 666B) and York the east fronts are great compositions all in one plane, the sides level with the centre. There are similar differences in the second kind; at Salisbury the Lady chapel, under its own gable, is embraced between the parallel roofs of the extended aisles which cover a processional path; at Hereford the eastern chapel projects as a separate block from the long wall of a low eastern transept, which similarly covers the ambulatory. Lichfield, although it is a high ridge example, is unusual in that it has a Lady chapel of three bays terminated by a polygonal apse only slightly lower than the main roof; at Wells an octagonal chapel is embedded in what is otherwise an unexceptional low east end. The choirs of Durham and Fountains (p. 570) both finish with a transept of nine bays roofed to full height.

The detailed internal arrangements of the east end were governed by two factors; the customary placing of the feretory (or principal shrine), if one existed, behind the high altar, and the extent and therefore position of the choir stalls, which normally faced east from about the position of the crossing tower. At Winchester (p. 650C) and S. Albans the feretory is located in the favoured position behind the main altar, separated from it by a solid stone screen. Further screens close off the aisles behind the stalls. The west end of the choir was almost always shut off from the nave by the great stone screen or pulpitum (p. 656B). Occasionally, these were of wood as at Hexham or Manchester (p. 657), and had one central or two side doors for access. Many have been removed, but splendid ones still remain at Exeter, York and elsewhere. The stalls at Westminster occupy the first four bays of the nave, leaving the space under the tower open as a Coronation Theatre, while at S. Albans they are similarly pulled back into the nave.

Eastern transepts, to admit extra light, occur very often, on either side of the choir at about the original position of the high altar. At Lincoln, Beverley (p. 650A) and Salisbury they are very pronounced, and aisled on their eastern sides; but at York the transepts are formed differently, by carrying up a one-bay section of the aisle wall as a tall traceried window to the full height of the main roof. A section of the triforium roof covering is omitted at Ely on either side of the sanctuary, and the upper arcade glazed to admit more light.

In a church served by many clergy extra chapels were always needed. Besides placing altars in available wall spaces, especially with an eastern orientation, other enclosures were made inside both naves and choirs. William of Wykeham's chantry chapel at Winchester is contrived in one bay of the rebuilt nave. Bishop Gower's tomb occupies a specially formed recess in the choir screen at S. David's, an arrangement also found at Exeter. The finest series of mortuary chapels are in Westminster Abbey, but the group in the retro-choir at Winchester are important; one, built for Bishop Stephen Gardiner (1531–55), shows marked Renaissance influence. Sumptuous chapels were added at Ely, in 1488 for Bishop Alcock, and in 1533 for Bishop West (p. 652C) by the extension eastwards of the choir aisles.

The west fronts of English churches hardly ever match the best French ones. The simplest, like Ripon (p. 659A) or Southwell, are barely the width of the nave and aisles with modest towers astride the outer end bays. Others are placed outside the line of the aisles to form a screen. Lincoln (p. 656A) is of colossal size, having fourteenth-century towers (once capped by spires) on top of a thirteenth-century screen which itself sits across a substantial Romanesque façade. Wells (p. 658B) is another wide one, largely thirteenth-century, a broad composition designed to display sculptured figures, to which towers were skilfully added in the fifteenth century. Peterborough (pp. 658A, 660A) has two dumpy towers (one is incomplete), flanked by short transepts fronted by a tall thirteenth-century three-bay arcade, into which a later porch has been inserted. The fourteenth-century cathedral at Exeter does without towers altogether, retaining the Norman ones at either end of the main transepts. York (p. 649) and Beverley were completed similarly with grand pairs of towers, when at other places they were omitted. Winchester and Bath Abbey are two very late perpendicular examples which anticipate the turreted wide-windowed fronts of S. George's Chapel, Windsor (p. 574A) and King's College, Cambridge (646, 694B).

The eventual construction of a central tower was an aspiration of most great church builders. Sometimes the flimsy construction of the crossing precluded anything but a slight projection above it (as at Westminster or Beverley). At others, shortage of funds or structural difficulties discouraged building, so that the superstructure of a tower is frequently later than its lower parts. At Wells (p. 660C) it was necessary to insert strainer arches between the main piers, before the great tower of 1321 was considered safe. The downward load of a central tower could help to stabilize the crossing by offering some resistance to the lateral pressures of the arcades. York's central tower (p. 666A), the largest of all, is carried on piers whose broad perpendicular cases enclose much thinner and much less secure masonry. The spire of Salisbury, 123 m (404 ft) high, was carried up in the fourteenth century from an inconsiderable lower stage built with the rest of the cathedral a hundred years before. The Octagon at Ely (pp. 645J, K, 652A, B) replaced the centre of the old church destroyed when the Norman tower fell in 1322. Perhaps the finest crossing towers of all are those at Lincoln (intended to have a spire) (p. 656A), and the Bell Harry tower at Canterbury (1493–1505), completed just a century after the building of Henry Yevele's superb nave (p. 651A). After King's College Chapel, Cambridge, it is the finest late Gothic building in the country.

Both the chapel at King's (1446–1515) (pp. 646, 694B) and that of S. George's, Windsor (1473–1516) demonstrate the late Gothic ideal church. They are long uniform structures with rather insignificant aisles, richly vaulted in stone over their whole length. S. George's has a small projection north and south, a pale reminder of transepts; both chapels are divided into two by means of massive screens closing

York Minster: west façade. See p. 667

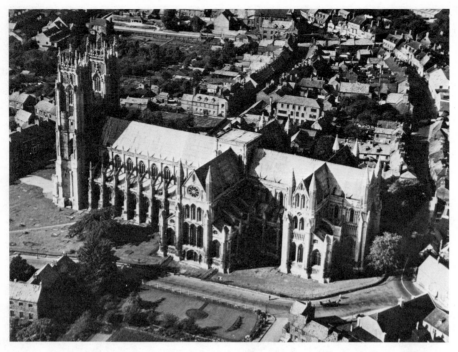

A. Beverley Minster (13th, 14th and 15th cents.): aerial view. See p. 653

B. Beverley Minster: Percy shrine
(c. 1370)

C. Winchester Cathedral: the reredos
(early 16th cent.). See p. 667

A. Canterbury Cathedral from S.W. See pp. 568, 653

B. Canterbury Cathedral: choir
(1174–85) looking E.

C. Norwich Cathedral: presbytery and
apse (11th–15th cents.). See pp. 568, 661

A. Aerial view of Cathedral from S.W. (vaulted Galilee porch 1198–1215)

B. Octagon (1322–40)

C. Bishop West's Chantry (1533)
See p. 648

Ely Cathedral. See p. 654

the choirs proper, one for scholars, the other for royal canons, from naves reduced to the status of processional spaces.

The comparative plans of thirty-one churches (pp. 640–3) are drawn to a uniform scale and indicate the work of successive periods. In the short notices which follow, Early English, Decorated and Perpendicular are abbreviated respectively to E.E., Dec., and Perp. The suffixes C., A., P. and C.C. indicate the original status of the Church or Cathedral, Abbey, Priory or Collegiate Church, irrespective of subsequent changes.

Bangor, C. (p. 642D). Repeatedly destroyed. Present church, which suffered much in the civil wars, is Dec. and Perp. Thoroughly restored by Sir George Gilbert Scott (1866).

Bath, A. (p. 659B). Benedictine, Norman church (1090–1120) with later additions, all demolished and replaced 1501–39 by a late Perp. building occupying the site of the nave only. Large clear-storeys, central tower and broad fan vaults designed by Robert and William Vertue, towerless west front. No cloisters. Extensive repairs by Sir George Gilbert Scott (1864–73).

Beverley, C.C. (p. 650A, B). Scant remains of Norman church. E.E. choir rebuilt with double transepts (1220–60). East window replaced 1416. Perp. nave and towers (c. 1308–1420). Superb canopies, Dec. tomb in north choir aisle (c. 1370), known as Percy shrine, perhaps used as an Easter sepulchre. Early sixteenth-century stalls (cf. Manchester and Ripon). Substantial eighteenth-century repairs; classical pavement and woodwork.

Bristol, A. (pp. 643K, 659C, D). Augustinian monastery. Rectangular Norman chapter house. E.E. 'Elder Lady Chapel'. Dec. choir (1306–32). Modern nave by Street to match choir. Peculiar in having nave and aisles of nearly equal height, with lofty aisle windows, as in German 'hall' churches, without triforium and clear-storey. Remarkable canopied wall recesses.

King's College Chapel, Cambridge, C.C. (pp. 646, 694B). Unlike most other college chapels, it is built in complete isolation from other buildings, and is one of the major monuments of English Mediaeval architecture. Built in three phases, 1446–62, 1477–84 and 1508–15, the first two are noticeable because of a change in the stone used, the latter being chiefly the construction of the great fan vault by the master mason John Wastell. The interior is one space 88 m (289 ft) long, 12.2 m (40 ft) wide with a height to the vault inside of 24.4 m (80 ft), divided only by a timber choir screen (c. 1531–6) in the style of the early Renaissance. There are no proper side aisles, but continuous north and south ranges of chapels and vestries occur between the deeply projecting walls of the main buttresses. The painted glass of the main windows is the most complete set to survive from the Tudor period, with an iconographical scheme still Mediaeval in tradition.

Christchurch, Hampshire, A. Norman nave and transepts completed by about 1130. Ambitious late Perp. choir added in two parts, a four-bay chancel and an ambulatory bay from which the tall Lady chapel projects; lierne vaulted. Solid Dec. reredos (c. 1350) with forceful sculpture separates the choir from the eastern chapels (cf. Winchester and S. Albans). Notable tombs, especially in the Draper chantry (1529) which combines Gothic and Renaissance motifs and stallwork. Massive Perp. west tower and north porch.

Canterbury, A.C. (pp. 641B, 651A, B). First Norman church was built 1071–7. Choir replaced and enlarged 1096–1126; choir rebuilt on the remains after fire and extended eastwards 1174–85 by master mason William of Sens and his successors. Original Norman work of singular interest (p. 564A). Contraction in width of choir, to preserve two earlier Norman chapels. At extreme east is 'Becket's Crown' and Patriarchal Chair. There are extensive crypts of 1100–25 under eastern portion.

Double transepts. Splendid late Perp. central tower (1490–1503). Perp. nave begun 1379 by Henry Yevele, west front and towers unimportant. Much thirteenth-century glass. Oblong chapter house (1400) with fine wooden ceiling. Perp. cloisters on north of great beauty. Numerous side chapels.

Carlisle, A.C. (p. 643B). Augustinian abbey. Only two bays of Norman nave remain. Dec. east end of beautiful design with fine traceried windows.

Chester, A. (p. 643F). Originally the convent of S. Werburgh, became Benedictine Abbey 1093. Built of red sandstone. Dec. nave; northern arcade has triforium and clear-storey combined. Perp. central tower. Cloisters on north. Lady chapel at east end.

Chichester, C. (p. 642G). Chief example of double aisles, resulting from former lateral chapels. Fine central spire. Norman nave. Transitional retro-choir. Bell-tower (fifteenth-century) only surviving detached example to an English cathedral.

Durham, A.C. (pp. 564D, 641E). Norman work (1093–1133). Massive. E.E eastern transept, known as the 'Chapel of the Nine Altars' (1242–80) and central Perp. tower (1465–90). A group of great dignity which has few rivals. Norman nave (1110–33) is finest in England with pillars, about the same width as the openings, channelled with chevrons, diapers and flutes. Norman north transept vaults (1128–33) first to incorporate pointed ribs.

Ely, A. (pp. 640A, 644E, F, 645J, K, 652). Norman nave and transepts with timber roof (modern painting). Choir remarkable for carving. Unique central octagon (1322–40), 21.3 m (70 ft) in diameter with unequal sides, by John Attegrene, master mason, has rich wooden vault with octagonal lantern by master carpenter William Hurley. This plan influenced that of S. Paul, London (p. 1014). Exceptional Lady chapel, 30.5 m × 14 m (100 ft × 46 ft) (1321–49) (cf. chapter house, Canterbury). Imposing west front 55 m (180 ft) wide with high tower, same width as nave, flanked originally both north and south by transepts with octagonal turrets. In front of the tower projects the E.E. vaulted Galilee porch (1198–1215).

Exeter, C. (pp. 642E, 655). Norman twin towers over north and south transepts. The finest specimen of the Dec. style and rich in varied tracery and carved stonework. Unusual Perp. sculptured screen to west façade.

Gloucester, A. (pp. 641C, 665B). Early Perp. south transept (1329–37) (p. 665A), Norman choir cased with Perp. (cf. Winchester). Perp. fan-vaulted cloisters of singular completeness. Choir has largest Perp. windows in England, with elaborate Lady chapel. Central tower 68.5 m (225 ft) high with flying buttresses.

Hereford, C. (p. 643H). Norman nave and choir, E.E. Lady chapel and Dec. central tower. Famous 'Mappa Mundi' in south choir aisle.

Lichfield, C. (pp. 643J, 645G, H). Built of reddish stone sited on sloping ground. Nave, transepts, chapter house and west front in E.E. style. Graceful central and western spires in Dec. style form the only triple group of spires in England. Bow-sided triangular clear-storey windows. No cloisters.

Lincoln, C. (pp. 640F, 656). Is situated on a steep hill dominating the town. Some Norman work of 1073 and later at west end. Rebuilt 1129–1320. Choir and lesser transepts 1192–1200, the earliest example of E.E. work of known date. E.E. main transepts, nave, central tower, Galilee porch and chapter house (1209–53). Dec. 'Angel Choir' (retro-choir) also of remarkably advanced design for its date (1256–80). Central tower heightened (1307–11, from the designs of Richard of Stow), the highest at 82.5 m (271 ft) in England. Cloisters on the north (1296). E.E. decagonal chapter house, vaulted to central pillar and surmounted by flying buttresses. Unusual west front consists of screen wall behind which rise two western towers.

Exeter Cathdral: nave looking E. (mid-14th century). See pp. 568, 654

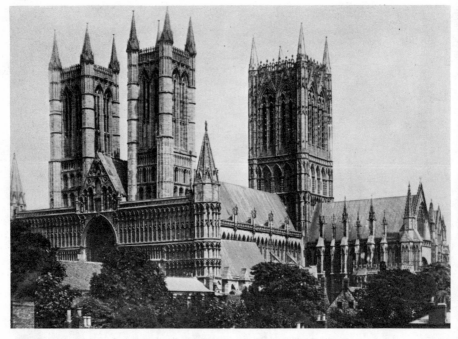

A. Lincoln Cathedral (11th–14th cents.) from S.W. See p. 654

B. Lincoln Cathedral: choir (1192–1200) looking W.

Manchester Cathedral (1422–1520): nave looking E. See p. 661

A. Peterborough Cathedral: west façade (*c.* 1193–1230). See pp. 568, 661

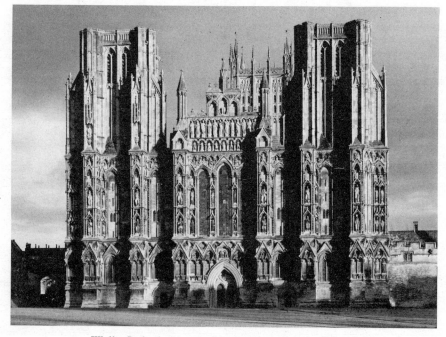

B. Wells Cathedral: west façade (*c.* 1206–42). See p. 662

A. Ripon Minster: west façade
(*c.* 1233). See p. 661

B. Bath Abbey (1501–39): west façade.
See p. 653

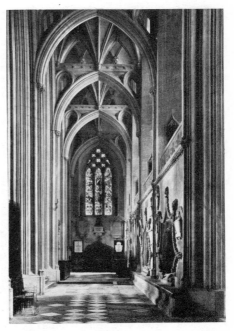

c. Choir looking E.

D. Choir aisle vault

Bristol Cathedral. See pp. 568, 653

A. Peterborough Cathedral: aerial view from S.E. (1117–93). See pp. 568, 661

B. Peterborough Cathedral:
retro-choir

C. Wells Cathedral (*c.* 1180–*c.* 1425):
nave looking E. with 14th-cent.
strainer arches under central tower.
See pp. 648, 662

Llandaff, C. (p. 643C). Begun 1120. A long low building situated at foot of hill, without transepts or side chapels, E.E. west front. Two western towers. Nave much restored. Square chapter house with central pillar. No triforium or cloisters. Had important classical repairs.

Manchester, C.C. (pp. 642B, 657). Perp. (1422–1520). Remarkable for double aisles obtained, as at Chichester, by inclusion of side chapels. Fine stalls.

Norwich, A.C. (pp. 641D, 651C). Long narrow Norman nave (1096–1145), aisleless transepts, and choir with apsidal chapels. Bold central spire, choir, clearstorey, some windows on south of nave and vaulting throughout are Perp. Remains of original bishop's throne behind High Altar. Eastern apsidal chapel replaced by Lady chapel, since destroyed. Chapter house, resembling Durham, also destroyed.

Oxford, P. (pp. 630B, 642C). Augustinian. Norman nave and choir (1158–80). E.E. chapter house and Lady chapel. Nave pillars, alternately circular and polygonal, support lofty Norman arches beneath which is triforium gallery—an unusual arrangement in order to give height. Norman central tower with E.E. upper part and short spire. Nave, shortened by Cardinal Wolsey when building his college of Christ Church, forms a vestibule to choir, which has fan vaulting with pendants.

Peterborough, A. (pp. 640D, 644A, B, 658A, 660A, B). Norman church (1117–93) with next finest interior after Durham. Nave timber roof is very probably the oldest in England, with painted wooden ceiling of lozenge-shaped compartments. Nave aisles vaulted (cf. Ely). Apsidal choir enclosed on the east by rectangular Perp. retro-choir, fan-vaulted, as at King's College, Cambridge. Grand E.E. western façade (c. 1193–1230), 48 m (158 ft) wide, has a portico of three gigantic arches, the full height of the cathedral. A gable crowns each arch, and angle abutments are carried up as small towers with spires. Other towers rise immediately behind, over western bays of the aisles. Central archway encloses two-storeyed Perp. porch.

Ripon, C.C. (pp. 643G, 644C, D, 659A). Begun c. 1179, but nave and much of choir rebuilt later. Central and two western towers. Saxon crypt. Rich choir stalls with tabernacle work. Perfect E.E. western façade (c. 1233) (restored by Sir George Gilbert Scott).

Rochester, A.C. (p. 642H). Norman and E.E. crypt, Norman nave and west doorway. E.E. walled-in choir and transepts. Perp. clear-storey and wooden roof.

S. Albans, A. (p. 642F). Much destroyed and altered in modern times. Norman nave (longest in England, 86.5 m—284 ft), transepts and choir. Western portion of nave is E.E. Dec. marble shrine of S. Alban discovered and re-erected by Sir George Gilbert Scott.

S. Asaph, C. (p. 642A). Rebuilt in Dec. style. Central tower, formerly with timber spire. No triforium. Perp. roof and choir stalls. Restored by Sir George Gilbert Scott.

ʿS. David's, C. (p. 643E). Central tower. Two-storeyed south porch. Transitional nave arches support a carved oak roof of Perp. design (1508). Dec. rood-screen. West front 1789 by John Nash, rebuilt again by Sir George Gilbert Scott.

Salisbury, C. (pp. 639, 640E). On a level site. Almost entirely in the E.E. style (1220–58). Characteristic of English Gothic as Amiens is of French (p. 601). Double transepts, central tower, Dec. spire 123 m (404 ft) high, the loftiest in England. West façade (1258–65) is unimpressive, but a fine vaulted north porch projects boldly. Dec. cloisters. Restorations by James Wyatt and Sir George Gilbert Scott. Vaulted octagonal chapter house (1263–84). Detached belfry pulled down.

Selby, A. (p. 666B). Norman nave begun after 1100 and continued westwards in Trans. E.E. style. Sumptuous Dec. choir rebuilt 1280–1340. South transept and central tower reconstructed 1909; west towers completed (1935) by Oldrid Scott.

Southwark (S. Saviour, or S. Mary Overie), A. (p. 628C). Restored nave, E.E. choir and retro-choir or Lady chapel.

Southwell, C.C. (p. 642K). Norman nave, transepts and three towers, E.E. choir. Dec. octagonal chapter house without central pillar, probably the model for York, has rich and well-preserved naturalistic carving. No cloisters.

Wells, C. (pp. 642J, 658B, 660C). c. 1180–c. 1425. E.E. nave, double transepts, and western bays of choir. The E.E. west front, 46 m (150 ft) wide, including buttresses, is flanked by towers arcaded and enriched with sculpture—the highest development in English Gothic of this type of façade. Central tower, eastern Lady chapel and octagonal chapter house. Unique triforium of close-set openings. As illustrating the comparative height to width of English and French cathedrals, Wells is 9.7 m (32 ft) wide and 20.4 m (67 ft) high (two to one), and Amiens is 14 m (46 ft) wide and 42.6 m (140 ft) high (three to one).

Westminster, A. (pp. 629H, 663, 664, 665C). Perhaps the single most important Mediaeval building in Britain. Traditionally on the same site as a church built in 616, the Benedictine monastery was founded by S. Dunstan in 960 and partly rebuilt by Edward the Confessor, 1055–65, but the greater part was reconstructed on a grander scale by Henry III. The present eastern arm, transepts and five bays of the nave were built between 1245 and 1269 and are E.E. The vault is 31 m (102 ft) to the ridge. The octagonal chapter house, vaulted from a central clustered pier is supported by bold flying buttresses, built in 1250. The nave, continued westwards between 1375 and 1506 adhered to the E.E. design but uses Perp. detail. The cloisters are of various dates, Dec. in character. The upper parts of the western towers were added 1736–45 by John James to a design by Nicholas Hawksmoor, in a mixed classical and Gothic style. The east end of the choir terminates in a polygonal apse, with an ambulatory and a cluster of surrounding chapels (pp. 664A, 665C). It is the only complete 'chevet' in England, and contains the shrine of Edward the Confessor and the Coronation Chair. Other Mediaeval monuments abound; notably those of Queen Eleanor (1290), Henry III (1272), Edward I (1307) and Aymer de Valence (1324). There are splendid Tudor and Jacobean examples; to Queen Elizabeth (1603) and Mary Queen of Scots (1587), and a whole range of others from the seventeenth century to the present day, which constitute the most complete and extensive collections of sepulchral art in the country. The choir stalls (nineteenth-century copies) are drawn back into the four easternmost bays of the nave (pp. 663D, 665C), leaving the crossing and sanctuary open for coronation ceremonials (as in Reims cathedral). Beyond the ambulatory is the Chapel of Henry VII (p. 664C), built by the brothers Robert and William Vertue between 1503 and 1519 on the site of the Lady chapel of 1220. The stone fan vault ranks with that over the choir at Christ Church, Oxford (c. 1478–1503), as the most elaborate achievement of the late Gothic period. Long pendants, apparently unsupported, are really elongated voussoirs of half-concealed transverse arches, from which the conoidal web is built up. The outer wall buttresses take the form of octagonal piers, between which multi-sided windows light the deep recesses of the side aisles. The tomb of the King and his Queen, Elizabeth of York (by Pietro Torrigiani) is enclosed by a metal screen with a fine range of stalls on either side.

Whilst the conventual buildings have undergone many changes, the whole complex is intact enough to give a good idea of the arrangements of the precinct of a great abbey. The dormitory, part of the refectory, infirmary and Abbot's house remain, in fragmentary form; only at Fountains and Chester are monastic buildings more completely preserved. In the adjoining **Palace of Westminster, S. Stephen's Chapel,** with its surviving undercroft, begun in 1292, was architecturally related to the Sainte-Chapelle in Paris. **Westminster Hall** (p. 634C),

WESTMINSTER ABBEY

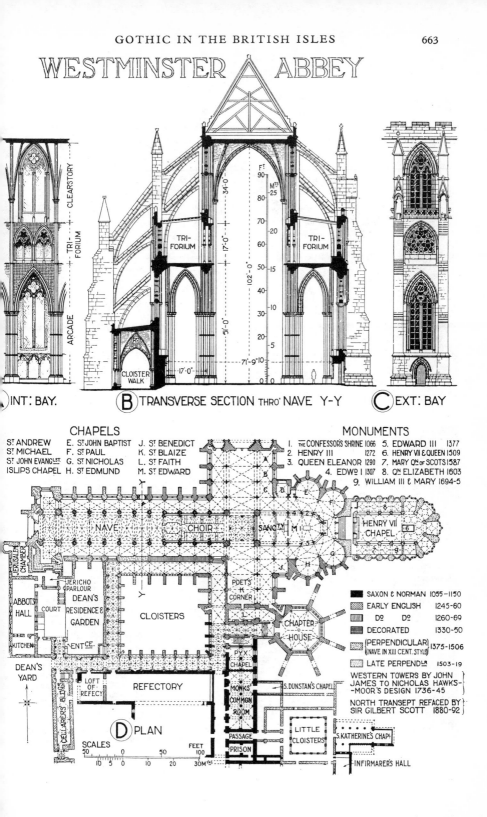

INT: BAY.

(B) TRANSVERSE SECTION THRO' NAVE Y-Y

(C) EXT: BAY

CHAPELS

ST ANDREW E. ST JOHN BAPTIST J. ST BENEDICT
ST MICHAEL F. ST PAUL K. ST BLAIZE
ST JOHN EVANGLST G. ST NICHOLAS L. ST FAITH
ISLIPS CHAPEL H. ST EDMUND M. ST EDWARD

MONUMENTS

1. THE CONFESSOR'S SHRINE 1066   5. EDWARD III 1377
2. HENRY III   1272   6. HENRY VII & QUEEN 1509
3. QUEEN ELEANOR 1290   7. MARY QN OF SCOTS 1587
    4. EDWD I 1307   8. QN ELIZABETH 1603
                9. WILLIAM III & MARY 1694-5

SAXON & NORMAN 1055-1150
EARLY ENGLISH 1245-60
DO   DO   1260-69
DECORATED   1330-50
(PERPENDICULAR) 1375-1506
(NAVE IN XIII CENT. STYLE)
LATE PERPENDLR   1503-19

WESTERN TOWERS BY JOHN }
JAMES TO NICHOLAS HAWKS- }
-MOOR'S DESIGN 1736-45 }

NORTH TRANSEPT REFACED BY }
SIR GILBERT SCOTT 1880-92 }

(D) PLAN

A. Westminster Abbey from S.E.: Henry VII's Chapel on right. See p. 662

B. Westminster Abbey:
Nave looking E.

C. Westminster Abbey: Henry VII's
Chapel (1503–19) looking west

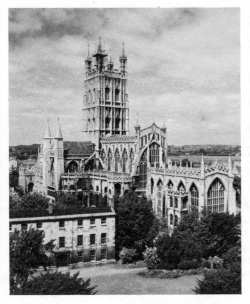

A. Gloucester Cathedral from S.E.
(14th–15th cents.). See pp. 568, 654

B. Gloucester Cathedral:
Lady Chapel looking W.

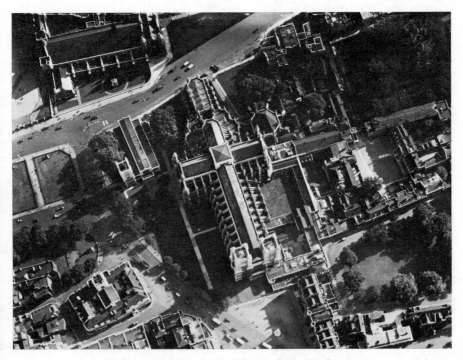

C. Westminster Abbey: aerial view from W. See p. 662

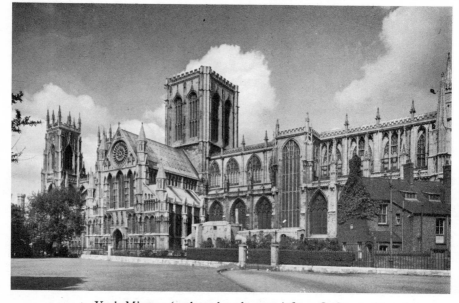

A. York Minster (14th and 15th cents.) from S. See p. 667

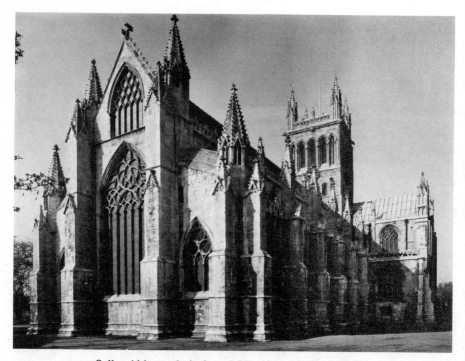

B. Selby Abbey: choir from N.E. (1280–1340). See p. 661

reconstructed between 1394 and 1402, is another major survival built into Sir Charles Barry's nineteenth-century Houses of Parliament.

Winchester, A.C. (pp. 640C, 645L, M, 650C). Greater total length—170 m (560 ft)—than any other Mediaeval cathedral in Europe. Norman transepts and tower (1079–95). Norman nave and choir (1079–93) transformed by veneer of Perp. on Norman core and a vaulted roof. Largest E.E. retro-choir (1202–c. 1235) in England. Dec. stalls (cf. Gloucester). Tombs and chantries. Timber vault (1510–28) to choir.

S. George's Chapel, Windsor, C.C. (pp. 574A, 629K). Begun in 1475 and continued east to west. Fourteen bays, seven on either side of a central oblong crossing (intended for a tower like that of Bath), a symmetrical arrangement 72 m (237 ft) in length. The short transepts have polygonal ends, and there are smaller chapels likewise east and west. The west front has no towers. The interior is splendidly vaulted and of complex design, divided into a flattened central ceiling with coved half-vaults either side in the choir, nave and transepts, with fan vaults proper under the crossing and in the lower aisles. There is a stone pulpitum (1790–2) and a set of wooden stalls (Perp.) (1478–85).

Worcester, A.C. (p. 641A). Level site on banks of the Severn. Norman crypt, transepts and circular chapter house (the only one in England). E.E. choir, Dec. and Perp. nave, cloisters and central tower, 60 m (196 ft) high. Interesting monuments, including royal chantries of King John and Prince Arthur.

York, C. (pp. 640B, 649, 666A). Largest in both area and width, 32 m (106 ft) within the walls, of any English Mediaeval cathedral. E.E. transepts remarkable for beauty of mouldings and the 'Five Sisters'—a name given to lancet windows of north transept, each 15 m (50 ft) high and 1.5 m (5 ft) wide. Unique fourteenth-century stained glass. Nave and octagonal chapter house, with wooden roof and without central columns, of Edwardian Gothic (1261–1324). Perp. towers. No cloisters. Nave—second in height to Westminster Abbey—and choir have wooden imitation of stone vault. West front of French type.

Other important churches include:

Abbey Dore, Herefordshire, A. The choir of this Cistercian abbey, now the village church, is E.E., built with a square ambulatory and five vaulted chapels about 1220. The nave is destroyed.

Boxgrove, Sussex, P. A fragment of the nave, crossing and the complete chancel. The latter added to the Romanesque parts about 1220. E.E.

Brecon, Breconshire, P. Large E.E. choir of three bays with close groups of tall lancets; vault renewed. Nave Dec., octagonal piers and squat clear-storey. Simple undecorated exterior; Lady chapel north of chancel; short central tower; extensive restorations since 1850.

Cartmel, Lancashire, P. Norman and E.E.; remodelled Perp. windows and curious upper stage to tower set diagonally on earlier base. Notable Dec. tomb (1347), and fifteenth-century stalls with Renaissance canopies (1618–23).

Edington, Wiltshire, C.C. An earlier church was replaced from about 1341 to house a new community founded by William of Edington, later Bishop of Winchester. The church demonstrates the change from the Dec. to Perp. styles (cf. Gloucester choir and Winchester Cathedral).

Great Malvern, Worcestershire, P. Six-bay Norman nave (c. 1085), with later clear-storey to bring the height up to that of the late Perp. choir built between 1420–60. Crossing vaulted and tower elaborately panelled rather like that of Gloucester Cathedral. Notable collection of Mediaeval floor tiles.

Hexham, Northumberland, A. Large cruciform church, mainly late E.E. and early Dec., with best-preserved internal night stair now extant, and ancient crypt.

Howden, Yorkshire, C.C. Good example of a church of intermediate size, mainly Perp., with very tall central tower in three stages. Choir and octagonal chapter house in ruins.

Ottery S. Mary, Devon, C.C. Twin transeptal towers (*c.* 1260), like those at Exeter; the remainder substantially Dec. (*c.* 1337–60).

Rievaulx, Yorkshire, A. After Fountains the best preserved ruin. Extensive conventual buildings and lavish E.E. choir (*c.* 1225–40). Transepts and nave enlarged upwards to match the new scale.

Sherborne, Dorset, A. Largely rebuilt in fifteenth century with fan vaults.

Tewkesbury, Gloucestershire, A. Sombre Romanesque church. Early fourteenth-century Dec. clear-storey and vault added to choir. Nave has low E.E. vault. Important range of canopied tombs of fourteenth and fifteenth centuries.

Tintern, Monmouthshire, A. Most perfectly preserved ruin of a Cistercian church, largely geometrical Dec. Low central tower, remains of lay-brothers' choir in nave. No eastern extension beyond the great east window, of spectacular size.

PARISH CHURCHES

The greater abbeys and cathedrals apart, parish churches are collectively of prime importance; there are still more than 9,000 Mediaeval examples in existence.

With a few exceptions (such as **S. Mary Redcliffe, Bristol,** p. 670A, B), parish church design uses the style of more sophisticated work without being in the fullest sense 'Gothic'—if by this term we mean structurally regulated by a bay system of vaulted compartments. Decorative devices, window tracery, even plans follow the precedent of more important buildings, but the functional and architectural development of the average parish church was related to such local factors as the available building materials, population and relative prosperity. For obvious reasons the most impressive churches are the later ones, built during the fifteenth century and enlarging or replacing earlier structures. After the mid-fourteenth century the great churches might be said to have lost some of their importance, since much more money was in the hands of middle class merchants and others who lavished it on local buildings. Large Perpendicular parish churches (pp. 657, 675A) were therefore often in the forefront of artistic development. They were the characteristic ecclesiastical buildings of their time, in the same way that the choirs of the cathedrals of Lincoln or Exeter had been in the thirteenth and fourteenth centuries.

It is convenient to use the progressive enlargement of the typical parish church to illustrate the development of vernacular church buildings over a period of more than three hundred years. There are examples where development was frozen at an early stage as at **Tilty** and **Southease** churches (pp. 669B, 671B); other churches were lavishly rebuilt in an intermediate style (e.g. **S. Andrew, Heckington, Lincs.,** p. 671A) and not changed afterwards. But the majority can show work of all periods from Romanesque (and occasionally Saxon) up to the late Perpendicular Gothic of the sixteenth century.

In the Norman period, when the majority of parish churches were located on their present sites, there was still a strong turriform (i.e. centrally planned) tradition of Celtic origin, as at **Breamore, Hants** (p. 669A). Square chancels soon replaced semicircular apses; sometimes a short tower bestrode the axial ridge between chancel and nave (as at Iffley, Oxfordshire), but most towers were built against the west wall of the nave, as at **S. Cuthbert, Wells** (p. 670C). An early tower in the centre of a church enlarged on all sides, might survive until the final rebuilding absorbed it vertically (e.g. Tamworth, Staffordshire). Only rarely does one find both central and western towers, but quite frequently a late Gothic church might have a quasi-cruciform plan (maybe a reminder of a vanished central tower), since one or two

A. Breamore Church, Hants (mid 10th century) from S.W. See p. 668

B. Tilty Church, Essex (13th and 14th cents.) from S.E. See p. 668

A. S. Mary Redcliffe, Bristol:
nave looking E. See p. 668

B. S. Mary Redcliffe, Bristol:
south porch

C. S. Cuthbert, Wells (15th century) from S.E. See p. 668

A. S. Andrew, Heckington, from
S.W. (14th cent.). See p. 668

B. Southease Church, Sussex
(15th cent.). See p. 668

C. All Saints Church, Stock,
Essex (15th cent.). See p. 637

D. S. John, Devizes, Wilts.
South Chapel from E. See p. 673

A. Ipplepen Church, Devon (mid-15th cent.): rood screen. See p. 673

B. Southwold Church, Suffolk (15th cent.): lower part of screen. See p. 674

C. S. Thomas of Canterbury, Salisbury, Wilts (early 16th cent.):
the Doom painting over chancel arch. See p. 674

bays of both the north and south aisle walls project under roofs running across the church (p. 671A).

During the thirteenth century first one and then another aisle would be added on to the nave. Usually the new outer walls were raised first, and then careful openings made through the old masonry into the church. One aisle might be added long after another, which explains many assymmetrical examples with arcades of two distinct dates. Later, still wider aisles might be made together with other enlargements or repairs, leaving an older arcade intact or replacing it in a style matching a super-imposed clear-storey. An old lower roof line is often apparent from raking marks on the eastern face of the west tower.

The elaboration of ritual, the popularity of processions, and the growth of the chantry movement all had profound effects on church planning during the four-teenth century. Chancels were rebuilt again, as they had been the century before. Aisles were enlarged or given new windows, extended eastward on either side of the chancel and united with it through wide arches. When a wealthy donor provided part of the structure, it might be absorbed into a general scheme of enlargement or remain as a conspicuous appendage, as at **S. John, Devizes** (p. 671D).

By the fifteenth century the walls of the nave were nearly always raised above those of the side aisles. If the windowed clear-storey was extended along the chancel also, the chancel arch became redundant, since it no longer marked a drop in outside roof level. Thus it was sometimes removed or not built at all in new churches. By this means the 'through church' of the fifteenth century was evolved: a nave and chancel of equal height flanked by wide, lower, aisles running the full extent from west to east. Other more superficial features were added, such as crenellated parapets (p. 670C), raised or rebuilt towers, especially in certain regions like Somerset (p. 670C), spires of stone or wood, wider traceried windows to accommodate stained glass, and sumptuous north and south porches (p. 670B).

A fully-developed church of the later Middle Ages would have an internal appearance very different from that which it has today. Good, finely-jointed masonry was used only in the best buildings. Rubble walls inside and out would be plastered and regularly coated with thin limewash. All but the finest ashlar would be treated in this way, unless there were costly or well-preserved wall paintings which were part of a comprehensive iconographical scheme. Internal movable fittings would be few. Pews and benches were introduced very late. There might be an elaborately decorated cover to the font, either opening at the sides or raised from above. Numerous parclose screens (p. 675B) enclosed separated chapels which housed the tombs of wealthy benefactors together with their attendant chantry altars, the scant remains of wall sinks (or piscinas) often indicating their former positions today.

In nearly every church, large and small, a Rood screen and loft divided the interior into two distinct parts. While certain liturgical practices were associated with them, the basic function of the loft was to provide access to the Rood figures above. Staircases were contrived, either within the thickness of the adjoining walls, or as a freestanding timber structure, at times little more than a ladder. Whilst the screen was usually contained by the chancel arch, in some later examples, notably in the south west, it continued across the full width of the church, having three doorways instead of the usual one as in **Ipplepen Church, Devon** (p. 672A). Often there were secondary altars, each with its own reredos, ranged against the western face. In its most characteristic form, the lower part of the actual screen widens out to the loft platform above, with an elaborate canopy of vaulted panels. Occasionally the parapet of the loft survives as at Kenton and Atherington in Devon, and **Dennington, Suffolk** (p. 675D). Above the suspended Rood figures there was a painted background (usually of the Last Judgement) on a canvas screen, on wooden boards or on the plaster surface of the surrounding arch, as in the **Church of S. Thomas of Canterbury, Salisbury** (p. 672C). Sometimes that part of the ceiling immediately overhead was given special decorative treatment. Particularly in East Anglia and Devon, there are substantial remains of original polychromatic painted decorations, which convey some idea of the sumptuous effect of a late Gothic interior in its original state (p. 672B).

Inside the chancel itself there might be a few wooden stalls, not unlike those of a conventual church, used by chantry priests and other dependent clergy at the main services. The high altar (of stone) would be placed against the east wall or a little way forward from it, raised up two or three steps in front of an elaborate stone or timber reredos. The roof might (like that over the Rood) be decoratively treated and have a bracketed ceilure and a boss, from which a pyx or sacrament house could hang. A three-seat sedilia and a mural wash basin (piscina) were often situated against the south wall. Opposite, an Easter Sepulchre was sometimes contrived, either in conjunction with a tomb or as an elaborate object in its own right, as at **All Saints Church, Hawton, Nottinghamshire** (p. 675C).

Local variations in architectural style and decoration are important and regional characteristics based on building materials and economic factors are easy to observe. In the many smaller fittings there is a marked similarity in the decoration applied to objects of all kinds. Perhaps at no other period has one style, in all aspects of design, been so pervasive. Constructional devices, essentially lithic in character, are used indiscriminately, so that they may generate the spire-like form of a late Perpendicular timber font-cover, the decoration of a silver ornament, or the arrangement of the tracery of a chantry screen (p. 675B).

CASTLES AND FORTIFICATIONS

The earliest defensive structures in Britain are the prehistoric earthworks, of which Maiden Castle in Dorset is perhaps the best known. Old Sarum in Wiltshire is another which was re-used in the feudal period. The Romans built forts and walled towns which were occasionally redeveloped. The Mediaeval town walls of Chester and York were enlarged on such foundations, and at Cardiff a Norman motte was raised within a Roman enclosure, strengthened by the addition of mural towers.

A simple classification may be made as follows:

(1) *Ancient earthworks*, e.g. Bratten, Wiltshire, and Oswestry, Shropshire.

(2) *Roman fortifications*, e.g. Caerwent, Monmouthshire, and Hadrian's Wall.

(3) *Feudal fortresses:* (*a*) Motte and bailey castles (p. 573C), (*b*) Curtain wall castles, (*c*) Concentric castles.

(4) *Artillery forts.*

(5) *Dismantled castles, domestic enlargements, fortified manor houses.*

The main strength of Norman motte and bailey castles had been either in the shell keep, or in the 'donjon' within the bailey. From the early thirteenth century, however, the outer encircling walls were strengthened, made thicker and higher, to bind together the whole castle as one defensive unit. Occasionally an old keep was retained, as at **Goodrich, Herefordshire,** embedded in later walls, or at **Helmsley, Yorkshire,** where it became one amongst a whole series of mural towers. At **Framlingham, Suffolk** (*c.* 1200) the wall towers are rectangular, but like the later keeps at **Orford, Suffolk** (1166–72) (p. 573B) or **Conisborough, Yorkshire** (*c.* 1190) (p. 573F), they were usually made polygonal or circular, so as to resist the dangers of mining more effectively.

The castle building programme of Edward I in Wales began in 1277 and was

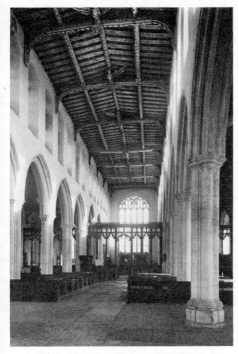

A. Holy Trinity Church, Blythburgh, Suffolk: nave looking E. See p. 668

B. Lavenham Church, Suffolk: screen to the Spryng Chapel. See p. 673

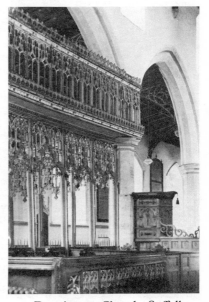

C. All Saints Church, Hawton, Notts. Easter Sepulchre. See p. 674

D. Dennington Church, Suffolk: rood loft. See p. 673

A. Conway Castle, Caernarvonshire (1283–9): town and walls. See p. 677

B. Caernarvon Castle from Coed Helen Hill (1283–1323). See p. 677

largely directed by the royal mason, Master James of S. George, who imported the latest techniques in fortification from the continent. Since the main strength of a curtain wall system was the outer wall itself, the gatehouse and entrance arrangements were of crucial importance; a pair of towers built close together would have several doors, drawbridges, pits and barbicans. There are particularly elaborate gatehouses at **Denbigh, Chepstow** and **Pembroke,** so massive that they are the equivalent of the old keeps. Where possible, some principal apartments were contrived in the towers, but the courtyard within was normally disposed with the larger residential rooms, great hall and stables leaning against the outer walls in such a way that there was access above along the whole length of the ramparts.

Three defensive principles affected the design of the great enclosure. Firstly, by making battered walls and spurs, where possible with ditches and water defences, the attackers were kept away from the base of the curtain. Secondly, maximum command of the intervening walls was secured by the generous projection of the mural towers and the construction of overhanging crenellations, although at first these might be wooden hoardings on galleries, and later machicolations of stone. Thirdly, it was desirable that each tower and sector of wall should be individually defensible. A tower would be accessible by stairs, having doors at each level to isolate one or more floors or section of rampart. Occasionally small surmounting turrets were placed on towers (already higher than the walls) to give extra command of the rooftops. This principle of limited internal defence was frequently extended, so that the bailey or ward was subdivided into parts defensible to some extent on their own, with a strong gate between them.

Conway (1283–9) (p. 676A) and **Caernarvon** (1283–1323) (p. 676B) are the most sophisticated examples of this type. A ring of eight towers in all, projecting well away from the walls, surrounds the natural crag on which Conway castle stands. The four towers nearest to the river are grouped closer together (with an upper turret apiece) and were approached by a further barbican and gatehouse from the waterside. The outer subsidiary towers and those of the town wall are backless, i.e. semicircular in plan, to prevent their use inwards by attackers who managed to gain the ramparts. Caernarvon has the added strength of several superimposed mural galleries between its polygonal towers, which allowed concentrated fire to be directed from the south face of the enclosure. At both places the courtyards were originally divided into two self-contained parts, and whilst their strength and grandeur are exceptional, at a host of other castles old walls were surrounded and strengthened by the construction of subsidiary outer lines of defence.

By this means the 'concentric' principle was developed which, at **Caerphilly** (1267–77), **Harlech** (1283–90) (p. 679B) and **Beaumaris** (1283–1323) (p. 679A) takes on a more systematic and symmetrical form. At Beaumaris a pair of large gatehouses (each composed of four towers, two large and two small) are centrally sited at the opposite ends of an enclosure linking six other major towers detached for three-quarters of their circumference. Outside this there is a narrow surrounding courtyard within a further wall lower than the first. A wide moat, originally linked to the sea by a channel, is crossed by an elaborate gatehouse itself associated with a strong town wall.

Settlement within a planned township, adjoining a castle, was frequently encouraged by the granting of chartered rights and privileges. Perfect examples of these 'bastides' are **Flint, Conway, Caernarvon, Beaumaris, Ludlow** and **Chepstow,** in which the original grid pattern of streets is apparent in spite of later encroachments. Later in the Middle Ages other towns, especially the wealthy merchant cities of York, Chester, Norwich and Southampton, enlarged their walls for self-defence. At **Chester** the walls right round the town are in good order to a height of about 3.7 m (12 ft), but all the old gates have gone. Two and a half miles of wall survives on both sides of the river Ouse at **York,** dating mainly from the mid-fourteenth century. There are numerous towers, and of the three remaining gateways, Bootham Bar, **Micklegate Bar** (p. 680B) and Walmgate, the latter retains substantial parts of its elaborate barbican.

By the end of the fourteenth century the military importance of the castle had declined as the character of warfare changed. A more polite society demanded higher standards of comfort, and fortified manors became popular alternatives to the old castles. Some great fortresses were rebuilt or substantially modified. **Kenilworth Castle, Warwickshire** is an example representing many periods of construction. To a Norman keep (1160–80) a large outer bailey was added (1200–60) surrounded by extensive water defences. In 1571 the Earl of Leicester added a new gatehouse and a range of modern apartments. In its weakened state it withstood a seige in the Civil War like the even more splendid **Raglan Castle, Monmouthshire** (c. 1430–60) (p. 680A), where the old defences consisted of a moated tower linked to a curtain wall enclosure. In the sixteenth century new apartments were made, windows enlarged, a new decorative gatehouse built and the moat spanned by a two-storey bridge. In its restored state Raglan perfectly illustrates the outlook of the later Middle Ages, when there was a curious revival of interest in feudal chivalry—a movement which found its most bizarre expression in the mock Mediaeval keep at **Bolsover Castle, Derbyshire** (1612–21) (p. 680C).

After 1400 obsolete castles rapidly fell into ruins, but as late as the sixteenth century there were a few new constructions, notably a series of artillery forts along the south coast. Two examples are **Deal** (p. 679C) and **Walmer,** both in Kent and started after 1540, which have spacious gun platforms and ammunition stores; gun ports replacing arrow-slits. Sometimes a castle was brought up to date by the reduction and filling of the old towers as a solid base for ordnance. Walled earth banks, their ends shaped like the more ambitious continental fortification schemes can be seen at **Carisbrooke, I.O.W.** (p. 573E) and elsewhere. They surrounded an older conventional curtain wall, part of a concentric system, pivoting about an ancient motte and shell keep. Five centuries of history are thus shown.

There is a group of buildings which, whilst not castles in the full sense, possess defensive features beyond those of a normal domestic manor house, which might be securely planned round a courtyard with nothing more than a strong gatehouse. **Stokesay Castle, Shropshire** (1285–1305) (p. 679E) is such an instance. Its plan is essentially domestic, with a great hall of a kind rapidly becoming typical, and the modest protection afforded by a crenellated polygonal tower, a moated curtain wall and a gatehouse (the latter rebuilt c. 1620–5). A northern tower erected in the thirteenth century has a jettied half-timbered storey of the period 1285–1305. **Maxstoke, Warwickshire** (1346) and **Wingfield, Derbyshire** (1441–55) are other good examples. **Tattershall Castle, Lincolnshire** (1436–46) (p. 679D) is a five-storey tower house about 34 m (112 ft) high, built of excellent brickwork, rectangular in plan with angle turrets. Its rooms are compressed into this single block, reminiscent of an old keep, standing on the edge of the moated inner bailey of a thirteenth-century castle.

Until well into the sixteenth century a dominant tower, astride a gateway, was a quasi-military feature common in domestic and collegiate buildings, for example at **Layer Marney Towers, Essex** (1520) (p. 689A), **S. John's College, Cambridge** (1511) (pp. 694B, 696A), and **S. James's Palace, London** (p. 689B).

A. Beaumaris Castle, Anglesey
(1283–1323). See p. 677

B. Harlech Castle, Merionethshire
(1283–90). See p. 677

C. Deal Castle, Kent
(c. 1540). See p. 678

D. Tattershall Castle, Lincs.
Keep (1436–46). See p. 678

E. Stokesay Castle, Shropshire (1285–1305): aerial view. See p. 678

A. Raglan Castle, Monmouthshire (*c.* 1430–60). See p. 678

B. Micklegate Bar, York.
S.W. elevation. See p. 678

C. Bolsover Castle, Derbyshire
(1612–21). See p. 678

MANOR HOUSES

At the beginning of the thirteenth century it was still necessary to retain some defensive character, and many licences to 'crenellate' or fortify manor houses were granted by Henry III. Most of the known examples, numbering about thirty-six, are found in the south-east or in central England, the ground-floor type of hall now being the more frequent and plainly gaining in favour. Plans varied, and had not yet settled down to what was to be the orthodox disposition in the later Middle Ages. Houses with the first floor hall might yet have only the single upper room, be subdivided to provide a solar, or have the solar as a conjoined room whether on the same axis or placed crosswise; sometimes a chapel is the sole adjunct or there is a latrine chamber too. There are other variants; but the most significant development is the alliance of the two-storey block with a ground-floor hall of stone or timber, in which case the upper room becomes a solar, and its undercroft provides 'service' rooms (for food preparation and storage and domestic utensils) to the great common hall. The more pretentious, though not all, of the ground floor halls remained aisled, and in some cases one end was partitioned to form a service room or rooms, with perhaps a solar above them, reached by stairs from the hall or externally, the whole being under one roof. Thus the two types of manor-house plan tended to merge. Kitchens normally were separate, outdoors at the inferior or 'lower' end of the hall. Late in the century, as illustrated again at Stokesay (p. 679E), by the 1285–1305 additions, there was a new and important move towards establishing the solar at the superior or 'upper' end of the hall, raised over a storage basement or 'cellar', leaving the service rooms at the lower end intact, along with what then became an extra private or sleeping chamber over. This scheme, double tier at either end of the hall, the whole under one roof, became very popular for the smaller mansions in the south-east after the middle of the next century. As in the Norman period, ground floor halls had a central hearth for an open fire or brazier—actually slightly nearer the upper end—the smoke escaping by a louvre in the roof timbers above, or through small gablets at the two ends of the roof apex in the case of hipped roofs. In the case of the two-floored manor houses, wall fireplaces had been in use since late Norman times. Windows, often transomed, grew larger, and there was some use of glass, though wooden shutters still were normal. Main floors were of stone or tiles, upper floors of wood (or stone, if over vaults), inferior apartments of rammed earth.

Little Wenham Hall, Suffolk (*c.* 1270–80) one of the best-preserved manor-houses of the period, is of brick, with stone and flint dressings. The plan is L-shaped, comprising a small chapel adjoining a first-floor hall, both standing over stone-floored storage undercrofts having quadripartite brick vaults carried on stone ribs. The hall has fine, two-light foliated 'sitting-windows' on each wall; its tiled floor and chestnut beamed ceiling are sixteenth century. The entrance to the vaulted chapel is flanked by traceried openings and from it opens a turret-stair in the re-entrant angle leading down to the undercrofts and up to a room over the chapel which was probably a solar.

Charney Basset Manor House, Berkshire (*c.* 1280) (p. 576), can only be definitely ascribed to the thirteenth century as regards the two-storey south wing, but it is clear that this has always been a solar block, originally built in relation to a ground-floor hall, perhaps aisled, occupying a position similar to that shown on the plan. Such a combination of hall and first solar represents an important development. The undercroft to the solar probably afforded the service accommodation to the hall; the kitchen, however, would be external, reached by a passage running across the nearer part of the hall. Solar and chapel are timber floored; the roof timbers of the chapel are not original; those over the solar are genuine, and interesting in that they demonstrate the fundamentals of south-eastern roof structure. There is no true principal; a cambered tie-beam supports a 'crown-post' (or 'king-post'— the first term is preferable for the type) which, with the aid of struts, carries a 'collar-purlin' running longitudinally to stiffen the ridgeless pairs of trussed rafters. The system is quite different from that at Stokesay Hall, which shows a north-western method by which arch-braced principals carry a ridge and side purlins on their backs.

Other examples are **Little Chesterford, Essex** (*c.* 1225), a stone, two-floor solar block, crosswise to an aisled, ground floor timber hall; and **Warnford, Hampshire** ('King John's House') (early thirteenth century), a flint-walled ground-floor hall, with columned aisles, with one end divided by a wall to form a service room.

The larger manor houses of the fourteenth century were generally castellated, and the greatest assumed a quadrangular plan, as did the castles of the period, and had a central courtyard entered through a gatehouse, protected by a portcullis and drawbridge over a moat around the whole group of buildings. The typical manor was smaller, and much more compact, nevertheless normally standing in its walled or moated enclosure. In all, however, the essentials were much the same, for a common type had now been established, centred on a ground-floor hall, and only the lesser manor houses maintained the former immature types of disposition. Typically, a porched entrance led to a passage which crossed the lower end of the hall to a second doorway in the opposite wall, the passage being separated from the hall by a screen with two doors or openings, while on its other side there were three doors into the service rooms. The term 'screens' is applied to the whole of this passage, which sometimes was ceiled, and allowed a minstrels' gallery above. Such galleries, popular from the fifteenth century, were often added to older buildings. The screens originated in projecting timber spurs or 'speres', giving protection against draughts from the doors; they were often connected to a roof principal which defined the passage, and which consequently is known as the 'spere-truss'. The hall was the whole height of the house, and at its further end was a shallow platform or dais, a feature which had made its appearance in earlier times. The solar block now regularly stood at the upper end of the hall, but the solar itself, on the upper floor, now became known as the withdrawing-room. In important houses, a lady's bower and additional rooms indicate an increased desire for privacy, and a chapel in this wing would have a gallery for the master and his family, while the retainers were below. The hall, which attained its greatest development in this century, was still a sleeping room for the retainers and had its floor strewn with rushes and its walls hung with tapestries and trophies of the chase. Glazed windows were as yet rare. Though wall fireplaces with hooded canopies were increasingly common, the hall sometimes still had a central hearth for an open fire or brazier, and a smoke louvre in the roof, as at **Penshurst, Kent** (1341–8) (p. 683). In this great hall the Lord of the Manor held his court and administered justice, and here too, on the dais, the family dined at the high table, while at long tables in the body of the hall his vassals took their meals. The dais sometimes had a lofty bay window which gave additional dignity to this part of the hall. Of the three doorways in the 'screens' on the side away from the hall, the central one led by a passage to the kitchen, still often detached from the main building, in case of fire, and in such case connected by a covered way. Another door gave on to the buttery (Fr. *bouteille* = bottle), and the third on to the pantry (Fr. *pain* = bread).

Other examples are **Ightham Mote, Kent; Baguley, Cheshire; Smithills, near Bolton, Lancs;** and **Sutton Courtenay, Berks.**

In spite of the Wars of the Roses, the fifteenth century witnessed an improvement in social conditions and commercial prosperity. This was duly reflected in the

PENSHURST PLACE, KENT.

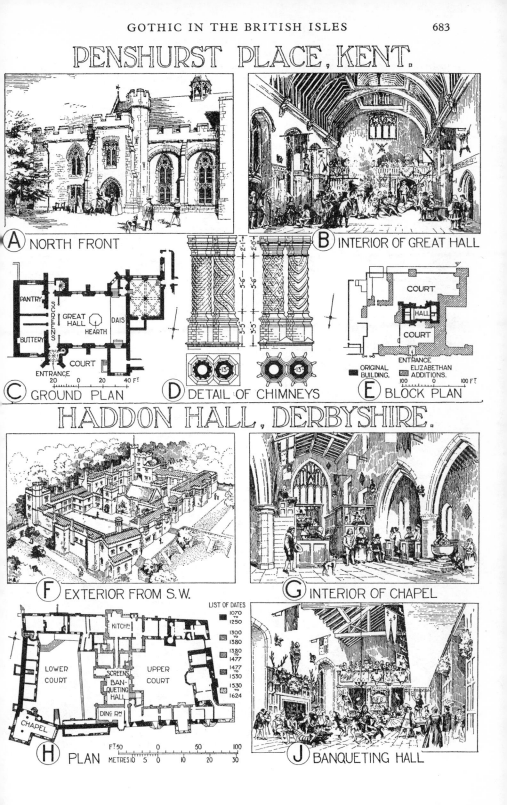

(A) NORTH FRONT

(B) INTERIOR OF GREAT HALL

(C) GROUND PLAN

(D) DETAIL OF CHIMNEYS

(E) BLOCK PLAN

HADDON HALL, DERBYSHIRE.

(F) EXTERIOR FROM S.W.

(G) INTERIOR OF CHAPEL

(H) PLAN

(J) BANQUETING HALL

A. Cothay Manor House, Somerset (1480). See p. 685

B. Athelhampton Hall, Dorset (c. 1485–1509): the courtyard. From a 19th-cent.
lithograph by Joseph Nash. See p. 686

architecture of manor houses by further provision for domestic comfort. The hall, with fine bay-window, canopied fireplace, and open timber roof, continued to be the principal feature; furniture was still scanty, trestle tables were in use, and the floor was only covered with rushes or matting. The withdrawing-room and lady's bower were now used only as sitting-rooms, while bedrooms increased in number, and the hall ceased to be the general dormitory. The kitchens at Stanton Harcourt, Oxon., and New College, Oxford, show the importance frequently given to this department, to which were now added a scullery, bakehouse, brewhouse and dairy, while corn mills, granaries and stables became more numerous. **East Barsham Manor House, Norfolk** (c. 1500–15), with a fine detached gatehouse, has turrets and ornate chimneys showing the early use of brick in England.

Oxburgh Hall, Norfolk (1482), is a fine specimen of brickwork, but it has been partly restored. The plan is quadrangular, with buildings round a court surrounded by a moat. The magnificent brick gatehouse is flanked by towers, seven storeys high, and is reached across a bridge which spans the moat, and leads to a courtyard and on to the great hall through the usual screens (destroyed 1778).

Haddon Hall, Derbyshire (p. 683) dates from the Norman period onwards, its plan somewhat resembling an Oxford or Cambridge college, since the hall occupies the centre of the range between the two courtyards with the screen passage joining them. The kitchens and service rooms are particularly complete; the entrance to the lower court is beneath a tower at the opposite corner from the chapel (which contains important mural paintings and a fine Mediaeval reredos of alabaster). Several interiors are later in date, notably the richly panelled Elizabethan Long Gallery, a room of great splendour.

Hever Castle, Kent (rebuilt 1462), equipped with moat and drawbridge, and **South Wraxall Manor House, Wiltshire** (1440), both illustrate the change from the fortified type to the later dwelling-house. **Rufford Hall, Lancs,** (fifteenth century), of which little survives except the wonderfully fine hall, is a rare instance in which a movable screen, shielding the approach to kitchen, still survives (p. 687A), and at its upper end has a canopied tester (p. 687B) which lent extra dignity to the high table. **The Bishop's Palace, Wells,** though a semi-ecclesiastical building, has a fortified wall with gatehouse and moat, while the old **Archbishop's Palace, Croydon,** still retains its fine timber roof. **Cothay Manor House, Somerset** (1480) is a perfect stone example, in which the tripartite division of hall, service rooms and private apartments is clearly apparent from the main façade (p. 684A).

Manor houses of the first half of the sixteenth century were principally erected by new and wealthy trading families, who were taking the place of the old nobility, while the suppression of monasteries by Henry VIII provided him with both money and lands with which to enrich his favourites, who vied with one another in the building of fine houses. The Tudor house, with its increased number and variety of rooms, was usually still built round a quadrangular court from which many rooms were entered direct. Under the changed conditions such features as battlemented parapets and fortified gateways were retained for ornament rather than defence, while the addition of numerous ornamented chimneys provides evidence of the increased comfort within (p. 688c). The entrance to the quadrangle was under a gatehouse, opposite which on the other side of the court was the porch leading to the 'screens' of the great hall, which now definitely declined in importance, owing to the addition of other rooms, and also to the reduction by legal enactments of military retainers. The hall, however, still remained a feature on which much artistic skill was lavished, and this is seen especially in the richly carved wall fireplace, oak-panelled walls and timber roof, while the furniture, which became more plentiful, followed, as in previous periods, the architectural style. We now first hear of such additional rooms as the study, summer and winter parlours, and private dining-rooms; while bedrooms, though often only 'thoroughfare' rooms, were increased. Gardens were now laid out on definite architectural plans, with paved alleys, yew hedges, stone steps and balustraded terraces.

Athelhampton Hall, Dorset (p. 684B), is a very fine Tudor structure, dating from the reign of Henry VII, and its notable features are the gatehouse (with oriel window), since destroyed, the beautiful octagonal bay-window of the hall, and the projecting porch, with its pointed archway. The hall, which measures nearly 12 m × 7 m (about 38 ft × 22 ft), is of the usual type, with bay-window, panelled walls and open timber roof.

Bramhall Hall, Cheshire (p. 687C). While dating from the fifteenth century, extensive modifications a hundred years later have obscured its old form. The hall, measuring 11 m × 8 m (36 ft × 26 ft) is barely 3.6 m (12 ft) high, probably because of the insertion of an intermediate floor, when the Elizabethan drawing-room was made in the upper part. There is a small domestic chapel and the so-called Banqueting Room (now half its old length) has a robustly fashioned timber-arched braced roof. There was formerly a Long Gallery precariously placed on the top floor, similar to that which still exists at Little Moreton Hall, Cheshire.

Compton Wynyates, Warwickshire (1520), one of the finest of Tudor mansions, was completed by Sir William Compton, a London merchant and favourite of Henry VIII. The entrance, under a low square battlemented tower, has a four-centred archway, surmounted by a three-light mullioned window. Opposite the entrance, on the other side of the court, are the screens, with the minstrels' gallery over, and these give access to the buttery and kitchens, and to the hall with its bay window. South of the court are the drawing-room and chapel, while numerous turret stairs communicate with upper rooms. East of the hall are the eighteenth-century additions.

Hampton Court Palace (pp. 688, 689C) is one of the most remarkable domestic buildings in this country, and much of it (p. 689C) still remains as built from *c.* 1520 for Cardinal Wolsey (1472–1530) from the designs of the chief mason, Henry Redman. Fitted with gorgeous furniture and tapestries, the palace seems to have excited so much royal envy that in 1526 the Cardinal made it over to Henry VIII, who between 1531–6 added north and south wings to the west front and the Great Hall and the Chapel, the designer then being John Molton, royal mason and successor of Redman at Hampton Court, who died in 1528. The eastern portion however, was pulled down by Sir Christopher Wren and rebuilt in the Renaissance style, with the grand avenue through Bushey Park intended as an approach to the Great Hall, and on the east the radiating avenues and Long Water. The original part of the palace is of mellow red brickwork, in diaper pattern, with battlemented parapets. There are two courts in the Tudor part of the palace; the first, Base Court, is entered through the impressive West Gate, across a shallow moat. There are angle turrets, an oriel window and important terra-cotta medallions of Roman Emperors obtained by Wolsey from the sculptor Majano. Beneath a second gateway, steps lead up to the Great Hall built by Henry VIII. Measuring 32 m × 12 m (106 ft × 40 ft) and 18 m (60 ft) high, it is entered as usual through screens. The hammer-beam roof by James Nedeham is of great splendour, and the bay window rising to the full height of the room at the south-east end, opposite the dais, forms a great feature of the exterior of the hall seen from the Clock Court, so called from a curious astronomical clock over one of its gateways. To the east of the Great Hall is the Watching Chamber, with its plaster ceiling, and still farther east is the Tudor chapel with linen-fold panelling, Renaissance altar-piece and coloured pendant roof. The Fountain Court, surrounded by cloisters, and the Ionic colonnade (1690)

A. Lower end, with movable screen   B. Upper end, with canopied tester

Rufford Hall, Lancs: interior (15th cent.). See p. 685

C. Bramhall Hall, Cheshire (15th cent. and onwards): courtyard. From a 19th-cent. lithograph by Joseph Nash. See p. 686

HAMPTON COURT PALACE

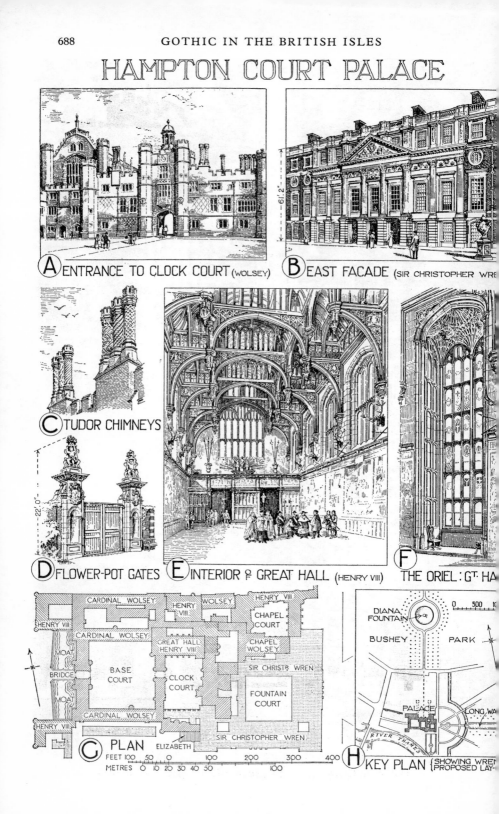

(A) ENTRANCE TO CLOCK COURT (WOLSEY)

(B) EAST FACADE (SIR CHRISTOPHER WRE

(C) TUDOR CHIMNEYS

(D) FLOWER-POT GATES

(E) INTERIOR ⁰ᶠ GREAT HALL (HENRY VIII)

(F) THE ORIEL: G.ᵀ HA

(G) PLAN
FEET 100 50   0   100   200   300   400
METRES 0 10 20 30 40 50   100

(H) KEY PLAN {SHOWING WRE
{PROPOSED LAY-

A. Layer Marney Towers, Essex:
entrance tower (*c.* 1520). See p. 678

B. S. James's Palace: Tudor gateway.
See p. 678

c. Hampton Court: the West Gatehouse (*c.* 1520). See p. 686

A. House and shop at Lavenham, Suffolk (Tudor). See p. 691

B. Farm at Bishop's Frome, Herefordshire. See p. 691
(Timber wing *c.* 1400, centre *c.* 1575, further wing *c.* 1625)

in the Clock Court are striking and restrained examples of the art of Sir Christopher Wren, and near the latter a grand staircase leads to the state rooms (now the picture galleries) in the east façade. On the south of the palace, extending as far as the river, are the Privy Garden, with its handsome iron gates by Tijou, and the Pond Garden, and to the north is the wilderness and Flower Pot Gates. Since the time of George II, Hampton Court has ceased to be a royal residence.

Sutton Place, Guildford (1523–5), was built by Sir Richard Weston, a trusted counsellor of Henry VIII. The plan was quadrangular, and was formerly entered through a central gateway which has been demolished. The entrance to the great hall, placed centrally on the axis of the former gateway, is an early instance of a desire for symmetry as opposed to convenience, and is flanked by bay windows in the corner of the façade. The terra-cotta work shows the influence of Italian Renaissance, as in the delicate flowering in the hollows of the mullions.

Other typical examples are **Layer Marney Towers, Essex** (c. 1500–25) (p. 689A), **Horham Hall, Essex** (1502–20), **Barrington Court, Somerset** (1514–48), and **Little Moreton Hall, Cheshire** (1550–9), with its long gallery, 23 m × 3.8 m (75 ft × 12 ft 6 ins), sometimes regarded as an early Renaissance building.

SMALLER HOUSES

Houses of the ordinary people were of the simplest kind, rude one-roomed shelters of wood and thatch; none of these have survived. Small houses, older than the seventeenth century, that still exist were often of greater social importance in their time than would appear today. The feudal system provided quarters for vassals and retainers within the castle walls and close to the manor house or monastery. In time some of these places became thriving trading towns. Elsewhere specially planned settlements were more regularly laid out, for example, as military bastides like Conway (p. 676A) or Ludlow.

Town houses were generally sited on 'burgages' or narrow strips of land, with a limited frontage on to the main street, often going back to another lane. Usually of timber, they would present to the street a series of sawtooth gables (sometimes visible today beneath later frontages). There might be one or two rooms (the one nearer the street used for trading) open at the front through a shuttered arch. Occasionally, by leaving part of the plot open, side lighting could be contrived to the rear apartments, and a simple gallery made to give access to the upper floor. Other dwelling rooms, stores, workshops and privies cluttered the back of the site. Unaltered examples are rare, since they are often buried beneath later erections. The plot width in a mediaeval town was usually of the order of 4.6–6 m (15–20 ft), the widest in the more prosperous streets. Subsequently, frontages might be rebuilt across two or more plot widths, and properties amalgamated or subdivided. Many old towns can show instances, notably parts of **York, Lewes, Sussex** (p. 693A) and **Ludlow, Shropshire.** Good individual survivals are at **Lincoln** (the Jew's House of the twelfth century in stone), **Lavenham** (p. 690A), **Colchester** and **Shrewsbury.**

In the country the homesteads of small freeholders or yeomen were based on the manor house model, having a centrally placed hall or 'house part', usually combining the function of kitchen later, flanked at one end by service rooms and at the other by private chambers. Wall fire-places, which did not become usual until Tudor times, gave more freedom to add an upper floor. Examples are many, and include those at **Abbey Dore** (p. 693B) and **Bishop's Frome** (p. 690B), both in Herefordshire, and **Maiden Newton, Dorset.** Smaller houses, as the one at **Putley, Herefordshire** (p. 693C), show different timber framing methods, in the latter case with 'crucks', a form of construction mainly confined to the mid-west and north-west of England.

COLLEGES, SCHOOLS AND ALMSHOUSES

The University of Oxford appears to have been formed by English scholars from the University at Paris, and it dates from about 1167, while that of Cambridge (1209) arose through a migration from Oxford. Colleges were similar in general equipment to monastic establishments, and were based on the plan of the Mediaeval house, with hall and rooms grouped round a quadrangle. Halls of residence, or colleges, for communities of teachers and students to promote discipline and common interests date from the thirteenth century. Whilst the buildings of nearly all colleges have been much altered, the normal arrangements would include a chapel, a communal dining hall, a library and living apartments arranged with considerable ingenuity in 'sets' of large and small rooms, entered from staircases. In addition there might be more ample provision for the head of the college and necessary domestic buildings—stores, brewhouses, etc. Entrance was usually through a gatehouse, giving security to the precinct.

Occasionally, as at **Jesus College, Cambridge,** monastic buildings were turned to collegiate use, the chapel formed in the old choir and domestic buildings added round the cloister. The building of the chapel choir and transepts of **Merton College, Oxford** (p. 696B) (begun in 1294), without the intended nave led to the adoption of the normal 'T' plan of choir and antechapel used by William of Wykeham in his model foundation at **New College, Oxford** (p. 694A).

The aerial view of **S. John's College, Cambridge** (p. 696A), taken from Loggan's *Cantabrigia Illustrata* published in 1690, gives a good idea of the layout of a large collegiate establishment, as it existed before some drastic nineteenth-century alterations. The First Court, built in 1511, is entered under the tall gateway directly from the street. To the left is the original library, while to the right the chapel occupies the whole of the north side. Facing, astride the main axis, are the Hall (to the right, as is clearly shown by the great bay window) and the service rooms, kitchens, butteries and pantries across the screens passage. The Second Court, added in 1598, gave more comfortable rooms to the master (at the right), and added further sets of undergraduate rooms to those already provided in the front court. In 1623 a new library and more rooms made two sides of a Third Court, completed in 1669 by a lateral wing in a full Renaissance style. An extension across the river in the early nineteenth century made a Fourth Court, and since then a larger chapel in the French Gothic style has been built by Sir George Gilbert Scott.

At both Oxford and Cambridge there are late Mediaeval buildings belonging to the University as a whole—notably the **Divinity School, Oxford** (1430–83) (p. 630C), and the **Bodleian Library** (rebuilt 1613–36) (p. 1000).

At first schools were usually attached to cathedrals, monasteries and collegiate churches, but later were often supported by chantry endowments or the trade guilds of the prosperous towns. **Winchester** (1382) (p. 695B) and **Eton** (1440) (p. 695A) were both founded to feed scholars to parent university colleges, which they resemble architecturally. After the Reformation other schools were refounded and sometimes housed in buildings which had belonged to disendowed religious corporations; **Chethams Hospital, Manchester** occupies the fifteenth-century domestic buildings of the former collegiate church.

Hospitals, or Almshouses, increased in numbers with the decline of the monasteries, some of whose services they were designed to meet. The **Hospital of S. Cross, Winchester** (1136), believed to be the oldest in England, was founded by

A. Late Mediaeval houses in High Street, Lewes, Sussex. See p. 691

B. Farm at Abbey Dore, Herefordshire (14th cent. and later). See p. 691

C. Small house with crucks, Putley, Herefordshire. See p. 691

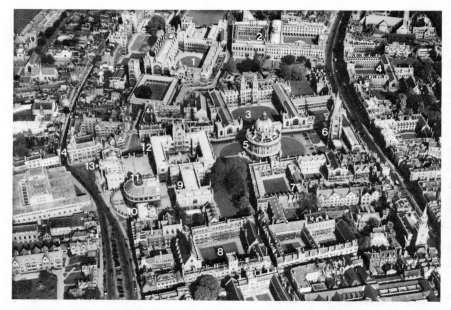

A. Oxford: aerial view from N.W. See p. 692

1. New College; 2. Queen's College; 3. All Souls' College; 4. University College; 5. Radcliffe Library; 6. S. Mary; 7. Brasenose College; 8. Exeter College; 9. Divinity School; 10. Old Ashmolean Museum; 11. Sheldonian Theatre; 12. Bodleian Library; 13. Clarendon Building; 14. Indian Institute.

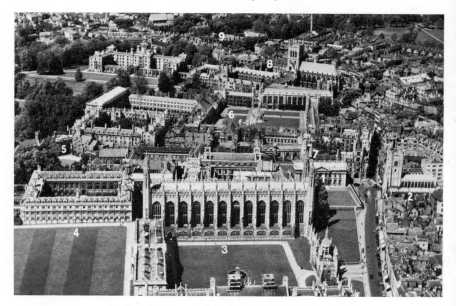

B. Cambridge: aerial view from S. See p. 692

1. Senate House; 2. S. Mary; 3. King's College; 4. Clare College; 5. Trinity Hall; 6. Trinity College; 7. Gonville and Caius College; 8. S. John's College; 9. Magdalene College.

A. Eton College: aerial view. See p. 692

1. Entrance; 2. Chapel; 3. College Hall; 4. Upper School; 5. Weston's Yard;
6. Provost's Lodge; 7. Headmaster's House.

B. Winchester College: aerial view. See p. 692

1. Entrance tower; 2. Outer Court; 3. Chamber Court; 4. Chapel; 5. Hall;
6. Cloisters; 7. Fromont's Chantry; 8. Old School; 9. Classrooms; 10. Headmaster's
House; 11. Moberley Library; 12. Warden's Lodging.

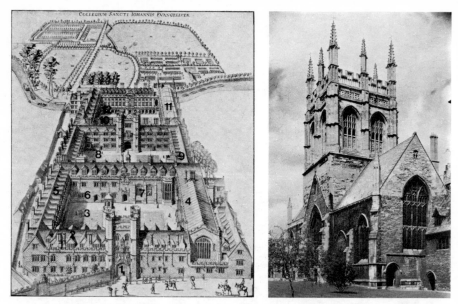

A (*left*). S. John's College, Cambridge, from E. (1511–). See p. 692. 1. Gateway; 2. Library; 3. First Court; 4. Chapel; 5. Chambers; 6. Kitchen; 7. Hall; 8. Second Court; 9. Master's Lodge; 10. Third Court; 11. Library; 12. Loggia.
B (*right*). Merton College Chapel, Oxford, from S.E. (1294). See p. 692

C. Old London Bridge, from Southwark, from a lithograph by Brewer. See p. 699

A. The George Inn, Glastonbury, Somerset (15th cent.). See p. 699

B. Market Cross, Salisbury, Wilts (14th cent.). See p. 699

c. Bridge and gateway, Monmouth (14th century). See p. 699

A. Exterior from S.W.　　　　　B. Interior: Master's pillar

Rosslyn Chapel (1447). See p. 700

C. Melrose Abbey from E. (1450–1505). See p. 700

Bishop Henry de Blois for thirteen aged and poor persons; a second foundation was added by Cardinal Beaufort in 1445. It is a remarkable group of massive gatehouse, cruciform Norman church and a quadrangle round which are the Master's house, refectory and dwellings.

The **Almshouses, Cobham, Kent,** founded in 1598, occupy the fifteenth-century buildings of the former College of Chantry Priests, which had been attached to the adjoining parish church in 1370.

The **Hospital, Ewelme, Oxfordshire** (1436), endowed by a Duke of Suffolk, consists of rooms round a quadrangle cloister. Steps through one range go up to the church in which are the sumptuous tombs of the founders.

The **Bede House, Stamford, Lincolnshire** (1490) was established by Alderman Browne for ten poor men and two nurses. An entrance porch leads from the street into a quadrangle, south of which is the dormitory arranged with cubicles on either side and a chapel at its far end, lit by tall traceried windows.

OTHER SECULAR BUILDINGS

The more important buildings usually have the character of contemporary ecclesiastical or domestic work; for example, the **George Inn, Glastonbury, Somerset** (p. 697A) or the **Guildhall, Cirencester, Gloucestershire,** both of the fifteenth century, compare favourably with Perpendicular churches, whilst the **Guildhall, Lavenham** is scarcely distinguishable from its domestic neighbours. Tithe barns, often of great size, are commonly found in rich agricultural areas (p. 634A). Two other classes of public buildings must be mentioned: Market Halls and Crosses survive in fair numbers, either as stone or timber structures, like that at **Ledbury, Herefordshire** with a raised building covering a market beneath, or more sophisticated designs for example at **Salisbury** (p. 697B) of the fourteenth century, and **Chichester,** built in 1500. Simple crosses of a more specifically religious character were put up in market places, churchyards or at crossroads. Two well-known ones are at **Northampton,** one of the celebrated 'Eleanor Crosses', and the **Bristol High Cross,** removed from its original site to **Stourhead, Wiltshire** in the eighteenth century.

Bridges are some of the most impressive structures of the Middle Ages to have survived. Very often they serve their original purpose today, repaired or widened from time to time. Timber must formerly have been the most common material, but from the thirteenth century the usual method was to build stout stone piers, with pointed ends, protected by 'starlings' to resist the scour of the current, connected by ribbed arches. **Old London Bridge,** like many others, even supported houses (p. 696C). Mills, water cisterns, chapels and defensive gateways were commonly associated with the structure itself, maintenance being imposed on civic or religious authorities. The **bridge at Monmouth** (p. 697C) retains an impressive military gateway, whilst that at Wakefield, Yorkshire supports the best surviving chantry chapel. Most curious of all is the bridge at Crowland, Lincolnshire, designed to carry three roads over three waterways.

LATE MEDIAEVAL ARCHITECTURE IN SCOTLAND AND IRELAND

Mediaeval architecture in Scotland followed on much the same lines as in England until the fifteenth century, when it assumed a more definitely national character. Inspiration was largely drawn from France, with which there was close political connection, especially after Robert Bruce (1306–29) secured the independence of

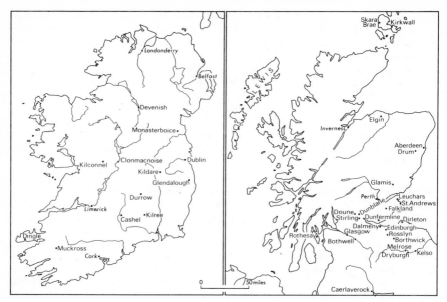

Ireland and Scotland in the fifteenth century

Scotland. Melrose Abbey (1450–1505) (p. 698C) shows French influence, while **Rosslyn Chapel** (1447) (p. 698A, B) bears a strong resemblance to the Portuguese church of Belém, near Lisbon (p. 770), though the latter is some fifty years later. Lancet windows either singly or in groups were used long after they had been discontinued in England, while the Flamboyant tracery of French Gothic was preferred to the Perpendicular style of English Gothic.

Glasgow Cathedral (1181–1508) (pp. 643D, 701A) is the best preserved Gothic building in Scotland, and, although of different dates, is uniform in appearance. It has an internal length of 86 m (283 ft), with nave and aisles, choir and aisles, eastern aisle with chapels beyond, and chapter house and sacristy. The fine vaulted crypt (1233–58), encloses the shrine of S. Mungo.

Other important cathedrals are those of Edinburgh, S. Andrews (1160–1318) Kirkwall (1138–1550), Dunblane (1230–60, with Romanesque tower), one of the finest Mediaeval buildings in Scotland, Aberdeen (*c.* 1357–1522) and Elgin. **S. Giles, Edinburgh** (mainly 1385–1416) (p. 701B) has a crown-like spire (–1495), while the abbeys of Kelso (1128–), Melrose, Dunfermline (nave, 1125–30), Holyrood (late thirteenth century) and Dryburgh are well known. **Dalmeny Church** (*c.* 1175) and **Leuchars Church** (p. 564B) are notable parish churches.

Castles and mansions in Scotland from the twelfth to the seventeenth century have a national character. Of about eight hundred instances of the castle or private stronghold, the Anglo-Norman type of earthwork of the twelfth century was some fifty years later than in England. While the orthodox motte-and-bailey arrangement was common, more frequently the motte and bailey were undivided by a ditch and stood together elevated on a great mound. On the motte was a wooden tower within a palisade; in the bailey, itself surrounded by palisaded ramparts, were other timber buildings forming chapel, kitchen, bakehouse, stables and storehouses.

In the thirteenth century, the bailey type of defended residence took firmer

A. Glasgow Cathedral (1181–1508). See p. 700

B. S. Giles's Cathedral, Edinburgh, from W. (1385–1416; spire 1495). Refaced
by W. Burn, 1829. See p. 700

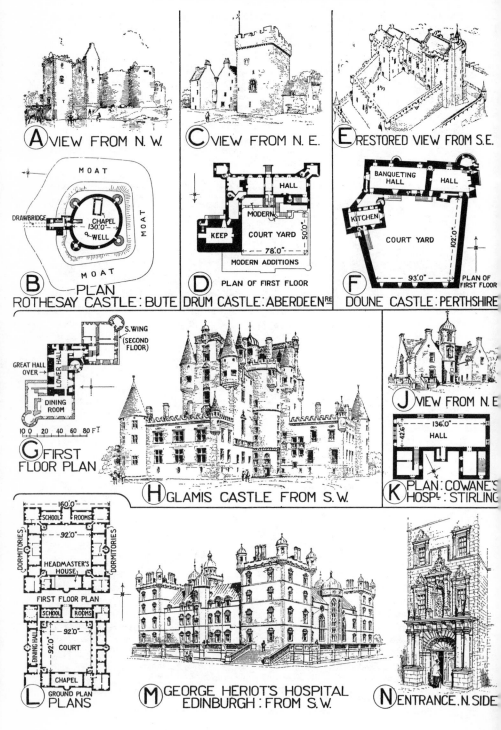

A VIEW FROM N. W.

C VIEW FROM N. E.

E RESTORED VIEW FROM S.E.

B PLAN
ROTHESAY CASTLE : BUTE

MOAT
MOAT
MOAT
MOAT
DRAWBRIDGE
CHAPEL
130'.0"
WELL

D PLAN OF FIRST FLOOR
DRUM CASTLE : ABERDEEN^RE

HALL
MODERN
KEEP
COURT YARD
50'.0"
78'.0"
MODERN ADDITIONS

F PLAN OF FIRST FLOOR
DOUNE CASTLE : PERTHSHIRE

BANQUETING HALL
HALL
KITCHEN
COURT YARD
102'.0"
93'.0"

G FIRST FLOOR PLAN

S.WING (SECOND FLOOR)
GREAT HALL OVER →
LOWER HALL
DINING ROOM
10 0 20 40 60 80 FT

H GLAMIS CASTLE FROM S. W.

J VIEW FROM N. E

K PLAN : COWANE'S HOSP^L. : STIRLING

136'.0"
HALL
42'.6"

L PLANS

160'.0"
SCHOOL ROOMS
92'.0"
DORMITORIES
DORMITORIES
HEADMASTER'S HOUSE
FIRST FLOOR PLAN
SCHOOL ROOMS
92'.0"
DINING HALL
92'.0"
COURT
CHAPEL
GROUND PLAN

M GEORGE HERIOT'S HOSPITAL
EDINBURGH : FROM S.W.

N ENTRANCE. N. SIDE

shape, yet still in 1300 most castles were wholly of timber, and the smaller ones in diminishing numbers afterwards; only the most important had acquired stone walls. These exceptions, of the latter part of the period, included Dirleton Castle, East Lothian, Bothwell, Lanarkshire and Caerlaverock, Lanarkshire, in their initial form.

Of fourteenth century instances, **Rothesay Castle, Bute** (1312–34) (p. 702A, B) is less advanced than the castles last named but representative in its girdle of high, towered walls (the gatehouse and chapel are later), though baileys were not usually so regular, being variously triangular, rectangular or polygonal, according to site circumstances. Sometimes there was nothing but a stone-walled enclosure; ordinarily, there were projecting round towers, and one, occasionally rectangular, was larger than the rest and thus reminiscent of the original motte with its special tower. The towers served for residential chambers and other uses, but most of the living and ancillary accommodation was still provided in separate buildings, irregularly dispersed in the bailey, the more important, such as the chapel and hall, increasingly tending to appear as stone structures. The hall was then almost invariably raised on an undercroft, often vaulted. The defended homes of the lesser gentry, sporadically changing to stone late in the period, were more compact, a single tower or 'fortalice' sufficing, with a restricted court or 'barmkin' at its foot, demarcated by a wall about 2.7–3.6 m (9–12 ft) high, and a ditch beyond. The first modest stone 'peles' of the border country belong to the same time.

Fifteenth-century prosperity produced a spate of building. Military traditions weakened; in the great houses the first-storey hall block, as much as 30 m (100 ft) long, now assumed higher importance than the great tower, and the two were often conjoined to form a frontispiece to the bailey or court behind. In this block the 'long gallery' made its appearance under direct French influence, as at Falkland Castle, Fife, in 1461, a long time before such a feature appeared in England. Crenellated and corbelled parapets were already normal, but machicolated parapets, with apertures between the corbels, are limited almost precisely to this century in the Scottish castle. The angle turret or 'bartizan' was another French borrowing which contributes to the special character of the national style. **Doune Castle, Perthshire** (early fifteenth century) (p. 702E, F) illustrates these points and the equally typical pitched roofs with their 'corbie' or 'crow-stepped' gables. Quite often, such roofs were carried on pointed barrel vaults; and the lowest floor of castles, under the main floor, too was usually vaulted, as well as intermediate floors in some cases. Of numerous tower houses (fortalices), **Borthwick Castle, Midlothian** (1430–) is a simple rectangular block with two shallow wings on one flank.

Sixteenth- and seventeenth-century major castles and mansions tended to become more elaborate; the number of storeys increased at times and wings thrown out behind the frontal block might enclose the entire court to form such a regular plan as that of **George Heriot's Hospital, Edinburgh** (c. early seventeenth century) (p. 702L, M, N), a fine building in the early Renaissance style of which the quality of detail is especially marked in the entrance gateway. **Drum Castle, Aberdeen** (p. 702C, D), shows a partial step in the same direction. The dwellings of simpler fashion persisted in their Mediaeval form with little consistent change, save that barmkins and parapets often were dispensed with, and angle turrets or bartizans, round or square, were roofed over. In general in the lesser dwellings, fortalice or border pele, the first-floor hall was a principal element just as in the mansions, and to provide minor rooms without impeding natural light, wings were often thrown out from the angles of the main block, giving plans approximating to L, Z, T or E forms, as at **Cowane's Hospital** or **Guildhall, Stirling** (1639) (p. 702J, K) or **Glamis Castle, Angus** (c. 1606) (p. 702G, H), which has a Z plan produced from an original L arrangement by low-wing extensions made later in the century.

In Ireland the influence of Continental art was felt during the Middle Ages, but few monuments of importance were erected. The cathedrals of **Dublin** (p. 643A), **Kildare** and **Cashel** are the most important. The absence of parish churches is remarkable, while those of monasteries and friaries (principally Franciscan) are small and usually have a nave and choir—probably once divided by a wooden screen—transept and southern aisle, cloisters, and a tower, often added in the fifteenth century. The best known are those at Cashel, Kilconnel and Muckross.

The earlier castles of the Irish chieftains are an interesting study, and the Anglo-Norman overlordship after 1171 has left its military traces; but there is little domestic architecture left of this period.

BIBLIOGRAPHY

See also Bibliography to Chapter 20 (p. 582).

ENGLAND AND WALES

BATSFORD, H., and FRY, C. *The Greater English Church*. London, 1940.
BLOXHAM, M. H. *The Principles of Gothic Ecclesiastical Architecture*. London, 1849.
BOND, F. *The Cathedrals of England and Wales*. London, 1912.
—. *Gothic Architecture in England*. London, 1905.
—. *Introduction to English Church Architecture*. London, 1913.
BOWMAN, H., and CROWTHER, J. S. *The Churches of the Middle Ages*. Manchester, 1894.
BRANDON, R., and J. A. *Analysis of Gothic Architecture*. Edinburgh, 1903. (1st ed. 1847.)
—. *Open Timber Roofs of the Middle Ages*. London, 1849.
—. *Parish Churches*. 2 vols. London, 1851.
BRAUN, H. *English Abbeys*. London, 1971.
—. *Parish Churches*. London, 1970.
BRITTON, J. *Architectural Antiquities*. 5 vols. London, 1807–26.
—. *Cathedral Antiquities*. 13 vols. London, 1817–35.
CLARK, G. T. *Mediaeval Military Architecture in England*. 2 vols. London, 1884.
COOK, G. H. *The English Cathedral through the Centuries*. London, 1957.
—. *English Collegiate Churches*. London, 1959.
—. *Mediaeval Chantries and Chantry Chapels*. London, 1947.
CROSSLEY, F. H. *English Church Craftsmanship*. London, 1941.
—. *English Church Monuments: A.D. 1150–1550*. London, 1921.
FRANKL, P. *The Gothic: Literary Sources and Interpretations through Eight Centuries*. Princeton, 1960.
GARDNER, S. *A Guide to English Gothic Architecture*. Cambridge, 1922.
GARNER, T., and STRATTON, A. *The Domestic Architecture of England during the Tudor Period*. 2 vols. London, 1929.
GODFREY, W. H. *The Story of Architecture in England*. London, 1928.
HARVEY, J. H. *English Mediaeval Architects: a biographical dictionary down to 1550*. London, 1954.
—. *Gothic England*. 2nd ed. London, 1948.
—. *Henry Yevele*. 2nd ed. London, 1946.
HOWARD, F. E., and CROSSLEY, F. H. *English Church Woodwork*. 2nd ed. London, 1927.
KNOOP, D., and JONES, G. P. *The Mediaeval Mason*. Manchester, 1933.
LETHABY, W. R. *Westminster Abbey and the King's Craftsmen*. London, 1906.
PALEY, F. A. *A Manual of Gothic Mouldings*. London, 1845–1902 (many editions).
PUGIN, A. C. *Specimens of Gothic Architecture*. 2 vols. London, 1821.
PUGIN, A. C., and A. W. N. *Examples of Gothic Architecture*. London, 1836–8.
PUGIN, A. W. N., *A Treatise on Chancel Screens and Rood Lofts*. London, 1851.
RICKMAN, T. *Gothic Architecture*. Oxford and London, 1881.
SALZMAN, L. F. *Building in England down to 1540*. Oxford, 1952.
SCOTT, G. G. *Lectures on Mediaeval Architecture*. 2 vols. London, 1879.
—. *History of English Church Architecture*. London, 1881.
SHARPE, E. *Seven Periods of British Architecture*. London, 1881.

—. *Architectural Parallels.* London, 1848.

—. *Mouldings of the Six Periods of British Architecture.* London, 1871-4.

—. *Rise and Progress of Decorated Window Tracery in England.* 2 vols. London, 1849.

STATHAM, H. H. (Ed.) *Cathedrals of England and Wales.* London, 1898. (The 'Builder' series, with large scale plans.)

SWARTOUT, R. E. *The Monastic Craftsman.* Cambridge, 1932.

THOMPSON, A. HAMILTON. *The Ground Plan of the English Parish Church.* Cambridge, 1911.

—. *Historical Growth of the English Parish Church.* Cambridge, 1913.

—. *English Monasteries.* Cambridge, 1913.

TIPPING, H. A. *English Homes.* Period I, 1066-1485; Period II, 1485-1558. London, 1921-37.

VALLANCE, A. *Greater English Church Screens.* London, 1947.

—. *Old Crosses and Lychgates.* London, 1933.

WICKES, C. *Spires and Towers of the Mediaeval Churches of England.* 3 vols. London, 1853-9.

WOOD, M. E. *The English Mediaeval House.* London, 1965.

SCOTLAND AND IRELAND

BILLINGS, R. W. *Baronial and Ecclesiastical Antiquities of Scotland.* 4 vols. Edinburgh and London, 1848.

DUNRAVEN, EARL OF. *Notes on Irish Architecture.* 2 vols. London, 1875-7.

Edinburgh Architectural Association, Sketch Book. 1878-94.

Glasgow Architectural Association, Sketch Book. 3 vols. 1885.

HILL, A. *Ardfert Cathedral, Co. Kerry.* Cork, 1870.

LINDSAY, I. G. *The Cathedrals of Scotland.* 1926.

National Art Survey of Scotland. *Scottish Architecture, 12th–17th Cents.* 4 vols. 1921-33.

PETRIE, G. *Ecclesiastical Architecture of Ireland.* Dublin, 1845.

PINCHES, F. *The Abbey Church of Melrose.* London, 1879.

SCOTT-MONCRIEFF, G. (Ed.) *The Stones of Scotland.* 1938.

ANTWERP CATHEDRAL

TOWER

(A) PLAN

AISLES — NAVE — AISLES
388·0
172·0

(C) SECTION a-a
92·0

50   0   50   100   150 FT
10   0   10 20 30 40 MTS

(B) INTERIOR LOOKING E.

(D) EXTERIOR FROM N.W.

23
GOTHIC ARCHITECTURE IN THE NETHERLANDS

Twelfth to sixteenth century

INFLUENCES

GEOGRAPHICAL

The Netherlands consists of the basins and delta·lands of the Rhine, Meuse (Maas) and Scheldt, the flat, low-lying coastal areas and the hills of the Ardennes. The fertile land and the great navigable rivers created and maintained a number of Mediaeval states and prosperous cities, dependent culturally on either France or Germany. Today, the area is divided between the kingdom of Belgium and the Netherlands, the latter popularly called Holland.

GEOLOGICAL

Belgium has marbles, limestone, sandstone and granite, and these were employed on the great churches of Brussels, Antwerp, Ghent, Liège and Tournai, and in the later Middle Ages, for palaces, houses and town halls in the prosperous cities. In Flanders, where clay is abundant, a characteristic and beautiful brick architecture developed; from the forests of the Ardennes and Fagnes came timber, not only for building, but also for wood-carving for which Belgium is famous.

Holland being wholly without stone except around Maastricht, and without forests too, had to import tufa, limestone and sandstone from Germany and Belgium. This deficiency early caused the Dutch to make bricks from the clay soil, and from them their buildings obtained a characteristic simplicity, texture and soft colouring which is enhanced by the reflected light of the seldom-distant water.

CLIMATIC

The climate of the Netherlands is similar to that of south-eastern England, but there are greater degrees of heat and cold. An often grey and rainy climate gave rise to many and large windows in houses and to great traceried windows in churches and town halls. Window-shutters against driving rain and belts of trees as wind screens are common in Holland and Flanders, while in the north-east, windows are fewer and smaller and buildings plainer, to withstand the winds which sweep across the sea and the level land.

HISTORICAL, SOCIAL AND RELIGIOUS

Celt and Roman, Frisian, Saxon and Frank made up the pattern of ruler and ruled until, in the Middle Ages, the Netherlands comprised many feudal states, such as the counties of Flanders, Holland and Guelders, the principality of Liège, the duchy of Brabant and the bishopric of Utrecht, all owing some sort of allegiance to France or the Empire. Though not united politically, these formed a growing cultural and economic unity by the thirteenth century, dependent on the common

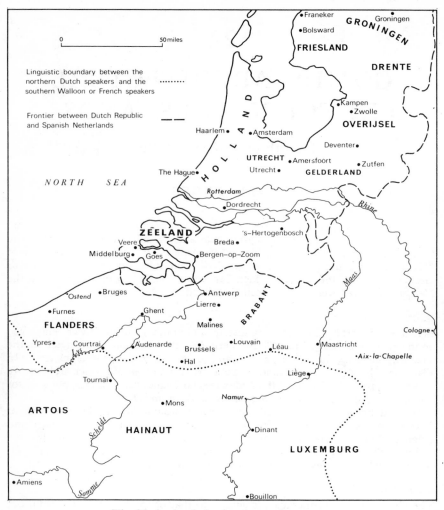

The Netherlands in the sixteenth century

interests and ambitions of the towns rather than on their rulers. Later on the cause of unification was also furthered by the high ambitions of the House of Burgundy. The chief cultural division was (and still is) represented by the linguistic boundary running from east to west a few miles south of Brussels. To the north Dutch was spoken, while to the south the Walloons spoke French.

Flanders passed to Burgundy in 1369, and under Charles the Bold (1433–77) formed, with most of the rest of the Netherlands, something approaching a national state. In 1482, through the marriage of Maximilian of Austria with Mary of Burgundy, the Netherlands became a Hapsburg domain. Charles V (1500–58), born at Ghent and a prince of the Netherlands, became king of Spain in 1516. Against the Spanish rule and against Philip II (1555–98) a movement of revolt began in

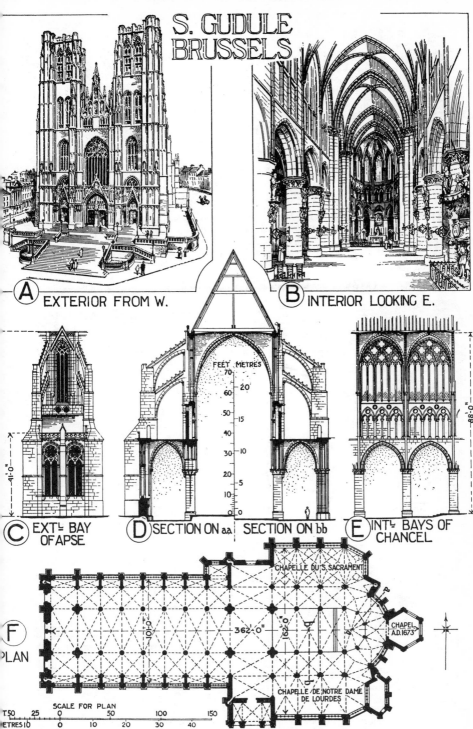

S. GUDULE
BRUSSELS

(A) EXTERIOR FROM W.

(B) INTERIOR LOOKING E.

(C) EXT⸍ BAY OF APSE

(D) SECTION ON aa   SECTION ON bb

FEET METRES
70
60   20
50
.50   15
40
30   10
20   5
10
0   0

(E) INT⸍ BAYS OF CHANCEL

CHAPELLE DU S. SACRAMENT

CHAPEL A.D. 1673

362'·0"

162'·0"

CHAPELLE DE NOTRE DAME DE LOURDES

(F) PLAN

SCALE FOR PLAN
FT 50 25   0   50   100   150
METRES 10   0   10   20   30   40

Ⓐ WINDOWS
TOWN HALL: LOUVAIN

Ⓑ S. APSE: TOURNAI

Ⓒ ARCHWAY
S. JACQUES: LIEGE

Ⓓ CHIMNEY-PIECE: TOWN HALL: COURTRAI

Ⓔ CHIMNEY-PIECE: TOWN HALL: AUDENARDE

Ⓕ ARCADE & VAULTING: THE BOURSE: ANTWERP

Ⓖ SCREEN: AERSCHOT

which William, Prince of Orange and Count of Nassau, took a leading part: by the end of the century the outcome was partition, with Protestantism supreme in the northernmost seven provinces, forming the Dutch Republic. Spain and Catholicism retained the south, including the Dutch-speaking provinces of Flanders and Brabant.

Mediaeval architecture followed closely on the social progress of these sturdy, brave and industrious peoples, and the independent towns rivalled each other for power and in the arts, much as they did in Italy. Guild houses and town halls of great magnificence, large in conception and rich in detail, reflect the prosperity and civic pride of such towns as Bruges, Antwerp, Louvain, Ghent, Ypres and Courtrai in the south, and Middelburg, Veere and Gouda in the north. The fame of these and many other cities is a record of the industry, of unending struggle against the waters, of ventures on land and sea, of commercial acumen and manufacturing enterprise which made the Netherlands among the first in commerce and sea power. The glory of Flemish weaving was immortalized by the establishment at Bruges in 1430, by Philip the Good, of the 'Order of the Golden Fleece'.

Until the year 1558, the bishoprics of Utrecht and Liège came under the jurisdiction of Cologne, and there were further connections with Münster; while those of Arras, Cambrai and Tournai all owed allegiance to Reims: through these affiliations came both German and French influences on the architecture. Later, the Spanish rule left its mark on Belgian architecture in the form of exuberant and florid decoration. Through the Benedictine, Cistercian and Premonstratensian Orders, the early styles of Italy, France and Germany were brought to the Netherlands and moulded to the local idiom. The Brabantine style, of mainly French origin, became the major national style; the architecture of Holland, while depending largely on Brabant and Flanders, developed other regional styles by assimilation of Westphalian and Rhineland characteristics.

ARCHITECTURAL CHARACTER

The Carolingian chapels of the Valkhof at Nijmegen, the eleventh- and twelfth-century churches at Nivelles, Soignies and Liège in Belgium, and Utrecht and Maastricht in Holland and, above all, the great triapsal and five-towered cathedral at Tournai, established the Romanesque in the Netherlands. The best surviving examples of this period are the nave and towers of Tournai Cathedral (p. 710B), the westblocks (see Glossary) of S. Denis and of S. Barthélémy at Liège, the churches of Our Lady and S. Servaas at Maastricht and S. Peter at Utrecht.

Gothic architecture of the Netherlands was governed by the same principles as applied to the rest of Europe, but owing to Rhenish conservatism, reached there only after 1220 through Hainault, Brabant and Flanders. Thus French cathedral Gothic of Sens, Senlis, Noyon and Laon formed its basis, and from this grew the Brabantine style which spread north in its pure form as far as 's-Hertogenbosch and Utrecht. From another direction, through Cologne, the Gothic of Reims and Amiens was the inspiration for the cathedral of Utrecht in the mid-thirteenth century, while the older traditions and the manners of Westphalia and the Rhineland were continued in the eastern and northern parts of Belgium and Holland. These latter include the long, narrow and low-set sanctuary windows and, later, the 'hall' churches, in which nave and aisles were approximately of equal height. In Flanders, a national variant adapted to brick, developed and spread northward along the coast of Zeeland, Holland and Friesland, and far beyond to Scandinavia and the Baltic. Adaptation to brick entailed simplification of detail and ornament, most evident in the Dutch churches; many of these lack vaults or the vaults are of timber, though sometimes the reason is instability of the ground.

Nonetheless, few Dutch or Flemish churches are without an immense, high and ornate tower, the product of civic rivalry in wealth and splendour.

Not only did the rich towns build vast churches and elaborate town halls, guildhalls and trade halls, but also, merchants built houses and warehouses, with stepped gables and many regular windows. Compared with the intricate elaboration of the town halls at Louvain, Audenarde and Alost, those of Gouda, Kuilenburg and Haarlem are simple.

EXAMPLES

ECCLESIASTICAL ARCHITECTURE

S. Gudule, Brussels (1220–1475) (p. 709), has a choir which is the earliest example of Gothic in the Netherlands, deriving from the north-eastern French style but with a triforium arcade still suggesting Romanesque. It expresses a mixture of influences which include those from Tournai, Valenciennes, Burgundy and Champagne, all of which go to create the Gothic of Brabant. Typical of the Netherlands is the plan, which lacks aisles to the transepts and a full chevet of chapels but includes wide chapels flanking the choir. The nave was added in 1425–75, still with the cylindrical piers and Brabantine foliage capitals, but with a blind triforium united to the clear-storey windows by tracery panelling. The western façade seems strangely English, flat and with a central window, though it is probably of German derivation.

Tournai Cathedral (1066–1340) is of three periods, and is built largely of black Tournai marble. The nave is Romanesque, the apsidal transepts (p. 710B) and the five towers Transitional (mid-twelfth century), while the choir, with a complete chevet, is of French Gothic design (1242–). The influence of Tournai was widely felt in Flanders and beyond. The Chapel of S. Piat is in the florid fifteenth-century style.

Notre-Dame de Pamele, Audenarde (1234 and after), of blue-black Tournai limestone, is by Arnould de Binche, partly in the local Scheldt Gothic style which soon afterwards established itself in Zeeland.

Notre-Dame, Bruges (1239–97) with its tall plain tower, and **S. Bavon, Ghent** (choir, 1274–1300), are characteristic of early Flemish Gothic adapting itself to brickwork.

Antwerp Cathedral (1352–1411) (p. 706), probably by Jean Amel de Boulogne, is in the mature Belgian style, with further outside influences. It is remarkable for its great width—a nave flanked by triple aisles—yet the transepts are aisleless and the spread of chapels each side of the choir is typical of the Netherlands. Tracery wall panelling, many slender pier shafts, often without capitals, and huge clear-storey windows mark the period. The west front was undertaken between 1422–74, but only the dominating north-west tower by D. van Waghemakere and others was completed (1519); it is 122 m (400 ft) high and capped by a three-stage lantern with pinnacle buttresses.

Malines Cathedral (begun c. 1217) has an unfinished tower (1452–1546) designed by Andries Keldermans, the finest in Belgium—97 m (318 ft) high—with strongly stressed verticals and stone detailing like lace.

The **Chapelle du Saint-Sang, Bruges,** is a reliquary shrine, its lower parts mid-twelfth century and the upper, fifteenth century, with a Flamboyant doorway and brick spiral-staircase.

S. Jacques, Liège (1513–38) (p. 710C), represents the extreme Brabantine Flamboyant.

Utrecht Cathedral (1254 to fourteenth century and later) (p. 713A) is the major

A. Utrecht Cathedral: choir
(1254–67). See p. 712

B. S. John, 's-Hertogenbosch: choir
(1370–1415). See p. 715

C. Castle of Muiden, near Amsterdam (13th cent.). See p. 715

(Renaissance, 1595–1622) (Gothic, 1515–28)

A. Town Hall, Ghent. See p. 715

1202–1304 Hôtel de Ville (1575–1621)

B. Cloth Hall, Ypres (rebuilt since 1914–18 war). See p. 716

example of French cathedral-Gothic in Holland, deriving from Amiens through Cologne; changing detail from the apse westward through the choir to the transepts is noticeable, especially in the omission of capitals. The nave collapsed in the seventeenth century and the western axial tower is isolated. Built between 1321–82 by Jan van Henegouwen (i.e. Hainault), it was an important Dutch prototype.

S. John, 's-Hertogenbosch (1370–1559) (p. 713B) is a rare instance of pure and rich Brabantine found in Holland, comparable with S. Peter, Louvain, and S. Waldru, Mons. The rectilinear wall-panelling resembles English Perpendicular; it is profusely decorated, with much sculpture by Alard van Hameel (1478–1529). The Great Churches of **Dordrecht** (1339 to sixteenth century) and **Haarlem** (1400–90) are more typically Dutch, being of brick and stone, spacious and plain. Both are simplified Brabantine, with Haarlem belonging to the local style of Aerschot, called Demer Gothic. Dordrecht has brick vaulting, but that of Haarlem nave is timber. In Zeeland the churches of **Middelburg, Goes, Hulst, Veere** and others followed the Scheldt and coastal Flemish-Brabantine traditions. **S. Michael, Zwolle** (c. 1350–1450) is a hall church deriving from Germany; these are common in east and central Holland but rare in Belgium—**Damme**, in west Flanders, is an exception.

The ruined **Abbey Church of Villers** (Belgian Luxemburg) (1216–67) and the **Dominican Church, Maastricht** (after 1260), represent early Maas (Meuse) Gothic with blind triforium arcades and typical leaf capitals, while **Meersen** (fourteenth century) is later and richer. This Maas style includes tall, narrow apse windows reaching to within a few feet of the ground.

In the north-east of Holland at **Bolsward, Franeker** and **Groningen** there are churches in provincial variants of the main styles. Here the parish churches in villages are of brick and very simple, with high domed vaults and much wall arcading—very different from those of other parts; examples are **Stedum** and **Zuidbroek.**

SECULAR ARCHITECTURE

At **Kampen,** three fifteenth-century gateways, white and capped by steep conical roofs, give an idea of a Dutch Mediaeval walled town, and at **Ghent**, the **Rabot Fort** (1488) remains of the fortifications together with the **Château des Comtes** (twelfth century); while at **Bouillon** is a castle more typical of the countryside. In Holland the **Castle of Muiden** (thirteenth century) (p. 713C), near Amsterdam, relied largely on water for its defence, and the **Binnenhof,** seat of the Counts of Holland at The Hague, has a knight's hall of 1250 with a typical large arch-braced roof.

The **Hospital,** the **Byloke, Ghent** (thirteenth century and later) and the **Béguinage** there, are examples of precinct planning and grouping. At Béguinage (Dutch Begijnhof) is an open Order for women, founded in Brabant in the thirteenth century, and peculiar to the Netherlands; the work of the Sisters is amongst the poor, and they live in houses grouped around a court containing a chapel. The establishments at **Bruges, Courtrai** and **Breda** are still in use, but not that at **Amsterdam**—few have much Mediaeval building left.

Belgium, and to a lesser extent Holland, are rich in Mediaeval town halls symptomatic of the wealth of her cities. **Bruges** (1376–) (p. 717F), **Louvain** (1448–1463) (p. 717G) by Mathieu de Layens, **Ghent** (1515–28 and later) (p. 714A) by D. van Waghemakere, **Audenarde** (1525–30) (p. 717A) by Jan van Pede and **Brussels** (1402–) (p. 717E) by Jakob van Thienen, with a tower (1448–63) by Jan van Ruysbroeck (1448–63), are magnificent and ornate; simpler is **Damme** (sixteenth century), near Bruges. Dutch examples in the Flemish-Brabantine style are **Middelburg** (1412–1599), by the Keldermans of Malines (rebuilt after 1945), and **Veere** (1474–1599). Weighhouses are also typical of Holland; the one at **Deventer,** of brick and stone, is late Gothic.

The greatest of the Cloth Halls was at **Ypres** (1202–1304) (p. 714B), outstanding not only because of its size, 134 m (440 ft) long, but also because of its majestic simplicity. It was destroyed in 1915, and the present one is a replica. That at **Bruges** (Halles, p. 717C) has a tower 80 m (260 ft) high (1282 with later lantern), and is typical of Flemish brick and stone civic architecture. The Guild Houses in the Grand' Place, **Antwerp** (p. 944A) though sixteenth century, have only a little Classical ornament, but those of **Brussels** (p. 944B) belong to the early Renaissance. The **Maison des francs Bateliers** ('Skipper's House'), **Ghent** (1531) (p. 717B) and the **Vieille Boucherie, Antwerp** (1501) are further examples of Guild Houses.

The **Maison Havart, Liège** (1594) and **S. Peter's House, Middleburg** (sixteenth century) are among the few surviving timber-framed houses; patrician and merchants' houses in stone such as some at Malines (p. 717D) and others in brick are more numerous. The **Zoudenbalch House, Utrecht** (1467) and **Het Lammetje, Veere** (House of the Scottish Merchants) (mid-sixteenth century) are stone houses of very different types. Typical brick houses are found at **Furnes** and **Goes** in the Flemish style, and in eastern Holland at **Zutfen.**

BIBLIOGRAPHY

DESSART, CHAS. (Ed.) *Images de Belgique.* 7 vols. Edition des Deux Mondes. *Pierres flamandes.* Paris.
FOCKEMA, ANDREAE, TERKUILE, and OZINGA. *Duizend Jaar Bouwen in Nederland.* Vol. i. Amsterdam, 1948.
LAURENT, M. *L'Architecture et la sculpture en Belgique.* Paris and Brussels, 1928.
LUYKX, THEO. *Atlas culturel et historique de Belgique.* 1954.
Ministry of Education, Arts and Science, The Hague. *Guide to Dutch Art.* 1953.
TIMMERS, J. J. M. *A History of Dutch Life and Art.* Amsterdam and London, 1959.
VRIEND, J. J. *De Bouwkunst van ons Land.* 3 vols. Amsterdam, 1942.

Ⓐ TOWN HALL : AUDENARDE

Ⓑ THE SKIPPER'S HO. GHENT

Ⓒ CLOTH HALL & BELFRY : BRUGES

Ⓓ OLD HOUSES MALINES

Ⓔ TOWN HALL : BRUSSELS

Ⓕ TOWN HALL : BRUGES

Ⓖ TOWN HALL : LOUVAIN

S. STEPHEN : VIENNA

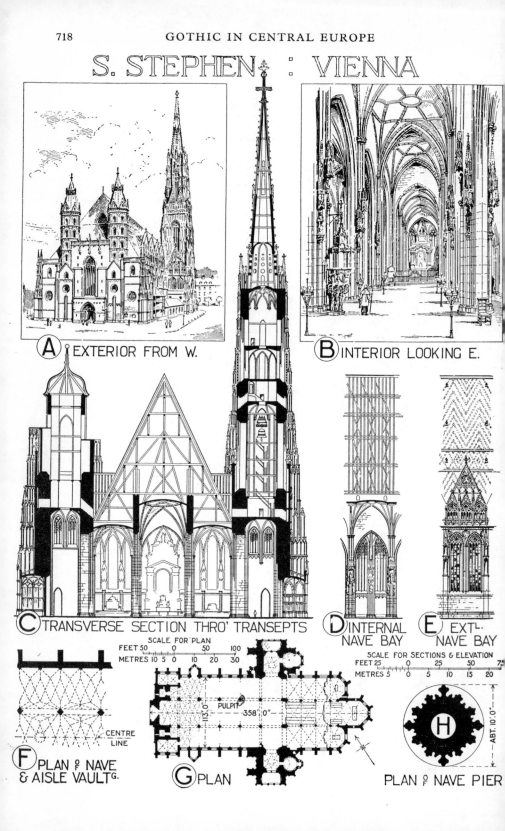

A EXTERIOR FROM W.

B INTERIOR LOOKING E.

C TRANSVERSE SECTION THRO' TRANSEPTS

D INTERNAL NAVE BAY

E EXT.L NAVE BAY

SCALE FOR PLAN
FEET 50 0 50 100
METRES 10 5 0 10 20 30

SCALE FOR SECTIONS & ELEVATION
FEET 25 0 25 50 75
METRES 5 0 5 10 15 20

PULPIT
—358'·0"—
113'·0"
CENTRE LINE

F PLAN OF NAVE & AISLE VAULT.G

G PLAN

H PLAN OF NAVE PIER
ABT. 10'·0"

24

GOTHIC ARCHITECTURE IN CENTRAL EUROPE

Thirteenth to sixteenth century

INFLUENCES

GEOGRAPHICAL

The former collection of states which became the German Empire, was inevitably in geographical touch with the architecture of neighbouring countries. The chief influence on German Gothic architecture came from France and is conspicuous in the Rhine Provinces and Westphalia, notably in Cologne Cathedral and other churches, castles, town halls and domestic buildings along the Rhine, which was always an important highway of commerce. Elsewhere in Germany geographical influence was of less consequence in the Gothic period.

GEOLOGICAL

The northern plains of Germany provide little building material but brick, which gives a special character to the architecture, particularly in the districts of the Oder and Elbe. In the centre and south and along the Rhine, excellent stone was found; while timber from the great forests in these regions gives an individuality to domestic buildings, as in wooded districts of England.

CLIMATIC

The climate, referred to in considering Romanesque architecture (p. 505), is without the fierce sun of the south, and therefore permitted large traceried windows, as in England and France, but the snows of severe winters rendered steep roofs a necessary and special characteristic.

HISTORICAL, SOCIAL AND RELIGIOUS

Central European history in this period is complicated by the successive rise and fall of imperial and royal dynasties, by the intrigues of princely and ducal houses of the various states to secure kingly power, and by the secular ambition of prince-bishops who combined the intolerance of ecclesiastical with the arrogance of secular tyrants. In the twelfth and thirteenth centuries Germany was the centre of the Western Empire, and under the Hohenstaufen emperors long wars were carried on with the Lombard league of the north Italian towns (p. 462). After the fall of the Hohenstaufen dynasty on the death of Conrad IV, the following years (1254–73), known as the 'Great Interregnum', were times of confusion and lawlessness, not conducive to progress in architecture. The house of Hapsburg came into power in 1273, and the general adoption of Gothic architecture from France coincides with that event and lasted till the reign of Maximilian I (1486–1519), which marks the end of the Middle Ages and the commencement of the Renaissance movement (p. 918).

Central Europe in the fifteenth century

For a right understanding of the types of architecture peculiar to different districts it must be remembered that Germany was not one, but many states, among which were the provinces under the Houses of Luxemburg, Wittelsbach and Haps-burg; ecclesiastical states, such as Münster; and Imperial cities like Nuremberg, Strasbourg and Ulm. The 'Hanseatic League', an alliance of the great commercial towns of north Germany, such as Lübeck and Hamburg, exercised considerable influence on the peaceful arts, and in the fourteenth century the power of the League secured to the larger towns comparative independence, which necessitated the erection of municipal buildings. Then there was the Rhineland on the French frontier, across which came the Gothic architecture which in castle, convent and church played its part in the folklore of the Rhine. Thus the style of architecture varies with the locality, just as does the constitution of the various states and cities. Trade guilds during this period acquired great importance and built elaborate halls, while Freemasons have been credited with much influence in the design and work-ing out of the Gothic style. The feudal system in Central Europe was so compli-cated by the existence of the many principalities of differing degrees of importance and independence that by the beginning of the sixteenth century relationships between rulers and vassals had often become merely nominal.

The most salient feature, apart from monastic establishments, in the religious life of Mediaeval Germany before the Reformation, was the exercise of civil power by prince-bishops, who included in their ranks Electors of the Holy Roman Empire, and whose principalities were only finally swept away by the European upheaval during the French Revolution. The activities of these powerful prelates are evidenced in numerous churches, and in costly palaces and tombs erected by them or in their honour. Ecclesiastical abuses and especially the sale of indulgences led to the revolt against the authority of Rome, until in 1517 Luther published at

S. ELIZABETH : MARBURG

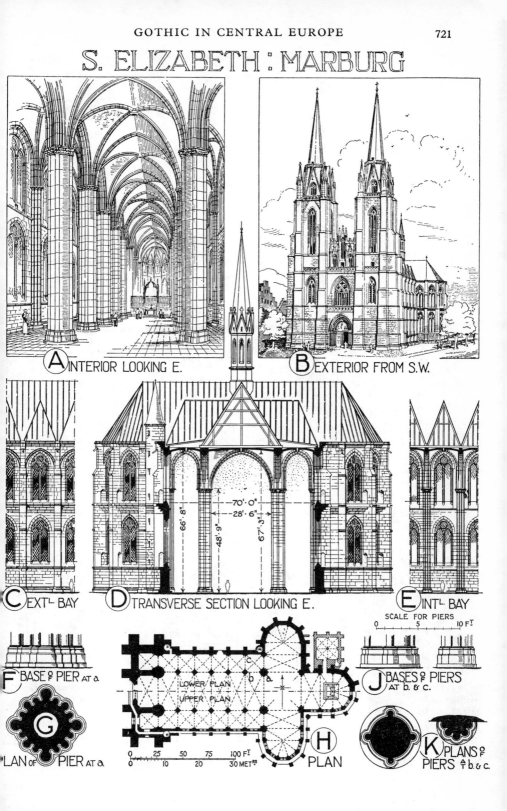

A INTERIOR LOOKING E.

B EXTERIOR FROM S.W.

C EXT.ᴸ BAY

D TRANSVERSE SECTION LOOKING E.

70' 0"
28' 6"
66' 8"
48' 9"
67' 3"

E INT.ᴸ BAY

SCALE FOR PIERS
0 5 10 FT

F BASE OF PIER AT a

G PLAN OF PIER AT a

LOWER PLAN
UPPER PLAN

H PLAN

0 25 50 75 100 FT
0 10 20 30 METRES

J BASES OF PIERS AT b. & c.

K PLANS OF PIERS AT b. & c.

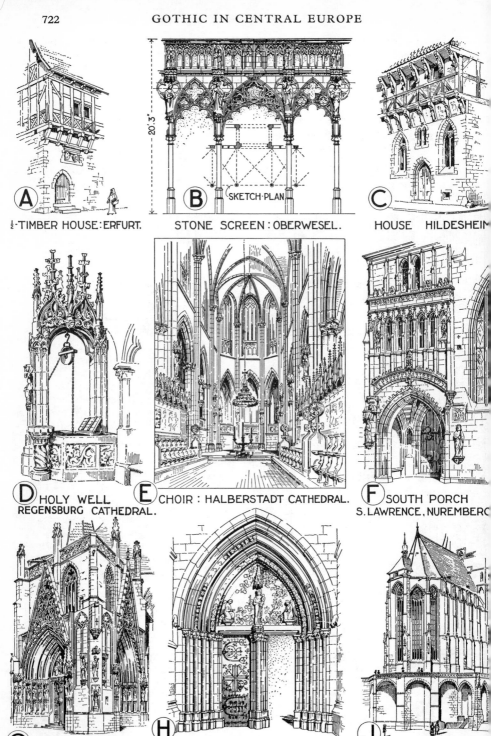

A. ½-TIMBER HOUSE: ERFURT.

B. STONE SCREEN: OBERWESEL.

20'.3"

SKETCH·PLAN

C. HOUSE HILDESHEIM

D. HOLY WELL REGENSBURG CATHEDRAL.

E. CHOIR: HALBERSTADT CATHEDRAL.

F. SOUTH PORCH S. LAWRENCE, NUREMBERG

G. PORCH: ERFURT CATH.

H. W. PORTAL: S. ELIZABETH, MARBURG.

J. CHOIR: ERFURT CATH

Wittenberg his famous theses against indulgences. The Reformation divided Germany into the Protestant north and Catholic south, but churches were not damaged, as in the Calvinist Netherlands and later on in Puritan England.

ARCHITECTURAL CHARACTER

Gothic architecture in Germany was similar in general character to that in other parts of Europe, and may be considered to have lasted from 1250–1550. The style, however, came direct from France and was not evolved from German Romanesque, and this method of its introduction may be due to the extent to which Romanesque building had been developed in Germany, where a preference for the ponderous Romanesque style had resulted in the adaptation of vaulting to new needs without resorting to the pointed arch and other Gothic features. The Gothic style was therefore only reluctantly adopted in the middle of the thirteenth century when it was near its zenith in France, but Romanesque precedents were long followed, and although the pointed arch appears in 1140 in Paderborn Cathedral, it was long before it supplanted the round arch of the Romanesque. In northern Germany and in the valley of the Elbe the architecture was carried out in brick, and at Lübeck even window mullions and tracery were of brick, and this brick architecture, although more meagre in design than that of Lombardy, has the character due to the material.

The 'hall' churches (*dreischiffige Kirchen*) are a special characteristic of German Gothic, more particularly in the north, and in these the nave and aisles are approximately the same height, with the consequent absence of triforium and clear-storey (p. 721A). The only English cathedral of this unusual type is Bristol, although it also occurs in the Temple Church, in London, and in some parish churches. Yet another marked feature is a single western tower or western apse in place of the wide, sculptured doorways of French cathedrals, thus giving a totally different external appearance (p. 727D). It has been suggested that this apse at the west end may have been derived from a detached baptistery; or it may have been for the use of the laity in cases where the eastern apse was devoted to conventual use.

EXAMPLES

ECCLESIASTICAL ARCHITECTURE

S. Gereon, Cologne (pp. 361, 504A, C, 725A), on the site of a tomb, 39 m (126 ft) in diameter, possibly erected by Helena, mother of Constantine, has an unusual grouping, recalling the tomb at Aix-la-Chapelle. The straight-sided choir with its sacristy dates from the Romanesque period (1075–). The eastern apse and towers were added in 1160, while the ten-sided nave, 20 m × 17 m (66 ft × 55 ft), oval on plan, was built (1219–27) in the Gothic style with pointed windows, eaves gallery and a pyramidal roof. The church was partly ruined in the 1939–45 war.

Limburg Cathedral (1213–42) (p. 508E–G, K), is a fine Transitional church, and with its seven towers forms an imposing group above the River Lahn.

The **Liebfrauenkirche, Trier (Trèves)** (1242–53) (pp. 515B, 725C, D), severely damaged in the 1939–45 war, forms part of the cathedral group (p. 516), and is a copy of Braine Abbey Church, near Soissons. It is a Transitional building with both round and pointed arches; the cruciform upper part has clear-storey windows and a fine vault, and there is an elaborately sculptured western doorway.

S. Elizabeth, Marburg (*c.* 1257–83) (p. 721), is the typical 'hall' church in which nave and aisles are of equal height, and thus there is no triforium or clear-storey. The plan has nave and aisles, western entrance between two towers, and apses at the ends of the transepts and sanctuary. The exterior is peculiar in having a continuous external walking way at the level of each stage of windows, carried right through the buttresses. Flying buttresses were unnecessary, and the interior has the appearance of a large columned hall (p. 721A).

Cologne Cathedral (1248 onwards) (p. 726A, B), is the largest Gothic church of Northern Europe, covering about 8,400 m² (91,000 square ft), and is a conspicuous instance of the adoption of the details of a style, without having assimilated the spirit that created it. The huge plan has a width out of all proportion to its length, 143 m (468 ft) long by 84 m (275 ft) wide, and the nave (1388), with a clear width of nearly 12.6 m (41 ft 6 ins), is 46 m (150 ft) high, almost as high as Beauvais; while the double aisles are equal in width to the nave and there are two enormous towers at the west end. The aisled transepts, with entrances, project one bay more than at Amiens, and the eastern half of the church, which is a reproduction of Amiens in plan and dimensions, has an apsidal end and processional aisle and chevet of seven chapels. The building, which was only finished, according to the original design, between the years 1824–80, displays an injudicious disposition of parts; it nevertheless makes an imposing monument, as, with its great twin-towers 152 m (500 ft) high, it stands on the level plain of the wide Rhine valley.

The **Frauenkirche, Nuremberg** (1354–61) (p. 727A, B), completely ruined in the 1939–45 war, was a 'hall' church in the market-place. Its immense roof covered nave and aisles, while its two-storeyed western porch was surmounted by a curious old clock with central figure of Charles IV and moving figures of the seven Electors, which appeared at noon. The interior (p. 727B) showed the equal heights of nave and aisles, separated by cylindrical piers with foliated capitals, encircled with figures, behind which sprang the vaulting ribs.

S. Lambert, Hildesheim, S. Stephen, Mainz (1257–1328) and S. Quentin, Mainz (1450), are also 'hall' churches, while Munich Cathedral (1468–88), S. Barbara, Kuttenberg and S. Martin, Landshut (1404), with a fine tower, 133 m (436 ft) high, are further instances of similar type.

Freiburg Cathedral (c. 1250–1360) (p. 725B) has Romanesque transepts and side towers and a remarkable single western tower and spire 117 m (385 ft) high, dating from 1310–50, similar to those of Cologne. The tower is square at the base, which contains the porch, octagonal in its second stage, and terminates in a lace-like spire (p. 725B), which completes a pleasing group.

Regensburg Cathedral (1275–1534) (p. 726C, D) is regular in plan with three eastern apses without ambulatory, in the German manner. The west front flanked by towers and open-work crocketed spires, added in 1859–69, has a beautiful little triangular porch in the centre (1482). The cloisters show a mingling of Gothic and Renaissance details.

Ulm Cathedral (1377–1492) (p. 727D), spacious and lofty, is an instance, not uncommon in Germany, of excellence in masonry and poverty in design, for the smallness of the ratio of the supports to the area produces an unpleasing interior. The polygonal eastern apse is without ambulatory. The exterior has an arcaded eaves gallery, due to Romanesque traditions, and a great western tower and spire, 161 m (529 ft) in height, the upper part of which was completed only in the nineteenth century, though to the original designs.

S. Stephen, Vienna (c. 1300–1510) (p. 718). The Stephansdom is a characteristic 'hall' church in Austria, without either clear-storey or triforium, for the three aisles are nearly equal in width and height, and the great roof covers the church in one span. The transepts serve as entrance porches, one of which is carried up as a

A. S. Gereon, Cologne: nave (1219–27), looking E. See p. 723

See p. 723

B. Freiburg Cathedral from S. (*c.* 1250–1360). See p. 724

See p. 724

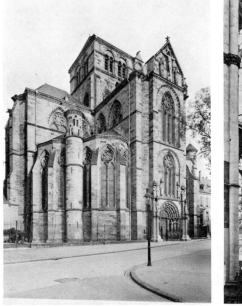

C. Exterior from S.E.   D. Interior
Liebfrauenkirche, Trier (Trèves) (1242–53). See p. 723

See p. 723

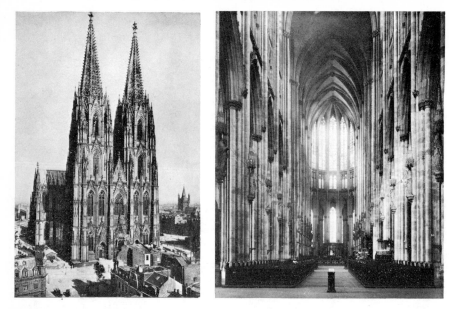

A. Façade   B. Nave
Cologne Cathedral (1284 onwards; completed 1824–80). See p. 724

c. Regensburg Cathedral   D. Regensburg Cathedral: nave.
(1275–1534). See p. 724   See p. 724

A. Exterior from S.W.   B. Interior looking E.

Frauenkirche, Nuremberg (1354–61). See p. 724

C. Prague Cathedral from E. (1344–96).
See p. 729

D. Ulm Cathedral (1377–1492;
upper part of tower 19th cent.).
See p. 724

A OLD HOUSE : BRUNSWICK

B KLINGENTOR ROTHENBURG

C THE KAISERWORTH : GOSLA

D OLD HOUSES : NUREMBERG

E THE CUSTOM HOUSE : NUREMBERG

F WINDOW : FÜRSTENBURG PALACE : INNSBRUCK

G RATHAUS REGENSBURG

H CHAPEL OLD RATHAUS : PRAGUE

tower terminated by a splendid spire, less open than usual in Germany. The vaults are traceried and the windows still contain some original stained glass. **Lübeck Cathedral** (1173–1335) (p. 516) and the **Marienkirche, Lübeck** (1251–1310), much damaged in the 1939–45 war, express the possibilities of design in brickwork, so usual in north Germany.

Prague Cathedral (1344–96), by Mathieu d'Arras (d. 1352) and Peter Parler (d. 1399), has often been described as the final flowering of French Cathedral Gothic, which it typifies in plan and many details (p. 727C).

SECULAR ARCHITECTURE

Castles were ubiquitous, with notable instances at **Marienburg** (1280–), **Meissen** (1471–) and **Rothenburg,** where the old fortified town still retains its mediaeval walls, with defensive towers (p. 728B).

Town Halls (Rathäuser) at Brunswick (Braunschweig), Hildesheim, Cologne, Halberstadt, Münster, Regensburg (Ratisbon) (p. 728G), Ulm, and Lübeck, are prominent and impressive buildings, and, like the town gates in the Baltic provinces, are evidence of the prosperity of those times.

The **Custom House, Nuremberg** (1498) (p. 728E), is remarkable, with three storeys in the walls and no less than six storeys in its high roof, finished with a fine traceried gable.

The **Old Houses, Brunswick (Braunschweig)** (p. 728A) and **Nuremberg** (p. 728D), and the **Kaiserworth, Goslar** (p. 728C), are characteristic examples of the secular architecture of the period, while timber houses, in which a lower storey of masonry supports a timber upper part, were frequent, as at **Erfurt** (p. 722A), **Hildesheim** (p. 722C) and elsewhere, but war has taken a heavy toll.

Domestic Architecture was marked by lofty roofs which frequently had more storeys than the walls, and were provided with dormer windows to make a through current of air for their use as a 'drying ground' for the large monthly wash. The planning of the roof-ridge, either parallel with or at right angles to the street, considerably influenced design; thus in Nuremberg, where the ridge is generally parallel with the street, dormer windows are plentiful and party walls are finished off at the roof level with artistic treatment, while at Landshut and elsewhere the ridge at right angles to the street results in gables of great variety of design, often with a hoist in the top gable to raise goods from the ground level.

BIBLIOGRAPHY

DEHIO, G., and BEZOLD, G. V. *Die kirchliche Baukunst des Abendlandes.* Folio. Stuttgart, 1884–.
DEHIO, G. *Geschichte der deutschen Kunst, II.* Berlin and Leipzig, 1921.
—. *Handbuch der deutschen Kunstdenkmäler.* 5 vols. Berlin, 1927–35.
Dehio-Handbuch: die Kunstdenkmäler Österreichs. 4th and 5th edns. 1954–8.
EYDOUX, H. B. *L'architecture des églises cisterciennes en Allemagne.* Paris, 1952.
HAHN, H. *Die frühe Kirchenbaukunst der Zisterzienser.* Frankfurt, 1957.
HARVEY, J. *The Gothic World.* London, 1950.
HOOTZ, R. (Ed.) *Deutsche Kunstdenkmäler.* 7 vols. Darmstadt, 1958–62.
LÜBKE, W. *Ecclesiastical Art in Germany during the Middle Ages.* Edinburgh, 1873.
MÖBIUS, H., and F. *Mediaeval Churches in Germany.* London, 1965. (Deals mainly with churches in the German Democratic Republic.)
STURGIS, R., and FROTHINGHAM, A. L. *A History of Architecture.* Vols. iii and iv. New York, 1915.
SWOBODA, K. M. *Peter Parler: der Baukünstler und Bildhauer.* Vienna, 1943.

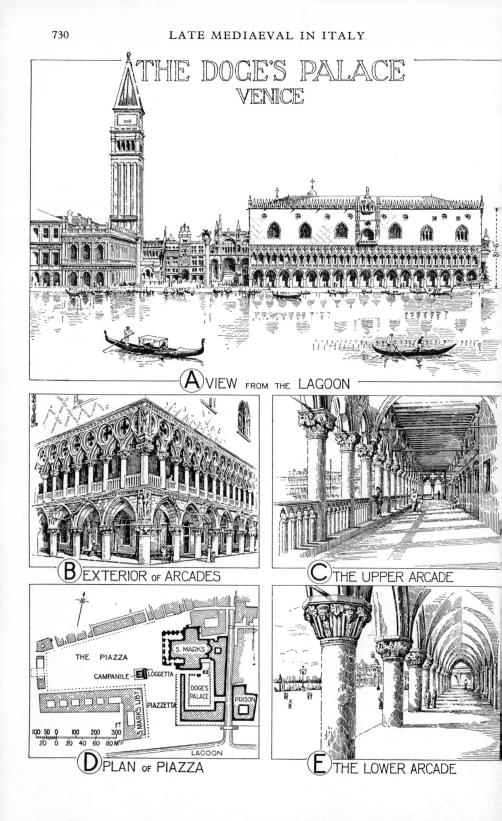

THE DOGE'S PALACE
VENICE

Ⓐ VIEW FROM THE LAGOON

Ⓑ EXTERIOR OF ARCADES

Ⓒ THE UPPER ARCADE

Ⓓ PLAN OF PIAZZA

Ⓔ THE LOWER ARCADE

THE PIAZZA

S. MARKS

CAMPANILE — LOGGETTA

DOGE'S PALACE

PIAZZETTA

PRISON

S. MARKS LIBY.

FT
100 50 0   100   200   300
20 0 20 40 60 80 Mᵗˢ

LAGOON

25

LATE MEDIAEVAL
ARCHITECTURE IN ITALY

Twelfth to sixteenth century

INFLUENCES

GEOGRAPHICAL

Geographical influence in Italy varied considerably in the north, centre and south of this long, narrow peninsula. North Italy includes the great Lombard plains and the islands of the Venetian Republic, and was brought into intercourse with Germany through Milan and Verona by the S. Gothard and Brenner Passes across the natural barrier of the Alps; while the Venetian state on the coast of the Adriatic was, through her overseas trade, in constant contact with the Byzantine sphere and the East. Thus seas and mountains, often regarded as nature's barriers, were turned, by an expanding civilization, into high-roads of art and commerce. Central Italy, although dominated by the enduring tradition of Old Rome, yet produced in the districts to the north and farther from Rome, magnificent Gothic churches of a type peculiar to this district, as at Florence, Siena and Assisi. South Italy and Sicily were exposed in the past to Greek and Byzantine influences on the east, Roman on the north and Moslem on the south, and these conflicting influences produced a peculiar blend of Mediaeval architecture, further emphasized by Norman rule.

GEOLOGICAL

North Italy is especially remarkable for the abundance of clay in the alluvial Lombard plains, from which were made the beautiful red bricks and terra-cotta used for many buildings, both ecclesiastical and secular, such as the Frari Church, Venice, the Certosa, Pavia and the Ospedale Maggiore, Milan; while lustrous white and coloured marbles from the mountains to the north were also employed, as at Milan, Genoa and Verona. Central Italy is characterized by the extensive use of coloured marbles, which are wrought into the fabric as colour decoration. South Italy and Sicily are both rich in coloured marbles.

CLIMATIC

North Italy has a climate similar to the temperate region of Central Europe, and this contributed to the development of those essentially Gothic features, such as large traceried windows, with the consequent necessity for buttresses instead of walls, as seen in Milan Cathedral and to a less extent in the buildings of Padua, Verona and Venice. In central and south Italy, the sunny climate and brilliant atmosphere naturally demanded small windows and thick walls to exclude the glare and heat of the sun. The preference, moreover, for opaque wall decoration, whether in mosaic, fresco or marble, handed down from the ancient Romans through the Romanesque period, counteracted any tendency to supersede walls of stone by transparent walls of glass and window tracery.

Italy in the fifteenth century

HISTORICAL, SOCIAL AND RELIGIOUS

In spite of internal turmoil, Italy led the way in Europe in arts, learning and commerce, and the cultural revival, known as the Renaissance, took place there nearly a century in advance of northern Europe, and effectually arrested the further evolution of the Gothic style in Italy. The Latin conquest of Constantinople (Istanbul) (1204) during the Fourth Crusade, in which the republic of Venice played a prominent part, and the subsequent years of the Latin occupation of the city (1204–61), were partly responsible for the immigration, in the thirteenth century, of Graeco-Byzantine artists into Italy. These skilled craftsmen, trained in Classical traditions, settled in Genoa, Venice, Pisa, Florence, Siena and many another town, and gave an impetus to the creative arts which enriched Italy, and then spread their influence throughout Europe. The rise of Venice was marked by the defeat of the Genoese off the Sardinian coast in 1353, and of the Turkish fleet

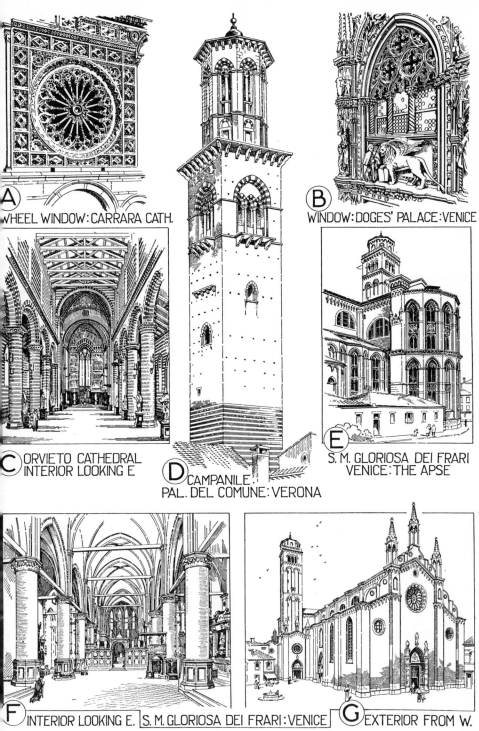

A WHEEL WINDOW: CARRARA CATH.

B WINDOW: DOGES' PALACE: VENICE

C ORVIETO CATHEDRAL INTERIOR LOOKING E

D CAMPANILE PAL. DEL COMUNE: VERONA

E S. M. GLORIOSA DEI FRARI VENICE: THE APSE

F INTERIOR LOOKING E. S. M. GLORIOSA DEI FRARI: VENICE

G EXTERIOR FROM W.

(A) THE FONTE GATTESCHI
VITERBO

(B) A TOMB OF THE SCALIGERS
VERONA

(C) ANGLE WINDOW
VENICE

(D) LA CERTOSA: CHIARAVALLE

(E) PORCH: S.M.MAGGIORE
BERGAMO

(F) PORCH: THE DUOMO
FERRARA

(G) LOGGIA DEI MERCANTI
BOLOGNA

(H) FACADE: S.AGOSTINO
BERGAMO

in 1416. These victories fired the Venetians with a desire to make the Doge's Palace a fit symbol of their success, and it was completed when Venice reached the zenith of her power and prosperity.

Italy had no national unity at this period, but was cut up into principalities and commonwealths, such as the republics of Venice, Florence and Genoa, the duchy of Milan, the kingdom of Naples and the Papal States. This absence of national unity is mirrored in the varied architectural treatment in different parts of the peninsula. Political life was full of rivalry and activity, and small wars were of constant occurrence. The erection of the cathedrals of Siena, Orvieto, Florence, Milan and Lucca was largely due to the vigorous civic pride of rival cities; while during the struggles between popes and emperors and their respective factions, the Guelphs and Ghibellines, both sides had to reckon with the increasing power of the townsmen who erected those numerous town halls which attest the growth of municipal institutions. Thus architecture was used more freely in the service of the people. Dante (1265–1321) presents a vivid picture of the age in his *Divina Commedia*, and this poem, which standardized the Italian language in literature, also coincided with the development of Italian Gothic architecture.

The power of the pope, as head of the Western Church, waned after the death of Boniface VIII (1303), for succeeding popes were under the influence of the kings of France, and for almost seventy years (1309–77), a period known as the 'Babylonish captivity', they resided at Avignon, losing authority and influence during their absence from Rome, in which city it is significant that there should be only one Gothic church. After the return of Gregory XI to Rome and his death in 1378, Western Christendom was plunged by rival popes into the religious turmoil of the 'Great Schism of the West' (1378–1417), which was only terminated by the Council of Constance and the accession of Martin V. It is not surprising that this period of confusion was unfavourable to the building of churches in Italy. S. Francis of Assisi (1182–1226) founded the Order of Franciscans or Grey Friars, which fired the religious imagination of the time and revolutionized religious life.

ARCHITECTURAL CHARACTER

The Gothic style in Italy dates approximately from the twelfth to the sixteenth century, but the influence of Roman tradition remained so strong that the conspicuous verticality of northern Gothic is generally neutralized in Italy by horizontal cornices and string courses. Churches are marked externally by the following features: flatness of roofs (pp. 738A, 749A), the screen wall of the west façade which masks the aisle roofs (p. 737A), the circular window of the west front (p. 733A, G), an absence of pinnacles and of flying buttresses (p. 749A), stripes of coloured marbles instead of mouldings, occasional frescoes and mosaics in panels, and small windows without tracery (p. 749A). The projecting entrance porches with columns, often resting on the backs of lion-like beasts (p. 734E), are in striking contrast to the cavernous porches of Northern Europe.

The sculpture and carving of the period, executed in the fine-grained marble of Italy, continued to be as refined as in the Classical period, and the influences of Old Rome is seen in modified Corinthian capitals with their acanthus leaves. The sculpture, although superior in technique to that of Northern Europe, is not such an essential part of a style which, as we shall see, never developed, as in France and England, into the highest form of Gothic. The brickwork and plastic terra-cotta of the Lombard plains resulted in a smallness of detail and intricacy of ornament natural to this material, as in the Frari Church, Venice (p. 733G), the Certosa, Pavia (p. 751F) and Chiaravalle (p. 734D), and many civic buildings. Colour effect and delicate detail were relied on, rather than depth of shadow and boldness of design; thus was the material allowed to give full expression to its own capabilities without forcing it beyond its limitations. The architecture of south Italy, and more especially of Sicily, owes its beauty to the combination of Greek inspiration, Roman construction and Byzantine decoration.

EXAMPLES

NORTH ITALY

Milan Cathedral (*c.* 1385–1485) (pp. 737, 738, 739A), initiated by the populace and the clergy of the city and sponsored by Giovanni Galeazzo Visconti, duke of Milan, is, with the exception of Seville, the largest Mediaeval cathedral, and is somewhat German in character, as among the fifty or so architects who had a part in it were consultants from north of the Alps. The choir and transepts were finished about 1450, and the nave and aisles were commenced in 1452. In plan (p. 738C) it consists of a nave 16.7 m (55 ft) wide between the piers, lofty double aisles and transepts terminated with a circlet of columns in the French manner, but enclosed in a German polygonal apse, while there is an absence of lateral chapels. The interior (pp. 737B, 738D) is vast, lofty and imposing, with fine perspective views, rendered all the more impressive by the dimness and mystery which result from lack of light. It has huge piers, 18 m (60 ft) high, surrounded by engaged shafts and surmounted by enormous capitals, 6.1 m (20 ft) in height, containing canopied niches and statues, from which spring the nave arches supporting the vault 45 m (148 ft) above the ground. It resembles S. Petronio, Bologna and owing to the excessive height of the aisles there is no triforium and the clear-storey is small, in striking contrast with French and English Gothic cathedrals. The exterior is a gleaming mass of white marble with lofty traceried windows, panelled buttresses, flying buttresses and pinnacles crowned with statues (p. 739A), the whole wrought into a soaring design of lace-like intricacy. The three magnificent traceried windows of the apse, 20.7 m × 8.5 m (68 ft × 28 ft), are the finest of their type in Italy (p. 738B). The flat-pitched roofs are constructed of massive marble slabs laid on the vaulting (p. 738A), and over the crossing is a domical vault, 65.5 m (215 ft) above the ground, designed by Amadeo and Dolcebuono in a competition in 1490, finishing in a lantern to which in 1750 an open-work spire was added, rising 107 m (350 ft) above the ground (p. 738D). The later façade (p. 737A), which has the wide-spreading gable lines of Romanesque churches, such as S. Michele, Pavia (p. 475F), was partly built from the designs of Carlo Buzzi after 1653, but only completed by Napoleon at the beginning of the nineteenth century. ·

The **Certosa, Pavia** (1396–1497) (p. 751D–F), a famous Carthusian monastery, was commenced by Giovanni Galeazzo Visconti, and forms a splendid memorial of the Milan dynasties. The monastic buildings were nearly completed at his death in 1492. The church was in progress by 1453. In plan (p. 751D) it is a Latin cross and similar to many German churches in the triapsal terminations to sanctuary and transepts, but the nave is in square, and the aisles in oblong bays, in the Italian manner. On the south are the two cloisters, richly wrought in terra-cotta. The exterior (p. 754O) is a fascinating instance of Lombard transitional Gothic-Renaissance style with arcading and terra-cotta ornament; while the monumental façade (1473–*c*. 1540) is wholly of Renaissance character (pp. 804, 805A).

· **S. Antonio, Padua** (1232–1307) (p. 740), is a seven-domed pilgrimage church resembling S. Mark, Venice (p. 389), in general conception. The nave is in square bays covered with domes on pendentives, which are also placed over the crossing,

MILAN CATHEDRAL

Ⓐ EXTERIOR FROM S.W.

Ⓑ INTERIOR LOOKING E.

MILAN CATHEDRAL

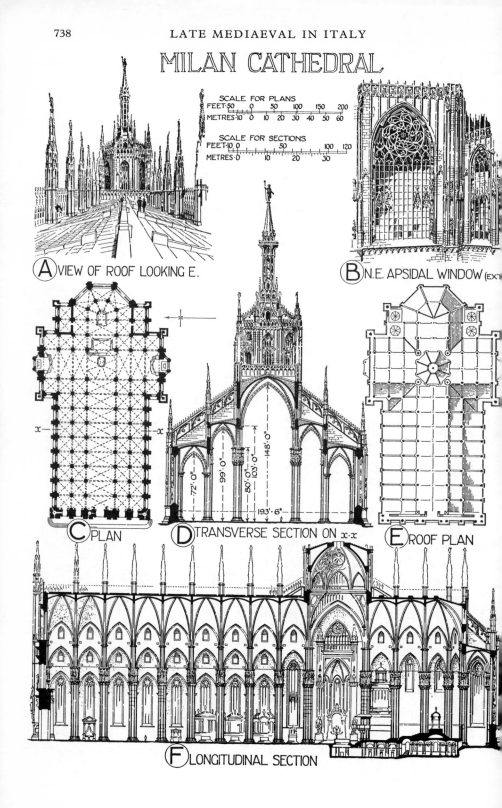

SCALE FOR PLANS
FEET·50 0 50 100 150 200
METRES·10 0 10 20 30 40 50 60

SCALE FOR SECTIONS
FEET·10 0 50 100 120
METRES·0 10 20 30

(A) VIEW OF ROOF LOOKING E.

(B) N.E. APSIDAL WINDOW (EX)

(C) PLAN

(D) TRANSVERSE SECTION ON x·x

(E) ROOF PLAN

(F) LONGITUDINAL SECTION

A. Milan Cathedral from N.W. (c. 1385–1485). See p. 736

B. SS. Giovanni e Paolo, Venice, from W. (1260–1385; façade 1430—unfinished; dome of later date). See p. 743

A. S. Antonio, Padua, from N.W. (1232–1307; domes heightened 1424). See p. 736

B. S. Antonio, Padua: nave

A. S. Anastasia, Verona (1261–).
See p. 743

B. Capella degli Scrovegni, Padua
(c. 1300–05). See p. 743

c. Palazzo Vecchio (1298–1314) and Piazza della Signoria, Florence with the
Loggia dei Lanzi (right) (1376–82). See p. 757

A. S. Petronio, Bologna, from N. (1390–1437). See p. 743

B. S. Petronio, Bologna: nave looking E.

C. SS. Giovanni e Paolo, Venice (1260–1385): interior

transepts and choir, beyond which is an apse and chevet with nine radiating chapels similar to contemporary churches in France. The interior also was obviously influenced by the Venetian church, but falls far short of the original, as it lacks the glamour of coloured mosaic decoration. The exterior has an arcade of pointed arches and an upper arcaded gallery, like the Romanesque churches of Lombardy. Also at **Padua**, the unpretentious **Cappella degli Scrovegni**, known, too, as Madonna dell'Arena (p. 741B), is a vehicle for Giotto's unsurpassed frescoes.

SS. Giovanni e Paolo, Venice (1260–1385) (pp. 739B, 742C), a Dominican church of imposing proportions and historic importance, contains the tombs of the Doges. The Latin cross of the plan is elaborated by pronounced transepts with eastern chapels, and by a polygonal apse to the choir. The interior is essentially Italian in the wide spacing of piers, the square bays of the nave vaulting, and the oblong bays of the aisles, and internal wooden ties take the place of external flying buttresses. The exterior is of beautiful brickwork with pointed windows and moulded cornices, and the clear-storey is loftier than usual in Italy, while a dome of later date crowns the crossing.

S. Maria Gloriosa dei Frari, Venice (1250–1338) (p. 733E, F, G), is a Franciscan church, designed by Niccolo Pisano, in which there are six eastern transept chapels. The interior (p. 733F) has lofty stone cylindrical piers tied together by wooden beams, supporting an arcade of pointed arches and brick vaulting in square bays with massive ribs resting on shafts rising from the pier capitals. The exterior (p. 733G) is in fine coloured brickwork, the plain west façade is set off by the sculptured central doorway and circular window above, and by small lateral windows, while along the aisles are pointed windows. The square campanile has vertical panels and a belfry of open arches, and is crowned with an octagonal lantern. The apse (p. 733E), with its double tiers of pointed tracery windows, flanked by the eastern transept chapels, is the great glory of the church.

S. Anastasia, Verona (1261–) (p. 741A), with its delightful portal and brick campanile, is a beautiful expression of Italian Gothic, and **S. Andrea, Vercelli** (1219–), has a character of its own derived from its two western towers and English type of plan.

S. Petronio, Bologna (1390–1437) (p. 742A, B), was designed for this famous university city by Antonio di Vincenzo to eclipse the cathedral at Florence. If completed it would have been one of the largest churches in Italy, but the eastern part was never built. The interior resembles Milan in having nave and aisles in diminishing heights, and the nave, with little ornamental detail, has widely spaced piers, resembling those of Florence. The chief feature of the entrance façade is the great doorway with its sculptured ornament designed in 1425 by Jacopo della Quercia. The exterior was never finished, although a competition was held about 1535 in which Palladio, Vignola and others took part and fifty designs are still preserved.

The **Doge's Palace, Venice** (pp. 730, 852), the façades of which date from 1309–1424, and are from designs by Giov. and Bart. Buon, is the grandest effort in civic architecture of the period, and is material evidence of the proud position of Venice as a great trading community, whose commerce was protected by the supremacy of her navy. The palace, started in the ninth century, several times rebuilt, and completed in the Renaissance period (p. 852), forms part of that great scheme of town-planning which was carried out through successive centuries (p. 730D). The façades, with a total length of nearly 152 m (500 ft), have open arcades in the two lower storeys, and the third storey was rebuilt after a fire in the sixteenth century, so as to extend over the arcades (p. 730B). This upper storey is faced with white and rose-coloured marble walls, resembling patterned brickwork, pierced by a few large and ornate windows (p. 733B) and finished with a lace-like parapet of oriental cresting. The arcade columns (p. 730E), which originally stood on a stylobate of three steps, now rise from the ground without bases, and the sturdy continuous tracery of the second tier of arcades lends an appearance of strength to the open arches, so heavily loaded by the solid walls above. The capitals of the columns, particularly the angle capital which was eulogized by Ruskin in *The Stones of Venice*, are celebrated for the delicate carving in low relief, which was made possible by the use of fine-grained marble. The whole scheme of columned and pointed arcades, with its combination of carved capitals and long horizontal lines of open tracery, is of that unique design which can only be termed Venetian Gothic. The 'Porta della Carta' gives entrance to the Cortile (p. 852).

The **Palazzo Pubblico, Cremona** (1206–45), the **Palazzo Pubblico, Piacenza** (1281–) and the **Mercanzia, Bologna** (1382–4) (p. 734G), are similar with pointed arcades and an upper storey, often with a projecting *ringhiera* or tribune, and there are the familiar forked battlements.

The **Broletto, Monza** (thirteenth century), possesses, like many another town hall, a *ringhiera* or balcony (p. 465D) on a level with the floor of the great hall, from which the magistrates were wont to address the citizens.

The **Ca d'Oro, Venice** (1424–36) (p. 745C), is another fine design by the two architects of the Doge's Palace. The windows are grouped together in the usual Venetian manner to form a centre for the façade which, however, in this instance seems to lack one wing. The arcaded entrance of five arches, lighting the deep central hall, is surmounted by an arcade divided into six openings, filled with characteristically Venetian tracery, and flanked by wider arches with projecting balconies, above which is another storey lighter in treatment, and there is a curious roof cresting of Saracenic design. The finished wing of the façade is of solid masonry, which sets off the intricate tracery of the centre.

The **Palazzi Foscari** (fifteenth century), **Contarini-Fasan** (fourteenth century), **Cavalli** (fifteenth century) and **Pisani** (fifteenth century) (p. 745B) are all on the Grand Canal. They display the concentration of traceried openings in the centre to light the hall, and have solid unbroken wings.

The **Ponte di Castel Vecchio** or **Scaligero, Verona** (1335), wholly destroyed in the 1939–45 war, was one of many bridges which were of such importance as means of intercommunication that they were considered sacred. It was a fortified bridge across the Adige, with a tower on either bank, and had segmental arches, a low octagonal tower at every pier, and forked Ghibelline battlements along its whole length (p. 753B).

The **Torre del Comune, Verona** (1172) (p. 733D), is one of those communal towers which sprang up as a result of Mediaeval civic life; for they served as bell towers to summon the citizens and as watch towers against fire and enemies. The square shaft of striped stone and brickwork has a belfry of three lights on each face; the crowning octagonal turret, in two stages, rises to a height of 83 m (272 ft), and was added after 1404, when the city lost its independence to Venice.

The **Torrazzo, Cremona** (1261–84), the highest at 122 m (nearly 400 ft) in Italy, and the celebrated **Campanile of S. Mark, Venice** (pp. 479, 730A, D), rebuilt since its collapse in 1902 in the form it had possessed since the early sixteenth century, add to the world-fame of Italian towers.

The **Ospedale Maggiore, Milan** (1457–c. 1624) (p. 819F–H), is unusual in that it was begun in transitional Renaissance style by Antonio Filarete of Florence (p. 803), but continued from 1465 in late Gothic. It is built of brick and terracotta, the use of which has resulted in delicacy of modelling in the broad frieze between the storeys and in the ornamental bands round the windows. It was the first lay hospital. The interior was severely damaged in the 1939–45 war.

A THE BIGALLO: FLORENCE

B PALAZZO PISANI: VENICE

PROJECTED EXTENSION

C PALAZZO CA D'ORO: VENICE

D PALAZZO PUBBLICO: SIENA

E BALCONY: VENICE

F PAL. DEI PRIORI: VOLTERRA

G MEDIÆVAL Hº: VITERBO

H PAᴸ PUBBLICO: MONTEPULCIANO

S. MARIA DEL FIORE: FLORENCE

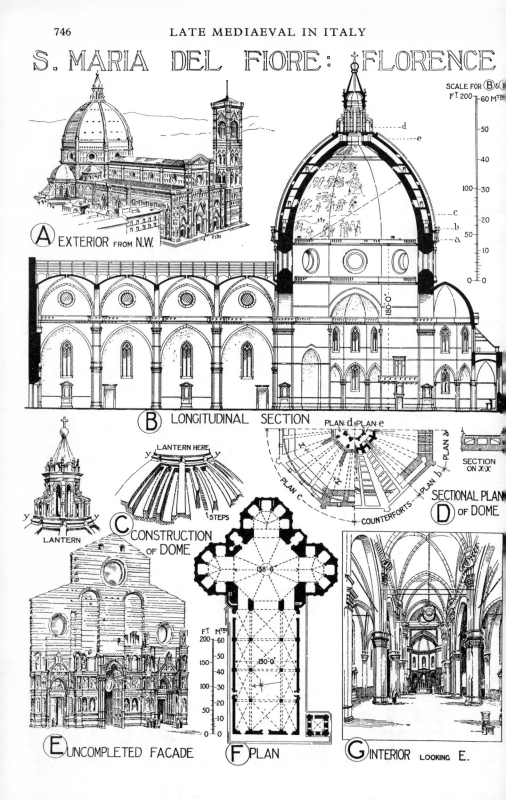

SCALE FOR Ⓑ &

Ⓐ EXTERIOR FROM N.W.

Ⓑ LONGITUDINAL SECTION

Ⓒ CONSTRUCTION OF DOME

LANTERN HERE

STEPS

LANTERN

PLAN d · PLAN e

PLAN c

PLAN b

COUNTERFORTS

SECTION ON X-X

Ⓓ SECTIONAL PLAN OF DOME

180'·0"

Ⓔ UNCOMPLETED FACADE

Ⓕ PLAN

138'·6"

150'·0"

Ⓖ INTERIOR LOOKING E.

CENTRAL ITALY

Florence Cathedral (1296–1462) (pp. 746, 749A, B), also known as **S. Maria del Fiore,** was designed by Arnolfo di Cambio, and is essentially Italian in character without the vertical features of northern Gothic. It was built around the old church of S. Reparata by the city council, and it forms there the centre of the group which emphasizes the importance of Florence and the ambition of her sons during the Middle Ages. On Arnolfo's death either in 1302 or 1310 the building was stopped until 1334, when Giotto was appointed master of the works, and he was followed by Andrea Pisano and Francesco Talenti, who in 1357 enlarged Arnolfo's scheme, while in 1365 a commission of architects laid out the choir and transepts. The three apses were completed in 1421, the dome was added by Brunelleschi (1420–34) as the result of a competition (p. 793), and the lantern was placed over it in 1462 by Giuliano da Majano, after Brunelleschi's death in 1446. The plan (p. 746F) is a peculiar type of Latin cross, and remarkable for the large central nave, 82 m (270 ft) long, and wide spacing of nave arcades, for there are only four square bays of 18 m (60 ft) (p. 749B). This vast nave forms an impressive though sombre approach to the majestic octagon (p. 746G), 42 m (138 ft 6 ins) in diameter, from which extended the three immense apses with fifteen radiating chapels. The piers have attached pilasters and unmoulded pointed arches; there is no triforium, but a small clear-storey of circular windows below the vaulted roof. The exterior (pp. 746A, 749A) is notable for its coloured marble panelling, small traceried windows, absence of buttresses and pinnacles, and for the horizontal lines of the design, the unique semi-octagonal apses, and the pointed dome. The marble facing of the west façade, partially completed under Arnolfo di Cambio (p. 746E) but destroyed in 1588, was recommenced in 1875 (p. 746A), with its panels of coloured marble, sculptures and mosaics, and finished in 1887.

The **Campanile, Florence** (1334–59) (pp. 746A, 749A), on the site of an earlier tower (888), is 14 m (45 ft) square and 84 m (275 ft) high, and was designed by Giotto on traditional Italian lines. Only the lowest stage was finished in Giotto's time, and the design was twice changed as it proceeded, first by Andrea Pisano and finally by Francesco Talenti. It rises sheer from the pavement without supporting buttresses, and all its four sides are panelled in coloured marble and embellished with sculptured friezes and marble inlay. It is divided into four principal stages, of which the topmost is the belfry, crowned by an arched corbel table, instead of the spire intended by Giotto.

The **Baptistery, Florence** (p. 749A), thought to have started as a fifth-century church, converted into a baptistery in the middle of the eleventh century, received various minor adornments during the thirteenth century and, standing to the west of the Cathedral, forms part of this world-famous group. The octagon is 27 m (90 ft) in diameter, covered with an internal dome, 31 m (103 ft) high, probably modelled on that of the Pantheon. The façades are in three stages of dark green and white marble, crowned with a low roof and lantern. The Baptistery is noted for the marvellous workmanship of its famous bronze doors, which were added in the fourteenth (1330–6) and fifteenth (1403–24 and 1425–52) centuries by Andrea Pisano and Lorenzo Ghiberti (p. 788). In 1514, in view of threatened collapse, Michelangelo introduced an iron chain around the base of the dome.

Siena Cathedral (*c.* 1226–1380) (pp. 750A, C, 751A–C), one of the most stupendous undertakings since the building of Pisa Cathedral, was largely the outcome of civic pride, and all the artists of Siena contributed their works to its building and adornment. The plan is cruciform, with an unusual irregular hexagon at the crossing, 17.7 m (58 ft) in diameter (p. 751C), covered by a dome and lantern of 1259–64;

while the sanctuary, owing to the slope of the ground, is built over the Baptistery of S. Giovanni, which thus forms a crypt, and is entered from the lower level. The interior is striking in its combination of unusual features (pp. 750C, 751B). The zebra marble striping on wall and pier, the squinch-arches of the strange hexagon, and the incised marble floor (fourteenth–fifteenth century), by the famous pavement-artists of Siena, form suitable surroundings for the famous sculptured pulpit by Niccolo Pisano (1265–9). Between 1339–48 a grandiose project for adding a new nave, to which the existing church would have formed transepts, was begun and abandoned. The building stands on a stepped platform (p. 751A) which gives dignity to the composition, and it has an elaborately sculptured western façade (lower part 1284–1300, upper, 1377–80) which is merely a frontispiece faced with white marble relieved with pieces of Siena red and Prato green marble and with three highly ornate recessed doorways (p. 750A). The shaft-like campanile, (thirteenth century) in striped marble, has six stages of windows which increase in size, and, rising from the south transept, it forms the central feature of the group.

The **Campo Santo, Pisa** (1278–83) (pp. 469A, 470B, 752A), by Giov. Pisano, consists of an open rectangle surrounded by a cloister with round-arched openings, filled with beautiful open tracery in 1463.

S. Maria della Spina, Pisa (1323) (p. 752B), is a miniature church on the banks of the Arno which has a shrine-like façade of crocketed gables and pinnacled canopies.

Orvieto Cathedral (1290–1330) (pp. 733C, 750B), of which the first architect was probably Arnolfo di Cambio, stands on an eminence in this isolated hill-city. Its plan is basilican with nave, aisles and projecting semicircular chapels. The interior (p. 750B) shows basilican influence, with its lofty cylindrical pillars in grey and white marble, which support semicircular arches surmounted by a striped clear-storey and pointed windows, all crowned by a timber roof of basilican type. The exterior also is of striped marble (basalt and travertine) carried round the aisle chapels, the windows of which are partly filled with alabaster. The façade (1310–30, not fully completed until 1580) resembles Siena with its three porches, gables and rose window, and is a glowing mass of symbolism carried out in coloured mosaic, carving and sculpture of great beauty, but is a mere frontispiece.

S. Maria Novella, Florence (1278–1350) (p. 753A), was designed by Fra Sisto and Fra Ristoro as a Latin cross of great size with transepts, chapels and beautiful cloisters. The nave has no triforium, but a low clear-storey with circular windows and a ribbed vault. The original design of the unfinished exterior is indicated by some blind arcading on the entrance façade, which was completed from designs by Alberti in the Renaissance period (p. 798).

S. Croce, Florence (1294–1442) (p. 754A), one of the largest churches in Europe, was by Arnolfo di Cambio, and contains many monuments to celebrated Italians. It is a Gothic version of a basilican church, with widely spaced columns and open timber roof. The western façade, left unfinished, was completed 1857–63, and is similar in character to that of Siena Cathedral.

Or San Michele, Florence (1337–1404), which was designed by Francesco Talenti and others, was originally called 'S. Michele in Orto', from its orchard site. It has a rectangular ground storey originally serving as a church of the trade guilds, which has fine three-light windows with slender columns and elaborate tracery enclosed in semicircular arches. These arcade infillings were an afterthought, dating from 1366–81. Externally, between the windows, are niches filled with statues by celebrated sculptors, such as Donatello and Ghiberti, as offerings from the twelve great trade guilds of Florence between 1428 and 1550. In the interior is a beautiful tabernacle and high altar by Andrea Orcagna (1349–59). There are two

Campanile (1334–59)

A. Florence Cathedral from S.E. (1296–1462). See p. 747

B. Florence Cathedral: nave looking E.

C. Loggia dei Lanzi, Florence (1376–82). See p. 757

A. Siena Cathedral: exterior.
See p. 747

B. Orvieto Cathedral (1290–1330):
nave looking E. See p. 748

c. Siena Cathedral: interior (c. 1226–1380). See p. 747

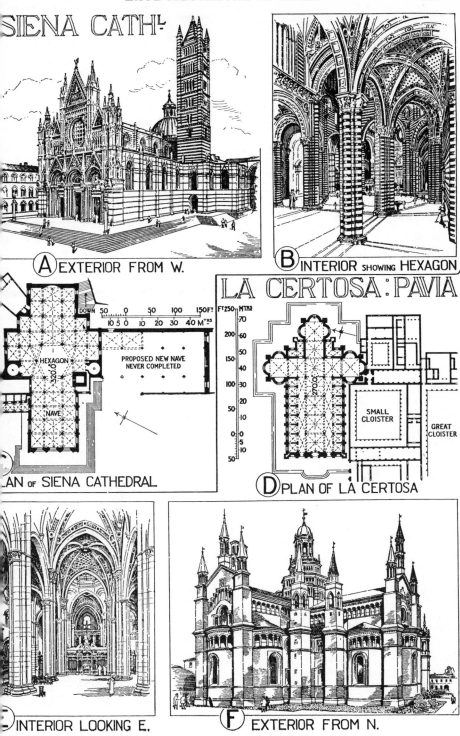

SIENA CATH^L

Ⓐ EXTERIOR FROM W.

Ⓑ INTERIOR SHOWING HEXAGON

LA CERTOSA : PAVIA

DOWN 50 0 50 100 150FT
10 5 0 10 20 30 40 M^{TRS}

HEXAGON

PROPOSED NEW NAVE
NEVER COMPLETED

NAVE

Ⓒ PLAN OF SIENA CATHEDRAL

SMALL
CLOISTER

GREAT
CLOISTER

Ⓓ PLAN OF LA CERTOSA

Ⓔ INTERIOR LOOKING E.

Ⓕ EXTERIOR FROM N.

A. Campo Santo, Pisa (1278–1463; tracery 1463). See p. 748

B. S. Maria della Spina, Pisa (1323). See p. 748

A. S. Maria Novella, Florence (1278–1350; façade 1456–70). See pp. 748, 798

B. The Ponte di Castel Vecchio, or Ponte Scaligero, Verona (1335). See p. 744

A. S. Croce, Florence: nave (1294–1442). See p. 748

B. S. Maria sopra Minerva, Rome: nave (*c.* 1285). See p. 757

A. S. Francesco, Assisi, from lower terrace on E. (1228–53). See p. 757

B. S. Francesco, Assisi: upper and
lower church and W. end of
Great Cloister

C. S. Francesco, Assisi: upper church

A. The Castle, Volterra (1343). See p. 757

B. The Ponte Vecchio, Florence (1345). See p. 757

C. San Gimignano: view of the Towers (13th–14th cent.). See pp. 480, 757

upper storeys over the church which have two-light windows; down to 1569 they formed granaries and are now used for State archives.

S. Francesco, Assisi (1228–53) (p. 755A–C), the great pilgrimage church situated on the hill above the historic plain, owes much of its imposing character to its lofty position, while the hill-slope facilitated the erection of an upper and lower church. The vast monastic buildings on their massive masonry substructures testify to the magnetic influence of the great Italian saint and founder. Both churches are vaulted, and the dim mystery of the aisleless interiors, terminated by a polygonal apse, ·gives a sense of solemnity to the brilliant frescoes of Cimabue and Giotto. These frescoes form a complete and consistent scheme of decoration, and make one of the most glowing church interiors in all Italy. The pulpit and the monuments are all of considerable interest. The doorways of both upper and lower church, the circular window of the nave, and the turret-shaped buttresses, with low flying arches, are the main features of the exterior. A sturdy campanile, which retains the Lombard Romanesque character, crowns this famous group.

S. Maria sopra Minerva, Rome (c. 1285) (p. 754B), designed by the two Dominican friars who were the architects of S. Maria Novella, Florence (p. 753A), is the only Gothic church in Rome—evidence of the impregnable fortress which the citadel of Classic Rome presented to the advance of Gothic art.

The **Palazzo del Podestà** or **Bargello, Florence** (1255–), the **Palazzo Vecchio, Florence** (1298–1314) (p. 741C), the **Palazzo Pubblico, Siena** (1289–1309) (p. 745D), the **Palazzo del Municipo, Perugia** (1281–), and the **Palazzo Pubblico, Montepulciano** (late fourteenth century) (p. 745H), represent the municipal life and enterprise of these Mediaeval cities, and stand, grave and severe, amidst the bustle of modern life, with their lofty watch towers and fortified façades, often finished with machicolations and battlements.

The **Palazzo dei Priori, Volterra** (1208–57) (p. 745F), is in four storeys with two-light windows, now irregularly placed. It is crowned with heavy battlements and the square tower rising above the front wall is capped with a belfry.

The **Castle, Volterra** (1343), high on its rocky site, is a typical Mediaeval stronghold of imposing outline with massive walls, small windows, central circular keep, round towers and machicolations (p. 756A).

The **Bigallo, Florence** (1352–58) (p. 745A), is a delicately arcaded little loggia, designed to shelter foundlings who were there displayed by the Capitane of S. Maria to appeal to the charity of the public.

The **Loggia dei Lanzi, Florence** (1376–82) (pp. 741C, 749C), with its bold semicircular arches and compound piers, forms part of a scheme embracing the piazza which would have made it the finest arcaded square in Italy.

The **Mediaeval House, Viterbo** (p. 745G), with its arcaded ground storey and traceried windows, is interesting among many such houses as evidence of a phase of civilization which has passed away.

San Gimignano (pp. 480, 756C) on its hill-top still retains thirteen towers built by rival local families—adherents of the Ghibellines and Guelphs—which vividly suggest the condition of the times when, as we are told, the municipality had to make building regulations to limit the height of the towers of these fortress-houses, mainly of the tenth and eleventh centuries, which still give a strangely mediaeval aspect to this picturesque hill-city.

The **Ponte Vecchio, Florence** (1345) (p. 756B), by Taddeo Gaddi, the oldest bridge in Florence, has three segmental arches springing boldly from massive piers to withstand the waters of the Arno when swollen with the melting snows of the Appenines, while along both sides of its roadway are the small shops of the goldsmiths' quarter. The corridor above the shops is by Vasari (1564).

SOUTHERN ITALY AND SICILY

Messina Cathedral (1092–1197), frequently altered after damage by fire and earthquakes until it was practically destroyed by the earthquake of 1908, was basilican in plan with timber roof in Moslem honeycomb work.

Palermo Cathedral (1170–85) (p. 759A) repeatedly altered, built on the site of an earlier Moslem mosque, is also basilican in plan and was commenced by King William the Good of Sicily. The open porch (c. 1480), with slender columns supporting stilted pointed arches of Moslem type, is reminiscent of the Alhambra, Granada; while the roof battlements recall those of the Doge's Palace. At the west end the Cathedral, which is Moslem in character, is connected across the street by two pointed arches to the tower of the Archbishop's Palace. Two slender minaret towers on either side resemble those at the east end, and in its vigour of skyline the whole group suggests Northern Gothic. The external decoration is in stone of two colours, and the apses are particularly fine in treatment with polychrome interlaced blind arcading. The dome is an addition of 1781–1801.

The **Castello Nuovo, Naples** (1279–83), built by Charles I of Anjou, is a lofty, rectangular structure, with three machicolated round towers and curtain walls, now pierced with Renaissance windows.

The **Palazzo S. Stefano, Taormina** (1330) (p. 759B)—one of many palaces in ancient precipice-city which have pointed two-light windows with trefoil heads and crowning machicolated cornices—and the **Palazzo Arcivescovile, Palermo,** designed with flamboyant tracery windows (15th century) (p. 759C)—now mostly blocked up—are typical secular buildings of the Mediaeval period.

BIBLIOGRAPHY

ARGAN, G. C. *L'architettura del Duecento e Trecento.* Florence, 1936.

CUMMINGS, C. A. *A History of Architecture in Italy from the Time of Constantine to the Dawn of the Renaissance.* 2 vols. New ed., 1928.

FRANKLIN, J. W. *The Cathedrals of Italy.* London, 1958.

JACKSON, SIR T. G. *Gothic Architecture in France, England and Italy.* 2 vols. London, 1915.

NESFIELD, E. *Specimens of Mediaeval Architecture.* London, 1862.

POPE-HENNESSY, J. *Italian Gothic Sculpture.* London, 1955.

PORTER, A. KINGSLEY. *Lombard Architecture.* 4 vols. New Haven, Conn., 1915–17.

—. *Mediaeval Architecture.* 2 vols. New York and London, 1909.

ROMANINI, A. M. *L'Architettura Gotica in Lombardia.* 2 vols. Milan, 1964.

RUSKIN, J. *Stones of Venice.* 3 vols. London (many editions).

STREET, G. E. *Brick and Marble in the Middle Ages.* London, 1874.

TOESCA, P. *Storia dell'Arte Italiana: Il Medioevo.* Vol. ii. Turin, 1927.

—. *Storia dell'Arte Italiana: Il Trecento.* Turin, 1951.

WAGNER-RIEGER, R. *Die italienische Baukunst zu Beginn der Gotik.* Graz and Cologne, 1956–7.

WHITE, J. *Art and Architecture in Italy: 1250–1400.* Harmondsworth and Baltimore, 1966.

Open porch *c.* (1480)

A. Palermo Cathedral from S. (1170–85; dome 1781–1801). See p. 758

B. Palazzo S. Stefano, Taormina
(1330). See p. 758

C. Window in Palazzo Arcivescovile,
Palermo (15th cent.). See p. 758

A. Salamanca: the Old Cathedral (1120–78) backed by the New Cathedral (c. 1509–1734). See pp. 534, 762

B. Salamanca: the dome of the New Cathedral from W. tower. See p. 762

C. Salamanca New Cathedral: nave (1512–38). See p. 762

26

GOTHIC ARCHITECTURE IN SPAIN AND PORTUGAL

Twelfth to sixteenth century

INFLUENCES

The geographical, geological and climatic conditions of Spain and Portugal have been described in Chapter 19.

RELIGIOUS, SOCIAL AND HISTORICAL

The establishment of the Spanish Inquisition (1477) in Castile and later in other provinces was designed to bring about national unity by first securing religious unity. This inquisitorial scheme resulted in the expulsion from Spain of both Jews and Moslems, who were important communities in commercial and industrial life, and Spain was thus materially weakened by their departure. During the whole of the Mediaeval period, until 1492, Spain was divided into different kingdoms under the independent rule of Christian kings and Moslem caliphs and emirs. The Catholic sovereigns Ferdinand (1479–1516) and Isabella (1474–1504) arrogated to themselves supreme power, making use of Church, nobles and cities as intruments of their government, establishing police against brigandage, annexing the power and money of the military Orders, and enforcing military service from the nobles. They even reduced the Cortes of Castile to a money-granting machine and gradually crippled commerce and industry through the control of officials and the imposition of excise duties, thus establishing an inquisition in commerce as well as religion.

ARCHITECTURAL CHARACTER

Despite the fall of the Moslem capital of Toledo in 1085, Moorish influence remained a salient aspect of Spanish art and architecture until the final expulsion of the Moors with the fall of Granada in 1492. The Gothic style (introduced *c.* 1210), was most highly developed in Catalonia where, though mainly on French lines, the grand scale of the single-span vaulted interiors gives it, as at Gerona (p. 768C), a specifically Spanish character, and the same may be said of León Cathedral, which surpasses its French prototype at Amiens both in the expanse of window openings and the tenuity of the piers (p. 766D). Moorish influence made itself felt in such Moslem features as the horseshoe arch and pierced stone tracery, and notably in rich surface decoration of intricate geometrical and flowing patterns (pp. 767, 773), for which Moslem art is remarkable, as in the Sinagoga del Transito, Toledo (1360–6), while the early Spanish churches seem to have been the work of Moorish craftsmen. Church exteriors are flat in appearance, owing to the chapels which are so frequently inserted between the buttresses (p. 768). Unlike French Gothic, large wall surfaces and horizontal lines are conspicuous, and generally

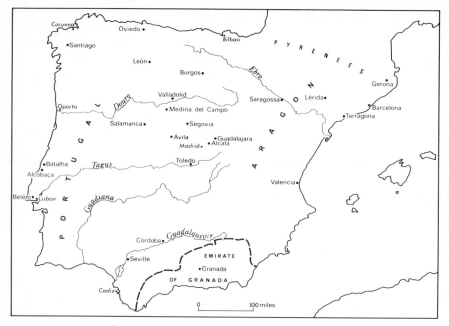

Spain and Portugal in the fifteenth century

there is excessive ornament, due to Moorish influence, without regard to its constructive character (p. 765B). The cloisters of many cathedrals, as Barcelona (p.
766A), Toledo, Segovia (pp. 764C, 767A) and Lérida, are very characteristic. In the
later period Classical detail was grafted on Gothic forms, producing most picturesque features, transitional in style (see Chapter 31).

EXAMPLES

ECCLESIASTICAL ARCHITECTURE

Ávila Cathedral (1160–1211 and later), with its chevet built astride the city walls,
is one of the most interesting in the Peninsula. The chevet has double aisles and
semicircular chapels in the thickness of the walls, whose slit windows indicate that
it was part of the city fortifications. The 'coro' or choir west of the transepts, the
fine cloisters, the widely spaced nave bays, twin western towers, and two unique
hammered-iron pulpits (p. 773A) are well-known features of this church.

Salamanca New Cathedral (1509/13–1734) (p. 760), by Juan Gil de Ontayon,
sited a little to the north of the (Romanesque) Old Cathedral, is a vast, magnificent
late Gothic and Plateresque church, 103 m (340 ft) long and 48.8 m (160 ft) wide.
Churrigueresque features, typical of Salamanca two centuries after the Gothic
period, are explained by the long-deferred completion.

Burgos Cathedral (1221–1457) (pp. 763, 765A, 968) is irregular in plan and the
most poetic of all the Spanish cathedrals. The two western towers, with open-work
spires (p. 763E), recall Cologne, and a richly treated central lantern or 'cimborio'
(p. 968) is a feature of the exterior (p. 763C). The interior has elaborate triforium

BURGOS CATHL

Ⓐ CAPILLA DEL CONDESTABLE

Ⓑ TRANSEPTS & CIMBORIO

Ⓒ EXTERIOR FROM S.E.

Ⓓ PLAN

Ⓔ EXTERIOR FROM W.

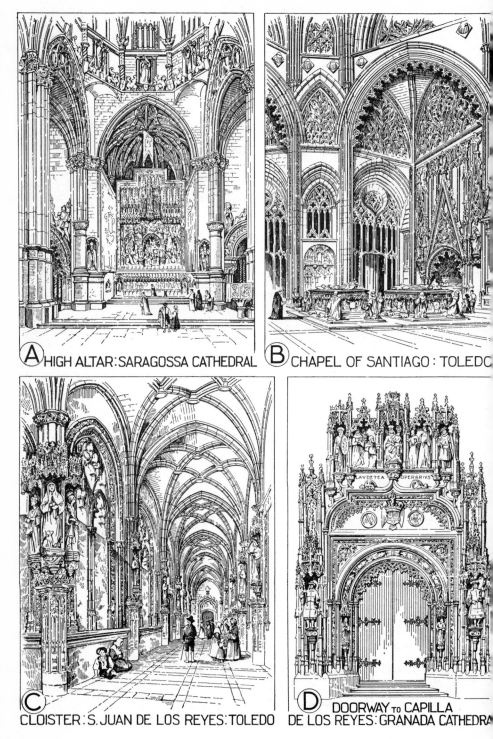

A HIGH ALTAR: SARAGOSSA CATHEDRAL

B CHAPEL OF SANTIAGO : TOLEDO

C CLOISTER : S. JUAN DE LOS REYES: TOLEDO

D DOORWAY TO CAPILLA DE LOS REYES: GRANADA CATHEDRAL

A. Burgos Cathedral (1221–1457): lantern from N. See p. 762

B. College of S. Gregorio, Valladolid (façade, 1492–6). See p. 769

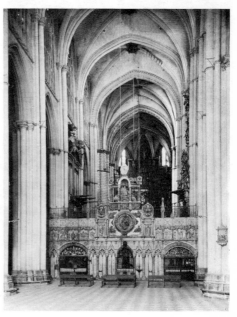

↑
Tower (17th cent.)

C. Toledo Cathedral from S.W. (1227–1493). See p. 769

D. Toledo Cathedral: interior looking E. See p. 769

A. Barcelona Cathedral: nave and towers
(1365–89); cloisters (1382–1448).
See p. 769

B. The Monastery, Batalha:
Capellas Imperfeitas (14th cent.).
See p. 770

C. S. Juan de los Reyes, Toledo:
choir from S.W. (1478–92). See p. 770

D. León Cathedral: interior
(1255–1303). See p. 770

A. CLOISTERS SEGOVIA

B. DOORWAY: S. CRUZ: SEGOVIA

C. APSE: COLLEGE OF S. ISIDORO: LEON

D. LANTERN (INT.) OLD CATH: SALAMANCA

E. DOORWAY: LA CARTUJA: BURGOS

F. LANTERN (EXT) OLD CATH: SALAMANCA

G. GALLERY ARCADE AT a

H. COURT: COLL. OF S. GREGORIO: VALLADOLID

J. CAPS. IN MUS. SARAGOSSA

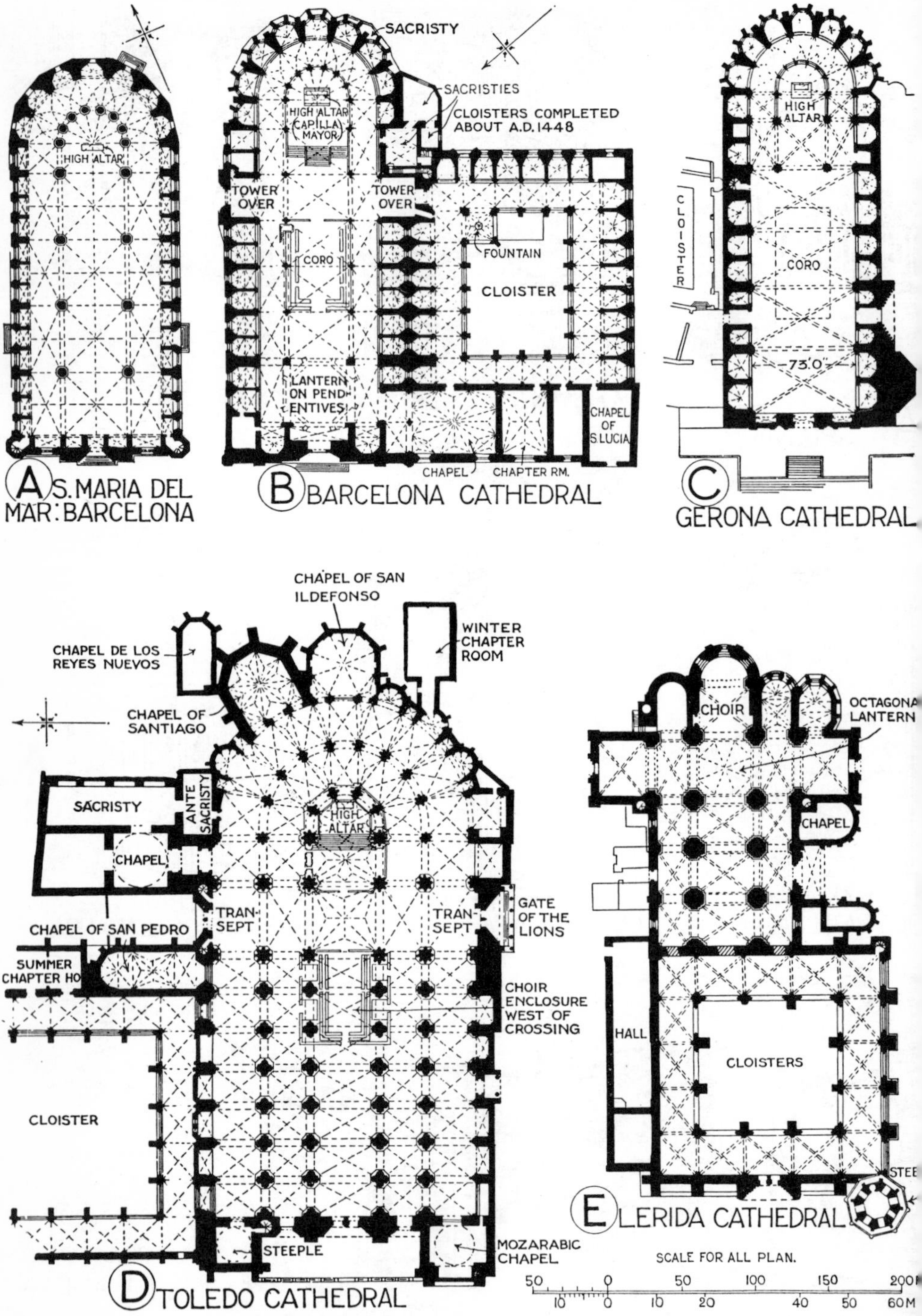

A. S. MARIA DEL MAR: BARCELONA

- SACRISTY
- HIGH ALTAR

B. BARCELONA CATHEDRAL

- SACRISTY
- SACRISTIES
- CLOISTERS COMPLETED ABOUT A.D. 1448
- HIGH ALTAR (CAPILLA MAYOR)
- TOWER OVER
- TOWER OVER
- CORO
- FOUNTAIN
- CLOISTER
- LANTERN ON PENDENTIVES
- CHAPEL OF S. LUCIA
- CHAPEL
- CHAPTER RM.

C. GERONA CATHEDRAL

- HIGH ALTAR
- CLOISTER
- CORO
- 73' 0"

D. TOLEDO CATHEDRAL

- CHAPEL OF SAN ILDEFONSO
- CHAPEL DE LOS REYES NUEVOS
- WINTER CHAPTER ROOM
- CHAPEL OF SANTIAGO
- SACRISTY
- ANTE SACRISTY
- CHAPEL
- HIGH ALTAR
- CHAPEL OF SAN PEDRO
- TRANSEPT
- TRANSEPT
- GATE OF THE LIONS
- SUMMER CHAPTER HO
- CHOIR ENCLOSURE WEST OF CROSSING
- CLOISTER
- STEEPLE
- MOZARABIC CHAPEL

E. LERIDA CATHEDRAL

- CHOIR
- OCTAGONAL LANTERN
- CHAPEL
- HALL
- CLOISTERS
- STEE

SCALE FOR ALL PLAN.

50　0　50　100　150　200ft
10　0　10　20　40　50　60M

tracery, massive piers rebuilt to support the high 'cimborio' which was added in 1539–67, and fine transeptal circular windows (p. 763B). The 'coro' is in the usual Spanish position west of the crossing, which reduces the nave to a vestibule (p. 763D). Among the side chapels, which are of extraordinary size, the octagonal Capilla del Condestable (1482–), over 15.2 m (50 ft) in diameter, is specially remarkable for the beauty and magnificence of its late Gothic detail (p. 763A), and the altar of S. Ana has an altar-piece which is a miracle of richness (p. 773B).

Toledo Cathedral (1227–1493) (pp. 765C, D, 768D), with five aisles and a range of side chapels, resembles Bourges Cathedral in general plan. It is about the same length, but it is considerably wider, with the choir enclosure, as is usual in Spain, west of the crossing (p. 768D). A singularly shallow sanctuary, with immense wooden 'retablo', flanked by tiers of arcaded statuary, is terminated by a chevet of double aisles and chapels completing a most impressive interior. The exterior has a low roof, usual in most Spanish churches, and has a fine ornamental north-west steeple. The Chapel of Santiago (1435) (p. 764B), in the chevet, has doorways with elaborate screenwork and great frilled arches, supporting the octagonal vault. There are fine stained-glass windows, beautiful carved choir stalls, and a treasury, rich even for Spain, containing the famous silver-gilt 'Custodia'— the flower of Spanish Gothic miniature art.

The **College of S. Gregorio, Valladolid** (1488–96) (p. 765B), now the town hall, has a sculptured façade (1492–6) embellished with statues, heraldic devices, and a genealogical tree of Ferdinand and Isabella, all framed with canopied niches and pinnacles, which show the influence of Moorish art in church ornament. The court (p. 767H) has arcades of the later period, with three-centred arches, twisted columns and intricate Moorish-type carving (p. 767G).

S. Pablo, Valladolid (1276–1492), has a façade (1486–92) (p. 771C) and internal doorways which, in intricacy of detail, also show Moorish influence.

Barcelona Cathedral (1298–1448) (pp. 766A, 768B) is remarkably fine, with nave vaulted in square and aisles in oblong bays, in the Italian manner, and with characteristic 'coro' west of the crossing (p. 768B). There is a fine western lantern on pendentives (c. 1420–48), slightly projecting transepts surmounted by towers, as at Exeter (p. 642E), and chevet of nine chapels. The thrust of the vault is counteracted by the deep internal buttresses which enclose chapels along the aisles, as at Albi in France (p. 609). The vault, as is usual in Spain, is exposed externally and roofed by tiles (p. 766A). The cloisters were completed c. 1448, with twenty-two chapels.

Gerona Cathedral (1312–1598) (p. 768C) is another instance where buttresses have internal chapels between them. There are no aisles, and the nave (1417–1598), 22 m (73 ft) wide, in four compartments, has the widest Gothic vault in Europe, and this, together with the length of 84 m (275 ft), produces a fine effect with the enclosed choir and chevet (1312–46) at the sanctuary end. The central hall of the Royal Courts of Justice, London, although less than 14.6 m (48 ft) wide, gives an idea of this interior, which resembles Albi (p. 609).

S. Maria del Mar, Barcelona (1328–83) (p. 768A), is a splendid town church, characterized both internally and externally by severe simplicity, and the front to the street is flanked by two octagonal pinnacles. The roof vaulting rests upon widely spaced octagonal granite piers. The nave and aisles are of great height; there is no triforium and only small clear-storey windows in the vault spandrels.

SS. Justo y Pastor, Barcelona (1345), has an aisleless nave 13.7 m (45 ft) wide, with chapels between internal buttresses. The altar stands in an unusual position in front of stalls ranged round the apse.

S. Maria del Pino, Barcelona (1453), similar in plan, has a fine heptagonal apse and western circular window.

Seville Cathedral (1402–1520) (p. 771A, B), is the largest Mediaeval cathedral in Europe, and, with the exception of S. Peter's, Rome, the largest church in the world. It owes its plan and size, with nave, double aisles and side chapels, to its erection on the site of a mosque. This also controlled its rectangular outline, about 122 m (400 ft) × 76 m (250 ft), and its square east end, unusual in Continental churches, to which is added a small apse. The Cathedral is indeed enormous, as may be realized by comparison with Westminster Abbey. The nave, about 13.7 m (45 ft) wide in the clear, is nearly half as wide again as Westminster nave; each of the four aisles is approximately equal in width to the Abbey nave, and in addition there are surrounding chapels as wide as the aisles, so that with the chapels, Seville Cathedral is about eight times the width of Westminster nave. The interior is impressive, although the nave vault, 40 m (130 ft) high has ribs which are somewhat confused in design and overloaded with bosses. The thirty-two immense clustered piers and numerous stained-glass windows produce an imposing effect, in spite of the absence of a triforium. The richness of the interior is enhanced by the sculptured stalls of the 'coro' occupying two nave bays, the fine 'reja' or grille (1518), the 'retablo', choir stalls and archbishop's throne. The exterior, owing to many additions, has a certain shapelessness and absence of skyline, but bears a general resemblance to Milan Cathedral, although of a simpler Gothic type and less fanciful in detail. The slender 'Giralda' (1184–96, upper part 1568–), originally the minaret of the mosque, gives this massive group a curiously Oriental aspect.

S. Juan de los Reyes, Toledo (1478–92) (pp. 764C, 766C), is a royal sepulchral chapel erected by Ferdinand and Isabella for a purpose similar to that of Henry VII's Chapel, Westminster. This late Gothic building, with traces of the incoming Renaissance, has a sculptured façade and 'cimborio' with lofty pinnacles. The interior (p. 766C) is chiefly notable for the raised galleries for the use of kings and nobles, surmounted by the characteristic octagonal 'cimborio' with its beautiful squinch arches. The two-storeyed cloisters (p. 764C), with their traceried windows and canopied statues, are held to be the most beautiful Gothic creations in Spain.

Valencia Cathedral (1262–c. 1356) and **León Cathedral** (1255–1303) (p. 766D) show French influence.

Lérida Cathedral (1203–78) (p. 768E), long used as barracks but now cleared, is an impressive early building with octagonal 'cimborio', three eastern apses, and adjacent cloisters, and the roofing slabs rest directly on the stone vaults.

The **Monastery of the Jerónimos, Belém, near Lisbon** (1499–1522), is a distinguished reminder of Portugal's former prominence. The cloisters have a two-storeyed arcade draped with delicate sculpture. The church is a richly ornamented late Gothic aisled hall of three bays. Much of the decoration is Renaissance or Manueline (see Chapter 31).

The **Monastery, Batalha, Portugal** (1387–1415), with its unique fourteenth-century church and octagonal tomb chapel (p. 766B), forms a fine architectural group.

SECULAR ARCHITECTURE

The finest secular architecture is found in Catalonia, as seen in the much altered **Palacio de la Audiencia, Barcelona,** with its remarkable court containing a picturesque external stairway (p. 772B); the **Casa del Ayuntamiento, Barcelona** (1373–); the **Alcázar, Segovia** (1410–55), an old Castilian castle with massive towers; the **Torre del Clavero, Salamanca** (1480); the **Gateway of S. Maria, Burgos,** and the remarkable **Puente de Alcantara, Toledo** (1258), which spans the Tagus and is protected by a defensive tower.

The **Ducal Palace, Guadalajara** (1480–92), had a very picturesque court

A. Seville Cathedral from S.W. (1402–1520). See p. 770

B. Seville Cathedral: nave
looking E. See p. 770

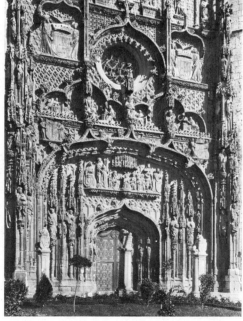

C. S. Pablo, Valladolid: principal
doorway (1486–92). See p. 769

A COURT: DUCAL PALACE GUADALAJARA

B COURT: THE AUDIENCIA BARCELONA

C DOORWAY: FOUNDLING HOSPITAL: CÓRDOBA

D LA LONJA: VALENCIA

E CASTLE: MEDINA DEL CAMPO

F PUERTA DE SERRANOS VALENCIA

G WINDOW IN BISHOP'S PALACE: ALCALA

H PUERTA DEL SOL: TOLEDO

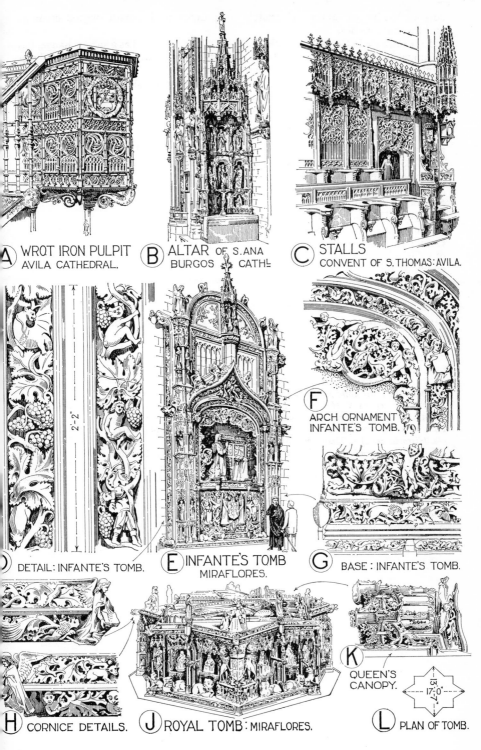

A. WROT IRON PULPIT AVILA CATHEDRAL.

B. ALTAR OF S. ANA BURGOS CATHL

C. STALLS CONVENT OF S. THOMAS: AVILA.

D. DETAIL: INFANTE'S TOMB.

E. INFANTE'S TOMB MIRAFLORES.

F. ARCH ORNAMENT INFANTE'S TOMB.

G. BASE: INFANTE'S TOMB.

H. CORNICE DETAILS.

J. ROYAL TOMB: MIRAFLORES.

K. QUEEN'S CANOPY.

L. PLAN OF TOMB.

surrounded by two storeys of ornately sculptured arcades, with twisted columns and multifoil arches.

La Lonja de la Seda, Valencia (1482–98) (p. 772D), used as a silk exchange, has an unbalanced façade of about 60 m (nearly 200 ft), with central tower, an east wing with large gateway and two pointed windows, and a west wing with two rows of square-headed Gothic windows surmounted by open galleries.

The **Castillo de la Mota, Medina del Campo** (1440–) (p. 772E), is stern in aspect, with circular towers, battlemented parapets, and windowless curtain walls, and a high tower commands the surrounding country.

The **Puerta del Sol, Toledo** (p. 772H), much repaired at various times, forms part of the town walls of the ancient city, and with its horseshoe arches, intersecting arcades, and Moorish battlements indicates that the Mediaeval Spaniard, with craftsman-like skill, applied the art of the time to all secular buildings.

The **Puerta de Serranos, Valencia** (1349) (p. 772F), with its mediaeval fortifications, has two polygonal towers flanking the gateway, above which is traceried wall panelling and a gallery on enormous corbels.

These and many more similar buildings reflect the power and position of the Catholic Church and of the Spanish grandee, while the well-preserved town walls of such old-world cities as **Ávila** and **León,** and the countless imposing castles in which Spain is singularly rich, indicate the unsettled conditions of those times.

BIBLIOGRAPHY

BALBAS, L. T. *Arquitectura Gótica* (Ars Hispaniae VII). Madrid, 1952.
BEVAN, B. *History of Spanish Architecture.* London, 1938.
BOOTON, H. W. *Oriel Architectural Guide: Spain.* Newcastle upon Tyne, 1963.
CALVERT, A. F. *Spain.* 2 vols. London, 1924.
DURLIAT, M. *Art Catalan.* Paris, 1963.
HARVEY, J. *The Cathedrals of Spain.* London, 1957.
LAMBERT, E. *L'art gothique en Espagne aux 12e et 13e siècles.* Paris, 1931.
LAMPÉREZ Y ROMEA, V. *Historia de la arquitectura Cristiana española.* 2nd ed. Madrid, 1930.
LAVEDAN, P. *L'architecture gothique religieuse en Catalogne.* Paris, 1935.
LOZOYA, J. DE CONTRERAS, MARQUÉS DE. *El arte gótico en España.* Barcelona, 1935.
—. *Historia del Arte Hispanico.* Madrid, 1940.
RAHLVES, F. *Cathedrals and Monasteries of Spain.* Paris, 1965; London, 1966.
SANTOS, R. DOS. *O estilo manuelino.* Lisbon, 1952.
STREET, G. E. *Account of Gothic Architecture in Spain.* London, 1874. Revised edition with notes by G. G. King, London, 1914.
STURGIS, R., and FROTHINGHAM, A. L. *A History of Architecture.* Vol. iii. New York, 1915.
UNAMUNO, M. DE. *Por Tierras de Portugal y España.* Madrid, 1941.
WASHBURN, O. *Castles in Spain.* Mexico City, 1957.
WEISMÜLLER, A. A. *Castles from the Heart of Spain.* London, 1967.

27

RENAISSANCE ARCHITECTURE IN ITALY

Fifteenth to nineteenth century

INFLUENCES

GEOGRAPHICAL

The Renaissance in Italy is best considered geographically under the three great distinctive cities of its activity, Florence, Rome and Venice, which, however, will be taken as centres of influence rather than localized schools. Each had its own regional traits, though these became less marked as time progressed, and gave way almost completely to universal characteristics during the Baroque period. At no time did South Italy and Sicily play more than a minor or subservient rôle.

Florence. The city-state of Florence, centrally situated, was one of the chief powers of Italy. Though its expanding dominions never included more than a small part of the peninsula, the Florentines not only exerted considerable influence over the whole of Tuscany but carried Renaissance architecture, which originated with them, much farther afield. Under Florence are included Genoa, a maritime republic, which was little affected by the new style until mid-sixteenth century, and Milan, centre of yet another powerful state and in which Florentine architects were the first to build in Renaissance style: Turin comes into the picture in later times.

Rome. The shrunken and distressed Mediaeval city began to recover its prestige and unique influence while the Renaissance was taking root in Florence, and soon popes and cardinals were reviving its glories in fine architecture. The ruins of ancient Rome, then better preserved than now, supplied the models for new buildings which, in their turn, became models for all Europe. The Popes claimed temporal rights over the Papal States, extending from the region of Rome northwards along the east coast to link with the Republics of Florence and Venice. In the more remote of the States papal authority was negligible until the early sixteenth century, and they were in fact in the hands of despots, who created their own individual artistic environments.

Venice. The greatness of Venice was founded during the Mediaeval period (pp. 461, 731) on her Oriental commerce, and this prosperity continued well into Renaissance times. By 1500 her territories in Italy extended westward almost to Milan, thus embracing Padua, Vicenza, Verona, Brescia, Bergamo and other cities along the valley of the River Po, while across the Adriatic she retained Dalmatia and enlarged her holding in Istria. The history of the Venetian State was always influenced by her impregnable location in the Venetian lagoon, protected by a belt of islands, and by her sea-power which secured her maritime trade with the East; when geographical discoveries opened up new routes she gradually sank into decline.

GEOLOGICAL

Florence. As shown previously (pp. 461, 731), the quarries of Tuscany yielded ample fine stone, obtainable, when needed, in large blocks. Siena, a rival republic until 1555, had her own local supplies, as well too of white and yellow marble. From Carrara and vicinity in the north-west of the modern province of Tuscany came the famed white marble—the Luna marble of Roman times—and also coloured, and from quarries at Fiesole, the Florentines won the 'pietra serena', a blue-grey stone of fine quality much employed in Early Renaissance buildings in the city, as well as the 'pietra forte', a brown stone more suitable for outside work. The Genoa district was equally well favoured, having ready access to the northward extension of the massif which includes Carrara, and to the green- and vari-coloured marbles of Liguria and Piedmont. In the Milan region, where brick and terra-cotta were normal, coloured marbles could be obtained, though with some difficulty, and therefore tended to be used in sparing, precious fashion.

Rome. Good building stone of many varieties was available within ready reach of the city (pp. 256, 345, 461), the finest being travertine, won from quarries around Tivoli, a stone much used by the Romans. But as in previous periods, Renaissance builders often found the decaying pagan buildings a much more handy source, as well too for the coloured marbles which the Romans had brought at such great pains from various parts of their mighty empire. The northerly Papal States also mostly lay in stone-producing districts, except around Bologna and the neighbouring lower Po valley, where brick was the natural material.

Venice. The site of the city was devoid of suitable materials, but brick-earths were accessible on the nearby mainland, and by easy water-carriage, stones, timber and marbles could be obtained according to need, as in the Mediaeval period (pp. 461, 731). Istrian cream-coloured stone continued to be used extensively in Venice, and red- and orange-coloured marbles were available near Verona. Westward, the cities under Venetian rule lay in the brick-producing zone, but stone from the neighbouring foothills of the Alps was accessible for the best work.

CLIMATIC

Florence. As elsewhere in Italy, the bright and sunny climate rendered large windows not only unnecessary but also unsuitable. The open 'cortile' or court, normal to palaces, and the sheltering colonnade or arcade are arrangements perpetuated from ancient times; while the low-pitched roof, natural in a country where snow was rare, lent itself to cornice and parapet or balustrade.

Rome. The effects of climate were much as in previous times (pp. 257, 461, 731). The narrow streets of Italian towns gave protection not alone against the blaze of summer sun but also against winter cold, severely felt in the indifferently-heated buildings. The cramped, bustling streets in their turn, along with the risks of faction fights, brawls and nocturnal depredations, led to living on upper floors of palaces, the first floor being the principal or 'piano nobile', while the ground floor was devoted to general service purposes.

Venice. As shown earlier (pp. 461, 731), the extreme heat of summer was here tempered by sea breezes, and to enjoy them, belvederes and balconies were usual, these all the more necessary in that the restricted island sites gave little room for gardens. On the other hand, the northern latitude and the winds that swept down from the snow-topped mountains, made fire-places almost essential, and the funnel-topped chimneys are a distinctive Venetian feature.

HISTORICAL, SOCIAL AND RELIGIOUS

Originating in Italy in the early fifteenth century, the Renaissance spread throughout all those countries of Europe which had formed the Western Roman Empire. For this reason, and before considering those influences of a specific nature affecting

Italy in the sixteenth century

the individual, principal Italian city-states, it may be useful to present a brief general survey of the many factors, not all of Italian provenance, contributing to an eventful movement which altered radically the political, philosophical, intellectual and artistic attitudes of the West.

By the beginning of the sixteenth century France, England and Spain had become strong national states, though some marked differences remained between the two chief Spanish kingdoms of Castile and Aragon. Elsewhere in Europe there obtained a rich variety of political structures and relationships. In Italy and in Germany no effective nation-states emerged, yet some of the component states of both countries were attaining greater power and efficiency. In Italy the city remained the effective social and cultural unit: only in moments of speculative idealism did Machiavelli and others proclaim an Italian patriotism. In Germany sentiment still attached to the Holy Roman Empire, but its fiscal and military organs scarcely functioned; the power of the Hapsburg Emperors arose not from the Imperial office but from their hereditary lands, now including not only Austria but most of the Low Countries. The attempt of the Dukes of Burgundy to resuscitate a Middle Kingdom collapsed in 1477, when the Swiss defeated and killed Charles the Bold. Switzerland, a loose confederation of cantons and city-states, detached itself decisively from the Empire and from Hapsburg rule. Bohemia continued to draw inspiration from the sense of Czech nationality which had arisen amid the politico-religious revolt initiated around 1400 by John Huss. Despite civic strife between the moderate and the left-wing parties among the Hussites, Prague remained a leading European cultural centre, while humanism also flourished at the courts and among the nobility of both Hungary and Poland. Nevertheless, despite all these varieties of political and social structure, in most regions of Europe princes, cities and noble families had great resources and, giving proportionately less to the Churches, extended their political and social prestige by lavish patronage and by building.

Three great inventions contributed to the general upheaval of this period. Gunpowder changed the character of warfare. The mariner's compass led to the discovery of the Cape of Good Hope by Diaz (1487), and of America by Christopher Columbus (1492). When, in 1453, the Turks took Byzantium (Constantinople) and conquered Syria and Egypt, the old trade routes between East and West were blocked, but a new route was opened up when Vasco da Gama sailed round the Cape to India (1497). Led by Cortez and Pizarro, the Spaniards conquered and colonized Mexico and immense areas of South America, while the Portuguese erected numerous trading stations and colonial settlements both in the East Indies and in Brazil.

The third invention, printing by movable types, was first made practicable by John Gutenberg and John Fust at Mainz in about 1450. It contributed greatly to the circulation of ideas, and underlay the rapid expansion of humanist studies, vernacular literature, and (from 1520) the Protestant Reformation. Copperplate engraving also came into use toward the end of the fifteenth century and helped to spread knowledge of architectural forms. The temporal and spatial perspectives of Europeans were enlarged through the discovery of ancient manuscripts and works of art, through contact with hitherto unknown civilizations overseas, and through the exploration of the extra-terrestrial universe. Led by Copernicus (1473–1543) and Galileo (1564–1642) the astronomers showed that the universe was vastly larger than had been supposed, and the earth merely a planet of the solar system.

The new intellectual movements manifested themselves earlier in literature than in architecture. In particular, classical humanism involved a historical attempt to see the Ancient World as it had actually existed, free from Christian trappings and adaptations. The effort to understand its values, its literary and artistic forms, helped in due course to promote a new creativity, a new intellectual independence and freedom. Petrarch (1303–74) was the first great literary figure among the humanists, though the rise of Greek (as distinct from Roman) studies, together with the discovery of 'lost' classical texts, occurred mainly after 1400. Amongst the Greek and Roman literature brought to light was the *Treatise on Architecture* by Vitruvius, written in the time of Augustine: it was first issued at Rome in 1486 and translated into Italian in 1521. A return to the forms and proportions of ancient Roman architecture naturally occurred first in Italy, where classical studies were most advanced and where surviving Roman buildings could be studied and measured.

Meanwhile the religious and intellectual unity of Christendom had begun to crumble in the fourteenth century, when Marsiglio of Padua (d. 1342), John Wycliffe (d. 1384) and John Huss (d. 1415) all attacked the temporal power and wealth of the Church. The Papacy, held captive at Avignon since 1309 by the

French kings, returned to Rome in 1377, only to be disputed for over half a century between two and sometimes three rival Popes, each supported by a group of nations. The Conciliar Movement, aimed to reform the Church and control the Popes through a series of General Councils, collapsed in 1449, leaving the Papacy to recover its independent power. The career of Julius II (1503–13) placed the Papacy in control of a relatively strong state stretching across central Italy. On the other hand, its moral authority throughout Europe sank to new depths under the vicious Alexander VI, the war-like Julius II and the aesthete Leo X (d. 1521). While the magnificent ecclesiastical art and architecture of Italy became in general less austere and spiritual in character, the Netherlands and north-western Germany saw the rise of new schools of mysticism, and the 'new piety' (*devotio moderna*) sought refuge in a withdrawn interior life. Clerical shortcomings were satirized not merely by the heretical followers of Wycliffe and Huss, but after 1500 by many humanists, especially in Germany and the Netherlands. Erasmus (1466–1536) used his literary reputation not only to ridicule abuses but to demand a return to the Christianity of Christ, based not on ecclesiastical tradition but on linguistic and historical study of the original Greek and Hebrew texts of the Bible.

Yet the revolt which effectively divided the Church was initiated in 1517–20 by Martin Luther (1483–1546), a professor of biblical theology at the Saxon university of Wittenberg. A prolific pamphleteer making full use of the printing presses, Luther gradually detached most of the German states and cities from the papal obedience. In Switzerland the Protestant Reformation was at first headed by Huldreich Zwingli (d. 1531), but then spread and systematized mainly by John Calvin (1509–64) from his stronghold at Geneva. The Counter Reformation—the effort to restore the Catholic Church from within, along papalist lines—did not acquire great momentum until after the foundation of the Society of Jesus (1540) by Ignatius Loyola. The Council of Trent, sitting intermittently from 1545 to 1563, defined doctrine along conservative lines while a reformed Papacy kept control of the process from Rome. Catholic fervour developed apace, especially in Italy, Spain and Portugal, while the new religious Orders built many churches in the Mannerist and Baroque styles. The latter, arising about 1600, has indeed been unduly identified with the Counter Reformation in general and the Jesuit Order in particular. The architectural activities of the Jesuits have recently been shown as deeply influenced by their wealthy patrons, especially the great noble families of Rome, where Baroque originally evolved.

FLORENCE

The grouping together of independent commonwealths in Italy is an important feature of this period when, as in ancient Greece, one city bore rule over another. In 1406 Florence conquered Pisa and thus obtained a seaport, and in 1421 she took Leghorn from the Genoese and was strong enough to challenge Milan and Lucca in war, and so became the chief power in Italy and the art centre of Europe. The feuds between nobles were aggravated by the warfare between the Guelphs and Ghibellines (pp. 462, 735). In 1494 Charles VIII of France occupied Florence during his brief invasion of Italy to enforce his claims to the Kingdom of Naples. The Republic then erected by Savonarola and his associates was overthrown in 1512 by the Spaniards, who restored the Medici. Though again ejected in 1527, the Medici were finally reinstated by the Emperor Charles V when he took the town in 1530, after a siege of eleven months, during which Michelangelo acted as engineer to the Republic. Political liberty was subsequently curtailed, especially under Cosimo I (1537–74), who, however, greatly extended the Florentine dominions and took

Siena in 1555. The Grand Dukes of Tuscany passed through varying fortunes until, in 1737, the House of Medici became extinct and the Duchy passed to Austria. In 1801 Florence again attained political freedom as a republic and afterwards as the Kingdom of Etruria. Between 1807 and 1814 she was incorporated with France, and in 1860 she was united to the Kingdom of Italy.

The rediscovery of classical literature produced a wave of enthusiasm throughout Italy for old Roman architecture. This new movement began in Florence about 1420, and was developed with enormous zeal. It was stimulated by the Medici family, founded in 1424 by Giovanni de' Medici (d. 1429), which acquired great wealth in the upsurge of commercial prosperity, and gradually assumed supreme authority in the State. Giovanni's son, Cosimo (d. 1464), founded the Medici Library and the Platonic Academy, and was a most generous patron of artists, such as Brunelleschi, Michelozzi, Donatello, Masaccio and Lippi. He in turn was succeeded by his son, Piero (d. 1469), followed by his grandson, Lorenzo 'the Magnificent' (1449–92), whose brilliant personal gifts and devotion to the arts marked the most glorious phase in Florentine history. Through banking activities, from which their riches sprang, the Medici family had considerable repute in other Italian cities and even abroad; it produced two Popes, Leo X (1513–22) and Clement VII (1523–34), and its fortunes long remained interwoven with those of Florence. For at least a century after the inception of the new architecture, Florentine social life exhibited intense vitality at every level, never quite paralleled elsewhere at this or any other time in Renaissance Italy. The profound individualism of Florentine society—the semi-fortified character of the palaces is witness to the feuds of rival political parties—never obliterated a deep concern for the welfare of the state or a public-spirited patronage of the arts. For artists to be distinguished in several rather than a single art was almost a commonplace, and social distinctions rested far more upon ability in commerce, craftsmanship, literature and the arts than upon class. The great artists achieved a status in society far higher than in any previous epoch. All the records of Florence indicate a city of vital, pulsating energy, its streets a bustle of purposeful activity. The powerful and well-organized craft guilds, which had religious and not merely lay connotations, had a considerable share in directing the activities of studios and workshops. Florentines soon began to carry the Renaissance to other fields, and their ardent spirit rapidly inspired rivalry in other Tuscan cities. The earliest architects to work in Renaissance style in both Rome and Milan were Florentines. Genoa was more tardy, and scarcely began to show architectural evidences of the movement before the sixteenth century.

The Dominican friar, Savonarola (1452–98), by his ardent piety and reforming zeal, changed the habits of the citizens, swayed the policy of the State, and even threatened the authority of the Pope, Alexander VI. He roused opposition to the subtle tyranny of the Medici and called for a general council to reform Church abuses. At one time banished from Florence by a Medici, at another excommunicated by a pope, and yet again forsaken by his own people, Savonarola, in spite of all, became the saviour and lawgiver of the Florentine Republic.

ROME

With the conclusion of the Great Schism, the recovery of political authority by the Popes and the decline of baronial influence resulted in more stable government, increasing wealth and a revival of building in Rome. The ambitious Julius II, besides extending the temporal power of the papacy, sought to aggrandize himself in the popular imagination, and thus his original intention of erecting a monumental tomb house for himself developed into the gigantic scheme for the rebuilding of

S. Peter's, as the greatest cathedral in Christendom (p. 839). In 1527 Rome was brutally sacked by an Imperial army which ran amok; this tragedy helped to promote a spirit of reform, but it did not long inhibit architecture and artistic creativity. After 1530 Spain stood firmly established in Naples and Milan, thus dominating Rome and Italy until the age of Louis XIV. Thenceforward France and Austria strove for predominance in Italy until under Garibaldi and Cavour the country achieved unity and independence.

Meanwhile, the city of Rome recovered from its mediaeval poverty, and it was the patronage of the Church, with its renewed temporal power, and of the great papal and noble families, that drew flocking to it aspirants of every description. Population increased enormously and building proceeded apace; splendid new palaces and churches were erected and embellished by eminent craftsmen and artists. Because of the special circumstances, the social structure in Rome was substantially different from that of Florence. Rome had no commercial importance, and therefore no close-knit burgher community, and subsisted largely upon its metropolitan functions, exercised by an aristocracy that, through papal favours, now became extremely rich and powerful, while the former meagre populace received a tremendous infusion of newcomers whose common bond was little more than that of ambition. Though as in ancient times in Rome their dwellings might be intermingled, there was here a much greater distance between the social classes and between patron and client. The great families held almost regal court in their palaces, vying one with the other in cultivated extravagance. The Popes, avaricious of their revenues outside the city, spent them prodigally within, and even ran up enormous debts. Before they were brought under effective papal authority in the time of Julius II or later, certain of the more northerly of the States of the Church held their own petty but brilliant courts of the leaders of the families which governed them, such as the Malatesta family of Rimini, the Montefeltri of Urbino or the Este of Ferrara; and thus for a while, architecture in these centres was more responsive to local factors than to developments in Rome.

VENICE

In the middle of the fifteenth century, when Byzantium (Constantinople) was conquered by the Turks in 1453, the supremacy of Venice, which had been her commercial ally, was undermined; while the discovery by Vasco da Gama in 1498 of the new route round the Cape to India diverted Venetian commerce to the Portuguese. From the early years of the fifteenth century the city compensated for the untoward change by winning a land-empire stretching westward across Lombardy to the Adda. This supplied her with grain and ensured control of the entrances to the eastern Alpine passes leading to central and northern Europe. The League of Cambrai (1508) failed to dismember the Republic which, though temporarily overrun, had recovered her territories by 1510. During the sixteenth and seventeenth centuries the Venetians were intermittently at war with the Turks, and eventually in 1718 Venice lost her Adriatic possessions.

During the fifteenth and sixteenth centuries Venice allowed virtual self-government to the subject-cities of Padua, Verona and Vicenza, although with Venetian governors. Venice's prosperity was due to the State commercial system, and was not the result of mere accident or of the enterprise of individuals. This successful trading community produced many commercial magnates, whose rivalry in display led to the erection of numerous fine palaces on the Grand Canal, which from their situation on the broad waterfront needed less protection against civic turmoil than was necessary in Florence and other inland cities, and so could be more splendid and open externally. John of Speyer established in 1469 the first of those printing presses for which Venice became so famous when, at a later time, the Aldine Press issued its editions of the Greek classics. Thus, though her prosperity was fading as the Renaissance advanced, Venice was far-famed for her artistry, her theatre and her joyous, luxurious life. No part of Italy remained unaffected by the recovery of Rome and the papacy, but the Venetians stubbornly resisted ecclesiastical controls and maintained a semi-independence of the Popes.

ARCHITECTURAL CHARACTER

The Renaissance in Italy may be divided broadly into three main periods, viz.:

Early Renaissance—fifteenth century
High Renaissance and Proto-Baroque—sixteenth century
Baroque—seventeenth and early eighteenth centuries

Thereafter, from c. 1750–1830, the Renaissance follows an 'Antiquarian' trend.

The salient characteristic of Renaissance architecture, in Italy as elsewhere, was the employment of the Classic Roman 'Orders', which were now introduced after lying in abeyance for nearly a thousand years. These Orders—Tuscan, Doric, Ionic, Corinthian and Composite—were standardised by Renaissance architects, such as Palladio, Vignola and Scamozzi, and used both rationally and decoratively.

It has been shown earlier (p. 735ff.) that the welter of influences upon Italian Gothic, including the ancient Roman, exerted by the still-numerous monumental remains, produced differing regional types, these mostly quite unlike the Gothic architecture of Western Europe. The round arch was never completely abandoned, and Byzantine structural and decorative practices, even more than the Western Gothic, were interwoven with those developed from the direct Roman and Romanesque succession. The Renaissance reversion to Ancient Roman architectural character was in fact more superficial than might at first appear, and indeed neither in their manner of construction nor in their building types nor purpose in planning did the Renaissance enthusiasts make the least attempt to turn back the hands of the clock. Roman mass construction had long been conclusively superseded by the more compact and scientific Mediaeval systems, and if there was some attempt to emulate the Roman grand manner of formal planning, it was for visual effect and not for the improvement of physical comfort and convenience. In all fundamental respects, from a threshold of its Gothic and Byzantine inheritance the Renaissance pursued its own individual and characteristic course. Thus for instance, in tracing its development we see a protracted struggle for favour between the Gothic longitudinal and the Byzantine centralized church plans, resolved in a happy marriage in the Baroque period when the Byzantine ordonnance was commonly adopted for the eastern half of a Latin-cross scheme, while without the aid of the Byzantine pendentive and the tie-bar system—which generated the hoop-tie principle (pp. 841C, 1018) —we probably never should have known the glories of the domes of S. Peter's, Rome (p. 842) or S. Paul's, London (p. 1019A).

In the Early Renaissance, regional character importantly survived; in the High Renaissance and Proto-Baroque period it was partially eradicated, owing to a widening dissemination of ideas fostered by travel and the convergence on Rome of so many architects for their training, while with the Baroque it almost wholly disappeared. By the High Renaissance, the stage of elementary learning of Roman decorative systems had been passed, and architects worked in the freedom of firmly acquired knowledge. The true nature of the Renaissance as a distinctive style then began to emerge. These relatively untrammelled adventures exposed the personal

A. CAPITAL IN CORTILE PAL. GONDI : FLORENCE

B. CAPITAL AND BRACKETS THE BADIA DI FIESOLE : Nᴿ FLORENCE

C. PILASTER CAPITAL S. SPIRITO : FLORENCE

D. WINDOW IN CORTILE PAL. QUARATESI : FLORENCE

E. NICHE : NATᴸ MUS : FLORENCE

F. WINDOW AND FOUNTAIN PALAZZO PITTI : FLORENCE

G. DOORWAY S. CROCE : FLORENCE

H. CHIMNEY PIECE NATIONAL MUS : FLORENCE

J. PORCH S. ALESSANDRO : LUCCA

A FRIEZE: PAL. VECCHIO: FLORENCE

A TABERNACLE S. CROCE: FLORENCE

B CANTORIA (SINGING GALLERY) MUSEUM OF S. MARIA DEL FIORE FLORENCE

C HOLY WATER STOU SIENA CATHEDRA

D 'LAVABO' S. M. NOVELLA FLORENCE

E ALTAR-PIECE: S. CROCE: FLORENCE

F PULPIT: S. M. NOVELLA FLORENCE

G BRACKET TO PULPIT S. CROCE: FLORENCE

H RELI-QUARY S. SALVA-DORE D' OGNISSANTI: FLORENCE.

J BALUSTRADE TO PULPIT SIENA CATHEDRAL

(A) FIRST FLOOR WINDOW PAL. FARNESE : ROME

(B) SECOND FLOOR WINDOW PAL. FARNESE : ROME

(C) BALCONY WINDOW : PAL. DELLA CANCELLERIA : ROME

(D) DOORWAY : PAL. GAGNATI MONTEPULCIANO

(E) ARCADE IN CLOISTER S. MARIA DELLA PACE : ROME

(F) DOORWAY : PALAZZO SCIARRA : ROME

(G) DOORWAY PAL. SACRATI : FERRARA

(H) FONTANA PAOLA : ROME

(J) TRICLINIUM OF LEO III : ROME

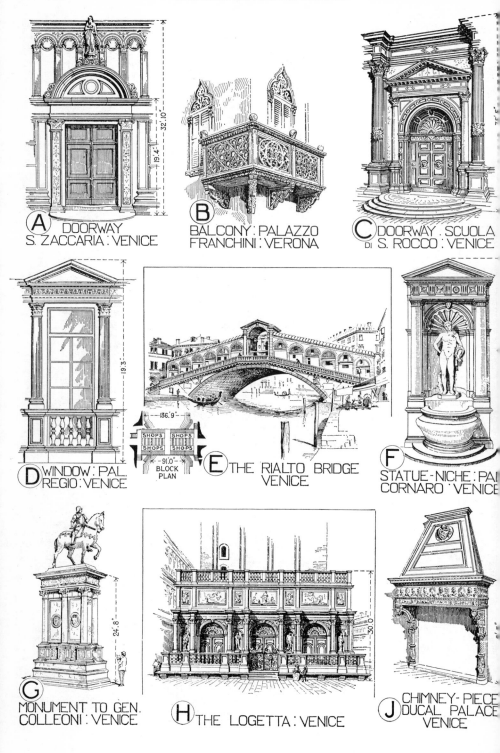

A DOORWAY
S. ZACCARIA : VENICE

B BALCONY : PALAZZO
FRANCHINI : VERONA

C DOORWAY . SCUOLA
DI S. ROCCO : VENICE

D WINDOW : PAL.
REGIO : VENICE

SHOPS
SHOPS
SHOPS
SHOPS
136'.9"
91'.0"
BLOCK
PLAN

E THE RIALTO BRIDGE
VENICE

F STATUE-NICHE : PAL
CORNARO · VENICE

G MONUMENT TO GEN.
COLLEONI : VENICE

H THE LOGETTA : VENICE

J CHIMNEY-PIECE
DUCAL PALACE
VENICE

A BRONZE STANDARD
PIAZZA of S.MARK:VENICE

B CAPITAL . S.M. DEI
MIRACOLI . VENICE

C BRONZE CANDELABRUM
S. ANTONIO : PADUA

ENLARGED A C
SKETCH

D MONᵀ of P. BERNARDO
THE FRARI CH: VENICE

E PANEL: S.M. DEI MIRACOLI: VENICE

F ALTAR of S. GIACOMO
S.MARK : VENICE

G PORTION of DOORWAY
ORFANI AI GESUATI: VENICE

H BALUSTRADE: S.M. MIRACOLI: VENICE

J PORTION of VENDRAMIN MONᵀ
SS.GIOVANNI E PAOLO: VENICE

style of individual designers, and hard on the heels of the High Renaissance came the phase known in art history as 'Mannerist', wherein practices which had no ancient Roman precedent were interspersed among those fully sanctioned, or whole buildings were conceived in a non-Roman way. Such exuberance in design was in many cases strongly marked by the mid-sixteenth century, and was encouraged by the rediscovery of hard-plaster stucco as an artistic medium, long ago exploited in ancient Roman art. Here, the term 'Proto-Baroque' is used for these non-conforming manifestations—though 'Mannerism' is convenient for the less obvious departures from Roman precedent—since they represent a genuine stage towards that ultimate fulfilment of the entire Renaissance movement in the Baroque, on the threshold of the seventeenth century. The High Renaissance and Proto-Baroque phases, together covering the sixteenth century, cannot readily be separated, as the latter is at first spasmodic in its incidence. Further, it is a phenomenon of the Renaissance movement that even in the 'High' Baroque phase (c. 1625–75), ancient Roman canons retained their prestige, and from time to time monuments were produced which were almost wholly Classical in character; and about 1750, architecture as a whole returned to a profound regard for the Roman and Greek antique, in what is known alternatively as the 'Neo-Classical' or 'Antiquarian' phase.

Below, the course of development is considered in the three main regions under the headings of the great cities which represent them, to the point where regional differences almost wholly disappear.

FLORENCE

The Renaissance of the fifteenth century in Italy had its birth in Florence, where, under unique conditions and influences, a type of palace-building was evolved, to which huge blocks of rusticated masonry give an unusually massive and rugged appearance. The typical palace was built round an internal court, similar to a mediaeval cloister, surrounded by an arcade supporting the walls of the upper storeys (pp. 800C, 808D). There is a general absence of pilasters as decorative features in the façades, which are therefore called 'astylar'; while sparing use of detail, together with concentration on pronounced features, produces boldness and simplicity of style. The imposing appearance of these massive palaces fronting on narrow streets is emphasized by boldly projecting roof cornices, which crown the walls and are proportioned to the height of the buildings, as in the Palazzo Riccardi (p. 800A, B). The columnar arcade is a favourite feature, not only in courtyards, but also in streets, as in the Foundling Hospital (p. 794A). Early Renaissance churches are conspicuous for refinement, in strong contrast to the rugged, fortress-like character of the palaces. The architectural character owes much of its interest to the contributions of sculptors and painters. Among others there were Luca della Robbia (1400–82), famous for his coloured glazed reliefs in terra-cotta, Lorenzo Ghiberti (1378–1455), who designed the Baptistery doors (p. 793), and also Donatello (1386–1466), Mino da Fiesole (1430–84), and Benedetto da Majano (1442–97), renowned for their bas-reliefs, carvings and statues. Florentine craftsmanship shows highly developed artistic perception and technical skill (pp. 783, 784). Not only does ornament depend upon the personality of the artist, but architectural design also now becomes the product of the individual architect rather than of a school of craftsmen working on traditional lines. The examples which follow will therefore be classified and considered under the names of the different architects.

Florence contains very many examples of Early Renaissance architecture, but fewer of the High Renaissance and Proto-Baroque period and almost none of the Baroque. In the second quarter of the sixteenth century Michelangelo led the Proto-

A. S. Peter, Rome. Michelangelo's entrance façade. See p. 839

B. 'School of Athens' by Raphael, possibly based on Bramante's design for the interior of S. Peter, Rome. See p. 839

A. Boboli Gardens, Florence (16th cent.). See pp. 791, 797

B. Villa Gamberaia, Settignano (c. 1550–). See p. 791

Baroque breakaway from academic formalism in design with his New Sacristy of S. Lorenzo (p. 836A) and the Laurentian Library (p. 836B), and was soon emulated by local architects such as Ammanati and others in Rome and Genoa. About this same time Florentine garden art was approaching its zenith. The earliest Renaissance villas (from c. 1450) in the neighbouring beautifully-diversified, undulating country-side, had retained something of mediaeval character; progressively they developed towards an intimate charm of formally related garden compartments of differing types, centred on a summer dwelling or 'casino', growing more natural as they merged at the fringe with the surrounding landscape. The Villa Gamberaia, Settignano (c. 1550-) (p. 790B) is a fine instance, while in the city itself are the Proto-Baroque Boboli Gardens (c. 1550-) (p. 790A).

In Milan, the Early Renaissance at first secured only a precarious hold, but there then appeared a very distinctive small-scale diversified architecture, in the local brick and terra-cotta, of a character often associated with the name of Bramante, who worked hereabouts before his great High Renaissance achievements in Rome. In Genoa, almost the first appearance of the Renaissance was at the Proto-Baroque stage, its palaces distinguished by the remarkable treatment of their airy, axial staircases, and there, as in Milan and Turin, the Baroque reached full flower.

ROME

The Early Renaissance in Rome is comparatively unimportant, though some gracious buildings were completed in the various Papal States. The High Renais-sance and later phases are splendidly represented. Roman palaces nearly always have a 'four-square' majesty and dignity (pp. 820A, 826B). At first the Classic Orders often were used in simple, direct arrangements in superimposed tiers on façades and in cortili (pp. 785E, 820, 826, 831F), but afterwards in a giant arrangement extending the whole height of a building (pp. 831J, 837). Bramante was the chief figure of the High Renaissance, of which his Tempietto at S. Pietro in Montorio (p. 823B) is a notable example, but other great architects, scarcely a generation younger than he, began to show Mannerism in their buildings, using architectural elements in a free, decorative, and sometimes illogical way unsanctified by antique precedent, particularly around wall-openings and in novel treatments of rustication (p. 831B, E, G), while large and small Orders were employed in juxtaposition (p. 837B). Michelangelo's Roman work is of this Proto-Baroque class (p. 837). Peruzzi, an architect of great discernment and taste, showed scholarly appreciation of ancient architecture and at the same time manifested individuality in such as the use of the coupled Order and jewel-like enframements to windows of the façade of his Palazzo Massimi (p. 824). He, like Romano and Vignola, carried Proto-Baroque traits afield (pp. 829A, 832). Domestic planning evidences great skill and ingenuity together with a Roman formalism (pp. 824H, 826G, J, 831A, D, 832D), and in churches the Byzantine-type centralized plan retained much of its popularity (pp. 825A, 841F). Civic design and the adornment of street and public open places made great strides, the pace increasing in the Baroque period (pp. 837, 838, 850A), and many splendid villas were created in the vicinity of the city. The Baroque flourished greatly in Rome. Carlo Maderna was its first successful exponent, and Bernini its most brilliant and versatile figure: among Bernini's several very able contemporaries was the eccentric Borromini, and together they mark the climax of the movement (c. 1625-75). Palaces maintained their cliff-like character, and generally were astylar, their planning now extremely adept and incorporating grand axial staircases and dignified ceremonial apartments, often of circular, elliptical or other regular geo-metrical shapes. Stylar treatment mostly was reserved for church façades, which are richly ornate with reiterated clusters of pilasters and columns, and have great vigour of expression, the front often being convex or concave on plan, to afford forceful contrasts of light and shade (pp. 847C, 849A, B). Unity is strongly marked, usually resolved in the entrance portal (p. 817A). Church plans were either centralized and compact, building up to a circular or elliptical dome (p. 849C), or the centralized plan served for the eastern half of a longitudinal scheme. The latter solution, originated with Vignola's Gesù church (1568–84) (p. 825D), became universally popular (p. 866H) and was eventually adopted for S. Peter's (p. 842G). The output of Rome diminished in quality, virility and bulk in the eighteenth century, and about 1750 the true Baroque gave place to a renewed and academic Classicism. As a whole, Roman Renaissance ornament displays great technical skill and fine craftsmanship (p. 785), and though it is exceptionally rich and even excessively exuberant in the Baroque period, shows a brilliant unity of all the arts.

VENICE

The Renaissance style in Venice is distinguished from that of the rest of Europe by features peculiarly Venetian, and it is coloured by the history and unique character of the sea-city, with its own beautiful type of Mediaeval architecture, impressed more by Near-Eastern Byzantine trends than by the normal current of Gothic or by Rome and her Classic traditions. So strongly marked an individuality responded grudgingly to the new movement, and the Early Renaissance was delayed and at first hybrid in character, manifested in buildings which retained intermingled Gothic features, as in the courtyard of the Doge's Palace (p. 853B). The architecture of Venice is, in general, lighter and more graceful than that of Florence. Its special character is in some part due to the fact that its gleaming buildings are built upon a hundred islets on a multitude of wooden and stone piles, the mundane brickwork of their walls often concealed by sparkling marble sheathing; the ubiquitous waterways, spanned by charming bridges (p. 786E), carry colourful reflections and throw back the brilliant light to expose every detail in crystal clarity. In such an ethereal setting, rustication, though frequently practised, seems far less appropriate than to the ponderous masonry façades of Florence. Marble sheating is typical of the Early Renaissance, used in panels decorated centrally (or intermittently, in the case of friezes and architraves) with coloured marbles in ribboned medallions or jewellike devices (pp. 853E, 855, 856C). A notable Venetian feature is the central grouping of windows, marking deep rooms behind the comparatively flat palace façades which outline the waterways (p. 855). Orders are used freely on exteriors at most times, and are usually confined to the main storeys of palaces, these being crowned by entablatures often containing a deep, windowed frieze (pp. 855C, 861A). Balconies (pp. 786B, 855B, D) are graceful and important features, their projections adding materially to the play of light and shade. Palace plans normally were compact, owing to the cramped and precious sites, while early churches were simple and mostly aisleless, resplendent with marble encrustation within and without (p. 854). The Lombardi family, particularly Pietro, contributed greatly in the early period; Sansovino, with his rich, sculpturesque style (pp. 786H, 861) heralded the High Renaissance and Proto-Baroque period. The latter phase is denoted by the use of large and small Orders together, coupled columns and 'tabernacle' windows (as p. 786D). Sanmichele and the famous Palladio, working mostly in the inland towns of the Venetian State, used rustication more legitimately and effectively (p. 860B, J), and Palladio made great play with the giant Order in his many palaces and villas (p. 865). The Venetian sixteenth-century churches are mostly longitudinal, but with the Byzantine-type centralized arrangement toward the eastern end (p. 866D,

H) in a kind of plan now popular everywhere. For western fronts a giant Order masking the nave was combined with a threaded lesser Order extending to the aisle ends, a treatment not wholly successful (pp. 866C, G, 867A). Venetian ornament is characterized by refinement and freedom of line, the sculptured carvings naturally having various maritime allusions.

Baroque architecture was adapted to the strict Venetian conditions, and there were few attempts to model frontages in curved plan advances and recessions. S. Maria della Salute (p. 856A), the masterpiece of Longhena, was a rare exception.

EXAMPLES

FLORENCE

EARLY RENAISSANCE

FILIPPO BRUNELLESCHI (1377–1446), one of the most famous sons of Florence, entered the competition in 1401 for the bronze doors of the Baptistery, Florence. Lorenzo Ghiberti, however, was successful, and the doors were executed between · 1403–24. Brunelleschi set out for Rome after the competition, to study Classic architecture at the fountain head. Returning to Florence, his career as an architect began in 1418. Most of his works were completed by others after his death.

The **Foundling Hospital, Florence** (1421–45) (p. 794A), the first of the kind in Europe and one of the first buildings undertaken by Brunelleschi, has a famous arcaded loggia (1421–4) of Corinthian columns supporting broad semicircular arches, with glazed terra-cotta medallions in the spandrels. In many respects the arcade maintains old Florentine traditions, as may be seen by comparing the west front of the Romanesque church of S. Miniato (p. 472A).

The **Dome of Florence Cathedral** (1420–34) (pp. 746A, B, C, D, F, 749A), which was entrusted to Brunelleschi as a result of a competition, is a miracle of design triumphantly blending a Renaissance dome with a Gothic building. It covers an octagonal apartment, 42 m (138 ft 6 ins) in width, and is raised on a drum, with circular windows to light the interior. This unique dome, pointed in form, consists of inner and outer shells constructed on the Gothic principle, with eight main and sixteen intermediate ribs supporting panels of herring-bone brickwork. It is said that it was erected without centering, but this may have been used to a limited extent. An entirely new departure in the history of building is the introduction of a hoop, made up of lengths of timber, secured with iron at the junctions, binding-in the base of the dome (p. 746D—plan C) to prevent its splitting outwards, thus obviating the need for buttresses and making it practicable to raise the dome on a drum. Tie-bars, a Byzantine invention, had long been used in Italian architecture, and indeed appear in the Mediaeval nave of the same building (p. 746G), but this is the first known example of the application of the tensional principle to domes. The domes of S. Peter's, Rome and S. Paul's, London are bound with iron chains (pp. 841C, 1017E, 1018). The interior was frescoed by G. Vasari.

S. Lorenzo, Florence (1421–60) (p. 795) is of the basilican type, with nave and aisles separated by Corinthian columns supporting entablature blocks, the earliest instance of such features in the Renaissance. The aisles have simple domes over each compartment, and the side-chapel openings are enframed with continuous mouldings, without imposts at the springing of the arches. At the crossing is a dome with pendentives, carried out by Antonio Manetti, who took over the work after Brunelleschi's death. The sanctuary is flanked by the Old Sacristy (1421–8), the earliest part of Brunelleschi's building, and the famous New Sacristy (1521–34)

A. The Foundling Hospital
(Ospedale degli Innocenti), Florence:
loggia (1421–4). See p. 793

B. S. Maria delle Carceri, Prato
(1485–91): façade. See p. 797

c. The Ducal Palace, Urbino
(1444–82): cortile. See p. 815

D. Palazzo Spannocchi, Siena (1469–).
See p. 803

PAZZI CHAPEL: FLORENCE

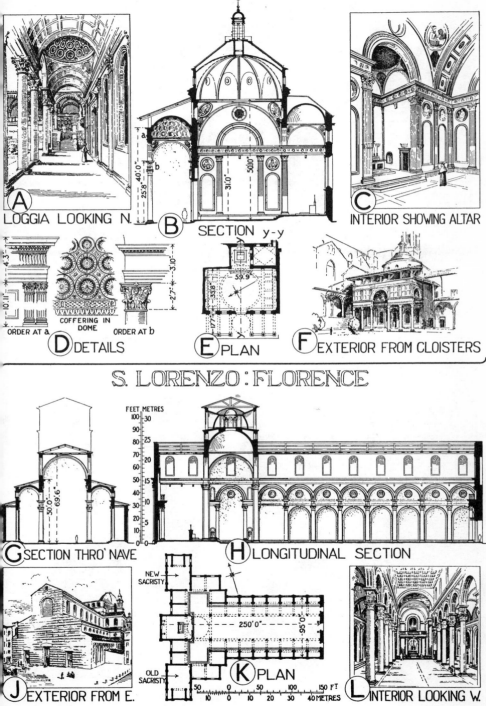

A LOGGIA LOOKING N.

B SECTION y-y

C INTERIOR SHOWING ALTAR

ORDER AT a
COFFERING IN DOME
ORDER AT b

D DETAILS

E PLAN

F EXTERIOR FROM CLOISTERS

S. LORENZO: FLORENCE

G SECTION THRO' NAVE

H LONGITUDINAL SECTION

J EXTERIOR FROM E.

K PLAN

L INTERIOR LOOKING W.

S. SPIRITO : FLORENCE

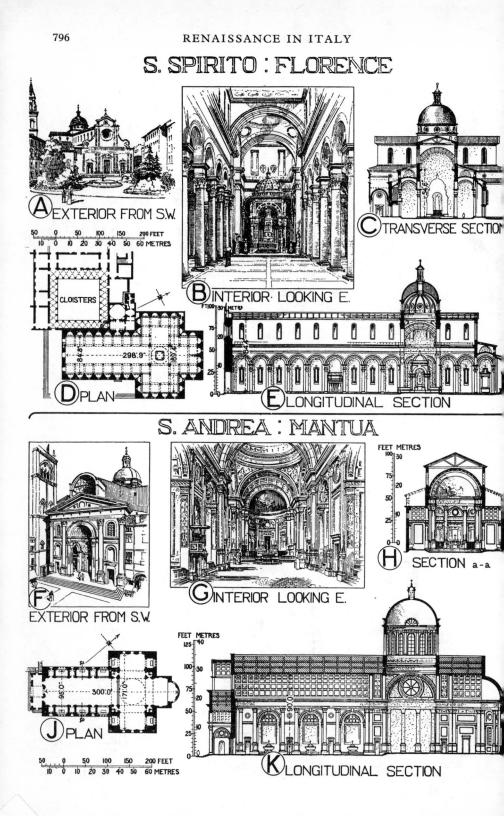

A EXTERIOR FROM S.W.

B INTERIOR · LOOKING E.

C TRANSVERSE SECTION

CLOISTERS

298'9"

D PLAN

E LONGITUDINAL SECTION

S. ANDREA : MANTUA

F EXTERIOR FROM S.W.

G INTERIOR LOOKING E.

H SECTION a-a

300'0"

J PLAN

K LONGITUDINAL SECTION

added by Michelangelo as described on p. 834 and illustrated on p. 836A. The west façade of the church was never built, and remains in rough brick.

S. Spirito, Florence (1445–82) (p. 796), barely begun in Brunelleschi's lifetime, is also of the basilican type, which Italians preferred through the Middle Ages, but has wide transepts making a Latin cross, and there are domical-vaulted aisles round nave, transepts and choir. The nave has arcades forming another early instance of columns supporting pieces of entablature interposed between them and the arches, while a flat timber ceiling covers the nave, and there is a dome over the crossing. The charming campanile (p. 796A) (*c.* 1506) is by Baccio d'Agnolo.

The **Pazzi Chapel, Florence** (1429–46) (p. 795) is an architectural gem which inspired many later buildings, such as **S. Maria delle Carceri, Prato** (1485–91) (p. 794B), by Giuliano da Sangallo, and is itself a developed version of the San Lorenzo Old Sacristy dispositions. It faces into the cloisters of S. Croce, and has a centralized plan covered in part by short barrel vaults but chiefly by a rib-vaulted dome on pendentives, capped by a lantern. The dome ribs support small barrel vaults diminishing towards the lantern; at their base, the lunettes allow circular windows in an upstanding drum, which, with its tiled conical roof, conceals the dome externally. A smaller pendentived dome covers the altar recess, and there is another of similar size, ornamented with coloured terra-cotta coffering, placed centrally in the stone barrel vault which spans the six-column portico. The stone-panelled front recalls the marble encrustations of the great Mediaeval monuments of the city. Indeed this miniature building may well be described as Byzantine in conception, Gothic in construction and Classical in decorative detail.

The **Palazzo Pitti, Florence** (1458–) (p. 799), designed for Luca Pitti, a friend of Cosimo de' Medici, is the largest palace in Italy except the Vatican. It was, however, erected piecemeal, and begun only after Brunelleschi's death from his designs. The original design comprised solely the central portion, and this had proceeded up to the top of the second tier (1458–65) in the charge of Luca Fancelli when the palace was left unfinished; until brought to initial completion under Ammanati, who added the great cortile, and gave the present character to the rear façade (1558–70). Extensions to the length, which included the small lateral cortili, were made (1620–40) under G. and A. Parigi, and the outer projecting wings were added (1764–83) by Ruggeri. Minor alterations and internal remodellings followed later. The grand façade, with three-storeyed centre 36 m (119 ft) high, is 201 m (660 ft) in length. It is of astylar treatment, bearing in its rugged simplicity a curious resemblance to the bold Claudian Aqueduct, with its massive blocks of masonry and arches of the ground storey (p. 783F). The windows within these arches are by Ammanati, and the lions' heads below the sills are relatively modern (p. 783F). The cortile (p. 799D), facing the Boboli Gardens (p. 790A), is unique in its rusticated treatment of Doric, Ionic and Corinthian attached columns. The palace became the grand-ducal residence and is partly occupied by the famous picture gallery, remodelled for Ferdinand II (1640–7) by P. Cortona with Baroque paintings set in elaborate stucco frames painted white and gold.

The **Palazzo Quaratesi, Florence** (1462–72) (p. 799E), formerly Pazzi, is believed to have been designed by Brunelleschi but its execution was mainly due to Giuliano da Majano. The Pazzi arms survive on the angle of the façade, which has channelled masonry and characteristic windows, each with a central shaft supporting sub-arches, perpetuating Mediaeval practice (p. 783D). There is an overhanging roof in place of the usual cornice. The cortile is especially fine.

MICHELOZZO MICHELOZZI (1396–1472) was a friend of Cosimo de' Medici, whom he accompanied in exile to Venice. He also at one time visited Milan, where he built the Portinari Chapel (1462-6) in S. Eustorgio, domed like Brunelleschi's Old Sacristy in S. Lorenzo, Florence.

The **Palazzo Riccardi, Florence** (1444-60) (p. 800), is Michelozzi's best known building. It was built as the Medici home, and here Lorenzo the Magnificent kept his brilliant court. The palace was sold in 1659 to the Riccardi family, and in 1680 it was extended to the north, adding seven new windows to the original ten of the first floor on the main front. The older portion of the plan (p. 800F) shows a typical arrangement of the period, the rooms arranged around an open cortile (p. 800C), the main apartments being those on the 'piano nobile', approached by an unpretentious but generous staircase, not symmetrically placed. The more intimate of the family rooms were on the second floor. The exterior is an admirable astylar example and shows the effect of graduated rustication. The ground storey has heavily rusticated masonry, with semicircular arches enclosing windows added from the designs of Michelangelo (p. 800E); the intermediate storey has channelled masonry, with bifurcated windows not very different in appearance from the type usual in Florentine Gothic palaces (p. 800G); and the upper storey, in plain ashlar masonry, has similar windows. The whole façade is crowned by a bold cornice, about one-eighth the height of the building and projecting 2.5 m (8 ft 4 ins) (p. 800A).

LEON BATTISTA ALBERTI (1404-72) was a student of classical literature, and his book on architecture, *De Re Aedificatoria*—the first architectural book published with movable type (1485)—helped the revival of the old Roman style. His writings are interesting as an early attempt to define the Renaissance aesthetic. Beauty was thought to be based on the harmony of numbers. Like Pythagoras, who drew the analogy between music intervals and mathematics, Alberti attempted to extend the principle to embrace the visual arts. Euclidian geometry was invoked to give absolute sanction to the use of basic shapes such as the square, cube, circle and sphere, while simple integral proportions were derived from these figures by doubling and halving. These ideals, especially with regard to church building, are epitomized in the perspective panels at Urbino (p. 807C).

The **Palazzo Rucellai, Florence** (1446-51) (p. 799G), ornamented externally with superimposed pilasters, is thus the first 'stylar' building of the Renaissance. The presence of the tiers of pilasters brought the difficulty that the crowning cornice could not be in scale with the whole height of the building as well as with the order immediately below it, a problem which did not arise in 'astylar' palaces. The quality of the detail is refined, and set standards for future buildings of the type. Alberti was the designer, but the work was carried out by Rossellino (see p. 803), an able architect in his own right.

S. Francesco, Rimini (1446-50) (p. 807A), a Gothic church, was remodelled for Sigismondo Malatesta, as a monument to himself and his wife, from the designs of Alberti externally but internally mainly by Agostino di Duccio (1418-81), a Florentine by birth, in charming and varied but somewhat naïve Renaissance details. The entrance façade, which was never complete, bears some resemblance to the Arch of Augustus in the same city; on the flank are arcaded recesses containing sarcophagi of scholars and poets who had figured at the Ducal court.

S. Maria Novella, Florence, a Gothic church (p. 748), has a Renaissance façade (1456-70) (p. 753A) designed by Alberti, and was one of the first churches in which flanking scrolls were used to connect aisles and nave into one composition.

S. Sebastiano, Mantua (1459) has suffered various misfortunes in the course of time and is ill preserved. It was the first church of the Renaissance to be designed on the Greek-cross plan, though chapels like Brunelleschi's Pazzi at Florence had already shown a development towards the Byzantine idea of 'centralized space'.

S. Andrea, Mantua (1472-94) (p. 796F-K), designed by Alberti, was begun only

PALAZZO PITTI : FLORENCE

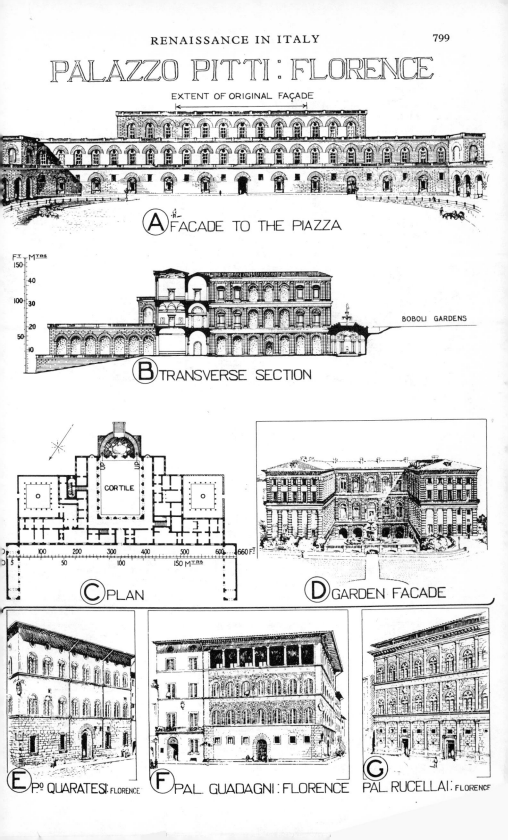

EXTENT OF ORIGINAL FAÇADE

(A) FACADE TO THE PIAZZA

(B) TRANSVERSE SECTION

BOBOLI GARDENS

CORTILE

(C) PLAN

(D) GARDEN FACADE

(E) Pᵒ QUARATESI: FLORENCE

(F) PAL. GUADAGNI : FLORENCE

(G) PAL. RUCELLAI: FLORENCE

PALAZZO RICCARDI : FLORENCE

A CROWNING CORNICE

10'0"

8'4"

B EXTERIOR

C CORTILE

FEET METRES

D TRANSVERSE SECTION ON a-a

80'0"

E GRᴰ FLOOR WINDOW

28'3"

F PLAN

OPEN COURT

CORTILE

190'0"

225'0"

50 25 0 25 50 75 100 150 175 FT
10 10 20 30 40 50 MTᴿˢ

G FIRST FLOOR WINDOW

15'0"

ANGLE OF (A) CORNICE AT a

(B) PLAN LOOKING UP AT y-y

(C) ANGLE OF CORNICE AT b

(D) DOORWAY: PAL. GAMBARO GENOA

(E) DOORWAY: PAL. CAREGA: GENOA

(F) LAVABO OLD CONVENT GENOA

SECTION THRO' COFFERS

(G) COFFERED CEILING: VILLA CAMBIASO IN ALBARO

(H) TYPICAL CAP.

(J) DOORWAY GENOA

(K) PILASTER VILLA CAMBIASO

(L) DOORWAY VERONA

PALAZZO STROZZI: FLORENCE

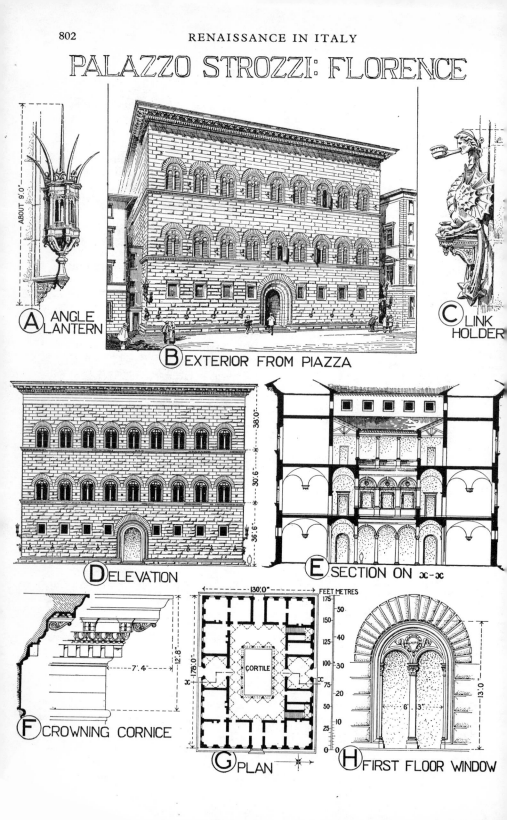

(A) ANGLE LANTERN

ABOUT 9'.0"

(B) EXTERIOR FROM PIAZZA

(C) LINK HOLDER

(D) ELEVATION

38'.0"　30'.6"　36'.6"

(E) SECTION ON x-x

(F) CROWNING CORNICE

7'.4"　12'.8"

(G) PLAN

130'.0"　178'.0"　CORTILE

FEET METRES
175　50
150
125　40
100　30
75
50　20
25　10
0　0

(H) FIRST FLOOR WINDOW

13'.0　6'.3"

in the year of his death. The grand entrance portico, looking rather like a Roman triumphal arch (p. 796F), leads into an imposing and finely-proportioned barrel-vaulted aisleless nave, flanked by side-chapels between chambered piers which are faced by pairs of Corinthian columns on pedestals. This arrangement of the chapels allows a stronger and more unified building than is possible with the columned basilican plan. Eastwards, the crossing, transepts and apsidal sanctuary reflect the wide and narrow alternations of the nave, and yet give the spaciousness of Byzantine 'centralized space', the whole church establishing a Latin-cross type of plan which was to be followed in very many later churches. The eastern portions, including the transepts and crossing, were built in 1597–1600 and later, and the dome added by Juvarra (p. 815) in 1732–82; but the general conception is due to Alberti.

BERNARDO ROSSELLINO (1409–64), Florentine architect and sculptor, was the creator of the Bruni tomb (1445) in S. Croce, Florence, which established a type for this class of mural monument. Rossellino was even more distinguished as an architect. From 1450 he, with Alberti, was employed for the reconstruction of the old S. Peter's at Rome. His work on the Palazzo Rucellai is described on p. 798.

The **Palazzo Piccolomini, Pienza** (c. 1460) (p. 807B) closely follows the design of the Rucellai, having three tiers of regularly-spaced pilasters enframing round-headed windows on its channel-rusticated walls, crowned with a bold cornice. Also in Pienza, the Cathedral, again by Rossellino, the Palazzo Pubblico and the Episcopio (episcopal palace), attributed to him, are all of about the same date.

The **Palazzo Spannocchi, Siena** (1469–) (p. 794D) shows a reversion to astylar design and to round-headed, bifurcated windows similar to those of the Riccardi at Florence, but the heights of the three storeys are less well graded and there is no differentiation of the rusticated stonework, which is channel-jointed throughout. Nevertheless, the palace has a fine, massive quality, the ground storey being especially forceful, and the cornice is quite novel in having a plain frieze below it, this affording an effective liaison with the façade and permitting a less ponderous cornice than would otherwise be necessary: small windows are inserted there.

IL CRONACA (1454–1508), properly Simone Pollaiuolo, had studied ancient architecture in Rome. Architect of the delightful Sacristy of S. Spirito (1489–92), conjointly with Giuliano da Sangallo, he is better known for the works below.

The **Palazzo Strozzi, Florence** (1489–1539) (p. 802), begun by Benedetto da Majano, was continued by Cronaca. It is the representative Florentine palace of the period. The chief features are a large central cortile with arcades on the three storeys, off which are the stairs and surrounding rooms. The astylar tripartite façade (p. 802B, D) is rusticated uniformly in bolster-like units which give the building a somewhat hard and mechanical appearance, and is capped by a grand cornice, projecting over 2.1 m (7 ft) and occupying about one-thirteenth of the height of the building, with a plain astragal frieze like that of Rossellino's Palazzo Spannocchi at Siena, though here not containing windows (p. 802F). The main windows (p. 802H), angle-lanterns and link-holders (p. 802A, C) are attractive features.

The **Palazzo Guadagni, Florence** (1490–1506) (p. 799F) has the two main storeys faced with 'sgraffito' of black plaster overlaid with white, cut away to show patterns, and an open loggia crowned with a widely-overhanging roof serving as a fourth storey.

ANTONIO FILARETE (1396–1465), a famous Florentine sculptor, was also an architect of note and is best known for his work in Milan, where he was among the first to introduce the Renaissance style, preceding Michelozzi there (p. 797).

The **Ospedale Maggiore, Milan** (1457–c. 1624) (p. 819F, G, H), the earliest municipal hospital (p. 744), has façades towards the grand cortili with delicate transitional detail, suitable to the plastic terra-cotta. These are the work of Filarete;

but the style reverted to Late Gothic in 1465 under his successor, Solari, and the building was completed about 1624 by Ricchini. It was very badly damaged by bombing in 1943.

GIOVANNI AMADEO (1447–1522), Lombard sculptor and architect, was a notable figure in the early Lombard Renaissance, and took part in the work proceeding in his day at the cathedrals of Milan and Pavia and at the Certosa di Pavia.

The **Certosa di Pavia** (p. 751D, E, F) was begun in 1396 with the monastic portions, and the body of the church probably was not seriously undertaken before *c.* 1453 (p. 736). The church is transitional from the Gothic in its main features, and except at the east end, the external expression is almost everywhere round-arched and bears little likeness to the western, pointed style. It is a brick and terra-cotta architecture, characteristically small in scale, and marble is used sparingly at important decorative points, while the crossing has the galleried cupola traditional in the Lombard region; the 'lanterns' at Chiaravalle (p. 734D) and Milan Cathedral (p. 738D) are versions rising to a spire. The church was finished by *c.* 1497 except for the west façade (p. 805A), constructed wholly in marble between 1473– *c.* 1540. In this Amadeo contributed both as a sculptor and in the design, having been given charge of the work in 1491. Several other sculptors took part. The upper half is simpler, owing to a halt in the progress of the work. The framework of the façade, with its canopied and pinnacled buttresses, still is partly Gothic, but filled in with Renaissance features, such as profusely ornamented windows, arcaded galleries and statues in niches, which, together with carved ornament and medallions, make it one of the most elaborate combinations of architecture and sculpture in Western history.

The **Colleoni Chapel, Bergamo** (1470–6) (p. 806A) is less sculptural externally than the Certosa di Pavia façade, but is extremely richly encrusted with white- and rose-coloured marbles, displayed in surface patterns, and profuse ornament. Lombard canopied pinnacles appear again, along with arcaded open galleries, medallions and many versions of the candelabrum motif. Indeed it is in this building that we find what are probably the earliest instances of the use of the true baluster, here occurring as alternating supports in the continuous arcade below the main cornice. The type came quickly into general use; in Rome, the first example is probably that found in the Singing Gallery of the famous Sistine Chapel (*c.* 1480). Hitherto, parapets had been made up of miniature columns (p. 784F, pulpit from design by Brunelleschi) or with low-relief or pierced panels (p. 787E, H) based on Byzantine precedents. The baluster thus is a Renaissance invention, derived from the candelabra ornament, and the subsequent development of baluster forms affords clues to the dating of monuments.

HIGH RENAISSANCE AND PROTO-BAROQUE

BARTOLOMEO AMMANATI (1511–92), sculptor and architect, worked in Lucca Montepulciano, Rome and his native Florence. He had considerable ability, and was responsible for a large number of buildings, one of the most important being the Collegio Romano, Rome (1582–4). In Florence or Tuscany in general, there was virtually no High Renaissance interlude following the vigorous early developments, and Ammanati's work shows most strongly that individualism or 'Mannerism' which is a first-found freedom from Classical restraints that presages the Baroque. He was thus a follower of Michelangelo, who, with Raphael, first evidenced in his architecture the new trend. Notable in much of Ammanati's work is the exploitation of rustication, and it is likely that the façades to his extensions of the Palazzo Pitti, referred to earlier (p. 797), influenced the design of the Luxembourg Palace, Paris, built for Marie de' Medici by de Brosse (p. 892).

A. The Certosa, Pavia, from N.W. (*c.* 1453–97; West façade 1473–*c.* 1540).
See pp. 736, 804

B. Palazzo Sauli, Genoa (*c.* 1555). See p. 809

A. The Colleoni Chapel, Bergamo
(1470–6). See p. 804

B. S. Maria dei Miracoli, Brescia
(1488–, 1522–). See p. 857

C. Palazzo Micheletti, Lucca
(c. 1550). See p. 809

D. Palazzo Durazzo-Pallavicini, Genoa
(1619–). See p. 810

A. S. Francesco, Rimini (1446–50).
See p. 798

B. Palazzo Piccolomini, Pienza (c. 1460).
See p. 803

C. Panel (possibly by Piero della Francesca) in the Ducal Palace, Urbino.
See p. 815

D. S. Maria in Carignano,
Genoa (1552–1603). See p. 809

E. Palazzo di Venezia, Rome (1455–64).
See p. 816

PALAZZO MUNICIPO : GENOA

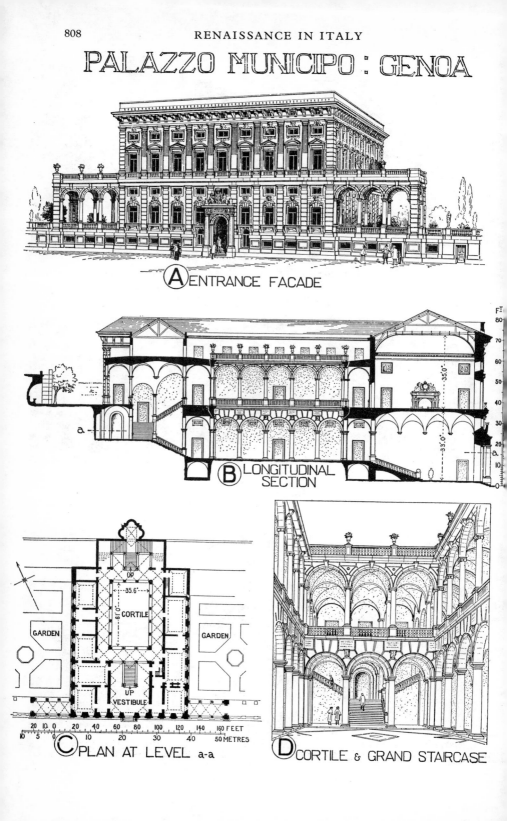

(A) ENTRANCE FACADE

(B) LONGITUDINAL SECTION

(C) PLAN AT LEVEL a-a

(D) CORTILE & GRAND STAIRCASE

The **Palazzo Micheletti, Lucca** (*c.* 1550) (p. 806c) is representative of Ammanati's earlier style, orthodox in most respects but showing Mannerist devices in the lower portion of the façade, especially in the use of rustication; the vertically-tooled cushion-like units are characteristic of his personal style.

The **Ponte S. Trinità, Florence** (1567–70), by Ammanati, is a bridge of brilliant design, profoundly Renaissance in spirit but quite un-Roman in its flat-elliptical arches, panelled spandrels and gay keystones and cartouches. The bridge was blown up in 1944 and rebuilt to the original design in 1957–8.

GALEAZZO ALESSI (1512–72), born in Perugia and trained in Rome, came under the influence of Michelangelo. Nearly all his buildings are in Genoa, where he settled about 1549. Up to that time the Renaissance had had little important effect there. The work of Alessi and the small band of architects that gathered about him is still more strongly inclined towards Mannerist freedom of expression than that of Ammanati, for the local traditions, like those of Lombardy, favoured elaborate ornamentation; and also, as in Rome at this time, hard stucco had been rediscovered as a plastic medium admirable for the architectural adornment of brick-carcassed buildings. In essentials, the ancient Classical principles are reasonably observed, but the lesser features commonly are brilliantly ornate, and superficial decoration sometimes is modelled in extremely high relief, externally as well as indoors. Panelling, strip-rustication, masks, cartouches and scrolled foliations repeatedly occur, and great decorative emphasis often is placed on focal features, such as entrance doorways. Alessi was an architect of great originality and distinction and had a prodigious output of palaces and villas; such as the **Palazzo Sauli** (*c.* 1555) (p. 805B), of which little remains. Mostly of brick faced with stucco, they are famous for their entrance vestibules, courtyards, and flights of steps, and the sloping sites were utilized to form beautiful vistas of terraces and hanging gardens. The façades frequently have rusticated basements surmounted by pilasters and a bold crowning cornice over attic windows between supporting consoles.

S. Maria in Carignano, Genoa (1552, completed 1603) (p. 807D) resembles Bramante's church of SS. Celso and Giuliano, Rome (destroyed) and his more elaborate scheme for S. Peter's (p. 841E), maintained in essentials by Peruzzi, in being of Greek-cross type filled out with angle bays so as to form a square plan, with no significant projection except at the sanctuary apse. The arms of this large church are barrel-vaulted and the crossing domed. Tall, staged campanili rise on the wings of the entrance front, and the central doorway, with its columned enframement following a recessed curve and the rich ornamentation above, is clearly Proto-Baroque.

The **Palazzo Marino, Milan** (1558–60) (p. 844D) is a sumptuous example of Alessi's style, in which the influence of plastic stucco ornamentation is plainly demonstrated. The lavish enrichments include garlands, cartouches, masks, enframed sculptured panels, niches with statues, scroll-ended 'broken' pediments and downward-tapering pilasters, either with double Ionic capitals or these replaced with human-headed grotesque figures. Especially noteworthy are the graceful arcades, one of the first instances of the arrangement, with wide-spaced paired columns, in place of the single columns usual in early Florentine arcades.

ROCCO LURAGO (d. 1590), a Lombard working in Genoa, was one of the more important and talented of the contemporaries of Alessi. In his palace designs he showed great appreciation of the potentialities of falling sites.

The **Palazzo Municipo, Genoa** (1564) (p. 808) has a magnificent plan (p. 808c) on axial lines, with central entrance leading to a large vestibule and cortile, beyond which stairs lead to the 'piano nobile' and terraced gardens. The cortile (p. 808c, D) established a type followed by many others in this city of opulent palaces.

The façade (p. 808A), a dignified composition about 60 m (200 ft) long by 24 m (80 ft) high, has Tuscan and Doric pilasters, each framing two storeys of windows, the lower Order being flanked by arcaded loggias giving breadth to the design.

BAROQUE

BARTOLOMEO BIANCO (c. 1589–1657) followed Alessi's lead at some distance of time, and is accounted Genoa's best Baroque architect. His palace work is much more pure and gracious than that of his predecessors, and freed of excessive sculptural ornamentation.

The **Palazzo Durazzo-Pallavicini, Genoa** (1619–) (p. 806D) follows the scheme used by Lurago for the Palazzo Municipo, the front being arranged in two double-tiered stages rising to a massive cornice over the centre block, with flanking shallow wings finishing in open loggias, though this time the loggias are on the level of the upper stage rather than on the lower. Comparatively, the treatment is grand and austere, though it is possible that the front was intended to be painted or frescoed in accordance with old local traditions.

The **Palazzo dell' Università, Genoa** (1634–6) (p. 818B, D), built as a Jesuit college and created a university in 1812, is Bianco's finest building. It improves upon the plan principle inaugurated by Lurago in the Palazzo Municipo; the cortile again is utilized in the stately stair approach to the 'piano nobile', but now the stairway beyond the cortile is duplicated to lead also to terraces above the arcades, while the lower tier of the latter is continued towards the street to form an airy enframement to the lofty vestibule (p. 818B). The light and gracious arcades stand upon columns more closely paired than in Alessi's Sauli and Marino palaces, surpassing in their airy simplicity those of the court of the **Palazzo Borghese, Rome** (1590–) (p. 844F), which otherwise they closely resemble.

The **Porta Pila, Genoa** (1633) (p. 811C), attributed to Bianco, a gateway now re-erected away from its original position, has the full power and vigour of the true Baroque, though its qualities are the less easy to appreciate in the lack of the contrasting plain walls within which it formerly stood. The massive entablature and heavily rusticated columns have precedents in gateways built for the defensive walls of Verona by Sanmichele more than a hundred years earlier; their impressive scale is emphasized by the relative delicacy of the shrine which stands aloft.

GIOVANNI BATTISTA ALEOTTI (1546–1636) is best known for his **Teatro Farnese, Parma** (1618–28) (p. 811D, F)—largely destroyed in the Second World War—showing an advance on the theatre at Vicenza (p. 811B) by Palladio and Scamozzi in having an elaborately-enframed proscenium spaced apart from a deep U-shaped auditorium by archways on each side. The superposed arcades surrounding the auditorium resemble those around Palladio's Basilica at Vicenza (p. 862). Both this theatre and that at Vicenza are fitted within rooms independently roofed.

FRANCESCO RICCHINI (1583–1658), studied in Rome and returned in 1603 to Milan, where such of his important Baroque work as has survived is to be found.

S. Giuseppe, Milan (1607–30) (p. 817A), the earliest Baroque building in the city, has a simple octagonal plan, 15.2 m (50 ft) across, covered by a pendentived dome. The façade is skilfully integrated with the staged octagonal cupola, and the whole makes a strongly unified composition comparable with Carlo Maderna's S. Susanna, the earliest Baroque church in Rome (p. 817B).

GUARINO GUARINI (1624–83), an extraordinary genius whose remarkable buildings show some influence of Borromini (p. 846), was born in Modena and became a Theatine monk. He was at various times in Messina, Paris and elsewhere, and a church from his designs was erected in Lisbon (Portugal); from 1666 he worked

A. Villa d'Este, Tivoli (1549-).
Water organ. See p. 834

B. Teatro Olimpico, Vicenza: interior (1580-4).
Scenery at back of stage. See p. 863

C. The Porta Pila, Genoa
(1633). See p. 810

D. Teatro Farnese, Parma: auditorium (1618-28).
See p. 810

E. S. Sindone Chapel, Turin
Cathedral: dome (1667-90).
See p. 815

F. Teatro Farnese, Parma: proscenium (1618-28).
See p. 810

A. The Superga, Turin (1717–31). See p. 815

B. Palazzo Carignano, Turin (1679). See p. 815

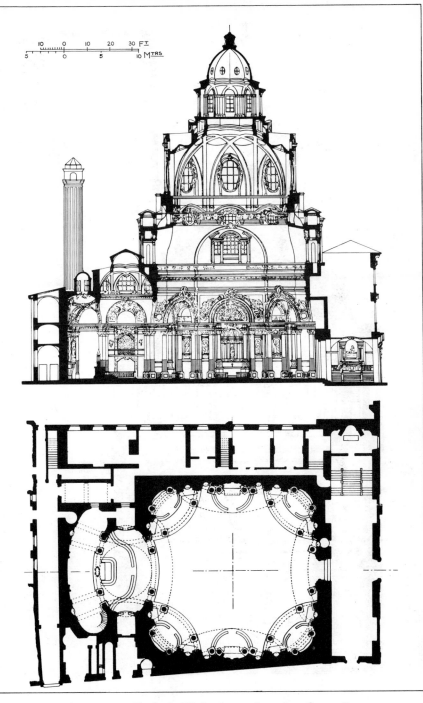

S. Lorenzo, Turin (1668–): plan and section. See p. 815

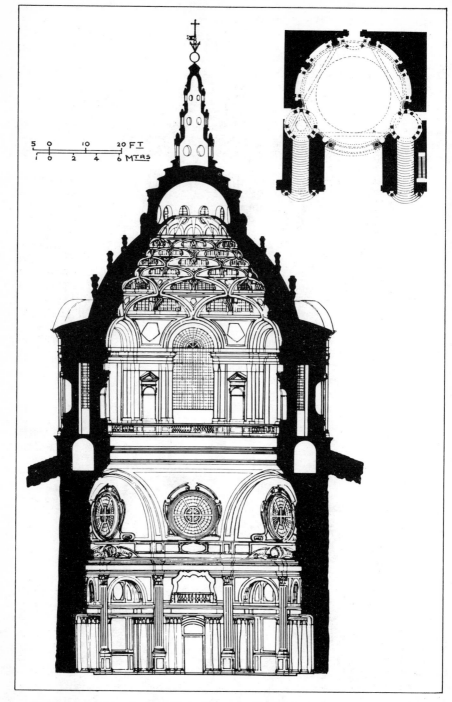

S. Sindone (Chapel of the Holy Shroud), Turin Cathedral (1667–90): plan
and section. See p. 815

mainly in Turin. The vaulting of his centralized churches there, such as **S. Lorenzo** (1668–) (p. 813) and the **S. Sindone Chapel** (1667–90) (pp. 811E, 814) are astonishing compositions of intersecting arched ribs carrying vertical windows instead of solid webs, both fabrics rising externally in a series of stages perpetuating the cupola form of covering to the crossing which so long had been a tradition in Lombardy and Piedmont. Schematically, his church planning is based upon overlapping circles or ovals, usually of minor curvilinear shapes intruding into larger ones, and from these there proceeds in the internal structure a spatial illusion of interrelated volumes; while externally, walls follow sinuous or undulating lines, ornamented superficially with thin and scratchy architectural detail or locally by clustered pilasters and detached columns. His buildings, in particular the longitudinal churches, had a considerable influence on Late Baroque architecture in Southern Germany (p. 920).

The **Palazzo Carignano, Turin** (1679) (p. 812B), is the best known of Guarini's domestic buildings. The undulating central part, masking paired grand staircases alongside a spacious oval hall, relieves this majestic mass from any danger of monotony that might arise from the regular fenestration, much more effectively than would any other means. The façades are almost wholly in brick and terra-cotta.

FILIPPO JUVARRA (1678–1736) is another outstanding personality in Piedmontese Baroque architecture, which flourished in the hundred years from about 1660, when initiative in Rome had begun to decline. A brilliant and prolific designer, Juvarra achieved great fame. Born in Messina, he studied in Rome under Carlo Fontana (p. 846), and thereafter was in demand in several countries abroad, working chiefly in and around Turin after 1714. There, he built many major structures; royal palaces, town residences and churches.

The **Superga, Turin** (1717–31) (p. 812A), a church and convent, is Juvarra's masterpiece. It stands on a hill overlooking the city; the domed church, with its columned portico and flanking campanile, precedes the monastic establishment of which the modest, window-studded façades lend emphasis to the majestic climax in the frontispiece. As simple, forceful and straightforward as the work of Guarini is complex, it is one of the greatest monuments of the whole Renaissance.

S. Annunziata, Genoa (p. 818E) has a fine portico (c. 1830) by Carlo Barabino (1768–1835), added to Giacomo della Porta's incomplete brick-faced façade (1587), which brings into contrast the strict Classical properties of the Antiquarian Phase and the free individualism of the Proto-Baroque.

B. A. VITTONE (1702–70) designed S. Michele Rivarolo at Canavese, about 30 km (20 miles) north of Turin, and the church at Grignasco, Valsesia (1750).

C. MICHELA, who designed **S. Marta, Agliè** (1740–58) (pp. 848D, 850C) displays like Vittone the influence of Guarini. The plasticity of S. Marta is remarkable.

ROME

EARLY RENAISSANCE

LUCIANO LAURANA (c. 1420/5–80). Before the Renaissance reached Rome significantly, it had spread to the more northerly of the Papal States, and some charming, delicate work had been done at the Ducal Palaces of Urbino and Gubbio. With the first of these at least, the name of Laurana is associated. He came from Dalmatia, was perhaps trained in Venice, and worked mainly at Urbino, where Bramante was one of his pupils, for both Bramante and Raphael were born in that neighbourhood.

The **Ducal Palace, Urbino** (c. 1444–82) (p. 794C), built for Federigo Montefeltro, is transitional in some ways, but after Laurana took charge c. 1465 it took on

Early Renaissance character. It is celebrated for the beauty and charm of its apartments, with their doorways, simple plaster vaults, marble-hooded chimneypieces and gracious windows. The cortile (p. 794C) shows Classic principles to have been well imbibed; the arcades stand on single columns like so many at Florence, though the arrangements for turning the angles on clustered piers are individual. The pilastered upper tier contains wooden, two-light transomed windows, with simple architrave surrounds and cap-moulds. In the palace is an interesting perspective panel (possibly by Piero della Francesca), depicting an imaginary ideal Renaissance town (p. 807C). The **Ducal Palace, Gubbio** (1474–80), also built for Montefeltro, is so similar in all respects that it safely may be ascribed to Laurana.

MEO DEL CAPRINO (1430–1501) was one of several Florentines who first brought the Renaissance to Rome, working there between 1462–89.

The **Palazzo di Venezia, Rome** (c. 1455–64) (p. 807E), built with stones from the Colosseum, was not designed by Caprino—it has been conjectured that Alberti was the designer—but he took part in the supervision of its erection, along with Francesco di Borgo di San Sepolcro. It is a transitional building, as the machicolations show, the Renaissance elements appearing mainly in the windows, those with transomes being distinctively Roman, and in the fine entrance doorway.

DONATO BRAMANTE (1444–1514) was Rome's first outstanding architect of the Renaissance, but he did not work there until 1499, and by then he had undertaken a number of important commissions in the Milan area. He was born near Urbino, and began as a painter. From 1467–72 he worked under Laurana at Urbino, settling in Milan c. 1477, practising still as a painter for a while. He was destined to have great influence on the development of Renaissance architecture, not only in Italy but also in Europe. It was he who made the first designs for the new S. Peter's at Rome, and inaugurated the rebuilding of the Vatican.

S. Satiro, Milan (1482–94) (p. 817C, D) was built alongside the old ninth-century small church—with campanile—of that name, which is now approached from the north transept of Bramante's church. The latter has aisled barrel-vaulted and coffered transepts and nave, but owing to the proximity of the street there was no room for a sanctuary arm, so Bramante rendered this in extremely shallow, modelled perspective, an art which was very much engrossing painters and architects at that time. The lunettes at the ends of the transept arms have each five 'wheel' windows forming a half circle around another semicircular shape, placed centrally; this was a favourite device with Bramante. The arcades are of the so-called 'Roman Order', here expressed as arches between pilasters. Above the crossing is a coffered dome carried on a deep entablature above pendentives, the exterior being concealed by a drum with conical tiled roof and a lantern, like Brunelleschi's Pazzi Chapel at Florence. Off the nave is a splendid octagonal sacristy (1488) (p. 817D), one of the most original of Bramante's designs.

S. Maria delle Grazie, Milan, is a fifteenth-century abbey-church to which in 1492–7 Bramante added the choir, transepts and crossing (p. 819). The crossing gives a Byzantine spaciousness, for it is a square the full width of the old church, covered by a dome, 19.8 m (65 ft) across, concealed externally by a sixteen-sided galleried cupola, with sloping roof and lantern, all in the tradition of this northern region. Light is cleverly admitted through circular windows in the dome and from a range of windows in the shallow drum on which it stands, while the lunettes of the crossing have circular decorative panels in lieu of the wheel windows used in S. Satiro in this position. The choir arm is covered by a 'cloister' vault (square dome) penetrated by minor vaults which allow light from circular windows at the east end, over an apsidal termination. Two other apses serve in lieu of transepts. The exterior is all in brick and terra-cotta, except the column shafts in the cupola, which are of

A. S. Giuseppe, Milan: façade (1607–30). See p. 810

B. S. Susanna, Rome: façade (1597–1603). See p. 845

C. In foreground 9th cent. church (restored externally in 1478) and old campanile

D. Sacristy: interior (1488)

S. Satiro, Milan (1482–94). See p. 816

A. Tempietto in S. Pietro in Montorio, Rome: detail (1502–10). See p. 821

B. Palazzo dell' Università, Genoa (1634–6): vestibule. See p. 810

C. Hemicycle, Giardino della Pigna, Vatican, Rome (c. 1503–13). See p. 821

D. Palazzo dell' Università, Genoa: cortile (1634–6). See p. 810

E. S. Annunziata, Genoa (church, 1587; portico, c. 1830). See p. 815

F. Casa Pollini, Siena (c. 1527). See p. 822

S. MARIA DELLE GRAZIE : MILAN

(A) EXTERIOR FROM S.W.

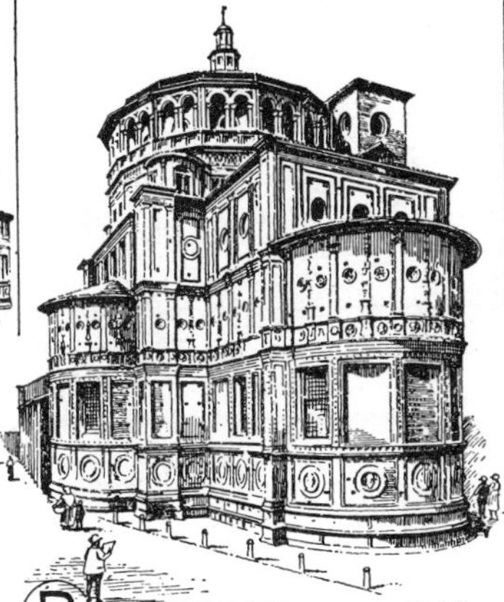

(B) EXTERIOR FROM S.E.

(C) THE CLOISTERS

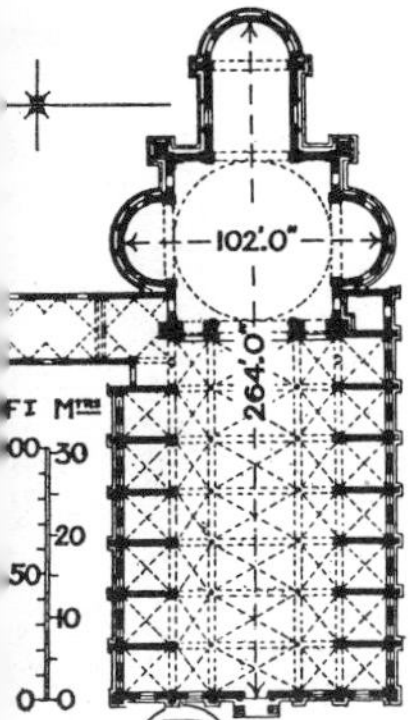

(D) PLAN

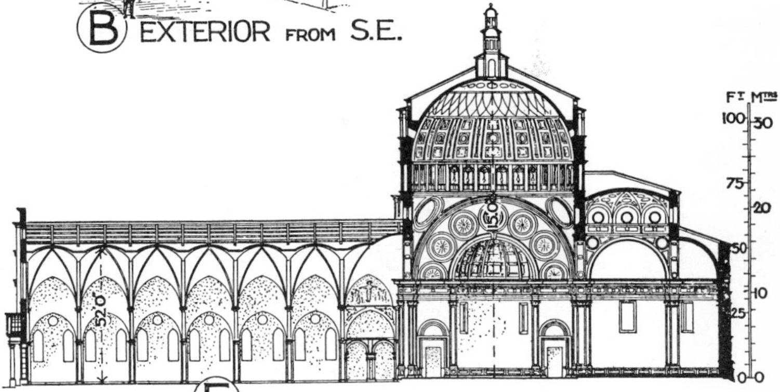

(E) LONGITUDINAL SECTION

THE OSPEDALE MAGGIORE : MILAN

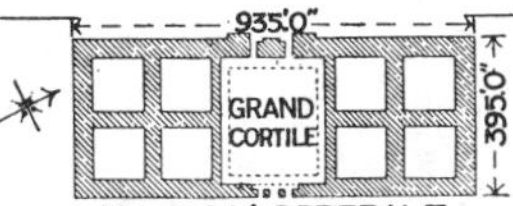

(F) BLOCK PLAN

GRAND CORTILE

VIA DELL' OSPEDALE

(G) EXTERIOR FROM VIA DELL' OSPEDALE

(H) GRAND CORTILE

PAL. DELLA CANCELLERIA : ROME

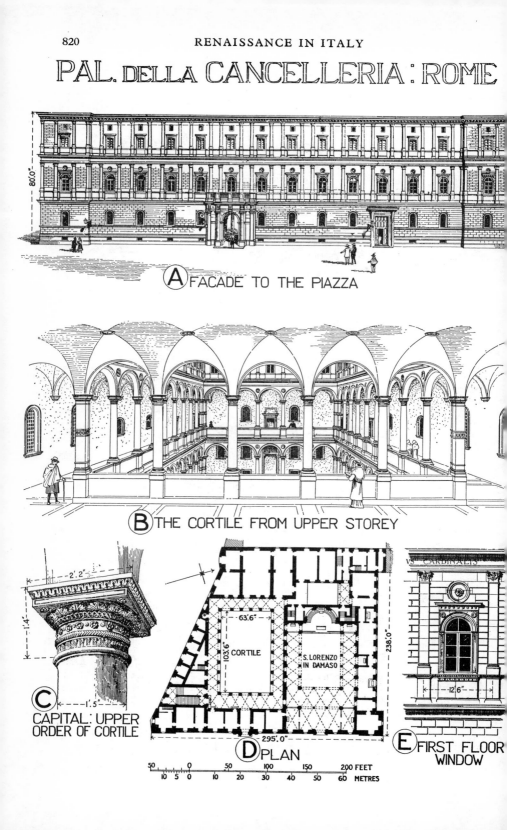

80'-0"

Ⓐ FACADE TO THE PIAZZA

Ⓑ THE CORTILE FROM UPPER STOREY

2'. 2"

1'. 4"

1'. 5"

Ⓒ CAPITAL: UPPER ORDER OF CORTILE

63'.6"

103'.6"

CORTILE

S. LORENZO IN DAMASO

295'.0"

Ⓓ PLAN

238'.0"

VS CARDINALIS

12'.6"

Ⓔ FIRST FLOOR WINDOW

50   0   50   100   150   200 FEET
10 5 0   10   20   30   40   50   60 METRES

marble. The panelled pilasters, candelabra, medallion and wheel ornaments are normal to Lombard practice of the day. Other works by Bramante in this area are the Canonry of S. Ambrogio, Milan (1492), recently restored after war damage; the west façade to the abbey-church at Abbiategrasso (1497); and additions to the Castle of Vigevano (c. 1494).

HIGH RENAISSANCE AND PROTO-BAROQUE

The **Palazzo della Cancelleria, Rome** (1486–98) (p. 820) has for long been considered a work of Bramante, and indeed in certain respects it recalls his Milanese style, but it was substantially complete before his arrival in Rome and the architect is unknown. Still slightly immature, it is the first really important Renaissance building in Rome, and was a rebuilt residence for Cardinal Riario, incorporating S. Lorenzo in Damaso, an ancient basilica which previously had been on another site (p. 820D). The façades are of travertine stone robbed from the Colosseum; they rise in three main tiers, the lowest in channelled masonry and the two upper each ornamented with plain Corinthian pilasters arranged in alternating spacings instead of the regular spacings of earlier stylar palaces. The intermediate full entablature is subdued, while that at the top has vertical modillions across the frieze, giving it all the vigour of the crowning cornice of the Colosseum. The shallow pilasters stand upon simulated pedestals, the corresponding 'blind' parapets serving as aprons to the main windows, which latter have arched openings on the first floor, fitted within square, corniced heads (p. 820E). The main doorway is an addition by Domenico Fontana (1589). The wings of the principal façades are advanced slightly, and round the corner to the left of the entrance front (p. 820A) is a first floor balcony with extremely delicate decoration (p. 785C). The imposing cortile, 31.5 m × 19 m (104 ft × 63 ft), is surrounded by two storeys of arcades (p. 820B) of Doric columns (p. 820C) carrying a third, solid, storey ornamented with pilasters spanning two tiers of small windows in height and carrying a bold cornice similar to that on the fronts.

S. Maria della Pace, Rome has a beautiful cloister (1500–4) (p. 785E) surrounded by a two-storeyed arcade designed by Bramante, in which, as in examples by him in the Milan area, the upper storey has twice as many openings as the lower. The church itself was reconstructed by Pietro da Cortona in 1656–7, to whom is due the skilfully designed plan and semicircular portico (p. 849B).

The **Tempietto in S. Pietro in Montorio, Rome** (1502–10) (pp. 818A, 823), erected to mark the spot where S. Peter was martyred, is a perfect architectural gem by Bramante, in full High Renaissance style, resembling in design a small Roman circular temple. It is only 4.5 m (15 ft) in diameter internally and is surrounded by a Doric peristyle, behind which rises the drum, pierced with windows alternating with shell-headed niches and carrying a dome. The crypt was superficially redesigned internally in 1628.

Cortili of S. Damaso and Belvedere, Vatican (pp. 838A, B, 843A). The home of the Popes contains the Court of S. Damaso, of which the lower arcades are by Bramante (p. 838A), and the much larger Belvedere Court which also he undertook for Julius II (1503–13). The latter court (pp. 838, 843A), extremely long and narrow, was later subdivided into two by other buildings on the line of a series of terraces, which had formed part of Bramante's scheme, and the one half, called the Giardino della Pigna (Garden of the Pine Cone), contains at its northern end a great, three-storeyed, half-domed hemicycle, with a terrace and pavilions over (p. 818C). The buildings flanking this feature are two-storeyed and ornamented with pilasters in alternating spacings; on the lower storey the wider spacings contain arches, and thus give an effect of a series of 'triumphal arch' motifs.

BALDASSARE PERUZZI (1481–1536) designed many buildings in Rome and his work shows great versatility and skill as well as a refinement often approaching the Greek. Born in Siena, he settled in Rome in 1503, studying ancient architecture and travelling extensively in Italy. A design by him in 1523 for the west front of S. Petronio, Bologna (p. 743), was not carried out.

The **Villa Farnesina, Rome** (1509–11) (p. 831H), built for Agostino Chigi, a Sienese banker, has two storeys of superimposed Orders and a central arcaded loggia between projecting wings on the rear side. The plan is an early example of the new villa type not based on a cortile. The famous ground-floor loggia is painted in trompe-l'œil by Raphael and G. da Udine with garlands to represent an arbour. The topmost storey has a deep ornamental frieze, in which windows are inserted, an idea originated by Rossellino in his astylar Palazzo Spannocchi at Siena (p. 803) and afterwards adopted by Sansovino in the Library of S. Mark, Venice (p. 861A).

The **Palazzo Pietro Massimi, Rome** (1532–6) (p. 824), refined both in design and detail, is especially interesting for the clever treatment of a convex façade to follow the line of the street. The plan (p. 824H) shows remarkable skill in arranging two separate palaces on an irregular site. The entrance to the right-hand palace is a recessed vestibule (p. 824C) which leads into a cortile (p. 824G) with portico (p. 824J) and steps to an upper loggia (p. 824F), whence the grand salon (p. 824E) is reached. The façade (p. 824B) relies for effect on the Doric Order of columns and pilasters stretching from end to end of the ground storey, contrasted with the severe astylar treatment of the upper storeys, with architrave-enframed windows, unadorned balconies and a vigorous crowning cornice. In several particulars the Massimi shows 'Mannerist' departures from strict Classical precedent, as do several other of the buildings of Peruzzi's later life. The chaste **Casa Pollini, Siena** (c. 1527) (p. 818F), and the **Palazzo Albergati, Bologna** (1519–40) (p. 830F), the latter only partially completed in his lifetime, are other buildings attributed to him.

S. Maria della Consolazione, Todi (1508–1604) (p. 825), designed by Cola da Caprarola, with Peruzzi as adviser, was a long time in building. It is another of the churches based on the popular Greek-cross plan, here with apses forming the four arms (p. 825A) of a square crossing 15.2 m (50 ft) in diameter. The exterior (p. 825B) has superimposed pilasters, surmounted by a low attic, above which semi-domes abut the dome on its high, windowed drum, the whole rising to a height of 55 m (180 ft). The interior (p. 825C) has a similar pilaster treatment, and the line of these is carried up in dome ribs. Giant pilasters mark the angles of the crossing, and carry arches between which span the dome pendentives.

The **Madonna di S. Biagio, Montepulciano** (1518–29) (p. 830A), built by Antonio da Sangallo the Elder (1455–1534), is another splendid Greek-cross church of confident High Renaissance design, here with four rectangular arms, that at the east end being extended to form an apse. Twin, free-standing campanili towers were intended to flank the west front, but only one was fully completed. The arms are barrel-vaulted, and the dome over the crossing is sustained on a high, windowed drum over pendentives. The one completed campanile has superimposed Doric, Ionic and Corinthian Orders paired at the angles of the square-planned tower, the inner shafts being in the round, and above them is a squat, staged octagonal spire. Also at Montepulciano is the **Palazzo Contucci**, begun by Sangallo and finished by Peruzzi about 1535 in thorough-paced Mannerist style.

ANTONIO DA SANGALLO the Younger (1485–1546) worked in Rome most of his life, and for a time after 1506 was an assistant of Bramante.

The **Palazzo Farnese, Rome** (1515–) (p. 826), the grandest palace of this period, was designed by Sangallo. The plan (p. 826G) is rectangular and symmetrically arranged on axial lines with main entrance, vestibule (p. 826H) and side colonnades.

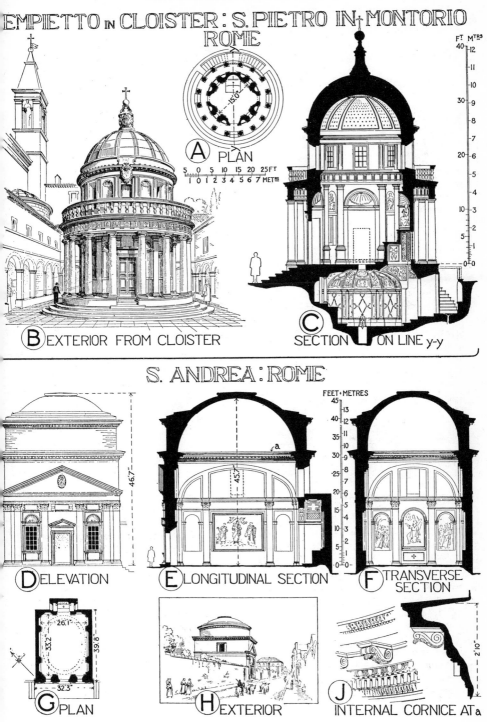

TEMPIETTO ɪɴ CLOISTER : S.PIETRO IN MONTORIO ROME

Ⓐ PLAN

5 0 5 10 15 20 25 FT
1 0 1 2 3 4 5 6 7 METRES

Ⓑ EXTERIOR FROM CLOISTER

Ⓒ SECTION ON LINE y-y

S. ANDREA : ROME

Ⓓ ELEVATION

Ⓔ LONGITUDINAL SECTION

FEET·METRES

Ⓕ TRANSVERSE SECTION

Ⓖ PLAN

Ⓗ EXTERIOR

Ⓙ INTERNAL CORNICE AT a

PALAZZO PIETRO MASSIMI : ROME

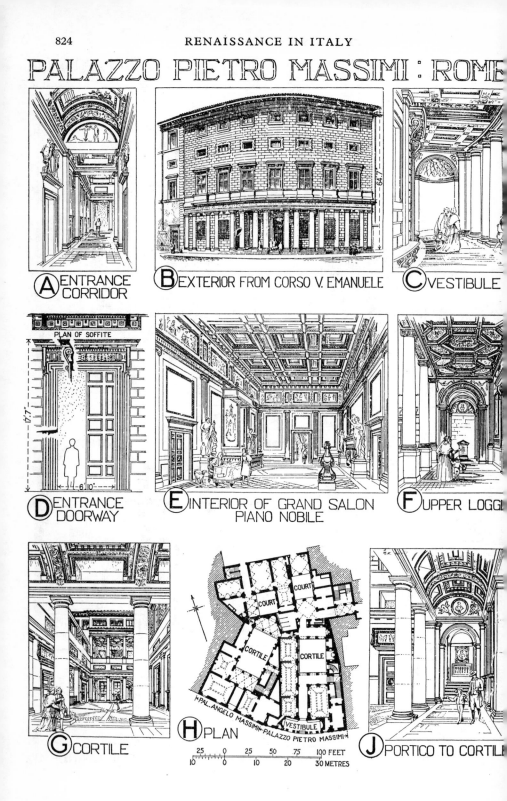

Ⓐ ENTRANCE CORRIDOR

Ⓑ EXTERIOR FROM CORSO V. EMANUELE

Ⓒ VESTIBULE

PLAN OF SOFFITE

Ⓓ ENTRANCE DOORWAY

Ⓔ INTERIOR OF GRAND SALON PIANO NOBILE

Ⓕ UPPER LOGGIA

Ⓖ CORTILE

Ⓗ PLAN

COURT · COURT · CORTILE · CORTILE · VESTIBULE
PAL. ANGELO MASSIMI · PALAZZO PIETRO MASSIMI

25   0   25   50   75   100 FEET
10   0   10   20   30 METRES

Ⓙ PORTICO TO CORTILE

S. MARIA·DELLA CONSOLAZIONE·: TODI

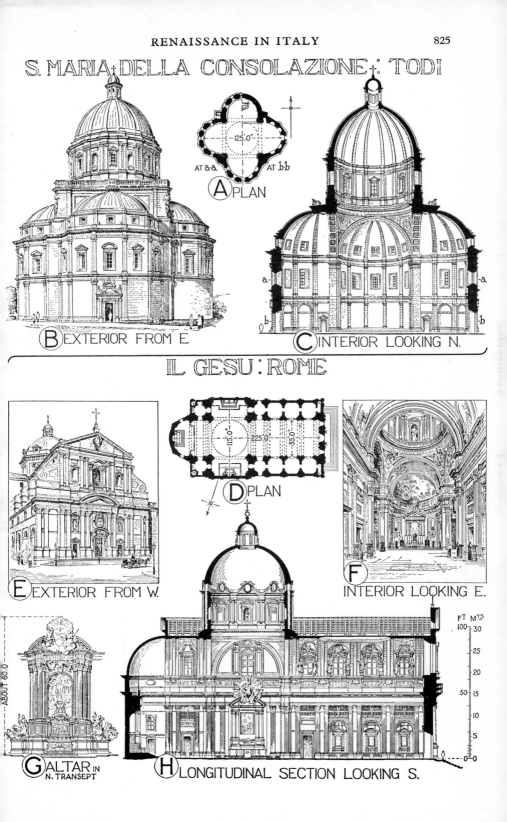

(A) PLAN

125'·0"

AT a·a · AT b·b

(B) EXTERIOR FROM E.

(C) INTERIOR LOOKING N.

IL GESU : ROME

(D) PLAN

115'·0" · 225'·0" · 55'·0"

(E) EXTERIOR FROM W.

(F) INTERIOR LOOKING E.

(G) ALTAR IN N. TRANSEPT

ABOUT 60.0

(H) LONGITUDINAL SECTION LOOKING S.

FT MTS
100 — 30
— 25
— 20
50 — 15
— 10
— 5
0 — 0

PALAZZO FARNESE : ROME

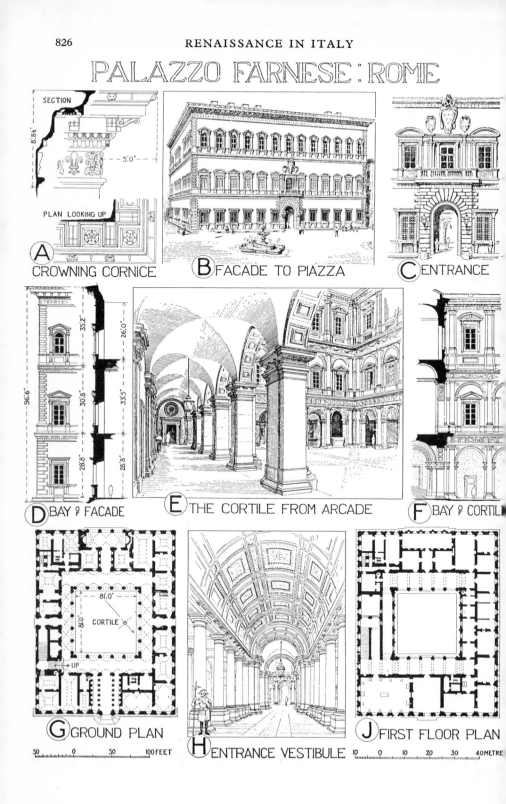

A CROWNING CORNICE

SECTION
8.8½"
5.0"
PLAN LOOKING UP

B FACADE TO PIAZZA

C ENTRANCE

D BAY OF FACADE

96.6" 35.2" 26.0" 30.8" 33.5" 28.8" 28.8"

E THE CORTILE FROM ARCADE

F BAY OF CORTILE

G GROUND PLAN

81.0" 81.0" CORTILE UP

H ENTRANCE VESTIBULE

J FIRST FLOOR PLAN

50 0 50 100 FEET

10 0 10 20 30 40 METRE

The cortile, 24.5 m (81 ft) square, is surrounded by arcades off which are the apartments and a fine staircase, not itself symmetrically aligned, leading to the 'piano nobile'. The ground floor loggia in the centre of the rear façade opens on to the garden. The façade to the piazza (p. 826B) is an imposing astylar composition without any break, 56 m (185 ft long) × 29.5 m (96 ft 6 ins) high, of three storeys of nearly equal height, of brick covered with stucco and stone dressings of travertine from the Colosseum. The ground storey has a fine central entrance (p. 826C), flanked by windows; the first floor has pedimented windows (p. 785A), alternately triangular and segmental, carried by a full Order, a regular and characteristic practice at this period. The top storey, added by Michelangelo (1546–), has windows of Proto-Baroque design (p. 785B), with columns on brackets, surmounted by triangular pediments, the window arch encroaching on the entablature. The great crowning cornice (p. 826A) is allied to the wall by an ornamental frieze, which allows it to be lighter than that of the Strozzi at Florence (p. 802F)—here about one-eighteenth of the height of the façade, or one-eleventh if the frieze is included. The façade was taken by Sir Charles Barry as the model for the Reform Club, London (p. 1138). In the cortile the storeys are marked by superimposed attached Orders, arcaded in the two lower tiers, while in the upper the overlying pilasters and the window enframements again evidence Michelangelo's Proto-Baroque style. Inside, the Galleria Farnese was decorated by Annibale Carracci between 1595–1604, and is a magnificent example of 'quadratura' or illusionistic art. Sculptural figures of marble and bronze reliefs frame easel pictures which show chinks of sky, thus creating a sense of infinite space. Michelangelo's Sistine ceiling must have been a formative influence.

RAPHAEL SANTI (1483–1520) of Urbino, one of the world's greatest painters and an architect of distinction, was active in Urbino, Perugia and Florence before being invited by Julius II to Rome in 1508, where his reputation as a painter had preceded him. Pope Leo X in turn employed him extensively, and it was he who called Raphael to advise as to the design of S. Peter's (p. 839) though Raphael does not appear to have taken any actual part in carrying it out. The exploration of such half-buried ruins as the Baths of Titus, Nero's Golden House and the ruins of other ancient buildings gave artists the opportunity of studying Roman mural decorations and frescoes, in which flowers and foliage, men and monsters, birds, vessels and trophies were all blended together in delicate colour schemes, and on these Raphael based his decoration of the world-famous Vatican Loggia. As Cellini tells in his fascinating *Memoirs*, the term 'grotesque' was coined to describe the Roman arabesques through their 'being found in certain subterranean caverns in Rome by students of antiquity; which caverns were formerly chambers, hot-baths, cabinets for study, halls and apartments of like nature', buried in the processes of time. Other architect-decorators were similarly inspired by these ancient mural decorations, and modelled stucco was enthusiastically exploited for the next few decades, sometimes to extravagant extremes (p. 835B), invading architecture externally as well as indoors.

The **Villa Madama, Rome** (1516–) (p. 831J), designed by Raphael and continued after his death by his assistant, Guilio Romano, was never completed, but the part executed became the model for nearly all the formal gardens of Italy. The charming loggia, which is virtually all now to be seen of the ambitious residence or 'casino' intended, was brilliantly decorated with stuccoes and frescoes by Romano and Giovanni da Udine.

The **Palazzo Pandolfini, Florence** (*c.* 1520–7) is one of Raphael's most famous designs, and was carried out jointly by two local architects. It inspired the design of the Traveller's Club, London (p. 1137). The stuccoed walls are set off with angle rustications, while the windows are the High Renaissance 'tabernacle' type, with flanking pilasters or attached columns carrying entablatures with alternating triangular and segmental pediments. The effective cornice, above an astragal frieze, is of wood. A low, one-storey wing gives asymmetry to the composition, and the portal giving access to the garden approach has the extremely deep voussoirs to the arched head favoured by Raphael in other palace designs.

GIULIO ROMANO (1492–1546), a pupil of Raphael, approached architecture through painting, and acquired great skill in combining stucco decoration with frescoes in panels, an art learnt from Roman remains. He assisted Raphael at the Villa Madama and at the Loggie and Stanze of the Vatican. In 1524 he left Rome for Mantua, where he was employed as painter, decorator, garden-designer and architect. At Mantua he had as a pupil Francesco Primaticcio (1504–70), who in 1532 joined Il Rosso in Fontainebleau, and thus spread the stuccoist art to France (pp. 872, 882).

The **Palazzo del Tè, Mantua** (1525–35) (p. 829A), a one-storey summer pleasure house for Duke Federico Gonzaga II, has a grim exterior for this class of building, but originally was only the chief feature in vast grounds, including subsidiary buildings, groves and avenues, mazes, fishponds and delightful formal gardens, furnished with pavilions, terraces, statues, fountains and pools. Primarily a decorator, Romano regularly shows himself impatient of Classical rules; here evidenced by the structurally-illogical distribution of the Doric pilasters on the façades, and the casual omission of triglyphs from the frieze to provide small windows. The palace is quadrangular on plan, with grand saloons and an arcaded garden vestibule around a central garden court, the rooms having splendid paintings and ornament by Romano and his pupils.

Giulio Romano's house, Mantua (c. 1544) (p. 830B) is among his latest and most accomplished architectural works, with rustications on two floors, pedimented, marble-enframed upper windows and marble and terra-cotta decorations. Departures from Classical principles are again notable; in the stressed and rusticated voussoired arches duplicating the window-enframements, the elliptical-arched doorway and its rusticated pediment breaking through the string-moulding line, and the location of the ornaments within the arches.

The **Villa Lante, Bagnaia** (p. 829B, C), near Viterbo, supposedly designed by Vignola in 1566 for Cardinal Gambera, was subsequently owned by Duke Ippolito Lante in 1656. Laid out on axial principles on a gently sloping site, this is the first Renaissance garden to make contact with wild nature. Instead of a grand climax, its upper terraces lose themselves in a source of water that gushes out from the wooded 'bosco'. The garden progresses from this stream to the basin of the open sun-lit parterre that commands a prospect over the town below. It is a movement from the natural to the sophisticated, from dark closed space to light and air; order emerging from chaos. The villa itself is divided in two, with identical casinos on each side of the axis and the garden between.

GIACOMO BAROZZI DA VIGNOLA (1507–73), born in Bologna, worked principally there and in and around Rome, apart from two years in the service of Francis I of France (1541–3). Author of *The Five Orders of Architecture* (published 1562), he was destined to have great influence upon the course of the Renaissance and especially in France, where his precepts were followed in preference to those of Palladio, favoured in England. He was more academic in his writings than in his architecture, which shows great versatility, elegance and originality of design.

The **Villa of Pope Julius III, Rome** (1550–5) (p. 831), as it now survives is the nucleus of what formerly was a much more extensive scheme. Even so, it is an architectural gem. Other famous architects had a hand in it, including Michelangelo

A. Palazzo del Tè, Mantua (1525–35). See p. 828

B. Villa Lante, Bagnaia (16th cent.): water garden. See p. 828

C. Villa Lante, Bagnaia: detail of water garden and casino

A. Madonna di S. Biagio, Montepulciano (1518–29). See p. 822

B. Giulio Romano's house, Mantua (c. 1544).
See p. 828

C. Garden Pavilion, Caprarola
(c. 1549). See p. 833

D. Palazzo Odescalchi, Rome (1664–).
See p. 846

E. Villa Medici, Rome (1574–80). See p. 834

F. Palazzo Albergati,
Bologna (1519–40).
See p. 822

VILLA OF POPE JULIUS: ROME

A GROUND PLAN

278'.0"

90'.0"

DOWN

UP

GRAND CORTILE

B ENTRANCE FACADE

55'0"

a

b

50 0 50 100 150 200 FT
10 0 10 20 30 40 50 60 MTS

C LOWER ORDER GRAND CORTILE

4'.0"

20'.2"

5'.10"

D UPPER FLOOR PLAN

E WINDOW AT a

8'.9" 4'.5"

F GRAND CORTILE

G WINDOW AT b

8'.10" 4'.4"

H VILLA FARNESINA: ROME

J VILLA MADAMA: ROME

PAL. FARNESE : CAPRAROLA : N⸰ ROME

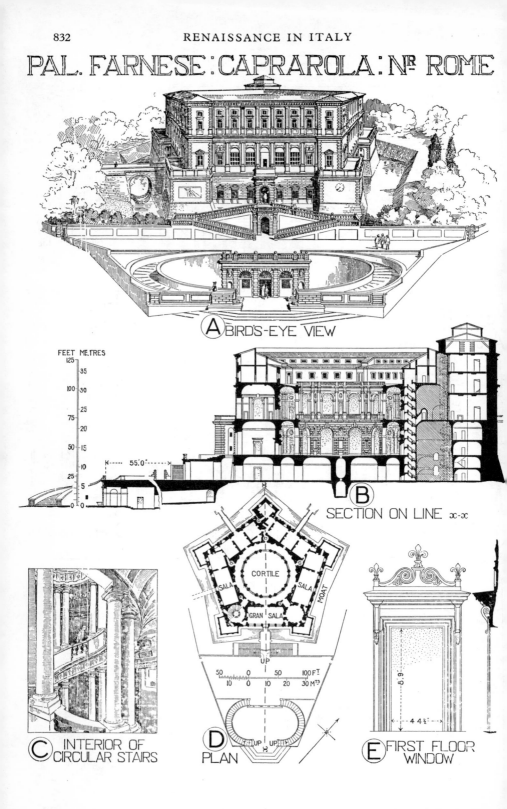

Ⓐ BIRD'S-EYE VIEW

FEET METRES

Ⓑ SECTION ON LINE x-x

Ⓒ INTERIOR OF CIRCULAR STAIRS

Ⓓ PLAN

Ⓔ FIRST FLOOR WINDOW

and Vasari, but essentially it is by Vignola and is his best-known work. Nowadays, it serves as the Etruscan Museum. The plan (p. 831A) shows a straight front with entrance leading to the semicircular portico; grand cortile with formal garden; sunken court embraced by summer rooms, approached by sweeping flights of steps and having a central fountain grotto with caryatid figures, rippling water and tiny cascades; and a further flower garden beyond. The whole forms a delightful piece of garden architecture. The façade (p. 831B) is a most pleasing composition and influenced later buildings. It has rusticated ground-floor windows (p. 831E) and crested first-floor windows (p. 831G) which together with the central feature show some Proto-Baroque departures from Classical precedent. The semicircular façade to the grand cortile (p. 831F) instances a clever and attractive interweaving of large-scale and small-scale Orders of architecture.

The **Palazzo Farnese, Caprarola** (1547–9) (p. 832), a semi-fortress of pentagonal form situated on a mountain spur, is one of the most magnificent of all Renaissance buildings, and incorporates many brilliant features which have inspired later designs. The plan (p. 832D) is a great pentagon, each side being 46 m (150 ft) long. Paired steps and staircases of varied patterns, interspersed with terraces and axial pavilions and grottoes, ascend on the main axis to the Gran Sala, beyond which is a circular cortile, 19.8 m (65 ft) in diameter, with façades of two arcaded storeys, rusticated below and above ornamented with attached columns in a 'triumphal arch' arrangement. In one angle of the plan is the famous circular open staircase (p. 832C) (cf. Château de Chambord, p. 880G). The general lay-out (p. 832A), with entrance portal, circular ramps, stairs and moat, makes a fine symmetrical and monumental group. Connected with the palace but a little distant from it there survives another famous formal garden, where a series of charming elements, including several kinds of water display, is arranged along a falling axis. Commanding them all, astride the axis, is a delightful garden house, single-storeyed on the upper side and double on the other, which is among Vignola's most original creations (p. 830C).

S. Andrea, Rome (c. 1550) (p. 823), on the Via Flaminia, is one of Vignola's smaller works, the very simple plan (p. 823G) being covered by an elliptical dome, borne on a normal Corinthian cornice (p. 823J) over pendentives, thus showing a new departure in Renaissance adventure. The method of buttressing the dome by a quasi-drum is the same as in the Pantheon, Rome (p. 288A). On the entrance front (p. 823D), a portico, with pediment, is simulated with pilasters.

The **Gesù Church, Rome** (1568–84) (p. 825), completed by Giacomo della Porta, who modified the scheme for the façade, is one of Vignola's best-known works. The interior was redecorated in 1674–9 by G. B. Gaulli and the walls lined with marble in 1860; the altar in the north transept (p. 825G), a superlative Baroque masterpiece by a great number of craftsmen, was designed in 1695–9 by Andrea Pozzo. Vignola's plan (p. 825D) is an improved version of that of Alberti for S. Andrea at Mantua (p. 796J), and became the type for very many later churches. It is the Byzantine centralized type, domed over the crossing, with short barrel-vaulted transept and sanctuary arms but an extended nave, where there are close-spaced chapels in lieu of aisles, and lunette windows over them in the base of the barrel-vault (p. 825H). The lunettes afford a much better lighted church than Alberti's. The Proto-Baroque façade has a centre-piece of two superimposed Orders, while the aisle roofs stop against large scroll brackets, as used by Alberti at S. Maria Novella, Florence (pp. 748, 753A).

The two small cupolas at S. Peter's (p. 839), and the Portico de' Banchi, Bologna (1562), were also from the designs of this master.

PIRRO LIGORIO (c. 1520–80) is remembered principally for his spectacular

Villa d'Este, Tivoli (1549–) (pp. 811A, 835A), with its remarkable formal gardens containing endless natural and artificial delights; and his charming **Villa Pia, Rome** (1561) (pp. 835B, 838), embodying ornate pavilions around a decoratively-walled oval court in the Vatican gardens. In the garden features of both of these, stucco is used extensively: the passion for modelled stucco at this time extends freely to the encrustation of building exteriors, where too, antique panels were often embedded, and is illustrated by several well-known palaces and villas, including the **Villa Medici, Rome** (1574–80) (p. 830E) by Annibale Lippi. Stucco was a cheap, tractable medium eminently suited to garden ornament, but used sculpturally on buildings tended to produce a restlessness conflicting with the architectural lines.

MICHELANGELO (1475–1564), the long-lived and world-famous Florentine sculptor and the painter of the vaulted ceiling of the Sistine Chapel (1508–), was no less distinguished in his later years as an architect, and is a most striking instance of the wonderful versatility of artists of this period.

The **Medici Chapel, Florence** (1521–34) (p. 836A) constitutes the New Sacristy (p. 795K) in S. Lorenzo, and was added by Michelangelo to correspond with the Old Sacristy built (1421–8) by Brunelleschi. The interior, 12 m (40 ft) square, approximates in design to its counterpart; pilasters of black Istrian stone carry the main entablature, which is surmounted by an attic with pilaster-enframed windows and niches. A deep, dome-crowned recess contains the altar. Yet in the architectural settings for the funerary elements of the ducal tombs which give the building its special renown, there are very significant differences of style, manifesting the first important Proto-Baroque departures from ancient Classical precedent. The white marble mural tombs are those of Giuliano de' Medici and, directly opposite, Lorenzo (II) de' Medici, each with a commanding sculptured figure of the deceased against a background of pilaster-enframed niches, over a marble sarcophagus bearing recumbent allegorical figures, representing in the first case Night and Day, and in the other, Evening and Dawn. The architectural settings are treated sculpturally, and in quite a few respects are illogical in structural implication, both within themselves and in relation to the fundamental architectural theme of the Chapel.

The **Laurentian Library, Florence** (1524–) (p. 836B), adjoining S. Lorenzo, was well advanced by 1534 but continued afterwards by Giorgio Vasari (1511–74), best known for his *Lives of the Painters*, who, with Ammanati, carried out the vestibule and staircase from 1559 (p. 836B), with some modifications of Michelangelo's plans. Proto-Baroque features are again notable, in the triple staircase itself and on the flanking walls, where coupled columns, supported on consoles, are set within recesses between protruding sections of wall ornamented by panels and pedimented niches flanked by downward-tapering pilasters. The library has walls bearing pilasters and a fine timber ceiling; it may have been the model for Wren's Trinity College Library, Cambridge (p. 1022).

The **Capitol, Rome** (p. 837), the reconstruction of which was planned by Michelangelo about 1546, was his most successful civic work and a fine town-planning achievement. He not only remodelled on symmetrical lines the approaches to the piazza, but also designed the great palace façades on the three sides. He superintended the erection only of the approach stairway, the monumental double flight of steps of the palace opposite and, at an earlier time (1538), of the statue of Marcus Aurelius (p. 837C) in the centre of the piazza, the remainder being executed from his designs by his successors. The **Palazzo dei Conservatori** (1564–8) (p. 837A, D, E) has a façade 20 m (66 ft) high. The **Palazzo del Senatore** (1592–), completed by Girolamo Rainaldi (1570–1655) with slight modifications of Michelangelo's designs, rises 27 m (90 ft) high and has a rusticated basement behind the

B. Villa Pia, Rome (1561): garden
pavilion. See p. 834

A. Villa d'Este, Tivoli (1549–).
See p. 834

C. Scala Regia, Rome (Vatican) (1663–6).
See p. 846

A. The Medici Chapel (New Sacristy), S. Lorenzo, Florence (1521–34).
See p. 834

B. The Biblioteca Laurenziana, Florence: entrance (1524–; staircase 1559–).
See p. 834

THE CAPITOL AT ROME

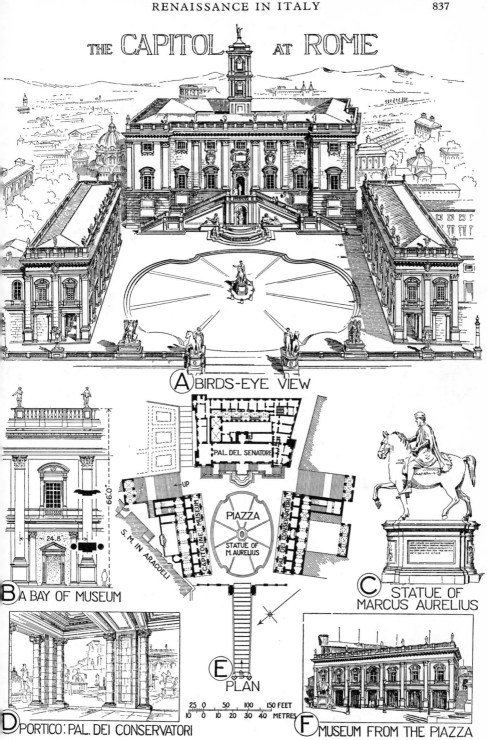

A BIRDS-EYE VIEW

B A BAY OF MUSEUM

C STATUE OF MARCUS AURELIUS

D PORTICO: PAL. DEI CONSERVATORI

E PLAN

F MUSEUM FROM THE PIAZZA

PAL. DEL SENATORE

PIAZZA

STATUE OF M. AURELIUS

S. M. IN ARACOELI

CAPITOLINE MUSEUM

PAL. DEI CONSERVATORI

25 0   50   100   150 FEET
10 0   10 20 30 40 METRES

S. PETER : ROME

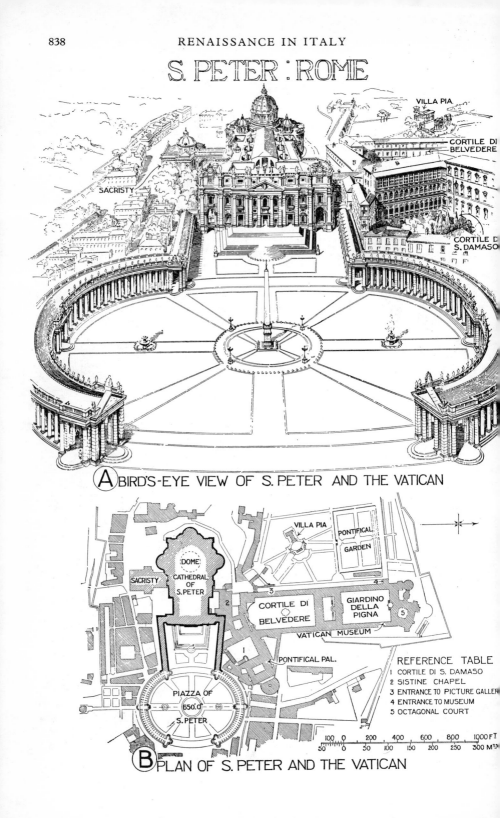

Ⓐ BIRD'S-EYE VIEW OF S. PETER AND THE VATICAN

Ⓑ PLAN OF S. PETER AND THE VATICAN

imposing staircases, and giant Corinthian pilasters carried through two storeys, while above the façade peers a campanile (1579), standing over the ancient Tabularium and overlooking the Forum Romanum. The 'Capitoline Museum' (1644–55) (p. 837A, B, E, F), which was again carried out by Girolamo Rainaldi, illustrates Michelangelo's method of securing unity by carrying up a giant Order, a feature of all three façades. The planning scheme is complemented by the fine flights of steps leading right and left to the triple-arched loggias designed (c. 1550–5) by Vignola.

S. Maria degli Angeli, Rome (p. 302A, D, F), was a daring experiment by which in 1563 Michelangelo converted the tepidarium of the Baths of Diocletian into a Christian church (p. 301). This hall 61 m × 24.4 m (200 ft × 80 ft) became the nave of the church, but in 1749 Vanvitelli transformed the nave into a huge transept, placed the entrance on the west side, and formed a deep chancel on the east. The actual bases of the ancient monolithic granite columns are over 2 m (7 ft) below the new floor constructed by Michelangelo.

Michelangelo was also responsible for many important features in the planning and final treatment of S. Peter, Rome, which is therefore dealt with under his name.

S. Peter, Rome (1506–1626) (pp. 838, 841, 842, 843), the most important building of this period, was the outcome of the work of many architects under the direction of many popes during a period of 120 years. The present Cathedral had its origin in the intention of Pope Julius II to erect a tomb house for himself (1505) (p. 780). This Pope was an outstanding personality as pontiff, statesman and patriot, with great ambitions for the papacy, the Church and Italy; so his initial personal project finally took the form of ruthlessly pulling down the old basilican church (p. 353) in order to erect such a monument as should enshrine all the magnificence which he wished to stand as associated with the papal power, the Christian religion, and the Latin race. A competition produced several designs, still preserved in the Uffizi Gallery, Florence, and that of Bramante was selected (p. 841E). In 1506 the foundation stone was laid of Bramante's church, planned as a Greek cross, and his proposed dome (p. 841B) was founded on that of the Pantheon, with the addition of a peristyle and lantern. In 1513, on the death of Julius II, Bramante was superseded by Giuliano da Sangallo, Fra Giocondo and Raphael, but the two former died in 1515. Raphael proposed a plan in the shape of a Latin cross, but, following his death in 1520, Baldassare Peruzzi, who was then appointed the architect, reverted to the Greek-cross plan. Ecclesiastical funds were now running short, there were troubles both in Church and State, and finally the sack of Rome (1527) disorganized all artistic projects. In 1536, on the death of Peruzzi, Antonio da Sangallo the Younger submitted a slightly altered plan, with an extended vestibule (p. 841G), lofty campanile, and elaborated central dome (p. 841D). On his death, ten years later, Michelangelo, then in his seventy-second year, succeeded him, and the present building owes most of its outstanding features to him. He used a Greek-cross plan (p. 841F), strengthened the piers of the dome, and redesigned the surrounding chapels and apses. Like others of Bramante's successors, Michelangelo reduced the original and indeterminate number of bays to each limb of the church from two to one. He further suppressed the proposed circumscribing ambulatories, producing thereby a more closely-knit pyramidal composition. The application of the giant order and the splaying off of the re-entrant angles furthered the external unity, while the elimination of the four campanili achieved a less sprawling mass. The effect was enhanced too by raising the level of the four minor subordinate domes to group more closely with the great central dome (p. 789A), which he planned and indeed began. The drum was completed before his death, in 1564, and he left models for this and for the lantern. From these models the dome was completed (1585–90) by Giacomo della Porta and Domenico Fontana. In 1564 Vignola had added side cupolas (pp. 838A, 842C), but these became ineffective when Carlo Maderna lengthened the nave to form a Latin cross (p. 842G), and added the gigantic façade (1606–12). Finally Bernini erected (1655–67) the noble entrance piazza, 198 m (650 ft) wide, surrounded by 284 columns forming the imposing fourfold Tuscan colonnades (pp. 838, 843A).

Cathedral, Piazza and Vatican (p. 821) form a world-famous group (p. 838A, B). The completed plan (p. 842G), of vast proportions, is a Latin cross with an internal length of 183 m (600 ft), and an internal width across the transepts of 137 m (450 ft), while the total external length, including portico, is 213.4 m (700 ft), or about half as much again as that of Salisbury Cathedral. The nave, 25.6 m (84 ft) wide, consists of four immense bays, and is about the same width as the Basilica of Constantine (p. 291E), but considerably longer. The crossing is covered by the majestic dome, 41.9 m (137 ft 6 ins) internal diameter, while the short transepts and the sanctuary are terminated by semicircular apses. The magnificent entrance portico, 71.3 m × 13.3 m (234 ft × 43 ft 6 ins), extends the whole width of the church (p. 842F, G), and leads to the interior (p. 843B), the walls of which are of brick faced with plaster coloured to imitate marble. The nave is flanked by great piers faced by a gigantic Order of Corinthian pilasters, 25.5 m (83 ft 6 ins) high, and entablature 6.1 m (20 ft) high, or nearly double the height of the Pantheon portico (p. 288), surmounted by a semicircular barrel vault, coffered, gilded and frescoed, 46 m (150 ft) above the marble pavement. The four stupendous piers, 18 m (60 ft) square which uphold the dome have colossal statues 4.9 m (16 ft) high, and the impression on gazing into the vast internal cupola, 102 m (335 ft) high, with its coloured frescoes and mosaics, is awe-inspiring and sublime. The planning of the supports of the dome and its four pendentives is in marked contrast with that of S. Paul's, London (p. 1018), with its eight piers. The Throne of S. Peter, in the western apse, is a Baroque work of Bernini, as is also the magnificent Baldachino (p. 843B), 30.5 m (100 ft) high, covering the High Altar, which stands over the alleged tomb of S. Peter in the crypt, beneath the dome.

The exterior (pp. 838A, 841A, 842C), roughly executed in travertine stone, has a giant Order of Corinthian pilasters carried round the entire building, giving unity to the design, with podium 5.5 m (18 ft), Corinthian columns and pilasters 27.5 m (90 ft 9 ins) diameter 2.7 m (9 ft), entablature 6.1 m (20 ft), attic and balustrade 11.5 m (38 ft 6 ins), which, excluding the statues, 6.1 m (20 ft) high, gives a total height of 51 m (167 ft 3 ins), or more than half as high again as the façade of S. Paul's Cathedral (p. 1018). The gigantic scale of this building can best be realized by comparison with Trajan's Column, Rome (p. 326), which is 29.7 m (97 ft 7 ins) high, with a diameter of 3.7 m (12 ft 2 ins), and is placed on a pedestal 5.5 m (18 ft) high. Thus the countless half-columns and pilasters which encircle the great Cathedral are actually only about 2.1 m (7 ft) less in height than the single column of Trajan. In no other building has an Order of such immense size been used. If Michelangelo's design for a portico of free-standing columns had been carried out, it would have been one of the most impressive features in all Christendom.

The great dome (pp. 838, 841A, C, 842), 2.7 m (9 ft) thick at base and upper part, formed of two shells of brickwork, with stone ribs supporting the crowning lantern, nearly equals that of the Pantheon in diameter, but Michelangelo set himself a very difficult problem, inasmuch as the base of his dome is nearly 76 m (250 ft) from the pavement, and depends for support only on four massive piers instead of on a continuous circular wall. No less than ten iron chains at the base have been inserted at different times to prevent the dome from spreading. Although the dome with the lantern is 137.7 m (452 ft) in height—more than twice that of the towers of Westminster Abbey—its dominating effect is impaired externally, except from a distance,

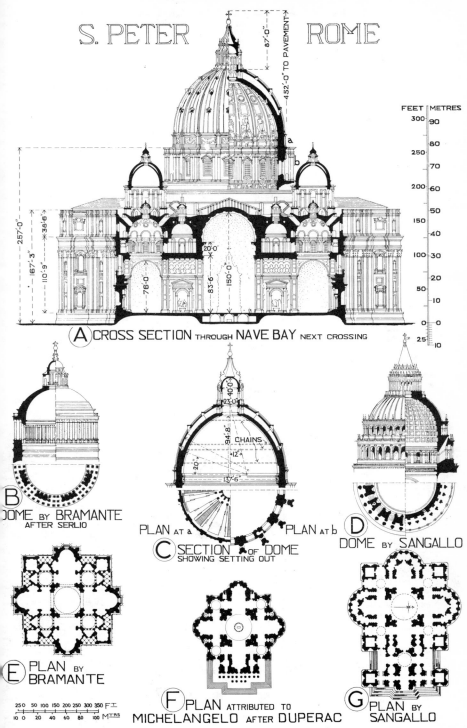

S. PETER — ROME

FEET / METRES
300 / 90
250 / 80 / 70
200 / 60
150 / 50 / 40
100 / 30
50 / 20 / 10
0 / 0
25 / 10

452'-0" TO PAVEMENT
87'-0"
257'-0"
167'-3"
110'-9"
38'-6"
76'-0"
20'-0"
83'-6"
150'-0"

A — CROSS SECTION THROUGH NAVE BAY NEXT CROSSING

B — DOME BY BRAMANTE AFTER SERLIO

PLAN AT a   PLAN AT b
40'-0"
23'-0"
94'-8"
CHAINS
20°   12°
137'-6"

C — SECTION OF DOME SHOWING SETTING OUT

D — DOME BY SANGALLO

E — PLAN BY BRAMANTE

250 50 100 150 200 250 300 350 FT
10 0   20   40   60   80   100 MTRS

F — PLAN ATTRIBUTED TO MICHELANGELO AFTER DUPERAC

G — PLAN BY SANGALLO

S. PETER : ROME

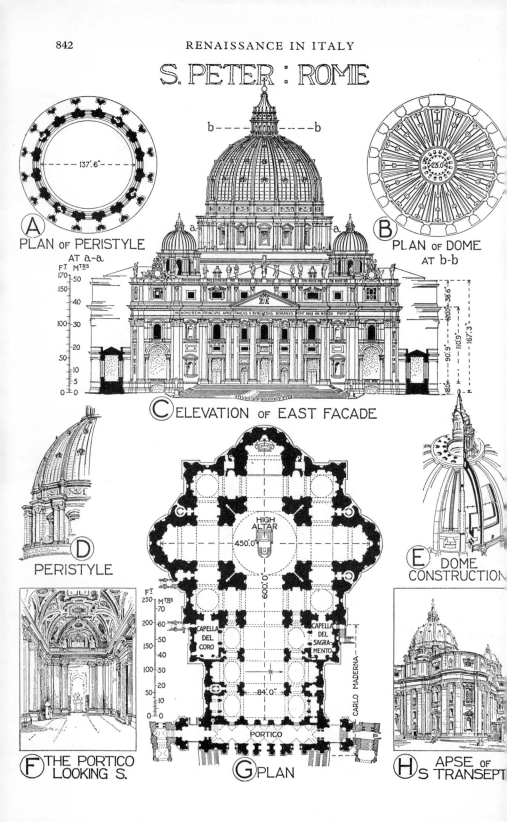

Ⓐ PLAN OF PERISTYLE
AT a-a

137′.6″

Ⓑ PLAN OF DOME
AT b-b

23.0″

b------b

a------a

Ⓒ ELEVATION OF EAST FACADE

18′.0″　90′.9″　110′.9″　167′.3″　200′-38′.6″

IN HONOREM PRINCIPIS APOST PAVLVS V BVRGHESIVS ROMANVS PONT MAX AN M DCVI PONT VII

Ⓓ PERISTYLE

Ⓔ DOME CONSTRUCTION

Ⓕ THE PORTICO LOOKING S.

Ⓖ PLAN

HIGH ALTAR
450′.0″
600′.0″
84′.0″

CAPELLA DEL CORO

CAPELLA DEL SAGRAMENTO

CARLO MADERNA

PORTICO

Ⓗ APSE OF S TRANSEPT

A. S. Peter, Rome: aerial view from E. showing Vatican on right, with covered approach from Castle of S. Angelo (1506–1626; colonnades 1655–67).
See p. 839

B. S. Peter, Rome: drawing of interior by Piranesi

A. General view, west side   B. Entrance block, west side

Palazzo Barberini, Rome (1628–38). See p. 845

C. Madonna di S. Luca, Bologna   D. Palazzo Marino, Milan:
(1723–57). See p. 851   cortile (1558–60). See p. 809

E. S. Maria Maggiore, Rome: F. Palazzo Borghese, Rome: cortile (c. 1590).
façade (1743). See p. 851   See p. 810

by Maderna's lengthened nave and additional portico, which latter is not only over 50 m (167 ft) high, but is also as much as 137 m (450 ft) from the centre of the crossing, and consequently hides the lower part of the dome from the near spectator.

DOMENICO FONTANA (1543–1607), born near Lake Lugano in Lombardy, came to Rome in 1563, where he received many commissions, including that for his share in S. Peter's, referred to above. He laid out new streets and palaces, with their ornaments and fountains, for the latter collaborating with his brother, Giovanni (1540–1614), a distinguished water-engineer. Towards the end of the century he moved to Naples, where he designed the Royal Palace (1592). Architecturally, his work is not greatly distinguished, and he represents the last stages of the Proto-Baroque in Rome.

The **Palazzo del Laterano, Rome** (1586), erected by Fontana on the site of the former palace, was, after being an orphan asylum, turned into a museum in 1843. The buildings are arranged round a court, and the astylar façade is a simple and tame version of the Palazzo Farnese treatment.

BAROQUE

CARLO MADERNA (1556–1629), also from Lake Lugano, came early to Rome and was trained under his uncle, Domenico Fontana. He is the chief figure of the early Baroque in Rome. His architecture has a vigour and robustness superior to that of his immediate predecessors, Michelangelo excepted, as is evident in the main work of his active life, the lengthening of S. Peter's.

S. Susanna, Rome (1597–1603) (p. 817B), has a façade virtually devoid of windows, their place being taken by enframed niches, comprised of two tiers of super-imposed Corinthian Orders, expressed in crisply-projecting pilasters except on the centre bays of the lower tier, where attached columns appear. The decorative interest is built up to centre strongly on the entrance doorway, the bay spacings being progressively increased in width towards it, and advanced in planes. The crowning, balustraded pediment over the nave is reflected in a lesser pediment breaking the lower cornice, and in others of segmental form serving to emphasize the upper and lower axial openings. The rich reiteration of features, as here in the theme of the pediments and in the clustered Orders, is typical Baroque practice.

The **Palazzo Barberini, Rome** (1628–38) (p. 844A, B), was only started the year before Maderna's death, but externally at least, was executed closely according to his designs by Bernini, with Borromini serving under him in a subordinate capacity: some novel features of the internal planning are due to Bernini. The plan of the palace is unusual for Rome, as it has no courtyard, and takes an 'H' shape, as, however, had been customary for some time for villas. The three-storey main façade is strongly rhythmical, like most Roman palaces, but unlike the majority is stylar, of fairly orthodox 'Roman Order' design except on the top floor, where there are overlaid pilasters, their lines carried up into the entablature, while the seven windows are treated in perspective. The elliptical staircase and the 'quadratura' paintings (1633) of the hall above by P. Cortona are noteworthy.

FLAMINIO PONZIO (1560–1613), another Lombard, was an excellent designer, though less advanced in his style than his contemporary, Maderna.

S. Sebastiano fuori le mura, Rome (1608–13) (p. 847A), completed by Vasanzio, has a chastely severe façade, of which the lower storey has arches standing on paired columns, a motif appearing also in the courtyard of the **Palazzo Borghese, Rome,** begun in 1590 by Martino Lunghi the Elder and finished by Vasanzio; and again later (1634–6) in Bianco's Palazzo dell' Università at Genoa (p. 810). Ponzio's **Fontana Paola, Rome** (1612) (p. 785H) is one of the city's finest monuments.

GIOVANNI LORENZO BERNINI (1598–1680) represents the Roman Baroque at its peak. Born in Naples, he was brought to Rome at a tender age (c. 1604), for his father was a sculptor of repute and followed his art in Florence, Naples and Rome in turn. In Rome, the father, Pietro Bernini (1562–1629) was the creator of the 'Barcaccia' (c. 1629), a boat-shaped fountain in the Piazza di Spagna, Rome, which attractively complements the spectacular 'Spanish Steps' (p. 850A). The son quickly achieved renown and social esteem. Primarily a sculptor, he was brilliant too as an architect and painter; being a facile and prodigious worker he executed a host of varied commissions in his long life, virtually all of them in and around Rome. His one and only foreign excursion was a short and abortive visit to Paris (1665) (p. 889). Much of Bernini's finest architectural as well as sculpturesque work was done for S. Peter's, where his colonnades for the piazza are world-famous (pp. 838A, 843A). He designed many altar pieces and also fountains, such as the 'Fountain of the Four Rivers' (1647–52) in the Piazza Navona, Rome (p. 849A).

S. Andrea del Quirinale, Rome (1658–70) (pp. 847B, 848A), is the best known of Bernini's churches, each of them small, but widely imitated later on. The exterior demonstrates the essential simplicity of Bernini's effects. The protruding vestibule comprises a pair of overlaid plain Corinthian pilasters, with pedimented entablature above, enclosing an archway and a semicircular two-columned porch, on which is a large, sculptured coat of arms. The church behind is a domed ellipse, 24 m (80 ft) × 16.8 m (55 ft) across, with the main axis at right angles to the approach, and from this centralized space open eight radiating chapels, making, with the entrance and sanctuary, ten recesses embedded in the very thick walls. The scheme thus is similar to that of the ancient Pantheon, Rome (p. 288); and the likeness is still more close in the case of his **S. Maria dell' Assunta, Ariccia, Rome** (1662–4), which has a domed circular plan, with eight radiating recesses in the walls. Another church at **Castel Gandolfo, Rome** (1658–61), has a simple Greek-cross plan, with a pendentived dome over the crossing.

The **Palazzo Odescalchi, Rome** (1664–) (p. 830D), has a stylar main block with a giant Corinthian pilastered Order embracing the two upper floors, in a composition which has the broad simplicity typical of Bernini. Large consoles bestride the entablature frieze, and they are paired over the line of the pilasters. The length of the central façade was doubled from the original seven bays by additions made in 1745 by Salvi and Vanvitelli.

The **Palazzo Montecitorio, Rome** (begun 1650), was completed by Carlo Fontana (1634–1714) several decades later, but much on the lines Bernini had planned.

The **Scala Regia, Rome** (1663–6) (p. 835C), a magnificent monumental stairway approach to the Vatican adjacent to the portico of S. Peter's, from which there is also an approach (p. 842G), is celebrated for its remarkable perspective effects.

FRANCESCO BORROMINI (1599–1667), born near Como and at first a sculptor, came to Rome about 1614 and trained under Carlo Maderna and Bernini. In temperament introspective and intense, his architecture is as tortuous and involved as Bernini's is direct and fundamentally simple. He committed suicide.

S. Carlo alle Quattro Fontane, Rome (1638–41, façade 1665–7) (pp. 847C, 848C), shows ingenious planning to meet the difficulties of a small and cramped site. Borromini here discards the typical Renaissance plan made up of clearly demarcated geometrical elements and adopts a scheme which, although resolving itself ultimately into an elliptical pendentived dome running east to west, begins at wall level internally as an undulated Greek cross, made up of four concave lobes passing into one another in convex curves. Undulating plan curves appear on the west front too, and henceforward Baroque architecture repeatedly exploits this kind of device.

S. Ivo della Sapienza, Rome (1642–50) (p. 847D), the church of the University,

A. S. Sebastiano fuori le mura, Rome (1608–13). See p. 845

B. S. Andrea del Quirinale, Rome (1658–70). See p. 846

C. S. Carlo alle Quattro Fontane, Rome (1638–41; façade 1665–7). See p. 846

D. S. Ivo della Sapienza, Rome: from cortile (1642–50). See p. 846

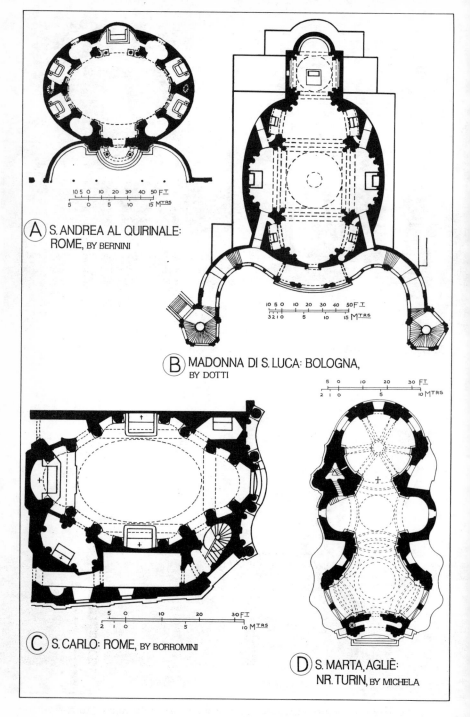

A S. ANDREA AL QUIRINALE: ROME, BY BERNINI

B MADONNA DI S. LUCA: BOLOGNA, BY DOTTI

C S. CARLO: ROME, BY BORROMINI

D S. MARTA, AGLIÈ: NR. TURIN, BY MICHELA

A. Fountain (1647–52) and S. Agnese (1652–), Rome. See pp. 846, 851

B. S. Maria della Pace, Rome: façade (1656–7). See p. 851

C. S. Maria di Monte Santo and S. Maria dei Miracoli, Rome (1662–79).
See p. 851

A. Scala di Spagna (Spanish Steps), Rome (1721–5). See p. 851

B. Fontana di Trevi, Rome
(1732–62). See p. 851

C. S. Marta, Agliè, nr Turin
(1740–58). See p. 815

the rest of which had been built by Giacomo della Porta in 1576, is another instance of the bizarre planning of Borromini, having a centralized plan contained by six lobes, of which three are semicircular and the alternate ones shaped as half-hexagons; Corinthian pilasters line the inner walls, and from their entablature springs a steep dome, retaining the plan shape internally, but masked externally by a six-lobed cupola and hexagonal lantern terminating in a corkscrew spire.

S. Agnese, Rome (1652–) (p. 849A), facing the Piazza Navona, was begun by Rainaldi, continued by Borromini from 1653–5 and completed by others by 1666. The plan is comparatively restrained, but the splendid composition, with recessed front, twin campanili and commanding dome is largely due to Borromini.

PIETRO DA CORTONA (1596–1669), distinguished painter and architect, was of the same generation as Bernini and Borromini; his early architecture had great vigour and originality, but became more commonplace in later life. He carried out very many commissions, both ecclesiastical and domestic.

S. Maria della Pace, Rome, the church to which Bramante had added the cloister (p. 785E), was rebuilt by Cortona, with a fine façade and semicircular portico (1656–7) (p. 849B) which well represent the vigorous modelling of this architect's schemes. He obtains forceful expression by the interplay of convex and concave plan forms at large and at small scale, or by advancing and receding planes, while securing richness by a lavish use of columns and pilasters. He rarely employed the giant Order, but expressed his buildings in distinct tiers. Similar characteristics appear in his **SS. Martina and Luca, Rome** (1634–47) and the façade of **S. Maria in Via Lata, Rome** (1658–62).

CARLO RAINALDI (1611–91), another High Baroque architect, is of only slightly less importance than the three last named. His extensive church work includes the commencement of S. Agnese, Rome, mentioned above, and the reconstruction (1673) of the east end of the old Basilica of S. Maria Maggiore, Rome.

S. Maria di Monte Santo and S. Maria dei Miracoli, Rome (1662–79) (p. 849C), are twin churches by Rainaldi dividing three main roads of central Rome as they leave the Piazza del Popolo, skilfully planned to present a fine civic effect towards the square. As there is a difference in width of their sites, the plans are not identical, and to give the illusion of symmetry externally, the central space and covering dome of S. Maria di Monte Santo are made elliptical in the depth of the church, while in the other church they are based on a circular plan. Both domes have faceted drums externally. When approaching completion, Bernini was given charge of the Monte Santo church.

CARLO DOTTI (1670–1759) represents the eighteenth-century Late Baroque at Bologna, in the north of the Papal territories, where the **Madonna di S. Luca** (1723–57) (pp. 844C, 848B), a finely-massed, hill-top pilgrimage church outside the city, is his masterpiece. In situation it resembles the Superga, Turin (p. 812A).

ALESSANDRO SPECCHI (1668–1729) was an able civic designer who, among other works, began the delightful **Scala di Spagna, Rome** ('Spanish Steps') (1721–5) (p. 850A), connecting in cleverly-varied curvilinear flights and landings the Piazza di Spagna with SS. Trinità de' Monti. It was, however, FRANCESCO DE SANCTIS (1693–1740) who took over in 1723 and completed the design.

ALESSANDRO GALILEI (1691–1737) carried out the principal façade of **S. Giovanni in Laterano, Rome** (1733–6) (p. 867B), entrusted to him as the result of an important architectural competition.

NICOLA SALVI (1697–1751) has claims to fame for his **Fontana di Trevi, Rome** (1732–62) (p. 850B), finished by Pannini.

FERDINANDO FÙGA (1699–1780), the designer of the entrance façade of **S. Maria Maggiore, Rome** (1743) (p. 844E), was the last notable Baroque architect of Rome.

FILIPPO RAGUZZINI (1680–1771) designed the **Piazza S. Ignazio, Rome** (1727–8); FERDINANDO SANFELICE (1675–1750) is renowned for the ingenuity of his staircase designs for various palaces in **Naples,** including the **Palazzo Serra Cassano;** while amongst the most notable buildings designed by LUIGI VANVITELLI (1700–73) is the **Palazzo Reale, Caserta** (1752).

VENICE

EARLY RENAISSANCE

PIETRO LOMBARDO (1435–1515) was one of a family who impressed their personality upon the architecture of the sea-girt city, where the Renaissance arrived much later than in Florence.

The **Doge's Palace, Venice,** commenced in the Mediaeval period (p. 743), was continued at this time. The Cortile (p. 853) was undertaken by Antonio Rizzo from about 1485, continued by Pietro Lombardo from 1499–1511, and completed by Antonio Scarpagnino in 1545–50. The Cortile façades are transitional in retaining series of pointed arcades, but are otherwise quite Renaissance in character (p. 853B, C, E), especially the upper tier of the south face of the small Court of the Senators (p. 853C). Inside the main entrance (Porta della Carta) is the famous 'Giants' Staircase (Scala dei Giganti) (1485–9), flanked by Sansovino's figures of Mars and Neptune (p. 853A, B). The Ducal Palace is equally renowned for its external Gothic arcades (p. 730) and its sumptuously-enriched apartments, with their elaborate chimney-pieces (p. 786J) and stucco-encrusted walls and ceilings enriched with paintings by Veronese and Tintoretto and many other famous artists. The **Bridge of Sighs** (c. 1595) (p. 853D), connecting the Palace and the prison, is a romantic feature, with its elliptical arch, rusticated pilasters and heraldic devices.

The **Palazzo Corner Spinelli, Venice** (c. 1480) (p. 855B), which may be by one of the Lombardi family, is a delightful example of the Early Renaissance, and has some fine apartments. The symmetrical elevation; the dignified axial entrance from the Grand Canal; the balconied windows, so disposed as to give extra light to the large rooms reaching the centre of the façade; the strong angle treatment; all are traditional features in Venice, carried on from the Mediaeval period (p. 745B, E).

The **Palazzo Vendramini, Venice** (1481) (p. 855), ascribed to Pietro Lombardo, has the customary three-floored scheme and window arrangement, but is stylar, the attached Corinthian Order, with varied designs for the capitals, being used for each floor (p. 855E, G). The top entablature is made abnormally deep so as to serve as a fitting termination for the whole front, and, as usual in Venetian palaces, the full architectural treatment is confined to the main façade. The bifurcated, traceried windows (p. 855F), retaining a Mediaeval note, are typical of the Early Renaissance in Venetia. The charming balconies (p. 855G) still retain the miniature columns in place of the true baluster by this time usual in Italy elsewhere.

S. Maria dei Miracoli, Venice (1481–9) (p. 854), designed by Pietro Lombardo, is a marvel of marble work, both within and without. This miniature church has an aisleless nave covered internally by a deep segmental wooden roof with gilded panels, and with a non-concentric semicircular roof showing externally. The recessed sanctuary and the choir over the sacristy are approached by a wide flight of steps, flanked by marble balustrades and twin pulpits, while the altar is enclosed with beautiful pierced screenwork (p. 787H). Above the sanctuary is a small pendentived dome with a shallow, windowed drum. The east end, with its adjacent circular staircase carried up as a domed turret, and the lead-covered, external timber dome over the sanctuary, forms a delightful composition as seen from the nearby

DOGE'S PALACE : VENICE

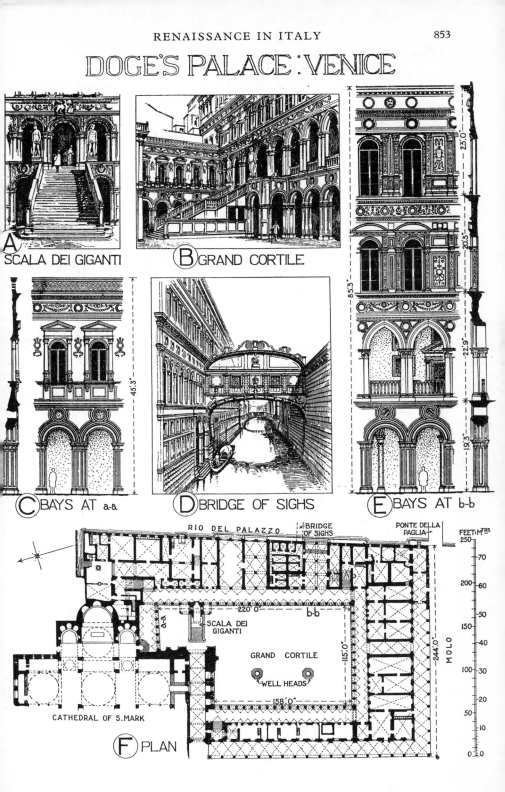

A SCALA DEI GIGANTI

B GRAND CORTILE

C BAYS AT a-a

D BRIDGE OF SIGHS

E BAYS AT b-b

45.3"

85.3"

23.0'

20.3'

22.9'

19.3'

RIO DEL PALAZZO

BRIDGE OF SIGHS

PONTE DELLA PAGLIA

220'0"

b-b

a-a

SCALA DEI GIGANTI

GRAND CORTILE

WELL HEADS

115.'0"

158.'0"

244.'0"

MOLO

CATHEDRAL OF S.MARK

F PLAN

FEET MTRS
250
200
150
100
50
0
70
60
50
40
30
20
10
0

S. MARIA DEI MIRACOLI : VENICE

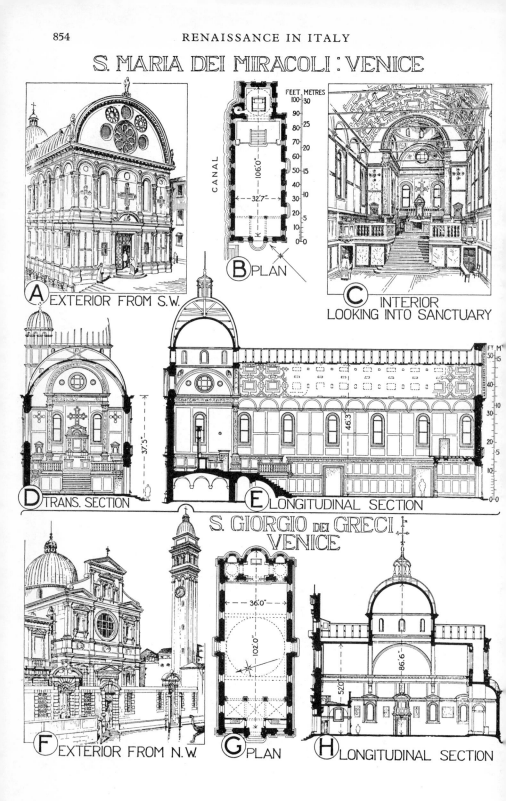

A EXTERIOR FROM S.W.

B PLAN

FEET METRES
100—30
90
80—25
70
60—20
50—15
40
30—10
20—5
10
0—0

CANAL

106'0"

32'7"

C INTERIOR LOOKING INTO SANCTUARY

D TRANS. SECTION

37'5"

E LONGITUDINAL SECTION

FT M
50—15
40—10
30
20—5
10
0—0

46'3"

S. GIORGIO dei GRECI : VENICE

F EXTERIOR FROM N.W.

G PLAN

36'0"

102'0"

H LONGITUDINAL SECTION

86'6"

52'0"

PAL. PESARO VENICE

PAL. CORNER SPINELLI: VENICE

PAL. CORNER DELLA CA' GRANDE: VENICE

A

B

C

PALAZZO VENDRAMINI : VENICE

D EXTERIOR FROM GRAND CANAL

BALCONY AT FIRST FLOOR LEVEL

E ORDERS TO FIRST & SECND FLOORS

F FIRST FLOOR WINDOW

G ORDER TO GROUND FLOOR

A. Exterior   B. Interior

S. Maria della Salute, Venice (1631–82). See p. 864

C. The Scuola di San Marco, Venice, from S. (1485–95). See p. 857

canal. The walls of the church are faced internally and externally with coloured marbles. The exterior (p. 854A), although clothing a one-storeyed structure, has two stages of superimposed pilasters, the upper as a blind arcade recalling Mediaeval treatment, while the roof runs through on the west front to a semicircular pediment, such as is seen at S. Zaccaria and the Scuola di S. Marco (p. 856C), probably borrowed from the Byzantines, with whom it represented the exterior of their vaults.

S. Zaccaria, Venice (1458–1515) and **S. Giobbe, Venice** (1451–93), are other early examples which have many interesting features, and show much the same character as the work of the Lombardi.

FRA GIOCONDO (1435–1515), a native of Verona, in later life worked in Rome, where for the two years before his death he was associated with the work at S. Peter's (p. 839).

The **Palazzo del Consiglio, Verona** (1476–92) (p. 860H), is notable for the delicate arcade, with columns directly supporting arches, after the manner of the Foundling Hospital, Florence (p. 793), but stiffened with a pilaster midway. The upper tier has paired segmental-headed windows of a Venetian type, and panelled arabesque decoration.

S. Maria dei Miracoli, Brescia (1488–) (p. 806B), was designed by Mastro Jacopo, but work continued slowly, and the scheme was altered in 1522. The delicately-sculptured marble façade of the earlier portion included a remarkably ornate porch.

S. Salvatore, Venice (1506–34), by Tullio Lombardo, a son of the famous Pietro, and Giorgio Spavento, has a Baroque façade (1663) and a plan somewhat similar to Alberti's S. Andrea, Mantua (p. 796J), but with a nave covered by two large domes, repeating, precisely, the dome over the crossing. In this manner of covering the church, the Byzantine influence is strongly apparent.

The **Scuola di S. Marco, Venice** (1485–95) (p. 856C), now the City Hospital, by Martino Lombardo, has a façade which echoes that of S. Mark. The ground storey has Corinthian pilasters between which are panels bearing some curious perspective reliefs. These are by Tullio Lombardo, and bear witness to the intense interest of artists in the science of perspective at this period, evidenced also in Bramante's S. Satiro, Milan (p. 816). The pediment over the doorway and those serving as cresting, again are semicircular, and bear acroteria decorations at base and apex.

S. Giorgio dei Greci, Venice (1538–), in which Sante Lombardo had a part, is a graceful little building in the style of the Early period, except the façade, which is mature Renaissance. It has an aisleless plan (p. 854G), somewhat resembling S. Maria dei Miracoli (p. 854B), and a triapsal sanctuary (p. 854G). A dome is placed centrally over the nave (p. 854H), while the exterior (p. 854F) has a rather unusual treatment, terminating in three pediments, and the group is completed with a lofty campanile (1587).

HIGH RENAISSANCE AND PROTO-BAROQUE

MICHELE SANMICHELE (1484–1559), born at Verona, was trained in Rome from the age of sixteen. He acquired distinction as a military engineer, and after 1527 was employed by the Venetian Republic in the design of fortifications. His work in architecture consequently has great vigour, and he often makes use of rustication, sometimes on the Orders themselves. His originality was not unduly restrained by observance of Roman precedent. The **Porta Nuova** (1533–40) and the **Porta del Palio** (1542–55), **Verona** (p. 868A) are excellent instances of his bold treatments. The **Palazzo Bevilacqua, Verona** (1527–) (p. 860J), has rustications carrying across the pilasters on the ground storey and spirally-fluted Corinthian attached columns on the upper tier, arranged in alternating spacings suggestive of the Roman 'triumphal arch' motif. These features of the upper floor, and the smaller arched openings capped by alternating triangular and segmental-headed pediments, all have direct precedents in Roman arches still existing in the city, but the sculptured spandrels and keystones are his own innovations.

The **Palazzo Pompeii, Verona** (1530–) (p. 860), is a stately composition on axial lines, with a simple arched portal leading to a cortile. A rusticated basement, with arched windows, supports the 'piano nobile', with its fluted Doric columns, tall semicircular-headed windows and carved masks on keystones (p. 860c).

The **Palazzo Grimani, Venice** (1556–) (p. 859), facing the Grand Canal, is Sanmichele's greatest work. The plan is most cleverly contrived on an irregular island site with three large openings to the columned vestibule and long hall, off which are the staircases. The symmetrical façade, 27.5 m (90 ft) long and 29.5 m (97 ft) high, has superimposed Corinthian Orders, the lower comprising two storeys and the whole bound together with a striking balcony stretching from end to end. By doubling the Order to demarcate the end windows, the customary Venetian fenestration is preserved. A crowning entablature, 2.6 m (8 ft 8 ins) high, is proportioned to the full height of the façade.

The **Palazzo dei Diamanti, Ferrara** (completed 1555) (p. 860G), has a façade showing some influence of Sanmichele, with faceted rustications, whence the name.

The **Gran Guardia Vecchia, Verona** (1610–) (p. 860), for public meetings, is the work of Domenico Curtoni, nephew and pupil of Sanmichele, and is more purely Classical than any of the buildings of the uncle. The façade, over 86.5 m (285 ft) long, has a rusticated ground storey with semicircular arches, and an upper tier graced with a stately line of coupled Doric columns, surmounted by an entablature, while the centre is emphasized by an upper storey.

JACOPO SANSOVINO (1486–1570), sculptor and architect, born in Florence and trained there and in Rome, settled in Venice in 1527, where all his most important work is to be found. He was among the first to react from the strict Classical rule, and shows himself a skilful assimilator, borrowing ideas from Peruzzi, Sanmichele and other contemporaries and blending them cleverly in a unique manner.

The **Zecca, Venice** (1536–) has a peculiar treatment of column rustication, giving a severe appearance in keeping with its purpose as a mint.

The **Library of S. Mark, Venice** (1536–53) (pp. 730A, 861) is the most outstanding of the buildings by Sansovino, finished with magnificent sculptural grace. It has arcades of superimposed Ionic over Doric Orders, the upper embracing minor Ionic columns sustaining the window arches. The use of a deep, windowed, frieze in the upper entablature (p. 861B, D) gives the necessary extra importance to allow it to command the whole height of the façade, while the rich ornament of reclining figures in the arch spandrels and of cherubs and festoons in the upper frieze, remains firmly subservient to the architectural lines. The adjacent building, facing into the Piazza di S. Marco, rising one storey higher than the Library, was commenced by Scamozzi in 1584. This and the corresponding structures on the opposite side of the Piazza once were a series of residences for the nine 'Procurators', the chief officials of the Republic after the Doge.

The **Palazzo Corner della Ca' Grande, Venice** (1537–56) (p. 855C) has excellent proportions and stands on an imposing site fronting the Grand Canal. The lower part is rusticated and has three central openings flanked by windows in two tiers, while the two upper storeys are faced with paired Ionic and Corinthian Orders, embracing circular-headed windows. The windowed frieze is used again, but the arrangement of the windows has now become completely regular.

PAL. GRIMANI : VENICE

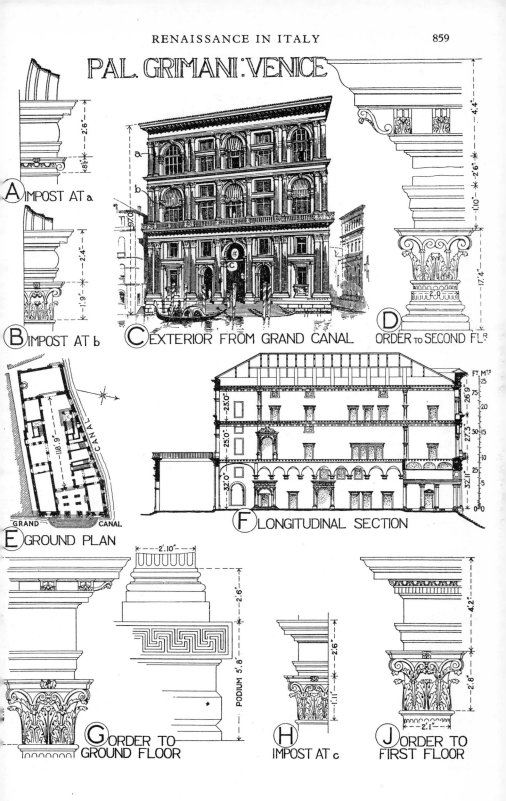

A IMPOST AT a

B IMPOST AT b

C EXTERIOR FROM GRAND CANAL

D ORDER TO SECOND FL.R

E GROUND PLAN

F LONGITUDINAL SECTION

G ORDER TO GROUND FLOOR

H IMPOST AT c

J ORDER TO FIRST FLOOR

PALAZZO POMPEI : VERONA

CORTILE

136'0"

70'3"

Ⓐ PLAN

Ⓑ EXTERIOR FROM W.

Ⓒ A BAY

44'0"

8'10"

18'0"

13'6"

GRAN GUARDIA VECCHIA : VERONA

285'10"

33'6"

38'7"

Ⓓ SECTION

Ⓔ VIEW FROM E.

Ⓕ SIDE BAY

72'1"

20'11"

13'6"

OTHER PALACES

Ⓖ PAL. DEI DIAMANTI

Ⓗ PALAZZO DEL CONSIGLIO

Ⓙ PAL. BEVILACQUA

LIBRARY of S.MARK: VENICE

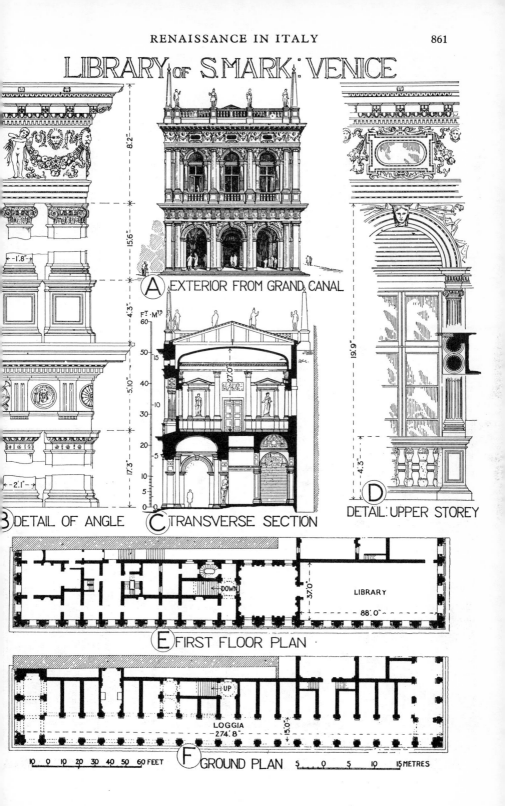

A EXTERIOR FROM GRAND CANAL

B DETAIL OF ANGLE

C TRANSVERSE SECTION

D DETAIL: UPPER STOREY

LIBRARY
37'0"
88'0"

E FIRST FLOOR PLAN

LOGGIA
274'8"
15'0"

F GROUND PLAN

10 0 10 20 30 40 50 60 FEET   5 0 5 10 15 METRES

THE BASILICA : VICENZA

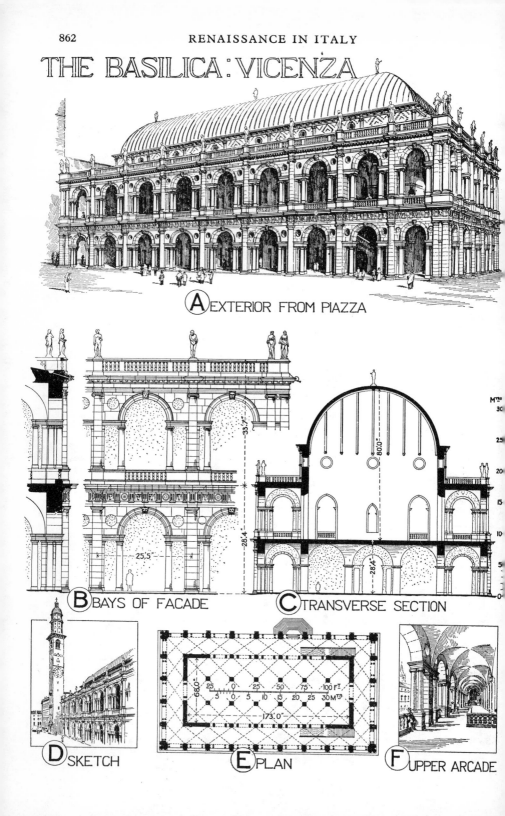

Ⓐ EXTERIOR FROM PIAZZA

Ⓑ BAYS OF FACADE

Ⓒ TRANSVERSE SECTION

Ⓓ SKETCH

Ⓔ PLAN

Ⓕ UPPER ARCADE

The **Loggetta, Venice** (1540–) (p. 786H), at the base of the great Campanile of S. Mark, is a light and graceful structure with detached Corinthian columns arranged in Sansovino's favourite 'triumphal arch' disposition, with a high attic and balustrade over. It is richly adorned with sculptures.

ANDREA PALLADIO (1508–80), the most influential architect of the whole Renaissance, was born in Padua and at first trained as a mason. Moving to Vicenza about 1524, his second home, where so much of his work was to be done, he secured the patronage of a connoisseur, with whom, after 1540, the date on which he first appears as an architect, he twice voyaged to Rome and made the intensive studies of ancient remains which led eventually to the publication of his famous book *I quattro libri dell' Architettura*. The results of his Classical research and his preoccupation with harmonic proportions can be traced in his designs for buildings both in Venice and Vicenza. They were unfortunately mostly in mean materials, such as brick faced with stucco, and the success he achieved is an instance of how genius can produce works of art out of commonplace materials. Some of his buildings were never completed, or were finished by others, but the publication of the designs in his book, first issued in Venice in 1570, and since published in every country in Europe, has had a far greater influence on architecture than have his buildings; especially in England, where Palladio had an ardent disciple in Inigo Jones (p. 980), who published an annotated edition of this book.

The **Palazzo Chiericati** (designed 1550, completed *c.* 1580), **Palazzo Thiene** (1556), **Palazzo Valmarana** (1566) (p. 865D), **Palazzo Barbarano** (1570), **Palazzo Capitanio** (1571) and **Casa del Diavolo** (1571) (p. 865G) at **Vicenza,** are some of the palaces exhibiting rusticated lower storeys supporting an Order often carried through the height of a building to give unity of design. He also built very many splendid villas in the Venetian countryside.

The **Teatro Olimpico, Vicenza** (1580–4), with a permanent stage built in perspective, is an interesting building, designed by Palladio but completed by Scamozzi (p. 811B), and inspired by ancient Roman theatres.

The **Basilica, Vicenza** (1549) (p. 862), is famous for its Renaissance arcades added by Palladio to the Mediaeval structure erected in 1444. The design was won in competition in 1545, and completed 1614. The plan (p. 862E) shows the large Mediaeval hall, 52.5 m × 20.7 m (173 ft × 68 ft), with its supporting piers which gave the lines for the Renaissance piers of the surrounding arcades, while the transverse section (p. 862C) shows the upper floor, which regulated the height of the surrounding Orders. The arcades showing the cross-vaults and the twin columns supporting the arches are very impressive (p. 862F). Palladio had to adjust the arcades as an outer husk to the width and height of the Gothic building. The end bays on each façade were unrestricted in width, so Palladio made them narrower in order to give an effect of strength at the angles, as had been previously done by the Greeks, e.g. the Parthenon (p. 194). These arcades (p. 862B), in fine hard stone which has beautifully weathered, consist of superimposed Doric and Ionic Orders which, under the main entablature, frame intervening arches supported on smaller free-standing twin columns, and there are circular openings in the spandrels. This grouping and combination of columns and arches has been termed the 'Palladian motif', and is exceedingly effective, especially when seen in conjunction with the slender campanile alongside (p. 862D).

The **Villa Capra, Vicenza** (1552–) (p. 865), known also as the Rotonda, is a square building with pillared portico on each face, leading to a central circular hall of which only the low dome appears externally above the tiled roof, which is hipped from the angles of the main building. This design was an important departure, and caught the popular taste. It was utilized by Lord Burlington at Chiswick (p. 1041B) and by Colen Campbell at Mereworth Castle, Kent (pp. 1041A, 1051G), and has often been copied both in England and on the Continent.

The **Villa Barbaro, Maser** (1560–8) has a central block with no portico, and is supported by arcaded wings of the attached farm buildings. The cruciform hall is famous for its trompe l'oeil paintings by Paolo Veronese.

S. Giorgio Maggiore, Venice (1565–) (pp. 866, 867A), has a cruciform plan with apsidal transepts. The interior has piers faced with Corinthian columns and the façade, completed by Scamozzi (1602–10), shows the adaptation of Classic Orders to a church of the basilican plan. The church, with pedimented façade, dome, turrets and campanile, stands on an island in the Lagoon (p. 866B).

Il Redentore, Venice (1577–92) (p. 866), is similar in plan, but there are side chapels in lieu of aisles. In the façade the principal and subsidiary Orders start from the same base, and the aisles are fronted with half-pediments. This church shows how impossible it is to judge a building from a geometrical drawing only, for in a near view (p. 866J) the dome over the crossing is dwarfed by the long arm of the nave, as in S. Peter, Rome.

BAROQUE

BALDASSARE LONGHENA (1598–1682), a pupil of Scamozzi and contemporary with Bernini, was by far the most distinguished Venetian architect of the period.

S. Maria della Salute, Venice (1631–82) (p. 856A, B), groups most effectively with the Dogana (Custom House) (1676) on the Grand Canal, and is sufficient to stamp the architect as a man of genius. The church is octagonal in form, with a central space, 20 m (65 ft) in diameter, with Corinthian columns in the angles (p. 856B), and the spacious surrounding ambulatory and radiating chapels make it one of the largest aisled, polygonal churches. The circular dome with high drum is connected to the outer walls by scrolled buttresses which contribute much to the effect (p. 856A). The second dome with its flanking turrets over the wide chancel adds to the picturesqueness of this majestic group, which, throned upon its measured steps above the canal, is the apotheosis of the Baroque style in Venice.

The **Palazzo Pesaro, Venice** (1663–79) (p. 855A) was not finished in Longhena's lifetime and the top floor was added by Gaspari (1710). It is similar to the Palazzo Corner della Ca' Grande (p. 855C) of 126 years previously, but the columns are fully detached and combined with minor Orders carrying the window archivolts. Also, there is here a return to the traditional demarcation of the central group and the flank windows of the main façade.

The **Palazzo Rezzonico, Venice** (1667–) (p. 868B) again was finished after Longhena's death, the top floor being added by Massari in 1752–6. Except that the decorative columns are single rather than coupled, it bears a still closer resemblance to Sansovino's Palazzo Corner della Ca' Grande, having a regular disposition of windows across the façade. In this case there is an attached Order on the ground storey too, the column shafts, as well as the walls, being rusticated.

The **Palazzo Labia, Venice,** has frescoes in the ballroom by Tiepolo (1745).

BIBLIOGRAPHY

ACKERMAN, J. S. *The Architecture of Michelangelo.* 2 vols. London, 1966.
—. *Palladio.* Harmondsworth, 1966.
ACTON, H. *Tuscan Villas.* London, 1973.
BALLO, A. *Torino barocco.* Rome, 1965.
BLUNT, A. *Artistic Theory in Italy: 1450–1600.* London, 1962 and 1966.

VILLA CAPRA: VICENZA

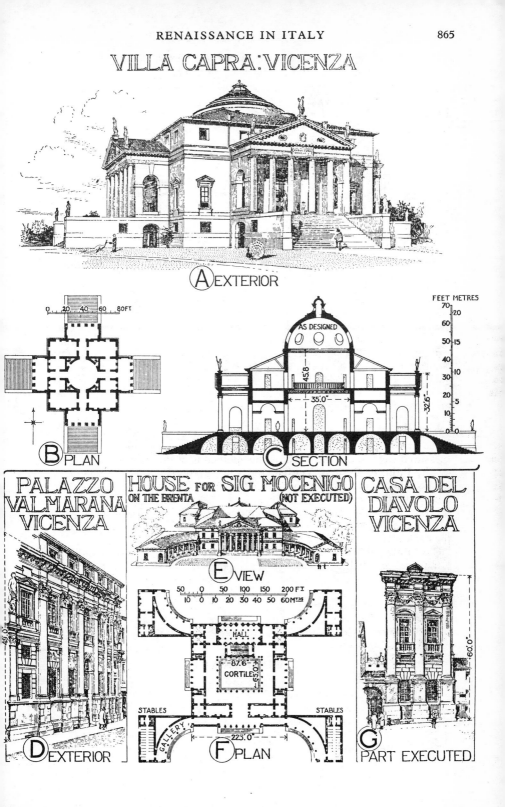

Ⓐ EXTERIOR

Ⓑ PLAN

Ⓒ SECTION

AS DESIGNED

FEET METRES

PALAZZO VALMARANA VICENZA

Ⓓ EXTERIOR

HOUSE FOR SIG. MOCENIGO
ON THE BRENTA (NOT EXECUTED)

Ⓔ VIEW

HALL

CORTILE

STABLES   STABLES

GALLERY

Ⓕ PLAN

CASA DEL DIAVOLO VICENZA

Ⓖ PART EXECUTED

S. GIORGIO MAGGIORE : VENICE

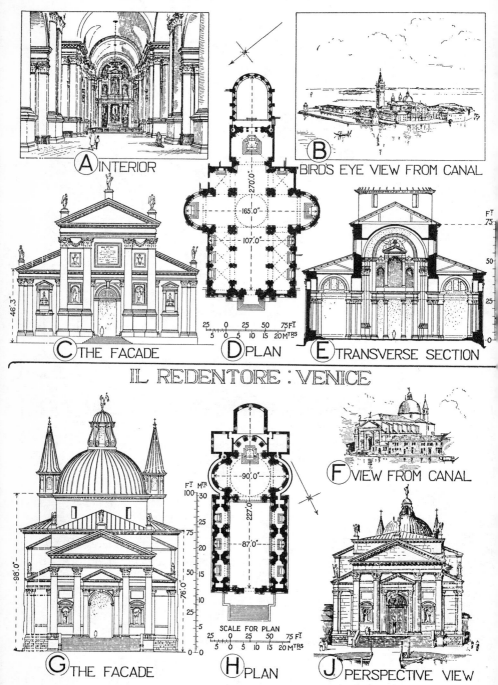

Ⓐ INTERIOR

Ⓑ BIRDS EYE VIEW FROM CANAL

Ⓒ THE FACADE

Ⓓ PLAN

Ⓔ TRANSVERSE SECTION

IL REDENTORE : VENICE

Ⓕ VIEW FROM CANAL

Ⓖ THE FACADE

Ⓗ PLAN

Ⓙ PERSPECTIVE VIEW

A. S. Giorgio Maggiore, Venice (1565–1610). See p. 864

B. S. Giovanni in Laterano, Rome: façade (1733–6). See p. 851

A. The Porta del Palio, Verona (1542–55). See p. 857

B. Palazzo Rezzonico, Venice (1667–1756). See p. 864

BRIZIO, A. M. *L'architettura barocca in Piemonte*. Turin, 1953.

BURCKHARDT, J. *The Civilization of the Renaissance in Italy*. London, 1955 (and many other editions).

CARLI, E. *Brunelleschi*. Milan, 1952.

CHASTEL, A. *Italian Art*. London, 1963.

CHIERICI, G. *Bramante*. Milan, 1954.

—. *Palladio*. Turin, 1952.

DONATI, C. *Carlo Maderna*. Lugano, 1957.

FRANCK, C. L. *The Villas of Frascati: 1550–1750*. London, 1966.

GADOL, J. *L.-B. Alberti, Universal Man of the Early Renaissance*. Chicago, 1969.

HAUPT, A. (Ed.) *Renaissance Palaces in Northern Italy and Tuscany*. 3 vols. London, 1931.

HUGHES, J. Q., and LYNTON, N. *Simpson's History of Architectural Development*. Vol. iv of new edition. London, 1962.

LEES-MILNE, J. *Roman Mornings*. London, 1956.

LETAROUILLY, P. M. *Student's Letarouilly illustrating the Renaissance in Rome*. London, 1948.

LOWRY, B. *Renaissance Architecture*. New York and London, 1962.

—. *Venice Observed*. New York and London, 1956.

MASSON, G. *Italian Gardens*. London, 1961.

—. *Italian Villas and Palaces*. London, 1959.

MAZZOTTI, G. *Palladian and other Venetian Villas*. London, 1966.

MCCARTHY, M. *Stones of Florence*. New York and London, 1958–9.

MILLON, H. A. *Baroque and Rococo*. New York and London, 1961.

MURRAY, P. *The Architecture of the Italian Renaissance*. London, 1963.

PEROTTI, M. V. *Borromini*. Milan, 1951.

PORTOGHESI, P. *Borromini*. London, 1968.

—. *Guarino Guarini*. Milan, 1956.

ROVERE, L., VITALE, V., and BRINCKMANN, A. E. *Fillipo Juvarra*. Milan, 1937.

SCOTT, G. *The Architecture of Humanism*. London, 1914.

SEMENZATO, C. *L'architettura di Baldassare Longhena*. Padua, 1954.

SHEARMAN, J. *Mannerism*. London, 1967.

SHEPHERD, J. C., and JELLICOE, G. A. *Italian Gardens of the Renaissance*. London, 1966.

WITTKOWER, R. *Architectural Principles in the Age of Humanism*. 3rd ed. London, 1952.

—. *Art and Architecture of Italy, 1600–1750*. Harmondsworth and Baltimore, 1966.

WÖLFFLIN, H. *Renaissance und Barock*. English trans. London, 1964.

REPRINTS OF HISTORICALLY IMPORTANT TEXTS

ALBERTI, L. B. *Ten Books of Architecture*. English trans. by J. Leoni of 1726. London, 1955.

BORROMINI, F. *Opera et Opus Architectonicum*. Ridgewood, N.J., 1965.

GUARINI, D. GUARINO. *Architettura civile* (1738). Ridgewood, N.J., 1964.

PALLADIO, A. *The Four Books of Architecture*. English trans. by Isaac Ware of 1738. New York, 1965.

VASARI, G. *Lives of the most eminent Painters, Sculptors and Architects*. London, 1964.

A. Château de Blois from N.W. (1515–24). See p. 878

B. Château de Chambord from N. (1519–47). See p. 881

28

RENAISSANCE ARCHITECTURE IN FRANCE

Fifteenth to nineteenth century

INFLUENCES

GEOGRAPHICAL

France had, since the Romanesque and Gothic periods (pp. 486, 585), become one united kingdom, with Paris as the centre, from which the new Renaissance influence radiated to all parts of the country. This new geographical condition conduced to a homogeneous development within her extended boundaries, in striking contrast to the variety displayed at this period in the independent city-states of Italy. The distance of Paris from the centre of the Renaissance movement in Italy helped to delay its adoption in France but Italian influences, long powerful in the southern commercial capital of Lyons, grew rapidly from 1500.

GEOLOGICAL

We have already seen in considering the Romanesque and Gothic periods (pp. 486, 585) that throughout France there was good building stone, easily worked; so much so that Paris, in which many of the finest buildings were erected under the influence of the now powerful court, is consequently a city of stone, just as, under different geological conditions, London is a city of brick. Iron, wrought and cast, came into use as a building material shortly after 1780.

CLIMATIC

The climate, as in previous periods (pp. 486, 585), asserted its influence on architecture in demanding a continuance of large windows, high-pitched roofs and lofty chimneys, which differentiated Renaissance architecture in France from that in Italy, the land of its birth.

HISTORICAL, SOCIAL AND RELIGIOUS

The chief factor in the process of building up the Kingdom of France was the struggle to expel the English, inspired by Joan of Arc's leadership (1429–31) and culminating in the expulsion of the English in 1453. A new national feeling was then created, which, as in other countries under similar conditions, gave a great impetus to architecture, and resulted in the erection of many fine buildings, which have since been held worthy to rank as national monuments. During the first half of the sixteenth century Italy became the battlefield of Europe, for in 1494 Charles VIII of France marched through Italy to claim the Kingdom of Naples, and in 1508 Louis XII joined the League of Cambrai against Venice, when Florence became the ally of France. Francis I also invaded Italy to substantiate his claim to the duchy of Milan, but was defeated and taken prisoner at the battle of Pavia, 1525. In these wars the French kings, while failing in their actual object, were brought into contact with the older civilization of Italy and were thus drawn into the Renaissance movement. Following the disturbances caused by the religious wars of the second half of the sixteenth century, there began a long period of firm government commencing with the reign of Henry IV (1589), first of the Bourbon dynasty, which endured for some two hundred years. France then achieved an unprecedented unity, power and splendour, establishing a prestige in Europe which was not secured without civil and religious tribulations and military and diplomatic clashes with her neighbours. The long reign of Louis XIV (1643–1715) marked the zenith of French power and influence in Europe, though its last years were clouded by military defeats. The advent of Louis XV (1715) heralded a decline, culminating in the Revolution of 1789; this being succeeded by republican governments soon in aggressive conflict with England and the majority of the European states. Napoleon Bonaparte emerged as an omnipotent national figure, establishing an Empire (1804–14) by feats of arms; but, facing reverses and the defeat of his marshals in France, abdicated and retired to the island of Elba. He returned again in 1815 to lead a brief campaign against his country's foes, only to meet disaster at the hands of Wellington at Waterloo in the same year. Bourbons (Louis XVIII and Charles X) reigned again until 1830.

Paris, as the capital of the newly consolidated kingdom of France and as the centre of the brilliant court of Francis I, attained pre-eminence in art and literature. This resulted in the adoption of one national architectural style which emanated from Paris and the schools in the vicinity; while the valley of the Loire became a highway along which, in response to new social conditions, the famous châteaux of kings and courtiers sprang up and formed models for other parts of the country. This influence was largely augmented by the presence of a number of Italian artists at the court and in the so-called 'schools', established first at Amboise by Charles VIII, and afterwards at Tours, Blois and, most importantly, Fontainebleau. Notable among the Italian artists were the following, the length of residence in France being given in parenthesis after each name: Giuliano da Sangallo (1495; a brief visit only) (pp. 797, 839) and Fra Giocondo (1495–1505) (p. 857), neither of whom has left much trace of his stay; Domenico da Cortona, known as Boccadoro (1495–1549), pupil of Giuliano da Sangallo, a woodworker who only emerged as an architect in 1519; the great Leonardo da Vinci (1516–19), who died at Amboise in the latter year; Giovanni Battista di Giacopo, known as Il Rosso (1530–40) and Francesco Primaticcio (1532–70) (p. 828), both being highly important in introducing Proto-Baroque or 'Mannerist' architectural practices, chiefly decorative, into France; Benvenuto Cellini (1537, and again, 1538–45), celebrated goldsmith and sculptor; G. B. Vignola (1541–3) (p. 828) and Sebastiano Serlio (1541–54), the latter having a profound influence in France rather by his writings than his architecture. These, and other artists, aided by Italian craftsmen, did much to further the spread of the Renaissance in the country. The kingly power was gradually becoming absolute, owing largely to the policy of Cardinal Richelieu and his successor, Mazarin, in the reign of Louis XIII (1610–43), so that Louis XIV (1643–1715) could declare with truth 'L'Etat c'est moi'. He was the great patron of the later Renaissance in France, and the palaces of the Louvre and Versailles are monuments of his lavish expenditure on architecture and the decorative arts. Under Louis XV (1715–74) the accumulated evils of despotism, bad government and the selfishness of the aristocracy had already become pronounced, when Voltaire and others voiced enlightened criticism in their writings. They prepared the way for the Revolution of 1789, when all architectural development was arrested until about 1794. In the interim, there occurred some destruction and defacement of existing monuments. Development was resumed thereafter, new trends showing themselves

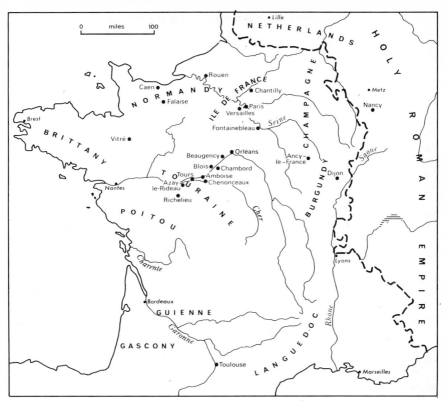

France in the sixteenth century

in response to the changed social conditions. Patronage passed from the hands of the aristocracy to the plutocracy of the new régime, which had tastes of a coarser and more pretentious kind. Ambitions mounted, however, and many new architectural works were carried out: Napoleon I continued the work of beautifying Paris. The Restoration of the monarchy fostered fresh tendencies once again, but while these were intensifying, the current practices in architecture continued to prevail with diminishing support until about 1830.

In south-western France and other limited areas the Huguenot gentry and cities attained considerable strength during the prolonged Wars of Religion (1562–98), yet by 1628 Richelieu had deprived them of political and military independence. Throughout most of France the supremacy of the Catholic Church remained unshaken until the Revolution. Many of the best Huguenot craftsmen were driven abroad by persecution, which was renewed in 1685 when Louis XV revoked the tolerant Edict of Nantes. At first the supply of Gothic churches sufficed, but in the seventeenth century the Jesuit Order—the chief influence on ecclesiastical architecture in France during the later Renaissance period—built great churches designed for preaching to large congregations, with the object of refuting Reformation heresies. The Revolution of 1789 was hostile to religion, but Catholicism reasserted itself with renewed vigour in the nineteenth century.

ARCHITECTURAL CHARACTER

The Renaissance style in France, which took root about seventy-five years later than in Italy, may be divided into three periods:

(a) *The Early Period* (1494–1589 or sixteenth century), comprising the latter part of the reign of Charles VIII (1483–98), beginning with his campaign through Italy against Naples, and the reigns of Louis XII (1498–1515), Francis I (1515–47), Henry II (1547–59), Francis II (1559–60), Charles IX (1560–74) and Henry III (1574–89). The special character of this transitional period lies in the combination of Gothic and Renaissance features to form a picturesque ensemble, and is best understood by noting how it differs from Italian Renaissance. Thus in Italy a return to Classic forms took place, though there was variety in the disposition of revived architectural features; whereas in France there was a period of transition, during which Renaissance details were grafted on to such Gothic features as flying buttresses and pinnacles (p. 911A). In Italy the principal buildings were erected in towns, such as Florence, Rome, Venice and Genoa, as palaces for popes, prelates, and nobles (pp. 800, 808, 826, 855); while the principal buildings in France were castles in the country round Paris and on the Loire for the king and his courtiers (pp. 883, 870, 885, 891). In Italy, moreover, the influence of ancient Rome is apparent in the Classical treatment of detail and ornament, while the influence of Rome was naturally less manifest in France than in Italy, and the influence of traditional Gothic craftsmanship was pronounced. Then, too, in Italy the predominant characteristics are stateliness and a tendency to Classical horizontality (p. 820A), but in France the salient features are picturesqueness and a tendency to Gothic verticality (p. 870B). Early buildings of the period in Italy were principally churches, in consequence of the comparatively small number erected in the Middle Ages, although there are also many Italian palaces of this epoch. Early buildings in France were principally châteaux for the nobility, as sufficient churches of the Middle Ages already existed.

Even before 1494 there were one or two instances of Renaissance architecture constructed in France, but they were wholly by Italians and evoked no French response. Through the majority of the reign of Francis I (to *c.* 1535), the French Renaissance was based upon the school of Amboise, which followed Lombard precedents; new buildings sometimes were designed in the general sense by the Italians, but mostly the Italians contributed the superficial effects to structures in the charge of distinguished French master-masons. After *c.* 1535 the school of Fontainebleau became the more prominent, and the Roman Renaissance provided the chief inspiration. Already the High Renaissance stage had been passed in Italy, and the character of architecture then in vogue was a moderately orthodox Classicism mingled with variously extreme instances of the Proto-Baroque. Primaticcio, in particular, carried the Mannerist decorative architectural arts of Rome via Mantua to Fontainebleau (p. 828). In this second phase too, Frenchmen were at length beginning to produce their own national version of the Renaissance style, the chief personalities being Jean Goujon (*c.* 1505–*c.* 1568), sculptor and architect, Pierre Lescot (*c.* 1510–78); Philibert de l'Orme (*c.*1512–70), a man of great ingenuity in construction and planning; Jean Bullant (*c.* 1520–78); and Jacques Androuet du Cerceau the Elder (*c.* 1520–85). It is significant that each of these visited Rome at some time in his career, usually in its earlier stages.

(b) *The Classical Period* (1589–1715 or seventeenth century) comprising the reigns of Henry IV (1589–1610), Louis XIII (1610–43) and Louis XIV (1643–1715). The period is notable for the dignity, sobriety and masculine quality of its foremost buildings, resulting from the subordination of plan, composition and

D PANEL: PALAIS DE FONTAINEBLEAU

A FRONT VIEW   B SIDE VIEW
CAP. PALAIS DE FONTAINEBLEAU

C CAP. CHATEAU DE CHAMBORD

E PANEL: PALAIS DE FONTAINEBLEAU

F CAP. CHATEAU DE CHAMBORD

PLAN OF NICHE

G DOORWAY CHATEAU DE CHENONCEAUX

SECTION   ELEVATION   PLAN

H DORMER WINDOW: CHATEAU DE CHAMBORD

ELEVATION   PLAN

ROOF

A — KEY STONE (LOUIS XV)

B — BALCONY (LOUIS XV) PARIS
27, RUE S. ANDRÉ-DES-ARTS
SIDE   SECTION

C — LEAD VASE   PALAIS DE VERSAILLES

D — DORMER WINDOW (LOUIS XV) LYCÉE NAPOLEON: PARIS
SIDE VIEW   14.8"

E — CONSOLE (LOUIS XV) PARIS
8'.0"

F — DOORWAY (LOUIS XVI)
HÔTEL DES MONNAIES
9'.9"   SEC

G — LOUIS QUATORZE STYLE of DECORATION

H — KEYSTONE (LOUIS XV)

J — FOUNTAIN (LOUIS XV) PARIS
S. GERMAIN-DES-PRÉS,
(ON SQUARE MONGE)
SECTION   ELEVATION   PLAN   15.6

K — DOOR & WINDOW (LOUIS XVI) PARIS
12, RUE DE TOURNON
SIDE ELEVATION   CONSOLE   39'.10"   SECTION   9'.6"

L — CORNICE & BALUSTRADE (LOUIS XVI)
SECTION

detail of the unity of the whole, and the clarity and simplicity with which the elements were used. Ornament, though somewhat coarse, is vigorous and reasonably restrained. Influences from Italy on the one hand and the Low Countries on the other are for the most part tempered by French taste, and the Baroque is chiefly of importance in imparting grandeur of ideas in architectural and civic design and in garden planning, the latter art making great strides. Very few buildings, and those mostly ecclesiastical, are readily recognisable as Baroque from their external effects, and the extreme forms of Baroque are rare indeed. Though the exteriors become Classical and straightforward, interior decoration remains rich and luxuriant. It is here that foreign Proto-Baroque and Baroque influences play an important part, though again, the outcome of the amalgam is characteristically French. In the earlier part of the period brick is much favoured as a building material, usually in conjunction with stone or stucco used for quoins and dressings and for 'chaînes', which in lieu of pilasters, rise vertically between the string-mouldings and cornice so as to form wall-panels (pp. 894B, 896B), these often having central framed ornaments or niches or being infilled with patterned brickwork. Windows grow increasingly large, and ride up into the steep roofs as dormers, while stone mullions and transoms tend to give place to wood. There is much play with rustication, on the Orders themselves when these appear; sometimes the Orders enframe dormers, as well as the windows aligned vertically below. Roofs at first mostly are steep and treated in separate pavilion units, and the 'mansard' roof of two different slopes is popular, but as the period develops, unified pitched roofs or flat roofs become increasingly common. The Orders figure much more frequently in the second half of the period, normally superimposed in the typical French manner, but with a little recourse to the giant Order. The Orders become much more strictly Classical in proportions and detail than formerly, and this relative simplicity of exterior design accentuates the contrast with interior decoration, which is brilliantly profuse in fanciful scrolls, nymphs, wreaths and shells, carried out in stucco and papier-mâché, forms of ornament also consistently applied to furniture and fittings. This was the great age of Renaissance architecture in France. The principal architects of the period are the accomplished Salomon de Brosse (c. 1562–1626), best known for his Palais du Luxembourg; Jacques Lemercier (1585–1654), François Mansart (1598–1666) and Louis Le Vau (1612–70), the latter three largely responsible for the inception of true Classicism; André Le Nôtre (1613–1700), France's outstanding garden architect; Charles Lebrun (1619–90), a painter, who practised and influenced all the visual arts; Jules Hardouin Mansart (1646–1708), master designer and brilliant interpreter of Louis XIV's architectural ambitions; Sébastien Vauban (1633–1707), a Marshal of France and great military engineer, whose fortified towns, such as Briançon, Hautes-Alpes and Neufbrisach, Alsace, reveal a sure grasp of the harmonic values of Classical architecture and urbanism.

(c) *The Late Period* (1715–1830 or eighteenth century), comprising the reigns of Louis XV (1715–74) and Louis XVI (1774–92) and the subsequent period of rapid political change, embracing the ascendancy of Napoleon Bonaparte, concluding with the reign of Charles X (1824–30). Architecturally, three stylistic phases may be distinguished. The first two are usually identified with the names of the sovereigns Louis XV and XVI, but in fact overlap considerably; the third is known as that of the 'Empire', approximately from 1790–1830. In the first phase there is a descent from the Classical grandeur of the previous, Louis XIV, era, towards a relative intimacy of effect, particularly marked in domestic planning and in interior decoration. Very many modest residences and town 'hôtels' were erected in which comfort and convenience were considered far more important than chilly dignity. Rooms were planned for independent approach rather than in sequence, now being interlocked in compact arrangements with many devices of circular, oval, curvilinear or polygonal shape to facilitate compression and produce diverting visual effects. Double-depth or deep, squarish plans became normal. Internal corners of apartments sometimes were rounded, and occasionally walls followed sinuous curves on plan, this type of planning being the especial forte of J. A. Meissonnier, who at the same time contributed much to the development of the exuberant style of decoration later to be known as Rococo, but in France generally described as 'rocaille'. Externally, however, except in church architecture, architecture became more simple but at the same time less Classically pure, the Orders often being substituted by pilaster 'chaînes' of rustication and sparse ornament in domestic buildings, while windows grew larger still, often absorbing the greater part of the wall. About the middle of the eighteenth century a romantic tendency made itself felt, leading to a return to the sober Classicism of Louis XIV's time and, more importantly, to a growing respect for the monuments of antiquity, stimulated by discoveries at Herculaneum (1719) and Pompeii (1748) and other sites in Italy, Asia Minor and Greece. Measured drawings and 'restorations' of ancient remains appeared in increasing volume. The puristic reaction was anti-Baroque and anti-Rococo, yet was more effective in cleansing exterior architecture of superfluities than in materially reducing the richness of interiors, which became austere and refined rather than simple, while new decorative motifs were drawn from widely divergent sources; from the art of neighbouring countries, the Orient, Egypt or from France's own antecedents as well as from Classical antiquity. Classicism, however, chiefly gained the day in the 'Empire' phase, when a frigid formality was the keynote, Graeco-Roman coalescing with Egyptian motifs to produce a distinctively French national decorative style. Externally, it was Roman character that was chiefly favoured, only slightly tinctured with the Greek; in France the Greek and the Gothic Revivals never achieved the popularity that they did in early nineteenth-century England. Constructively, cast and wrought iron were exploited from the late eighteenth century, a dome and bridges having been erected in the material before 1810. Among the notable architects of the Late period are Jacques Jules Gabriel (1667–1742); Germain Boffrand (1667–1754); Jean Nicolas Servandoni (1695–1766), an Italian, designer of the S. Sulpice, Paris, façade; Jacques François Blondel (1705–74), more famous than his namesake, F. Blondel, of almost a century previously, as a writer and teacher, author of *Cours d'architecture*, an influential theoretical work; Jacques Germain Soufflot (1713–80), whose studies of Roman and Greek monuments in Italy produced their effects on his Panthéon, Paris; Étienne Louis Boullée (1728–99) and Claude Nicolas Ledoux (1736–1806), each responsible for several fine houses and fertile of progressive ideas; Jacques Denis Antoine (1733–1801), designer of the Hôtel des Monnaies, Paris; Jean Francis Chalgrin (1739–1811), best remembered for his scheme for the famous Arc de Triomphe; Bernard Poyet (1742–1824) author of the frontispiece to the Chambre des Députés, Paris; the inseparables Charles Percier (1764–1838) and Pierre F. L. Fontaine (1762–1853), joint designers of the Arc du Carrousel, Paris, and virtual inventors of the 'Empire' decorative style; and Pierre-Alexandre Vignon (1763–1828), known for his Madeleine church, Paris.

EXAMPLES

SECULAR ARCHITECTURE

The **Château de Blois** (1498–1524 and later) (pp. 870A, 879), begun in the thirteenth century (p. 617), was continued (1498–1504) by Louis XII in an addition

CHATEAU DE BLOIS

A STAIRCASE TOWER (FRANCIS I)

B BIRD'S-EYE VIEW

C STAIRCASE TOWER (FRANCIS I) AT C

D CHIMNEY STACK (FRANCIS I)

13TH CENTURY
15TH CENTURY
LOUIS XII (1498-1504)
FRANCIS I (1515-1524)
GASTON D'ORLEANS (1635-1638)

ENTRANCE

E PLAN

50 0 50 100 150 200 FT
10 0 10 20 30 40 50 60 MTS

F CHIMNEY-PIECE (FRANCIS I)

CHATEAU DE BURY

MOAT
CHAPEL
GARDEN
GARDEN
160.0
MOAT
COURT
50 0 50 100 FT
10 0 10 20 30 MTS
MOAT
MOAT
ENTRANCE

G PLAN

H BIRD'S-EYE VIEW (RESTORED)

CHATEAU DE CHAMBORD

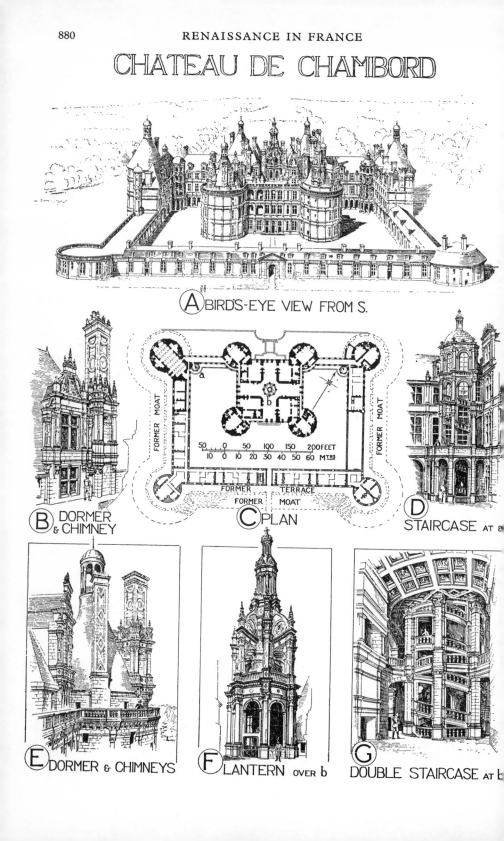

A BIRD'S-EYE VIEW FROM S.

B DORMER & CHIMNEY

C PLAN

FORMER MOAT

FORMER MOAT

50　0　50　100　150　200 FEET
10　0　10　20　30　40　50　60 MᵀᴿˢES

FORMER TERRACE

FORMER MOAT

D STAIRCASE AT a

E DORMER & CHIMNEYS

F LANTERN OVER b

G DOUBLE STAIRCASE AT b

to the east wing which shows very little Renaissance influence, and by Francis I shortly afterwards (1515–24), being finally completed (1635–8) by François Mansart for Gaston d'Orléans in the reign of Louis XIII. The buildings belonging to these successive periods are grouped around an irregular quadrangle (p. 879B, E), with central entrance, enriched with statuary, through the Louis XII block. The façades of the time of Francis I have windows with panelled instead of moulded mullions (p. 879C), ornate crowning cornices, and carved roof dormers and chimney stacks (p. 879D), which together make a pleasing and characteristic combination, further enhanced by the famous spiral staircase of Francis I in its open tower (p. 879C), in which the letter F and the Salamander, emblems of Francis I, are introduced as heraldic decoration among the carving on the balustrades and vault bosses. The staircase (p. 879A) has a beautiful architectural treatment, founded on the Mediaeval corkscrew stair (p. 614E), similar to a spiral shell. The chimney-pieces (p. 879F), with columns, niches and carving are ornate, and show that internal fittings were elaborated more than in the Gothic period. The part for Gaston d'Orléans was designed by François Mansart, and its stately formality forms a contrast with the Early Renaissance work of the time of Francis I (p. 879B).

The **Château de Bury** (1520) (p. 879), a few miles from Blois, but now in ruins, consisted of a large square court fronted by a screen wall, one storey high, with internal colonnade and terminated by circular towers. The central entrance is contained between minor circular towers. The courtyard is flanked by two-storeyed wings containing servants' apartments on one side and offices and stabling on the other, connected with the three-storeyed 'corps de logis'—the block forming the residence of the family. Beyond this main building was the walled garden with the chapel at the centre of the further side facing the garden entrance of the house. In French country houses of this period, of which the Château de Bury is typical, the internal court, originally designed for security, was retained; whereas in England, after the time of Henry VII, the closed court had become an exception. This description applies also to French town houses even up to recent times, with modifications dependent on site and local conditions.

The **Château de Chambord** (1519–47) (pp. 870B, 880), designed by an Italian architect, Domenico da Cortona—though much modified by French masons—is the most famous in the Loire district. It is semi-fortified in character and has a plan reminiscent of a Mediaeval 'concentric' castle, being made up of two rectangles one within the other, but with the façade of the smaller on the same line as that of the outer court, which thus protects it on three sides, while the fourth is protected by the moat (p. 880C). This inner block or 'donjon', 67 m (220 ft) square, corresponds to the keep of an English castle, and has four lofty halls on each floor, finished by elliptical barrel vaulting (p. 880G); at the junction of these halls is the world-famous double spiral staircase, by which people can ascend and descend simultaneously without being visible to each other. It is built up in a cage of stone (p. 880G), crowned with a storeyed lantern which forms the central feature of the exterior (pp. 870B, 880A, F). There is much waste of space, as rectangular rooms are formed in the circular towers. This remarkable pile has many Gothic features clothed with Renaissance detail, and a vertical Gothic effect is produced by wall pilasters with unique carved capitals (p. 875C, F), and angle towers with domes or with conical roofs (p. 880A); while the high-pitched roof with ornate dormers (p. 875H) and lofty chimneys (p. 880B, E) make the variegated skyline of this Early French Renaissance building (p. 870B). It may be contrasted with the palace at Caprarola by Vignola (p. 832).

The **Château de Chenonceaux** (1515–23) (p. 883B) stands on piles in the River Cher, and was originally a simple rectangular block with typical entrance doorway

(p. 875G), and steep roof crowded with the conical tops of angle turrets, dormers and chimney stacks, but was picturesquely extended (1556–9) by Philibert de l'Orme by a five-arched covered bridge reaching across the Cher, to which an upper gallery was added (1576) by Jean Bullant in a much more ornate style. Philibert de l'Orme (1515–70) was appointed as surveyor to the royal works, and was the first professional French architect to have studied in Italy. Though his elevational ordonnance is often immature, the concept and scale of his planning is truly Classical. His projected design of Chenonceaux included vast hemicycles symmetrically disposed about a 'cour d'honneur' axially approached by a trapesoidal 'basse-cour'. Among his other regular and extensive schemes were those for the Tuileries (p. 888B) and the Château of Anet (1548) for Diane de Poitiers.

The **Château d'Azay-le-Rideau** (1518–27) (p. 883A) is an attractive building, built on an island, with similar characteristics to the original at Chenonceaux, yet with the features much more sedately disposed. It retains a heavy machicolated cornice of Mediaeval type, which can also be seen on the enchanting **Château du Lude, Sarthe** (c. 1520). In the same district is the **Château de Villandry** (1536), where the early Renaissance gardens of unique extent and quality have been restored to their sixteenth-century design.

Ancy-le-Franc, Burgundy (c. 1546) (p. 885C) was designed by the Italian architect Serlio, but modified by French masons. It illustrates the trend towards Classicism in the continuous cornices, uninterrupted by dormers, which now become roof features divorced from the face of the wall. The lowering of the ridge levels by the use of flats gives a better proportion between wall and roof, and the chimneys are more regularly disposed. The square angle pavilions with their more constructively used pilasters proclaim this to be an advanced example of the Fontainebleau school. The square internal court is still surrounded on all sides to the same height, and displays the alternate rhythms of the Roman arch motif as deployed by Bramante. Inside, the hall is painted with frescoes of the mannerist type (1578), with Roman emperors depicted in the lunettes.

Other châteaux in traditional style are those of **Écouen** (1531–8), to which the north wing was added (c. 1555) by Jean Bullant, and three mostly carried out by the master-mason, Pierre Chambiges (d. 1544); **S. Germain-en-Laye, La Muette** and **Challuau** (all c. 1539–49), of which only S. Germain survives. The **Châtelet, Chantilly** (c. 1560) (p. 884A) is in Bullant's typical Proto-Baroque manner, while J. A. du Cerceau I's sons Jean-Baptiste and Jacques II probably both worked on the extraordinarily perverse château of **Verneuil-sur-Oise** (1565–c. 1590).

The **Palais de Fontainebleau** (1528–40) (pp. 884B, 885A, B, 886), by the master-mason Gilles Le Breton for Francis I, has subsequent alterations by Primaticcio (1568) and others which account for its irregular plan. Unlike the Château de Blois, the exterior is remarkably ineffective in composition, and the palace depends for its attraction on the courts (pp. 884B, 885B), formal gardens, terraces, lakes and radiating vistas, while the chief interest lies in the architectural features of the interior (p. 875A, B, D, E) and in the sumptuous salons (p. 886A, B) decorated by Rosso, Primaticcio and later masters. The type of mural decoration practised here by the Italians, of boldly-modelled stucco varied with painted panels, had tremendous repercussions in Western Europe, particularly in the case of the modelled strapwork originated by Rosso in the Galerie de François Ier.

The **Palais du Louvre, Paris** (1546–1878) (pp. 887, 888A, 890) was in course of construction from the time of Francis I to Napoleon III in the nineteenth century, and thus exhibits a complete history of the progressive stages of French Renaissance art carried out in successive periods (p. 890E). The Louvre, together with the Tuileries, constituted one of the most imposing palaces in Europe, and enclosed an

A. Château d'Azay-le-Rideau (1518–27). See p. 882

B. Château de Chenonceaux (1515–23; bridge 1556–9; gallery over bridge 1576).
See p. 881

A. The Châtelet, Chantilly (*c.* 1560). See p. 882

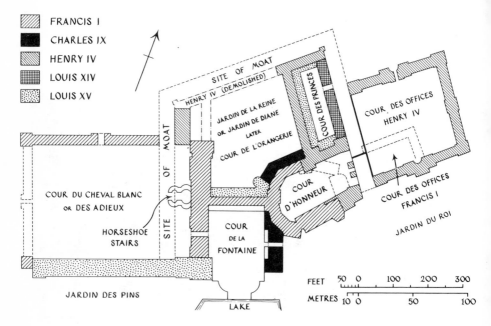

FRANCIS I

CHARLES IX

HENRY IV

LOUIS XIV

LOUIS XV

SITE OF MOAT

HENRY IV (DEMOLISHED)

JARDIN DE LA REINE
OR JARDIN DE DIANE
LATER
COUR DE L'ORANGERIE

COUR DES PRINCES

COUR DES OFFICES
HENRY IV

SITE OF MOAT

COUR DU CHEVAL BLANC
OR DES ADIEUX

HORSESHOE
STAIRS

SITE OF MOAT

COUR
DE LA
FONTAINE

COUR
D'HONNEUR

COUR DES OFFICES
FRANCIS I

JARDIN DU ROI

JARDIN DES PINS

LAKE

FEET   50 0   100   200   300

METRES 10 0   50   100

B. Palais de Fontainebleau: plan showing dates of erection

A. Palais de Fontainebleau: Cour du Cheval-Blanc (1528–40 and later). See p. 882

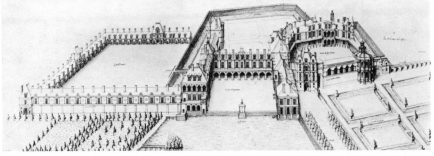

B. Palais de Fontainebleau looking N.: drawing by J. A. du Cerceau I

C. Ancy-le-Franc, Burgundy (c. 1546). See p. 882

A. Palais de Fontainebleau: Galerie de François Ier (1533–40). See p. 882

B. Palais de Fontainebleau: Galerie de Henri II (*c.* 1540, decorations *c.* 1552–).
See p. 882

A. The Louvre, Paris: courtyard façade, with Pavillon de l'Horloge (1546–1654).
See p. 882

B. The Louvre, Paris: east façade (1667–74). See p. 882

A. Palais du Louvre, Paris: Galerie d'Apollon (decorated by Lebrun 1662).
See p. 882

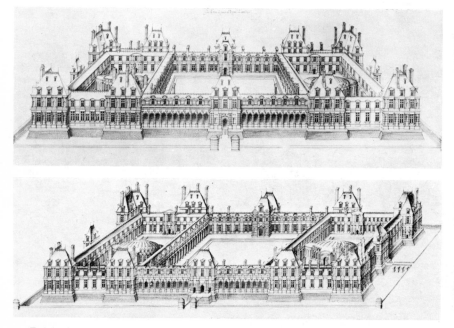

B. Palais des Tuileries, Paris (destroyed): drawings by J. A. du Cerceau I made in
1579. (*Above*) view from W.; (*below*) view from E. See p. 892

area of over 45 acres. Pierre Lescot was employed by Francis I to design a palace in the new style on the site of the old Gothic château which occupied the south-west quarter of the present court, and he commenced the west side of the Renaissance palace (1546) (p. 890E). The façade of this early design consists of two storeys with Corinthian and Composite pilasters surmounted by an attic storey, and is enriched with beautiful sculptured detail by Jean Goujon (pp. 887A, 890A B,). Catherine de' Medici continued Lescot's design round the south of the court, and conceived the idea of connecting the Louvre and the Palais des Tuileries by a gallery along the Seine, a scheme not realized for some 300 years. Henry IV, the last monarch to live in the Louvre, instructed J. A. du Cerceau II (1550–1614) to erect (1600–9) the gallery facing the Seine, in which pilasters including two storeys were surmounted by alternately triangular and segmental pediments (p. 902C), remodelled under Napoleon III (1860–5). Louis XIII, with Cardinal Richelieu, enlarged the original scheme, and in 1624 the north and east sides of the old château were pulled down. Lemercier then commenced the present court, which, measuring 122 m (400 ft) square, is four times the area of the Mediaeval court, but he only completed (1624–54) the north-west part, including the Pavillon de l'Horloge, which became the centre of the enlarged façade on the west. Louis XIV, with Cardinal Mazarin, commissioned Louis Le Vau to complete the north, east and south sides of the enlarged court (1650–64), and with his minister, Colbert, employed Claude Perrault to erect (1667–74) the eastern façade, after consideration of designs by several other notable French architects and even of two famous Italian Baroque masters, Carlo Rainaldi (p. 851) and the great Lorenzo Bernini (p. 846), the latter travelling to Paris (1665) specially for the purpose of presenting his schemes. The selected design was by Perrault, who was associated with Le Vau and Lebrun in the project. This eastern façade (p. 887B) is of a much more monumental character than the court façades. It is 183 m (600 ft) in length, and consists of a solid-looking basement which supports a colonnade of coupled Corinthian columns, stretching between the pedimented centre-piece and the side wings, instead of the usual and more effective pavilion blocks. A pilaster treatment is carried round part of the north and south external façades. As Perrault's design was higher than the portions already erected, a third Order was now substituted for the attic storey on the east side and on the eastern half of north and south sides of the court, which, as completed with the three storeys of Orders (p. 890B), contrasts with the portion with two storeys and an attic as designed by Lescot. The courtyard of the Ospedale Maggiore, Milan (p. 819G, H), with its open arcades, is the only one in Italy that is comparable to the completed court of the Louvre, which has arcading in the French version on the wall surfaces.

In 1675 the work was suspended, as Louis XIV was directing his energies to his palace at Versailles, and very little appears to have been done to the building until Napoleon I employed Percier and Fontaine to continue the Order to the third storey on the western half of the north and south sides of the court, and a small portion at the north-east angle of the Place Louis Napoléon. Between 1806 and 1813 the same architects commenced the north wing from the Pavillon de Marsan to the Pavillon de Rohan, to connect the Louvre to the Palais des Tuileries, but this wing lost its significance when the latter was destroyed in 1871.

The later nineteenth-century history of these twin palaces may be conveniently added here. Napoleon III conceived the idea of effecting a satisfactory junction between the Louvre and the Tuileries, and in order to mask the converging sides of the connecting wings he employed (1850–7) Visconti and Lefuel to erect the building known as the 'Nouveau Louvre' on the north and south sides of the Place Louis Napoléon. Lefuel refaced (1860–78) the Pavillon de Flore and the adjacent

THE LOUVRE PARIS

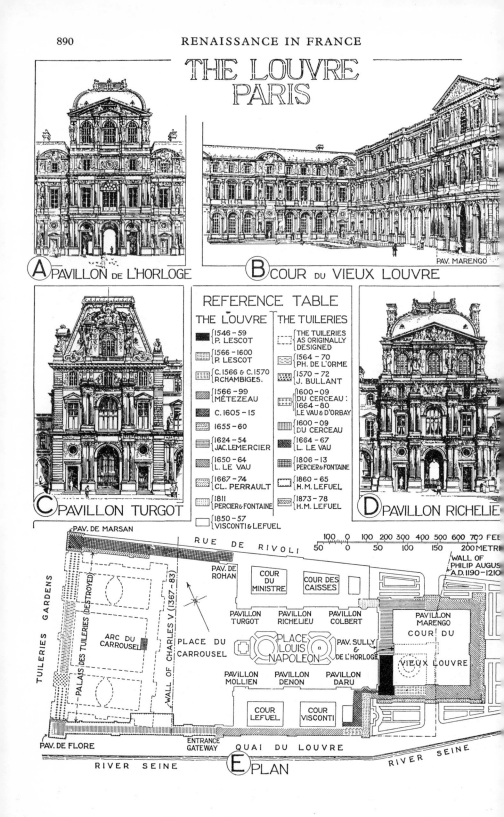

A PAVILLON DE L'HORLOGE

B COUR DU VIEUX LOUVRE

PAV. MARENGO

REFERENCE TABLE

THE LOUVRE	THE TUILERIES
1546–59 P. LESCOT	THE TUILERIES AS ORIGINALLY DESIGNED
1566–1600 P. LESCOT	1564–70 PH. DE L'ORME
C.1566 & C.1570 R.CHAMBIGES.	1570–72 J. BULLANT
1566–99 MÉTEZEAU	1600–09 DU CERCEAU: 1664–80 LE VAU & D'ORBAY
C.1605–15	1600–09 DU CERCEAU
1655–60	1664–67 L. LE VAU
1624–54 JAC.LEMERCIER	1806–13 PERCIER & FONTAINE
1650–64 L. LE VAU	1860–65 H.M.LEFUEL
1667–74 CL. PERRAULT	1873–78 H.M.LEFUEL
1811 PERCIER & FONTAINE	
1850–57 VISCONTI & LEFUEL	

C PAVILLON TURGOT

D PAVILLON RICHELIE

E PLAN

PAV. DE MARSAN

RUE DE RIVOLI

100 0 100 200 300 400 500 600 700 FEE
50 0 50 100 150 200 METR

WALL OF PHILIP AUGUS A.D.1190–1210

PAV. DE ROHAN

COUR DU MINISTRE

COUR DES CAISSES

TUILERIES GARDENS

PALAIS DES TUILERIES (DESTROYED)

WALL OF CHARLES V (1367–83)

ARC DU CARROUSEL

PLACE DU CARROUSEL

PAVILLON TURGOT

PAVILLON RICHELIEU

PAVILLON COLBERT

PAVILLON MARENGO

COUR DU VIEUX LOUVRE

PLACE LOUIS NAPOLEON

PAV. SULLY & DE L'HORLOGE

PAVILLON MOLLIEN

PAVILLON DENON

PAVILLON DARU

COUR LEFUEL

COUR VISCONTI

PAV. DE FLORE

ENTRANCE GATEWAY

QUAI DU LOUVRE

RIVER SEINE

RIVER SEINE

CHATEAU DE MAISONS: NEAR PARIS

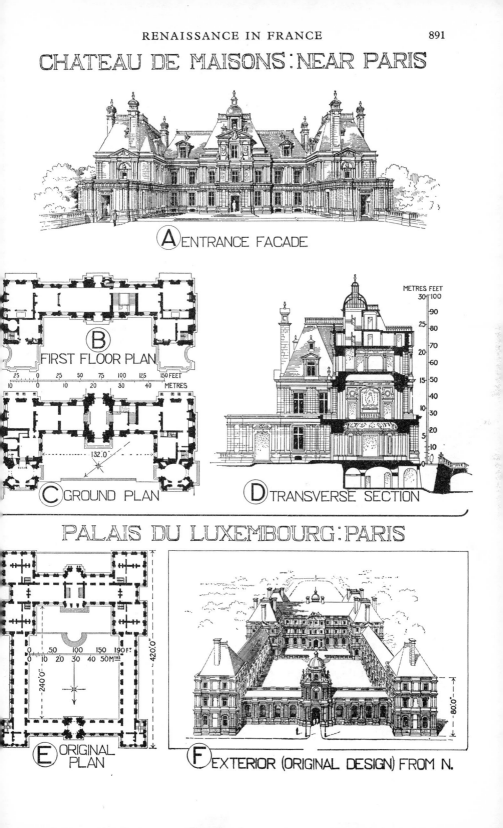

Ⓐ ENTRANCE FACADE

Ⓑ FIRST FLOOR PLAN

25 0 25 50 75 100 125 150 FEET
10 0 10 20 30 40 METRES

Ⓒ GROUND PLAN

132.0

Ⓓ TRANSVERSE SECTION

METRES FEET
30 ┬ 100
   ├ 90
25 ├ 80
   ├ 70
20 ├ 60
   ├ 50
15 ├ 40
10 ├ 30
   ├ 20
5 ├ 10
0 ┴ 0

PALAIS DU LUXEMBOURG: PARIS

Ⓔ ORIGINAL PLAN

0 50 100 150 190 FT
10 20 30 40 50 M™S

240'0"   420'0"

Ⓕ EXTERIOR (ORIGINAL DESIGN) FROM N.

80.0

wing towards the Seine, and also the Pavillon de Marsan and a small portion adjacent, and at the same time the facing of the north wing fronting the Rue de Rivoli was taken in hand. The Pavillon de l'Horloge (pp. 887A, 890A), designed by Lemercier, is a fine composition, obviously derived from the high towers of the Mediaeval period, and gave the keynote for the subsequent Pavillon Turgot (p. 890C) and the Pavillon Richelieu (p. 890D), built two centuries later. The sumptuous interiors (p. 888A) for which the Louvre is famous, are replete with decorations by all the best painters of the day.

Within the ambit of the Louvre, Percier and Fontaine were also the designers of the **Arc du Carrousel** (1806) (p. 890E), largely copied from the Arch of Septimius Severus, Rome (p. 323). Three kilometres (about two miles) to the west and forming part of the same grandiose conception, the contemporary and much more celebrated **Arc de Triomphe de l'Étoile** (1808-) (p. 904A), by Chalgrin and others, is less inhibited by archaeological precedent.

The **Palais des Tuileries, Paris** (1564-1680) (pp. 888B, 890E), was begun for Catherine de' Medici by Philibert de l'Orme, who only erected a domical central pavilion, flanked by low wings (1564-70). The central court measured 112 m × 88 m (370 ft × 290 ft). A wing was added (1570-92) by Jean Bullant, and further extensions were begun by J. A. du Cerceau II (1600-9), but not completed till 1680 by Le Vau and D'Orbay. The Palace was rich in historical associations, especially in connection with the overthrow of the French monarchy in 1792, and from the time of Napoleon I, who erected the Arc du Carrousel to serve as a monumental entrance, it was the constant residence of the French rulers, till its destruction in 1871. There is a small portion of the façade still preserved in the Tuileries gardens.

There are also throughout France numerous Early Renaissance buildings, such as the **House of Agnés Sorel, Orléans** (c. 1520), the later portion of the **Hôtel de Bourgtheroulde, Rouen** (1501-37) (p. 617), the **Hôtel de Ville, Orléans** (1503-13) and a much humbler one of very similar design, the **Hôtel de Ville, Beaugency** (1526) (p. 893A), a beautiful instance of municipal architecture. More mature in character are the **Hôtel d'Assézat, Toulouse** (1555) (p. 893C), by an able local architect, Nicolas Bachelier, an advanced design of tiered, paired columns embracing shallow, windowed arcades; the **Maison Milsand, Dijon** (c. 1561) (p. 893B), by Hugues Sambin, its façade bearing an abundance of surface ornament; and the **Hôtel Lamoignon, Paris** (1584) (p. 893D), by Jean-Baptiste du Cerceau (1544-90), instancing the use at this time of the giant Order.

The **Palais du Luxembourg, Paris** (1615-24) (p. 891E, F), was erected for Marie de' Medici by Salomon de Brosse, one of the ablest architects of the century, in a bold and simple style designedly echoing Ammanati's rusticated garden façade to the Palazzo Pitti, Florence (p. 799D). The plan (p. 891E) and composition admirably typify the French hôtel, consisting of a one-storeyed entrance screen with 'porte-cochère', two-storeyed side wings for service and stabling, and the three-storeyed 'corps de logis', forming a court, 73 m × 58 m (240 ft × 190 ft). The palace is now used as the Senate House. De Brosse also built the **Château de Coulommiers** (1613-) (ruined), of similar character and plan and almost equally attractive, and the **Château de Blérancourt** (1614-19) (destroyed), which lacked wings to the forecourt.

The **Château de Richelieu** (1631-7), south-west of Tours, a vast scheme by Lemercier, survives only in a few small elements, but there still exists the walled town of Richelieu, also by Lemercier, which the Cardinal at the same time caused to be built in replacement of the former village. The 'gridiron' plan of streets and squares was filled out with appropriate buildings and houses of brick with stone dressings.

A. Hôtel de Ville, Beaugency:
façade (1526). See p. 892

See p. 892

B. Maison Milsand, Dijon (*c.* 1561):
upper part of façade. See p. 892

See p. 892

C. Hôtel d'Assézat, Toulouse: courtyard façade (1555). See p. 892

See p. 892

D. Hôtel Lamoignon, Paris (1584).
See p. 892

See p. 892

A. Château de Grosbois, Seine-et-Marne (*c.* 1600). See p. 897

B. Château de Balleroy (1626–36). See p. 897

A. Palais de Versailles: park façade (1678–88). See p. 897

B. Palais de Versailles: Galerie des Glaces (1678–84). See p. 897

C. Palais de Versailles: the entrance façade (1678–1756)

A. Palais de Versailles: aerial view from the park (1661–1756). See p. 897

B. Place des Vosges, Paris (1605–12). See p. 898

The **Château de Cheverny, near Blois** (1634–46) has a fine Louis XIII interior and absolute architectural symmetry, rare at this date, the simple horizontal emphasis of the façades contrasting with the varied, almost Baroque, handling of roof and skyline.

The **Château de Maisons**, near Paris (1642–6) (p. 891A–D), is one of the most pleasantly harmonious of all the châteaux. It was designed by François Mansart on a symmetrical E-plan with central entrance and twin oval-shaped side vestibules. It is notable externally for the effective use of the Classic Orders and the high roofs with prominent chimney stacks, of the three pavilions, and internally for the refinement of detail of the balustraded stairs, carved chimney-pieces and ornamental ceilings. The same fine quality as at Maisons is notable in the Orléans wing at Blois (p. 879B) which Mansart had added to the Château a little earlier (1635–8). Before this again, he had built the **Château de Balleroy** (1626–36) (p. 894B), an excellent composition in shale with stone dressings. François Mansart (1598–1666) purified and consolidated the French tradition. All his compositions have a dominant centre pavilion, and he shows a tendency to link up the roofs of separate blocks. Whilst conservative in the handling of superimposed Orders, he modulated them with meaning and subtlety. At Blois the opening at first-floor level in the ceiling vault over the staircase allows the eye to range to the top floor—a Baroque device. The main flight stops at the first floor, and further upward progress is continued elsewhere. Also Baroque are the 'aperçus' cut into the dome of S. Marie, rue S. Antoine, Paris (1633).

The **Château de Grosbois**, Seine-et-Marne, 19 km (12 miles) south-east of Paris (*c.* 1600) (p. 894A) has a front typical of the Lous XIII period. The stone dressing of its brick façade, forming vertical 'chaînes' of rusticated quoins and horizontal string courses over the window heads, frame and bind the elevation in the same way that the Orders were used to compartment the surface in the time of Henry II. The concave sweep of the 'corps de logis' is unusual.

The **Château of Vaux-le-Vicomte** (1657–61), by Louis Le Vau, with its magnificent formal gardens, is one of the most spectacular in France. There are no wings, only a balustrade, to define the forecourt, and the apartments are consolidated in a double-depth arrangement in a symmetrical composite block, of which the transverse axis is strongly accentuated by a colonnaded entrance vestibule on the forecourt side leading directly to a grand oval salon dominating the garden front, capped with a dome and lantern consorting awkwardly with the steeply-pitched roofs of the broad angle pavilions. Flat pilasters rise through the two main storeys, enframing large windows differentiated to stress the 'piano nobile'.

The **Palais de Versailles** (1661–1756) (pp. 895, 896A) was built for Louis XIV by Le Vau, who designed a palace round the old hunting château (1624–6) erected by de Brosse for Louis XIII. Louis XIV later employed Jules Hardouin Mansart to extend the palace north and south, to form a building of 402 m (1,318 ft) long. Other portions were added (1756) by J. A. Gabriel (1698–1782) for Louis XV. The park façade (p. 895A), has a rusticated ground storey supporting an Order of pilasters, high attic and balustrade, producing a monotonous effect with unbroken skyline. The sumptuous apartments form in themselves a veritable museum of the decorative art of the period. The magnificent 'Galerie des Glaces' (p. 895B), by Mansart, is 73 m × 10 m (240 ft × 33 ft) and 13 m (43 ft) high, and may be compared with the Galerie d'Apollon at the Louvre (p. 888A). Decorated by Lebrun in 1680, its walls are ornamented with Corinthian pilasters of green marble, supporting an entablature surmounted by trophies, and a fine ornamental vault with painted panels representing the apotheosis of 'Le Roi Soleil'. This royal residence is typical of the period to which it belongs, both in the magnitude of its lay-out and in the enormous expenditure in money and labour which it involved. The magnificent formal gardens laid out by Le Nôtre, on axial lines cleverly manipulated to give vistas of avenues and water canals, are liberally adorned with fountains, terraces and arbours, set off with statues and vases in the Antique style (p. 905D, F).

The great garden designs of André Le Nôtre (1613–1700) were among France's finest contributions to European culture. Based on traditional forest rides (avenues) and the use of ornamental water (moats), Le Nôtre's formal schemes used these elements in conjunction with the parterre. The latter, laid out with low-level topiary and coloured earths, produced the 'parterre de broderie', a geometrical pattern resembling Genoese velvets when seen from the upper windows of the châteaux. Broad vistas stretch axially away punctuated by vases and statuary to form pleasing promenades, while on either hand closely-planted trees frame the view. Far from the châteaux, canals reflect the broad open skies. The conception of these vast schemes is social in intent, and more Baroque in spirit than any other manifestation of French art.

Among the very many important urban dwellings constructed during the Classical period, especially in Paris, seat of the highly-centralized government of the country, are those built around the **Place des Vosges, Paris** (1605–12) (p. 896B), perhaps by Claude Chastillon, in a comprehensive scheme of private 'hôtels' fronting the arcaded square, forming an excellent example of the early (Henry IV) brick and stone style; also, the **Hôtel de Sully, 66 rue S. Antoine, Paris** (1624–9) (p. 900A), by Jean du Cerceau, dignified in scale and proportions but over-elaborated with the coarse ornament typical of the day; the **Hôtel Lambert, S. Louis en l'Île, Paris** (1640–) (p. 900B), by Louis Le Vau, exhibiting the Classical character and restraint of the later phase of the period; and the **Place Vendôme, Paris** (1698–) (p. 901A), by J. H. Mansart, another group of private dwellings organized into a fine, unified Classical scheme, comprising a giant Order over a rusticated arcaded basement. The **Hôtel de Beauvais, 68 rue François Miron, Paris** (1656) (p. 899A), by Antoine le Pautre, illustrates a typical and ingenious plan of the seventeenth-century town house, with a row of shops facing the street at ground-floor level. Triumphal arches include the single-arched **Porte S. Denis, Paris** (1671–4) (p. 900C), by François Blondel and the sculptor-brothers François and Michel Anguier, while among public buildings there is the **Collège des Quatre Nations, Paris** (1662), by Louis Le Vau, Classical in detail but Baroque in its bold conception.

In the Late period, châteaux and town houses at first follow the preceding trends, whilst showing an increasingly simple yet less pure external style, ornament being concentrated at nodal points. Keynotes are intimacy of scale; compact planning, leading to an abandonment of the courtyard approach in châteaux; and the use of many varieties of rich and delicate interior decoration (p. 903B). About mid-century, Antiquarianism begins to show positive and widespread effects.

The **Hôtel de Matignon, 57 rue de Varenne, Paris** (1721) (p. 899B), by J. Courtonne, shows the sophistication of planning achieved by the eighteenth century. The shift of axis from the courtyard to the garden front is adroitly accomplished. The side stepping of the staircase and the 'dégagements' of the small offices make this an eminently workable plan.

The **Hôtel de Soubise, 60 rue des Francs Bourgeois, Paris** (1706–) (p. 903A), is now the Archives Nationales. Designed by Pierre Alexis Delamair, the interior is by Germain Boffrand, and the salon (1735) shows Rococo style of the period of Louis XV. The elliptical plan, the use of mirrors, and the fusion of wall and ceiling with the use of scroll work in place of the Orders make this elegant painted room an outstanding example.

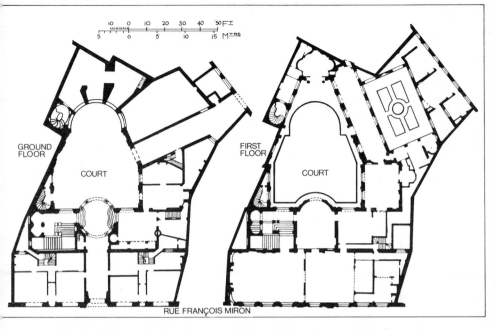

A. Hôtel de Beauvais, Rue François Miron, Paris: plans (1656). See p. 898

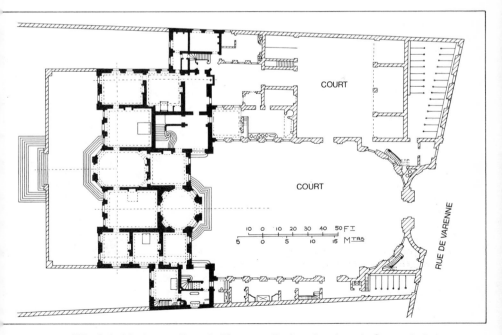

B. Hôtel de Matignon, Rue de Varenne, Paris: plan (1721). See p. 898

A. Hôtel de Sully, Paris (1624–9). See p. 898

B. Hôtel Lambert, Paris: court
(1640–). See p. 898

C. Porte S. Denis, Paris (1671–4).
See p. 898

A. Place Vendôme, Paris (1698–). See p. 898

B. Place de la Carrière, Nancy (1750–7). See p. 907

A. Palaces in Place de la Concorde, Paris: angle pavilions (1753–70). See p. 907

B. Hôtel des Monnaies, Paris: centre block (1771–5). See p. 907

C. Palais du Louvre: gallery facing Seine by J. A. du Cerceau II (since refaced) and Pavillon de Flore (1600–9). See p. 882

A. Hôtel de Soubise, Paris: salon (1735).
See p. 898

B. Panel centre by J. Verberckt in
Louis XV's apartments at Versailles (1753).

C. Barrière de la Villette, Paris (1785). See p. 907

A. Arc de Triomphe de l'Étoile, Paris (1808–). See p. 892

B. Château Moncley, Franche-Comté (1778). See p. 907

A THE PETIT TRIANON : VERSAILLES FROM S.

B LUCARNE (DORMER WINDOW) HOTEL DES INVALIDES PARIS

C LUCARNE (DORMER WINDOW) HOTEL DES INVALIDES PARIS

D MARBLE VASE VERSAILLES

E HOTEL : RUE DU CHERCHE-MIDI : PARIS

F MARBLE VASE VERSAILLES

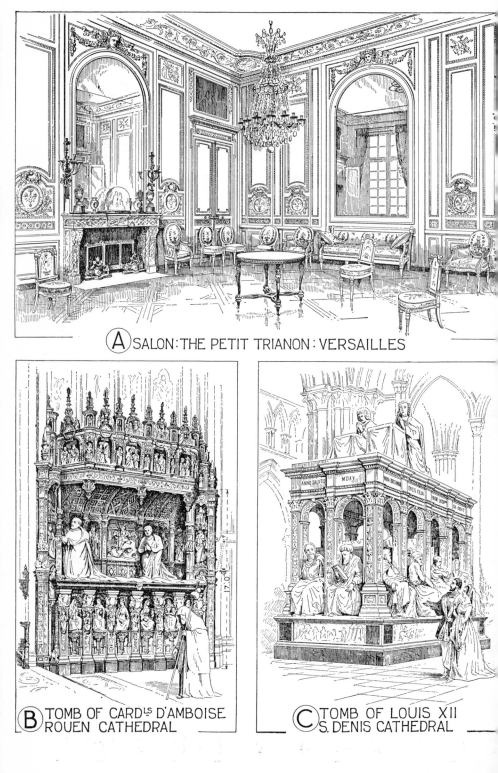

Ⓐ SALON: THE PETIT TRIANON: VERSAILLES

Ⓑ TOMB OF CARDᴸˢ D'AMBOISE ROUEN CATHEDRAL

Ⓒ TOMB OF LOUIS XII S. DENIS CATHEDRAL

The **Grandes Écuries, Chantilly** (1721–36), by Jean Aubert, extend their single storey (and attic) for 183 m (600 ft) before a great lawn. Designed to house the Prince de Condé's 240 horses, his hounds and hunt servants, the stables of the Château de Chantilly make sober, elegant, harmonious architecture.

The **Château de Ménars, near Blois**, with gardens gently sloping towards the Loire, still recreates in every external aspect the atmosphere of a great country house (in this case, Madame de Pompadour's) in the mid-eighteenth century. The terrace and orangery are by Soufflot.

The **Petit Trianon, Versailles** (1762–8) (pp. 905A, 906A), erected by J. A. Gabriel for Louis XV, who presented it to Madame du Barry, is one of the most superb pieces of domestic architecture of the century. It has a gracious air, resulting from the clarity of its ordonnance and the sedate proportions. The south front (p. 905A) has a basement treated with the smooth-faced rustication of the period, while the ashlar of the upper floors is ornamented with flat, Corinthian pilasters rising through two stages between architraved windows differentiated in height to accentuate the 'piano nobile'. As the plan is nearly square, the four façades are similar, except that there are no pilasters on the eastern front, and on the western, they are substituted by columns. The building is related to an exquisite formal-garden setting by quadrant wing-walls and terraced staircases. The salon (p. 906A) also is typical of the period, with its panelled walls, large mirrors, double doors, consoled chimney-piece, coved ceiling and elaborate chandelier, while the chairs and the table with its Hermes legs complete this interesting interior.

The **Hôtel de Brunoy, Paris** (1772), by E. L. Boullée, and the **Hôtel de Thélusson, Paris** (1780: destroyed), by C. N. Ledoux show most strongly the archaeological reversion to ancient precedents, though still at this time many town residences continued to follow French national traditions in design.

Château Moncley, Franche-Comté (1778) (p. 904B), by C. A. Bertrand (1734–97), has an unusual plan, with mediaeval circular towers linked to the main 'corps de logis' by open screens.

The **Place Louis XV**, now **Place Stanislas, Nancy**, a city which was formerly the capital of Lorraine, formed part of an ambitious civic scheme laid out (1750–7) by the architect Emmanuel Héré de Corny (1705–63), linking with two small 'hôtels' built earlier by G. Boffrand and with the Governor's Palace so as to form a series of squares of varying shape and character. The Place Stanislas, nearly square, is surrounded by public buildings which on the north side turn outwards to bridge a moat and frame a vista passing successively through a triumphal arch and the long **Place de la Carrière** (p. 901B), flanked symmetrically by Boffrand's two hôtels and rows of simple terraced houses, to close on the Place du Gouvernement and Governor's Palace lying transversely at the northern end. Hemicycle screens bind the façade of the Governor's Palace to the northern ends of the terraced houses, and the Place de la Carrière is attractively laid out with alleys of trees and embellished with balustrades and statues. The principal buildings have that simple ordonnance yet rich detail which is found at an earlier time in the rest of France.

The **Place de la Concorde, Paris** (1753–70), by J. A. Gabriel, has twin palaces on the north side (p. 902A), now turned to other uses, which in their impressive monumental character evidence the sobering influence of archaeological research; as also do the **École Militaire, Paris** (1752–), by the same architect, the **Hôtel des Monnaies (Mint), Paris** (1771–5) (p. 902B), by J. D. Antoine and the **Palais de Justice, Paris** (rebuilt 1776), by J. D. Antoine and others.

The **Barrière de la Villette, Paris** (1785) (p. 903C), by C. N. Ledoux, is one of the four survivors of the forty-five toll houses built in a ring around Paris, which were torn down by the mob during the Revolution. Ledoux was an 'Architecte du Roi', and nearly went to the guillotine. Visionary and romantic, he used a vocabulary based on values of association. His main work was 'La Saline de Chaux', an early ideal industrial city built for the chemical workers at **Arc-et-Senans, Doubs** (1775–9).

Neo-Classicism was given impetus by the writings of Abbé Laugier. Reacting to Baroque and Rococo décor, the Abbé's *Essai* (1753) called for reform by architects. He required that antiquity should be re-assessed and maintained that structural purity should inform, and the log hut inspire. Neo-Classical buildings display many of these qualities: external colonnades, and basilica-type interiors aim at a noble simplicity that was once Greek. Even the effect of mediaeval arcades was not lost to appreciation, but no attempt was made to revive the Gothic style in France.

The **Théâtre, Bordeaux** (1773–80), by Victor Louis, stands behind a peristyle of twelve giant Corinthian columns. Supremely elegant inside and out, it was regarded for more than a century as the model—both technically and architecturally—for all theatres.

The **Chambre des Députés, Paris,** south of the Place de la Concorde, received its dodecastyle (twelve-columned) portico (1807; architect, B. Poyet) (p. 909A) in the final (Empire) phase of the Late period. This façade shows the uncompromising Classical severity common in important monuments at that time. The whole composition is based on Roman principles, and comprises a broad flight of steps, flanked by statuary, preceding a temple-like pedimented front standing forward of plain wings decorated only with slight angle pilasters and isolated ornamented panels. The windowless walls are textured with plain-faced rustication.

ECCLESIASTICAL ARCHITECTURE

The earliest indications of Renaissance in France, as in England, occur in sepulchral monuments, pulpits, portals and fittings of existing Gothic churches, such as the **Tomb of Louis XII** (1515) in S. Denis Cathedral (p. 906C), the **Tomb of the Cardinals d'Amboise, Rouen** (1522) (p. 906B), the **portals of La Trinité, Falaise,** the **Château de Vitré pulpit** (p. 909C) and the apsidal chapels of **S. Pierre, Caen** (1528–45) (p. 909B).

S. Étienne du Mont, Paris (1517–60) (p. 910A, B), has nave piers crowned with Doric-like capitals supporting ribbed vaulting, and there is an unusual ambulatory above the nave arcade. The famous 'jubé' or rood screen (*c.* 1545) (p. 910A), probably by Philibert de l'Orme, has double staircases with ornate balustrades of Renaissance detail. The screen was extended across the aisles in 1606. The centre of the façade, added 1610–25, has an entrance doorway framed with Composite columns, supporting an entablature and sculptured pediment. Above is a circular window with quasi-Gothic tracery, crowned with a steep-pitched gable to the nave, while beyond is a lofty tower.

S. Eustache, Paris (1532–89) (p. 911A), not completed till 1654, may have been designed with the aid of the Italian-born Domenico da Cortona (p. 872). It is planned like a five-aisled Mediaeval church with apsidal end, high roofs, window tracery, flying buttress, pinnacles and deeply-recessed portals, all clothed with Renaissance details, and is a remarkable evidence of how the Mediaeval plan lingered on into the Renaissance period. The west front dates from 1772–87.

S. Gervais, Paris (1616–21) (p. 910C), a façade added to the Late Gothic church by Salomon de Brosse, has three tiers of coupled columns of the Doric, Ionic and Corinthian Orders arranged to give the direct straightforward expression which is typical of this architect's work. It is the earliest wholly Classical church façade of importance of the French Renaissance.

A. Chambre des Députés, Paris: portico (1807). See p. 908

B. S. Pierre, Caen: apsidal chapels
(1528–45). See p. 908

C. Château de Vitré: external pulpit
(16th cent.). See p. 908

A. S. Étienne du Mont, Paris (1517–60): showing jubé (*c.* 1545; screens across aisles 1606). See p. 908

B. S. Étienne du Mont, Paris (1517–1560; centre of façade 1610–25).

C. Church of S. Gervais, Paris (1616–21). See p. 908

A. S. Eustache, Paris (1532–89). See p. 908

B. Church of SS. Paul and Louis,
Paris (1625–34). See p. 915

C. Church of the Sorbonne, Paris
(1635–42). See p. 915

A. Church of the Val de Grâce, Paris (1645–67). See p. 915

B. S. Sulpice, Paris (façade 1733–49; N. tower finished 1778). See p. 915

C. The Panthéon, Paris: interior looking towards apse (1755–92). See p. 915

D. The Dome of the Invalides, Paris (1680–91). See p. 915

A. The Panthéon, Paris (1755–92). See p. 915

B. The Madeleine, Paris (1806–42). See p. 916

DOME OF THE INVALIDES: PARIS

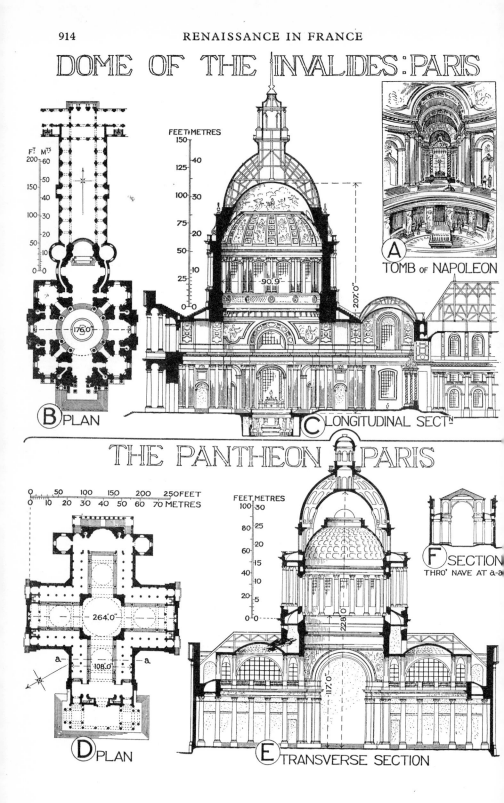

FEET METRES

A TOMB of NAPOLEON

176.0"

B PLAN

90.9"

207.0"

C LONGITUDINAL SECTN

THE PANTHEON PARIS

50 100 150 200 250 FEET
10 20 30 40 50 60 70 METRES

FEET METRES

F SECTION
THRO' NAVE AT a-a

264.0"

108.0"

228.0"

117.0"

D PLAN

E TRANSVERSE SECTION

SS. Paul and Louis, Paris (1625–34) (p. 911B), by François Derand, built as the church of the Jesuit College, has the type of plan and richness of effect usually associated with Jesuit churches. Like S. Gervais, it is unusual, however, in having three tiers of Orders in its façade, which in the multiplication of its lines and features and abundant ornament is undisguisedly Baroque.

The **Church of the Sorbonne, Paris** (1635–42) (p. 911C), designed for Cardinal Richelieu by Lemercier, bears evidence of his training in Rome, yet has the restraint typical of the French Classical period as a whole, ornament being effectively subordinated to the comprehensive architectural effect. The plan has a double-axis symmetry, the crossing crowned with a fine dome, 12 m (40 ft) in diameter. The façade has superimposed Orders, only the lower being in the round, and finishes above with an unbroken pediment, while the aisles are linked to the nave by extended scrolls.

The **Church of the Val de Grâce, Paris** (1645–67), begun by François Mansart, formerly attached to a monastery, now forms part of the Military Hospital. Lemercier took over the work when Mansart was dismissed in 1646, and the design of the upper part is due to him. It is for this reason that the exterior (p. 912A) has some resemblance to the Church of the Sorbonne, though it is bolder and more successfully composed. It has a fine projecting portal, by Mansart, and the aisles are connected to the nave by vigorous scrolled consoles, while in the distance rises Lemercier's massive and ornate dome, retained by sixteen buttresses faced with pilasters and capped with inverted consoles above the serrated entablature. The interior, with wide nave flanked by piers faced with Corinthian pilasters, vaulted roof and dome, 17.1 m (56 ft) diameter, and the saucer-domed aisles, undoubtedly influenced Sir Christopher Wren in his design for S. Paul's, London (p. 1014).

S. Sulpice, Paris (p. 912B), was commenced in 1646 but the scheme was refashioned by Le Vau in 1655, while others took a hand before the body of the church was finished in 1745. It is a church of vast size, with no less than eighteen chapels, and with domical vaulting borne by Corinthian columns. The famous façade (1733–49) (p. 912B), designed by Servandoni, is 62.5 m (205 ft) wide and forms a great two-storeyed narthex screen with superimposed Doric and Ionic Orders flanked by towers, the northernmost having been finished by Chalgrin in 1778.

The **Dome of the Invalides, Paris** (1680–91) (pp. 912D, 914A–C), by J. H. Mansart, completed the scheme of the Hôtel des Invalides undertaken by Bruant during the years 1670–7, and is one of the most impressive Renaissance domes in France (p. 912D). It has an internal diameter of 27.6 m (90 ft 9 ins), and is placed over the centre of a Greek-cross plan, resting on four piers in which openings lead by steps to four angle chapels (p. 914B) which fill in the angles of the cross, making a square of 60.3 m (198 ft) externally. It has a high drum with coupled columns and lofty windows, and the dome proper is triple in construction (p. 914C). The inner dome, 53.3 m (175 ft) high, has a wide central opening, through which are seen the painted decorations of the middle dome, lighted by windows at its base. The external dome is framed of timber covered with lead, and crowned by a high lantern and cross, rising to a height of 106.5 m (350 ft). The construction differs considerably from that of S. Paul's, London (pp. 1014, 1018), where an intermediate brick cone supports the external stone lantern.

The **Panthéon, Paris** (1755–92) (pp. 912C, 913A, 914D–F), erected from designs by Soufflot, has a fine portico with unusual arrangement of columns leading to the main building, which is a Greek cross on plan (p. 914D). The four piers which support the central dome were originally so slight as to threaten the stability of the structure, and were afterwards strengthened by Rondelet. The dome, 21 m (69 ft) in diameter, is triple in construction (p. 914E), as in the Invalides, but has an outer dome of stone covered with lead (p. 913A). The interior (p. 912C) owes much of its elegance to the unusually slender piers, the fine Corinthian columns, and the large clear-storey windows, invisible externally (p. 914F), surmounted by the domical vaulting. The general effect is enhanced by the coloured frescoes of foremost French artists. The exterior (p. 913A) is striking by reason of its magnificent hexastyle portico of Corinthian columns, thrown into relief by the unbroken, windowless walls, whose only decoration is a continuous entablature with carved festoons. The Panthéon was originally the church of S. Geneviève.

The **Madeleine, Paris** (1806–42) (p. 913B), designed by Vignon in imitation of an octastyle peripteral Roman temple, 106.5 m × 44.5 m (350 ft × 147 ft), has a 'cella' or nave divided into three bays, covered by saucer domes with central openings for lighting the church, which has a most impressive interior, while the apse at the sanctuary end has a semi-dome. The imposing exterior depends largely for its effect upon its island site, which is further accentuated by the podium, 7 m (23 ft) high, on which the building stands, and by the magnificent rise of the approach up the wide expanse of steps. The Corinthian columns of the grand surrounding peristyle are built up in thin drums, the joints of which somewhat confuse the lines of the fluting. This peristyle supports an entablature in which the architrave is formed of voussoirs instead of a series of horizontal lintels, and the principal pediment has a sculptured tympanum.

BIBLIOGRAPHY

BASDEVANT, D. *L'Architecture française*. Paris, 1971.

BLOMFIELD, R. *A History of French Architecture, 1494 to 1661*. 2 vols. London, 1921.

—. *A History of French Architecture, 1661 to 1774*. 2 vols. London, 1921.

BLONDEL, J. F. *L'Architecture française* (known as the 'Grand Blondel'). 4 vols. Folio. Paris, 1752–6.

BLUNT, A. *François Mansart*. London, 1941.

—. *Art and Architecture in France, 1500–1700*. Harmondsworth and Baltimore, 1953.

—. *Philibert de l'Orme*. London, 1958.

DESHAIRS, L. *Le Petit Trianon et le Grand Trianon*. 2 vols. Paris, 1909–.

DU CERCEAU, J. A. *Les plus Excellents Bastiments de France*. 2 vols. Paris, 1868–70 (date of original work, 1576–9).

FELS, E. FRISCH, COMTE DE. *Jacques-Ange Gabriel*. Paris, 1912, 1924.

GALLET, M. *Paris Domestic Architecture* (of the eighteenth century). London, 1972.

GANAY, E DE. *Châteaux de France*. Paris, 1948–50.

GÉBELIN, F. *Les Châteaux de la Loire*. Paris, 1927.

—. *Les Châteaux de la Renaissance*. Paris, 1927.

—. *Le style Renaissance en France*. Paris, 1942.

GEYMÜLLER, H. VON. *Die Baukunst der Renaissance in Frankreich*. Stuttgart, 1898–1901.

GROMORT, G. *L'architecture de la Renaissance en France*. Paris, 1930.

GUÉRINET, A. *L'Architecture française: extérieurs et intérieurs*. 12 vols. Paris, 1900–.

HAUTECOEUR, L. *L'Architecture française de la Renaissance à nos jours*. Paris, 1941.

—. *Histoire de l'architecture classique en France*. 7 vols., sixteenth century to 1900, some of which have been revised. Paris, 1943–65–.

HERMANN, W. *Laugier and Eighteenth-Century French Theory*. London, 1962.

JESTAZ, B. *Le Voyage d'Italie de Robert de Cotte*. Paris, 1966.

KALNEIN and LEVEY. *Art and Architecture of the Eighteenth Century in France*. Harmondsworth and Baltimore, 1972.

KAUFMANN, E. *Architecture in the Age of Reason*. Cambridge, Mass., 1955, paperback 1968.

KIMBALL, F. *The Creation of the Rococo*. Philadelphia, 1943, paperback 1964.

KRAFFT, et RANSONNETTE. *Plans . . . des plus belles Maisons . . . construites à Paris*, etc. Paris, c. 1810.

LAVEDAN, P. *L'Architecture française.* Paris, 1944, paperback in English 1956.

MITFORD, N. *The Sun King.* London, 1966.

NOLHAC, P. DE. *La création de Versailles.* Paris, 1925.

—. *Versailles and the Trianons.* London, 1906.

—. *Histoire du château de Versailles.* Paris, 1911–18.

PÉROUSE DE MONTCLOS, J. M. *Étienne-Louis Boullée.* Paris, 1969.

PETZET, M. *Soufflots Sainte-Geneviève und der französische Kirchenbau des 18. Jahrhunderts.* Berlin, 1961.

RAVAL, M. *C.-N. Ledoux.* Paris, 1945.

REUTERSWÄRD, P. *The Two Churches of the Hotel des Invalides.* Stockholm, 1965.

ROSENAU, H. *Boullée's Treatise on Architecture.* 1953.

WARD, W. H. *Architecture of the Renaissance in France, 1495–1830.* 2 vols. London, 1926.

—. *French Châteaux and Gardens in the Sixteenth Century.* Illustrated with facsimiles of original drawings by J. A. du Cerceau. London, 1909.

29
RENAISSANCE ARCHITECTURE
IN GERMANY
AND CENTRAL EUROPE

Sixteenth to nineteenth century

INFLUENCES

GEOGRAPHICAL

By reason of their central position in Europe the Teutonic peoples absorbed Renaissance art from Italy to the south and from France to the west, but the distance from the centre of the movement deferred its arrival until some 125 years after its emergence in Italy. The states of Prussia, Hanover, Saxony, Bavaria, Wurtemberg and Baden, together with Silesia, Bohemia, Switzerland and Austria, were distinguished by different geographical conditions, and these differences were reflected in the architecture.

GEOLOGICAL

Timber, brick and stone continued to impart their particular character to architecture, according to local usage. Moulded and ornamental brickwork was used in great variety in the northern alluvial plains, while stone and timber were handled in the vernacular manner of the locality.

CLIMATIC

The revived Classic forms were modified from those of Italy to suit a more northern temperature. Thus windows continued to be large, roofs to be steep to throw off snow, and chimneys, necessary for heating, to be prominent features.

HISTORICAL, SOCIAL AND RELIGIOUS

The succession of Charles V (Charles I of Spain) to the possessions of the Houses of Castile, Aragon and Burgundy, including the Low Countries, marks the climax of the German Renaissance. In 1516 he gained the two Sicilies, and on the death of Maximilian in 1519 he became, as Emperor, the most powerful ruler of his day. Various invasions by the Turks between the years 1529 and 1562 further complicated matters in Germany, increased the difficulties of the House of Hapsburg, and were inimical to architectural activities. The wars of Charles V and the Catholics against the Protestant princes (1547–55) were brought to an end by the Peace of Augsburg, which allowed each state to set up what religion it pleased, and to exile individuals who were of different religion from that of the prevailing government. The growing maladjustment and the political incapacity of both sides culminated in the famous 'Thirty Years' War' (1618–48) between Catholic and Protestant princes. Frederick, the Elector Palatine, son-in-law of James I of England, Christian IV of Denmark and Gustavus Adolphus of Sweden fought on the Protestant

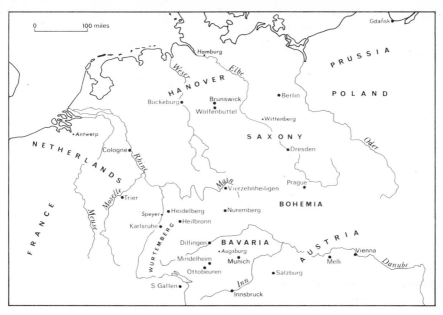

Central Europe in the Renaissance period

side. Under Cardinals Richelieu and Mazarin, France backed the Protestant side in order to weaken the Hapsburgs; and when the Peace of Westphalia (1648) brought the long struggle to an end, the war had impoverished Germany, depleted her population, and left France the leading nation in Europe. These wars not only arrested the development of architecture during the period of their actual prosecution, but also retarded building activities for some time after the conclusion of peace. In the latter part of the seventeenth century many German princes allied themselves with Louis XIV, but under the Hohenzollerns Brandenburg-Prussia became powerful in the north, its Elector being crowned Frederick I, King of Prussia in 1701. His grandson Frederick II ('the Great') raised Prussia to predominance among the German states, a position which it lost in the Napoleonic era but regained after 1815.

Renaissance Germany was composed of divers margravates, palatinates, electorates, duchies, ecclesiastical states and imperial cities, subject to the different reigning houses of Hapsburg, Hohenzollern, Wittelsbach and Wettin. There obtained a great diversity and rivalry in social life and institutions, which also made for a corresponding diversity in artistic development. The Holy Roman Empire still failed to function effectively, even though in 1556 it was separated from Spain and assigned to Ferdinand, brother of Charles V. Feudalism began to disappear; gunpowder changed military methods and bands of mercenaries replaced feudal troops. There were also various internal influences at work, such as the power of the great trading towns of the Hanseatic League, the position of the Guilds in civic government, and the attempt of the peasants to secure their freedom. The principal Renaissance factor was the influence of the universities, notably of Heidelberg, the chief seat of the Humanist movement. This was further strengthened by the invention of printing, while in the eighteenth century the literary works of Winckelmann, Goethe and others aroused interest in the architecture of ancient Greece. Martin Luther (1483–1546) towers above all other Germans of his time as the dominating figure of the Reformation in Germany, and the day in 1517 on which he published in Wittenberg his famous theses against indulgences inaugurated a revolution in the religious life of Germany. He subsequently burnt the Bull of Excommunication issued against him by the Pope, winning support from the rulers of Saxony, Hesse and numerous German cities. Luther's choice of High German for the translation of the Bible led to its adoption as the basis of the literary language of Germany, while the anti-Roman movement derived support from the longstanding nationalist emphasis of the German humanists. A decree of the Diet of Speyer (1529), forbidding ecclesiastical changes, called forth the protest from Luther and his adherents which originated the name of Protestant. This was followed in 1530 by the Confession of Augsburg and by the Schmalkaldic League of Protestant princes and cities for mutual defence against the House of Hapsburg. The stress and turmoil in religious thought of this period of upheaval allowed little opportunity for the erection of new churches, but it resulted in the transformation of those of previous periods to meet the needs of the reformed religion, in the ritual of which preaching became a powerful factor, and necessitated that increased space for seated congregations which brought about the introduction of galleries. The strife between Protestants and Catholics was followed by the Counter-Reformation, reinforced by the arrival of the Jesuits and by the Council of Trent (1563).

ARCHITECTURAL CHARACTER

The Renaissance style appeared in Germany about 1550. Approximately, the successive periods were: (a) *Early Renaissance* (1550–1600), chiefly consisting of the introduction of Renaissance elements into Gothic buildings or of additions to them, though some examples, such as the Heinrichsbau, Heidelberg, are of great size; (b) *Proto-Baroque* (1600–60), in which Italian architects themselves carried the Renaissance from north Italy to Switzerland, Austria and Germany, while native architects began successfully to emulate them and produce national versions of the style; (c) the *Baroque* (1660–1710), in which architects, principally of native origin but who often had received part of their training in Rome or elsewhere in Italy, brought German architecture to a splendid culmination; (d) the *Rococo* (1710–60), an extension of the Baroque period wherein architecture and decoration show great refinement and technical mastery but less vigour and force; and (e) the *Antiquarian* (1760–1830), in which there is a progressive return to ancient Classical models, the Greek Revival being a manifestation within and somewhat beyond the period 1790–1830.

Broadly speaking, the greatest works of the German Renaissance date from the hundred years 1660–1760, i.e., the Baroque period, including the Rococo. In no other part of Europe outside Italy was there so joyous and picturesque a flowering of Renaissance architecture, and indeed, the Baroque of Austria and neighbouring Bavaria, Switzerland and Bohemia appears as a natural, superlative, culmination of the Italian Renaissance, intimately related to and an outgrowth of the Baroque of Rome and Lombardy. The German Baroque suited the people, peasant and patrician alike, in its intensely visual appeal; the rich profusion of ornamentation in church interiors was not wilful display but told the Bible story much as hieroglyphs, mural reliefs or stained glass had carried the religious message in other times and places. Church and palace interiors may sometimes appear over-ornate, even gaudy, but the opulent magnificence that frequently resulted was a direct response to

Ⓐ WINDOWS & NICHE with DIANA: HEINRICHSBAU, HEIDELBERG CASTLE

Ⓑ CHARLES THE GREAT: FRIEDRICHSBAU, HEIDELBERG CASTLE

Ⓒ WINDOWS & NICHE with SATURN: HEINRICHSBAU, HEIDELBERG CASTLE

Ⓓ CAPITAL. FOUNTAIN of S.JEAN: FREIBURG: SWITZᴰ

Ⓔ GABLE HEILBRONN

Ⓕ CAPITAL. FOUNTAIN of THE SAMARITAN: FREIBURG: SWITZᴰ

Ⓖ WINDOW · ERFURT

Ⓗ CARTOUCHE · HEILBRONN

Ⓙ DOORWAY S.MICHAEL: MUNICH

HEIDELBERG CASTLE

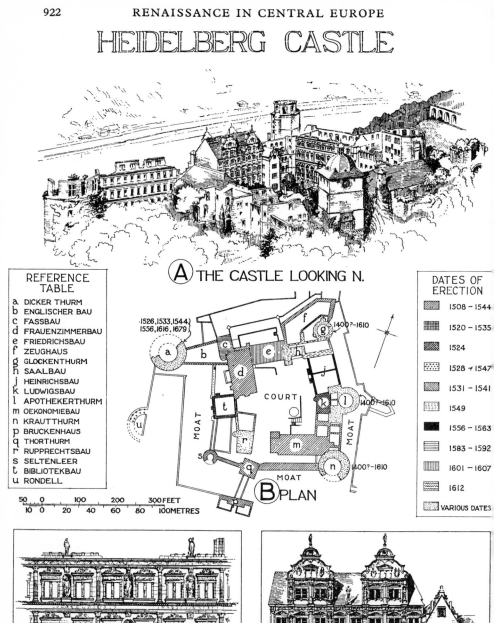

(A) THE CASTLE LOOKING N.

REFERENCE TABLE

a DICKER THURM
b ENGLISCHER BAU
c FASSBAU
d FRAUENZIMMERBAU
e FRIEDRICHSBAU
f ZEUGHAUS
g GLOCKENTHURM
h SAALBAU
j HEINRICHSBAU
k LUDWIGSBAU
l APOTHEKERTHURM
m OEKONOMIEBAU
n KRAUTTHURM
p BRUCKENHAUS
q THORTHURM
r RUPPRECHTSBAU
s SELTENLEER
t BIBLIOTEKBAU
u RONDELL

·1526,1533,1544)
1556,1616,1679

1400?-1610

COURT

MOAT

MOAT

1400?-1610

1400?-1610

MOAT

(B) PLAN

DATES OF ERECTION

▨	1508 – 1544
▦	1520 – 1535
▩	1524
▨	1528 – 1547
▨	1531 – 1541
▨	1549
■	1556 – 1563
▤	1583 – 1592
▥	1601 – 1607
▧	1612
▨	VARIOUS DATES

50 0   100   200   300 FEET
10 0   20   40   60   80   100 METRES

(C) HEINRICHSBAU

SAAL BAU

(D) FRIEDRICHSBAU

social, religious and political circumstances, and just as spontaneous as the gaiety universally manifested in peasant art. Ornamentation was deliberate and purposeful, and had a greater part to play in ecclesiastical, particularly Jesuit, buildings than in secular architecture, which was relatively plain, except in the case of the mansions and country residences of the nobility, where it was appropriate to express gracious living.

Notable Baroque architects were Johann Bernhard Fischer von Erlach (1656–1723), also a sculptor and writer on architectural history, who trained under Carlo Fontana (p. 846) in Rome and worked principally in Vienna; Jakob Prandtauer (1660–1526), designer of the monastery at Melk, an architectural masterpiece (p. 932B, C); and the Thumb family of Vorarlberg, Christian (1683–1726), Michael (1640–90) and Peter (1681–1766). Contemporary with these last were the brothers Asam (Cosmas Damian, 1686–1739 and Egid Quirin, 1692–1750), gifted fresco painters and stuccoists who also practised as architects; Balthasar Neumann (1687–1753), the most brilliant of the group; Lukas von Hildebrandt (1688–1745), who began as a military engineer but whose buildings nevertheless are cheerfully lively in mien; the Dientzenhofer family, native to Bavaria but working principally in Prague, of whom Christopher and Kilian Ignaz (1689–1751) were perhaps the most distinguished; and Johann Michael Fischer (1692–1766), second in ability only to Neumann among south German architects. No less talented were Dominikus and Johann Baptist Zimmermann (the latter 1680–1758) and their sons Franz Dominikus and Joseph.

A feature of the Baroque and Rococo periods was the collaboration of artist-craftsmen with the designers of the buildings. They were to be found in every town, often a family group working together in different crafts. Usually these men worked for fashionable architects; but some, like the Asam brothers, already mentioned, and the Zimmermann family, painters, carvers and stuccoists, were themselves the architects of some of the finest buildings of their age. Not only were Baroque buildings enhanced by their furnishings—organs by Gabler and Greiff at Weingarten, or by Riepp at Ottobeuren, pulpits by F. Sporer at Weingarten or by J. Früholzer at Steinhausen, figures by A. Sturm at Wies, stalls by M. Hörmann at Zwiefalten, or similar works in any church of the period—but the architecture itself was largely the work of these craftsmen. Trompe l'œil, as practised by Italian painters such as Baciccio at the Jesuit Church in Rome, reached its peak in Germany. Painters such as J. Michael Rottmayr, Paul Troger, Johann Georg Bergmüller, Christof Thomas Scheffler, Johann Baptist Zimmermann, Cosmas Damian Asam, the Wink family, Johann and Januarius Zick, Matthäus Günther, Johann Jakob Zeiller and, perhaps the greatest of them all, Franz Anton Maulbertsch, to select only a few of the great number practising at the time, framed their frescoes with architectural forms, painted in perspective and with cast shadows, so as to continue the actual architecture of the building. From the ground it is not possible to tell what is two-dimensional paint and what is three-dimensional stucco. The illusion is complete. That collaboration between artist and architect was equally complete can be seen, for instance, in the work of Johann Zick for Balthasar Neumann, and of Januarius Zick, in the next generation, in his frescoes at Wiblingen Abbey Church, which he painted after his return from Paris in the Neo-Classical manner to blend with the architecture executed in the same style several years before.

EXAMPLES

Some of the examples to be named were destroyed or severely damaged in the 1939–45 war; in some cases they have since been repaired or rebuilt.

SECULAR ARCHITECTURE

Heidelberg Castle (1531–1612) (p. 922) well exemplifies progressive developments of the Early Renaissance in the various additions to the Mediaeval castle (p. 922B). The later of them suffer from over-ornamentation. There is a great watch tower (1531–41) and an irregular court around which are grouped the Renaissance buildings (p. 922A). The Saalbau (1549) in the north-east corner shows Gothic features mingled with those of the incoming Renaissance: this is relatively plain (p. 922D). The Heinrichsbau (1556–63), long ago fallen into a ruined state, has superimposed Ionic and Corinthian pilasters and half-columns, two-light windows showing Venetian affinities, and symbolic statues in niches (pp. 921A, C, 922C). The Friedrichsbau (1601–7), on the north side, is more mature in design, again showing borrowings from early Venetian Renaissance in the round-headed traceried windows of the ground floor and the two tiers of pedimented two-light windows above them, while two picturesque windowed and scrolled gables and a steep roof indicate some slight retention of native Mediaeval traits (p. 922D). Niches containing statues of the Counts Palatine are distributed on each of the tiers (pp. 921B, 922D).

The **Rathaus, Heilbronn** (1535–96) (p. 925A) (severely damaged), is an attractive and quaint building still essentially Gothic in character. Its arcade of stumpy columns encloses a market, and side steps lead up to the upper storeys; while a central panel bears the signs of the zodiac and a clock with figures and a bell; the steep roof has three stages of dormer windows and an open turret.

The **Gewandhaus, Brunswick (Braunschweig)**, the body of which is Gothic, has an eastern façade (1592) (p. 926B) illustrating typical north-German early Renaissance characteristics, introduced via the Low Countries rather than directly from Italy. An arcade of three-centred arches is surmounted by three storeys of Ionic, Corinthian and Composite three-quarter columns, and above rises an immense gable of four storeys of Hermes pilasters, so much used in Elizabethan architecture, framed in by the customary side-scrolls of the stepped gables.

The **Rathaus Portico, Cologne** (1569–71) (p. 926E) (destroyed) designed by W. Wernickel, was an exquisite structure remarkably advanced for its day, showing marked north Italian traits. An arcade of semicircular arches with free-standing Corinthian columns was surmounted on the first storey by slightly-pointed arches flanked by Composite columns, while Gothic tradition was also evident in a 'rib-and-panel' vault within. The crestings and steep roof similarly showed mixed Mediaeval and Lombard Renaissance ideas.

The **Pellerhaus, Nuremberg** (1605) (p. 926D) (destroyed), one of the finest examples of the earlier Renaissance in the city, was of Proto-Baroque design externally, the influence of the stucco medium being clearly apparent in the busy ornament lavishly used in its upper parts. The main dispositions, however, were still of the native type, resembling Belgian practice rather than Italian, tiers of large windows rising into a stepped and scrolled gable ornamented with pinnacles and a sculptural centre-piece at the apex. The basement and pilasters of the lower two window tiers were rusticated, and the gable windows divided by Hermes pilasters.

The **Zeughaus, Gdańsk, Poland** (1605) (p. 926A) (rebuilt), a good example of the brick architecture of the north, showing kinship with Belgian Early Renaissance, was designed by a Flemish architect, Anton van Obbergen. The tall, mullioned-and-transomed windows were of the plain early type, ornament being confined to doorways and to local features, except on the third storey, broken into scrolled and pinnacled gables and enlivened with strapwork decoration.

The **Rathaus, Bremen** (façade 1612–) is mainly Gothic (1405–10). The chief

A. The Rathaus, Heilbronn (1535–96). See p. 924

B. The Loggia, Waldstein Palace, Prague (1621–30). See p. 929

A. The Zeughaus, Gdańsk (1605).
See p. 924

B. The Gewandhaus,
Brunswick (1592).
See p. 924

C. The Residenz, Würzburg (1722–).
See p. 929

D. The Pellerhaus, Nurem-
berg (1605). See p. 924

E. The Rathaus, Cologne: Renaissance
portico (1569–71). See p. 924

F. The Kinsky Palace, Vienna
(1709–13). See p. 929

A. The Troja Palace, Prague: garden front (1679–96). See p. 929

B. The Zwinger, Dresden (1711–22). See p. 929

C. The Schloss, Karlsruhe (1751–6 and later). See p. 929

A. The Brandenburg Gate, Berlin (1789–93). See p. 930

B. The Neumünster-Stiftskirche,
Würzburg (façade 1710–19).
See p. 937

C. The Frauenkirche, Dresden
(1726–40). See p. 937

frontage has a light arcade, large windows, scroll gables and many statues.

The **Loggia, Waldstein Palace, Prague** (1621–30) (p. 925B) by Antonio and Pietro Spezza, is of Italian design, like the palace as a whole. Paired Tuscan-Doric columns support the triple arches of the porch in a gracious scheme showing expert knowledge of the classical elements. The fenestration is Proto-Baroque, as are the subsidiary details, while the stucco decorations are the work of the famous Genoese architect, Bartolomeo Bianco (p. 810).

The **Troja Palace, Prague** (1679–96) (p. 927A), by J. B. Mathey, is a fine instance of the Baroque period, a restrained design of a single giant Order, the lines of the Composite pilasters being carried into the entablature as far as the bed-mould of the cornice. The central intercolumniation is wider than the rest. While the façade proper has a Palladian dignity and simplicity, a profusion of rich sculptural detail is concentrated about the upper and lower portals and the double, horseshoe, staircase giving access to the 'piano nobile'.

The **Palace of the Hungarian Guard, Vienna** (1710–12) (p. 932A) by J. B. Fischer von Erlach, was originally (and is today commonly) known as the **Trautson Palace**. A giant Order of paired Composite pilasters stands over a horizontally-rusticated basement storey; the decoration is rich, but is not allowed anywhere to intrude upon the main elements of the architectural composition. While the modelling of the chief masses is vigorous, the modelling of the detail is finer and shallower than in typical Baroque architecture, and in fact tends towards the Rococo expression. Other notable secular buildings by Fischer von Erlach are the **Clam Gallas Palace, Prague** (1701–12), the **Ministry of the Interior, Vienna** (1716) and the **Schwarzenberg Palace, Vienna** (1705–20). He collaborated with Lukas von Hildebrandt in the design of the **Ministry of Finance, Vienna** (1702–10).

The **Kinsky Palace, Vienna** (1709–13) (p. 926F) (half-ruined), by Lukas von Hildebrandt, is very representative of this architect's style. The windowed frieze in the main entablature is an interesting feature.

The **Belvedere, Vienna** (1693–1724), a summer residence, is one of Hildebrandt's most famous works. It has an upper (1721–4) (p. 931A) and a lower palace, and splendid gardens stretching between.

The **Zwinger, Dresden** (1711–22) (p. 927B) (rebuilt), by M. D. Poppelmann (1662–1736), is one of the most curious and bizarre constructions of the German Renaissance, built as a resort for the princely court for pageants, festivals and tournaments, structures of one and two storeys being arranged around an open enclosure. The entrance is particularly extravagant, seething with a congestion of columns, pilasters, fragmented entablatures and incoherent ornament, crowned with a bulbous, crested 'helm'.

The **Residenz, Würzburg** (1722–) (p. 926C), by Balthasar Neumann, but in consultation with other architects, including de Cotte and Boffrand (who was largely responsible for the plan) from France and Hildebrandt from Vienna, is an immense palace built for the Prince Bishop Philip Franz von Schönborn. In the garden room is an early ceiling by Johann Zick, superseded by G. B. Tiepolo who painted the staircase ceiling, which includes a portrait of Neumann and his dog. Plasterwork in the state rooms is by Antonio Bossi and other paintings are by J. Rudolf Byss.

The **Schloss Bruchsal**, north-east of Karlsruhe (1730s) includes the Grand Staircase and state rooms by Neumann. The main wings are by Franz Freiherr von Ritter (1715), the stucco by Johann Michael Feichtmayr, and the frescoes by Johann Zick. Almost totally destroyed during the Second World War, it has been restored using, as far as possible, original techniques and similar materials.

The **Schloss, Karlsruhe** (1751–6 and later) (p. 927C) (badly damaged) has a fan-shaped plan which determined the arrangement of the whole town, laid out earlier in the century with thirty-two streets radiating from it.

The **Brandenburg Gate, Berlin** (1789–93) (p. 928A) (damaged), by C. G. Langhans, is in Greek Revival style and imitates the Propylaea at Athens (p. 197); it illustrates the Antiquarian trend of the later part of the century in Europe. The Glyptotek, Pinacothek and Propylaea, all in Munich, and the Walhalla, Regensburg, were designed by Leopold von Klenze (1784–1864); the New Theatre, the Museum and the Polytechnic School, Berlin, by Karl Friedrich von Schinkel (1781–1841).

ECCLESIASTICAL ARCHITECTURE

Of the few new sixteenth-century churches the Jesuit church of **S. Michael, Munich** (1583–97) was among the first to show Renaissance features (p. 921J).

The **Marienkirche, Wolfenbüttel** (1608–23) is an essentially Gothic structure, adorned with quite unassimilated Proto-Baroque detail concentrated strongly in stepped and scrolled gables ranged together on the two long sides.

The **Church, Bückeburg** (1613) has an extravagantly ornate Proto-Baroque west front, but the windows still are Gothic: the interior has Corinthian columns supporting a pointed arcade and rib-and-panel vault.

The **Cathedral, Salzburg** (1614–28) by Santino Solari, an Italian, and the Jesuit churches at **Dillingen** (1610–17), **Mindelheim** (1625–6), **Vienna** (1627–31) and **Innsbruck** (1627–40) were among the first to be expressed wholly in the Renaissance manner.

The **Theatine Church, Munich** (1663–90) (p. 931B), by A. Barelli and H. Zuccali, is an instance of the developed Baroque style. It is based upon the church of S. Andrea della Valle at Rome. The west façade has two tiers of Orders, the aisles being linked to the nave by swept buttresses, while twin western towers rise through three storeys of Orders to oddly coarse scroll-buttressed helms. The features are not as vigorously modelled as in contemporary Italian Baroque, nor is the focal emphasis on the west door so strongly marked. A lanterned dome over the crossing completes the impressive scheme.

The **Monastery, Melk** (1702–14) (p. 932B, C) by Jakob Prandtauer, with frescoes by J. Michael Rottmayr, is one of the most striking monuments of the Baroque period. The abbey buildings mount in stages at the crest of a steep-sided rocky ridge, riding high above the wood-fringed river Danube; western towers with helms of intriguing profile serve as foil to the softly-moulded contours of the crowning dome. The grand effect arises principally from the disposition of the building-masses on the rising site. Ornament is used sparingly in the most effective locations, and the abbey main buildings are relatively severe. There are other great monasteries at **S. Florian** (1686–1715), near Vienna, to which Jakob Prandtauer contributed after 1708, and **Klosterneuburg** (c. 1750), where the church is an old foundation of 1136.

Brevnov Monastery Church, Prague (1710–15) (p. 933A) by Christopher Dientzenhofer is a splendid illustration of what Baroque architects could achieve without recourse to elaborate ornamentation. This modest building has most of the Baroque qualities, showing play with richly curved forms in plan, elevation and detail, varied expressions of condition and spacing of the Orders and the vigorous modelling of masses which distinguishes the Baroque proper from the Rococo.

S. Nicholas, Prague (1703–52) (p. 934C, D), the finest Baroque church in the city, has a nave designed by Christopher Dientzenhofer (1703–11) (p. 934D) of which the interior has all the dramatic power of which the style was capable. Giant clustered pilasters are set diagonally to form an arcade embracing aisle and

A. The Upper Belvedere, Vienna (1721–4). See p. 929

B. The Theatine Church, Munich (1663–90). See p. 930

A. Palace of the Hungarian Guard,
Vienna (1710–12). See p. 929

B. The Monastery, Melk (1702–14).
See p. 930

C. The Monastery, Melk: interior of church

A. Brevnov Monastery Church, Prague (1710–15). See p. 930

B. Karlskirche, Vienna (1716–37). See p. 937

A. Entrance front   B. Interior

The Church of the Holy Ghost, Munich (1724–30). See p. 937

C. Entrance front   D. Interior (1703–11)

S. Nicholas, Prague (1703–52). See p. 930

A. West front

B. Interior

S. Michael, Berg-am-Laim, Munich (1738–51). See p. 937

c. West front

D. Interior

The Pilgrimage Church, Vierzehnheiligen (1744–72). See p. 937

A. S. Paulin, Trier (1732–54).
See p. 937

B. Wiblingen Abbey Church
(1772–81): nave. See p. 938

C. The Wieskirche, Steinhausen
(1746–54): interior. See p. 938

D. Zwiefalten Monastery Church
(1738–62): N. side of nave. See p. 938

clear-storey in such wise as to produce an undulated vault which, with the help of its painted decoration, seems less to contain than to free the upper space and open up the heavens. Most of the architectural lines are curvilinear; the voids seem to interweave, the lesser into the greater, and the whole effect is one of swirling movement totally different from the serene static character of Palladian architecture.

The **Neumünster-Stiftskirche, Würzburg** (façade, 1710–19) (p. 928B), by V. Pezani and J. Dientzenhofer, is truly Baroque with its concave modelling, clustered and variously-disposed Orders, and vigorous, dramatic effect. Also at Würzburg, is the **Käppele Pilgrimage Church** (1747–50), by Neumann, with frescoes by Matthäus Günther.

Karlskirche, Vienna (1716–37) (p. 933B), by J. B. Fischer von Erlach, is this famous architect's masterpiece, finished after his death. In some respects it resembles S. Agnese, Rome. The hexastyle entrance porch leads up to a mighty dome, and the nave façade has quadrant links with scroll-topped, symmetrical angle pavilions beyond mighty replicas of Trajan's column at Rome (p. 326). The composition is grand and impressive, yet this instance of Fischer von Erlach's later architecture is quieter and shallower in modelling than his earlier work, thus partaking more of the Rococo than the true Baroque quality.

The **Church of the Holy Ghost, Munich** (1724–30) (p. 934A, B) by J. G. Ettenhofer, itself a rebuilding of an earlier hall-church, was extended westwards by three bays in 1885 and the west front re-fashioned after the former design. The Rococo interior is essentially the work of the brothers Asam.

The **Frauenkirche, Dresden** (1726–40) (p. 928C) (destroyed) was the prime example of eighteenth-century Protestant church architecture. It had a highly centralized plan, contained within a square of 43 m (140 ft) sides. The stone dome was oval, about 24 m (78 ft) across, and so excessively stilted as to appear slightly onion-shaped. The strong modelling and pyramidal arrangement made a powerful composition.

S. Paulin, Trier (1732–54) (p. 936A) by Balthasar Neumann, is one of a number of fine works by this distinguished architect. It is an aisleless church, high in proportions, with a helm-topped axial western tower and an eastern apse. Internally (p. 936A) it is aglow with colour and lively with the play of form; clustered pilastered piers, some with sinuous cornices, contrast effectively with the relatively plain walls, while the compartmented domical vaults are enriched with refined stuccowork and brilliant frescoes. The columned and coroneted baldachino, the elaborately fretted woodwork and metalwork of the fitting, contribute to the effect.

S. John Nepomuk, Munich (1733–5) by the brothers Asam, a small church designed and built by the architects at their own expense, is a very representative example of the Rococo phase of Baroque architecture. The ceiling paintings are by T. Scheffler, and the High Altar by F. Tietz.

S. Michael, Berg-am-Laim, Munich (1738–51) (p. 935A, B), by J. M. Fischer, with stucco and frescoes by Johann B. Zimmermann and altars by Johann B. Straub, has a west front typical of the period, a bow-fronted, convex-faced nave flanked by tall, staged and helm-crested western towers.

The **Abbey Church of Ottobeuren** (1748–67), also by J. M. Fischer, the largest Rococo church in Germany, has a similarly arranged west front. The ceiling frescoes are by Jakob Zeiller and the stalls by F. X. Feichtmayr. There is simplified Rococo detailing throughout the Abbey buildings, and there are elaborate state rooms, with frescoes by E. Zobel and Christopher Voght. Similar west fronts with twin towers can be seen in the **Pilgrimage Church, Vierzehnheiligen** (1744–72) (p. 935C, D) by Neumann, with frescoes by Appiani and stucco by Johann M. Feichtmayr; in neighbouring Switzerland at the **Abbey Church, Einsiedeln** (1719–23), by H. G. Kuen and Casper Moosbrugger (who also acted as stone-mason on the Abbey buildings), with frescoes by C. D. and E. Q. Asam; and at **S. Gallen Cathedral** (1755–86) by Peter Thumb and G. G. Bagnato. Other churches by J. M. Fischer include **Zwiefalten Monastery Church** (1738–62) (p. 936D), with frescoes by J. Spiegler and stucco by Johann M. Feichtmayr, and the **Monastery Church** at **Rott-am-Inn** (1760), which has frescoes by M. Günther, figures by Ignaz Günther and stucco by F. X. Feichtmayr.

Wiblingen Abbey Church (1772–81) (p. 936B) was completed, after the death of J. M. Fischer, by Johann Specht in the Louis XVI style of serene Neo-Classicism. Januarius Zick painted his frescoes to match the architecture. The magnificent Rococo library is by C. Wiedemann, with an undulating gallery and ceiling by Franz Martin Kuen (1744).

The **Pilgrimage Church, Steinhausen** (1723–33) is by Dominikus Zimmermann, with Rococo decorations by Johann B. Zimmermann. The **Wieskirche** (1746–54) (p. 936C) is by the same designers, with sculptures by Anton Sturm and J. Verhelst, and altar paintings by B. Albrecht and I. G. Bergmüller. Wies is the most celebrated Rococo church, but has an exterior as simple as a village barn. Both churches have an elliptical plan, but Wies has a rectangular chancel.

BIBLIOGRAPHY

BOURKE, J. *Baroque Churches of Central Europe.* 2nd ed. London, 1962.
BURROUGH, T. H. B. *South German Baroque: an Introduction.* London, 1956.
CHARPENTRAT, P. *Living Architecture: Baroque.* Fribourg and London, 1967.
DEHIO, G. *Handbuch der deutschen Kunstdenkmäler.* Berlin, 1927.
Dehio-Handbuch: die Kunstdenkmäler Österreichs. 4th and 5th eds. Vienna, 1954–8.
FISCHER VON ERLACH, J. B. *Entwurf einer historischen Architektur.* Vienna, 1721.
FRANZ, H. G. *Bauten und Baumeister der Barockzeit in Böhmen.* Leipzig, 1962.
GRIMSCHITZ, B. *Johann Lucas von Hildebrandt.* Vienna, 1923.
HANFSTAENGL, E. *Die Brüder . . . Asam.* Munich, 1955.
HEMPEL, E. *Baroque Art and Architecture in Central Europe.* Harmondsworth and Baltimore, 1965.
—. *Geschichte der deutschen Baukunst.* 2nd ed. Munich, 1956.
HITCHCOCK, H.-R. *German Rococo: The Zimmermann Brothers.* London, 1968.
—. *Rococo Architecture in Southern Germany.* London and New York, 1968.
KUNOTH, G. *Die historische Architektur Fischers von Erlach.* Düsseldorf, 1956.
LIEB, N., and DIEDL, F. *Die Vorarlberger Barockmeister.* Munich and Zurich, 1960.
POWELL, N. *From Baroque to Rococo.* London, 1959.
REUTHER, H. *Die Kirchenbauten Balthasar Neumanns.* Berlin, 1960.
SEDLMAYR, H. *Österreichische Barockarchitektur.* Vienna, 1930.

30

RENAISSANCE ARCHITECTURE IN BELGIUM AND THE NETHERLANDS

Sixteenth to nineteenth century

INFLUENCES

GEOGRAPHICAL

The Netherlands is a term which formerly embraced the whole of the 'Nederland' (Holland) and Belgium. The physical similarity of the low-lying parts did not result in the maintenance of political unity, chiefly owing to the intrusion of external powers. The movement of power and commerce from the Mediterranean to the Atlantic and northern seas of Europe placed the Low Countries in a favourable central position to share in the new sea power, trade, world exploration and colonial expansion; at the same time they were directly in the path of conflicts between the major powers. The period opens with Antwerp, following the decay of Bruges due to the silting up of her waterways, as the richest city and greatest port in northern Europe. After the establishment of the Dutch Republic (1588) the ports of Zeeland, the Zuider Zee, and especially of Amsterdam and Rotterdam, rose to supremacy. Through them and through constant warfare the Dutch developed as an energetic and courageous seafaring nation, with extensive trade and colonial possessions. In the seventeenth century the Dutch began their great engineering feats of draining and reclaiming land, of building polders, dykes and canals, and erecting windmills for pumping water, for all of which they have long been famous.

GEOLOGICAL

Stone and marbles, because they were readily available, and brick continued to be the chief building materials of Belgium, together with the timber of the Ardennes which the craftsmen used with such skill and flourish, especially in the exuberant mature architecture of the seventeenth century. In Holland, bricks (smaller than in England) made from her clay soil created her relatively sober national architecture, and by the seventeenth century the influence of this was felt in England, Denmark and Sweden.

CLIMATIC

In addition to the remarks on p. 707, it should be noted that there are two main climatic zones in the Low Countries, the one relating to the highlands of eastern Belgium and Dutch Limburg, which share the characteristics of continental France and Germany, and the other to the low-lying parts of the Flemish and Dutch coastal areas. The architecture of Holland is greatly influenced by its sea-girt, river intersected and low-lying, fen character, where the frequent driving rains, the winds and clear light produced a simplicity of façade and large windows, with compositions conceived in terms of planes rather than sculptural form. Such circumstances apply less strongly to lowland Belgium, and scarcely at all to its eastern parts.

HISTORICAL, SOCIAL AND RELIGIOUS

Through the marriage of the Emperor Maximilian with Mary of Burgundy the Low Countries became a Hapsburg domain. Hence, on the abdication of Charles V in 1556, the Netherlanders came under the fanatically rigid rule of Philip II of Spain (1556-98). A long and bitter revolt, led by William the Silent, Prince of Orange (1533-84), was ruthlessly opposed by the Spanish who by 1590 had reconquered the ten southern provinces, roughly the modern Belgium. Yet aided by geography and seapower the seven northern provinces won their independence and became the Dutch Republic.

The seventeenth century in Belgium was not a peaceful one, and, with the decay of Antwerp's trade her prosperity suffered greatly. In the eighteenth century, Spanish authority was followed by a period of French rule (1700-6), and under the Treaty of Utrecht (1713) the country passed to Austria. Later, it became involved in the struggle against Louis XV's ambitions (1740-8), only to be returned to Austrian rule. In 1789 there was an internal revolt, and soon after came occupation by the French Revolutionary Forces (1794), this a prelude to her absorption into Napoleon's Empire.

Though equally plagued by wars in the seventeenth century, the Dutch Republic, dominated by the rich and highly urbanized province of Holland, became a great naval power and maritime trading nation with overseas colonies. So great was this prosperity that it survived almost to the end of the next century, despite further major wars, and finally, a middle-class revolt. The shrunken and ramshackle Batavian Republic which followed received French acquiescence in 1795, but expired in 1806 when Napoleon decided to make his brother Louis King of Holland, and in 1810 Dutch independence was eclipsed for a while when Holland became a French province.

The Kingdom of the Netherlands, including Belgium, Holland and Luxembourg, was created in 1815 with William I of Orange as its head. The rule of the Dutch king was unwise, and the situation so disadvantageous to the Belgians that they revolted and became a separate kingdom in 1830; Luxembourg too was made independent.

During the sixteenth century, power and wealth in the Low Countries were mainly in the south, the Court residing at Brussels or Malines, while trade was concentrated on Antwerp. Sacked by the Spaniards in 1576, Antwerp lost its mercantile supremacy to Amsterdam, the Scheldt being closed to commerce from 1648 by the Treaty of Westphalia. The result was catastrophic, since there were no other good ports in the south. For a short time, within the period of Austrian rule in the eighteenth century, prosperity revived, but Belgium remained poor compared with the Dutch Republic.

As the prosperity of the south waned, the fortunes of the north grew and reached a climax in the 'Golden' seventeenth century, with the Dutch Republic as a great European power; the power of wealth through trade was largely in the hands of the burgher class, principally of the provinces of Holland and Zeeland. Within the semi-monarchical Republic, the Princes of Orange had a court which increasingly looked to France for a lead in taste and fashions. The burghers followed the Court in its patronage of art, and their houses were richly decorated and furnished, giving a lively market for the many artists of this great period of Dutch art. The prosperity of the seventeenth century did not last and, by comparison, the next century was one of consolidation, and later, of stagnation.

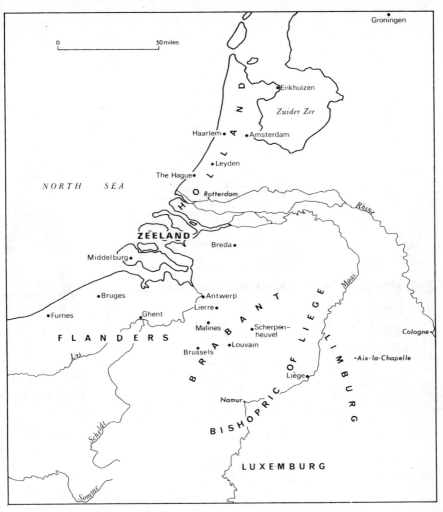

The Netherlands in the seventeenth century

The beliefs of Luther and Calvin were received early in the Low Countries, but since Charles V and Philip II, rulers during the greater part of the sixteenth century, regarded the Catholic Church and the State as indivisible, Protestants were persecuted. However, the revolt and war against the Spaniards became more political than religious: indeed the Protestant Prince of Orange led armies which included a minority of Catholics. The Spanish Netherlands (later Belgium) remained almost wholly Catholic and followed the lead of Rome in church building, wherein as elsewhere, the Baroque style was favoured by the Jesuits. The Dutch, after first adapting and even copying the old churches and setting an enormous pulpit halfway along the side of the nave, arranging pews to face it, experimented with a variety of central plans which were developed to suit the Reformed religion and national taste.

A PINNACLE HAARLEM

B FINIAL HAARLEM

C GABLE ANTWERP

D SPIRE TOWN HALL LEYDEN

E SPIRE NEW CHURCH HAARLEM

F PILASTER UTRECHT CATHᴸ

G TOWN HALL: LEYDEN

H PILASTER UTRECHT CATHᴸ

WOOD

STONE

A, B ENCH-ENDS: DORDRECHT

C GABLE END WITH IRON TIES

D DOOR THE MUSEE PLANTIN ANTWERP

E DOORWAY: ANTWERP

F FROM CHIMNY PIECE: MUSEUM: BRUSSELS

G CAPITAL FROM THE MONUMENT OF GUILLAUME DE CROY, L'EGLISE DES CAPUCINS: ENGHIEN

H STAIRCASE: MUSEE PLANTIN: ANTWERP

J ORNAMENT TO COLUMN L'EGLISE DE CAPUCINS:ENGHIEN

K FIGURES FROM CHIMNEY PIECE IN THE PALAIS DE JUSTICE AT ZALTBOMMEL

A. The Town Hall (1561–6) and Guild Houses, Grand' Place, Antwerp. See p. 946

B. Guild Houses, Grand' Place, Brussels (1690–1752). See p. 946

ARCHITECTURAL CHARACTER

The Early Renaissance becomes notable in the Low Countries about 1515, at first in the southern zone, which continued to enjoy a prodigious prosperity, the factors at work on this Belgian architecture producing that same rich and often extravagantly ornate expression, and that same zest for ornamentation, that had created the Brabantine Gothic. To some extent the nature of this style can be explained by the circumstance of the distance from the Italian source, and Spanish, French and German influence during transmission, but its strong individuality is mainly due to national conditions and characteristics. It is rich externally and internally, is rarely grand in scale and, due to the northern climate, windows in domestic work are even larger than the French and may occupy almost as much space as wall. Architectural details progressively assume a more authentic Italian character, but methods of composition and decoration are in a variety of ways unique. The Early Renaissance was centred on Flanders and Brabant, and at first, pseudo-Classical detail was applied to Gothic forms. The Parma Palace (now the Palais de Justice) at Malines (1503) was perhaps the first instance in Northern Europe; but more typical is the Old Chancellery, Bruges (1530–5) (p. 947A). Several Italians were then working in the Low Countries, Donato di Boni on the fortifications of Antwerp (1543) and Tommaso Vincidor at Breda Castle (1536). Antwerp was the chief centre, with its great school of painters and sculptors who were often also architects. There, Pieter Coecke van Aalst (1502–50) published translations of Alberti and Serlio, and Cornelius Floris (or de Vriendt) (1504–75) established a style with his Town Hall (p. 944A). This style was widely spread by the books of Hans Vredeman de Vries (1527–1606) throughout northern Europe. The Early Renaissance of Belgium continued to the end of the sixteenth century, though owing to political reasons little was done in the last thirty years. The northern provinces (Holland) followed the southern lead, but at a little distance of time, since they were as yet economically less robust, but from the first, Dutch architecture was simpler and more restrained. It was the books of Vredeman de Vries and the example of the Antwerp Town Hall that guided Lieven de Key (1560–1627), a Flemish refugee, in designing the buildings in Holland that first soundly established the Renaissance there (p. 942G).

For the seventeenth century and later it is essential to speak separately of Belgium and Holland. Belgium progressed with its individualistic interpretation of the Italian Proto-Baroque flourishing at that time, to a style which may be described as Baroque, though it is more profuse and less bold and grand than its Italian counterpart; apart from Jesuit and other church architecture which affords a closer parallel. The best period of the Belgian version of the Baroque falls in the first half of the seventeenth century, after which it loses some of its virility though none of its exuberance; and with the eighteenth, shows in its decoration the influence of Austrian and French Rococo, while from the mid-century it took the Antiquarian turn notable also in Italy, France and England. Towards the end of the same century, occasional Greek Revival manifestations appeared. Meanwhile, Dutch architecture took a substantially different course. Lieven de Key and Hendrik de Keyser (1565–1621) developed the early Dutch style, usually plainer than the Belgian, until c. 1625 when it matured in a 'Palladian' phase of considerable dignity and quality, the principal exponents being Jacob van Campen (1595–1657) and Pieter Post (1608–69). The Palladian phase passed about 1670, merging easily into another of some twenty years' duration of positive austerity, external decoration being almost wholly excluded. Next, Daniel Marot (1661–1752), a Huguenot refugee, introduced the masculine style of Louis XIV to the Dutch court, effective in influencing interior decoration rather than architecture proper, and thenceforward French fashions continued to be followed, though with sober external expression and bold and effective planning. As in France and England in the eighteenth century, plain exteriors often belie lavish but tasteful interior decoration. Minor and provincial architecture remained more strongly Dutch. Eighteenth-century architects of note were P. de Swart (1709–72) in Holland and J-P. van Baurscheit the Younger (1699–1768) in Belgium.

Dutch architectural influence spread far beyond the boundaries of the Netherlands. As will be seen in Chapter 32, the early English Renaissance owed much to Dutch influence, and in Scandinavia too it was very strong. Dutch architects, such as Joost Vingboons, Caspar Panten and the Tessin family (who came originally from Flanders), practised in Sweden; and in Denmark, Dutch architects were employed in the 1570s to design the new castle-palaces of Frederick II, while later the Charlottenborg Palace was designed with a garden in the Dutch manner (see Chapter 33).

EXAMPLES

BELGIAN SECULAR ARCHITECTURE

The **Chancellery (Maison de l'Ancien Greffe), Bruges** (1535) (p. 947A), a town house, has seemingly precocious Baroque qualities which are in fact due to the perpetuation of the Flamboyant Gothic spirit. It has a two-storeyed façade with quasi-Doric Orders, mullioned and transomed windows, and central gable with side-scrolls, crockets and figures.

The **Musée Plantin-Moretus, Antwerp** (1550) (pp. 943D, 947C), once the house of Christopher Plantin, printer to Philip II, is more authentically Classical, and in its extent and character illustrates the opulence and social status of a highly successful Flemish burgher.

The **Town Hall, Antwerp** (1561–6) (p. 944A), by Cornelius Floris (or de Vriendt), the most distinguished architect and sculptor of the century in the Netherlands, as already mentioned (p. 945) is an important prototype of Belgian Early Renaissance, signalling the conclusion of the experimental stage. It has superimposed Orders between closely-spaced large windows, a rusticated basement storey and a galleried upper storey. While in the main straightforward and plain, its centre-piece is highly characteristic of the phase, with its freely manipulated classical detail and generous use of plastic ornament.

The **Guild Houses, Grand' Place, Brussels** (p. 944B), erected by various guilds, Archers (1691), Shipmasters (1697), Carpenters (1697), Printers (1697), Mercers (1699), Butchers (1720), Brewers (1752), Tailors and Painters, are late Belgian-Baroque and Rococo fantasies which with their serried gable fronts and large window areas follow types established by the late sixteenth-century **Guild Houses in the Grand' Place, Antwerp** (p. 944A), and indicate the wealth of Flemish and Brabantine guilds of craftsmen and tradesmen.

The **Hôtel d'Ansembourg, Liège** (1740) (p. 947B), now a museum, is an example of French fashions in Belgium, while the **Town Hall, Lierre** (1740) (p. 947D), by J-P. van Baurscheit the Younger, is similarly an instance of the Rococo period.

The **Place Royale, Brussels** (late eighteenth century) (p. 948B), together with the Rue Royale, by Barnabé Guimard, a Frenchman, show the Antiquarian trend in evidence at this time. Guimard was also the designer of the church of **S. Jacques sur Coudenberg** (1773–6) in the Place Royale (p. 948B).

A. The Old Chancellery,
Bruges (1535). See p. 946

B. The Hôtel d'Ansembourg, Liège (1740).
See p. 946

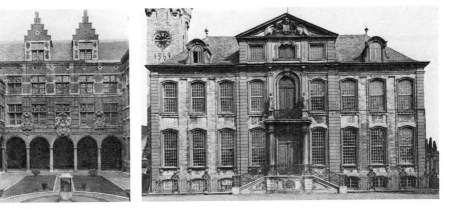

C. The Musée Plantin-
Moretus, Antwerp (1550).
See p. 946

D. The Town Hall, Lierre (1740).
See p. 946

E. The Trippenhuis, Amsterdam
(1662). See p. 951

F. The Mauritshuis, The Hague (1633).
See p. 951

A. The Royal Palace, Amsterdam (1665). See p. 951

B. The Place Royale, Brussels (1776–). See p. 946

A. The Town Hall, Enkhuizen (1686–8). See p. 951

B. The Royal Library, The Hague (1735). See p. 951

A. S. Michel, Louvain (1650–70). See p. 951

B. The New Church, Haarlem (1645–9): interior, drawn by Pieter Saenredam in 1652. See p. 952

C. The Church at Scherpenheuvel (1607). See p. 951

D. The New Church, The Hague (1649–56). See p. 952

DUTCH SECULAR ARCHITECTURE

The **Town Hall, Leyden** (1594) (p. 942D, G), by Lieven de Key, a religious refugee from Antwerp, owes something of its inspiration to Antwerp Town Hall, but is especially noteworthy as an example of the strapwork, fretwork and other petty ornament (p. 942G) typical of the Early Renaissance in the Netherlands generally, and popularized there as in Germany and Elizabethan and Jacobean England (p. 978) by the books of Vredeman de Vries, principally those appearing in 1565 and 1568. The Butchers' Hall, Haarlem (1602), also by de Key, again has the profusion of pseudo-Classical detail normal to the Netherlands Early Renaissance.

The **Mauritshuis, The Hague** (1633) (p. 947F), built by van Campen and Pieter Post for Prince Maurice of Nassau, instances the Dutch Palladian phase in its flattened temple-like front in a harmonious façadal treatment of brick and stone. Buildings of this class may have influenced Hugh May's Eltham House, Kent (p. 1013), and hence the tradition which succeeded it in Georgian England. The **Cloth Hall, Leyden** (1640), by Arent van 's-Gravensande, is a further example of Dutch Palladianism.

The **Royal Palace, Amsterdam** (originally the Town Hall) (1648–65) (p. 948A), by Jacob van Campen, is a major example of Dutch civic architecture on an unusually large scale. Its style is Palladian in the sense that it is of clear, simple ordonnance with no important departures from strict Classical rule and that there is no intrusion of ornament on to the architectural lines. There is, however, a greater freedom in the design of an open cupola-turret over the central, shallowly-projecting pavilion of the two-tiered pilastered façade, standing on a low basement storey, and the crowning pediment has an infilling of petty sculpture.

No. 46, Singel, Amsterdam (1662), by J. Vingboons, is representative of a type of tall, narrow house in that city, usually adorned with the Classic Orders, in the development of which first de Keyser and then the Vingboons played an important part. The **Trippenhuis, Amsterdam** (1662) (p. 947E), also by J. Vingboons, is a larger example of such houses for the merchant class.

The **Town Hall, Enkhuizen** (1686–8) (p. 949A), by Steven Vennecool, represents the later stage of the Palladian phase, achieving a soft plastic quality despite its being almost completely devoid of decoration.

No. 8, Lange Vijverberg, The Hague (1715), now the Federal German Embassy, by Daniel Marot, a Frenchman, is of undecorated, Italianate character inclining to the Baroque; but the building now used as the **Royal Library, The Hague** (1735) (p. 949B), also by Marot, shows in its Rococo ornament the influence of French taste upon the Dutch court.

The **Town Hall, Groningen** (1774–92, built 1802–10), by J. Otten-Husby, belongs to the Antiquarian phase.

BELGIAN ECCLESIASTICAL ARCHITECTURE

The **Church at Scherpenheuvel** (near Louvain) (1607) (p. 950C), by Wenzel Coeberger, was the earliest centrally-planned and domed church in the Low Countries, and is among the exceptions in Belgium to the basilical 'altar' churches normal there. Its style is Proto-Baroque.

S. Pierre, Ghent (1629–1749), **S. Michel, Louvain** (1650–70) (p. 950A) and the tower of **S. Charles, Antwerp** (1620), all by Pieter Huyssens, who belonged to the Jesuit Order, typify the Catholic Baroque style in Belgium. In its west façade, with its superimposed Ionic and Composite columns, broken pediments and enormous side scrolls masking the aisle roofs, S. Michel shows a close approach to the Baroque of Rome, except that its portal is mean and less focal than it would be there, while the banded Orders show some French influence and the ornament has native, Netherlands, characteristics.

DUTCH ECCLESIASTICAL ARCHITECTURE

The **West Church, Amsterdam** (1610–30), by Hendrik de Keyser, is Classical in decoration though its form is based on Gothic precedent adapted to Protestant needs. Its dominant tower (1638), with that of the **South Church** (1614) also by Keyser, are among the best examples in Holland of the adaptation of the native Gothic tradition to Classical themes and elements, this development beginning with de Key's towers (p. 942D, E), which have an affinity with those of Wren's City churches (p. 1021). The **North Church, Amsterdam** (1620), by de Keyser, has a Greek Cross plan typical of the Dutch central-space 'pulpit' churches.

The **New Church, Haarlem** (1645–9) (p. 950B), by van Campen, has the Greek-Cross-in-square plan popular in Holland, the arms of the cross being covered by wooden barrel vaults meeting at a cross vault, the corner squares by flat ceilings —a scheme similar to S. Martin's, Ludgate, London (p. 1021) by Wren. The tower (1613) (p. 942E), from an earlier church, was designed by de Key. The Baroque elongated church normal to Belgium is occasionally represented in Holland, as in the **New Church, The Hague** (1649–56) (p. 950D), by P. Noorwits and B. van Bassen, comprising two interlocking squares with six apsidal bays.

The **East Church, Middelburg** (1647–67), by Frans Drijfout and Pieter Post, centrally-planned, has some resemblance to the Scherpenheuvel church in the Belgian zone; the **Marekerk, Leyden** (1639–49), by 's-Gravensande, though smaller, is more original and refined.

BIBLIOGRAPHY

BURKE, G. L. *The Making of Dutch Towns*. London, 1956.

EDWARDS, T. *Belgium and Luxembourg*. London, 1951.

FOCKEMA ANDREAE, S. J. and others. *Duizend Jaar Bouwen in Nederland*, vol. ii. Amsterdam, 1957.

GERSON, H. and TER KUILE, E. H. *Art and Architecture in Belgium, 1600–1800*. Harmondsworth and Baltimore, 1960.

GEYL, P. *The Revolt of the Netherlands, 1555–1609*. London, 1958.

MINISTRY OF EDUCATION, ARTS AND SCIENCES. *Guide to Dutch Art*. The Hague, 1953.

OZINGA, M. D. *De Protestansche Kerkenbouw in Nederland*. Amsterdam, 1929.

PARENT, P. *L'architecture aux Pays-Bas méridionaux aux XVI–XVIII siècles*. Paris and Brussels, 1926.

PLUYM, W. van der. *Vijf eeuwen Binnenhuis en Meubels in Nederland*. Amsterdam, 1954.

ROSENBERG, J., SLIVE, S., and TER KUILE, E. H., *Dutch Art and Architecture, 1600–1800*. Harmondsworth and Baltimore, 1966.

SITWELL, S. *The Netherlands*. London, 1948.

TIMMERS, J. J. M. *A History of Dutch Art and Life*. Amsterdam and London, 1959.

VRIEND, J. J. *De Bouwkunst van ons Land*. Amsterdam, 1949.

YERBURY, F. R. *Old Domestic Architecture in Holland*. London, 1924.

YSENDYCK, J. J. van. *Documents classiques de l'art dans les Pays-Bas*. 5 vols. Antwerp, 1954.

31

RENAISSANCE ARCHITECTURE IN SPAIN AND PORTUGAL

Sixteenth to nineteenth century

INFLUENCES

GEOGRAPHICAL

In the middle ages, Spain and Portugal formed no more than the Iberian Peninsula, a distant rugged country in the extreme south-west of Europe, torn by constant strife between Moor and Christian. In the Renaissance period, with the vast hereditary possessions and military conquests of the Spanish monarchy, and her power greatly enhanced by the discovery of America, Spain was the leading country of Europe. Her dominions, under the Emperor Charles V, embraced the Netherlands and much of Central Europe, but after the Peace of Westphalia (1648) her prestige declined. There remained, however, the colonies in America—Mexico, Peru, Chile and, for Portugal, Brazil—naturally allied in so many respects with the sunny European homelands. Spanish pre-eminence was initially rivalled by Portuguese achievements in exploration, and in the exotic newly-discovered lands Spanish and Portuguese architects and their colonial-born descendents found ample scope for the exercise of their talents.

GEOLOGICAL

As in the past, granite was the principal material. Its hard severe nature had much to do with the grim aspect of the Escorial. Stone and semi-marbles also abounded and were in general use. Brick was employed with stone in bonding courses, mainly in former Moorish centres such as Toledo, and the iron ore of the northern mountains gave an impetus to the development of 'rejas', decorative wrought-iron screens. In Portugal a grey-green granite produced most sympathetic effects, especially in association with stucco.

CLIMATIC

The climate varies from severe winter cold on the high central table-lands to tropical summer heat in the south and, owing to the general sunny character of the Peninsula, there is a prevalence of small windows, flat roofs and open 'patios', or courtyards. In many of the new Spanish colonies in America, the climate was not unlike that of Spain, and was thus favourable to the reproduction of similar architectural features. The effects aimed at by the Baroque style were peculiarly adapted to the clear air, intense sunlight and strong shadows of Spain and many parts of America.

HISTORICAL, SOCIAL AND RELIGIOUS

In the latter part of the fifteenth century the power of Spain gradually increased until, under the Hapsburg Emperor Charles V (1516–56), it became the chief power in Europe. The Turkish occupation of the Levant, which closed the usual

Spain and Portugal in the seventeenth century

trade routes to the East, had promoted that spirit of maritime enterprise in Spain and Portugal which led to the great discoveries of new lands in the West and thus brought increased riches to the Peninsula. In 1487 Diaz discovered the Cape of Good Hope; in 1492 Columbus discovered the West Indies, and in 1497–9 the continent of America, bringing consequent riches to Spain. In 1497 Vasco da Gama carried Portuguese trade to India. The extent of the Hapsburg dominions in Europe was due to a succession of marriages, as a result of which the Emperor Charles V reigned over Spain, the Netherlands, Sardinia, Sicily, Naples, Franche-Comté, Milan and Germany. To this European Empire, greater than any since that of Charlemagne, Charles added by conquest Mexico, Peru, Chile and Central America, before he abdicated in 1556. This vast empire was held together by his political tenacity and by the excellence of the Spanish army, of which the infantry was the finest in Europe. Philip II checked the power of the Turks in 1571 by winning the naval battle of Lepanto. Yet, his harsh and despotic rule alienated the Netherlands while the expedition against England ended in the defeat of the Armada in 1588. Provinces were gradually lost, until in 1659 the power of Spain was shattered by the Peace of the Pyrenees. Trade and industry continued to languish, and by 1700 Spain had become a protégé of Louis XIV, who upon the death of the last Hapsburg king placed his own grandson on the Spanish throne as Philip V. The resultant war of the Spanish succession (1701–13), terminated by the Peace of Utrecht, resulted in the loss of Gibraltar as well as of the Spanish dominions in Italy and the Netherlands. At the commencement of the nineteenth century Napoleon's invasion led to an outburst of national resistance, when, with the powerful aid of the armies of Great Britain under Wellington, the French were finally driven out of Spain after the battle of Vittoria (1813). From the period of the Peninsular War the Spanish colonies in America had revolted and eventually won their independence.

The marriage in 1469 between Ferdinand of Aragon and Isabella of Castile began that fusion of the different states which resulted in the consolidation of the Kingdom of Spain. In 1512 Ferdinand conquered the Kingdom of Navarre, which was incorporated with Castile, and thus the whole of Spain was joined under one rule, and during the annexation of Portugal (1580–1640) the Spanish monarchy ruled the whole peninsula. From the days of Ferdinand and Isabella Jews and heretics were steadily persecuted. Under Philip III (1598–1621) the Moriscos (Moorish converts to Christianity) were driven out of the country, and this proved a great loss, both in handicrafts and commerce, for their industry had contributed much to its prosperity.

The Protestant Reformation obtained few adherents in Spain, for the religious and racial struggle between Christianity and Islam formed a bond of union amongst all Christians. The final conquest of the Moors, after the fall of Granada (1492), resulted in a revival of ecclesiastical building, and many fine Renaissance churches were erected in the hitherto Moorish districts. Spain was the country of Ignatius Loyola, the founder of the Society of Jesus, which received Papal recognition in 1540, and the religious zeal of this and other religious Orders is responsible for many magnificent Baroque churches and convents throughout the country.

ARCHITECTURAL CHARACTER

SPAIN

Renaissance Spain was heir to two civilizations, Moslem and Christian, and not herself possessing much political and cultural unity, particularly in the Christian regions, tended to conservatism while being at the same time locally susceptible to external influences. Hence, although in general the Renaissance advanced by stages similar to those in other European countries, there was considerable diversity in the manner of expression and in the rates of progression in different parts of the country. Individualism was strongly marked. Keeping these matters in view, the Renaissance may be divided into four tolerably distinct phases, determined by the characteristics predominant in the different periods.

The Early Period (1492–1556), which begins with the fall of Granada, is notable for the grafting of Renaissance details on to Gothic forms, and was influenced by the exuberant fancy of Moorish art. Thus there had been produced by this time a style as rich and poetic as any in Europe, commonly known as the Plateresque (*Plateria* = silverwork), from the minuteness of its detail and its similarity to silver-smiths' work which itself had received a great impetus through the importation of precious metals from the New World. The Plateresque is extremely florid and decoratively involved, and has its fundamentally Gothic versions, carrying on until mid-sixteenth century, as well as those in which Renaissance detail substantially appears.

The Classical Period (1556–1650) was marked by a closer adherence to Italian Renaissance art, and under the influence of the sculptor Alonso Berruguete (*c.* 1488–1561), the Spanish Donatello, and the notable architect Juan de Herrera (*c.* 1530–97), who had visited both Flanders (1547–51) and Italy (1551–9), for a while took a more classical and austere turn.

The Baroque Period (1650–1750) was characterized by a reaction from the correct and frigid formalism observed by Herrera and his followers. As in the earlier phases of the Renaissance there was no single version to which all designers of the day adhered, but several, and among them one which is considered as being peculiarly Spanish in its extraordinary virility, opulence and disregard of strict classical rules.

While the earlier Baroque examples show some relationship to Lombard, Central Italian or Neapolitan precedents, a fantastically extravagant expression, the 'Churrigueresque', developed in the late seventeenth century and continued to mid-eighteenth; due to a family of architects led by José de Churriguera (1650–1723), though he was not himself the most extreme of the exponents of the style. There were also followers, including the brilliant Narciso Tomé, active between 1715–42, whose work, however, is mainly sculptural. The Spanish Churrigueresque is well seen in the Cathedral of Santiago de Compostela (west front, 1738–49) (p. 970A), several buildings at Seville, at Valladolid, and above all at Salamanca. The style inspired many buildings in the Spanish colonies. French and Italian fashions intruded strongly into Spain in the eighteenth century.

The Antiquarian Period (1750–1830). As in general in Central and Western Europe, architecture turned more and more towards ancient Classical models at this time.

PORTUGAL

The Manueline style, a peculiarly Portuguese phenomenon, was contemporary with the 'Early Period' of the Spanish Renaissance. Taking its name from King Manuel I, who reigned from 1495–1521, it is decorative rather than structural in character and, because it was generally superimposed upon Gothic forms—the great monasteries of Belém and Batalha (p. 766B) are notable examples—it is often classified as mediaeval. Manueline drew its exuberant inspiration from the voyages of the discoverers, exploiting in fantastic patterns the symbols of the armillary sphere, ropes, corals and the Cross of the Order of Christ, which Vasco da Gama and his fellow navigators bore on the sails of their ships. It is seen at its most bewildering in the group of buildings of the Convent of Christ at Tomar. Apart from the Manueline, Portuguese architecture showed few distinctive characteristics during the Renaissance period until the splendid phase of Baroque and Rococo in the first half of the eighteenth century, when sudden wealth deriving from the discovery of gold and diamonds in Brazil led to a spate of building. The exquisitely beautiful interior of the University Library of Coimbra, a poem of chinoiserie, is of this date. In 1755 occurred the appalling disaster of the Lisbon earthquake, and from the rubble of destruction emerged some fine, if rather monotonous, town planning, exemplified at its best by the formal splendour of the Praça do Comercio, one of Europe's most impressive squares.

The style of the rehabilitated capital, in particular of the important quarter of the Baixa, with the regular grid of the street plan, and the plain, nearly uniform, façades and standardized building elements, is sometimes called Pombaline, after the Marquis of Pombal, the ruthlessly efficient minister who directed the reconstruction programme with the able assistance of the engineers and architects Manuel de Maia, Carlos Mardel and Eugénio dos Santos. Their sober work here was in marked contrast to the contemporary high Rococo of Queluz (see p. 968) and the imposing Roman Baroque of the vast convent-palace of Mafra (begun in 1717 by J.-F. Ludovice), which reflect the royal manner of the Joanine period (so called after the king Dom João V). But, if the explanation of the sobriety of rebuilt Lisbon lay partly in the need for economy, a dichotomy has generally been apparent in Portuguese architecture between an instinct for simple elegance in the form of buildings and a love of sumptuous embellishment. In the north the local granite proved an appropriate vehicle for the rich flamboyant Baroque of Nicolau Nasoni, a Tuscan architect, painter and sculptor, who worked in Malta before emigrating to Oporto, where in thirty years of the mid-eighteenth century he transformed the

A. The Casa de las Conchas, Salamanca (1512–14). See p. 961

B. The University, Salamanca (façade 1514–29). See p. 961

C. Casa de Ayuntamiento, Seville: detail of façade (1527–64). See p. 961

A. Palace of Charles V, Granada (1527–68): detail of façade. See p. 961

B. Casa de Miranda, Burgos (1543). See p. 961

C. Palace of Charles V, Granada: central court

A. The University, Alcalá de Henares (façade 1537–53). See p. 961

B. The Alcázar, Toledo: the patio (c. 1537–53). See p. 961

A. Tavera Hospital, Toledo: façade (1542–79). See p. 967

B. Tavera Hospital, Toledo: patio

face of the city. Nasoni's death in 1773 was followed by a revived interest in Palladianism, to which the British colony of vintners certainly contributed, notably in the spacious hospital of S. António, built to the designs of John Carr of York (1723–1807).

EXAMPLES

SECULAR ARCHITECTURE

The **Casa de las Conchas, Salamanca** (1512–14) (p. 957A) takes its name from the curious treatment of its façade, which is covered with carved scallop shells. The windows are few in number; the small lower ones are guarded with grilles of elaborate Moorish ironwork, while the upper ones have carved panels in lieu of balconies and are enriched with heraldic carvings.

The **University façade, Salamanca** (1514–29) (p. 957B) is a masterpiece of Plateresque design of admirable craftsmanship and embodying, within a Gothic frame, a number of Italianate motifs such as amorini, panelled pilasters infilled with arabesques, portrait roundels and candelabra as well as the arms of Ferdinand and Isabella and of Charles V, all embedded in a wealth of surface ornament of Moorish inspiration.

The **Casa de Ayuntamiento, Seville** (1527–64) (p. 957C), designed by Diego de Iano (active 1517–34), has a symmetrical front of two and three storeys, fully ornamented with the Orders, spaced into bays by single or paired pilasters or on the upper storeys by attached columns treated as candelabra. The design is very reminiscent of Italian Lombard architecture, of mixed Early and Proto-Baroque character, but has the excessive elaboration stamping it as Plateresque.

The **University façade, Alcalá de Henares** (1537–53) (p. 959A), by Rodrigo Gil de Hontañon (c. 1505–77), whose earlier work was Gothic, has the characteristically ornate centre-piece and paucity of windows, except for an arcaded third-storey window series bracketing the greater part of the front. The main windows, on the first floor, have side scrolls, excessive enframements and iron grilles, while the angle treatment and pinnacles strike a Gothic note. Nearby is the **Archbishop's Palace**, its staircase and fine 'patio' being by Alonso de Covarrubias (1488–1570), the patio having spreading bracket capitals.

The **Casa de Miranda, Burgos** (1543) (p. 958B) has a noted two-storey patio with bracket capitals to the columns, so usual in Spain.

The **Casa Polentina, Ávila** (c. 1550) (p. 962B) also has an attractive patio, the columns on each of two storeys carrying bracket capitals and richly-carved architraves, and having heraldic shields above the capitals.

The **Alcázar, Toledo** (c. 1537–53) (pp. 959B, 962A), a castle of mixed Moorish and Gothic character, was remodelled by Alonso de Covarrubias for Charles V. It was largely destroyed in the Civil War (1936–9). The well-designed patio (p. 959B) had superimposed Corinthian columns in light arcades of the Early Italian type, the arches standing upon the column caps, and like the façade which formed a new front to the old castle (p. 962A), was not richly sculptured, since the material was granite. The central entrance was flanked by Ionic columns surmounted by statues, and the elaborate overdoor had a panel carved with the arms of Charles V. The first storey windows of the façade, with iron balconies, were set off by plain walling, while the top storey had an unusual rusticated treatment, with a small Order on pedestals, surmounted by a flat balustraded roof.

The **Palace of Charles V, Granada** (1527–68) (p. 958A, C), adjoining the Alhambra (p. 430), was designed by Pedro Machuca (active 1517–50) and continued

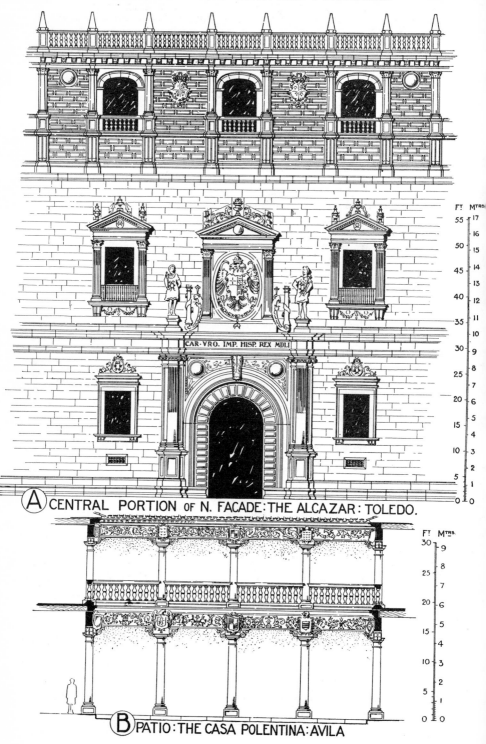

CAR·VRO. IMP. HISP. REX MDLI

FT   MTRS.
55   17
      16
50   15
45   14
      13
40   12
35   11
      10
30   9
25   8
      7
20   6
      5
15   4
10   3
      2
5   1
0   0

(A) CENTRAL PORTION OF N. FACADE: THE ALCAZAR: TOLEDO.

FT   MTRS.
30   9
      8
25   7
20   6
      5
15   4
10   3
      2
5   1
0   0

(B) PATIO: THE CASA POLENTINA: AVILA

THE ESCORIAL : Nᴿ MADRID

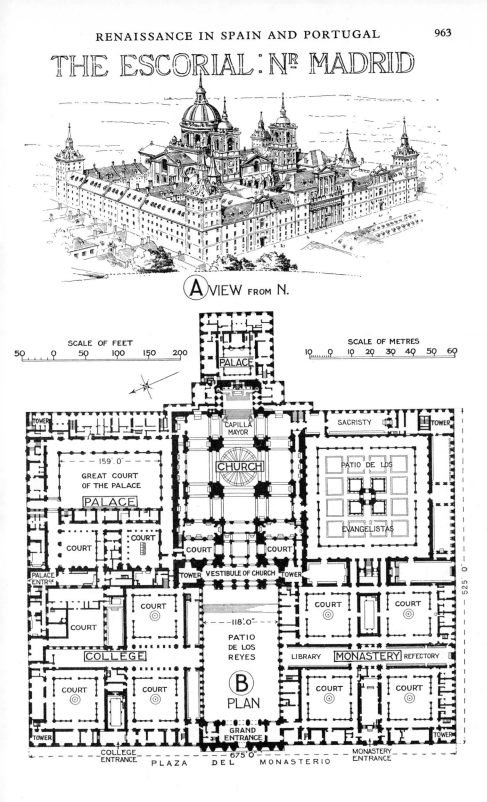

Ⓐ VIEW FROM N.

SCALE OF FEET
50 0 50 100 150 200

SCALE OF METRES
10 0 10 20 30 40 50 60

PALACE

PALACE

TOWER

CAPILLA MAYOR

SACRISTY

TOWER

159'.0"

GREAT COURT OF THE PALACE

CHURCH

PATIO DE LOS

PALACE

COURT

COURT

EVANGELISTAS

COURT

COURT

COURT

PALACE ENTRᶜᴱ

TOWER VESTIBULE OF CHURCH TOWER

COURT

COURT

COURT

COURT

COURT

118'.0"

PATIO DE LOS REYES

COLLEGE

LIBRARY MONASTERY REFECTORY

525'.0"

COURT

COURT

Ⓑ
PLAN

COURT

COURT

TOWER

GRAND ENTRANCE

TOWER

COLLEGE ENTRANCE

MONASTERY ENTRANCE

675'.0"

PLAZA DEL MONASTERIO

A. The Escorial, near Madrid (1559–84): south front. See p. 967

B. The Escorial, near Madrid:
façade of church

C. The Palácio Nacional, Queluz, near
Lisbon (1758–94). See p. 968

A. Casa de los Guzmanes, León (*c.* 1560). See p. 968

B. The University, Valladolid: façade (1715–). See p. 968

A. The Hospicio Provincial, Madrid: portal (1722–). See p. 968

B. The Palace of the Marqués de Dos Aguas, Valencia (1740–4). See p. 968

C. The Royal Palace, La Granja, near Segovia: garden façade (1735–9). See p. 968

after his death by his son Luis. It equates with the Italian High Renaissance in character, and is thoroughly classical in spirit. It is a square mass of building about 61 m (200 ft) each way, enclosing a fine, majestic open circular patio. The external façades are two storeys in height, the lower of which has rusticated Doric columns, except in the centre-piece, where they are fluted, and the upper has Ionic columns (p. 958A). In both storeys there are circular windows above the main ones, to light mezzanine floors, their place being taken by sculptured panels on the centre-piece. It is built in golden-coloured stone. The circular patio (p. 958C) is a grand architectural conception, 30.5 m (100 ft) in diameter, with superimposed Doric and Ionic colonnades, and forms the chief feature of this monumental building, which, however, was never completed for occupation.

The **Tavera Hospital, Toledo** (1542–79) (p. 960), designed by Bartolomé de Bustamente (c. 1500–70) is again strongly Italianate and unusually restrained for Spanish Renaissance architecture. It has a rectangular plan, 106.5 m (350 ft) long, and a powerfully severe façade, with vigorously protruding rusticated quoins at the angles of the building and around the sparse windows, in addition to channelled rustications covering the two principal storeys as a whole (p. 960A). There is, however, the usual Spanish centre-piece, rising through three tiers. The patio (p. 960B), with its two storeys of graceful arcades, Ionic over Doric, is as classically faultless as any Florentine Renaissance cortile, apart from the varied span of the arches.

The **Escorial** (1559–84) (pp. 963, 964A, B), about 48 km (30 miles) from Madrid, was commenced by Juan Bautista de Toledo (d. 1567) for Philip II, but in 1552 Juan de Herrera was given charge of the work. This austere group of buildings on a lonely site, 206 m × 209 m (675 ft × 685 ft), consists of monastery, college, church and palace with state apartments (p. 963B). The grand entrance in the centre of the west front opens into the 'Patio de los Reyes', which, lying between the great courts of the monastery and the college, forms the atrium of the church, the latter measuring 100 m × 64 m (330 ft × 210 ft). To the right of the atrium is the monastery, with its four courts, each 18.3 m (60 ft) square, surrounded with arcades in three storeys, beyond which is the 'Patio de los Evangelistas'. To the left of the atrium is the college, with its four courts, and beyond this the great court of the palace is connected with the state apartments, which project behind the church and make the plan into the form of a gridiron. The church is similar in type to S. Maria di Carignano, Genoa (p. 809), and shows Italian influence on the work of Herrera, but the Spanish character is seen in the position of the choir over a vaulted vestibule at the west end, which shortens the long arm of the Latin cross, so that the main building is a Greek cross on plan. The simple church façade (p. 964B) has noble Doric columns, surmounted by granite figures of the Kings of Judah, and the windows between the statues light the raised choir within. The interior, although cold, is impressive by reason of its simplicity, and the granite walls are in strong contrast to the frescoed vaults, while the magnificent reredos, with its quiet blending of colour, further emphasizes the general subdued effect. This world-famous pile owes much of its character to the yellowish-grey granite of which it is built, both within and without, a material which imposed restraint upon the architect, and may indeed have accorded with the ascetic taste of Philip II. The external façades, five storeys high (p. 964A), are in great blocks of granite, of such a size that the door architraves are in one stone, 3 m (10 ft) high, and there is no attempt at window grouping, as in the Alcázar façade (p. 962A), and openings generally are devoid of ornament. The external effect of the Escorial is remarkably dignified, with its plain façades and angle towers, the whole group culminating in the great western towers of the church and its central dome, 95 m (312 ft) in height. The impressiveness of this group of buildings, grand in its security (p. 964A), is enhanced by the lonely austerity of its mountain background.

The **Casa de los Guzmanes, León** (c. 1560) (p. 965A) is a representative building of the Classical period, the architectural elements being used with discretion and restraint. The special Spanish note is struck by the angle pavilions—normal to domestic architecture—the columned doorway flanked by statues, small windows protected by iron grilles, and continuous arcaded upper storey in the deep shadow of wide-spreading eaves.

The **Casa Lonja, Seville** (1583–98), from designs by Juan de Herrera, shows in its patio of Ionic-over-Doric arcades, in which the attached Orders enframe the arches in the Roman manner, the cold academic character widespread at this time.

The **Hospicio Provincial, Madrid** (1722–) (p. 966A), designed by Pedro Ribera (1683–1742), provides in its period an instance of the Churrigueresque version of the Baroque. In secular architecture externally, it was often solely upon portals that this kind of almost riotous elaboration was concentrated, as again too, though with greater discipline, in the façade of the **University, Valladolid** (p. 965B), begun in 1715 by Narciso Tomé. The **Palace of the Marqués de Dos Aguas, Valencia** (1740–4) (p. 966B) shows a later development in which the tortuous and involved ornament around the openings has something of the character of a viscous efflorescence.

The **Royal Palace, La Granja, near Segovia** (1719–39) (p. 966C) has an eastern or garden façade built by foreign architects, the centre part (1735–9) from the designs of the Italian, Filippo Juvarra (p. 815); and this, having a giant Corinthian Order embracing the two main floors, has most of the qualities associated with Italian Baroque architecture. The splendid gardens were laid out between 1727–43. The **Royal Palace, Madrid** (1738–64) by the Italian, G.B. Sacchetti, similarly is in classical heavy Baroque style, having little distinctive Spanish character.

The **Palácio Nacional, Queluz** (1758–94) (p. 964C), by the Frenchman J.-B. Robillon and the Portuguese M. Vicente de Oliviera, is an exquisite Rococo country house, a typical if elaborate example of the 'quinta'. The superb gardens, also designed by Robillon, include a canal, which is lined with panels of 'azulejos', the traditional coloured tiles, a decorative feature of all periods of Portuguese architecture, though of Moorish origin.

ECCLESIASTICAL ARCHITECTURE

S. Esteban, Salamanca (1524–1610) is mainly a Gothic building, influenced by Moorish art, but has a rich Plateresque western front: a great arch, with superimposed pilasters, half-columns and baluster shafts, encloses sculptured figures of saints in high canopied niches carried right across the elaborate façade, which is further enriched with heraldic shields and finished off with a truncated pediment.

Burgos Cathedral (pp. 763, 765A) is made conspicuous externally by its magnificent central tower, added 1539–67, with quasi-Gothic windows and lofty angle pinnacles emphasizing the old Gothic tradition which lingers throughout. Internally, four massive circular piers, built after the collapse of the previous Gothic piers in 1539, support pointed arches, elaborate squinches, high octagonal drum, and the open-work vault or 'cimborio'. The Escalera Dorada (1519–23) in the north transept is a unique Plateresque feature of the interior.

Granada Cathedral (1528–63 and later) (p. 969A, B), undertaken by Diego de Siloe (c. 1495–1563), is one of the grandest Renaissance churches in southern Spain, and a remarkable example of the Plateresque period. The interior (p. 969B) is a translation of Seville Cathedral into the Renaissance style, and the great piers of the

A. Façade (1667–1703)   B. Interior, looking W.

Granada Cathedral (1528–1703). See p. 968

C. Jaén Cathedral: façade (1667–88). See p. 971

D. El Pilar Cathedral, Saragossa (1677–1766). See p. 971

A. The Cathedral of Santiago de Compostela: façade (1738–49). See p. 956

B. The Sacristy, la Cartuja (Charterhouse), Granada (1727–64). See p. 971

C. Valladolid Cathedral: façade (lower part 1580–; upper, 1730–3). See p. 971

D. Church of the Clérigos, Oporto (Porto) (1731–63). See p. 971

nave (completed between 1667–1703) are faced with the Classic Orders, while the radiating piers, supporting the dome of the circular 'Capilla Mayor', show an ingenious and novel treatment. The Capilla Real, to the south of the transept, is late Gothic (1504–21) and earlier than the Cathedral itself. It is entered through a magnificent wrought-iron 'reja' and contains the famous tombs of Ferdinand and Isabella and other kings and queens of Spain. The unfinished west front shows a change of design, due to Alonso Cano (1601–67) and erected 1667–1703: it is an instance of Baroque architecture, a type in which the use of the Orders is largely evaded (p. 969A).

Jaén Cathedral (1540–) is mainly of the Classical period but has an impressive Baroque west front and towers (1667–88) (p. 969C); **Malaga Cathedral** (1528–) continued in building into the eighteenth century, though without considerable departure from the early design.

Valladolid Cathedral (1580–), begun on the plans of Juan de Herrera, the Spanish Palladio, was never finished to his designs or it would have been just about as large as Seville, and among the largest cathedrals in the world. Nevertheless Herrera's design had great influence on other cathedrals in Spain and Spanish America. It was finished at a much reduced size in 1730–3, the upper part of the west front (p. 970C) being by Alberto Churriguera (1676–1750), whose style is here a vigorous Baroque, instead of having the intricacy usually found in the work of the Churriguera family of architects.

El Pilar Cathedral, Saragossa (Zaragoza) (begun 1677; extensively altered 1753–66) (p. 969D) has a rectangular plan similar to that of Herrera's Valladolid, with a fine enclosed western 'coro'. The exterior, as seen across the River Ebro, forms an imposing pile, of many domes, the two angle towers having been completed in modern times and the other two yet awaiting completion. The principal material is orange-brown brickwork, and the roofing is finished in colour-patterned tilework. Moorish influence is apparent.

The **Sacristy of la Cartuja (Charterhouse), Granada** (1727–64) (p. 970B) is famous as an extreme instance of Churrigueresque architecture, designed by F. Manuel Vasquez. The windows are at a high level and leave the walls free for the bizarre fretted plasterwork enclosing picture-panels and inlaid doors and cupboards.

S. Francisco el Grande, Madrid (1761–84), built on the model of the Pantheon, Rome (p. 286), to contain the tombs of famous Spaniards, and the façade of **Pamplona Cathedral** (1780–83), severely formal in design, illustrate the Neo-Classical revival in the Antiquarian period.

The **Church of S. Francisco, Oporto (Porto)**, a late mediaeval church remarkable for its grotto-like interior, is completely faced with extravagant eighteenth-century carved and gilded woodwork. Grotesque in the original sense of the word, such treatment of surfaces, which is known as 'talha', is typical of Portuguese architectural ornament.

The **Pilgrimage Church of Bom Jesus do Monte, near Braga,** was rebuilt from 1784 in a Neo-Palladian manner by C.-L. Ferreira da Cruz Amarante. Set in superb gardens, it stands at the head of a steeply-rising ceremonial granite staircase (1723), adorned with fountains and sculptured figures at each successive 'landing' of the long hillside ascent. Some of these figures appear to anticipate the statues of the prophets at Congonhas do Campo, carved by Aleijadinho in colonial Brazil (p. 1108).

The **Church of the Clérigos, Oporto** (1731–63) (p. 970D), by Nicolau Nasoni, is a skilful pastiche of seventeenth-century Italian Baroque. The plan, curiously attenuated owing to the exigencies of the site, incorporates an elliptical nave, entered at the sides and not through the monumental doorway of the richly decorated façade, which is blind. The tower, rising to 76 m (over 250 ft), is of granite and beautifully proportioned. It has been compared, but with insufficient reason, to that of the Palazzo Vecchio in Florence (p. 741C).

BIBLIOGRAPHY

BEVAN, B. *History of Spanish Architecture*. London, 1938.
BRADFORD, S. *Portugal and Madeira*. London, 1969.
BRIGGS, M. S. *Baroque Architecture*. London, 1913.
BYNE, A., and STAPLEY, M. *Provincial Houses in Spain*, New York, 1925.
CALZADA, A. *Historia de la arquitectura española*. Barcelona, 1933.
CHAMOSO LAMAS, M. *La arquitectura barroca en Galicia*. Madrid, 1955.
FRANCA, J.-A. *Une Ville des Lumières, La Lisbonne de Pombal*. Paris, 1965.
GALLEGO Y BURIN, A. *El barroco granadino*. Madrid, 1956.
HARVEY, J. *The Cathedrals of Spain*. London, 1957.
KUBLER, G. *Arquitectura española 1600–1800*. (Ars Hispaniae, XIV). Madrid, 1957.
—., and SORIA, M. *Art and Architecture in Spain and Portugal*. Harmondsworth and Baltimore, 1959.
MAYER, A. L. *Architektur und Kunstgewerbe in Alt-Spanien*. Munich, 1920.
PRENTICE, A. N. *Renaissance Architecture and Ornament in Spain*. 1893.
SCHUBERT, O. *Geschichte des Barocks in Spanien*. 1908.
SITWELL, S. *Spanish Baroque Art*. London, 1931.
SMITH, R. C. *The Art of Portugal 1500–1800*. London, 1968.
—. *Nicolau Nasoni, Arquitecto do Porto*. Lisbon, 1966.
VILLIERS-STUART, C. M. *Spanish Gardens*. 1929.
WARING, J. B., and MACQUOID, T. R. *Examples of Architectural Art in Italy and Spain*. 1950.
WYATT, SIR M. DIGBY. *An Architect's Note-book in Spain*. 1872.

32

RENAISSANCE ARCHITECTURE IN BRITAIN

Sixteenth to nineteenth century

INFLUENCES

GEOGRAPHICAL

The island influence still continued, as in previous periods (p. 546), to produce those pronounced modifications which stamp all English architecture with an essentially national character. Owing to the distance from Italy, the birthplace of the Renaissance, England was the last country to fall under the influence of the movement, which naturally reached this island by way of France and the Netherlands. The friendly relations which, at different times, marked its intercourse with these countries may be seen faithfully reflected in English architecture. The great wars, however, at the end of the eighteenth and beginning of the nineteenth century closed Continental travel to Englishmen, though contacts were at once renewed after 1815. Internal communications began to improve in Britain about the mid-eighteenth century, the first important step as regards good road-making having been taken by General George Wade in Scotland from 1726; the really important developments were due to Thomas Telford and James Loudon Macadam in the first quarter of the nineteenth century. Bridge-building necessarily improved at the same time. The peak period of canal and navigable inland waterway construction was between 1760 and 1800, and the extensive system created greatly facilitated the transport of heavy goods, including building materials, with the result that the surviving local character in minor architecture tended to disappear.

GEOLOGICAL

This influence has been considered in the mediaeval period (p. 637), and, as one of the natural influences, it is continuous, and still gives a special character to the architecture of various districts; though other elements have modified its operation. Timber, for instance, gradually fell into disuse for building purposes, partly because of the growing scarcity of the material as forests were cleared for the needs of the rising population, or because of the risk of fire in crowded towns, but particularly because stone, and in due course, brick, provided more stable, permanent and weather-proof structures. Timber-frames, exposed externally, were still normal throughout Elizabethan times, and under various forms of external sheathing, such as plaster or tile-hanging, persisted in the smaller buildings of the countryside even until the opening of the nineteenth century in regions where building-stone was not readily available. In the latter regions, as in East Anglia, buildings of note not infrequently were being built in brickwork as early as *c.* 1500. Stone, however, was the natural successor to timber, and in favoured areas became usual in the seventeenth century. Inigo Jones first made use of Portland stone in his London buildings. Sir Christopher Wren also adopted it for his many churches and secular buildings, and it has been largely used up to the present day. Bath stone of the soft oolitic formation, which crosses England diagonally from Somerset to Lincoln, gives a charming character to the manor and other houses of these districts, just as the Yorkshire gritstone, which did not lend itself to carving, caused the adoption there of a plain and unornamented style. The geological map (p. 623) gives a rough indication of the building materials available in the different districts. By the eighteenth century, brick was becoming almost universal for domestic architecture and the less important classes of building. Bricks, thinner than today, were at first bonded irregularly in a loose form of 'English bond', but after mid-seventeenth century 'Flemish bond' became usual. Terra-cotta, introduced in the Tudor period, was not much used even for architectural details until Victorian times (p. 1127). Roofing-tiles accompanied the use of bricks in the eastern and southern parts of the country, while stone slates or flags replaced thatch in the upland midland, western and northern regions. The employment of thin slates extended greatly after mid-eighteenth century, their distribution made practicable by the improvement of inland waterways and roads and the construction of canals. A consequence of the exploitation of mineral resources as the Industrial Revolution gathered force was the appearance of cast iron as a structural material, well before 1800.

CLIMATIC

When the new style was introduced here from Italy, the dull English climate caused it to be adapted to our northern use. In order to admit abundant light, large windows still continued, especially in the early period, in striking contrast to those of Italy. A growing desire for comfort, coinciding also with the more general use of coal as fuel in the reign of Charles I, brought about the introduction of a fireplace in each room; while chimneys continued, as in the Tudor period, to be prominent symmetrical features of the external design, instead of being disguised as in Italy.

HISTORICAL, SOCIAL AND RELIGIOUS

Henry VIII had been firmly established on the English throne, and the security of his position at home enabled him to interest himself in affairs on the Continent. His famous meeting with Francis I on the Field of the Cloth of Gold in 1520, with all its resplendent accessories, helped to attract foreign artists to his court, and they largely determined the manner of the adoption of the Renaissance style in England, alike in architecture, sculpture and painting. Henry VIII avoided prolonged warfare until the last years of his reign, but he would brook no interference from Rome with his royal prerogative. Continental Protestantism began winning English converts around 1520, but although in 1535 Henry granted access to the English Bible, he sanctioned no doctrinal changes. Yet on the failure of the Pope to nullify his marriage, he excluded Papal jurisdiction from his kingdom. In 1534 he became Supreme Head of the English Church by Parliamentary statute. Through the same instrument he dissolved the monasteries (1536–9) and sold a large part of their estates. The ministers of his young son Edward VI (reigned 1547–53) decisively Protestantized the English Church, replacing the Latin Mass by the *Book of Common Prayer*. This trend was temporarily halted during the reign of Mary who, through her marriage with Philip II, came under Spanish influence, though it did not extend much beyond her own immediate surroundings. French influence had been at work in Scotland, and there French architectural features were popularized, owing to the long-standing alliance of France and Scotland which Henry VIII and Edward VI failed to break by making war on the Scots.

Queen Mary's reaction was cancelled by the accession in 1558 by her sister Elizabeth I. By a new Act of Supremacy (1559) an Anglican Church was restored

England in the Renaissance period

with the Queen as its Supreme Governor and the *Book of Common Prayer* as its Liturgy. At once peace-loving and economical, Elizabeth postponed for three decades war with Spain. When it came, the defeat of the Spanish Armada (1588) confirmed the independent position of England. The sense of security and the prosperity which followed found material expression in the splendid mansion-building of the period. Monasteries either fell into ruin or emerged as national cathedrals; while others again were cleared away for the erection of country houses, or were even incorporated in the mansions of the new nobility. During this period men's minds were turned rather to Church reform than to church building. Moreover, the great church-building era of the Middle Ages had left an ample supply of churches, and not until the latter part of the seventeenth century was there a renewal of church building.

The Stuarts brought England into closer touch with the Continent, more especially with France and Italy. James I was not only a disciple of the new learning, but also a patron of Inigo Jones, the great architect who studied in Italy and introduced the Palladian Renaissance into England. Charles I inaugurated a period of intrigue, politics and war, when the King found himself embroiled both with France and Spain. Architecture, painting and the minor crafts were fostered by the fine artistic sense of the King, but the Civil War arrested progress in architecture. The Commonwealth, with its Puritan reaction, was essentially a period when the connection between England and the Continent was marked rather by the power of Cromwell in asserting the position of England than by the operation of foreign influences upon English art. Soon after the Restoration (1660) of Charles II, the Great Fire (1666) gave Sir Christopher Wren an unparalleled opportunity for church-building in London. Charles had lived at the court of Louis XIV, and there imbibed French ideas in art, which were introduced into England at the Restoration and predominated till the Great Rebellion and the flight of James II (1688). William of Orange brought over Dutch influences which were so long predominant in English domestic architecture. The later Stuart period saw the carrying trade of the world largely transferred from Holland to England, while English victories over the French, followed by the Peace of Utrecht (1713), secured to England the chief trade of Europe and made her rich enough to build up a navy which gave her supremacy at sea, both over France and Holland. England still depended largely on the manufactured products of those countries, but Huguenot weavers from France helped English workmen in the towns to develop their industries, and engineers from Holland taught agriculturists to convert swampy fenlands into corn-growing country. Thus there was an increase in general prosperity which naturally produced a still greater demand for more and better dwelling-houses.

The first half of the eighteenth century saw Dutch influence on architecture gradually anglicized, and the houses that were now built were of the convenient and comfortable type known as Queen Anne and Georgian, well suited to the needs of the increasing middle classes, both in town and country.

Renaissance Humanism, with its recognition of the inherent human right to the enjoyment of life, appealed strongly to a community which had thrown off ecclesiastical domination and was rapidly developing a free national and domestic life along more secular lines. The Wars of the Roses (1454–85) had already decimated the old nobility, but expanding commerce was constantly supplying a new class of wealthy merchants and traders to take the place of former feudal lords. The new men who, as we have seen, had acquired land—often former monastic estates—now required houses suitable to their wealth and to the standing in the country which their enterprise or good fortune had conferred upon them. These then were the men who were ready to adopt the new style which, in its grandness of scale, exactly suited their ideas. The printers, led by Caxton, with his press at Westminster (1477), had brought the hoarded knowledge of the privileged few within the reach of common humanity. The printed and picture book also served to make artists and craftsmen familiar with the plans and details of Classic buildings. An Englishman, John Shute, published the *First and Chief Groundes of Architecture* in 1563, this owing much to the writings of the Italian, Serlio; while the great work of Vitruvius, the ancient Roman architect, was also translated and circulated.

Foreign artists, imbued with Renaissance ideas, had already flocked to the court of Henry VIII, and to these were added, in the reign of Elizabeth, Flemish and German craftsmen, who settled principally in the eastern counties, and there influenced the style of the new mansions. Finally, civil war and persecution in France drove to England many skilled Huguenot craftsmen who contributed to the efficient execution of the new style in their new home. The changed social conditions, together with practical considerations resulting from new methods of warfare and the increasing use of gunpowder, had rendered the fortification of dwelling-houses useless. The progressive development in domestic comfort and the increase of hospitality during the reign of Elizabeth (1558–1603) were responsible for an era remarkable for the erection of those great and commodious houses which are still the special pride of England. It also became fashionable for young men to visit Italy, and thus Renaissance ideas and tastes were brought to England. Despite the dissolution of the monasteries, the period as a whole saw a considerable growth of education and of charitable endeavour. Though the government of Edward VI abolished the chantries, the schools attached to them were preserved, while in addition many new schools were founded by prelates, gentry and citizens throughout the Tudor and Stuart periods. At Oxford and Cambridge additional colleges were founded by both royal and private benefactors.

During the reigns of James I and his son, English colonizing enterprise, unequalled by any other country, led to the expansion of English trade, with a consequent further accession of numbers to the wealthy classes who, following the King's example, lived much in the country and there erected many stately houses. Though Charles I was a patron of art, the disturbed condition of the country during his ill-starred reign, culminating in the Civil War, arrested the progress of architecture, as exemplified in the abandonment of the great scheme for the projected Palace of Whitehall (p. 1003). During the Stuart period the colonies of North America and the West Indies, together with Indian and African trade, established English overseas prestige. This growing trade also gave increased consideration to all questions of home commerce and a greater importance to the trading classes.

The Bank of England was established in 1694; the economic situation underwent a marked change, and the 'mercantile system' secured a surplus of exports over imports, which naturally resulted in an increase of home manufactures. Thanks to numerous innovations, agriculture was in a more thriving condition, and pauperism consequently decreased; while the settlement laws of the period helped to equalize the poor relief of different districts and to arrest vagrancy. There was a greater sense of security, which created better conditions for general architectural enterprise. The general increase in wealth and the rise in the standard of comfort are seen in the number of plain comfortable Georgian houses of our country towns. As late as the end of the eighteenth century there were still only some eight million inhabitants in England and Wales; while London, with almost a million, far exceeded any other town in size, and correspondingly influenced public opinion and national policy. Norwich, with its weaving and banking community, and Bristol, with its West Indies trade and sugar refining, were next in importance to the capital. The increase of population in London did not, however, induce the City to extend its boundaries, and thus a new town grew up to the westward, which gave a further opportunity to Renaissance architects.

ARCHITECTURAL CHARACTER

Not until a century after its birth in Florence did the Renaissance style make its first appearance in England in the Tomb of Henry VII (1509) (p. 989A), a tentative display of a style which afterwards secured a firm footing, as suitable for the magnificent country mansions and stately town houses of the substantial professional and trading families which were rapidly forming England's new nobility.

English Renaissance architecture may be divided as follows:

Early Renaissance	Elizabethan	(1558–1603) (pp. 978, 987)
	Jacobean	(1603–25) (pp. 978, 996)
Late Renaissance	Stuart	(1625–1702) (pp. 979, 1003)
	Georgian	(1702–1830) (pp. 981, 1032)

EARLY RENAISSANCE

Elizabethan Architecture. The reign of Elizabeth (1558–1603) witnessed the establishment of the Renaissance style in England. Elizabethan architecture, which followed the Tudor, was a transition style with Gothic features and Renaissance detail, and in this respect it bears the same relation to fully developed English Renaissance as the style of Francis I does to fully developed French Renaissance. But in character it was quite individual, fundamentally still Mediaeval yet affected superficially by influences which had been transmuted in the course of their passage from the source in Italy. Italian or French books on architecture, notably the writings of the Italian, Sebastiano Serlio (1475–1552), in various editions, had some importance, but particularly, the Renaissance influences reached England from Flanders, which at the time was practising a decoratively-exaggerated style of 'strapwork' and grotesques mainly based on the work of the Italian stuccoists, such as Il Rosso and Primaticcio at Fontainebleau (p. 882). As we have seen, Antwerp was a highly important commercial and artistic centre at this period, and from that locality and neighbouring Germany came not only architectural pattern books of various kinds but also craftsmen and artisans displaced by political disturbances or religious persecution. The zeal for church building in the Middle Ages in England had provided churches which remained sufficient for popular needs, and thus Elizabethan architecture was secular rather than ecclesiastical in its nature, and was the outcome of the needs of a time when powerful statesmen, successful merchants, and the enriched gentry required mansions suitable to their new position, and these were built in England, as in France, mainly in the country, in contrast to the churches and palaces of the cities in Italy. These great houses were not designed comprehensively by a single person but were rather the conceptions jointly of the owner and his chosen master-craftsmen (for large buildings, the chief was usually a mason), and subordinate specialist craftsmen might be employed to execute decorative features like entrance-doorways, porticoes, fireplaces, staircases and panelling, to their own designs. The mansions displayed many new combinations of features. Externally, towers, gables, parapets, balustrades and chimney-stacks produced an effective skyline, and walls were enlivened by oriel and bay-windows with mullions and transoms (p. 990), while internally the same style, when applied to fittings, furniture, and decoration, made for repose, dignity and uniformity. Elizabethan mansions looked outwards rather than inwards towards courtyards as in the Mediaeval period, so that there now could be formal settings related to each front, a forecourt, perhaps with decorative gateway and angle pavilions, on the entrance side, and on the others, formal gardens with beds of plants arranged in intricate geometrical knots and a central fountain marking converging paths, or balustraded terraces, topiary gardens and walks, or terraces and orchards.

Jacobean Architecture. The architecture of the reign of James I (1603–25) inherited Elizabethan traditions; but as Roman literature and models became better known, a subtle change crept in, and the sober regularity of Classic columns and entablatures gradually supplanted the irregularity of Elizabethan architecture, although the main lines of the design remained much the same in both periods. There was a greater tendency, however, for new structures to be designed by a single hand. Buildings still continued to be for domestic rather than religious use, and thus the style developed along lines suited to popular needs, with considerable latitude in detail and ornament, not only for buildings, but also for fittings and furniture, which now became more abundant in quantity and more decorative in quality, and were supplied both for mansions and churches. As also in the Elizabethan period, it was in the screens, pulpits and monuments, which were freely added to mediaeval churches, that Jacobean art found its outlet in ecclesiastical architecture, and much of the human interest of English Gothic churches is due to the historical continuity supplied by these Jacobean monuments.

The drawings collected by John Thorpe (1563–1654) and Huntingdon Smithson (d. 1648), the former collection now being preserved in Sir John Soane's Museum and the latter at the R.I.B.A., London, are very informative about the houses of the period c. 1570–1633. The buildings represented are not by any means all their own personal designs, but in many cases represent the work of others. There were two notable generations of Thorpes and three of Smithsons. Thomas Thorpe (d. 1596) was probably the principal mason and virtual designer of Kirby Hall, Northants (p. 988), while his son John, a land surveyor and officer of the King's works, made drawings of notable contemporary structures without himself contributing any buildings of special merit. Robert Smithson (c. 1536–1614) was an outstanding figure. Probably the chief mason-designer of Longleat House, Wilts (p. 995), he was certainly the architect of Wollaton Hall, Notts (p. 988), his chief work, and importantly concerned with Hardwick Hall, Derbyshire (p. 995) and other great houses in the Midlands, besides originating plans for smaller houses which became established types. His son John (d. 1634) designed Bolsover Castle, Derbyshire (p. 997), and he with his son, Huntingdon Smithson, made important additions to the same building later on.

LATE RENAISSANCE

Stuart Architecture. The term 'Stuart' is used for the architecture of Charles I (1625–49), the Commonwealth (1649–60), Charles II (1660–85), James II (1685–8), and William and Mary (1689–1702).

The period readily falls into two phases, dominated respectively by two great personalities, Inigo Jones and Sir Christopher Wren: but in the first, lasting to about 1660, the majority of buildings showed little response to the striking innovations of Inigo Jones in his courtly circles, and maintained a consistent trend on the basis of the Jacobean. The designers mostly were working masters of the respective crafts, rising from the ranks of the masons, carpenters or bricklayers. The latter term may today suggest a more lowly social status than was sometimes attained by the more gifted of such master-craftsmen. Influences still came mainly via the Netherlands, but also from France; the former were evidenced at this time by the so-called 'Dutch gables', shaped with ogee parapets crowned with semicircular or triangular pediments (p. 1012C). Brickwork, very often with stone dressings, became increasingly popular as the century advanced, and stone and brick mullions progressively gave place to wooden windows. Notable master-masons were Nicholas Stone (1586–1647), who received part of his training in Amsterdam; the younger Smithsons, still working in this phase; and, among master-bricklayers, Peter Mills (1600–70). In the second or 'Wren' phase of the period, from c. 1660 onwards, the national character of English architecture was becoming more firmly established, in commonplace buildings as well as in those of prime importance. Dutch influences, now much more authentically Classical, were reinforced towards the end of the century, while increased travel brought a surer knowledge of French practices and genuine Italian precedents. By this time Italy had nearly passed the peak of the Baroque. Thus it will be seen that in the Stuart period the influences upon English architecture became increasingly complex, and they remained so in the next, the Georgian period. Development throughout the Late Renaissance was importantly determined by the fortunes, training and preferences of distinguished individuals referred to in the short notices which follow.

Inigo Jones (1573–1652) was a man of dominating personality and brilliance who produced an architecture which was far in advance of that of his contemporaries, so much so that its revolutionary nature was not at once fully recognized, and it was only after his death that its importance began fully to be appreciated. His prolonged studies in Italy, more especially of the works of Palladio but also of contemporary Italian architecture as well as the antique, caused him to become an ardent disciple of the Italian Renaissance style. Born of an undistinguished London family, he apparently had first visited Italy about 1601, and emerges in 1605 as the designer of costumes and scenery for court masques, an activity which he continued until the outbreak of the Civil War. It is known that he visited Paris in 1609, and had an important nineteen-months further tour in Italy in 1613–14 in the retinue of the Earl of Arundel. His attractive personality, together with his skill and ingenuity in stage-craft, seem to have brought him favour, for in 1611 he was appointed Surveyor to Prince Henry, and in 1613, Surveyor of the King's Works. Yet it was only in the latter year that his notable work in architecture began. His principal buildings are mentioned on pp. 1003–13. A pupil and assistant of Inigo Jones from 1628 to 1652 was John Webb (1611–72), who naturally absorbed his master's ideas; Webb's own personality emerges in a small number of houses which he erected on his own account after c. 1648. His greatest work and only public building was the King Charles's block at Greenwich (p. 1004). Sir Roger Pratt (1620–85) spent six years studying on the Continent (1643–9) and brought back ideas directly from Italy. He knew Jones, who served as adviser for the first of the five considerable houses which represented Pratt's total architectural output, all completed before 1672, and shared Jones's taste for architecture as interpreted by the Italian writers, Palladio, Serlio and Scamozzi; thus being similarly in advance of the general run of practice of the day. Pratt secured his knighthood for his services as one of the three Royal Commissioners appointed for the control of the city after the Great Fire of London of 1666, the other two being Hugh May and Sir Christopher Wren. Hugh May (1622–84) is less readily classed with the Inigo Jones group, as his architecture had a Dutch inclination, due to his strong contacts with Holland, which at this time was practising its own brick-and-stone interpretation of Palladianism.

Sir Christopher Wren (1632–1723) was the supreme figure of the second phase of the Stuart period. Scholar, mathematician, astronomer, his scientific training at Oxford developed his constructive power, and largely counterbalanced his lack of early architectural training; for he did not start the study and practice of architecture until somewhat late in life, when in 1663 he was made a member of the Commission for the repair of S. Paul's Cathedral. In the same year he was asked to prepare a design for Pembroke College Chapel, Cambridge (p. 1014). As Inigo Jones had come under Italian, so Sir Christopher Wren came under French influence. He was in Paris in 1665, when the Palais du Louvre was in course of extension, and he then became associated with the group of architects and artists, such as Bernini (the great Italian master of the Baroque, invited to Paris by Louis XIV to prepare a design for the Louvre), Mansart, Louis le Vau and others, and he not only studied Renaissance buildings in Paris but also saw the royal and other châteaux in the surrounding country: he may have visited the Netherlands. As he never went to Italy, the force of this French influence was further accentuated, and, moreover, his royal patron, Charles II, had been an exile at the French court, and had there imbibed similar ideas. The destructive ravages of the Great Fire of London (1666) offered Wren an immediate opportunity for practising his art on a grand scale in the rebuilding of S. Paul's and the city churches, although it was found not possible to execution his plan for the rebuilding of the City of London. As mentioned one of three Royal Commissioners charged to consider the problems of rebuilding the city after the Fire, and one outcome of their recommendations was an Act (1667) which laid down standards for the new houses, which were to be in brick and follow one or other of three types, each with specified wall-thicknesses and floor-heights. These prescriptions had ramifications in other cities and towns. In 1669, Wren was appointed Surveyor-General of the King's Works. With the exception of his work on the palaces at Hampton Court and Greenwich (p. 1022), Wren does not appear to have been responsible for much domestic building, and such as survive of his lesser houses show some influence of the mature Dutch style. He produced his effects, not by expensive elaboration, but by careful proportion of the various parts, by concentration of ornament in the most telling position, or by one outstanding feature in the design. His buildings, too, owe much of their character to the use of Portland stone, which proved to have such good weathering properties; while in his domestic buildings, and some of his city churches, he made an effective use of brick with stone dressings, as at Hampton Court and S. Benet, Paul's Wharf, London. Whether in the graded greys of quarried stone or in the warm reds of hand-made bricks, Wren's buildings seem native to the site for which they were designed, and his influence was of the greatest importance to subsequent developments. His principal buildings are referred to and are illustrated later (pp. 1014–32). Wren's work is individual, but its character in the later stages gave rise to a brief phase of English Baroque, this spanning the thirty or so years concluding about 1725. As the main buildings of this nature were in course of erection in the early eighteenth century, the phase may be regarded as introductory to Georgian architecture.

Georgian Architecture. Under this title is classed the architecture of the reigns of Anne (1702–14), George I (1714–27), George II (1727–60), George III (1760–1820), George IV (1820–30).

Reference has been made to the English Baroque, the rare examples of which fall mainly between 1695–1725; Georgian architecture in general otherwise may be divided into two phases, the Anglo-Palladian and the Antiquarian, the latter commencing about 1750 and comprehending almost completely the so-called 'Greek Revival' and the formative stages of the 'Gothic Revival'—which only matured in Victorian times —as well as a variety of other manifestations of a developing retrospective outlook.

As to the English Baroque; we have seen that the arrival of the Renaissance in England was much belated and its nature transformed by practice in the countries through which it had passed from the fountain-head in Italy, as well as by circumstances in England itself. Yet as there was always some direct intercourse between England and Italy, increasing as time passed, and published works which gave fairly recent accounts of what was transpiring at the source, the influences on England were bound to be somewhat confused, the more recent being superficially imposed upon those of longer standing, already partly or wholly assimilated. In Italy, the 'High' Baroque of c. 1625–75 had been passed, and though in the main it was little to the English taste it would have been remarkable if it had not been reflected in some degree. A comparatively early response is demonstrated in the south porch of S. Mary the Virgin, Oxford (1637), with its twisted columns and broken pediment. It is not known who designed it, but the mason was a John Jackson. Besides the echoes in the later works of Wren and in those of William Talman (1650–1719), who built Thoresby House, Notts (1671; destroyed by fire, 1745) of remarkably advanced character, and the south and east fronts of Chatsworth House (1687–96) (p. 1014), famous for its art treasures and grounds laid out by Paxton, the English Baroque appears outstandingly in the architecture of three great personalities, and, to a diminished extent, in some few buildings designed by admiring followers. The three were Vanbrugh, Hawksmoor and Archer.

Sir John Vanbrugh (1664–1726) was a writer of dramas as well as a designer of palaces, besides being a military officer, a wit and a courtier, who became Controller of the Royal Works (1702). Monumentality is the keynote of his architecture. His was a personal, not recognizably Italian, interpretation of the Baroque, depending on plasticity of mass; that is, a bold advance or recession of parts, or 'movement' as it was called. At least as regards the detail a good deal of the eventual character of his buildings must have been due to Nicholas Hawksmoor (1661–1736), his distinguished assistant from the outset, possessing highly-developed practical abilities, for previously he had been a right-hand man to Sir Christopher Wren from the age of about eighteen. Hawksmoor assisted Wren with the city churches, and again at Greenwich Hospital, where he was Clerk of Works or Assistant Surveyor for his whole life after 1698. He also did important work on his own account, including six London churches, some buildings at Oxford and Cambridge, as well as designs for the western towers of Westminster Abbey (1734) (p. 663), completed after his death. Hawksmoor's varied interpretations of the Baroque seem to have been based partly on Wren and partly on books; he was much interested in antiquity. Thomas Archer (c. 1668–1743), designer of a small number of churches and houses, studied for four years on the Continent. His buildings are the closest approximation to the Italian Baroque ever achieved in England, showing a leaning in taste towards Borromini (p. 846). Archer influenced provincial vernacular building, particularly in Somerset, Dorset and Devon, as in the work of the Bastard brothers (John, 1688–1770; William, c. 1689–1766) at Blandford, Dorset, in the rebuilding of the town after a disastrous fire in 1731. Outside the London region there was little new church building, and thus so much the less room for the Baroque to take hold: we have seen that, in Italy, churches were the chief vehicle for the more florid expressions of the style. In the eighteenth century, domestic architecture continued to be the chief type of building, though there was an expansion in public building too. The spread of wealth brought fewer opulent great houses but many more of comparatively modest dimensions, sited in the countryside or at the fringes of towns, while the smaller houses reached new standards of comfort and convenience, and even cottages passed into permanent, solidly-built form.

The English phase of the Baroque, acclimatized and restrained though it was, was short-lived and already being supplanted by a 'Palladian' phase before it had run its course. The change is illustrated by the professional career of James Gibbs (1683–1774), born near Aberdeen, who, having travelled extensively on the Continent and studied under Carlo Fontana (p. 846) in Rome, returned to England in 1709, imbued with the Baroque. In this vein he built S. Mary-le-Strand, London (1714–17) (p. 1056), but thereafter his very great output of building was accommodated to the prevailing Palladian mode, which from about 1710 to 1750 came to affect building comprehensively in the country down to the most modest dwelling. Gibbs himself contributed to the diffusion of Palladian principles in his many writings, of which the principal was *Rules for Drawing the Several Parts of Architecture* (1732), used as a copy-book by builders not only in England but also in America. Foundational in the Palladian movement was a growing recognition of the virtues of the buildings of Inigo Jones, together with the influence of books such as the *Vitruvius Britannicus* (1717 and 1725) of the Scot, Colen Campbell (d. 1729), architect of a score of houses between 1712–27, and a new edition (1715–16) of Palladio's *I quattro libri dell' Architettura*, by Giacomo Leoni (1686–1746)— a Venetian working in England—under the title of *The Architecture of A. Palladio*.

Palladio's restrained Classicism was readily adaptable to the English taste. Its most influential advocate was the Earl of Burlington (1694–1753), who in the part he played typifies the interest now displayed in architecture by the social élite.

Attracted by Colen Campbell's *Vitruvius Britannicus*, Burlington visited Italy a second time in 1719 expressly for the study of Palladio's architecture, particularly that at Vicenza (p. 863). He was accompanied on his return by William Kent (1684–1748), who had long been studying in Italy as a painter-stuccoist and who turned architect under Burlington's patronage from about 1732. Lord Burlington at first employed Campbell's services for the buildings he undertook, but after about 1721 began himself to assume the position of designer, with or without the help of Campbell, Kent and others, but with Henry Flitcroft (1697–1769) as his personal assistant. After *c.* 1729, Flitcroft designed a number of houses and one or two churches in his own right, including S. Giles-in-the-Fields, London. Kent is worthy of his fame as a decorator, and as a prolific architect is celebrated especially for his Horse Guards building, Whitehall (p. 1062). He is almost more famous as a landscape architect, for he practised the doctrines of irregularity first preached by Lord Temple in his dissertation 'Upon the garden of Epicurus' (1685), where the beauty of informality is opposed to the geometrical contrivance of the Baroque garden. Following the third Earl of Shaftesbury in the belief that harmony, balance and proportion are alike the basis of morality and beauty, Kent adopted a 'Platonic idealism' to be voiced later by Pope, where contrast, surprise and concealment of the boundary were the formative notions. Preceded by Bridgeman at Stowe (1718) in the use of the 'Ha ha', he carried out modifications here in 1740–50, as he had done at Chiswick (1736). The shifting point of view and the element of surprise were the inspiration of Rousham, Oxon (1741), where landscape first became a visual extension of the grounds.

Another protégé of the Earl of Burlington was Isaac Ware (d. 1766), whose fame rests mainly on his writings; he made his own translation of Palladio, published a collection of *Designs of Inigo Jones and Others* and, much more important, *The Complete Body of Architecture*. The two latter went through several editions, and became much-used copy-books. Important, too, as a writer, was John Vardy (d. 1765). There was a veritable flood of such books at this period, laying down the standard parts of the Orders, ostensibly according to the revered masters, Alberti, Palladio, Jones, etc., giving ranges of designs for doorways, windows, fireplaces and other features and reproducing buildings designed by famous contemporary personages; not, of course, excluding the works of the author himself, where forthcoming, for the books of the eighteenth century served as a chief means of advertisement. Books were directed now, not solely towards the well-informed patron or connoisseur, but increasingly towards the master-builder, the working craftsman, artisan and even gardener, like those of 'William Halfpenny', an alias for Michael Hoare (d. 1755) and Batty Langley (1696–1751), both of whom were enormously prolific writers. Langley's *The Builder's Jewel, or the Youth's Instructor, and Workman's Remembrancer* (1746), and *New Principles of Gardening* (1728) are typical. He attracted much ridicule by attempting to standardize Gothic elements into Orders in his book *Gothic Architecture improved by Rules and Proportions* (1742), a topic significant of a coming change in architectural development. Another contemporary was Roger Morris (1695–1749), designer of the Palladian bridge at Wilton House, Wilts (1736) (p. 1013), and of several other works of comparable excellence, including Marble Hill House, Twickenham (1728–9).

Palladianism thus entered the bloodstream of the architecture of England, and also that of Scotland and Ireland. Formal Palladian principles were applied not alone to individual buildings but to the relationship of buildings one to another in schemes of civic design. The work of the Woods at their native town of Bath (John the elder, 1704–54; John the younger, 1728–81) serves as an illustration, and demonstrates the link between successive generations of designers practising Palladian principles. There, town houses were drawn together to afford collectively a 'palatial' effect. The Circus, Bath, begun 1754 by the elder Wood and completed by the younger, and the Royal Crescent (1767–75) by the latter, are famous instances (p. 1048A). Notable London architects at this time were Sir Robert Taylor (1714–88), who began as a sculptor and studied in Rome, and James Paine (1716–89), each enjoying a very large practice. It was said that they 'divided the practice of the profession between them until Robert Adam entered the lists', though in fact, John Carr (1723–1807), a provincial architect, of York, only a few years younger, was equally if not more prolific of country houses. This great increase in the employment of architects, who now began to engage pupils, led to the consolidation of the profession. As well as the proliferation of a wealthy capitalist class, due to the incipient industrialization of the country, urban development proceeded apace and created demands for an augmented number of public buildings. The luxury of internal decoration in dwellings, often contrasted with grandly simple exteriors, bears witness to the influx of wealth from fresh sources. Landscape art reached its climax in the work of Lancelot Brown (1716–83), known as 'Capability' Brown from his habitual reference to the capabilities of the site. He designed very many gardens and converted old formal gardens into the new style, besides in his later days adventuring in architectural design.

While Palladian architecture proceeded, a new trend became clearly apparent about mid-century: there had been signs long before of an Antiquarian movement, which was on the one hand romantic and vocative, and on the other archaeological. Indeed Palladianism itself was in some sense a reversion to practices of an earlier time, but now, designers began to turn to more distant architectural antecedents, to the Gothic and to ancient Rome and to Greece. The Roman grafted itself almost imperceptibly on to the Palladian—one important outcome was the 'Adam' manner —and to a less extent so did the Greek, though the latter and the Gothic emerged as plainly recognizable 'styles' after the end of the century. Each of the latter styles, as also some quaint interpretations of the Chinese and Indian, was superficial rather than fundamental, and building plans remained essentially Renaissance in character. Gothic architecture had never been wholly abandoned: Wren, Vanbrugh, Kent and others, occasionally had produced their personal versions of it, usually, but not invariably, to match existing structures, while country builders in stone-producing districts like the Cotswolds might continue to preserve the old traditions uninterruptedly. The new tendency of mid-eighteenth century was a deliberate looking-back to bygone times. Whimsical, decorative 'Gothick' was popularized particularly by Horace Walpole (1717–97), 4th Earl of Orford, who from 1747 to 1776 progressively extended and decorated his house at Twickenham, which he named Strawberry Hill (p. 1046A), in Gothic conceits. Sanderson Miller (1717–80) was another amateur with kindred tastes, who, however, was himself the actual designer of one or two buildings in the new Gothic mode.

Books, French, German and British, particularly those reporting archaeological investigations, were important in stimulating the various antiquarian movements; like Robert Wood's (1716–71) Ruins of Palmyra, published in 1753, and his Ruins of Balbec (1757); or the series due to James Stuart (1713–88) and Nicholas Revett (1720–1804), beginning some years after their visit to Greece with The Antiquities of Athens in 1762. Both Stuart and Revett did a little designing in full-blooded Greek style, but their volumes, appearing intermittently over a long span of years, had much the greater influence.

The famous Robert Adam (1728–92) emulated Stuart and Revett. He left his native Scotland for Italy in 1754, studying in Paris on the way, and after a long period centred on Rome, where he met Piranesi, the accomplished draughtsman and etcher, whose imaginative restorations of Roman monuments are world-renowned. Adam went with a small party to Dalmatia in 1757, where he made the measurements which led to the publication of his *Ruins of the Palace of Diocletian at Spalatro* (now Split) in 1764. He returned to England in 1758 to found with his brother James an enormous practice, advertising it very soon with the first two volumes of his *Works in Architecture of Robert and James Adam* (1773, 1779). Adam's light and gracious style owed little to the Palace of Diocletian, and was due to his discreet selection among Roman precedents and the Italian Renaissance interpretations of them, particularly of methods of stucco ornamentation. He captured the Greek Hellenistic spirit in Roman work, and justly claimed to have introduced depth of 'movement' and a calculated variety of effect in his buildings, inside as well as out. Sir William Chambers (1723–96), on the other hand, abhorred his rival Adam's light style, and practised a robust and correct Classicism tinctured with the contemporary French; for he too, studied abroad for a considerable period. Not only did he visit the nearer European countries, including a five-years stay in Italy (1750–5), but in his earlier days had twice been to China. An outcome of the latter voyages was a book on *Design of Chinese Buildings*, etc. (1757). Of more far-reaching importance was his *Treatise on Civil Architecture* (1759), enlarged in subsequent editions. The range and quality of his architectural work vied with that of the Adams.

The 'Grand Tour' on the Continent became a regular procedure, followed by Robert Mylne (1734–1811), another Scottish architect, who also gained an extensive practice, and, a decade later (1762–8) by James Wyatt (1746–1813), a much more colourful personality. Wyatt's Classical style had a strong resemblance to that of Adam, of which the latter complained; like Adam and other of his predecessors and contemporaries, some of his country houses were Gothic, but whereas theirs were usually Classical conceptions tricked out with battlements, turrets and towers, Wyatt's were imaginative decorative creations in the succession of Walpole's Strawberry Hill. A growing respect at this time for the old Mediaeval buildings led to a general move for their repair, and Wyatt got into trouble with knowledgeable antiquarians for his too-drastic 'improvements' to several of the great cathedrals; Salisbury, Lichfield, Hereford and Durham. A lesser light practising a frail and decorative Gothic was the provincial architect, Francis Hiorne, of Warwick (1744–89) (p. 1056). The better-known contemporaries of Wyatt include the younger George Dance (1741–1825), most of whose work, often highly original and sometimes showing a strong Greek note, has been destroyed or drastically remodelled; Thomas Cooley (1740–84) and James Gandon (1742–1823), the latter a pupil of Sir William Chambers, both famous for their Dublin buildings; Thomas Hardwick (1752–1829), another pupil and somewhat colourless follower of Sir William Chambers; and Henry Holland (1745–1806), son-in-law of 'Capability' Brown, whose style was the now-current 'Graeco-Roman'. Humphrey Repton (1752–1818), has more importance in the history of landscape art than in that of architecture, being a designer of 'Picturesque' gardens, but sometimes he himself designed the related mansions also, at others he deputed the latter function to his collaborator, John Nash, who struck a new note by introducing the informality of the Picturesque into the buildings too.

John Nash (1752–1835) is an outstanding figure. He acquired extensive commissions and the royal favour, and designed many mansions as well as civic schemes, and some churches and public buildings. In his day the English Renaissance movement came to a close, succumbing to the rising tide of stylistic revivalism, to which Nash himself contributed. A brilliant if superficial designer, with grand ideas, his urban style was mostly Neo-Classical, a compound of the notions of his contemporaries, cleverly organized on Picturesque lines. Hard plaster stucco was his favourite medium, in which at relatively low cost his external effects were secured. But he also worked in the Gothic, and some of his houses, villas and estate cottages were informal versions of this or were pretentiously based on English vernacular homesteads. He even essayed the 'Hindoo' at the Royal Pavilion, Brighton (p. 1049D), with internal decorations veering to the Chinese. Much of an age with Nash was Sir John Soane (1753–1837), following the Neo-Classical expression with many personal idiosyncrasies. His interiors had fine and remarkable qualities, yet externally, his innovations were not invariably successful. The uncertainties of his style illustrated this period of change. He made the famous collection of models, casts, drawings and fragments of ancient architecture in his house in Lincoln's Inn Fields, which he left to the nation as a museum.

The work of the next generation of architects falls almost wholly in the early nineteenth century, and much of it after the Napoleonic wars; it tends more definitely to be revivalist, either Greek or Gothic, though some maintain the older cast. Despite a number of eighteenth-century precursors, both the Greek and the Gothic Revivals were only consolidated about 1805, and neither gained real force until after 1815. Meantime, books on Greek architectural precedents continued to appear, while antiquaries such as the draughtsmen John Carter (1748–1817) and A. C. Pugin (1762–1832) made faithful drawings of Mediaeval monuments which gave greater authority to the Gothic Revival. Thomas Rickman (1776–1841) was author of a momentous book *An Attempt to Discriminate the Styles of English Architecture from the Conquest to the Reformation* (1817) which did much to turn the Gothic Revival from a wayward caprice into a definite and protracted movement. He himself built only three Classical churches, but some fifty-seven in the Gothic, all in the provinces, including four 'iron' churches at Liverpool, of which S. George's (1812–14) was said at the time to be 'nearly the first iron church erected in the kingdom; the framework of the windows, doors, pillars, groins, roofs, pulpit and ornamental enrichments are of cast iron'. Other early adherents to the Gothic Revival now were John Shaw (1776–1832), designer of S. Dunstan-in-the-West, Fleet Street, London (1831) (p. 1060D), with a fine steeple; James Savage (1779–1852), author of S. Luke, Chelsea (1820) (p. 1060C); Francis Goodwin (1784–1835), who built a number of churches in the provinces; and Francis Bedford (1784–1858), whose work, a few churches, is mostly in London. Each of these built in the Classical style too, still strongly favoured for public buildings; Goodwin's Old Manchester Town Hall (demolished 1912) (p. 1066C), in Greek Revival style, was especially fine.

The Greek Revival had passed its best by *c.* 1830, and by 1840 was definitely dead in England, though it lingered in Scotland until after mid-century. William Wilkins (1778–1839), designer of University College, London (1827–8) (p. 1067B) and the National Gallery (1834–8) (p. 1067A) was a notable figure, practising the style extensively from about 1806 onwards. He, and Sir Robert Smirke (1781–1867), a prolific though not particularly gifted architect, who used the Greek principally for public buildings such as the British Museum (1823–47) (p. 1068D), had both undertaken Continental tours and studied architecture in Greece and South Italy, and thus their work has an archaeological correctness of detail. Wilkins was the author of *Antiquities of Magna Graecia* (1807) and several other writings on archaeological themes. Among the chief provincial architects adopting the Greek Revival importantly were David Hamilton (1768–1843) of Glasgow, John Foulston (1772–1842) of Plymouth, John Foster (1786–1846) of Liverpool, and Thomas Hamilton (1785–1858) and W. H. Playfair (1789–1857) of Edinburgh. In London, a slightly younger group included H. W. Inwood (1794–1843), who, with his father, William Inwood (*c.* 1771–1843), designed several churches of varying merit, including, however, S. Pancras Church, London (1819–22) (p. 1060B), the finest ecclesiastical building of the whole Revival. In the Greek character were also certain of the earlier buildings of Decimus Burton (1800–81), whose triple archway at Hyde Park Corner, London, is famous (1825–46) (p. 1068E), and of Sir Charles Barry (1795–1860), whose best design of the type was the Royal Manchester Institution building (1824–35), now the City Art Gallery.

By no means all architecture fell into the Greek or Gothic Revival categories. Sober Graeco-Roman continued to be a popular expression, the Georgian succession reached its final phase in the spare and refined delicacy of many a suburban or town house or terrace, while some buildings were so mixed in their characteristics as to defy classification. Architects might betray leanings in a particular direction, but changed freely from one expression to another as seemed to them best to meet the occasion. The scholarly and much-travelled Professor C. R. Cockerell (1788–1863), despite the extent of his archaeological knowledge, was no exception; he at times practised the Gothic, and in the Classical, had his own personal vein, favouring Graeco-Roman rather than Adam character while admitting some influence from contemporary French architecture. His buildings have quality of detail. Contemporary with him was John Dobson (1787–1867) of Newcastle-on-Tyne, who built up a considerable practice in north-east England, and designed the lay-out of the expanding city. While his public buildings were Classical, in his country mansions and churches he was among the first to introduce the Gothic into that region.

Churches in general were the more likely to be expressed in Gothic. Apart from a flurry of Classical works in the later seventeen-eighties and early nineties there had been comparatively little church building in the forty years before 1810; but by 1820 activity had become intense, partly as a result of the Church Building Act of 1818, which devoted a million pounds to contributions to the building of cheap churches and chapels to serve the fresh congregations of expanding towns. The aged John Nash and Sir John Soane, and the much younger Sir Robert Smirke, were advisers to the Commissioners discharging the Act, and each himself built one or two churches. By 1837 the 'Commissioner' churches totalled about 230, and the advance of the Gothic is indicated by the fact that scarcely a fifth of these were in the Classical styles. The Greek Revival was especially favoured in the London area at the outset, the provinces meanwhile having turned in force to the Gothic, but after 1827 the fashion passed and the very few churches afterwards built in the Greek style were almost all in the provinces. Classical churches of any sort became rare after 1827; but whatever the style externally, plans followed Classical lines. Being for congregational worship, they usually were simple rectangular boxes, lacking transepts or chancels, and had galleries inside. Nearly all had an axial 'western' tower, spire, cupola or bell-turret, unlike Victorian churches (Chapter 36), of which the towers normally were asymmetrically placed. For cheapness, they were mostly of brick with stone dressings.

EXAMPLES

EARLY RENAISSANCE

(Elizabethan Architecture, 1558–1603)

MONUMENTS, TOMBS, AND FITTINGS

The early Renaissance was heralded by a number of smaller monuments and fittings erected in existing churches, as in other countries.

The **Culpepper Tomb, Goudhurst,** the **wall tablets at Peterhouse,**

Cambridge and also **All Hallows, Barking, London,** the **pulpit, North Cray,** and the **chapel screen, Charterhouse,** are examples of many features found in churches throughout the country, while the **stalls, King's College, Cambridge** (1531–5), are amongst the earliest examples of the newly introduced style.

The **Tomb of Henry VII** (1509) (pp. 662, 977, 989A), in Westminster Abbey, by Torrigiani, is an early and exquisite example of Renaissance art. It is a black marble table tomb, with angle Corinthian pilasters, between which are the royal arms, while above are winged cherubs and effigies of Henry VII and his queen, enclosed in a Chantry Chapel with a fine Gothic screen by Ducheman (p. 664c).

ELIZABETHAN MANSIONS

Well-known Elizabethan mansions are: **Charlecote, Warwickshire** (1558); **Pitchford, Shropshire** (1560–70) (p. 989E); **Loseley Park, Surrey** (1562–8) (p. 992B); **Longleat House, Wilts** (1567–80) (pp. 991A, 994D) probably by Robert Smithson; **Kirby Hall, Northants** (1570–5) (pp. 993A, 1013), perhaps by Thomas Thorpe; **Penshurst Place, Kent** (portion) (1570–85) (p. 683); **Burghley House, Northants** (1577–87) (pp. 989D, 994A, 1001B); **Montacute House, Som.** (1580–99) (pp. 989B, 994B); **Wollaton Hall, Notts** (1580–8) (pp. 991B, 994C), by Robert Smithson; **Longford Castle, Wilts** (1580) (p. 994E); **Haddon Hall, Derbyshire** (long gallery) (1567–84) (pp. 685, 992A); **Westwood Park, Worcester** (1590); **Bramhall Hall, Cheshire** (additions 1590–1600) (p. 686); **Hinchingbrooke Hall, Hunts** (1602) (p. 1001C); **Sizergh Castle, Westmorland** (1558–75), enlarged in this period, and **Waterston Manor, Dorset** (1586).

These mansions show a general similarity in their arrangement with those of the Jacobean period, and so we give here detailed descriptions of the plan and usual features, which were evolved from those of the Tudor period (p. 685). The smaller mansions had a central hall flanked at one end by kitchen and offices, and at the other by withdrawing- and living-rooms; while the larger type was quadrangular with similar accommodation, but with additional rooms grouped round the court, and with a gatehouse in the centre of the entrance side, as at Oxburgh Hall, Norfolk, Compton Wynyates, Warwicks, and Sutton Place, Surrey. Elizabethan and Jacobean architects adhered to the Tudor plan for smaller mansions, but they evolved the E-shaped plan from the quadrangular plan by omitting one side, as at Hatfield, thus admitting sunlight and air (p. 994F), and for this reason one side of the court at Caius College, Cambridge, was removed. The H-shaped plan was used also in this period. The gatehouse often became a detached building, as at Burton Agnes, Yorkshire; Charlecote, Warwicks; Cranborne, Dorset (p. 1003) and Stanway, Glos. Features, such as the great hall, grand staircase, and long gallery, are common to the typical houses mentioned above. As houses began to look outwards, instead of into courts, surrounding gardens developed, on formal lines.

The Great Hall (pp. 990D, 994) still retained its central position, but became more than ever a hall of state, connecting the various parts of the mansion. The walls were cased internally in oak panelling to a height of 2.4 m or 3 m (8 or 10 ft), surmounted by ancestral portraits, armour and trophies of the chase. The fireplace, with its huge dog-grate, was an elaborate feature flanked by columns, while above were ranged heraldic devices of the owners. The hall was covered either by an open timber roof, as that over the Middle Temple Hall, London (p. 993C) or with elaborately moulded plaster panels (p. 998B). At the entrance end the carved oak screen supported the minstrels' gallery and also screened off the kitchen department beyond; while at the other end of the hall was the lofty bay window and raised dais, from which were reached the living-rooms of the family. A similar arrangement of plan was

A. Westminster Abbey. Tomb
of Henry VII (1509) and his
Queen (1503). See pp. 662, 988

B. Montacute House, Somerset (1580–99).
See p. 988

C. Benthall, Shropshire:
staircase. See p. 995

D. Burghley House, Northants (1577–87).
See p. 988

E. Pitchford, Shropshire (1560–70). See p. 988

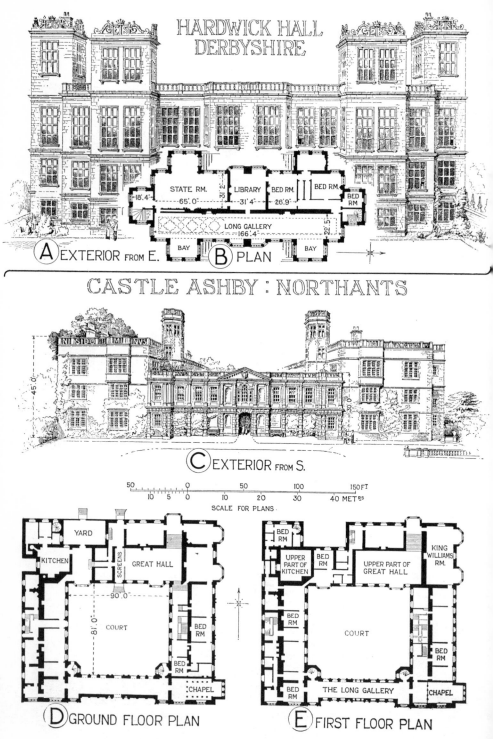

HARDWICK HALL
DERBYSHIRE

STATE RM.
18'.4"
65'.0"
31'.2"
LIBRARY
31'.4"
BED RM.
26'.9"
BED RM.
BED RM.
LONG GALLERY
166'.4"
22'.5"
BAY
BAY

Ⓐ EXTERIOR FROM E.   Ⓑ PLAN

CASTLE ASHBY : NORTHANTS

45'.0"
30'.0"

Ⓒ EXTERIOR FROM S.

50   0   50   100   150 FT
10 5 0   10   20   30   40 METRS
SCALE FOR PLANS

YARD
KITCHEN
SCREENS
GREAT HALL
90'.0"
COURT
BED RM.
BED RM.
CHAPEL

Ⓓ GROUND FLOOR PLAN

BED RM
UPPER PART OF KITCHEN
BED RM
UPPER PART OF GREAT HALL
KING WILLIAMS RM.
BED RM
COURT
BED RM
BED RM
THE LONG GALLERY
CHAPEL

Ⓔ FIRST FLOOR PLAN

A. Longleat House, Wilts (1567–80). See p. 995

B. Wollaton Hall, Notts (1580–8). See p. 988

A. Haddon Hall, Derbyshire: long gallery (1567–84). See p. 988

B. Loseley Park, Surrey: drawing room (1562–8). See p. 988

A. Kirby Hall, Northants: courtyard (1570–5). See p. 988

B. Gray's Inn Hall: interior (1556–60).   C. Middle Temple Hall, London: interior
See p. 996   (1562–70). See p. 996

EARLY RENAISSANCE PLANS
(ELIZABETHAN & JACOBEAN)

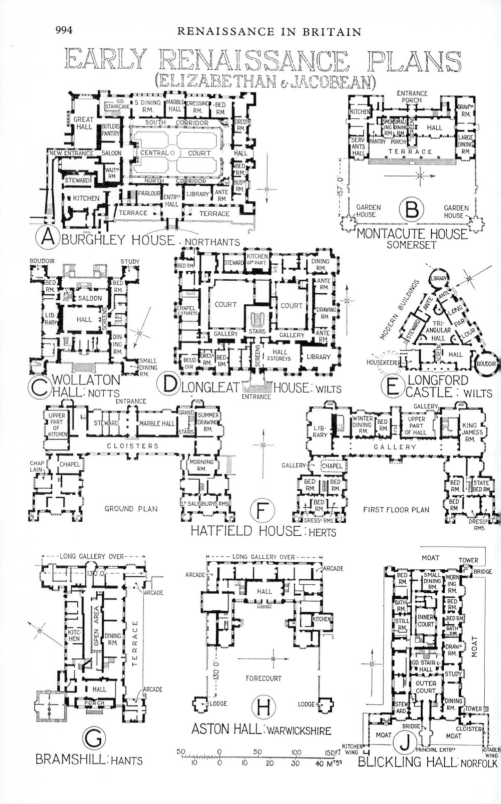

A BURGHLEY HOUSE : NORTHANTS

B MONTACUTE HOUSE SOMERSET

C WOLLATON HALL : NOTTS

D LONGLEAT HOUSE : WILTS

E LONGFORD CASTLE : WILTS

F HATFIELD HOUSE : HERTS
GROUND PLAN   FIRST FLOOR PLAN

G BRAMSHILL : HANTS

H ASTON HALL : WARWICKSHIRE

J BLICKLING HALL : NORFOLK

adopted in the colleges of Oxford (p. 998C) and Cambridge, and the Inns of Court, London, as Gray's Inn Hall (p. 993B) and Middle Temple Hall (p. 993C).

The Grand Staircase, as at Benthall, Shropshire (p. 989C), Aston Hall and Blickling Hall (p. 1002B, C), with carved newels and pierced balustrades, and usually adjacent to the hall, forms a dignified approach to the rooms above, and its prominence as a feature is in marked contrast with tne inconvenient corkscrew stairs of the Mediaeval period.

The Long Gallery (pp. 990B, E, 992A, 994) is perhaps the most striking feature of an Elizabethan mansion, with ornamental chimney-pieces, panelled or tapestried walls, large mullioned windows and modelled plaster ceiling. Long, low and narrow, though varied as at Haddon by room-like bays (p. 992A), the gallery often ran the whole length of the upper floor of the house and connected the wings on either side of the central hall (p. 994F). Its original purpose is somewhat doubtful; it may have been designed merely as a connecting corridor, as a covered promenade, or as a 'picture gallery' used to display the art treasures which it had now become the fashion to collect. It would almost seem as if the aristocracy of Elizabethan times in England rivalled one another in the length of their galleries, even as did the nobility of Mediaeval Italy in the height of their towers (p. 757). Some of the finest of these galleries are: Haddon Hall (1567–84) (p. 992A), 33 m × 5.5 m (109 ft × 18 ft); Montacute House (1580–99), 52 m × 6 m (170 ft × 20 ft), and Hardwick Hall (1590–7) (p. 990B), 50.5 m × 6.7 m (166 ft × 22 ft).

The Withdrawing-room or 'solar' of previous times was often elaborately finished with carved chimney-pieces and panelled walls, as at Loseley Park, Surrey (1562–68) (p. 992B), Crew Hall, Cheshire (1636) and Stockton House, Wiltshire (1610) (p. 1002A), where it even rivalled a long gallery in treatment.

Bedrooms were multiplied and were often elaborate, as at Sizergh Castle, and a private chapel was frequently incorporated in the building (p. 994D, F).

Longleat, Wilts (1567–80) (pp. 991A, 994D), for which R. Smithson had begun the design of the elevations in 1546, before fire necessitated rebuilding. The pilastered bays thus date from before the corrupting influence of German copybook mannerism. It owes much to Old Somerset House in London, where the owner of the Longleat estate, Sir John Thynne, had worked as secretary to the Duke of Somerset, Lord Protector during the brief reign of Edward VI. It is interesting to compare the elevations with the courtyard front of the Château of Écouen, France (p. 882).

Hardwick Hall, Derbyshire (1590–7) (p. 990), designed by Robert Smithson, is unusual in plan (p. 990B), consisting of a rectangular block with projecting bays. The exterior is famous for its large mullioned and transomed windows, giving rise to the saying 'Hardwick Hall, more glass than wall', while bay-windows, carried up as towers, relieve the skyline and are terminated by open scroll-work with the initials 'E.S.' for Elizabeth, Countess of Shrewsbury, known as 'Bess of Hardwick'.

Castle Ashby, Northants (1572–) (p. 990C-E), added to from time to time, is situated on high ground, and was originally in the form of a three-sided court, which included the great hall, 18 m × 9 m (60 ft × 30 ft), with screens, bay-window, and staircase turrets. The lettered balustrade displays the words 'Nisi Dominus Ædificaverit', etc. (Ps. cxxvii). The fourth side (*c.* 1635), with the long gallery 27.7 m × 4.7 m (91 ft × 15 ft 6 ins), attributed to Inigo Jones, illustrates the difference between the Elizabethan and Later Renaissance styles (p. 990C).

ELIZABETHAN COLLEGES

During the Mediaeval period many colleges had been founded at the universities (p. 692), and as the day of the pious founder had not yet passed, new colleges were still endowed both at Oxford and Cambridge. These were, of course, built in the Elizabethan style, which retained many Gothic features; while additions were also made to Mediaeval colleges. Thus revival of learning and Renaissance in architecture went hand in hand in the old universities. At **Cambridge** there is **Emmanuel College** (1584), with its dignified façade; the beautiful little **Gate of Honour, Caius College** (1572–3) (p. 1000B), designed by the founder, Dr Caius; **Nevile's Court, Trinity College** (1593–1615), and new quadrangles to **Sidney Sussex College** (1596–8) and **S. John's College** (1598–1602) (p. 692), by Ralph Simons. At **Oxford** there is a fine example of Renaissance work in **Jesus College** (1571) by Holt. Other colleges and additions at both universities belong to the later periods (pp. 997, 1069). Among the **Inns of Court, London, Gray's Inn Hall** (1556–60) (p. 993B), **The Temple,** with its church, halls, libraries, chambers and the famous **Middle Temple Hall** (p. 993C), with its magnificent hammer-beam roof (1562–70), partly date from this period. Much damage was caused at Gray's Inn and the Temple by bombing between 1941–5.

ELIZABETHAN TOWN HOUSES

Many interesting houses were built, not only in London, but also in country towns; for in days of slow and difficult travelling by coach, many of the landed gentry, especially in parts remote from London, found it convenient to have their town residences close at hand. York, Chester, Shrewsbury, Ludlow, Coventry, Canterbury, Exeter, Truro and many another town bear testimony to the fine design and craftsmanship of the houses of this period. In London there remain, in spite of the Great Fire, the half-timber building of Staple Inn (1581), with its fine hall and hammer-beam roof, and portions of the **Charterhouse,** including the great hall (1571, mutilated by war damage), added by the Duke of Norfolk; while the façade of Sir Paul Pindar's House (1600) is now preserved in the Victoria and Albert Museum, as is also a panelled room from the Palace of Bromley-by-Bow (1606), which, with its plaster ceiling, recalls the glories of such palatial buildings although it actually dates from the Jacobean period.

EARLY RENAISSANCE
(Jacobean Architecture, 1603–25)

JACOBEAN MANSIONS

Hatfield House, Herts (1607–11) (pp. 994F, 998A, B, 1002E), built for Robert, first Earl of Salisbury, stands pre-eminent among many noble piles of this period in displaying the special characteristics and elaboration of treatment considered suitable for the country mansion of a nobleman. The house is E-shaped in plan (p. 994F), with central hall and projecting symmetrical wings, and is set off by formal gardens, designed with the same care as is displayed in the planning of the house itself. The entrance front, 68.5 m (225 ft) long, is of daringly plain brickwork with stone mullioned windows, relieved by a projecting central entrance; while the bay-windows of the wings are taken up as small lateral towers, and the building is finished by a flat roof and balustrade and dominated by a central clock-turret. The south front (p. 998A) is much more ornate in treatment, with Doric, Ionic and Corinthian Orders superimposed to form a centre-piece flanked by an arcaded ground storey, mullioned windows and pierced parapet. The two-storeyed hall (p. 998B), with mullioned windows, minstrels' gallery, and modelled plaster ceiling, is a Renaissance development of the traditional Mediaeval hall, but there is an unusual connecting gallery at the dais end. The long gallery, chapel, grand staircase and suites of private rooms all contribute to the completeness of this Jacobean mansion, designed, at least in part, by Robert Lyming, who was also the designer of the whole of Blickling Hall (see below).

Holland House, Kensington (1607), was erected for Sir Walter Cope and afterwards inherited by the Earl of Holland, and was the residence of many famous men. It was burnt out in 1940. The plan was H-shaped, with the entrance at one end, as at Bramshill (p. 994G), and with arcades on the south bordering a fine terrace. The central porch was carried up as a tower with an ogee roof, and was flanked by bay-windows and curved gables. The entrance had been intended to be central on the south front, and the change to the east side required an encroachment on one of the arcades. The doorway and the typical chimney-piece and oak-panelled walls in the White Parlour are noticeable features.

Bramshill House, Hampshire (1605–12) (pp. 994G, 1001A, D, J) was designed for Lord Zouche. Its unusual plan (p. 994G), partly due to an older building, is of the H-type, with entrance through an arcaded porch direct into the hall, which thus loses its feudal character, but still retains the dais. An odd feature is the long narrow internal area. The long gallery, 39.6 m (130 ft) long, the terrace with its arcades (p. 994J), and the oriel window (p. 1001A) are among the many beautiful features of this building.

Blickling Hall, Norfolk (1626) (pp. 994J, 995, 1001G, 1002B, C, F) by Robert Lyming, is built in brick and stone, usual in Norfolk, and the plan resembles that of Bramshill. It has two small internal courts, the outer court giving entrance to the hall, which is a thoroughfare room, as at Aston Hall (p. 994H); at the external angles of the building are square towers. The principal entrance (p. 1001G), reached across the moat, has an arched opening with carved spandrels, framed with Doric columns and entablature, surmounted by the arms of Sir Henry Hobart. The staircase (p. 1002B, C), rearranged in its present position in 1770, with the upper part in two opposite flights—unusual in this period—has boldly carved newels surmounted by figures, and an arched balustrade. The chimney-piece (p. 1002F) has flanking pilasters diminishing towards the base and surmounted by Hermes figures which frame heraldic devices.

Other Jacobean mansions of interest are: **Chastleton House, Oxon** (1603–14); **Audley End, Essex** (1603–16) (p. 999A), by Bernard Johnson; **Knole House, Kent** (1605) (re-modelled); **Charlton House, Wilts** (1607); **Stockton House, Wiltshire** (1610) (p. 1002A); **Aston Hall, Warwickshire** (1618–35) (p. 994H); **Bolsover Castle, Derbyshire** (1612–), by John Smithson, which has later additions made (1629–33) by John and his son, Huntingdon Smithson; **Quenby Hall, Leicestershire** (–1621); and **Charlton House, London** (1607–12) (p. 999D).

JACOBEAN COLLEGES

The **Bodleian Library, Oxford** (1613–36) (pp. 694A, 1000A), formerly the Old Schools, attributed to Thomas Holt (d. 1624), is a conspicuous instance of the work of the period, for the tower over the gateway is a curious but effective mixture of traditional Gothic and new Renaissance, with mullioned windows and canopied niches flanked by the five Orders of architecture, one above the other; while the whole is capped by Gothic pinnacles.

Thomas Holt is equally dubiously credited with several other works at the older University at this time. At **Merton College** he is said to have designed the entrance, with superimposed Orders (1610) (p. 1000D), and library (p. 1000C); **Wadham College,** frontispiece of 'Orders' (1610–13), and fine hall (p. 998C), besides additions to

A. Hatfield House, Herts: south façade (1607–11). See p. 996

B. Hatfield House, Herts: hall (1607–11).
See p. 996

C. Wadham College, Oxford: hall (1610–
1613). See p. 997

A. Audley End, Essex (1603–16). See p. 997

B. Fountains Hall, Yorkshire (1611).
See p. 1003

C. S. Peter's Hospital,
Bristol (1610). See p. 1003

D. Charlton House, London: west façade (1607–12). See p. 997

A. Tower of the Bodleian Library, Oxford (1613–36). See p. 997

B. Gate of Honour, Caius College, Cambridge (1572–3). See p. 996

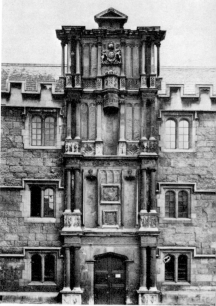

C. Library (additions c. 1600–24)

D. Entrance (1610)

Merton College, Oxford. See p. 997

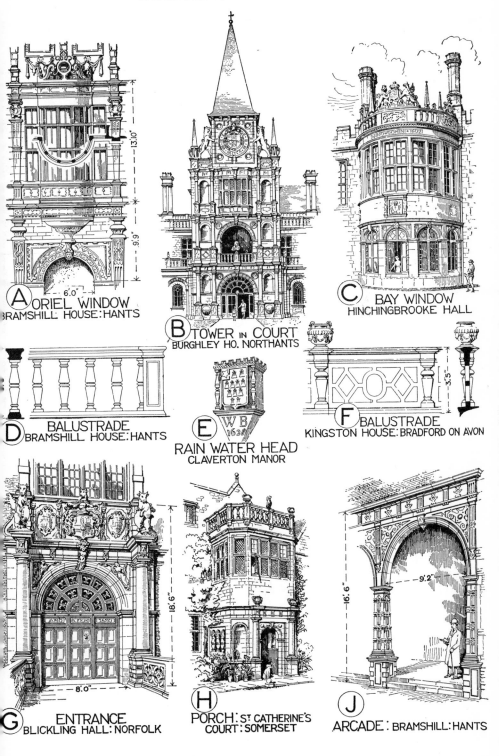

A ORIEL WINDOW
BRAMSHILL: HOUSE: HANTS

B TOWER IN COURT
BURGHLEY HO. NORTHANTS

C BAY WINDOW
HINCHINGBROOKE HALL

D BALUSTRADE
BRAMSHILL HOUSE: HANTS

E RAIN WATER HEAD
CLAVERTON MANOR

F BALUSTRADE
KINGSTON HOUSE: BRADFORD ON AVON

G ENTRANCE
BLICKLING HALL: NORFOLK

H PORCH: St CATHERINE'S
COURT: SOMERSET

J ARCADE: BRAMSHILL: HANTS

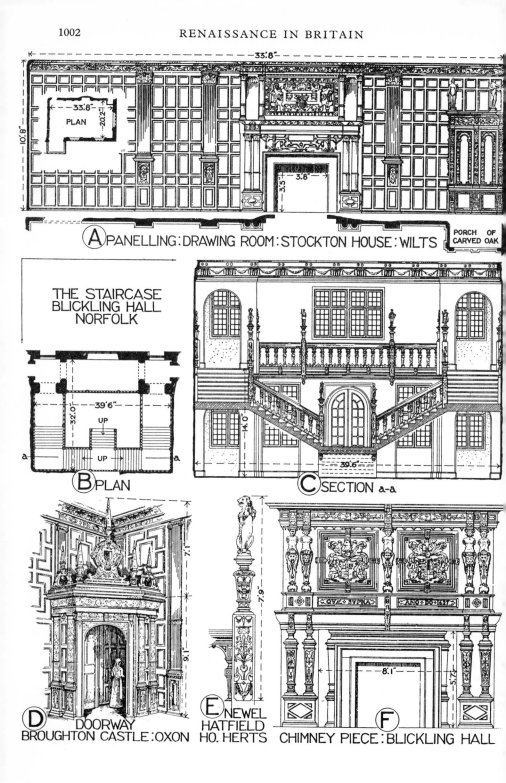

Ⓐ PANELLING : DRAWING ROOM : STOCKTON HOUSE : WILTS   PORCH OF CARVED OAK

THE STAIRCASE BLICKLING HALL NORFOLK

Ⓑ PLAN

Ⓒ SECTION a-a

Ⓓ DOORWAY BROUGHTON CASTLE : OXON

Ⓔ NEWEL HATFIELD HO. HERTS

Ⓕ CHIMNEY PIECE : BLICKLING HALL

Oriel and Jesus Colleges (1612). Pembroke College (1624) is certainly by another hand. At Cambridge the quadrangle of **Clare College** is later (1638–).

JACOBEAN MANOR HOUSES

Mediaeval manor houses supplied a good ground-work for Jacobean architects to elaborate with Renaissance additions and fittings, such as we see in South Wraxall Manor, Wilts (p. 685), and Cranborne Manor House, Dorset (1601–12)—a Tudor building with a Jacobean casing; while **Fountains Hall, Yorkshire** (1611) (p. 999B), is a complete example, built largely with material from the Mediaeval abbot's house (p. 571).

JACOBEAN TOWN HOUSES

The building known as **S. Peter's Hospital, Bristol** (1610, totally destroyed in the war of 1939–45) (p. 999C), was a fine half-timbered house of this period, with over-hanging upper storey and panelled 'Court Room' with carved chimney-piece and modelled plaster ceilings.

JACOBEAN MARKET HALLS

Market halls, as at Shrewsbury (1595) and Chipping Campden (1627), are frequently built of stone or brick, while the Market Hall, Wymondham, Norfolk (1617), is a half-timbered example.

JACOBEAN HOSPITALS AND ALMSHOUSES

The need for hospitals and almshouses became greater after the Dissolution of the Monasteries, and many hospitals were erected in this period.

The Whitgift Hospital, Croydon (1596–9), with its fine quadrangle, common hall, and living-rooms, still carries on the uses for which it was founded. Sackville College, East Grinstead (1619), Weekley Hospital, Northants (1611), Chipping Campden Almshouses (1610), Trinity Hospital, Greenwich (1613), Trinity Hospital, Castle Rising (1614), Eyre's Hospital, Salisbury (1617), Abbot's Hospital, Guildford (1619), and somewhat later, Berkeley Hospital, Worcester, are a few of these buildings which have a similar arrangement of hall, kitchen, chapel and rooms for the inmates.

LATE RENAISSANCE
(Stuart Architecture, 1625–1702)

INIGO JONES (1573–1652) (p. 980). The court masques (1605–40) during the reigns of James I and Charles I, for which Inigo Jones designed the scenery, showed his intimate acquaintance with Italian Renaissance architecture. He was the first man in England to appreciate and put into practice modular design, whereby the part is made the measure of the whole: the whole is equal to the sum of its integral units. He was the leader of the Stuart connoisseurs.

The **Banqueting House, Whitehall, London** (1619–22) (pp. 1005, 1006B) was erected by Inigo Jones on the site of the old Jacobean Banqueting House burnt down in 1619. It was afterwards intended by John Webb, Inigo Jones's talented pupil, to incorporate this Banqueting House in a design for a royal palace which is shown on the plan (p. 1005B). This palace-scheme would have formed one of the grandest architectural conceptions of the Renaissance in England, both in extent and in the finely adjusted proportions of its various parts (p. 1005A). The complete plan of the palace (p. 1005B), with its seven courts, shows the position the Banqueting House would have occupied on the Grand Court 243 m × 122 m (800 ft × 400 ft), twice the size of the court of the Louvre, Paris (p. 890E); across its intended site now runs the thoroughfare of Whitehall. The façade of the Hall pays overt tribute to Palladio's Palazzo Porto-Colleoni. The two storeys are enriched with superimposed Corinthian and Ionic Orders fully modelled about the three central bays. There is a rustic basement and an upper frieze of festoons and masks. The pilasters are doubled at the angles and the walls are rusticated behind the plain shafts of the Orders. Wren used this ordonnance as a model for S. Paul's. Originally the windows were of the 'croisée' leaded type set in alternating triangular and segmental pedimented frames, the upper tier having straight cornices. Designed for the performance of court masques, all but the end and the centre windows were originally dummies. The severely Classic treatment here employed for the first time in England was the natural result of Inigo Jones's study of the correct Palladian architecture of Italy, and constituted an architectural revolution following directly, as it did, on the free and picturesque Jacobean style. The fine interior occupies the entire height of the building, with a gallery at the level of the upper Order (p. 1005D). Converted into a Chapel Royal by George I, it was then variously misused until its restoration in 1973 to a modern semblance of its intended function.

The **Queen's House, Greenwich** (1616–35) (pp. 1007A, 1008) (now National Maritime Museum), by Inigo Jones for the Queen of James I, shows the influence of Palladian architecture. It has a lofty cubic two-storeyed entrance hall (p. 1006A), with a ring gallery leading across a former road by bridge to a central Ionic loggia set at first-floor level. The sills of the ground-floor windows have since been lowered and sashed. Extra bridges were added by Webb, and later colonnades date from 1811.

Greenwich Hospital had its commencement as a palace by the erection of 'King Charles's Block' designed 1663–7 by John Webb, the pupil of Inigo Jones. The façade (p. 1008F) has a lofty Corinthian Order showing a close study of Inigo Jones's work. The building was completed as a Hospital by Sir Christopher Wren, who included the Queen's House and King Charles's Block in one grand symmetrical scheme (pp. 1007B, 1008, 1022).

York Water-Gate, London (1626) (p. 1009A, B, C) seems to have been designed by Sir Balthazar Gerbier (c. 1591–1667) as an element in the scheme for York House, residence of the Duke of Buckingham. It was executed by the mastermason, Nicholas Stone, to form the river entrance, in days when the Thames was used as a highway for the pleasure barges of the nobility, but it now stands isolated in the Embankment gardens. This is a charming little piece of monumental architecture, with rusticated masonry and Tuscan Order surmounted by a pediment with armorial bearings flanked by 'lions couchants'.

S. Paul, Covent Garden, London (1631–5) (p. 1009G, H, J), was designed by Inigo Jones to be the 'handsomest barn in England', for he was told by the Earl of Bedford to erect a church as simple and inexpensive as a barn, and he here showed, in the Tuscan portico, wide-spreading eaves and simple pediment, how it was possible to produce dignity by the simplest means. Actually, the present building is merely a close copy, for the original was burnt in 1795 and rebuilt by Thomas Hardwick (1752–1829) in 1795–8. The church was part of a scheme for Covent Garden—which soon began to develop in a small way as a market—standing on the west side of the square, which for the rest was lined with uniform terraced houses, arcaded on the ground floor, the whole forming the earliest instance in London of

WHITEHALL PALACE : LONDON

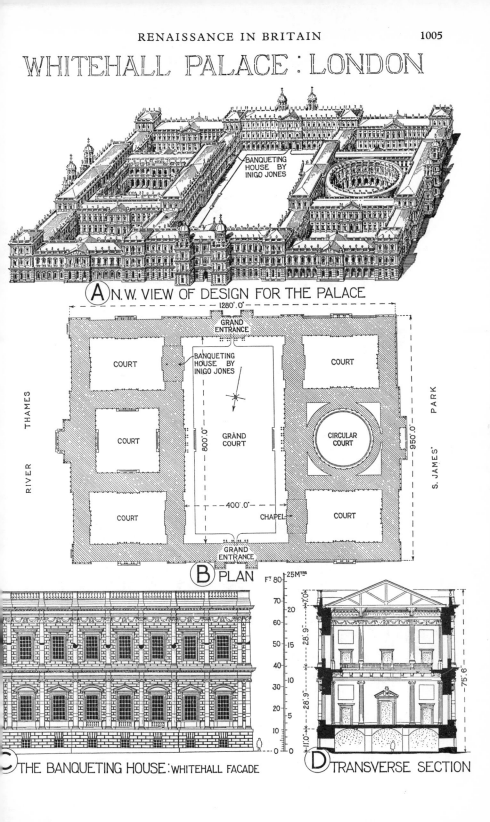

A N.W. VIEW OF DESIGN FOR THE PALACE

BANQUETING HOUSE BY INIGO JONES

—— 1280'.0" ——

GRAND ENTRANCE

BANQUETING HOUSE BY INIGO JONES

COURT

COURT

RIVER THAMES

COURT

GRAND COURT

CIRCULAR COURT

COURT

S. JAMES' PARK

950'.0"

800'.0"

COURT

— 400'.0" —

CHAPEL

COURT

GRAND ENTRANCE

B PLAN

C THE BANQUETING HOUSE : WHITEHALL FACADE

D TRANSVERSE SECTION

FT 80
70
60
50
40
30
20
10
0

25 MTRS
20
15
10
5
0

7'.0"
28'.9"
28'.9"
11'.0"
75'.6"

A. Queen's House, Greenwich: the Great Saloon (1616–35). See p. 1004

B. The Banqueting House, Whitehall, London: west façade (1619–22). See p. 1003

A. Queen's House, Greenwich (begun 1616): north façade. See p. 1004

B. Greenwich Hospital (1663–1814) from the river (N.), with the Queen's House in the background. See p. 1004

GREENWICH HOSPITAL

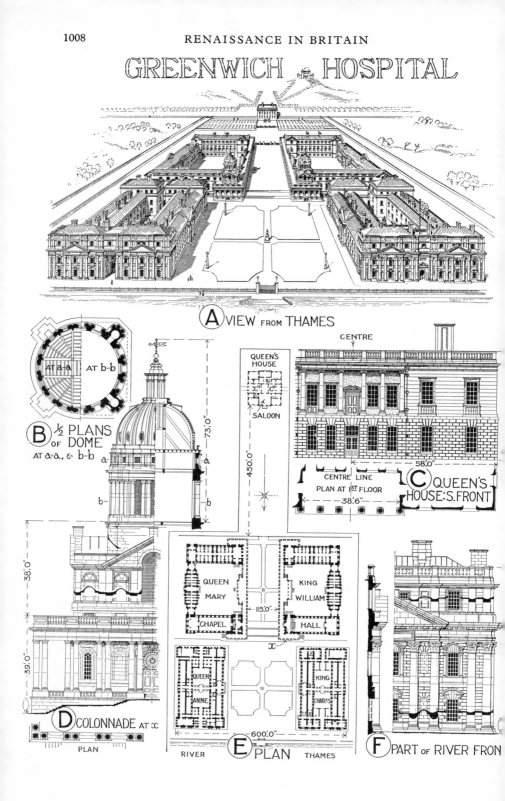

(A) VIEW FROM THAMES

(B) ½ PLANS OF DOME AT a-a, & b-b

AT a-a   AT b-b

73'·0"

450'·0"

QUEEN'S HOUSE

C'   C'

SALOON

CENTRE

58'·0"

CENTRE LINE
PLAN AT 1ST FLOOR
38'·6"

(C) QUEEN'S HOUSE: S. FRONT

38'·0"

39'·0"

(D) COLONNADE AT ∝

PLAN

QUEEN MARY   KING WILLIAM

115'·0"

CHAPEL   HALL

∝

QUEEN ANNE   KING CHARLES

600'·0"

RIVER   (E) PLAN   THAMES

(F) PART OF RIVER FRONT

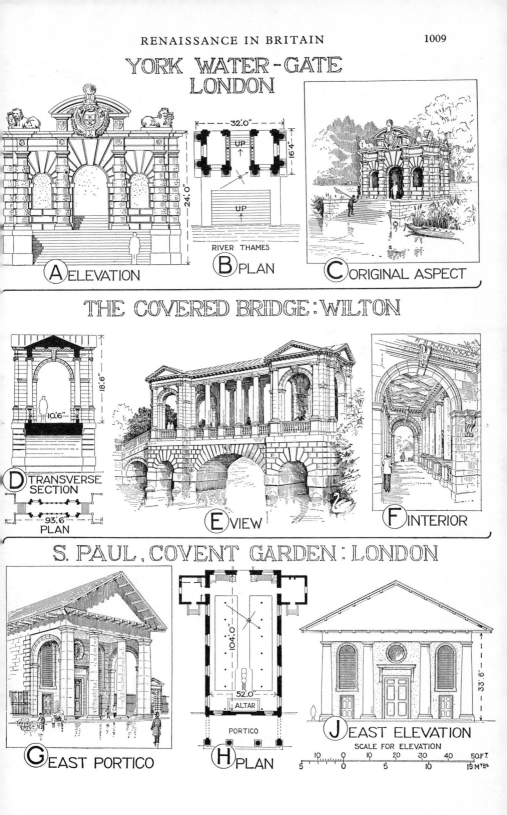

YORK WATER-GATE LONDON

A ELEVATION

B PLAN

RIVER THAMES

C ORIGINAL ASPECT

THE COVERED BRIDGE: WILTON

D TRANSVERSE SECTION

PLAN

E VIEW

F INTERIOR

S. PAUL, COVENT GARDEN: LONDON

G EAST PORTICO

H PLAN

ALTAR

PORTICO

J EAST ELEVATION

SCALE FOR ELEVATION

A STAIRCASE: ASHBURNHAM HOUSE: LOND.

B CHIMNEY PIECE: STOKE HALL: DERBYSHIRE

C DINING ROOM: BELTON HOUSE: GRANTHAM: LINCS.

A. Wilton House, Wilts: south façade (*c.* 1632–49). See p. 1013

B. Saloon   C. Entrance façade

Coleshill House, Berks (1650–62): destroyed by fire 1952. See p. 1013

D. Eltham House, Kent: the
staircase (1664). See p. 1013

E. Belton House, Lincs (1685–8).
See p. 1013

A. Honington Hall, Warwickshire (c. 1685). See p. 1013

B. Groombridge Place, Kent (late 17th cent.). See p. 1013

C. Raynham Hall, Norfolk (1635–8).
See p. 1013

D. Thorpe Hall, Northants (1653–6).
See p. 1013

this class of civic planning. The houses, too, have been replaced, in a character different from the original.

Stoke Bruerne Park, Northants (1629–35) (p. 1051N), by Inigo Jones, consisted of a central block containing the living-rooms connected by quadrant wings for library and chapel—a Palladian type of plan which influenced the larger Georgian houses (p. 1035). Of the inordinate number of further houses and other buildings ascribed to Inigo Jones there is possibility for **Chevening Place, Kent** (1630) (p. 1051H), much altered, and lately ably restored; certainty for part of **Wilton House, Wilts** (south façade, c. 1632–49) (p. 1011A), in the grounds of which is the later, very fine ornamental Palladian bridge (1736) (p. 1009D, E, F); and near certainty for **Raynham Hall, Norfolk** (1635–8) (pp. 1012C, 1033E), plainly built under his close influence. Less likelihood attaches to **Kirby Hall, Northants** (additions, 1638–40) (p. 988); **Lindsay House, Lincoln's Inn Fields** (1640); and Barber-Surgeons' Hall (1636) (destroyed). The Queen's (now Marlborough) Chapel in S. James's Palace, London (1623–7) (much altered later) is among his earliest designs.

Ashburnham House, Westminster (–1662) probably by John Webb (1611–72), pupil and assistant of Inigo Jones from 1628–52, is notable for its fine staircases (pp. 1010A, 1027J).

Coleshill House, Berks (1650–62) (pp. 1011B, C, 1035, 1051C), by Sir Roger Pratt in consultation with Inigo Jones, was a work of fine quality representative of the small output of this able designer. It was destroyed by fire in 1952.

Ashdown House, Berks (c. 1650) (p. 1015A), built for Lord Craven, is a tall cubiform house designed to face four ways, with the characteristic hipped roof, cupola and quoins common at the time.

Belton House, Grantham (1685–8) (pp. 1010C, 1011E, 1051B), by the mason William Stanton (1639–1705) for Sir John Brownlow, very strongly shows the influence of the domestic designs of Sir Roger Pratt. It is of the H-type plan (p. 1051B) double depth in the centre, with central steps up to the hall and rooms on the principal floor. There is a main staircase to the right of the hall, and in each wing service stairs from the kitchen in the basement. The exterior (p. 1011E) has a projecting pedimented centre, hipped roofs, dormers, belvedere and central turret. The dining-room (p. 1010C) has Late Renaissance decorative treatment with walls panelled from floor to ceiling, doors with large panels and pediments, and chimney-piece surmounted by elaborately carved birds, fruit and flowers probably by the famous woodcarver Grinling Gibbons (1648–1720), while the plaster ceiling has a fine geometrical design.

Groombridge Place, Kent (late seventeenth century) (pp. 1012B, 1051F), similar in many respects to Belton House, has an H-type plan and a central hall serving as a thoroughfare room, although the entrance is across one end, in the old tradition. Externally it has the same essentially English character. It is reached by a bridge across a moat (p. 1012B) and is of red brick with sash windows, divided by stout bars, with Ionic portico, hipped roofs, dormers and tower-like chimney stacks.

Honington Hall, Warwickshire (c. 1685; with later additions) (p. 1012A) is another example of a country house of the period, of brick with stone dressings, projecting wings and hipped, low-pitched roof.

Thorpe Hall, Northants (1653–6) (pp. 1012D, 1051M) is similar to Chevening Place in its deep rectangular plan and to both this and Coleshill House in its external character. But it is by no means equal to either in quality, and is indeed a coarser rendering of the type, suited to the average country house and soon in popular favour. It was designed by Peter Mills (c. 1600–70), a master-bricklayer of London who attained considerable repute as a surveyor and architect.

Eltham House, Kent (1664) (pp. 1011D, 1051E), by Hugh May (1622–84),

Paymaster (Surveyor) to the King's Works from 1660 to 1668, externally evidences the influence of a Palladianism which had recently developed in Holland, where he had resided. He also erected some buildings at Cornbury House, Oxfordshire (1663–8) and did some remodelling at Windsor Castle (1675–83), besides designing Berkeley House, Piccadilly (1665) and Cassiobury Park, Herts (c. 1677–80).

Chatsworth, Derbyshire (1681–96) (p. 1039A) was designed for the Duke of Devonshire by William Talman, who exercised the office of Comptroller under Wren. His firm handling of the south front shows his ability in the grand manner. The cascade and water temple in the grounds are by Thomas Archer.

SIR CHRISTOPHER WREN (1632–1723) (p. 980). Though an alumnus of the 'Experimental School of Philosophy', Wren relied like his contemporaries on antique authority and example for his aesthetic, and quoted freely from the precedents of Serlio and Vitruvius.

Pembroke College Chapel, Cambridge (1663–5), designed for his uncle, the Bishop of Ely, was Wren's first essay in architecture, and though a daring innovation, shows restraint in design, with its Corinthian pilasters, central window flanked by niches and hexagonal cupola (pp. 1015C, D, 1027A).

S. Paul's Cathedral, London (1675–1710) (frontispiece, pp. 1016–1019, 1020A, B), occupying the site of the Mediaeval cathedral destroyed in the Great Fire, is Wren's masterpiece. The first design, of which there is a model in the north triforium, was a Greek cross in plan, with projecting vestibule (p. 1016A, B), but the influence of the clergy, who desired a long nave and choir suitable for ritual, finally caused the selection of a Latin cross or Mediaeval type of plan (p. 1016D). The interior has a length of 141 m (463 ft) including apse, a breadth including aisles of 30.8 m (101 ft), and an area of about 6,000 m² (64,000 square ft). This plan, in which Wren wisely so spread the weight of the structure that in the crypt solids and voids are approximately equal, consists of a great central space at the crossing suitable for vast congregations, like Ely Cathedral, crowned by a dome painted by Sir James Thornhill; choir and nave in three bays, north and south transepts with semicircular porticoes, and projecting western portico of coupled columns. The western bay of the nave is, unlike the other bays, square on plan, and is flanked by chapels, which project externally. This bay (p. 1016D) has coupled columns supporting lateral arches, through the northern of which is visible the Chapel of S. Dunstan, with its fine columnar screen of carved woodwork. The Corinthian pilasters of the nave (pp. 1016C, 1019B) support an attic concealing the aisle roofs over the triforium, and the nave is crowned by ingeniously designed saucer-like domes, 27.7 m (91 ft) high, (p. 1017B), beneath which the clear-storey windows (not visible from the exterior) (pp. 1016C, 1017F, 1020A) have lunette vaults. The choir is enriched with fine stalls and organ case by Grinling Gibbons, and beautiful hammered iron gates by Tijou, while it terminates in the modern reredos, the vaulting being decorated by Sir William Richmond with coloured glass mosaics. The dome (pp. 1016C, D, 1019B, 1020A) and its support presented a complicated structural problem (p. 1018). The dome is carried on eight piers, and is 34 m (112 ft) in diameter at the base of the high drum, at the level of the Whispering Gallery, diminishing to 30.8 m (101 ft) at the top of the drum, and is of triple construction. The inner dome of brick, 457 mm (18 ins) thick, has its eye 65.3 m (214 ft 3 ins) above the floor, while the intermediate conical dome, of brick 457 mm (18 ins) thick, strengthened by a double chain of iron (pp. 1017E, 1018A), supports the stone lantern, ball and cross; besides which the outer dome also rests on this intermediate cone and is formed of timber covered with lead (pp. 1016C, 1017E). Eight openings are formed in the summit of the outer dome to admit light to the inner dome (p. 1017D, E).

A. Ashdown House, Berks (*c.* 1650).
See p. 1013

B. Winslow Hall, Bucks (1700). See p. 1032

c. Façade   D. Interior

Pembroke College Chapel, Cambridge (1663–5). See p. 1014

S. PAUL : LONDON

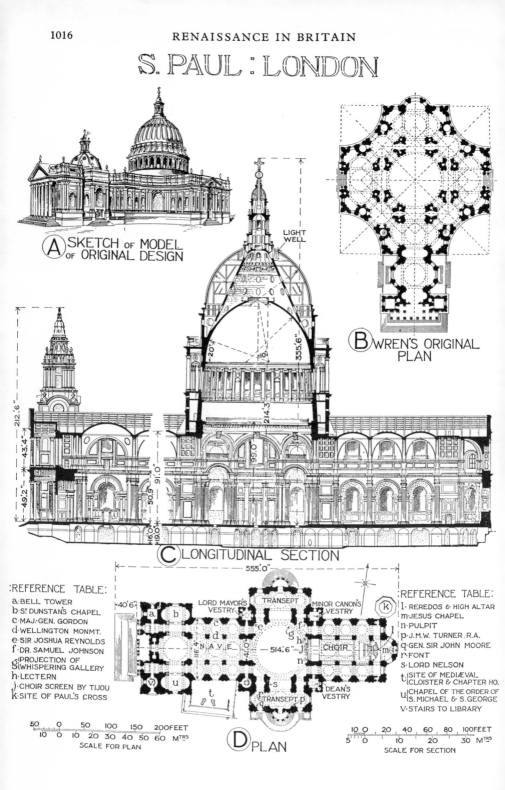

Ⓐ SKETCH of MODEL of ORIGINAL DESIGN

Ⓑ WREN'S ORIGINAL PLAN

LIGHT WELL

Ⓒ LONGITUDINAL SECTION

Ⓓ PLAN

:REFERENCE TABLE:
a· BELL TOWER
b· S! DUNSTAN'S CHAPEL
c· MAJ·GEN. GORDON
d· WELLINGTON MONMT.
e· SIR JOSHUA REYNOLDS
f· DR. SAMUEL JOHNSON
g· PROJECTION OF WHISPERING GALLERY
h· LECTERN
j· CHOIR SCREEN BY TIJOU
k· SITE OF PAUL'S CROSS

REFERENCE TABLE:
l· REREDOS & HIGH ALTAR
m· JESUS CHAPEL
n· PULPIT
p· J. M. W. TURNER. R.A.
q· GEN. SIR JOHN MOORE
r· FONT
s· LORD NELSON
t· SITE OF MEDIÆVAL CLOISTER & CHAPTER HO.
u· CHAPEL OF THE ORDER OF S. MICHAEL & S. GEORGE
v· STAIRS TO LIBRARY

LORD MAYOR'S VESTRY
TRANSEPT
MINOR CANON'S VESTRY
NAVE
CHOIR
DEAN'S VESTRY
TRANSEPT

50   0   50   100   150   200 FEET
10   0   10   20   30   40   50   60 M^TRS
SCALE FOR PLAN

10   0   20   40   60   80   100 FEET
5   0   10   20   30 M^TRS
SCALE FOR SECTION

S. PAUL · LONDON

366'0" TO PAVEMENT

A PERISTYLE

SAUCER DOME
GROIN LINE
PENDENTIVE
LUNETTE

B SKETCH OF NAVE BAY

67'0"
53'0"

C ¼ PLAN OF PERISTYLE

212'6"

43'4"

49'2"

D WEST ELEVATION

EIGHT WELLS TO LIGHT INTERIOR OF CONE

ESTIMATED WEIGHT OF LANTERN 850 TONS

1'6"

1'6"

WREN'S CHAIN

E SECTIONAL VIEW OF DOME

110'6"

43'4"

91'0"

47'0"

41'0"

59'2"

58'2"

16'0"

F SECTION THRO' NAVE. LOOKING W.

25 0 25 50 75 100 FT
10 0 10 20 30 MTRS

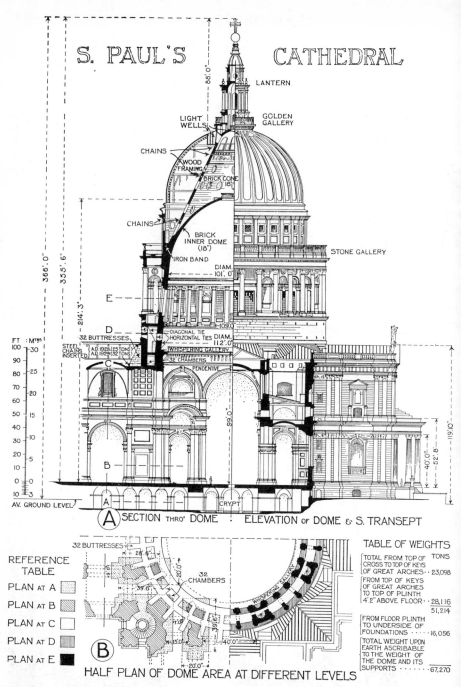

S. PAUL'S CATHEDRAL

SECTION THRO' DOME : ELEVATION OF DOME & S. TRANSEPT

LANTERN

LIGHT WELLS

GOLDEN GALLERY

CHAINS

WOOD FRAMING

BRICK CONE 18"

CHAINS

STONE GALLERY

BRICK INNER DOME (18")

IRON BAND

DIAM 101'.0"

E ———— 109.0

D ———— DIAGONAL TIE
HORIZONTAL TIES DIAM. 112.0'
32 BUTTRESSES

STEEL CHAINS INSERTED
A.D. 1928 (25 TONS)
A.D. 1929 (32 TONS)

WHISPERING GALLERY
32 CHAMBERS

C

PENDENTIVE

B

99.0'

A

CRYPT

AV. GROUND LEVEL

366'.0"
355'.6"
214'.3"
88'.0"

FT : M^{TRS}
100 — 30
90
80 — 25
70
60 — 20
50 — 15
40
30 — 10
20
10 — 5
0 — 0
10 — 3

119.10
52'.8
40'.0"

A

B HALF PLAN OF DOME AREA AT DIFFERENT LEVELS

32 BUTTRESSES

28'.6"

20'.0"

32 CHAMBERS

39'.6"

39'.6"

51'.0"

15'.0"

40'.0"

20'.0"

WHISPERING GALLERY

REFERENCE TABLE

PLAN AT A
PLAN AT B
PLAN AT C
PLAN AT D
PLAN AT E

TABLE OF WEIGHTS

TONS

TOTAL FROM TOP OF CROSS TO TOP OF KEYS OF GREAT ARCHES · · 23,098

FROM TOP OF KEYS OF GREAT ARCHES TO TOP OF PLINTH 4'2" ABOVE FLOOR · · 28,116
51,214

FROM FLOOR PLINTH TO UNDERSIDE OF FOUNDATIONS · · · · · 16,056

TOTAL WEIGHT UPON EARTH ASCRIBABLE TO THE WEIGHT OF THE DOME AND ITS SUPPORTS · · · · · · 67,270

The Table of Weights was calculated by J. E. Drower for the S. Paul's Commission. The thrusting weight of the inner and outer drums is extended over a larger area by thirty-two radiating buttresses, assisted at a lower level by four great bastions. When cracks in the masonry appeared, £400,000 was collected publicly between 1914 and 1930 and spent in strengthening the piers carrying the dome, the surrounding bastions, and in the insertion of chains in the triple dome.

A. S. Paul's Cathedral, London, from S.W. (1675–1710). See p. 1014

B. S. Paul's Cathedral, London: nave looking E.

A. The Crossing

B. S. aisle looking W.

S. Paul's Cathedral, London (1675–1710). See p. 1014

C. S. Mary-le-Bow, Cheapside, London (1670–3): steeple (1680). See p. 1021

D. S. Bride, Fleet Street, London (1671–8): steeple (1701–3). See p. 1021

The vaulted crypt, extending under the whole church, is the last resting place of many famous men, including Nelson, Wellington and Wren himself.

The exterior is exceedingly effective and groups well with the central dome. The façades have two Orders, the lower Corinthian and the upper Composite, totalling 33.6 m (110 ft 6 ins) in height (p. 1017F). The aisles are only one storey high, so the part above them is a screen-wall introduced to give dignity and to act as a counter-weight to the flying buttresses concealed behind it, which receive the thrust of the nave vault. The western façade, 54 m (177 ft) wide (frontispiece, p. 1017D), approached by a broad flight of steps which give scale to the building, has a central two-storeyed portico of coupled Corinthian and Composite columns superimposed, surmounted by a pediment sculptured with the Conversion of S. Paul. The portico is flanked by two beautifully proportioned campanile, 64.7 m (212 ft 6 ins) high above the nave floor, that on the north containing bells and that on the south the clock, while the fine semicircular porticoes to the transepts are also notable. The external dome (frontispiece) is probably the finest in Europe, for the projecting masses of masonry at the meeting of nave and transepts, forming the vestries and stairs to dome, express support from the ground upwards (pp. 1016D, 1019A). The peristyle round the drum, with an external diameter of about 42.5 m (139 ft 6 ins), is particularly effective with threequarter columns attached to radiating buttress-walls, every fourth intercolumniation being filled with masonry. Above the colonnade is the 'Stone Gallery', and attic supporting the dome, which is crowned with lantern, ball and cross, weighing 850 tons, rising to a height of 111.5 m (366 ft) above the pavement.

The **London City Churches** (p. 1023), 52 in number, supervised 1670–1711 by Wren in the Renaissance style to replace those destroyed by the Great Fire, are models of simplicity and restraint in treatment. Many have been destroyed or war-damaged but the towers and steeples still remaining help to make the City of London one of the most picturesque metropolitan settings in the western world. Many are most skilfully planned on cramped and awkward sites (p. 1023), and are among the first churches actually designed to meet the requirements of Protestant worship, in which a central preaching-space usurps the nave and aisles suitable for the processions of Roman Catholic ritual, while galleries were frequently added.

S. Stephen, Walbrook (1672–9, damaged in 1941) (p. 1024), is famous for original and ingenious planning which produces a wonderful effect within a limited area. Enclosed in a rectangle are sixteen columns, of which eight are arranged in a circle to carry a central cupola, with the judicious disposition of single-columns so as to produce a church with five aisles. The fine pulpit, organ (p. 1024E) and reredos (p. 1024F) are typical of Grinling Gibbons's influence.

S. Mary-le-Bow, Cheapside (1670–3, damaged in 1941) (pp. 1020C, 1023G, 1026), is specially notable not only for 'Bow Bells', but for its graceful Renaissance steeple (completed 1680), the masterpiece of that particular type which Wren may be said to have evolved. With the Gothic spire as his prototype, he surmounted a square tower with a pyramidal spire in receding stages of encircling columns, all unified by a clever use of inverted consoles.

S. Bride, Fleet Street (1671–8, gutted 1940) (pp. 1020D, 1025, 1026), has a similar but less successful steeple (1701–3), in which the absence of the inverted consoles give a telescopic effect to the series of columned stages.

S. Martin, Ludgate (1677–84) (p. 1023D), has an interior with four Corinthian columns to the central vault, but is best known for its beautiful little steeple, consisting of a square tower connected by side scrolls to the façade and surmounted by an octagonal stage with timber spire and weather vane, all grouping well with views of S. Paul's Cathedral.

S. Clement Danes, Strand (1680–2) (gutted 1941, partly restored 1958) with a graceful spire in diminishing stages added by Gibbs in 1719–20, and **S. James, Piccadilly** (1682–4) (p. 1025) (damaged 1941, restored 1952) are remarkable for their two-storeyed aisles in which galleries are supported by square piers surmounted by Corinthian columns and a barrel-vaulted roof, intersected by semi-cylindrical vaults at right angles over the gallery bays (p. 1025C).

S. Mary Abchurch (1681–6) (p. 1023A) (damaged, 1940) is a square church in a cramped position with the dome on pendentives as a principal feature, while the steeple is neither fine nor well placed; but the Grinling Gibbons altarpiece and the excellent organ case, pulpit and pews help to produce an attractive interior, which even appears spacious under its painted dome.

S. Mildred, Bread Street (1677–83) (destroyed, 1941) was a rectangle in three compartments with central dome on pendentives, and was quite a gem in the perfection of its parts and in the beauty of its carved woodwork.

S. Lawrence Jewry (1671–7) (p. 1023B); **S. Benetfink** (1670–3) (p. 1023C) (destroyed, 1842); **S. Mary-at-Hill** (1670–6) (p. 1023E), a vaulted and domed church formed into a cross by four columns; **S. Anne and S. Agnes** (1677–80, steeple c. 1714) (p. 1023F); **S. Swithin, Cannon Street** (1677–85) (p. 1023H) (gutted, 1941); **Christ Church, Newgate Street** (1677–87, steeple 1704) (p. 1023J) (gutted, 1940), and **S. Magnus-the-Martyr, London Bridge** (1671–6, steeple 1705) (p. 1023K), all show Wren's subtle adaptation of plan to site.

S. Alban, Wood Street (1682–5) (wrecked, 1940); **S. Dunstan-in-the-East** (1670–1, steeple 1697–9) (gutted, 1941); **S. Mary Aldermary** (1681–2, tower 1702–44) and **S. Michael, Cornhill** (1670–2, tower completed by Hawksmoor 1718–22), offer examples of his treatment of Gothic towers and spires.

Wren designed a number of collegiate buildings in Oxford and Cambridge which display his peculiar power of adapting the design to meet the exigencies both of site and purpose. At Oxford there is the **Sheldonian Theatre** (1664–9) (p. 694A) designed after the Theatre of Marcellus with the roof on the lines of a velarium, since altered, while the **Library, Queen's College** (1693–6) (p. 1028C), **Tom Tower, Christ Church** (1682) and the **Garden Quadrangle, Trinity College** (1668, north wing; 1682, west wing; 1728, south wing) exhibit Wren's mastery of design. The **Old Ashmolean Museum** (1679–83) (p. 694A) was designed by T. Wood under Wren's influence. The designer of **Trinity College Chapel, Oxford** (1691–4) (p. 1028B) is not definitely known. At Cambridge, in addition to **Pembroke College Chapel** (p. 1014), there are **Emmanuel College Chapel** (1668–73), and **Trinity College Library** (1676–84) (p. 1028A).

Among Wren's secular works are the **Monument, London** (1671–6), to commemorate the Great Fire of 1666; the Fountain Court and garden façades (1689–94) of **Hampton Court Palace** (pp. 686, 1029A) which have been described in connection with the Tudor portion of Henry VIII (p. 686); **Chelsea Hospital** (1682–91) (pp. 1029B, C) with a fine chapel (p. 1029C); Marlborough House, Pall Mall (1709–11); additions to Kensington Palace (1690–1704); and the Greenwich Observatory (1675–6). There is no evidence, however, that he designed **Temple Bar, London** (1672) (p. 1030C), (now at Theobald's Park, Herts), often ascribed to him, which was built by two master-masons, Thomas Knight and Joshua Marshall; and he was only indirectly concerned with the **Orangery, Kensington Gardens** (1704) (p. 1030A), probably designed by Vanbrugh (p. 982). Again, there is no documentary proof that Wren had directly anything to do with **Morden College, Blackheath** (1694) (pp. 1031A, 1051K).

Greenwich Hospital (1696–1715) (pp. 1004, 1007, 1008) is a splendid palace scheme devised by Wren to include the Queen's House and King Charles's Block,

WREN'S CITY CHURCHES

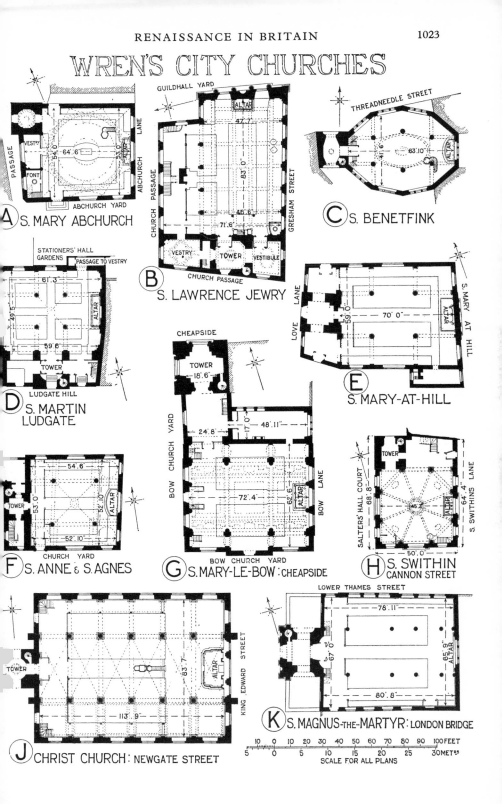

A S. MARY ABCHURCH

B S. LAWRENCE JEWRY

C S. BENETFINK

D S. MARTIN LUDGATE

E S. MARY-AT-HILL

F S. ANNE & S. AGNES

G S. MARY-LE-BOW : CHEAPSIDE

H S. SWITHIN CANNON STREET

J CHRIST CHURCH : NEWGATE STREET

K S. MAGNUS-THE-MARTYR : LONDON BRIDGE

SCALE FOR ALL PLANS

S. STEPHEN, WALBROOK : LONDON

Ⓐ INTERIOR LOOKING S. W.

Ⓑ SKETCH OF STEEPLE

Ⓒ SECTION a-a

Ⓓ PLAN

Ⓔ INTERIOR WEST DOOR & ORGAN

Ⓕ THE REREDO

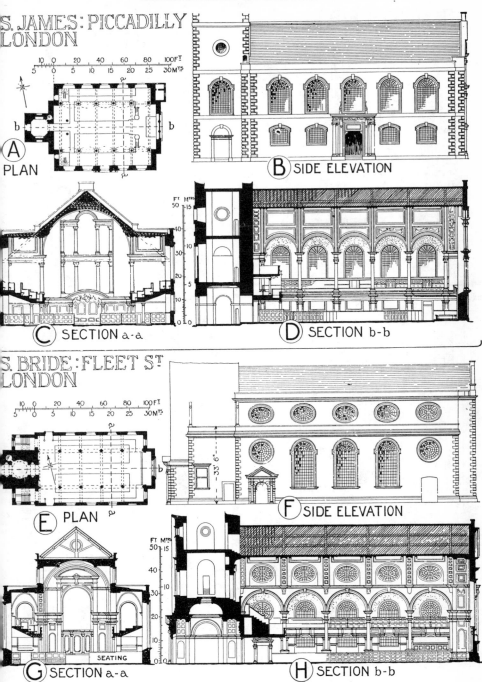

S. JAMES: PICCADILLY LONDON

(A) PLAN

10 0 20 40 60 80 100 FT
5 0 5 10 15 20 25 30 MTS

b b

(B) SIDE ELEVATION

(C) SECTION a-a

(D) SECTION b-b

FT MTRS
50 15
40
30 10
20 5
10
0 0

S. BRIDE: FLEET ST LONDON

(E) PLAN

10 0 20 40 60 80 100 FT
5 0 5 10 15 20 25 30 MTS

b

(F) SIDE ELEVATION

33' 6"

(G) SECTION a-a

SEATING

FT MTRS
50 15
40
30 10
20 5
10
0 0

(H) SECTION b-b

S. MARY·LE·BOW LONDON

PLAN AT a

WEIGHT & THRUST OF UPPER PORTION TAKEN BY INVERTED TRUSSES

PLAN AT b

CORBEL OR PEND^TVE

25'·9"

STAIRS

16'·3"

(A) SECTION

(B) ELEVATION

S. BRIDE LONDON

PLAN AT g

PLAN AT h

CORBELS OR PENDENTIVES

20'·10"

16'·0"

(C) ELEVATION

(D) SECTION

33'·10"

17'·9"

19'·0"

104'·6"

111'·7"

103'·8"

226'·11"

FT MTRS
100 — 30
90 —
— 25
80 —
70 — 20
60 —
50 — 15
40 —
30 — 10
20 —
— 5
10 —
0 — 0

½ PLAN AT c

½ PLAN AT d

½ PLAN AT e

½ PLAN AT j

½ PLAN AT k

½ PLAN AT l

20'·6"

(E) PLAN AT f

19'·1"

(F) PLAN AT m

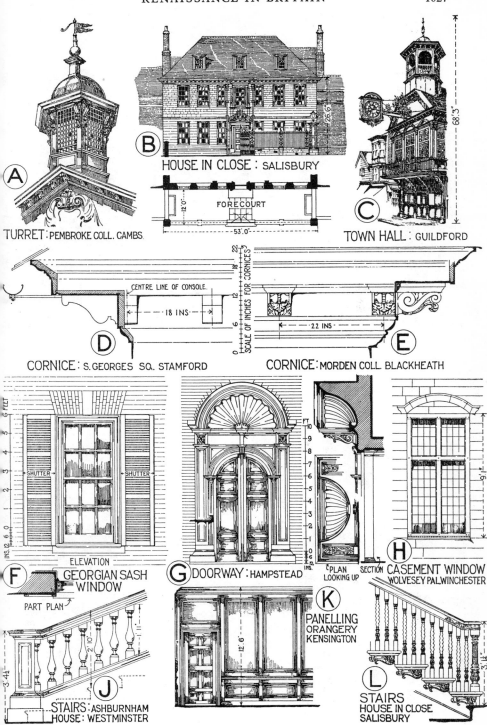

A TURRET: PEMBROKE COLL. CAMBS.

B HOUSE IN CLOSE: SALISBURY

FORECOURT

26.6

12.0

53.0

C TOWN HALL: GUILDFORD

68.3

D CORNICE: S. GEORGES SQ. STAMFORD

CENTRE LINE OF CONSOLE.

18 INS

E CORNICE: MORDEN COLL. BLACKHEATH

SCALE OF INCHES FOR CORNICES

22

18

12

6

0

22 INS

F GEORGIAN SASH WINDOW

ELEVATION

SHUTTER SHUTTER

PART PLAN

G DOORWAY: HAMPSTEAD

PLAN LOOKING UP   SECTION

H CASEMENT WINDOW WOLVESEY PAL WINCHESTER

9.1

J STAIRS: ASHBURNHAM HOUSE: WESTMINSTER

3.4½

2.10

K PANELLING ORANGERY KENSINGTON

12.6

L STAIRS HOUSE IN CLOSE SALISBURY

3.4

A. Trinity College, Cambridge: Nevile's Court (1593–1615), looking towards the Library (1676–84). See pp. 996, 1022

B. Trinity College Chapel, Oxford (1691–4). See p. 1022

C. Queen's College, Oxford: library (1693–6). See p. 1022

A. Hampton Court Palace: south façade (1689–94). See pp. 686, 1022

B. Portico   C. Chapel

Royal Hospital, Chelsea (1682–91). See p. 1022

A. The Orangery, Kensington Gardens, London (1704). See p. 1022

B. Custom House, King's Lynn (1683).
See p. 1032

C. Temple Bar, Strand, London:
looking E. (1672). See p. 1022

A MORDEN COLLEGE : BLACKHEATH : KENT

168'.6

B BUTTER MARKET
BARNARD CASTLE : DURHAM

C GARDEN HOUSE
POUNDISFORD PARK : SOM.

D BUTTER MARKET
BUNGAY : SUFFOLK

E TOWN HALL : MONMOUTH

F TOWN HALL : ABINGDON : BERKS

respectively by Inigo Jones and John Webb (p. 1004), with which he incorporated the great court and Queen Anne's Block, and the two intermediate blocks of King William and Queen Mary with the Hall, Chapel, two majestic domes, and fine colonnades.

Winchester Palace (1683–5), designed by Wren, was left unfinished at the death of Charles II, and burnt down in 1894.

Middle Temple, London; the cloisters in Pump Court (1680–1) (p. 996) (destroyed 1941) were from Wren's design.

Winslow Hall, Bucks (1700) (p. 1015B) is a rare instance of a domestic building by Wren. Particularly noteworthy are the grouped stacks regularly displayed above the hipped roof.

Abingdon Town Hall (1677–80) (p. 1031F), with its open market and assembly-room over, is a bold design with pilasters including two storeys, of a character strongly suggesting the influence of Wren.

The **Custom House, King's Lynn** (1683) (p. 1030B), by Henry Bell (1653–1717), is an example of effective grouping.

Guildford Town Hall (1682) (p. 1027C) is a bold, picturesque building of the period, partly vernacular in that it retains timber-frame structure, with carved brackets supporting the overhanging storey; above are large pedimented windows separated by pilasters, consoled cornice, hexagonal turret and projecting clock with wrought-iron stays.

LATE RENAISSANCE
(*Georgian Architecture*, 1702–1830)

GEORGIAN HOUSES

We have seen that the course of Renaissance architecture depended largely upon the leadership exercised by the Crown and its surveyors. So far as domestic architecture is concerned, the Low Countries still had continued mainly to be favoured in the Stuart period, influences proceeding therefrom through trade, political expatriates or pattern books. But about 1630 Dutch architecture itself changed to a straightforward Palladianism, expressed in brick with stone dressings, reflected in England after the Restoration in 1660. These fresh influences were in turn assimilated, and by the present period an English national character was being firmly established. There was a great expansion in domestic building. Mansions for the aristocracy grew more numerous, if progressively less grand in scale, but the really significant increase was in the houses of the middle and working classes. Already before 1800, villas were being erected on the fringes of towns, and even humble cottages mostly had achieved lasting form. In towns, terrace building in rows, a mark of the Industrial Revolution, became an increasingly common practice.

The Georgian house was generally planned as a simple symmetrical square or rectangular block with or without wings. The grander winged examples were the seats of the more well-to-do and the aristocracy. The centre third of the main block in both types was usually occupied by the entrance hall, which in the larger houses was carried up the full height of two storeys. The staircase, also designed for show, was either axially beyond or to one side of the hall and was seen through columned or arched screens. In the simple block type a single staircase sufficed, but in winged mansions two staircases became necessary on account of the high hall. Communication was then achieved at first-floor level by a gallery. Winged types often had light wells. The precedent for this type was Stoke Bruerne Park, Northants (p. 1013). In the simple block type the ancillary rooms were grouped

A SWAN HOUSE CHICHESTER

B STONE VASE WREST PARK: BEDS.

C SUNDIAL: WREST: BEDS 3' 9¾"

D DOORWAYS LAURENCE POUNTNEY HILL: LOND.

E DOORWAY RAYNHAM HALL: NORFOLK

A. The Moot House, Downton, Wilts
(1650; remodelled 1720). See p. 1035

B. Eagle House, Mitcham, Surrey
(c. 1700). See p. 1035

C. Mompesson House, Salisbury (1701). See p. 1035

round the hall and stair nucleus within the compact rectangular envelope. The kitchen, stores and offices were relegated to the basement. This type recalls Coleshill House, Berks (pp. 1013, 1051C) and Thorpe Hall, Northants (p. 1013).

(a) Examples of the simple block plan

Swan House, Chichester (1711) (p. 1033A) is built wholly in gauged and rubbed brickwork, the centre third thrust forward to frame narrow lights on either side of the pilastered and segmentally pedimented door case. Above the dentil and moulded brick cornice is a panelled parapet partly concealing the hipped and tiled roof. Exposed sash boxes and thick glazing bars enliven the front. As this is a town house it is set back from the pavement edge and has a wrought-iron balustrade on a low wall with gate piers and steps.

The **Moot House, Downton, Wiltshire** (1650, remodelled 1720) (p. 1034A) has a Flemish bond brick elevation with stone dressings, the centre projecting to form a tall, narrow, pedimented feature. It has a hipped roof with hipped dormers, and a moulded and modillioned eaves cornice and alternate quoins. The sash boxes are exposed to view, with thick glazing bars, and there is a pedimented door case.

Mompesson House, Salisbury (1701) (pp. 1027B, L, 1034C, 1051A) is similar to the Moot House, but is in stone without pediment or quoins. The proportions and spacings are generous, the sparing use of carved detail rich and satisfying.

Other examples are **Eagle House, Mitcham, Surrey** (c. 1700) (p. 1034B), **Penton House, Hampstead** (p. 1051D). **Bradford-on-Avon, Wilts; Burford, Oxon; Chichester; Farnham, Surrey; Painswick, Glos.** and **Trowbridge, Wilts** are all rich in examples.

(b) Examples of the central block with wings

Castle Howard, Yorkshire (1699–1712) (p. 1037) has the distinction of being Sir John Vanbrugh's first essay in architecture, at the age of 35. Hitherto he had been a soldier and playwright, and it was through his kinsman William, who held office at the Board of Works at Greenwich, that he owed his preferment. With a typical gesture, he had the village of Henderskelfe swept bodily away to provide the site. The building is coeval with Blenheim, and the two houses have points in common. Vanbrugh's amanuensis was Nicholas Hawksmoor. The north front, with its ordonnance of paired Doric pilasters spaced closely about superimposed niches for statuary, may owe something to d'Orbay's remodelling of Versailles, while the dome and lantern recall Le Vau's Collège des Quatre Nations, Paris, which Vanbrugh must have seen while serving abroad. The hall under the dome had its pendentives painted by Pellegrini (damaged by fire 1940). Its composite clusters of pilasters in the angles, and the pierced openings above the fireplaces yield dramatic glimpses of the staircases going up on either side. The west wing, built in 1753–9 by the Palladian Sir Thomas Robinson, is somewhat of an anticlimax. In the grounds Vanbrugh erected the four-porticoed 'Belvedere' temple, while Hawksmoor was responsible for the **Mausoleum** (1736), of whose close inter-columniations the Palladians were critical.

Blenheim Palace, Oxfordshire (1704–20) (pp. 1038, 1039B), by Sir John Vanbrugh, is the most monumental mansion in England. Vanbrugh's bold and forceful personality stamped itself on all his designs, which are characterized by his love of projecting porticos, twinned-column supports for trophies and the contrast of light and shade. He had a keen eye for a good site, and Blenheim, lined up on axis with Blaydon's village spire, was placed on a rise which necessitated a grand approach by bridge across the dammed waters of the river Glyme. The stable and kitchen wings soon became imposing courtyard groups punctuated by clock turrets.

Vanbrugh's compositions were symphonic, if diffuse, and the attendant outworks of gateways, pyramids and temples add yet another octave to his formal keyboard. The palace itself centres on a grand entrance hall, the ceiling painted by Thornhill, 21.3 m × 13.7 m (70 ft × 45 ft) and 20.5 m (67 ft) high, which leads directly to the saloon painted by Laguerre, the centre-piece of a suite of rooms on the south side. From the hall—its 'proscenium' arch echoes Vanbrugh's sometime Haymarket Theatre—corridors lead right and left and pass internal courts. The staircases (only one of which was built) on either side of the hall were designed to be seen through the openings of the superimposed arcades. As Blenheim was a monument for show, the bedrooms are insignificant. The main apartment was the gallery, 54.5 m × 6.7 m (180 ft × 22 ft), on the western side. The four corner pavilions are rusticated, in contrast to the central Corinthian ordonnance, and have attic storeys bearing trophies (some carved by Grinling Gibbons) symbolic of Marlborough's victory over the French. The formal hexagonal parterre raised on bastions at the corners, by London and Wise, was swept away when 'Capability' Brown remodelled the park.

Seaton Delaval, Northumberland (1720–8) (p. 1040A), by Sir John Vanbrugh, is more tightly articulated than the preceding examples, and more intensely dramatic. The service wings are closer together and extend forward from the main block to make an impressive approach. The rusticated entrance on the north front is framed by be-ringed Doric columns set in pairs on either side as supports for heraldic devices. The hall is arcaded in a dour Roman manner, and the chimney-pieces have 'terms' which focus the attention on the saloon door at the far end, over which the stair landing is returned so as to form a bridge. Seaton was gutted by fire in 1822.

Sutton Scarsdale, Derbyshire (1724) (p. 1040B) was designed by Francis Smith of Warwick, a prolific Midland builder of Georgian Baroque houses, and was his most magnificent work. The plan was of the simple block type, and the building was destroyed by fire, and ultimately by neglect, in 1924.

Mereworth Castle, Kent (c. 1722–5) (pp. 1041A, 1051G), by Colen Campbell, is based very closely on the Villa Capra, Vicenza (p. 865), by Palladio, whose precepts the English Palladian followed with slavish zeal. The elevations are the same on all four fronts, and the principal apartments are ranged around a great circular hall, 10.6 m (35 ft) in diameter, crowned by a dome which commands the whole composition. Chimney flues ascend the shell of the dome, and meagre circular windows afford the only natural light which the hall receives. The kitchen and offices are in the basement, which is only partially below ground. Two separate pavilions flank the main entrance front, the one containing bedrooms and the other stables.

Chiswick House, Chiswick (1725–) (p. 1041B), by Lord Burlington and William Kent, is a second and better version of the Villa Capra, Vicenza, having again the raised 'podium' sustaining the principal apartments, these ranged around a high, domed hall, the dome being octagonal and having arched windows in the drum. This type of plan is not well suited to the English climate, but was also followed in **Nuthall Temple, Notts,** a house designed by Thomas Wright in 1754 (demolished 1923). Chiswick House has only one grand portico and impressive flights of entrance steps.

Holkham Hall, Norfolk (1734–) (p. 1051J), was designed by William Kent in collaboration with Lord Burlington and the owner, Thomas Coke, Earl of Leicester, but executed by Matthew Brettingham (1699–1769), and is a representative mansion of Palladian character in the present class. Unlike Vanbrugh's principal houses, the plan (p. 1051J) shows no deliberate framing of the entrance court by the wings, which here number four instead of two and give symmetrical elevations on all four fronts. A grand feature of the central block is the hall, adorned by Ionic colonnades which turn in an apse to enclose an axial flight of steps rising to the 'piano nobile'

CASTLE HOWARD : YORKSHIRE

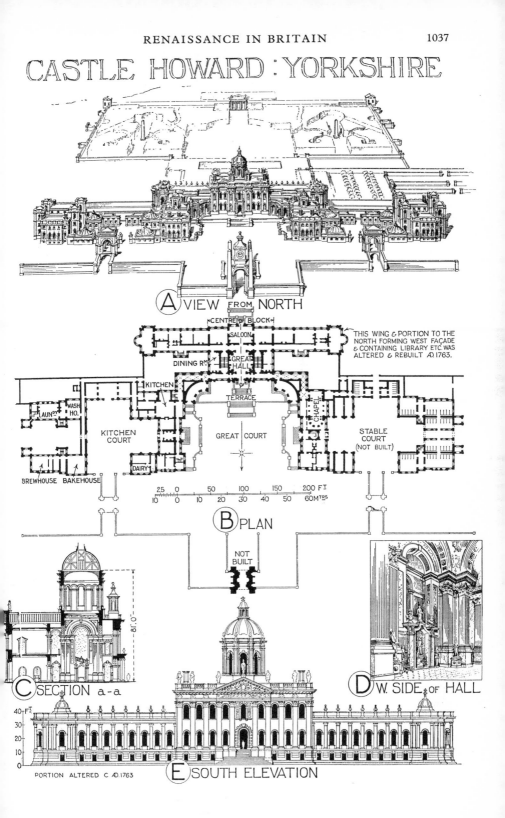

Ⓐ VIEW FROM NORTH

◄ CENTRE BLOCK ►

SALOON

THIS WING & PORTION TO THE
NORTH FORMING WEST FAÇADE
& CONTAINING LIBRARY ETC. WAS
ALTERED & REBUILT A.D. 1763.

DINING RM

GREAT
HALL

KITCHEN

TERRACE

CHAPEL

WASH
HO.

LAUNDY

KITCHEN
COURT

GREAT COURT

STABLE
COURT
(NOT BUILT)

BREWHOUSE BAKEHOUSE

DAIRY

25 0   50   100   150   200 FT
10 0   10   20   30   40   50   60 MTRS

Ⓑ PLAN

NOT
BUILT

18'.0"

Ⓒ SECTION a-a

Ⓓ W. SIDE OF HALL

40 FT
30
20
10
0

PORTION ALTERED C AD.1763

Ⓔ SOUTH ELEVATION

BLENHEIM PALACE : OXON

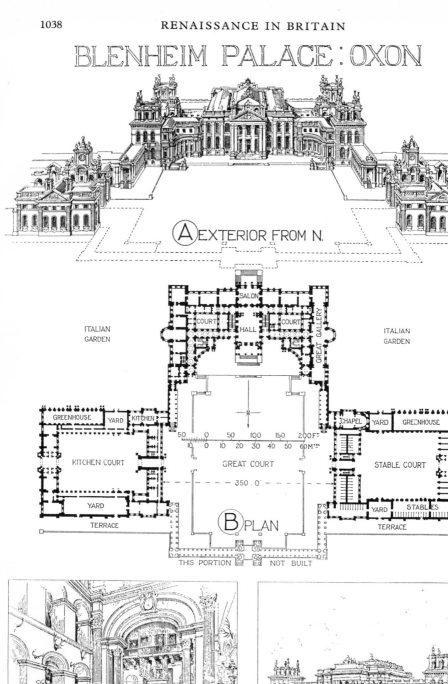

A EXTERIOR FROM N.

B PLAN

ITALIAN GARDEN

ITALIAN GARDEN

SALON

COURT

HALL

COURT

GREAT GALLERY

GREENHOUSE YARD KITCHEN

CHAPEL YARD GREENHOUSE

KITCHEN COURT

GREAT COURT

STABLE COURT

50 0 50 100 150 200 FT
10 0 10 20 30 40 50 60 M.

350.0

YARD

YARD STABLES

TERRACE

TERRACE

THIS PORTION NOT BUILT

C GREAT HALL

D EXTERIOR FROM S.E.

A. Chatsworth, Derbyshire (1681–96): south front. See p. 1014

B. Blenheim Palace, Oxon: north front (1704–20). See p. 1035

A. Seaton Delaval, Northumberland: north front (1720–8). See p. 1036

B. Sutton Scarsdale, Derbyshire (1724). See p. 1036

A. Mereworth Castle, Kent (*c.* 1722–5). See p. 1036

B. Chiswick House, Chiswick, Middlesex (1725–). See p. 1036

C. Houghton Hall, Norfolk (1722–6): the Grand Saloon. See p. 1043

KEDLESTON HALL : DERBYSHIRE

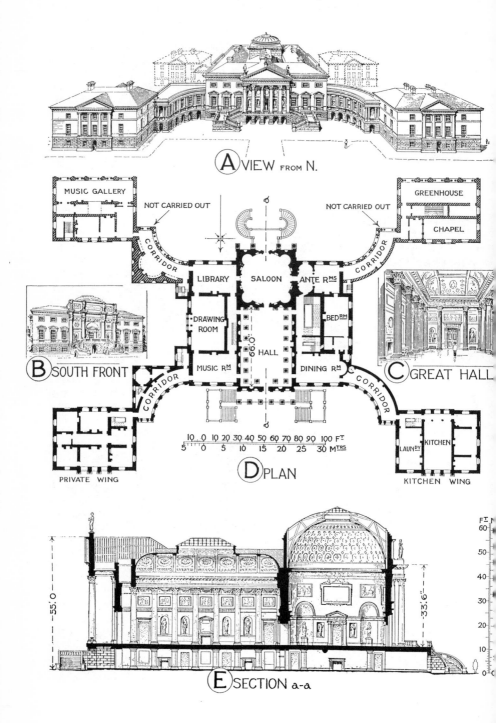

A VIEW FROM N.

MUSIC GALLERY   GREENHOUSE

NOT CARRIED OUT   NOT CARRIED OUT   CHAPEL

CORRIDOR   CORRIDOR

LIBRARY   SALOON   ANTE RMS

DRAWING ROOM   BED RM

66.0   HALL

B SOUTH FRONT   MUSIC RM   DINING RM   C GREAT HALL

CORRIDOR   CORRIDOR

10 0 10 20 30 40 50 60 70 80 90 100 FT
5 0 5 10 15 20 25 30 MTRS

D PLAN

PRIVATE WING   LAUNDY   KITCHEN   KITCHEN WING

55.0   33.6   FT
60
50
40
30
20
10
0

E SECTION a-a

or principal floor; the chief apartments include a stately gallery of three related rooms. Externally, on the south front there is the inevitable Palladian portico, while the angles of the main block are raised by attic storeys into pavilions, each of which has as a chief feature a 'Venetian' window (p. 1053C), of a type deriving from the so-called 'Palladian motif' (p. 863). The elevations in general are typically Palladian in that considerable play of form is contrived by simple means of advance and recession of the planes, which mostly comprise local symmetrical and focalized features though subordinated to the general composition: there is little recourse to identical rhythms in the fenestration as a means of binding the elements visually together. The similarity of the Holkham exterior to that of the Horse Guards, Whitehall (p. 1064A), also by Kent, is noteworthy.

Other Palladian mansions with wing blocks are **Ditchley, Oxon** (1720–5) by James Gibbs, who formerly had been an exponent of the Baroque; **Moor Park, Herts** (c. 1720), by Sir James Thornhill (1675–1734), of which the wings were rebuilt by Robert Adam in 1763 and demolished c. 1785; **Houghton Hall, Norfolk** (1722–6) (p. 1041C) by Colen Campbell; **Prior Park, Bath** (1735–48), designed by John Wood the elder, in the grounds of which there is a delightful version of the Palladian bridge (perhaps by 'Capability' Brown, c. 1765) originated by Roger Morris at Wilton House, Wilts (p. 1013); **Wentworth Woodhouse, Yorkshire,** as remodelled from the dull and tasteless designs of Henry Flitcroft, c. 1735; **Buckland House, Berks** (1755–7) (p. 1051L), by John Wood the younger, with its central block on the model of his father's Prior Park, Bath, with corridors right and left leading to the octagonal chapel and library; **Wrotham Park, South Mimms, Middlesex** (c. 1754) by Isaac Ware, and **Spencer House, London** (1756–65) by John Vardy, both less strictly modelled on the Palladian precept; **Woburn Abbey, Beds** (c. 1747), by Henry Flitcroft; and **Harewood House, Yorkshire** (1759–71) by John Carr of York, which in some sense is transitional to the next phase, since substantial amendments by Robert Adam were incorporated in the design, and Adam was responsible for the interior. John Carr designed and built the adjacent Harewood village.

Kedleston Hall, Derbyshire (p. 1042) was designed by James Paine and its erection supervised by Matthew Brettingham between 1757–61, but then Robert and James Adam succeeded them and completed the work, including the south front, the saloon, and the interior decoration as a whole (c. 1765–70). It is thus, like Harewood House, Yorkshire, partly Palladian, yet in many respects the whole building exhibits the Antiquarian tendency. The plan (p. 1042D) consists of a central block, 41.1 m × 32 m (135 ft × 105 ft), having on its principal floor the great hall, 20 m × 12.8 m (66 ft × 42 ft), and saloon on the central axis, with drawing-room and other apartments on either side. Quadrant corridors connect the main building with the kitchen and private wings, but the southern wings, which would have completed a general likeness to the plan of Holkham Hall, Norfolk, were not carried out. The hall·(p. 1042C, E) is a most imposing apartment, being the whole height of the mansion and having the appearance of an ancient basilica, with colonnades of alabaster Corinthian columns, 7.6 m (25 ft) high, surmounted by a coved ceiling in the Adam style, while the walls have statue niches. The drawing-room is a fine example of Adam's style. The general lay-out (p. 1042A) shows the usual basement storey, the external steps to the principal floor, with its fine Corinthian portico, and on either side the wings which, being lower, give scale and importance to the central block. The south front (p. 1042B), by Adam, has curved steps to the garden.

Further examples of the mansion with linked wings in the second half of the eighteenth century, during which time the type was becoming rare, are **Mersham-le-Hatch, Kent** (1762–5), by Robert Adam, for once wholly from his designs, for so many of his country domestic works were remodellings; **Wardour Castle, Wiltshire** (1770–6), by James Paine; **Heaton Hall, Lancashire** (1772), and **Castlecoole, Co. Fermanagh, Ireland** (1790–7), both designed by James Wyatt, a rival of Adam; and **Stowe House, Buckingham,** where the south front (1771–9) was a remodelling from the designs of Robert Adam, carried out by J. B. Borra and others. The grounds of Stowe, where the famous 'Capability' Brown first developed his art as a landscape gardener, are exceedingly rich in garden temples and other ornamental buildings, variously by Sir John Vanbrugh, James Gibbs, William Kent and Giacomo Leoni, who each contributed a number. Ornamental garden buildings, including bridges, arches, grottoes and the like, were normal embellishments of the grounds of eighteenth-century mansions (pp. 1009D–F, 1037A, 1048C, 1054D, G). The **Garden House, Poundisford Park** (c. 1675) (p. 1031C) near Taunton, Somerset, is an earlier homely and pleasing example.

Syon House, Isleworth, Middlesex, a square-planned Jacobean house which was remodelled 1762–9 by Robert Adam, affords some of the finest instances of his methods of interior decoration, while **Osterley Park, Middlesex,** a similar remodelling (1761–80) by the brothers Adam, and **Luton Hoo, Beds** (1768–75), wholly built by Robert but reconstructed in later times, are yet other examples of Adam domestic works. Later houses of the same class include **Althorp, Northants** (p. 1046C), reconstructed internally and cased externally (1787–9) in white 'mathematical tiles' (these are brick-tiles nailed to timber, brick, stone or flint walls through a flange which is hidden when the tiles are mortared into position, giving a very convincing cheap imitation of brickwork), by Henry Holland; **Heveningham Hall, Suffolk** (1778–99), begun by Sir Robert Taylor and completed after his death by James Wyatt, which shows Wyatt's interior decoration at its best (p. 1045B) and as being very similar to that of Adam; **Dodington Park, Glos** (1798–1808), by James Wyatt, designed in a style tinctured with the Greek, then coming into popular favour; the **Casino at Marino,** near Dublin (p. 1053E) designed by Sir William Chambers in 1759 and built in 1769, a dwelling in miniature, neatly contained in a Greek-cross plan: the design was originally intended for an end pavilion at Harewood House, Yorkshire, and is a fine early example of the Antiquarian phase; and **Stratton Park, Hants,** comprehensively remodelled in 1803–6 by George Dance II, wholly in Greek Revival mode.

It is ironic that the first foothold of 'Gothick' was in the domestic field. Fashioned by literary taste and Batty Langley's pattern books (p. 983), early examples such as **Waynflete's Tower, Esher, Surrey** (1730), by William Kent; a temple at **Stowe, Bucks** (1740) by James Gibbs; **Adlestrop, Glos** (1750) by Sanderson Miller (the creator of 'true rust' for sham ruins); **Alscot Park, Warwickshire** (1751), and the Hall of **Lacock Abbey, Wilts** (1753–5), also by Miller, show an irreverence for scholarship. Horace Walpole's **Strawberry Hill, Middlesex** (1747–63) (p. 1046A) pioneered an irregular plan and displayed an abandoned travesty of mediaeval technique that shocked and delighted its critics. Before 1760 the 'Gothick' style exhibited all the qualities associated with Rococo—light, gay and playful. Only a few churches were infected, such as **Shobden, Herefordshire** (1753) and **Tetbury, Glos** (1777) (p. 1059B), by F. Hiorne. Examples towards the end of the century tended to stress the qualities of gentility and refinement, such as **Donnington Grove, Newbury, Berks** (1760–85), by J. Chute, and **Arbury, Warwicks** (1776) (p. 1048B), by Henry Keene, which amused a society bored by Palladianism. Later followed **Lee Priory, Kent** (1785–90); **Fonthill Abbey, Wilts** (1796–) (p. 1047A) with a tower 84.5 m (278 ft) high (collapsed 1807), and **Ashbridge Park, Herts** (1803–13) (p. 1046B), all designed by James Wyatt in a melodramatic idiom calculated to awe the spectator. **Downton, Shropshire**

A. Home House, 20 Portman Sq., London (1775–7): music room. See p. 1055

B. Heveningham Hall, Suffolk (1778–99): saloon. See p. 1044

A. Strawberry Hill, Twickenham (1747–63). See p. 1044

C. Althorp, Northants: house cased
in white brick-tile (1787–9). See p. 1044

B. Ashridge Park, Herts (1803–13):
hall and staircase. See p. 1044

D. Cronkhill, Salop (1802).
See p. 1050

A. Fonthill Abbey, Wiltshire (1796–). See p. 1044

B. Culzean Castle, Ayrshire (1777–90). See p. 1050

A. Bath, Somerset: aerial view showing Circus and Royal Crescent (1754–75).
See pp. 984, 1050

B. Arbury, Warwickshire: drawing room (1776).
See p. 1044

C. Wadsworth, Yorks: gateway by
James Paine (1749). See p. 1044

A(*left*). Soane Museum, London (1812–13). See p. 1055

B(*right*). Cumberland Terrace, Regent's Park, London (*c.* 1827) See p. 1055

C. Ely House, London (1772). See p. 1055

D. Royal Pavilion, Brighton (1815–21): centre of E. front. See p. 1050

(1774–8), by R. P. Knight, was deliberately 'picturesque'; **Culzean Castle, Ayrshire** (1777–90) (p. 1047B), by Robert Adam, was symmetrical, as was **Eastnor Castle, Herefordshire** (1814), by Robert Smirke. A remarkably spiky version with cast-iron tracery was **Eaton Hall, Cheshire** (1804–12, remodelled 1870) by William Porden. The nouveaux riches and the eccentrics of the Regency commissioned buildings like **Ravensworth, Northumberland** (1808), by Nash and **Belvoir, Leicestershire** (1801) by Wyatt. **Luscombe, Devon** (1800–4) by Nash was typically classic within and battlemented without, set in grounds landscaped by Humphrey Repton. The eclecticism of the Regency period indulged in extravaganzas, such as **Sezincote, Glos** (1803–15), for which S. P. Cockerell employed the 'Indian style', and the **Royal Pavilion, Brighton** (1815–21) (p. 1049D), in which Nash did not scruple to mix Indian and Chinese motifs in an orgy of refinement and bad taste. Nash brilliantly developed picturesque cottage architecture, using barge boards, thatch and quaint chimneys, while at **Cronkhill, Salop** (1802) (p. 1046D) he produced an Italianate villa. It was not until the reforming zeal of A. W. N. Pugin (p. 1128) that this engaging if bizarre period in English architecture yielded to the forces which created Victorian society.

GEORGIAN TOWN HOUSES

The constant making-up of the street raised the level of the town house frontage above its garden at the back. A short flight of steps up to the entrance thus made it possible for offices to be accommodated in the basement (coal cellars reached out under the pavement). Areas for light and air were required, so that the house stood back some 3 m (10 ft) from the traffic. The consequent need for protective wrought-iron railings thus gave a special character to the domestic street. Terrace houses were frequently speculatively built. In 1774 their size was graduated on a scale of affluence in six 'rates' in descending order of magnitude. Plans were on narrow frontages and went deep; generally there was only width enough for a vestibule hall alongside a parlour or dining room. Beyond, the staircase climbed at the back to the principal floor occupied by a balconied drawing room across the entire front. Above were the bedrooms, and over them the attics. A formative consideration was the gathering of chimney flues into the party walls. Ingenuity in planning was expended more on formal alignments and tricks of concealing irregularity than on the provision of sanitary offices. Only the very grand had stabling and mews.

It has been noted that speculation was a factor in developing the terrace house. A seventeenth-century initiator of several such schemes in London was N. Barbon, while Inigo Jones introduced the house-lined square, as at **Covent Garden,** where he built 'row' houses over ground-floor arcades, reminiscent of the Place Royale (now Place des Vosges), Paris, and at **Lincoln's Inn Fields.** After the Restoration the speculators were generally aristocratic landlords, **S. James's Square** being an early enterprise. **Schomberg House, Pall Mall** (c. 1700), was part of this scheme, but the most interesting relic of very early eighteenth-century terrace architecture is **Queen Anne's Gate.** This type of domestic building evolved remarkably during the succeeding hundred years, culminating at the very end of our period in Thomas Cubitt's majestic townscape in Belgravia.

At Bath, John Wood senior contrived to impart a palatial unity by the application of a giant Order with a pedimented centre-piece to seven large houses built as a terrace on the north side of **Queen's Square** (1728). His ideas were extended to the creation of domestic squares, crescents and circuses; also at **Bath** his **Circus** (1754) and the **Royal Crescent** (1767–75) (p. 1048A) by his son were copied at **Buxton, Derbyshire,** by John Carr, and later by Robert Adam in Edinburgh.

LATE RENAISSANCE PLANS
(STUART & GEORGIAN)

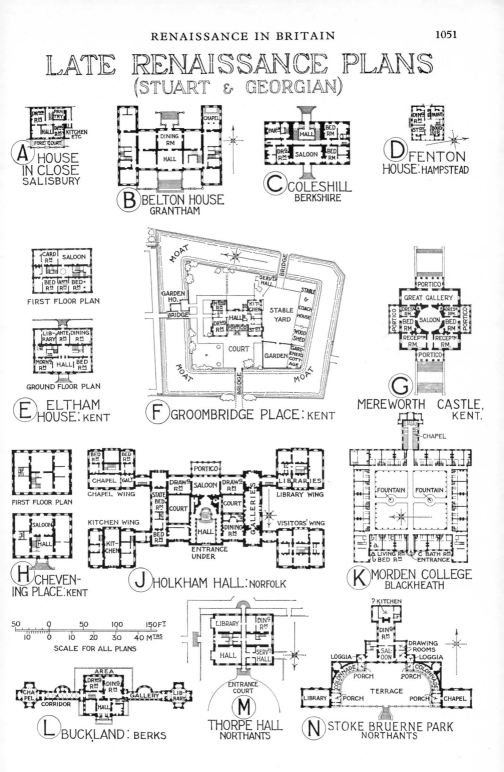

A HOUSE IN CLOSE SALISBURY

B BELTON HOUSE GRANTHAM

C COLESHILL BERKSHIRE

D FENTON HOUSE: HAMPSTEAD

E ELTHAM HOUSE: KENT

F GROOMBRIDGE PLACE: KENT

G MEREWORTH CASTLE, KENT.

H CHEVENING PLACE: KENT

J HOLKHAM HALL: NORFOLK

K MORDEN COLLEGE BLACKHEATH

SCALE FOR ALL PLANS
50 0 50 100 150 FT
10 0 10 20 30 40 MTRS

L BUCKLAND: BERKS

M THORPE HALL NORTHANTS

N STOKE BRUERNE PARK NORTHANTS

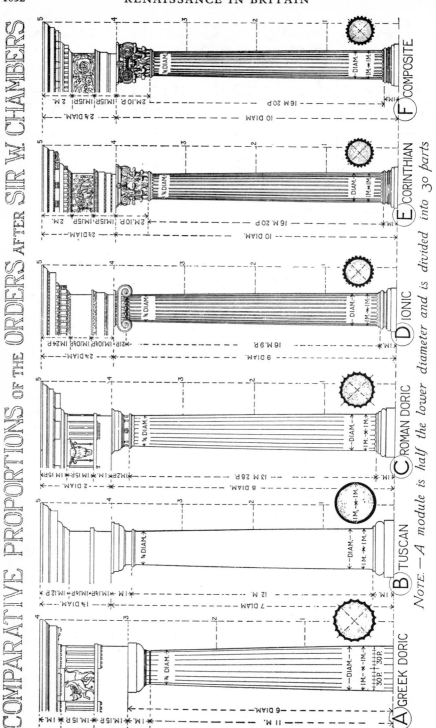

COMPARATIVE PROPORTIONS of the ORDERS after SIR W. CHAMBERS

A GREEK DORIC B TUSCAN C ROMAN DORIC D IONIC E CORINTHIAN F COMPOSITE

NOTE.—A module is half the lower diameter and is divided into 30 parts

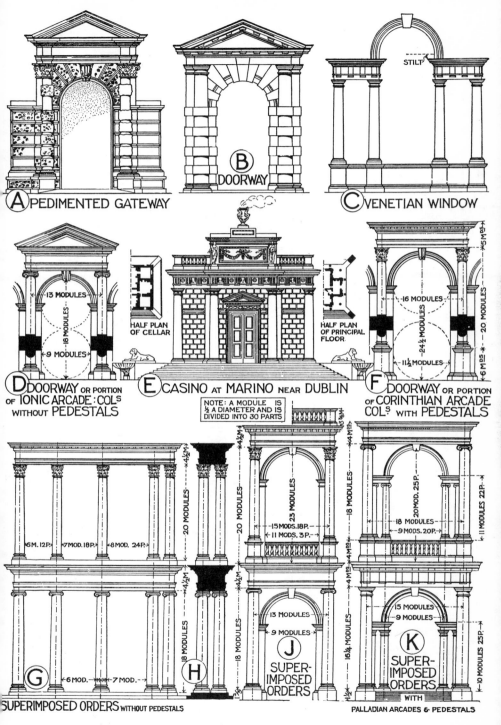

(A) PEDIMENTED GATEWAY

(B) DOORWAY

(C) VENETIAN WINDOW

STILT

(D) DOORWAY OR PORTION OF IONIC ARCADE : COLS WITHOUT PEDESTALS

13 MODULES
18 MODULES
9 MODULES

HALF PLAN OF CELLAR

(E) CASINO AT MARINO NEAR DUBLIN

HALF PLAN OF PRINCIPAL FLOOR

NOTE: A MODULE IS ½ A DIAMETER AND IS DIVIDED INTO 30 PARTS

(F) DOORWAY OR PORTION OF CORINTHIAN ARCADE COLS WITH PEDESTALS

16 MODULES
24½ MODULES
11½ MODULES
20 MODULES
6 MDS
5 MDS

(G) SUPERIMPOSED ORDERS WITHOUT PEDESTALS

6M. 12P.
7MOD. 18P.
8 MOD. 24P.
6 MOD.
7 MOD.
18 MODULES

(H)
20 MODULES
4½ M
4½ M
18 MODULES

(J) SUPER-IMPOSED ORDERS

4½M
20 MODULES
15 MODS.18P.
11 MODS. 3P.
23 MODULES
13 MODULES
9 MODULES
4½M
18 MODULES
16½ MODULES
4 M PS

(K) SUPER-IMPOSED ORDERS WITH

20MOD. 25P.
18 MODULES
9 MODS. 20P.
15 MODULES
9 MODULES
11 MODULES 22 P.
10 MODULES 25P.
5 MDS
4 M PS
4 M PS
4 M PS

PALLADIAN ARCADES & PEDESTALS

A DOORWAY: TYPE WITH RUSTICATED ARCHITRAVE

4'.6"

B TYPICAL HORSE GUARDS WINDOW BY KENT LONDON

C DOORWAY: WITH RUSTICATED ¾ IONIC COLS

D ARCH WILTON 9'.1" KEY PLAN 25'.0"

APERNATUS MARCUS AURELIUS PONT MAX MAXIMUS VXI PXI ARC XXX

INSCRIPTION

E TYPICAL CIRCULAR WINDOW: S.MARTIN: LONDON

F MONUMENT TO SIR JOHN BRIDGMAN ASTON: WARWICKSHIRE

G GATE PIERS 18'.11" 10'.0"

FRAME FOR PICTURE

H CHIMNEY PIECE BY GIBBS

J MONMT TO DUKE OF NEWCASTLE WESTMINSTER ABBEY 30'.0" ABOVE GROUND

FRAME FOR PICTURE

K CHIMNEY PIECE BY GIBBS

No. 44 Berkeley Square, London (1742–4), by William Kent, is distinguished for its remarkable staircase. **Chesterfield House, South Audley Street, London** (1766, demolished 1937) by Isaac Ware, and **Ely House, Dover Street, London** (1772) (p. 1049C) by Sir Robert Taylor, with its elegant, dignified front, are notable examples of their type. But the markedly Palladian **Mansion House, London** (1739–52), by the elder George Dance, is exceptional in that it was built as the official mayoral residence, and thus has the qualities of a public building.

The Antiquarian phase is represented by many fine houses, including a number in London by Robert Adam: **Lansdowne House, Berkeley Square** (1762–8, now demolished), **No. 20, S. James's Square** (1772–4), **Apsley House, Piccadilly** (c. 1775, much altered) and **Home House, No. 20, Portman Square** (1775–7; now the Courtauld Institute) with its splendid interior decoration (p. 1045A). Adam also carried out a considerable venture at the **Adelphi, London** (1768–72), a speculative undertaking which failed and of which very little now is left, and a scheme for **Charlotte Square, Edinburgh** (1791, built 1792–1807). Henry Holland developed **Hans Town, Chelsea** (1771–), covering a number of streets, but of which only a house or two remain, and built individual houses such as **Carlton House, Pall Mall, London** (1783–5, demolished 1827) and **Dover House, Whitehall** (1787). **No. 13 Lincoln's Inn Fields** (1812–13) (p. 1049A), by Sir John Soane, is now the Soane Museum, housing a collection of drawings, antiquities and works of art which he left to the nation. The most extensive work of the whole career of the prolific John Nash was his grand scheme of civic design for frontages extending through Regent St., London, to Regent's Park. The **Quadrant, Regent Street** (1818–20) was rebuilt between 1906–23, but much remains of the terraces (1821–30) facing the Park, one of the best being **Cumberland Terrace** (c. 1827) (p. 1049B).

GEORGIAN CHURCHES

A number of churches of this period were designed by followers of Wren, whose influence was paramount, with central space and surrounding galleries, suitable for the preaching requirements of the Protestant faith. The first to be noted are several having a character as nearly approaching the Baroque as was ever achieved in ecclesiastical architecture in Renaissance England.

S. Mary Woolnoth, London (1716–26) (p. 1057A), by Nicholas Hawksmoor, who had been assistant both to Wren and Vanbrugh, is remarkable for its rusticated façade and curious oblong tower with Composite columns surmounted by two low turrets, forming a very original treatment. It was one of six built by him under the Act of 1711 for the erection of fifty new churches (only a dozen materialized), others of his being **S. Alphege, Greenwich** (1712–14, later steeple); **S. Anne, Limehouse** (1712–14, restored 1851) (p. 1057D); **S. George-in-the-East** (1715–23, gutted 1941); **S. George, Bloomsbury** (1720–30) (p. 1057B), with a pyramidal spire; and **Christ Church, Spitalfields** (1723–9) (p. 1057C), with a lofty and unusual steeple. **S. Philip, Birmingham** (1709–25) (p. 1058A), now the Cathedral, shows the strong Baroque leanings of its gifted designer, Thomas Archer. The much-weathered western tower, with its concave sides, is unique in the country. A chancel was added in 1883–4. Similar though less pungent qualities are observable in two of the 'fifty churches' by Archer; **S. Paul, Deptford** (1712–30), a compact, centralized structure with a western spire and a columned semicircular porch embracing its base, and **S. John, Westminster** (1714–28, gutted 1742 and again in 1941), a less attractive composition. The influence of Archer was traceable in **S. Paul, Sheffield** (1720–1, demolished 1937), by John Platt I, an attractive composition with a western tower completed by a nephew, John Platt II, in 1769.

S. Mary-le-Strand, London (1714–17) (p. 1058B), by James Gibbs, one of the 'fifty churches', shows evidence of his studies in Rome, where he had been a pupil of Carlo Fontana (pp. 846, 982), but although it is florid it is not of thorough-paced Baroque character. Situated conspicuously on an island site in the Strand, it is notable for its fine proportions, with façades of superimposed Ionic and Corinthian Orders, a semicircular portico and storeyed western steeple, oblong on plan.

S. George, Hanover Square, London (1712–25) (p. 1058C), by John James, another of the 'fifty churches', is progressive in many ways while being massive and indecisively Baroque in external character. Its ponderous Corinthian portico, 21.3 m (70 ft) long, serves as a shelter in connection with the numerous weddings solemnized within. Here for the first time is found a steeple rising from the roof, without apparent support from the ground. **S. Martin-in-the-Fields, London** (1722–6) (p. 1058D), by James Gibbs, shows the developing mature manner of the architect after he had tempered his Baroque inclinations and adopted a more orthodox style, based on the characteristic work of Wren yet paying deference to current English-Palladian trends. Here, all the rich architectural features are a logical expression of the plan. A straightforward rectangular building, roofed from end to end, it has a great Corinthian portico approached by a broad flight of steps and a western steeple of singular beauty. Gibbs also designed (1719–20) the upper part of the steeple of Wren's **S. Clement Danes** (p. 1022).

S. Giles-in-the-Fields, London (1731–4), is by Henry Flitcroft, protégé of Lord Burlington, the architect being both designer and contractor for the building. It is an impoverished version of S. Martin-in-the-Fields, except that its steeple is at the side and not on the axis at the west.

A few privately built churches of the latter half of the century exist, such as at **Brandsby Hall, Yorkshire,** where the church interior (1768) (p. 1059A) by T. Atkinson shows how a basic box form can be modified by columnar screens to yield interesting results.

Other churches about this time were **All Hallows-on-the-Wall, London** (1765–7) by George Dance II, showing internally 'Neo-Classical' purity by the elimination of the cornice member of the entablature between the column and the springing of the vault; **All Saints, Newcastle-upon-Tyne** (–1796), by David Stephenson (b. 1757) and **S. Chad, Shrewsbury** (1790–2) (p. 1059C), by George Stewart (d. 1806), the latter two with circular naves and storeyed western towers.

Tetbury Church, Gloucestershire (rebuilt 1777–81, except steeple) (p. 1059B), by Francis Hiorne, is one of the precursors of the Gothic Revival. The nave is dull externally but internally amazingly light and delicate, with slender piers of lapping timbers which carry nothing but a lath and plaster vault, for the roof is supported from the side walls.

S. George, Liverpool (1812–14), by Thomas Rickman is the earliest of about forty-seven churches built by this influential author-architect, all in the provinces and all but three being in the revived Gothic style. Here, as in other cases, he used cast-iron extensively for the structural and decorative elements.

S. Marylebone Parish Church, London (1813–18) (p. 1060A), by Thomas Hardwick, was the first London church of importance in the new century. A dignified hexastyle pedimented portico, said to be 'after the Pantheon', fronts a transverse vestibule and stair block carrying a cupola supported by a tholos on a rusticated base. Inside are galleries carried on cast-iron pillars, and there are two vestries set angle-wise to frame the altar, behind which is a mahogany reredos screen, ornamented with Ionic pilasters, carrying the organ. Originally there were private galleries at the sides of the organ, fitted with fireplaces, but these were altered to normal open galleries in 1826.

A. S. Mary Woolnoth, London (1716–26).
See p. 1055

B. S. George, Bloomsbury, London
(1720–30). See p. 1055

C. Christ Church, Spitalfields (1723–9).
See p. 1055

D. S. Anne, Limehouse (1712–14;
restored 1851). See p. 1055

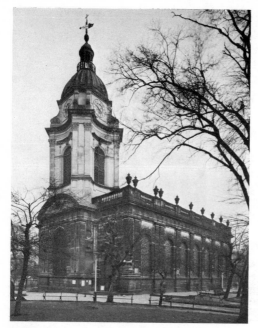

A. S. Philip, Birmingham (1709–25).
See p. 1055

B. S. Mary-le-Strand, London
(1714–17). See p. 1056

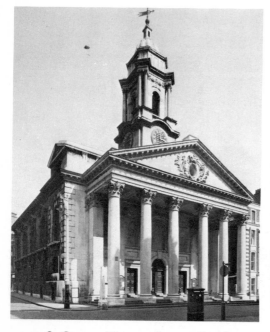

C. S. George, Hanover Square, London
(1712–25). See p. 1056

D. S. Martin-in-the-Fields, London
(1722–6). See p. 1056

A. Brandsby Hall, Yorkshire: interior of church (1768). See p. 1056

B. Tetbury Church, Glos (1777–81).
See p. 1056

c. S. Chad, Shrewsbury (1790–2).
See p. 1056

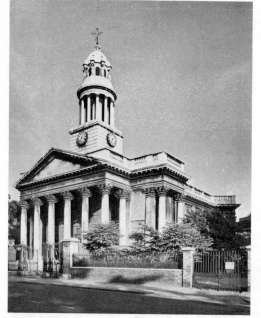

A. S. Marylebone Parish Church, London
(1813–18). See p. 1056

B. S. Pancras, London (1819–22).
See p. 1061

C. S. Luke, Chelsea (1820–4).
See p. 1061

D. S. Dunstan-in-the-West, London
(1831–3). See p. 1061

S. Pancras, London (1819–22) (p. 1060B), by William Inwood and his father, H. W. Inwood, is the best-known example of the Greek Revival, a fine design based very closely upon the Erechtheion at Athens (p. 230). It has a hexastyle portico, vestries resembling the Caryatid porch and an axial western steeple which is a two-storeyed version of the Tower of the Winds, Athens (p. 239). By the same architects is **All Saints, Camden Town** (1822–4), also in Greek Revival style.

All Souls, Langham Place, London (1822–5), by John Nash, is one of about 230 churches built under the Church Building Act of 1818, devoting one million pounds to providing churches to serve the new populations of expanding towns. It is a simple Bath stone box, of Classical design, elaborated by a western circular Ionic portico from which springs an acute conical spire, itself having a ring of Corinthian columns at its base, concentric with the portico below but of a reduced diameter. Severely damaged in 1941, it has been sensitively restored by H. S. Goodhart-Rendel.

S. George, Camberwell (1822–4), by Francis Bedford, and **S. Mark, Kennington** (1822–4), by D. R. Roper assisted by A. B. Clayton, are typical churches built for the Commissioners administering the Act of 1818, here expressed in the Greek Revival style, which was strongly favoured in the London area in the years 1821–7, but rarely used thereafter; they are simple rectangular boxes with western, Doric, porticoes and axial, storeyed western towers riding the ridge, over the vestibule.

S. Mary, Wyndham Place, London (1822–4, remodelled internally 1874), by Sir Robert Smirke, has a semicircular columned Ionic portico in a sober Classical style, like his **S. Philip, Salford, Lancashire** (1822–5, altered 1895).

S. Luke, Chelsea (1820–4) (p. 1060C), by James Savage, is the earliest, and one of the best, Commissioner churches in London in the Gothic Revival style, having a nave and aisles forming the usual plain rectangular composition and with an axial tower which here visually reaches the ground to contain the principal portal of the western entrance porch. It is unusual for its class in having vaults over the nave, with flying buttresses spanning the aisles. **Holy Trinity, Bordesley, Birmingham** (1820–3), by Francis Goodwin, is a provincial example without a tower.

S. Dunstan-in-the-West, Fleet Street, London (1831–3) (p. 1060D), by John Shaw I and his son, John Shaw II, is a fine town church, with a steeple which recalls in form, if not in height, that of S. Botolph, Boston, Lincs, a local landmark since 1515, known as 'Boston Stump'.

GEORGIAN PUBLIC BUILDINGS

Civic, social, government and collegiate requirements had all to be provided for during this period. **Town Halls** arose, as at Liverpool (1748–55), by John Wood and son of Bath, at Monmouth, where the Shire Hall (1724) (p. 1031E) is a well-balanced building, and at Salisbury, where the Council House (1788–95) is from designs by Sir Robert Taylor though executed after his death by his pupil W. Pilkington; **Exchanges,** as at Rochester (1706) (p. 1063A), Bristol (1741–3), by John Wood I, and Liverpool (1749–95), by John Wood I but burned and rebuilt (1795–1802) by John Foster, a portico being added in 1811; **Law Courts,** as the 'Four Courts', Dublin (1776–1802, damaged 1922) (p. 1063C), by Thomas Cooley and James Gandon; **Custom Houses,** as in London (1813–17) (p. 1063D), by David Laing, partly rebuilt by Sir Robert Smirke in 1825, and Dublin (1781–91, damaged 1921) (p. 1063E), by James Gandon; **Prisons,** such as Newgate (1770–8, demolished 1902) (p. 1064D), by George Dance II; **Hospitals,** such as (in London) S. Bartholomew's (1730–, gateway of 1702 by E. Strong), by James Gibbs, S. Luke's Hospital (1782–4), by George Dance II. Many **Banks** were erected throughout the country.

The Bank of England, London (1788–1833), by Sir John Soane, is unique by reason of its windowless façades in which he employed the Corinthian Order as used for the Temple at Tivoli (p. 283), while he obtained light and shade by columned recesses. It was reconstructed (1930–40) by Sir Herbert Baker, rising to a much greater height than formerly, though within the original shell of Soane's façades.

Butter Markets at Barnard Castle (1747) (p. 1031B), Bungay (1789) (p. 1031D), and Ludlow, are examples of the civic buildings on a smaller scale which abound throughout the country towns, and show the full corporate and commercial life of the period.

Clubs and similar social institutions developed greatly in the period, particularly in the latter part. **The Assembly Rooms, York** (1731–2) (p. 1064C), by Lord Burlington, is a fine example of Anglo-Palladian art; the entrance front was re-modelled in 1828 by J. P. Pritchett and W. Watson. Clubs were developed from coffee-houses, which originally were almost indistinguishable from private houses. Examples in London are Almack's Club, S. James's (1764–5, demolished 1863), by Robert Mylne; **Boodle's Club** (1775) (p. 1063C), by John Crunden; the Royal Society of Arts (1772–4), by Robert Adam; Brooks's Club (1776–8), by Henry Holland; the 'Pantheon', Oxford St. (1770–2), by James Wyatt, a famous fashionable resort, eventually demolished (c. 1936) after much reconstruction and change of function; United University Club (1822–6, demolished 1902), by William Wilkins and J. P. Deering; United Service Club (1827, altered later), by John Nash; and the Athenaeum Club (1827–30, attic 1899), by Decimus Burton.

Theatres were liable to rapid change, often due to fire, as Covent Garden, London (1732), by E. Shepherd, reconstructed (1792) by Henry Holland, rebuilt after a fire (1809–10) by Robert Smirke and A. Copland, and again rebuilt after fire (1857–8) by E. M. Barry; also Drury Lane Theatre, London (1672–4), by Wren, refronted (1775–6) by Robert Adam, rebuilt (1791–4) by Henry Holland, rebuilt after fire (1811–12) by B. D. Wyatt, altered (1822) by Samuel Beazley. Beazley (1786–1851) was responsible for much other theatre building in London, and theatres at Birmingham (Royal, 1820), Dublin (Royal, 1821, burned 1880), Leamington (Royal Music Hall, 1821) and abroad in South America, Belgium and India.

Hospitals and Almshouses continued to reflect the wishes of the pious founders, as we have seen in **Morden College, Blackheath** (1694) (p. 1022). Many of these buildings date from the seventeenth century, and amongst them may be mentioned Smyth's Almshouses, Lewisham (1664), Bromley College, Kent (1666), Corsham Almshouses (1668), **College of Matrons, Salisbury** (1682) (p. 1064B), Trinity Almshouses, Mile End, London (1695), Trinity Almshouses, Salisbury (1702), Fishmongers' Almshouses, Yarmouth (1702) and Somerset Hospital, Petworth (1748).

Government Buildings of the period in London include the Old Admiralty, Whitehall (1723–6), by Thomas Ripley, and its enclosing street screen (1759–61), by Robert Adam; the unexecuted design for the Houses of Parliament; the Treasury Buildings (façade to S. James's Park) (1734–6), and **Horse Guards** (1750–8) (pp. 1054B, 1064A), from designs by Kent. The Register House, Edinburgh (1774–92), is by Robert Adam.

Somerset House, London (1776–86, east and west wings completed 1834 and 1856) (p. 1066B), by Sir William Chambers, is a grand and dignified building, with a river façade, 183 m (600 ft) long, in which rusticated walls carry a Corinthian Order rising through two storeys pleasingly relieved by colonnades which emphasize the open courts.

The British Museum, London (1823–47) (p. 1068D) by Sir Robert Smirke,

Corn Exchange, Rochester (1706). See p. 1061

B. 'Four Courts', Dublin (1776–1802). See p. 1061

C. Boodle's Club, London (1775). See p. 1062

D. The Custom House, London (1813–17). See p. 1061

E. The Custom House, Dublin (1781–91). See p. 1061

A. The Horse Guards, Whitehall, London: west façade (1750–8). See p. 1062

B. College of Matrons, Salisbury (1682). See p. 1062

C. Assembly Rooms, York (1731–2). See p. 1062

D. Newgate Prison, London (1770–8, demolished 1902). See p. 1061

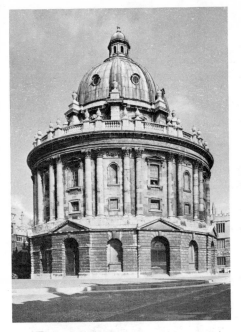

A. Radcliffe Library, Oxford (1737–49).
See p. 1069

B. Queen's College, Oxford
(1709–38): gateway. See p. 1069

c. Clarendon Building, Oxford: north front (1712–15). See p. 1069

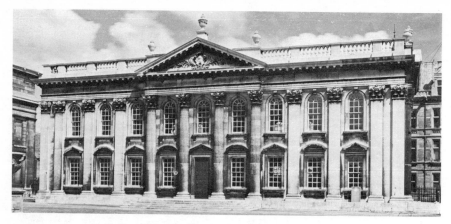

A. Senate House, Cambridge (1722–30). See p. 1069

B. Somerset House, London (1776–86): waterfront. See p. 1062

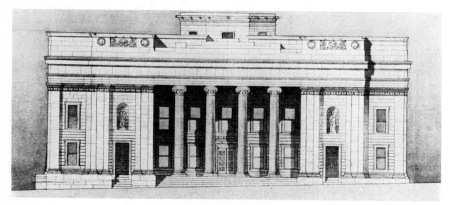

C. The Old Town Hall, Manchester (1822–4). See p. 1070

A. The National Gallery, Trafalgar Square, London (1834–8). See p. 1069

B. University College, London (1827–8). See p. 1069

A. Radcliffe Observatory, Oxford (1772–94). See p. 1069

B. The Old University Library, Cambridge (1754–8). See p. 1069

C. Guildhall, Worcester (1721–3). See p. 1070

D. The British Museum (1823–47). See p. 1062

E. Triple Archway, Hyde Park Corner, London (c. 1825). See p. 1069

continued in building into the Victorian era. Its southern front has an octastyle pedimented portico and projecting wings, around which the portico is continued. The massive and impressive scale of the Greek Ionic Order is reinforced by the reiteration of the columns. The domed reading room, 42.6 m (140 ft) in diameter, was added (1854–7) by Sydney Smirke. The General Post Office (1824–9), by the same architect, also a Greek Revival building in the Ionic Order, was demolished in 1912.

The **National Gallery, London** (1834–8) (p. 1067A), by William Wilkins, occupies a magnificent position in Trafalgar Square. Its southern façade is much broken into pavilions and parts, which insufficiently subscribe to the central octastyle Corinthian portico (formerly at Carlton House), pedimented and crowned with an inadequate dome, while the principal floor is raised upon a high podium.

Ornamental buildings in London include the Marble Arch (c. 1825), by John Nash, built to front the architect's half-realized scheme for Buckingham Palace, and moved to its present position at the north-east corner of Hyde Park in 1847. Also connected with the scheme for Buckingham Palace was the arch on Constitution Hill (1828), a composition by Decimus Burton similar to the Arch of Titus, Rome (p. 318), in the Composite Order. It is not now in its original position, its alignment having been changed in 1883 from one axial with the nearby magnificent **Ionic screen at Hyde Park** south-east corner (c. 1825) (p. 1068E), a Greek Revival masterpiece which Decimus Burton had intended to be a complementary feature.

Collegiate buildings received many important additions, and numerous effective examples of the period are to be seen in the universities.

The **Radcliffe Library, Oxford** (1737–49) (pp. 694A, 1065A), by J. Gibbs—probably his finest work—is monumental in character, with a rusticated sixteen-sided ground storey, having alternately pedimented arch openings and niches, while the upper portion is circular, 30.5 m (100 ft) in diameter, with two storeys of windows and niches included in one Order of coupled Corinthian columns, supporting entablature and balustrade, behind which a high drum with eight buttresses supports the lead-covered dome.

Queen's College, Oxford (1709–38) (pp. 694A, 1065B), by Nicholas Hawksmoor, a pupil of Wren, is a fine example of a late Renaissance college with quadrangle, hall, and chapel, and the library designed by Wren (p. 1028C) with a dignified Order. The gateway (p. 1065B) is an effective composition with an archway flanked by Tuscan columns and entablature, surmounted by an open cupola, enclosing a statue of Queen Caroline.

The **Clarendon Building, Oxford** (1712–15) (p. 1065C), by Hawksmoor, is a pleasing structure with a fine Doric portico.

The **Senate House, Cambridge** (1722–30) (pp. 694B, 1066A), is by J. Gibbs. Two storeys are included in a single Order of Corinthian pilasters, coupled at ends, and centre-piece of four half-columns surmounted by a sculptured pediment, flanked by balustrades, while the sash windows of the ground storey are headed by alternately triangular and segmental pediments, the upper windows being round-headed. The whole has a unity of composition and is rich yet reposeful in effect.

Among collegiate buildings of this period may be mentioned: at **Oxford** (p. 694A), Worcester College (planned c. 1720, Hawksmoor participating), the **Radcliffe Observatory** (1772–94) (p. 1068A), by Henry Keene and James Wyatt, and the North Quadrangle, All Souls College (1715–40), by Hawksmoor. At **Cambridge** (p. 694B), the **Old University Library** (1754–8) (p. 1068B), by Stephen Wright, and Downing College (1807–20), an early instance of the Greek Revival by Wilkins. Trinity College, Dublin (1752–98), was altered by Chambers, and Edinburgh University (1789–91) is substantially by Robert Adam, completed (1815–34) by W. H. Playfair. **University College, London** (1827–8) (p. 1067B), by William

Wilkins, assisted by J. P. Deering, is a fine Greek Revival design with an axial Corinthian portico with dome over (destroyed 1941, rebuilt 1950), elevated on a high podium and approached by grand flights of steps.

The **Guildhall, Worcester** (1721-3) (p. 1068C), by Thomas White, is a fine civic example, while the **Guildhall, High Wycombe** (1757) by Henry Keene, is an interesting building of which there are many in English country towns by provincial architects whose names and works are now becoming more generally known.

The (Old) **Town Hall, Manchester** (1822-4) (p. 1066C), by F. Goodwin, was demolished in 1912 and set up in part in the grounds of Heaton Hall, Lancashire. The Greek disposition of the columnar screen 'in antis' and the ante of the terminal blocks will be noted.

Bridges of architectural character, as Pulteney Bridge, Bath (1769-74), by Robert Adam; Richmond Bridge (1774-7) and Kew Bridge (1783-9, rebuilt 1903), both designed by James Paine, now joined up the busy districts on either side of the Thames and other bridges of this period are at Chertsey and Walton. Waterloo Bridge (1811-17, demolished 1938), designed by John Rennie, showed the influence of the Greek Revival.

BIBLIOGRAPHY

BEARD, G. *Georgian Craftsmen*. London, 1966.

BELCHER, J. and MACARTNEY, M. E. *Later Renaissance Architecture in England*. 2 vols. London, 1897–1901.

BOLTON, A. T. *The Architecture of Robert and James Adam*. 2 vols. 1922.

CLARK, K. *The Gothic Revival*. 2nd ed. London, 1950.

COLVIN, H. M. *Biographical Dictionary of English Architects 1660–1840*. London, 1954.

DALE, A. *James Wyatt, Architect 1746–1813*. Oxford, 1936.

DOWNES, K. *Hawksmoor*. London, 1959.

—. *English Baroque Architecture*. London, 1966.

DUTTON, R. *The English Country House*. London, 1935.

—. *The English Interior*. London, 1948.

FLEMING, J. *Robert Adam and his Circle*. London, 1962.

GIROUARD, M. *R. Smythson and the Architecture of the Elizabethan Era*. London, 1966.

GOTCH, J. A. *The English Home from Charles I to George IV*. London, 1919.

HARRIS, J. *Sir William Chambers*. . . . London, 1970.

HILL, O., and CORNFORTH, J. *English Country Houses, 1625–1865*. London, 1966.

HUSSEY, C. *English Country Houses, 1715, 1760, 1800*. 3 vols. London.

—. *The Picturesque*. London, 1927, reprinted 1967.

—. *English Gardens and Landscape 1700–1750*. London, 1967.

ISON, W. *The Georgian Buildings of Bath*. London, 1947.

—. *The Georgian Builders of Bristol*. London, 1952.

JOURDAIN, M. *English Decoration and Furniture, 1760–1820*. London, 1922.

—. *English Decorative Plasterwork of the Renaissance*. London, 1926.

—. *The Work of William Kent*. London, 1948.

KNOOP, D., and JONES, G. P. *The London Mason in the 17th Century*. Manchester, 1935.

LENYGON, F. *Decoration in England from 1660–1770*. London, 1927.

MORDAUNT CROOK, J. *The Greek Revival*. London, 1972.

PILCHER, D. *The Regency Style*. London, 1947.

RAMSEY, S. C. *Small Houses of the Late Georgian Period*. 2 vols. London, 1919–23.

RICHARDSON, SIR A. E. and EBERLEIN. *The Smaller English House, 1660–1830*. London, 1925.

SMALL, T., and WOODBRIDGE, C. *Houses of Wren and Early Georgian Periods*. London, 1928.

STEEGMAN, J. *The Rule of Taste*. London, 1936.

STROUD, D. *Henry Holland*. London, 1950.

—. *Capability Brown*. London, 1950.

—. *Humphrey Repton*. London, 1962.

—. *The Architecture of Sir John Soane*. London, 1961.

—. *George Dance the Younger*. London, 1970.

STUTCHBURY, H. *The Architecture of Colen Campbell*. Manchester, 1967.

SUMMERSON, SIR J. *John Nash*. London, 1935.

—. *Georgian London*. London, 1945.

—. *Sir John Soane*. London, 1952.

—. *Inigo Jones*. Harmondsworth, 1966.

—. *Sir Christopher Wren*, London, 1953.

—. *Architecture in Britain 1530–1830*. Harmondsworth, 1963 and other editions.

TIPPING, H. A. *English Homes: Periods III, IV, V, VI, 1558–1820*. 6 vols. London, 1920–8.

Vitruvius Britannicus, by Campbell, Woolfe and Gandon. 5 vols. London, 1715–71.

WHIFFEN, M. *Stuart and Georgian Churches*. London, 1947–8.

—. *Thomas Archer*. London, 1950.

WHINNEY, M. *Renaissance Architecture in England*. London, 1952.

WHISTLER, L. *Sir John Vanbrugh*. London, 1938.

—. *The Imagination of Vanbrugh and his Fellow Artists*. London, 1954.

WREN SOCIETY. Publications, vols. I–XX. 1924–43.

33

RENAISSANCE ARCHITECTURE IN SCANDINAVIA

Sixteenth to nineteenth century

INFLUENCES

GEOGRAPHICAL

By derivation, the word 'Scandinavia' applies only to the southern part of Sweden
—Skåne—but it has come to apply to the whole group of nations north and west of
the Baltic: Denmark, Norway, Sweden and Finland, and also Iceland. Geographically, the present boundaries are not as logical as those which generally persisted
for a thousand years before 1660 when, with minor exceptions, the present frontiers
were established. The natural barrier of lakes and forests which runs across Sweden
roughly on the line of the Göta Canal was more significant than the small strip of
water between Sweden and Denmark; similarly, the mountains between Sweden
and Norway were a greater barrier than the water separating Norway and Denmark.
Throughout this period, Denmark was master of South Sweden and of Norway, as
well as—depending upon the ebb and flow of successive wars—the plains of north-
west Germany. Norway, with her communities in the fjords so isolated as to be
almost independent, looked westward and southward, while Sweden looked eastward and to her south, to the southern shores of the Baltic, which for much of her
history she has controlled. Finland, a land of forests and lakes, was for most of her
history a colony of Sweden.

GEOLOGICAL

Sweden has very important deposits of iron and copper, both more significant to
her economic well-being than to her building crafts. She also has granite, marble
and, in the south, suitable clay for bricks. The Danish earth-crust, like that of
Skåne and north Germany, is predominantly boulder clay, and it is not surprising
that in all these regions brick is the principal building material. Norway, Sweden
and Finland have vast tracts of forest, and wood is the basis of vernacular architecture in the three countries. In 1666 Norway supplied the timber for the rebuilding of London after the great fire.

CLIMATIC

Owing to the proximity of the sea throughout Scandinavia, and to the influence of the Gulf Stream and the effects of the prevailing west and south-west
winds, the climate almost everywhere is less harsh than in countries further
east of similar latitude, although the winters are habitually long and severe.
The wide availability of timber, with its effective insulation and weather-
resistant properties, and the early development of ingenious wood-construction
techniques counteracted to some extent the rigours of domestic life in the
protracted cold season.

HISTORICAL, SOCIAL AND RELIGIOUS

From Viking times until the accession of Gustavus Vasa to the Swedish throne in 1523, Denmark had been the dominant Scandinavian power. Thereafter Denmark's influence waned, though her kings continued to rule Norway and to draw lucrative tolls from shipping entering the Baltic. Lutheran missionaries were winning converts in Denmark as early as 1523, and in Sweden from 1526. Much as in England, a genuine religious movement proceeded alongside its political exploitation by the monarchies. On the one hand, the Bible was translated into the northern vernacular languages (including Finnish); on the other hand monastic and other ecclesiastical lands were appropriated by kings like Gustavus Vasa of Sweden and Christian III of Denmark.

Both Sweden and Denmark were deeply involved in the politico-religious conflicts of the seventeenth century. Under Gustavus Adolphus (1611–32) Sweden built up an empire which encircled the shores of the Baltic, including much of the German littoral, and it was her emissaries who, with the French, dominated the negotiations which led to the Treaty of Westphalia at the end of the Thirty Years' War. Axel Oxenstierna, Gustavus Adolphus's adviser and Regent during the minority of his daughter Christina, has been described as the greatest minister of a century which included Richelieu and Mazarin. Not surprisingly, French influence on Swedish manners, art and architecture was paramount at this time, and became even more apparent during the reign of Queen Christina, an extravagant, unpredictable, brilliant monarch, one of the most learned women of her day and a staunch Francophile. First defeated by Brandenburg-Prussia in 1675, Sweden won some impermanent victories under the unbalanced militarist Charles XII, who was killed in 1718 after suffering heavy defeats by Peter the Great of Russia. In the eighteenth century Swedish prestige continued to wane, a succession of unsuccessful attempts being made to recapture past glories in campaigns against Russia in 1741–3, Prussia in 1757–62, and Russia again in 1788–90. As in other countries, the French Revolution provoked restiveness in Sweden, and in 1792 Gustavus III, an enlightened despot, was assassinated at a masked ball (the subject of Verdi's opera *Un Ballo in Maschera*) by a group of nobles.

In Denmark the eighteenth century was marred by the plague of 1711 and a series of fires which destroyed much of old Copenhagen, while further fires in the early 1880s devastated the city, so little of the old part now remains. The early years of that century also saw the rise of the puritanical cult of Pietism in both Sweden and Denmark. This was followed in the latter country by a period of unprecedented licence, and then by the foundation of a system of social services unique in its time. These reforms, which included the provision of homes for illegitimate children, hospitals for the treatment of venereal disease, and the like, were continued by the controversial German-born statesman Struensee, who ultimately fell foul of the entrenched forces of privilege and was executed. Nevertheless, Denmark emerged from the eighteenth century as a progressive country— she abolished her slave trade in 1792—and one with a strong sense of national identity. The nineteenth century was soon to be marked by a remarkable flowering of intellectual life, especially in the field of literature. Norway remained under the Danish crown until she was united with Sweden in 1814, and did not become a fully independent state until 1905. Finland, dominated by Swedish noble landowners, belonged to the Swedish monarchy until ceded to Russia in 1809. She obtained independence in 1917, acquiring at the same time a corridor to the Arctic Ocean through the port of Petsamo. The Russians, however, took this back again during the Second World War, together with the Carelian Isthmus north of Leningrad. Iceland declared herself independent of Denmark in 1944.

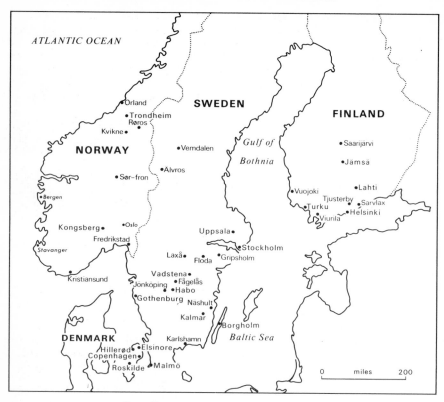

Scandinavia in the Renaissance period

ARCHITECTURAL CHARACTER

In spite of its geographical isolation, the architecture of Scandinavia has developed along the lines of other European nations, major influences, as in other countries, reflecting the political allegiances of the time. Even in Iceland and the remoter parts of Finland the functional vernacular timber buildings carry suggestions of current or recent fashions in countries further south. Thus, in the Stave churches of the twelfth century, timber braces took the unfunctional form of Norman stone arches, complete with false keystones, and the functional posts carried collars cut in the shape of Norman stone capitals. The interiors were painted in the iconographic manner of the mosaics in Byzantine churches, and the tradition was maintained in Renaissance and Baroque times. Fågålas and Habo, both in Västergötland, are typical. Every inch of the walls of these churches, pillars, altar rails, even the balcony front and pews, is painted to represent marble, and the ceiling and reredos to represent frescoes of conventional religious scenes, with putti and draperies carved or painted in the decorations. The result is not unlike south-German Baroque, but through the painting the joints in the timbers can be clearly seen, and externally the churches in their red- or brown-painted clap-boarding and shingle roofs have the unsophisticated look of village barns.

In Finland there was a church-building programme during the seventeenth century for the inland areas. All these churches were of wood with painted interiors.

Externally, Classical details were reproduced in wood—pilasters, architraves, cornices, even channelled rustication. This superimposition of current Classical fashions appeared in the humblest buildings, the protruding ends of log-built barns being treated as rusticated quoins, and false pediments provided over entrances and Classical surrounds to windows, simplified to be easily constructed by the estate carpenter. Thus from the most rural farmyard to the greatest church (perhaps the great church of Kongsberg in Norway is the most pretentious example) the timber vernacular was adapted to the reigning style.

It is interesting to note that the oval plan-shape, current during the Baroque period (cf. Steinhausen in Germany, S. Agnese in Rome, Karlskirche in Vienna or S. Benetfink in London, p. 1023C) also appeared at Jokkmokk in Lappland, Näshult in Småland, and Vemdalen in Härjedalen, all timber churches of the mid-eighteenth century. It is doubtful, however, whether this was due to a desire to keep pace with architectural fashion: a more likely reason was the practical need to provide more space, while limited by the length of timber available.

One characteristic of Scandinavian vernacular architecture cannot be overlooked: the free-standing bell-tower. This varies from the simple shingle-clad pyramid to the Classically-detailed white-painted tower complete with pediments, pilasters and cupola, or a simple skeleton-pole structure supporting the bells under a pitched or ogee roof. Whatever their form, it is they, and the tall crowned maypole on the village green, which give the northern villages their peculiar character.

In the following paragraphs the more sophisticated architecture of the Renaissance period will be considered country by country. For this purpose it will be assumed that the Scandinavian countries have their present boundaries.

SWEDEN

The Malmöhus, the Citadel of Malmö, built in 1536 by the Dutch architect Martin Bussaert, must count as one of the first major Renaissance buildings still surviving in Sweden. The castles of Gripsholm (by the German Heinrich von Cöllen) of 1537, and Vadstena (by the Pomeranian Joachim Bulgerin) of 1545, have less Renaissance character, but a new Gripsholm was built in 1572 for the future Charles IX with a classically ordered arrangement of rooms and painted walls. In 1576 the astronomer T. Brahe built a palace on the Sound, Uranienborg (of which only the foundations remain), with a plan very like the central block of Chambord (p. 880C), except that the circular towers are in the centre, not at the corners, of the building. In Kalmar Castle there is classical panelling with fluted Corinthian columns and full entablature with intarsia panels (p. 1077B). The most prominent architects of this period were the four Pahr brothers from Milan who, in addition to Vadstena, worked on Kalmar, Uppsala and Borgholm, but Dutch influence was very strong, and vernacular buildings such as those in the Old City of Stockholm (Gamla Stan), tended to have tall stepped gables facing the street.

In 1639 the French engineer Simon de la Vallée was appointed Royal Architect, and designed (c. 1650) the Oxenstierna Palace in Stockholm, the first 'Roman' building (p. 1077C). His son Jean (1620–96) and the Fleming, Nicodemus Tessin, studied under him and abroad, while Tessin's son visited Rome to study the work of Bernini. It was the latter, Nicodemus Tessin the Younger (1654–1728) who, under Bernini's inspiration, prepared designs for the Louvre and for a proposed new palace in Copenhagen, neither of which were executed, as well as for the new Royal Palace in Stockholm (1690), which also included a large church (Storkyrka), a bridge (Norrbro) and formal square (Norrmalmstorg), and a Baroque sepulchral church on the axis. The last was never built, and if the remainder of the scheme was not carried out in full, it demonstrated that Swedish planners had absorbed the current European philosophy.

A purely Swedish development, which spread to other parts of Scandinavia, was the so-called 'säteri' (manor house) roof. This is basically two roofs, with a small break or clear-storey between, the lower roof being usually curved in section. The first major building to adopt this form was the Riddarhus (House of Lords) in Stockholm (p. 1077D), as completed by Jean de la Vallée in 1656, after the Dutchman Joost Vingboons had drastically altered the design of the elder de la Vallée. This roof-type became almost universal in Sweden, as can be seen in the engravings of drawings by the Swedish architect Eric Dahlberg (1625–1703), assembled in his *Suecia Antiqua et Hodierna*. These volumes reveal the wealth of Sweden in the seventeenth and eighteenth centuries, with page after page of great country houses standing in their forest estates, with formal gardens leading down to landing-stages on the lakes or archipelago. Dahlberg himself was responsible for the town hall at Jönköping, and the 'Old Town Hall' in Stockholm, as well as Laxå and Karlshamn churches, both with Greek-cross plans and säteri roofs.

The first Palladian building, in the Dutch manner of the Mauritshuis (p. 947F), was the de Geer House of 1646 in Stockholm (now Ebba Brahe's House), probably by Vingboons, but the Palladian plan appeared in Vibyholm Castle in 1622, by the Dutchman Caspar Panten. Drottningholm, designed by Tessin the Elder in the 1660s, had a symmetrical plan with a central 'Grand Staircase' and a säteri roof, while Tessin the Younger designed Steninge Castle (1694), also symmetrical in plan, but with a large oval salon projecting in the manner of Vaux-le-Vicomte (p. 897). Variations of Palladian plans and exteriors with giant Orders and Classical cornices below säteri roofs can be seen all through Dahlberg's collection of engravings. The interpretation, however, is perceptibly French.

Kalmar Cathedral, on a large scale, and the mausoleum at the mediaeval Riddarholms church in Stockholm, both by Tessin the Elder, and that at Floda (p. 1085A, B), by Dahlberg, on a small scale, display a rich Classicism merging into the Baroque, which came to full flower in the completion of the Royal Palace, Stockholm in the mid-eighteenth century. Hårleman's East India Company warehouse (1740) in Gothenburg is the Swedish equivalent of English quayside architecture, strong and simple, with a rusticated ground floor and pediment over the central five bays, but with the säteri roof (p. 1084B). In Stockholm, Eric Palmstedt's Exchange of 1767 shows a transition to Neo-Classicism (p. 1086A), apparent also in the Botanicum at Uppsala in 1788 by the Frenchman Desprez (p. 1084C). Apart from the country houses already mentioned, comparable in quality with those of England of much the same period, the buildings of rural Sweden were generally simple two-storey structures of wood, with occasional concessions to the prevailing style in the provision of rudimentary Classical detailing in windows, doors and cornices.

DENMARK

The earliest important Renaissance buildings in Denmark were the castles of Frederick II (1559–88). Kronborg, at Elsinore (p. 1086B), formerly the stronghold controlling the Sound, was transformed in the 1570s into that typical Renaissance building type, the luxury castle-palace. The bastions were moved away from the palace and reconstructed in the Italian manner suited to the newer artillery. The vast building, the largest palace in Scandinavia, is Dutch in character with curvilinear gables and polygonal decorative spires. The architects were Flemish, and the costs were met from tolls levied from ships passing through the Sound. Frederiksborg, at Hillerød (p. 1078A), was also built for Frederick II, but much enlarged and

A. Timber 'Palladian' house, near Skansen, Stockholm (1833)

B. Kalmar Castle, Sweden: King Eric XIV's room (16th cent.). See p. 1075

C. Oxenstierna Palace, Stockholm (c. 1650). See p. 1081

D. The Riddarhus, Stockholm (c. 1653). See p. 1081

A. Frederiksborg Castle, Hillerød (1602). See p. 1087

B. Fredensborg Castle (Peace Palace) (1670 and 1718): garden room. See p. 1087

altered by Christian IV in 1602. This palace, too, has the rich curvilinear gables and complicated spires which became the trade-mark of early Renaissance palace-building in Denmark. A peculiar Danish feature is the 'breaking' of the spires in the middle and the supporting of the upper section on large golden balls. Christian IV (1577–1648) was an amateur architect of ability, and was largely responsible for the design of Frederiksborg; of Rosenborg in Copenhagen, also with rich gables and spires; the Copenhagen Exchange with its long low two-storeyed range, gabled bays and spire of twisted dragons' tails (p. 1086E); the University and the Trinity Church. As a town planner, he prepared the scheme adapted in the eighteenth century by N. Eigtved (1701–54) for the Amalienborg area.

In the seventeenth century Denmark became the leading Scandinavian country architecturally. Generally, the current French style was adopted for country houses, and Italian for town, but with the Swedish säteri form of roof. In the 1660s Frederick III built the Citadel (Castellet) of Copenhagen as a refuge (p. 1087). It was never needed for that purpose, but the area within the bastions was used for barracks, and the ranges of painted wooden buildings which still survive are reminders of what much of Copenhagen must have been like before the succession of disastrous fires and bombardments. The noble Classical gateways, of the same period (p. 1086C), were designed by Henrik Rúse. The other group of timber buildings to survive is in the Nyboder area. These were designed for naval crews in 1631–41, and are now much in demand as small town houses. Rúse was also responsible for the layout of the Bredgade-Adelsgade area of the city.

In the late seventeenth century the Charlottenborg complex of palace, town square (Kongens Nytorv) and Dutch garden was created by the king's half-brother, Gyldenløve. In 1697 the Swedish architect Tessin the Younger submitted a model for a palace and later, with H. Scheel, the design for Frederiksberg (just outside Copenhagen), both in the Roman Baroque manner, the latter with a park modelled on Versailles. Both park and palace at Frederiksberg have been much altered.

At the end of the Nordic War, with the Treaty of Nystad in 1721, Frederick IV built his 'Peace Palace', Fredensborg, a country retreat in the form of an Italian villa. Although also much altered, it reflects an aspect of the back-to-nature cult which in Denmark culminated in the Hermitage, a royal hunting lodge by Laurids Thurah (1706–59) in 1734. The middle of the century saw a strengthening of the French Classical influence with the appointment of N.-H. Jardin as Director of the Royal Academy, and the beginning of the Amalienborg scheme, similar in date and conception to that of Nancy.

With the succession to the Academy of C. F. Harsdorff (1735–99), who had studied under Soufflot in Paris, a Neo-Classical phase began. In his own house in Kongens Nytorv, designed as an example to students, he displayed a strange aberration by placing the volutes on the Ionic capitals end-on (p. 1089A). A truer Neo-Classicism came with C. F. Hansen (1756–1845) who, in 1803, designed the Town Hall and Law Courts (Raad- og Domhus) in Copenhagen with a severe Ionic portico, and Vor Frue Kirke with its richer Doric portico against a plain front wall and, inside, an uninterrupted coffered vault carried on a lofty colonnade, itself on an arcade leading the eye to Thorvaldsen's figure of Christ in an apse (p. 1089C).

The history of Danish architecture can perhaps best be seen in the cathedral of Roskilde. The main structure in brick of the twelfth century succeeded a tenth-century timber building, and since that time the royal burial chapels have been built around it. Renaissance monuments of the mid-sixteenth century can be seen in the Christian I Chapel, while the Frederik V Chapel was designed by Harsdorff in the 1770s in the purist Neo-Classical style (p. 1089B). The work of leading sculptors of all periods can be seen in the many sarcophagi.

NORWAY

In comparison with the same period in Denmark and Sweden, less of architectural note was built in Norway in the seventeenth and eighteenth centuries. Grid-iron street plans were laid out in many towns within star-shaped fortifications: Frederikstad in 1567 (improved in 1665), Oslo (then Kristiania) in 1624, Kristiansund in 1641, and Trondheim, by Johan Caspar de Cicignon from Luxembourg, in 1708 (after the great fire of 1681). The period, however, also produced many formal buildings in wood, with central gables in the form of pediments, and Classical or Baroque details superimposed for doors and windows, and pilaster strips. Two notable instances are Damsgård, near Bergen (p. 1090C), and the residence (now royal) of Stiftsgården, Trondheim, the largest wooden building in Scandinavia (p. 1090B), both dating in their present form from the 1770s. As in Sweden and Finland, unsophisticated Renaissance buildings in timber can be seen in the country districts, often with richly detailed features. The acanthus leaf was widely adopted by local craftsmen.

Pre-Reformation churches sufficed until after 1660. After the log church had superseded the stave-church, plans became narrow for structural reasons, so that enlargement entailed transepts and a cruciform plan (cf. Kvikne Lutheran Church in Hedmark, dating from 1652 and retaining its painted decorations from the 1730s). This plan-type remained popular, even for later brick and stone churches. Thus Oslo Cathedral (1697) was cruciform. Later, the elongated octagon was adopted at Røros, probably by S. Aspaas (1784), on the long axis, and at Sør-fron, Gudbrandsdal, on the cross axis (1786). Kongsberg Church, by J. A. Stuckenbrock (1761), is in brick and timber with superimposed galleries, a dramatic Baroque altar-piece surmounted by an organ loft (p. 1090D), and a flat wooden ceiling painted in Rococo trompe-l'oeil.

In 1814, when Norway (united with Sweden) became independent of Denmark, a capital was needed. Kristiania (Oslo), founded by Christian IV, was chosen. H. D. F. Linstow, trained in Scandinavia, was the architect for the new palace, traditionally Classical with a central colonnaded portico on a rusticated arcaded base. The University, more Neo-Classical in feeling, the Exchange (1826–) (p. 1090E), the Norwegian Bank (1828) (p. 1090F), the Magistrature and the Maternity Hospital were designed by the principal architect of the day, Christian Heinrich Grosch, who also applied Romanesque motifs in a romantic vein to the Market Halls in Oslo in the 1840s. The German Alexis de Châteauneuf added a spire to the Cathedral (of 1697) and also built a Neo-Gothic church at Trefoldighet, and a Dane, J. H. Nebelong, built the romantic castellated Oscarshall palace of 1848. Throughout Norway, buildings reflect the styles of the day, sometimes with precision and polish, as in the development of Oslo after unification with Sweden, but more usually in a manner wholly delightful and original, varying from the ultra-simple to the over-elaborate, and commonly with an added vernacular flavour that comes from the use of timber, instead of stone or brick, for the external walls.

FINLAND

Finland's major contribution to Scandinavian architecture was the development of Helsinki after she became a Russian Grand Duchy in 1809. A plan for the new city had been drawn up following the disastrous fire of 1808. As in Russia, wide streets were the custom, because of the fire hazard, but the new plan, by J. A. Ehrenström, incorporated a succession of squares with public buildings. The principal feature is an immense square, the largest in Scandinavia, bounded by the

Senate House on one side and the University on the other, and dominated by the Cathedral at the top of a great flight of steps between two pavilions, all by C. L. Engel (1778–1840). The square is separated from the waterfront by another long range of buildings, incorporating the City Hall. Engel, from S. Petersburg, who had been a fellow-student of Schinkel in Germany, had also studied in Italy, and his work reflects this catholic background. Other buildings in Helsinki by Engel include the University Library (1836) (p. 1091B) and the Observatory, the Guards' Barracks, and the old Military Hospital. His personal version of Neo-Classical architecture gives the city its unique character.

Finnish churches have much in common with those in Sweden, and are similarly distinguished for their Baroque furnishings, so that, within a mediaeval shell of the simplest form, the building may have a richness comparable with that of a church by Asam or Fischer. Generally churches were rectangular with a simple high-pitched roof and low eaves. The main external feature was the bell-tower, sometimes finished with a spirelet, and sometimes, as at Jämsä or Hollola, the tower is a fully-developed Renaissance building, with pediments, entablatures, parapets and pilasters.

There is a dearth of good domestic architecture. The social structure did not call for great country mansions; the castles were purely defensive, and the few manor houses were modest by Scandinavian standards. One of the most pretentious is Sarvlax (1619), with wide pilaster strips and bracketed cornice. Engel designed others at Viurila and Vuojoki, and C. T. Heideken designed the manor house at Tjusterby in a form of 'Nash-Gothick', but as late as 1867.

The great bulk of building is timber vernacular, more Russian than Scandinavian, grey-painted, with overhanging eaves and fretted verges, and looking somewhat monotonous in the wide streets of towns, because of the almost uniform height of two storeys. Gradually, however, these timber streets, which give Finland her peculiar character, are giving way to the universal brick and stucco of the modern chain-store and office block.

EXAMPLES

SWEDEN

Oxenstierna Palace, Stockholm (c. 1650) (p. 1077C), by S. de la Vallée, the first town house in Sweden in the Roman manner, has three storeys and a mezzanine over a rusticated ground floor, and a bold cornice under a low-pitched roof. The windows have segmental pediments on the first floor and triangular on the third, both on brackets, and the second-floor windows have 'picture-frames'.

The **Riddarhus, Stockholm** (c. 1653) (p. 1077D) was begun under the direction of Joost Vingboons, who was responsible for the tall smooth pilasters, pedimented windows and attic floor with the central pediment of the façade. He was succeeded by Jean de la Vallée, who designed the attic windows and the säteri roof, the first for a major building.

Drottningholm Castle, near Stockholm (c. 1660) (p. 1083A), was designed by Nicodemus Tessin the Elder for the Dowager Queen Hedvig Eleonora in the French manner as a reflection of Versailles. An almost Palladian plan was adopted with a central domed block round a monumental staircase, and small corner pavilions linked with connecting wings. Nicholas Millich was responsible for the sculptural decorations of the staircase. The Castle stands on a superb lake-side site with extensive gardens and park. The private theatre of 1764, virtually unchanged, is still used for performances. The **Kina Slott** (China Castle) (p. 1083B) was built in the gardens in the 1760s by Cronstedt and Adelcrantz in a whimsical Chinese Rococo style, echoing the work of Swedish-born Sir William Chambers.

The **Royal Palace, Stockholm** (1690–1753) (p. 1084A), was designed by Tessin the Younger, an architect of international stature. After a start had been made on the new palace, fire ravaged the old one and work was therefore accelerated, with the result that designs were being prepared while the work was in progress. This accounted for the differences in treatment of the elevations to the four sides of the palace, which is basically a large square round a courtyard, with four lower projecting wings. Unlike the Riddarhus or Drottningholm, there is no visible roof, but a balustraded parapet.

The **East India Company building, Gothenburg** (1740) (p. 1084B), by Carl Hårleman (1700–53), is a massive building of nineteen bays and three floors over a channelled ground floor with arched openings giving access to storage spaces. The central five bays project and carry an ornamented pediment and, in the centres of the side wings, one bay slightly projects and is crowned by a segmental pediment. The detailing is austere, the quoins being simply channelled, and only seven windows on the first floor have pediments or any decoration. There is a säteri roof.

The **Exchange, Stockholm** (1767–76) (p. 1086A), by E. Palmstedt, foreshadowing the Greek revival, stands in a prominent position facing the only large open space in the Old Town, and has a central feature of a pedimented projecting portico with three arches on the ground floor and framed windows on the first floor between columns, Doric and Ionic respectively. The ground floor is channelled, and there is a balustraded parapet and urns on the central pediment. The roof is concealed, but there is a shallow dome and lantern in the centre.

The **Botanicum, Uppsala** (1788) (p. 1084C), designed by the Frenchman L.-J. Desprez, is a simple, unadorned and severe building dominated by a portico with exaggerated low-pitched pediment carried on eight widely-spaced columns, Doric in conception, but of idiosyncratic detail, and with large chunky mutule blocks giving a tough, brutal character, similar in feeling to much of the work of the contemporary French architect, C.-N. Ledoux (p. 907).

The **Church of S. Katarina, Stockholm** (1656), designed by Jean de la Vallée, represents the Greek-cross plan then becoming fashionable. It has a dome on a lofty octagonal drum and small towers over the corner chapels. These towers, and the high central lantern, are completed with spirelets. Also with a Greek-cross plan, but with the addition of apses at either end of one axis, is **Kalmar Cathedral** (1660s), by Tessin the Elder.

The **Lars Kagg Mausoleum, Floda, Södermanland** (1661) (p. 1085A, B), was added by E. Dahlberg to the old church (twelfth century), which incorporates some remarkable paintings over walls and vaulting in the north aisle by Albertus Pictor. The mausoleum has a symmetrical Greek-cross plan with pediments on the exposed sides and a low dome and lantern over the body of the chapel. The treatment of the exterior is unusual in that each projecting wing has three pilasters, one in the middle under the apex of the pediment. There are panels of florid carving on the sides of the exterior, and the inside is richly stuccoed by Carlo Carove.

The **Caroline Mausoleum, Riddarholms Church, Stockholm** (1671), designed by Tessin the Elder, has a Greek-cross plan and is more orthodox in having twin Tuscan columns at each corner supporting, over a fully detailed entablature, simpler attics and a gadrooned dome designed later by Carl Hårleman in the 1740s.

Älvros Church, Härjedalen (sixteenth century and 1741) is typical of many up-country Swedish village churches. It is on a fine site by a great river and is of the utmost simplicity outside, with a steep-pitched roof and tall free-standing

A. Drottningholm Castle, near Stockholm (*c.* 1660). See p. 1081

B. The Kina Slott, Drottningholm (*c.* 1760). See p. 1081

A. Royal Palace, Stockholm (1690–1753). See p. 1082

B. The East India Company building, Gothenburg (1740). See p. 1082

C. The Botanicum, Uppsala (1788). See p. 1082

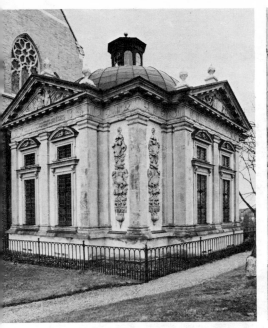

The Lars Kagg Mausoleum, Floda, Södermanland (1661). See p. 1082

B. The Lars Kagg Mausoleum,
Floda, Södermanland: interior

C. Habo Church, Västergötland (1720).
See p. 1087

D. Habo Church, Västergötland: interior

A. The Exchange, Stockholm (1767–76). See p. 1082

B. Kronborg Castle, Elsinore (1577; destroyed and rebuilt 1629). See p. 1087

C. The Royal Gate, Copenhagen (c. 1663). See p. 1087

D. Amalienborg Palace, Copenhagen (1754). See p. 1087

E. The Exchange, Copenhagen (1619–30). See p. 1079

belfry with a helmet roof, both church and belfry being built of timber. It is unusual in being an early example of a cruciform plan, and the wooden vault is painted all over to represent clouds; much of the furnishing is marbled, the pew doors are painted with bunches of flowers, a different design for each pew, and there is some rich decorative carving.

Habo Church, Västergötland (1720) (p. 1085C, D) is also typical, but is the only example in Sweden of an aisled timber church. The aisles have galleries. As is customary, every inch of the interior is painted, the structural members being marbled, and the pulpit and altar are richly designed in the Baroque manner with barley-sugar columns, swags and putti. The exterior is shingled and boarded, and there is a free-standing belfry. There are over 160 timber churches in Sweden built before 1800.

DENMARK

Kronborg Castle, Elsinore (p. 1086B), which contains the heart of the old mediaeval castle, is basically a square structure, disposed round a courtyard, with four corner towers. These vary in height, design and richness, so that the castle has an asymmetrical air, emphasized by contrasting plain walls and richly detailed surfaces pierced by many windows. Elaborate Dutch gables enhance the intricate effect, but a certain consistency is achieved by facing all walls in sandstone and roofs in copper (done at the King's insistence in 1580). Occupying a commanding site at the narrowest part of the Sound (a reminder of its original strategic purpose), the castle was rebuilt in 1629 after a fire, by Hans van Steenwinckel, a Dutch architect, but in appearance it remains largely as it was created in 1577 by Antonius van Opbergen, a Flemish architect. The immense banqueting hall is one of the longest rooms in Europe.

Frederiksborg Castle, Hillerød (1602) (p. 1078A), designed by H. and L. van Steenwinckel, occupies three sides of a quadrangle. Excluding attics and basements, it is four storeys high with corner towers and spires, and gables in the Dutch manner, and with a free-standing gate-house with helmet dome and spire. In plan the castle, divided into two symmetrical sections for summer and winter use, contains an audience chamber and three-aisled church. The walls are brick with sandstone ornamentation, and the roofs and towers are covered in copper. The interiors are very elaborate.

The **Citadel, Copenhagen** (c. 1663), designed by H. Rúse, was intended as a residence for Frederick III, who feared that he might need a defended refuge. The star-shaped and moated fortifications date partly from the previous reign, when they acted as a defence system for the city from the Baltic. The **Royal Gate** (p. 1086C), the Norway Gate, and the six barracks and two large magazines were completed in 1665. The Citadel buildings were used as a State prison until 1869.

Fredensborg Castle (1670 and 1718) (p. 1078B), originally a hunting lodge on Lake Esrom, was enlarged when the war with Sweden came to an end. At this time (1723), it comprised the main building under a dome, with an octagonal courtyard, and stable wing and servants' quarters on either side. The architect was J. C. Krieger, succeeded in 1733 by L. Thurah, who raised the mezzanine to a full storey, after the chimneys had been moved from the roof peak to the dome corners. In 1750 the banqueting hall was rebuilt and then later, towards the end of the century, the accommodation was doubled under the direction of the neoclassicist C. F. Harsdorff. In spite of its size, the castle retains the simple, homely quality appropriate to a country retreat.

The **Amalienborg Palace, Copenhagen** (1754) (p. 1086D) was designed by N. Eigtved as four similar palaces placed across four angles of an octagonal piazza, to form the cardinal features of an ambitious scheme, which was only partly realized and some of that much later in a different style. The interiors of the palaces are rich Baroque. M. Tuscher was responsible for breaking the façades into four separate structures, and the colonnades are by C. F. Harsdorff.

Other palaces are **The Hermitage, near Copenhagen**, by L. Thurah, a diminutive French 'château' with segmental gables and a säteri roof; **Jaegerspris, west of Elsinore**, a mediaeval castle enlarged and modified in the Renaissance style; **Bernsdorff, Gentofte** (1760), a Neo-Classical palace by N.-H. Jardin; and **Pederstrup, near Nakskov** (1813), a Neo-Classical country house by C. F. Hansen.

The **Frelserkirke, Copenhagen** (1682) has a Greek-cross plan similar to that of the Katarina church in Stockholm, but Lambert van Haven has not expressed it externally. The central space is covered by intersecting pitched roofs, and the building is dominated by the tall tower and helical spire designed by L. Thurah.

The **Frederik V Chapel, Roskilde Cathedral** (1774) (p. 1089B), is the finest example of the Neo-Classical style in Denmark. The entrance is between unfluted columns while fluted columns panel the walls. Shallow transepts have coffered barrel vaults, and there is a central dome of semi-elliptical section. The architect was C. F. Harsdorff.

Vor Frue Kirke, Copenhagen (1810) (p. 1089C), by C. F. Hansen, is a large church, externally plain, the front consisting of a blank wall against which is placed a Doric portico. Above is a three-tiered tower. The interior is lit from above through openings in the coffered barrel-vault supported on an arcade of Roman Doric columns. These are carried on a range of simple semicircular arches with a balustraded cornice. The figure of Christ by Thorvaldsen completes a conception at once grand and restful.

NORWAY

Austråt, Orland, Trøndelag (1654) (p. 1090A) is a most unusual Renaissance building. Embracing a courtyard with open cloisters and galleries, it has Classical columns on the ground floor, but strange naturalistic figures standing on the balustrade plinths to support the roof of the floor above.

Damsgård, Bergen (p. 1090C), is a rebuilt timber building and the best example of Rococo architecture in Norway. The architect (if any) is unknown; the building owes its present form to its owner from 1770–95, J. C. Geelmuyden. The formal arrangement of the façade—central pediment and lantern, two gabled side pavilions —contrasts with a fanciful use of Classical motifs.

Stiftsgården, Trondheim (1774) (p. 1090B) was built for a Fru Schøller, whose son-in-law, General Friedrich von Krogh, may have been the architect (an alternative possibility is J. D. Berlin). A very large, austere wooden building, with nineteen bays to the main block, its solid mass is relieved only by a small pediment gable in the centre. Interest is afforded, however, by the odd arrangement of windows— evenly spaced, with segmental and triangular pediments, not alternating, but in pairs. Vertical strips between the bays suggest pilasters.

The **Exchange, Oslo** (1826, but not completed until 1852) (p. 1090E), was designed by C. H. Grosch in association with the eminent K. F. von Schinkel, whose influence is apparent in the broad, low look, fashionable at the time, with widely-spaced Greek Doric columns, a simplified entablature, and heavy mutule blocks to the cornice and pediment. It is a building of great charm.

The **University, Oslo** (1840), by C. H. Grosch, is built in a simplified Empire style, with a central block with portico and pediment, and projecting side wings round an entrance court. It stands at the lower end of the boulevard leading to the palace, designed by the Danish architect Linstow.

A. C. F. Harsdorff's house in Kongens Nytorv, Copenhagen. See p. 1079

B. Frederik V Chapel, Roskilde Cathedral (1774). See p. 1088

C. Vor Frue Kirke, Copenhagen (1810). See p. 1088

A. Austråt, Orland, Trøndelag (1654). See p. 1088

B. Stiftsgården, Trondheim (1774). See p. 1088

C. Damsgård, near Bergen (rebuilt 1770–95). See p. 1088

D. Kongsberg Church, Norway (1740–61). See p. 1093

E. The Exchange, Oslo (1826; completed 1852). See p. 1088

F. The Norwegian Bank, Oslo (1828). See p. 1080

A. The Old Academy, Turku (1802). See p. 1093

B. The University Library, Helsinki (1836), exterior and interior. See p. 1093

A. The Old Church, Helsinki (1826). See p. 1093

B. S. Nicolai Church (Cathedral),
Helsinki (1830). See p. 1093

C. S. Nicolai Church (Cathedral),
Helsinki: interior

The **Market Halls, Oslo** (1840), also by C. H. Grosch, form a neo-romantic building group along the lower slopes of a hill. Covered space for stalls is provided behind an arcade which, in its rugged, almost Byzantine quality, foreshadows Scandinavian architecture of sixty years later.

Kongsberg Church (1740, but not completed until 1761) (p. 1090D), about 75 km south-west of Oslo, is one of the most remarkable Scandinavian churches. The architect was J. A. Stuckenbrock, Director of the local silver mines which financed the building. Externally a plain brick building, internally exuberant timber Baroque, it is much wider than long in plan and, with two tiers of galleries, seats over 2,000 people, despite its relatively small size.

FINLAND

The **Old Academy, Turku** (1802) (p. 1091A), by C. C. Gjörwell, is the first build-ing of a Neo-Classical group round the old cathedral. Simple and austere, with a very wide central pediment over eighteen bays, it has two storeys, the lower rusticated. The **New Academy** (1823), by C. F. Bassi, is rather more pretentious, with a projecting colonnaded portico. Adjacent is a house (1829), by P. J. Gylich, now part of the Academy, with a façade of eleven bays, the central three between giant pilasters under a richly detailed pediment.

The **Russian Military Hospital, Helsinki** (1826), by C. L. Engel, now part of the civil hospital, comprises three buildings with giant Ionic pilasters, linked by low portals with unfluted pairs of Doric columns and simplified basic entablatures.

The **University, Helsinki** (1828), plays a very important rôle in the scheme planned by Ehrenström and designed by C. L. Engel for the Senate Square which, measuring 171 m × 101 m (560 ft × 330 ft), slopes to the south down towards the harbour. The **Senate House** (1818) has a four-storey frontage, with central, Corinthian portico, facing the University. The latter, badly damaged in the war, has been restored, retaining an impressive three-storey staircase with Doric columns. The **University Library** (1836) (p. 1091B), also by Engel, to the north of the University, has two-storey unfluted, square-section, Corinthian pilasters, and an attic storey with semicircular windows at the ends, and plain on the eleva-tion facing the cathedral. The interior (p. 1091B) has a richly detailed coffered dome and vaults supported on unfluted Corinthian columns.

Hollola Church, near Lahti, is a mediaeval village church, which has a bell-tower (1848) reputedly designed by C. L. Engel, but built fourteen years after his death. Erected on a sophisticated Classical base, it has a small dome and drum very much in the manner of Helsinki cathedral. Other examples of strictly Classical bell-towers, usually of painted wood, are at **Jämsä** and **Saarijärvi.**

The **Old Church, Helsinki** (1826) (p. 1092A) stands apart from the main civic centre, laid out at about the same time, in a pleasant green city park. The cruciform wooden building, with pedimented portico, and pediments and pilasters to the full height of the end walls, has a central tempietto as a lantern, square, with Doric columns carrying a cupola. A charming church, it lacks the pompousness of so much of Engel's work.

S. Nicolai Church (Cathedral), Helsinki (1830) (p. 1092B, C), by C. L. Engel, standing at the top of an immense flight of steps extending almost the full width of Senate Square, is the focal point of a grand design. Cruciform, with hexastyle porticoes on each arm, the church is a square block with towers and cupolas at each corner with a small dome at the centre on a tall circular colonnaded drum. Within the Greek-cross plan, the interior is quatrefoil, with four apses round semicircular colonnades. Two tall pedimented pavilions with corner pilasters stand at either end of the flight of steps. The whole treatment is very academic.

BIBLIOGRAPHY

ABRAHAMSEN, H. *Building in Norway*. Oslo, 1959.

ALNAES, E., and others. *Norwegian Architecture*. Oslo, 1958.

BUGGE, A. *Norske Stavkirker*. Oslo, 1953.

CORNELL, H. *Den Svenska Konstens historia*. 2 vols. Stockholm, 1944–6.

DAHLBERG, E. *Suecia antiqua et hodierna*. Stockholm, 1716.

FABER, T. *Dansk Arkitektur*. Copenhagen, 1964. English ed. 1964.

HAHR, A. *Architecture in Sweden*. Stockholm, 1938.

KAVLI, G. *Norwegian Architecture past and present*. Oslo, 1958.

LANGBERG, H. *Danmarks Bygningskultur*. Copenhagen, 1955.

LUNDBERG, E. *Svensk bostad*. Stockholm, 1942.

NORDIN, E. *Swedish Timber-churches*. Stockholm, 1965.

PAULSSON, T., *Scandinavian Architecture*. London, 1958.

RICHARDS, J. M. *A Guide to Finnish Architecture*. London, 1966.

THURAH, L. de T. *Den danske Vitruvius*. Copenhagen, 1749.

VREIM, H. *Norsk Trearkitektur*. Oslo, 1947.

34
RENAISSANCE ARCHITECTURE IN RUSSIA

Sixteenth to nineteenth century

INFLUENCES

GEOGRAPHICAL

West of the Urals, Russia covers 5,500,000 km² (2,100,000 square miles); including
the vast regions to the east, the area becomes more than four times as great. In a
land of such enormous distances, and with a highly centralized government,
Renaissance architecture was established in the capital city as an importation from
abroad. Provincial buildings then followed suit, and in the nineteenth century their
design seems actually to have been dictated from S. Petersburg.

GEOLOGICAL

Except in the Vladimir region in the twelfth century, building in stone has never
been a feature of Russian architecture. The forests of the north provided ample
supplies of wood, which was in almost universal use for smaller domestic buildings
and influenced the design of churches. But throughout the vast plain which is
Russia proper, the main material of Renaissance buildings is brick.

CLIMATIC

The severe northern climate called for high-pitched roofs and the onion domes on
buildings which are indigenous to the country. Such considerations were ignored,
however, in S. Petersburg, where the aesthetic of Western styles prevailed in the
design of secular buildings.

HISTORICAL AND SOCIAL

The history of Russian architecture is not one of continuous development, but of
separate phases, each resulting from political events and associated with the arrival
of foreign architects on Russian soil. Early mediaeval church architecture derives
from Byzantine culture, which was brought to Kiev with Orthodox Christianity in
the tenth century. In the third decade of the thirteenth century Russia was overrun
by the Tartars and cut off from the rest of Europe, with an almost complete cessa-
tion of artistic activity for a century and a half. When the new Russia emerged,
centred on Moscow, Ivan III (1462–1505; the first ruler to take the title of Tsar)
sent for Italian architects to reconstruct the Kremlin. A third dramatic change of
direction occurred with the founding of S. Petersburg by Peter the Great in 1703,
and the construction of his new capital as a window on the West. This third period
merits more recognition than it usually receives, as a major achievement of Baroque
and Classicism on a scale unequalled in any other city.

The Italian architects brought to Moscow by Ivan III succeeded in re-establishing
the techniques and craftsmanship almost lost during the period under the

Tartars. Following the union of the Ukraine with Russia in 1667, Baroque idioms from Poland and Lithuania found their way to Moscow by way of Kiev, and were applied as decoration to structures of genuinely Russian character. But the building of S. Petersburg represented a complete break with Russian popular and traditional architecture, and the imposition of styles dictated by the most absolute and autocratic monarchy in Europe. Coinciding with the social upheaval caused by Peter the Great's reforms, the new styles were resented as un-Russian and Western, an attitude still apparent in Dostoievsky's description of 'the most abstract and artificial city in existence'. Baroque and Classical S. Petersburg has survived both the 1917 October Revolution, commemorated in its new name of Leningrad, and the terrible siege of 1941–4 by the German armies. Neither the eclectic buildings of the later nineteenth century, nor the massive expansion of industry and housing by the Soviet government have intruded upon the scale and character of the Renaissance core of the city.

ARCHITECTURAL CHARACTER

The brick walls and towers of the Moscow Kremlin, and the Cathedral of the Dormition (the coronation church of the Tsars), were built by Italian architects in the last quarter of the fifteenth century, but deliberately related to mediaeval Russian prototypes. In the sixteenth century, side by side with the many domes of monastic foundations, a new type of votive church appeared in the form of an octagonal tower crowned with a tent-shaped roof. Baroque ornament applied in contrasting colours to these varied forms produced a picturesque blend of Russian and Western architecture, the 'Moscow' or 'Naryshkin' Baroque.

S. Petersburg, the first great city of modern times to be built to a pre-determined plan, reflects the taste of Peter the Great and his successors, and their choice of architects throughout the eighteenth and first half of the nineteenth century. Although largely designed by foreigners, the buildings show a vastness of scale, an exuberance and use of colour which are essentially Russian. Secular architecture is predominant, and the granite quays of the Neva, the intersecting canals and the immense squares are lined with great palaces and public buildings of brick, plastered and painted yellow, blue or green, to offset the white of Classical Orders and decoration. The design of all buildings was controlled and none were allowed higher than the Winter Palace, except for the occasional gilt needle-spire or church dome punctuating the skyline. Such interiors as have survived are resplendent with glittering chandeliers and marble columns.

EXAMPLES
MOSCOW

The **Cathedral of the Archangel Michael** (1505–9) by Alevisio Novi, the latest of the three main Kremlin Cathedrals, is a traditional five-domed church except for the two-storey façades, which have Italian Renaissance pilasters surmounted by scallop-shell niches.

The **Facets Palace** (1487–91) in the Kremlin, built by Pietro Solari and Marco Ruffo for Ivan III, is the earliest remaining secular building in Moscow. Its name refers to the faceted patterning of the façade, resembling some palaces in northern Italy. Inside is a vaulted throne room, and the windows, now straight-headed, were once arched.

The **Church of the Intercession of the Virgin** (1693) (p. 1099A), at **Fili,** was built for an uncle of Peter the Great, Prince Lev Kirillovich Naryshkin, whose name is given to the Naryshkin Baroque. Basically, it is a church of the sixteenth-century pyramidal type to which Ukrainian Baroque ornament is applied. The subtleties of Baroque three-dimensional design appear in the upward progression through a cube with apsidal projections on four sides, a simple cube, and two octagons diminishing in size. The walls are of pink brick, with colonnettes, window surrounds and parapets of white stone, a bulbous gilt cupola at the summit, and four others at mid-height.

The **Church of the Resurrection** (1687) in the Kadashi district, has the same pink and white Naryshkin decoration as at Fili, but only the tall octagonal belfry is pyramidal and the church is the usual cube with five domes.

S. PETERSBURG (LENINGRAD)

The examples in this section are grouped under the names of their architects.

DOMENICO TRESSINI (1670–1734), a Swiss-Italian, was put in charge of building operations by Peter the Great in 1705. He had worked in Denmark and belongs to the Dutch-inspired school of Northern Baroque.

The **Peter and Paul Fortress,** on the Peter Island which was the first site of the new city, is practically all that remains of Tressini's work. The **Cathedral** (1714–25), which has been partly reconstructed, lies behind the brick bastions of the fortress. Its high tower of 122 m (400 ft) and slender gilt spire symbolizes a defiant break with the domed churches of old Russia.

BARTOLOMEO RASTRELLI (1700–71), the son of an Italian sculptor, came to Russia as a boy, studied in France, probably visited Austria and Italy, and was entrusted with all her important commissions by the Empress Elizabeth (1741–62). His architecture is powerfully Baroque in form, with Rococo decorative motifs apparently derived from Austria, and shows an uncanny ability to assimilate essentially Russian qualities.

Peterhof (1747–53), now named Petrodvorets, was intended by Peter the Great to be the Russian Versailles. Alexandre Le Blond, a French architect engaged in 1716, built a plain two-storey palace, which Elizabeth ordered Rastrelli to double in length. He retained Le Blond's main block, with an extra storey added and on either side a low wing terminating in a pavilion. The most striking feature is the pavilion roofs, elaborate Rococo versions of traditional Russian domes and lanterns. Peterhof is noted for its fountains, waterfalls and statues, and smaller palaces and pavilions in the great park. All the Imperial palaces near Leningrad suffered in the Second World War, but Peterhof was the most completely destroyed and the first to be reconstructed.

Smolny Convent (1748–55) has as its central feature the high dome of a great cathedral, flanked on the diagonal axes by four towers with cupolas and lanterns. The lower convent buildings spread around it in a cruciform layout, with four subsidiary domes. The contemporary symmetrical plan and white-on-blue Rococo ornament combine with the fantasy of a silhouette evocative of an old Russian monastery. Rastrelli did not complete the work; some changes were made in his design and a belfry tower which would have been the highest in the city was never built.

The **Cathedral of S. Andrew, Kiev** (1747–8) (p. 1099B), completed by Rastrelli, is similar to that of Smolny Convent, but is a detached building. It demonstrates to the full his success in applying three-dimensional Baroque forms to the needs of the Orthodox Church.

During the later years of Elizabeth's reign Rastrelli was occupied with the two greatest of the Imperial palaces, each posing the formidable problem of designing an immensely long façade of uniform height.

The **Ekaterininsky (Catherine) Palace** (1749–56) (p. 1099C), formerly the Great Palace, at Tsarskoe Selo (Tsar's Village), now re-named Pushkin, is no less than 298 m (978 ft) in length. As at Peterhof, Rastrelli had to incorporate an existing building. Above a basement storey, the giant Corinthian Order of the principal and attic storeys carries a balustrade and broken pediments. The façade is broken down into sections, with groups of columns supported by caryatids, and varied treatment of the windows. The huge scale, the white columns and blue walls, the gilt domes of the chapel, are all unmistakeably Russian. Originally the external Rococo ornament was gilt, and the effect of overpowering richness can still be savoured in some interiors which have been restored.

The **Winter Palace** (1754–62) is the most important building in S. Petersburg, and has its long façades towards the Neva and Palace Square. It replaced three earlier palaces and has suffered from a disastrous fire in 1837, the famous storming during the October Revolution, and damage in the Second World War. The palace now houses the State Hermitage Museum, and the only surviving Rastrelli interior is the magnificent white marble stairway, but the exterior is essentially as he designed it. The façades are painted green and white, and have three main storeys and two superimposed Corinthian Orders. The elongated giant columns of the upper storeys support a heavy entablature, and balustrades and pediments adorned with statues and vases.

The Empress Catherine II (the Great) (1762–96) shared Elizabeth's passion for building, but not her taste, and she immediately sought to replace the Rococo with a plainer and more Classical style. Not surprisingly, the architects already working in S. Petersburg could not entirely adapt themselves to the change.

ANTONIO RINALDI (c. 1709–after 1790), an Italian, came to Russia in 1755.

The **Marble Palace** (1768–72), the only palace remaining unaltered of several built by Rinaldi, was so named because of its marble facing, an innovation in S. Petersburg. The three-storey façade is of Classical proportions, with giant pilasters above a rusticated base, but a central round-headed niche with a coat of arms on an attic above it is one of several Baroque overtones from the previous reign.

CHARLES CAMERON (c. 1740–1812/20), a Scotsman of whose early life little is known, except that he travelled in Italy and published a book on The Baths of the Romans, was in Russia by 1778. He enjoyed the full confidence of Catherine and satisfied her taste for interiors more intimate in scale and decorated in the style of Classical antiquity. The influence of Robert Adam and of Clérisseau is apparent in his work, but translated into a more exuberant and luxurious idiom.

Tsarskoe Selo was the main scene of Cameron's employment by the Empress. He redecorated three suites of rooms in Rastrelli's Great Palace, and added a wing consisting of the Agate Pavilion leading to the Cameron Gallery (1783–6), an open Ionic colonnade at first-floor level overlooking the park and lake, to which there is access by a spectacular double-flight staircase. Cameron's interiors made use of such exotic materials as agate, jasper and bronze, also of coloured glass and Wedgwood plaques. Whereas the walls of Adam's Etruscan rooms were painted in the manner of Herculaneum, Cameron designed similar motifs in relief and with slender columns of polychrome porcelain.

The **Pavlovsky Palace, Pavlovsk** (1781–96) was built by Catherine for her son, the future Tsar Paul. A square block with a low central dome and curved service wings, it is somewhat marred by later additions. Cameron's share in the sumptuous interior decoration is not always distinguishable from that of Brenna, Voronikhin

Church of the Intercession of the Holy
Virgin, Fili (1693). See p. 1097

B. S. Andrew's Cathedral, Kiev (1747–8).
See p. 1097

C. The Ekaterininsky (Catherine) Palace (formerly the Great Palace), Pushkin
(1749–56). See p. 1098

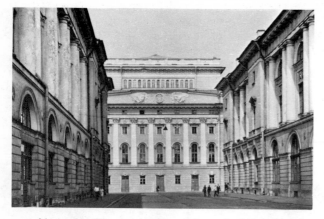

A. Alexandra Theatre (1828–32) from Architect Rossi Street, Leningrad. See p. 1102

B. Pavlovsky Palace, Pavlovs nr Leningrad (1781–96): th Grecian Hall. See p. 1098

C. Former General Staff Headquarters, Leningrad (1819–29). See p. 1101

D. The Academy of Sciences, Leningrad (1783–7). See p. 1101

E. The Admiralty, Leningrad (1806–15). See p. 1101

and others. The Grecian Hall (p. 1100B) seems to be modelled on Adam's Great Hall at Kedleston (p. 1042C), but many of the rooms are surprisingly domestic in scale. The round Temple of Friendship (1780) is one of several delightful garden pavilions by Cameron, and the first building in Russia with Greek Doric columns.

GIACOMO QUARENGHI (1744–1817), of Bergamo, arrived in Russia in 1780. He had made a close study of both Roman and Italian Renaissance architecture, particularly the work of Palladio.

The **Academy of Sciences** (1783–7) (p. 1100D) is a rectangular block which has three ranges of plain windows and a central portico with columns and pediment, depending for its effect on scale and proportion. The basic design and severe Palladian manner were repeated by Quarenghi in many important buildings up to the end of Catherine's reign.

The **Hermitage Theatre** (1782–5) was built with its axis parallel with the Neva and reveals at one end the curved wall of a tiered semicircular auditorium. Corinthian columns and statues in niches are the main ornament of the interior and also of the façades, imparting the more festive character suited to a theatre.

The **Smolny Institute** (1806–8), adjoining Rastrelli's convent, was Quarenghi's last and largest commission. The long façade has a central portico and two projecting wings, and Ionic columns are the only ornament.

The first half of the nineteenth century saw an even greater extension of S. Petersburg, still in the Classical style at a time when it was declining elsewhere in Europe. The impetus was given by Tsar Alexander I (1801–25) and continued into the earlier years of his successor, Nicholas I (1825–55).

ADRIAN DMITRIEVITCH ZAKHAROV (1761–1811), one of several Russians worthy to rank with the best foreign architects, is remembered for one building as conspicuous as the Winter Palace, and even larger.

The **Admiralty** (1806–15) (p. 1100E), a monumental rebuilding of Peter the Great's foundation, is no less than 408 m (1,340 ft) long. Although Zakharov was influenced by French Academic architecture and the new fashion for Greek rather than Roman Classicism, his design is unprecedented and eminently Russian. The central courtyard is entered under a round-headed archway in a square pavilion, above which are piled up the Mausoleum of Halicarnassos, a Baroque dome and lantern, and a Gothic spire! On either side a long plain wing leads to a portico and ends in a square block with a low dome. The massive but simple shapes give a coherent and integrated form to the vast building.

CARLO ROSSI (1755–1849), the main agent in the great building programme which followed Napoleon's retreat of 1812, has left his imprint on S. Petersburg more than any other architect. Like his contemporary John Nash, Rossi excelled less in the detailed design of buildings than in their disposition to form an architectural panorama extending over whole districts of the city.

The **Mikhailovsky Palace** (1819–23), built for the Tsar's brother Grand Duke Michael, occupies one side of a large square (now Arts Square) entirely designed by Rossi. The central block has a rich Corinthian Order and pedimented portico, and faces a courtyard formed between two wings in plainer Doric style. Rossi's decorative features are white and his walls yellow, the standard colouring of nineteenth-century Russian Neo-Classicism. The Palace, now the Russian Museum, has retained its original grandiose staircase.

The former **General Staff Headquarters** (1819–29) (p. 1100C) is a huge three-storey crescent, quite plain but for the central feature, a triumphal arch surmounted by a quadriga. It forms the perfect foil to Rastrelli's Winter Palace facing it across the immense Palace Square, and must rank as Rossi's masterpiece and the swan-song of Classical townscape on the grandest scale.

The **Alexandra Theatre** (1828–32), now the Pushkin Theatre, is at the centre of a whole complex of buildings around a street linking two squares. The rectangular block of the theatre, with Corinthian columns and pilasters, closes the vista along a street with identical façades and coupled Doric columns, now named Architect Rossi Street (p. 1100A).

AUGUSTE RICARD DE MONTFERRAND (1786–1858), a previously little-known French architect, designed two prominent features of the S. Petersburg townscape which represent the final and declining phase of Neo-Classicism.

The **Cathedral of S. Isaac** (1818–58) combines huge scale with costly materials, such as the Corinthian red granite columns and bronze capitals of four porticoes, and the drum of the gilt central dome. But S. Isaac's does not compare well with other great European domed cathedrals, because of a general heaviness and a failure to integrate its parts to a unified composition.

The **Alexander Column** (1834), a gigantic monolith of red granite weighing 600 tons, carries an angel holding aloft a cross. Although not the most graceful of monuments, its siting and scale make it an essential and successful element in the grand composition of Palace Square.

BIBLIOGRAPHY

AKADEMIA ARKHITEKTURY SSSR. *Istorija Russkoi Arkhitektury*. 2nd ed. Moscow, 1956.

ARKIN, D. *Rastrelli*. Moscow, 1954.

BRONSHTEIN, S. S. *Arkhitektura Goroda Pushkina* (Architecture of the town of Pushkin). Moscow, 1940.

EGOROV, I. A. *The Architectural Planning of St Petersburg*. Cleveland, Ohio, 1969.

HAMILTON, G. H. *The Art and Architecture of Russia*. Harmondsworth and Baltimore, 1954.

HAUTECOEUR, L. *L'Architecture classique à Saint-Pétersbourg à la fin du XVIIIe siècle*. Paris, 1912.

HOFER, P. 'Montferrand and the Alexandrine Column' (at Leningrad). *Gazette des Beaux-Arts*, 6e pér., XXVI, 1944.

LUKOMSKI, G. K. *Mobilier et décoration des anciens palais impériaux russes*. Paris, 1928.

MARSDEN, C. *Palmyra of the North, the First Days of St Petersburg*. London, 1942.

PETROV, A. N. and others. *Pamiatinki Arkhitektury Leningrada* (Architectural Monuments of Leningrad). Leningrad, 1969. (Has English summary.)

PILJAVSKI, V. I. *L'Attivitá artistica di Giacomo Quarenghi in Russia*. Bergamo, 1967.

RAE, I. *Charles Cameron, Architect to the Court of Russia*. London, 1971.

RÉAU, L. *L'Art russe de Pierre le Grand à nos jours*. Paris, 1922.

TALBOT RICE, T. *A Concise History of Russian Art*. London, 1963.

35

RENAISSANCE
AND POST-RENAISSANCE
ARCHITECTURE OUTSIDE
EUROPE

The rediscovery of the Classical world, which inspired the Renaissance in art and architecture, coincided with the awakening of colonial aspirations in European nations, stimulated perhaps by the military, maritime and commercial enterprises of their forbears of Classical Antiquity. It was therefore a variously interpreted amalgam of Renaissance ideas which the British, French, Spanish and Portuguese took to the Americas; the Dutch to South Africa; the British, French, Portuguese, Danes and Dutch to India and South-East Asia, and the British to Australia.

THE AMERICAS

ARCHITECTURAL CHARACTER

In general, the architecture of a particular region reflected that of the settlers' homeland, with modifications occasioned by climate, the types of building material obtainable, and the quality of labour available. Thus in seventeenth-century New England building followed the pattern of English weather-boarded, heavy timber-frame prototypes (p. 1105A), while in eighteenth-century Virginia we find a 'Georgian' architecture, often almost indistinguishable from that of eighteenth-century England (p. 1105C). Colonial architecture of Latin America followed the pattern of Spanish and Portuguese work. Early examples show derivation from Spanish Mediaeval prototypes (p. 1107), and Moorish influences (p. 1111) are apparent. The Plateresque, Churrigueresque, Baroque and Antiquarian phases of the architecture of the Spanish homeland are all mirrored in the work of Spanish America (pp. 1107, 1111). Architecture of Portuguese Brazil in the second half of the eighteenth century had much in common with the Rococo of Central Europe (p. 1108).

EXAMPLES

DOMESTIC BUILDINGS

Capen House, Topsfield, Mass. (1683) (p. 1105A), an excellent example of seventeenth-century colonial architecture in New England, is of heavy timber-frame construction, the first floor and gables being carried forward as 'jetties' as in antecedent English examples, while the central, clustered brick chimney is reminiscent of similar features in England. Externally, the house is clad in weatherboarding and has a wood shingle roof. Internal walls and partitions are faced with vertical boarding, beams are left exposed and decoration is sparse, being confined to such details as the stair balusters. Windows are small, leaded casements. The ground floor is divided into two rooms by a central brick core, incorporating two fireplaces back-to-back. An entrance lobby is at one end of the brick core, from which a staircase leads to the upper floor. Other houses of a similar character are: **Whipple House, Ipswich, Mass.** (1639); **Scotch-Boardman House, Saugus, Mass.** (1651); **Fairbanks House, Dedham, Mass.** (*c.* 1637); **Whitman House, Farmington, Connecticut** (1664); **Paul Revere House, Boston, Mass.** (*c.* 1676); **John Ward House, Salem, Mass.** (1684); **House of the Seven Gables, Salem, Mass.** (*c.* 1670).

Bacon's Castle, Surry County, Virginia (*c.* 1655) (p. 1105E) is cruciform in plan. Built in brick, with its curved Flemish gables, high clustered chimneys and Classical details in the brickwork over its entrance, the house has much in common with Jacobean examples in England.

Abraham Ackerman House, Hackensack, N.J. (1704) shows Dutch influence. Its roof is of the 'gambrel' or mansard type with widely projecting eaves, covered in wood shingles, as also are the gables and dormer cheeks. The walls of the ground floor are of roughly-dressed, coursed masonry. Other houses showing Dutch influence are: **Dyckman House, New York, N.Y.** (*c.* 1783); **Terheun House, Hackensack, N.J.** (*c.* 1709); **Vreeland House, Englewood, N.J.** (1818) and **Jan Ditmars House, Brooklyn, N.Y.** (*c.* 1700).

Parlange, Pointe Coupée Parish, Louisiana (1750) (p. 1105B), a French plantation house, has an open, colonnaded verandah running round the house on both floors, a feature providing protection from the hot sun and heavy rains of the area. The high-pitched, hipped roof is covered in shingles and, because of the dampness of the site, the ground floor is constructed of brick, although the first floor is of timber. Other examples showing a similar character are: **Connelly's Tavern, Natchez, Mississippi** (*c.* 1795); **Keller Mansion, St. Charles Parish, La.** (*c.* 1801).

Westover, Charles City County, Va. (*c.* 1730–4) (p. 1105C), one of the most distinguished eighteenth-century Virginian plantation houses, has a close affinity with English Georgian work. A seven-bay brick structure of two storeys, there are further rooms in the steeply-pitched hipped roof, which is punctuated with elegant dormer windows. The central entrance to the main front is accentuated by a Baroque-like broken pediment, finely carved in Portland stone, probably shipped specially from England for this purpose. The house is flanked symmetrically by (though originally not physically linked with) two minor structures, one providing kitchen and servants' quarters, the other serving as the plantation office. Internally the house has finely proportioned rooms, with their superbly executed details ranking with the best contemporary work of the mother country. Some ceilings have applied designs, cast in composition and almost certainly imported from England where they were currently fashionable.

Other colonial houses of Georgian character are: **Mount Pleasant, Philadelphia** (1761–2), built in stuccoed rubble, its stone details probably derived from a contemporary English pattern book like those of Batty Langley (p. 983), has a low-pitched, lead-covered roof, truncated to form a flat terrace or deck, a feature of many American houses of this period known as a 'captain's walk'; **Miles Brewton House, Charleston, South Carolina** (1765–9) has a fine two-storeyed pedimented, colonnaded porch and similar features are to be found at **Shirley, Charles**

Capen House, Topsfield, Massachusetts (1683). See p. 1103

B. Parlange, Pointe Coupée Parish, Louisiana (1750). See p. 1104

C. Westover, Charles City County, Virginia (c. 1730–4). See p. 1104

D. Drayton Hall, South Carolina (1738–42). See p. 1107

E. Bacon's Castle, Surry County, Virginia (c. 1655). See p. 1104

A. Ecala Palace, Querétaro (*c.* 1785).
See p. 1107

B. S. Pedro dos Clérigos,
Recife (1729–). See p. 1108

C. Mercedarian Monastery, Quito (*c.* 1630–).
See p. 1108

D. The Sanctuary, Ocotlán
(*c.* 1745–). See p. 1108

E. The Cathedral, Mexico City (1563–1667).
See p. 1107

F. Casa del Alfeñique, Puebla
(*c.* 1780). See p. 1107

City County, Va. (*c.* 1769), **Drayton Hall, S.C.** (1738–42) (p. 1105D) and in Thomas Jefferson's first design for his own house, **Monticello, near Charlottesville, Va.** (1770–5).

Brandon, Prince George County, Va. (*c.* 1765) has a more monumental plan arrangement showing Palladian influence, and the house is flanked on either side by minor buildings to which it is joined by low linking elements. A similar plan arrangement is found at **Mount Vernon, Fairfax County, Va.** (1757–87), **Mount Airy, Richmond County, Va.** (1758–62), **Tulip Hill, Anne Arundel County, Maryland** (*c.* 1756) and the **Hammond-Harwood House, Annapolis, Md.** (1773–4).

The **Ecala Palace, Querétaro, Mexico** (*c.* 1785) (p. 1106A), with its richly decorated façade, heavy Baroque pediments over the first-floor windows with their lace-like wrought-iron balconies, deep, arcaded loggia on the ground floor and, under the roof cornice, a wide frieze of blue and white tiles, provides a fine example of a Spanish colonial palace.

The **Casa del Alfeñique, Puebla, Mexico** (*c.* 1780) (p. 1106F) is particularly noteworthy on account of its lavish use of 'azulejos' (glazed tiles) as a facing. Its façade is covered with large, octagonal, unglazed, red tiles and chequered with smaller, white glazed tiles, decorated with blue flowers.

Other important houses in colonial Latin America are: **Torre Tagle Palace, Lima, Peru** (*c.* 1730) showing pronounced Moro-Spanish characteristics; **Quinta de Presa, Lima, Peru** (1766), with its pink colour-washed, adobe walls, evocative of Austrian Rococo work; and the **Saldanha Palace, Salvador, Brazil** (*c.* 1720) with a richly carved entrance incorporating flanking caryatids.

RELIGIOUS BUILDINGS

The **Cathedral, Santo Domingo (now Ciudad Trujillo), Dominican Republic** (1521–41), an important example of the use of late Gothic forms in colonial architecture, has chevet and lateral chapels, and Gothic ribbed vaulting over its square nave bays. The west façade is in the Plateresque style.

The **Cathedral, Mexico City** (1563–1667) (p. 1106E) replaced an earlier primitive, flat-roofed structure (1525–). The building shows a curious mingling of Baroque and more severely Classical features. With three aisles to both nave and chancel, and rows of side chapels filling the length of the building on both sides, the church measures 54 m (177 ft) in width and is 118 m (387 ft) long. The nave and shallow transepts are covered by barrel vaults pierced by lunettes, while each bay of the side aisles is domed. The clustered piers of the nave are each made up of four engaged Roman-Doric columns, the fluting of which is continued round the nave arches. Externally, the west façade is flanked by twin towers rising 62 m (203 ft), but these and the remainder of the elevational detail (carried out in buff-coloured limestone with statues and other detail in white marble, to the designs of José Damián Ortiz de Castro) date from 1786 and are Neo-Classic in character. The present dome and lantern and some of the decorative work on the west front are by Manuel Tolsa, and date from the early nineteenth century.

The **Cathedral, Lima, Peru** (1543–51; altered and enlarged *c.* 1570–; rebuilt *c.* 1750–) provides a fascinating story of the battle against earthquakes. After the collapse of the original stone vaults in the early seventeenth century, these were rebuilt in brick. Further earthquakes caused the latter to be replaced by vaults of wood, reed and plaster in the mid-eighteenth century and this form of construction has been retained for various later rebuildings. Externally, the church with its twin west towers and enriched central entrance bay (although heavily restored in 1940) retains original work by the sculptor Juan Martínez de Arrona (1562–1635) and, despite its Baroque flavour, has much in common with the work of Juan de Herrera, architect of the Escorial (p. 967).

Among numerous examples, the following Latin American colonial religious buildings are particularly noteworthy: the **Cathedral, Puebla, Mexico** (1562–1664); the **Cathedral, Monterrey, Mexico** (1630–1800); **Mercedarian Monastery and Cloister, Cuzco, Peru** (1650–69); **Mercedarian Cloister, Mexico City** (1634–); **Mercedarian Monastery, Quito, Ecuador** (c. 1630–) (p. 1106C) and **College of San Francisco Javier, Sucre, Bolivia** (c. 1624–).

S. Pedro dos Clérigos, Recife, Brazil (1729–) (p. 1106B) by Ferreira Jacome is an example of Portuguese colonial work. Characterized by the tall, elegant proportions of its west front, the church is generally evocative of mid-European Baroque. The same qualities are seen in the churches of the **Rosário** (1725–77) and **S. Antonio** (1750–3), both at Recife.

S. Francisco de Assis, Ouro Preto, Brazil (1766–) (p. 1109A), is probably by Antonio Francisco Lisbôa (known as Aleijadinho), a mulatto architect-sculptor of genius, who certainly carved the exquisite 'pedra-sabão' of the Borrominesque façade of this Brazilian church. Aleijadinho is better known for the striking series of statues of the prophets which line the steps leading to the church at **Congonhas do Campo** (1800–5) (p. 1109B).

The **Sanctuary, Ocotlán, Mexico** (c. 1745–) (p. 1106D), marking a famous pilgrimage site, has a façade of gleaming white stucco shaped into fantastic Churriguresque forms, flanked by slender twin towers covered with bright red tiles in a scale-like pattern. The interior is equally rich, much of its carving being by the eighteenth-century Indian sculptor, Francisco Miguel.

S. Luke's Church, Smithfield, Va. (1682–) (p. 1109D) shows the influence of English Mediaeval parish churches. Built in brick, the church consists of a simple, rectangular nave with a squat, square tower at the west end. The gables to the nave have stepped parapets reminiscent of Dutch work, while the side walls are strengthened by mediaeval-like buttresses. With their crudely-formed brick tracery, the windows also indicate a Mediaeval prototype.

Bruton Parish Church, Williamsburg, Va. (1711–15) (p. 1109F), a simple brick structure of cruciform plan, has round-headed windows lighting the nave and transepts and an internal west gallery. The square west tower was added in 1769; this is surmounted by a timber steeple, a much-simplified version of an English eighteenth-century spire like that by Gibbs at S. Martin-in-the-Fields, London (p. 1056).

S. Michael's Church, Charleston, S.C. (1752–61) (p. 1109C), a beautiful example of a fully-developed English colonial church in the style of James Gibbs, has a Classical entrance portico, surmounted by an elegant timber steeple built up of a series of diminishing octagonal drums with pilasters, entablatures and arched openings to each stage, all reminiscent of S. Martin-in-the-Fields, London (p. 1056). The main body of the church is of stuccoed brick; there is a gallery around three sides of the interior, carried on timber Ionic columns.

Christ Church (Old North), Boston, Mass. (1723), a simple brick building with an internal gallery and box-pews, has a square western tower surmounted by a timber steeple, a simplified version, perhaps, of that of Wren's S. Dunstan-in-the-East (1693) (p. 1022).

King's Chapel, Boston, Mass. (1749–54) (p. 1109E), a stone church, considerably grander than most English colonial examples with an unpedimented Ionic portico surmounted by a square tower (the latter uncompleted); **Christ Church, Cambridge, Mass.** (1759–61) built in timber; and **Touro Synagogue, Newport,**

A. S. Francisco de Assis, Ouro Preto, Brazil (1766–). See p. 1108

B. Congonhas do Campo, Brazil (1800–5). See p. 1108

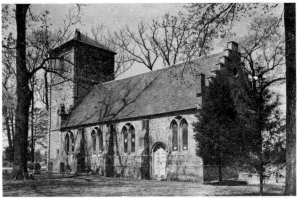

C. S. Michael's Church, Charleston, South Carolina (1752–61). See p. 1108

D. S. Luke's Church, Smithfield, Virginia (1682–). See p. 1108

E. King's Chapel, Boston, Massachusetts (1749–54): interior. See p. 1108

F. Bruton Parish Church, Williamsburg, Virginia (1711–15). See p. 1108

A. The Capitol, Williamsburg, Virginia
(1701–5). See p. 1112

B. Independence Hall, Philadelphia
(1731–91). See p. 1112

C. The Cabildo, New Orleans, Louisiana (1795–). See p. 1111

Rhode Island (1759–63) were all designed by Peter Harrison (1716–75), an English sea-captain from York.

The **First Baptist Meeting House, Providence, R.I.** (1774–5); **Christ Church, Philadelphia, Pennsylvania** (1727–54) and **S. Paul's Chapel, New York, N.Y.** (1764–6) are other important examples of English colonial churches and show the influence of the work of Wren and, more particularly, James Gibbs through his *Book of Architecture* (1728) and his other publications (p. 982).

The **Parish Church of Lacadie, Quebec** (1810) is a rare surviving example of the traditional church of French Canada, externally austere, internally exuberant and Baroque. It was designed by the Abbé Pierre Conefroy, who was responsible for several similar buildings reflecting the attitudes of an earlier generation.

EDUCATIONAL, CIVIC AND PUBLIC BUILDINGS

The **Governmental Palace, Guadalajara, Mexico** (1751–75), by Nicholas Enriquez del Castillo and José Conique, presents a rich mixture of Churrigueresque, Baroque and Neo-Mudéjar elements, while the patio of the **University, Antigua, Guatemala** (rebuilt in 1763) is an important example of Neo-Mudéjar design in Latin America.

The **Real Cabildo (Town Hall), Antigua, Guatemala** (1743–), an example of the more strictly Classical style favoured for colonial government buildings at this time, has arcaded loggias to both floors of its nine-bay façade.

The **Vizcaínas, (formerly Colegio de San Ignacio), Mexico City** (1734–53) by Pedro Bueno, a school for poor girls, is a good example of the current idiom for public buildings in Spanish America, while the **Cabildo (Town Hall), New Orleans, La.** (1795–) (p. 1110C), built to house the Spanish administrative council during its period of control in this area, shows the academic trend of late eighteenth-century Spanish design. The open arcaded ground floor, the arcaded first floor with its pilasters, the central pedimented feature, the weight and richness of the stone detail and the academic use of classical motifs, relate the building closely to contemporary Spanish work. The mansard roof was a later addition (*c.* 1850).

The **Penitentiary, Ouro Preto, Brazil** (1784–8) by Francisco Pinto de Abreu, combined the functions of town hall and prison, and despite its purpose, has a Rococo elegance in its façade.

The **Governor's Palace, Santa Fé, N.M.** (1610–14) was the dominating building in the original walled 'presidio' or administrative enclosure of this outpost of the Spanish Empire. The building, a long single-storeyed structure, constructed by local Indian labour in adobe brick, is approached from the 'plaza' of Santa Fé through an open loggia or 'portal' running the length of the palace and terminated at each end by simple adobe pavilions. The flat roof of the building is formed of round logs, supported along the portal by crude columns, hewn from whole tree trunks, with carved bracket-heads.

The **Governor's Palace, San Antonio, Texas** (1749), built in stone, with fine wrought-iron window grilles, possessed a ballroom and grand reception rooms overlooking its internal patio, and evinces the high standard of life even in remote parts of the Spanish Empire.

William and Mary College, Williamsburg, Va. (1695–1702) may have been designed by Sir Christopher Wren in his capacity of Royal Surveyor of England. If this were so, the drawings provided by Wren must have been largely diagrammatic, for records state that they were 'adapted to the nature of the country by the gentlemen there'. The plan is U-shaped, the three-storeyed central block containing classrooms, while two projecting wings house, respectively, the college chapel and refectory. On the west side of the building, an open arcaded loggia extends between the two projecting wings. The building is Georgian in character, its central block surmounted by an elegant cupola.

Harvard University, Cambridge, Mass., founded as Harvard College in 1636, is the oldest university in the U.S.A. Nothing remains of the first buildings, constructed largely of timber, but the following are important: **Massachusetts Hall** (1718–20); **Holden Chapel** (1742–4); **Hollis Hall** (1762–3); and **Harvard Hall** (1764–6), with its pedimented gables, full cornice and comparatively massive cupola, representing an early attempt to introduce a more monumental character into North American collegiate architecture.

Other important colonial university buildings include: **Nassau Hall, Princeton University, N.J.** (1754–6) (much altered); **University Hall, Brown University, Providence, R.I.,** (1770–1) and **Connecticut Hall, Yale University, New Haven, Conn.** (1750–2).

The **Capitol, Williamsburg, Va.** (1701–5; rebuilding completed 1934) (p. 1110A) is an accurate reconstruction of the Capitol as it was completed in 1705. The latter was replaced after a fire in 1747 by another building, which was in turn burned down in 1832. The plan is H-shaped, with two apsidal-ended wings. The entrance is through a central linking block which, on the ground floor, takes the form of an open arcaded loggia and, on the first floor, housed a conference room for joint meetings between the Governor's Council and members of the House of Burgesses. Built of brick and basically Georgian in character, the building shows the effect of climate on architectural style; because of the heat of the Virginian summers the proportion of solid to void is considerably higher than in English examples. The open entrance loggia, permitting the free circulation of air, is similarly explained.

The **Governor's Palace, Williamsburg, Va.** (1706–20; reconstructed 1932) is a particularly fine piece of Georgian design, evocative of the work of Wren. With its magnificent gardens and fine ballroom (a later addition) it provides evidence of the sophistication of life in early eighteenth-century Virginia.

Independence Hall, Philadelphia, Pa. (1731–91) (p. 1110B) was the scene of the signing of the Declaration of Independence on July 4th, 1776, and is therefore a monument of great significance to Americans. Work on the State House, as it was called, commenced in 1731, and the central block was completed by 1745. The tower with its fine steeple was built 1750–3; becoming unsound, this was demolished in 1781 and rebuilt on the original lines by William Strickland in 1832. The two-storeyed flanking buildings, connected with the central block by arcaded links, were erected in 1736 and 1739 respectively and have recently been restored. In 1789 and 1791 further buildings were added, completing the seven-unit complex and providing a civic centre perhaps unequalled in eighteenth-century America. The buildings, essentially Georgian in character, are in brick with white stone quoins and other dressings. The central block is surmounted by a balustraded roof-deck, above which rises the tower and its elaborate timber lantern, a rich piece of design forming one of the finest Georgian towers in America or Britain.

Carpenters Hall, Philadelphia, Pa. (1770–1), built as the headquarters of the 'Carpenters Company', i.e. the master carpenters, of Philadelphia, is a simple Georgian building of cruciform plan, its four gables being treated as pediments. A timber lantern surmounts the building which to Americans is of particular importance, since it was here that the First Continental Congress gathered on September 5th, 1774.

Province House, Halifax, Nova Scotia (1811–18) by John Merrick, a simple sturdy Classical building in stone, is strongly evocative of English Georgian work and set the pattern for other English administrative buildings in Canada.

SOUTH AFRICA

ARCHITECTURAL CHARACTER

Cape Town was founded by the Dutchman Jan van Riebeck in 1650, and from that time Dutch influence has been strong. Colonial buildings had much in common with contemporary examples in Holland (p. 939). Flemish gables, often of a curvilinear form, decorated with scrolls and 'strapwork' (p. 942), are found in surviving seventeenth- and eighteenth-century examples, while some eighteenth-century work incorporates charming Rococo details. Brick and stucco were popular building materials, and thatch, tiles and shingles were used for roofs.

EXAMPLES

Burgher Watch House, Cape Town (1755–) (p. 1116A); **Lutheran Parsonage, Cape Town** (c. 1780); **Government House, Cape Town** (1682; much altered 1798–; considerable later additions); **Rhone, Groot Drakenstein** (1795–); **Groot Constantia** (1691; rebuilt c. 1780); **Groot Schuur** (restored by H. Baker in 1898); and the **Koopman de Wet House, Cape Town** (c. 1790).

INDIA AND SOUTH-EAST ASIA

ARCHITECTURAL CHARACTER

The Portuguese were the first of the seafaring Europeans to be drawn to India. The discovery of the sea route round the Cape of Good Hope by Vasco da Gama in 1498 was quickly followed by the establishment (1510) of a commercial enclave at Goa, on the west coast, 640 km (400 miles) south-east of Bombay, and for the next hundred years Portugal enjoyed a virtual monopoly of the lucrative Indian trade with Europe. Velha Goa (the old capital), basking in picturesque decay, eloquently recalls in elaborate 'baroque' churches and fading imperial splendour the glories of Portugal overseas. Vasco da Gama himself still presides over the great arch through which the Viceroy passed on ceremonial occasions.

The seventeenth century saw the arrival of British, French and Danish trading enterprises at various points along the west and east coasts of India, and there began a gradual extension of European and, ultimately, of predominantly British influence throughout the sub-continent. At first the buildings of the immigrant companies were inevitably primitive, but between the first half of the eighteenth century and the early middle years of the nineteenth a Neo-Classical idiom evolved, which differed only in small details in the towns and cantonments of the various nations. Such was (and is) a white-walled flat-roofed architecture of plaster-faced brick, with spacious porticoes, and colonnaded verandahs often completely embracing the building, the inter-columnar spaces usually occupied by Venetian blinds or the traditional 'tatties'. This climatically-adjusted Classicism produced no masterpieces, but in a setting of bougainvillaea and gold-mohur trees, as in the prosperous streets of the Chowringhee district of Calcutta, the effect could be very striking. Few of its interpreters were professional architects: many were engineer officers in the army, and it seems to have been an engineer, Dumont, who designed what was reputedly the finest European structure in India, the French Governor's residence (1752) at Pondicherry. This was a magnificent formal palazzo with a two-storey open gallery extending the full length of the principal façade, decorated throughout in the 'rocaille' manner of the style Louis XV, and completely destroyed by British troops in 1761. G. D. Coleman, a trained architect who had worked in Calcutta, applied the Neo-Classical vocabulary of European India with marked distinction to many buildings in the new city of Singapore in the early nineteenth century.

Bitter rivalry with Portugal over the spice trade lured the Dutch to the islands of Indonesia before the end of the sixteenth century, and in 1619 a township which the Dutch called Batavia came into being close to the mouth of the Tjiliwoeng river, on the north coast of Java. The city which took shape here in the seventeenth and eighteenth centuries, described by a traveller in 1770 as 'the queen of the towns of the East Indies', and now the principal business section of Djakata, was laid out with squares and interrelated canals, characteristic of the Netherlands and of the urban pattern generally followed in the Dutch colonies. Many seventeenth-century houses and a number of Protestant churches of the same period, all reminiscent of contemporary work in Holland, have survived. The impressive Town Hall and Governor-General's Residency date from 1710 and 1708 respectively.

Until thirty years ago the Philippines could offer many well-preserved examples of Spanish architecture of the sixteenth and seventeenth centuries. Intramuros, the old walled stronghold of Manila, the capital, which was once a treasure-house of ultramarine Hispanic art, suffered irreparable damage in the Second World War. Only the sixteenth-century church of S. Pablo (see below) has emerged relatively unscathed.

EXAMPLES

RELIGIOUS BUILDINGS

The **Basilica of Bom Jesus, Velha Goa, India** (1594), with a tiered frontispiece framed with coupled fluted columns and pilasters, which extends as a single composition to form the façade of the Convent of the Jesuits (1590) and contains in a side chapel the shrine of S. Francis Xavier, is one of a number of buildings of extraordinary merit lining the great square.

S. Pablo de los Agustinos Calzados, Manila, Philippines (*c.* 1590), by J. A. de Herrera (perhaps related to Juan de Herrera, the architect of the Escorial), is a three-aisled church of sober Classical lines and, inside, of ornate Proto-Baroque decoration, the side-aisles occupied by inter-communicating chapels. The resistance of this handsome building to repeated earthquakes, typhoons and, latterly, high explosives, bears witness to sound construction.

S. James's Church, Delhi (*c.* 1830) (p. 1115A), probably designed by the legendary Anglo-Indian, Colonel James Skinner (of Skinner's Horse), is a part-Baroque, part-Neo-Classical, domed structure built on a Greek-cross plan. The architectural effect of this seemingly small, actually spacious church, currently painted yellow ochre and white, is wholly satisfying.

S. John's Church, Calcutta (1784–7) (p. 1115B), by (Lieutenant) J. Agg, is considerably influenced in plan by S. Martin-in-the-Fields in London, but there is no pedimented portico. The Doric Order, popular in Calcutta, is used throughout. Other churches of the same period or a few years later, which followed the guidance of James Gibbs, are S. Andrew, Calcutta; S. Olav, at (Danish) Serampore; and S. Andrew, Madras, the last by T. de Havilland, all three in their various ways accomplished works.

A. S. James's Church, Delhi (*c.* 1830). See p. 1114

B. S. John's Church, Calcutta (1784-7). See p. 1114

C. Government House (now Raj Bhawan), Calcutta (1799-1803). See p. 1117

A. The Burgher Watch House, Cape Town (1755-). See p. 1113

B. S. James's Church, Sydney (c. 1824). See p. 1117

CIVIC AND CIVIL ARCHITECTURE

Government House (now Raj Bhawan), Calcutta (1799–1803) (p. 1115C), by (Lieutenant) C. Wyatt, who may have been a member of the Wyatt dynasty of architects, is an ostentatious residence built for the governors of Bengal in six acres of 'park'. The plan is that of Kedleston Hall, Derbyshire (p. 1042D), and the impressive gates are clearly modelled on the West Road entrance to Syon House, Middlesex, another Adam work.

Barrackpore House (1805–23), apparently by T. Anbury, the country seat of the Governor-General (subsequently Viceroy), stands in superbly landscaped grounds on the east bank of the Hooghly, 22 km (14 miles) north of **Calcutta** and facing, across the river, the once Danish settlement of Serampore. The dazzling white Tuscan-Ordered building, typical of its time and place, with formal porticoes to south and north, rises only one lofty storey's height above an arcaded basement, but there is a shallow attic beneath the parapeted flat roof to improve insulation and ventilation.

Serampore College, Serampore (c. 1820), certainly based on English precedents, although built in a Danish colony, presents an elegant Palladian exterior, and was designed to have two symmetrically opposed and identical wings, of which only one was erected.

Among smaller buildings of historical and architectural interest, **Hastings House, Alipur, near Calcutta** (1775), which is recorded in Zoffany's portrait of Warren Hastings and his wife, has been well preserved, but two single-storey wings and a portico have been added to the original two-storey cube.

The 1820s saw a Greek revival, exemplified by the **Town Hall, Bombay,** by (Colonel) T. Cowper, and **The Mint, Calcutta,** by W. N. Forbes.

AUSTRALIA

ARCHITECTURAL CHARACTER

Discovered in 1606 by the Portuguese navigator Luis de Torres, Australia had no permanent European settlement until after Captain James Cook took possession of New South Wales in the name of the British Crown in 1770. The colony was initially a penal settlement, but in 1793 it was opened to free immigration. The city of Sydney was founded in 1788, and Melbourne in 1835. Australia's first important architect was a convicted felon, Francis Greenway (1777–1837), transported from his native Bristol to Botany Bay for forgery in 1813, but also an artist in building of acute sensibility and, perhaps surprisingly, high professional integrity. Apart from some not very successful experiments in the Gothic taste, most of Greenway's work is Georgian in feeling and noteworthy for restraint in decoration and sensitive handling of stone and brick.

EXAMPLES

In Sydney and its surroundings Greenway was responsible for a number of distinguished buildings. Among the survivors are three finely proportioned brick Georgian churches: **S. James, Sydney** (c. 1824, impaired by late nineteenth-century restoration) (p. 1116B); **S. Luke, Liverpool** (1819); and **S. Matthew, Windsor** (1817); the **Hyde Park Barracks, Sydney** (1817), another nicely balanced design, Palladian in conception (much altered); and the **Stables, Government House, Sydney** (1817), an uncharacteristic exercise in (English) Regency 'castellated' architecture.

A rare instance in **Melbourne** of the Georgian (or Colonial) manner is **S. James's Old Cathedral** (begun 1839), by Robert Russell, which has been moved from its original site.

BIBLIOGRAPHY

AZEVEDO, C. DE. *Arte Christã na India Portuguesa*. Lisbon, 1959.

BAKER, H. *Architecture and Personalities*. London, 1944.

BAZIN, G. *L'Architecture religieuse baroque au Brésil*. 2 vols. Paris, 1956–8.

BRIDENBAUGH, C. *Peter Harrison, First American Architect*. Chapel Hill, 1949.

DIAZ-TRECHUELO SPINOLA, M. D. *Arquitectura española en Filipinas (1565–1800)*. Seville, 1959.

ELLIS, M. H. *Francis Greenway: His Life and Times*. Sydney, 1953.

FAIRBRIDGE, D. *Historic Houses of South Africa*. London, 1922.

FORMAN, H. C. *Architecture of the Old South; The Mediaeval Style*. Cambridge, Mass., 1948.

GOWANS, A. *Building Canada*. Toronto, 1966.

HANCOCK, T. H. 'Coleman of Singapore', *Architectural Review*, London, March 1955.

HERMAN, M. *The Early Australian Architects and Their Work*. Sydney, 1954.

JOHNSTON, F. B. and WATERMAN, T. T. *The Early Architecture of North Carolina*. Chapel Hill, 1941.

JORGE, F. *O Aleijadinho: sua vida, su obra* . . . São Paulo, 1966.

KELEMEN, P. *Baroque and Rococo in Latin America*. New York, 1951.

KELLY, J. F. *The Early Domestic Architecture of Connecticut*. New Haven, 1948.

KIMBALL, F. *Domestic Architecture of the American Colonies and of the Early Republic*. New York, 1922.

KUBLER, G. and SORIA, M. *Art and Architecture in Spain and Portugal and their American Dominions: 1500–1800*. Harmondsworth and Baltimore, 1959.

LIVERMORE, H. V. (Editor) *Portugal and Brazil: An Introduction*. Oxford, 1953.

MORRISON, H. *Early American Architecture*. New York, 1952.

NAVARRO, J. G. *Religious Architecture in Quito*. New York, 1945.

NEWCOMB, R. *Spanish Colonial Architecture in the United States*. New York, 1937.

—. *Architecture in Old Kentucky*. Urbana, Ill., 1953.

NILSSON, S. *European Architecture in India: 1750–1850*. London, 1968.

PEARSE, G. E. *The Cape of Good Hope: 1652–1833; An account of its buildings* . . . Pretoria, 1956.

—. *Eighteenth Century Architecture in South Africa*. London, 1933.

Revista do Patrimonio Histórico e Artístico Nacional. Ministerio da Educação e Cultura, Rio de Janeiro. A long series.

SANTOS, P. F. *O Barroco e o Jesuitico na Arquitetura do Brasil*. Rio de Janeiro, 1951.

TAPIÉ, V. L. *The Age of Grandeur*. London, 1960.

WATERMAN, T. T. *Domestic Colonial Architecture in Tidewater Virginia*. New York, 1932.

—. *The Mansions of Virginia*. Chapel Hill, 1946.

—. *The Dwellings of Colonial America*. Chapel Hill, 1950.

WETHEY, H. E. *Colonial Architecture and Sculpture in Peru*. Cambridge, Mass., 1949.

WHIFFEN, M. *The Public Buildings of Colonial Williamsburg*. Williamsburg, 1958.

36

ARCHITECTURE IN BRITAIN
1830-1914

INFLUENCES

The 'Age of Revivals' is a common descriptive title for the years covered by this chapter in British architectural history, and yet it could with equal truth be described as the 'Age of Innovation'. Paradoxically, it was one in which major new developments in the construction and planning of buildings were often combined with stylistic revivalism, varying in character from the purely antiquarian to the free interpretation of assumed historical principles.

Social and technological influences, both in unprecedented forms, were of major architectural significance. They arose from the demands of a rapidly growing population within a society in the throes of the Industrial Revolution. There is no agreed date for the beginning of industrialization, but major inventions in metallurgy, cotton manufacture and the development of steam-power in the latter half of the eighteenth century ordained the course of the nineteenth. An increased birth-rate and a reduction in infant mortality contributed to the rise in population, which in England and Wales increased from almost 9 millions in 1801 to about 18 millions in 1851 and over 32.5 millions in 1901. Urbanization developed similarly: the greater part of the population was rural at the beginning of the century, but by 1851 half, and by 1901 three-quarters, had become urban. The population of London more than quadrupled in the hundred years from 1801, and some provincial industrial cities expanded with similar prodigality.

The housing of the new urban population created acute social problems and threatened public health through overcrowding, inadequate sanitation and impure water supply. In the late 1840s public attention was drawn to these deficiencies by reformers such as Edwin Chadwick (1800–90), whose arguments were savagely underlined by several cholera epidemics between 1831 and 1866. The worst evils were mitigated, but the design of large-scale housing was left principally to speculative builders, although a few 'improved' or 'model' dwellings designed by architects appeared from the 1840s. The dreariness and overcrowding of the monotonous rows of terraced houses, the standard expedient in housing, inspired reactions expressed in the creation of a number of model villages, such as Port Sunlight in 1888 and Bournville, from 1895; in the rather visionary exposition by Ebenezer Howard (1850–1928) of the garden city ideal in his book of 1898 now known as *Garden Cities of Tomorrow*; and in the legislation of the 1909 Town Planning Act.

The growing industrial areas were supported by new transport systems. A canal network was constructed from 1757 which eventually linked London to Kendal and the Mersey to the Humber. It was most dense in the industrial areas of the North-West and the Midlands and provided access to major ports. Railways prematurely terminated the canals' profitability and the first major rail link between cities, the Liverpool to Manchester line, opened in 1830. Within twenty years 5,000 miles of railway existed and the major cities were interconnected, further speeding transport and commercial development. One architectural effect of canal and railway facilities was that the cheapest building materials, common brick and Welsh slate, became readily available anywhere and displaced local materials, causing a marked decline in local crafts and vernacular traditions of building from 1840 onwards. On the positive side, the canal and railway engineers were often architect-engineers, such as Thomas Telford (1757–1834), John Rennie (1761–1821) and Isambard Kingdom Brunel (1806–59), who created severely practical structures of almost Roman grandeur. The two former introduced a functional manner of building which itself, for a few decades, became a vernacular tradition of the new age.

The expansion of the towns meant that greater numbers of conventional buildings were required, such as houses, theatres and churches. Parliament, for instance, voted a million pounds in 1818 for the construction of churches in the new populous districts. In addition, entirely new types of buildings were necessary, such as the railway station, and many existing building types were transformed by new requirements; the town hall had to serve greatly expanded municipal business; the hospital had to meet new medical practice requiring the pavilion plan, and commercial organizations also evolved new methods, as when those in banking produced the public bank, and those in the textile trade the warehouse as a prestige building of architectural, social and commercial significance, while changes in the retail trade led to the evolution of the department store. National legislation also reflects social change and several Parliamentary Acts involved architectural provision. The Poor Law Amendment Act of 1834 resulted in the construction of many workhouses; various Acts from 1845 enabled museums to be supported from public funds, and the Education Act of 1870 led to the building of Board Schools giving wider access for elementary education (p. 1121). Innovations of type or function include almost all classes of buildings: town and country houses, swimming baths, fire and police stations, exhibition halls, university buildings, prisons, art galleries and many examples of buildings for transport and industry. Prime architectural examples of the age are often found outside London, because the new commercial centres were ambitious to express their importance. Manchester Town Hall, built by Alfred Waterhouse (1830–1905) (p. 1153A, B) at a cost of over one million pounds between 1868 and 1877, is one notable instance.

Although secular influences were predominant in determining the architectural requirements of the age, religious buildings are amongst its most significant works; The Nonconformist revival of the eighteenth century continued as one important factor of religious life, but the Catholic Emancipation Act of 1829 in extending religious tolerance sanctioned church building of greater influence in work by A. W. N. Pugin (1812–52), the theorist and designer. The Anglican Church, resuscitated by evangelical example and the Oxford Movement controversy of the 1830s, energetically laboured in 'a missionary spirit to meet the spiritual needs of the population, building on a lavish scale in the towns and restoring many neglected country churches, frequently ruthlessly, in accordance with the strict tenets of the Cambridge Camden Society, later called the Ecclesiological Society. These, published in its periodical *The Ecclesiologist*, first issued in 1841, adopted many of the principles preached by Pugin, the Catholic apologist, the essence being that the modern church should follow both the principles and precedents of the Mediaeval church. Modern needs often made strict Mediaeval precedent impracticable, but the attempted interpretation of principle produced some remarkable buildings by men like William Butterfield (1814–1900) and G. E. Street (1824–81).

As has already been indicated, advances in scientific knowledge and technology were fundamental to nineteenth-century progress. Steam-power generated many

A. West Street School, London Fields (*c.* 1870). See p. 1127

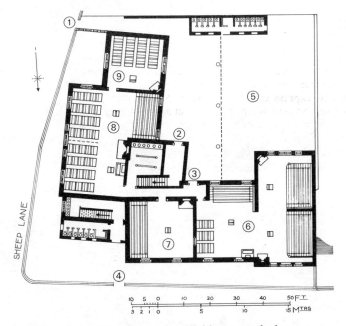

B. West Street School, London Fields: ground plan

1. Girls' and infants' entrance
2. Girls' entrance
3. Infants' entrance
4. Boys' entrance
5. Girls' and infants' playground
6. Junior infants' school
7. Babies' room
8. Senior infants' school
9. Classroom

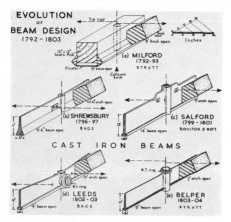

A. Development of beams from timber to cast-iron. See p. 1123

B. The Iron Bridge at Coalbrookdale, Shropshire (1779). See p. 1123

C. The Clifton Suspension Bridge, Bristol (1830–63). See p. 1134

D. Benyon, Bage and Marshall's Mill at Shrewsbury (1796–7). See p. 1123

uses, providing motive power for transport, and innumerable industrial purposes, thus leading to the enlargement of industrial buildings to take full advantage of the capacities of expensive equipment. The invention of the process of making coal-gas about 1800 led to gas-lighting in factories from about 1807 and thereby made extended working hours more feasible. It was adopted for street lighting shortly afterwards. Electrical power was made possible by Faraday's discovery of electromagnetic induction in 1831, and the telegraph, telephone and wireless telegraphy followed in 1837, 1878 and c. 1896 respectively. Commercial application inevitably followed such major scientific inventions and developments.

Equally far-reaching innovations in building were often related to progress in general technology, e.g. in metallurgy, and some were of great architectural importance. Although originating outside this immediate period, one was the development of structural iron, dramatically illustrated by the construction of the Iron Bridge at Coalbrookdale, Shropshire, in 1779 (p. 1122B) by the iron-founder Abraham Darby III (1750–91), probably based on a design by the architect T. F. Pritchard (d. 1777). Cast-iron was soon adopted on a growing scale for structural purposes and in the 1790s a millowner, William Strutt, erected several mills at Belper, Derbyshire, partly supported internally by cast-iron columns (p. 1122A). The first known building with a consistent internal cast-iron column and beam system (previously mill floors had been supported on heavy timber beams) is the Benyon, Bage and Marshall spinning mill at Shrewsbury (1796–7) (p. 1122D). The advantages of such a system were considerable, since the structure required little floor area, allowed greater flexibility in design through the bay system and a greater number of storeys than was practicable with masonry alone. Mills of this type, constructed eight or nine storeys high, were not uncommon in the textile towns by 1830. An example of great modernity, the Phillips, Wood and Lee mill at Salford, Lancashire, built in 1801 by William Fairbairn (1789–1874), was powered by a Boulton and Watt steam engine and heated by steam transmitted through the hollow cast-iron columns. Gas-lighting was added in 1807. Cast-iron framed buildings of this type were frequently made more fire-resistant than hitherto by constructing the floors on shallow segmental brick arches (jack arches) spanning between the floor beams. A further refinement, lightening the weight of the structure, was the substitution of hollow pots for bricks in the arches. Cast-iron was seldom used in Britain as an external cladding, but a few examples occur, with several in Glasgow (p. 1155B). However, the manufacture and export of cast-iron buildings of all descriptions became a thriving business.

The combination of cast-iron and glass, a material also produced by new methods, led to the development of a novel building technique derived from the construction of greenhouses, the most spectacular example being the Crystal Palace, erected in Hyde Park, London, for the Great Exhibition of 1851 (p. 1144A). Hybrid buildings combining traditional masonry structures and iron and glass elements became popular, as in that highly serviceable Victorian building, the shopping arcade.

Wrought-iron, twice as expensive as cast-iron, was not used as much as the latter for structural purposes for this reason, but its tensile properties were exploited to provide ties, bolts and trusses and to meet special requirements, as at S. Pancras Station, London (1863–7), with a clear span of 74 m (243 ft) (p. 1155C). Steel was produced in quantity through the Bessemer process from 1855, but it was not used for general building until the 1880s, when rolled sections were manufactured and replaced wrought-iron in the construction of wide spans. Fully steel-framed buildings of any significance occurred later in Britain than elsewhere in Europe and America and the first, the Ritz Hotel, London, by Mewès and Davis, dates from 1905. There was no expression of the frame in most similar early examples, partly because the reduction of the external wall thickness was not permitted until after the 1909 London Building Act, but in a few buildings the new technique was exploited before 1914, one example being Kodak House, London, of 1911, by Sir John Burnet (p. 1177).

The advent of reinforced concrete, mass concrete incorporating steel bars, introduced a material capable of withstanding great compressive and tensile loads, like steel, but with the further important advantage of a high degree of fire-resistance. Further, the materials could be cast in any form, theoretically freeing architects from the traditional constraint of the rectilinear plan. The technique of reinforcing concrete became practicable after the invention of Portland cement, which was shown at the Great Exhibition in 1851 and proved to be much stronger than others then available and also water-resistant, therefore giving iron reinforcement greater protection from corrosion. The development of reinforced concrete construction was pioneered on the Continent by the French, notably by Joseph Monier, François Coignet and François Hennebique, and by the German firm of Wayss and Freitag (see p. 1189). Hennebique and Coignet opened offices in London in 1897 and 1904 respectively. Early contracts were for dock buildings and warehouses, but within a decade of its introduction into England concrete was being tentatively exploited architecturally, although its potentialities were not fully realized until after the First World War.

Although structural advances are perhaps the most dramatic innovations in building technology, there were others of great consequence. Gas-lighting was sufficiently refined to be introduced into houses in the 1840s and began to be superseded by electricity in the 1890s, the first electric lighting installation in England being at the Gaiety Theatre, London, carried out by French contractors in 1878. Central heating became an accepted part of the equipment of public buildings and large houses from 1860, although the coal fire remained ubiquitous. Central heating made larger windows possible, and the repeal of the burdensome excise on glass in 1845 made them cheaper and resulted in an increased use of plate glass, produced by a new mechanical process. These influences on fenestration produced lighter interiors. Great improvements in urban life also occurred through advances in drainage and sanitation, with the introduction of the water-closet, effective main drainage, and the provision of pure water, with the latter often piped from major catchment areas. Of greater significance to the actual form of buildings was the invention of the lift or elevator. Earliest lifts operated on a counter-weight system and were used for goods only, but in 1854 the American Elisha Graves Otis (1811–61) invented a rachet-and-pawl safety system, and in 1857 the first public lift was installed in a store in New York. The possibilities brought about by cheap steel, the concrete fire-resistant floor, the electric lift, and improved services wrought within two decades the most profound and unprecedented changes in building form.

Not only were nineteenth-century buildings shaped by new, complex requirements, social and technical, but they were commissioned by new types of patron. The growth of a strong middle class of professional and business men created a type of patron no longer likely to be familiar with matters of taste and architectural values. Nor was the architectural profession prepared to meet the inexorable tide of change described. In the first decades of the nineteenth century it could hardly answer to the title of profession at all. The custom of the eighteenth century had either placed the architect under direct patronage or had made him virtually synonymous with the master-mason, in which capacity it was common practice for the architect to act as contractor, an arrangement leading to abuse and giving ample cause for the low reputation of such practitioners. By forming an effective professional association architects endeavoured to rectify this state of affairs. In 1834 the

Institute of British Architects was founded and classes of membership and a code of professional conduct were created; three years later a Royal Charter of Incorporation was granted. The establishment of close-professionalism with entrance by examination was a contentious process which advanced slowly: in 1882 admission to Associateship became subject to examination, but the principle of a closed profession was debated for decades before being instituted in 1931. Growing with these concerns was that of architectural education. Articled pupilage was the standard practice of the nineteenth century and initially the Royal Academy of Arts was the only body offering instruction in the form of lectures to architectural students, but from 1841 university courses in architecture were offered in London. The Architectural Association was founded in 1847 to encourage the study of architecture, and towards the end of the century the provincial universities, led by Liverpool in 1894, began to establish architectural chairs and courses. Pupilage, part-time courses and self-help, however, appear to have been the prime means of architectural education, with the latter facilitated by a voluminous technical press. The most celebrated architectural magazine of the century, *The Builder*, appeared in 1842, with professional and technical information, and excellent illustrations of major works of the period. The influence of such journals was immense; they were disseminators of styles as well as of news and technical matters, and linked London and the provinces architecturally as effectively as had the railways physically.

Wealth, commerce and technical inventiveness characterize Victorian Britain and were principal architectural influences, associated with her position as the leading industrial nation, until rivalled by Germany and America in the 1880s. The possession of an empire with vast natural resources, and the enjoyment of stable government at home and freedom from major wars abroad, all contributed to the creation of the material prosperity of which Victorian architecture is so significant an expression. However, this prosperity was not uniform; there were periods of economic depression and, as has been indicated, the social cost of industrialism was blatantly conspicuous. Nor were contemporaries unaware of this. The basis of society was seriously questioned and criticized not only by political theorists such as Karl Marx and Friedrich Engels, but by such writers as Thomas Carlyle, John Ruskin and William Morris, who, directly and indirectly, had considerable architectural influence upon fundamental attitudes to design and society. Their theories contributed to a radical stream in architectural thought which is reflected in the work of many important architects, such as A. W. N. Pugin, William Butterfield, Philip Webb and W. R. Lethaby, constituting a vital source of influence.

Although English architecture from 1830–1914 is frequently loosely described as Regency, Victorian or Edwardian, it does not conform to the royal chronology, but may best be divided into three phases, which also broadly correspond with other events and developments in social and political life: *Early Victorian*, c. 1830 to c. 1850; *High Victorian*, c. 1850 to c. 1870, and *Late Victorian and Edwardian*, c. 1870 to 1914. Each phase has a distinctive architectural character, reflecting the different contemporary emphases of the material, social and cultural influences of this vigorous and diverse age.

ARCHITECTURAL CHARACTER

The most conspicuous characteristic of Victorian and Edwardian architecture is its diverse use of historic styles. Since architectural development is a continuum, it is not surprising that major influences were inherited from the eighteenth century in the forms of Classical and Gothic Revivals, in the inspiration drawn from 'Picturesque' values, often reflected in multi-coloured, strongly textured buildings of highly informal design, and in the spirit of eclecticism which informed its taste for exotic forms of architecture. Nineteenth-century eclecticism knew few bounds, and examples of native and foreign styles of almost all periods were brought into service and, not infrequently, were combined in the same design. Revivalism and eclecticism were by no means always wilful. They were often rationally flexible to contemporary needs, expressive of the imagination and attitudes of their day, and in this sense were entirely modern. There is no mistaking any Victorian Classical or Gothic Revival building as anything but the product of its age, as distinctive as the contemporary iron-and-glass structures which appear modern to twentieth-century eyes. Paradoxically, from the late 1840s concern was expressed over the need for an original style, although it was not until the last two decades of this period that a less derivative general architecture appeared, first as a result of the Aesthetic and Arts and Crafts Movements and, later, of the new technology, which made new forms of expression possible.

In many respects the architecture illustrates this rapidly changing era, with its critical problems of expansion, tradition and innovation. New functions and techniques produced new forms, but orthodox materials remained prevalent, stone and brick being used externally until towards the end of the century when, probably as an answer to the severe atmospheric pollution, the use of faience became common. Because external walls were load-bearing, a conventional arrangement of windows was followed, although these became larger and had fewer glazing-bars after *c.* 1845, with the coming of plate-glass. The cast-iron frame, another characteristic device of the period, was used internally and resulted in larger buildings, with more storeys than previously, to meet practical requirements and make the maximum use of urban sites. Customarily, urban commercial buildings were constructed four or five storeys high until the introduction of steel-framing about 1905, and between then and 1914 eight or nine storeys became more general. As could be expected from a largely raw and unsystematically trained profession and a greatly extended building industry, the quality of buildings, both in design and execution, was exceedingly uneven. The worst type of jerry-building co-existed with technical excellence, and architectural bathos with high achievements.

In the nineteenth century the Classical tradition showed astonishing resilience. During the first decades the Greek Revival flourished (see Chapter 32) and was followed in the 1840s and '50s by a Graeco-Roman phase of great magnificence, used for public buildings such as S. George's Hall, Liverpool (1840–54) (p. 1137), and the Fitzwilliam Museum, Cambridge (1837–47) (p. 1137). The former was designed by H. Lonsdale Elmes (1814–47), the latter by G. Basevi (1794–1845), and both were completed by C. R. Cockerell (1788–1863). The Italian Renaissance 'palazzo', of Classical derivation, was adopted as a vehicle for Classical order by Sir Charles Barry (1795–1860) in several influential designs, two for London clubs, the Travellers' Club (1829–31) and the Reform Club (1837–41) (pp. 1137–8), and one for the Athenaeum at Manchester (1837–9), not a club but an adult educational institute. The palazzo style was a triumph of rational eclecticism; it did not require symmetry or the Classical Orders, allowed unrestricted size, permitted a wide range of fenestration, perfectly accommodated a cast-iron frame system, and provided a powerfully expressive architectural form with flattering social connotations. It is little wonder that it was widely adopted by the merchant princes of the industrial north for their warehouses, and it found fullest expression in a High Victorian building, the memorial to the Anti-Corn Law League, the Free Trade Hall, Manchester (1853–4) (p. 1146), by Edward Walters (1808–72).

Parallel with but less general than the Italian mode, a revival of French

Renaissance precedents occurred from the mid-50s, the time of the Anglo-French alliance during the Crimean War. Its most prominent characteristics were the mansard roof and rather florid ornament, and it was particularly popular for hotels and the more lavish town houses. The Grand Hotel, Scarborough (1863-7), by Cuthbert Brodrick (c. 1822-1905), represents the former and the design of the now demolished Alford House, London (1872) (p. 1151), by M. D. Wyatt (1820-77), the latter. Brodrick's Leeds Town Hall (1853-9) (p. 1146) reflects French influence in the design of the cupola to the tower, but combines this with the grandeur of a colonnade based on S. George's Hall, Liverpool (p. 1137), and ranks as a major High Victorian civic monument in civic architecture.

In Scotland Classicism survived more overtly in the longevity of the Greek Revival, as witnessed in the National Gallery of Scotland, Edinburgh (1850-4) (p. 1137), by W. H. Playfair (1789-1857), and other coeval buildings such as the works of Alexander 'Greek' Thomson (1817-75) in Glasgow (p. 1146).

Even at the nadir of Classicism and the height of the Gothic Revival in the 1860s, at Lord Palmerston's insistence Gothic was rejected for a Renaissance design for the Foreign Office, London (1860-75) (p. 1151), despite the objections of the architect, Sir George Gilbert Scott (1811-78), the renowned Gothicist. During this stormy affair, the cardinal event of the 'Battle of Styles', Classicism appeared in a new form, now recognized as indicative of the future Georgian Revival, in the house in Kensington which the novelist Thackeray built for himself in 1861. Shortly afterwards the seventeenth-century English vernacular mode, with its Renaissance features (see Chapter 32) was adopted and popularized by W. Eden Nesfield (1835-88) and R. N. Shaw (1831-1912). Kinmel Park, Denbighshire (1868-74) (p. 1158), a country house by Nesfield is an example, anticipated in some respects by his more transitional Cloverley Hall, Shropshire (1864-8), in which the new style, known as 'Queen Anne', merges with Gothic. Like the 'palazzo' mode, it permitted either symmetry or asymmetry, but gave great flexibility and combined Renaissance with native associations. It is characterized by mullioned windows, segmentally pedimented windows, door-cases and dormers, handsome brickwork and imposingly grouped chimneys. Lowther Lodge, Kensington (1873-4) (p. 1158) by Shaw is a mature example devoid of formal classicism. Renaissance details are arranged in a picturesque composition simulating the absorption of classical details in vernacular architecture. Terra-cotta decorative details and Dutch gables were also part of the Queen Anne idiom, which became the hallmark of the London Board Schools designed in the 1870s, many by E. R. Robson (1835-1917), and a national mode for the new elementary schools, of which West Street School, London Fields (c. 1870) (p. 1121) is an example.

More formal English Renaissance modes were introduced by the versatile R. N. Shaw in houses at 170, Queen's Gate, London (1888) (p. 1158), and at Bryanston, in Dorset (1890): later Shaw was to readopt the Classical Orders in his design for Chesters, Northumberland (1891) (p. 1158), and their fashionable return was also heralded by John Belcher (1841-1913) in his rich, almost Baroque design for the Institute of Chartered Accountants, London (1890). This resurgence of Classicism persisted well into the twentieth century on a national scale and was expressed in two principal forms. One, more literal than the other, reproduced the Orders and Classical and Renaissance detail, as is seen at Colchester Town Hall (1898-1902) (p. 1161) by Belcher; the other, which became ascendant after 1920, was introduced by architects such as Charles Holden (1875-1960) in the early 1900s and primarily observed Classical principles of composition without reproducing revivalist detail. Holden's extension to the Law Society building, London (1902-4) (p. 1161) is an early example of this form, but the London County Hall, Westminster (1912-22)

(p. 1161), by Ralph Knott (1878-1929), represents the conclusion of the more orthodox classical theme in the Edwardian 'grand manner'.

The taste for Gothic was part of the legacy of the eighteenth century. Its romantic and antiquarian character in the succeeding thirty years is evident from some of Sir Walter Scott's novels, such as *Ivanhoe* (1819), and the publication of numerous books on Mediaeval architecture including *An Attempt to Discriminate the Styles of English Architecture from the Conquest to the Reformation* (1817) by Thomas Rickman (1776-1841), in which he introduced the now familiar terms of classification 'Norman', 'Early English', 'Decorated' and 'Perpendicular'. The Houses of Parliament or Westminster New Palace, London (1836-68) (p. 1138), is the most magnificent example of romantic antiquarianism, and a turning point in the Gothic Revival. Its architect was Sir Charles Barry, appointed as the result of a major architectural competition whose terms stipulated that the style of the building should be 'either Gothic or Elizabethan'. Although Barry had previously worked in the Gothic style, he was by inclination and experience a Classicist, and to help him with the detailing of this important building he obtained the assistance of A. W. N. Pugin (1812-52), who responded brilliantly. Pugin was the agent in the drastic change in the attitude to Gothic design which is apparent in Early Victorian architecture. Architect, propagandist and zealous Catholic, in his book *Contrasts; or, a Parallel between the Noble Edifices of the Fourteenth and Fifteenth Centuries, and Similar Buildings of the Present Day; Shewing the Present Decay of Taste*, published in 1836, he compared architecture and life as he saw them with what he imagined to be their Mediaeval counterparts, invariably to the detriment of contemporary design and its utilitarian character. In a subsequent book, *An Apology for the Revival of Christian Architecture in England* (1843), he urged the adoption of Gothic architecture as the only appropriate architecture for Christian Englishmen, while in *The True Principles of Pointed or Christian Architecture* (1841) he advanced a rationalist theory of design derived from his profound knowledge of Gothic architecture; 'there should be no features about a building which are not necessary for convenience, construction or propriety', he asserted, also claiming that each part of a building should be distinctly expressed and 'not masked or concealed under one monotonous front', and that construction should be revealed, observing that 'Pointed architecture does not conceal her construction, but beautifies it'.

Both architects and clients were ripe for conversion to Pugin's architectural gospel, if not to its ecclesiastical authority, and the Gothic Revival acquired the impetus of moral force and cogent architectural principles. Up to 1850, the Anglican zeal for Mediaevalism was led by the small but influential minority of Anglican churchmen within the Oxford Movement and the Cambridge Camden Society (later renamed the Ecclesiological Society), both being sympathetic towards Catholic usage. It was shared by a number of rising architects, including William Butterfield, R. C. Carpenter (1812-55), George Gilbert Scott and G. E. Street. All the latter became potent sources of architectural influence, and all except Scott served the Ecclesiological Society professionally. The Protestant majority remained untouched and, indeed, suspicion of Catholicism was part of the contemporary scene. In 1849 John Ruskin (1819-1900), a Protestant of unimpeachable authenticity, published *The Seven Lamps of Architecture* in which he, like Pugin, vehemently attacked contemporary standards, but cited as his authorities Nature, the Bible and Mediaeval architecture. He denied Pugin's influence, but acknowledged that of Carlyle, who was also one of Pugin's sources. Social and architectural criticism, poetic allusion and brilliant natural description, biblical knowledge and the Christian ethic are all compounded in Ruskin's eloquent prose; his influence was less direct architecturally than Pugin's, but he made the Gothic Revival an issue for the majority, and a style for secular as well as religious purposes.

Early Victorian Gothic, up to 1850, had been expressed principally in native forms. From mid-century, and partly because of *The Seven Lamps*, much English Gothic was thought mean and considerable attention was paid to Continental models, which became the typical inspiration of High Victorianism. First Italian, then Venetian, precedents were followed, the latter especially after Ruskin's *Stones of Venice* was published (1851–3); later French, and to a lesser extent German, were favoured. William Butterfield (1814–1900) a principal architect of the Ecclesiological Society, designed All Saints, Margaret Street, London (1849–59) (p. 1151) as an exemplar for the Society. Built of brick on a confined site, he introduced into its design bands and patterns of differently coloured brick as permanent decoration, emulating the decorative effects obtained by the use of different marbles in the North Italian churches admired by Ruskin. Keble College, Oxford (1867–83) (p. 1151) affords an excellent illustration of what is known as Butterfield's 'constructional polychromy'. G. E. Street (1824–81), equal in importance to Butterfield, was also demonstrably attracted by Italian colourfulness, as may be seen in his church of S. James-the-Less, Westminster (1858–61). He also wrote *Brick and Marble in the Middle Ages* (1855), containing notes and drawings of his tours in North Italy.

Many Venetian-Gothic style buildings bear witness to Venice as revealed by Ruskin. Polychrome patterning, contrasted materials in general, pointed arches with non-concentric extradoses, short columns with heavily foliated capitals, and ornamental medallions and billet mouldings on elevations of a flat character, all point to this source. Two notable illustrations are the Oxford Museum (1855–9) (p. 1151) by Deane and Woodward, and the design of the now demolished Manchester Assize Courts of 1859 (p. 1151), by Alfred Waterhouse.

The causes of the French Gothic influence are less clearly defined, but one factor may have been the Crimean War (1854–6) which stimulated closer relations between England and France generally. Another of more direct significance is the French architect Viollet-le-Duc (1814–79), awarded the R.I.B.A. Gold Medal in 1864. His famous *Dictionnaire raisonné de l'Architecture Française du XIe au XVIe Siècle* (1854–68), published in ten volumes, provided a further fund of details of Christian architecture. In 1855 attention was focused on French Gothic architecture by the competition for a cathedral at Lille, won by the English architects Henry Clutton (1819–93) and William Burges (1827–81), with G. E. Street gaining second place. The chevet, the flèche, the hip-roofed tower and other French details became common, and young architects returned from travels abroad in the 1850s armed with sketch books of French architecture: R. N. Shaw's were published in 1858. Street's church of S. Philip and S. James, Oxford (1862) (p. 1152), exhibits French characteristics and combines them with touches of polychromy, as does Congleton Town Hall (1864–7) (p. 1152), by E. W. Godwin (1833–86), and Waterhouse's Manchester Town Hall (1868–77) (p. 1152) is a powerful civic example. The house Burges built for himself in Melbury Road, Kensington (1875–80) is a notable domestic example and Philip Webb's Red House, built for William Morris in 1859–60 (p. 1151), hints at the French vogue.

The high tide of the Gothic Revival was in the 1860s and early '70s. Burges's dramatic reconstruction of Cardiff Castle (1868–85) (p. 1157) and the nearby Castell Coch (1875–91) (p. 1157) are important examples, and the works of George Gilbert Scott (1811–78) cannot be omitted. He was responsible for the Albert Memorial, Kensington (1863–72) (p. 1152), the S. Pancras Hotel (1865–71) (p. 1152), and a vast number of churches, cathedral restorations and secular buildings throughout the country. His self-justifying memoirs, his unfortunate encounter with Lord Palmerston, and the proliferation of his works, have become standard butts for gibes, but he was by no means without architectural talent. An admirer of Pugin who remained outside the Ecclesiological circle, his striking design for the Nicolaikirche, Hamburg (p. 1200), won in competition in 1846, brought recognition on the Continent for what had until then been an essentially English movement. Scott wrote several architectural books and his *Remarks on Secular and Domestic Architecture, Present and Future* (1857) made some valuable points on the suitability of vernacular modes for adaption to modern needs, a further illustration of Victorian rational eclecticism rather than historicism. By the early 1870s younger architects were questioning the basis of the Gothic Revival, but its climax appears to have been reached with G. E. Street's design for the Law Courts, London (1871–82) (p. 1157). Many controversial charges of inconvenience have been levelled against the building, and it proved to be the last major public building of the Gothic Revival, fittingly ending the era of High Victorian Gothic design, although not that of the Gothic Revival.

In the 1880s Gothic Revivalists endeavoured to develop the more rational procedure of emulating Gothic principles rather than inventing stylistic adaptations, however original. This produced one of the characteristic forms of the Late Victorian phase, a freely interpreted version of Gothic. In churches the nave became the dominating feature by its great height, breadth and a clearly defined bay system. Decorative detail was much simplified and made subservient to mass, and was often Gothic in name only. Two notably inventive examples are Holy Trinity, Sloane Street, London (1888–91) (p. 1165), and All Saints, Falmouth (1887–90), both by J. D. Sedding (1837–91). Simultaneous with this development and having some features in common with it, was a more conventional reversion to English Gothic forms, seen in the work of G. F. Bodley (1827–1907), Basil Champneys (1842–1935), and J. L. Pearson (1817–97). The latter had a notable sense of structural form, expressed in the fine vaulting of S. Augustine, Kilburn, London (1870–80) (p. 1165). That the Gothic style still enjoyed wide support is indicated by two cathedrals begun in this period. Truro (1879–1910) (p. 1165) is by Pearson, and Liverpool (1903–) (p. 1165) by Sir Giles Gilbert Scott (1880–1960), grandson of Sir George Gilbert Scott, but these were almost the final manifestations of the Gothic Revival. Guildford Cathedral (1936–61) (p. 1178), by Sir Edward Maufe (b. 1883) is perhaps the very last major building of this character.

A third important influence from the eighteenth century was the taste for the 'Picturesque', reflected in the predilection for highly textured, colourful materials, asymmetry and informality. These features appear in some degree in all phases of Victorian Gothic, and the penchant for asymmetry appears to have affected even Alexander 'Greek' Thomson in his designs for Glasgow churches (p. 1146). Three particular instances of Picturesque influences are the cottage orné, the small country house affecting rural simplicity, which provided a model for the mid-Victorian detached suburban villa; the 'Jacobethan' style house, composed of elements borrowed from Elizabethan and Jacobean prototypes, e.g. carved barge-boards, twisted chimneys, half-timbering and irregular bays and gables (p. 1156), which was popular in some form throughout this whole period; and thirdly, the vernacular revival in domestic architecture, which on both functional and stylistic grounds developed in the latter half of the century, encouraging the use of local materials and traditional crafts, especially in the '80s and '90s in the Arts and Crafts Movement (see p. 1132). R. N. Shaw's Leys Wood, at Groombridge, Sussex (1868) (p. 1157), aptly illustrates vernacular and Jacobethan characteristics, which proved to be a particularly appealing combination and enjoyed a wide following.

Structural and technical developments have been described under 'Influences', and their early expression is mostly found in utilitarian structures. Cast-iron, however, was used decoratively, as in the iron fan-vaulting in the conservatory of Carlton House, London (1811–12) (p. 1141), by Thomas Hopper (1776–1856). On occasions structural and decorative uses were combined, as in several churches in Liverpool by Thomas Rickman, such as S. George, Everton (1812–14) (p. 1141), but such use of iron was disapproved by the Ecclesiologists and similar churches do not occur in the Early Victorian decades. In secular works the new technology knew no such restraints and notable instances of its bold expression are not uncommon. King's Cross Station, London (1850–2) (p. 1145), by Lewis Cubitt (1799–1883) is one instance of the directness of such works, and the Clifton Suspension Bridge (1830–63) (p. 1134) is another spectacular example. It was designed by I. K. Brunel, but long delayed in construction and completed after his death. The pylons have an Egyptian character, demonstrating that historicism and structural adventurousness were not incompatible. The Crystal Palace, designed by Sir Joseph Paxton (1801–65) for the Great Exhibition of 1851 (p. 1145), is the most famous in the line of great iron-and-glass structures. Its predecessors were the Great Conservatory at Chatsworth, Derbyshire (1836–40) (p. 1141), also by Paxton, and the more elegant Palm House at Kew (1845–7) (p. 1145), designed by Decimus Burton (1800–81) in association with the engineer Richard Turner. The Chatsworth conservatory incorporated Paxton's ridge-and-furrow principle in its external treatment, as did the Crystal Palace, whereas Burton's Palm House is remarkable for its continuous smooth surface. The design and construction of the Crystal Palace in nine months was by any standard an astonishing achievement, and the construction methods employed were direct, logical and efficient. The building was excellent for its specialized purpose, and a forerunner of twentieth-century concepts.

The extensive use of cast-iron externally is uncommon in British architecture, but the instances of its occurrence are of considerable interest. A boat-store built at Sheerness Dockyard in 1858–60 is a utilitarian but entirely consistent statement in cast-iron and glass (p. 1158). More urbane and equally unequivocal is Gardener's warehouse in Jamaica Street, Glasgow (1855–6) (p. 1158), and close to it is Paisley's warehouse (1854–5), which is as direct in expression but has stone spandrels. An effect of fine elegance is obtained in a Liverpool example, Oriel Chambers (1864–5) (p. 1158), designed by Peter Ellis (1804–84).

In the more numerous hybrid buildings combining masonry and iron-and-glass structural elements, the architectural character of the latter is frequently the principal point of interest. At the recently demolished Coal Exchange, London (1846–9) (p. 1145), by J. B. Bunning (1802–63), an orthodox exterior contained a circular hall roofed by an ingenious iron-and-glass dome, with the frame fully expressed. More conventional in treatment and character, the dome over the circular Reading Room of the British Museum was constructed in wrought-iron in 1852–7 by Sydney Smirke (1798–1877), brother of Sir Robert, the architect of the original building. An instructive comparison with these is provided by the Oxford Museum (1855–9) (p. 1151) by Deane and Woodward, where the entire building is in the Gothic style, including the iron frame of the exhibition hall which, because of its distinctly articulated jointing, seems curiously sympathetic to the skeletons exhibited.

The use of wrought-iron on a large scale for expressly architectural purposes appears to have been chiefly decorative rather than structural. There are some notable exceptions, such as the train shed at S. Pancras Station, London (1863–7) (p. 1158), designed by the engineer W. H. Barlow (1812–1902), and Paddington Station, London (1852–4) (p. 1157), designed by I. K. Brunel in collaboration with the architect M. D. Wyatt (1820–77), who designed the decorative screens and the motifs within the main structural frames. In Britain, however, wrought-iron appears to have played a secondary rôle to cast-iron.

The direct expression of structure, with a close inter-relationship between structural form and decoration, attracted admiration to Byzantine architecture, especially in the late nineteenth century. Like Gothic architecture, it symbolized a society in which art and life were integral. Westminster Cathedral (1895–1903) (p. 1165), by J. F. Bentley (1839–1902), is the only major example of a modern interpretation of Byzantine principles and a further expression of the outlook which animated the Late Victorian attitude to Gothic already described.

The final nineteenth-century themes to be discussed stem from the reactions of writers and artists to the more commonplace traits of contemporary art and life. Their most positive expression was in Aestheticism, which originated in French literature in the 1830s, and manifested itself in architecture and design as Art Nouveau, which appeared under different names in almost all European countries at the end of the century (see Chapter 38). The principal British contribution seems to have been the development of such characteristic features as the reflex S-curve, attenuated vertical forms and asymmetry. These have complex derivations, but one important source was the introduction of Japanese art, partly through Japanese exhibits in the International Exhibition in London in 1862. A number of architects of advanced views adopted Japanese taste: W. Eden Nesfield decorated his buildings with sunflower motifs, E. W. Godwin (1833–86) designed spindly furniture and interiors with plain walls. He also built the White House, Tite Street, Chelsea, in 1878–9 for the artist J. A. M. Whistler, and although this draws on historical motifs, it uses them in a highly unorthodox manner, and undoubtedly reveals a modern spirit. A. H. Mackmurdo (1851–1942), an architect, was also an artistic innovator. He founded the Century Guild in 1882 which exhibited furniture to his design with pronounced Art Nouveau characteristics, anticipating Belgian and French examples by over a decade. C. F. A. Voysey (1857–1941), an associate of Mackmurdo for a period, also produced what amounted to a personal and largely original mode of design in his neat, carefully planned, unostentatious white houses, with rigorously simple detail, mullioned windows, attenuated interior detail and heart-shaped decorative motifs. The Cottage, Bishop's Itchington (1888–9) (p. 1166), is a representative example. Other British architects who made significant stylistic innovations were Charles Rennie Mackintosh (1868–1928), whose several houses and brilliant design of Glasgow School of Art (1897–1909) (p. 1171) make him pre-eminent amongst a group of highly individualistic architects, including C. R. Ashbee (1863–1942), M. H. Baillie Scott (1865–1945), C. H. Townsend (1852–1928), George Walton (1867–1933) and Edgar Wood (1860–1935). All gained recognition on the Continent and produced designs of a conscious modernity which constitutes the more restrained British architectural equivalent to Art Nouveau, but they each added their personal stylistic inventiveness to a general stock of ideas and design principles then current in the Arts and Crafts Movement.

The inauguration of societies such as the Century Guild, the Art-Workers', Guild and the Arts and Crafts Exhibition Society, in 1882, 1884 and 1888 respectively, marks the formal appearance of the Arts and Crafts Movement. Its ideals can be traced to Ruskin and William Morris (1834–96), the founder of the famous firm which became Morris and Company. From 1877 Morris had been extremely active in lecturing on art, design and architecture and their relation to society, and had powerfully influenced the generation born in the 1860s. He became the public figure associated with the Arts and Crafts Movement. Its aims were to revive the crafts and revitalize design by reuniting it with the crafts, basing it on function and the appropriate use of material. The kinship with the Puginesque ideals of the Gothic Revival are readily apparent. Architects were closely associated with the formation of the different societies and rapidly developed the architectural implications of the movement, particularly in domestic architecture. Houses were planned with careful regard to convenient use and aspect, and the layout of the site and garden was governed by these principles rather than by conventional practice. Local materials and crafts were used whenever possible to produce a building harmonious with the landscape. Materials were used in such a way as to bring out their inherent qualities, and pattern and ornament were used only to enhance salient features of design, while ostentatious overall ornament was rejected. Importance was attached to technical developments leading to improved convenience, sanitation and hygiene. Historical styles were eschewed and it was considered that style would evolve 'organically' from meeting the requirements of the site and the building. The most characteristic architects of the Arts and Crafts Movement were W. R. Lethaby (1857–1931), an outstanding theorist and teacher, and E. S. Prior (1852–1932); but many of the architects born about 1860 and previously mentioned in connection with Aestheticism produced works unmistakably affected by Arts and Crafts ideals.

Many Arts and Crafts buildings, by painted friezes, carvings, stained glass, gesso work, metalwork and a rather more ebullient display of building craft than normal, palpably justify their title, but a number include significant technical innovations too. In E. S. Prior's church of S. Andrew, at Roker, Sunderland (1906–7) (p. 1172) the roof is carried on reinforced concrete purlins; more boldly, Lethaby's All Saints Church, Brockhampton, Herefordshire (1902), has a pitched roof of concrete, supported on stone arches, although externally it is clad in thatch; and Edgar Wood incorporated concrete flat roofs into his houses from 1906 onwards.

The Arts and Crafts Movement, and particularly its domestic architecture, attracted wide attention abroad between 1895 and 1910, especially in Germany and Scandinavia. It is undoubtedly important as a source of modern concepts of design, architecture and town-planning. Perhaps its most socially significant achievement was in the design and layout of low-cost housing, most clearly seen in the work of Barry Parker (1867–1947) and Sir Raymond Unwin (1863–1940). Their design of 1902 for the model village of New Earswick, York (p. 1172), built for Joseph Rowntree, was a significant, imaginative advance, rapidly followed by their work at Letchworth in 1903 and Hampstead Garden Suburb in 1906. Such developments, and Unwin's *Town-planning in Practice* (1909) long remained influential.

The new architectural concepts of the 1880s and 1890s combined with the possibilities produced by the introduction of steel and reinforced concrete led to the design of a heterogeneous group of buildings of strikingly progressive character between 1900 and c. 1914. Nearly all have some historical connotations stylistically, but their innovatory features in other respects outweigh these, and consequently they are not treated thematically here. H. B. Creswell (1869–1960), more famous as the author of *The Honeywood File*, etc., was architect of an early building in this group, the starkly functional factory of 1901 for Willans and Robinson at Queensferry, near Chester (p. 1172). If its battered walls are reminiscent of Egyptian architecture, they are also highly expressive of the massive, load-bearing strength required for their engineering purpose, as are the exposed cast-iron beams which span the openings in the brickwork. J. H. Sellers (1861–1954) was an early exponent of concrete flat-roof construction who worked in association with Edgar Wood of Manchester from about 1904. Their practice was mainly domestic. Sellers was by inclination a Classicist and Wood's previous practice was consistent with the avantgarde of the 1890s. Designing independently, both produced works of remarkable modernity with concrete flat roofs. Amongst other buildings Sellers designed the small but distinguished office block for Dronsfield Bros at Oldham (1906–7) (p. 1172) in a severely restrained but basically classical idiom, and Wood produced a series of houses between 1907 and 1916 planned on highly original lines and built with concrete flat roofs, plain brickwork and Tudorish mullioned windows arranged asymmetrically, of which Upmeads, at Stafford (1908) (p. 1177) is an example. Several larger-scale works expressively exploit the new structural systems. Lion Chambers, Hope Street, Glasgow (1906) (p. 1172) was designed by James Salmon, junior (d. 1924) and built by Mouchel in reinforced concrete on the Hennebique system. At Manchester, Woodhouse, Corbett and Dean produced the Y.M.C.A. building (1908–9) (p. 1177), designed by A. E. Corbett (d. 1916) with the American engineering firm of Julius Kahn. It is a concrete structure clad in faience and completely devoid of historicism or traditional associations. Sir J. J. Burnet (1857–1938) of Glasgow, like Sellers, was fundamentally a Classicist with a strong interest in modern structure. He is most famous for the Kodak building on Kingsway, London (1911) (p. 1177), but several of his Glasgow buildings are notably adventurous, e.g. McGeogh's warehouse (1905) and the Wallace Scott factory, Cathcart (1913), which is architecturally superior and no less expressive than the Kodak design. The buildings in this group do not amount to a movement, so much as a collection of memorable examples revealing a direction of architectural development before 1914. With the exception of Burnet, their architects do not appear to have been influential subsequently, when the Neo-Georgian and Classical Revivals made taste rather than structural logic or radical expression the arbiter of success, but these designs are the fruit of the search for a style, which is such an important aspect of the architectural development of this turbulent period.

EXAMPLES

EARLY VICTORIAN (1830–1850)

The **Clifton Suspension Bridge, Bristol** (1830–63) (p. 1122C), designed by Isambard Kingdom Brunel, a versatile and imaginative engineer, was carried out contrary to the recommendation of Thomas Telford who, as a result of the near destruction of his recently-built Menai Suspension Bridge (1819–26) by crosswinds, doubted the advisability of erecting a suspension bridge of this size in such an exposed position. The principal span of 214 m (702 ft) over the 76 m (250 ft) deep gorge, is suspended on chains from a previous bridge by Brunel, the Hungerford Bridge, London, taken down in 1862. The pylons supporting these are Egyptian in character and Brunel intended that they should be faced with metal plates stamped with hieroglyphics. Antiquarianism and the idea of grandeur matching grandeur are characteristic Early Victorian attitudes. The work proceeded with many delays, but the bridge was completed in 1863, after Brunel's death, by W. H. Barlow, the engineer of S. Pancras Station (see p. 1157).

The **Entrance Screen, Euston Station, London** (1835–7) (p. 1135A), designed by Philip Hardwick (1791–1870) as a triumphal arch in the form of a massive Greek Doric propylaeon, marked the terminus of the London and Birmingham Railway. It was destroyed in 1962 for the reconstruction of the station. The Greek Order chosen by Hardwick represented an already dying fashion in London, and in the later station building of 1846–9 Hardwick, assisted by his son P. C. Hardwick (1822–92), employed the Graeco-Roman style. The Great Hall, now demolished also, was a notably effective example of this style.

A. Entrance Screen, Euston
Station, London (1835–7).
See p. 1134

B. The Fitzwilliam Museum, Cambridge
(1837–47). See p. 1137

c. S. George's Hall, Liverpool (1840–54). See p. 1137

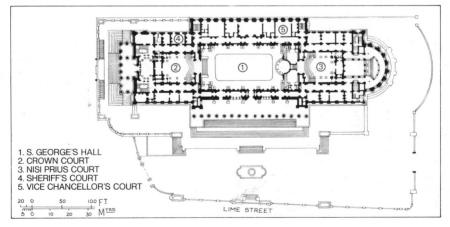

1. S. GEORGE'S HALL
2. CROWN COURT
3. NISI PRIUS COURT
4. SHERIFF'S COURT
5. VICE CHANCELLOR'S COURT

LIME STREET

D. S. George's Hall, Liverpool: ground plan

A. Bristol branch, Bank of England (1844–6). See p. 1137

B. Bridgewater House, London (1847–57). See p. 1138

C. The Reform Club, Pall Mall, London (1837–41): exterior. See p. 1138

D. The Travellers' Club, Pall Mall, London (1829–31): front façade. See p. 1137

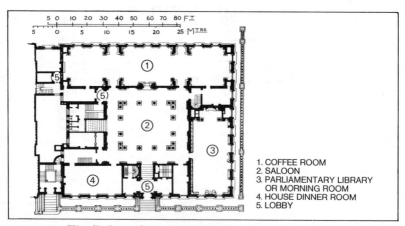

1. COFFEE ROOM
2. SALOON
3. PARLIAMENTARY LIBRARY OR MORNING ROOM
4. HOUSE DINNER ROOM
5. LOBBY

E. The Reform Club, Pall Mall, London (1837–41): plan

S. George's Hall, Liverpool (1840–54) (p. 1135C, D), by Harvey Lonsdale Elmes, is the most magnificent Neo-Classical monument in Britain. Elmes succeeded in winning two separate competitions for a concert hall and for assize courts for Liverpool in 1839 and 1840. Subsequently the accommodation was combined in this one design. The planning is strongly axial, but satisfies the complex requirements ingeniously, and the different elements are freely expressed externally. The main portico (south) has a double row of eight Corinthian columns, and the east and west elevations are essentially symmetrical. Elmes died in 1847, aged only thirty-three, and the structure was completed by the engineer Sir Robert Rawlinson and, later, C. R. Cockerell designed much of the interior detail, including the circular concert room.

The **Fitzwilliam Museum, Cambridge** (1837–47) (p. 1135B) is the work of George Basevi and was completed after his death by C. R. Cockerell. The latter was a fastidious and scholarly architect and it is revealing to compare the character of his works with this more florid work by Basevi. The Fitzwilliam Museum is more orthodox in relation to archaeological prototypes, with its giant Corinthian portico, but is decidedly brash. The portico and heavily pilastered wings make an impressively showy front, which is in marked contrast to the plain side elevations.

The **Ashmolean Museum (University Galleries) and Taylor Institution, Oxford** (1841–5), by C. R. Cockerell, who was a confirmed Classicist, is an extensive, southward-facing building breaking forward at the ends into wings. It is ornamented with a giant Ionic Order, pilastered mostly, but with free-standing or attached columns at the principal points. The monumental qualities are most apparent on the east front of the east wing, where the Order is the Ionic of the Temple of Apollo Epicurus, Bassae (p. 220C), with its extraordinarily deep capitals, which Cockerell had studied in Greece in his youth. The entablature returns above the columns, which carry only statues.

The **Bristol Branch of the Bank of England** (1844–6) (p. 1136A), was designed by C. R. Cockerell, who was appointed architect to the Bank of England in 1833, in succession to Sir John Soane. He carried out alterations to the Bank of England, London, in 1834–5 and 1845 and also built branches at **Plymouth** (1835), **Manchester** (1845–6) and **Liverpool** (1845–58). They are similar and equally distinguished in character, combining Classical and Renaissance elements in a highly original way. Each design is dominated by a pediment, contains a Classical Order and entablature, and employs Renaissance devices to provide means of introducing windows to give light in a multi-storey building. All of these elements conform to a powerful, strongly modelled, geometrical arrangement which Cockerell executed with great precision and masterly clarity.

The **National Gallery of Scotland, Edinburgh** (1850–4) (p. 1139A), by W. H. Playfair, is one of the numerous monumental Greek Revival buildings with which the city was endowed in the early decades of the nineteenth century. This, with the **Royal College of Physicians** (1850–4) by Thomas Hamilton (1785–1858), is a remarkably late example of the style for a major work. The National Gallery is in the Ionic style, whilst the adjacent Royal Scottish Institution (1833–6), also by Playfair, is a rather overladen essay in Greek Doric.

The **Travellers' Club, Pall Mall, London** (1829–31) (p. 1136D), by Sir Charles Barry, is one of the designs in which he initiated the Renaissance Revival and the 'palazzo' mode in England. The two-storeyed façade of five regular bays is made asymmetrical by the location of the main entrance in an end bay. The storeys are divided by a deep string-course and capped by a projecting cornice. The external corners are emphasized by toothed quoins and the windows are framed, the upper ones being made dominant by balustrades, pediments and flanking pilasters.

All the Renaissance apparatus, said to be derived here from the Palazzo Pandolfini, Florence (p. 827), is deployed with refined skill.

The **Reform Club, Pall Mall, London** (1837–41) (p. 1136c, e) by Sir Charles Barry, adjoins his Travellers' Club and is a similar but more imposing design, being larger, three-storeyed, and symmetrical. It is planned around a central saloon (in place of the Italian cortile), with rooms opening from it in such a way that the saloon and the rooms conform to axial principles. In the exterior design the link to the Travellers' Club is managed neatly by a recessed two-storey bay containing an entrance. The Renaissance features previously described are repeated, but the windows to the uppermost storey are framed by astragal mouldings and embraced in a frieze below the cornice. Barry's **Athenaeum, Manchester** (1837–9) is a similar variant on the palazzo theme, which he further developed at **Bridgewater House, London** (1847–57) (p. 1136b), now demolished, a town house of grand scale. It was planned on the cortile principle and was distinguished externally by a more vigorous expression of rustication, especially at the quoins, than was normal in Barry's earlier works, giving an effect of massiveness and strength.

Westminster New Palace (Houses of Parliament), London (1836–68) (p. 1139b, c). The Old Palace of Westminster was destroyed by fire in 1834 and in 1836 the design by Sir Charles Barry was selected from those submitted in the architectural competition for the New Palace. A non-Classical design had been forced upon Barry by the competition conditions (see p. 1128 above), and he had obtained the expert assistance of A. W. N. Pugin for the Tudor detail of the building. Three important trends emerged from the design: the authentic Gothic detail, supplied by Pugin, reflects the antiquarian character of the contemporary Gothic Revival; the formal, but not fully symmetrical planning by Barry, which had to accommodate the surviving Westminster Hall, reveals the continuing potency of Classicism; and the informal, irregular grouping of the towers and skyline, especially when seen from the riverside, is eloquent testimony to the value still attached to the concept of the Picturesque. Because these three strands are so inextricably combined, the Houses of Parliament summarises the developments of several previous decades, and one could consider the Early Victorian phase to begin after this architectural landmark. The formal approach from the west or landward side is via S. Stephen's Porch, which also gives access to Westminster Hall and leads into the Central Hall, where a cross-axis leads south to the House of Lords and north to the House of Commons. Subsidiary suites of chambers are arranged around a series of courts. In the south-west corner the massive Victoria Tower rises 102 m (336 ft) high, and at the northern end is the Clock Tower, 96 m (316 ft) high, housing 'Big Ben'. There is a further 'Middle Tower' or spired lantern over the Central Hall, rising to 91 m (300 ft) in height. This great complex of buildings, with its intricate Tudor detail, is significant as the first major public building of the Gothic Revival.

S. Wilfred, Hulme, Manchester (1839–42) (p. 1140c), by A. W. N. Pugin, was designed in accordance with the architect's ecclesiological principles, and was described by him in his book *The Present State of Ecclesiastical Architecture in England* (1843). It differs from the 'Commissioner' Gothic Revival churches built under the 1818 Million Pound Act in having separately articulated parts—nave, aisle and south porch, together with eastern lateral chapels divided from the aisles and chancel by ornamentally-painted screens. It was to have had a tower at the north-west corner, which would have made it the first Gothic Revival church to depart from the axial principle, but funds gave out. Intended to demonstrate that a Gothic 'Correct' church need not be more costly than a Classical one, it is of red brick with stone dressings, and although unimpressive as a monument, it makes its point architecturally.

A. The National Gallery of Scotland, Edinburgh (1850–4). See p. 1137

B. Westminster Palace (Houses of Parliament), London (1836–68). See p. 1138

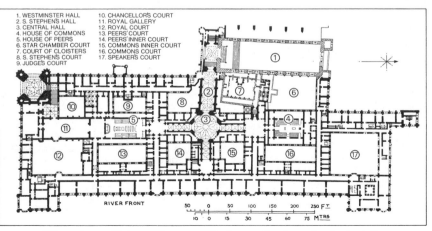

1. WESTMINSTER HALL	10. CHANCELLOR'S COURT
2. S. STEPHEN'S HALL	11. ROYAL GALLERY
3. CENTRAL HALL	12. ROYAL COURT
4. HOUSE OF COMMONS	13. PEERS' COURT
5. HOUSE OF PEERS	14. PEERS' INNER COURT
6. STAR CHAMBER COURT	15. COMMONS INNER COURT
7. COURT OF CLOISTERS	16. COMMONS COURT
8. S. STEPHEN'S COURT	17. SPEAKER'S COURT
9. JUDGES' COURT	

RIVER FRONT

C. Westminster Palace (Houses of Parliament): plan of principal floor

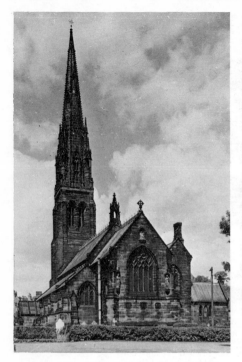

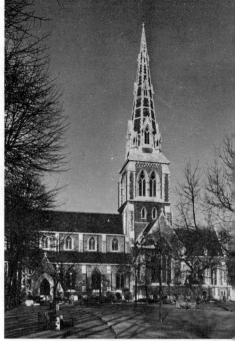

A. S. Giles, Cheadle, Staffs (1841–6). See p. 1141

B. S. Giles, Camberwell Church Street, London (1842–4). See p. 1141

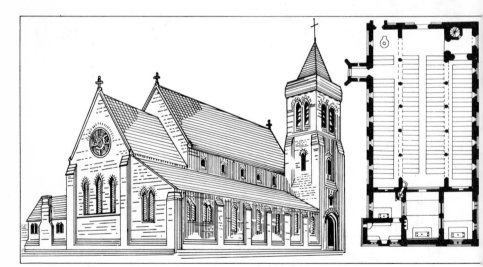

C. S. Wilfred, Hulme, Manchester (1839–42): perspective and plan. See p. 1138

S. Giles, Cheadle, Staffs (1841–6) (p. 1140A), by A. W. N. Pugin, is a handsome, stone-built and finely finished church. Its composition profits by the presence of a commanding axial western tower and spire. Not unduly ornamented externally, its interior rejects the 'Puginian' canon, but is sumptuously painted and decorated.

S. Giles, Camberwell Church Street, London (1842–4) (p. 1140B), by Scott and Moffatt, was won by them in competition before Sir George Gilbert Scott had set up on his own account. It is a large stone structure seating 1,500 persons; cruciform in plan, it rises to an impressive spire-crowned central tower 60 m (200 ft) high. Designed in the Geometrical Gothic style of the thirteenth century, it demonstrated Scott's powers and also provided a model for certain of his own later churches as well as for those of fellow architects. Other comparable Gothic Revival churches are **S. Paul, Brighton** (1846–8), by R. C. Carpenter; **S. Stephen, Rochester Row, London** (1847–50), by Benjamin Ferrey (1810–80); and **Holy Trinity, Bessborough Gardens, London** (1849–52), by J. L. Pearson.

The **House at Ramsgate, Kent** (1841–3) (p. 1142B), was built for himself by Pugin in his own version of Gothic (he had built an earlier residence of eccentric design, S. Marie's Grange, near Salisbury, in 1835–6, which he had occupied for the previous five years). It is of flint with stone dressings on the road elevation, and grey-yellow brickwork for the toothed quoins and for the walling elsewhere. Notable features are the studied asymmetry, the steep, barge-boarded gables and the general informality of the arrangements. Only the more important windows have label-moulds, transoms and traceried heads, and there is a first-floor oriel of timber of quite unorthodox design.

The **Vicarage, S. Saviour, Coalpitheath, Gloucestershire** (1844–5) (p. 1142A), an early design of William Butterfield, is a freely-planned composition of stone rubble with ashlar dressings. The main rooms are reached from the living-hall, as was normal in the traditional yeoman's house. The roofs, which have gabled parapets, are steep, and there are casually-disposed angle-buttresses as well as a square, shallow bay.

Harlaxton Hall, Lincolnshire (1834–55) (p. 1142C), by Anthony Salvin (1799–1881), demonstrates that combination of Elizabethan and Jacobean features which gained the nickname 'Jacobethan'. Although the main block is substantially symmetrical, its ogival cupolas, spiky pinnacles, banks of chimneys and gables create, from any non-axial view, a picturesque effect which was undoubtedly not unintentional. **Scotney Castle, Lamberhurst, Kent** (1837–40), was also by Salvin and is a much plainer but pleasant building.

Highclere Castle, Hampshire (1842–4) (p. 1142E), is a refacing by Sir Charles Barry of an existing mansion. Also 'Jacobethan', it is formal and severe in its modelling, if not in its detail. It is a four-square block with serried two-light transomed windows in three tiers, demarcated by pilastered Orders and crowned by pinnacled pierced parapets. Its angle towers rise a storey higher, and a massive principal tower rises a further stage to command the whole.

The **Conservatory, Carlton House, London** (1811–12) (p. 1142D), although pre-dating this period, illustrates in the elaborate design of Thomas Hopper the use of cast-iron for structural and decorative purposes; structural in the columns and decorative in the fan-vaulting and tracery.

S. George, Everton, Liverpool (1812–14) (p. 1142F), by Thomas Rickman and with iron-work by the ironmaster John Cragg, is one of the two churches which were built in this manner in the locality, representing a potentially systematic use of the material for architectural purposes. The character of the Gothic design is reminiscent of the eighteenth rather than expressive of the nineteenth century.

The **Conservatory, Chatsworth, Derbyshire** (1836–40, demolished 1920)

A. The Vicarage, S. Saviour, Coalpitheath, Gloucestershire (1844-5). See p. 1141

B. Pugin's House, Ramsgate (1841-3). See p. 1141

c. Harlaxton Hall, Lincolnshire (1834-55). See p. 1141

D. Carlton House, London: Conservatory (1811-12). See p. 1141

E. Highclere Castle, Hampshire (1842-4). See p. 1141

F. S. George, Everton, Liverpool (1812-14). See p. 1141

A. The Conservatory, Chatsworth, Derbyshire (1836–40). See p. 1141

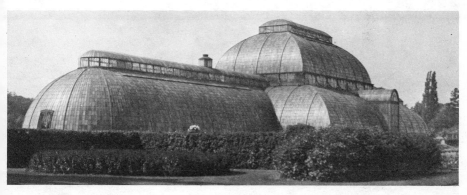

B. The Palm House, Royal Botanic Gardens, Kew (1845–7). See p. 1145

C. King's Cross Station, London (1850–2). See p. 1145

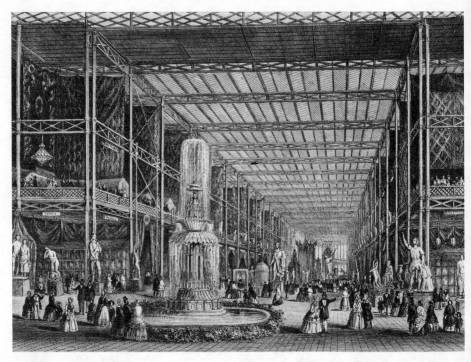

A. The Crystal Palace at completion in Hyde Park, London (1851): interior

B. Revised structure, erected (1852-4) at Sydenham, London

The Crystal Palace, London. See p. 1145

(p. 1143A), was an early venture in iron and glass by the gardener Sir Joseph Paxton, assisted by Decimus Burton in the grounds of the sixteenth- and late seventeenth-century mansion (p. 1014). It was not the first of its kind, except in its extraordinary magnitude, being 84 m (277 ft) long and 37 m (123 ft) wide, rising to a height of 20.4 m (67 ft) in the form of a double vault, one cloister vault being raised upon another. The timber and glass ridge-and-furrow sections anticipated those of the famous Crystal Palace.

The **Palm House, Royal Botanic Gardens, Kew** (1845-7) (p. 1143B), by Decimus Burton and Richard Turner, resembles the Chatsworth design in its central part—except that all the glass smoothly follows the double vault section, which is crowned by a shallow, continuous apex feature. Two single-vault arms, rounded at the ends, extend from the central portion which spans 32 m (106 ft) and rises 18.9 m (62 ft): the wings span 17 m (56 ft) and rise 10 m (33 ft).

The **Coal Exchange, Lower Thames Street, London** (1846-9, demolished) (p. 1147A), by J. B. Bunning, was a corner block presenting Italian Renaissance masonry façades linked by a tower over the angle entrance. It was notable for an internal iron-framed glass dome over the circular court; the dome was 18 m (60 ft) in diameter and 22.5 m (74 ft) high, with cantilevered access balconies serving each of its three upper tiers. This structural element, walls and dome, was entirely metal-framed, and no masonry at all appeared. A comparable domical building is the **Reading Room, British Museum** (1852-7), added by Sydney Smirke, of which the main ribs are of wrought-iron, but the structure of greater dimensions, the room being 42.6 m (140 ft) across and 32.3 m (106 ft) high. The architectural treatment, however, is more orthodox than Bunning's.

King's Cross Station, London (1850-2) (p. 1143C), by Lewis Cubitt, has an entrance façade which is a part of the train sheds, which it completes with a pair of vast brick arches in receding orders set between massive piers, but with a slightly incongruous Italianate clock-tower rising from the central one. Cubitt's design included the triple-arcaded porticoes below each of the great arches which lent a Roman scale and dignity to the unpretentious composition. The two iron-and-glass barrel vaults over the tracks were carried on laminated-timber arches rising 21.7 m (72 ft) to bridge the 32 m (105 ft) spans, but were replaced by steel arches in the identical positions in 1869.

The **Crystal Palace, London** (1850-1) (p. 1144), designed by Sir Joseph Paxton, was one of the most remarkable buildings in nineteenth-century Britain. Although the Great Exhibition, for which it was built, is generally considered to belong to the High Victorian epoch, the building of the Crystal Palace rests firmly on Early Victorian technology and is here regarded as its culminating example. It was erected originally in Hyde Park and was moved to Sydenham in 1852-4. The idea of holding a great exhibition was conceived in 1849, and public subscriptions were invited. An international competition was launched in 1850 and 245 designs were received. None was acceptable, and with limited time available all were set aside in favour of an idea of Paxton's, after an attempt to combine the best features of the more promising of the competition designs in a single official project. The working drawings were hurriedly prepared in a seven-week period after the letting of the contract in August 1850, and the structure was wholly completed nine months later on 1 May 1851, each structural component having been tested before erection. Paxton's idea, arising from his experience at Chatsworth and elsewhere, was for a giant conservatory with a cast-iron frame and the ridge-and-furrow glazing system he had developed for the Chatsworth conservatory. In cross section the building somewhat resembled a double-aisled basilica, rising in three tiers, the lowest 124.4 m (408 ft) wide, the next (the inner aisles) 80.4 m (264 ft) and the nave or topmost 36.5 m (120 ft). However, the 'aisles' and 'nave' were divided from one another by tiered open galleries 7.3 m (24 ft) wide, so that the actual span of the 'nave' was only 22 m (72 ft) (the same as its height). Symbolically, the total width was made up of fifty-one of the 2.4 m (8 ft) wide bay units, and the length was 563 m (1,848 ft), this being as near to 1,851 as the 8-ft units would allow. About the middle of the length a 'transept' was introduced, as a last-minute modification of the working design, to allow the enclosure of a growing tree. The transept had the same width as the nave but was barrel-vaulted. In this colossal project of prefabricated building, requiring vast quantities of iron and glass and other materials, as well as scrupulous organization to allow the work to be completed in so short a time, Paxton had as engineer-associates Sir Charles Fox (1810–74) and his partner, while Owen Jones, author of the book *Grammar of Ornament* (1856), was responsible for the decoration. Changes were made when the Palace was re-erected at Sydenham, the nave then being given a barrel roof, like the transepts (p. 1144B). The entire structure was destroyed by fire in 1936.

HIGH VICTORIAN (1850–1870)

The **Town Hall, Leeds** (1853–9) (p. 1147C), by Cuthbert Brodrick, is the masterpiece of High Victorian Classicism. Grandiose in conception, rugged and massive in outline and opulent in detail, it asserts the independence and pride of an important and prosperous industrial city. The colonnade owes a debt to S. George's Hall, Liverpool (p. 1135C), and the cupola reveals the contemporary French influence, but such elements are fully assimilated in so original and bold a design. Other notable works by Brodrick are the **Corn Exchange, Leeds** (1851–3) and the **Grand Hotel, Scarborough** (1863–7).

The **Free Trade Hall, Manchester** (1853–4) (p. 1147B), by Edward Walters, is a powerful design in the 'palazzo' style. It differs from Barry's earlier 'palazzo' designs (pp. 1137–8) by the High Victorian character expressed in the bold mouldings and the rich details. It was built to commemorate the success of the Anti-Corn Law League, but of the original structure only the two principal elevations survive, owing to war damage. The lowest storey of the main façade forms a handsome, open arcade with massive piers and carved spandrels. The 'piano nobile' is also arcaded and its bays are divided by paired Ionic columns. In each bay a sculptured panel, each representing by a seated figure some branch of world trade, is placed within the intrados of the arch and surmounting a framed and pedimented window. Above the arcade a swagged frieze is succeeded by a cornice and balustrade. The arcading to the piano nobile is deeply inset and the whole façade is strongly and decisively modelled; the Renaissance cornucopia was never more generously filled. Walters designed several other excellent 'palazzo' style buildings in Manchester, mainly warehouses. His last work, the Manchester and Salford District Bank (now Williams and Glyn's), Moseley Street, of 1860, is also an exceptional work.

The **Caledonia Road Free Church, Glasgow** (1856–7) (p. 1147E), by Alexander Thomson, an admirable if belated example of the Greek Revival (a style which survived much longer in Scotland than in England) has the asymmetrically placed western tower normal to High Victorian Gothic in an impressively massive structure terminating rather weakly above an open belfry in an inset, heavily-corniced attic. The hexastyle west porch, of faultless classical proportions, is raised upon a high podium adorned only with lateral entrance doors. The interior of the church was gutted by fire in 1965 and, regrettably, has not been restored. Two other Glasgow churches by Thomson, also in Greek Revival style, are in S. Vincent Street (1859) and Queen's Park (1867).

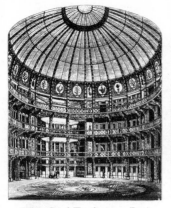

A. The Coal Exchange, Lower
Thames Street, London:
interior (1846–9). See p. 1145

B. The Free Trade Hall, Manchester
(1853–4). See p. 1146

C. The Town Hall, Leeds
(1853–9). See p. 1146

D. The Foreign Office, London (1860–75).
See p. 1151

E. Caledonia Road Free
Church, Glasgow (1856–7).
See p. 1146

F. Alford House, London (1872).
See p. 1151

A. Church, Choir School and Parsonage   B. Interior: nave and chancel

All Saints, Margaret Street, London (1849–59). See p. 1151

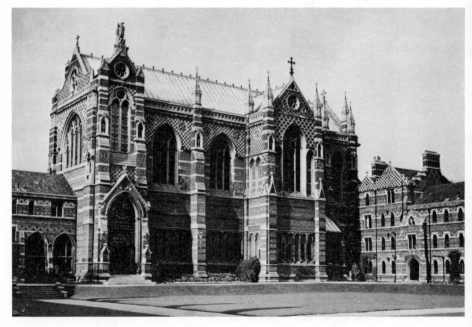

C. Keble College, Oxford: chapel (1867–83). See p. 1151

A. The University Museum, Oxford (1855–9). See p. 1151

B. The University Museum, Oxford: interior

C. Church of SS. Philip and James, Oxford (1860–2). See p. 1152

A. View from S.

B. Interior   C. Plan

Red House, Bexleyheath, Kent (1859–60). See p. 1151

The **Foreign Office, London** (1860–75) (p. 1147D), by Sir George Gilbert Scott, is his only work in the Italian Renaissance manner, but it is by no means ineffectual. In the controversy of the 'Battle of the Styles' over this project, Scott was obliged to provide a non-Gothic design, but some approximation of his original intentions may be seen in his S. Pancras Station and Hotel (p. 1152).

Alford House, London (1872, now demolished) (p. 1147F), by Sir M. D. Wyatt, was French in character, with a mansard roof, and luxuriant terra-cotta dressings, derived from the 'Second Empire' mode then popular.

All Saints, Margaret Street, Westminster (1849–59) (p. 1148A, B), by William Butterfield, is a turning-point in the Gothic Revival and the first church to incorporate polychromy in its construction. It stands with a parsonage and choir school on an extremely cramped site, creating a striking effect by its unusual character and lofty spire. It was built as a model church of the Ecclesiologists in the 'Middle Pointed' or fourteenth-century Gothic style then favoured. Typical but not invariable Butterfieldian features are the harsh, angular forms, the brick construction and the highly durable materials used to form permanent decoration in 'constructional polychromy'. Internally, geometrical patterns decorate the walls and fittings in multi-coloured marbles and tiles and alabaster. Stained glass and gilded ironwork add to the rich effect. The church was a potent source of influence for secular and ecclesiastical architecture. Among many other works by Butterfield are **S. Mathias, Stoke Newington** (1849–53), **S. Alban, Holborn** (1859–62, now altered internally), **Rugby School** (1858–84), **Keble College and Chapel, Oxford** (1867–83) (p. 1148C), and numerous churches, parsonages and church restorations, some of which assume the unobtrusive character of vernacular forms.

The **University Museum, Oxford** (1855–9) (p. 1149A, B), designed by Benjamin Woodward (1815–61), of Deane and Woodward, is a landmark of High Victorian Gothic architecture, regarded by C. L. Eastlake as 'one of the first fruits of Mr. Ruskin's teaching'. The main front (p. 1149A) has a narrow, steeply-roofed central feature, containing the entrance door, flanked by two-storey wings in which there are regularly-spaced windows of Italian Gothic type. In the steep roofs of the wings there are triangular dormers in two series, the upper extremely small. The walls are of cream-coloured Bath stone, with inset marbles around the doorway head and upper-window arches, and the roofs are patterned in purple and grey-green slates. Internally, there is a quadrangle roofed with iron and glass (p. 1149B); the ironwork is decoratively 'Gothicized' with elaborate ornament. The roof is carried upon clustered and banded iron pillars, from which spring arcade ribs and steeply-pointed transverse ribs, the latter reaching to the apex of the glazed, pitched roof. The covered quadrangle is itself walled about by polychrome arcades. The selection of stones used in the construction and the naturalistic carvings of foliage, etc., relate to the building's scientific purpose. Woodward was also the architect of the **University Union, Oxford** (1856–7).

The **Assize Courts, Manchester** (1859–64), designed by Alfred Waterhouse, and demolished in 1959 after war damage, was particularly marked by Ruskin's influence. It was by this building, won in competition, that Waterhouse first made his name and it was said to 'unite considerable artistic merit with unusual advantages in regard to plan and internal arrangement'. A symmetrical two-storey building, over a windowed basement, with an arcaded central entrance block, slightly projecting angle pavilions and a bell-tower rising axially behind, it was typical High Victorian Gothic in its mixture of English, Lombard and French characteristics, the latter shown especially in the high-pitched and pavilioned roofs.

Red House, Bexleyheath, Kent (1859–60) (p. 1150), built by Philip Webb (1831–1915) for William Morris, so named because its materials, red brick and tiles, represent a striking change from the normal pretentious and heavily stylized dwelling of the period. The design is rationally eclectic rather than stylistically pure Gothic, although the general effect of high-pitched roofs and pointed arches is Gothic in character. Nevertheless, sash windows were used for practical reasons as were the pointed arches which span them. The planning is informal and unconventional, but met the practical needs of its singular owner. The different elements of plan and structure are expressed in accordance with Puginesque principles. The remarkable interior decoration and furnishings presage the Arts and Crafts Movement of the 1880s. Other works by Webb include **Arisaig, Inverness-shire** (1863, now much altered), the **Green Dining Room** at the **South Kensington Museum** (1866) with William Morris's firm of Morris, Marshall, Faulkner & Co., and **1, Palace Green, Kensington** (1868).

The **Church of S. Philip and S. James, Oxford** (1860–2) (p. 1149C), by G. E. Street, is a fine composition on an essentially English cruciform plan. The design illustrates French influence in the semicircular apse to the chancel and the repetition of wheel windows. Polychromy appears in the bands of red sandstone inserted into the creamy-yellow masonry, in the alternating colours of the voussoirs and by similar means in the interior, which is richly decorated with stained glass. Street, a member of the Ecclesiological Society, was principally a church architect and his importance and influence is similar to that of Butterfield. Other church commissions he executed include **S. Peter, Bournemouth** (1845–79), **All Saints, Boyne Hill, Maidenhead** (1854–7), **S. James-the-Less, Thorndike Street, London** (1858–61), and **All Saints, Bolton, Lancs** (1870).

The **Albert Memorial, London** (1863–72) (p. 1154A), by Sir George Gilbert Scott, is highly representative of High Victorian Gothic design. The seated bronze figure of the prince, elevated on a pedestal, is placed within an elaborate, spired and pinnacled ciborium, built of polished granite and marbles and embellished by mosaic, which crowns a high, sculptured base and an imposing stepped platform. The memorial was the subject of a competition won by Scott in 1863. His use of the ciborium theme was anticipated by Thomas Worthington (1826–1909), the designer of the **Albert Memorial, Manchester** (1862–4) (p. 1153A).

The **Town Hall, Congleton, Cheshire** (1864–7) (p. 1153C), by E. W. Godwin, is a modest, pleasant building embodying Italian and French Gothic influences in a remarkably successful way. It is two-storeyed, arcaded at street level, and has a central, machicolated and battlemented tower rising flush with the façade, and in general is reminiscent of a building such as the Palazzo Pubblico at Montepulciano (p. 745H). Northern Gothic character is evident in the flèche to the clock turret and the steeply-pitched roof pierced by sharp dormers. A further High Victorian characteristic is the polychromy of the roof and other details. Godwin was also responsible for the Town Hall at Northampton (1861–4).

S. Pancras Hotel and Station block, London (1865–71) (p. 1154B), by Sir George Gilbert Scott, is a prime example of High Victorian secular Gothic. Won in competition, the building allowed free rein to Scott's predilection for this style. The frontages rise through tiers of crowded pointed-arched openings to a steeply-pitched roof serrated by jagged dormers, massive chimney stacks and soaring pinnacled and spired towers. Scott originally intended that his design for the Foreign Office (p. 1151) should be in this vein, but more Italian in character, and this was the source of the contention. Other major secular works by Scott include **Leeds Infirmary** (1863) and **Glasgow University** (1864).

The **Town Hall, Manchester** (1868–77) (p. 1153A, B), by Alfred Waterhouse, has been described as a classic of the age. It is ingeniously planned on a difficult, triangular site and resolves the awkward external angles by skilful devices of

A. The Town Hall, Manchester (1868–77) with Albert Memorial (1862–4) on left.
See p. 1152

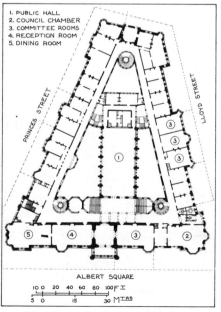

1. PUBLIC HALL
2. COUNCIL CHAMBER
3. COMMITTEE ROOMS
4. RECEPTION ROOM
5. DINING ROOM

PRINCES STREET

LLOYD STREET

ALBERT SQUARE

10 0   20   40   60   80   100 F I
5   0   15   30 M RS

B. The Town Hall, Manchester: plan

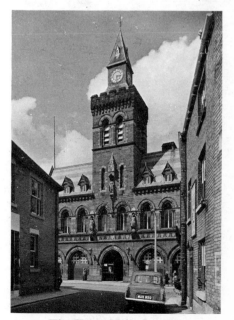

c. The Town Hall, Congleton,
Cheshire (1864–7). See p. 1152

A. The Albert Memorial, London
(1863–72). See p. 1152

B. S. Pancras Station, London (1865–71).
See p. 1152

C. Cardiff Castle (1868–85).
See p. 1157

D. Castell Coch, Cardiff (1875–91).
See p. 1157

A. The Royal Courts of Justice, London (1871–82). See p. 1157

B. Gardener's Warehouse, Jamaica Street, Glasgow (1855–6). See p. 1158

C. Train shed at S. Pancras Station, London (1863–7). See p. 1158

D. Oriel Chambers, Liverpool (1864–5). See p. 1158

E. Boatstore, Royal Naval Dockyard, Sheerness (1858–60). See p. 1158

A. Glen Andred, Groombridge, Sussex (1866–7). See p. 1157

B. Leys Wood, Groombridge, Sussex (1868–9). See p. 1157

projecting bays and blocks. The internal treatment is imaginative and effective. Open arcades and different levels produce constantly changing vistas and spatial relationships. The building is consistently well detailed and appropriately decorated. It represents the peak of Waterhouse's long career. His practice became vast and included **Owens College, Manchester University** (1870–1902), the **Natural History Museum, London** (1868–80), the headquarters in Holborn, London (from 1876) and numerous buildings for the Prudential Assurance Company. For the latter client he built in red brick and terra-cotta, materials which he increasingly adopted in his later career for their serviceability.

Cardiff Castle (1868–85) (p. 1154C) and **Castell Coch, near Cardiff, Glamorganshire** (1875–91) (p. 1154D), were reconstructed for the Marquess of Bute in a fantastic and highly personal version of the Gothic Revival by William Burges. The work at Castell Coch was militarily realistic to the point of providing a working drawbridge and portcullis, and apertures through which boiling liquids could be poured, but in addition to such novelties it possesses magnificent formal qualities which display on the largest scale Burges's exceptional talent. Both buildings are exotically detailed and decorated internally and in this respect Cardiff Castle is its author's chief work. Sculptures, mural painting, painted and carved friezes, stencilled patterns and decorated tiles create an incredibly rich but never uncontrolled profusion of ornament. In these buildings the Gothic Revival was a vehicle for an unusually vivid and exuberant imagination.

The **Royal Courts of Justice, London** (1871–82) (p. 1155A), by G. E. Street, one of the last important buildings to be erected in the High Victorian Gothic style, is a vast, vigorously modelled and romantic composition, planned with considerable ingenuity to meet complex requirements, with the courts arranged about a huge, vaulted Gothic concourse. The design is highly personal to Street, who executed 3,000 drawings by his own hand and completed the building in the face of dogged official parsimony.

Glen Andred, Groombridge, Sussex (1866–7) (p. 1156A), illustrative of the vernacular revival, was the first wholly personal design by Norman Shaw, though he was still at that time in partnership with W. Eden Nesfield. Shaw's style was not then fully formed, and the effect is somewhat crowded, yet the house has an honesty and freedom of expression which compares favourably with the work of his contemporaries. Much more romantic is his **Leys Wood, at Groombridge, Sussex** (1868–9) (p. 1156B), a large, brick and partly tile-hung structure arranged round three sides of a court, embodying Mediaeval motifs, including half-timber elements. Half-timber also appears in a number of houses that followed: **Grim's Dyke, near Harrow** (1872); **Wispers, Midhurst, Sussex** (1875); and **Cragside, Northumberland** (1870), a dramatically sited romantic pile in the Cheviots, where Shaw's vernacular vocabulary appears incongruously out of context. Shaw continued to develop his vernacular manorial manner for a further twenty-five years, but in simpler forms.

Paddington Station, London is of interest principally for its station sheds (1852–4) designed by Isambard Kingdom Brunel and the architect Sir M. D. Wyatt, and not for the Great-Western Hotel, forming its frontispiece. The sheds are of three spans totalling 72.5 m (238 ft), the centre one being wider than the others. Each of the coverings is carried on semi-elliptical wrought-iron ribs, without principals, glazed only over the central third. The three are joined together by cross vaults at two points in the length. Wyatt was responsible for the decorative aspect of the scheme, and notably the Gothic and Saracenic motifs integral within the structural members and wrought-iron screens. **S. Pancras Station, London,** like Paddington, was conceived independently of the (former) Midland Hotel and offices fronting it. The **train shed** (1863–7) (p. 1155C), by the engineer W. H. Barlow (1812–1902), is the largest and most spectacular of the High Victorian period, being a single span of 74 m (243 ft), rising 30 m (100 ft) high in a slightly pointed wrought-iron arch. The total length is 213 m (700 ft). At the base the arched vault is secured by rods 76 mm (3 ins) in diameter under the platforms.

Gardener's Warehouse, Jamaica Street, Glasgow (1855–6) (p. 1155B), by John Baird I, with its cast-iron façades, illustrates the great popularity of the material at this time, even if it was seldom used as external cladding in Britain. The material lends itself to easy repetition, and it is significant that each storey varies in this design, in which the lower ranges of arches are made progressively flatter for purely architectural reasons. A similar building, Paisley's warehouse (1854–5), stands nearby.

The **Boatstore, Royal Naval Dockyard, Sheerness** (1858–60) (p. 1155E), by G. T. Greene, who from 1850–64 was Director of Engineering and Architectural Works to the Admiralty, is among the earliest known tiered iron-framed buildings, particularly advanced in the details of its construction. Being a utilitarian building, the external panels could be lightly infilled with sheeting. It is 64 m (210 ft) long and 41 m (135 ft) wide, arranged internally as a top-lit 'nave' running the whole length of the building, and double 'aisles' with floors on each side at each of the four storeys. The stanchions already have the 'H' section which came to be adopted regularly later on.

Oriel Chambers, Liverpool (1864–5) (p. 1155D), by Peter Ellis, is another remarkably advanced building for the period, both in construction and architectural character. It has a complete cast-iron frame, stone-clad on the front in thin masonry piers, between which are iron frames carrying delicately detailed shallow oriels in each panel. There is little or no historical allusion in the forms employed, save a suggestion of collegiate Gothic in the cresting. No. 16, Cook Street, Liverpool (c. 1866), also by Ellis, is of similar construction and equally original.

LATE VICTORIAN AND EDWARDIAN (1870-1914)

Kinmel Park, Denbighshire (1868–74) (p. 1159A), by William Eden Nesfield, illustrates a re-awakening interest in Classical architecture, but although the house exhibits Renaissance components, e.g. segmental pediments, pilasters, sash windows, consoles and mouldings, it is not planned on the axial principles of Classical architecture (p. 1167A). It was the free and picturesque arrangement of such features that came to be known as the 'Queen Anne' style.

Lowther Lodge, Kensington (1873–4) (p. 1159B), by R. N. Shaw, who as well as building romantic vernacular-style houses (p. 1156B), designed in this informal mode of the Queen Anne style, which permitted Gothic freedom in planning and arrangement without Gothic associations. In this picturesque example the connection with Classicism is extremely tenuous, but individual details (see Kinmel Park, above) reveal the inclination of current taste. Shaw's **Old Swan House, Chelsea** (1876) and **170, Queen's Gate, London** (1888) (p. 1159D) approach a more orthodox Classical arrangement in their symmetrical elevations. The formality of 170 Queen's Gate is more truly akin to the original seventeenth-century Queen Anne house than the numerous examples supposedly originating from its example. Both designs were influential and are in marked contrast to the elaborations of the Jacobean, Flemish and French Renaissance styles then prevailing.

Bryanston, Dorset (1890) and **Chesters, Northumberland** (1891) (p. 1160), also by R. N. Shaw, both illustrate a positive return to Classic principles of axial design in plan and symmetry in elevation, further reinforced by the introduction of

A. Kinmel Park, Denbighshire (1868–74). See p. 1158

B. Lowther Lodge, Kensington (1873–4). See p. 1158

c. Extension to the Law Society Building, London (1902–4). See p. 1161

D. 170, Queen's Gate, London (1888). See p. 1158

E. Heathcote, Ilkley, Yorkshire (1906). See p. 1161

A. Chesters, Northumberland (1891). See p. 1158

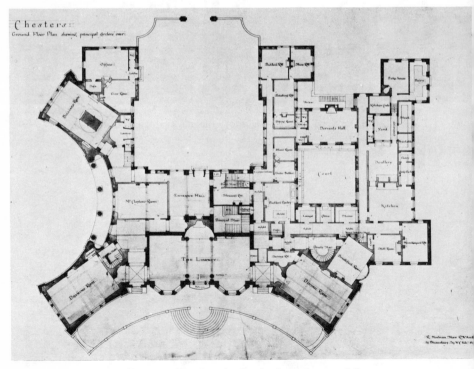

B. Chesters, Northumberland: plan of ground floor

an Ionic colonnade at Chesters. Both houses are highly accomplished works attempting to continue and extend the English country house tradition of the seventeenth and eighteenth centuries. Bryanston has features in common with Coleshill House, Berkshire (p. 1013), especially in the treatment of the main block, but the striation is of nineteenth-century assertiveness. Chesters incorporates an older house to which Shaw added wings to create the concave frontages to the south and west.

The **Town Hall, Colchester** (1898–1902) (p. 1164A), by J. Belcher, is a fine example of Neo-Baroque, of which there are quite a few notable instances of about this period, including the **City Hall and Law Courts, Cardiff** (1897–1906) and the **Methodist Central Hall, Westminster** (1906–12), both by Lanchester and Rickards.

Law Society, Chancery Lane, London (1902–4) (p. 1159C), an extension by Charles Holden when an assistant to H. Percy Adams, reveals the trend towards a modern Classicism, shorn of historicist detail but conforming to Classical rules of composition. In this design, dominated by the Venetian windows at first-floor level superimposed over a rusticated base, Holden played down historical detail and introduced such modern contemporary touches as the exaggeratedly attenuated keystone and, over the side windows, the 'eyebrow' shallow hood moulds. Holden became partner to Adams about 1907, L. Pearson joined them in 1912, and their firm subsequently achieved a considerable reputation and an extensive practice.

The **Piccadilly Hotel, London** (1905–8) (p. 1162A), by R. N. Shaw, was the architect's last major work. It is one of the best instances of the Neo-Baroque mode which, along with other expressions, was current over the turn of the century. A series of grand, vigorously-rusticated arches embodies shops at pavement level, and with a shallow balconied tier immediately over serves as a podium for an open Ionic colonnade linking pavilions, behind which rises the main mass of the building.

Heathcote, Ilkley, Yorkshire (1906) (p. 1159E), by Sir Edwin Lutyens (1869–1944), follows R. N. Shaw's excursion into the English Renaissance, but adapts its more grandiose features for a house of modest dimensions in this instance. Its pavilioned plan had many imitators. Lutyens designed country houses, large and small, on Renaissance lines, including **Temple Dinsley, Herts** (1908) and **Great Maytham, Sussex** (1909). An inventive and accomplished stylist, Lutyens also designed houses of a charming vernacular character (p. 1168B).

The **London County Hall** (1912–22) (p. 1162C), by Ralph Knott, is a Thames-side building of strong Free-Classical design showing French Renaissance influence.

New Delhi, India (1913–30) (p. 1162D), a grandiose administrative centre laid out by Sir Edwin Lutyens, who also designed the principal buildings concerned, is a scheme far more ambitious than any carried out during the same period in Britain. The new city, which follows Classical axial principles, lies some 5 km (3 miles) south of the walls of Delhi proper, and about 6 km (4 miles) south of the 'Red' Fort of Shah Jehan. The axis runs east and west for some 3 km (2 miles) in the form of a very wide tree-lined avenue, flanked by green spaces and canals. At the 'foot' (east end) stands the colossal All India War Memorial Arch and, to the west, below the natural ridge carrying the Secretariat, there extends an open square ornamented with six fountains, to the north of which is the circular Council Chamber, by Sir Herbert Baker (1862–1946). The axis now rises westward between the twin buildings of the Secretariat, designed by Baker, towards the vast President's (formerly Viceroy's) House (1920–31) which, despite its size, remains hidden until almost the last moment, an effect certainly not intended by Lutyens and presumably attributable to a misinterpretation of the lie of the site. Nevertheless, his combination of domes, minarets and Renaissance details produce a monument of originality and genuine Anglo-Indian character.

A. The Piccadilly Hotel, London (1905–8). See p. 1161

B. New Scotland Yard, Victoria Embankment, London (1887–8). See p. 1166

C. London County Hall, Westminster (1912–22). See p. 1161

D. New Delhi: aerial view looking W. (1913–30). See p. 1161

A. Truro Cathedral, Cornwall
(1879–1910). See p. 1165

B. Holy Trinity Church, Sloane Street,
London (1888–91). See p. 1165

c. S. Augustine, Kilburn, London (1870–80): vaulting. See p. 1165

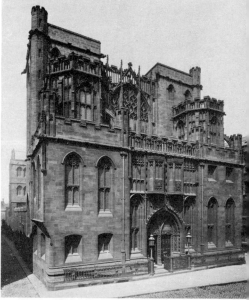

A. The Town Hall, Colchester
(1898–1902). See p. 1161

B. The Rylands Library, Deansgate, Manchester
(1890–9). See p. 1165

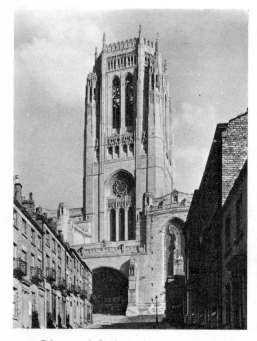

C. Liverpool Cathedral (1903–): central
tower from S. See p. 1165

D. Westminster Cathedral (1895–1903):
exterior from west. See p. 1165

Truro Cathedral, Cornwall (1879–1910) (p. 1163A), by J. L. Pearson, was not completed at his death and was continued by his son. A granite structure, it is typical of the architect's style: grand, plain and bold. There are spired central and western towers, and powerful vertical emphasis is given to the transept fronts and east end. Pearson was expert in vaulting, not often used in churches in his time. His **S. Augustine, Kilburn, London** (1870–80) (p. 1163C) is particularly notable in this respect.

Holy Trinity, Sloane Street, Chelsea (1888–91) (p. 1163B), by J. D. Sedding, is built in a free version of the Decorated and Perpendicular styles in red brick with stone dressings and striations. It confounds historicism by using Gothic motifs symbolically, for example in the spandrels to the nave arcades, and by simultaneously introducing Italian Renaissance elements such as in the pulpit and baldachino. Many of the furnishings and fittings of the church were installed after Sedding's death by notable artists associated with the Arts and Crafts Movement, including Burne-Jones, who designed the east window, and Henry Wilson (1864–1934), who was responsible for metalwork including the exterior railings, gate and altar rails. The interior was altered after war damage. Amongst Sedding's other works are **S. Clement, Boscombe, Hants** (1873–93), **All Saints, Falmouth** (1887–90) and **S. Peter, Ealing** (1889–92).

The **Rylands Library, Deansgate, Manchester** (1890–9) (p. 1164B), designed by Basil Champneys (1842–1935), is a splendid if belated example of secular Gothic. It is a much lighter and more gracious version than was normal in the High Victorian era, reverting to the English Decorated period for inspiration, but expressing it with a topical Art Nouveau piquancy. The richly ornamented centrepiece and the great bay windows of the recessed upper stage contrast effectively with the relatively plain walls on the lower flanks, in which deep, traceried windows are set in studied asymmetry. For the materials and the craftsmanship in stone, wood and bronze no expense was spared. Champneys carried out many commissions for Oxford and Cambridge Universities, including the **Indian Institute** (1884) and **Mansfield College** (1889) at **Oxford** and **Newnham College** (1875–1935) at **Cambridge.**

Liverpool Cathedral (1903–) (p. 1164C), by Sir Giles Gilbert Scott, who won the commission in competition aged twenty-two, is still incomplete, although it has progressed from the east end beyond the central tower to the west front. In many ways original, it is essentially a Free Gothic interpretation of the Decorated period, untraditional in having a double-axis symmetry—apart from the relatively minor masses at the east end—and dominated by a great central tower, on either side of which lie double transepts. The spaces between these double transepts are bridged by arches to form northern and southern porches. The material is mostly red sandstone, the vaults being covered by upper roofs of reinforced concrete. The eventual floor area will be greater than any existing cathedral in England, the internal length being 146 m (480 ft) and the width, including the aisles, 26.5 m (87 ft), the vaults rising to 52.7 m (173 ft).

Westminster Cathedral (1895–1903) (p. 1164D), by J. F. Bentley, is the one great work based on the revival of Byzantine architecture. There is a spacious nave, 18 m (60 ft) wide, covered by three pendentived domes, 34 m (112 ft) above the floor to the crown, flanked by aisles with side chapels—or, as in the case of the easternmost dome, by transepts—which bring the full width to nearly 30 m (98 ft). A fourth, slightly smaller dome covers the sanctuary and choir, and the full length to the apse is 104 m (342 ft). The grey-brown bricks of the walls are being progressively sheathed with similar marbles to those used in S. Sophia (p. 383), chapel by chapel, and the vaults covered with mosaics. Over the altar is a white marble baldachino supported on yellow marble columns. Externally the brick walls are patterned horizontally with stone, and near the north-west angle rises the sheer campanile known as S. Edward's Tower. Bentley built many churches in the Gothic style, including the **Church of the Holy Rood, Watford, Herts** (1887).

New Scotland Yard, London (1887–8) (p. 1162B), a famous London landmark, is entirely individual, a brilliant pastiche by R. N. Shaw. For reasons of convenience the fenestration follows a regular pattern in the Queen Anne style, as is openly expressed elevationally on the upper floors, but with the addition of bold stone striations in the brickwork. The roof treatment and lofty gables apparently borrow from the same source. The lower three storeys, however, faced in hard grey granite, assume a different, more aptly severe character, which is instantly dispelled by the punning of the Scottish Baronial corner turrets with their inconsequential ogival caps. Finally, Shaw's exuberance excels all else by lavish Baroque flourishes at the entrance and at the gable terminals. No public building before or since has ever presented such an extraordinary display of architectural sleight-of-hand, and High Victorian pomp is here treated with Late Victorian levity.

The White House, Tite Street, Chelsea (1878–9; demolished), by E. W. Godwin, was built as a studio-house for the artist J. A. M. Whistler, and was as unconventional as its owner. It was designed to be built in white brick with a green tiled roof. The windows were placed where light was required and the walls were intended to be plain. The Metropolitan Board of Works insisted that ornamental panels should be added, but despite this the design is remarkably spartan, and marks a distinct and significant break with historical precedent. Both Whistler and Godwin were prominent Aesthetes.

The Cottage, Bishop's Itchington, Warwickshire (1888–9) (p. 1168A), by C. F. A. Voysey, was his first house to be built and, although using traditional materials and forms, it combines them in an original and non-revivalist way. Voysey created a distinctly individual style of house by means of massive hipped roofs, plain, white, rendered walls with sloping buttresses, continuous ranges of mullioned windows, with those at first-floor level placed immediately below the eaves, and wide doorways, often decorated with simple cut-out heart shapes. Internally, the houses were equally elemental in treatment, with plain surfaces contrasted against attenuated verticals and exaggeratedly shallow mouldings, where mouldings were permitted at all. Voysey enjoyed a considerable practice and his work was widely published in Britain and Germany. **Broadleys, Windermere** (1898–9) (p. 1167B) is one of his best houses. Situated on the east side of the lake, it is planned so that the gardens and main rooms overlook the shore and gain good orientation, and the east-west service wing shelters the entrance court from the north. The principal living-room is a two-storeyed hall, a common feature of contemporary domestic planning, and a first-floor gallery links suites of bedrooms. Other Voysey houses include **The Orchard, Chorley Wood, Herts** (1899) (p. 1169E), built for his own use, **The Pastures, North Luffenham, Rutland** (1901) and **The Homestead, Frinton, Essex** (1905).

The Barn, Exmouth, Devon (1895–6) (pp. 1167D, 1169A) is by E. S. Prior, one of the most thorough-going of the architects of the Arts and Crafts Movement. The plan (p. 1167D), consisting of two diagonal arms linked by a central two-storeyed hall, is unusual but practical. The verandah and terrace, enclosed in the southern angle, overlook the coastline, as do the principal rooms, which are all placed on that side of the house, with the entrance and service rooms disposed on the opposite side. Windows occur where required but not entirely at random. The house is built of richly textured, vernacular materials appropriate to the region: the wall bases are of heavy sandstone blocks and the upper sections are of beach pebbles with sandstone

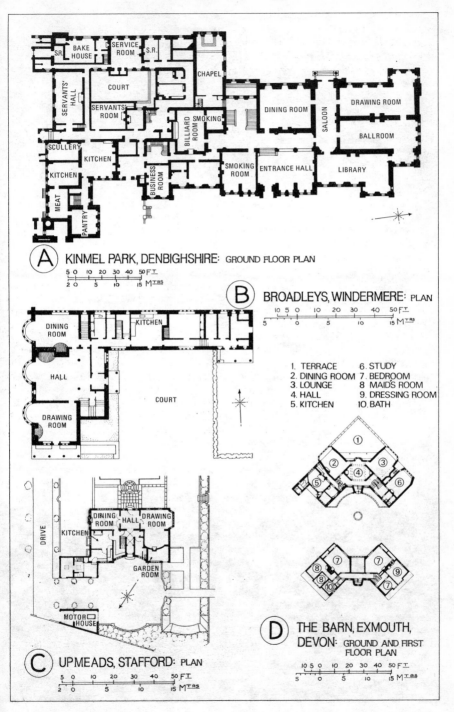

A KINMEL PARK, DENBIGHSHIRE: GROUND FLOOR PLAN

5 0 10 20 30 40 50 FT
2 0 5 10 15 MTRS

B BROADLEYS, WINDERMERE: PLAN

10 5 0 10 20 30 40 50 FT
5 0 5 10 15 MTRS

1. TERRACE 6. STUDY
2. DINING ROOM 7. BEDROOM
3. LOUNGE 8 MAIDS ROOM
4. HALL 9. DRESSING ROOM
5. KITCHEN 10. BATH

C UPMEADS, STAFFORD: PLAN

5 0 10 20 30 40 50 FT
2 0 5 10 15 MTRS

D THE BARN, EXMOUTH, DEVON: GROUND AND FIRST FLOOR PLAN

10 5 0 10 20 30 40 50 FT
5 0 5 10 15 MTRS

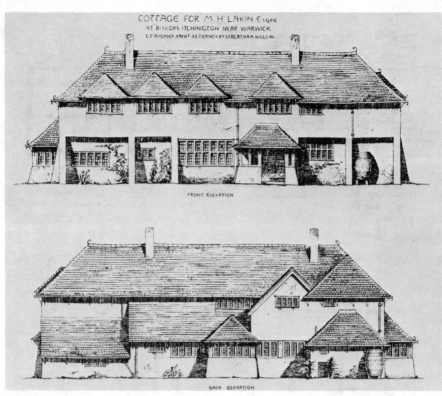

A. The Cottage, Bishop's Itchington, Warwicks (1888–9). See p. 1166

B. Deanery Garden, Sonning, Berks (1900–1). See p. 1171

A. The Barn, Exmouth, Devon (1895–6).
See p. 1166

B. House at New Earswick,
York (c. 1902). See p. 1172

C. Exterior

D. Entrance hall

Hill House, Helensburgh (1902–3). See p. 1171

E. The Orchard, Chorley Wood, Herts
(1899). See p. 1166

F. Eagle Insurance
Building, Birmingham
(1900). See p. 1171

A. North front (1897–9)   B. West end (1907–9)
The School of Art, Glasgow (1897–1909). See p. 1171

c. School of Art, Glasgow: the library   D. The Whitechapel Art Gallery,
            (1907–9)   London (1897–9). See p. 1171

inserts. The gable is boarded in oak and the roof, now slated, was originally thatched until destroyed by fire. The house perfectly illustrates both the progressive and the anachronistic elements of the Arts and Crafts Movement. Other characteristic works of Prior are **Winchester College School of Music** (1904) and **Home Place, Kelling, Norfolk** (1904).

The **Whitechapel Art Gallery, London** (1897-9) (p. 1170D), by C. H. Townsend, is an essay in abstract design and the contemporary modernism which the Aesthetic Movement inspired. The façade is the notable feature of the building: the massive, off-set, semicircular arched entrance, perhaps owing a debt to the American architect H. H. Richardson (see p. 1228), is balanced by an area of blank wall and contained by a continuous horizontal line of windows. Above this the façade divides into two turrets flanking a recession; the base of each is decorated by a deep band of foliage, forming further geometrical elements in the composition, and each is finished by paired pinnacles with novel, upswept gablets. All of this is executed in buff-coloured faience. Historicism and past associations, even by materials, are therefore avoided. Townsend also designed the **Horniman Museum, Forest Hill, London** (1902), and the church of **S. Mary the Virgin, Great Warley, Essex** (1904).

The **School of Art, Glasgow** (1897-1909) (p. 1170A, B, C), by C. R. Mackintosh, is one of the most notable examples of contemporary modernity and expresses a complete fusion of Aestheticism and the Arts and Crafts Movement. The former inspired the asymmetry, the slender verticals, the unusual disposition of ornament and the novel decorative forms for which the building is famous; to the latter belong the traditional character of the body of the building, the echoes of Scottish vernacular architecture, the expression of plain, substantial materials, and the simple and direct expression of function. The artistry of the amalgam and the complex, imaginative spatial relationships, however, are the personal creation of Mackintosh himself. The main building was constructed between 1897 and 1899 and houses studios and offices. The west wing, containing the magnificent library, was added in 1907-9 and is Mackintosh's supreme work. He was responsible for several other works of original character, including the houses **Windyhill, Kilmacolm** (1900), **Hill House, Helensburgh** (1902-3) (p. 1169C, D), and **Hous' Hill, Nitshill, Glasgow** (c. 1906); the **Scotland Street School, Glasgow** (1904) and the decoration and furnishing of some remarkable Glasgow tea-rooms. Mackintosh had a wider following in Germany and Austria, particularly Vienna, than in England, and in this respect is the most significant British architect of his generation.

The **Eagle Insurance Building, Birmingham** (1900) (p. 1169F), by W. R. Lethaby and J. L. Ball, highlights the predicament of a purist of the Arts and Crafts Movement when faced with a building in an urban situation. With historicism and the stylism of Aestheticism rejected, and vernacular modes patently inappropriate, there was a hiatus. Lethaby compromised between a vague Tudor, as in the ground floor windows, strict practicality, seen in the fenestration of the upper floors, and abstract patterns of primary forms, evident in the frieze. Honest intentions and nagging doubt could not be expressed more clearly than in this revealing design. Other more confident works by Lethaby are **Avon Tyrell, Christchurch, Hants** (1891), **Melsetter House, Hoy, Orkney** (1898) and the church of **All Saints, Brockhampton, Herefordshire** (1902).

The **Deanery Garden, Sonning, Berks** (1900-1) (p. 1168B) is one of many fine works by Sir Edwin Lutyens in which vernacular materials and forms are handled with imagination, artistic sensibility and consummate skill. As with R. N. Shaw, of whom he is the logical successor, he was too much a stylist to accept the sterner principles of the Arts and Crafts Movement, but he appreciated and captured their effect. Typical of the inventiveness of Lutyens is his constantly varying use of the semicircular motif at the Deanery Gardens. Other similarly characteristic works by him are **Tigbourne Court, Witley, Surrey** (1899) and the restoration of **Lindisfarne Castle, Holy Island, Northumberland** (1903–4).

New Earswick Model Village, York (1902–*c.* 1931) (pp. 1169B, 1173), by R. Barry Parker and Sir Raymond Unwin, was commissioned by the philanthropic Quaker manufacturer Joseph Rowntree to provide good housing in a satisfactory environment at economic rents with a 4% return. The aim was social improvement and the houses were not restricted to Rowntree's employees. The layout is spacious, informal and seeks to emulate the organic principle of the traditional village, but with the terraces of the cottages designed to obtain good orientation for each individual dwelling. A profusion of gables, dormers and chimneys added to the picturesque and attractive effect. The village includes a folk-hall, for communal activities, and an open-air school, which was designed in 1911, with south-facing classrooms, each fitted with large sliding-folding windows and an overhead sun-blind; the concrete flat roofs over the corridors on the north side are to enable clear-storey windows to be introduced in classrooms to ensure cross-ventilation. In concept and character New Earswick is as heavily indebted to the Arts and Crafts ideology as to Quaker social attitudes. It has several antecedents, including Port Sunlight and Bournville, and its successors include Letchworth (from 1903) and Hampstead Garden Suburb (from 1906), both laid out by Parker and Unwin.

S. Andrew, Roker, Sunderland (1906–7) (p. 1174A, B), the masterpiece of E. S. Prior, is a fine, strong and vigorous design strictly in accordance with Arts and Crafts ideals. Although nominally Gothic, it is far from revivalistic and fearlessly adapts Gothic features to modern needs and materials. The nave is spanned by massive, stone, pointed arches, which support reinforced concrete purlins carrying the roof, and openings tunnel through their bases for the aisles. The window tracery is vestigially Gothic, but only in barest rudiments. Some interior fittings are of very high quality and include examples by Ernest Gimson and others, who with Prior were exponents of the Arts and Crafts Movement.

The **Willans and Robinson Factory, Queensferry, Flintshire** (1901) (p. 1176A), by H. B. Cresswell, built for making water-tube boilers, is of a severely functional character. It is a long, single-storey block, built of a hard engineering brick and divided into bays by massive piers. The external walls and piers are battered, adding to the fortress-like appearance. Workshops are lit by a line of clear-storey windows and all openings are spanned by exposed cast-iron joists. There is no ornament, but brick dentils carry an oversailing parapet and some gables are stepped. It is a building of the most unequivocal and forceful expression.

Lion Chambers, Hope Street, Glasgow (1906) (p. 1174C, D), by James Salmon, junior, combines traditional and innovatory features in a remarkable way. The main frontage is orthodox in character, although in no way historicist; the north elevation, however, is highly unconventional and consists of a series of splayed and glazed bays rising through eight storeys. Technologically the building is important as an early example of the Hennebique system. It has a reinforced concrete frame and external walls only 100 mm (4 ins) thick of the same material.

Offices of Dronsfield Bros, Oldham, Lancs (1906–7) (p. 1176B), by J. H. Sellers, is neat, two-storeyed, symmetrical, elaborately modelled to articulate the separate parts of the building, and not at all revivalist in character. It has a concrete flat roof and is faced with impermeable materials, glazed green bricks and grey granite, to resist Oldham's atmospheric pollution. The front railings and the entrance doors are particular distinguished. Sellers, who was a scholarly architect, worked in association with Edgar Wood, and Dronsfield's may be usefully compared with **Upmeads, Stafford** (p. 1177). Other works attributed to Sellers,

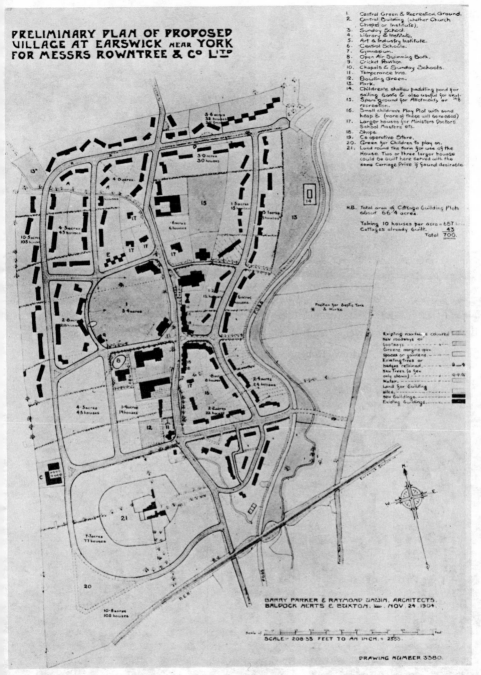

Plan of Model Village at New Earswick, York (1902). See p. 1172

A. East front, showing tower over chancel

B. Interior, looking east

S. Andrew, Roker, Sunderland (1906–7). See p. 1172

C. Front

D. Rear

Lion Chambers, Hope Street, Glasgow (1906). See p. 1172

A. Upmeads, Stafford (1908). See p. 1177

B. Gledstone Hall, Skipton, Yorkshire (1923–7). See p. 1178

A. The Willans & Robinson Factory, Queensferry, Flintshire (1901). See p. 1172

B. Offices of Dronsfield Bros, Oldham, Lancs (1906-7). See p. 1172

c. Town Hall Extension, Manchester (1934-8) with Central Library (1931-4) to left. See p. 1178

although executed in association with Wood, are two remarkable **schools at Elm Street and Durnford Street, Middleton, Lancs** (1910).

Upmeads, Stafford (1908) (pp. 1167C, 1175A), by Edgar Wood, is one of a series of houses he designed with reinforced concrete flat roofs, plain brick elevations and eclectic details, Tudor and Classical. Upmeads stands at the northern end of a site which falls to, and is entered from, the south. The garden is south of the house and the drive skirts its length and turns into a forecourt to the north of the house, giving access to the main entrance, which is situated in a curved recess. The main rooms face south and overlook the gardens. The layout of the house and site reflect the careful attention to orientation, aspect and site conditions which is typical of the advanced thinking of the leading architects of the day, and in Wood's case it derives from Arts and Crafts influence. Upmeads informally follows axial principles, but studiously avoids symmetry. Other similar works by Wood are **Dalny Veed, Barley, Herts** (1907) and **Royd House, Hale, Cheshire** (1914), a house designed and decorated for his own use.

The **Y.M.C.A. Building, Manchester** (1908–9) (p. 1179A), by A. E. Corbett of Woodhouse, Corbett and Dean, provides complex accommodation for social, residential and physical recreational purposes on a confined city site. For its date it is an extremely advanced reinforced concrete structure carrying a swimming pool, located on the top storey to obtain natural top-light, and an auditorium involving wide spans. Parliamentary sanction had to be obtained before construction could proceed, because there was no provision for such a structure within the existing building regulations. The elevations, clad in buff terra-cotta, combine the windows and the surface modelling in an abstract design entirely modern in spirit.

Kodak House, Kingsway, London (1911) (p. 1179B), by Sir John Burnet. Although the Ritz Hotel, London (1905–6), by Mewès and Davis, was the first non-utilitarian building in Britain constructed with a steel frame, this major innovation remained unexpressed in the external design and was absorbed in the Classical façade. Burnet's Kodak House expresses the frame boldly enough, but combines it with a feeble and debased Classicism that was to become all too familiar in the following thirty years. Other works in Glasgow by Burnet are equally demonstrative of his sense of structural expression and more representative of his wide abilities, e.g. **McGeogh's Warehouse, West Campbell Street** (1905), and the **Wallace Scott Factory, Cathcart** (1913).

AFTERMATH

After the First World War, although the content of architectural practice changed, the pattern of architectural development continued initially along lines established previous to 1914. The Gothic Revival, then obsolescent, was regarded as a historical anachronism and its practice became a rarity. The radical aspect of the Arts and Crafts Movement was unappreciated and left undeveloped, although its more romantic, vernacular associations continued to be exploited for some domestic architecture. In spite of growing modernism, Classical formalism gradually changing from elaborate historical to modern and elemental varieties, continued in Britain to be the representative architectural mode of the age.

The **Cenotaph, Whitehall, London** (1920) (p. 1179C), by Sir Edwin Lutyens, the principal instance amongst great numbers of memorials erected to commemorate the dead of the First World War, and a prototype for many of the others, is a tall, simple monument of Portland stone, of classical character, mounting in slightly receding stages and bearing an elevated and symbolic stone tomb. Other notable memorials are the **Menin Gate,** at **Ypres** (1923–6), by Sir Reginald Blomfield (1856–1942), and the **Scottish National War Memorial** (1918–27), by Sir Robert Lorimer (1864–1929) in Edinburgh Castle.

The **War Memorial Chapel, Charterhouse School** (1922–6) (p. 1179D), by Sir Giles Gilbert Scott, is an original composition in the Gothic Revival mode. Rectangular in plan and high-proportioned, the severity of the longitudinal walls is relieved by angle turrets and tall, slot-windows in buttress-like projections. It has some of the grandeur of Scott's Liverpool Cathedral (p. 1164C).

The **Town Hall Extension, Manchester** (1934–8) (p. 1176C), by E. Vincent Harris (1879–1971), is one of the few large contemporary public buildings to be designed with pronounced Gothic associations, here made unmistakable by the steeply-pitched roofs, tall narrow gables and mullioned Tudor windows. Waterhouse's neighbouring masterpiece was, no doubt, the reason for this departure from the prevailing Classicism. The **Central Library** (1931–4) (p. 1176C), immediately adjacent to the Town Hall Extension, also by Harris, is full-bloodedly Classical and based on the Pantheon at Rome. Harris designed many large municipal buildings including **Sheffield City Hall** (1920), **Leeds Civic Hall** (1926), and **Nottingham County Hall** (1935).

The **Cathedral, Guildford** (1936–61) (p. 1180A), by Sir Edward Maufe, was the subject of a competition. Traditional in its cruciform, central-towered composition, and Gothic Revival in theme, it is extremely broad and bold in scale, the massive simplicity of the towering brick walls contrasting powerfully with the tall traceried windows.

Ashley Chase, Dorset (1929), designed by Sir Guy Dawber (1861–1938), follows the traditional materials and forms of building made popular by the Arts and Crafts Movement. The scale of the house is large, but the spreading plan, dividing into irregular wings and bays, prevents the building from assuming too imposing a mass, and a variety of hips, gables, dormers and chimneys adds to the informal, casual character of the house. Dawber, who had made a special study of building in the Cotswolds, built many houses of vernacular character.

Gledstone Hall, Skipton, Yorkshire (1923–7) (p. 1175B), by Sir Edwin Lutyens, is a smaller country house, symmetrical in form, with an Ionic portico, projecting wings and flanking pavilions linked to the house by screen walls. The main block, with the portico omitted, provided a perfect and flexible model for the Neo-Georgian house, and with good proportions, pleasing brickwork and neat joinery it proved to be a practical as well as a popular success.

The **Carlton Club, Pall Mall, London** (refaced 1921, destroyed 1940) (p. 1181A). In refacing this building, Sir Reginald Blomfield converted a two-storeyed, arcaded, Italianate design of 1847 by Sydney Smirke, modelled on Sansovino's Library at Venice, to this completely different reproduction of eighteenth-century Renaissance forms. This exemplifies the scholarly revival of Classicism as opposed to its free interpretation, to be seen in the next example by Lutyens.

The **Midland Bank, Poultry, London** (1924) (p. 1180B), is by Sir Edwin Lutyens, who built several important branches for the Midland Bank including those at Piccadilly (1922) and Leadenhall Street (1928), London, and King Street, Manchester (1929). In this design for the Bank's headquarters Lutyens, in his idiosyncratically brilliant manner, avoided the large-scale use of the Orders and the conventions of orthodox Classicism. The major elements are an arcaded, rusticated base, surmounted by what is virtually a deep frieze pierced by a line of windows. Above this the major component of the composition, a block arcaded through three storeys and also rusticated, supports a superstructure set back from the frontage except where a miniature triumphal arch occurs on the centre line of the elevation.

A. Y.M.C.A. Building, Manchester (1908–9). See p. 1177

B. Kodak House, Kingsway, London (1911). See p. 1177

C. The Cenotaph, Whitehall, London (1920). See p. 1177

D. War Memorial Chapel, Charterhouse School, Surrey (1922–6). See p. 1178

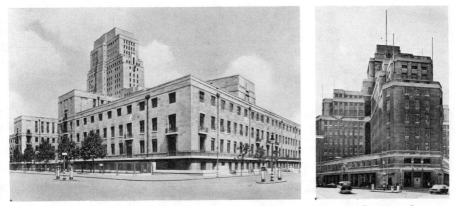

E (left). The Senate House, University of London (1933–9). See p. 1182

F (right). The London Passenger Transport Building, Westminster (1929). See p. 1182

A. The Cathedral, Guildford (1936–61). See p. 1178

B. The Midland Bank, Poultry,
London (1924). See p. 1178

C. The Municipal Buildings, Norwich
(1938). See p. 1182

A. The Carlton Club, Pall Mall, London (refaced 1921). See p. 1178

B. R.I.B.A. Building, Portland Place, London (1932–4). See p. 1182

C. The Gillette Factory, Isleworth, Middlesex (1936). See p. 1182

D. The City Hall, Swansea (1930–4). See p. 1182

Similar features crown the end elevations. The masonry detailing is remarkably imaginative; sweeping lines of rustication delineate abutting planes, arches contain arches, and pilasters that never materialize are implied by capitals and bases; and all has the assurance of sheer virtuosity. **Britannic House, Finsbury Circus** (1920), is an equally inventive and important London commission by Lutyens and similarly reflects the vitality of this late classicism.

The **Senate House, University of London** (1933–9) (p. 1179E), by Charles Holden, consists of two large four- and five-storey rectangular blocks, 75.5 m × 50.6 m (248 ft × 166 ft), joined together by a massive tower 36.5 m (120 ft) wide at the base and 64 m (210 ft) high. Forecourts on the east and west sides of the tower lead to a vestibule in its base, above which are the libraries and stack rooms. The southern block contains the administrative rooms and the northern certain other University elements. All the walls are load-bearing, being of stone-faced brickwork, although there is a steel frame in the tower to take the weight of the book stacks. In elevational character the building recalls the **London Passenger Transport Building, Westminster** (1929) (p. 1179F), by Adams, Holden and Pearson.

Gillette Factory, Great West Road, Isleworth, Middlesex (1936) (p. 1181C), by Sir Banister Fletcher (1886–1953), represents the numerous industrial buildings created on formal, axial lines in these decades. The slim, central tower, contrasted with a long horizontal block, divided into regular bays, and with a grandiose central entrance, amounted to a standard architectural formula.

The **City Hall, Swansea** (1930–4) (p. 1181D), by Sir Percy Thomas (1883–1969), the **R.I.B.A. Building, Portland Place, London** (1932–4) (p. 1181B), by G. Grey Wornum (1888–1957), and the **Municipal Buildings, Norwich** (1938) (p. 1180C), by S. Rowland Pierce (1896–1966) in partnership with C. H. James (1893–1953), are leading examples of Classical formalism in modern guise, shorn of the Orders and Classical mouldings, but implying modern construction by thin walls and flat roofs. The last is clearly influenced by Ragnar Ostberg's City Hall for Stockholm (p. 1212).

BIBLIOGRAPHY

ASLIN, E. *The Aesthetic Movement.* London, 1969.
BARRY, A. *The Life and Works of Sir Charles Barry.* London, 1867.
BELL, Q. *Ruskin.* Edinburgh, 1963.
BLOMFIELD, SIR R. *Richard Norman Shaw.* London, 1940.
BOASE, T. S. R. *English Art: 1800–1870.* London, 1959.
BRANDON-JONES, J. *C. F. A. Voysey 1857–1941.* Journal of the Architectural Association, May 1957.
BRIGGS, M. S. *Everyman's Concise Encyclopaedia of Architecture.* London, 1959. (Contains useful biographical entries.)
CHADWICK, G. F. *The Works of Sir Joseph Paxton.* London, 1961.
CLARK, G. K. *The Making of Victorian England.* London, 1962.
CLARK, SIR K. *The Gothic Revival.* 2nd ed. London, 1950.
COLLINS, P. *Changing Ideals in Modern Architecture 1750–1950.* London, 1965.
COLVIN, H. M. *A Biographical Dictionary of English Architects 1660–1840.* London, 1954.
CREESE, W. L. *The Search for Environment.* Newhaven, Conn., and London, 1966.
CROOK, J. M. *The Greek Revival.* London, 1973.
EASTLAKE, C. L. *A History of the Gothic Revival.* London, 1872 (reprint, Leicester, 1970, edited by J. M. Crook).
FERGUSSON, J. *History of the Modern Styles of Architecture.* 2 vols. 3rd ed. revised by R. Kerr. London, 1891.
FERRIDAY, P. *Victorian Architecture.* London, 1963.
GIROUARD, M. *The Victorian Country House.* London, 1971.

GOODHART-RENDEL, H. S. *English Architecture since the Regency*. London, 1953.

HARBRON, D. *Amphion, or the Nineteenth Century*. London, 1930.

HITCHCOCK, H.-R. *Architecture: Nineteenth and Twentieth Centuries*. 3rd ed. Harmondsworth and Baltimore, 1970.

—. *Early Victorian Architecture*. 2 vols. London, 1954.

HOWARTH, T. *Charles Rennie Mackintosh and the Modern Movement*. London, 1952.

HUSSEY, C. *The Life of Sir Edwin Lutyens*. London, 1953.

JENKINS, F. I. *Architect and Patron*. London, 1961.

KAYE, B. *The Development of the Architectural Profession in Britain*. London, 1960.

LETHABY, W. R. *Philip Webb and His Work*. London, 1935.

MACLEOD, R. *Style and Society: Architectural Ideology in Britain 1835–1914*. London, 1971.

MADSEN, S. T. *Art Nouveau*. London, 1967.

MUTHESIUS, H. *Das englische Haus*. 3 vols. Berlin, 1904–5.

MUTHESIUS, S. *The High Victorian Movement 1850–1870*. London and Boston, 1972.

NAYLOR, G. *The Arts and Crafts Movement*. London, 1971.

PEVSNER, SIR N. *Pioneers of Modern Design from William Morris to Walter Gropius*. London, 1936, Harmondsworth, 1960, and other editions.

PUGIN, A. W. N. *Contrasts, or a Parallel between the Noble Edifices of the Fourteenth and Fifteenth Centuries* . . . Salisbury, 1836. (Reprint of 1841 edition, Leicester, 1969.)

RICHARDS, J. M. *The Functional Tradition in Early Industrial Buildings*. London, 1958.

RICKMAN, T. *An Attempt to Discriminate the Styles of English Architecture* . . . 4th ed. London, 1835.

RUSKIN, J. *The Seven Lamps of Architecture*. London, 1849.

—. *The Stones of Venice*. 3 vols. London, 1851–3.

SCOTT, SIR G. G. *Personal and Professional Recollections* . . . , edited by G. G. Scott. London, 1879.

SINGER, HOLMYARD, HALL and WILLIAMS. *A History of Technology*. Vols. 4 and 5. London, 1958.

SKEMPTON, A. W. 'The Boat Store, Sheerness (1858–60) and its Place in Structural History', *Newcomen Society Transactions*, vol. 32, pp. 57–78; and (with JOHNSON, H. R.) 'William Strutt's Cotton Mills (1793–1812)'. *Op. cit.*, vol. 30, pp. 179–205.

STANTON, P. *Pugin*. London, 1971.

STREET, A. E. *Memoir of George Edmund Street* . . . London, 1888.

SUMMERSON, SIR J. N. *Architecture in Britain 1530–1830*. 5th ed. Harmondsworth and Baltimore, 1970.

—. *Heavenly Mansions*. London, 1949.

—. *Victorian Architecture: Four Studies* . . . New York, 1970.

THOMPSON, P. *William Butterfield*. London, 1971.

THOMSON, D. *England in the Nineteenth Century*. Harmondsworth, 1950.

A. The Houses of Parliament, Melbourne (1856–80). See p. 1185

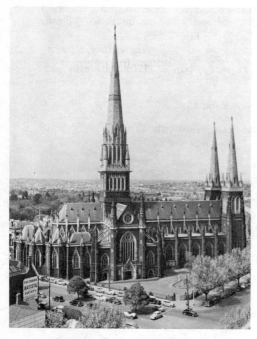

B. Catholic Cathedral of S. Patrick, Melbourne (1860–1939). See p. 1185

C. S. John's Anglican Cathedral, Brisbane (1901–). See p. 1185

37

ARCHITECTURE IN AUSTRALIA
AND NEW ZEALAND 1830-1914

ARCHITECTURAL CHARACTER

In the first half of the nineteenth century Australian domestic buildings were in general low, often of one storey only, with wide, spreading eaves. Covered, colonnaded verandahs were characteristic features, sometimes contained under the main roof and often displaying great sensitivity in their elegant columnar supports. Cast-iron lace-work, imported from England until the establishment of the Russell foundries in Sydney (c. 1843), which were quickly followed by similar manufactories elsewhere, proved widely popular for railings and screens. Later in the century two-storey houses were developed with decorated ironwork verandahs and tall upper windows opening on to spacious balconies. Fine examples of this type, which came to be recognized as specifically Australian, survive in Melbourne and district. Although the first colonial structures were of timber, the use of stone and brick (the latter often stucco-faced) soon became common, while for roofs, usually of low pitch, tiles, wood shingles and corrugated iron were employed.

From the middle to the end of the century, the architecture of Australia and New Zealand—the latter had been formally annexed to the British Crown only in 1840—accurately and punctually reflected in structure and decoration the virtues, failings, preferences and prejudices current in the Victorian age in Britain, from which most of the more prominent architects had of course emigrated.

EXAMPLES

S. Mark's Church, Darling Point, Sydney (1848–75), by E. Blacket, a sandstone Gothic Revival parish church, gracefully exploiting a hill-top site; **Sydney University** (1854–60), also by Blacket, a formal Gothic design, finely detailed, making an impressive nucleus of the present campus; **The Houses of Parliament, Melbourne** (1856–80) (p. 1184A), by J. C. Knight and Peter Kerr, a monumental, Classical building, surmounted by a stately cupola; **The Treasury Buildings, Melbourne** (–1862), by J. Clark, also in the Classical manner; **The Church of S. John the Evangelist, Toorak** (1860–73) by W. W. Wardell (1823–1900) in the English Gothic style and the same architect's great **Catholic Cathedral of S. Patrick, Melbourne** (1860–1939) (p. 1184B), also Gothic but of a continental European character. From designs by Wardell, too, is **Government House, Melbourne** (1872–6) (allegedly modelled on Queen Victoria's Osborne House in the Isle of Wight), a noble, beautifully sited, Italianate palace in ivory-painted stucco. The **Catholic Cathedral, Adelaide** (1870–) is based on designs prepared by A. W. N. Pugin (p. 1128), while the **Anglican Cathedral, Melbourne** (1850–1934) was designed by William Butterfield (p. 1129). **S. John's Anglican Cathedral, Brisbane** (1901–) (p. 1184C) was carried out by F. L. Pearson to the designs of his father, J. L. Pearson (p. 1130). The **Public Library, Melbourne** (1909–13) by Bates, Peebles and Smart, provides a significant and early example of reinforced concrete construction in its great dome, 35 m (115 ft) in diameter.

William Mason, politician, farmer, auctioneer and architect, is generally accepted as the first New Zealand member of the last profession. Working, like most of his contemporaries, in all the nineteenth-century styles, he was a competent interpreter of Gothic Revival theory. His most satisfying work is probably **S. Matthew's Church, Dunedin** (1873), a typical example of nineteenth-century Gothic.

BIBLIOGRAPHY

BEIERS, S. *Homes of Australia*. Sydney, 1948.

BOYD, R. *Australia's Home*. Carlton, 1952.

CASEY, M. *Early Melbourne Architecture: 1840–1888*. Melbourne, 1953.

HERMAN, M. *The Architecture of Victorian Sydney*. Sydney, 1956.

SHARLAND, M. *Stones of a Century*. Hobart, 1952.

STACPOOLE, J. *William Mason: The First New Zealand Architect*. London and Auckland, 1972.

TURNBULL, C. and JACK, C. *The Charm of Hobart*. Sydney, 1949.

38

ARCHITECTURE IN CONTINENTAL EUROPE 1830-1914

INFLUENCES

The French Revolution of 1789 and the Napoleonic Empire left indelible marks upon Europe. At its zenith, in 1810, the Empire comprised the whole of France, Belgium, the left bank of the Rhine, Holland and the German coast as far as the western Baltic, as well as those states which retained individual governments under the authority of the French Emperor: Switzerland, Spain, the Kingdom of Naples and the Illyrian Provinces. Inevitably French influence was paramount and affected most aspects of life, a factor of especial consequence being the Code Napoléon which laid the foundations of modern Continental law.

On the fall of Napoleon, the Congress of Vienna (1814-15) had tried to impose upon Europe its previous political structure without regard for the new feelings of nationalism stimulated, at least in part, by the internationalist system enforced by Napoleon, while memories of 1789, with its intoxicating ideals of liberty, fraternity and democracy, were impossible to erase. In 1830, almost the whole of the Continent erupted in revolt—in France where the Bourbon monarchy (restored after the eclipse of Napoleon) tottered, but found brief uneasy survival under the more liberal Louis-Philippe; in Belgium, which achieved national identity and independence; and in Poland, Germany, Italy, Switzerland, Spain and Portugal. Greece, for centuries part of the Ottoman Empire, regained her freedom in 1829.

Although for the most part outwardly at peace for the next eighteen years, thanks in large measure to the political dexterity of the Austrian Chancellor, Prince Klemens Metternich (1773-1859), by 1848 Europe was once more in the throes of revolution. The outcome was a strengthening of constitutional liberty in Denmark, Holland, Belgium and Switzerland; emancipation of the peasants in the Austrian Empire and German states and universal (male) suffrage in France, where the Second Republic was inaugurated. The same year saw the publication of the 'Communist Manifesto' of Karl Marx (1818-83) and Friedrich Engels (1820-95). The French Second Republic lasted only until 1852, when it was succeeded by the initially repressive Second Empire of Napoleon III, and the next twenty years saw the unification of Italy (between 1859 and 1870).

In the German states the seeds of nationalism had been sown before the Napoleonic era. Books like J. G. Herder's *Ideas on the Philosophy of the History of Mankind* (1784) had emphasized 'Volksgeist' or national character, and the great flowering of romanticism which produced Beethoven (1770-1827), Goethe (1749-1832), and Schiller (1759-1805) glorified it. However it was not until the second half of the nineteenth century that German national yearnings were realized through the single-minded opportunism of the Prussian Chief Minister, Otto von Bismarck

(1815–98), who, between 1866 and 1870, formed the German states into a cohesive nation. In France the brief and ill-starred Franco-Prussian War (1870) ended the Second Empire and marked the beginning of the Third Republic, which survived until the Second World War. In 1871 the German Empire was created: dominated by Prussia, it endured until the dissolution of Imperial Germany in 1918. In Austria Franz Joseph succeeded to the throne in 1848, and his long reign, marked by reactionary conservatism, lasted until 1916.

In general terms it can be said that between 1830 and 1870 Europe was imbued by liberal and national movements, while after 1870 she was increasingly dominated by power politics, based largely on the economic rivalry of France and Germany, which led eventually to the First World War, in which Germany was allied with Austria, and France with Belgium, Britain, Russia, Italy and later the U.S.A. Both France and Germany were administered by bureaucratic systems; the former retaining the liberal and democratic traditions she had pioneered, the latter, although in theory democratic, marked by a particularly harsh militarism.

Although Britain succeeded in retaining her leadership in commerce and technology during the nineteenth century, the countries of north-west Europe became serious rivals. In the early part of the century Belgium was the most enterprising, but France and later Germany developed prodigiously. By 1870 the latter was producing 50% more pig iron than France, and by 1880 she had doubled her output, overtaking Britain at the end of the century. In 1858 improvements were made in the Bessemer method of steel production by the Swede, G. F. Göransson (1819–1900), and by 1866 an alternative to the Bessemer process had been developed by Friedrich Siemens (1826–1904) and Pierre-Émile Martin (1824–1915).

Technological developments were reflected in the growth of communications, particularly railways. The Brussels–Malines line was opened in 1835, and the railway between Vienna and Trieste in 1853. In 1871 the Paris–Lyon railway was extended through the Alps to Turin by the Mont-Cenis Tunnel (begun 1857) and 1882 saw the completion of the S. Gotthard Tunnel. Work began on the Trans-Siberian Railway in 1891, and in 1898 on the Simplon Tunnel.

Just as England had built up an empire to provide outlets for manufactures and capital, in due course Belgium, Holland, France and later Germany acquired substantial colonies. In this way, aided by advances in ship design including the introduction of steam-power, new and wide communication links were formed. Particularly important as a link with the East was the Suez Canal, the work of the engineer Ferdinand de Lesseps (1805–94). Opened in 1869, within a decade the canal was carrying three million tons of shipping annually.

The enthusiasm of the age for technical progress and commercial endeavour was expressed in the series of international exhibitions of science and industry held in Paris in 1855, 1867, 1878, 1889 and 1900. Their prototype was the British Great Exhibition in London of 1851, and in all cases the exhibition buildings exploited metal and glass construction, and included special galleries for the display of machinery, that for the 1889 Exhibition, by the engineer Victor Contamin (1840–93) and architect C. L. F. Dutert (1845–1906), being specially noteworthy. It was for the same exhibition that the engineer Gustave Eiffel (1832–1923) designed the famous 300-metre (985-foot) high Eiffel Tower (1887–9), a monument to nineteenth-century technology as much as to the French Revolution, of which the exhibition marked the centenary. Eiffel had already been responsible for the entrance pavilion of the 1878 Exhibition (destroyed 1910), the bridge over the River Douro in Portugal (1875) with a single arch span of 160 m (525 ft), and the Garabit Viaduct (1880–4) with an arch span of 165 m (542 ft).

Throughout the century France made important contributions in structural design and also in the development of reinforced concrete construction. Joseph Monier (1823–1906), whose pioneer work included a system for reinforced concrete beams (1877), was followed by François Coignet (1814–88), and François Hennebique (1842–1921), who substituted steel for iron and developed hooked connections for reinforcing bars (1892). In Germany significant work was done by the firm of Wayss and Freitag of Frankfurt-am-Main, who commissioned the engineer Mathias Koenen (1849–1924) to write the important theoretical work *Das System Monier*. From the 1870s reinforced concrete was increasingly used for bridge construction, Hennebique completing a 57-metre (187-foot) arch across the River Vienne at Châtellerault in 1898.

French pre-eminence in civil engineering was partly the result of her highly developed technical education which was rooted in the eighteenth-century École des Ponts et Chaussées. In 1793, when the old schools were suppressed, Jean-Baptiste Rondelet (1743–1829)—who later published a famous work on building construction, *Traité théorique et pratique de l'art de bâtir* (1802–17)—set up the École Centrale des Travaux Publiques, with three-year courses in civil engineering and architecture, and in 1895 this became the École Polytechnique, the first school of general engineering. The École served as a model for other polytechnic schools —at Prague (1806), Vienna (1815), Karlsruhe (1825) and later Braunschweig, Stuttgart, Hanover, Dresden and Darmstadt. The creation of the 'ETH', the Swiss Federal Polytechnic at Zurich (1854), with status equivalent to a university, inspired the German 'technische Hochschulen' of the 1870s, and the establishment of the world-famous Charlottenburg Technical High School at Berlin in 1884. In addition numerous universities were founded during the century.

In religious matters the period was generally marked by tolerance. With the growing concern for national sovereignty and the increasing competition between the European nations, authority in the Catholic Church became more and more centred on Rome, and ultramontanism prevailed. The first ecumenical council since that of Trent was assembled in 1870 (Vatican I) and the dogma of papal infallibility proclaimed, the same year marking the end of the temporal power of the papacy with the final unification of Italy. In 1891 Pope Leo XIII published the encyclical *Rerum Novarum*, which offered an alternative to the remedies proposed by communism for the social evils which had grown up with industrialization. During the century the mainly middle-class Protestant Churches lost much of their earlier vigour and after 1850 tended to fall into two groups—the fundamentalists, who accepted the Bible as literal truth in spite of the theories of Darwin and others, and the modernists, who attempted to adapt Christian beliefs to the views of contemporary science. Science and secularism had a disintegrating effect on Orthodox Judaism and at the same time brought about a greater involvement of Jews in society generally, many like Karl Marx and Sigmund Freud (1856–1939) making notable contributions.

The achievements of the nineteenth century, especially in science and technology, were great and the pride and self-confidence of the age understandable. Coupled with the 'heroic' view of man, inherited from romanticism, it seemed that all things were possible and that man—European man, that is—was indeed 'master of his fate'. The German philosopher Hegel (1770–1831) saw history evolving through the interaction of opposites, encouraging a belief in evolutionary progress: in economic terms, his dialectic was adopted by Marx, and the theories of Charles Darwin (1809–82) on biological evolution have an affinity with it. Both Marx and Darwin appeared to deny the metaphysical nature of man, as did Friedrich Nietzsche (1844–1900), who between 1878 and 1889 wrote a series of works advocating a form of paganism centred on the concept of the superman, the natural leader who was 'beyond good and evil'. Although in his lifetime Nietzsche was regarded as a crank, in retrospect his ideas reflect only too clearly the underlying attitudes of many late-nineteenth-century industrial and political leaders.

ARCHITECTURAL CHARACTER

The architecture of the period can be considered in three phases more or less corresponding to Europe's political history: 1830–50, 1850–70 and 1870–1914.

1830-1850

In spite of widening eclecticism, the Roman and Greek forms popular during the Napoleonic era continued to be used. The round arch, Florentine, Romanesque and Byzantine as well as Roman, was a popular motif especially in Germany, where the term 'Rundbogenstil' was coined to describe buildings employing it. France was particularly influential, especially through the publications of E. L. Boullée's pupil, Jean-Nicolas-Louis Durand (1760–1834) who, after serving as an engineer in Napoleon's army, had been appointed Professor of Architecture at the École Polytechnique on its establishment in 1795. His *Recueil et parallèle des édifices en tout genre, anciens et modernes* (1801), known as 'Le Grand Durand', was influential in the development of eclecticism, while his *Précis des leçons d'architecture données à l'École Polytechnique* (1802–5) explained his system of design. Based on the repetition of standard bays, both in plan and elevation, which could be enriched with Classical, Mediaeval or Renaissance motifs as desired, it provided a convenient, though often dull, formula for the design of the large, complex buildings required by the age. In principle it had an affinity with the bay system, pragmatically adopted with the introduction of iron construction, in English industrial buildings. Durand's influence was wide and particularly marked in the work of the German architects Karl Friedrich von Schinkel (1781–1841) and Leo von Klenze (1784–1864).

As in Britain the period was marked by a revival of Italian Renaissance forms, already used in the Rundbogenstil but seen in a much more developed way in the work of F. L. J. Duban (1797–1870), and in the exterior of Henri Labrouste's Library of S. Geneviève, Paris (p. 1208A), designed in 1843 and perhaps the most distinguished European building of the decade. Although Gothic did not achieve the popularity it had in contemporary Britain, there was a growing interest in the style which, as in England, was seen as having strong national associations, particularly in Germany. Schinkel had designed the cast-iron Kreuzberg War Memorial (1819–21) in the style, and the brick and terra-cotta Werder Church, Berlin (1825), and a concern with the mediaeval past is seen in the completion of Cologne Cathedral, where work was resumed in 1824 by F. A. Ahlert (1755–1833), continued by A. F. Zwirner (1802–61), and completed in 1880 by R. Voigtel (1829–1902). In France the writer Prosper Mérimée (1803–70) was appointed Inspector General of National Monuments and Historical Antiquities in 1834, and under him the restoration of Carcassonne (1855–79), and the cathedrals of Laon, Vézelay and Saint-Savin was carried out by Viollet-le-Duc (p. 1191).

The use of iron in building increased, notable examples being the Galerie d'Orléans, Paris (1829–31), by P. F. L. Fontaine; the Dianabad, Vienna (1841–3) by Karl Etzel; S. Isaac's Cathedral, S. Petersburg (1818–58) by A. de Montferrand, with a remarkable cast-iron dome completed in 1842; and the interior of Labrouste's Library of S. Geneviève, Paris (1843–50) (p. 1206).

By mid-century the Renaissance had become the dominant style in France, eclecticism flourished in the German states, while in Italy and Spain generally Neo-Classicism continued.

1850-1870

Covering roughly the period of the French Second Empire, this phase is comparable with the High Victorian in Britain. During it the Renaissance revival became more firmly established and took on a new richness. Pavilions and high mansard roofs with elaborate metal crestings added sky-line interest, while wall surfaces were relieved with often opulent decoration of a *cinquecento* character. The fashion can be attributed at least in part to the building of the New Louvre (1852–7) (p. 1206), while the Paris Opera (1861–74), marked a step towards further richness in design, initiating a form of Neo-Baroque. The École des Beaux-Arts played an increasingly important part, being placed under direct state control by Napoleon III in 1864, and its influence extended far beyond France. Less 'rationalist' than the École Polytechnique, its greatest concern was with Antique and Renaissance precedents, reflected also in P. M. Letarouilly's *Édifices de Rome Moderne* (1864), finely engraved measured drawings of Renaissance and post-Renaissance buildings in Rome. Inspired by the study of Roman examples great emphasis came to be placed on axial planning, as exemplified in the Paris Opera (p. 1206).

The phase was marked by a number of major town-planning undertakings, the most important being the replanning of Paris by Baron Eugène Georges Haussmann (1809–91) between 1853 and 1868. Apart from improving living conditions in the city where the population approached a million, the intentions were to provide a capital worthy of the Second Empire and, with memories of the 1848 Revolution still fresh, to ensure that it could be adequately controlled by police and troops. Haussmann's enormous, seemingly endless avenues, cutting ruthlessly through the old city, and in the process destroying many splendid architectural relics of the 'ancien régime', reflect a preoccupation with national prestige. The same is true of the Ringstrasse, in Vienna (begun 1858), built by the Emperor Franz Joseph, on the site of the old city walls to the plans of Ludwig Förster (1797–1863), and punctuated by public buildings in various styles, including the polychromatic and ornate Army Museum (1856–77) by Förster and Theophil von Hansen (1813–91), in a style reminiscent of Byzantine, the enormous red-brick Neo-Gothic Rathaus (1872–83) by Friedrich von Schmidt (1825–91), and Hansen's Neo-Greek Parliament Building (1873–83). Budapest, the second capital of the Austro-Hungarian Empire, was also much enriched by Franz Joseph; while in Rome, the capital of the newly united Italy, civic improvements included the Via XX Settembre and the Via Nazionale, the latter terminating in the splendid Esedra, designed by Gaetano Koch (1849–1910), on the site of one of the exedra of the Baths of Diocletian.

So far mention has been made of work in what can be described as the 'academic stream' of the period, but parallel with this there were other currents which as far as the future was concerned were of considerable importance. In great measure they stemmed from the French rationalist tradition as represented in the École Polytechnique, and were associated with the growing interest in Gothic architecture and the structural use of iron. Labrouste had employed iron construction in his Library of S. Geneviève, and in the National Library, Paris (1862–8) (p. 1206) he made more extensive use of the material, and it was his associate, Eugène-Emmanuel Viollet-le-Duc (1814–79) who became one of the most important influences of the second half of the century. Significantly he was a student of A.R.F. Leclerc (1785–1853), who in turn had studied under Durand. Of his numerous writings particularly important were the *Dictionnaire raisonné de l'architecture française du XIme au XVIme siècle* (1854–68), which interpreted Gothic architecture in terms of structural rationalism and set a new standard for speculative archaeology, and the *Entretiens sur l'architecture* (1863–72), which developed the thesis that rational construction was the basis of all good design and advocated the use of iron and other new materials as a means of achieving a truly nineteenth-century architecture. Viollet-le-Duc designed few buildings but was responsible for an enormous amount of restoration and reconstruction work on French mediaeval monuments, including S. Chapelle (1840), Notre-Dame, Paris (1845–56) and the Château of Pierrefonds (1859–70). Examples of iron construction included the demolished buildings for the Paris Exhibitions of 1855 and 1867, the former by F.-A. Cendrier (1803–92) and J.-M.-V. Viel (1796–1863), with adventurous iron and glass interiors masked externally by a masonry shell, the latter, by J. B. Kranz and Eiffel, planned as a series of concentric ellipses, expressing more frankly its iron construction; the Halles Centrales, Paris (1853–9, demolished 1971) (p. 1219); and the Galleria Vittorio Emanuele, Milan (1865–77) (p. 1219). Iron was used in the Neo-Gothic S. Eugène, Paris (1854–5), and more conventional examples of Gothic include the Votivkirche, Vienna (1856–79) (p. 1200) by Heinrich von Ferstel (1828–83), and S. Epvre, Nancy (1863–) by M.-P. Morey (1805–78). Of considerably more interest is Viollet-le-Duc's S. Denys-de-l'Estrée, Paris (p. 1200).

To generalize, it can be said that during this phase France maintained her leadership in both academic and innovatory architecture; Prussia and Italy tended to follow her in the former, while in Austria and southern Germany a wide eclecticism prevailed, leaning towards the purely imitative as in Dollmann's elaborately pretty Schloss Linderhof (p. 1194).

1870–1914

Enthusiasm for metallic construction intensified and was audaciously displayed in the Paris Exhibitions of 1878, and especially 1889 (p. 1220), while for the 1873 International Exhibition at Vienna an iron cupola, 107 m (350 ft) in diameter, was built, the largest structure of this sort of the century. The Paris department store, the Bon Marché (1876) (p. 1220), which had a floor area of over 2,500 square metres (30,000 square ft), was almost entirely of iron and glass; and what was probably the first fully iron-framed building in France, the turbine house of the Menier Chocolate Factory, Noisiel-sur-Marne, was erected in 1871–2 (p. 1220).

Academic architecture as represented by the École des Beaux-Arts prevailed through most of the continent. There was a tendency to turn increasingly to Antique as opposed to Renaissance forms, as in the Victor Emanuel II Monument, Rome (begun 1885) (p. 1212), but a Baroque scale and 'imperial' richness were maintained, sometimes in an excessively ponderous way, as in the Berlin Reichstag Building (1884–94) (p. 1215A) by P. Wallot (1841–1912). Gothic was still employed for churches and, less frequently, for public buildings, as well as the Romanesque and sometimes Byzantine styles, as at Le Sacré Coeur, Paris (p. 1200). In Holland and Scandinavia, inspired by mediaeval examples and the ideas of Viollet-le-Duc, there was a movement towards a less pretentious, more humane and at the same time rational, architecture. In both cases brick, which was the traditional material of the regions, was extensively used. Initiated by P. J. H. Cuijpers (1827–1921) and developed by H. P. Berlage (1856–1934) in Holland, and represented by Martin Nyrop (1849–1923) in Denmark, Ragnar Östberg (1866–1945) in Sweden and Eliel Saarinen (1873–1950) in Finland, the movement had an affinity with the contemporary British vernacular revival. The movement was of considerable importance and laid the foundations for the fine architectural traditions which developed in those countries during the twentieth century and have had widespread influence. In Spain in the 1880s there was a sudden and extraordinary creative flowering in Barcelona in the work of Antoni Gaudí (1856–1934). In its plasticity of form, his work might appear to be linked to, and indeed anticipate, Art Nouveau, but the latter has more likely connections with the linear forms of metal construction and the malleable properties of wrought iron and steel, as well as the ideas contained in the second volume of Viollet-le-Duc's *Entretiens*. A remarkable self-conscious movement, manifested chiefly in the decorative arts, Art Nouveau emerged in Belgium in the 1890s in the work of Victor Horta (1861–1947), though the term itself was derived somewhat later from Samuel Bing's decorative arts shop in Paris, Maison de l'Art Nouveau, opened in 1896. Short-lived and without lasting influence though it was, the style spread rapidly, especially after the Paris Exhibition of 1900, and became in Germany the 'Jugendstil', in Italy the 'Stile Liberty' (after the London shop of that name), while in France it was sometimes called 'Le Moderne Style'. Enthusiasm for it among aesthetes and intellectuals seems to have been coloured by a consciousness of the approaching new century, and a somewhat desperate feeling that the nineteenth century had so far failed to produce a style specifically its own.

From the end of the century until the war, Europe was a ferment of new ideas in architecture. The Darmstadt Art School was founded in 1899 with Joseph Maria Olbrich (1867–1908), a pupil of Otto Wagner (1841–1918), as its head. In 1907 the influential Deutscher Werkbund was established, and in 1914 the Werkbund Exhibition took place in Cologne (see p. 1246).

EXAMPLES

DOMESTIC BUILDINGS

Rue de Rivoli (west), Paris (1811–35) (p. 1195A), by Charles Percier (1764–1838) and P. F. L. Fontaine (1762–1853), forms part of a larger planning scheme initiated by Napoleon I. The five-storey houses are in terrace blocks of a restrained Classical character, and are unified horizontally by elegant iron balconies at first- and third-floor levels, the continuous open arcades at street level being reminiscent of the much earlier Place des Vosges (p. 898). The group was extended to the east in the same design in 1852–5, when high mansard roofs were added.

Schottenhof, Vienna (1826–32), by Joseph Kornhäusel (d. 1860), is a large housing scheme built round a series of square internal courtyards. The stuccoed street elevations have shops at ground level and rise through five main storeys, unified by shallow projecting giant Ionic pilasters, which form central pedimented 'temple fronts' to each elevation.

Feilner House, Berlin (1829), by Karl Friedrich von Schinkel, a three-storey, nine-bay house constructed of brick and terra-cotta for a manufacturer of those products, has a Greek Revival severity in its overall forms, although its sparse but fine terra-cotta detail suggests Early Renaissance sources. In its simple and regular window arrangement the house is reminiscent of early industrial buildings in northern England, which Schinkel would have seen on his visit in 1826.

Court Gardener's House, Charlottenhof, Potsdam (1829–31) (p. 1195C), by Schinkel, is a remodelling of an existing building in a highly picturesque way, inspired by contemporary English taste. Its low-pitched roofs, overhanging eaves and asymmetrically placed belvedere-like elements derive from Italian vernacular sources. With the same architect's **Tea House and Roman Bath** (1833–4), the house forms an evocative, romantic group.

No. 10, Place de la Bourse, Paris (1834), a block of flats by A. J. Pellechet (1789–1871), provides an example of Parisian street architecture of the period. Stucco-faced, the seven-bay, six-storey building is roofed by a mansard, from which pedimented windows open to a delicate iron balcony supported by the main cornice. At street level there are shops which, with a mezzanine floor, form a base for the façade of well-proportioned windows with carefully detailed architraves, the whole being unified horizontally by string courses.

The **Old Palace, Athens** (1837–41) (p. 1195D), by Friedrich von Gärtner (1792–1847), was designed for Otto von Wittelsbach on his accession to the Greek throne. The three-storey building achieves a forceful effect by a simple incisive fenestration pattern, on the principal façade a three-bay pedimented central element with, at entrance level, a sturdy unpedimented single-storey Greek Doric decastyle portico, being flanked by seven-bay wings.

Flats, Rue de Liège, Paris (1846–8) (p. 1195B), the first executed design of Viollet-le-Duc, is a highly original essay in the use of mediaeval detail. At street level openings are simple and have shallow segmental arches; above, bold, projecting string courses, and labels and sills continued between the windows tie the façade together. **Flats, Rue de Douai, Paris** (c. 1860), by the same architect, is more severe in treatment and again represents an attempt to apply mediaeval forms in a way appropriate to nineteenth-century needs. The façade of clean-cut, rectangular openings has at fourth-floor level a continuous iron escape balcony carried on ponderous stone brackets. The second floor, where the windows are emphasized by heavy stone hoods, has a shorter balcony, borne on three massive corbels.

The **Boulevard de Sébastopol, Paris** (1860) is architecturally typical of Haussmann's Second Empire Paris (p. 1191). Above street-level shops are commonly five or six floors of flats. Despite their height, the result of exploiting the economic potential of the sites, the retrained elevations, with their judicious ornamental accents and disciplined emphasis on a regular, unifying vertical rhythm, give an excellent answer to the problem of repetitive street architecture. Another typical example is illustrated on p. 1196A.

No. 11, Rue de Milan, Paris (c. 1860) (p. 1198A), by A.-F. Mortier, represents a more opulent treatment for flats in Paris at this date. The seven-bay, four-storey façade provides a sumptuous array of baroque elements which enrich its entire surface. Strongly projecting string courses at each floor unify the composition.

Heinrichshof, Vienna (1861–3, demolished 1939–45) (p. 1197A), by Theophil von Hansen, was an example of the grandiose developments in the city under the Emperor Franz Joseph. A vast, five-storey block of dwellings, its façades were covered by a bewildering assortment of string courses, balustrades and elaborate window surrounds from various Renaissance sources, giving a general impression of restless, facile opulence.

Schloss Linderhof, near Oberammergau (1870–86) (p. 1197B), by Georg von Dollmann, was built for Ludwig II of Bavaria in the South-German Rococo style. It is superbly sited with delightful formal gardens and sumptuous and finely executed Rococo interiors. Dollmann's **Herrenchiemsee** (begun 1878), an extraordinary island château based on Versailles, was also built for Ludwig II, as was the fantastic, Wagnerian mountain schloss, **Neuschwanstein** (1869–81), by Eduard Riedel (1813–85) and Dollmann. Together the buildings exemplify, in an extreme form, the penchant for imitative eclecticism characteristic of south German and Austrian architecture during the nineteenth century.

Nos. 24–26, Carrer de les Carolines, Barcelona (1878–80), a suburban villa, the first building of Antoni Gaudí, is based on Spanish traditional and mediaeval forms and constructed of rubble masonry banded with polychrome tiling.

A. Rue de Rivoli (west), Paris (1811–35).
See p. 1193

B. Flats, Rue de Liège, Paris
(1846–8). See p. 1194

C. Court Gardener's House, Charlottenhof, Potsdam (1829–31). See p. 1193

D. The Old Palace, Athens (1837–41). See p. 1194

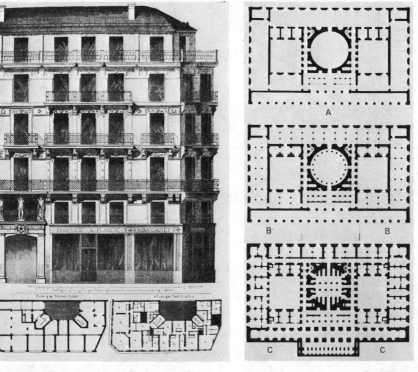

A. Typical Paris apartment house of the Second Empire. See p. 1194

B. Altes Museum, Berlin (1824–8), plans: A first floor, B ground floor, C basement. See p. 1205

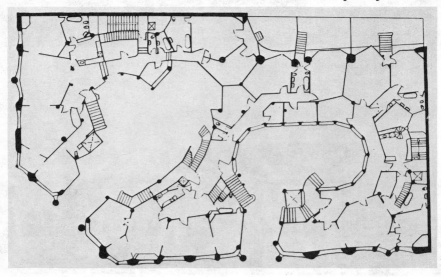

c. The Casa Milà, Barcelona (1905–10): ground floor plan. See p. 1199

A. Heinrichshof, Vienna (1861–3). See p. 1194

B. Schloss Linderhof, near Oberammergau (1870–86). See p. 1194

A. No. 11, Rue de Milan, Paris (c. 1860). See p. 1194

B. The Palau Güell, Barcelona (1885–9). See p. 1199

C. The Casa Batlló, Barcelona (1905–7). See p. 1199

D. The Casa Milà, Barcelona (1905–10). See p. 1199

E. No. 6, Rue Paul-Émile Janson, Brussels (1892–3): staircase. See p. 1199

F. No. 40, Linke Wienzeile (The Majolica House), Vienna (c. 1898). See p. 1199

The **Palau Güell, Barcelona** (1885–9) (p. 1198B), also by Gaudí, seems to presage Art Nouveau in its forms. Among the building's many novelties, especially interesting are the twin parabolic portals with their grilles of curvilinear ironwork, the cantilevered first floor, and the conscious asymmetry in the placing of elements. The **Casa Batlló, Barcelona** (1905–7) (p. 1198C), is an important example of Gaudí's mature work. The stone dressings of the lower part of the façade are modelled plastically in sinuous and ovoid forms, echoed in the metal balustrades above, while around the rectangular upper windows, the wall surface is studded with fragments of coloured glass. Gaudí's **Casa Milà, Barcelona** (1905–10) (pp. 1196C, 1198D), represents a further development. Undulating stone façades enclose an irregular mesh of polygonal rooms, no two alike, and none with right-angled corners, externally swept into heavy brows over the tiers of roll-edged, round-angled windows with intricate iron balconies.

No. 6, Rue Paul-Émile Janson (Hôtel Tassel), Brussels (1892–3) (p. 1198E), by Victor Horta, is generally regarded as the first complete building in fully-fledged Art Nouveau style. It is narrow-fronted and deep, the rooms planned rather more freely than was normal at this time and with some exploitation of floor levels. The main element of the generally unobtrusive façade is a segmental oriel bay with metal mullions and window heads and decorative iron balustrades. The interior, particularly in the staircase-hall and salon, provides striking examples of Art Nouveau. Iron is widely used for both structure and decoration and is developed into free-flowing, linear plant-like forms, echoed in the mosaic floor decoration. Other houses by Horta in Brussels are **No. 224, Avenue Louise (Hôtel Solvay)** (1895–1900), with a façade characterized by a flowing plasticity and attenuated linear forms, and **No. 4, Avenue Palmerston (Hôtel van Eetvelde)** (1895), with externally a series of arched bays in metal, and internally a superb salon, where a circle of iron columns flowing into elliptical arches, supports a shallow glass dome.

No. 40, Linke Wienzeile (The Majolica House), Vienna (c. 1898) (p. 1198F), a block of flats by Otto Wagner, has a six-storey tile-faced façade punctuated by regularly-spaced, rectangular window openings reminiscent of Schinkel's Feilner House (p. 1193). Here, however, in deliberate conflict with the generally severe rectangular forms, intricate coloured curvilinear patterning expands across the tile-facing, and delicate ironwork is introduced in the continuous first and second-floor balconies, and elsewhere.

RELIGIOUS BUILDINGS

Ludwigskirche, Munich (1829–40), by von Gärtner, is modelled on Romanesque prototypes somewhat loosely interpreted, its west end, with rose window and arcaded porch, flanked by attenuated towers and round-arch screen arcades.

Friedenskirche, Potsdam (1845–8), by Ludwig Persius (1803–45), a pupil of Schinkel, is a highly romantic copy of an Early Christian basilica, complete with atrium and arcaded campanile. Picturesquely sited at the edge of an artificial lake, out of which the apsidal west end and one side rise sheer, the building is characterized by exceptionally refined detail.

S. Vincent-de-Paul, Paris (1824; 1831–44), was designed and commenced by J.-B. Lepère (1761–1844), the work being taken over and completed by J.-I. Hittorff (1793–1867). A five-aisled basilica in plan, the church has a fine timber roof and its inner aisles are continued around the western apse, giving a spatial effect of great power. Entered through a grand, pedimented hexastyle Ionic portico, flanked by tall towers articulated by cornices at each stage, the church is approached by elaborate and monumental external stairs.

Nikolaikirche, Hamburg (1845–63) (p. 1201A) was built in the Gothic style from the winning competition designs of Sir G. G. Scott (p. 1127). Almost completely destroyed in the Second World War, the grandly proportioned and richly decorated west tower, combining English and German Gothic details, remains.

S. Clotilde, Paris (1846–57) was designed by F. C. Gau (1790–1854), the first project being prepared in 1839, and completed by Théodore Ballu (1817–74) after Gau's death. The church is in the style of French fourteenth-century Gothic, of cathedral proportions, and noteworthy for the iron construction of its roof.

S. Eugène, Paris (1854–5) (p. 1201D), by L.-A. Boileau (1812–96), also in the Gothic style, makes further use of iron in its construction and details, and is the first French iron-framed church. Extensive use of iron occurs also in **S. Eugène, Le Vésinet, S.-et-O.** (1863), by Boileau; **S. Augustin, Paris** (1860–71), by Victor Baltard; and **Notre-Dame-du-Travail, Paris** (1899–1901), by Astruc.

The **Votivkirche, Vienna** (1856–79) (p. 1201C), by Heinrich von Ferstel, a rich and elaborate essay in Gothic with tall, slender western towers with open belfries and crocketted steeples, was the result of a competition held in 1853. Also in Vienna, the **Fünfhaus Parish Church** (1868–75), by Friedrich von Schmidt, an important exponent of the Gothic Revival in Austria, is unusual for its aisled octagon plan. Above this rises a dome surmounted by a tall finial, while the west entrance is flanked by towers linked by flying buttresses to the drum of the dome.

S. Denys-de-l'Estrée, S. Denis, near Paris (1864–7) (p. 1202A), by the influential restorer Viollet-le-Duc, is comparable with the work of Butterfield and Burges (p. 1129) in England. The stone-vaulted nave has wide, square bays lit by groups of clear-storey windows, and above the western porch there is a sturdy tower, capped by a tall slated roof. Wall and vault surfaces are stencilled with coloured decoration and generally the detailing is tough and vigorous.

Mole Antonelliana, Turin (begun 1863), by Alessandro Antonelli (1798–1880), was initially intended as a synagogue, but was taken over for use as a municipal museum in 1876. The building is structurally audacious, especially in the great vaulted cupola covering the main mass, from which rises a tall spire-like feature, decorated with Neo-Classical elements in its lower stages, making a total height for the building of 167 m (548 ft). Antonelli's cupola of **S. Gaudenzio, Novara** (begun 1840), is similar in character, with two circular Corinthian peristyles supporting a dome, above which further colonnaded tiers rise to form a steeple with a total height of 125 m (410 ft).

The **Church of the Sacré Coeur, Paris** (p. 1202B), begun in 1875–7 to the design of Paul Abadie (1812–84), largely completed by the end of the century, but not wholly finished until 1919, stands with a cluster of white domes on the heights of Montmartre. It reflects Byzantine influence by way of the mediaeval cathedral of S. Front, Périgueux (p. 393).

S. Jean-de-Montmartre, Paris (1897–1905) (p. 1201B), by G.-E.-A. de Baudot (1836–1915), is the first building of major architectural importance to have been designed in reinforced concrete, although the architect had already completed some houses and a school in the material. In the system used the compression elements were of reinforced brickwork and the tension elements of reinforced cement, without a stone aggregate. The design is mediaeval in feeling generally, yet with many novel forms and with considerable use, both internally and externally, of interlaced arches, those of the gallery being decorated with mosaics.

The **Church of the Sagrada Familia, Barcelona** (crypt 1882–91; chevet 1887–91; transept façade designed 1891–1903 and built 1903–26) (p. 1203A), by Antoni Gaudí, who took over the work in 1884, still largely unfinished, has the

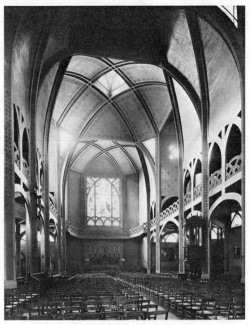

A. The Nikolaikirche, Hamburg
(1845–63). See p. 1200

B. S. Jean-de-Montmartre, Paris
(1897–1905). See p. 1200

C. The Votivkirche, Vienna (1856–
1879). See p. 1200

D. S. Eugène, Paris (1854–5).
See p. 1200

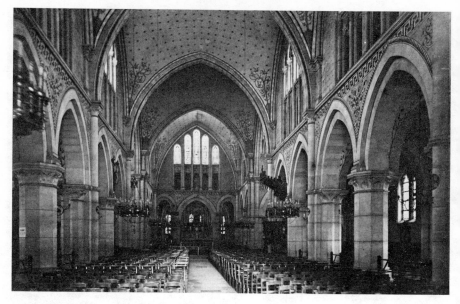

A. S. Denys-de-l'Estrée, S. Denis, near Paris (1864–7). See p. 1200

B. The Church of the Sacré-Coeur, Paris (begun in 1875–7). See p. 1200

A. The Church of the Sagrada Familia, Barcelona: 'south' transept (1903–26) seen from the inner side. See p. 1200

B. The Engelbrecht Church, Stockholm (1904–14). See p. 1205

C. The Högalid Church, Stockholm (1918–23). See p. 1205

D. The Grundtvig Church, Copenhagen (1921–6). See p. 1205

A. The Schauspielhaus, Berlin (1819–20). See p. 1205

B. Altes Museum, Berlin (1824–8). See p. 1205

same fantastic qualities seen in other buildings by this architect. The 'south transept' façade (the church is abnormally orientated) comprises a trio of steeply gabled, deeply recessed porches, the two lesser on the flanks corresponding to the transept aisles, dominated by four skittle-shaped openwork spires. The porches are profusely ornamented with sculptured naturalistic floral and figure ornament which, although in stonework, has the effect of soft, melting snow. Enormous faceted finials, studded with broken coloured tiles, cap the four towers. The inner arcades were to have been inclined towards one another and were intended to give the semblance of weird, angular trees, stark branches reaching upwards to sustain a stalactite vault over the nave and flat roofs over the double aisles, again with stalactites, between which scores of circular 'eyes' would admit shafts of daylight. Art Nouveau was never so plastic, dramatic or eccentric.

The **Grundtvig Church, Copenhagen** (designed 1913, completed 1921–6) (p. 1203D), by P. V. Jensen Klint (1853–1930), has an impressively composed western front which represents the progressive architecture of its day, yet retains something of the traditional Baltic flavour. The traditional note is present too in the **Engelbrecht Church, Stockholm** (1904–14) (p. 1203B), by L. I. Wahlman (b. 1870), which has a brick parabolic vault; and the fine **Högalid Church, Stockholm** (1918–23) (p. 1203C), by Ivar Tengbom (1878–1968).

PUBLIC BUILDINGS

The **Schauspielhaus, Berlin** (1819–20) (p. 1204A), by K. F. von Schinkel, a powerful work in the Greek Revival style, is marked by the strong, geometric control of its elements, the building taking the form of a series of boldly articulated rectangular masses. The entablature of the pedimented hexastyle Ionic portico is continued around the building, binding together its main forms. A high, pedimented attic, expressing the central auditorium, dominates the building with, on each of its faces, openings grouped together as continuous bands, divided by rectangular, pilaster-like mullions. The building, a masterpiece of Neo-Classicism, was extensively damaged during the Second World War.

The **Altes Museum, Berlin** (1824–8) (pp. 1196B, 1204B), by Schinkel, is Greek Revival in style and an example of the application of Durand's planning principles (p. 1190) to a new nineteenth-century building type. Four long, two-storeyed gallery wings, each planned on a regular bay system, form the sides of a square, in which is inscribed a large, circular hall rising the full height of the building, with an ambulatory at first-floor level communicating with the upper galleries, and surmounted by a Pantheon-like dome, the latter expressed externally as a simple attic. The museum is entered through a deep Ionic colonnade of eighteen columns, embracing the full two storeys of the building and extending across its entire width, contained by flank walls treated as antae. The entablature of the colonnade is continued around the building's perimeter, emphasizing the massive simplicity of its broad, rectangular form.

Thorwaldsen Museum, Copenhagen (1839–48) (p. 1207A), by M. G. B. Bindesbøll (1800–56), a pupil of C. F. Hansen (1756–1845) and architect of the Neo-Classic **Palace of Justice, Copenhagen** (1805–15), was built to house the work and collections of the Danish sculptor Bertil (Alberto) Thorwaldsen (1770–1844). Greek Revival in style, the bold severity of its astylar forms recalls the work of Schinkel, and to some extent Egyptian architecture, especially in the internal courtyards. The barrel-vaulted ceilings of the galleries are decorated in the Pompeian style, while on the external walls murals by Jørgen Sonne (1801–90) depict the transportation of the contents of the museum from Rome.

The **Library of S. Geneviève, Paris** (designed 1843, built 1845–50) (p. 1208), by Henri Labrouste, was the first French library to be designed as an individual building and, externally, is a brilliant example of Neo-Renaissance design. Internally, it has a complete iron frame, the metal double roof being supported by three rows of iron columns, the outer rows embedded in the masonry walls. A long, rectangular building, 80 m × 23 m (263 ft × 75 ft), with a rear projection containing a double staircase, the lofty main floor stands above a shallow ground floor, and is covered by two longitudinal barrel vaults with iron arch-ribs springing from the central line of columns, with panels between of thin, reinforced plaster. A low-pitched, metal outer roof spans the full width of the building, which served as a model for the Boston Public Library, U.S.A. (p. 1239).

The **National Library, Paris** (1862–8) (p. 1209), also by Labrouste shows further advances in planning and structure. The Reading Room (p. 1209A) is covered with a series of nine pendentived simple domes of terra-cotta, each pierced at its crown with an 'eye' providing natural top light, supported by twelve slender columns of iron, arranged in four rows, the outer columns standing close to the walls. The vaults, arch-soffits and the wall surfaces above book-stack level are enriched with delicate decoration. The Stack Room (p. 1209B, C) has tiers of top-lighted stacks with open gridded metal floors to allow light to pass to lower levels, flanking a central space, bridged at intervals by communicating gangways.

The **New Louvre, Paris** (1852–7) (p. 1207B), initiated by Napoleon III, was designed by L.-T.-J. Visconti (1791–1853), the work being taken over and much developed in details by H.-M. Lefuel (1810–80) on Visconti's death. Two extensive wings, each built around twin internal courtyards, extend from either end of the west front of the Old Louvre to form the Place Louis-Napoléon (since renamed Square du Carrousel). The buildings, intended for ministerial and other offices, are in the Second Empire style and had considerable influence in Britain and the U.S.A. A fuller account is given on p. 882.

Palace of the Congress, Madrid (1843–50), by Narciso Pascual y Coloner (1808–70), represents the conservative tendencies of Spanish architecture at this time. A Palladian composition, the main façade is dominated by a powerful Roman Corinthian hexastyle portico which is flanked by two wings with rusticated ground floors, string courses, main cornices and low attic storeys, the general character being one of sombre dignity.

The **Opera House, Paris** (1861–74) (pp. 1210, 1211), by J.-L.-C. Garnier (1825–98), shows a development of the Baroque in the New Louvre. The plan is a noteworthy example of the application of Beaux-Arts principles, its elements and spaces related and held together by a strongly controlled axial system. An enormous foyer (p. 1210B), sumptuously enriched with brightly gilded sculpture and Baroque architectural elements, with a vaulted painted ceiling from which hang candelabra, leads to the magnificent *escalier d'honneur* (p. 1210C), beyond which lie the auditorium and extensive stage area. Characterized throughout by opulent grandeur, the building is marked by a fine sense of architectonic control. Externally it is treated in a highly plastic, sculptural way and makes imaginative use of a wide range of Classical details and, on the main façade, some fine sculptural groups by J. B. Carpeaux (1827–75).

The **Opera House, Cologne** (1870–2) (p. 1213B), by J. Raschdorf (1825–1914), a building of modest dimensions destroyed in the Second World War, had affinities with French Neo-Baroque, recognizable in the steep mansard roof, the 'lucarne' or dormer windows and the disposition of the highly decorative, pavilion-like features on the otherwise astylar façades. The almost contemporary **Hoftheater, Dresden** (1871–8), by Gottfried Semper (1803–79) is essentially Neo-Baroque in character, and owes more to German sources than French or Italian.

A. Thorwaldsen Museum, Copenhagen: internal courtyard (1839–48). See p. 1205

B. The New Louvre, Paris (1852–7). See p. 1206

A. The Library of S. Geneviève, Paris (1845–50). See p. 1206

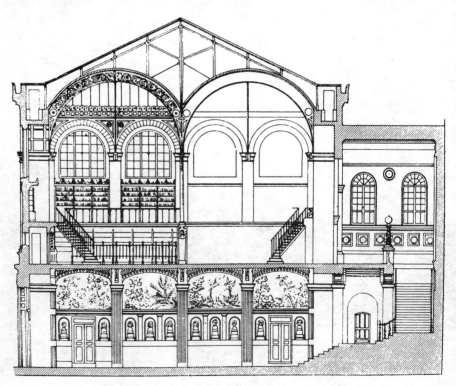

B. The Library of S. Geneviève, Paris: section

A. Reading room

B. Stack room   C. Detail of stacks

The National Library, Paris (1862–8). See p. 1206

A. Façade

B. Foyer　　　　　　　　　C. Grand staircase: upper flight

The Opera House, Paris (1861–74). See p. 1206

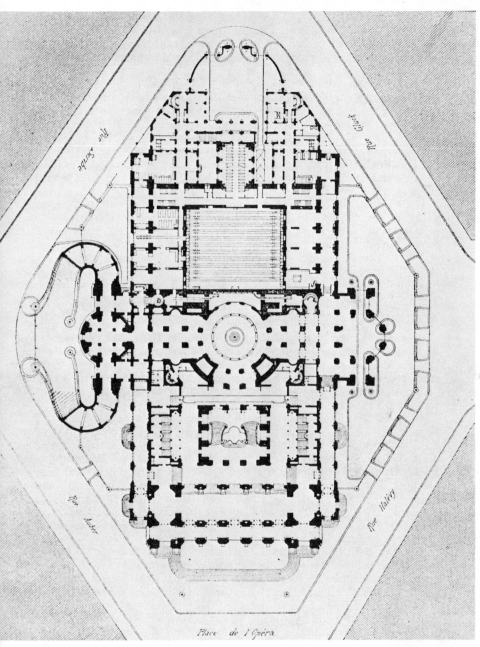

The Opera House, Paris (1861–74): ground floor plan. See p. 1206

The **Palais de Justice, Brussels** (1866–83) (p. 1213A), by Joseph Poelaert (1817–79), stands weightily on a height overlooking the city, and builds up pyramidally to a massive central tower. Vast, heavy and coarse in its ragged, overcrowded classical rhythms, it compares unfavourably with the brilliantly ornate Paris Opera House.

The **Rijksmuseum, Amsterdam** (1877–85) (p. 1214A), designed by P. J. H. Cuijpers has a French quality about its massing, with steep roofs, which are pyramidal over the end pavilions and the twin towers flanking the central entrance feature. An example of the large and complex planning problems which confronted nineteenth-century architects, the building is organized in a highly rational geometric way, its detail derived from sixteenth-century Gothic sources. The **Town Hall, Copenhagen** (1893–1902) (p. 1214B), by Martin Nyrop, is similar in its use of brick and in emulating transitional Gothic forms, the latter used with great imagination and authority.

The **Victor Emanuel II Monument, Rome** (1885–1911) (p. 1215B), on the slopes of the Capitol, was designed by Giuseppe Sacconi (1854–1905) and completed by others after his death. It consists of a vast platform with a terrace supporting an equestrian statue of the king, backed by an enormous, slightly concave Corinthian colonnade, supporting an elaborately decorated attic, and terminated at each end by porticoed pavilions bearing great bronze sculptural groups. The building has a total height of 61 m (200 ft) and completely dwarfs its surroundings.

The **Petit Palais, Paris** (1897–1900) (p. 1215C), an art gallery by Charles Girault, was designed for the International Exhibition of 1900, along with the neighbouring Grand Palais and the Pont Alexandre III. It has a finely balanced trapezoidal plan and a Neo-Baroque exterior which was much imitated abroad. Between the end and central domed pavilions, the latter abutted by an imposing entrance portal, are regular Ionic colonnades, standing on a shallow windowed basement. Internally two subsidiary semicircular staircases are in reinforced concrete, an early and successful experiment.

The **Stock Exchange, Amsterdam** (1898–1903) (p. 1216A), designed by H. P. Berlage, brought the architect renown far beyond his own country. It is of red brick with restrained stone dressings and, despite strong Romanesque overtones, has a character of honesty and simplicity. Internally, the glass and metal roof is frankly exposed, as also are the brick and stone of the galleried tiers rising from the hall floor. The same architect's **Diamond Workers' Union Building, Amsterdam** (1899–1900) (p. 1218C) has similar qualities. It is again largely of brick, the somewhat severe forms being handled with conviction. Berlage's work can be related to that of his near contemporaries, for example C. R. Mackintosh in Britain (p. 1132), and Louis Sullivan in the U.S.A. (p. 1228).

The **Post Office Savings Bank, Vienna** (1904–6) (p. 1216B), by Otto Wagner, retains internally, in the semi-elliptical form of its metal and glass roof, a trace of the lightness associated with Art Nouveau, but otherwise the building bears no readily identifiable historical associations, its character proceeding entirely from the essential structure.

The **Hochzeitsturm ('Wedding Tower'), Darmstadt** (1907) (p. 1218A), by J. M. Olbrich, dominates the buildings of the artists' colony of Mathildenhohe and was prophetic of future developments. Olbrich, a pupil of Otto Wagner and co-founder of the Vienna Sezession, whose exhibition building he designed in 1898–9, was appointed head of the Darmstadt Art School on its foundation in 1899.

The **City Hall, Stockholm** (1911–23) (p. 1217), by Ragnar Östberg, although highly eclectic, its motifs drawn from many historical sources, is composed with

A. The Palais de Justice, Brussels (1866–83). See p. 1212

B. The Opera House, Cologne (1870–2). See p. 1206

A. The Rijksmuseum, Amsterdam (1877–85). See p. 1212

B. The Town Hall, Copenhagen (1893–1902). See p. 1212

A. The Reichstag Building, Berlin (1884–94) (restored). See p. 1192

B. The Victor Emanuel II Monument, Rome (1885–1911). See p. 1212

C. The Petit Palais, Paris (1897–1900). See p. 1212

A. The Stock Exchange, Amsterdam (1898–1903). See p. 1212

B. The Post Office Savings Bank, Vienna (1904–6). See p. 1212

A. Exterior

B. The Golden Chamber

The City Hall, Stockholm (1911–23). See p. 1212

A. The Hochzeitsturm (Wedding Tower), Darmstadt (1907). See p. 1212

B. The Caffè Pedrocchi, Padua (1816–31). See p. 1219

C. The Diamond Workers' Union Building, Amsterdam (1899–1900). See p. 1212

D. The Turbine Building, Menier Chocolate Factory, Noisiel-sur-Marne, near Paris (1871–2). See p. 1220

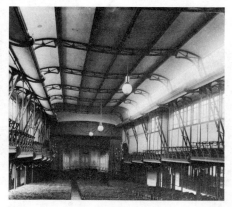

E. The Halles Centrales, Paris (begun 1853). See p. 1219

F. The Maison du Peuple, Brussels (1896–9). See p. 1220

remarkable skill and striking originality, and is the last romantic traditionalist building of importance in Sweden. Superbly sited, its south and east façades overlooking the lake, the building is arranged as a slightly wedge-shaped rectangular block around two unequal courts, the larger of which opens through the arcaded ground floor of the south range to a broad lakeside terrace. The smaller court is covered over and forms the 'Blue Hall', from which a ceremonial staircase leads to the main formal apartments, located on the first floor of the wing separating the two courts, the largest being the Assembly Room or 'Golden Chamber', richly decorated with mosaic murals. The Council Chamber is on the first floor of the south side. Externally the building has a dramatic and romantic silhouette, dominated by a massive tower (with slightly battered walls of rich brickwork) which links the south and east façades and rises to a height of 70 m (230 ft), above which extends a cylindrical open lantern with copper roof and three delicate crowns, making a total height of 108 m (354 ft). The main material throughout is brick, used with great understanding, but a limited amount of dressed stone is incorporated, for instance, in the column shafts of the south arcade. The steep roofs and elegant turret finials are of copper, weathered green.

COMMERCIAL BUILDINGS

The **Caffè Pedrocchi, Padua** (1816–31) (p. 1218B), by Giuseppe Jappelli (1783–1852) and Antonio Gradenigo (1806–84), is an inventive and elegant Neo-Classic design with an open, two-storeyed Corinthian loggia at first-floor level and, at street level, flanking twin pavilions in the Greek Doric style. Later Jappelli designed for the building a small but elaborate Neo-Gothic wing, **Il Pedrocchino** (completed 1837), an unusually early example of this style in Italy.

The **Halles Centrales, Paris** (begun 1853; demolished 1971) (p. 1218E), by Victor Baltard (1805–74) assisted by F.-E. Callet (1791–1854), were part of Haussmann's plan for Paris and the main markets of the city. Of the twelve pavilions, six formed the initial scheme, four were added later in the nineteenth century, and two in the 1930s. Planned as a series of broad circulation routes, intersecting at right angles, with the areas between occupied by stalls, the complex was constructed of iron and glass and completely covered. Light was admitted mainly through clear-storeys between the eaves of the pitched roofs of the circulation routes and the lower roofs over the stall areas.

Gare du Nord, Paris (1862–3) (p. 1221B), by Hittorff, a fine early railway station, has a superb iron and glass train shed and, externally, it shows a development of the Neo-Classic character seen in the architect's earlier work (p. 1199). More important was the **Gare de l'Est, Paris** (1847–52) (p. 1221A), by F.-A. Duquesney (1800–49), which has been greatly altered and enlarged, where the main front with two projecting Neo-Renaissance wings linked by a one-storey arcade, flanked a great central gable pierced with a large central semicircular window, eloquently expressing the idea of a communications 'gateway', and providing the focal point for Haussmann's Boulevard Sébastopol.

Galleria Vittorio Emanuele, Milan (1865–77) (p. 1222A), by G. Mengoni (1829–77), is a fine example of the many iron-and-glass roofed arcades that have been built since the late eighteenth century, mainly in England and France, and of which an early and influential example was the long-since destroyed **Galerie d'Orléans, Paris** (1829–31) by Fontaine, which formed part of the Palais Royal. At Milan, the gallery is a large and ambitious project arranged on a cruciform plan with a high, domed octagon at the intersection. Its internal façades, with giant pilasters embracing two of the three main storeys, have a Baroque richness and add to the general feeling of grandeur. The **Galleria Umberto I, Naples** (1887-90), by E. Rocco, provides a later less ambitious example of the same building type.

The **Bon Marché, Paris** (1876), a famous departmental store designed by Eiffel and L. A. Boileau, was almost entirely constructed of iron and glass, now hidden behind masonry façades.

The **Maison du Peuple, Brussels** (1896-9, demolished 1965) (p. 1218F), designed by Victor Horta for the city authorities, was remarkable for its skilful planning on an irregular site (a segment of a circular *place*) and for its brilliant use of glass and iron, the undulating external wall being almost entirely glazed and broken only by slender stanchions and transoms at floor levels.

The **Wertheim Department Store, Berlin** (1896-1904) was designed by Alfred Messel (1853-1909) in two stages. The first (1896-9), of which nothing remains, was a pioneer work making extensive use of metal and glass. The second stage (1900-4) was essentially Neo-Gothic in character.

The **Innovation Store, Brussels** (1901, destroyed by fire 1967), by Horta, was flamboyantly Art Nouveau in character, every detail of the façade, which was almost completely glazed from street level to the scroll-like eaves line, bearing the stamp of the style. The **Samaritaine Department Store, Paris** (1905-6) (p. 1222C), by F. Jourdain (1847-1953), also employs uninhibited Art Nouveau in its façade, where knots of metal foliage swirl sinuously over the functional structure, softening the strictness of its lines, unglazed panels being filled with boldly patterned, coloured faience.

Turbine Building, Menier Chocolate Works, Noisiel-sur-Marne (1871-2) (p. 1218D), by Jules Saulnier, offers probably the earliest French example of a full skeleton-frame in iron. It stands upon massive stone piers over the river Marne, borne on double girders which carry an iron frame incorporating the floors and pitched roof. The stanchions and their bracing enclose, externally, brick panels of polychromatic patterning, the effect somewhat resembling half-timber work.

The **Entrance Pavilion, International Exhibition, Paris** (1878, destroyed) (p. 1222D), by Gustave Eiffel, made extensive use of glass and iron, adapting these materials to currently fashionable architectural taste. Similar in the broad lines of its composition to the later Petit Palais (p. 1212), the domes of the central and end pavilions had large glazed lunettes, one on the central dome being projected downwards to form a deep, arched portal. Between the three pavilions, the walls were punctuated by enriched metal stanchions and fully glazed.

The **Galerie des Machines, International Exhibition, Paris** (1889, demolished 1910) (p. 1222B), by the engineer Victor Contamin (1840-93) and the architect C. L. F. Dutert (1845-1906), was 427 m (1,400 ft) long, 45 m (150 ft) high and spanned 114 m (375 ft). Its constituent steel principals formed four-centred arches, hinged at the apex and the base, where they tapered to their bearings. These principals were steel-braced longitudinally and the hall was completely glazed.

Metro Station, Place de la Bastille, Paris (1900) (p. 1222E), by H. Guimard (1867-1943), a metal and glass construction, well illustrates the characteristics of Art Nouveau. The linear expression of the metal, curved, sinuous or convoluted wherever structure allowed; the naturalistic, vegetal nature of the ornament; the lack of imposts on arches, as here on the dual horseshoe entrance; and the exclusion of historial references, are all typical of the style.

The **Railway Station, Stuttgart** (begun 1914, completed 1919-27) (p. 1222F), by Paul Bonatz (1877-1951) and F. E. Scholer (b. 1874), is in its basic composition reminiscent of Neo-Classicism, but all superfluous decoration is rigorously excluded and the building, constructed of strongly rusticated stonework, makes a considerable impact through the boldness and simplicity of its clearly articulated forms.

A. Gare de l'Est, Paris (1847–52). See p. 1219

B. Gare du Nord, Paris (1862–3). See p. 1219

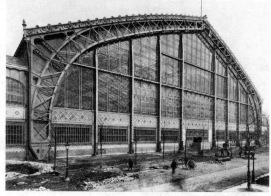

A. The Galleria Vittorio Emanuele, Milan (1865–77). See p. 1219

B. The Galerie des Machines, International Exhibition, Paris, 1889. See p. 1220

C. The Samaritaine Department Store, Paris (1905–6). See p. 1220

D. The Entrance Pavilion, International Exhibition, Paris, 1878. See p. 1220

E. The Metro Station, Place de la Bastille, Paris (1900). See p. 1220

F. The Railway Station, Stuttgart (1914–27). See p. 1220

BIBLIOGRAPHY

BARTHES, R. *La Tour Eiffel.* Paris, 1961.

BEENKEN, H. *Schöpferische Bauideen der deutschen Romantik.* Mainz, 1942.

COLLINS, P. *Changing Ideals in Modern Architecture 1750–1950.* London, 1965.

—. *Concrete: The Vision of a New Architecture.* London, 1959.

GIEDION, S. *Space, Time and Architecture.* Cambridge, Mass., 1941; London, 1968 and other editions.

HITCHCOCK, H.-R. *Architecture: Nineteenth and Twentieth Centuries.* 3rd ed. Harmondsworth and Baltimore, 1970.

KAUFMANN, E. *Von Ledoux bis Le Corbusier.* Vienna, 1933.

MADSEN, S. *Sources of Art Nouveau.* Oslo and New York, 1956.

MEEKS, C. L. V. *Italian Architecture 1750–1914.* New Haven and London, 1966.

—. *The Railroad Station.* New Haven, 1956.

MUTHESIUS, H. *Stilarchitektur und Baukunst: Wandlungen der Architektur im XIX. Jahrhundert.* Mülheim-Ruhr, 1902.

PEVSNER, N. *An Outline of European Architecture.* Harmondsworth, 1942 and many subsequent editions.

—. *Pioneers of Modern Design from William Morris to Walter Gropius.* London, 1936, Harmondsworth, 1960, and other editions.

PUNDT, H. G. *Schinkel's Berlin.* Cambridge, Mass., and London, 1973.

RAGON, M. *Histoire mondiale de l'architecture et de l'urbanisme modernes.* Vol. I: *Idéologies et pionniers, 1800–1910.* Paris, 1971.

RAVE, P. O. (Editor) *Karl Friedrich Schinkel: Lebenswerk.* Berlin, 1939–.

RÉAU, F. L. *L'Oeuvre du Baron Haussmann* . . . Paris, 1954.

RICHARDSON, E. P. *The Way of Western Art, 1776–1914.* Cambridge, Mass., 1939.

SWEENEY, J. J. and SERT, J. L. *Antoni Gaudí.* London, 1960.

A. The Larkin Soap Building, Buffalo, New York (1904–5). See p. 1243

B. Pennsylvania Railroad Station, New York (1906–10): main concourse. See p. 1244

C. Woolworth Building, New York (1911–13). See p. 1243

D. Empire State Building, New York (1930–2). See p. 1243

39

ARCHITECTURE OF THE AMERICAS 1790-1914

INFLUENCES

The European colonies, which formed a substantial part of the continent, gained their independence during this period and developed into distinct nations, a movement initiated in the British colonies of the eastern seaboard of North America.

In 1774 representatives of the colonies met in Philadelphia as the First Continental Congress to discuss their relationship with Britain, especially with regard to taxation and trade, an event precipitated by the decision of the British government to close the port of Boston, after angry colonists had refused to permit the landing of a shipment of tea on which they considered the tax unfair. The following year discontent flared up into open revolution which, with the adoption by the thirteen colonies of the Declaration of Independence, became in 1776 the American War of Independence. Peace came in 1783 and, with it, recognition of the independent status of the former colonies.

These at first formed a loose federation of separate republics, but in 1787 a constitution was drawn up whereby individuals became, for certain purposes, citizens of the federation itself and, for others, citizens of a particular state. The constitution, which remains in force today, was ratified in 1789. George Washington, the famous general of the War of Independence, was installed as first President of the United States of America in the same year.

From this point the history of the country was one of expansion. In 1803 the vast area between the Mississippi and the Rockies was purchased from France (the Louisiana Purchase), and in 1819 Florida was similarly acquired from Spain. Texas was annexed in 1845 and, as a result of the ensuing war with Mexico, the south-western part of the country as far as the Californian coast was absorbed in 1848. Oregon territory in the north-west was ceded by Britain in 1846, and small areas of Mexican territory added by the Gadsden Purchase of 1853. Finally, Alaska was bought from Russia in 1867.

Canada, which had remained loyal to Britain during the War of Independence, consisted of the four colonies of Upper and Lower Canada (both created in 1791), Nova Scotia and New Brunswick. Antagonism between Lower Canada, predominantly French, and Upper Canada led to a revolt in 1840, as a result of which Britain granted the colonies a broad constitution, providing for a parliament and the appointment of responsible ministers, the British Governor assuming a purely legal and symbolic rôle. With the passing of the British North American Act in 1867, the country was granted full Dominion status, which it retains within the British Commonwealth today. The Canadian Parliament and Ministries were set up at Ottawa, the national capital, on the lines of those at Westminster. To the original four provinces of Ontario (Upper Canada), Quebec (Lower Canada), Nova Scotia and New Brunswick, were added Manitoba (1870) and British Columbia (1871), former territories of the old Hudson Bay Company, and finally in 1905 the prairie provinces of Saskatchewan and Alberta.

In Latin America the vice-royalties of Spain and Portugal came to an end during the first quarter of the nineteenth century; and, after the failure of efforts to unite the former colonies into a federation similar to that of the U.S.A., the subcontinent became separated into a complex of independent states, which has survived geographically unchanged to this day. During these stormy years of revolution and formation important rôles were played by Simón Bolivar (1783-1830) in Colombia, Venezuela and Ecuador; by San Martín (1788-1850) in the Argentine and Peru; and by Bernardo O'Higgins in Chile. For a variety of reasons, mainly economic, the more stable countries were the Argentine, which owed much to its president General B. Mitre (1862-8) for his encouragement of railway building; Chile with its vast nitrate deposits; and Brazil. Modernization of the last began under the Portuguese Regent (later John VI), forced by Napoleon's invasion of Portugal to move his capital to Rio de Janeiro in 1808. In 1821 John returned to Portugal and Brazil became a separate kingdom under his son, Pedro I. The latter abdicated in 1831 in favour of his infant son, who as Pedro II took over the throne in 1840. His long reign was marked by much material progress and reform, including the abolition of slavery in 1888. In 1889 an army revolt established a republic, which in 1891 adopted a federal constitution as the United States of Brazil.

Mexico obtained her independence in 1821, but in 1858 was involved in bitter civil war. Supported by France, the Austrian Archduke Maximilian was installed as Emperor in 1864, but three years later, following the withdrawal of French troops, he was shot and the patriot Benito Juarez (1806-72), a Zapotec Indian, reassumed leadership of the country. But the creation of modern Mexico was left to Juarez's successor Porfirio Diaz (1830-1915), who ruled from 1876 to 1911.

Economically and socially the most advanced nation of the continent was the U.S.A., where a sense of national identity had been reinforced by the war with Britain of 1812-14. By 1840 the country's trade was worth 250 million dollars per year, almost half being earned by the State of New York. Pennsylvania developed rapidly as her extensive coal and iron resources were exploited, but the main wealth of the country still lay in cotton, of which Louisiana's exports in 1840 were valued at 33 million dollars.

The presidency of Andrew Jackson (1829-37), a representative of the new frontier men, gave impetus to wider democratic ideals and greatly encouraged individual enterprise, while the farming prospects of the great tracts of land beyond the Alleghenies attracted increasing numbers of settlers, the westward movement being dramatically accelerated by the discovery of gold in California in 1848.

The coming to power in 1861 of an anti-slavery government under Abraham Lincoln (1809-65) brought to a head the rivalry between the more dynamic northern states and the cotton-producing southern states, with their long-established plantation system based on slavery, and kindled the tragic Civil War (1861-5), during the course of which, in 1863, slavery was abolished. The victory of the northern states, and of the union, was decisive for the future of the country and encouraged industrial development, which in turn greatly increased the rate of immigration.

Generally the period following the Civil War was one of continuing commercial expansion, an age offering great opportunities and high material rewards to individual industrialists, bankers, farmers and railway owners. This situation, clearly reflected in the architecture of the time, continued until the financial crash of 1929 and the ensuing depression. The opening-up of the country by railways was essential to development, and the continent was finally traversed by rail from coast to coast in 1869. Alexander Graham Bell's invention of the telephone in 1876 further facilitated communications across the vast country which, in 1865, had been linked to Europe by Trans-Atlantic cable. Finally the mass-production of the motor car between the two World Wars further extended communications and movement.

As far as industry was concerned, Canada's development was much less rapid, her economy being based almost entirely on the export of lumber and wheat. As in the U.S.A. communications were of utmost importance: in 1847 improvements were completed on the S. Lawrence between Montreal and Lake Ontario, while the Canadian Pacific Railway had straddled the continent by 1885.

Like Canada, the countries of South America relied on the export of natural products rather than on manufacturing, and the opening of the Panama Canal in 1914 was of great significance in the development of the countries of the Pacific coast.

ARCHITECTURAL CHARACTER

European influence in both North and South America remained strong throughout the period, although materials, local skills, social customs and especially climatic conditions played their part, and buildings continued to possess strong regional characteristics. In South America French influence was particularly marked, with immigrant architects like A. J. V. Grandjean de Montigny in Rio de Janeiro (p. 1236) and C. F. Brunet-Debaines (1799–1855) in Santiago making important contributions, not only as practioners but also as teachers. In Canada a similar situation prevailed and architecture was much influenced by trends in England and, in the French-speaking part of the country, France; in addition the U.S.A., with a now firmly established building tradition, played an important part.

In the U.S.A. itself, while Europe continued to provide models and inspiration, a conscious striving for a truly 'national' architecture became evident soon after the War of Independence, and architecture in that country can be considered as passing through three broad and loosely-defined phases: (a) Post-colonial, c. 1790–c. 1820; (b) First eclectic, c. 1820–c. 1860; (c) Second eclectic, c. 1860–c. 1930.

(a) Post-colonial Phase (c. 1790–c. 1820). Architecture of this period moved away from the English Georgian idiom which had become established along the eastern seaboard of the country. Neo-Classic elements were introduced (p. 1235) and, while there was influence from the English architects the Adam brothers (p. 984) and Sir John Soane (p. 986), American architects tended to look more to France for inspiration.

(b) First Eclectic Phase (c. 1820–c. 1860). During this period the revived Greek style was predominant (p. 1228), receiving a more whole-hearted acceptance than it did in England and developing specifically American characteristics. The Gothic (p. 1232) and Egyptian (p. 1236) styles found some popularity but, compared with the Greek Revival, these were minor streams, and the American Gothic Revival did not develop the strength of the parallel movement in Britain (see Chapter 36).

The type of timber-framing known as the 'balloon-frame' came into use during this period (c. 1830) and revolutionized timber construction. Requiring relatively unskilled labour and obviating the elaborate joints of the traditional heavy timber structures built in colonial times, the balloon-frame has played an important part in American building and is still widely used in domestic work. As its name suggests, rather than relying on an essentially post-and-lintel construction, the balloon-frame owes its strength to the walls, roof, etc., acting as diaphragms. Comparatively light timber sections are employed which are nailed together, floor and ceiling joists forming ties, the whole stiffened by the external timber sheathing.

As in Britain and Europe (pp. 1119, 1187) the period saw considerable developments in the use of cast-iron as a building material.

(c) *Second Eclectic Phase* (c. 1860–c. 1930). American architecture achieved international significance during this period and followed two main streams. The first, related to the Gothic Revival and initiated as a Romanesque Revival with H. H. Richardson (1838–86) as its first important exponent (pp. 1231, 1232), gained considerable momentum and reached great vigour and vitality in the work of Louis Sullivan (1856–1924) (pp. 1240, 1243). In some respects the movement in its later stages can be equated with that of the Arts and Crafts in Britain (p. 1132) and it culminated in the work of Frank Lloyd Wright (1867–1959) (pp. 1231, 1243).

The second stream was more academic in character. Influenced by the École des Beaux-Arts in Paris, its architecture was inspired by the great periods of the past, the Italian (p. 1231) and French Renaissance (p. 1231), Ancient Greek (p. 1239) and Roman (p. 1244) and Late Gothic (p. 1243).

Two important and influential exhibitions belong to this period: the **Centennial Exposition** (Philadelphia, 1876) and the **World's Columbian Exposition** (Chicago, 1893). The Classical buildings and formal layout of the latter did much to reinforce the popularity of the academic architectural stream.

The period is noteworthy for structural experiment and achievement. The sky-scraper, often regarded as America's greatest single contribution to architectural development, was a product of this phase and was closely related to metal frame-construction, the non-load-bearing 'curtain' wall and the lift or elevator. The period saw also the establishment of many schools of architecture in the U.S.A., the first at Massachusetts Institute of Technology in 1868, under W. R. Ware.

EXAMPLES

DOMESTIC BUILDINGS

The **White House, Washington, D.C.** (1792–1829) (p. 1229A), the official residence of the Presidents of the U.S.A., was designed by James Hoban (c. 1762–1831) an Irish architect, in the English Palladian style. After damage sustained in the War of 1812, it was restored and considerable restoration has been carried out in the present century. The porticoes were designed by B. H. Latrobe (1807–8).

Monticello, nr. Charlottesville, Va. (1770–8; remodelled 1796–1808) (p. 1229B) was designed by Thomas Jefferson (1743–1826), third President of the U.S.A., for his own use. The first house, an elegant example of colonial Georgian, was completely remodelled in a free and imaginative Palladian manner (1796–1808).

Tontine Crescent, Boston, Mass. (1793–; dem. 1858) by Charles Bulfinch (1763–1844), was the first example in America of speculative terrace or 'row' housing and had much in common with contemporary English. Fine examples of early nineteenth-century brick terrace houses are also to be found in Philadelphia, again similar to English prototypes. A more monumental terrace is the brown-stone **Colonnade Row, New York** (1832) by A. J. Davis (1803–92), where a screen of Corinthian columns rises through two storeys above a rusticated ground floor.

Arlington, Va. (nr. Washington, D.C.) (1802–), at one time the home of General Robert E. Lee, is an interesting example of a Greek Revival mansion, particularly in the great hexastyle Doric Portico (added 1826), with its squat, sturdy Order.

Other major Greek Revival houses are: **South End House, Sapelo Island, Georgia** (1810–12), a fine and unusual example, especially interesting in that its walls are made from 'tabby' (concrete made from oyster shells); **Gaineswood, Demopolis, Alabama** (1842–9), a large house recalling the domestic work of Decimus Burton in England (p. 987); The **Hermitage, Nashville, Tennessee**

A. The White House, Washington, D.C. (1792-1829). See p. 1228

B. Monticello, near Charlottesville, Virginia (1770-1808). See p. 1228

A. Trinity Church, Boston, Massachusetts (1872–7). See p. 1232

B. Belle Grove, nr White Castle, Louisiana (1857). See p. 1231

C. Biltmore, Ashville, North Carolina (1890–5). See p. 1231

D. Stoughton House, Cambridge, Massachusetts (1882–3). See p. 1231

E. Robie House, Woodlawn Avenue, Chicago (1908–9). See p. 1231

(1819; rebuilt 1835), a characteristic example of a Tennessee plantation house with six Corinthian columns rising through two storeys across its main front, providing covered loggias at ground- and first-floor levels; **Polk Mansion, Rattle and Snap, Ten.** (*c.* 1845) with a grand, pedimented tetrastyle Corinthian portico projecting from its main front and rising through the building's two storeys; **Ralph Small House, Macon, Ga.** (*c.* 1835), a typical plantation house of the area, with a simple double-storeyed unpedimented hexastyle Doric portico; and **Belle Grove, near White Castle, La.** (1857) (p. 1230B) a grand example with 75 rooms and a superb portico with the Corinthian capitals of its columns carved in cypress wood.

Itamarati Palace, Rio de Janeiro, Brazil (1851–4), by J. M. J. Rebelo, now the Brazilian Foreign Office, is a delightful villa reminiscent of buildings in Paris of a somewhat earlier date. Elegant arched window openings, extending to floor level on each of its two storeys, encourage the free circulation of air throughout the building, which is marked generally by sophistication and refinement.

Vanderbilt Mansion, 5th Avenue, New York (1879–81; dem. 1925) was by R. M. Hunt (1827–95), the first American architect to be trained at the École des Beaux-Arts in Paris, in the style of an early French Renaissance château. An example of the academic stream of late nineteenth-century American architecture, it provided a prototype for other buildings, among them **Biltmore, Ashville, N.C.** (1890–5) (p. 1230C), also by Hunt.

Villard Houses, New York (1883–5) by McKim, Mead and White (C. F. McKim (1849–1909), W. R. Mead (1848–1928) and Stanford White (1856–1906), are in brown stone and were based on 'palazzi' of the Italian High Renaissance.

Stoughton House, Cambridge, Mass. (1882–3) (p. 1230D) by H. H. Richardson (1838–86) is a timber-framed house, its walls clad externally with wood shingles, providing an important example of the so-called 'Shingle Style'. An external cladding of wood shingles over a timber frame became popular in domestic building during the second half of the nineteenth century. Internally, the plan arrangement shows a loosening and foreshadows the 'free plan', to be developed later by Frank Lloyd Wright.

Winslow House, River Forest, Illinois (1893), the first important work of Frank Lloyd Wright (1869–1959), is a simple structure, basically symmetrical, but its hipped roof, wide projecting eaves and emphatic horizontal lines foreshadow the architect's later work and what was to become known as the 'Prairie House'.

Robie House, Chicago, Ill. (1908–9) (p. 1230E), also by Wright, is dominated externally by its strong horizontal lines which seem to make it almost one with the land on which it is built. Constructed of fine, small brick with low-pitched hipped roofs, the house is planned in an open and informal manner, interesting use being made of changes of level internally, the flowing internal spaces being generated by a central core containing staircase and fireplaces.

Other Wright houses of this period are: **Willitts House, Highland Park, Ill.** (1902); **Ross House, Delavan Lake, Wis.** (1902) and **Coonley House, Riverside, Ill.** (1908); and his own home, **Taliesin East, Spring Green, Wis.** (1911–).

Gamble House, Pasadena, California (1908–9), by C. S. Greene (1868–1957) and H. M. Greene (b. 1870), has much in common with the work of Wright in its sympathetic use of natural materials, and owes something also to the vernacular tradition of the west coast of America. Another Californian of similar inspiration, Bernard R. Maybeck (1862–1957), built a number of houses of marked individuality in and around Berkeley, where he designed also the **First Church of Christ Scientist** (1910–12) (p. 1233A). Such buildings provided an antidote to the epidemic of Old-Spanish-Mission revivalism, which was threatening to engulf architecture in California.

RELIGIOUS BUILDINGS

The **Catholic Cathedral, Baltimore, Md.** (1805–21), probably the most important work of Benjamin H. Latrobe (1764–1820), was the first major Roman Catholic Cathedral in the U.S. The plan is in the form of a Latin cross; over the crossing there is a great, coffered Pantheon-like dome more than 18 m (60 ft) in diameter while the nave is roofed by lesser saucer domes. Internally, the building is characterized by a wide spaciousness and is reminiscent of the work of Sir John Soane (p. 986) and of contemporary French examples. Externally, it has a fine pedimented portico (intended in the original design but added only in 1863), flanked by twin west towers, while the main dome springs from an octagonal drum.

Notre-Dame, Montreal, Quebec (1824–43) by James O'Donnell (1774–1830), an important early Canadian Gothic Revival building, has twin west towers and a triple-arched west entrance. Somewhat naïve in its detail, which is derived mainly from English sources, it originally had double internal galleries. The interior was completely remodelled c. 1870.

S. Andrew's Presbyterian Church, Niagara-on-the-Lake, Ontario (1831) is a rare example of the Greek Revival in Canada. A simple brick building, its 'west end' takes the form of a Greek Doric hexastyle temple-front and is surmounted by a timber cupola and spire.

Trinity Church, New York (1839–46) by Richard Upjohn (1802–78), now dwarfed by the commercial buildings of the modern city, was the third church of this name on the site. Comparable with the better examples of Gothic Revival Commissioners' Churches in nineteenth-century England (p. 987), it is in the Decorated style and in its day was the most important Gothic Revival building in the U.S.

Grace Church, New York (1843–6) and **S. Patrick's Cathedral, New York** (1858–79) were both by James Renwick Jr. (1818–95) and are important examples of American Gothic Revival architecture. The former was based on English examples, while the latter has continental sources.

The **Church of the Assumption, Montreal, Quebec** (1863–5) by Victor Bourgeau (1809–88), with elegant twin west towers, is a charming example based on Baroque prototypes, while the **Church of Notre-Dame-de-Grâce, Montreal** (–1851) by John Ostell (1813–92) provides another example of the Baroque Revival which found favour for churches in this area in the mid-nineteenth century.

The **Cathedral of S. James, Montreal, Quebec** (1875–85), designed by Joseph Michaud (1822–1902) and Victor Bourgeau, was (at the direction of the Bishop of Montreal) based on S. Peter's Basilica, Rome (p. 839). Despite great differences in scale, the west façade, the dome and general plan arrangement are clearly derived from S. Peter's. Nevertheless, the church possesses its own strong and specifically Canadian character.

The **Episcopal Cathedral of S. John the Divine, New York,** was originally designed in the Romanesque style (1892) by Heins (1860–1907) and Lafarge (1862–1938) who completed the choir in 1907. It was remodelled (commencing 1910) by Cram, Goodhue and Ferguson, in a mixture of Late English and French Gothic, and five aisles, together with a double clear-storey, great central tower, twin west towers and eastern chevet termination were incorporated.

Trinity Church, Boston, Mass. (1872–7) (p. 1230A), by H. H. Richardson, is one of the key monuments of American architecture. The design, chosen in competition, although basically Romanesque in character is handled in a masterful and imaginative way and established Richardson's reputation. A Greek cross in plan, the building is dominated by a square central tower with round corner turrets, and is constructed mainly of red granite, the rock-faced texture of which is exploited.

A. The First Church of Christ Scientist, Berkeley, California (1910–12).
See p. 1231

B. Unity Temple, Oak Park, Ill. (1905–7). See p. 1235

A. The State Capitol, Richmond, Virginia (1789–98). See p. 1235

B. The United States Capitol, Washington, D.C. (1793–1867). See p. 1235

Internal decoration in encaustic colour was carried out by J. Lafarge, while the west porch was added in 1897 to the designs of Shepley, Rutan and Coolidge.

Unity Temple, Oak Park, Ill. (1905-7) (p. 1233B) by Frank Lloyd Wright, is characterized by the sturdy simplicity of its external massing, on which the design relies rather than eclectic detail. In the building, as in all his work, the architect displayed a knowledge of and sympathy with the natural qualities of materials, which are here exploited both externally (in the pebble-faced concrete of the walls) and internally (in the sand-lime plaster work and natural timber details).

EDUCATIONAL, CIVIC AND PUBLIC BUILDINGS

The **State Capitol, Richmond, Va.** (1789-98) (p. 1234A) by Thomas Jefferson, was based on a Roman temple prototype, the Maison Carrée, Nimes (p. 276). An Ionic order was used by Jefferson, while for the fenestration of the 'cella' he had recourse to Palladian formulae. The building may be regarded as the first truly Neo-Classic monument in the U.S. and had much influence on later American buildings. Classical temple forms, both Greek and Roman, were adapted for banks, schools and other buildings, accommodation being sometimes ruthlessly crammed into the 'cella' in order to retain, at all costs, the external lines of the antique form. The appendages to the flanks of the Richmond Capitol are additions dating from 1904-6, when the building was refurbished and the portico steps added.

Palace of the Mint, Santiago, Chile (1788-99), now the executive residence and cabinet building, was designed by the Italian architect Joaquin Toesca and reflects civic architecture towards the end of Latin America's colonial period. Neo-Classical in style, the main façade of two storeys, with a three-storey central entrance pavilion, is divided into regular bays by giant pilasters and surmounted above the cornice by a somewhat heavy balustrade.

The **State House, Boston, Mass.** (1795-8), by Charles Bulfinch, shows the influence of French and English Neo-Classicism in its elevational treatment, particularly in the projecting central feature, with its simple arcade at entrance level and colonnaded loggia above, and in the Adam-like detail of the windows at the extremities of the main façade. The building is surmounted by a dome, a feature frequently to be incorporated in later American governmental buildings.

The **United States Capitol, Washington, D.C.** (1793-1867) (p. 1234B), seat of the United States Government, has become, with its great crowning dome, one of the world's best-known buildings. The first building, erected to the designs of Dr. William Thornton (1759-1828), an amateur architect from England, was planned on Palladian lines with a central rotunda; this has survived in essentials, despite numerous modifications and additions. Thornton's work, in which he was assisted by a French architect, E. S. Hallet (1755-1825), was continued (1803-11) by B. H. Latrobe, who had been trained in England under Samuel Pepys Cockerell (1754-1827) (p. 1050). After the War of 1812, Latrobe was responsible for rebuilding the structure (1815-17), badly damaged by the British. Charles Bulfinch continued the work which was completed in 1829. Between 1851 and 1867 additions were made by Thomas Ustick Walter (1804-88), who designed the flanking wings and great dome over the central rotunda. The latter replaced an earlier Pantheon-like dome, and was constructed largely of cast iron, with an internal diameter of 30 m (98 ft) and a total height of 68 m (222 ft).

The **University of Virginia, Charlottesville, Va.** (1817-26) (p. 1242A), was designed by Thomas Jefferson, aided by Thornton and Latrobe, as an 'academical village'. Set in the plain overlooked by Jefferson's own home, Monticello (p. 1228), it established a pattern for later American universities in their campus layouts. The plan consists of a wide, rectangular, tree-lined open space, on each of the longer sides of which are ranged five double-storeyed pavilions with Classical, columned porticoes. These housed teaching staff and lecture rooms and are linked to one another by low colonnades from which opened the students' rooms. The central space is terminated at one end by the university library (modelled on the Roman Pantheon), burned down in the early part of the present century and rebuilt by Messrs. McKim, Mead and White. Behind the ranges of teaching and living accommodation and separated from them by gardens, accommodation was provided for the slaves whom the students brought to the university as personal servants. Each of the buildings in the scheme was intended to illustrate some famous Classical work, and thus provide architectural exemplars to the students.

Founders' Hall, Girard College, Philadelphia, Pa. (1833–47), by T. U. Walter, is in the form of a giant, peripteral octastyle Corinthian temple, and in the grandeur of its conception is an important monument of the Greek Revival in America. Its external form bears little relation to its internal planning.

The **County Record Office, Charleston, S.C.** (1822–3), the **Patent Office** (1836–40) and the **Treasury Building** (1836–42), **Washington, D.C.** by Robert Mills (1781–1855) were all designed as 'fire-proof' buildings, making extensive use of vaulted construction. Like most work by Mills, they are characterized by their constructional ingenuity and a vigorous and highly personal interpretation of the Greek style.

The **Customs House, Rio de Janeiro, Brazil** (1826), by A. J. V. Grandjean de Montigny (1776–1850), reflects contemporary French influence. Trained in France, de Montigny became the first Professor of Architecture at the Imperial Academy of Fine Arts established in Rio de Janeiro in 1816, and was responsible for the design of the Academy building as well as the Market in Rio de Janeiro.

City Prison (The Tombs), New York (1838), by John Haviland (1792–1852), was in the Egyptian style, while the same architect's **Eastern State Penitentiary, Philadelphia, Pa.** (1821–35), planned with radiating cell blocks, was regarded in its day as a model prison.

Washington Monument, Washington, D.C. (designed 1836; built 1848–54; 1879–84), a slender 170 m (555 ft) high obelisk in white granite, designed by Robert Mills as a monument to the great general of the War of Independence, was the highest structure in the world, until the erection of the Eiffel Tower in 1889.

The **Smithsonian Institution, Washington, D.C.** (1847–55), by James Renwick Jr., is a romantic and picturesque structure in the Norman style.

University College, Toronto, Ontario (1856–8), by W. C. Cumberland (1821–1881), an essay in the Romanesque style, is comparable with the Smithsonian Institution.

The **National Academy of Design, New York** (1862–5) (p. 1237C), by P. B. Wight (1838–1925), Venetian Gothic in style and making full use of polychrome masonry patterning, shows the influence of the writings of John Ruskin.

The **Pennsylvania Academy of the Fine Arts, Philadelphia, Penn.** (1871–6) by Frank Furness (1839–1912), a highly individualistic building, makes imaginative use of forms of diverse stylistic origin and polychromatic masonry. Its architect is of particular interest for he employed the young Louis Sullivan as an assistant in his office in Philadelphia. The **Provident Trust Company Building, Philadelphia** (1879; destroyed) was another characteristic building by Furness.

Dominion Parliament Buildings, Ottawa, Ontario (1861–7) (p. 1238A), by Thomas Fuller (1822–98), an English architect who moved to Canada in 1856, and F. W. Stent, provided a superb example of Victorian Gothic with an ebullient silhouette of towers, pinnacles and crestings. Most of the original buildings were

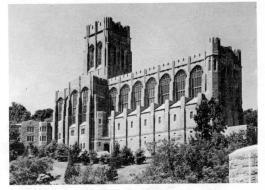

A. The Lincoln Memorial, Washington, D.C. (1911–22). See p. 1239

B. The Chapel, U.S. Military Academy, West Point, New York (1904–). See p. 1239

C. The National Academy of Design, New York (1862–5). See p. 1236

D. The Temple of Scottish Rite, Washington, D.C. (–1916). See p. 1239

E. The Public Library, Boston, Massachusetts (1887–93). See p. 1239

A. Dominion Parliament Buildings, Ottawa, Ontario (1861–7). See p. 1236

B. The City Hall, Philadelphia (1874–1901). See p. 1239

C. Merchants' Exchange, Philadelphia (1832–4). See p. 1240

D. Cast-iron façade, S. Louis, Missouri (c. 1850). See p. 1240

E. The Marshall Field Wholesale Warehouse, Chicago (1885–7). See p. 1240

F. The Monadnock Building, Chicago (1889–91). See p. 1240

destroyed by fire in 1916 and the present structure (largely based on the original but lacking much of its decorative richness) and the soaring Neo-Gothic **Peace Tower** (1919–) were by J. A. Pearson (1867–1940) and J. O. Marchand (1873–1936).

The **City Hall, Philadelphia, Pa.** (1874–1901) (p. 1238B), by John McArthur (1823–90), in the French Second Empire style (p. 1191), provides an example of fashions prevailing in the late nineteenth century. Its central tower, 156 m (512 ft) is crowned by a 11.3 m (37 ft) high bronze statue of William Penn.

The **Public Library, Boston, Mass.** (1887–93) (p. 1237E), by McKim, Mead and White is a beautifully detailed building, representative of the best in the academic stream of late nineteenth- and early twentieth-century architecture in America. Elevationally it is based on the Library of S. Geneviève, Paris (1843–50) (p. 1206) by Henri Labrouste.

The **Public Library, New York** (1897–1910), by J. M. Carrère (1859–1911) and Thomas Hastings (1860–1929) is also noteworthy as another example of academic Classical architecture.

The **Lincoln Memorial, Washington, D.C.** (1911–22) (p. 1237A), by Henry Bacon (1866–1924), is in the form of an unpedimented Greek Doric peripteral temple, set on a high podium and surmounted by a simple attic. Executed in white marble, its detail is superlatively refined and in its scholarship and execution marks a peak in academic architecture.

The **Temple of Scottish Rite, Washington, D.C.** (–1916) (p. 1237D), a masonic temple designed by John Russell Pope (1874–1937), is in the same tradition as the Lincoln Memorial. Externally, it takes the form of a reconstruction of the Mausoleum at Halicarnassos (p. 249), but is somewhat ponderously handled.

The **Chapel** (p. 1237B) **and Post Headquarters, U.S. Military Academy, West Point, N.Y.** (1904–), romantically sited on a steep escarpment overlooking the Hudson River, are the work of Cram, Goodhue and Ferguson, and provide examples of academic architecture in the Gothic style.

The **Allegheny County Courthouse and Gaol, Pittsburgh, Pa.** (1884–7), by H. H. Richardson, is a fine and vigorous piece of work which, despite its overtly Romanesque character, is indicative of the virility of a rising movement. The building relies largely on the inherent qualities of the materials in which it is constructed and these are exploited in an imaginative yet highly disciplined manner, particularly the great, rock-faced slabs of granite forming the gaol walls.

The **City Hall, Toronto, Ontario** (1890), by E. J. Lennox (1856–1933), has a sturdy, Romanesque character and owes much to the work of H. H. Richardson, particularly his Allegheny County Courthouse, Pittsburgh (above).

COMMERCIAL AND INDUSTRIAL BUILDINGS

The **Second Bank of the U.S. (Old Customs House), Philadelphia, Pa.** (1817–24), by W. Strickland, carried out in brick and white Pennsylvanian marble, was the result of an open architectural competition. With octastyle Doric porticoes to the front and rear, modelled on those of the Athenian Parthenon (p. 213), the building is rectangular in plan. Internally the central banking hall, with its fine barrel-vaulted ceiling springing from Ionic colonnades, is particular noteworthy.

The **Providence Arcade, Providence, R.I.** (1828), by James Bucklin (1801–90) and Russell Warren (1783–1860), provides, as in European arcades, a covered avenue for business premises, and is entered from either end through superbly detailed Ionic columnar screens carried out in granite. Internally the arcade is lighted by skylights, while the first-floor premises are entered from elegant iron balconies.

Merchants' Exchange, Philadelphia, Pa. (1832–4) (p. 1238C), by William Strickland, is in the Greek Revival style and is noteworthy for the grand, apsidal treatment of its rear elevation, enriched externally by a screen of Corinthian columns rising from first-floor level through two storeys, and crowned by a cupola based on the Choragic Monument of Lysicrates, Athens (p. 237).

The **Farmers' and Mechanics' Bank, Pottsville, Pa.** (1830), by John Haviland, is important since it was probably the first building in America to make use of a cast-iron façade. Here iron sheets, moulded to simulate masonry, were fixed to a brick backing; but later pre-fabricated iron units were to be used for complete structures.

James Bogardus (1800–74) played an important part in the development of this type of construction, which he employed in many buildings, among them his own factory, New York (1848–9); **Laing Stores, New York** (1849) and **Harper Bros. Printing Works, New York** (1854; razed 1920). He also put forward a scheme for the **New York Exhibition Building** (1853) but this was not realized. Other buildings using the same constructional technique were the **Penn Mutual Life Insurance Building, Philadelphia, Pa.** (1850–1; demolished), by G. P. Cummings, and some particularly fine examples in the dock area of S. Louis, Mo. (c. 1850–c. 1880) (p. 1238D).

The **A. T. Stewart Store (later Wanamaker's Store), New York, N.Y.** (1862; burned 1956), by John Kellum (1807–71), was another noteworthy example of iron construction using prefabricated units. Elevationally the building was made up of repeated bays, each of its five floors being treated as a 'Renaissance' arcade or, in the case of the ground floor, colonnade. Internally the building was framed with iron stanchions (cast in the form of Classical columns) and girders.

The **Montauk Building, Chicago, Ill.** (1881–2; demolished), by D. H. Burnham (1846–1912) and J. W. Root (1850–91), the first of a series of extremely important buildings in Chicago, made use of spread foundations to carry its ten-storey load-bearing walls and heralded the advent of the skyscraper.

The **Home Insurance Co. Office Building, Chicago, Ill.** (1883–5), by W. Le B. Jenney (1832–1907) and W. B. Mundie (1893–1939), a ten-storey building, was the first in Chicago to make full use of metal skeleton construction.

The **Tacoma Building, Chicago, Ill.** (1887–8), by W. Holabird (1854–1923) and M. Roche (1855–1927), also had its external walls carried by a metal skeleton.

The **Marshall Field Wholesale Warehouse, Chicago, Ill.** (1885–7; demolished c. 1935) (p. 1238E), by H. H. Richardson, had seven storeys and was of load-bearing wall construction. A remarkably powerful design, with its great arched openings and the vigorous texture of its masonry, it had considerable influence on later buildings in Chicago and elsewhere.

The **Auditorium Building, Chicago, Ill.** (1886–9) (p. 1241A), by Dankmar Adler (1844–1900) and Louis Sullivan (1856–1924), combined an opera house with hotel and office accommodation and owes much of its external character to Richardson's Marshall Field Warehouse (above). Ten storeys high, it is of load-bearing wall construction built on spread foundations. Settlement has occurred to one side of the structure, in the tower which rises nearly 30 m (100 ft) higher than the main building. Internally, the details are of a high order, many showing a Byzantine character and some probably designed by Frank Lloyd Wright, who entered Sullivan's office as a draughtsman in 1887.

The **Monadnock Building, Chicago, Ill.** (1889–91) (p. 1238F), by D. H. Burnham of Burnham and Root, has sixteen storeys. The building derives distinction from the simplicity of its elevational treatment and was the last tall building in Chicago for which load-bearing walls were employed.

A. The Auditorium Building, Chicago (1886–9).
See p. 1240

B. The Reliance Build-
ing, Chicago (1890–4).
See p. 1243

C. The Second Leiter Building, Chicago
(1889–90). See p. 1243

D. The Schlesinger-Mayer Store,
Chicago (1899–1904). See p. 1243

E. The Gage Building, Chicago (*right*)
(1898–9). See p. 1243

F. Wainwright Building, S.
Louis, Missouri (1890–1).
See p. 1243

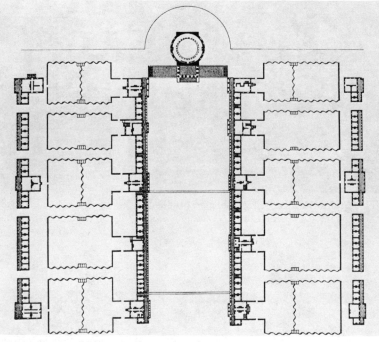

A. University of Virginia, Charlottesville, Va. (1817–26): plan. See p. 1235

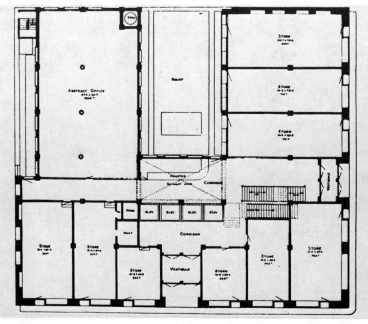

B. Wainwright Building, S. Louis, Missouri (1890–1): ground floor plan.
See p. 1243

The **Second Leiter Building, Chicago, Ill.** (1889–90) (p. 1241C) (now occupied by Messrs. Sears Roebuck), by W. Le B. Jenney, is an eight-storey metal-framed building with a simple and effective elevational treatment, the stone façade reading as a sheath over the internal metal structure.

The **Reliance Building, Chicago, Ill.** (1890; extended 1894) (p. 1241B), by Burnham and Root, was originally built as a four-storeyed structure but was later extended to sixteen floors. The terra-cotta facing to the metal frame was reduced to a minimum and in its simple yet carefully-detailed elevation the building marks an important advance in skyscraper design.

The **Gage Building, Chicago, Ill.** (1898–9) (p. 1241E), by Louis Sullivan and Holabird and Roche, is a three-bay, eight-storey framed structure, and fore-shadows the elevational treatment of the Schlesinger-Mayer Store.

The **Schlesinger-Mayer Store (now Carson, Pirie, Scott and Co.), Chicago, Ill.** (1899–1904) (p. 1241D), by Louis Sullivan, was originally a nine-storey structure, a twelve-storey section being added in 1903–4 and further additions in 1906 by D. H. Burnham, following Sullivan's original design. The building was originally crowned by a rich overhanging cornice. The white terra-cotta facing to the building's steel frame truthfully follows its structure, and horizontal lines are emphasized. The ground and first floors have cast-metal friezes richly decorated in low relief, providing first-rate examples of Sullivan's decorative work, in some ways suggestive of European Art Nouveau.

The **Wainwright Building, S. Louis, Mo.** (1890–1) (pp. 1241F, 1242B), by Adler and Sullivan, a ten-storey steel-framed building, provided an answer to the elevation problem of the skyscraper. Vertical members of the frame are emphasized externally as brick piers, and the building is capped by a deep, richly decorated frieze, pierced by circular windows lighting the top floor, while the recessed panels between floors are similarly decorated.

The **Guaranty (now Prudential) Building, Buffalo, N.Y.** (1894–5), also by Adler and Sullivan is similar in general character to the Wainwright Building but rises through thirteen floors and is faced externally in terra-cotta.

The **Larkin Soap Co. Building, Buffalo, N.Y.** (1904–5; destroyed) (p. 1224A), by Frank Lloyd Wright, was designed around a central circulation court, lit from the roof and sides by windows sealed from noise and dirt. Offices were approached from galleries around the court, borne on brick piers. Externally, the building was characterized by the simplicity and scale of its massing, which relied entirely on the relation of clearly articulated rectangular forms.

The **National Farmers' Bank, Owatonna, Minnesota** (1907–8), a virile and characteristic building by Louis Sullivan, is particularly noteworthy for its inventive decorative detail and the bold geometry of its simple but powerful forms.

The **Woolworth Building, New York** (1911–13) (p. 1224C), by Cass Gilbert (1859–1934), 241 m (792 ft) high with fifty-two storeys, was carried out in the Gothic style, and provides an important landmark in the story of high building.

Soon after the completion of the Woolworth Building, the New York City Zoning Ordinance (1916) became law. This had a profound effect on the form of New York skyscrapers which, for reasons of light and ventilation, were now required to have certain minimum set-backs, related to their height. The effects of the ordinance can be seen in J. M. Howells' (b. 1868) **Panhellenic House** (–1928), with twenty-seven storeys, and more clearly in the **Empire State Building** (1930–2) (p. 1224D) by Shreve, Lamb and Harmon, which rises through eighty-five storeys.

Later Chicago buildings to be noted include: **Tribune Tower** (1923–5) a news-paper office block by J. M. Howells and Raymond Hood (1881–1934). In the Gothic style, the skyscraper was the result of an architectural competition in which

Eliel Saarinen and Walter Gropius also took part. **Palmolive Building** (1929) and **333 North Michigan Avenue** (1928) are both by Holabird and Roche and provide interesting and typical examples of Chicago skyscrapers of the 1920s.

Among numerous examples of railway stations, the following are particularly important: **Grand Central Station, New York** (1903–13), by Reed and Stem (later replaced by Warren and Wetmore), provides a fine example of American academic architecture, particularly in its great concourse. Based on antique Roman sources, it shows the influence of the École des Beaux-Arts. **Pennsylvania Railroad Station, New York** (1906–10; demolished *c.* 1965) (p. 1224B), by McKim, Mead and White, was in the same tradition. Overtly based on Roman 'thermae' designs, its concourse, both in scale and detail, recalled the central hall of the Baths of Caracalla, Rome (p. 297).

BIBLIOGRAPHY

CONDIT, C. *The Rise of the Skyscraper.* Chicago, 1952.

—. *The Chicago School of Architecture.* Chicago and London, 1964.

FITCH, J. M. *American Building: the Historical Forces that shaped it.* New York, 1966.

HAMLIN, T. F. *Greek Revival Architecture in America.* New York, 1944 and 1964.

—. *The Architecture of H. R. Richardson and his Times.* New York, 1936 and 1965.

HITCHCOCK, H.-R. *Architecture: Nineteenth and Twentieth Centuries.* 3rd ed. Harmondsworth and Baltimore, 1970.

JORDY, W. H. *American Buildings and their Architects.* Vols 3 and 4. New York, 1970–73. Covers the later nineteenth and twentieth centuries: see also under Pierson below.

PIERSON, W. H. *American Buildings and their Architects.* Vols 1 and 2. New York, 1970–73. Deals with the Colonial and Neo-Classical styles.

SCULLY, V. J. *American Architecture and Urbanism.* New York and London, 1969. An important bibliographical source.

—. *The Shingle Style and the Stick Style.* New York, 1971.

TALLMADGE, T. *Architecture in Old Chicago.* Chicago, 1941.

WHITE, T. (ed.) *Philadelphia in the Nineteenth Century.* Philadelphia, 1953.

Monographs on individual architects:

GALLAGHER, H. M. P. *Robert Mills.* New York, 1935.

GILCHRIST, A. A. *William Strickland: Architect and Engineer.* Philadelphia, 1950.

HAMLIN, T. F. *Benjamin Henry Latrobe.* New York, 1955.

HITCHCOCK, H. R. *In the Nature of Materials.* New York, 1942. (On Frank Lloyd Wright.)

KAUFMANN, E. and RAEBURN, B. *Frank Lloyd Wright: Writings and Buildings.* Cleveland and New York, 1960.

KIMBALL, F. *Thomas Jefferson, Architect.* Boston, 1916.

MAGGINIS, C. *The Work of Cram and Ferguson, Architects.* New York, 1929.

Monograph of the Work of McKim, Mead and White. 4 vols. New York, 1914–25.

MORRISON, H. *Louis Sullivan.* New York, 1935, 1952 and 1962.

NEWTON, R. H. *Town and Davis: Architects.* New York, 1942.

NORTH, A. T. *Raymond M. Hood.* New York, 1931.

PLACE, C. *Charles Bulfinch: Architect and Citizen.* Boston, 1925 and 1968.

REILLY, C. H. *McKim, Mead and White.* London, 1924.

SULLIVAN, L. H. *The Autobiography of an Idea.* New York, 1956 and earlier editions.

UPJOHN, E. *Richard Upjohn: Architect and Churchman.* New York, 1939.

VAN RENSSELAIER, M. G. *Henry Hobson Richardson and his Works.* New York, 1888, reprinted 1969.

40

INTERNATIONAL
ARCHITECTURE SINCE 1914

In the social history of the West it is logical to regard the year 1914, and the cataclysm of the First World War, as the grand watershed which, for better or for worse, separated the relatively still waters of the old conditions of society from the turbulent currents of the new. In the closely related field of architectural history, the date is more a matter of convenience than of logic, for the story of the building arts is one of gradual evolution, in which abrupt changes of direction rarely occur. Thus the so-called 'Modern Movement' was no sudden flash of divine inspiration, as some of its most respected chroniclers seem to imply. Many of the features which are most readily associated with the new architecture have a long pedigree. Skeleton frame construction, which first came to fruition in the work of the Chicago School of late Victorian times, can trace its descent from the eighteenth-century iron founders, although it was immeasurably advanced in the late nineteenth century by the development of steel, with its vastly increased tensile strength. Reinforced concrete is largely a late nineteenth-century material, but not entirely, for a mortar and rubble aggregate with metal reinforcement had been used in France in the eighteenth century, notably by J.-B. Rondelet, Soufflot's collaborator (and successor) in building the church of Sainte-Geneviève (now the Panthéon) in Paris.

The curtain wall is a development of techniques exemplified in the Crystal Palace (1851) in London, and in earlier glass-houses and conservatories, but the principle was at least embryonically present in the mediaeval Gothic cathedral. Steel—unless we include plate-glass—was the only truly new building material evolved in the nineteenth century, but European and American architects, with remarkably few exceptions, were happy to dress it in the time-honoured clothes; and it was this belief that architecture was simply a matter of certain pre-ordained styles which, more than any other factor, induced the first stirrings of protest.

But, if a variously expressed antipathy to the historic styles was a principal motive among late nineteenth-century rebels, and the possibilities offered by expanding industrial technology a constant inspiration in the early 1900s, there were other important contributory influences. The asymmetrical plan, evident at first only in domestic architecture, the house growing organically out of its internal requirements (the basis of the future 'plan libre' of Le Corbusier) seems to have originated with architects later to be associated with the Arts and Crafts Movement in England (1887), whose ideas were also certainly absorbed by the young Frank Lloyd Wright in the U.S.A. The same movement, which strongly affected Art Nouveau, played a major part in arousing a new social conscience among architects, turning their attention to areas hitherto largely neglected by the profession, in particular to the housing of the underprivileged, and to town planning.

The Art and Crafts Movement succumbed to the Georgian Revival. Art Nouveau, which was never much more than a fashion in decoration, flourished briefly and flamboyantly at the turn of the century, before its peculiar susceptibility to vulgarization and its essentially transitional character forced it to give place to forms more appropriate to the emergent age of mechanization. Its most potent manifestation had been in Belgium, and its most distinguished exponents, Victor Horta and Henri van de Velde, both Belgian-born, remained faithful to its principles. Other leading architects of the period immediately before the First World War were not so loyal. Peter Behrens, who had begun his career as a protagonist of Jugendstil, the important German counterpart to Art Nouveau, was among those who changed course to geometrical forms in architecture and functionalism in industrial design, a field which now attracted some of the best brains. In 1910 Adolf Loos built the Steiner House in Vienna (p. 1251C), simple geometrical forms devoid of all ornament. Auguste Perret, never appreciably influenced by Art Nouveau, introduced reinforced concrete in Paris in 1903 with the house in the Rue Franklin (p. 1251A), and in 1905 with the garage in the Rue de Ponthieu (demolished 1968, due for partial re-erection) (p. 1262C), both of which, although basically Classical in conception, suggest the exposed frame construction that was to become an architectural cliché fifty years later. In Italy Futurism made its appearance, expressed in Sant' Elia's vision (1914) of the Città Futurista. Peter Behrens built the AEG Turbine Factory, Berlin, in 1909 (p. 1265A), in which structural elements define architectural form. In 1907 the Deutscher Werkbund, an association of architects, artists and designers concerned with the improvement of industrial products, was formed, and was quickly followed by similar societies in other European countries.

Historical ties, however, still held firm. The Werkbund Exhibition of 1914 in Cologne revealed a muted Neo-Classicism (with the exception, perhaps, of Bruno Taut's curious helmet-like glass house), and leading designers appeared to have taken several cautious steps backward from their pioneering position of the previous decade. Behrens was by now turning to the restrained, monumental Classicism which characterizes his later work. A staunch opponent of this incipient reaction was the young Walter Gropius (b. 1883), who had acquired the elements of 'Modern' architecture when working as an assistant in the office of Behrens himself.

Gropius built the Fagus Works (1911–16) (p. 1265B), with Adolf Meyer, for Karl Benscheidt in Alfeld/Leine, and with it created the accepted prototype of modern architecture. There was nothing original about the structural system—columns in front and load-bearing masonry at the back. The novelty lay in the conception of form: the apparently free-standing glass sheath, suspended on a framework across the face of the building. The first true example of this idea, later to be known as the curtain wall, may well have been the Hallidie Building, San Francisco, completed in 1918 (p. 1276A). In 1919 Gropius succeeded van de Velde as Director of the School of Applied Art at Weimar, where he founded the 'Bauhaus', developing a form of training intended to relate art and architecture to technology and the practical needs of modern life. In 1925 he moved to Dessau, where he re-established the Bauhaus, erecting new buildings to house the school (p. 1261C), based on his own principles, and attracting in due course many leading artists as teachers and visiting lecturers. His book The New Architecture and the Bauhaus (1935, but not published in German until 1965), had wide international influence. From 1934 to 1937 he was in England, subsequently living in the U.S.A., where he continued to teach and practice until his death in 1969.

Meanwhile, progress in steel and reinforced concrete construction continued. Tony Garnier (1867–1948), who also applied some of the principles of modern urbanism in his unrealized plan for a 'Cité Industrielle', achieved with steel a span of 80 m (262 ft) in a hall for a cattle market and abattoirs at Lyon (1913), and Max Berg (b. 1870) designed the glazed dome of 65 m (213 ft) diameter of the Centennial

Hall at Breslau (1912–13) (p. 1259B) with reinforced concrete. The latter has massive radial and concentric ribs almost of masonry proportions. Eugène Freyssinet (1879–1962) used concrete very much more economically in his parabolic-vaulted airship hangar at Orly, near Paris (1916) (p. 1268A), destroyed in the Second World War, which in the thin zig-zag section of its enormous ribs inaugurated the principle of the 'folded slab', a technique widely adopted later on. Another engineer, the Swiss Robert Maillart (1872–1940), employed the 'flat slab' method in his splendidly simple bridge designs (p. 1267A), the first in 1906, or in the case of tiered buildings, used the slab in conjunction with pillar supports in an arrangement known as 'mushroom' construction (1908). However, the parabolic vault, folded slab and slab-and-pillar or mushroom types of reinforced concrete construction did not come into general use until the inter-war period, the normal early system being that of the simple box-frame outlining the space to be enclosed.

Other outstanding personalities of the years after the First World War were Mies van der Rohe (1886–1969), Le Corbusier (1887–1965) and J. J. P. Oud (1890–1963). Mies van der Rohe, German-born like Gropius and much influenced, like him, by Behrens, whose office he entered in 1908, became the Director of the Bauhaus in 1930, but emigrated to America in 1937. His personal interpretation had matured by 1919: in a competition that year he designed a glass-sheathed, twenty-storey Berlin skyscraper, and in 1920–1 a model of another, thirty storeys high, designed as a cluster of interpenetrating circularly-planned elements sustained by an inner steel skeleton supporting cantilevered floors, the whole entirely glass-faced. The unrealized towers anticipated by very many years his forty-storeyed Seagram Building in New York (1956–8), planned in collaboration with Philip Johnson (p. 1278C). All his mature work is characterized by extreme simplicity, clarity of form and richness of materials. Externally, glass is widely used, and he normally adhered to the rectangular steel frame. Interior accommodation is organized by freely-disposed light partitions, interwoven with the inner pillars of the structural frame.

'Le Corbusier' (a pseudonym for Charles-Edouard Jeanneret), of French origin, Swiss birth and, later, French nationality, dominated the European scene for nearly half a century. In his formative years he worked in Paris with Perret, from whom he learned the structural possibilities of reinforced concrete, and very briefly with Behrens in Berlin. Also a painter and sculptor, he became closely associated with Cubism and its more prominent exponents, Ozenfant, Fernand Léger and Picasso. His earlier architectural work was domestic, and his philosophy at this period may be summed up in his dictum, far too often quoted and certainly misinterpreted by his critics, that 'the house is a machine to live in', by which he implied no more than that the programme for building a house should be set out with the same precision as that for building a machine. A prolific writer, his books, particularly *Vers une Architecture* (1923, English translation 1927) had enormous influence. He advocated that the structural frame should be separately identified from the space-enclosing walls, that a house should be lifted on pillars ('pilotis') so that the garden might spread under it, a device incidentally used in 1792 by Ledoux in one of several houses he built for the American philanthropist Hosten; that roofs should be flat, capable of use as a garden, as pitched roofs disturbed the cubic or rectilineal form; that the interior accommodation should be freely planned, each floor according to the need, since all loading could be taken by the structural frame. The latter was not a new notion, for Perret had conceived it in 1903, nor indeed were most of the others, but collectively they constituted a fresh conception, entirely opposed to the traditional principles still generally obtaining. Le Corbusier went on to produce buildings of virtually all principal classes and schemes for town-planning, ever provoking curiosity and controversy yet ultimately securing general confidence in the tenability of his many stimulating ideas.

J. J. P. Oud was as much representative of Holland at this time as Berlage had been in the pre-1914 period. Oud was a member of the important Dutch 'De Stijl' group of geometric-abstract artists formed in 1917 by Theo van Doesburg, whose tenets concerned the manipulation of geometrical forms. Architecturally, they rejected the rigid enclosure of buildings in their enveloping walls in favour of the free interplay of spatial volumes. Oud softened the jagged asperities of the early architectural ventures of the group and developed a clean, sedate style, markedly horizontal in stress but with emphasis on the sheer wall, rather than upon the banded windows. Another coming under the influence of the De Stijl was W. M. Dudok (b. 1884), designer of many fine buildings, who went less quickly and less far towards Modern architectural principles, and chose to work almost exclusively in brickwork, thus allying himself to some extent with an Amsterdam group of architects who exploited fine brickwork, the traditional material of Holland, in a dramatic and romantic manner. Notable among the latter were Michael de Klerk (1884–1923) and Piet Kramer (b. 1881). Yet Holland's greatest building of the period is the Van Nelle Factory, Rotterdam (1927–30) (p. 1268B), unique at the time in the measure of its fulfilment of Modern principles, by J. A. Brinkman, L. C. van der Vlugt, and (principally) Mart Stam. Stam was one of the architects, including Mies van der Rohe, Le Corbusier, Gropius, Behrens, Oud, the Taut brothers and Scharoun, who took part in the 'Weissenhof' Exhibition (1927) at Stuttgart, organized by the Werkbund as a combined practical exercise in the design and construction of low-cost housing. Some of this modest and fascinating scheme, one of the landmarks of the Modern Movement, survives in inhabited and recognizable form. Two other pioneer designers, not often remembered today, are R. Mallet-Stevens, who built several houses in a street in Auteuil, Paris (1926–7) which exploit the formal possibilities of the cube and the cylinder; and Eileen Gray, an inventive and scrupulous craftsman in furniture who also designed buildings, among the few executed being a house by the sea at Roquebrune, near Monte Carlo (1927–9), which anticipates in plan and architectural treatment the expertise of her more publicized contemporaries.

Another considerable figure among the pioneers was Erich Mendelsohn (1887–1953), a German who left his own country for England in 1933, then spent five years in Israel before settling in the U.S.A. His buildings have a dynamic, sculptural quality and a marked horizontal emphasis. Scandinavia produced many outstanding personalities. In Sweden, Ragnar Östberg (1866–1945) (p. 1192) and Ivar Tengbom (p. 1205) also showed that the traditional mode could vie in brilliance with the new, as pursued so effectively by Sven Markelius (b. 1889) and by Erik Gunnar Asplund (1885–1940), who effected the transition from historicism superbly in his own professional span. Asplund helped by his example to quicken the pace in Denmark too, where Neo-Classicism held sway almost to 1930. Finland came into the picture fairly early, due to the endeavours of Eliel Saarinen (1873–1950), though he settled in the U.S.A. after 1923. After him Alvar Aalto (b. 1898), an incomparable artist in his country's traditional material, wood, has remained the dominant Finnish figure. As we have seen, Italy made tentative steps towards Modernism in the visionary schemes of Antonio Sant' Elia (1888–1917), but no real beginning until the formation in 1927 of 'Gruppo 7', this once again an association of progressive artists and designers such as had led the revolt against revivalism in so many other countries. Fascism tolerated the Modern Movement, but the new architecture developed in the late inter-war period was largely impersonal, apart from that of Pier Luigi Nervi (b. 1891), who had already begun the remarkably distinguished career in which he was to prove the supreme artist in architectural engineering.

Since about 1930 the architectural contribution of the Americas has been of great significance. Not only the U.S.A., but also Canada and the countries of Latin America have produced notable buildings, which have had much influence throughout the world. With the rise of Nazism many of the leaders of European architecture went to the U.S.A., including Gropius, Mies van der Rohe and Mendelsohn. Others were Marcel Breuer (b. 1902), who had studied and taught at the Bauhaus, and the Austrians Richard Neutra (1892–1970) and Rudolf Schindler (1887–1953), whose glass and white-walled architecture has left a lasting imprint on the West Coast. Schindler was briefly associated with, and certainly influenced by, Frank Lloyd Wright, the American-born genius who began his long career in the Chicago office of Louis Sullivan, an architect of immense originality (p. 1228). Wright's reputation was soon to spread to Europe, where such buildings as the Robie House (1908–9) (p. 1230E) had a profound effect on contemporary and subsequent architectural thinking, especially on the De Stijl movement. In both Mexico and South America the greatest contribution has been in reinforced-concrete building, and work in these areas is often characterized by its daring structural forms. The use of colour is also noteworthy, and in Mexico whole façades are sometimes treated as rich mosaic mural decorations.

It has often been said that the seeds of the new architecture were sown in England, and there is no doubt that Britain contributed seminal ideas, as well as industrial skills, to the development of the Modern Movement. Two architects of considerable influence upon contemporary thinking on the Continent were C. F. A. Voysey and Charles Rennie Mackintosh (p. 1132), but it was not until the early 1930s that the physical forms of Modern architecture found recognition in the British Isles. Among the very few pioneer buildings that appeared before this was the house at Northampton altered and extended in 1916 by Mackintosh (p. 1280A). In 1931 a number of British architects founded the Mars Group, in close association with C.I.A.M. (Congrès Internationaux des Architectes Modernes), an international union formed three years earlier by leading architects including Le Corbusier. In the immediately succeeding years Gropius, Breuer and Mendelsohn practised briefly in England before emigrating to the U.S.A. Their influence was beyond question crucial.

After the Second World War, the new architecture evolved rapidly, while under its influence the buildings still designed on traditional lines tended to shed stylistic ornament and mouldings and to share its directness and simplicity. Steel and reinforced-concrete frames became common for all but the smallest structures. Multifarious fresh departures were made in the servicing and equipment of buildings and in the methods of cladding and weather-proofing. Synthetic materials played a large part in these developments. In the field of structure, 'shell' vaulting offered—and continues to offer—the greatest opportunities for architectural exploration. Long ago, and independently, Perret and Freyssinet had appreciated that the need for bulk is greatly diminished when reinforced concrete is used for arched vaults, particularly those of parabolic section, since the stresses are then mainly compressional, with a consequent saving in the load to be supported. In domes, the conditions are especially favourable, as was discovered by Walter Bauersfeld in 1922. After experiments, the first sizeable shell-dome was constructed at Jena, Germany, in 1925, spanning 25 m (82 ft), with the concrete not more than 60 mm ($2\frac{3}{8}$ ins) thick. An octagonal dome at Basle market hall spans 60 m (197 ft), at a thickness of barely 80 mm ($3\frac{1}{8}$ ins). After hemispherical domes, segmental domes and then barrel vaults were tried, the latter sometimes running with the length and sometimes in a series, side by side, across a hall; and with these too, enormous unobstructed spans were at length achieved. Sometimes the transverse barrel vaults were allowed to protrude beyond their seating on the longitudinal walls, cantilevered to provide a serrated crest or awning. In the case of all these types there were problems of stiffness to be resolved, for arches or vaults, however light, exert thrust, which has to be buttressed, contained or countered.

Before the Second World War the shell vault was used mainly for utilitarian structures. It was in the post-war world that it emerged as a reputable feature in 'polite' architecture, and remarkable feats of roofing have been accomplished with it. Thus the curvilinear note was restored to organic architecture after decades of rectilinear geometry, bringing with it a charm, even a delicacy, hitherto lacking. But it was not only in reinforced concrete that further potentialities had been discovered, for steel, while remaining the most suitable structural material for the framing of high-rise and other cellular buildings, was now often used over great halls in unified space-frame arrangements, composed in three dimensions instead of as a series of principals or trusses supporting longitudinal members on the age-old method. It had been found, too, that lamination, the glueing together of overlapping layers of wood, provided beams and arches with calculable capacities vastly beyond the range of timber in its natural state.

EXAMPLES

EUROPEAN CONTINENT

DOMESTIC BUILDINGS

The **Apartment Block, No. 25b, Rue Franklin, Paris** (1903) (p. 1251A), by Auguste Perret, is the earliest instance of frank architectural expression of reinforced-concrete framed construction in an important secular building. The block is trapped between other frontages, and to avoid internal light wells, the centre of the façade is deeply recessed, the wings having projecting bays. The concrete is faced externally with ceramic slabs, plain where the essential frame was to be expressed and around the windows, but ornamented with floral or pebble patterns on the non-load-bearing panels between. Glass bricks, invented about 1890, were used on the staircase outer wall at the rear. The floor loads are taken upon internal pillars instead of the dividing walls, and this innovation had an important influence upon later domestic architecture.

The **Stocklet House, Brussels** (1905–11) (p. 1251B), by Josef Hoffmann, is an opulent asymmetrically-composed mansion, lavishly marbled internally and elegant externally, with white walls patterned by rhythms of neat windows. A feature much imitated later on is the tall staircase window running the full height of the house, accentuating the vertical lines of the dominant tower.

The **Steiner House, Vienna** (1910) (p. 1251C), by Adolf Loos, is the first wholly Modern dwelling. It is strictly functional, the designer being strongly opposed to ornament in whatever form. Elevationally it is symmetrical and flat-roofed, its plain white walls broken by stark windows, carefully proportioned to give a balance and restfulness to the whole façade.

The **Dageraad Housing Estate, Amsterdam** (1918–23), by Piet Kramer, is distinguished by the tenement blocks built in 1922–3 (p. 1251D), which show the clever and ornamental treatment of fine brickwork evidenced by the Amsterdam school of architects at this time. The block of **Flats on the Henriette Ronnerplein, Amsterdam** (1920–2) by Michael de Klerk, offers a further example.

B. The Stocklet House, Brussels (1905–11).
See p. 1250

A. Apartment Block, No. 25b, Rue
Franklin, Paris (1903). See p. 1250

C. The Steiner House, Vienna (1910). See p. 1250

D. The Dageraad Housing Estate,
Amsterdam (1922–3). See p. 1250

E. Workers' Houses, Hook of Holland (1926–7).
See p. 1252

The **Workers' Houses, Hook of Holland** (1926–7) (p. 1251E) by J. J. P. Oud, comprising two terraces, represent the Dutch Rotterdam school, more genuinely functional and progressive than the foregoing. The white façades are linked by long balconies which curve to form canopies over shops at the ends. The plinths are of yellow brick.

The **Villa 'Les Terraces' at Garches, near Paris** (1926–7) (p. 1253A) by Le Corbusier and Pierre Jeanneret (Le Corbusier's cousin, who practised with him until 1943) is the most famous of his many houses, and embodies his principles. There are two main floors, the first floor providing the kitchen and living accommodation and the second the bedrooms. The ground or entrance floor includes the garage and remaining domestic offices, while the roof has terrace gardens, a guest suite and servants' bedroom quarters. As a whole, the villa forms a rectangle, the concrete floors being carried on the end walls and sparse internal pillars, but projecting forward on the two long sides as cantilevers, so that none of the main structural supports is visible in the long horizontal 'ribbon' windows. Since there are no internal load-bearing walls the accommodation could be freely planned. The living floor is treated as a single lightly-divided space, the elements being demarcated by doorless and movable curved or straight partitions. Each main floor includes a covered garden, that of the first floor being related to the external garden by a projecting terrace, supported on a squat round column, and a flight of steps.

The **Villa Savoye, Poissy, S.-et-O., France** (1928–31) (p. 1253B), by Le Corbusier, follows similar principles, but differs in design. The main floor is raised upon 'pilotis', approached by a long dog-legged ramp instead of a staircase. Most of the accommodation is on the first floor, which also includes a large covered terrace. Above, there is a roof garden, with curvilinear screens to the access stair and small pavilions. The ground floor is cored by a spacious, round-fronted hall, from which the ramp leads. The upper floors are cantilevered at the two ends, but on the sides of the rectangular house-block the pillar supports pass immediately behind the first-floor screen-walls, which have almost continuous horizontal ribbon windows.

The **Tugendhat House, Brno, Czechoslovakia** (1930) by Ludwig Mies van der Rohe, is celebrated for its internal open planning. The house stands on a southern steep slope, and is entered from the top partial storey, which contains the entrance hall, bedrooms and guest suite, besides the garage block at the west end. The stair descends to the main floor, of which an area of about 24 m × 12 m (80 ft × 40 ft) is lightly divided by free-standing partitions. One of the screens is of pale onyx marble, and another, forming a semicircle around the dining space, is of ebony, while the steel pillars supporting the upper floor are finished in chrome bronze. The continuous great windows on the cantilevered south and east sides of the block may be lowered electrically into the storage basement which elevates the main floor above the terrace and hillside. Externally, the house has that grand elegance which distinguishes the work of the designer.

The **Swiss Hostel, Cité Universitaire, Paris** (1931–2) (p. 1254A) by Le Corbusier, is a dormitory block standing impressively upon enormous double 'pilotis' of concrete which leave the site almost completely open at ground level. Above, the building is steel-framed, faced with concrete slabs, with bands of large windows facing south-west to light the single-banked study-bedrooms. The ends of the block are devoid of windows, as also is the concave north-east face of a rear wing which juts out to contain the communal rooms.

The **Unité d'Habitation, Marseilles** (1946–52) (p. 1254B) by Le Corbusier, is an enormous apartment block designed to house a complete community. It stands on massive coupled 'pilotis', and is concrete framed, faced with prefabricated slabs or units. Near the centre of the height is a floor devoted to shops and communal

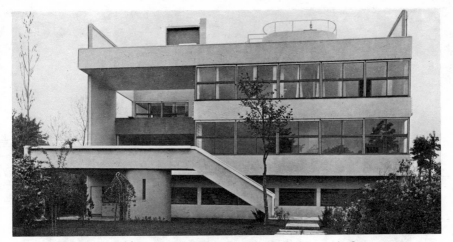

A. The Villa 'Les Terraces', Garches, near Paris (1926–7). See p. 1252

B. The Villa Savoye, Poissy, S.-et.-O., France (1928–31). See p. 1252

A. The Swiss Hostel, Cité Universitaire, Paris (1931–2). See p. 1252

B. The Unité d'Habitation, Marseilles (1946–52). See p. 1252

C. The Champs-Elysées Theatre, Paris (1911). See p. 1258

services, complemented by other facilities on the roof—swimming bath, gymnasium, nursery school and play and sun-bathing areas. The apartments are ingeniously interlocked between front and back of the block so that each dwelling can occupy a floor and a half of height, including a two-storey living room. Covering the front and back faces of the block are concrete frames, which shield the rooms from glare and provide balconies on both fronts to each dwelling.

The **Terrace of small houses at Søholm, near Copenhagen** (1950) (p. 1270A), by Arne Jacobsen, is a modest scheme of striking originality. Built to a stepped plan, the angular pattern of the roofs conforming to the layout of the two-storey interiors, the row contrasts pleasantly with the cubic designs habitual at the time. The construction is traditional, the principal facing material being yellow brick.

CHURCHES

The **Church of Notre Dame, Le Raincy, S.-et-O.** (1922–3) (p. 1256A, B) by Auguste Perret, is the first in which reinforced concrete finds direct architectural expression. The simple, single-aisled 'hall-church' plan, 56 m (185 ft) × 19 m (63 ft) wide, is formed by four rows of slender, vertically-reeded tapering pillars, 11.3 m (37 ft) high, supporting a flat segmental concrete vault, 50 mm (2 ins) thick, over the nave, and transverse shallow segmental vaults over the bays of the aisles. Being so thin, the nave vault is stiffened by transverse fins protruding above the vault, themselves covered by large, curved tiles. The church floor falls towards the east. The slight walls clasp the outer lines of columns, and are constructed of precast concrete elements forming trellis-like 'claustra', glazed with stained glass to their full height over a plain dado. There is a shallow segmental apse at the east end, and the chancel is raised 1.5 m (5 ft) above a basement containing vestries and sacristies, eastward of a flight of steps extending across the church. At the west end, where there is an organ gallery, a tower rises from cruciform pillars, each compounded of four columns similar to those supporting the vaults. All the structural concrete in the church is left as it came from the formwork, without facing. **S. Thérèse, Montmagny, S.-et-O.** (1925–6) (p. 1257B) by Perret, is a similar if less attractive church.

S. Antonius, Basel, Switzerland (1926–7) (p. 1256C) by Karl Moser (1860–1936) owes its inspiration to the Le Raincy church. It is plainer and much less subtle, its square, tall pillars supporting a concrete barrel vault over the nave and flat ceilings over the narrow aisles, all heavily ribbed into square coffers.

The **Steel Church, Presse, Cologne** (1928) (p. 1257C), by Otto Bartning (1883–1959), with steel and glass walls, and **S. Matthew, Düsseldorf** (1930–1), by Wach and Roskotten, are other interesting examples of the inter-war period.

After the Second World War, traditional character in church design was almost entirely abandoned, yet the many new churches built were extraordinarily diverse in the nature of their plans, structural systems, forms of construction and materials.

The **Chapel of Notre Dame, Ronchamp, Haute Saône** (1950–5) (p. 1257A), by Le Corbusier, stands on the crest of a hill. The chapel is compact and massively walled, the south wall battered inwards and containing an intriguing pattern of slot windows of varying dimensions and proportions, some square and inert, others with vertical or horizontal trends. Round, soft-contoured angle towers contain minor chapels, and with the help of a south-eastern great spur-buttress sustain a billowing roof, sweeping outwards and upwards to form an enormous canopy. On the east wall is an outdoor pulpit. Internally, the deep-set, jewel-like splay-jambed windows send shafts of richly-coloured light across the crepuscular gloom, while at the wall top a thin band of light demarcates wall from roof, the latter being slightly elevated on metal supports.

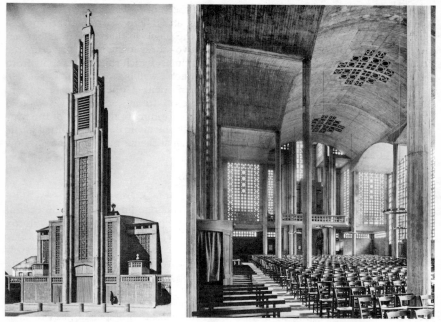

A. Exterior   B. Interior, looking W.

The Church of Notre Dame, Le Raincy, S.-et-O. (1922–3). See p. 1255

C. S. Antonius, Basel (1926–7). See p. 1255

A. The Chapel of Notre Dame, Ronchamp, Haute Saône (1950–5).
See p. 1255

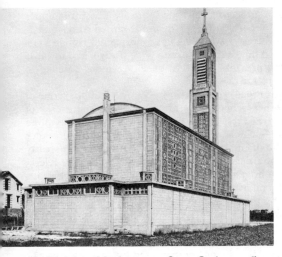

B. S. Thérèse, Montmagny, S.-et-O. (1925–6).
See p. 1255

C. The Steel Church, Presse,
Cologne (1928). See p. 1255

PUBLIC BUILDINGS

The **Champs-Elysées Theatre, Paris** (1911) (p. 1254C) was in the first place designed by Henri van de Velde, but as completed is almost wholly due to the Perret brothers. It is of reinforced concrete, faced externally with thin slabs of marble. Internally, the actual structural frame determines the essentials of the effect, the concrete merely being covered with plaster. The building has the Classical dispositions and character normal to Auguste Perret's work. The façades, with relief sculpture by Bourdelle, are a modification of van de Velde's original design.

The **Centennial Hall, Breslau** (1912–13) (p. 1259), by Max Berg, one of the most daring structures erected before the First World War, is covered by a vast concrete dome (p. 1259B), 65 m (213 ft) diameter, springing from the ground, its upper part comprising a series of heavy radial ribs, serving to carry tiers of continuous windows, which mask the dome externally and give it the much lighter appearance of a stepped cupola. Here, reinforced-concrete structure itself makes the design. The approach and entrance porches however, are fashioned into slender colonnades of Classical complexion (p. 1259A).

The **Einstein Tower, Potsdam, near Berlin** (1920–1) (p. 1260B), by Erich Mendelsohn, an observatory and astrophysical laboratory, is a wholly plastic expression, completely devoid of historical allusions, its forms being symbolic of optical instruments. Designed for poured concrete, it is actually executed in cement-covered brickwork.

The **City Library, Stockholm** (1924–7) (p. 1260A), by E. Gunnar Asplund, has a high cylindrical lending hall rising above a contrasting rectilinear arrangement of lesser apartments, the whole making a very dignified, reticent composition, showing only the barest trace of Classical historical allusion.

The **Bauhaus, Dessau** (1925–6) (p. 1261A, C), by Walter Gropius, was erected to provide studio-dormitories, assembly and dining-hall, workshops, administrative and social rooms and the school of design for this famous pioneer establishment, and is itself expressive of the Bauhaus aims of uniting art with industrial production. The various elements of the accommodation are linked together into an asymmetrical composition, the living quarters projecting towards the rear. The three upper of the four floors of the workshop block are cantilevered, and sheathed with a metal-and-glass curtain, while the administrative wing has long, horizontal ribbon windows. Between them is a two-floored link standing over a wide bridge, and towards the rear the projecting hostel wing presents a pattern of wide windows joined to individual cantilevered balconies (p. 1261A).

The **Vondelschool, Hilversum** (1926) (p. 1261D), by W. M. Dudok, is one of his many buildings, including other schools, at this new town, south-east of Amsterdam, founded shortly before the First World War, of which he was appointed chief architect. The Vondelschool—which received an extension at the entrance end in 1931—is very characteristic of his mature style, and still echoes his early contact with the 'De Stijl' group of artists (p. 1248). Like the architects de Klerk, Kramer and the Amsterdam group in general, he adheres to fine brickwork as his principal medium, but unlike them avoids fanciful effects, instead giving his buildings a serene dignity, stressing the horizontal lines and opposing the restfulness of large plain areas of brickwork to the pungent rhythms of long, banded windows. There is usually an element of cubism in his compositions, as is plainer to see in his **Town Hall, Hilversum** (1929) (p. 1261B), and they are normally asymmetrical, their essential horizontality being compensated by a strong tower or other vertical feature.

The **Tuberculosis Sanatorium, Paimio, Finland** (1929–33) (p. 1260C), by

A. Exterior

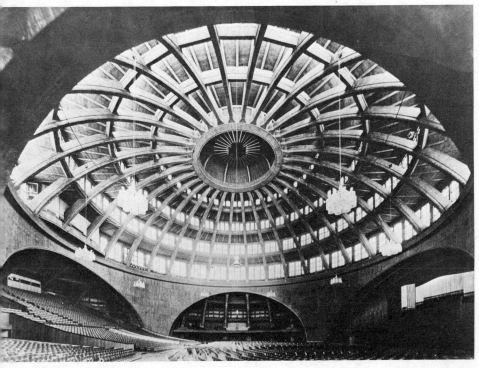

B. Interior
Centennial Hall, Breslau (1912–13). See p. 1258

A. The City Library, Stockholm (1924–7). See p. 1258

B. The Einstein Tower, Potsdam (1920–1). See p. 1258

C. The Tuberculosis Sanatorium, Paimio, Finland (1929–33). See p. 1258

A. The Bauhaus, Dessau:
Hostel wing. See p. 1258

B. The Town Hall, Hilversum (1929).
See p. 1258

C. The Bauhaus, Dessau (1925–6). See p. 1258

D. The Vondelschool, Hilversum (1926 and (*right*) 1931). See p. 1258

A. The Casa del Popolo, Como (1932–6). See p. 1264

B. The Musée des Travaux Publics, Paris (1938–). See p. 1264

C. Garage, Rue de Ponthieu, Paris (1905–6). See p. 1246

A. The Palazzetto dello Sport, Rome (1956–7). See p. 1264

B. The UNESCO Secretariat Building, Paris (1958). See p. 1264

C. The CNIT Building, Paris (1959). See p. 1271

Alvar Aalto, is an early and advanced demonstration of the adaptation of modern structural resources to the design of hospitals. Of reinforced concrete, this large establishment is freely and openly planned, the various units receiving the ideal orientation for them, the wings running on different alignments, with widely-projecting balconies, ample windows, and a light, cheerful appearance.

The **Casa del Popolo, Como** (1932–6) (p. 1262A) by Giuseppe Terragni (1904–1942), a member of the original 'Gruppo 7', shows Italian Modern architecture already reaching maturity. Finely finished and studiously proportioned, this reinforced-concrete building achieves a distinctively Mediterranean character.

The **Musée des Travaux Publics, Paris** (1938–) (p. 1262B), by Auguste Perret, stands on a wedge-shaped island site, entered at the narrow end, where the entrance vestibule surrounds a semicircular auditorium. The composition in reinforced concrete is symmetrical about the long axis, and the design clearly bears Perret's personal stamp, being conceived throughout on Classical lines. The elements of the design, however, are carefully attuned to the material, both in the decorative and structural sense. Externally there are concrete colonnades, their shafts tapering downwards for logical reasons, and these correspond with similar columns internally, together carrying the load of the coffered ceiling and superstructure, the thin outer walls carrying nothing but their own weight.

The **Palazzetto dello Sport, Rome** (1956–7) (p. 1263A), by P. L. Nervi and Annibale Vitellozzi, is of circular plan, 61 m (200 ft) diameter, covered by a shell-concrete shallow dome with a rippled edge, the thrusts at the base taken by forked flying buttresses. The stadium was designed to accommodate about 5,000 spectators and to serve the Olympic Games of 1960. It was made of prefabricated elements, the dome proper having been erected in the space of forty days. The much larger **Palazzo dello Sport, Rome** (1959), also designed by Nervi and for the 1960 Olympic Games, is again circular and domed, capable of accommodating 15,000 people in three tiers of seats, one of them descending below ground level, along with the arena. The construction and the method of lighting are also similar, there being a large central 'eye' and peripheral vertical windows near the base. Externally it differs in having a surrounding open, skeletal colonnade.

The **UNESCO Secretariat Building, Paris** (1958) (p. 1263B), by M. Breuer, P. L. Nervi and B. Zehrfuss, Y-shaped on plan, has a reinforced-concrete frame (supporting seven glass-fronted storeys) carried on seventy-two pilotis. Connected to a handsome trapezoidal congress hall, with a folded-slab roof, it was ingeniously extended below ground level, with sunken patios (1965), by Zehrfuss, who also designed another UNESCO block, Rue Miollis (1970), remarkable for its curtain wall of white-enamelled laminated steel and aluminium brise-soleil.

INDUSTRIAL AND COMMERCIAL BUILDINGS

The **Turbine Factory, Berlin** (1909) (p. 1265A), by Peter Behrens, is important in having shown that industrial buildings can make good architecture solely by meticulous organization of the structure and materials, without recourse to ornament. Great windows provide the flood of light needful, set between steel uprights, exposed externally, to which the metal roof principals are framed, and taper downwards on to hinged base-plates. Apart from the metal and glass the walls are of concrete, with horizontal striations on the angle masses.

The **Fagus Factory, Alfeld-an-der-Leine** (1911–14) (p. 1265B), by Walter Gropius and Adolf Meyer, is of brick, but on the main fronts tall windows project beyond the intervening piers and give the impression of continuous curtain walls, an impression heightened by the use of angle windows.

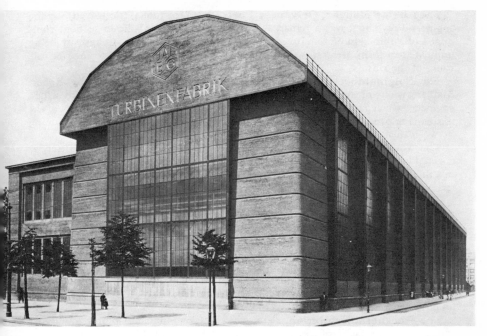

A. Turbine Factory, Berlin (1909). See p. 1264

B. The Fagus Factory, Alfeld-an-der-Leine (1911–14). See p. 1264

The **Airship Hangar, Orly, near Paris** (1916) (p. 1268A) (destroyed), by the engineer Freyssinet, was a remarkable concrete vault, parabolic in section, comprised of a thin skin of reinforced concrete given stiffness and strength by being undulated to form great ribs, lattices of window apertures being formed on the backs of the ribs.

The **Salginatobel Bridge, Switzerland** (1929–30) (p. 1267A) by Robert Maillart, is one of the many fine reinforced-concrete bridges by this distinguished engineer, which gain their elegance and beauty from the functional simplicity of the means employed, here a curved slab supporting a flat one, other slabs spanning between them vertically.

The **Market Hall, Leipzig** (1928) (p. 1267B) by Dischinger and Ritter, is covered by two octagonal shell-concrete domes of 75.5 m (248 ft) span, 90 mm (3½ ins) thick. The earliest shell-concrete dome was that of the Jena Planetarium (1925), spanning 25 m (82 ft).

The **Van Nelle Factory, Rotterdam** (1927–30) (p. 1268B), by J. A. Brinkman, L. C. van der Vlugt and Mart Stam, for a firm of tobacco, tea and coffee merchants, is Holland's finest Modern building of the first half of the century. Of reinforced concrete, the main eight-storey block is in 'mushroom' construction (a system used by Maillart as early as 1908), the respective floors being carried on internal pillars which fan outwards at the top, the outer walls being non-load-bearing and supported by the floors. Externally, the horizontal ribbon windows are admirably balanced by the flow of form of the projecting tower blocks, and afford an effective contrast of panels of plain wall.

The **Stockholm Exhibition, 1930** (p. 1268C), by Gunnar Asplund, admirably illustrated the capacity of modern architectural forms, aided by colour, to produce gay, graceful and delicate effects.

The **Station, Amstel suburb, Amsterdam** (1939) (p. 1269A), by H. G. J. Schelling, is an attractive, economical structure built of brick, with very large panels of glass on the two long sides, and a low-pitched roof.

The **Aircraft Hangars** (1935 and 1939–40) (p. 1269B) (destroyed) which were located on various sites, several of a standard type designed by P. L. Nervi, 100 m × 41 m (330 ft × 135 ft) internally, involved a three-dimensional conception of structure, a segmental barrel vault of precast reinforced-concrete ribs forming a diagonal lattice being sustained on only six buttressing supports. The lower edges of the hipped roof were stiffened by triangular 'space-frames' on the open side.

The **Exhibition Hall, Turin** (1948–9) (p. 1270C), by P. L. Nervi, is the larger and slightly the earlier of two constructed there, and is a rectangular building of 95 m (312 ft) span, bridged by a segmental vault of concrete springing from the ground. Forked buttresses fan into ribs near the base, and these support corrugations of 2.4 m (8 ft) interval carrying precast shell units 50 mm (2 ins) thick, braced fins and embodying shallow, strip windows. This remarkable structure took only eight months to build.

The **Stazione Termini, Rome** (1947–51) (p. 1269C), by E. Montuori and associates, includes a vast concourse, of imposing simplicity, fronting a 'slab' office block with narrow, horizontal ribbon windows. The concourse ceiling, finished in white glass mosaic, stands on multiple slender pillars of granite-faced concrete, and undulates in logical accord with the stresses resisted; the latter are asymmetrical, since the ceiling continues externally to form a great, cantilevered canopy over the entrance front, ending in a thin fascia slab.

The **Jespersen Office Block, Copenhagen** (1956) (p. 1270B), by Arne Jacobsen, has a façade of ultimate simplicity, a curtain wall fronting cantilevered floors being divided uniformly into panels. Each of the windows reproduces the proportions

A. The Salginatobel Bridge, Switzerland (1929–30). See p. 1266

B. The Market Hall, Leipzig (1928). See p. 1266

A. Airship Hangar, Orly, near Paris (1916). See p. 1266

B. The Van Nelle Factory, Rotterdam (1927–30). See p. 1266

C. The Stockholm Exhibition, 1930. See p. 1266

A. The Station, Amstel suburb, Amsterdam (1939). See p. 1266

B. Aircraft hangar, Orbetello, Italy (1939–40). See p. 1266

C. The Stazione Termini, Rome (1947–51). See p. 1266

A. Terrace at Søholm, near Copenhagen (1950). See p. 1255

B. The Jespersen Office Block,
Copenhagen (1956). See p. 1266

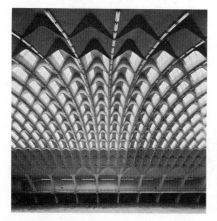

C. Exhibition Hall, Turin: interior
(1948–9). See p. 1266

D. The Pirelli Office Block, Milan
(1957–60). See p. 1271

of the block as a whole. The opaque panels underneath the ribbon windows are differentiated from them solely by change of colour. The **Pirelli Office Block, Milan** (1957–60) (p. 1270D), by P. L. Nervi, Gio Ponti and others, with its thirty-two storeys above ground, towers to such a height as to constitute a skyscraper. Skyscrapers were as yet fairly few in Europe, though subsequently in all European cities there has been a general tendency for commercial and apartment buildings to reach far greater heights than ever before.

The **Centre National des Industries et Techniques (CNIT), Paris** (1959) (p. 1263C), by R. Camelot, J. de Mailly and B. Zehrfuss, is a vast exhibition hall with the longest span for a thin-shell vaulted structure, 206 m (676 ft) at the façades, 238 m (780 ft) at the groin.

NORTH AND SOUTH AMERICA

DOMESTIC BUILDINGS

Falling Water, Pa. (1936–7) (p. 1272A), by Frank Lloyd Wright, is of stone and reinforced concrete. The free plan makes good use of level changes and in its woodland site, its structure partly cantilevered over a waterfall, the house presents a superbly balanced composition of rectilinear masses. Wright's **Friedman House, Pleasantville, N.Y.** (1948–9), is based in plan on circular forms and built mainly in rubble walling, with mushroom-like concrete roofs over the circular elements. Circular plan forms are used also in his **Jacobs House, Middleton, Wisconsin** (1948) and the **David J. Wright House, nr. Phoenix, Arizona** (1952).

Farnsworth House, nr. Plano. Ill. (1950) (p. 1272B), by Ludwig Mies van der Rohe, is remarkable for the simplicity of its form and the precision of its detail. The plan of this flat-roofed, single-storey building is rectangular, with a central core (comprising bathrooms, heating plant and a fire-place) around which space flows freely, the various areas for eating, sleeping, etc., being indicated simply by partitions and fittings which do not connect with the ceiling. Structurally the house is a cage of white-painted welded steel (with large areas glazed in plate glass) carried on a concrete slab, lifted above the ground on low supports.

Nos. 845–60 Lake Shore Drive, Chicago, Ill. (1949–51) (p. 1278B), two 26-storey blocks of flats by Mies van der Rohe, are characteristic of his work. Like glazed cages of steel, lifted from the ground on 'pilotis' at entrance level, the services, lifts, etc., are contained in a central core, thus permitting completely glazed elevations. The designs rely on the careful proportioning of the rectangular grid formed by vertical and horizontal structural steel members and refinement of detail. Between the main vertical structural members, intermediate uncased steel I-sections are introduced, running the height of the building and stiffening the structure.

Promontory Apartments, Chicago, Ill. (1949), also by Mies van der Rohe, are twenty-two storeys high and of reinforced-concrete construction, vertical structural members being emphasized externally. The plan is U-shaped and consists of two self-sufficient blocks, each with its own lifts and staircase, joined as one. The detail is severe but carefully considered.

Among numerous examples of first-rate domestic work, the following are particularly noteworthy: **Houses at Wayland, Mass.** (1940) and **Lincoln, Mass.** (1938), by Walter Gropius and Marcel Breuer; work by Richard Neutra; **Boissonas House, New Canaan, Conn.** (1955–6) and **R. S. Davis House, Wayzata, Minnesota** (1954), by Philip Johnson.

Among interesting examples of domestic architecture in South America are: **Parque Guinle Flats, Rio de Janeiro** (1948–54), by Lúcio Costa, the designer

A. Falling Water, Pennsylvania (1936–7). See p. 1271

B. Farnsworth House, near Plano, Illinois (1950). See p. 1271

of Brasilia, the new Brazilian city; and blocks of flats (1954) in the **Cerro Piloto Housing Estate, Caracas, Venezuela,** by Guido Bermudez. Built of reinforced concrete and making good use of colour, in the liveliness of their conception these represent characteristic examples of modern South American design.

EDUCATIONAL AND RELIGIOUS BUILDINGS

Illinois Institute of Technology, Chicago, Ill. (1939–) (p. 1274A). In 1939, a year after settling in the U.S., Mies van der Rohe was commissioned to design an entire campus layout together with its buildings, which include **Crown Hall,** housing the School of Architecture (1956); **Administration Building** (1944); **Chemical Engineering and Metallurgy Building** (1949); **Mineral and Metal Research Building** (1943); the **Alumni Memorial Hall** (1946) and the **Chemistry Building** (1946) (p. 1274A). Like all Mies van der Rohe's work, the beauty of these buildings lies in their proportions, refined and appropriate detail and first-rate craftsmanship. Exposed structural steel (painted black), large areas of glass reflecting the trees and landscaping of the campus, and a buff-coloured brick are the basic materials used in the scheme. Internal planning is generally open, particularly in the Alumni Memorial Hall and Crown Hall, the main floor of the latter being completely unimpeded by walls or partitions.

Baker House (Dormitory Block), Massachusetts Institute of Technology, Cambridge, Mass. (1947–9), by Alvar Aalto, has a serpentine plan and is carried out in a rich, red brick, the walls punched with simple but finely-detailed windows on its six residential floors.

The **Graduate Center, Harvard University, Cambridge, Mass.** (1949–50) (p. 1275B), by Walter Gropius and his associates, is a fine and characteristic example of the former's work. Seven dormitories, housing altogether some 300 students, and the Commons Building form the scheme which, although basically in two loose courts, is informal in layout and most attractively landscaped. The higher dormitory buildings have reinforced-concrete frames and the predominant facing material is a yellowish brick. Horizontal lines are emphasized, particularly in the Commons Building, the interior of which is enriched with work by Hans Arp and others.

The **Auditorium Building, Massachusetts Institute of Technology, Cambridge, Mass.** (1952–5) (p. 1274B), by Eero Saarinen, has a great shell-concrete roof, springing from the ground at three points like a billowing sail, the three elevations being glazed up to the soffit of the shell.

University City, Mexico (1950–) is a vast complex of buildings mainly constructed in reinforced concrete. Particularly notable are the **Olympic Stadium** (1951–2), by A. P. Salacios and others, and the **Central Library** (1951–3) (p. 1275A) by Juan O'Gorman and others. The latter is dominated by a massive tower housing the library stacks and covered in brilliant mosaic, incorporating decorative and symbolic devices from the pre-Columbian civilizations of Mexico.

The **Church of S. Francisco, Pampulha, Brazil** (1943) (p. 1275C), by Oscar Niemeyer (b. 1901), an example of (perhaps excessive) virtuosity in reinforced concrete, is roofed by a series of concrete vaults. Its flank walls are faced with murals in 'azulejos' and to one side there is a concrete bell-tower, tapering towards its base.

The **Chapel, Illinois Institute of Technology, Chicago, Ill.** (1950), by Mies van der Rohe, is a simple, box-like structure in black-painted steel and buff brick, its west end entirely glazed.

Marial Chapel, Lac Bouchette, Quebec (1952), by Henri Tremblay, is intended to form part of a larger church. Billowing shell-concrete vaults are used in interesting juxtaposition to solid rubble walls.

A. Chemistry Building, Illinois Institute of Technology, Chicago (1946).
See p. 1273

B. The Auditorium Building, Massachusetts Institute of Technology,
Cambridge, Mass. (1952–5). See p. 1273

A. University City, Mexico: Central Library (1951–3). See p. 1273

B. The Graduate Center, Harvard University, Cambridge, Mass. (1949–50).
See p. 1273

C. S. Francisco, Pampulha (1943). See p. 1273

A. The Hallidie Building, San Francisco (1918). See p. 1277

B. Rockefeller Center, New York (1930-). See p. 1277

C. Lever House, New York (1952). See p. 1277

D. The Johnson Wax Co. Buildings, Racine, Wisconsin (1936-49). See p. 1277

E. The Ministry of Education and Health, Rio de Janeiro (1937-42). See p. 1279

F. General Motors Technical Institute, Warren, Michigan (1946-55). See p. 1277

The **Chapel, Massachusetts Institute of Technology, Cambridge, Mass.** (1954–5), by Eero Saarinen, is in the form of a cylinder of beautifully-laid, rich red brick rising on low arches from a shallow pool, through which diffused and flickering light enters the building. In addition, partially-baffled light enters from above, producing a most effective atmosphere.

COMMERCIAL, INDUSTRIAL AND GOVERNMENTAL BUILDINGS

The **Hallidie Building, San Francisco, California** (1918) (p. 1276A), by W. J. Polk, was remarkably prophetic of techniques to become widely used forty years later. The main façade is in the form of a great glass 'curtain', broken only by the grid of the horizontal and vertical glazing members and enriched at its crown and base by bands of intricate, fretted metal-work. Behind, and free from the glass 'curtain', rise the main structural supports of the building.

The **Saving Fund Society Building, Philadelphia, Pa.** (1932), designed by G. Howe and W. Lescaze, with no external adornment, is completely modern in feeling. The vertical elements of the frame are strongly emphasized on the long sides of the rectangle. The narrow sides have continuous ribbon windows.

Rockefeller Center, New York (1930–) (p. 1276B), is a complex of impressive buildings set amid a series of related open spaces. The focus of the centre is the **R.C.A. Building**, 260 m (850 ft) high with seventy storeys, a sheer slab-like structure with its vertical lines strongly emphasized. Around it are grouped thirteen lesser buildings, including the **Time and Life Building** (thirty-six storeys) and the **International Building** (forty-one storeys). In the early stages of the scheme a number of architects, including L. A. Reinhardt, Henry Hofmeister, H. W. Corbett and Raymond Hood, seem to have played some part, but the chief executive of the grand design was Wallace K. Harrison, who (with his partner, Max Abramovitz) has also had overall responsibility for the subsequent architectural work.

The **Johnson Wax Co. Buildings, Racine, Wis.** (1936–49) (p. 1276D), by Frank Lloyd Wright, consist of two main units, the **Administration Building** (1936–9) and the **Laboratory Tower** (1946–9). Carried out principally in red brick, the buildings are characterized by the plasticity of their forms, generated by the curvilinear plan shapes. The interior of the Administration Building presents a forest of reinforced-concrete mushroom columns, with elegant shafts tapering towards bases set in steel shoes and surmounted by wide, circular concrete discs. The interstices between the discs are glazed with glass tubes laid in patterns through which light filters, providing an unusually dramatic effect. The Laboratory Tower is constructed on what Wright called the 'tap-root' principle, a massive concrete core with deep foundations providing a structural spine for the building and anchorage for the floors which are cantilevered from it. The external walls carried by the floors are merely screens giving protection from the elements: they consist of brick and glazing (made up from horizontal glass tubes) which wrap around the building in wide alternating bands.

The **General Motors Technical Institute, Warren, Michigan** (1946–55) (p. 1276F), designed by Eliel Saarinen and his son, Eero Saarinen, a complex of twenty-five laboratory and other technical buildings, grouped about a formal lake, is comparable with the work of Mies van der Rohe in the clear-cut precision of its forms. Stainless steel, black oxidized aluminium, glass and brightly-coloured glazed brick are used in the buildings, which admirably express their functions.

Lever House, New York (1952) (p. 1276C), by Gordon Bunshaft of the firm of Skidmore, Owings and Merrill, is completely sheathed in glass and stainless steel

A. The United Nations Headquarters, New York (1947–50): the Secretariat Block. See p. 1279

B. Nos. 845–60 Lake Shore Drive, Chicago (1949–51). See p. 1271

C. Seagram Building, New York (1956–8). See p. 1279

curtain walling. A sheer slab block rises from a low structure mounted on pilotis, through which one enters a small patio, a delightful oasis in busy Park Avenue.

The **Seagram Building, New York** (1956–8) (p. 1278C), by Mies van der Rohe and Philip Johnson, is another notable skyscraper office block, clad externally in glass and bronze.

The **Alcoa Building, Pittsburgh, Pa.** (1952), by W. K. Harrison and Max Abramovitz, is an instance of the structural frame of the skyscraper sheathed in prefabricated, pressed aluminium panels with relatively small window areas.

The **United Nations Headquarters, New York** (1947–50) (p. 1278A), was designed with the advice of an international committee including Le Corbusier, Oscar Niemeyer and Sir Howard Robertson, with Harrison and Abramovitz of New York as executive architects. Sited by the East River, the scheme is dominated by the towering slab · block of the Secretariat Building which, with its narrow end walls rising like sheer white cliffs and its longer sides clad in glass curtain walling, has had considerable influence on subsequent high buildings throughout the world.

The **Ministry of Education and Health, Rio de Janeiro** (1937–42) (p. 1276E), was designed by Lúcio Costa and Oscar Niemeyer with Le Corbusier as consultant. A skyscraper in reinforced concrete borne on pilotis, the deep reveals of the building's vertical structural members, aided by horizontal louvres, control sunlight and provide an example of the influence of climate on modern architecture.

The **Edificio Polar, Caracas, Venezuela** (1953–4), by M. Vegas Pacheco and J. M. Galia, has a fifteen-storey tower rising above a lower structure and shows strong influence of the work of Mies van der Rohe.

BRITAIN

DOMESTIC BUILDINGS

No. 78, Derngate, Northampton (1916) (p. 1280A), an alteration and extension of an existing terrace house by C. R. Mackintosh, is a remarkable anticipation of the Modern architecture of the future, with its forthright geometrical composition, white walls, enclosed balcony, plain vertical balusters and, in general, genuine structural expression, unencumbered with ornament.

The **Sun House, Hampstead, London** (1935) (p. 1280B), by E. Maxwell Fry, is an early instance of English 'Modern' domestic architecture. The flat roof, white walls, metal-and-glass ribbon windows, metal handrails, balustrades and gates, concrete canopies and balconies, are all significant features. The main rooms on the first floor have a virtually unimpeded glass wall, while the bedroom windows are appropriately reduced in height. The house is attractive in its play of form and contrast of solid and void. A still earlier example is **'High and Over', at Amersham, Bucks** (1928–9), a beautifully sited house on a triangular plan, by Amyas Connell, who soon afterwards went into partnership with Basil Ward (both were New Zealanders), and Colin Lucas. In the few remaining years before the Second World War, Connell, Ward and Lucas were responsible for a succession of interesting exercises in reinforced concrete and 'floating' glass, based to a considerable extent on Le Corbusier's structural concepts, in which floor slabs, roof slab and walls are all reinforced and rigidly 'fused' into a monolithic framework. Examples are **'Aldings'** (originally 'New Farm'), **Haslemere, Surrey** (1932), and, perhaps their best work, a London house at **66 Frognal, Hampstead** (1938) (p. 1280D). Of the same period are a **House near Halland, Sussex** (1938) (p. 1288A), by Serge Chermayeff, a simple, two-floored, timber box-frame structure standing in

A. Derngate, North-
hampton (1916).
See p. 1279

B. The Sun House, Hampstead, London (1935).
See p. 1279

C. House in Newton
Road, Paddington, Lon-
don (1939). See p. 1281

D. 66 Frognal, Hampstead, London (1938).
See p. 1279

E. Alton Estate, Roehampton,
London (1954–6). See p. 1281

F. Highpoint I, Highgate, London (1934–5).
See p. 1281

park-like spacious grounds, and an urban **House in Newton Road, Paddington, London** (1939) (p. 1280C), by Denys Lasdun.

Highpoint I, Highgate, London (1934–5) (p. 1280F), is by Tecton, a team founded by Berthold Lubetkin (b. 1901), to which Anthony Chitty, Lindsey Drake, Michael Dugdale, Val Harding and Denys Lasdun belonged. It is an eight-storey group of flats, standing on 'pilotis', made up of wings thrown outward to catch the sun and air, with generous windows and balconies on each storey.

After the Second World War flats were a much more common form of civic housing than formerly. Among the many fine flat blocks, erected in the first years of the post-war period are the **Spa Green Estate, London** (1949), by Tecton; the **Churchill Gardens Development, Pimlico, London** (1951), by Powell and Moya; the **Tower Block, Harlow New Town** (1951), by Sir Frederick Gibberd; the **Alton Estate, Roehampton, London** (1954–6) (p. 1280E), by Sir H. Bennett, Sir J. L. Martin, Sir R. H. Matthew, H. J. Whitfield Lewis and others.

EDUCATIONAL AND RELIGIOUS BUILDINGS

Impington Village College, Cambridgeshire (1936) (p. 1282A), by E. Maxwell Fry and Walter Gropius, represents a new departure in school design. An attractively informal and mainly one-storey structure, it caters for adult education whilst also serving the normal purpose of a school.

The **Pentley Park Primary School, Welwyn Garden City, Herts** (1948–50) (p. 1282C), by C. H. Aslin, instances the trend away from institutional formality and towards a domestic intimacy of scale and character. The individually-arranged classrooms are generously lighted and the walls are of precast concrete slabs on a light steel frame. The **Day Nursery, Garston, Herts** (1951–2) also designed by Aslin, admirably fulfils similar objectives. The structure is a light steel frame, the supports being within the thin walls of metal and glass and laminated plaster, these protected above by a deep fascia of fluted asbestos. The **Hallfield Primary School, Paddington, London** (1955), by Drake and Lasdun, possesses excellent qualities. Built on a well-treed site, its concrete buildings are diversified in character and shape, presenting many intriguing and attractive facets.

S. Nicholas, Burnage, Manchester (1931), designed by Welch, Cachemaille-Day and Lander, instances the endeavours made at this time to break away from revivalism. The interior effects are contrived by simple means: the wall openings are skilfully disposed, certain of the pillars within them being left in exposed brick-work. Equally original for the period is S. Saviour, Eltham, Kent (1932), by the same architects.

The **Cathedral, Coventry** (1951–62) (p. 1283), by Sir Basil Spence, lies on a N.S. axis at right angles to the former church, of which the spired tower and ruined walls are preserved. The Cathedral is a modern version of a hall-church, 76 m (250 ft) long by 24.4 m (80 ft) wide, the high-proportioned nave and aisles being divided by slender, downward-tapering pillars, fanning out at the head into a faceted vault, pierced with decorative patterns (p. 1283A). The side walls are formed in oblique short sections, joined by tall stained-glass windows running the full height, which throw the incoming light towards the altar. Behind the altar is the Lady Chapel, the rear wall of which is clothed with a vast tapestry designed by Graham Sutherland. A 'Chapel of Unity', of circular plan, projects westward near the entrance end, and a smaller, circular 'Chapel of Christ the Servant' lies beyond the east side of the Lady Chapel.

The **Church at Tile Hill, Coventry** (1957), designed by Sir Basil Spence, is one of three churches built to serve a new community. It is a simple rectangle,

A. Impington Village College, Cambridgeshire (1936). See p. 1281

B. The Finsbury Health Centre, London (1938–9). See p. 1284

C. The Pentley Park Primary School, Welwyn, Herts (1948–50). See p. 1281

A. Interior looking north

B. East side and Chapel of Christ
the Servant

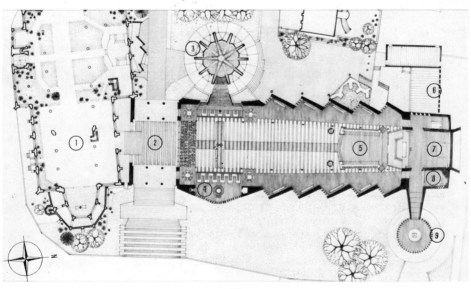

c. Plan

1. Ruins of old cathedral; 2. Entrance porch; 3. Chapel of Unity;
4. Baptistery; 5. Chancel; 6. Refectory; 7. Lady Chapel;
8. Chapel of Christ in Gethsemane; 9. Chapel of Christ the Servant.

Coventry Cathedral (1951–62). See p. 1281

walled in 'no-fines' concrete, the low, open timber roof being sustained on concrete frames. Adjacent to the church is a church hall and a concrete, openwork belfry.

PUBLIC, COMMERCIAL AND INDUSTRIAL BUILDINGS

The **Royal Horticultural Hall, London** (1923–6) (p. 1285A), by Murray Easton and Howard Robertson, shows development towards Modern architecture. Tall, diaphragm arches span the hall and support a series of concrete flat decks, stepped inwards concentrically with the arches and connected vertically with ribbon windows, diminishing in height towards the top of the hall.

The **Shakespeare Memorial Theatre, Stratford-upon-Avon** (1928–34) (p. 1285C), by Scott, Chesterton and Shepherd, was the outcome of a competition won in 1928 by Elizabeth Scott. Brick is the main material, chosen to harmonize with the architectural character of the small town, and a gracious and dignified effect is contrived without recourse to historical sources for inspiration.

Boots Chemical Factory, Beeston, Notts (1930–2) (p. 1285B), by Sir Owen Williams, employs on a vast scale the 'mushroom' type of concrete construction first used on the Continent by Robert Maillart in 1908 (p. 1247). The supporting concrete pillars swell outwards at the top of each storey in a form like an inverted pyramid and support a continuous slab floor.

The **Penguin Pool, Regent's Park Zoo, London** (1933–5) (p. 1286C), by B. Lubetkin, is a spatial adventure in form, an early and wholly modern design demonstrating that the most improbable subjects are capable of yielding high-quality architecture. The somewhat earlier **Gorilla House** (1933) has comparable virtues.

The **'Daily Express' Offices, Fleet Street, London** (c. 1933) (p. 1286A), by Ellis and Clarke, with Sir Owen Williams, is a concrete-framed building with horizontal ribbon windows and a facing, most unusual for the period, of polished black glass, the joints of the sheets being covered with strips of silver-coloured metal. There is a similar *Daily Express* building in Manchester.

The **De la Warr Pavilion, Bexhill, Sussex** (1935), is by Erich Mendelsohn and Serge Chermayeff. The long body of the hall, its sheer white walls perfectly plain apart from a circular, decorative inscription, forms a striking contrast with the semicircular bay (p. 1286B) at the restaurant end, with tiers of balconies and translucent walls through which the convolutions of the staircase can be seen.

The **Peter Jones Store, Sloane Square, London** (1935–6) (p. 1287A), by William Crabtree, J. A. Slater and A. H. Moberly, with Sir Charles Reilly as consultant, gains much from the undulations of its façade and the close-spaced vertical ribs which counter the insistence of the long, horizontal windows. An incisive crowning member gains in effectiveness by the recession of the storey immediately below it, giving a band of deeper shadow.

The **Royal Corinthian Yacht Club, Burnham-on-Crouch, Essex** (1930) (p. 1287B), by Joseph Emberton, is one of the earliest English buildings to reject stylistic expression, the south front towards the river Crouch being wholly functional. Of steel-framed construction, the walls of the main block are of stucco-faced cavity brickwork.

The **Finsbury Health Centre, London** (1938–9) (p. 1282B), by Tecton, is unaffectedly symmetrical in mass. A 'Modern' design in the full sense, it has a concrete frame and façades faced with glazed tiles, the windows of the two-storey wing blocks being linked vertically with opaque glass panels.

The **Brynmawr Rubber Factory, South Wales** (1945–51) (p. 1287C), by the Architects' Co-Partnership, with Ove Arup and Partners, Consulting Engineers,

A. The Royal Horticultural Hall, London (1923–6). See p. 1284

B. The Boots Chemical Factory, Beeston, Notts (1930–2). See p. 1284

C. The Shakespeare Memorial Theatre, Stratford-upon-Avon (1928–34): river front with later additions. See p. 1284

A. The *Daily Express* Offices, Fleet Street, London (*c.* 1933). See p. 1284

B. The De la Warr Pavilion, Bexhill, Sussex (1935). See p. 1284

C. The Penguin Pool, Regent's Park Zoo, London (1933–5). See p. 1284

A. The Peter Jones Store, London (1935–6). See p. 1284

B. The Royal Corinthian Yacht Club, Burnham-on-Crouch, Essex (1930). See p. 1284

C. The Brynmawr Rubber Factory, South Wales (1945–51). See p. 1284

D. The 'South Bank' Exhibition, London (1951), general view. See p. 1289

E. The Royal Festival Hall, London (1951). See p. 1289

A. House near Halland, Sussex (1938). See p. 1279

B. Arnold High School, Nottingham (1963). See p. 1290

is a large industrial scheme covering almost three acres, in which the main factory area is roofed by nine concrete shell-domes, each of a rectangular plan, 25.5 m × 19 m (85 ft × 62 ft) clear span, arranged in a three-by-three block and standing on pillars at the corners. The general ceiling level is 4.3 m (14 ft) above the floor, raised higher locally by shallow segmental domes, sufficiently spaced apart to allow clear-storey lighting through the lunettes below the domes.

The **'South Bank' Exhibition, London** (1951) (p. 1287D), for which Sir Hugh Casson was Director of Architecture, served to popularize the Modern movement in Britain. Many architects and designers contributed. The whole site was planned on informal lines and enlivened with flowers, trees, shrubs, water gardens, garden ornaments, statuary and variegated pavings.

The **Royal Festival Hall, London** (1951) (p. 1287E), by Sir R. H. Matthew, Sir J. L. Martin, Peter Moro and Edwin Williams, originally formed part of the South Bank Exhibition, and brought an entirely new kind of architecture to the Thames river front. It contains a large auditorium to seat 3,000, primarily for orchestral and choral concerts, and a smaller hall for recitals, chamber music, ballet, etc., together with promenades, foyers, refreshment bars, a spacious restaurant facing the river, an exhibition gallery, and meeting rooms. The structural frame is of reinforced concrete, and the auditorium is suspended above a grand foyer approach. There are no solid load-bearing walls, all the work being done by reinforced-concrete pillars, the interior partitions and outer sheath being of glass and metal or light materials.

CONTINUATION

With the great advances in steel and reinforced-concrete construction, structure is no longer so decisive a design factor as in the past. It is possible nowadays to cover very large areas with one unbroken span. For multi-cellular buildings, a steel or reinforced-concrete frame is general, the plan of each floor being defined merely by the structural grid, and these framed buildings can be raised completely from the ground on pilotis, thus providing the equivalent of a covered loggia at ground level. By incorporating all services, such as lifts, stairs, plumbing, heating equipment, etc., within a central core, it is now possible to free external walls from the elevational restrictions imposed in earlier times. The wall itself may be a skin of glass, sheet-metal, plastic or a sandwich material, playing no part in its stability, inside which air-conditioning provides an artificial climate. The concept of environmental control has now been extended to embrace whole districts. In 1961 the American engineer, Buckminster Fuller, whose experiments with private climates and in many other areas of potentially trouble-free living can be traced back to his Dymaxion house of 1927, designed a hemispherical dome, 2 miles in diameter, to enclose a large part of Manhattan, which could theoretically be assembled in 5-ton sections by helicopters in three months. Less ambitious exercises in pre-fabrication have lately become the normal practice of the building industries in all technologically advanced countries. In the field of housing, in particular, the majority of dwellings are wholly or partly system-built in quantity from standard factory-made components. In England, as elsewhere, the need for many new schools after the Second World War encouraged the development of rapid-assembly systems of construction. An outstandingly successful example was one evolved initially in the office of the County Architect of Nottinghamshire, and subsequently by the CLASP group of city and county councils (CLASP = Consortium of Local Authorities Special Programme), which allowed considerable freedom to the architect within a range of predetermined items and a square grid for buildings and components of about 1 m (3 ft 4 ins). The **Arnold High School, Nottingham** (1963) (p. 1288B), is a typical example.

To many architects, however, technical and functional excellence, although very important, no longer seemed enough. The past decade has seen certain changes in attitude among the profession towards 'modern' architecture, while also witnessing the almost universal acceptance of its principles and formal vocabulary, often at the cost of total rejection of national and regional building traditions. The heroic age of the masters is certainly well past. Almost all the major pioneers have disappeared and there has been no second (or third) generation of titans to replace them, even if cult-figures attract attention now and then, such as Louis Kahn (1901–74). The **Richards Medical Research Center, Philadelphia, Pa.** (1957–61) (p. 1291A), a cluster of square-plan laboratory towers with conspicuous externally-placed service shafts, exemplifies in striking visual terms his distinction between 'served' and 'servant' spaces, and his thesis that a building must not only fulfil its purpose, but be seen to do so. If Kahn has brought an extremely individual quality to the architectural expression of functionalism, another American, Philip Johnson (b. 1906), sometime partner of Mies van der Rohe and the protagonist of rectilineal simplicity, has been increasingly concerned with what he himself once described in a particular context as 'pure form—ugly or beautiful—but pure form', whether in designing the mushroom domes of the engaging little **Dumbarton Oaks Art Gallery, Washington, D.C.** (1962–4) (p. 1291B), or the heavily monumental cylindrical brick columns of the massive **Kline Science Center, Yale University, New Haven, Conn.** (1962–5) (p. 1293A). Eero Saarinen (1910–61), who died so tragically at the height of his career, showed extraordinary resource in the handling of symbolic form, witness the contrast between two works of similar purpose completed in 1962: the **TWA Passenger Reception building at Kennedy Airport, New York,** and the **Dulles International Airport building, Washington, D.C.** (p. 1292A). The first is a graphic shell-concrete representation of a soaring bird (although the architect denied the analogy), the second is dominated by its huge suspended roof, buoyant and resilient, and both, in Saarinen's contention, identifying structure, form and function. The **Yale University Art and Architecture building, New Haven, Conn.** (1963) (p. 1292B), by Paul Rudolph (b. 1918), much admired in the mid-60s when Yale became an architectural Mecca, stands on a confined street-corner site. Externally it presents an unlikely combination of Wright (cf. the Larkin Building, Buffalo, N.Y., p. 1243) and Le Corbusier (in the sculptural exploitation of 'béton brut', but here the coarse-textured finish is bush-hammered not board-marked), and internally an ingenious sequence of interrelated spaces enclosed by galleries. Skidmore, Owings and Merrill, usually loyal to the Mies van der Rohe aesthetic of immaculate precision and rectilineal simplicity, ventured abroad to build the handsome (and expensive) **Banque Lambert in Brussels** (1962) (p. 1293C), in which they abandoned their usual glass sheath, placing the containing membrane of the offices behind a structural frame of cruciform precast concrete elements, a practice which they have followed in principle in several subsequent buildings in the U.S.A.

It would be wrong, of course, to suggest that American architects have made most of the running in the recent past. In accepting 'modern' architecture, almost the entire world also accepted the influence of one architect in particular, Le Corbusier, who was responsible for (or collaborated in) the design of more buildings outside his own country than in it, and whose ideas, practical and theoretical, are reflected and more or less faithfully interpreted in such diverse realizations as the **Roehampton (Alton) Housing Estate** (p. 1280E), by architects of the Greater London Council; Brazil's new federal capital, **Brasilia** (p. 1294A), by Lúcio Costa and Oscar

A. Richards Medical Research Center, Philadelphia, Pa. (1957–61). See p. 1290

B. Dumbarton Oaks Art Gallery, Washington, D.C. (1962–4). See p. 1290

A. Dulles International Airport building, near Washington, D.C.
(completed 1962). See p. 1290

B. Yale University Art and Architecture building, New Haven, Conn.
(1963). See p. 1290

A. Kline Science Center, Yale University, New Haven, Conn. (1962–5). See p. 1290

B. The Supreme Court, Chandigarh (1951–6). See p. 1295

C. Banque Lambert, Brussels (1962). See p. 1290

A. Parliament Buildings, Brasilia (1960). See p. 1290

B. Maisons-Jaoul, Neuilly, Paris (1954–6). See p. 1295

C. Park Hill housing scheme, Sheffield (1961). See p. 1295

D. Cistercian Monastery of La Tourette at Éveux, near Lyon (completed 1960). See p. 1295

Niemeyer; and a host of buildings in Japan, by Kenzo Tange, Kunio Mayekawa and others. Of his own works, **Chandigarh** offered both the opportunity of a lifetime and the culmination of a lifetime's 'patient' quest. Le Corbusier (in association with the British architects Maxwell Fry and Jane Drew) began to build the new capital of the Punjab in 1950 on a virgin site, intended ultimately to accommodate 500,000 people. Three principal features dramatizing the vast, open, artificially undulating expanse of the 'Capitol', with its concealed roads and traditional 'tanks', were completed before his death in 1965. These are **the Secretariat, the Assembly** and the **Supreme Court** (p. 1293B), each an abstract of formal and spatial planning theories developed over forty years: roof-terraces, under-roof ventilation ways, vertical circulation by ramps, horizontal circulation by 'rues intérieures', infinite variations on the theme of the 'brise-soleil'. The exuberant freedom of Chandigarh contrasts with the self-effacing, austere **Cistercian Monastery of La Tourette at Éveux,** near Lyon (completed 1960) (p. 1294D), one of Le Corbusier's last major works in France.

Although probably declining, his influence has been ubiquitous in Europe. In Switzerland, the country of his birth, it is still understandably pervasive. A typical instance is the **Halen housing estate** of low-rise dwellings, near Berne (1961), by a group of young architects known as Atelier 5; while in Britain acute perception is not needed to see that James Stirling and James Gowan had the **Maisons-Jaoul,** a modest undertaking by Le Corbusier at Neuilly, Paris (1954-6) (p. 1294B), very much in mind when designing the **Langham development at Ham Common, Richmond,** near London (1958), although the resemblance here is more apparent than real, i.e. the inverted L-shaped windows and handling of materials, but not the interior planning. The very large **Park Hill housing scheme, Sheffield** (1961) (p. 1294C), by J. L. Womersley, J. Lynn, Ivor Smith and F. Nicklin, offers another example of Le Corbusier's inspiration, in this case less in the elevational treatment than in the planning of the maisonette-type flats and the introduction of internal street-decks. His extraordinary sensibility in the plastic manipulation of 'béton brut' is almost rivalled in the part-subterranean **Church of the Atonement** on the site of the concentration camp at Dachau (1967), by H. Striffler.

The growing significance of leisure in contemporary society, which has immeasurably extended the potential sphere of the architect's work, was one of the factors contributing to the ultimate rejection of the somewhat limited objectives of the Athens Charter (1933), for long the sacred writ of the Modern Movement, and to the dissolution of C.I.A.M. (p. 1249), over both of which the tutelary spirit of Le Corbusier had hovered for thirty years. The Olympic Games, if not typical of this phenomenon, afforded in Tokyo (1964), Mexico (1968) and Munich (1972) (p. 1297B), opportunities to local architects for experiment. For the Tokyo games, K. Tange (in association with U. Inoue and Y. Tsuboi) designed two elegant tensile structures as sports halls, the larger comprising twin steel cables suspended between two masts, from which two doubly-curved saddle-form membranes are stretched to two reinforced-concrete curvilinear edge-members. The smaller is similar, but simpler, in conception. Both trace their ancestry to the cable-hung roof of the Sports Arena, Raleigh, N.C. (1954), by M. Nowicki and F. Severud (the structural engineer who collaborated with Eero Saarinen on the Dulles International Airport building and many other jobs). Nowicki's work has encouraged much research in the field of tensile structures, notably by Frei Otto, who designed the 'roof' of the **German Pavilion at Expo 1967, Montreal,** and the huge tent of pvc-coated polyester fabric suspended over part of the stadium, the sports hall and swimming pool of the **Olympic Games complex, Munich** (1972) (p. 1297B), by G. Benisch and his partners, and J. Joedicke. In both these enterprises the part played by the structural engineer, F. Leonhardt, was manifestly crucial.

The progress made in recent years in the techniques of display is mirrored in the design of museums, although the tendency of architects to stress the visual qualities of the building at the expense of those of the exhibits has been a common failing. A spectacular instance, which seems to equate the designer's inclinations with the visitor's needs, is the **Solomon R. Guggenheim Museum in New York,** by F. Lloyd Wright, finished in 1959 (p. 1298A). The building is conceived as a continuous spiral ramp embracing an open well, the diameter of the spiral increasing towards the dome, a principal source of natural light 28 m (92 ft) above ground. The gently curving walls, entirely unadorned inside and out, are slightly inclined towards the interior, a device which Wright believed provided the ideal surface for showing pictures. It is probably in Italy, however, that some of the best work has been done in the design of new museums or in extending and rehabilitating older galleries. The **Castello Sforzesco, Milan,** is characteristic of the flexible approach of Italian architects to museum design, in this case exemplified in a building of great historical interest, severely damaged in the Second World War, and of the unobtrusive native capacity to make the objects exhibited mould their own appropriate environment. The work, by L. B. Belgiojoso, E. Peressutti and E. N. Rogers, was carried out in two stages over ten years (1954–64). A somewhat similar programme was accomplished for the Civic Museum in the fourteenth-century **Castel Vecchio, Verona** (1961), by C. Scarpa, who has been responsible for a number of other museum schemes in Italy. In **Lisbon** the **Headquarters and Museum of the Fundação Calouste Gulbenkian** was completed in 1970 (p. 1298B). This large group of interrelated buildings of emphatic horizontal character—comprising an administrative block, a gallery for temporary exhibitions, the museum of the Gulbenkian Collection, a library, various auditoria, conference rooms and an amphitheatre—is disposed with great skill in a pleasantly landscaped park. Of its many qualities, one is beyond question technical excellence, the gamut of international expertise in the environmental sciences, so far as they affect the presentation and protection of works of art, being comprehensively applied. The architects were A. Pessoa, P. Cid and R. Athouguia, while the team of consultants included Sir J. L. Martin, Carlos Ramos, Franco Albini and William A. Allen. Memories of 'De Stijl' are revived in the **National Vincent van Gogh Museum, Amsterdam** (1973), by Gerrit-Thomas Rietveld, who had largely completed the design before his death in 1964. Alvar Aalto (in association with J.-J. Baruël) has been responsible for the **Nordjyllands Kunstmuseum, Ålborg, Denmark** (1972) (p. 1299A). Both are noteworthy for the excellence of the lighting, and an informal, hospitable atmosphere, uncommon in the museums of the past.

Since 1950 there has been more activity in theatre construction than at any period since the late nineteenth century. In Federal Germany, where generous public expenditure on the performing arts is an established characteristic of local patriotism, some thirty major theatres and concert halls have risen, the majority replacing war-destroyed buildings. An especially successful realization is the **Hall of the Berlin Philharmonic Orchestra, Berlin** (completed 1963) (p. 1300A), by Hans Scharoun (1893–1972), which achieves a rare unity between orchestra and audience by ranging the seats in relatively small open compartments about an arena 'stage'. Among the more interesting theatres are those at **Münster** (1956) (p. 1300B) and at **Gelsenkirchen** (1959), both designed by M. von Hausen, O. Rave and W. Ruhnau, who were associated with H. Deilmann in the initial phase of the Münster programme. The Münster playhouse makes effective use of a constricted site, on which it was placed diagonally in order to preserve (and incorporate as a freestanding sculptural feature) the Classical façade of the ruined Schloss Romberg. The Gelsenkirchen 'double-house', with its vast glass show-case front, brilliantly

A. German Pavilion, Brussels Expo, 1958. See p. 1308

B. Part of the suspended roof of the Olympic Games Stadium, Munich (1972).
See p. 1295

A. Solomon R. Guggenheim Museum, New York (1959). See p. 1296

B. Headquarters and Museum of the Fundação Calouste Gulbenkian, Lisbon (1970). See p. 1296

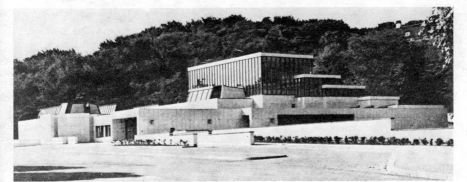

A. The Nordjyllands Kunstmuseum, Ålborg, Denmark (1972). See p. 1296

B. Festival Theatre, Chichester (1962). See p. 1301

C. The Playhouse, Nottingham (1964). See p. 1301

A. Hall of the Berlin Philharmonic Orchestra, Berlin (completed 1963).
See p. 1296

B. Münster Civic Theatre (1956). See p. 1296

lit at night, is a deliberate piece of flamboyant gaiety in a mournful expanse of industrial townscape. Another striking municipal theatre was completed in 1966 at **Ingolstadt,** a picturesque historic town on the Danube. Designed by the H.-W. Hämer and M.-B. Hämer Büro, K. Meyer-Rogge and N. Weber, it is an uncompromising example throughout of the board-marked concrete aesthetic. These theatres are generally of a high technical standard, as is the **City Theatre of S. Gallen** (1968), in Switzerland, by C. Paillard and H. Gügler, a successful if doctrinaire composition of interrelated hexagons, beautifully sited in a park. The hexagon is also the basic plan of the **Festival Theatre, Chichester** (1962) (p. 1299B), by A. J. P. Powell and J. H. Moya, a strictly functional building, in which all technical equipment is exposed and none of the 1,300 seats is more than 18 m (60 ft) from the stage. P. Moro and Partners have designed several remarkable theatres in Britain, including the **Playhouse, Nottingham** (1964) (p. 1299C), a well-balanced blend of humanity and efficiency, with an elegant inviting auditorium, its black slatted-wood wall-face contrasting with the gilded balcony parapet and bright blue seats. Other recent European theatres of high quality are: the **Folketshus, Stockholm** (1961), by S. Markelius; the **National Theatre, Helsinki** (1967), by T. Penttilä; the (new) **Abbey Theatre, Dublin** (1966), by M. Scott and Partners; the **Deutsche Oper, Berlin** (1961), by F. Bornemann and others; the two houses of the **Maison de la Culture, Grenoble** (1968), by A. Wogenscky, a disciple and colleague of Le Corbusier.

In the United States all else in theatre building pales before the sheer opulence of the **Lincoln Center, New York** (completed 1966) (p. 1302A), a showpiece in the monumental tradition and, perhaps, a logical expression of the richest society in history, comprising four major buildings, of which three—the New York State Theater, by Philip Johnson, the 4,000-seat Metropolitan Opera House, by Wallace K. Harrison, and the Philharmonic Hall, by Max Abramovitz—are symmetrically disposed about a formal plaza. The fourth, the Vivian Beaumont Theater, by Eero Saarinen, occupies a corner site. In a less conspicuous way, the universities of America have continued to make an extremely important contribution to the theatre and to theatre architecture. Many colleges have built theatres adaptable to every form of dramatic experiment. A typical instance is the **Loeb Drama Center, Harvard University, Cambridge, Mass.** (1960), by Hugh Stubbins and Associates. The Canadian firm of architects, Affleck, Desbarats, Dimakoupolos, Lebensold and Sise, have designed and carried out three large theatre schemes in less than a decade: the **Salle Pelletier,** an opera house and concert hall in **Montreal** (1964); the playhouse of the **Confederation Centre, Charlottetown** (1964); and the three theatres incorporated in the **National Arts Centre, Ottawa** (1969). In Australia the saga of **Sydney Opera House** is apparently over. The beautiful sail-like shells, designed in 1957 by Jørn Utzon of Denmark (p. 1302B), billow over a complex building opened to the public in 1973.

A notable step towards the provision of a comprehensively planned, architect-designed, environment for popular leisure has been taken in Languedoc-Roussillon, since some 180 km (110 miles) of the Mediterranean littoral, extending eastward from the Spanish border, were scheduled by the French government in 1961 for development as a holiday zone. This hitherto neglected region will have six major resort towns and be able to accommodate nearly half a million people simultaneously in hotels, flats, single-family housing and on camping sites. Two of these towns, the marina ports of **La Grande-Motte,** by J. Balladur and **Leucate-Barcarès,** by G. Candilis and partners, are already in being and a third, **Le Cap d'Agde,** by J. Le Couteur, is well advanced. Candilis headed the multi-disciplined team, who prepared the regional development plan, and with A. Josic and S.

A. The Lincoln Center, New York (completed 1966). See p. 1301

B. Sydney Opera House (1957–73). See p. 1301

Woods has been responsible for planning the overspill town of **Le Mirail at Toulouse,** now under construction, which will eventually house 100,000 people, and for much housing throughout the Communauté française far above the average architectural level of low-rent dwellings. The **holiday flats at Le Grau-du-Roi** (1973–) (p. 1304A) are typical of the work of Candilis, Josic and Woods for the scheme.

The success of Scandinavia, and especially of Sweden, in shaping the urban environment has generally been due to foresight in land acquisition. In the case of **Stockholm,** the City Council embarked more than sixty years ago on a policy of systematic land purchase and by 1952, when the first Greater Stockholm Plan was introduced, they already owned all the sites required for orderly expansion outside the city boundaries and for carefully planned renewal of the central areas. The development of the satellite towns of **Vällingby, Farsta** and **Täby** was closely co-ordinated with a highly organized public transport network. The guidance of Sven Markelius, both as town-planner and City Architect, was of great consequence to the programme. The **garden city of Tapiola** (p. 1304C), 10 km (6 miles) from the centre of Helsinki, spaciously planned for 17,000 residents in a traditional Finnish landscape of forest and water, has little difficulty in qualifying as the most enticing of all the new (or satellite) towns built since the Second World War. The natural surroundings were the principal architects, but others who have helped are Alvar Aalto, (the late) Viljo Revell, Aarne Ervi, Kaija and Heikki Siren, A. Blomsted and M. Tavio. A wide variety of housing types are exploited at Tapiola, and there is no evidence of the architectural monotony which so disappointingly characterizes many new towns elsewhere.

Two special problems have concerned the Netherlands, hindered by a constantly-growing overabundant population: the continual need to reclaim land from the sea and convert it to economically effective and habitable use, and the remoulding and renewal of war-destroyed urban environments, a task made more difficult by the Dutch preference (shared with the British) for low-rise low density housing and by the need to preserve green spaces in a country where the distinction between town and country threatens to disappear. The second problem has been admirably solved in **Rotterdam,** which suffered terrible damage in 1940 and 1944, and in its satellite communities (e.g. Pendrecht, Hoogvliet, etc.). Of Rotterdam's many exemplary features, the **Lijnbaan** (1954) (p. 1304E), designed by J. B. Bakema and J. H. van den Broek, a pedestrian shopping way extending from the railway station to the commercial centre and over 600 m (700 yards) in length, subsequently became a model for all traffic-free precincts.

In different circumstances, there have been spectacular instances of urban renewal in other countries. In downtown **Montreal** a focal point of development is the **Place Ville-Marie,** where a forty-eight-floor block, cruciform in plan (1967) (p. 1304D), by I. M. Pei and H. Cobb, in association with Affleck, Desbarats, Dimakoupolos, Lebensold and Sise, presides amid a spaciously disposed cluster of commercial towers above an elaborate system of subterranean communications, including half a mile of sheltered shopping promenades which will eventually extend to 6 miles. **Australia Square, Sydney** (1970) (p. 1304F), crowned by a fifty-storey circular office-tower, largely composed of lightweight concrete elements and with a revolving restaurant on the 47th floor, by H. Seidler and partners, has been compared with the Place Ville-Marie, which by intention was planned for completion simultaneously with the Montreal International Exposition of 1967. This event offered copious opportunities for architectural experiment, none of which caused more controversy than **'Habitat',** by M. Safdie, a composition of 354 precast concrete dwelling boxes, each weighing 85 tons, lifted into place by crane to form 158 apartments of various sizes and combinations (p. 1304B). Quite another

A. Holiday flats, Le Grau-du-Roi (1973–).
See p. 1303

B. 'Habitat', Montreal Expo
1967. Dwelling boxes.
See p. 1303

C. Houses at the garden city of Tapiola,
near Helsinki (1955–). See p. 1303

D. Place Ville-Marie, Montreal
(1967). See p. 1303

E. The Lijnbaan, Rotterdam (1954).
See p. 1303

F. Office tower, Australia
Square, Sydney (1970).
See p. 1303

A. The City Hall, Boston, Mass. (1969). See p. 1307

B. Falmer House, Sussex University, Brighton (1966). See p. 1307

C. University of East Anglia, near Norwich (1967). See p. 1307

A. S. Bride, East Kilbride, Lanarkshire (1964). See p. 1307

B. S. Anne, Düren (1956). See p. 1308

C. Engineering Building, Leicester University (1963). See p. 1307

sort of development is demonstrated in the **City Hall, Boston, Mass.** (1969) (p.
1305A), by G. Kallmann, N. M. McKinnell and E. F. Knowles, a stark impressive
trapezoid of exposed concrete and brick, apparently doorless and therefore open to
the public by night and day. It is an architectural extension of the huge brick-paved
City Square and the *pièce de résistance* of a new civic centre, which has given space
and a measure of unity to a district badly in need of regeneration, while also, if
indirectly, stimulating schemes for restoring the historically important Faneuil
Hall, Quincy Market and the waterfront nearby.

A promising experiment in the provision of a civilized urban environment has
been undertaken for and by the **City of London** on thirty-five bomb-scorched
acres north of London Wall. Known as the **Barbican,** the area is developed as a
'genuine residential neighbourhood' of mixed and pleasantly varied high- and
medium-rise flats and maisonettes, primarily for people who work in the 'City'.
The scheme, which is substantially completed, includes a large school, a 1,250-seat
theatre, a 2,000-seat concert hall, public library, art gallery, shops and restaurants,
as well as the Guildhall School of Music. Historic features, such as the church of
S. Giles, are ingeniously and sensitively woven into the fabric of the design.
Pedestrian and wheeled traffic are segregated by introducing an extensive 'podium'
or artificial ground level. Chamberlin, Powell and Bon are the architects.

The 1960s saw many new towns, generated in Britain since the New Towns' Act
of 1946, reach an appreciable state of maturity. Fruit of the garden city concept of
Ebenezer Howard, first proclaimed in 1898 and exemplified soon afterwards at
Letchworth and Welwyn, and exponents of the neighbourhood-unit theory (Cum-
bernauld, by Sir Hugh Wilson and partners, is an exception), they have had great
influence on the thinking of urbanists throughout the world. In terms of design,
however, a balance between architectural unity and variety of townscape has
proved hard to attain, although there is no lack of good individual buildings. One
example is the Catholic church of **S. Bride, East Kilbride, Lanarkshire** (1964)
(p. 1306A), by Gillespie, Kidd and Coia, the interior recalling Ronchamp despite
the use of a coarse-textured brick in place of concrete.

Enterprise in developing new towns in Britain has been followed in the past
decade by radical planning for higher education. Since 1960 the number of university students in the British Isles has more than doubled and the number of universities has risen from twenty-two to nearly fifty. Many of these are civic universities
or greatly expanded colleges of advanced technology, but seven are independent
self-contained communities of the American campus-type and present interesting
and strikingly dissimilar interpretations of the concrete academic environment. At
York, where Sir Robert Matthew, Johnson-Marshall and partners were the architects (with Andrew Derbyshire in charge of the programme) a modified version of
the CLASP system of prefabricated building was widely used; **Sussex,** near
Brighton, is spaciously sited, sympathetic in scale and architecturally uniform in
the well-established sculptural idiom of the university's architects, Sir Basil Spence,
Bonnington and Collins, of pale-red fair-faced brick, cast concrete panels and
rhythmic patterns of segmental arches (p. 1305B) (cf. the Guards Barracks, Knights-
bridge, London, 1970); **Lancaster,** by P. Shepheard and G. Epstein and others, is
characterized by coherence, concentration, urbanity and visual diversity; and **East
Anglia,** close to Norwich, which is memorable for the stepped, six- and seven-level
residential terraces, designed by Denys Lasdun to face open parkland and the river
Yare (p. 1305C), is among the most appealing buildings of the present century. A
number of equally interesting additions to existing universities have been made.
The composite structure designed for the **Engineering Department, Leicester
University** (1963) (p. 1306C), by J. Stirling and J. Gowan, attracted great attention,

an immaculate instance of functionalism, as it was understood by protagonists of the machine aesthetic half a century ago.

In the last few years, 'modern' architecture has suffered many losses from among its leading practitioners: André Lurçat, especially remembered for the **school at Villejuif, Paris** (1933), an early French interpretation of the Bauhaus manner and model for much subsequent architecture; Egon Eiermann, an architect of many facets, author of the **German Pavilion, Brussels Exposition** (1958) (p. 1297A), the curious flat-roofed octagonal **Gedächtniskirche, Berlin** (1961) in its rebuilt inward-looking form, the **Federal German Embassy, Washington, D.C.** (1964) and many buildings marked by simplicity, precise detailing and discreet elegance; Arne Jacobsen, an artist in the Danish brick tradition (of which Kay Fisker had also been a master in the 1920s and 1930s), who became the curtain wall's most accomplished executant (p. 1266); the Catholic mystic Rudolf Schwarz, designer of a number of austere, but inspiring churches, in which the plan often assumes symbolic forms (**S. Michael, Frankfurt-am-Main,** 1954; **Mary the Queen, Saarbrücken,** 1959; **S. Anne, Düren,** 1956, p. 1306B); F. R. S. Yorke, who had worked with Marcel Breuer in the early 1930s and later, in partnership with E. Rosenberg and C. Mardall, realized a long line of undramatic buildings of consistently high quality, of which **Gatwick Airport, Surrey,** is best known to the public; Wells Coates, another early champion in Britain of the Modern Movement, who perhaps achieved more success as an industrial designer than in architecture; Ernst May, already a leader in the 1920s, architect of the **Römerstadt housing development, Frankfurt-am-Main** (1925-30), much studied at the time and since, who returned to West Germany (after many years of self-chosen exile) to become a key figure in post-war urbanism; and Hugo Häring, a principal designer of the very admired **Siemensstadt housing scheme, Berlin-Charlottenburg** (1928), who—unlike so many of his contemporaries—remained in Germany during the baleful years of National Socialism. As a result he built little, although he influenced many in his lifelong advocacy of organic principles in architecture.

An organic building can mean different things to different people. To Häring it had implied an organism growing out of the nature of its function, a concept not conflicting widely with the current inclination to exploit in formal terms the apparatus of environmental technology in preference to that of structure, i.e. to turn to architectural account the mechanical services, which are a building's arteries and ensure the performance of function in the parts and the whole. We have seen the characteristic dramatized by Kahn in the Richards Medical Research Center (p. 1290): it then reappeared in the lift towers of a remarkable, if unrealized, project by Alison and Peter Smithson for Sheffield University (1953), and is fundamental to the Utopian urban space-frame proposals of the 1960s of Yona Friedman, Schulze-Fielitz, Richard Dietrich and the authors of 'Metastadt', and the Japanese 'Metabolists', if only because it cannot be hidden. In England a group of young architects, some of whom were working in the Architectural Department of the London County (now Greater London) Council, formulated the theory of 'Plug-in City', and featured it in their own periodical *Archigram*, which was soon to enjoy an international vogue. They were also members of the team of designers who clothed in vigorous configurations of concrete the pipe-runs and heating and ventilation ducts of the Queen Elizabeth Concert Hall (1967) on London's South Bank (Architect to the Council, Sir Hubert Bennett).

Parallel phenomena, and potentially more significant, are an absolute rejection by younger architects everywhere, of monumentality and—in the fields of domestic work—an ardent interest in vernacular building and the simplest forms of habitat (e.g. man's 'natural' home, 'drop-out' shelters, etc.). The rigours of the latter, however, are presumably to be preferred when tempered by the technological paraphernalia supposedly ensuring minimal drudgery and an unpolluted life. Inherent in these attitudes, and not least in the Utopian systems mentioned above, as the names of two indicate, is a ready adaptability to change. Future historians will no doubt take pleasure in assessing their validity.

BIBLIOGRAPHY

BANHAM, R. *The Architecture of the Well-tempered Environment.* London, 1969.
—. *Theory and Design in the First Machine Age.* London, 1960.
COLLINS, P. *Changing Ideals in Modern Architecture, 1750–1950.* London, 1965 and 1967.
—. *Concrete: the Vision of a New Architecture.* London, 1959.
DOXIADIS, C. A. *Ekistics: an Introduction to the Science of Human Settlements.* London, 1968.
FITCH, J. M. *American Building: The Environmental Forces that shape it.* New York, 1972.
GIEDION, S. *Space, Time and Architecture.* 5th ed. Cambridge, Mass. and London, 1968.
GROPIUS, W. *The New Architecture and the Bauhaus.* London, 1935.
HATJE, G. *Encyclopaedia of Modern Architecture.* London, 1963.
HITCHCOCK, H.-R. *Architecture: Nineteenth and Twentieth Centuries.* Harmondsworth and Baltimore, 1958 and 1970.
HITCHCOCK, H.-R. and JOHNSON, P. C. *The International Style.* New York, 1932.
HOWARD, E. *Garden Cities of Tomorrow.* 1898. Reprinted, London, 1964–5.
HOWARTH, T. *Charles Rennie Mackintosh and the Modern Movement.* London, 1952.
JACOBUS, J. *Twentieth-Century Architecture 1940–65.* London and New York, 1966.
JAFFÉ, H. L. C. *De Stijl 1917–31.* Amsterdam and London, 1956.
JOEDICKE, J. *Architecture since 1945.* London, New York and Stuttgart, 1969. (Has very good bibliography.)
—. *A History of Modern Architecture.* London and New York, 1959 and 1962.
—. *Shell Architecture.* London and New York, 1963.
LE CORBUSIER. *Vers une Architecture.* Paris, 1923, English editions 1927 and 1947.
—. *My work.* London, 1960.
—. *Oeuvre Complète.* 7 vols, Zurich, 1935–65.
MUMFORD, L. *Art and Technics.* New York and London, 1952.
—. *Technics and Civilization.* London, 1934.
NAYLOR, G. *The Bauhaus.* London, 1968.
PEVSNER, N. *Pioneers of Modern Design from William Morris to Walter Gropius.* London, 1936, Harmondsworth, 1960 and other editions.
RICHARDS, J. M. *An Introduction to Modern Architecture.* London, 1962, and many other editions. (Has very good bibliography.)
SHARP, D. C. *Modern Architecture and Expressionism.* London, 1966.
SIEGEL, C. *Structure and Form in Modern Architecture.* London, 1962.
WRIGHT, F. L. *A Testament.* New York, 1957.

COMPARATIVE ARCHES

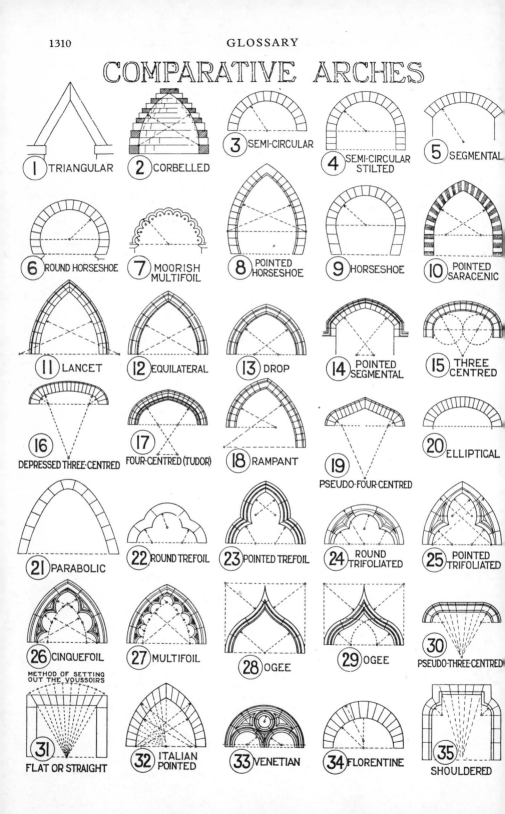

1 TRIANGULAR

2 CORBELLED

3 SEMI-CIRCULAR

4 SEMI-CIRCULAR STILTED

5 SEGMENTAL

6 ROUND HORSESHOE

7 MOORISH MULTIFOIL

8 POINTED HORSESHOE

9 HORSESHOE

10 POINTED SARACENIC

11 LANCET

12 EQUILATERAL

13 DROP

14 POINTED SEGMENTAL

15 THREE CENTRED

16 DEPRESSED THREE-CENTRED

17 FOUR-CENTRED (TUDOR)

18 RAMPANT

19 PSEUDO-FOUR-CENTRED

20 ELLIPTICAL

21 PARABOLIC

22 ROUND TREFOIL

23 POINTED TREFOIL

24 ROUND TRIFOLIATED

25 POINTED TRIFOLIATED

26 CINQUEFOIL

27 MULTIFOIL

28 OGEE

29 OGEE

30 PSEUDO-THREE-CENTRED

METHOD OF SETTING OUT THE VOUSSOIRS

31 FLAT OR STRAIGHT

32 ITALIAN POINTED

33 VENETIAN

34 FLORENTINE

35 SHOULDERED

GLOSSARY

Abacus (Lat. *abacus*=table, tablet). A slab forming the crowning member of a capital. In Greek Doric, square without chamfer or moulding (pp. 205A, 207). In Greek Ionic, thinner with ovolo moulding only (p. 224B). In Roman Ionic and Corinthian, the sides are hollowed on plan and have the angles cut off (pp. 275J, 288C). In Romanesque, the abacus is deeper but projects less and is moulded with rounds and hollows, or merely chamfered on the lower edge (pp. 561B, C, E, 562A, B). In Gothic, the circular or octagonal abacus was favoured in England (pp. 561L, Q, U, 562), while the square or octagonal abacus is a French feature (p. 619A, C).

Abutment. Solid masonry which resists the lateral pressure of an arch (pp. 271, 378, 589).

Acanthus. A plant whose leaves, conventionally treated, form the lower portions of the Corinthian capital (p. 236).

Acropolis (Gk., upper city). Most ancient Greek cities were on hills, the citadel on the summit being known as the Acropolis, containing the principal temples and treasure-houses (p. 198).

Acroteria (Gk., summits or extremities). Blocks resting on the vertex and lower extremities of the pediment to support statuary or ornaments (p. 211A–D).

Adobe (Sp.). Sun-dried (i.e. unbaked) brick, often used as the core of a wall behind a facing of stone bricks.

Adyton or **Adytum.** The most sacred room of a Greek temple. Usually approached from the naos by a doorway.

Aedicule (Lat. *aedicula*=a little house). A small temple-like arrangement originally limited to shrines but which became a common motif in the Classical system: columns or pilasters carry a pedimented entablature and enframe a niche or a window. The term 'tabernacle' sometimes is used to convey a similar meaning (p. 786D, F).

Agora. The Greek equivalent of the Roman forum, a place of open-air assembly or market (p. 248C).

Aisles (Lat. *ala*=wing). Lateral divisions parallel with the nave in a basilica or church (pp. 353, 356J, 590, 1016D).

Alabaster. A very white, fine-grained, translucent, gypseous mineral, used to a small extent as a building material in the ancient Middle East, Greece, Rome, the Eastern Empire of Byzantium and, nearer to our own day, by certain Victorian architects for its decorative qualities (and Biblical associations). In Italy a technique was evolved many centuries ago (and still survives) of treating alabaster to simulate marble, while there seems little doubt that in the past marble was often mistakenly described as alabaster.

Alae (Lat. *ala*=wing). Small side extensions, alcoves or recesses opening from the atrium (or peristyle) of a Roman house (pp. 332B, 333).

Alure (Fr. *aller*=to go). An alley, walk or passage. A gallery behind a parapet (pp. 528, 575A).

Ambo (Gk. *ambōn*=stage, pulpit). A raised pulpit from which the Epistle and the Gospel were read (pp. 349C, H, K, 350A).

Ambry or **Aumbry.** A cupboard or recess in a church to contain sacred vessels.

Ambulatory (Lat. *ambulare*=to walk). The cloister or covered passage around the east end of a church, behind the altar (pp. 590B, 591A–F).

Amorino (pl. **amorini**). Diminutive of Amor, the Roman god of love, identified with the Greek Eros. Amorini were usually represented by Renaissance artists as cherubs.

Amphi-antis. A temple with columns between antae (i.e. a recessed portico) at both ends. None such survives (pp. 202, 203B).

Amphi-prostyle. A temple with portico at both ends (pp. 203D, 228A).

Ancones (Gk., elbow or hollow). Consoles on either side of a doorway supporting a cornice (pp. 801L, 824D). Also, projections left on blocks of stone such as drums of columns for use in hoisting and setting in position (p. 205G).

Annulet (Lat. *annulus*=a ring). A small flat fillet encircling a column. It is several times repeated under the ovolo or echinus of the Doric Capital (p. 205A).

Anta (pl. **antae**). A pilaster terminating the side wall of a Greek temple, with base and capital differing from those of adjacent columns; also seen in Egyptian temples (*see* Pilaster) (pp. 11L, 228B, E, F).

Antefixae (Lat. *ante*=before+*figo*=I fix). Ornamental blocks, fixed vertically at regular intervals along the lower edge of a roof, to cover the ends of tiles (p. 205H).

Anthemion (Gk., a flower). A honeysuckle or palmette ornament of several varieties, in cornices, neckings of Ionic capitals and elsewhere in Greek and Roman architecture (pp. 222R, S, 254G).

Antiquarian. The phase in Western European Renaissance architecture, *c.* 1750–1830, when renewed inspiration was sought from ancient Greek and Roman and from Mediaeval architecture. Its more concrete manifestations were the Greek and Gothic Revivals (q.q.v.), both continuing further into the 19th century.

Apodyterium (Gk.). A room for undressing in a Roman bath-house (pp. 296B, 302D).

Apophyge (Gk., a flying off). The cavetto or concave sweep at the top and bottom of the column shaft connecting it with the fillet (p. 222R, S).

Apse (Lat., an arch). The circular or multangular termination of a church sanctuary, first applied to a Roman basilica. The apse is a Continental feature, and contrasts with the square termination of English Gothic churches (pp. 291B, E, 353C, E, 465E–G, 590).

Apteral (Gk., without wings). A temple without columns on the sides (p. 203 A–D).

Arabesque. Surface decoration, light and fanciful in character, much used by Arabic artists, in elaborate continuations of lines. Applied also to the combination of flowing lines interwoven with flowers, fruit, and figures as used by Renaissance artists (pp. 423C, 429B, 943J).

Araeostyle. A term used when the space between two columns is more than three diameters (p. 207A).

Arcade. A range of arches supported on piers or columns, attached to or detached from the wall (pp. 306A, 730).

Arch (Lat. *arcus*=an arc of a curve, an arch). A structure of wedge-shaped blocks over an opening, so disposed as to hold together when supported only from the sides. *See* p. 1310.

Arch-braced Roof. *See* **Collar-braced Roof.**

Architrave (Gk., chief beam). The beam or lowest division of the entablature, which extends from column to column (p. 205A). The term is also applied to the moulded frame round a door or window (pp. 234C, D, 801J, L).

Archivolt. The mouldings on the face of an arch, and following its contour (pp. 296A, 320, 489K).

Arcuated (Lat. *arcuatus*=bent like a bow). A building, building system or style of architecture, of which the principal constructive feature is the arch (e.g. Roman). Cf. **Trabeated.**

Arris. The sharp edge formed by the meeting of two surfaces (pp. 207E, 242J).

Art Nouveau (Fr., new art). A decorative movement in European architecture, heralded in the 1880s and flourishing 1893–1907, characterized by flowing and sinuous naturalistic ornament and avoidance of historical architectural traits (p. 1193). *See also* **Moderne Style, Jugendstil, Stile Liberty.**

Asbestos. A fibrous mineral, used as a building material, which has high resistance to fire.

Ashlar. Masonry of smooth squared stones in regular courses, in contradistinction to rubble work.

Astragal (Gk., knuckle-bone). A small semicircular moulding, often ornamented with a bead or reel (p. 241B). Torus is the name applied to large mouldings of similar section (p. 241L).

Astylar. A treatment of a façade without columns (pp. 800, 802).

Atlantes. Carved male figures serving as pillars, also called Telamones (p. 209J).

Atrium. An apartment in a Roman house, forming an entrance hall or court, the roof open to the sky in the centre (p. 332A, B, D, F). Sometimes the rim of the roof aperture (compluvium) was supported by four or more columns. In Early Christian and later architecture, a forecourt (pp. 353C, E, 384G).

Attic. A term first applied in the Renaissance period to the upper storey of a building above the main cornice; also applied to rooms in a roof.

Attic base. A base to a Classic column, so named by Vitruvius, and formed of upper and lower torus and scotia joined by fillets, and the most usual of all column bases (p. 242H, S).

Aumbry. *See* **Ambry.**

Aureole (Lat. *aurum* = gold). A quadrangular, circular, or elliptic halo or frame surrounding the figure of Christ, the Virgin, or certain saints. Also known as the Mandorla or Vesica Piscis (q.v.). When a circular halo envelops only the head, it is called a Nimbus.

Bailey. Open area or court of a fortified castle (p. 679D).

Baldac(c)hino. A canopy supported by columns, generally placed over an altar or tomb, also known as a 'ciborium' (p. 843B).

Ball-flower. The ornament of Decorated Gothic architecture, possibly from a flower form or a horse-bell.

Balloon Frame. A method of light timber framing, long established in the United States for domestic buildings, in which the corner posts and studs (intermediate posts) are continuous from sill to roof plate, the joists carried on girts (ties) spiked to, or let into, the studs, and all these elements secured by simple nailing.

Baluster. A pillar or column supporting a handrail or coping, a series forming a balustrade (pp. 1001D, 1027J, L).

Baptistery. A separate building to contain a font, for the baptismal rite (pp. 470B, E–G, 472C).

Barbican. An outwork of a mediaeval castle, of which the object was to protect a drawbridge or the entrance (p. 679A, B).

Barge board. A board fixed to the verge of a pitched roof (p. 1142B).

Baroque. A term applied to design during the late Renaissance period (1600–1760 in Italy), when architecture reached a characteristic, non-Roman expression; rich, bold and vital.

Barrel Vault. A continuous vault of semi-circular section, used at most periods and in many countries from Roman times to the present (p. 627A–C). Also called a **Tunnel Vault, Wagonhead Vault,** or **Wagon Vault.**

Bartizan. A small, overhanging turret (p. 680B).

Bar Tracery. *See* **Tracery.**

Base (Gk. *basis* = that on which one stands). The lower portion of any structure or architectural feature.

Basement. The lowest stage of a building; also an underground storey.

Basilica (Gk. *basileus* = a king). A hall for the administration of justice.

Bas-relief (It. *basso rilievo*). Carving in low or shallow relief, on a background.

Basse-cour or **Base Court.** An inferior court or service yard, generally at the back of a house.

Bath Stone. Oolite building stone, not confined to the area of Bath, Somerset, used throughout English architectural history.

Batter. A term applied to a wall with an inclined face.

Battlement. A parapet having a series of indentations or embrasures, between which are raised portions known as merlons (p. 680A).

Baulk-tie. A tie-beam joining the wall-posts of a timber roof and serving also to prevent walls from spreading (p. 635). Cf. **Tie-bar.**

Bays. Compartments into which the nave or roof of a building is divided (p. 589). The term is also used for projecting windows (p. 687C).

Bead. A small cylindrical moulding often carved with an ornament resembling a string of beads (pp. 241B, 242P, Q) (*see* Astragal).

Beak-head. A Norman enrichment like a bird's head and beak.

Belfry (Old Fr. *berfrei* = a tower—not connected with 'bell'). A term generally applied to the upper room in a tower in which the bells are hung, and thus often to the tower itself.

Bell Capital. The solid part, core or drum of a capital, especially of the Corinthian and Composite Orders or of a Corinthianesque character in French and English Gothic. So-called 'bell' capitals, moulded and without foliated ornament, occur frequently in the Mediaeval ecclesiastical architecture of both countries (p. 561L, Q, U).

Belvedere (It., beautiful view). A roofed but open-sided structure affording an extensive view, usually located at the roof-top of a dwelling but sometimes an independent building on an eminence in a landscape or formal garden (pp. 799F, 830E).

Bema (Gk., a raised platform). A raised stage reserved for the clergy in Early Christian churches; it forms the germ of the transept when expanded laterally in later architecture (p. 353C, E).

Billet. A Norman moulding of short

cylinders or square pieces at regular intervals.

Bipedales (Lat. *bipedalis*=two feet long). Tiles, 2 ft square, used by the Romans for bonding masonry.

Bird's Beak. A moulding used in Greek architecture, which in section is thought to resemble the beak of a bird (pp. 241K, 242E).

Bit-hilâni. Syrian porched house (pp. 65F, G, 71).

Blind Storey. *See* **Triforium.**

Boss (Fr. *bosse*=lump or knob). A projecting ornament at the intersection of the ribs of ceilings, whether vaulted or flat. The term is also applied to the carved ends of weather-mouldings of doors and windows (pp. 628C, 630C).

Bouleuterion. A Greek Senate building or council house (p. 199).

Bowtell (perhaps from its resemblance to an arrow shaft or bolt). A Norman convex moulding (usually three-quarters of a circle in section) applied to an angle—a form of roll moulding (p. 563B, C, D). Pointed bowtell is a roll moulding in which two faces meet in a blunt arris.

Brace. In framed structures, a subsidiary member placed near and across the angle of two main members in order to stiffen them, as in carpentry roofs.

Brace-moulding. *See* **Bracket Moulding.**

Bracket. A projecting member to support a weight, generally formed with scrolls or volutes; when carrying the upper members of a cornice, brackets are generally termed Modillions or Consoles (*see also* Ancones) (pp. 278B, C, 783B).

Bracket Moulding (also called 'brace' or 'double ogee'). A late Gothic moulding consisting of two ogee mouldings with convex faces adjoining, resembling a printer's 'brace' or bracket (p. 563V).

Branch Tracery. A form of tracery characteristic of German Gothic, suggesting the branches of a tree.

Brise Soleil (Fr., sun break). A screen to break the glare of sunshine upon windows. In recent architecture such screens often take the form of louvres (q.v.), and are usually made a permanent and effective part of the architecture (p. 1276E).

Brochs. A vernacular term for primitive Scottish forts.

Broach Spire. An octagonal spire rising without a parapet above a tower, with pyramidal forms at the angles of the tower, as in Early English churches.

Brownstone. A brown sandstone found in New Jersey, Connecticut, Pennsylvania and elsewhere. A popular building material in the 19th century in New York and the eastern United States.

Buttress (Old Fr. *bouter*=to bear against). A mass of masonry built against a wall to resist the pressure of an arch or vault. A flying buttress is an arch starting from a detached pier and abutting against a wall to take the thrust of the vaulting (p. 589).

Byzantine Architecture. The style evolved at Constantinople (Byzantium, now Istanbul) in the 5th century, and still the style of the Eastern or Greek Church.

Cable. A Norman moulding enrichment like a twisted rope (p. 562A, B).

Caen Stone. A building stone from Caen, Normandy, sometimes used in the construction of English mediaeval buildings, despite difficulties of transport.

Caisson. *See* **Coffer.**

Caldarium or **Calidarium.** A chamber with hot water baths in a Roman baths building (pp. 296B, 302D).

Camber. Slight rise or upward curve of an otherwise horizontal structure.

Cames. Slender strips of lead, grooved at the sides for the reception of pieces of glass, in casement, stained glass and other types of window.

Campanile (It. *campana*=bell). An Italian name for a bell-tower, generally detached from the main building.

Cancelli (It. *cancello*=barrier). Low screen walls enclosing the choir in Early Christian churches, hence 'chancel' (q.v.) (p. 349K).

Canephorae (Gk., basket-carriers). Sculptured female figures bearing baskets on their heads (p. 254D).

Cantoria (It., choir, chantry). In the Renaissance the term was generally used to denote a singers' gallery, often elaborately carved, in a major church (p. 784B).

Capital (Lat. *caput*=head). The crowning feature of a column or pilaster.

Carrara Marble. A snow-white marble from the Carrara district of Tuscany, although the band of rock also extends far to the north of this area. It was the favoured medium of Michelangelo. It was known to the Romans as *Luna*.

Caryatids. Sculptured female figures used as columns or supports (p. 233).

Casemate. A vaulted chamber contrived in the thickness of a fortress wall, usually with embrasures for defence. The term is often applied nowadays to other forms of armoured enclosure (e.g. gunturret). Hence 'casemated', meaning strongly fortified.

Casement. A wide hollow used in late Gothic (p. 563W, X), so called as it encased bunches of foliage.

Casement Window. A window of which the opening lights are hinged at the side and open in the manner of a door.

Casino. A summer- or garden-house of ornamental character.

Castellation. Fortifying a house and providing it with battlements.

Cast-iron. Iron shaped by pouring into moulds. Cast-iron was used to a rapidly increasing extent in building works from the late 18th century (e.g. the Iron Bridge, Coalbrookdale, p. 1122B) until superseded by steel in the mid-19th.

Caulicoli (Lat. *caulis* = a stalk). The eight stalks supporting the volutes in the Corinthian capital (p. 236).

Cavetto (It., from Lat. *cavus* = hollow). A simple concave moulding (p. 241D).

Cella (Lat.). The chief apartment of a temple, where the image of a god stood (p. 275).

Cenotaph (Gk., an empty tomb). A sepulchral monument to a person buried elsewhere.

Chaînes (Fr. *chaîne* = a chain). Vertical strips of rusticated masonry rising between the horizontal string-mouldings and cornice of a building, and so dividing the façades into bays or panels (p. 894B). A popular mode of wall-ornamentation in French 17th-century domestic architecture.

Chaitya. A Buddhist meeting-hall (p. 97).

Chamfer (Fr. *chanfrein* = channel). A diagonal cutting off of an arris formed by two surfaces meeting at an angle. Hollow chamfer, the same but concave in form, like the cavetto.

Chancel (Lat. *cancellus* = a screen). The space for clergy and choir, separated by a screen from the body of the church, more usually referred to as the **Choir** (pp. 590, 591).

Chantry (Fr. *chanter* = to sing). A small chapel, usually attached to a church, endowed with lands or by other means, for the maintenance of priests to sing or say mass for whomever the donor directs.

Chapels Places for worship, in churches, in honour of particular saints. Sometimes erected as separate buildings.

Chapter House (Lat. *capitulum* = council). The place of assembly for abbot, prior and members of a monastery, often reached from the cloisters (p. 663D). In England, it was usually polygonal on plan, with a vault resting on a central pillar (pp. 639C, 640E, F), but sometimes oblong (p. 641B).

Chattri (Hindi, *chatta* = umbrella). An umbrella-shaped cupola (p. 443C).

Chevet (Fr. *chef* = head). A circular or polygonal apse when surrounded by an ambulatory, off which are chapels (p. 663D).

Chevron (Fr., rafter). A zigzag moulding used in Norman architecture, and so called from a pair of rafters, which gave this form (p. 562B, C).

Choir. *See* **Chancel.**

Churrigueresque. An expression of Spanish Baroque architecture and sculpture associated with the Churriguera family of artists and architects (p. 956), characterized by a lavish, even fantastic, but not inharmonious, decorative exuberance. In architecture a recurrent feature was the richly garlanded spiral column.

Ciborium. *See* **Baldachino.**

Cimborio. The Spanish term for a lantern or raised structure above a roof admitting light into the interior (p. 767D, F).

Cinquefoil (Fr. *cinq feuilles* = five leaves). In tracery an arrangement of five foils or openings, terminating in cusps.

Cladding. An outer veneer of various materials applied to a building façade.

Classic, Classical. The architecture originating in ancient Greece and Rome, the rules and forms of which were largely revived in the Renaissance in Europe and elsewhere. **Classicism,** a classic idiom or style.

Claustra. A term sometimes used in the late 19th and early 20th century to describe panels, pierced with geometrical designs, as employed by the French architect Auguste Perret in certain of his reinforced-concrete buildings (p. 1256 A, B).

Clear-storey, clere-story, clearstory or **clerestory** (probably from Fr. *clair* = light). An upper stage in a building with windows above adjacent roofs; especially applied to this feature in a church (p. 589).

Clepsydra (Gk., a stealing away of water). A water-clock or instrument for measuring time by the discharge of water through a small opening (p. 238F–H).

Cloisters (Lat. *claustrum* = a secluded place). Covered passages round an open space or garth, connecting the church to the chapter house, refectory, and other parts of the monastery. They were generally south of the nave and west of the transept, probably to secure sunlight and warmth (p. 663D).

Coemeteria. Underground burial places, in ancient Rome often taking the form of vaults each containing a number of interments in funerary receptacles (p. 313).

Coffers. Sunk panels, caissons or lacunaria formed in ceilings, vaults, and domes (p. 289C).

Collar-braced Roof. A logical development of the cruck-type timber frame (*see* **Crucks**), in which the principal rafters are raised upon walls (instead of rising from the ground) and linked close to the ridge by a short tie-beam (also called a collar-beam) to form an A-shaped truss or collar. When this collar is additionally stiffened underneath by braces extending from the principal rafters, the roof is described as arch-braced (pp. 633D, 635).

Collar-purlin. A purlin (longitudinal member) laid centrally and stiffening the collars (*see* Collar-braced Roof) of an open timber-framed roof, and supported by a crown-post rising from a tie-beam. If the roof was long, more than one crown-post (and, therefore, more than one tie-beam) might be needed (p. 635).

Column (Lat. *columna* = a post). A vertical support, generally consisting of base, circular shaft, and spreading capital.

Compartment. A division or separate part of a building or of an element of a building (*see* **Bays** and **Severy**).

Compluvium (Lat. *pluvia* = rain). A quadrangular opening in the atrium of a Roman house, towards which the roof sloped so as to throw the rain water into a shallow cistern or impluvium in the floor.

Composite. *See* **Order.**

Concrete (Lat. *concretus* = compounded). A mixture of water, sand, stone and a binder (today generally Portland cement). The Romans used pozzolana in place of sand, and lime (p. 268). **Reinforced concrete,** nowadays universally used, is concrete with a reinforcement of steel rods or mesh (often bamboo in eastern countries). **Prestressed concrete** is concrete in which cracking (an inherent charac-

teristic) and tensile force are counteracted by compressing it. Two principal methods are applied to achieve this, post-tensioning and pre-tensioning, both using bars or wires. Prestressed concrete is reliable and relatively economical for large spans (e.g. the CNIT Building, Neuilly). In the past decade **precast concrete,** in which various concrete elements are cast on site or in a factory before assembly, has been much used for many building types. In **board-marked concrete,** made fashionable by Le Corbusier, a supposedly pleasing effect is created by leaving the marks of the wood shuttering on the exposed concrete. Among many other methods of treating a concrete surface is **bush-hammering** (e.g. Art and Architecture Building, Yale University), by which a roughened, 'rusticated' appearance is attained with the aid of a bush-hammer, a mechanically operated percussive tool.

Conoid. Having the form of a cone. The term is usually applied to the lower part of a Mediaeval vault where the ribs converge against the outer wall and form an approximation of an inverted half-cone or half-pyramid (p. 655).

Console. *See* **Bracket.**

Coping. The capping or covering to a wall.

Corbel (Fr. *corbeau* = crow, hence a beak-like projection). A block of stone, often elaborately carved or moulded, projecting from a wall, supporting the beams of a roof, floor, vault, or other feature.

Corbel Table. A plain piece of projecting wall supported by a range of corbels and forming a parapet, generally crowned by a coping (pp. 466H, 489C, G).

Corbie Gable (Fr. *corbeau* = crow) or **Crow-step Gable.** A gable with stepped sides (p. 703).

Corinthian. *See* **Order.**

Cornice (Fr. *corniche*). In Classic or Renaissance architecture, the crowning or upper portion of the entablature, also used for any crowning projection (p. 205A).

Coro (Sp., choir). In Spain the choir usually occupied two or more bays of the nave, the *Capilla Mayor* (comprising sanctuary, high altar and presbytery) filling the east end (p. 768B, D). Rejas (q.v.) often served as dividing screens.

Corona. The square projection in the upper part of a cornice, having a deep vertical face, generally plain, and with its soffit or under-surface recessed so as to form a 'drip', which prevents water from running down the building (p. 242A, N).

Corps de Logis (Fr.). That part of a substantial house which forms a self-contained dwelling, i.e. without the service quarters (*communs*), stables, etc.

Cortile. The Italian name for the internal court, surrounded by an arcade, in a palace or other edifice (p. 808C, D).

Cove, Coving. A large hollow, forming part of an arch in section, joining the walls and ceilings of a room. Often decorated with coffering or other enrichment (p. 1042C, E).

Cosmati. The name given to craftsmen in mosaic and marble working in Rome in the 12th to 14th centuries, many of whom belonged to a family of that name. Hence **Cosmato work.**

Cour d'honneur (Fr.). The finest, most handsome, court of a château or other great house, where visitors were formally received.

Credence. A small table or shelf near the altar, on which the Eucharistic elements were placed.

Crenellation (Old Fr. *crenel*=a notch). An opening in the upper part of a parapet. Furnished with 'crenelles', or indentations (p. 697A). In Britain, a licence to crenellate was necessary before houses could be fortified.

Crepidoma. The steps forming the base of a columned Greek temple (p. 205A).

Cresting (Old Fr. *creste*=crest or summit). A light repeated ornament, incised or perforated, carried along the top of a wall or roof (p. 64E).

Crocket (Fr. *croc*=a hook). In Gothic architecture a projecting block or spur of stone carved with foliage to decorate the raking lines formed by angles of spires and canopies (pp. 592H, 593A).

Croisée (Fr., crossing). (1) Transept; (2) the French term for the type of casement window preferred for the last three centuries in France; (3) *croisée d'ogives*= intersecting ribs of a vault. Rarely used in English.

Crossing. Area at the intersection of nave, chancel and transepts.

Cross Vault or **Groined Vault.** Vaults characterized by arched diagonal arrises or groins, which are formed by the intersection of two barrel vaults (p. 628).

Crown-post. A post standing upright on the tie-beam of a timber roof and by means of struts or braces giving support to a central collar-purlin and adjacent rafters (p. 635) but not reaching the apex of a roof, as in the case of a king-post (q.v.).

Crow-step Gable. *See* **Corbie Gable.**

Crucks. Pairs of timbers, arched together and based near the ground, erected to form principals for the support of the roof and walls of timber-framed small houses (p. 693C): in use in the western half of England until the 16th century or later.

Crypt (Gk. *kryptos*=hidden). A space entirely or partly under a building; in churches generally beneath the chancel and used for burial in early times.

Crypto-porticus (Lat., concealed or enclosed portico). A passage way wholly or mainly below ground.

Cubiculum (Lat.). A bedroom in a Roman house, but sometimes used in a less specific sense to denote other rooms.

Cunei (Lat. *cuneus*=wedge). The wedge-shaped sections into which seats are divided by radiating passages in ancient theatres (p. 244B).

Cupola (Lat. *cupa*=cup). A spherical roof, placed like an inverted cup over a circular, square, or multangular apartment. *See* **Dome.**

Curtain Wall. The logical outcome of skeleton-frame construction, in which the external walls serve no load-bearing purpose, but are suspended on the face of the building like a curtain (pp. 1228, 1245). Not to be confused with the curtain wall of mediaeval military architecture, denoting a defensive (usually outer) wall linking towers and gatehouses.

Cushion Capital. A cubiform capital, the angles being progressively rounded off towards the lowest part (p. 561C).

Cusp (Lat. *cuspis*=a point). The point formed by the intersection of the foils in Gothic tracery (p. 560).

Cyma (Lat. *cyma*=wave or billow). A moulding with an outline of two contrary curves—either the cyma recta or cyma reversa (pp. 241G, H, 242Q).

Cymatium. The crowning member of a cornice generally in the form of a cyma (above) (p. 220G).

Dado. The portion of a pedestal between its base and cornice. A term also applied to the lower portions of walls when decorated separately.

Daïs. A raised platform at the end of a Mediaeval hall, where the master dined apart from his retainers; now applied to any raised portion of an apartment.

Decastyle. A portico of ten columns (p. 203N).

Decorated. The style of English Gothic architecture prevalent during the 14th century (p. 625).

Demi-columns. Columns semi-sunk into a wall.

Dentils (Lat. *dentes*=teeth). Tooth-like blocks in Ionic and Corinthian cornices (pp. 241J, 242N, P).

Diaconicon (Gk.). The vestry, or sacristy, in Early Christian churches.

Diaper. A term probably derived from tapestry hangings of Ypres, and applied to any small pattern, such as lozenges or squares, repeated continuously over the wall surface.

Diastyle. A term used when the space between two columns is three diameters.

Diazoma. A horizontal passage dividing upper and lower levels of seats in an ancient theatre or amphitheatre (p. 244B).

Die. The part of a podium or pedestal between its cap-mould and base.

Dipteral (Gk. *dipteros*=double-winged). A temple having a double range of columns on each of its sides (p. 203H, N).

Distyle in antis. A portico with two columns between antae (p. 203A).

Dodecastyle. A portico of twelve columns (rare).

Dog-tooth. An ornament resembling a row of teeth specially occurring in Early English buildings.

Dome (It. *duomo*=a cathedral, from Lat. *domus*=a house). The custom in Italy was to erect cupolas over churches, and the word 'dome' has passed in English and French from the building to this form of roof (*see* **Cupola**).

Donjon. *See* **Keep.**

Doric. *See* **Order.**

Dormer. A window in a sloping roof, usually that of a sleeping-apartment, hence the name (p. 900A).

Dosseret. A deep block sometimes placed above a Byzantine capital (p. 401B–E) to support the wide voussoirs of the arch above. Perhaps a survival of the piece of entablature similarly placed in Roman architecture (pp. 269J, L, 291C, F).

Double Cone Moulding. A characteristic Norman (Romanesque) motif, formed by the continuous horizontal juxtaposition of cones, alternately base to base and vertex to vertex.

Dripstone. In Gothic architecture, the projecting moulding over the heads of doorways, windows and archways to throw off rain; also known as 'hood-moulding' or, when rectangular, a 'label'.

Dromos. A long, uncovered narrow passage leading to an underground tholos or chamber tomb (p. 190B, C).

Drum. The upright part below a dome or cupola, in which windows might be placed to light the central area of a building.

Dutch Gable. A shaped gable surmounted by a pediment (p. 1012C).

Early English. The style of English Gothic architecture prevalent during the 13th century (p. 624).

Eaves. The lower part of a roof projecting beyond the face of the wall.

Echinus (Gk. *echinos*=sea-urchin). The convex or projecting moulding, resembling the shell of a sea-urchin, which supports the abacus of the Greek Doric capital; sometimes painted with the egg and dart ornament (pp. 205A, 207).

Egg and Dart or **Egg and Tongue.** Alternating oval (*see* **Ovolo**) and pointed motifs, originating in Greece and widely applied to mouldings in the Renaissance (p. 241F).

Elizabethan. A term applied to English Early Renaissance architecture of the period 1558–1603 (p. 978).

Embattled. Furnished with battlements: occasionally applied to an indented pattern on mouldings.

Embrasure. An opening in a parapet between two merlons (p. 680A); the inward splaying of a door or window.

Encaustic. The art of mural painting in any way in which heat is used to fix the colours. **Encaustic tiles;** ornamental tiles of different clays, producing colour patterns after burning. Used in the Middle Ages and revived in the 19th century.

English Bond. Brickwork with alternate courses of stretchers and headers.

Enneastyle. A portico of nine columns (p. 203K).

Entablature. The upper part of an Order of architecture, comprising architrave, frieze and cornice, supported by a colonnade (p. 205A, B).

Entasis (Gk., distension). A swelling or curving outwards along the outline of a column shaft, designed to counteract the optical illusion which gives a shaft bounded by straight lines the appearance of curving inwards (p. 193D).

Entresol. See **Mezzanine.**

Ephebeion (Ephebeum). A room connected with an ancient Greek or Roman gymnasium, or with the gymnasium element of a baths building (pp. 296B, 302D, H).

Epinaos. See **Opisthodomos.**

Eustyle. A term used when the space between two columns is 2¼ diameters.

Exedra (Gk., out-door seat). In Greek buildings, a recess or alcove with raised seat where the disputations of the learned took place. The Romans applied the term to any semicircular or rectangular recess with benches, and it is also applied to an apse or niche in a church.

Extrados (Lat. *extra* = without + *dorsum* = back). The outer curve of an arch.

Façade. The face or elevation of a building.

Faience. Glazed earthenware, often ornamented, used for pottery or for building. Originally made at Faenza in Italy from about 1300.

Fan Vault. Vaulting peculiar to the Perpendicular period, in which all ribs have the same curve, and resemble the framework of a fan (pp. 631, 660B).

Fascia (Lat. *facies* = face). A vertical face of little projection, usually found in the architrave of an Order. The architrave of the Ionic and Corinthian Orders is divided into two or more such bands (pp. 254J, 278C). Also, a board or plate covering the end of roof rafters.

Feretory (Lat. *ferre* = to carry). A shrine for relics designed to be carried in processions.

Fielded panels. Panels of which the surface projects in front of the enclosing frame.

Fillet. A small flat band between mouldings to separate them from each other; also the uppermost member of a cornice (p. 241A).

Finial (Lat. *finis* = end). The upper portion of a pinnacle, bench-end, or other architectural feature.

Flamboyant (Fr. *flambeau* = flame). Tracery in which the bars of stonework form long wavy divisions like flames (pp. 593D, 606D).

Flèche (Fr., arrow). A slender wooden spire rising from a roof (p. 592C, H).

Flemish Bond. Brickwork with alter-nate headers and stretchers in the same course.

Fluting. The vertical channelling on the shaft of a column (p. 224).

Flying Buttress. See **Buttress.**

Foil (Lat. *folium* = leaf). The small arc openings in Gothic tracery separated by cusps. Trefoil, quatrefoil, cinquefoil, etc., signify the number of foils (p. 1310).

Folded Slab. A development of the reinforced-concrete thin slab, which has both aesthetic and structural advantages in spanning large halls and buildings of similar type, while also facilitating the provision of good natural and artificial lighting. So-called because in section the resultant ribbed roof assumes the form of pleats or folds (pp. 1247, 1268A).

Formeret. In a Mediaeval vault, the half-rib against the wall, known in England as the 'wall rib' (p. 628C).

Formwork. Temporary casing of woodwork, within which concrete is moulded.

Fortalice. A small fortification, often a tower (p. 703).

Forum. The public open space, for social, civic or market purposes found in every Roman town (p. 272).

Fresco (It. *fresco* = fresh). The term originally applied to painting on a wall while the plaster is wet, but is often used for any wall painting not in oil colours.

Fret (Old Fr. *frettes* = grating). An ornament in Classic or Renaissance architecture consisting of an assemblage of straight lines inersecting at right angles, and of various patterns (p. 859G). Sometimes called the **Key Pattern.**

Frieze (It. *fregio* = ornament). The middle division of the Classic entablature (p. 205A). See **Zoophorus.**

Frigidarium. An apartment in a Roman baths building, equipped with a large, cold bath (pp. 296, 302B, D).

Gable. The triangular portion of a wall, between the enclosing lines of a sloping roof. In Classic architecture it is called a pediment.

Gadroon. One of a series of convex curves, like inverted fluting, used as an ornamental border.

Galilee. A porch used as a chapel for penitents, etc., in some Mediaeval churches. The origin of the term is conjectural: perhaps from the Latin *galeria*, a long porticus or porch, or possibly from Mark xvi, 7, 'He goeth before you into Galilee: there shall ye see him,' suggesting a meeting-place (pp. 640A, F, 641E).

Gallery. A communicating passage or wide corridor for pictures and statues. An internal and external feature in Mediaeval buildings (p. 511A, C). An upper storey for seats in a church (p. 356A, C, D, E).

Garbha-griha. The small unlit shrine of a Hindu temple.

Gargoyle (Lat. *gurges* = whirlpool). A projecting water-spout grotesquely carved to throw off water from the roof (p. 618B).

Georgian. English Late Renaissance architecture of the period 1702–1830 (p. 981).

Glyph (Gk., a groove). A carved vertical channel. *See* **Triglyph.**

Glyptotheca (Gk. *glypton* = carving + *theke* = repository). A building to contain sculpture.

Gopuram. A gateway tower of a Hindu temple, ornate, pyramid-shaped, and sometimes very large (p. 106D).

Gorge Cornice. The characteristic hollow-and-roll moulding of an Egyptian cornice (p. 11J). Also found in Persian architecture.

Gothic. The name generally given to the pointed style of Mediaeval architecture prevalent in Western Europe from the 13th to the 15th century.

Gothic Revival. A manifestation first evident in the late 18th century, but belonging principally to the 19th. The countries most affected were England, France and Germany and, less strongly, the U.S.A.

Greek Revival. Like the Gothic Revival, this had its beginnings in the late 18th century. In England it culminated in the 1820s and had concluded by 1840 (later in Scotland), while in France it similarly was at its most evident in the early 19th century. In Germany it endured to mid-19th century. In the U.S.A. it was the especial characteristic of the architecture of the period 1815–60.

Groin. The curved arris formed by the intersection of vaulting surfaces (p. 269M).

Groin Vault. *See* **Cross Vault.**

Guilloche. A circular interlaced ornament like network, frequently used to ornament the 'torus' moulding (p. 241L).

Guttæ (Lat. *gutta* = drop). Small cones under the triglyphs and mutules of the Doric entablature (p. 205A).

Gymnasium (Gymnasion). In ancient Greece, a place for physical exercises and training, larger than the palaestra (q.v.).

Gynaeceum. The women's apartments in a Greek (or Roman) house; also the women's gallery in a Byzantine church.

Hagioscope (Gk. *hagios* = sacred + *skopein* = to view). An oblique opening in a Mediaeval church wall giving a view of the altar, sometimes known as a 'squint'.

Half-timber Building. A building of timber posts, rails and struts, and interspaces filled with brick or other material, and sometimes plastered (p. 722A).

Hall Church. Church in which nave and aisles are of, or approximate to, equal height.

Hall-keep. Early type of keep, rectangular in form, in which the great hall and private bed-chamber were placed side by side.

Hammer-beam Roof. Late Gothic form of roof without a direct tie (pp. 633, 634C).

Hecatompedon (Gk., a hundred-foot temple). The name given to the naos of the Parthenon, Athens, inherited from a former temple of 566 B.C. upon the site, of which the length was exactly 100 Doric feet (1 Doric foot = 12.88 ins) and the width 50 Doric feet.

Helix (Gk., a spiral or tendril). One of the 16 small volutes (helices) under the abacus of a Corinthian capital (p. 236).

Helm. Bulbous termination to the top of a tower, found principally in central and eastern Europe (p. 931B).

Helm Roof. Type of roof in which four faces rest diagonally between the gables and converge at the top (p. 508K).

Hemicycle Buttress. Half-moon-shaped buttress, sometimes very large, often masked by other masonry or designed to perform utilitarian tasks additional to its purely structural purpose, widely used by the Romans (p. 271).

Henostyle-in-antis. A portico with one column between antae.

Heptastyle. A temple having seven columns on the front (p. 203G).

Hermes. A Greek deity. A bust (Hermes, Herm or Term) on a square pedestal instead of a human body, used in Classic times along highways and to mark boundaries, and decoratively in Roman and Renaissance times (p. 801K).

Heroum. In Greek architecture, a

small shrine or chapel dedicated to a semi-deified person or to the memory of a mortal.

Hexastyle. A portico having a row of six columns (p. 203J).

Hieron (Gk., a holy place). The sacred enclosure surrounding a temple.

Hippodrome. In ancient Greece, a course for horse and chariot racing, the equivalent of the Roman circus.

Honeysuckle Ornament. *See* **Anthemion.**

Hood Moulding. *See* **Dripstone.**

Hoop-tie Principle. A method developed in the Renaissance period, by which a pieced ring of timber, or a metal chain or hoop, binds the lower part of a dome or cupola to prevent splitting outwards or to minimise the burden on external buttresses having a similar purpose (p. 841C).

Hypæthral (Gk., under the sky). A building or temple without a roof or with a central space open to the sky.

Hypocaust (Lat. *hypocaustum* = a fire chamber). A system of ducts by which heat from the furnace was distributed throughout the building (p. 296).

Hypogeum. In ancient times, all parts of a building underground.

Hypostyle (Gk. *hypo* = under + Lat. *stylus* = pillar). A pillared hall in which the roof rests on columns. Applied to the many-columned halls of Egyptian temples.

Hypotrachelion (Gk., under the neck). The channels or grooves beneath the trachelion at the junction of capital and shaft of a column (p. 205B). *See* **Trachelion.**

Iconostas. A screen between nave and chancel of a Byzantine church.

Imbrex. In Classical architecture, a roofing cover tile over the joint between flat or hollow tiles (p. 205H).

Imbrication. An overlapping, as of one row of scalloped roofing tiles breaking joint with the next (p. 238D).

Impluvium. In Greek and Roman houses, a shallow tank under the Compluvium, or opening in the roof of an atrium (p. 332B).

Impost (Lat. *imponere* = to lay upon). The member, usually formed of mouldings, on which an arch rests (p. 320).

In Antis. A covered colonnade at the entrance to a building is 'in antis' if recessed (p. 203A). Cf. **Prostyle.**

Incrustation. The facing of a wall surface, generally marble, with a decorative overlay. An Italian, predominantly Venetian, craft.

Indent. A notch. **Indented moulding.** A moulding cut in the form of zig-zag pointed notches (p. 562B, abacus of left capital).

Intarsia. In furniture, a decorative inlay of various materials in another, usually wood.

Inter-columniation. The space between the columns (p. 207A).

Intrados (Lat. *intra* = within + *dorsum* = back). The inner curve of an arch.

Ionic. *See* **Order.**

Insula (Lat., island, i.e. a house not joined to another by a common wall). A block of flats in a Roman town.

I'rimoya Gable. A traditional type of Japanese gable, placed vertically above the end walls and marked by roofs of varying pitch (p. 162A, H).

Islamic Architecture. For terms used in Islamic architecture (Bab; Chattri; Iwan; Jami; Kibla; Madrassah, Medrese; Masjid, Mesjid; Mihrab; Mimber; Sahn; Saray, Serai; Selamlik) *see* p. 411.

Jacobean. English Early Renaissance architecture of the period 1603–25 (p. 978).

Jambs (Fr. *jambe* = leg). The sides of doors and windows. The portion exposed outside the window-frame is the 'reveal'.

Jubé (Fr.). The equivalent of the English rood-screen between nave and chancel (p. 910A).

Jugendstil. The movement in Germany contemporary to **Art Nouveau** (q.v.). The name derives from the periodical *Jugend* (= youth) (p. 1193).

Kalasa. *See* **Sikhara.**

Keel Moulding. A moulding like the keel of a ship formed of two ogee curves meeting in a sharp arris (p. 563J, K); used rounded in form in the 15th century. The word 'keel' is also applied to the ogee form of arch (p. 1310, Nos. 28, 29).

Keep. The inner Great Tower or Donjon of a castle (p. 573A, B, F).

Key Pattern. *See* **Fret.**

Keystone. The central stone of a semi-circular arch, sometimes sculptured (pp. 319, 320).

Khans. Caravanserais or inns, especially in large Moslem cities.

Kheker Cresting. A decorative motif used by the Egyptians (p. 19B).

King-post. A vertical post extending from the ridge to the centre of the tie-beam below (pp. 633B, E, 635).

Kiosk. A light, open pavilion.

Knapped Flint. A traditional East-Anglian craft of splitting flints, so that they present a smooth black surface on a wall-face. The arrangement of knapped flints in patterns is sometimes called 'flushwork' (p. 637).

Label. See **Dripstone.**

Laconicum. A dry sweating room in a Roman baths building.

Lacunaria. See **Coffer.**

Lancet Arch. A sharp pointed arch, chiefly in use during the Early English period (pp. 560B, C, 1310, No. 11).

Lantern. A construction, such as a tower, at the crossing of a church, rising above the neighbouring roofs and glazed at the sides (pp. 746C, 880F).

Lararium. A room or niche in a Roman house, in which the effigies of the household gods (Lares) were placed (p. 328B).

Later. A Roman unburnt brick.

Lath. See **Stambha.**

Lavabo. Ritual washing-basin for celebrant; monastic washing-trough (p. 784D).

Leaf and Tongue. In Greek architectural ornament, a conventional motif of the cyma reversa (p. 241H).

Lesene. An undecorated pilaster without base or capital (p. 551C).

Lich or **Lych Gate** (A.-Sax. *lic* = body). A covered gateway to a churchyard, forming a resting-place for a coffin where portion of the burial service is often read.

Lierne (Fr. *lien* = tie). A short intermediate rib in Gothic vaulting which does not rise from the impost and is not a ridge rib (pp. 631, 659C, 670A).

Linenfold. A type of relief ornament, imitating folded linen, carved on the face of individual timber panels. Popular in the late 15th and the 16th century.

Lintel. The horizontal timber or stone, also known as the architrave, that spans an opening.

Loculi (Lat. *loculus* = a little place). Recesses for corpses in Roman burial vaults.

Loggia. A gallery behind an open arcade or colonnade (p. 824F).

Long and Short Work. In Anglo-Saxon building, a method of laying the quoins or angles, in which the stone slabs are superposed vertically and horizontally in alternate courses (p. 551C).

Louvre. A series of inclined slats in a vertical frame, allowing ventilation without admitting rain or direct sunlight; a roof ventilator embodying the principal. Sometimes applied to roof ventilators in general.

Lucarne. A window with a sloping roof (p. 905B, C). See also **Dormer.**

Luna Marble. See **Carrara.**

Lunette (Fr. *lune* = moon). A semicircular window or wall-panel let into the inner base of a concave vault or dome (p. 1017B).

Machicolation (Fr. *mache* = melted matter + *coulis* = flowing). A projecting wall or parapet allowing floor openings, through which molten lead, pitch, stones, etc., were dropped on an enemy below (pp. 611C, 680A, 745H).

Maeander. Running ornament in the form of a fret (q.v.) or key pattern.

Mandapa. The porch-like hall of a Hindu temple.

Mandorla (It., almond). See **Aureole.**

Mannerism. A term coined to describe the characteristics of the output of Italian Renaissance architects of the period 1530–1600. Architecture of this character, which in fact is common to the European Renaissance as a whole, is for that reason herein distinguished as 'Proto-Baroque' (p. 782), the Baroque being the ultimate outcome.

Mansard Roof. A roof with steep lower slope and flatter upper portion, named after Mansart (p. 1213B). Also known as a 'gambrel' roof.

Marquise (Fr.). A projecting canopy over an entrance door, often of metal and glass (p. 1222E).

Masons' Mitre. The treatment in masonry and sometimes in joinery for mouldings meeting at right angles, when the diagonal mitre thus formed does not coincide with the joint, but is worked on the face of the one piece which is carried straight through and simply butts on the other (pp. 234C, D, 369R).

Mastaba. An ancient Egyptian, rectangular, flat-topped, funerary mound, with battered (sloping) sides, covering a burial chamber below ground (p. 15A–G).

Mathematical Tiles. Brick tiles designed to imitate facing bricks (pp. 1044, 1046C).

Meander Fret. See **Maeander.**

Mediaeval. A term taken to comprehend the Romanesque and Gothic periods of architectural development.

Megaron. The principal room of an early Anatolian or Aegean house (pp. 68, 188A).

Merlon. The upstanding part of an embattled parapet, between two 'crenelles' or embrasure openings (p. 680A).

Metope (Gk. *meta* = between + *ope* = an opening). The space between Doric triglyphs, sometimes left open in ancient examples; afterwards applied to the carved slab (pp. 205A, 215A, B, M).

Mezzanine. An intermediate floor formed within a lofty storey (Fr. *entresol*).

Minaret. A slender tower, rising above (or otherwise connected with) a mosque, from which the muezzin (crier) calls the faithful to prayer.

Misericord (Lat. *misericordia* = pity). A hinged seat, made to turn up to afford support to a standing person, with the underside frequently grotesquely carved.

Mitre. The term applied, especially in joinery, to the diagonal joint formed by the meeting of two mouldings at right angles.

Moderne Style, Le. A term once used in France to denote **Art Nouveau** (q.v.), but nowadays the latter is preferred.

Modillion. See **Bracket.**

Module (Lat. *modulus* = measure). A measure of proportion, by which the parts of a Classic Order or building are regulated, being usually the semi-diameter of a column immediately above its base, which is divided into thirty parts or minutes (pp. 207, 1052, 1053).

Monopteral. A temple, usually circular, consisting of columns only.

Mosaic. Decorative surfaces formed by small cubes of stone, glass and marble; much used in Hellenistic, Roman and later times for floors and wall decoration (pp. 369A, B, Q, S, T, 392B, 394A).

Motte. The earthen conical mound of a castle; usually has a related **Bailey**, thus a courtyard or ward (p. 573C).

Mouldings (Lat. *modulari* = to be measured). The contours given to projecting members (pp. 241, 242, 563).

Mudéjar. A Spanish Moslem under Christian rule. A vernacular style of Spanish architecture, particularly of Aragon and Castile, of 12th–16th century, blending Moslem and Christian characteristics: its influence survived into the 17th century.

Neo-Mudéjar. A perpetuation or revival of features of the style in the 16th–19th century in Latin America (p. 1111).

Mullions. Vertical members dividing windows into different numbers of lights (p. 560).

Mushroom Construction. A system of reinforced-concrete construction without beams, in which the floor-slabs are directly supported by columns flared at the top (p. 1247).

Mutules. Projecting inclined blocks in Doric cornices, derived from the ends of wooden beams (p. 205).

Nail-head. A Norman (Romanesque) motif, carved in the form of a small pyramidal stud or nail-head (p. 562E).

Naos (Gk., dwelling). The principal chamber in a Greek temple, containing the statue of the deity (p. 217G).

Narthex. A long arcaded entrance porch to a Christian basilican church, originally appropriated to penitents (p. 353C, D, E).

Naumachia (Gk., a battle of ships). A lake for the exhibition of sea fights, encircled by seats for spectators; sometimes refers to the spectacle itself.

Nautilus Shell. A decorative motif used by the Greeks, especially for the spiral of the Ionic volute (p. 222D).

Nave (Gk. *naos* = dwelling, or more probably Lat. *navis* = ship, a symbol of the Church, in which the faithful are borne safely over the sea of life to the haven of eternity). The western limb of a church, as opposed to the choir; also the central aisle of the basilican, Mediaeval, or Renaissance church, as opposed to the side aisles.

Necking. The space between the astragal of the shaft and the commencement of the capital proper in the Roman Doric (p. 820C).

Necropolis. (Gk., a town of the dead). A burial ground.

Newel. (1) The central shaft of a circular staircase; (2) also applied to the post into which the handrail is framed (pp. 879A, 1002C, E).

Niche (It. *nicchio* = shell). A recess in a wall, hollowed like a shell, for a statue or ornament (p. 786F).

Nimbus. See **Aureole.**

Norman. The style, also termed English Romanesque, of the 11th and 12th centuries.

Nymphæum (literally a sanctuary of the nymphs). A building in Classic architecture for plants, flowers and running water, ornamented with statues.

Obelisk. A tall pillar of square section tapering upwards and ending in a pyramid.

Octastyle. A portico with a range of eight columns (p. 203H, M).

Odeion (Gk., music-room). A building, resembling a Greek theatre, designed for musical contests (p. 198B).

Oecus. The main room of a Greek house, the successor of the megaron.

Ogee. A moulding made up of a convex and concave curve. Also an arch of similar shape (pp. 241H, 131O, Nos. 28, 29).

Ogival (Fr., pointed). The traditional term in France for Gothic architecture. Not commonly used today.

Opaion. A Greek term for a clear-storey or top light.

Opisthodomos (Gk., a back room). The rear porch of a temple (p. 217G).

Opus (pl. **Opera**). A work.

Opus Alexandrinum (Lat., Alexandrian work). Mosaics inlaid in a stone or marble paving (p. 369Q).

Opus incertum, — quadratum, — reticulatum, — testaceum, etc. see p. 268.

Order. An Order in architecture comprises a column, with base (usually), shaft, and capital, the whole supporting an entablature. The Greeks recognized three Orders: Doric, Ionic and Corinthian. The Romans added the Tuscan and the Composite (the latter also known as Roman), while using the Greek Orders in modified form. The **Doric Order** is unique in having no base to the column. The capital is plain; the shaft fluted (pp. 202, 205). The **Ionic Order** is lighter, more elegant, than the Doric, with slim columns, generally fluted. It is principally distinguished by the volutes of its capital (pp. 221, 222, 224). The **Corinthian Order** has a bell-shaped capital, from which eight acanthus stalks (caulicoli) emerge to support the modest volutes. The shaft is generally fluted (pp. 235, 236). The **Tuscan Order** resembles the Doric in all but its very plain entablature. The shaft is properly unfluted (p. 266J, K). The **Composite** (or **Roman**) **Order** combines the prominent volutes of the Ionic with the acanthus of the Corinthian on its capital, and is thus the most decorative. The shaft may be fluted or plain (p. 319G).

Ordinates. Parallel chords of conic section (in relation to the bisecting diameter) describing an ellipse; a principle followed by Renaissance builders to adjust cross-vaults of equal height, but unequal span (p. 628D).

Ordonnance (Fr.). The disposition of the parts of a building.

Oriel. A window corbelled out from the face of a wall by means of projecting stones (p. 688F).

Orthostats. Courses of large squared stones at the base of a wall.

Osiris Pillars. Pillars incorporating the sculptured figure of Osiris, Egyptian God of Death and Resurrection (p. 10H).

Ovolo. A convex moulding much used in Classic and Renaissance architecture, often carved with the egg and dart or egg and tongue (pp. 241F, 242L, Q).

Pai-lou. A Chinese ceremonial gateway, erected in memory of an eminent person (p. 153C). Also found in Japan.

Palæstra (Gk. *palaistra* = wrestling school). A public building for the training of athletes (p. 199A, B).

Palladian Motif. An arched opening flanked by two smaller, square-headed openings (p. 862).

Palmette. See **Anthemion**.

Palm Vaulting. Similar to **Fan Vaulting** (q.v.).

Panel. A compartment, sunk or raised, in walls, ceilings, doors, wainscoting, etc. See also **Coffer**.

Papyrus (Gk.). Aquatic plant used by the Egyptians for a great variety of purposes, including the construction of primitive 'reed' huts. A recurrent motif in Egyptian architectural sculpture (p. 11A–C).

Parabolic Vaulting. A thin shell covering, normally of reinforced concrete, of parabolic section (i.e. a shape made by cutting a cone parallel to one edge). Such structures are comparatively light, and not subject to tensional stresses under conditions of uniform loading (p. 1247). Cf. **Shell Vaulting**.

Parapet (Lat. *parare* = to guard + *pectus* = breast). The portion of wall above the roof-gutter, sometimes battlemented; also applied to the same feature, rising breast-high, in balconies, platforms and bridges.

Parclose (Old Fr. *parclose* = an enclosure). A screen enclosing a chapel, as a shelter from draughts, or to prevent distraction to worshippers; also the screen around a tomb or shrine.

Pargetting (pargeting, parging). External ornamental plasterwork having raised, indented or tooled patterns; used from Tudor times onward chiefly in East Anglia and the south-east of England.

Pastas or **Prostas**. A vestibule in front of a Greek house, with a part of one side open to a forecourt (p. 253B).

Paterae. Flat circular ornaments which resemble the Classical saucers used for wine in sacrificial libations (p. 234C, D).

Patio. A Spanish arcaded or colonnaded courtyard.

Pavilion (Fr. *pavillon* = little house, for pleasure or recreation). A prominent structure, generally distinctive in character, marking the ends and centre of the façade of a major building (p. 890). A similarly distinctive building linked by a wing to a main block. An ornamental building in a garden.

Pavimentum (Lat. *pavire* = to ram down). A pavement formed by pieces of tile, marble, stone, flints or other material set in cement and consolidated by beating down with a rammer.

Pedestal. A support for a column, statue or vase. It usually consists of a base, die and cornice or cap-mould.

Pediment. In Classic architecture, a triangular piece of wall above the entablature, enclosed by raking cornices (p. 205A). In Renaissance architecture used for any roof end, whether triangular, broken or semicircular. In Gothic, such features are known as gables.

Pele-towers. Small square towers of massive construction, built in the border country of England and Scotland until the late Middle Ages.

Pendant. An elongated boss projecting downward or suspended from a ceiling or roof.

Pendentive. The term applied to the triangular curved overhanging surface by means of which a circular dome is supported over a square or polygonal compartment (pp. 83H, 269N, 378).

Pentastyle. A temple front of five columns.

Peribolus (Gk. *peribole* = an enclosing). The enclosing wall or colonnade surrounding a temenos or sacred enclosure, and hence sometimes applied to the enclosure itself (p. 279B).

Peripteral. A term applied to an edifice surrounded by a single range of columns.

Peristyle. A range of columns surrounding a court or temple.

Perpendicular. A phase of English Gothic evolved from the Decorated style, and prevalent during the 15th and 16th centuries (p. 625).

Perron (Fr.). A landing or platform outside the portal of a domestic or public building, approached in a dignified way by a single or double flight of steps (p. 947D).

Piano Nobile (It., noble floor). The principal floor of an Italian palace, raised one floor above ground level and containing the principal social apartments.

Piazza (It.). A public open place, surrounded by buildings: may vary in shape and in civic purpose.

Picturesque. The term is used in a specialized sense to describe one of the attitudes of taste towards architecture and landscape gardening in the late 18th and early 19th century (*c.* 1785–1835); buildings and landscape were to have the controlled informality of a picture. Influential publications of the period were *An Essay on the Picturesque* (1794) by Sir Uvedale Price and *An Enquiry into the Changes of Taste in Landscape Gardening* by Humphrey Repton.

Pier (Lat. *petra* = rock). A mass of masonry, as distinct from a column, from which an arch springs, in an arcade or bridge; also applied to the wall between doors and windows (p. 490K). The term is sometimes given to a pillar in Gothic architecture.

Pilaster. A rectangular feature in the shape of a pillar, but projecting only about one-sixth of its breadth from a wall, and the same design as the Order with which it is used (*see* Anta) (pp. 817B, 867B).

Pilotis (Fr., stilts). Posts on an unenclosed ground floor carrying a raised building (p. 1254A).

Pinacotheca (Gk., picture gallery). A building to contain painted pictures.

Pinnacle. In Gothic architecture, a small turret-like termination on the top of buttresses, parapets, or elsewhere, often ornamented with bunches of foliage called crockets (p. 589).

Piscina (Lat., a reservoir of water). A stone basin in a niche near the altar, to receive the water in which the priest rinses the chalice. Also applied to the tank or fountain in Roman baths.

Plateresque (Sp. *plateria* = silverwork). A phase of the Early Period of Spanish

Architecture of the later 15th and early 16th century, an intricate style named after its likeness to silverwork (p. 955).

Plate Tracery. *See* **Tracery.**

Plinth. The lowest square member of the base of a column; also applied to the projecting stepped or moulded base of any building (pp. 224E, F, 288E).

Plough-share Twist. The irregular or winding surface in a vault, where the wall ribs, owing to the position of the clear-storey windows, start at a higher level than the other ribs (p. 628C).

Podium. A continuous pedestal; also the enclosing platform of the arena of an amphitheatre (pp. 275, 308D).

Polychromy. A term originally applied to the art of decorative painting in many colours, extended to the colouring of sculpture to enhance naturalism, and very loosely used in an architectural context to describe the application of variegated materials to achieve brilliant or striking effects. As such, it is a characteristic of the High Victorian phase (p. 1129) and of Art Nouveau (q.v.).

Poppy-head (Lat. *puppis*=poop or raised stern of a ship). The ornamental termination of a bench-end, frequently carved with fleur-de-lis, animals or figures.

Porphyry (Gk., purple). A hard rock, red or purple in colour, used as a building stone or for sculpture, especially by the Egyptians, Greeks and Romans.

Portcullis (Fr. *porte*=a gate +*coulisse*= a groove). A heavy lattice grating of timber or iron, sliding in vertical grooves in the jambs of a portal of a defended building.

Portico. A colonnaded space forming an entrance or vestibule, with a roof supported on at least one side by columns (p. 281A, B, E, F).

Posticum. The Latin term for the rear porch of a temple. *See* **Opisthodomus.**

Prato Marble. A green marble from the district of Prato in Toscana.

Presbytery (Lat. *presbyter*=elder). The space at the eastern end of a church for the clergy, but often applied to the whole sanctuary (pp. 640–3).

Pronaos. The part of a temple in front of the naos often synonymous with portico (p. 217G).

Propylæum (pl. **Propylæa**) (Gk., a front portal). An important entrance gateway or vestibule, in front of a sacred enclosure (pp. 197, 198).

Proscenium (Gk. *proskenion*). In ancient Greek theatres, a colonnade standing in front of the scene building (*skene*), the top of which eventually became the stage (*logeion*=a speaking place): thus all of the stage works in front of the ornamental back-stage. Nowadays, the term means only the frontispiece of the stage.

Prostyle (Gk., a column in front). An open portico of columns standing in front of a building (p. 203C, D).

Prothesis. That part of a church where the credence table (q.v.) stands.

Prytaneion (**Prytaneum**). The public hall and state dining room of a Greek city.

Pseudo-dipteral (Gk., false double-winged). A temple which is planned as a dipteral building, i.e. two columns in depth around the naos, but from which the inner range is omitted (p. 203L).

Pseudo-peripteral (Gk., falsely peripteral). A temple lacking a pteroma and having the flank columns attached to the temple walls (pp. 203G, 275A–C).

Pteroma (Gk., a wing). The space between the lateral walls of the naos of a temple and the peristyle columns (p. 203).

Pulpitum (Lat.). A stone gallery or rood-loft (q.v.) over the entrance to the choir of a cathedral or church.

Pulvinated (Lat., a cushion). A term applied to a frieze whose face is convex in profile (pp. 284H, J, 859A, B).

Pumice. Igneous rock derived from volcanic lava. As a building stone, it was used by the Romans and, later, is present in Byzantine and Romanesque work: it had the advantage of extreme lightness.

Purbeck Marble. A fine hard limestone from Purbeck, Dorset.

Purlin. A horizontal beam in a roof, resting on the principal rafters and supporting the common rafters and roof covering.

Pycnostyle (Gk., close columned). A term given when the space between two columns is 1½ diameters.

Pylon (Gk., a gateway). A term applied to the mass of masonry with central opening, forming a monumental entrance to Egyptian temples (pp. 39B, 42A).

Quadrangle. A broad enclosure or court, defined by buildings.

Quadriga. A four-horsed chariot, in sculptured form, often surmounting a monument (pp. 250, 319F).

Quadripartite Vaulting. A vault in which each bay is divided by intersecting diagonal ribs into four parts.

Quatrefoil (Fr. *quatre feuilles*=four leaves). In tracery, a panel divided by cusps into four openings (p. 560D).

Quirk. A sharp V-shaped incision in a moulding, such as that flanking the Norman bowtell (p. 563B, E).

Quoin (Fr. *coin*=angle). A term generally applied to the corner-stones at the angles of buildings and hence to the angle itself.

Rampart. Defensive earthen bank surrounding a castle, fortress or fortified city (p. 573C). May have a stone parapet.

Rath. Hindu rock-cut temple, especially in South India (p. 104A, B).

Rebate. A rectangular sinking, channel or groove cut longitudinally in a piece of timber to receive the edge of another, or a recess in the jambs of an opening to receive a door or window.

Reeding. A series of convex mouldings of equal width, side by side: the inverse of fluting (p. 11J). The fluting of the lower third of column shafts was sometimes infilled with reeds to strengthen them (p. 287B).

Refectory. The dining-hall in a monastery, convent or college.

Regula (Lat., a rule). The short band, under the triglyphs, beneath the tenia of the Doric entablature, and to which the guttæ are attached (p. 205A).

Reja (Sp.). An ornate iron grille or screen, a characteristic feature of Spanish church interiors (p. 763B).

Reliquary. A light portable receptacle for sacred relics (p. 784H).

Renaissance (Fr., a new birth). The term applied to the reintroduction of Classic architecture all over Europe, in the 15th and 16th centuries.

Rendering. Plaster or stucco applied to an external wall; a first coat of plaster internally.

Repoussé Work (Fr. *repousser*=to emboss). Ornamental metal work, hammered into relief from the reverse side.

Reredos. The screen, or ornamental work, rising behind the altar (p. 650C).

Respond. A half-pillar at end of an arcade.

Retable. A ledge or shelf behind an altar for holding vases or candles. The

Spanish **retablo** (p. 764A) is a sumptuously ornate form of reredos (above).

Retro-choir. The parts of a large church behind the high altar (p. 640D).

Reveal. The surface at right angles to the face of a wall, at the side of an opening cut through it; known as a 'splay' when cut diagonally. Especially applied to the part outside the window-frame.

Rib. A projecting band on a ceiling, vault or elsewhere (p. 628).

Ridge. The apex of a sloping roof, running from end to end.

Ringhiera. A balcony on the main front of an Italian Mediaeval town hall from which decrees and public addresses were delivered (p. 465D).

Rococo (Fr. *rocaille*=rock-work). A term applied to a type of Renaissance ornament in which rock-like forms, fantastic scrolls, and crimped shells are worked up together in a profusion and confusion of detail often without organic coherence, but presenting a lavish display of decoration (pp. 876, 936A).

Roll Moulding. A plain round moulding (p. 11J). In Mediaeval architecture, sometimes known as the Bowtell (q.v.).

Romanesque. The style of architecture, founded on Roman architecture, prevalent in Western Europe from the 9th to the 12th century.

Rood Loft (A.-Sax., rod, hence cross or crucifix). A raised gallery over the **Rood Screen** (pp. 672A, 675D), a name given to the chancel screen when it supports the 'rood' or large cross erected in many churches in Mediaeval times. Reached by stairs in the chancel wall it was also used as a gallery for minstrels and singers on festival days.

Rose Window. *See* **Wheel Window.**

Rostrum (Lat., the prow of a ship). The plural 'rostra' denoted the raised tribune in the Forum Romanum (p. 273B), from which orators addressed the people, and was so called because decorated with the prows of ships taken in war, as were **Rostral Columns** (p. 326G).

Rotonda. A round building.

Rubble. Stone walling of rough, undressed stones.

Rustication. A method of forming stonework with roughened surfaces and recessed joints, principally employed in Renaissance buildings (pp. 800, 802).

Sanctuary. A holy or consecrated

place. The most sacred part of a church or temple (p. 640D).

Sarcophagus. Richly carved coffin (pp. 251G, H, 266C, 369H).

Sash Window. A double-hung, usually wooden, glazed frame (or sash), designed to slide up and down in grooves with the aid of pulleys (pp. 1027F, 1033).

Säteri Roof (Swedish, *säteritak* = manor-house roof). A form of hipped roof, interrupted by a smaller vertical part sometimes provided with windows. This low perpendicular break forms a middle portion between the lower part of the roof and its considerably smaller continuation above the break. It is characteristic of the great houses of the Swedish nobility and gentry of the 17th and 18th centuries (pp. 1076, 1077D).

Scena (Gk. *skene*). The back scene of an ancient theatre (p. 244).

Scholae (Lat., but derived from Gk. *schola* = leisure). Places of leisure, which to the classical mind meant places for learned conversation or instruction; hence 'lecture rooms of the philosophers'.

Scotia (Gk. *skotia* = darkness). The concave moulding between the two torus mouldings in the base of a column, throwing a deep shadow (pp. 241E, 242H, T).

Screen. A partition or enclosure of iron, stone or wood, often carved; when separating choir from nave, it is termed the choir screen. Cf. **Chancel.**

Scroll Moulding. A moulding resembling a scroll of paper, the end of which projects over the other part (p. 563M).

Section (Lat. *sectus* = cut). The representation of a building cut by a vertical plane, so as to show the construction.

Sedilia (Lat., seat). The seats for the priests, generally of masonry, in the south wall of the chancel.

Severy. A compartment or bay of a vault (pp. 627F, H, 589C, F).

Sexpartite Vaulting. A vault where each bay is divided into six parts by the intersection of two diagonal ribs and one transverse rib (pp. 627E).

Sgraffito (It., scratched). A method of decoration by which an upper coat of white stucco is partially cut away to expose a dark undercoat and so form a design.

Shaft. The portion of a column between base and capital (p. 205A); also applied in Mediaeval architecture to a small column, as in a clustered pier, supporting a vaulting rib (p. 561).

Shell Vaulting. A thin curved plate-like form of roofing, generally of reinforced concrete and often of striking elegance, widely used nowadays for spanning large halls (p. 1302B). Cf. **Parabolic Vaulting.**

Shingle Style. The cladding of external walls with shingles (wooden tiles) over a timber frame (p. 1231).

Shrine. A sacred place or object, e.g. a receptacle for relics.

Sikhara. A spire-like structure, conical or pyramidal in shape, erected above the shrines of Hindu temples. A finial, called a **kalasa**, is generally the crowning feature (p. 93).

Soffit. The ceiling or underside of any architectural member.

Solar (Lat. *solarium* = a sunny place or balcony). A Mediaeval term for a private chamber on the upper floor.

Space Frame. A frame which is three-dimensional and stable in all directions.

Span. The distance between the supports of an arch, roof or beam.

Spandrel. The triangular space enclosed by the curve of an arch, a vertical line from its springing, and a horizontal line through its apex (p. 319B, D, E, F). In modern architecture, an infill-panel below a window-frame in a curtain wall.

Specus. The duct or channel of a Roman aqueduct, usually rectangular in section and lined with a waterproofing of successive coatings of hydraulic cement, and covered by stone slabs or by arched vaults (p. 324B).

Spere (also **Speer** or **Spur**). A fixed timber screen, sometimes elaborately carved, shielding the entrances of Mediaeval houses and large halls. When directly attached to a roof-principal, the resultant structure became a **spere-truss** (p. 682).

Spina. The spine wall down the centre of an ancient hippodrome or circus (p. 312A, D).

Spire (A.-Sax. *spir* = a stalk). The tapering termination of a tower in Gothic. or Renaissance architecture, which was the result of elongating an ordinary pyramidal or conical roof (p. 593B).

Splay (short form of 'display', cf. **Reveal**). The diagonal surface formed by the cutting away of a wall, as when an opening is wider inside than out or conversely.

Springer. The lowest unit or voussoir of an arch, occurring just above the springing line (pp. 269F, 628).

Squinch. A small arch, bracket or similar device built across each angle of a square or polygonal structure to form an octagon or other appropriate base for a dome or spire (pp. 475A, C, 764A). Sometimes known as a **squinch arch.**

Stalls. Divisions with fixed seats for the clergy and choir, often elaborately carved, with projecting elbows, 'misericords' and canopies (p. 773C).

Stambhas. Free-standing monumental pillars, characteristic of Buddhist architecture. Also called **Laths** (p. 100A).

Stanchion. A vertical steel support. Cast-iron was used until relatively cheap steel became available.

Starling. The pointed mass of masonry projecting from the pier of a bridge, for breaking the force of the water, hence known also as a 'cutwater'.

Steeple. The term applied to a tower crowned by a spire (p. 1024B, C).

Stele. An upright slab forming a Greek tombstone or carrying an inscription (p. 254G).

Stellar Vault. A vault in which the ribs compose a star-shaped pattern (pp. 631, 665B, 670A).

Stepped Gable. A gable with stepped sides, especially characteristic of the Netherlands.

Stijl, de (Dutch, the Style). A short-lived geometric-abstract movement in Holland (1917–31), which had a lasting influence on the development of 'Modern' architecture and of industrial design (p. 1248).

Stile Liberty. In Italy the contemporary equivalent of **Art Nouveau** (q.v.), named after the London store.

Stilted Arch. An arch having its springing line higher than the line of impost mouldings, to which it is connected by vertical pieces of walling or stilts (pp. 663B, 1310, No. 4).

Stoa. In Greek architecture, a portico or detached colonnade (pp. 199B, 200A).

Storey (pl. **Storeys**). The space between two floors.

Strapwork. A type of relief ornament or cresting resembling studded leather straps, arranged in geometrical and sometimes interlaced patterns; much used in the Early Renaissance architecture of England and the Low Countries (p. 1001A, J).

String Course. A moulding or projecting course running horizontally along the face of a building (p. 802B).

Stuart. A term applied to English Late Renaissance architecture of the period 1625–1702 (p. 979).

Stucco (It.). A fine quality of plaster, much used in Roman and Renaissance architecture for ornamental modelled work in low relief (pp. 315B, C, 835B). In England, it was extensively employed in the late 18th and early 19th century as an economical medium for the modelling of external features, in lieu of stone.

Stupa or **Tope.** A mound forming a Buddhist sacred monument (p. 95A).

Stylobate. In Classic architecture, the upper step forming a platform on which a colonnade is placed (p. 205A). Collectively, the three steps of a Greek Doric temple constitute a crepidoma.

Sudatorium. The sweating room in a Roman baths building (p. 296B).

Systyle. A term used when the space between two columns is two diameters.

Tabby. A form of concrete made from oyster shells (p. 1228).

Tabernacle. A recess or receptacle—usually above an altar—to contain the eucharistic Host, and is also applied to a niche or arched canopy. 'Tabernacle work' is the name given to elaborately carved niche and canopy work.

Tablet-flower. A variation of the ball-flower ornament of Decorated Gothic architecture in the form of a four-petalled open flower.

Taenia or **Tenia** (Lat., but of Gk. derivation, *taenia* = band). A flat projecting band capping the architrave of a Doric entablature (p. 205A).

Tegula. The Latin term for a large flat tile.

Telamones. *See* **Atlantes.**

Temenos. A sacred precinct in which stood a temple or other sanctuary.

Tempera (It.). In painting, the same as distemper.

Tempietto. A small temple. The term is usually reserved for Renaissance and later buildings of an ornamental character, compact circular or temple-like structures erected in the parks and gardens of country houses, although the most famous instance is Bramante's chapel in the cloisters of S. Pietro in Montorio, Rome (p. 823A–C).

Tepidarium. An apartment in a Roman baths building equipped with warm baths (pp. 296B, 302B).

Terra-cotta. Earth baked or burnt in

moulds for use in construction and decoration, harder in quality than brick.

Tessera. A small cube of stone, glass or marble, used in making mosaics.

Tetrastyle. A portico of four columns (p. 203C, D).

Tholos. The dome (cupola) of a circular building, hence the building itself (p. 203E).

Thrust. The force exerted by inclined rafters or beams against a wall, or obliquely by the weight of an arch, vault or dome.

Tie-bar. A beam, bar or rod which ties parts of a building together, and is subjected to tensile strain. Sometimes of wood, but usually of metal. Tie-bars are especially notable in Byzantine, Italian Gothic and Renaissance architecture to stiffen arcades or to contain the outward thrust of vaults.

Tie-beam. Normally the lowest member of a roof truss, extending from wallplate to wall-plate and primarily intended to prevent the walls from spreading. A secondary function may be to carry a kingpost or crown-post (pp. 633B, E, 635).

Tierceron. An intermediate rib between the main ribs of a Gothic vault.

Tope. See **Stupa.**

Torana. A ceremonial gateway to a Buddhist stupa (pp. 94, 105A).

Torii. The characteristic entrance gateways to Shinto temples, comprising upright posts supporting beams (p. 164).

Torus (Lat., a swelling). A large convex moulding, used principally in the bases of columns (pp. 241L, 242H, S). See **Astragal.**

Trabeated (Lat. *trabs*=a beam). A style of architecture such as the Greek, in which the beam forms the constructive feature.

Tracery. The ornamental patternwork in stone, filling the upper part of a Gothic window; it may be either 'plate' or 'bar' tracery. **Plate tracery** appears to have been cut out of a plate of stone, with special reference to the shape of the lights, whereas **bar tracery** was designed principally for the pleasing forms produced by combinations of geometrical figures. It is also applied to work of the same character in wood panelling (pp. 560, 593, 738B).

Trachelion. The neck of a Greek Doric column, between the annulets and the grooves or hypotrachelion (p. 205B).

Transept. The part of a cruciform church, projecting at right angles to the main building (p. 590A, B).

Transoms. The horizontal divisions or cross-bars of windows (pp. 560D, M, 875H, 993).

Transverse Rib. A rib which extends at right angles to the wall across a bay or other vaulted space (p. 628C).

Travertine Stone (It. *travertino* = limestone). A calcareous deposit from springs, yellowish in colour, used since Roman times as a building stone, especially in Italy where there are large accumulations. In modern architecture, often seen as a decorative facing material, in thin panels.

Trefoil (Fr. *trois feuilles* = three leaves). A term applied to this distribution in Gothic tracery (pp. 560D, E, H, 1310).

Triangulation. The principle of the design of a roof-truss, in which every panel or space enclosed by its members is triangular.

Triclinium. A Roman dining room with couches on three sides (p. 332B).

Triforium (Lat. *tres* = three + *fores* = openings). The space between the sloping roof over the aisle and the aisle vaulting. The term was first applied to the Norman arcades at Canterbury which had triple openings towards the nave, and was afterwards used for any passages and galleries in this position. It occurs in large churches only, and, from having no windows to the open air, is often called a 'blind-storey' (p. 589C, F).

Triglyphs (Gk., three channels). Blocks with vertical channels which form a distinguishing feature in the frieze of the Doric entablature (p. 205A).

Tristyle-in-antis. A portico having three columns between antae.

Trussed-rafter Roof. A form of roof composed of pairs of rafters, closely spaced and without a ridge-piece. To contain the outward thrust, the rafters were joined by collars and further stiffened by braces (pp. 633A, 635).

Tudor. A term applied to English Late Gothic architecture of the period 1485–1558 (p. 624).

Tufa. A building stone of rough or cellular texture, of volcanic or other origin (travertine may be described as calcareous tufa).

Tunnel Vault. See **Barrel Vault.**

Turrets. Small towers, often containing stairs, and forming special features in Mediaeval buildings (p. 575D).

Tuscan. See **Order.**

Tympanum. The triangular surface

bounded by the sloping and horizontal cornices of a pediment (p. 205A); also the space enclosed between the lintel and the arch of a Mediaeval doorway (p. 490B).

Unctuaria (Lat. *unctura* = anointing). Rooms for oils, unguents and various forms of treatment in Roman public baths.

Undercroft. In Mediaeval architecture, vaulted chambers upon which the principal rooms are sometimes raised.

Vault. An arched covering in stone or brick over any building (pp. 269, 627, 628).

Velarium. A great awning drawn over Roman theatres and amphitheatres to protect spectators against the sun.

Vesica Piscis (Lat., bladder of a fish). A pointed oval form, so called from its shape (p. 490B). *See* **Aureole**.

Vestibule. An ante-room to a larger apartment of a building (p. 824C, H).

Vihara. A Buddhist monastery (p. 97).

Vimana. The sanctuary of a Hindu temple (p. 93).

Vine Ornament. Variations on the theme of the vine-leaf, a characteristic motif of the Gothic Decorated style.

Volute (Lat. *voluta* = scroll). The scroll or spiral occurring in Ionic, Corinthian and Composite capitals (pp. 222, 236, 319G).

Voussoirs. The truncated wedge-shaped blocks forming an arch (p. 1310).

Wagon or **Wagonhead Vault.** *See* **Barrel Vault.**

Wave Moulding. A typical moulding of the Decorated period consisting of a slight convexity flanked by hollows (p. 563P, R, S).

Weathering. The slope given to offsets to buttresses and the upper surface of cornices and mouldings, to throw off rain.

Westblock. A multistorey gallery at the west end of some German and Netherlandish churches, surmounted by towers or turrets.

Wheel (or **Rose**) **Window.** A circular window, whose mullions converge like the spokes of a wheel (pp. 569A, C, 593E, H, 733A).

Ziggurat or **Ziqqarat.** A high pyramidal staged tower, of which the angles were orientated to the cardinal points, which formed an important element in ancient Mesopotamian temple complexes. The number of stages rose from one to seven in the course of time, and in the Assyrian version the stages were developed into a continuous inclined ramp, circulating the four sides in turn (pp. 54, 65A).

Zigzag. *See* **Chevron.**

Zoophorus. A frieze in which reliefs of animals are introduced (p. 215N).

Among the many sources consulted in revising and extending the glossary, the following works have been of especial value:

AHLSTRAND, J. T. and others. *Arkitekturtermen.* Lund, 1969.
HARRIS, J. and LEVER, J. *Illustrated Glossary of Architecture: 850–1830.* London, 1966.
SCOTT, J. S. *A Dictionary of Building.* Harmondsworth, 1964.
——. *A Dictionary of Civil Engineering.* Harmondsworth, 1958.

INDEX

Page numbers in *italic type* refer to illustrations, and are listed separately following text references. Where illustration pages interrupt a passage of text, this is ignored in the index. For example, if text at the foot of page 1 were continued at the top of page 4, the subject of that passage would be cited as appearing on pages 1–4, even if the illustrations on pages 2 and 3 were not related to that subject. When a subject is mentioned more than once on a page, in separate passages, this is indicated by a number in brackets immediately after the page number.